DATE DUE		
REF.	REF.	REF.	
			REF.
	REF.	REF.	
			REF.
REF.			

A Dictionary
of
AMERICAN
SOCIAL
CHANGE

Other Writings in History and Literature by Louis Filler

Books

The Muckrakers (1976 ed.)
Appointment at Armageddon: Muckraking and Progressivism in the American Tradition (1976)
Randolph Bourne (1965 ed.)
The Crusade against Slavery, 1830-1860 (1960 ff.)
A Dictionary of American Social Reform (1963, Greenwood ed. 1970)
The Unknown Edwin Markham (1966)
Muckraking and Progressivism: an Interpretive Bibliography (1976)
Voice of the Democracy: a Critical Biography of David Graham Phillips (1978)
Vanguards and Followers: Youth in the American Tradition (1978)

Edited Works

The New Stars: Life and Labor in Old Missouri. Manie Morgan (1949)
Mr. Dooley: Now and Forever, Finley Peter Dunne (1954)
From Populism to Progressivism (1978), anthology
The Removal of the Cherokee Nation: Manifest Destiny or National Dishonor? (1977 ed.)
The World of Mr. Dooley (1962)
The Anxious Years (1963), anthology of 1930s literature
Horace Mann and Others, Robert L. Straker (1963)
A History of the People of the United States, John Bach McMaster (1964)
The President Speaks (1964), major twentieth-century addresses
Horace Mann on the Crisis in Education (1965, Spanish translation (1972)
Wendell Phillips on Civil Rights and Freedom (1965)
The Ballad of the Gallows-Bird, Edwin Markham (1967)
Old Wolfville: the Fiction of A. H. Lewis (1968)
The Rise and Fall of Slavery in America (1981)
Abolition and Social Justice (1972)
A Question of Quality (1976)
Seasoned Authors for a New Season (1980)
Contemporaries by David Graham Phillips (1981)

Introductions

Chatterton, Ernest Lacy (1952)
Plantation and Frontier, Ulrich B. Phillips, in new edition, John R. Commons et. al.
    A Documentary History of American Industrial Society (1958)
The Acquisition of Political, Social and Industrial Rights of Man in America, John Bach McMaster, (1961)
My Autobiography, S. S. McClure (1962)
A Modern Symposium, G. Lowes Dickinson (1963)
A Statistical History of the American Presidential Elections, Svend Petersen (1963)
Samuel Gompers, Bernard Mandel (1963)
The Political Depravity of the Founding Fathers, John Bach McMaster (1964)
Democrats and Republicans, Harry Thurston Peck (1964)
A Political History of Slavery, W. H. Smith (1966)
Georgia and States Rights, Ulrich B. Phillips (1967)
The Pantarch: a Biography of Stephen Pearl Andrews, Madeleine B. Stern (1968)
Forty Years of It, Brand Whitlock (1970)

A Dictionary

of

AMERICAN
SOCIAL
CHANGE

By

LOUIS FILLER

ROBERT E. KRIEGER PUBLISHING CO., INC.
MALABAR, FLORIDA 32950

Original Edition 1982
(Based upon "A DICTIONARY OF AMERICAN SOCIAL REFORM")

Printed and Published by
ROBERT E. KRIEGER PUBLISHING COMPANY, INC.
KRIEGER DRIVE
MALABAR, FL 32950

Printed in the United States of America

Library of Congress Cataloging in Publication Data

Filler, Louis
  A dictionary of American social change.

  Originally published as: A dictionary of American social reform. 1963.
  1. Social sciences—Dictionaries.   2. Social problems—Dictionaries.
  I. Title.
H41.F5   1982   300'.3   82-10036
ISBN 0-89874-242-0 Cloth   AACR2
ISBN 0-89874-564-0 Paper

For
EMILY ARMA HOWARD FILLER
*to help see our American
people as they have been and
are; and to follow through
with them*

INTRODUCTION
ON THE DYNAMICS OF CHANGE

Finley Peter Dunne's (*q.v.*) immortal "Mr. Dooley" once opined that he saw great changes every year, and no change at all every fifty years. Certainly, we are inclined to exaggerate our problems as greater than any which came before. Yet a judicious modern can claim an urgency in his affairs that many in the past could not. Yes, there have been plagues and catastrophes which confound the mind. But they did not loosen the human being from his or her physical and psychological moorings quite so decisively as do nuclear fission, the finality of oil, or the unchartable nature of space probes.

All of these have redeeming qualities of excitement and hope. We may master the temperamental nucleus. We may make our transition to an oil-less world with less anguish than we sometimes suppose. Our space experiences can prove a sublime adventure.

Certainly, there is *change*, some unprecedented, and that is the theme of this dictionary. Our education must, to some degree, be based on established principles, at least in science and the practical arts. It is in the area of civilization, of culture, and social science that we must ask why we study this or that *in* books, media, education: what we can do with them, and what they can do for us. *Relevance* is a legitimate feature of our work and study. While pondering topics and treatments for this dictionary, I have considered relevance often. With some leeway for variation and experiment, I have asked what anyone should know, regardless of his or her specialty, who wished to think and act in a modern context.

The student, the instructor, the reader of newspapers and magazines has an endless field of choices on the table, while thinking of work or preparations in the liberal arts. Even the seeker of entertainment knows that questions have been raised, for example, about the value of television (*q.v.*). That television is inevitable in our lives, there can be no doubt. That it produces communication invaluable to our thoughts and feelings is certain. But what of its actual program?—its boring, mind-softening foolishness, hypnotic waste, which all but drives friends of democracy to despair?

What defenses have we against the dangers and frustrations television, or, for that matter, communication and education generally, create? Abraham Lincoln's (*q.v.*) belief that we must trust democracy is consoling. We may yet master the media, rather than be wasted by them. But, meanwhile, to some extent, we must fend for ourselves. It is one purpose of this dictionary to aid the reader to reach out to the resources of the world we have, and not be overwhelmed by them.

Relevance, yes. But none of these topics has come from nowhere. They have taken their shape from feelings and experiences in the past. This can be noted sharply in the experiences of "under-developed" countries which have been brought willy-nilly into the twentieth century, with leaders, novel conditions, and complex languages to make their place among civilizations with longer modernizing experiences. In the last several years *Iran* (*q.v.*), under-developed in a special way, has been a dramatic example of what can occur when efforts are made to tear human beings out of old ways with insufficient skill and attention to their history and human nature.

Continuity, then, a respect for the formidable past, is as vital a factor in understanding as is relevance in estimating the status of a topic, or the qualities which go into making it meaningful. It may or may not be in the headlines, but it must be grasped on its own terms. Accordingly, much of this dictionary is concerned not only with what Americans must understand and respect, but what Americans *are* who must do this understanding. Our own history and culture is endless and fascinating to the initiate. Because of their roots in the history and culture of all our minorities—a mixture without parallel in the world—they require special care in handling. Those of British background, of African background, of Irish, Indian, Hispanic, Jewish, (*qq.v.*) Continental background must reconcile their instincts to produce an *American* grasp of where they are. This nub of relevance, then, this projec-

tion into the past and future is an art which must be studied, if we are not as a people to stumble blindly from Vietnams into Irans—if we are not to learn about communist and Third World (*qq.v.*) worlds only through pain and humiliation.

Relevance and continuity, within the limits of choice. The language of change cannot efficiently cover all topics, even though they may erupt for a day with new aspirants to glory and power. All dictators are not Stalins (*q.v.*), all Prime Ministers Churchills, all intellectuals Orwells, all minority leaders Paynes (*qq.v.*). All inventors have not created xerox (*q.v.*) machines. Moreover, all change has not been toward novelty, but sometimes toward older modes of thought and action, involving conservatism, cooperatives, fundamentalist goals (*qq.v.*). Communism under Brezhnev is not what it was under Lenin, and it thus becomes a question how it can be most usefully investigated, at least as a shibboleth. With half the nations in the world claiming "Marxist" principles something must be said on the subject and something is.

But also something about the desire to make things better. Emerson (*q.v.*) said that man was born to be a reformer. The problem here is that no one any longer knows just what constitutes reform. Our post-World War II leaders have struggled with welfare, poverty, urban deterioration, and acute ethnic and ethical confusions. How much of this has involved reform?—how much mere appeasement of interest groups? America in 1982 struggles at the edge of social bankruptcy to give form to its citizens's needs, while holding itself as best it can together as a nation and as a people.

It is not clear, as we enter into the last phases of the twentieth century, how much of our program involves mere technique for handling relevance and continuity, how much reform of our ways of living and thinking. But so much is true:

America has had a long tradition of generous ideals, a faith in progress, and a will to better conditions, for individuals, for society as a whole. The nation gave up a million men, the hope of its civilization, to end the tragedy of slavery—a tragedy which shadows the world today in the millions, in many guises. (See Slavery.) It created a long tradition of world famous reformers, from Thomas Jefferson to Linus Pauling. They, by example, by eloquence urge us on to better ourselves, and better the lot of others. *Reform*, then, is not all of the world of change. It needs also regard for permanent things as well as innovations. But reform enters into our complex of action and ideas. Reform is therefore amply represented in the following pages.

Finally, there is the student, the instructor, the reader, himself and herself. It would be a poor program for our rounding out of the twentieth century, which asked nothing of us, asked only that we do what someone else suggests or tells us to do. This *Dictionary of American Social Change*, then, is in part a protracted essay in independent thinking. Its purpose is to be suggestive. For example, I have in due place a number of significant dates, from 1900 on. But, obviously, all years are significant. I note a few of them for pivotal circumstances; but the reader can profitably work up others, from elections, key innovations like the Ford car, special events, and others symbolizing important change.

The reader is here given entree into topics, personalities, events, connotative phrases which have affected us not only here in America, but in the world. They have pressed upon us in the past, and they press upon us today. They are likely to do so tomorrow, in some form. The bibliography which accompanies the text is not intended to be exhaustive. It is planned to open subjects wider, and to indicate that they can be widened still further, in accordance with the student's or investigator's interests or concerns.

LOUIS FILLER

The Belfry, Ovid, Michigan

Publisher's Note: Some variation in type may be noted for material representing the latest entries.

A

A.A.A., see Agricultural Adjustment Administration.

ABBOTT, EDITH (1876-1957), AND GRACE (1878-1939), pioneers in social work, associated with Hull House (q.v.) and related enterprises. Edith was a professor, and became dean of the School of Social Service Administration of the University of Chicago; her books included *Women in Industry* (1910); *Crime and the Foreign Born* (1931); *The Tenements of Chicago* (1936). Grace served as director of the Immigrants Protective League (1908-17). In 1917-8, she administered the newly-passed Child Labor Law, until it was struck down by the Supreme Court as unconstitutional. She later served (1921-34) as head of the Children's Bureau, in the United States Department of Labor. Edith Abbott, *Women in Industry* (1913); Grace Abbot, *From Relief to Social Security* (1941).

ABLEMAN vs. BOOTH (1859), concluding decision in the battle of Wisconsin Free Soilers (q.v.) to defy the Fugitive Slave Act (q.v.). In 1854, abolitionists, led by Sherman M. Booth, had forcibly freed a fugitive slave, seized by Federal officials. Booth was jailed, but let out of prison by the state Supreme Court decision that the Fugitive Slave Act was unconstitutional; the Court invoked the doctrine of concurrent powers (q.v.) for this purpose. The U. S. Supreme Court denied this view. Booth was sought and imprisoned, later pardoned by outgoing President James Buchanan.

ABOLITIONISM, a radical permutation of anti-slavery, it claimed status among Americans on grounds that it expressed their essential interests. Anti-slavery could be, and often was, an aspiration, rather than a program; seen thus, it was possible to be both anti-slavery in theory, pro-slavery in practice. Thus, Henry Clay professed anti-slavery views, but, after 1798, did little to advance its program. "Gradual" abolitionism won out with relative ease, in the North, thanks in part to the fact that social and economic conditions were not receptive to slave labor, but abolition as a reform was partly dependent on a moral attitude attending it. Thus, John Woolman (q.v.), though a Friend who sought mild approaches toward his compatriots, in persuading them to oppose slavery, is a true precursor of later abolitionists, because of the strongly moral attitude he sustained. Colonization (q.v.), though supposedly an arm of anti-slavery, was partly enervated because of its inability to build its moral component. The greatest loss to abolitionism was its failure to take root in the South, where the majority of slaves actually were. It has been argued that the rise of "immediatist" abolitionism in the North—the demand, first fostered by William Lloyd Garrison (q.v.), that slaveholding be treated as sin, and immediate emancipation be demanded—drove the South to defending slavery as good. This may be questioned; the roots of southern anti-slavery were shallow, those of pro-slavery deep. Although northern industry had a practical stake in opposing slavery extension, the north was not tolerant of abolitionists, who were required to suffer a "martyr age" during the 1830's. The abolitionists increasingly won status because they were able to equate their crusade with the civil rights of white northerners. The Negro was, in large measure, a pawn in this North-South struggle, but his efforts in his own behalf are a factor in the anti-slavery crusade yet to be adequately appreciated. To an extent, abolitionism was a reform separate from, and even opposed to, that of "Jacksonian reform" (q.v.), which held the poor, white worker to be worse enslaved than the black, and more deserving. It has even been suggested, though without evidence of any kind, that abolitionism was part of a plot to divert attention from the Jacksonian program

(A. M. Schlesinger, Jr., *Age of Jackson* [1945]). This artful, though absurd, suggestion derives a shadow of substance only from its failure to distinguish between abolitionism and political abolitionism (q.v.). The latter moved toward free soil party (q.v.) goals, and thus brought into the scene politicians who were less concerned for slavery in the south than for free land in the west. A strange work, measuring abolitionism by modern "women's lib" (q.v.) standards reproved abolitionists for allegedly not recognizing women's rights, thus condemning Lewis Tappan (q.v.) as "authoritarian" and of aid to pro-slavery forces; see A. Kraditor, *Means and Ends in American Abolitionism* (1969); for a balanced approach, R. B. Nye, *William Lloyd Garrison and the Humanitarian Reformers* (1955); see also Louis Filler, *The Crusade against Slavery* (1960 ff.); Benjamin Quarles, *Black Abolitionists* (1969).

A-BOMB, see Atom Bomb.

ABORTION, a vital issue of the 1970s, made a priority by Youth eruptions, Family controversies, and Woman issues and debates. Dominant forces in the nineteenth century were actively anti-abortion. Women's changing roles, and crusades such as Margaret Sanger's favoring contraceptive information and aid helped weaken defenses against pro-abortion arguments. The Supreme Court ruled in 1973 that abortions were legal prior to six months pregnancy. The use of state funds for abortions was seen as aiding poor women, but were fought on moral, religious, and pro-fetus grounds by various social groups and elements. ERA proponents actively propagandized for "women's choice," beyond the widely-accepted "health reasons," as, for example, determining the number of weeks before which a fetus could be legitimately aborted; Catholic spokesmen held that it was a human being on conception. Jimmy Carter's approval of ERA, and its funding, was seen as aiding pro-abortion forces; the Republican triumph of 1980 as retarding their cause (qq.v. for the above). Linda Bird Francke, *The Ambivalence of Abortion* (1978); B. N. Nathanson and R. N. Ostling, *Aborting America* (1979); L. R. Sass, *Abortion: Freedom of Choice and the Right to Life* (1978); J. C. Mohr, *Abortion in America: The Origins and Evolutions of National Policy* (1978). See also Birth Control.

ABRAHAM LINCOLN BRIGADE, a volunteer element organized in the United States which went to Spain during its civil war (q.v.) to help defend the Madrid government. It was one of a number of such units organized, in Great Britain, France, and elsewhere. The Abraham Lincoln Brigade, despite its name, was influenced by communist partisans and sympathizers.

ABRAMS vs. UNITED STATES (1919), famous opinion by Justice Holmes (q.v.) in connection with war-time limitations on free speech. Though affirming the right of the government to defend itself and its purposes, Holmes failed to see that the leaflets of the defendant constituted a threat to the government, and affirmed that the twenty-year sentence imposed upon him was out of all proportion to his alleged crime: and that his appeal to the First Amendment (q.v.) was justified: "[The] ultimate good desired is better reached by free trade in ideas. . . . That at any rate is the theory of our Constitution. It is an experiment, as all life is an experiment. . . . [We] should be eternally vigilant against attempts to check the expression of opinions that we loathe. . . . " See also Gitlow vs. People of New York.

ABSCAM, see CORRUPTION

ABSENTEE LANDLORDS, who derive incomes from lands to which they hold no allegiance, for which they take no responsibility; notoriously British holders of Irish lands, but invidiously perceived in many other areas of the world.

ABSENTEE OWNERSHIP, an urban equivalent of the preceding. Shareholders in a company have little regard for conditions in the plant, they spend their profits elsewhere, the town gains nothing from them as individuals, families, civic personages.

ABSENTEEISM, a strike tactic, employed by policemen, teachers, and other categories of labor, who, in large numbers are taken "ill," and unable to attend to their regular duties.

ABSTINENCE, a concept in Puritan ethics which assumes that worldly advance is a product of doing without, self-denial, that worldly failures have been unwilling to deprive themselves of trifling, immediate pleasures in their drive toward success. The concept assumed that worldly success went along with honesty in business endeavors, and did not always observe that successes were not uniformly abstemious. The word was also applied, in a special sense, as describing the non-use of liquor. The concept contradicts assumptions of the Welfare State, and of controlled depreciation (qq.v.).

ABSTRACT ART, a modern permutation among art movements, avoiding direct representation, emphasizing personal feeling, quintessence, impression, utilitarianism. To the extent that it resisted social reform as confining, it contributed to anti-reform tendencies; to the extent that it repudiated discipline, as, notoriously, in the work of Jackson Pollock, it was reactionary in product. But to the extent that it represented individualistic effort it played its role in opposing totalitarianism. Hitler Germany denounced abstract art as decadent, and rallied friends for it. Communist Russia also scorned abstractions, but rallied somewhat fewer friends against its program: many sympathizers of abstract art hoped to influence Russians toward greater tolerance; they noted, too, that Russians were less concerned for the artistic tenets of artists elsewhere than for their willingness to cooperate with communists, who, for example, made Pablo Picasso's "Dove of Peace" world-famous. Abstract art as escapism seemed to have passed its peak by 1960; people were distinguishing more clearly between designs for walls, and pictures to hang on walls, and some artists were willing to experiment with representation.

ABSTRACT TERMS, including Freedom, Truth, Beauty have been sometimes held, especially by Marxists, but also by Pragmatists (qq.v.), to derive from minds incapable of dealing with social realities. "Democracy" has been considered by such social critics as meaningless unless implemented by economic opportunities. Constitutional rights, they insisted, were by themselves no more than the right to starve. Others have held that abstract terms constitute ideals which ought not to be forgotten, and, indeed, that apparently more concrete thinking can lead one into slavery, rather than well-being; in A. P. Herbert's epigram, the communists had sold their birthright "for a pot of message."

ABSURD, THE LITERATURE OF THE, a modern tendency derived from older philosophical and literary responses to questions about irrational life and society. Catastrophes of world war and possible wholesale destruction by nuclear warheads affected works in many fields, and made famous Jackson Pollack in art, Samuel Beckett, Peter Weiss, Harold Pintner in drama, William Burroughs, Joseph Heller in fiction. They saw life as unfair but offered no means for improving it; see works by Thomas Pynchon, E. L. Doctorow, Jean-Paul Sartre (q.v.), Bertolt Brecht.

ACADEMIC FREEDOM, see Education and Free speech.

ACEN, see Assembly of Captive European Nations.

ACHESON, DEAN (1893-1971), New Deal Stalwart, United Nations advocate and influential in formulating international relief programs, following World War II. He was appointed Secretary of State in 1949 by President Truman. His public statement, early the next year, that he would not turn his back on Alger Hiss (q.v.), was a milestone in public tolerance of communist co-workers. He was an architect of NATO, but would not support nationalist China (qq.v.). See his autobiographical Present at the Creation (1969).

A. C. L. U., see American Civil Liberties Union.

ACTIONIST, one dissatisfied with theory, or hopes for "inevitable" social improvement; one determined upon early efforts and results.

ACTIVIST PRESIDENT, political science term created in the 1950s during Democratic criticism of Eisenhower's alleged inactivity, and reinforced by subsequent crises requiring Presidential decisiveness; see R. Neustadt, Presidential Power (1960); L. C. Kerpelman, Activists and Non-Activists: a Psychological Study of American College Students (1972), for a broader view of the concept.

ACTON, LORD, see Machiavelli, Niccolo di.

A.D.A., see Americans for Democratic Action.

ADAMIC, LOUIS (1899-1951), author and pioneer advocate of ethnic (q.v.) diversity. He traced violence (q.v.) in America, in Dynamite (1931); the rise of Yugoslavia, his native land, in The Eagle and the Roots (1952); ethnicity, in From Many Lands. See his My America 1928-1938 (1938).

ADAMS, BROOKS (1848-1927), like his brother Henry (q.v.), a theoretician of society, and like him concerned for aristocratic values in a civilization which welcomed ambitious nonentities and capitalists. His suspicion of the latter directed him toward theories which seemed to put him at one with reformers, though the interests he defended were removed from theirs. Thus, he supported free coinage of silver (q.v.), but was no Populist (q.v.). In his Theory of Social Revolution (1913) he was critical of the competence of the capitalist class to direct society. He was a proponent of the initiative and referendum (q.v.). His gloomy predictions respecting the future of society derived from his fear of unbridled democracy; he believed that the coming of World War I bore out his prophecies. See also his lengthy introduction to Henry Adams's The Degradation of the Democratic Dogma (1919).

ADAMS, CHARLES FRANCIS, JR. (1835-1915), like his brother Henry Adams (q.v.), more concerned for the fact that increasing democratization threatened the social establishment of which his family was a part than for the challenge to reformers which the untidy democracy of post-Civil War decades presented. Adams's Chapters of Erie (1871) offered a classic display of the corruption by which the upstart financiers of the era lived. As a railroad executive, Adams was unable to cope with the ruthless methods of Jay Gould (q.v.). As chairman of the first railroad commission, in Massachusetts, Adams acted as a regulator, rather than a reformer. See his Autobiography (1916).

ADAMS, FREDERICK UPHAM (1859-1921), inventor and engineer, in the 1890's, of radical temperament, and editor with Benjamin Orange Flower (q.v.) of the firmly reformist The New Time (1896). He later changed his views to become sweepingly conservative.

ADAMS, HENRY (1838-1918), offers striking contrasts with his grandfather, John Quincy Adams (q.v.), like him having numerous intellectual interests, but unlike him a total failure as a social and political figure. His major significance to reform lies in his critical view of post-Civil War America, which he held to be operating with principles which had been debased by irresponsibly-augmented democracy. His novel, Democracy (1880), anonymously published, was a mordant view of Washington politics. Adams's outlook was pessimistic, rather than reformistic, but his complex and probing mind offered ideas and materials which could serve reformers as well as conservatives, and also manifest reactionaries.

ADAMS, JOHN (1735-1826), second President of the United States, a Deist (q.v.), and a principled conservative, as depicted in his own Discourses on Davila (1791); however, he not only served the country during the American Revolution with distinction—Jefferson credited his eloquence with having ensured the ratification of the Declaration of Independence—but refused to be panicked by conservative prejudice into a belief in the existence of an Illuminati (q.v.), or to join the agitation in support of an all-out war with revolutionary France. His determination to negotiate differences with that country prevented what might have been an unprincipled and otherwise disgraceful military adventure.

ADAMS, JOHN QUINCY (1767-1848), sixth President of the United States, and chiefly notable as a nationalist, rather than as a reformer. However, as a representative from Massachusetts in Congress, 1831-48, he attained a unique position as a defender of northern liberties. He was the outstanding opponent of the "Gag Rule," intended to stop discussion of slavery in the legislature. In the course of his battle to have it overthrown, from 1836 to 1844, when it was defeated, he was the impassioned spokesman for free speech, the right to petition Congress, and other Constitutional guarantees. Seeking support for his campaign, he made common cause with numerous reformers, including Benjamin Lundy, Joshua Leavitt, Lewis Tappan (qq.v.), and others who were more particularly identified with reform causes and attitudes. He led the final effort to free the Amistad captives (q.v.). His essential conservatism helped give respectability to reformers whose unconventional qualities made them more vulnerable to criticism.

ADAMS, SAMUEL (1722-1803), Revolutionary patriot, second cousin of John Adams, notable for the persistence with which he maintained revolutionary principles during the long crisis between the British and the colonies, when many of his compatriots sought compromise and satisfaction. Adams, in Massachusetts, like Patrick Henry (q.v.), in Virginia, worked consciously to foster discontent and to keep resentment against British policy alive. Explanations have been sought in his father's business failures for his deep-seated bitterness and resourceful antagonism. He symbolized Boston independency, in his resistance to British taxes, in his organization of the Non-Importation Association (1768), and in his brilliant use of the Boston "Massacre" to whip up colonial rebellion. Having created the Sons of Liberty (1765), he later set up the Massachusetts committee of correspondence (1772): extra-legal measures which culminated, appropriately, in the Boston Tea Party (1773). He was a delegate to the Continental Congress. Why the revolutionary firebrand should have become a conservative governor of Massachusetts (1794-7) is one of the mysteries of his personality and social role.

ADAMS, SAMUEL HOPKINS (1871-1958), muckraker and popular novelist, a writer for McClure's (q.v.), author of The Great American Fraud (1906), exposing patent medicines. Revelry (1926) was a more shoddy, fictional "expose" of the Harding Administration; but The Incredible Era (1939) told in round, revitalized prose the same tale. Under the pseudonym "Warner Fabian," Adams perpetrated another shabby novel, with, however, a memorable title: Flaming Youth (1923).

ADAMSON ACT (1916), one of the pieces of reform legislation passed during the first administration of Woodrow Wilson. It established an eight-hour work day for interstate carrier employees. A factor which hastened its passage was the threat of a national strike of railroad workers.

A.D.C., see Aid to Dependent Children.

ADDAMS, JANE (1860-1935), founder of Hull House, in Chicago, a pioneer settlement house which concerned itself with the problems of the poor, the immigrants, and other components of the urban problem (q.v.). She was concerned for the philosophy of social reform, as well as for practical accomplishments, in such works as Democracy and Social Ethics (1902) and The Spirit of Youth and the City Streets (1909). She was also an outstanding pacifist, though as chairwoman and conscience, rather than activist.

ADULT EDUCATION, a modern permutation of nineteenth century efforts to expand opportunities for intellectual growth, including the Lyceum, Mechanics, Institutes (qq.v.), the Chautauqua Movement, and university extension work. The Lyceum had a relationship to reform, to the extent that it offered reformers a platform to speak from. The purpose of the Mechanics' Institutes was to advance their patrons economically, at least as much as intellectually, but moral and social purposes were asserted as well. The Americanization Movement of World War I (q.v.), along with vastly expanded systems of public lectures and extension school offerings created the concept of adult education; in 1926, the American Association for Adult Education was instituted. Only a small portion of the field can be identified with reform. "Night school" education has been memorialized in Leonard Q. Ross's, The Education of H*y*m*a*n K*a*p*l*a*n (1937).

"AFFIRMATIVE ACTION," slogan of Negroes and their white

co-workers, in the 1970s. They argued that Negroes having been long oppressed, they ought to receive opportunities, if necessary at the expense of equally sound or better equipped applicants; such inequities in the present would pay social dividends in the future. The New York Times urged such action as constituting "Reparations" (q.v.). Another protagonist believed "affirmative action" might "require action for the general good which impinges on the freedom of the individual." See American Enterprise Institute, Affirmative Action: the Answer to Discrimination? (1975); also, Robert Calvert, Affirmative Action: a Comprehensive Recruiting Manual (1979), and Walter B. Connelly, Jr., et al., Affirmative Action after Bakke (q.v.) (1978).

A.F. of L., see American Federation of Labor.

AFFLUENCE, early conspicuous in America, as in Joseph G. Baldwin, The Flush Times of Alabama and Mississippi (1853). Mark Twain and Charles Dudley Warner, The Gilded Age (1873) was critical of the insubstantial goals "good times" created. Nineteen Twenties affluence was notorious for its excesses, though a close study of the times would have shown achievements in research, philanthropy, and democratic expansions, as in education. These contrast strongly with the Great Depression (q.v.) record. With the world become smaller, and made more dangerous by nuclear energy (q.v.), America's use of its resources came under new critical scrutiny. Eugene Linden, Affluence and Discontent...[in] Consumer Societies (1979); Stephen Goode, Affluent Revolutionaries: a Portrait of the New Left (1974); J. K. Galbraith, The Affluent Society (1976).

AFGHANISTAN, a factor in the continuing movements of West and Eastern powers to advance their influence and positions in world geopolitics. The Soviet military assault on this quasi-"Marxist" state, and the resistance it met, raised questions of how Russian resort to arms, as, earlier, in Hungary, Czechoslovakia, (q.v.) and elsewhere, could be discouraged or resisted. Also, Russian limited success in quelling the Afghan tribes suggested the Soviets might be suffering a modified Vietnam (q.v.). T. F. Rodenbaugh, Afghanistan and the Anglo-Russian Dispute (1885); Peter G. Franck, Afghanistan between East and West (1960); Peter M. King, Afghanistan: Cockpit in High Asia (1966).

AFRICA, UNION OF SOUTH, has been a land which passed through two major crises significant to reformers. The Boer War (q.v.) stirred them in opposition to imperialism and made the Boer leaders famous as fighters for hearth and home in opposition to British expansionists. When, however, rapport was achieved under British auspices, they turned to protecting white supremacy against the equalitarian demands of Negroes of various classes, who demanded better treatment, facilities, work conditions, and against their white sympathizers. The principle of Apartheid—of separation of Negroes from white people—corresponded roughly with the similar principle pronounced by white leaders in the American South. Like them, too, South African leaders have argued that they sought the Negro's good, and would offer him "equal, but separate" facilities; but surrounded by many more Negroes than the American South had to cope with, they felt it necessary to be more ruthless in enforcing segregation principles. The demonstrations and strikes of 1959-60 were ruthlessly suppressed; symbolic was the Sharpeville massacre of March 21, 1960, in which 69 Negroes were killed, most of them by rifle-fire from the rear, and 186 wounded; see Ambrose Reeves, Shooting at Sharpeville: the Agony of South Africa (1961). Alan Paton's (q.v.) conciliatory approach has seemed too radical to South Africa's political leaders. The independence drive which created numerous black nations north of South Africa produced a do-or-die psychology among its leaders. In 1961 it voted itself a republic and left the British Commonwealth. Twenty years later it faced not only blacks and the disapproval of the West, but restless members of its "colored" population, of mixed blood and Indians. It moved resolutely to maintain law and order with weapons and politics. After Rhodesia had become Zimbabwe (q.v.) and other pressures developed, there were hints South Africa might modify aspects of its rigid Apartheit. Ann and Neva Seidman,

South Africa and U.S. Multinational Corporations (1979); Robert W. Peterson, ed., *South Africa and Apartheit* (1975); Richard E. Bissell, ed., *South Africa into the 1980's* (1979); Alan Paton, *South African Tragedy: the Life and Times of Jan Hofmeyl* (1965); Christian N. Barnard, *South Africa: Sharp Dissection* (1977).

AFRICAN NATIONALISM, long suppressed by force af arms, by paternalistic programs, by tribal rivalries, was unleashed by agitations in the United Nations encouraging to nationalist groups in North Africa, by world interest and sympathy for the Negroes of the Union of South Africa to improve their status, by the resultant excitement and ambition stirred among Negro populations in Central Africa, and by their ability to profit from the international duel for support of the under-developed nations by the communists, on the one hand, the democracies, on the other. The struggle of Algerian nationalists against French rule was aided by the struggle which continued between Algerian French and the French at home over national policy. The struggle between Kenya nationalists and their British masters, a similar situation in Rhodesia, and, in 1960, the unleashing of Congolese Negroes into the difficulties of self-rule, shook the entire continent. Reformers faced the question of how to cope with a Union of South Africa determined to maintain white supremacy (*q.v.*) under any conditions. Their problem for middle Africa was how to help its multiplying Negro overlords to develop democratic measures and institutions to resist demagogues, military adventurers. Weapons in the war were education, means for fighting disease, malnutrition, unclean habits, technical assistance for raising standards in housing, transportation, and other social requirements. To an extent the continent became a vast area in which world competition between the West and communist-influenced nations struggled for materials including oil in Nigeria and Libya, strategic connections, and cultural impress. The struggle involved, too, the progress of the Union of South Africa (*q.v.*), and the future of irresponsible dictators like Colonel Gaddafi in Libya, who practiced murder for social control, and Idi Amin (*q.v.*) who wrecked Uganda. More promising was the heritage of Sir Seretse Khama (*q.v.*) of Botswana, whose death was widely mourned. Nigeria, too, with its ninety million people, and despite a tragic civil war, gave promise of progress. But mainly Africans needed food, shelter, and hope; and both European advisors and African heads of state had gambled recklessly for modernization at the expense of agriculture and clan unity. Africans, cried a famous agronomist, needed oxen, not tractors; see Rene Dumont, *The Growth of Hunger* (1980); Patrick Marnham, *Fantastic Invasion: Dispatches from Contemporary Africa* (1980); C. A. Diop (of Senegal), *Black Africa: the Economic and Cultural Basis for a Federated State* (1979); Philip D. Curtin, ed., *Africa and the West* (1972); Z. K. Brzezinski, *Africa and the Communist World* (1963); W. G. Cartey, *The Africa Reader* (1970).

AGE OF REASON, THE (1794), see Paine, Thomas.

AGED, see OLD AGE

AGENT PROVOCATEUR, used by anti-labor agencies to foster violence during a strike or other social crisis, in order to give police and troops an occasion for intervening and arresting strike and radical leaders. See also Stool Pigeon.

AGITATOR, used invidiously by defenders of the *status quo* (*q.v.*), with approval by those who believe that "stirrers-up of the people" merit appreciation. Daniel O'Connell (*q.v.*) was known as "The Great Agitator." "Immediatist" abolitionists (*q.v.*) were agitators, though the preferred epithet was "incendiary." Agitators increasingly flourished under post-Civil War industrial conditions, as difficult living and working circumstances called up spokesmen; following their organization in 1905, the I.W.W. (*q.v.*) created many. Since the development of "Big Labor" and the N.L.R.B. (*qq.v.*), they have been fewer, none famous.

AGNEW, SPIRO (1918-   ), "a heartbeat away from the Presidency," he was a poverty-to-riches American success, in whom Republicans and Greeks everywhere could take pride. He rose swiftly in Baltimore County, Maryland, from Zoning Board of Appeals in 1957 to governor in 1966. Two years later he was Richard M. Nixon's (*q.v.*) running mate for national election, conspicuous for his firm stand against rioters and agitators and his rotund eloquence. Nixon contributed an introduction to *Where He Stands: the Life and Opinions of Spiro T. Agnew* (1968). Years of speech-making before excited partisans and opponents ended abruptly in the shocking revelation that he had received payoffs from special interests even when governor and as Vice-President. His resignation from office *October 10, 1973*, with its implicit admission of guilt, shook the conservative establishment and helped push the Nixon Administration toward catastrophe, as well as made Gerald R. Ford (*q.v.*) his successor. It also helped reveal dangers in democratic processes. J. R. Coyne, Jr., *The Impudent Snobs: Agnew vs. the Intellectual Establishment* (1972); Joseph Albright, *What Makes Spiro Run* (1972); Theo Lippman, *Spiro Agnew's America* (1972); R. M. Cohen and Jules Witcover, *A Heartbeat Away* (1974).

AGNOSTICISM, see Ingersoll, Robert G.

"AGRARIAN DEMOCRACY," a concept developed in ideal form by those who followed Thomas Jefferson (*q.v.*) in believing that agriculture was the mainstay of society: that it alone produced wealth, that the city was the demesne of manipulators who, at best, had less to contribute. It envisioned a nation of small landowners, having a minimum of obligation to their central governments, living in peace and plenty. The dream persisted through the Jackson "Revolution" (*q.v.*), which honored the farmer, though it emphasized more than Jefferson had done, the city worker, newly enfranchised. In the post-Civil War era, the manifest rise of the city weakened the effectiveness of the concept on a national basis; it maintained considerable strength in the midwest, inspired the Populist Revolt and continued to show potency in the operations of the Nonpartisan League (*qq.v.*).

AGRARIAN REVOLT, see Populist Revolt. Agrarianism gained by being compared with problems elsewhere; see Solon J. Buck, *The Agrarian Crusade* (1921); R. J. Alexander, *Agrarian Reform in Latin America* (1974); S. M. Radwan, *Agrarian Reform and Rural Poverty, Egypt, 1952-1975* (1977); C. F. Estrella, *Agrarian Reform in the New Society* (1974); Kyle Steenland, *Agrarian Reform under* [*Salvador*] *Allende* (*q.v.*) (1977).

AGRICULTURAL ADJUSTMENT ADMINISTRATION, created 1933, as a New Deal (*q.v.*) measure. It was intended to help the farmer out of depression by restricting crop production, thus raising commodity prices, and paying him a bounty for his cooperation. Though reformist in purpose, and perhaps in ultimate results, the A.A.A.'s immediate effect was to encourage large landholders to put their less fertile acres out of production, and to expel their tenants who had been working them; in this way the "Okies" were created. One of the A.A.A.'s most remarkable features was the authority it received to levy a tax on the processing, or manufacturing, firms which handled the farmer's raw products and profited excessively from his labors. This tax, which provided the funds for subsidizing the farmer, was held unconstitutional by the Supreme Court in 1936 (United States v. Butler *et al.*), and the decision overthrew the "first" A.A.A. Its essential purposes were rescued by the Soil Conservation and Domestic Allotment Act of 1936 and the A.A.A. Act of 1938.

AGRICULTURAL COOPERATIVES, include marketing, farm, supply, irrigation, farming, live stock, breeding, and other cooperatives.

AGRICULTURAL WHEEL, an early permutation of the Order of Patrons of Husbandry in the southern states. It began in Arkansas in 1882, and spread in influence to some seven other states. In 1886 a National Wheel was projected, and the concept helped give a sense of the several sectional farmer interests, including those of the northwest and of the south. It is probably the source of the phrase: "he is a big wheel."

AGRICULTURAL WORKERS, see Migratory Agricultural Labor.

AGUINALDO, EMILIO (1869-1964), national hero of the Philippines. He plotted against Spanish rule (1896), and was exiled; during the Spanish-American War, he assisted United States troops to quell the Spanish, but when his expectations were frustrated that he could set up an independent government, he began a guerrilla war against the American troops. Anti-imperialists praised him as a fighter for the right. His insurrection quelled, he lived on as a national hero, finally concluding the American victory had been for the best; without it the Philippines would have been partitioned; see his *A Second Look at America* (1957); also, Simeon A. Villa, *Aguinaldo's Odyssey* (1963).

AID TO DEPENDENT CHILDREN, see Social Security Legislation.

AKRON RUBBER STRIKE (1936), the first major action of the C.I.O. (*q.v.*). It launched the United Rubber Workers of America, which, employing the "sit down" (*q.v.*) turned Akron into a union town.

"ALABAMA CLAIMS," see TREATY OF WASHINGTON (1871).

ALBERTA, most westerly of Canada's central agricultural provinces, and noted for its social credit (*q.v.*) government, concerned for a program which reformers have found of interest.

ALCOHOLICS ANONYMOUS, resulted from a meeting in 1935 in Akron, Ohio, between a well-known surgeon and a New York broker whose experiences with fellow-alcoholics permitted them in 1939 to issue the volume, *Alcoholics Anonymous*. This became the rallying phrase for persons needing advice and moral support. By 1953, they numbered some one hundred thousand persons, widely distributed, who had "banded together to solve their common problem and to help fellow sufferers in recovery from that age-old, baffling malady, alcoholism." Like the Washingtonians (*q.v.*) of earlier years, they emphasized helpful, rather than moral or religious tenets, though they employed these as circumstances warranted. An aid, rather than a crusade, they emphasized individual needs, rather than society's needs. See also Temperance.

ALCOHOLISM, a problem in social goals and perspectives. Although wars, religious skepticism, and weakened family structures diminished the temperance (*q.v.*) crusade, the devastation caused by drunkenness forced reconsideration of whether it was a "disease," and the responsibility of the individual before law and society. New efforts appeared likely, to control liquor, as to the young. Particular groups required help; thus Eskimoes, incorporated into the larger society, were being decimated by liquor. Women were seen as suffering in particular ways, as a result of wide-spread drinking. It was a factor in crime and sexual misadventures. Research was but one step in defining social action, and lagged behind it. See Hugh Brody, *Indians on Skid Row* (1971); Anne Pinder, ed., *Women: Their Use of Alcohol* (1976); Marian Sandmier, *The Invisible Alcoholics* (1980); Tom Alibrandi, *Young Alcoholics* (1978); R. Fox, ed., *Alcoholism: Behavioral Research, Therapeutic Approaches* (1967).

ALCOTT, AMOS BRONSON (1799-1888), educational pioneer and transcendentalist, a failure in all his projects, whose ideas were nevertheless respected by his peers among Boston reformers and honored by posterity, for the most part. In his schools, which even reformers did not help sustain, he attempted to treat children as individuals; he did, however, win the admiration and loyalty of Elizabeth Palmer Peabody (see Peabody Sisters). His Fruitlands cooperative community (1844-5) consisted of no more than his family and two Englishmen, and nevertheless failed to achieve practicality. His great success was in a family which held that he could do no wrong. He was the prototype of the progressive educator. His daughter, Louisa May Alcott (1832-88) rescued her family from meagre circumstances with her successful book for children, *Little Women* (1868), and herself endorsed the woman's suffrage reform. Alcott is satirized in Henry James' *The Bostonians* (1886), but is secure in the good opinion of litterateurs and reformers.

ALIEN AND SEDITION ACTS (1798), a result of bitter differ

ences between Federalists and Democratic-Republicans over attitudes toward the French Revolution (*q.v.*). The Federalist Congress passed three acts aimed at anti-Federalist intellectuals of English and French birth which jeopardized their tenure or freedom in America, and a sedition act intended to curb Jeffersonian editors who ridiculed and denounced the Administration. The alien acts were not enforced, though a number of visitors to the United States were frightened away; the sedition act resulted in the arrest of twenty-five ardent Jeffersonians, and roused their party to the defense of their liberties. Accordingly, Jefferson and Madison drafted the Kentucky and Virginia Resolutions of the same year, respectively, and had them introduced in the appropriate legislatures. They argued "that the several States composing the United States of America, are not united on the principle of unlimited submission to their general government"; in effect, arguing for the right to defy laws they deemed unconstitutional, they (albeit in the interests of civil liberties) created a precedent for defying decisions of the central government. It is true that the Supreme Court (*q.v.*) had not yet established its right to interpret the Constitution, but Jefferson's own attack on that body, during his Administration, established his readiness to sacrifice constitutional forms to what he deemed social necessities. See also Sedition Act of 1798; John C. Miller, *Crisis in Freedom* (1951); James M. Smith, *Freedom's Fetters* (1966).

ALIEN REGISTRATION ACT, see Smith Act.

ALLIANCE FOR PROGRESS, a Kennedy (*q.v.*) enterprise, intended to raise to a higher level United States-Latin American relations through economic aid and cooperation, within the Organization of American States. It was to be integrated with land and tax reform measures in the various nations, and so increase democracy as well as lift the level of Latin American production and more equitable distribution of goods. Basic to the program was American financing which, by the end of the 1970s, was stagnant, partly owing to revolutionary upsets and changes of government, and world conditions. H. S. Perloff, *The Alliance for Progress* (1969); Jerome Levinson and Juan de Onis, *The Alliance that Lost Its Way: a Critical Report* (1970).

ALLIANCES, see Farmers' Alliances.

"ALMIGHTY DOLLAR, THE," phrase first used in Washington Irving's *Wolfert's Roost and Other Papers* (1837); though used to refer to persons who esteem money above worthier considerations, it has taken on a more reformistic meaning than Irving originally intended.

ALLENDE, SALVADOR (1908-1973), known as the first "freely elected" Marxist president in the Western Hemisphere, he symbolized problems which the United States would increasingly have to meet. Allende, a long-time socialist, won his place in Chile, 1970, by a narrow margin, and, in his drive toward nationalization of industries, roused many foes, among them the C. I. A. (*q.v.*). Overthrown in September 1973, he committed suicide; partisans in Chile and in the United States claimed he was murdered. He was praised by Fidel Castro (*q.v.*), derogated by anti-Marxists, as in J. B. Gayner and L. D. Pratt, *Allende and the Failure of Chilean Marxism* (1974). See also Regis Debray, *The Chilean Revolution: Conversations with Allende* (1971).

A.L.P., see American Labor Party.

ALPHABET AGENCIES, popular term for bureaus or departments set up during the New Deal (*q.v.*) era which were recognized in their abbreviated form; see, N.R.A., A.A.A., C.C.C., W.P.A., F.H.A., T.V.A., R.E.A., H.O.L.C., among others.

ALTGELD, JOHN P. (1847-1902), an immigrant who rose from poverty to become a wealthy lawyer and governor of Illinois (1892-6). A humanitarian, he expressed advanced views in *Our Penal Machinery and Its Victims* (1884); see also his *Live Questions*, the two volumes of which (1890, 1894) reflect his causes and opinions, and were published together, with additional matter in 1899. As governor, Altgeld fought for anti-monopoly and pro-labor laws. He inspired numerous reformers, notably Clarence Darrow, Brand Whitlock, and Jane Addams (*qq.v.*). His freeing of the survivors of the Haymarket Riot (q.v.) in 1893 earned him the opprobrium of conservatives throughout the land. The next year, he was again accorded national attention when he sought to keep Federal troops out of the Pullman Strike (q.v.), averring that his state militia could maintain order. He was a power at the Democratic Convention of 1896 which nominated William Jennings Bryan, but his persistent reformism turned business associates against him. By his death, he was poor, and the "Eagle Forgotten" of Vachel Lindsay's (q.v.) poem, and of H. Barnard's book, *Eagle Forgotten* (1938). A curiosity was the plagerization of this work to feed popular exploitation of American themes by H. Fast, in *The American* (1946).

A.M.A., see American Medical Association.

AMALGAMATED ASSOCIATION OF IRON, STEEL AND TIN WORKERS OF THE UNITED STATES, founded 1876, a once-strong trade union, centered in and about Pittsburgh, which, however, deteriorated in prestige as it found itself unable to rise to the organizational and other needs of the workers. The failure of the Homestead strike (q.v.) put back organization for a generation, and the failure of the Steel Strike of 1919 (q.v.) for another. Not until the organization of the C.I.O., in 1935, and the subsequent operations of the Steel Workers' Organizing Committee (q.v.) was labor in the industry firmly established, becoming the United Steelworkers of America. J. S. Robinson, *The Amalgamated Association of Iron, Steel and Tin Workers* (1920); W. Z. Foster, *Unionizing Steel* (1936); Stewart Holbrook, *Iron Brew* (1939).

AMALGAMATED CLOTHING WORKERS OF AMERICA, formed in 1914 by a secession of labor leaders under Sidney Hillman (q.v.) from the United Garment Workers. It fought the American Federation of Labor leadership to establish itself as one of the notable unions in the country, a "showcase" of concern for the educational, welfare, and recreational needs of its members, and a leading unit in the organization of the C.I.O. (q.v.). J. B. S. Hardman, ed., *The Amalgamated, Today and Tomorrow* (1939); George Soule, *Sidney Hillman* (1939); H. H. Bookbinder, *To Promote the General Welfare* (1950).

AMENDMENTS TO THE CONSTITUTION have represented an avenue of expression for reformers, though requiring momentous social circumstances for attainment. Even the great depression of the 1930's, though it resulted in a wide range of New Deal (q.v.) legislation, resulted in no amendments adding securities or privileges for women, children, incapacitated persons, or others. Such radical amendments as the Fifteenth and the Nineteenth (qq.v.) resulted from critical changes in social circumstances and relations. The Eighteenth Amendment (q.v.) was a phenomenon resulting from long agitation and special conditions. Reformers have gained more by concentrating on changes in municipal ordinances, and the passage of state and Congressional enactments, as well as on general agitation intended to influence public feeling; see also Bill of Rights.

"AMERICA, YOUNG," see "Young America."

AMERICA FIRST COMMITTEE, an isolationist (q.v.) body formed in 1940 to influence public opinion in favor of keeping the United States out of World War II. Its most famous adherent was Charles A. Lindbergh, Jr. (q.v.). Its Congressional support included Burton K. Wheeler and Gerald P. Nye (qq.v.), as well as influential publishers. Their fear of communists inclined them toward elements which were not merely anti-communist, but pro-fascist as well. The Committee, undermined by the War effort, quickly declined; Wayne S. Cole, *America First: the Battle against Intervention, 1940-1941* (1971).

AMERICAN AND FOREIGN ANTI-SLAVERY SOCIETY, a relatively small group, largely activated by Lewis Tappan (q.v.), which maintained a moderate but firm abolitionist position, after it had separated from Garrison and his group. Tappan maintained correspondence with British abolitionist sympathizers, and sponsored a variety of publications.

AMERICAN ANTI-SLAVERY SOCIETY, formed in Philadelphia, in 1833, following several years of agitation, highlighted by the pioneering efforts of William Lloyd Garrison (q.v.). It brought together such notables as Arthur and Lewis Tappan, John Greenleaf Whittier, and Samuel J. May (qq.v.), as well as Garrison. The Society led a loosely organized body of local and state societies which by 1838 numbered about 1300, with perhaps a membership of 250,000. There were serious differences in program and perspective between the Garrison-led New England societies, and those dominated by the national office in New York. The latter feared that Garrison harmed their work by his extreme denunciations of slavery and its alleged supporters, by his attacks on the church, and by his willingness to use women as active members and public speakers. Differences culminated at the 1840 meeting in New York, which the Garrisonians dominated by bringing down delegates in great number from New England. The moderates therefore seceded, and formed the American and Foreign Anti-Slavery Society (q.v.). As the slavery issue became politicalized in the 1840's, both societies declined as institutions, though individual members continued to be influential as moral and even political forces.

AMERICAN ASSOCIATION FOR INTERNATIONAL CONCILIATION, organized 1907, an educational agency affiliated with a world body, chiefly notable for several of its publications. It published William James's *The Moral Equivalent of War* (1910), and several of the pamphlets of Randolph Bourne (q.v.), as well as his symposium, *Towards an Enduring Peace* (1916).

AMERICAN CIVIL LIBERTIES UNION, grew out of a Civil Liberties Bureau, established in 1917 as an adjunct to the American Union against Militarism, set up two years before. The C.L.B. then became a separate entity, with a board of its own. Department of Justice suspicions resulted in a raid on the National Civil Liberties Bureau's offices, in 1918. Its founder, Roger N. Baldwin (q.v.), a conscientious objector, resigned from the Bureau when called by the draft board, and served time in prison. Albert deSilver, a lawyer, served as director in his stead. In 1920, the A.C.L.U. was set up on a permanent basis, attracting, in addition to Baldwin, Rev. Harry F. Ward, Jeannette Rankin, Oswald Garrison Villard, Robert Morss Lovett, among others (qq.v.). The Union then began a distinguished record of service, opposing the Palmer Raids, conducting the Scopes defense, the Sacco-Vanzetti appeal, the protest against the Bonus Army eviction, the vindication of James Joyce's *Ulysses*, among many other notable actions (qq.v.). The A.C.L.U. refused to aid the defendants of the Sedition Trial of 1944 (q.v.). It had, in 1937, defended the rights of employers to express their anti-union sentiments, when unaccompanied by coercion. Its emphases were affected to a degree by current trends and understandings. In 1940, it took a stand against having totalitarians in its councils; as a result, Ward resigned from the organization. Its program for 1961 emphasized free speech and association, due process of law (q.v), equality before the law, and international civil liberties. For an informal account of its operation, by its secretary, see Lucille Milner, *Education of an American Liberal* (1954). In 1979 the ACLU antagonized some supporters by defending the right of Nazi-type persons to march through a section inhabited by Jews; see Skokie Case; Aryeh Neier, *Defending My Enemy* (1979).

AMERICAN COLONIZATION SOCIETY, formed in 1816 with impressive sponsorship which included Henry Clay and other persons of distinction, north and south. Its presumed aim was to advance anti-slavery. It was to build up Liberia (q.v.) as a bastion of freedom for Negroes, using free Negroes and freed slaves. It received much cooperation and financial assistance, including that from the Federal government. It became apparent to serious anti-slavery partisans that the Society emphasized sending free Negroes out of the country, rather than the freeing of slaves. Many militantly pro-slavery spokesmen emphasized this purpose. William Lloyd Garrison (q.v.) attacked the Society effectively in his *Thoughts on African Colonization...*(1832). The Society rapidly declined; see P. Staudenraus, *The African Colonization Movement* (1961).

AMERICAN COMMONWEALTH, (1888), see Bryce, James.

AMERICAN DREAM, like "Land of Opportunity," once widely pointing to hope, prosperity, satisfaction, and so seen by refugees and immigrants (*qq.v.*) even into the 1980s. In Norman Mailer, *An American Dream* (1965) reflected youth (*q.v.*) preoccupations: a caricature of its original meaning. See also D. Madden, ed., *American Dreams, American Nightmares* (1970), and R. C. Miller, ed., *Twentieth Century Pessimism and the American Dream* (1961). In R. J. Ringer, *Restoring the American Dream* (1979), the welfare state (*q.v.*) is indicted.

AMERICAN FEDERATION OF LABOR, a product of conservative labor thinking, founded in 1886, it determined to avoid the errors, as it saw them, of such organizations as the Knights of Labor (*q.v.*). The Federation, as directed by Samuel Gompers (*q.v.*) conceived of labor not as a moral crusade but as a practical means of acquiring material gains. Thus, its task was not to seek a new society, not to aid the unemployed and unorganized worker (*qq.v.*), or the incompetent, but to conserve the assets of established labor, and to fight from day to day for more, and to reward its friends and punish its enemies. However, since the Federation was a congeries of unions, it included such radical elements as the Western Federation of Miners, as well as shoddy and "racketeer" (*q.v.*) unions, and cooperated with both as union politics required. The Federation was composed of craft unions, rather than industrial unions (*qq.v.*), for the most part. It cooperated with the National Civic Federation (*q.v.*), seeking mediation between labor and capital, rather than conflict. Its methods, persisting into the depression of the 1930's, drove discontented groups to form the Committee for Industrial Organization, in 1935, reorganized three years later as the Congress of Industrial Organizations (*q.v.*). The two organizations engaged in jurisdictional disputes over the right to organize various parts of the labor force, but joined in 1955; Philip H. Taft, *The American Federation of Labor* (1957-9); W. Galenson, *The CIO Challenge to the AFL...1935-1941* (1960).

AMERICAN FRIENDS SERVICE COMMITTEE, organized in 1917 following entrance by the United States in World War I, it projected peaceful aid in the midst of war, and in post-War Europe cooperated in relief activities. In succeeding years, it attempted to develop programs making for peace, and to act as a mediating agency for clarifying contrasting points of view among nations. In the 1930's, it began to further work-camps, at home and abroad, which would serve needy people, enlist young people interested in serving others, and set an example of peaceful labor as an alternative to war. These work-camps, in the post-World War II period were administered by the Quaker International Voluntary Service. Though never numerous, they attracted much sympathetic regard, especially from pacifist-minded youth. Their activities were one precedent for the Peace Corps (*q.v.*). G. Jonas, *On Doing Good* (1971).

AMERICAN FUND FOR PUBLIC SERVICE, INC., established in 1922, the most important of all funds to support social reform and radical activities. Charles Garland, of Massachusetts, a libertarian in views, received some nine hundred thousand dollars for an inheritance, and turned it over for disbursement to a committee originally consisting, among others, of Roger N. Baldwin, William Z. Foster, Sidney Hillman, James Weldon Johnson, and Morris L. Ernst (*qq.v.*). The money grew, as a result of interest and investments; by 1930, about a million and a quarter dollars had been contributed to causes, about three-quarters of a million loaned out. Since principal as well as income could be disbursed, the Garland Fund was soon after exhausted. Aid was given for innumerable projects and organizations, including the A.C.L.U., the L.I.D., to aid such strikes as that in Gastonia, N.C., for I.L.G.W.U. ventures, and for the establishment of the Vanguard Press.

AMERICAN INSTITUTE OF PUBLIC OPINION, see Gallup Poll.

AMERICAN JOURNAL OF ECONOMICS AND SOCIOLOGY, THE, see George, Henry.

AMERICAN LABOR PARTY, organized in New York (1936), by independent and labor elements. It contributed to the success of the Democratic Party in New York State in that year's elections. An inter-party quarrel in 1944 resulted in a split, the moderate elements reorganizing as the Liberal Party (*q.v.*). The A.L.P. declined in significance. Its major policies included dissatisfaction with President Truman's Administration and the support of Henry A. Wallace in 1948.

AMERICAN LABOR YEAR BOOK, issued, 1916-1932, thirteen volumes, by the Labor Research Department of the Rand School of Social Science (*q.v.*). It made efforts to provide information impartially for the benefit of those concerned for labor and radical movements. It was a curious fact that it should have disappeared just when labor, under the effects of deep economic crisis, should have begun to proliferate ideas and developments, but that the *Labor Fact Book* (*q.v.*), first issued 1931 and committed to the communist view of affairs, should have enjoyed a lively career, continuing until 1953.

AMERICAN LEAGUE AGAINST WAR AND FASCISM, organized 1934, and dominated by the communists, mobilized much public opinion in favor of its program and tendencies. In 1937, its name was changed to the American League for Peace and Democracy; much of the attitude and many of the expectations whipped up by the League embarrassed the communists, in some degree, when the Nazi-Soviet Pact and the Russo-Finnish War (*qq.v.*) took place.

AMERICAN LEGION, THE, organized in 1919, became the most powerful veteran's lobby since the G.A.R. During the "Red Scare" (*q.v.*), elements of the American Legion engaged in vigilante (*q.v.*) activity. It emphasized veterans benefits and patriotic attitudes, through its spokesmen and through its publication, *The American Legion Magazine*. Its opposition to communism, and to those who cooperated with communists, whether consciously or unconsciously, was intense and undeviating. Notable among the Legion Posts was the Willard Straight Post, in New York City, which was liberal in its viewpoint. Victor Lasky, ed., *The American Legion Reader* (1953); Raymond Moley, *The American Legion Story* (1966).

AMERICAN LIBERTY LEAGUE, organized in 1934 by influential persons, including John J. Raskob, of the Democratic Party and the Du Pont organization, in order to resist what it conceived to be the radical program of the New Deal (*q.v.*). It campaigned for nineteenth century individualism and a defense of the leadership offered by such industrial combinations as Du Pont and General Motors. Its spokesmen included Alfred E. Smith (*q.v.*), among other distinguished names of the time. The League was unable to influence the humbler ranks of society, and operated largely on rarefied levels of press releases. It was disbanded in 1940. See Frederick Rudolph, "The American Liberty League, 1934-40," *American Historical Review*, October 1950.

AMERICAN MAGAZINE, revitalized in 1906 by writers and editors for *McClure's* (*q.v.*) who were dissatisfied with the amount of experiment and bold writing which was being permitted them. Lincoln Steffens, Ida M. Tarbell, Ray Stannard Baker, Finley Peter Dunne, and William Allen White (*qq.v.*) made the publication one of the best of the muckraking publications. In 1912, it was transformed by business interests into a more innocuous publication.

AMERICAN MEDICAL ASSOCIATION, the powerful group representing the interests of the practitioner. Its strength has been in its contention that it was protecting standards of competence in the field, and in the quality of medical products. Its battle against "quacks" (*q.v.*) was sincere, if only because they competed with physicians for clients. The adequacy of its standards, however, was challenged in such books as Arthur Kallet and F. J. Schlink, *100,000,000 Guinea Pigs* (1933), Oliver Garceau, *The Political Life of the American Medical Association* (1941), and James Rorty, *American Medicine Mobilizes* (1939). Reformers have principally worried over its monopolistic tendencies and its antipathy to "socialized medicine" (*q.v.*). It was sued in 1940 by Group Health Associates of Washington, D.C., on the grounds that it had interfered with their physicians's practice; the Supreme Court upheld a token fine against the A.M.A. in 1943. It is a major opponent of extended government health services.

AMERICAN MISSIONARY ASSOCIATION, formed in 1846 in protest against the policy of the powerful American Board for Foreign Missions, which was unwilling to offend its pro-slavery supporters. Several vigorous anti-slavery groups, including the Committee for the West Indian Missions, the Western Evangelical Missionary Society, and the group which had been formed to aid the defendants in the Amistad case (q.v.), united under the leadership of Lewis Tappan (q.v.) to send out missionaries to promote anti-slavery evangelical efforts. The A.M.A's greatest work was in the post-Civil War period, when it founded Berea College, Fisk University, and Hampton Institute (qq.v.), among other establishments.

AMERICAN PARTY, the name for minor political parties other than the more famous Know-Nothings (q.v.). Members of the National Christian Association organized such a party in 1872, opposing secret societies, closing of the saloons, Sabbath observance, among other measures, some less restrictive, as in their endorsement of justice for the Indian. In 1884, they merged with the Prohibition Party (q.v.). Another party organized under its name in 1887, emphasizing a limitation on immigration, exclusion from citizenship of radicals, and nationalistic tenets. See also North Americans, South Americans.

AMERICAN PEACE SOCIETY, see Peace Crusade.

AMERICAN PLAN, THE, a concept of American industry which emphasized the freedom of the entrepreneur (q.v.) to run his business without interference by organized labor. This view of business management arose in post-World War I days, and in reaction to what were deemed the excesses of labor and radicalism at home and abroad. Associated with the "American Plan" were the open shop (q.v.) and "welfare capitalism": an effort among industrialists to find alternatives to union-based demands.

AMERICAN PROTECTIVE ASSOCIATION, organized March 13, 1887, founded in Clinton, Iowa; similar to Know-Nothing Party of 1851-1856, except that any American citizen was eligible, whereas Know-Nothings accepted only native Americans. It grew rapidly to some two million members in 1896, thanks to the "new" immigration (q.v.), but with much less influence than the Know-Nothings with their 900,000 members. It did, however, in 1894, elect some twenty members to Congress. The "APA" advocated separation of church and state, had a belligerent suspicion of Catholics, and was concerned for free, non-sectarian education. It continued in existence into the twentieth century, though on a more local and sectional basis. D. L. Kinzer, An Episode in Anti-Catholicism: the APA (1964).

AMERICAN PURITY ALLIANCE, organized 1895, a federation of moral education societies which continued the work of the New York Committee for the Prevention of State Regulation of Vice, operating since 1876. It published The Philanthropist, fought "white slavery," as they designated prostitution, and interested themselves in permutations of the subject. The Alliance became the American Social Hygiene Association (q.v.) A. M. Powell, ed., National Purity Congress (1896). See also Spencer, Anna Garlin.

AMERICAN RAILWAY UNION, founded in Chicago in 1893 by Eugene V. Debs (q.v.) of the Brotherhood of Locomotive Engineers. The Union met its trial by fire in the Pullman Strike (q.v.), and then reorganized as a secret society aiming to unite all the railroad Brotherhoods: the Order of Railway Conductors, the Brotherhood of Railway Carmen, the Brotherhood of Railway Trainmen, the Brotherhood of Locomotive Firemen, the Order of Railway Telegraphers. For a chart of organizations, see Stevens, Cyclopedia of Fraternities (1907), p. 381. In 1897, the A.R.U. formally dissolved.

AMERICAN REVOLUTION, THE, was a movement in social reform which unleashed revolutionary forces and implications. Its original purpose was not to change the nature of American society, but to preserve its autonomy. England's traditional policy of "salutary neglect"—of permitting the colonies to administer their own internal affairs, of not enforcing Parliamentary acts directing and restricting colonial trade—had worked well: the colonies had almost no anti-Empire traditions; theoretically, they appreciated the virtues of mercantilism (q.v.). However, the end of the French and Indian War (1763) made it desirable for Great Britain to reorganize her establishment, after long and expensive sacrifices. Her Proclamation Line of 1763 stopped American settlement west of the Appalachian Mountains, ensuring an end to Indian quarrels and frontier massacres. Her taxation policy was intended to distribute the costs of the late war equitably. However, the Proclamation Line frustrated the poor who longed for their own land, and the rich who, by speculation, could profit from their efforts with rifle and axe. The taxing program not only threatened pocketbooks, but also a vigorous colonial career in economic growth and free enterprise. "Taxation without representation" was not an entirely accurate slogan, since members of Parliament were supposed to represent all Britishers everywhere, but Parliament's inability to soothe ruffled colonial feelings exposed differences which had grown up between Great Britain and her colonies. It is evident that all colonials had no equal stake in revolution, or even social reform. American slaves had nothing to gain by any taxation policy, white indentured servants as little. Governors and their entourages, conservative businessmen and planters might be irritated by one or another law or program, but had a stake in law and order. Thus, the revolutionary war, when it came, was, in large measure, a civil war. The colonial dissidents learned to resist official policy over a long period, using the arguments of James Otis (q.v.), learning from the philosophers of natural rights (q.v.), and organizing forces by means of the Stamp Act Congress, the voluntary Committees of Correspondence and Sons of Liberty, and, finally, the Continental Congresses (qq.v.). What all these tactics and instruments accomplished was to create a common denominator of goals which, using the great abstractions of liberty and equality promised gains to the depressed elements of the population, as well as the well-to-do. Primogeniture (inheritance by the oldest son) fell a victim to the revolutionary spirit. Land-grants were offered to the patriot soldiers. Though slavery was maintained in the south, the freeing of slaves increased, and slavery as a system was optimistically seen as on the way out. British military policy was so inept that, although slavery had been ended in Great Britain, the generals did not take advantage of their ability to embarrass the southern revolutionists by calling slaves to revolt and promising them freedom for so doing. Many slaves manifested loyalty toward their masters, and a few were granted freedom for so doing. Northern Negroes saw promise in the revolutionary slogans, and supported them with arms. Poor whites, like their social superiors, responded to mixed motives, sometimes serving with courage and persistence, as at Valley Forge (1777-8), sometimes darkening revolutionary hopes with demands for full rations and salary arrears, and threats of mutiny, such as General George Washington experienced at Morristown, N.J. (1780). Although the colonial patriots attracted Dutch, Spanish, and French aid, its purpose was malice toward Great Britain, rather than sympathy for her revolting colonists; the European nations were not hoping that their own people would be inspired with liberation sentiments. Nevertheless, some of them were, notably in the case of the Marquis de Lafayette (q.v.), and the American Revolution became the forerunner of later republican upheavals. Its first immediate fruit was the French Revolution (q.v.), offering similarities and differences to the social reformer.

AMERICAN REVOLUTION CONSIDERED AS A SOCIAL MOVEMENT, THE (1926), by J. F. Jameson, was an effort by an historian to see beneath the surface to the forces which had a stake in a revolutionary effort. For a critical analysis of this classic, Frederick B. Tolles, "The American Revolution Considered as a Social Movement: A Re-evaluation," American Historical Review, LX (October, 1954).

AMERICAN SOCIAL HYGIENE ASSOCIATION, organized 1914, an outgrowth of the American Purity Alliance (q.v.), it has sought to inform the public about the need for community action to curb prostitution and its attendant diseases, as well as to deal with the circumstances which create them and their abettors. It has emphasized sex education, the dissemination of relevant publications, and the encouragement of meetings to deal with aspects of the problem.

AMERICAN SOCIETY FOR THE PREVENTION OF CRUELTY TO ANIMALS, American Society for the Prevention of Cruelty to Children, see Bergh, Henry.

AMERICAN-SOVIET RELATIONS, see Russia, American Attitudes toward.

AMERICAN STANDARD OF LIVING, see Standard of Living.

AMERICAN STUDENT UNION, founded 1935, in a merger of the National Students League and the Student League for Industrial Democracy. It was emphatically social-minded, and subject to communist influence. It disintegrated under the pressure of selective service operations and war, in the '40's.

AMERICAN SUNDAY SCHOOL UNION as anti-reform; see Gallaudet, Thomas H.

AMERICAN SYSTEM, THE, a program conceived by Henry Clay for binding the several sections of the country into a national enterprise, in the period following the War of 1812. A protective tariff (q.v.) was to put native manufactures at an advantage with foreign competition. Roads and canals were to bring together the north and south, as well as the west, a national bank was to make the American financial structure more efficient. The raw materials from the south and west were to be equitably exchanged with the manufactured goods from the east. The program was one for prosperity, and emphasizing nationalism and individual enterprise.

AMERICAN TARIFF REFORM LEAGUE, see Free Trade.

AMERICAN TEMPERANCE SOCIETY, see Temperance.

AMERICAN VETERANS COMMITTEE, organized 1945 to act as a lobby for veterans' interests. It attracted, however, a more liberally-oriented type of veteran than did the American Legion (q.v.), as indicated by its slogan: "Citizens first, Americans second." Its organization and purposes were described in Charles G. Bolte, *The New Veteran* (1945). In 1961, its program was described by its Executive Director as being: "pro-UN, civil rights, governmental reform such as state constitutional revision, and reapportionment." The A.V.C. helped originate the World Veterans Federation, made up of non-government-sponsored veterans organizations around the world, with headquarters in Paris, France. It refuses to charter segregated local units, and opposes veterans special class legislation, as well as censorship in general. As opposed to the Veterans of Foreign Wars, who once presented their legion of Merit to Senator James Eastland of Mississippi, the A.V.C. gave an Americanism award to the nine Negro students who attended the Central High School of Little Rock, Arkansas (q.v.).

AMERICAN WARS, see Wars of the United States.

AMERICAN WOMAN SUFFRAGE ASSOCIATION, see Woman Suffrage.

AMERICAN YOUTH CONGRESS, formed in 1934 to organize the young for social action, was a lobby for youth benefits, social legislation, and anti-war agitation. Though exploited by the communists, whom it gave a forum, it attracted earnest energies, convinced that they were uniting with persons whose goals they shared, and whose means were not markedly different from their own. The Congress succumbed to the conscription policy instituted by the government in 1940. Its last significant effort was the Emergency Peace Mobilization, intended to resist the new Selective Service policy. The purposes of the A.Y.C. were described in Leslie A. Gould, *American Youth Today* (1940). See also, Youth Movement, The.

AMERICANISM, a controversial concept embodying important issues, as indicated in the very name of the House Un-American Activities Committee (q.v.). Martin Dies (q.v.) assumed Americanism meant belief in the present form of the American government, and his statement of his position showed strong partialities, couched rhetorically, thus offering little leeway for opponents of his views. Whether communism could indeed be seen as Earl Browder (q.v.) saw it: as twentieth-century Americanism was doubtful, but between Dies and Browder was the ground over which conceptions of Americanism had to be fought. "Americanism" also referred to language nuances, which disturbed some foreigners, but were accorded respect by others; see H. L. Mencken, *The American Language* (1919 ff.). See also Anti-American Feeling, Patriotism.

AMERICANIZATION MOVEMENT, a product of the entrance of the United States into World War I, and its fear that some immigrant elements might be inadequately apprized of "American" ideals. In effect, it was an adult education movement (q.v.). Its intention was to turn foreigners into "Americans"; the problem lay in determining what an American was. An idealistic immigrant like Mary Antin (*The Promised Land* [1912]) saw it as freedom and opportunity. Americanization classes tended to emphasize the Anglo-Saxon heritage at the expense of other traditions. The effort of Louis Adamic (q.v.) to formulate a multiple approach did not attract an equal amount of civic support.

AMERICANS FOR DEMOCRATIC ACTION, organized in 1947, in Washington; it has attracted the interest and leadership of such liberals as Leon Henderson, former administrator of the Office of Price Administration, Hubert H. Humphrey, Emil Rieve, president of the C.I.O. Textile Workers, and others. The A.D.A. supported Adlai Stevenson for president in the 1952 elections. It continued to act as a left-wing educational force. In 1957, it was belittled by the Governor of Massachusetts, Furcolo, whom it had invited to address its sessions, and who advised them to disband as no longer serving a significant purpose. However, the victory of John F. Kennedy (q.v.) in 1960 brought into his administration a number of A.D.A. leaders. Clifton Brock, *Americans for Democratic Action* (1962).

AMISTAD CASE (1839), involved a ship-load of Negro slaves, in a Spanish vessel, who mutinied, but, in attempting to return to Africa, found themselves in United States waters. The Democratic Administration made efforts to have them returned to captivity, but abolitionists publicized the case, roused general interest in the fate of the defendants, and provided legal counsel which ultimately secured their release.

AMNESTY, an effort to heal the wounds of internecine struggle; the major American effort involved removing disabilities against those who had supported the Confederacy; both President Lincoln and President Johnson issued proclamations to that effect. The Fourteenth Amendment to the Constitution (q.v.) deprived certain persons of the right to hold public office, but Congress was granted the right, by two-thirds vote, to remove such disabilities. Amnesty was an issue resulting from large evasions of conscription during the Vietnam war (q.v.). *Amnesty Action* was begun in 1966. *Amnesty Trumpet* was intended to win amnesty for Smith Act (q.v.) violators. Amnesty International was alert to a wide range of world civil rights violations; see its *Report on Torture* (1975). The 1980 draft (q.v.) registration promised further activity for those concerned. See Egon Larsen, *A Flame in Barbed Wire, the Story of Amnesty International* (1979).

ANARCHIAD, THE (1786-7), a satirical poem directed at what were deemed to be the disruptive values in French libertarian thought, and in defense of American values. It was essentially a conservative writing, as produced by the "Connecticut Wits" (q.v.), including Timothy Dwight, John Trumbull, and Joel Barlow (q.v.), among others. The vigor of their argument typified conservatism as an active force; see the poem with introduction and index by W. K. Bottorff (1967).

ANARCHISM, the principle of industrial liberty as supreme and superior to the value of the state. Anarchism can be "philosophical" or dependent on the "deed." The philosophical anarchist can be of any class or station. Thoreau was a philosophical anarchist; John D. Rockefeller was accused of being an anarchist; that is, of placing his individual views and will above those of society. The anarchist of the deed, on the other hand, has tended to be of the lower classes, sympathetic to the needs of oppressed and needy minorities. He has produced the bomb-throwers, the individual protestants, of the species of Alexander Berkman. Although the impulse of anarchism survives, even among such groups as the "beatniks" (*q.v.*), it has produced no such notables as the nineteenth century offered, in the form of Bakunin, Prince Kropotkin, and Emma Goldman (*qq.v.*). Anarchism and Socialism (*q.v.*) have met at points of idealism, the anarchist resenting private property as a suppression of individual rights, the socialist denouncing it as an infringement on social rights. See also Radicals, Terrorism.

ANCIEN RÉGIME, in French, the Old Regime, before the French Revolution, identified in the minds of reformers and revolutionists with the irresponsibility of the ruling class, its indifference to popular opinion and social need, its arrogant absorption in pleasures and intrigue; compare, Bourbon Democrat.

ANDERSON, JACK (1922-   ), an associate of Drew Pearson (*q.v.*), he succeeded him as a muckraker (*q.v.*) of contemporary corruption in high places. Despite numerous sensational revelations, his impact was limited, for lack of a philosophic base; see his *Confessions of a Muckraker* (1979).

ANDREWS, STEPHEN PEARL (1812-1886), a New Englander who moved to Texas; he became an outstanding lawyer, and made impressive efforts to persuade the state to abandon slavery. In 1844, he went to England where he tried to acquire a government loan which would permit the compensated emancipation (*q.v.*) of the Texas slaves. In 1847 he moved to New York, interested himself successfully in shorthand, and also advocated spelling reform. He developed complex theories involving social organization and sex harmony, which give him status as a pioneer sociologist. Although his "Panarchy" hypotheses have not been influential, they merit understanding. An outstanding linguist, he was master of thirty-two languages, and invented Alivato, a pioneer effort at a universal language. See M. B. Stern, *The Pantarch* (1968).

ANGLO-AMERICAN RELATIONS have long influenced American reform. Romantic democratic ideas and attitudes influenced the thinking and works of Charles Brockden Brown, Philip Freneau and other early writers. British and American anti-slavery workers learned from one another, and British Emancipation in the West Indies, in 1833, spurred abolitionist efforts in America. The humanitarian labors of Shaftesbury (*q.v.*) echoed among Americans disturbed by the negative features of the rising factory system. Chartists (*q.v.*) not only worked significantly in England, but not a few came to America to agitate in behalf of labor and land reform. Free trade (*q.v.*) was an important issue in both lands, though complicated by the fact that anti-reform Southerners favored free trade, and a reformer like Horace Greeley (*q.v.*) favored protection. Not a few later reformers, especially those from the midwest like Charles Edward Russell (*q.v.*), identified Great Britain with aristocracy, and scorned both. James Bryce (*q.v.*) was a genteel reformer at home with American genteel reformers, but rank and file Americans were inclined to recall the American Revolution, and to approve President Cleveland's stand on Venezuela (*q.v.*). England's patience in this crisis paid her off, in the long run, with the United States' decision to join the Allies during World War I (*q.v.*). American "isolationism" of the 1920's affected Anglo-American relations, though H. G. Wells (*q.v.*) was at home on both sides of the water; "isolationism" (*q.v.*) largely continued on the governmental level during the 1930's. However, the increasing power of the Labour Party influenced American reformist thought, as did its nationalization program after World War II. The later battle in Britain against inflation, low productivity, and diminished status among nations took similar form in America.

ANNE FRANK, a Dutch-Jewish schoolgirl, whose family hid in an Amsterdam house for over two years, seeking to avoid being seized by the Nazis who controlled the city. They were finally detected; Anne died in the concentration camp of Belsen. Her *Diary of a Young Girl*, first published in Holland in 1947, quickly achieved universal translation, and was hailed as a classic statement of the tragedy which afflicted Europe, the Jews, and her own appealing personality. Its fame was aided by stage and screen triumphs. However, it was claimed by Meyer Levin (*q.v.*) that his truer version of the intention of the diary had been withheld from the stage, in order to dampen the Jewish component in the tale, in the version which was accepted. See *Tales from the House Behind* (1962).

ANTHONY, SUSAN B. (1820-1906), militant woman suffrage leader and symbol, and associate of Elizabeth Cady Stanton (*q.v.*). She began her career as a school teacher, temperance advocate and anti-slavery speaker, during the 1850's, but increasingly emphasized women's right to vote. In 1869, she was one of the organizers of the National Woman Suffrage Association (see Woman Suffrage). In 1872, she defied state statutes by attempting to vote, and in a test case was able to speak memorably for her sympathizers. She was president of the National American Suffrage Association (1892-1900), representing a reunited movement. Female "activists" of the 1970s exploited her name; see Rheta Childe Dorr, *Susan B. Anthony* (1928).

ANTHRACITE COAL STRIKE (1902), a landmark in the growth and organization of the United Mine Workers of America (*q.v.*). Headed by John Mitchell (*q.v.*), it appealed successfully for public sympathy. It called forth the immortal remark from the leader of the coal operators, George F. Baer that "the rights and interests of the laboring man will be protected and cared for, not by the labor agitators, but by the Christian men to whom God in His infinite wisdom, has given control of the property interests of the country." President Theodore Roosevelt labored to mediate the conflict. The miners won a ten-percent increase in pay but no union recognition.

ANTI-AMERICAN FEELING has varied in purpose and expression, at home and abroad. Wealthy Americans who "married titles" (as satirized in David Graham Phillips' *The Golden Fleece* [1903]), were anti-democratic as well as anti-American in feeling. Ezra Pound's (*q.v.*) anti-Americanism had its source in bitterness and frustration. There was some anti-Americanism, or, at least, indifference to the American equation, among some immigrant groups: those Irish who were sufficiently dedicated to an independent Ireland to attempt to capture Canada, and hold it as hostage (1866, 1870); Germans in Minnesota and elsewhere whose patriotism suffered as a result of being mistreated by vigilante groups; and others. The expatriates (*q.v.*) of the 1920's were not so much anti-American, as cosmopolitan in feeling. Those who accepted Marx's view that patriotism was a snare leaned backward to establish their internationalism, but often found it expedient to avow their ardent love of America, and to exploit its flag as belonging more truly to them than to those they deemed harmful to its best interests. Probably as many foreigners have "liked" the Americans they have met, as being good-humored, generous, and fun, as have disliked them for being arrogant, over-familiar, and oblivious to local mores. The most significant anti-American feeling has been political. It has been possible to portray American democracy as a fraud, American policy-makers as a combination of fools and knaves, where it has served political purposes to do so. The American tradition of reform is little appreciated abroad; such figures as Thoreau, Bellamy, George, Debs, and Upton Sinclair (*qq.v.*) are known as individuals, if at all, rather than as representative Americans. Luigi Barzini, *Americans Are Alone in the World* (1953) was one of many such works, well received in America. The youth (*q.v.*) revolt of the 1960s and Seventies unleashed a torrent of anti-Americanism, as did the "hostages" crisis in Iran in 1979 and after. Former U.S. Attorney General Ramsey Clark abased himself before the Iranians, expressing unofficial shame and guilt for "his" country, and was approved by former U.S. ambassador to the United Nations Andrew Young. There were no conspicuous counter-expressions of patriotism (*q.v.*).

ANTI-CAPITAL PUNISHMENT CRUSADE, an American reform since the establishment of the new nation. Colonial America had had relatively few capital offenses, mainly because of the scarcity of labor; in England more than two hundred offenses could result in the death penalty, people there being less valuable than social order. The American Revolution opened the way for generous, humanitarian sentiments, and in subsequent years, contributions to the anti-capital punishment argument (or to related arguments calling for more effective laws and prisons) were made by Benjamin Rush (q.v.), William Bradford, and Edward Livingston, among others. During the era of reform (1830-60), anti-capital punishment advocates became numerous and articulate; notable reformers in the field included Robert Rantoul, Jr., and Rev. Charles Spear (qq.v.). Moreover, anti-gallows societies were set up, notably in New York and Massachusetts, but also in Pennsylvania and other states, and Michigan, Rhode Island, and Wisconsin abolished the death penalty. The outstanding reformer of the era in the field was Marvin H. Bovee (q.v.). In the post-Civil War era (the cause suffered a major set-back during hostilities), prison reform went hand in hand with the agitation favoring an end to the death penalty, and was aided by objective evidence, presented by competent observers, that it was an inadequate deterrent to crime. Alfred H. Love, of the Pennsylvania Prison Society, was a pacifist, as well as an energetic opponent of the death penalty. During the reform movement of the pre-World War I era, capital punishment was deplored, most effectively by Brand Whitlock (q.v.), who also contributed a novel, The Turn of the Balance (1907) to the argument. In the 1910's, it appeared that anti-capital punishment might sweep the land; American entrance into World War I put an abrupt stop to promising conditions. The Loeb-Leopold case (1924) revitalized interest in the subject. Its popularity rose and fell with such factors as fear of violent crime and radical suspicion of the law. The Chessman case (q.v.) roused major public excitement about capital punishment, as did, later, Gary Gilmore who, in opposition to those who pled for his life, asked and received execution; see Norman Mailer, The Executioner's Song (1979), T. Sellin, ed., Capital Punishment (1967).

ANTI-CATHOLICISM was always a factor in a nation built largely by dissidents: Anglican in Virginia, Congregationalist in Massachusetts, Quaker in Pennsylvania, Dutch Reform in New York, among other elements and persuasions. Maryland was founded by Catholics, and an effort to avoid distressing clashes permitted the passage of its Toleration Act of 1649 (q.v.). Nevertheless, Catholics continued in low esteem among the majority groups in the colonies and, in time, the new nation. The influx of Catholic Irish in the pre-Civil War period brought nativism to the fore, and created the Know-Nothing movement (qq.v.). After the Civil War, the coming of the Italians, the Poles, and other Catholic people, resulted in the phenomenal growth of the American Protective Association (q.v.). Anti-Catholic feeling continued to live, particularly in the rural areas. It contributed to the drastic defeat of Alfred E. Smith, in the Presidential campaign of 1928. Social reformers found little in common with the Catholic Church, though it produced its quota of reformers (see Catholic Church and Reform). Blanshard, in American Freedom and Catholic Power (1949) denounced what he saw as its authoritarian and anti-reform features, as did the latter-day Independent. The victory of John F. Kennedy, in the Presidential campaign of 1960, resulted not so much from a routing of anti-Catholic opinion, as from its failure to dominate other domestic and foreign issues.

"ANTI-CHAIN STORE ACT," see Robinson-Patman Act (1936).

ANTI-CIGARET LEAGUE, incorporated in 1901 and active in the early part of the century. It introduced bills in state legislatures, and maintained contact with the International Anti-Cigaret League, founded in London. See also Anti-Tobacco Crusade.

ANTI-COMMUNISM, in modern times, was a continuation of the fears and revulsion occasioned by the Paris Commune (q.v.). Those dedicated to the concepts of free enterprise and democracy denounced the "proletarian dictatorship" set up by the Bolsheviks in the course of the Russian Revolution of 1917 (q.v.) as the inevitable result of socialist principles. Moderate socialists, however, of the stamp of John Spargo (q.v.) denounced it as a perversion of socialist principles. During the 1920's, there was considerable popular and official prejudice against the communists in the United States. A typical work exploiting this feeling was R. M. Whitney, Reds in America, the Present Status of the Revolutionary Movement . . . together with Descriptions of Numerous Connections and Associations of the Communists among the Radicals, Progressives and Pinks (1924). During the 1930's, because of the depression and such second thoughts as the Sacco-Vanzetti case (q.v.) had inspired, communism was less unfashionable. Nevertheless, it continued to attract determined enemies, including Elizabeth Dilling and Martin Dies (qq.v.), as well as the numerous political and quasi-political types described in John Roy Carlson's Under Cover (1943). The U.S.-U.S.S.R. military alliance during World War II made anti-communism less popular, and native communists and their allies could assert their true Americanism with less contradiction. However, the break-up of the Grand Alliance, the continued activities of the Un-American Activities Committee (q.v.), the revelations and implications of efforts which could be accounted treasonable, gave new strength to anti-communist voices; the "McCarthy era" (q.v.) was the high point of such expression. Detente (q.v.) made obsolete the old anti-communism, and forced discrimination between actions, like treason (q.v.) which threatened national security, and others which did not.

ANTI-CORN LAWS, see Corn Laws.

ANTI-CRUELTY, see Bergh, Henry.

ANTI-DUELING, a reform which did not enlist crusaders and create a movement in the fashion of most reforms. Duels in colonial times and after were conceived of as a function of society, to be administered according to a "code," and to comport with standards of individual honor and decency. Since persons of no marked honor and sensibility often found duels advantageous, and since they resulted in such tragedies as the death of Alexander Hamilton, in 1804, responsible leaders like George Washington derogated them. Laws were passed opposing them, after the American Revolution, and, for the most part, they were honored, especially in the North. In 1838 Congress prohibited challenges in the District of Columbia. Dueling persisted in the cowboy West.

ANTI-EXPANSIONISTS, see Anti-Imperialism.

ANTI-HERO, a phenomenon of the 1970s. Disillusionment created scorn or indifference to heroes, of whom George Washington was a symbol, and also of heroes of the anti-slavery and Progressive struggles (qq.v.). Honored, instead, were such persons as Jerry Rubin and Abbie Hoffman, of the youth (q.v.) eruption of the time. See Debunking; also E. Z. Friedenberg, The Anti-American Generation (1971).

ANTI-FASCISM, see Fascism and Reform.

ANTI-IMPERIALISM has been tied in with the question of expansionism and "Manifest Destiny" (q.v.). Were the English in America, and the Americans after the Revolution, imperialistic in their relations with the Indians, or simply expanding upon terrain to which the Indians could scarcely claim title? Was the government policy toward the Cherokee Indians (q.v.) imperialistic, or did it recognize the facts of nature? Were Mexican-United States relations (q.v.), culminating in the Mexican War. imperialistic, or a function of expansionism?

Protests against government policy were posed not so much in anti-imperialistic terms, as in anti-war, pro-Indian terms. The Anti-Imperialist League, organized 1898, was in protest against the Spanish-American War (q.v.) and its results. It attracted such scions of gentility (q.v.) as Moorfield Storey (q.v), as well as anti-war partisans and humanitarians. Socialists, too, were anti-imperialistic in principle, as were isolationists (q.v.). These elements continued to represent anti-imperialism until the growth of nationalism in the under-developed countries (q.v.)

and the duel for their support between the U.S. and the U.S.S.R. made official imperialism disreputable. E. B. Tompkins, *Anti-imperialism in the United States: the Great Debate 1890-1920* (1970). See also Imperialism.

ANTI-LABOR LEGISLATION has always found its justification in the defense of freedom and the rights of property. In pre-Civil War decades combinations of workers and artisans, especially when employing the strike to persuade employers to raise wages and improve labor conditions, were held to be in conspiracy and liable to penalties. A milestone was the ruling by Chief Justice Lemuel Shaw of the Massachusetts Supreme Court, in *Commonwealth v. Hunt* (1842), that unions were legal instruments and strikes within the law. Nevertheless, aspects of legality would be contested over the years. Thus, during the Railroad Riots of 1877 (*q.v.*), it was made illegal in several states for engineers to take their trains out in the open fields, and there abandon them. The Sherman Anti-trust Act (*q.v.*) was supposedly directed at businesses acting illegally; it was interpreted as a weapon against the Pullman Strike (*q.v.*). "Yellow dog" contracts (*q.v.*) were held legal in the case of Adair v. U.S. (1908). The increasing power of labor unions, especially as a result of C.I.O. organization during the 1930's and the need for labor during World War II raised some question as to whether laws curbing labor unions were the same as laws curbing labor; passage of the Taft-Hartley Act (1947) (*q.v.*) brought this issue to a head. Development of "Right to work" laws (*q.v.*) was interpreted by liberals and reformers as an anti-labor movement. However, dramatic exposes of labor racketeering suggested the need for curbing irresponsible labor bosses, as a reform measure.

ANTI-LYNCHING BILLS, see Lynch Law.

ANTI-MASONRY, arose in the 1830's in protest against the secret methods and organization of the fraternal order of Freemasons. Although many conservatives, including George Washington, had been Masons, anti-masonry attracted conservatives antagonistic to the Jacksonians. It resulted in the first major third party (*q.v.*), the Anti-Masonic Party, which nominated for President in 1832 the Maryland lawyer William Wirt. Anti-masonry offered a stepping-stone into politics to such anti-slavery notables as John Quincy Adams, Thaddeus Stevens (*qq.v.*), and William Slade, of Vermont. Although denounced as secret and subversive of a free society, Masonry did offer opportunity for sociability and togetherness; see the pro-Mason John C. Palmer, *The Morgan Affair and Anti-Masonry* (1924), and William A. Muraskin, *Middle-class Blacks in a White Society: Prince Hall Freemasonry in America* (1975).

ANTI-MILITARISM was a facet of the anti-war movement, concentrating on the uselessness of a military establishment, being critical of the type of person it attracted and molded, its cost, its incentive to war, the false ideals it allegedly sustained; see George R. Kirkpatrick, *War—What For?* (1910). The voluntary nature of American enlistment, and the meager establishment maintained between wars, made it difficult to denounce its cost persuasively or to create effective symbols of defiance. Thoreau's symbolic refusal to pay a poll-tax in protest against the prosecution of the Mexican War is more famous in literary annals than historical events. Conscription (*q.v.*) during World War I and World War II produced its quota of dissidents. However, the emphasis became less upon the military than upon the government which directed them. Socialists who detested "capitalist warmongers" were often sympathetic to the Red Army of the U.S.S.R. defending the "Workers' Fatherland." The possibilities unleashed by the atom bomb (*q.v.*) turned thoughts away from the military to peace, "a moral equivalent for war," Moral Re-armament (*q.v.*), "high echelon" meetings, and other formulations. See also Peace Crusade,The.

ANTI-MONOPOLY, a cause based on concern for individual rights and social democracy. Monopolies were, under the colonial system, administered by the Crown; following the American Revolution, they continued to be granted by state and federal governments. The Jacksonian Revolution was, in part, a protest against a system of special favors to the established elite. In post-Civil War decades, private businesses, under such ambitious and powerful leaders as John D. Rockefeller, Sr., Andrew Carnegie, J. P. Morgan, among others, used secret agreements, the bribery of politicians, and even brute force to crush competitors, prevent laborers from organizing, and otherwise move toward the real mastery of the country. They and their organizations were resisted by combinations of smaller business people, in legal actions, in political action symbolized by the Populist Party (*q.v.*), and by such reform writers as Henry Demarest Lloyd (*q.v.*). Their problem was that Americans desired the results of mass production. Hence, it became utopian to attempt to end the trust; the proper goal was to control it. Instruments of control were the Interstate Commerce Commission, the Sherman Anti-Trust Act, and the Clayton Act, as well as the Federal Trade Commission (*qq.v.*), and other agencies. But the "little man" found it difficult to use them. Labor did not fight monopolies vigorously; it sought a monopoly of its own. With Big Business and Big Labor established, the hope of reformers lay in the "regulatory agencies": The Federal Communications Commission, the Federal Power Commission and others, as well as the Anti-Trust Division of the Department of Justice.

ANTI-MONOPOLY PARTY, THE, organized in 1884 and nominating Benjamin F. Butler (*q.v.*) for the Presidency, was notable for its name, which underscored growing public fears of developing trusts, and its program, including demands for a graduated income tax, the direct election of Senators, and the regulation of monopolies, which would reappear in the Populist Platform (*qq.v.*).

ANTI-NUKE, slogan of protesters against nuclear installations, in the United States and elsewhere. They feared accidents of leakage or explosion which might destroy or cripple local populations, and harm fetuses. They feared also that nuclear plant development could contribute to the threat of nuclear war. All such protests originated in countries not dominated by communists. See Nuclear Question, The.

ANTI-POVERTY PROGRAM, one of the efforts by Lyndon B. Johnson (*q.v.*) to out-New Deal the New Deal (*q.v.*) by settling all social problems through grants of money. The largesse failed to create the army of dedicated workers the program required, and accomplished little more than an augmented bureaucracy, and an increase in official corruption (*qq.v.*) and demands for more; see Robinson O. Everett, ed., *Anti-Poverty Programs* (1966).

ANTI-REFORM, see Reform.

ANTI-RENT WAR, THE, culminated decades of resistance by up-state New York tenants to the rule of the patroons (*q.v.*), who would not permit them to purchase their lands but insisted upon their perpetual lease and rent system. Thus, the tenants had the basic characteristics of farmers (*q.v.*): though extreme individualists, concerned for private profit, they were driven by need to cooperation and apparently "radical" solutions. When, in 1839, the patroons made efforts to enforce rent collections and evictions, the tenants united, and, using horns and disguises, prevented law enforcement officers from doing their duty. Blood was shed, martial law was invoked, and the strength of the farmers at the polls resulted in a new state constitution on 1846. See Henry M. Christman, *Tin Horns and Calico* (1945).

ANTI-SALOON LEAGUE, the most effective single agency in organizing forces which brought on the Volstead Amendment (*q.v.*). It first organized in Ohio, in 1893; the next year it became the Anti-Saloon League of America. Well organized, and practical in its approach to politics and publicity, it worked to curb the freedom of saloons, secured local option prohibition, agitated for state controls and state prohibition, and so built the national organization which carried its cause to national victory. It sought to secure its triumph by rooting it in an international crusade, and made common cause with other national movements in a World League against Alcoholism. Its success in this area was much less marked, and the Anti-Saloon League itself went into marked decline. For an authoritative statement of purposes and activities at its height, see "Anti-Saloon League," in E. H. Cherrington, ed., *Standard Encyclopedia of the Alcohol Problem* (1925), I, 175 ff.

ANTI-SEMITISM, a recurrent phenomenon, arising from religious or ethnic impulses, stirred by social or economic imbalances. It was relatively insignificant before the Civil War, because of the fewness of the Jewish people. A small number of clergymen concerned themselves for the conversion of the Jews, with little success. There was a clear thread of anti-semitism among Populists (*q.v.*), who laid their troubles to "Wall Street," and equated this, with little reason, with Jews. However, such anti-semitic impulses, though emotional, had little force nor program. The muckrakers, though a projection of Populism, were actively in favor of the Jews, as seen in writings by Lincoln Steffens, Hutchins Hapgood, David Graham Phillips, and others. The Russian-Jewish immigration of the 1890's and after, fleeing the pogroms (*q.v.*), brought a notable intelligentsia which influenced reform and aggravated antireformers. Leo Frank (*q.v.*) was a victim of anti-Jewish feeling. The Dearborn *Independent* (*q.v.*) featured anti-semitism, in the 1920's, as did the Ku Klux Klan (*q.v.*). Fascist movements of the 1930's made much of "Jewish plots" against the country's well-being, and sought to emulate fascism abroad. The war against fascism forced anti-semitism into the shadows, where it could take the form of discrimination (*q.v.*). Antisemitism persisted in the Soviet Union, despite its lipservice to brotherhood, and could be traced in official persecutions. A complex anti-semitism found in Arab countries, themselves semitic, summed up to antagonism toward Jews. See L. J. Levinger, *Anti-Semitism in the United States* (1972), and Paul Lendvai, *Anti-Semitism without Jews: Communist Eastern Europe* (1971).

ANTI-SLAVERY, see Abolitionism, Slavery.

ANTI-SUFFRAGE has persuaded a relatively few men and women to convene, during crises of suffrage agitation, in order to present the arguments in opposition to the suffrage, almost entirely with respect to votes for women. For the most part, however, those concerned for a restricted suffrage found it more profitable to sustain the *status quo*, than to engage prosuffragists in debate. See *Anti-Suffrage Essays*, by Massachusetts Women; with an introduction by Ernest Bernbaum (1916).

ANTI-TOBACCO CRUSADE, a minor but earnest evangel during the Era of Reform (1830 ff.). It continued to stir reformers who condemned the use of tobacco on many grounds: extravagance, the spitting induced, in particular by chewing tobacco, the stains to mouth, teeth, fingers, the odors resulting, the tension and other threats to health resulting. A useful summary of arguments was contained in Meta Lander (pseudonym for Margaret Woods Lawrence) *The Tobacco Problem* (1886), endorsed by the New York physician, Dr. Willard Parker. The book strove for objectivity, noting the use of tobacco in destroying vermin, among other benefits. However, such a work as James M. Barrie's *My Lady Nicotine* (1890) suggested that tobacco had other properties which would continue to make it sought. The possibility that cigarettes might be cancer-inducing, as raised in the 1950's, threw a different light on the situation. Despite the fact that the possibility was supported by laboratory tests on the highest medical levels, the use of cigarettes *increased*. Thus, the question of the nature of reform, and its relationship to the public will be raised. Temperance reformers have generally also opposed the use of tobacco.

ANTI-TRUST LAWS, see Monopoly, Anti-Monopoly.

ANTI-UTOPIA, see Utopia.

ANTI-VACCINATION, see Vaccination.

ANTI-VIVISECTION, see Vivisection.

ANTI-WAR LITERATURE has often been obscurely defined because of the will of reformers to read their intentions into creative writings. Thus, it is not clear that Ambrose Bierce's *Tales of Soldiers and Civilians* (1891) and Stephen Crane's *The Red Badge of Courage* (1895), though works of genius, oppose war. John Dos Passos's *Three Soldiers* (1921) carries an anti-war message, but Ernest Hemingway's *A Farewell to Arms* (1929) does not. Humphrey Cobb's *Paths of Glory* (1935) was one of the best American novels dealing with World War I, and a bitter footnote to it, but the most successful play and motion-picture on the theme, Maxwell Anderson and Laurence Stalling's *What Price Glory?* (1924) clearly saw it as more fun than folly. Norman Mailer's *The Naked and the Dead* (1948) sought to disrobe war of glamor, but whether its great popular audience were able to distinguish it from James Jones's thoughtless *From Here to Eternity* (1951) may be doubted.

ANTI-WAR ORGANIZATIONS have been of two types: which appealed for peace on principle and in theory solicited aid from all elements of society, and those which identified particular enemies of peace and sought to organize against them. The Carnegie Peace Foundation illustrates the first type; it sought to act as a mediating and educational force. The League to Enforce Peace, on the other hand, as established in 1915, contained within its tenets possibilities making for war; in effect, it helped to create a preparedness psychology, leading to American participation in World War I. The Socialist Party was actively anti-war; such a publication by one of its members as *War—What For?*, by George R. Kirkpatrick (1910) identified war with ignorance, industrial cupidity, callous leaders, and was a storehouse of anti-war arguments. The failure of the giant peace petitions, pacifist organizations, and socialist parties to prevent the war made such works largely obsolete. Revolutionists opposed capitalist wars but felt confident that wars would be necessary to end them. The League against War and Fascism, in the 1930's, crystallized their approach. The Society of Friends has sought to be a reasoning force among belligerents. The great danger posed by atomic weapons has, however, focussed attention on the United Nations and major government negotiations, at the expense of rank-and-file movements and pacifist groups. Warren F. Kuehl, *Seeking World Order: the United States and International Organization to 1920* (1969). See also Peace.

ANTIOCH COLLEGE, founded 1853 by the Christian Church, in Yellow Springs, Ohio, with Horace Mann (*q.v.*) as president. It was co-educational, anti-slavery, and concerned for educational principles which could demonstrate vitality. Mann's death in 1859, the Civil War, and post-war quarrels reduced the college in size and consequence. It was revived by Arthur E. Morgan (*q.v.*) during the 1920's, and emphasized educational experiments, a relationship between work and study, and student-faculty responsibility for college aims and operations. In the 1960s and 1970s changing times and issues separated the school from the Mann and Morgan traditions. Louis Filler, ed., *Horace Mann on the Crisis in Education* (1965).

A.P.A., see American Protective Association.

APARTHEID, see Negro, Abroad.

APPEAL TO REASON, THE, outstanding socialist publication begun in 1895 by Julius A. Wayland, and read not only by dedicated socialists but by numerous other discontented Americans who appreciated its salty appeal to folk wisdom, irony, realistic commentary on current affairs. Its most famous issue was the four-million copy "Rescue Edition" of April 28, 1906, in defense of William D. Haywood (*q.v.*) and others charged with the death of former governor of Idaho Frank Steunenberg. The *Appeal* later became the *American Freeman*, the *New Appeal*, and, finally, *Haldeman-Julius Weekly*.

APPEASEMENT POLICY, identified with the efforts of the democracies to avoid a war with Hitler Germany. The height of this policy, which included toleration of its destruction of democracy at home, its racial war against the Jews, its terrorization of anti-Nazi elements in the Saar, its Anschluss (union) with Austria, reached its climax in its demand that part of Czechoslovakia be "returned" to Germany as rightfully hers (the Sudetan area). Neville Chamberlain, Prime Minister of Great Britain, flew to Germany to negotiate the crisis. This was followed by the Munich Conference (September 29, 1938), attended by Chamberlain and the French Premier, Edouard Daladier, at which, in effect, Czechoslovakia was dismembered. Chamberlain returned, bearing his umbrella, which became a symbol of appeasement. He stated that he believed he had won "peace in our time"; an opinion which soon returned to mock him. See Alfred L. Rowse, *Appeasement: a Study in Political Decline* (1961); Ritchie Overdale, *Appeasement and the English-Speaking World* (1975); W. L. Kleine-Ahlbrandt, *Appeasement of the Dictators: Crisis Diplomacy?* (1970).

APPRENTICESHIP SYSTEM, see Indentured Servitude.

ARABS IN THE CHANGING WORLD confused by their dual problems of developing relations between themselves and the great powers, and by their need for internal reform. In the post-World War II era, the Arab nations were faced with two significant facts: the creation of the State of Israel *(q.v.)* in 1948, and the mounting competition between the two worlds headed by the United States and the U.S.S.R. Arabian oil was a major goal for both, but with old-style imperialism outmoded, new means for attaining Arabian cooperation became necessary. Although the Arab states, headed by Egypt, preached democracy and their people's needs, they continued to function in the interests of small parties of social and religious castes, which found it convenient to appeal demagogically to the passions of the ignorant and frustrated masses. Thus, the Anti-Slavery and Aborigines Protection Society and the United Nations were constrained to note the rise of slavery in the Arabian world, with oil-rich Saudi Arabia as a center, at a time when Arabian leaders demanded increased freedoms and aid, pitted communist strategists against democratic strategists, and sought to drive the Israelis into the sea. Their drastic 1973 raising of the price of oil, creation of OPEC *(q.v.)*, and mounting demands on western society created a financial and cultural crisis. The PLO *(q.v.)* grew in status from a terrorist gang to a force demanding international respect. Iran *(q.v.)*, Persian rather than Arabic, but part of the Mideast complex, presented as much danger to itself as threat to others. Arab wealth made it a force in western society. Arab influence was seen in Saudi Arabia's attempt to stop the showing of a film depicting the beheading of a Saudi princess for illicit sex with a commoner. Saudi Arabia sheltered the infamous Idi Amin *(q.v.)*. A bright spot in the Mideast was Anwar Sadat *(q.v.)* of Egypt, who determined upon peace and broke all rules to open dialogue with Israel. H. Hopkins, *Egypt the Crucible* (1969); J. Waterbury, *Egypt, Burdens of the Past, Options for the Future* (1978); R. W. Baker, *Egypt's Uncertain Revolution* (1978); C. E. Dawn, *From Ottomanism to Arabism: Essays on the Origins of Arab Nationalism* (1973).

ARBITRATION of labor-industry differences have been of two types: *voluntary and compulsory*. Both have involved the use of a third party; arbitration is distinguished from *conciliation*, which takes place solely between employed and employers, striving to reach an agreement by means of discussion and concessions. Samuel Gompers *(q.v.)* feared compulsory arbitration as a threat to union power, and opposed the Erdman Arbitration Bill of 1896, in Congress, which would have provided for compulsory arbitration of disputes respecting railroads and ships in interstate and foreign commerce, and imprisonment for those not abiding by the decision. The American Arbitration Association became a major organization for voluntary arbitration proceedings. The National Mediation Board in 1934 superseded an older United States Board of Mediation dealing with railroad problems. The Federal Mediation and Conciliation Service, created in 1947, though possessing no law enforcement authority, became influential, utilizing persuasive techniques. The fact that the country could ill-afford work-stoppages in its cold-war competitions with the U.S.S.R. gave incentives to Administrations and to their Secretaries of Labor to keep work-stoppages at a minimum. See also NLRB. W. E. Baer, *Strikes* (1975); D. L. Cole, *The Quest for Industrial Peace* (1978); F. and E. A. Elkouri, *How Arbitration Works* (1973); J. J. Lowenberg et al., *Compulsory Arbitration* (1976).

ARBITRATION, PERMANENT COURT OF INTERNATIONAL, established by the First Hague Conference (1898), for the voluntary settlement of disputes between nations. The United States cooperated in the creation of the Court, but maintained reservations about questions involving national honor and the Monroe Doctrine *(q.v.)*. Secretary of State Elihu Root *(q.v.)* in 1908-9 negotiated 25 arbitrary treaties which stipulated use of the Court as the mediating agency, but the qualifying phrases respecting national honor and interests confined them to minimum significance.

ARCHANGEL EXPEDITION (1918-1919) involved some 5,000 American troops sent to the Arctic port cities of Archangel and Murmansk, during the Bolshevik Revolution *(q.v.)*. Americans sympathetic with its aims, and fearful that allied cooperation with Russian counter-revolutionary forces might lead to the overthrow of the Bolshevik regime, resented United States cooperation with the Allied forces and the White Russians. Although American policy was antipathetic to the Bolsheviks, and hoped for its collapse, it did not commit itself to an all-out anti-Bolshevik offensive. The presence of the troops was, at least in part, intended to forestall a possible movement of Japanese forces into Siberia. Nevertheless, Americans engaged in battle with revolutionary detachments, and some five hundred Americans were killed or wounded. See E. M. Halliday, *The Ignorant Armies* (1960).

ARGENTINA, a leading nation in South America, and, like the others, seeking to cope with mighty problems of poverty and potential dictatorship. The long rule of Juan Perón (1946-56) pointed up the dangers to democratic hopes in Argentina; his fall did not dispel them. The national appeal continued to be to democratic goals, as shown by the party names: Radical Intransigents, Peoples Radicals, Party of Work and Progress, and Democratic Progressive Party. However, the strength of the outlawed communists was indeterminate, and the strength of the outlawed Peronistas continued admittedly great. The world-wide rise in terrorism *(q.v.)* affected Argentina acutely, and desperate forays between right-wing and left-wing guerrillas resulted in the 1976 coup which put the military in control. Their assault on the left became conspicuous with the disappearance of foes and suspects estimated by Amnesty *(q.v.)* International at 10,000. The government's General J. R. Videla defended its policies as necessary in its fight against subversion. V. S. Naipaul, *The Return of Eva Peron* (1980); H. F. Peterson, *Argentina and the United States* (1964); David Rock, ed., *Argentina in the Twentieth Century* (1975); K. F. Johnson, *Argentina's Mosaic of Discord* (1969).

ARISTOCRACY, traditionally seen as a block to social reform, and concerned for the perpetuation of outmoded social forms and privileges. However, the cooperation of aristocrats with socialist, labor, and even communist movements has modified the effect of this view. "Labor lords" in England have sustained socialist pretensions. See also, Elite, The, and Reform. That there has been an "aristocracy of labor" has been a recognized fact, involving the skilled and artisan classes, but it has not been emphasized by labor itself, requiring as it has, from time to time, the friendship and cooperation of the unskilled, and the sympathy of the general public.

ARMINIANISM, a "heresy," from the Calvinist *(q.v.)* point of view, in that it took a more benign and hopeful view of human destiny, not accepting total predestination, and maintaining a broader view of the possibilities for redemption through Christ than Calvinists would allow. Jonathan Edwards *(q.v.)* was a bitter critic of the Arminian theology.

ARMS EMBARGO, see Neutrality Acts, (1935, 1937).

ARMY OF LABOR, a propaganda concept which saw labor as "on the march," as leading the battle for a better social order; allied with "industrial democracy" *(q.v.)*.

ARMY OF THE COMMONWEAL OF CHRIST, THE, see Coxey, Jacob S.

ART AND SOCIETY, their relationship has been sought by political-minded intellectuals, and by others in times of stress. Such world artists as Michelangelo and Rembrandt were not reformers, except, perhaps, in their original techniques, but it has seemed a worthy social aim to make their art better available to more people. Such an artist as the French satirist, Daumier, had a manifestly libertarian direction in his work. William Morris (q.v.) sought to add an artistic component to ordinary life, to oppose machine design with artistry. Edwin Markham (q.v.) was inspired in his humanitarian verse by Jean Francois Millet's painting, *The Man with the Hoe*. The "Ash-Can School" of painters (q.v.) found beauty and fresh vision in democratic subject-matter. George Grosz's piercing drawing, the work of Diego Rivera (qq.v.), and others, offered insight into human possibilities without avoiding political content, or, at least, social content. The same could be said of the Americans Thomas Hart Benton and Grant Wood (qq.v.). The Federal Art Project (q.v.) attracted democratic spectators and many of the outstanding talents of its time; following its demise, it received the scorn of those opposed to "mere representation" and social content; abstract art (q.v.) proliferated in the late 1940's and in the '50s, in reaction to the austerities and compulsions of World War II. Whether the above artistic experiences would be given renewed use, brought into any relationships, in any social framework was unclear in 1982.

ARTICLE TEN, see Covenant of the League of Nations.

ARTICLES OF CONFEDERATION (1781), the constitutional framework for the new nation created by the American Revolution. It is notorious for having been weak, for having been led by insignificant presidents, for having tottered through a "critical period," in the historian John Fiske's phrase. However, its first president, John Hanson (q.v.) was not chosen to be a figurehead. The Articles were weak by design; the colonies had just fought to free themselves from too strong a central government. Democracy was at its height in the states, Virginia, for example, having drawn up a Bill of Rights for its constitution which would be a model for the later Constitution of the United States. Moreover, the Northwest Ordinance of 1787 (q.v.) was a major achievement of the Confederation. It is evident that the concept of a "critical period" was fostered by the constitution-makers; from the Whisky Rebellion to the Hartford Resolutions (qq.v.) life did not cease to be "critical" in America, following the abrogation of the Articles. The purpose of the Philadelphia convention of 1787 was to *revise* the Articles to make them more effective, not to overthrow them; it is evident that the constitution makers were revolutionists; see Constitutional Conventions, *Economic Interpretation of the Constitution, An*.

ARTISTS IN UNIFORM (1934), see Eastman, Max.

ARTS, see Abstract Art, Anti-War Literature, Art and Society, Federal Arts Projects, Cinema, Folk Arts, Literature and Social Reform, Theater, and individuals.

ASH-CAN SCHOOL, a group of artists who, after the turn of the twentieth century, under the leadership of Robert Henri, worked to develop a more democratic art than that sponsored by the official academies. John Sloan, William J. Glackens, George Luks, and Everett Shinn, though ridiculed by their foes as "apostles of ugliness," broke the convention of imitating classical models by seeking interest and variety in the ordinary and the unpretentious. George W. Bellows, too, in such canvasses as *Stag at Sharkey's* (1907), which depicted a prizefight, contributed to urban and unhackneyed subject matter and method. See also Art and Society.

ASIA, a massive area not readily defined, with nations working between ancient heritages and industrial developments, with raw materials or strategic positions important in the continuous struggles of advanced nations. Thus, Afghanistan (q.v.), though without known significant resources, stood among nations which did have them. China and Asian Russia engrossed terrain making tiny that surrounding them, but even such countries as Nepal, Bhutan and Bangladesh created problems which could harm them in world opinion or strategic choices. See also, Southeast Asia, China. R. A. Scalapino, *Asia and the Major Nations* (1972); Leon Howell and M. Morrow, *Asia, Oil Politics, and the Energy Crisis* (1974); Gunnar

Myrdal, *Asian Drama: an Inquiry into the Poverty of Nations* (1968); H. B. Melendy, *Asians in America* (1977).

ASIATIC BARRED ZONE, a stipulation of the Immigration Act of 1917, it barred from entry into the United States natives of an area within specific longitude and latitude, including such areas as India, Ceylon, and parts of Arabia, with exceptions made of persons in the upper classes; a problem in "immigration" (q.v.).

ASSASSINATION, abjured as a weapon of social reform in the United States; several of the relatively few efforts have involved patently non-reformers. The Molly Maguires (q.v.) made an instrument of terrorism, but under special conditions of group suppression. The McNamaras and Harry Orchard (qq.v.) represented terrorism in trade union affairs. Even during the post-Civil War period, which might have been most amenable to assassination, because of disorderly social circumstances, it was practiced with relative infrequency. President Garfield was shot by a disappointed office-seeker, President McKinley by a confused person who had heard anarchist doctrine, but not been an anarchist. A comparatively fluid society has made it difficult for a tradition of terrorism to flourish; unlike Czarist Russia, where those in power were clearly distinguished, it has never been clear who was in charge. One of the most famous assassination attempts was that of Alexander Berkman, and not on Carnegie, but on his lieutenant, Frick. The most notorious, if undiscriminating, effort at violence directed at a symbol of power was the explosion of a bomb (September 16, 1920) before the Wall Street offices of J. P. Morgan, which killed thirty-eight persons and wounded many more. The attempt on President-elect Franklin D. Roosevelt's life (February 15, 1933), at Miami, Florida, by Giuseppe Zangara was irrational and unpolitical, and resulted in the death of Mayor Anton Cermak of Chicago. An attempt to assassinate President Truman (November 1, 1950) was made by two nationalists from Puerto Rico (q.v.). The assassination of President Kennedy (q.v.) stunned admirers of his youth (q.v.), and his brother Robert's assassination cast a pall of alarm for American ways, as did that of Martin L. King (q.v.). See Terrorism.

ASSEMBLY, RIGHT OF, see First Amendment.

ASSEMBLY OF CAPTIVE EUROPEAN NATIONS, made up of exiles from countries absorbed into Soviet territory, or under its domination, including Albania, Bulgaria, Czechoslovakia, Estonia, Hungary, Latvia, Lithuania, Poland, and Romania. The Assembly was organized in 1951 in Independence Hall, Philadelphia, where it issued a Declaration of Aims and Principles of Liberation of the Central and Eastern European Peoples. It maintains a propaganda in favor of democracy and the need for refusing to accept as a *fait accompli* the actions of the Soviets. It publishes *ACEN News*.

ASSEMBLY-LINE, associated with mass production (q.v.), and presenting industrial dangers of shoddy production, unchallenging labor and dehumanization, as satirized in Charles Chaplin's *Modern Times*, and other problems, social and economic. See also, Taylorization, Ford, Henry, Speed Up.

ASSIMILATION, identified with the "melting pot" (q.v.) and the general process of receiving immigrants into the body politic; distinguished from "integration" (q.v.), directly identified with the problem of diminishing social differences and separations mainly between Negroes and whites (qq.v.).

ATATURK (family name of Mustafa Kemal Pasha), see Turkey.

ATELIERS NATIONAUX, national workshops established by French Provisional Government in 1848. Louis Blanc (q.v.), who sponsored them, quickly became disillusioned; they were abolished four months following that inauguration. The decree which created them declared that citizens had a "right to work" (q.v.).

ATHEISM asserts the non-existence of God; agnosticism affirms that it does not know. However, Thomas Henry Huxley, who coined the word Agnostic, appears to have doubted that life existed beyond the grave. Robert G. Ingersoll (q.v.) took essentially the same position. Atheism has been of militant and non-militant varieties. The Soviet League of the Godless is subsidized to oppose religious activity. The American Association for the Advancement of Atheism in the 1930's attracted political radicals and also non-radicals. Joseph Lewis had been the most active of atheists, as leader of the Freethinkers of America and editor of *The Age of Reason.* He had emphasized separation of church and state, opposed religious instruction in the schools, the necessity for religious oaths under civil auspices, and similar causes. The American Humanist Association opposed supernaturalism, but believed itself concerned for the "religion of humanity." Madalyn Murray O'Hair in 1963 ended prayer in public schools by way of suit. In 1980 her son, the child-plaintiff, rejected his mother's teachings in favor of religion. Observers of the religious scene noted many evasions of the law. See also Deism, Freethought. Peter Gay, ed., *Deism* (1968); M. G. Brown and G. Stein, eds., *Freethought in the United States* (1978).

ATLANTIC CHARTER (1941), though not a legal instrument, constituted a set of principles to which social reformers could refer in evaluating their country's actions and perspectives. It was prepared by President Franklin D. Roosevelt and Prime Minister Winston Churchill, August 9-12, 1941, and created a new bond between Great Britain, fighting for life against the Axis Powers (*q.v.*) and the United States, which was not yet embroiled. The Charter repudiated territorial ambitions, emphasized the right of people to have such governments as they preferred, approved international trade cooperation, the improvement of conditions for people everywhere, freedom from want, freedom of the seas, and the disarmament of aggressor nations. The Soviet Union, now at war with her recent ally, Germany, approved the Charter, as did fourteen other nations.

ATOM BOMB, THE, first exploded at Alamogordo, July 16, 1945, dropped on Hiroshima, August 6, destroying the city and some 160,000 persons, and, four days later, dropped on Nagasaki, a naval base. Arguments were maintained, among social reformers, whether it had been necessary to drop the bombs on people: whether a warning might not have sufficed. Yet the bomb on Hiroshima did not end the war; only the second bomb did. In addition, the government had no bombs to spare, at this point. America's monopoly of the bomb seemed to concentrate moral responsibility in the United States; Russia's attainment of the bomb, in 1949, raised the possibility that mankind might destroy itself, unless a rapprochement was discovered between communist and non-communist worlds. Programs for an international control of atomic energy proliferated, while its potentialities continued to be explored. See also Nuclear Question, The.

ATOM-BOMB SPIES were a particularly malignant result of a devious and frustrated radicalism. Liberals, in the 1920's and 1930's, were wont to quote Voltaire on Rousseau: that he disagreed with him entirely in what he believed, but that he would fight to the death for his right to speak his mind. Similarly, they supported the right of radicals to free speech, and, in considerable quantity, to free action. The revelation that communists had put the well-being of the Soviet Union above that of the United States, shook the faith of liberals and the tolerance of the general public. During 1947, some 830 persons were dropped from government agencies for suspected disloyalty. Nevertheless, a vigorous argument persisted whether they had received ample consideration. The Hiss case (*q.v.*) shook still further the public sense of how much leeway could be permitted, in matters of national security, to the individual conscience. Thus, relatively little sympathy supported Harry Gold, when he was revealed to have been an American collaborator with German-born physicist, Klaus Fuchs, who turned over British and American atomic secrets to the agents of the Soviet Union. The sentencing of Gold to prison, December 9, 1950, served as a prelude to the trial, conviction and death of the Rosenbergs (*q.v.*). Although the communists denounced the trial and executions to the world with consider-

able success, they achieved no propaganda victories in the United States; see Oliver R. Pilat, *The Atom Spies* (1952).

ATROCITIES, usually applied to noisome events abroad, as in the Kishenev massacre, the concentration camp excesses, and the Katyn Forest murders (*qq.v.*). However, events at home have had similar characteristics, though rarely, as in the Ludlow Massacre (*q.v.*) on a large basis. More typical have been such incidents as the Wesley Everett affair, the Leo Frank killing, and a variety of types of lynching (*qq.v.*). Atrocities abroad multiplied, and were difficult to condemn or believe when they affected politics, as with the P.L.O. (*q.v.*). North Ireland atrocities were mainly a British-Irish problem. Cambodian and Ugandan horrors, among others, were too remote and vast to be retained by western people. Amnesty International (*q.v.*) made efforts to call them to public attention.

ATTAINDER, BILL OF, a legislative act which assumes the guilt of an individual without permitting him a trial in which he could attempt to demonstrate his innocence. Employed in Parliament before the Puritan Revolution (*q.v.*), it was specifically forbidden in the Constitution (Art. I, sec. 9). A notable case involved Robert Morss Lovett (*q.v.*), who was accused of being a communist; as a result, he was separated from his position as Governor General of the Virgin Islands, and his salary withheld. President Franklin D. Roosevelt protested the action of Congress, but accepted it because it also involved war appropriations. The Supreme Court, however, found for Lovett.

ATTORNEY-GENERAL'S LIST OF SUBVERSIVE ORGANIZATIONS, drawn up in 1947 by Tom C. Clark, later Associate Justice of the Supreme Court. From time to time, organizations have been added to the list, or withdrawn from it. Liberals and others have protested that the list exposed groups and individuals to contempt and discrimination with inadequate evidence. Harry P. Cain of the Subversive Activities Control Board argued in 1955 that no organization should be listed unless it was simultaneously announced that prosecution would be initiated within several months.

ATTUCKS, CRISPUS (1723?-1770), a Negro who died in the "Boston Massacre," and who was therefore memorialized by the revolutionists. He entered into the lore of Negroes who emphasized the services to America by persons of their race, and who sought inspiration for their own efforts.

AUBURN PRISON, see Prison Reform.

AUSCHWITZ, Germany, site of a concentration camp in which during World War II numerous Jews perished; symbol of the National Socialist drive to exterminate them as a "final solution" to the racial problem they were alleged to present. Auschwitz was often referred to by social reformers who decried racism and fascism (*qq.v.*).

AUSTRALIA has been in the fore of radical government thought and experimentation. Its Labour Party, its Socialist Party, and its Communist Party have formalized the feelings and views of its lower classes and reformist circles. Somewhat less appreciated was its relationship to the natives of the South Seas whose affairs it administered, and who were subject to exploitation, as well as social and political repression. Notable in this connection were Papua and New Guinea. The future of the aborigines and other darker-skinned people in Australia proper was also a subject for the concern of reformers. See also New Zealand. R. W. Cameron, *Australia* (1971); Norman Bartlett, *Australia and America* (1976); J. Greenway, *Australia: the Last Frontier* (1973).

AUSTRALIAN BALLOT, first used in the several states of that Commonwealth, in the 1850's, brought to England in 1872, and to other English terrain thereafter. It was proposed by Henry George (*q.v.*) in 1882. It was first adopted by Massachusetts in 1888, and in subsequent years by other American states. Its essential purpose was to ensure the secret ballot; this was accomplished by printing the names of candidates and parties on one ballot, and the voter being enabled to vote for his preferred candidate by placing a check after his name, or in some other anonymous fashion indicating his choice.

AUSTRIA developed a socialist movement in the 1890's, under the leadership of Dr. Victor Adler. In following decades, it furthered programs of socialist housing and services. During the 1920's, following the split-up of the Austro-Hungarian Empire, it became the center for the so-called "Two and a Half International": a moderate attempt to maintain socialist principles tied neither to the Second or Third International. It was resisted by the so-called Christian Socialists, who were Catholic nationalists, for the most part, and who sought to curb the socialists without capitulating to those who sought *anschluss* (union) with Germany. In the 1930's, with Hitler in power in Germany, Dr. Engelbert Dollfuss sought, first, to control native Nazis, and, more successfully, to crush the socialists. In February, 1934, his government declared all parties but his own dissolved. His troops bombed the great Karl Marx Hof, center of socialist living and leadership, and drove the party from the scene. The event is celebrated in Stephen Spender's poem *Vienna* (1934), written from a communist perspective. Dollfuss was assassinated by the Nazis July 25 of that year. Efforts to keep Austria independent ended March 14, 1938 when Hitler rode triumphantly, standing in an open car, into Vienna. Following World War II, Austria undertook an enigmatic role of neither offending her "Iron Curtain" neighbors, Czechoslovakia and Hungary, nor defying them. See Joseph Buttinger, *In the Twilight of Socialism: a History of the Revolutionary Socialists of Austria* (1953).

AUTHORITARIANISM, emphasizing authority over the rights of the individual; theoretically opposed by reformers, except when they have identified their individual or corporate interests with those of society as a whole. Thus, the *Nation* deemed it proper to sue a writer for libel, in 1951, despite its libertarian principles, and its own dwindling influence. Thus, too, professed liberals deemed it proper to "defend the Soviet Union" against charges of dictatorship presented by its foes.

AUTOBIOGRAPHY OF AN EX-COLORED MAN, THE (1912), by James Weldon Johnson, a notable novel by a Negro poet and leader which dealt with the career of a Negro who had "passed," that is, had taken advantage of his light complexion to pass in society as a white person.

AUTOMATION, an industrial process involving highly developed machinery which displaced many workers who were previously necessary to the given industry. Automation presented itself as both a promise and a threat: a promise in that it could free workers for greater leisure and self-improvement, a threat in that, pending social circumstances which ministered to the individual, automation could simply throw workers into the industrial discard. Thus, automation, coupled with the declining use of coal, created chronically depressed areas in West Virginia, in the 1950's; it contributed to the growing economic depression of that period, despite a permanent state of military preparedness, which culminated in a sense of economic crisis in 1960, which contributed to the Presidential victory of John F. Kennedy (*q.v.*); in 1961, an Office of Automation was created in the U.S. Department of Labor; see also Leisure and the Work-day. Simon Marcson, *Automation Alienation, and Anomie* (1970); G. W. Ferborgh, *The Automation Hysteria* (1966).

A.W.O., see Agricultural Workers' Organization.

AXIS POWERS, term applied to Germany, Japan, and Italy. In 1936, Japan joined in a treaty with Germany. The latter had already cooperated with Italy in the Spanish Civil War (*q.v.*). In 1937, Italy joined the German-Japanese Anti-Comintern Pact. These powers and their satellites constituted a species of international, opposed to the Communist International (*q.v.*), but because of their heavily nationalistic and antagonistic content could never organize for concerted action.

A.Y.C., see American Youth Congress.

A.Y.D., see American Youth for Democracy.

BABBITT, a character in the novel by Sinclair Lewis (*q.v.*) by that name. George Follansbee Babbitt is a symbol of middle-class crassness and confused social understanding; as such, he was scorned by American social reformers as one symbol of what they opposed. However, it was observed, as in John Howard Lawson's play, *Roger Bloomer* (1923), that "Babbitts" could learn to incorporate in their thought sophisticated cultural and social references, and by Peter Viereck, in *Shame and Glory of the Intellectuals* (1953) that a "New Babbittry" had been created, consisting of persons who could say: "I go for art and progress in a big way. If there's one thing I can't stand, it's a Babbitt." Since the essence of such Babbittry was conformity, many "radicals" and "individualists" could rate as Babbitts.

BACKLASH, coined 1963 by columnist Eliot Janeway to describe how automation (*q.v.*) might affect black-white relations; made popular by Governor George Wallace's (*q.v.*) invasion of northern states, seeking votes in 1964. It was further identified with Negroes, as they were singled out for "affirmative action" and "reparations" (*qq.v.*) by government, some Negro leaders fearing "blacklash" actions by discontented whites. Retrospectively, it could be seen as violence or propaganda directed at any minority (*q.v.*) group which had become visible enough to rouse resentment. There were backlashes by labor (*q.v.*) against early Chinese settlers in California and elsewhere. Japanese also suffered backlash of discrimination and riot, as did Catholics, Jews, Poles, and others (*qq.v.*).

BACON, LEONARD (1802-1881), pastor of the First Congregationalist Church, New Haven, Conn., from 1825 till his death. Conservative in temper, he opposed the agitation of abolitionists and favored colonization (*q.v.*). However, his *Slavery Discussed in Occasional Essays* (1846) influenced the thought of Abraham Lincoln (*q.v.*) and in 1848, he became an editor of the *Independent* (*q.v.*), which spoke for a strategic class of Free Soilers. He made an effort to persuade Governor Henry A. Wise, of Virginia, that John Brown (*q.v.*) was insane and ought not to be prosecuted; they had been youths together in Ohio. This effort helped persuade the North that southerners were intransigent in their views.

BACON'S REBELLION, an uprising in 1676 by Virginia frontiersmen against the colonial leaders in Jamestown, headed by Governor William Berkeley. The revolt was headed by Nathaniel Bacon, who complained against the lack of adequate representation for frontiersmen in the Virginia legislature, the House of Burgesses, and against the government policy of appeasing the Indians, whom the settlers outside Jamestown feared and detested. Branded as a traitor by the governor, Bacon proclaimed himself the proper leader of the colony, and set out to create a more democratic order in Virginia. He died suddenly, and his followers were harshly punished. The rebellion, though denounced by the constituted authorities as revolutionary, had moderate aims. It initiated a tradition of frontier and western agitations. See T. J. Wertenbaker, *Torchbearer of the Revolution* (1940).

BAILEY, GAMALIEL (1807-1859), anti-slavery editor of the *Philanthropist* (*q.v.*), he sought a program which would enlist a majority of the North. Despite his moderation and appeal to reason, he was subject to assaults in Cincinnati, which he left in 1847 in order to edit the new anti-slavery *National Era* (*q.v.*). He himself became a leader of the anti-slavery elements in the national Capital, where the *Era* was published. In 1856, he was one of the organizers of the Republican Party. However, the rapid infiltration of conservatives into the Republican alliance increasingly rendered him less necessary to them; by the last year of his life, he had become obscure among them, while intransigents like William Lloyd Garrison (*q.v.*) became increasingly conspicuous, though they wielded little practical power.

BAILEY V. DREXEL FURNITURE COMPANY, see Child Labor

BAKER, NEWTON D. (1871-1937), known as both a pacifist and a worthy follower of Tom L. Johnson (*q.v.*), when mayor of Cleveland, 1912-16; as U.S. Secretary of War under Woodrow Wilson, he was one of the pre-World War I liberals who helped persuade Americans to turn from peace-time pursuits to war-time pursuits. As such, he was subjected to critical estimation by post-War reformers who believed American intervention in the war unnecessary. His defense appears in *Why We Went to War* (1936).

BAKER, RAY STANNARD (1870-1946), one of the most famous of the reform journalists of the pre-World War I period; like other *McClure's* (*q.v.*) journalists, he esteemed himself better than such "sensationalists" as Upton Sinclair and Thomas W. Lawson (*qq.v.*). He joined the "secessionists" from *McClure's* on the *American Magazine*. He wrote notably on labor racketeering, railroad monopoly operations, and other topics, with apparently impressive objectivity and grasp. *Following the Color Line* (1908), and *The Spiritual Unrest* (1910) were outstanding books of the time. He enjoyed another type of popularity under the name "David Grayson," writing a series of "Adventures in Contentment" which thoroughly escaped from social woes and challenges. He took Woodrow Wilson (*q.v.*) as a leader, served him during World War I, and wrote a multi-volumed life of him after. Baker's *The New Industrial Unrest* (1920) was intended to revive his role as a public commentator, but stirred no interest.

BAKKE CASE (1978), a landmark Supreme Court decision which held that a non-Negro who ranked higher than a Negro in medical school examinations ought not to be rejected because of "affirmative action" (*q.v.*) tenets. Although the Court elsewhere approved Negro opportunities when they did not transgress others's civil rights, the case signalled a turn from *New York Times*-termed "reparations" (*q.v.*) to Negroes. *Reverse Discrimination and the Supreme Court . . . Records and Briefs . . .* (1977); T. Eastland and W. J. Bennett, *Counting by Race: Equality from the Founding Fathers to Bakke and Weber* (1980); J. C. Livingston, *Fair Game? Inequality and Affirmative Action* (1980).

BAKUNIN, MICHAEL (1814-1876), Russian anarchist leader, involved in the revolutionary thought and crises of the 1840's and 1850's. His anarchist principles made him a political foe of Marx's, within the First International, and his idealist view of human associations gave him authority among impatient working class elements and radical intelligentsia. In fleeing European police, he came to the United States by way of Japan, in 1860, but went on to London to enter into socialist controversies. He gained considerable popularity among revolutionary elements in such agricultural lands as Spain, Italy, Russia (where his views precipitated "Nihilism" [*q.v.*]), and even in France. The break between Marx's followers and his own came to a head in 1872, when Bakunin was deliberately prevented from attending the meeting of the First International. His best-known work was *God and the State* (1882).

BALCH, EMILY G. (1867-1961), professor of economics and social worker, co-winner with John R. Mott (*q.v.*) of Nobel Prize for Peace, 1946. She was a pioneer in such organizations as the Women's Trade Union League, and in the work of Boston civic organizations. Her major energies went into the peace crusade. She wrote several of the essays in *Women at the Hague* (1915), following attendance at the International Congress of Women. For her pacifist activities, she was dismissed from Wellesley College. She later protested American Caribbean policy, championed Jewish victims of Nazism, and denounced Japanese Relocation (*qq.v.*). M. M. Randall, *Beyond Nationalism: the Social Thought of Emily Greene Balch* (1972).

BALDWIN, ROGER N. (1884-1981), after a professional career concerned in large measure for juvenile delinquency (*q.v.*), became a founder of the National Civil Liberties Bureau, precursor of the A.C.L.U. (*q.v.*), of which he served as long-time director and chairman of the Board. He was a conscientious objector during World War I, and associated with numerous reform and civil liberties organizations, including the Urban League (*q.v.*), the International League for the Rights of Man, and the Robert Marshall Civil Liberties Trust. His writings included *A New Slavery: Forced Labor* (1953).

BALL, JOHN (1338-1381), revolutionary English priest, supporter of the Wat Tyler (*q.v.*) Rebellion, for which he was hanged. A symbol of revolutionary aspiration, memorialized in William Morris' (*q.v.*) *The Dream of John Ball* (1888).

BALLAD OF READING GAOL, THE, by Oscar Wilde (*q.v.*), one of the great compassionate poems of the world, by an author whose own fall from fame to prison inspired a wide literature, only partially related to sexual scandal.

BALLINGER AFFAIR, THE (1909-1910), a major incident in the history of American conservation policy and democratic government. A young field worker in the Interior charged that Guggenheim and Morgan (*q.v.*) interests (soon known as the "Morganheims") had conspired to preempt important tracts of land in Alaska, then believed to involve coal-sites strategic to the future development of Alaska. Louis R. Glavis, the Interior employee, urged the Secretary of his Department, Richard A. Ballinger, to withhold clearance on the so-called "Cunningham Claims," pending investigation. Told to stop his interference, he passed over his chief's head to President Taft, who, stating that he had read the report on the situation which proved Glavis's unwarranted insubordination, recommended Glavis's dismissal. Gifford Pinchot (*q.v.*), too, for making a public protest, was dismissed as Chief Forester. A Congressional investigation brought in Louis D. Brandeis (*q.v.*) as counsel for the dismissed men; the popular magazines raised a hue and cry charging corruption. Brandeis proving that Taft had not read the report on which his judgment was allegedly based cast a shadow on his sincerity; although the majority report of the investigating committee exonerated Ballinger, the public preserved its skepticism, and though Ballinger resigned, the Congressional elections of that year resulted in a Democratic victory, foreshadowing that of 1912. The affair gave evidence that an alert public could prevent the sacrifice of little people in government; see A. T. Mason, *Bureaucracy Convicts Itself* (1941).

BALLOT REFORM was a phase in the modernization of ballots which were originally susceptible to cheats and capable of infringing on the citizen's privacy. Thus, a party ballot could be printed in a distinctive color, thus enabling the watcher at the polls to know how the citizen had voted, or to bribe him and be able to determine whether he had carried out his bargain by utilizing the party ballot. The Australian ballot (*q.v.*) did much good, but still permitted a bewildering number of names to appear on it which could cut to a minimum the effectiveness of his vote. The *short-ballot reform* argued for a minimum of elective appointments, which could concentrate the attention of the voter on the major candidates, they to be free to exercise their responsibility for appointing lesser stipendiaries.

BALLOU, ADIN (1803-1890), Universalist clergyman and a notable experimenter in cooperative living. He helped found the Massachusetts Association of Universal Restorationists during the 1830's. In 1841, he set up the Hopedale Community in Milford, Mass. It attracted over two hundred persons. Ballou himself edited *The Practical Christian*. In 1860 the Community merged with Hopedale Parish, and he became its pastor till 1880. Hopedale was one of the more successful "utopian" communities. Ballou's writings helped explicate his principles; see *Practical Christian Socialism* (1854), *Primitive Christianity and Its Corruptions* (1870), and *History of the Hopedale Community* (1897).

BANCROFT, GEORGE (1800-1891), distinguished American

historian, educator, U.S. Secretary of the Navy (1845-6), and Minister to Great Britain (1846-9); an ardent Jacksonian who added intellectual eminence and conviction to the democratic asseverations of his political associates. His *History of the United States* (1834-40, and ff.; revised 1876) asserted his belief that the hand of God (*q.v.*) was plainly to be observed in the course of American affairs, and was notable for intensive and original research. His belief in the people was somewhat platonic, but sincere. See R. B. Nye, *George Bancroft, Brahmin Rebel* (1944).

BANKS, NATHANIEL P. (1816-1894), Massachusetts politician and opportunist, architect of the Free Soil-Democratic alliance of 1849-53, which put Charles Sumner (*q.v.*) in the U.S. Senate. Banks was esteemed as a Democratic leader, a founder of the Republican Party, and a Free Soil partisan, though his unscrupulous career compares oddly with the numerous honors he was accorded. In 1856, he was made a symbol of northern liberties, because the southern bloc in the House of Representatives was unwilling to have him elected Speaker. His elevation to that post was treated as a northern victory. He was later a "political general," during the Civil War, of the highest rank and no distinction.

BANKS, often a symbol of capitalism and conservative principles; a symbol of anti-democratic operation, as in Andrew Jackson's battle against the Second Bank of the United States (*q.v.*). Their purposes and methods can be contrasted with those of the credit union (*q.v.*), and other cooperative institutions. Although they have been identified with the most serious anti-social purposes, as in the charge that bankers's loans to Great Britain and France helped to involve us in World War I, their conservatism has also made them reluctant to engage in adventures which might upset the *status quo*; thus, bankers were reluctant to involve us in a war with Spain during the Cuban crisis of 1895-1898, Spain's weakness not being fully known; it was popular and other opinion which forced the issue; Theodore Roosevelt (*q.v.*) denounced bankers, among others, whom he accused of frustrating our imperial destiny. See also Pet Banks, Second Bank of the United States, Federal Reserve System, Panic of 1907.

BANNEKER, BENJAMIN (1731-1806), free Negro astronomer of Maryland; though not a reformer, his accomplishments redounded to the credit of his race. He has been better known for Thomas Jefferson's apparent appreciation of his talent, than for the skepticism which Jefferson unfairly expressed as to whether or not he had been helped in his work. See S. A. Bedini, *Life of Benjamin Banneker* (1972).

BARBARY PIRATES, a humiliating arrangement whereby the United States paid tribute to the Barbary States ranging northern Africa, and involving the American War with Tripoli which extended from 1801 to 1805, and ended successfully, though the United States continued to pay tribute to other of the Barbary states; sometimes thought to involve the happy, though legendary slogan of "Millions for Defense, but not one cent for tribute" (*q.v.*).

BARBUSSE, HENRI (1874-1935), French pacifist and idealist, his *Under Fire* (1916) made him internationally famous for its sensitive account of the life of a soldier. Following the War, he became one of the most important spokesmen against war, his stories and essays being translated into many languages. His socialistic sympathies were exploited by the communists; his *Stalin* (1935) was written with unqualified admiration.

"BARGAIN AND CORRUPTION," demagogic slogan employed by the Jackson faction; see "Corrupt Bargain, The."

BARLOW, JOEL (1754-1812), many-sided American poet, businessman, diplomat, notable for his evolution from conservatism to liberalism. One of the Hartford Wits (*q.v.*), he contributed to their *Anarchiad* (*q.v.*), and wrote the pretentious *Columbiad* (1807), hailing his country in epic verse. However, it is his salute, in spontaneous verses, to *Hasty Pudding* (1796) which continued to be read. He published Thomas Paine's (*q.v.*) *Age of Reason*, and was sympathetic to the French Rev-

olution. He is one of the heroes of Dos Passos's (*q.v.*) *The Ground We Stand On* (1941), Dos Passos's career being the reverse of Barlow's, going from radicalism to conservatism.

BARNBURNERS, radical faction of the Democratic Party, especially strong in New York, accused by their more conservative confreres of being willing, like the legendary Dutch farmer, to burn down their political barn in order to rid themselves of the rats. They rose to prominence about 1844, and considered their leader to be Martin Van Buren, whom they followed out of the Democratic Party, when, in 1848, the Presidential nomination was withheld from him. They followed Van Buren (*q.v.*) into the Free Soil Party of that year's elections, and rejoined the Democratic Party with him, in 1852. Compare, Loco-Focos.

BARNES, HARRY ELMER (1889-1968), a vigorous, if somewhat over-prolific writer, editor, and college teacher who was particularly active in the 1920's and 1930's. His major causes were prison reform (*q.v.*), as exemplified by his *Evolution of Penology in Pennsylvania* (1922), *The Story of Punishment* (1931), and *Prisons in War Time* (1944), and opposition to war (*q.v.*), as shown in his *Immediate Causes of the World War* (1926). He became a leader of the "revisionists" (*q.v.*) who, like Charles A. Beard (*q.v.*), among others, attempted to show that American entrance into World War II was engineered in bad faith by Franklin D. Roosevelt (*q.v.*); see the Barnes-edited *Perpetual War for Perpetual Peace; a Critical Examination of the Foreign Policy of Franklin Delano Roosevelt and Its Aftermath* (1953).

BARUCH, BERNARD M. (1870-1965), American financier and political adviser, noted as having been welcomed by Democratic Party statesmen from Woodrow Wilson through and beyond Franklin D. Roosevelt. He was "economic dictator" during World War I and was called by Roosevelt to recommend legislation calling for orderly industrial mobilization in war time. As an "elder statesman" he was popular with journalists. His precise services to liberalism have not been defined. The "Baruch Plan" for international control of atomic energy was repudiated by the U.S.S.R. as a means for undermining its authority in the field.

"BASIN OF DEMOCRACY," see Turner, Frederick Jackson.

BASTILLE, a Paris fort exploited as a prison, destroyed in a mass assault, in the early stages of the French Revolution (*q.v.*), on July 14, 1789; a symbol of oppression.

BAY OF PIGS INCIDENT, a shocking miscalculation of the new Kennedy Administration (1961). It permitted Cuban exiles to attempt Castro's overthrow, with inadequate preparation and capacity to win, no air cover, for example, being permitted. The defeat heightened communist prestige and lost the United States respect only partially recovered by Kennedy's firm stand against Russian missile bases being set up in Cuba in 1962. The Bay of Pigs catastrophe may have begun American education in world realities. Peter Wyden, *The Bay of Pigs* (1980).

BEARD, CHARLES AUSTIN (1874-1948), historian and social critic, he acquired his ideals of Jeffersonian democracy (*q.v.*) in his native Indiana. His classic *An Economic Interpretation of the Constitution* (1913) was a remarkable exercise in method, undertaken to strike a relationship between alleged ideals and economic interests. His resistance to the war fever in 1917 contributed to his separation from Columbia University. Beard contributed to establishing the New School for Social Research (*q.v.*), he helped plan reconstruction projects following the Japanese earthquake of 1923, published with his wife their influential *The Rise of American Civilization* (1927). He despised Woodrow Wilson idealism as accomplishing no more than Mahan (*q.v.*) imperialism, and was a bitter critic of Franklin D. Roosevelt's foreign policy: with other "revisionists" (*q.v.*) he held that it had been calculated to bring us into war.

BEARD, MARY R. (1876-1959), historian, involved in labor and suffrage movements, wife and collaborator of Charles A. Beard (*q.v.*). Her works included *Woman's Work in Municipalities* (1915); *A Short History of the American Labor Move-*

ment (1920): *Woman as Force in History* (1946) (*q.v.*).

BEAST BUTLER, see Butler, Benjamin F.

BEATLES, THE, a rock music phenomenon of the 1960s and after, on whom fame and fortune poured continuously despite intense international musical competition outside communist-dominated countries, competition intended to outdo the Beatles in sex, drugs, peace and other themes and rhythms. When John Lennon, one of the most talented of the group and a writer of many of their songs, died in 1980 he was said to have possessed an estimated $365 million, and the music stores were immediately emptied of his records and tapes, with more being manufactured to meet the unslakeable demand. The Beatles phenomenon was comparable to that of Beaumarchais, whose *The Marriage of Figaro* (1784), "the firecracker which set off the French REvolution," first seemed a mere entertainment, but helped reveal the decay in the foundations of the French aristocracy; see Filler, *Vanguards and Followers: Youth in the American Tradition* (1978). Similarly, the Beatles, singing irreverent and inciteful songs, and wearing Edwardian garb and hair at unfashionable length, first appealed to a groping German youth whose enthusiasm for Beatles rhythms and their casual scorn and ridicule of established society carried back to their native Liverpool and nation and over to the United States. Although they had no political concerns in their first wave, other than their good humored contempt for those who had fought the Battle of Britain and held off the Nazi invasion, their dedication to sex, drugs and easy living appealed not only to "drop out" youth, but to revolutionaries, and also to the bored and directionless among their elders. They were followers rather than leaders in the advancing youth crisis, turning their wit and harmonies to peace and other conventional causes, but were gratefully received when they sang their "socially significant" *Rubber Soul* (1965) and *Revolver* (1966). Their indirect utterances made them useful to disciples, who ranged from earnest dissidents to such as Charles Manson (*q.v.*), who studied their *Magical Mystery Tour* (1967) and their cartoon *Yellow Submarine* (1968). As one of them, Paul McCartney said, they wrote songs with no purpose, "But in a week someone else says something about it,...and you can't deny it. Things take on millions of meanings." The killing of John Lennon by an infatuated admirer called forth an unprecedented outbreak of grief and gatherings, particularly in the United States and Great Britain, not matched by the mourning evoked a few years earlier by the death of Elvis Presley whom they had first sought to emulate. Although a large number of fan clubs and purchasers of records kept the flame of Presley lit, he did not draw out such innermost feelings of adorers as those sentiments which appeared on a placard at an enormous New York gathering: "Why?" The Beatles's influence with elements of the general public, including youth, promised to continue, though perhaps not in the same way as *The Marriage of Figaro*. *John Lennon in His Own Write* (1964); J. Phil Di Franco, *Beatles: a Hard Day's Night* (1977); R. Carr and T. Tyler, *Beatles: an Illustrated Record* (1978); N. Schaffer, *The Beatles Forever* (1977); Joe Washington, *The Beatles for Classical Guitar* (1975).

"BEATNIKS," a term coined in 1957 by Herb Caen, *San Francisco Chronicle* columnist, to describe the group of bohemians and social rebels who were making themselves apparent, especially in the North Beach section of the city; their emergence coincided with that of the *Sputnik* (*q.v.*). Taking off from the current concept of the "beat generation," Beatniks practiced apathy, resentment, a vague, unhappy yearning for self-expression, free-verse and random music in combination, a general distaste for the politics and mores of the post-World War II America, and, in due course, some religious groping, notably in Zen Buddhism. They also attracted a fair sampling of homosexuals and degenerates, on one end of the social scale, and, on the other, jaded middle-class housewives and their consorts who came to see them in their native regalia. Though similar elements could be found, in one recipe or another, in many American cities, and though some of them migrated from place to place, as depicted in Jack Kerouac's *On the Road* (1957), San Francisco remained headquarters for

a manifestly vigorous protest against stultifying social patterns. Although New York probably contained more such types, the city absorbed them without difficulty, The Beatnik milieu became increasingly artificial, drinking-places importing beatnik types to add decor to their surroundings. By 1960, little remained of the impulse but the faithful degenerates. See also Drop Outs, Hippies, Youth Movement and Reform.

BEAUTY, see Abstract Terms.

BEAUVOIR, SIMONE DE, see Sartre, Jean Paul.

BEBEL, AUGUST (1840-1913), German socialist theoretician, associate and successor to Wilhelm Liebknecht (*q.v.*), and leader of the Social Democratic Party in Germany. He suffered persecution and imprisonment, which stirred sympathy and support. He was the influential editor of the *Vorwärts*. His denunciations of imperialism and militarism were world-famous. His works included *Woman in the Past, Present and Future* (1886).

BECCARIA, CESARE BONESANA (1738?-1794), Italian humanist whose *Treatise on Crimes and Punishments* (1764) exerted an international influence on prison reformers and anti-capital punishment theoreticians.

BEECHER, CATHERINE ESTHER (1800-1878), the eldest of Rev. Lyman Beecher's nine children, and a pioneer in women's higher education. She developed advanced curricula for them, found women teachers for western and southern schools, and set up several female colleges. Although her writings, example, and industry had progressive results, her social views were conservative; *An Essay on Slavery and Abolitionism, with Reference to the Duty of American Females* (1837) argued, in effect in opposition to the work of the Grimké sisters (*q.v.*): it was women's place, she believed, to stay out of such controversies. For Beechers, C. M. Rourke, *Trumpets of Jubilee* (1927); L. B. Stowe, *Saints, Sinners and Beechers* (1934); see also Stowe, Harriet Beecher.

BEECHER, HENRY WARD (1813-1887), a popular preacher and spokesman on public issues; his sermons at the Plymouth Congregational Church in Brooklyn drew great audiences, and his articles on all topics in the *Independent* (*q.v.*) were widely read. Though a follower, rather than a leader, in the rising northern opinion favoring anti-slavery, guns sent to keep Kansas free, following passage of the Kansas-Nebraska Act (1854), were called "Beecher's Bibles." His speeches in England, in 1863, were thought to have aided the Union cause. Woman suffragists appreciated his statements in their behalf. A vent for suppressed middle-class feelings, he was not abandoned by his congregation or public when his sordid dealings with the wife of a fellow-editor and reformer, Theodore Tilton, were made public in 1874.

BEECHER-TILTON CASE, a notorious legal action which involved reputed reformers. Henry Ward Beecher was accused of committing adultery with the wife of Theodore Tilton, once his protegé, later his successor on the *Independent,* and famous in his own right as a social and religious liberal in the Reconstruction period. Tilton and Beecher were both supporters of woman suffrage, and friends of the movement's leaders. An article by Victoria Woodhull (*q.v.*), November 2, 1872, in *Woodhull and Claflin's Weekly* brought the scandal into the open. Tilton's ultimate suit against Beecher, August 20, 1874, resulted in a six-months' trial which stirred the country, but also in an indecisive conclusion. Beecher's "liberal" theology, his support of Grover Cleveland for election to the Presidency in 1884 (Cleveland had openly confessed to an illicit affair), and other deviations from an old-time fundamentalism could be taken as Beecher's rationalizations for deviating from an old-time morality, and the loyalty of his congregation as an obscure sympathy with them.

"BEEF TRUST," a major monopoly, target of exposes by liberal journalists of the muckraking (*q.v.*) era, notably Charles Edward Russell's (*q.v.*) *The Greatest Trust in the World* (1905). It was centered in the Chicago stockyards. Upton Sinclair's *The Jungle* (*qq.v.*) made a scandal of the industry and forced major government reform, though cooperation between the great houses, Armour, Swift, and Morris persisted.

20

B. E. F., see Bonus Marchers.

BELGIUM, created by a popular revolution in 1830, proved sympathetic to republicans and revolutionists, and received them from other lands. Its labor and socialist elements grew strong, in time. A major battle in 1890 took place over the socialist demand for the universal suffrage· The assumption by King Leopold, in 1885, of sovereignty over the Congo and its subsequent exploitation created a contrast between democratic Belgium, and its imperialist control of its African possessions. The "rape" of Belgium during World War I was a propaganda weapon in the hands of the Allies, in their duel with Germany. Belgium developed a strong paternalistic policy in the Congo, intended to quell nationalistic feeling, while maintaining white supremacy. Its sudden freeing of the Congo (q.v.) in 1960 created a major crisis.

BELLAMY, EDWARD (1850-1898), story-teller and reformer, whose *Looking Backward* (1888) changed him from an alleged successor to Nathaniel Hawthorne (q.v.) to a force in politics. His vision of an America operated for use, not profit, in the twentieth century, inspired his hundreds of thousands of readers, many of whom formed Bellamy Clubs to carry out the suggestions implicit in his novel. They sought the nationalization of public utilities, and succeeded in writing this plank into the Populist (q.v.) Platform of 1892. Bellamy became a theoretician of the new time coming; some have even seen his vision as having been translated in the New Deal (q.v.). He wrote a sequel to his best-selling work, called *Equality*, which was published posthumously. It spelled out many matters which *Looking Backward* treated in general terms. His earlier stories help explain the content and direction of his thought; see Louis Filler, "Edward Bellamy and the Spiritual Unrest," *Jour. of Econ. and Sociology*, April 1948. For an overall study, Arthur E. Morgan (q.v.), *Edward Bellamy* (1944).

BELSEN, one of the most notorious of concentration camps (q.v.), an "exchange" camp for Jews. Anne Frank (q.v.) died here.

BEMIS, EDWARD W. (1860-1930), economist and municipal reformer, he made studies of cooperatives and municipal ownership, and developed a career as a professor, also helping to organize the American Economic Association. He was an early academic freedom case, being, for his courageous views, dismissed from the University of Chicago, in 1895, and, in 1899, dismissed with other liberals, including its President, Thomas E. Will, from the Kansas State Agricultural College. He served as Superintendent of the Water Works under Tom L. Johnson, in Cleveland, and filled other municipal posts. His writings included *Municipal Ownership of Gas Works in the United States* (1891), and *Municipal Monopolies* (1899).

BENEFITS, paid to workers under stipulated conditions from trade union funds, by mutual aid societies (q.v.), or by the state or federal government operating under specific laws. Benefits cover a wide spectrum of circumstances, including death, sickness, accident, maternity, old age, marriage, medical needs, unemployment or "lay offs" (q.v.) and strike circumstances.

BENES, EDUARD (1884-1948), associate and co-founder of Czechoslovakia (q.v.) with Thomas G. Masaryk (q.v.). During the Nazi occupation of the country, following the Munich (q.v.) capitulation and subsequent dismemberment of the Czech confederation, Beneš, in 1940, organized a government-in-exile in London. He was unable to resist the communist succession to power, following his return, but refused to give up the democratic principles he had maintained.

BENEVOLENCE, abjured by reformers as connoting condescension and an inadequate sense of the rights of people; echoed in President McKinley's concept of "benevolent assimilation" as a proper policy to be taken toward the Philippines (q.v.). See Charities and Reform.

BENEVOLENT FEUDALISM, an unfriendly view, by reformers and radicals, of paternalistic welfare work sponsored by dominant elements of industry and government, and seen as intended to dissipate labor and reformist energies intended to accomplish more fundamental changes in the social structure; state socialism; the name of a notable book by William J. Ghent (q.v.), *Our Benevolent Feudalism* (1902).

BENEZET, ANTHONY (1713-1784), Huguenot Quaker, associate of John Woolman (q.v.) in antislavery work. He issued pamphlets opposing the slavery system and corresponded with antislavery leaders abroad; his most important publication was *A Caution and Warning to Great Britain and Her Colonies on the Calamitous State of the Enslaved Negroes* (1766). He also taught in and endowed schools, opposed war and intemperance, and sought justice for the Indians.

BENTON, THOMAS HART (1889-1975), painter and advocate of an American approach to art. His murals and lithographs exploited American themes, sometimes echoing classical themes, and sought to express American vitality and variety. Like Grant Wood, Benton could offer the reformer inspiration, rather than reform commentary. Benton was the grand-nephew of Thomas Hart Benton (1782-1858), energetic Jacksonian, famous for his "hard money" policies, as reflected in the Specie Circular (q.v.), and, though from a slave state, Missouri, his unwillingness to countenance secession from the Union in defense of slavery.

BEREA COLLEGE, Kentucky, developed from a school started in 1855, thanks to the interest and cooperation displayed by Cassius M. Clay, Lewis Tappan (qq.v.) and Oberlin and Lane Seminary graduates (qq.v.). Geographic and other circumstances permitted the founders to hope they could maintain an anti-slavery and non-segregated policy; the Civil War all but destroyed the school; in the post-Civil War era, it became a college emphasizing democratic education and ideals, work and study, and offering opportunities to the mountain youth to attain education. It has maintained this policy, and developed distinctive crafts and agricultural techniques as well as the liberal arts. E. Peck, *Berea's First Century* (1955).

BERGER, VICTOR L. (1860-1929), born in Austria-Hungary, became a worker and teacher in the United States of America, and soon after an influential and moderate leader of the Socialist Party in this country, editor of the Milwaukee *Vorwärts* and author of works including *Municipal Socialism* (1902). The first socialist to be elected to the United States Congress, he served in the House of Representatives in 1911-13, and was elected again in 1918; thanks to the war spirit, he was debarred from Congress in 1919. He was sentenced to prison in 1918 for treason, but the decision was reversed by the Supreme Court. He was returned to Congress, 1923-9.

BERGH, HENRY (1823-1888) was revolted, while in Russia as an attaché to Cassius M. Clay (q.v.) to observe the cruelty practiced there toward animals. Later, he was impressed with the work in England of the Royal Society for the Prevention of Cruelty to Animals. He began his American campaign single-handed, often making personal efforts to stop draymen and others from mistreating their animals. In 1866, he received a state charter in New York incorporating the American Society for the Prevention of Cruelty to Animals, of which he became president. In 1875, he joined others in forming the Society for the Prevention of Cruelty to Children; but his major interest continue to be brutes; A. F. Harlow, *Henry Bergh* (1957).

BERLE, A. A. (1895-1971), influential New Deal (q.v.) economist, whose *The Modern Corporation and Private Property* (1932), written with Gardiner C. Means, became a bible to those concerned with regulation of the corporation. The evidence Berle and Means amassed was calculated to show corporations as powerful beyond public control, and requiring regulation. Berle, as part of the New Deal "Brains Trust" (q.v.) helped fashion such safeguards as the Securities and Exchange Commission, the Public Utility Holding Company Act, and others. Berle saw a "revolution" in the enlarged powers of the corporation and its managers which required such special intervention as Federal chartering of interstate corporations, which he was not able to obtain. He was much involved in U.S.-Latin American relations, and helped to create the Alliance for

Progress (*q.v.*). Berle's long prominence in the field of corporation role and legislation was challenged in John D. Glover, *The Revolutionary Corporations* (1981), which argued that corporations had been fluid, subject to public interest and response, and were a force for growth, service, and changing social needs.

BERLIN AIRLIFT (1948-9), maintained by United States forces stationed in West Germany; an effort to cut off Berlin from contact and supplies by Soviet agencies was frustrated by the all-out program of keeping West Germany and West Berlin united by air, despite the intervening Soviet-dominated terrain. The Russian blockade heightened western-Soviet post-War differences. In September, 1949, both west and east Germany set up separate republics. *Berlin Wall* (1961), built by the Russians to prevent East German escape to the West. It gave some visible advertisement to freedom, but also displayed Soviet might; the United States disappointed its allies by inability to match Russian decisivness and action.

BERNSTEIN, EDUARD (1850-1932), German socialist, leader of the "revisionist" (*q.v.*) school which preached evolutionary, as opposed to revolutionary ideas; his most notable work was *Die Voraussetzungen des Sozialismus und die Aufgaben der Sozial-demokratie* (1899). He was denounced by Bebel (*q.v.*), who declared for class war. Kautsky (*q.v.*) replied to him in *Bernstein und das Sozialdemokratische Programm; eine Anti-kritik* (1899).

BEVERIDGE, ALBERT J. (1862-1927), a midwesterner who worked his way up, and was elected to the United States Senate in 1899, as it seemed, in the tradition of Abraham Lincoln. He distinguished himself for his big navy and rampant imperialist sentiments, and, embodying the contradictions of some Progressives of his era, his sponsorship of pure food, anti-trust, anti-child labor legislation. His increasing liberalism cost him his Indiana seat in 1911. He supported Theodore Roosevelt's Bull Moose campaign in 1912. He was author of one of the great American biographies, his four-volume *Life of John Marshall* (1916-19), and of an unfinished, two-volume *Life of Abraham Lincoln* (1928).

BIG BROTHER, see *1984*.

"BIG BUSINESS," a favorite term among reformers and non-reformers (though not of anti-reformers), during the reform era of pre-World War I days. It was intended to suggest businesses of unusual or monopolistic proportions, and avoided the question of how large a business ought legitimately to be; the solution arrived at was "regulation" (*q.v.*). See P. I. Blumberg, *The Megacorporation* (1975); O. Demaris, *Dirty Business* (1974); R. A. Liston, *Who Really Runs America?* (1974); *Ralph Nader's (q.v.) Conference on Corporate Accountability* (1971).

"BIG LABOR," see Anti-Monopoly.

BIG NAVY, an imperialistic (*q.v.*) slogan, it developed in post-Civil War years as the United States looked more intensively outward. Grover Cleveland's Secretary of the Navy, William C. Whitney, modernized the American fleet. A. T. Mahan (*q.v.*) was the major propagandist favoring a powerful Navy as a requisite to becoming a world power; his ideas influenced Theodore Roosevelt (*q.v.*). The problem of the role of the Navy in foreign affairs influenced policy from the Washington Conference of 1922 to the London Naval Conference of 1930. Since World War II, the role of planes, missiles, and, finally, the Polaris submarine, a death-dealing instrument of high potential, have complicated the question of the role of the Navy.

BIG STICK POLICY, so called for a speech by Theodore Roosevelt in Chicago in which he advocated that America "Speak softly and carry a big stick." Although his admirers fancied that this technique applied to his domestic operations as well as to foreign affairs, the phrase became associated mainly with the latter, in the minds of reformers; the first part of the phrase tended to be forgotten. See "I Took the Canal Zone."

BIGOTRY, condemned by social reformers, and identified with such activities as those sponsored by the Know-Nothings, the A.P.A. and the Dearborn Independent (*qq.v.*); see Gustavus

Myers, *History of Bigotry in the United States* (1943). Essentially a racist (*q.v.*) idea, it was hurt by Kennedy's (*q.v.*) accession to the Presidency. See also Jews, Catholics. Glenn E. Tinder, *Tolerance: Toward a New Civility* (1975).

BILL OF RIGHTS, the first ten Amendments to the Constitution of the United States, ratified in 1791, over two years following adoption of the Constitution. It is not always realized that many partisans of the Constitution were not partisans of the Bill of Rights. They guaranteed freedom of religion, speech, press, "the right of the people peaceably to assemble," to be secure in their persons, not to be compelled to be witnesses against themselves in criminal cases, and others; see the individual Amendments; see also Civil Liberties.

BILLION-DOLLAR CONGRESS, THE, name given to the Fifty-First Congress of the United States because its appropriations during the period 1889-1891 totalled more than a billion dollars. The remark by Speaker Thomas B. Reed that "This is a billion-dollar country" is a notorious Republican *non sequitur*.

BIRCH SOCIETY, a political phenomenon which burst upon popular attention in 1961, when brought to public scrutiny by U.S. Senator Milton R. Young, of North Dakota. The rapidly growing and influential society was founded by Robert H. W. Welch, Jr., a retired candy maker of Massachusetts, who named it for a Baptist missionary killed by communists in China ten days after the close of World War II. The Society engaged in such activities as circulating a petition to impeach Chief Justice of the U.S. Supreme Court Earl Warren, and imputing communist sympathies and aims to a wide variety of American political leaders. It attracted the cooperation of legislators and industrialists, and seemed to be complex enough to include various wings of opinion, as well as a national membership. See B. R. Epstein and Arnold Forster, *The Radical Right* (1967); Gene Grove, *Inside the John Birch Society* (1961).

BIRNEY, JAMES GILLESPIE (1792-1857), noted "gradualist" abolitionist, he became famous as a "rehabilitated" slaveholder; his effort to persuade other slaveholders to set free their slaves for colonization purposes exposed the inadequate premises of the colonialization (*q.v.*) cause. His effort to begin a Kentucky anti-slavery society, which was frustrated by his neighbors, helped reveal the tenacious nature of slavery, even in the Border States. *The Philanthropist*, which he published in Cincinnati, Ohio, maintained his cause against serious resistance. In 1837, he left the *Philanthropist* to Gamaliel Bailey (*q.v.*) and joined the executive Committee of the American Anti-Slavery Society. In 1840, he was put up for President by an *ad hoc* group of political abolitionists, though he himself was out of the country. In 1844, as Liberty Party candidate, his relatively few votes decided the election against Clay. He was an outstanding anti-slavery lawyer and, until 1847, an influence in anti-slavery circles; however, a severe accident incapacitated him for the most part and he figured little in anti-slavery councils after 1848. His most notable writing was *American Churches the Bulwarks of American Slavery* (1840). In 1852, discouraged with the course of affairs, he grieved abolitionists by urging the Negroes to return to Africa. His son William's *James G. Birney and His Times* (1890) is a valuable defense of "gradual" abolitionism.

BIROBIJAN, autonomous region in Siberia which was set aside by the U.S.S.R. as a national home for the Jews, was taken by admirers of the Soviets to be their contribution to easing the problems of beset Jews (*q.v.*). They were, however, given limited opportunities to maintain or develop their culture, or the means to develop this region: an area of some 14,000 square miles.

BIRTH CONTROL, a reform associated with several causes: Free speech and press (in the right to impart information on the subject), opposition to church strictures and social customs, women's rights, and pro-labor determination to lighten the burden of poor families and women. Various freethinkers and individualists made contributions to clarifying the issues involved, throughout the nineteenth century, in the United States and abroad. However, in 1873, Anthony Comstock (q.v.) persuaded Congress to make obscene literature, vaguely described, illegal, and thus debarred contraceptive writings from the mails. Possession of such materials was, in some states, made illegal. In 1880, D. M. Bennett, founder of the atheistic Truth Seekers was imprisoned for mailing a pamphlet on the subject. In 1912, Margaret Sanger (q.v.) was stirred to awareness of the problem; in 1915 the first National Birth Control League was organized. Its purposes were educational and legislative. The Voluntary Parenthood League, formed 1919, had essentially the same aims, emphasizing federal law. In 1921, Sanger organized the American Birth Control League, which worked toward offering clinical services. Contraceptives became more readily attainable, technically as a health measure. By 1960, there was a "birth control pill," approved by the U.S. Food and Drug Administration, to aid in "family planning." The only major antagonist to this trend and development was the Catholic Church, within which critics like Andrew M. Greeley commented. See also Abortion, Pill, The, Sex.

BISBEE DEPORTATIONS (July 12, 1917), a product of wartime vigilante enterprise, in the Arizona copper mines; some 1200 workmen were rounded up by the "Loyalty League" in the area and deported to New Mexico. The action was drastic enough to elicit condemnation from the United States government, for all that it, too, was eager to discourage strikes, especially in time of national emergency.

BISMARCK, PRINCE OTTO VON (1815-1898), symbol of Prussian military tradition and German nationalistic ambitions; he encouraged social reform where it contributed to national unity and strength, as in nationalizing the railroads, and tolerated social democracy to the extent that it helped divide republican forces in Germany. He did, however, in 1878, undertake an anti-socialist campaign, and in 1881 (following the assassination of Czar Alexander of Russia) attempt to organize an anti-socialist coalition, which failed. More successful was his persecution of social democrats for harboring revolutionists among them; in 1886, his government instigated a trial of nine socialist leaders, including August Bebel (q.v.).

BITTER-ENDERS, THE, applied to the group of Senators who, following World War I resisted President Woodrow Wilson's efforts to enlist the United States into the League of Nations, especially to those who in March 1919 signed a Round Robin which opposed acceptance of the Covenant of the League.

BLACK, HUGO (1886-1971), Alabama United States Senator and New Dealer, appointed in 1937 to the Supreme Court, but the center of much Congressional debate when it was revealed that he had earlier been a member of the Ku Klux Klan. The argument in his favor was that to begin a political career at the time he had, it was necessary for an individual from his part of the country to cooperate with the Klan, and that he had not long maintained his associations among them. With more vigorous pro-Negro elements adhering to socialist and quasi-communist tenets, it was relatively easy to hold together the fabric of the Democratic Party on the issue of Black's liberalism. As an Associate Justice, he revealed a concern for civil liberties, arguing, for example, for an interpretation which gave added strength to the Bill of Rights (q.v.). However, he also defended Japanese Relocation (q.v.). G. T. Dunne, Hugo Black and the Judicial Revolution (1972).

BLACKS, a phenomenon of the 1960s, when militant Caribbean Negroes, mainly of dark complexion, forced the word on the Negro community, largely many-complected, as part of their drive for new status in the American spectrum. "You're Black!" became a phrase difficult to resist, though it had been used as an epithet (q.v.) by bigots (q.v.), resisting the "color blind" judgment of the Supreme Court. The new meaning appeared to have a future, in America as abroad.

BLACK AND TANS, the union of carpetbaggers, scalawags (qq.v.), and Negroes, which constituted the ruling caste in southern states during the Reconstruction (q.v.). Black and Tan conventions revised the southern constitutions and their alliances dominated the legislatures.

BLACK CAUCUS, a group of Negro Congressional Representatives who worked for legislation servicing their constituents, using the bargaining power of black votes. Realists, they were untroubled by internal corruption, arguing it was racist when applied to themselves. Their senior member, Rep. Charles Diggs, Jr. (D., Mich.) being convicted in 1978 of mail fraud and false pay vouchers, they asserted he would be missed in their councils.

BLACK CODE, THE, state laws intended to keep Negroes inferior in status to the white people, to prevent them from entering the state, and make it easy to drive them out. Although these laws are popularly identified with states of the South following the Civil War, and with their attempt to control their freed populations, such laws also flourished in the pre-Civil War era, and in the North as well as the South. The "Black Code" originated in Louisiana under the French, it was retained by the Spanish, and set an example of laws regulating Negro-white relations. See also Negro Civil Rights, Freedmen. See Theodore B. Wilson, Black Codes of the South (1966).

BLACK ENGLISH, by J. L. Dillard (1972), an attempt to claim legitimacy for Negro dialect in the black ghettoes (q.v.). Some Negro spokesmen were made anxious by such arguments, fearing it would justify black children's ignorance in the schools. However, a Federal court in Ann Arbor, Mich. agreed in 1980 "Black English deserved special regard and educational consideration." It was hoped such empathy would help lower the Negro drop-out school record. Some leaders among Negroes, though approving the decision, deplored "native tongue" education for Puerto Ricans, and "Chicanos" in California, as making difficult their adjustment to American conditions.

BLACK FRIDAY, September 24, 1869, a day which followed a speculative frenzy in the course of which the adventurers Jay Gould and Jim Fisk (q.v.) sought to gain a "corner" on gold. Their plans required the United States Treasury to stand by without action, but the desperation created in business circles was such that President Ulysses S. Grant on the abovementioned date ordered the sub-treasury, in New York, to make gold available by sale. Although this "broke the corner," the disorder created was such as to shake up business and speculative circles violently.

"BLACK HUNDREDS," see Pogroms.

BLACK MOUNTAIN COLLEGE, established 1933, was a bold effort in cooperative living as well as learning, and intended to cut through shams and shibboleths. It attracted to its campus near Asheville, North Carolina, enthusiastic teachers and students, some talented, and some foundation and other aid. It was accepted as a four-year accredited liberal college. Its deterioration in the post-World War II era resulted in a demoralized campus, a rapid misuse of assets and social credit, and a final exodus of the few devout hangers on. The causes of its failures were personal and programatic, both of which factors merited study. See M. Duberman, Black Mountain (1972).

BLACK NATIONALISM, sometimes attempted in the American context, by Negroes with no intention of surrendering their civil rights (q.v.), but more seriously related to changes and reorganizations in Africa. It involved both nationalist efforts and attempts to create black-loyalty attitudes between separate black nations. See R. Chrisman and N. Hare, comp., Black Nationalism (1974).

BLACK REPUBLICAN, BLACK REPUBLICANISM, antagonistic epithets employed by the foes of Republicans, notably Democrats, in the pre-Civil War period, to indicate supposed Republican sympathy for Negroes, though a majority of the new Party maintained a dislike for Negroes; see also Republican Party, Radical Republicans.

BLACK SHIRTS, one of the distinguishing articles of Fascisti wear, and thus identified with Mussolini's (*q.v.*) dictatorship; also emphasized their military organization and purposes. Compare Red Shirts, Descamisados.

BLACKLIST IN SHOW BUSINESS, mainly associated with Hollywood (*q.v.*) concerns. Since many involved were highly verbal, a considerable amount of writing on the subject accrued; e.g., G. Kahn, *Hollywood on Trial* (1948); A. Bessie, *Inquisition in Eden* (1965); Eric Bentley, *Thirty Years of Treason* (1971); Stefan Kaufer, *A Journal of the Plague Years* (1973).

BLACKWELL, ANTOINETTE L. (BROWN) (1825-1921), was a resident of New York state, who early began speaking in public. She attended Oberlin College (*q.v.*), completing the theological course, in 1850. Refused a license because of her sex, she preached wherever she could before becoming a recognized pastor of the Congregationalist Church of South Butler, New York. She spoke eloquently in favor of abolitionism, temperance, and woman's rights (*qq.v.*). Her theological convictions, however, caused her to resign from her church in 1854, when she announced her acceptance of Unitarian tenets. Her most famous crisis took place in 1853, when she was refused permission to speak at the "World's" Temperance Convention in New York. Sister-in-law of Lucy Stone (*q.v.*).

BLAINE, JAMES G. (1830-1893), American politician, leader of the Republican Party, and Secretary of State, noted for his interest in developing Pan-American relations, but more for the scandal which attended revelations that he had had a personal interest in advocating private railroad interests, as exposed in the "Mulligan Letters" (*q.v.*). That he should nevertheless have become the standard-bearer of the Republican Party, in 1884, when he all but won the election has impressed reformers concerned for fathoming the American psychology and potential. See also Ingersoll, Robert G.

BLANC, JEAN J. C. LOUIS (1811-1882), French historian and revolutionary thinker. His most famous idea was to create National Workshops (*Ateliers Nationaux [q.v.]*) which would obliterate unemployment. As a member of the Provisional Government, set up during the February Revolution of 1848, they were established, but he soon turned against them; their abolition helped bring on further revolutionary uprisings. His writings contributed to socialist thinking; see his *Le Socialisme, Droit au Travail* (1849), and *Histoire de la Révolution Française* (1847-1862).

BLAND-ALLISON ACT (1878), a milestone in the development of the Silver Issue (*q.v.*). The price of silver being down as compared with gold, the Act instructed the U.S. Treasury to purchase from two to four million dollars worth of silver each month (the minimum was purchased, in fact), the same to be coined into standard dollars. Under the Act, more than two hundred million silver dollars were coined. The intention of the silver-miners was to raise the value of their silver, of the farmers to increase the presence of cheap money which could affect the value of gold and be more readily available. The silver, however, was purchased at market prices, little affecting them, and not placed largely in circulation; the government stored the greater mass of the silver. Accordingly, it accomplished little more than to indicate that silver was a politically effective issue on which battle would have to be joined.

BLANKET INJUNCTION, see Injunction.

"BLEEDING KANSAS," so termed because, during the struggle between pro-slavery and anti-slavery partisans, following the passage of the Kansas-Nebraska Act in 1854, various organized assaults took place, during which the "free" town of Lawrence was sacked, counter-actions notoriously including those of John Brown. (See Pottowatomie Massacre.) In reality, little occurred in Kansas which did not also occur in other newly-organized territories, but the term, "Bleeding Kansas," reflected the excitement which the slavery issue engendered in eastern minds, fearful that it might become a free or a slave state.

BLIND, THE, see Institutional Reform.

BLISS, W. D. P. (1856-1926), born in Turkey, the son of a Christian missionary; one of the founders of the Society of Christian Socialists, and a notable educator in the field. His *Encyclopedia of Social Reform* (1897, 1908, 1909-10 eds.) is a monument of information on the experiences and expectations of moderate socialists of his era. See also his *Handbook of Socialism* (1895).

"BLOOD AND IRON," Bismarck's (*q.v.*) notorious recipe for a successful foreign policy, reprobated by reformers, but turning up oddly in Herbert Croly's (*q.v.*) *The Promise of American Life,* and not noted, or ignored, by like-minded reformers enamored of Croly's approach.

"BLOODY SHIRT, WAVING THE," a demagogic oratorical technique employed by Republican spokesmen, in post-Civil War decades; when at loss for a more effective argument, they would attack their Democratic opponents by weaving florid tributes to the Federal soldiers who had died in the late war, and suggesting, more or less directly, depending on the circumstances—since some Republicans had not fought in the war, and some Union Democrats had—that the Democrats were traitors, unworthy of the suffrage of the people; see Foraker, Joseph B. S. P. Hirshson, *Farewell to the Bloody Shirt* (1962).

BLOOMER, MRS. AMELIA J. (1818-1894), an early American postmistress, editor of *The Lily* (1848-1854) which favored suffrage, temperance, and other reforms. Most famous for having popularized the bloomer costume, a combination of trousers and dress intended to give more freedom to women; a step in dress reform (*q.v.*). D. C. Bloomer, *Life and Writings of Amelia Bloomer* (1893).

BLOWING THE WHISTLE, a Ralph Nader (*q.v.*) concept, intended to encourage civil servants to inform, when they became aware of fraud or bungled work in government. However, individuals who did do their duty were sometimes harassed or separated from jobs, rather than praised or rewarded. Questions were also raised as to whether exposing secret materials served the public interest or provided information to the nation's enemies, or improperly diminished public respect for government. See Corruption, Ellsberg, Daniel, F. B. I. Charles Peters and T. Branch, *Blowing the Whistle* (1972).

"BLUE EAGLE," symbol of the New Deal (*q.v.*) in its first major effort to right the economy through the operations of the National Recovery Administration (*q.v.*). It depicted a vigorous eagle holding in one claw a bolt of lightning; the posters bearing the symbol proclaimed that the store owner who placed it in his window was "Member N.R.A. We Do Our Part." To those who feared the Administration as exhibiting "fascist" tendencies, the Blue Eagle looked like a Blue Buzzard, and the campaign it symbolized totalitarian in essence.

"BLUE LAWS," first drawn up in Connecticut, though in time identified with New England theocratic government intended to restrict personal liberty and expression in the interest of a Puritan view of life. The first collection, in 1650, was bound in blue covers, from which the popular term derived. "Blue Noses," describing a Prohibitionist, during the 1920's, may have been an extension of the original phrase, and perhaps contrasted with red noses, signifying merriment and vivacity.

BOER WAR, (1899-1900), the raid of Dr. Leander S. Jameson, administrator of Rhodesia, into the Boer-dominated Transvaal, January 1, 1896; impressed Americans as the actions of a great nation imposing itself upon a small one. The determined battle which the Boers later put up against British forces, under the dour and inflexible leadership of their president, Paul Kruger, roused sympathy and admiration in the United States, though there was official unwillingness to become committed to giving the Boers aid directly. The Boer War entered into anti-imperialist lore. However, it failed to include an analysis of Boer social attitudes, which would later emerge in their determined attempt to suppress Negroes who resisted segregation or inferior status. See Union of South Africa, Imperialism and Reform.

BOHEMIANS, malcontents with artistic inclinations, often, as G. K. Chesterton observed, living the poems they cannot write, but often, too, including persons of genius, from the fifteenth century French poet and criminal, François Villon, to the twentieth century artist and dissolute personality, Modigliani. They have in common with reformers an unwillingness to meet current fashions and standards, a criticism of mere conformity. The classic statement of Bohemia is in Henri Murger (1822-1861), *Scènes de la Vie Bohème* (1847). They are often too individualistic and self-centered to serve society directly, but their romantic temperament can give them an idealistic empathy with the "people"; Bohemians offered their breasts to the soldiery, in France, during fighting in the streets in the 1830 and 1848 revolutions. In the United States, Albert Parry's *Garrets and Pretenders* (1931), traces the development of Bohemia, and its classic period, the 1910's, which produced *The Masses* (*q.v.*), and such figures as John Reed (*q.v.*) who grew out of bohemianism into radicalism. Bohemians tend to sow wild oats and then settle down to conformity; those who do not tend toward demoralization, as youth and associates depart; compare Youth Movement, The, "Beatniks." See Louis Filler, *Vanguards & Followers: Youth in the American Tradition* (1978).

BOLÍVAR, SIMON (1783-1830), known as "The Liberator," one of the great South American figures in their struggle for independence from Spain. Born in Caracas, Venezuela, he was raised in comfort and study, and broadened his understanding with travel in Europe and philosophic studies. He was instrumental in the freeing of Peru and the area which was named for him, Bolivia. A great struggle extending over a decade established independent Venezuela with Bolívar at its head. His military and political hand was present, too, in the freeing of Colombia. A thinker as well as a man of action, he struggled with the problem of governments proper to so complex a social and racial pattern as that which South America presented. G. Masur, *Simon Bolívar* (1969).

BOLSHEVISM, resulted from a split in the Russian Social Democratic Party following a meeting in London in 1903. Lenin, heading the majority (the Bolsheviki), denounced democratic aims and perspectives and favored a dictatorship of the proletariat; the more moderate socialists were then in a minority (the Mensheviki), but felt it historically necessary to tolerate and cooperate with democratic tendencies in Russia. By 1917, the Bolsheviks, despite their name, were in a minority, but were able to carry their program in Russia.

BONUS MARCHERS (1932), were composed of veterans of World War I who sought to persuade the government to permit them to cash in their deferred bonuses granted by the Adjusted Compensation Act (1924). About 15,000 veterans, who included some ardent radicals, camped in shabby huts near the Capitol while striving to put pressure on Congress to pass the Patman Bill, which dealt with their demands. Their shelters were razed, and they were dispersed with tear-gas bombs. The incident harmed the Republican administration, and contributed to Hoover's overwhelming defeat in the fall election. See also Coxey, Jacob S. Donald J. Lisio, *The President and Protest* (1974).

BOODLE, a term popular in the late 1880's and 1890's, and still heard; designating the gains from illegal or more directly thievish activities, and associated with politics; the word expanded its meaning, popularly, to refer to all gains; a *boodler* was more directly a person dealing in bribes.

BOONDOGGLE, a New England rural term which surfaced early in the Great Depression (*q.v.*) as critical of relief (*q.v.*) measures intended to help the unemployed without depriving the employed. Hence, "leaf-raking" (*q.v.*) and other economically unfruitful labor was devised to give empty-handed people work.

BOOTH, SHERMAN, see Ableman v. Booth.

BORAH, WILLIAM E. (1865-1940), Senator from Idaho 1907-1931, prosecutor in the Steunenberg murder trial (*q.v.*) and a proponent of western individualism. However, he fought for the Seventeenth Amendment to the Constitution, (*q.v.*) and other Progressive legislation. He was one of the irreconcilables who fought entrance into the League of Nations, but he also introduced a Senate resolution, December 1920, calling for an international conference to stop the naval armaments race. He was honored with a write-up in Dilling's *Red Network* (*q.v.*), which waxed indignant over his protest (1926) against the landing of U.S. Marines in Nicaragua, and his advocacy of recognition of the U.S.S.R. (*q.v.*).

BORDER RUFFIANS, name applied to pro-slave Missourians by Free Soilers, when the former crossed over into Kansas in order to vote for pro-slave measures or cow the Free State partisans. The Kansas-Nebraska Act (*q.v.*) of 1854 resulted in a "Border War" which brought emigrants from North and South in their anxiety to help decide the issue in fashion favorable to their cause. S. A. Johnson, *The Battle Cry of Freedom* (1954).

BORDER STATES, THE, a momentous consideration throughout the crisis which ended in the secession of the Confederacy (*q.v.*), since the secession of almost any one of the Border States—Maryland, Kentucky, Tennessee, Missouri—would have ensured the stalemate the south needed for the success of its plans. There were stars in the Confederate flag for all of these states. The Border States continue to be significant for any program looking to the melioration of sectional tendencies in the south.

"BORING FROM WITHIN," a communist tactic widely employed during the 1930's: communists entered an organization which they did not control, and thanks to their firm party discipline and preparation, and the sympathy and cooperation of elements within the organization, "captured" its leadership and directed it according to their program. Compare Dual Unionism.

BOSS RULE, refers to political control centering about a strong party leader, the Boss. William Marcy Tweed (*q.v.*) was the prototype of such personalities, and in the decades following his fall, practically all cities developed comparable systems, which became a major target of attack during the pre-World War I era of reform. "Boss" from the Dutch *baas*, a foreman or master; also in connection with labor, not with the highest respect: "labor boss."

BOSTON MASSACRE (1770), an incident attending growing differences between British policy-makers and resentful colonial patriots. Soldiers brought into Boston were received with bitterness by the townspeople, and small clashes occurred. On March 5, a group of soldiers were jeered and pelted with snowballs by aggressive men and children. The tension created resulted in the possibly inadvertent firing of a volley which killed five persons, including Crispus Attucks (*q.v.*). John Adams (*q.v.*) and Josiah Quincy, though Boston patriots, defended the soldiers and secured the acquittal of most of them, the mild punishment of two. Samuel Adams (*q.v.*) seized upon the incident to rouse patriot indignation throughout the colonies, his greatest success being to fix the stigma of a "massacre" on the event. It revealed that the soldiers had no status among those who were technically their compatriots, and that snowballs could be an occasion for shooting. Many individual accounts of experiences associated with the "Massacre" are contained in Frederic Kidder, *History of the Boston Massacre, March 5, 1770; Consisting of the Narrative of the Town, the Trial of the Soldiers, and an Historical Introduction, Containing Unpublished Documents of John Adams and Explanatory Notes* (1870).

BOSTON TEA PARTY, THE, most famous of several similar actions: on December 16, 1773, a group of colonists, dressed as Indians, boarded three East India Company ships, broke open the three hundred and forty-two tea chests they carried, and dumped some £18,000 worth of tea into the harbor. This act was theoretically in retaliation for the fact that the British Parliament had laid a threepence tax on every pound of tea; in actuality the tea was being offered at bargain prices and would have undercut the market of Boston smugglers, notably John Hancock. Justification for the act must be found for its undercutting of the Non-Intercourse Agreement (q.v.).

BOTKIN, BEN A. (1901-1975), folklorist and author, who, while teaching at the University of Oklahoma, gathered folk materials and worked with such authors as Carl Sandburg, who were responsive to how the people thought and felt. He coined the word *Folk-Say* in 1928, and published a "regional miscellany" with that title, 1929-1932. He became Folklore editor of the Federal Writers Project, and gathered huge quantities of folk reminiscence, from which he drew his own pioneer *Lay My Burden Down: a Folk History of Slavery* (1945). His *A Treasury of American Folklore* (1944) was the first of a shelf of volumes capturing the essence of Americans in different eras and from coast to coast, aided by his literary sensibility and wide knowledge. He tutored his cousin George Gershwin in the folklore employed in the latter's *Porgy and Bess*. See Bruce Jackson, ed., *Folklore and Society: Essays in Honor of Ben A. Botkin* (1966).

BOURGEOIS, French noun and adjective, signifying middle-class, tradesman, of commonplace or uncultured qualities; invidiously used by upper-class elements offended by upstarts, who had acquired money, and sought acceptance. The word was adopted by liberals who deemed themselves sensitive to the finer or deeper facts of life, and, more technically, by socialists and communists, to designate persons who were unable to understand or accept the necessity or inevitability of social revolution, or who consciously sought to impede its advance. In sufficiently active situations, the "bourgeoisie" could be held to be "counter-revolutionary."

BOURNE, RANDOLPH S. (1886-1918), pacifist, literary man, and leader of the Youth Movement (q.v.) of the 1910's; a talented young man frustrated by a crippled physique, he graduated with honors from Columbia University, but sought more satisfying social fare. His *Youth and Life* (1913) called on youth to create the future. *The Gary Schools* (1916) and *Education and Living* (1917) called for experimentalism in and out of the schools. His symposium, *Towards an Enduring Peace* (1916) sought an answer to World War I. He wrote for the *New Republic* and the *Dial* (qq.v.), but his opposition to the war turned him against the state; he was investigating extreme individualism and communism when he died. *Untimely Papers* (1919) and *The History of a Literary Radical* (1920) helped make him a legend to later radicals; see Louis Filler, *Randolph Bourne* (1965 edition).

BOVEE, MARVIN H. (1827-1888), anti-capital punishment crusader, who beginning his career as a Wisconsin legislator, carried his campaign to abolish the death penalty to New York, Illinois, Massachusetts, and elsewhere, his speeches and legislative labors resulting in various reforms. In 1869, he published *Christ and the Gallows; or, Reasons for the Abolition of Capital Punishment*, a major work in the field.

BOWDITCH, HENRY I. (1808-1892), abolitionist and public health advocate, who edited the *Latimer Journal and North Star* in 1842-3, a striking example of journalistic enterprise and propaganda in behalf of a runaway slave whose case was a first test of the Prigg (q.v.) decision. His *Brief Plea for an Ambulance System for the Army of the United States* (1863), among other works, focused attention on it and related issues.

BOXER REBELLION (1900), an abortive effort on the part of frustrated Chinese elements to expel the "foreign devils" from their homeland; they occupied Peking and attacked the foreign legations. Suppressed, the Department of State under John Hay (q.v.) asserted views intended to discourage efforts on the part of any of the greater powers to dismember China. The Chinese government was forced to pay damages for the assault on foreigners; the money paid to the United States was used for the education of Chinese students in American institutions of higher learning. Richard O'Connor, *The Boxer Rebellion* (1973).

BOYCOTT, a labor tactic first employed in 1880 against a Captain Charles Boycott, agent of an Irish landholder; he was refused all services and others were prevented from offering him cooperation. As used in the United States, it involved labor seeking to bring a company to terms by stopping all intercourse with it, and urging others to do so. The major case was that involving the United Hatters of North America, who, in 1902, instituted a secondary boycott (q.v.) against the Dietrich Loewe firm in Danbury, Connecticut; by decision of the United States Supreme Court in 1908, the hatters involved were ordered to pay $250,000 damages as having engaged in restraint of trade under the Sherman Anti-Trust Act (q.v.). Another major case involved the Buck Stove and Range Company of St. Louis, boycotted in 1906 by the Iron Molders' and Metal Polishers Union. An injunction issued by the Supreme Court of the District of Columbia was challenged by the American Federation of Labor. Its leader, Samuel Gompers (q.v.), was sentenced to jail (1909) and appealed. The company's determined head died the next year, and his successor chose to arbitrate. Actions in the courts continued till 1914, when the statute of limitations ended the case, with no conclusion reached.

BRAIN TRUST, THE, applied to a group of men who gathered about Franklin D. Roosevelt (q.v.) during his first campaign for the Presidency in 1932. Originally, it was "Brains Trust," as coined by Dr. James M. Kieran, then president of Hunter College. The group was composed largely of academic and other professional men, and represented an innovation in that technical understanding was being added to the processes of national government over older political and social competencies; compare Wisconsin Idea. Notables among the original group—some of whom were sooner or later dissociated from it—included Rexford G. Tugwell, Arthur E. Morgan (qq.v.), Hugh S. Johnson, George N. Peek and Harcourt A. Morgan; see Kitchen Cabinet.

BRAINWASHING, somewhat similar to "thought control" (q.v.), in some aspects, but a more urgent and expedient means for neutralizing foes and achieving propaganda advantages. It was made notorious in the United States by the success which the Communists attained in persuading American prisoners of war, captured during the Korean War, to "confess" that the United States was engaged in disseminating germs among their captors, to declare the justice of the communist cause, and otherwise to repudiate their homeland and prior opinions. Brain washing was a flexible method which utilized flattery and terror, psychological techniques (such as exploiting fatigue, loneliness, confusion) and direct appeals to special circumstances: a Negro's sense of having been abused by white Americans, the sense a soldier from a poverty-filled home had of having been unjustly treated. The care which the Chinese communists took to refine brainwashing into an instrument they could use with mastery suggested the need for counter-measures which would enable Americans to anticipate its use with confidence that it could be resisted. See Edward Hunter, *Brainwashing: the Story of Men Who Defied It* (1956), Peter Watson, *War on the Mind: the Military Uses and Abuses of Psychology* (1978). See also Germ Warfare, Chemical Warfare.

BRANDEIS, LOUIS D. (1856-1941), a product of Progressive thinking, he was attorney for the policyholders during the 1905 investigation of the Equitable Life Insurance Company (see Insurance Investigation). His pioneer brief in Muller v. Oregon (1908) opposed Supreme Court practice of interpreting laws which reformed working conditions as unconstitutional, on the grounds that they contradicted the Fourteenth Amendment (q.v.). Brandeis marshalled facts which revealed the actual harm to workers, as a result of noxious shop conditions, and thus established that an abstract theory of constitutional rights ought not to be used to defend oppressive practices. Brandeis defended the rights of small business over large; his *Other People's Money* (1914) was a powerful, as well as popular, expose of the methods by which control over finance had been won by banking interests. A valued adviser of President Wilson, he was appointed to the Supreme Court in 1916 over strong conservative protests; there he served, with Justice Holmes (q.v.), as a part of a great team of dissenters, defending the right of government to experiment in the interests of the public. A. L. Todd, *Justice on Trial: the Case of Louis D. Brandeis* (1968); Iris Noble, *Firebrand for Justice* (1969).

BRANNAN PLAN, see Farmers and Reform.

BRASS CHECK, THE, (1919), by Upton Sinclair, one of the author's important analyses of American institutions, this one concerned for American communication, notably through the newspapers. Citing his own experiences and others's, he concluded that American journalism was not free, but linked to high finance. Written without scholarly caution, and containing errors of fact and interpretation, it was nevertheless a formidable piling up of evidence respecting the capitalist bias of American journalism of the time. Sinclair did not apply a similar combination of candor and inquiry into socialist and other journalism. He concluded early editions of the book with an appeal for funds to start an "impartial" news service, but soon dropped this idea.

BRAZIL, a giant land of 120 million people, it boasted a history looking back to Portuguese roots, eastward to Africa which brought it slaves, and north and west to Latin American countries whom it diminished with its vast resources and complex society. Only Argentina (q.v.) to the south could challenge its claims to civilization and authority. Nevertheless, Brazil's Portuguese tongue separated it from the Spanish speaking peoples of Central and South America. Despite its assimilation of Indian, Negro, and white peoples, its dazzling capital city of Brazilia, modern and hewn out of the wilderness, it displayed glaring contrasts of rich and poor, made acute by a continuing and all but insufferable inflation. Coffee continued to be the mainstay of its economy, a slender reed for a nation of three and a quarter-million square miles. Foreign loans kept it going, though in the 1970s it faced the problem of a shortage of oil from a vulnerable base. Harry Bernstein, *Contemporary Brazil* (1968); Euclides da Cunha, *Rebellion in the Backlands* (1957); Gilberto Freyre, *The Master and the Slaves* (1946); Samuel Putnam, *Marvelous Journey…Four Centuries of Brazilian Writing* (1948); E. B. Burns, ed., *A Documentary History of Brazil* (1966).

BREAD RIOTS, an incident of the depression of 1837 (q.v.). Unemployment and need caused the poor to gather in New York in protest against high prices. An agitator reminded them of the flour which was being stored in the city warehouses, which the mob proceeded to break into and plunder. Such suffering as attended early depressions qualify the fiction of a frontier (q.v.) which made want impossible in the New World.

BREADWINNERS, THE (1883), see Hay, John, 1887, Railroad Riots of.

BREST-LITOVSK, TREATY OF, see Versailles Treaty.

BRETHREN, CHURCH OF, a Christian sect, numbering some 200,000 communicants; like the Quakers and the Mennonites (qq.v.) concerned to a notable extent for peace and social service, as in Castañer, where the church maintains a public health and educational center high in the mountains of Puerto Rico.

BRIBES, identified with municipal, industrial, federal, and other corruption (q.v.), thought of by reformers as inseparable from the profit motive. However, there are bribes other than pecuniary; David Graham Phillips (q.v.) asserted that the one bribe no one can resist is the social bribe, that is, status offered in exchange for acquiescence before injustice. Thus, a person remaining silent in the face of cheats or frauds perpetrated by reformers would be as substantially a bribe-taker as a councilman accepting favors in exchange for his cooperative vote.

BRIDGES, HARRY (1900-   ), controversial labor leader, organizer of the great General Strike (q.v.) of San Francisco in 1934. He capped a career as a seaman by becoming an organizer of the International Longshoremen's Association in San Francisco in the 1920's, and later worked to organize a labor offensive in behalf of recognition of the union, a thirty-hour week, control of hiring halls by the union, and other demands. This resulted in what the antagonistic press called a "revolution." The government National Longshoremen's Board granted the union its demands. In 1937, another great strike reaffirmed the union's strength. Bridges became West Coast Regional Director of the C.I.O. (q.v.). In January 1940, Bridges was officially cleared of being a communist. That year, the House of Representatives passed a bill singling him out for deportation without specifying his crime. (Bridges was born in Australia.) An intensive F.B.I. (q.v.) investigation to determine whether he was, or ever had been, a communist —which would have made him subject to deportation under the Smith Act (q.v.)—failed to establish effective evidence. He continued to trouble those who held that his policies tallied with those of the communists, but West Coast sailors appeared unwilling to give up their loyalty to him. A late conservatism had him in 1960 negotiating a contract which traded a job cut for high wages and retirement. C. P. Larrowe, *Harry Bridges: the Rise and Fall of Radical Labor in the United States* (1972).

BRIGHT, JOHN (1811-1889), with Richard Cobden (q.v.) a leader of the free trade agitation in England which resulted in the repeal of the Corn Laws (q.v.). He was a Quaker and a pacifist, and, like Cobden, a Member of Parliament, where he supported a variety of liberal measures. H. Ausubel, *John Bright, Victorian Reformer* (1966); G. M. Trevelyan, *Life of John Bright* (1913).

BRISBANE, ALBERT (1809-1890), American follower of Fourier (q.v.), whose *Social Destiny of Man* (1840) influenced the "associationists" of the time, including Horace Greeley, William Henry Channing, and Charles A. Dana (qq.v.). Greeley allowed him to pay for a column in the *Tribune*, in which he preached (1842-1844) his views of the organization of human society, which also became those of Brook Farm (q.v.) in its last phase. His son Arthur (1863-1936) was an associate of William Randolph Hearst (q.v.), a master of the platitude who believed that it was impossible to under-rate the ignorance of the masses, and who became a multi-millionaire.

BRITISH EMANCIPATION took a different course from that in the United States, partly because slavery and exploitation were so widely scattered, and affected social and political interests differently. Slavery was ended in Great Britain proper in the 1770's. The slave trade in foreign terms was ended in both Great Britain and the United States in 1807, being largely a matter of Parliamentary and Congressional action. The British anti-slavery leaders, including Wilberforce (q.v.), Zachary Macaulay, Granville Sharp, Thomas Clarkson, Henry Brougham, Joseph Sturge, and others, rallied behind Thomas F. Buxton to form the Anti-Slavery Society and develop their campaign to end slavery. The West Indies planters found themselves opposed not only by moral reformers but by commercial interests, for example in the East Indies. The losing battle which the planters fought was weakened further by the readiness of the British to compensate them for their lost slave property. Emancipation was achieved in 1833, the final blow being the Reform Bill of 1832 which tripled the number of British voters. The planters of Jamaica, Barbados, Trinidad, and other Caribbean possessions received twenty million pounds for their slaves. An "apprenticeship" system intended to acclimate the freed Negroes to their new status was anxiously watched by abolitionists, who could report many acts of bad faith in the islands. One of the most influential reports, *The West Indies in 1837* (1837), by Sturge and Thomas Harvey, publicized notorious situations. British emancipation was an inspiration to American abolitionists, who defended it with pamphlets, celebrated emancipation annually, and appealed to the British for aid in their own work. Southerners claimed island commerce had deteriorated, and that emancipation concealed the realities of "white slavery" in England. See W. L. Mathiesson, *British Slavery and Its Abolition* (1926).

BRITISH LABOUR PARTY, founded in 1900 as the Labour Representation Committee, it was given its more permanent designation in 1906. It received the support of the Independent Labour Party (q.v.), the Trade-Union Congress, and other related organizations. Its major figure was J. Ramsay MacDonald, who, in 1924, organized Great Britain's first Labour Ministry. Prime Minister again in 1929-31, he was finally denounced as a traitor to labor for joining the National Coalition Government in the later year, and was expelled from the Party. It cooperated in the prosecution of both World Wars; in 1945, following the second, it took power from the Conservatives, under the leadership of Clement R. Attlee. Before being turned out in 1951, it had carried out major nationalization policies and given India its independence. In 1979, turned out of power by a determined Conservative Party headed by Margaret Thatcher (q.v.), it found itself both fighting for unity and to prevent a massive challenge to its traditions and work.

BRITISH REFORM differed markedly from that which absorbed the Americans, but the differences were motivated by circumstances rather than ultimate objectives. Thus, a major aim of British reform was an extended suffrage. In the United States, white male suffrage was largely achieved by 1830, except in Rhode Island. (See Dorr Rebellion.) In Great Britain, the Reform Bill of 1832 was but one long step in a struggle for democracy which continued far into the century. Catholic Emancipation was attained in 1829, Negro emancipation in 1833. Lord Shaftesbury (q.v.) was a one-man reform institution, concerning himself for all the victims of poverty and oppression. The municipal corporations, seedbeds of corruption, were reformed. In 1838, the Anti-Corn Law League was organized to cope with the Corn Laws (q.v). Criminal laws were revised, the press gang for the Navy being abolished. Free Trade was achieved in 1846. British reform developed such figures as Cobden and Bright (qq.v.), Henry Brougham whose reforms took in anti-slavery as well as education, and others who were as radical as the Friend and businessman, Joseph Sturge, and as conservative in essentials as Sir Robert Peel. The great Chartism (q.v.) agitation of 1849 capped a period of reform and modernization. These developments were punctuated by such events as the revolutions of 1830 and 1848 (qq.v.) See E. L. Woodward, The Age of Reform (1949), and Elie Halévy, The Triumph of Reform (1950). World War I and II (qq.v.) extended the suffrage, welfare, and nationalization (q.v.).

BROOK FARM (1841-1845), cooperative effort in living, organized and directed by Rev. George Ripley and religious in its inception, the intention being to provide an example of Christian living. It attracted as guests the intellectual elite of New England, and as residents, if only briefly, Theodore Parker, Margaret Fuller, and Nathaniel Hawthorne (qq.v.). It was at first a cooperative, in which all contributed to manual as well as intellectual labor, and comprising some one hundred and fifteen members. After some two years, it was captured by Fourierites (q.v.), including Charles A. Dana and William H. Channing (qq.v.); they joined with others to organize an American union of "associationists" who were to convert Americans to the phalanx principle. The Harbinger was begun at Brook Farm as the organ of Fourierite principles, and a huge phalanstery was built which was to house much of their project. The religious principle of unity was considerably weakened. On March 3, 1845, the almost completed phalanstery was burned to the ground, and the members, much of their original spirit dissipated, departed in various directions.

BROTHERHOOD OF SLEEPING CAR PORTERS, see Randolph, A. Philip.

BROTHERHOODS, chiefly associated with railway employee organizations. The curious feature of the railroad industry—that its employees were strung out along the line—suggested various organizational devices, which Eugene V. Debs sought to resolve with his consolidated American Railway Union (q.v.). Its failure, following the Pullman Strike (q.v.), revitalized the movement of employees back to their individual crafts, and brought about a renewed growth of the individual Brotherhoods. See also Railway Brotherhoods.

BROUN, HEYWOOD (1888-1939), columnist and reviewer, notably for the New York World-Telegram, famous for his good-humor, dramatic comment, and, increasingly, his liberal views of American affairs. His most famous columns were those denouncing the Sacco-Vanzetti trials as a travesty on justice; his dismissal from the World-Telegram for bold expression of opinion was cherished by proponents of free speech. His Anthony Comstock (1927) (see "Comstockery") was an indirect appeal for free speech. In the 1930's, he was a founder of the Newspaperman's Guild and a front man for liberal and even radical journalists who sought unionism and a permissive milieu. His sudden turn to Catholicism, shortly before his death, and burial from St. Patrick's Cathedral in New York was a sensation. Se H. H. Brown, ed., Collected Writings of Heywood Broun (1941).

BROWDER, EARL (1891-1973), an American phenomenon, born in Wichita, Kansas, he became a radical and general secretary of the Communist Party in 1929, when he strove to emulate Stalin in manners and wooden prose. He was "the Party's" candidate for President in 1936 and 1940, and, when World War II made the U.S. and the U.S.S.R. allies, warmly embraced Americanism and gladly dissolved his party in 1944. However, the revival of antagonism between communism and democracy, in the post-War period, demanded a scapegoat, and Browder was ousted from leadership and then from fellowship. Nevertheless, though now an exponent of capitalism, he was able to visit Russia and arrange to market Russian publications in the United States. An astounding revelation was that, while leader of the communists and calling American youth to rise against capitalist oppression, he had raised his own son along conventional lines and with conventional expectations.

BROWN, JOHN (1800-1859) crowned a long and enigmatic career as a businessman and family patriarch by involving himself in the struggles in Kansas resulting from the passage of the Kansas-Nebraska Act (q.v.). There, on May 24, 1856, he led the notorious Pottawatomie massacre. His career in Kansas is analyzed with effect in James C. Malin, John Brown and the Legend of Fifty-Six (1942). Following several years of individualistic plotting, and having received the support or sympathy of notable northerners, he, with a small band of white and Negro followers, seized the United States armory at Harpers Ferry. His plan was to build up an insurrectionary movement among Negroes throughout the South. His group either killed or overpowered, he was brought to trial in Charlestown, Virginia (now West Virginia), on October 25, 1859. He behaved with dignity, and wrote and spoke with eloquence, rousing much northern sympathy. The court refused the opportunity offered it to prove him insane, and he was hanged December 2. The grief expressed in the North over the event indicated how far it had come since the "incendiary" speeches of Garrison (q.v.) had been received with antagonism. A classic pro-Brown study in a vast literature is O. G. Villard, John Brown (1910); strong modern statements are in S. B. Oakes (1970) and J. Abels (1971). An elaborate effort to demean not only Brown, but reform generally is O. J. Scott, The Secret Six: John Brown and the Abolitionist Movement (1979).

BROWN, NORMAN O. (1913-   ), 1960s guru (q.v.), a classical scholar whose explorations in Freud (q.v.) led him to advocate, in Life against Death, a radical appeal for love as opposed to the sordid and material. His collage of quotations, Love's Body (1968) became a bible for social dissidents.

BROWN, OLYMPIA (1835-1926), woman's rights advocate and the first woman in the country to hold a pulpit on terms comparable to male ministers. She contributed her efforts to the famous campaign of 1867 in Kansas, intended to win the vote for women in that state, and continued active in that crusade elsewhere. See her Acquaintances, Old and New, Among Reformers (1911).

BROWN, WILLIAM MONTGOMERY (1855-1937), Protestant Episcopal Bishop of Arkansas who, in 1925, was unfrocked for heresy (*q.v.*): the first such case since 1906, when Algernon Crapsey was deprived of his Rochester, New York, charge for having denied the Virgin Birth. He was beside Brown at his trial. The occasion was Brown's book *Communism and Christianity* (1920); it denied Christ's existence and equated communism with morality and religion. Brown varied lectures in behalf of atheism with a bishopric in the Old Catholic Church, an offshoot of Rome. His well-known slogan was: "Banish Gods from skies and capitalists from earth." See also his *The Crucial Race Question* (1907), and *My Heresy* (1926).

BROWN v. BOARD OF EDUCATION OF TOPEKO (1954), a landmark case in efforts to hasten desegregation, and equality in educational opportunity. Implementation of the Brown decision resulted in massive busing (*q.v.*), "affirmative action," and "Black English" (*qq.v.*) decisions, aided by HEW and Democratic Presidents Johnson and Carter offering particular assistance in furthering these programs. Protracted legal and social duels over busing as wounding neighborhood schools and family preferences, and as retarding education generally, absorbed much social time and energy. Some paradoxes disturbed observers, such as black children being bused outside their neighborhoods into other Negro neighborhoods. Carter's resounding 1980 election defeat alarmed liberals and black leaders as signally a decline in the busing effort by the incoming administration. See R. Kluger, *Simple Justice: the History of Brown v. The Board of Education and Black America's Struggle for Equality* (1976). See also "Separate but Equal."

BROWNSON, ORESTES A. (1803-1876), religious seeker and controversialist, he investigated many sects, including Congregationalism, Methodism, Presbyterianism, Unitarianism, Universalism, and the free thought of Frances Wright (*q.v.*). In 1836, he edited the *Reformer*, then became an evangelical Democrat. His Boston *Quarterly Review* was one of the distinguished periodicals of the time, and he was an inspirer of Brook Farm (*q.v.*). His essays on "The Laboring Classes" in his *Review* (July, October, 1840) maintain a type of Marxian thought. However, it was not based on sound grounds, and Brownson was intemperately disillusioned by the victory of the Whigs over the Democrats, that year. His quest for inner security brought him into the Catholic Church in 1844, and ended his general influence. He survives as a figure of the transcendental (*q.v.*) impulse.

BROZ, JOSIP, see Tito, Marshal.

BRUCE, EDWARD (1879-1943), artist and lawyer, engaged in the Far East trade, he made collections of Chinese painting and a reputation for his own work, many of his canvases being purchased by museums. He was a representative for Far Eastern business interests, and from 1933 till his death was in the Treasury Department, in the Procurement Division, which, among other functions was responsible for the procurement of art work for public buildings. Bruce was Chief of the Section of Fine Arts, and, being a friend of the Roosevelts, as well as such influential artists as George Biddle, was able to persuade New Deal planners to expand the art services in the white collar projects as well as in the Treasury Department. Bruce was one of the most important pioneers in creating what ultimately became the Federal Art Project of the W.P.A.

BRYAN, WILLIAM JENNINGS (1860-1925), Nebraska lawyer, orator, and statesman, was raised to fame by his "Cross of Gold" speech at the Democratic convention in Chicago in 1896; "you shall not crucify mankind upon a cross of gold" was an image borrowed from Edward Bellamy's *Looking Backward* (*q.v.*). Gaining the support of left-wing Democrats and the bulk of the Populists (*q.v.*), he conducted a powerful, if unsuccessful campaign for the Presidency. His policy on imperialism (*q.v.*) was confused: he opposed war with Spain in 1898, but himself accepted a colonelcy which he was inept in exploiting; he directed the Democrats to accept the onerous treaty forced upon Spain, but campaigned in 1900 as an anti-imperialist, while insisting on holding on to the moribund

Free Silver issue. During the reform era of the 1900's, he developed a clear program for nationalizing the railroads, but could not develop political strength favoring it; his 1908 campaign was a failure. Still strong in the Democratic Party, he became Woodrow Wilson's Secretary of State, and though clear on the need for avoiding intervention in World War I, maintained interventionist policies in the Caribbean. He opposed the teaching of evolution in the public schools, and maintained his convictions during the Scopes Trial (*q.v.*). A tribune of the people, rather than a thinker, his strengths and weaknesses were those of his constituents. See Paolo E. Coletta, *William Jennings Bryan* (1964).

BRYANT, WILLIAM CULLEN (1794-1878) began his career as the son of Federalists (*q.v.*); his satire, *The Embargo*, was published when he was thirteen. Following his relatively brief career as the first great American poet, he became the long-time editor of the New York *Evening Post*, and, as such, one of the great American editors: he improved standards for journalistic writing as well as journalistic principle. A Jacksonian Democrat, he was not vigorously anti-slavery until 1848, when he supported the Free Soil Party (*q.v.*). He favored free trade and humanitarian principles.

BRYCE, JAMES (1838-1922), an English peer, historian, ambassador to the United States, 1907-13. A liaison figure between genteel (*q.v.*) elements at home and in the United States, his *The American Commonwealth* (1888) was a vital analysis of the American social and political system, in the spirit of a seeker of "good government."

BUCHENWALD, with Auschwitz and Belsen, among the most notorious names emerging from revelations attending the work of the concentration camps (*qq.v.*). The disorderly abandonment of the camp by the Nazis before the oncoming American troops, leaving cartloads of unburied corpses as well as "human lampshades" made for the female Nazi Ilse Koch seemed particularly memorable.

BUCHMAN, FRANK (1878-1961), founder of the Moral Rearmament (*q.v.*) movement, he began his work of moral uplift following experiences in many parts of the world centering about Christian work. In the 1920's, he developed the Oxford Group; in 1938 he undertook the campaign of which he became the leader and symbolic figure, and published a number of works which were highly esteemed by his followers and admirers.

BUCKLEY, WILLIAM F. (1925-   ), author, editor, and conservative spokesman. He attacked academic liberalism in *God and Man at Yale* (1951), and in 1955 founded the *National Review*, which became an influential center for social and cultural writings. As a columnist and television personality he carried his views widely and was involved in numerous polemics. His *McCarthy and His Enemies* (1954) was an elaborate defense of the Senator. Increasingly, his wit and variety attracted foes as well as admirers, who read his fiction, essays, and collections as well as constant flow of commentary. *Four Reforms* (1973) was indicative of his unwillingness to be categorized.

BUDGET OF THE UNITED STATES, of progressively increased importance as defense and social welfare measures preempt a larger portion of the national economy. Reformers and anti-reformers study its components to determine whether their hopes are being better or less well regarded. Great expenditures combined with inflation, the oil crisis, crisis in the automobile industry, welfare costs, and other factors made budget priorities vital to elements of the public. One of Jimmy Carter's (*q.v.*) promises was to balance the budget; his reverse accomplishment contributed to his defeat. The internationalization of American economic decisions promised to keep the American budget in the news. See R. D. Lee, *Public Budgeting Systems* (1973). President Reagan's (*q.v.*) budget victories of 1981 were a milestone of change in American economic affairs.

BUFORD INCIDENT, a culminating point in the Palmer Raids (*q.v.*), it gave substance to the often-voiced cliché: Why don't you go back where you came from? Two hundred and forty-nine persons with alien status, some with family and other American commitments, and including Emma Goldman (q.v.) and Alexander Berkman were placed on the famous "leaking boat," the U.S.S. transport *Buford,* and sent to Russia. Since over a third of the aliens rounded up in the raids were later released for lack of evidence, it appears reasonable to assume that some of the deportees were also innocent.

BULL MOOSE PARTY, THE, popular name for the Progressive Party of 1912, derived from Theodore Roosevelt's response to queries about his health, at the time he arrived in Chicago to receive the nomination: "I feel as fit as a Bull Moose." The emphasis upon energy was in line with the general emphasis of his faction upon extrovert qualities. See also Progressive Party. Amos R. E. Pinchot, *History of the Progressive Party* (1958).

BUND, see German-American Bund.

BUNK, see Debunking

BUONAPARTE, NAPOLEON (1769-1821), conqueror of Europe, self-proclaimed Emperor (1804), he profited from the deterioration of the French Revolution (q.v.); cited by social reformers as typical of the dangers social upset creates, sometimes defended for the allegedly positive achievements of his rule, notably the Code Napoleon (1804). He has seemed less offensive to social reform ideals when contrasted with another "Little Corporal," Adolf Hitler; see Hitlerism.

BUREAUCRACY, identified, invidiously, for the most part with federal government rather than municipal operations, and with political developments in the communist world as elements of it emerge from their revolutionary experiences. It suggests the triumph of organization over principles. Reformers criticize its inflexible or shoddy nature, the "red tape" which prevents action or accomplishment, the "channels" which substitute for individual responsibility. See also *Managerial Revolution, The.*

BURLEIGH BROTHERS, contributed verse, eloquence, and editorial services to the abolitionist and other campaigns; Charles C. Burleigh (1810-1878) abandoned law to join Garrison (q.v.) and gain fame by his personal appearances in behalf of reform causes and his editing (1838 and following) of the *Pennsylvania Freeman;* George S. Burleigh (1821-1903) wrote verses and edited the *Charter Oak;* and William Henry Burleigh (1812-1871) edited a number of publications, like his brothers, lectured on temperance as well as in behalf of the slaves, and published poems.

"BURNED-OVER DISTRICT," area in western New York, in the vicinity of Rochester which, in the early decades of the nineteenth century, became famous for the great numbers of enthusiasts it produced or attracted. A combination of social factors made it a seed-bed for revivalists, notably Charles G. Finney (q.v.). Here, too, were to be found the Shakers, the Noyes community at Oneida, the Mormons at Palmyra, spiritualism (qq.v.), among other phenomena. Whether enthusiasm produced more social good than ill has been the subject for discussion; see Whitney R. Cross, *The Burned-Over District* (1950).

BURNHAM, JAMES, see *Managerial Revolution, The.*

BURNS, ANTHONY, CASE (1854), notable in abolitionist annals: the major effort of the Franklin Pierce Democratic administration to carry out the Fugitive Slave Law (q.v.). Burns was a Negro slave who had escaped to Boston. Arrested, the abolitionists made desperate efforts to free him, forcibly or by law, but were repelled by the courts, and the great masses of volunteer militia who were recruited. Burns was placed on ship under armed guard, in defiance of the 20,000 Bostonians gathered in protest. This was the last major effort to enforce the Fugitive Slave Act in Massachusetts.

BURRITT, ELIHU (1811-1879), one of the greatest of all American pacifists; a self-instructed linguist, "the learned blacksmith" mastered many languages, ancient and modern, and used his fame to further peace, through the *Christian Citizen*

(1844-51), and organizational efforts in the United States and abroad which attracted idealists and notables. He integrated his cause with temperance, penny postage, and other humanitarian causes, and published *Sparks from the Anvil* (1846ff.), which discussed many of them.

BUSINESS AND REFORM, often considered to be in opposition, but often associated; thus the American Revolution (q.v.) was, to a degree, one against the Mercantilist System (q.v.) and led by such businessmen as John Hancock. Lewis Tappan (q.v.), an outstanding businessman of the reform era preceding the Civil War was also an outstanding reformer. To be sure, he was a Whig reformer, rather than a Democratic reformer, concerned for moral problems like slavery, rather than such issues as the Second Bank of the United States (q.v.), fought by Andrew Jackson (q.v.), who was a slaveholder. The development of trusts in post-Civil War times seemed to threaten democracy, in that it created a business system which was more effective than government in its operations, and raised such reformers as Henry George, Edward Bellamy, and Ignatius Donnelly (qq.v.) who attempted to stay the Goliath; business was a target, too, of the muckrakers (q.v.), and the subject of legislation, from the Sherman Anti-Trust Act to the Clayton Act (qq.v.). In the 1920's, it juxtaposed the American Plan (q.v.) to reform; the 1930's, however, produced partisans of the New Deal (q.v.), as well as opponents, and with World War II, business seemed indispensible to American affairs, and no more big than Big Labor. With business subject to the mediation services, anti-trust actions, and controls resulting from defense contracts and defense needs, and itself concerned for society, as indicated by the Ford Foundation (q.v.), the question was raised whether business had any more relationship to reform than any other element of society. See also Small Business Administration.

BUSINESS CONSOLIDATIONS, see Monopoly.

BUSINESS, CRITICS OF, particularly identified with the Muckrakers (q.v.); they inaugurated a tradition of conceiving of business as suspicious in essence. Sinclair Lewis's *Babbitt* (q.v.) topped the portrait by defining him as oafish, and to be distinguished from more vital artistic and social-minded types. During World War II, the necessity for businessmen became established, especially as elements of the reformers were demoralized by war circumstances, and artistic types retreated into esoteric byways. It became evident that critics of business were as vulnerable to criticism as their subjects. Mink-coat scandals, payola (q.v.) and other breaches in the integrity of business raised the possibility that their new social leadership might be threatened again. The N.A.M. reaffirmed its code of ethics, Henry Ford II warned the business community, smarting in 1961 over revelations of price-fixing (q.v.) in high places, that it must look to its gains of recent decades, which could be lost. See also Organization Man, The.

BUSINESS CYCLES, a fatalistic view of social economics which saw economic prosperity inevitably to be followed by economic depression: speculators and entrepreneurs were bound to develop the economy and to over-extend themselves; depressions necessarily eventuated. The post-Civil War brought the depressions of 1873, 1883, 1893, all of which took three to four years to work themselves out, depending on definitions of the crises. The "money panic" of 1907, the depression of 1913, and the Great Depression of 1929, created patterns, rather than "cycles," which reformers tended to see as implying doubtful analyses and grasp of factors.

BUSINESS UNIONISM, see Social Unionism.

BUSING, a determined effort aided by court actions (see April 20, 1971 Supreme Court decision: Swann v. Charlotte-Meckelburg) to force integration in education (q.v.) as the law and practice of the land. Black and white parents were often disheartened by busing and resistance to it, which impeded study and created dangers to children. The movement of white people out of the increasingly black cities—"white flight"—was not diminished when desegregation proceedings continued to follow it. Lillian

Rubin, *Busing and Backlash* (1972); Virginia Trotter, *Busing: Constructive or Divisive?* (1976).

BUTLER, BENJAMIN F. (1818-1893), politician and demagogue, practiced law and engaged in business in Massachusetts, and spoke the language of labor's demands. He was one of Lincoln's Army appointees: a "political general" who acquired great popularity by attempting to free Negroes in Virginia on the grounds that they were "contraband of war"; Lincoln overruled him. His attempt to enforce courtesy from New Orleans women by ordering that those who were disrespectful of Federal soldiers would be treated as women of the streets earned him the sobriquet of "Beast Butler." His popularity in the North was such that Lincoln may have offered him the vice-presidency in 1864, which he refused hoping for the higher opportunity. He helped manage Andrew Johnson's impeachment *(q.v.).* He was the Presidential candidate for both the Anti-Monopoly and Greenback Parties *(qq.v.),* in 1884.

BUTLER, NICHOLAS MURRAY (1862-1947), president of Columbia University, and of the Carnegie Endowment for International Peace *(q.v.).* He founded the American Association for International Conciliation *(q.v.).* Before America's entrance into World War I, he officially installed a peace representative on the campus; following the declaration of war, he refused to graduate students who opposed the draft. Among his books was *The Faith of a Liberal* (1924). In 1931, he and Jane Addams *(q.v.)* were awarded the Nobel Peace Prize. Following his death, his reputation plummeted.

BUTLER, SMEDLEY D. (1881-1940), first won attention because of spectacular generalship in command of Marines in Panama, later in Nicaragua. He won the Congressional Medal of Honor for his capture of Ft. Riviere, Haiti. In 1924, he acted as director of the Department of Safety, in Philadelphia, where he upset the local political machine with his honesty and decisive action. In 1934, he testified before the House Committee on Un-American Activities that he had been approached by conservatives fearful of the New Deal, and desirous of having him lead an American fascist party. He wrote *War Is a Racket* (1935). His cure for war was isolationism.

BUTTONS, containing the emblems of the union, were treated with pride by dedicated unionists, who "wore their button," and urged others to do the same, and who pointed with pride to their "working-class button." Such loyalty diminished with decreased "class" differences and loss of the labor heritage. The union label *(q.v.),* however, maintained its usefulness.

C

CA' CANNY, a slow-down by workers on the job, intended to keep production down and bring employers to terms; one of the techniques employed by the Wobblies, in the United States originating in Scotland. See Sabotage.

CABLE, GEORGE W. (1844-1925), southern author who fought in the Confederate Army, during the Civil War; he concluded that the one way of keeping the Negro in the gutter, as he said, was by joining him there. His fine ear for Creole language, and the subtleties of fiction permitted him to write the famous *Old Creole Days* (1879) and *The Grandissimes* (1884) which harbored equalitarian implications without creating a scandal. However, Cable's forthright denunciation of Negro repression and of the convict system which helped support the white supremacy program, in his *The Silent South* (1885), resulted in expressions of anger and contempt which caused him to take up residence in the North. Despite the friendliness of his neighbors and readers, the major phase of his career ended; A. Turner, ed., Cable, *The Negro Question* (1958).

CAHAN, ABRAHAM (1860-1951), socialist leader and intellectual, among Jews who had left unfriendly Czarist Russia for the United States; founder and editor of *Jewish Daily Forward,* outstanding socialist paper (1897), and author of works describing the adaptation of Jews to the American environment, notably *The Rise of David Levinsky* (1917).

CALAMITY HOWLERS, THE, a derogatory phrase with which Republicans in particular, during the Presidential campaign of 1888, attacked members of the Farmer's Alliance, the Grange, the American Federation of Labor, and other groups which deplored the economic state of the country: a phrase which demanded an optimistic view of its defenders.

CALDWELL, ERSKINE (1903-   ), one of the most successful of all American story-tellers, selling to low-brow and high-brow *(qq.v.)* alike, and, remarkably, in lands on both sides of the "Iron Curtain" *(q.v.).* The reason was his bold use of elemental sexual themes, leavened, however, with literary talent, and, on occasion, power. His depiction of degraded lives in the southern backwoods appealed to reformers and revolutionaries as an expose of negative American conditions. His most notable literary quality was his effort to treat Negroes as individuals and as victims of injustice, and to deal with "poor whites" *(q.v.)* in terms of their fascist and also their equalitarian potentials. His *Complete Stories of Erskine Caldwell* (1953) contained the worst and the best of his writings.

CALHOUN, JOHN C. (1782-1850), states-rights advocate and slavery defender whose nationalistic thought (and Presidential aspirations) envisioned a union between slave-holders in the south and mill-owners and other capitalists in the north. As a leading Democrat, he also attracted the cooperation of pro-labor advocates, while many of the capitalists, advocating "free soil" moved, instead, towards opposition to him and his principles; see also Nullifier, Nullification.

CALVINISM AND REFORM, appear, at first glance incompatible. Calvinism posited a wrathful God, disturbed over the fall of Adam. It assumed the majority of mankind predestined to eternal damnation, because of his sin in the Garden of Eden. It denied that "good works" entitled individuals to remission of sins; to believe this was a heresy. God saved a tiny remnant of humanity from hell-fire because it pleased Him to do so. However, one could never entirely know that he had been saved; therefore, one could only labor endlessly to prove to himself that he was deserving of grace. Though

Puritans and Pilgrims (*qq.v.*) were intolerant of other sects, they were in themselves examples of dissidence, and their rigidity did give occasion for the efforts of Anne Hutchinson and Roger Williams (*qq.v.*). Their congregational form of church did create the rudiments of social action, and the institution of the town meeting (*q.v.*). Although their theocratic (*q.v.*) government was repressive on personal liberty, and deteriorated into witchcraft (*q.v.*) frenzy, it inspired its opposite: unitarianism, which posited a God of love. As theocracy declined in strength, Calvinists found themselves competing with other denominations for public support, and many of them, in effect, sought to separate themselves from sinful pursuits and to reassure themselves with respect to their deservingness. Hence the success of such a latter-day Calvinist as the Rev. Charles G. Finney (*q.v.*), and the activity of his followers in such causes as temperance, anti-slavery, and woman's rights, as well as the universal reformers (*q.v.*) who planned a total revolution in human behavior, thus ensuring their freedom from sin.

CAMELOT a shallow musical, based on the King Arthur legend, which opened a month after the election of John F. Kennedy (*q.v.*), and which he was said to have admired. It posited a happy land of good will and justice, with simple tunes and words, and, as such, was enjoyed by countless auditors and spectators. The assassination of Kennedy seemed to many of them a defeat for "Camelot."

CAMPANELLA, TOMMASO (1568-1639), Italian monk and patriot, whose *Civitas Solis* (City of the Sun) (published 1623), is one of the utopias (*q.v.*) which reformers have pondered for hints respecting a more perfect society. A city is described in which wives and goods were held in common, all worked for the state, which carefully administered customs and education. Campanella influenced Fourier and St. Simon (*qq.v.*).

CANADIAN-AMERICAN RELATIONS have affected social reform less than circumstances might have suggested; better remembered have been fisheries and land-boundary disputes. The largest exception was the Rush-Bagot Agreement which followed the War of 1812, and which demilitarized the Great Lakes region. Although the general impression that the entire border was demilitarized is not quite accurate, since it was rather the result of a lengthy process extending to 1870, the Agreement inspired reformers with ambitions to extend disarmament elsewhere. The United States expended little thought on her "neighbor." The Northwest thought of her mainly in fear of her agricultural products, and helped to kill the reciprocity agreement which President Taft sponsored in 1911, which might have put American wheat in competition with Canadian wheat. A major source of relationship was the Canadian labor movement, which worked in association with the American Federation of Labor and later the C.I.O. (*qq.v.*). Canada provided social experiments of interest to reformers; like New Zealand (*q.v.*), her commitment to agricultural staples forced troubled farmers to be receptive to radical solutions, like social credit (*q.v.*), and to support the Cooperative Commonwealth Federation (*q.v.*); during the Great Depression of the 1930's, it sponsored "New Deal"-type legislation. The major project binding the United States and Canada was the St. Lawrence Seaway, which, by a system of channels and locks, opened the inland area between the two countries to deep-sea navigation in 1959, and further suggested possibilities of international cooperation. Canadian films, Montreal separatism, Toronto, Trudeau (*q.v.*) were reasons for following, among others, Canadian developments, yet to be fulfilled.

CANAL RING, THE, a conspiracy of entrepreneurs in New York State to receive money for the construction of canals, the terms of the contract not being fulfilled. The exposure of the Ring was carried through by Governor Samuel J. Tilden (*q.v.*) in 1874, who profited politically from the situation.

CANAL ZONE, see Panama Canal.

CANDIDE (1759), Voltaire's famous satire on optimists, who insist on seeing good where none exists. Dr. Pangloss's fatuous insistence that "All is for the best in this best of all possible worlds" has served the irony of reformers better than has the novel's philosophic close: "It is necessary that we cultivate our own garden."

CANNON, JOSEPH G. (1836-1926), known familiarly as "Uncle Joe," from 1903 to 1910 a firm would-be dictator and anti-reform Speaker of the House of Representatives. In the latter year, a revolt headed by George W. Norris (*q.v.*) overthrew his control of the powerful Rules Committee in the House and retired him from the Speakership. Blair Bolles, *Tyrant from Illinois* (1951).

CAPITAL, the villain of Karl Marx's analysis in *Das Kapital*, not seen by social reformers as a legitimate element in social operations, except when they require it for their own efforts. Capital is seen as a pawn in the hands of capitalists, who manipulate it for their own interests, to the detriment of society. It is seen as an "exploitative" device. See Value Theory, Private Enterprise, *Kapital*.

CAPITAL PUNISHMENT, see Anti-Capital Punishment.

CAPITALISM, seen by Marx as a product of decayed feudalism, the latter based on fixed social relations and limited economic efforts centered about the farm and castle, the former emphasizing individualism, speculation, adventures abroad, and more efficient technology and production, at the expense of a labor force increasingly reduced to specialized functions. Its inevitable expropriation of workers' rights, its constant substitution of machines for man, its inability to pay its laborers for work done, were seen as creating "contradictions" which only revolution could neutralize. Ludwig Von Mises, *The Anti-Capitalistic Mentality* (1956).

CAPITALISM AND REFORM, sometimes imagined to be antithetical, by socialist-minded reformers, but with a long history of concern for reform causes, of which the American Revolution (*q.v.*) was one. The Jacksonian (*q.v.*) reform movement in part represented "liberal capitalism," that is free enterprise demanding increased opportunities held in restraint States. However, the Jackson Administration was also pro-slavery, and, as such, opposed by northern Whig reformers who not only favored free enterprise, but also a firmer sense of freedom, including civil liberties. They also advocated Free Soil (*q.v.*) in the west: itself a reform. It was a paradox of the time that the pro-slavery south should have become a partisan of Free Trade (*q.v.*), opposing such reform capitalists as Horace Greeley (*q.v.*), who favored the protection of American industry from outside competition. In post-Civil War decades, capitalism moved toward monopoly, and though it opposed reform, it spawned reformers, many of whom did not plan to overthrow capitalism but to strengthen its free enterprise component. Thus, the Populists and the Progressives (*q.v.*) did not so much oppose capitalism as insist on a new capitalism: one more responsive to human and public demands. This they sought to achieve by regulatory devices. The rise of fascism and communism, and their totalitarian behavior, gave capitalism new credit with Americans. It claimed to operate in the public interest. It was indispensable in World War II and to the Post-War "free world." Such institutions as the Ford Foundation (*q.v.*) seemed strategic to American advance. Reformers might criticize its workings, or the workings of government, but capitalism maintained its status as representative of the American "way." Reformers concerned for American problems would have to cope with it in their programs and formulations. Oddly, communist administrators in Russia, China, and elsewhere were fascinated by capitalist production, and showed interest in emulating its successes. See Seymour Melman, *The Permanent War Economy; American Capitalism in Decline* (1974); L. Silk and D. Vogel, *Ethics and Profits: the Crisis of Confidence in American Businss* (1976).

CAPTAINS OF INDUSTRY, a concept intended to underscore the responsible role of businessmen and others in society as well as commerce, to suggest, too, their priority to labor, whom they presumably captain. It was treated with irony by labor elements and reformers who failed to discern the requisite social responsibility manifested by the people concerned. Compare Robber Barons.

CAPTIVE NATIONS, see Assembly of Captive European Nations.

CARIBBEAN NATIONS AND AMERICAN REFORM have been somewhat more related than the latter has been with Central America (q.v.). Revolutionists have operated industriously in both areas, but aspects of the former have also disturbed reformers. Thus, the policies of Trujillo (q.v.) in the Dominican Republic troubled Americans who had not been troubled by dictatorship in Central America. Puerto Rico (q.v.), an American possession, has been a trouble or encouragement to reform-minded Americans. The British West Indies (q.v.) were an inspiration to American abolitionists in the nineteenth century, and promised to interest their twentieth century counterparts. (See David Lowenthal, ed., *The West Indies Federation* [1961].) Cuba (q.v.) unexpectedly emerged as the most formidable challenge to American reformers, in 1961, as well as to the entire area. R. Millett and W. M. Will, eds., *The Restless Caribbean* (1979); Fred Phillips, *Freedom in the Caribban* (1977).

CARLSON, JOHN ROY (pseud.), author of first-hand investigations into the ramifications of anti-American alliances. Although opposed to communist machinations, as well as fascist machinations, Carlson found the latter more profitable to investigate in detail, and, in *Under Cover: My Four Years in the Nazi Underworld of America* (1943) and *The Plotters* (1946), traced in great detail their personalities and multifarious programs. Notable were their connections with some of the most respectable and famous citizens, not ordinarily identified with subversive and malicious plans.

CARLYLE, THOMAS (1795-1881), Scottish-born controversialist and historian, of humble background and aristocratic views. He made a fetish of work and of heroes, scorned the civilization of the machine. His style was startling, individual, but he disciplined himself to produce a *History of the French Revolution* (1837) which was vivid and yet responsible, and which saw the event as a grim result of a corrupt society. Though contemptuous of uninspired capitalists, he was fearful of the organized underprivileged, and exalted personal responsibility in *Chartism* (1839), *Past and Present* (1843), *Latter Day Pamphlets* (1850), among other writings. Some of his views, such as those on the Negro, whom he held inferior, disappointed admirers, who equated his Transcendentalism with that of Ralph Waldo Emerson (qq.v.); some modern students consider him a precursor of fascism (q.v.). Yet much of his work, seen in historical context, continues to seem useful and inspiring. Philip Rosenberg, *The Seventh Hero: Thomas Carlyle and...Radical Activism* (1974); D. A. Wilson, *The Truth about Carlyle* (1913); Julian Symons, *Thomas Carlyle* (1952).

CARMAGNOLE, a song and dance identified with the French revolutionists of 1789.

CARNEGIE, ANDREW (1835-1919), industrialist whose course to power was viewed critically in James H. Bridge's *The Inside History of the Carnegie Steel Company* (1903). Although he avoided having to assume responsibility for his company's conduct during the Homestead Steel Strike (q.v.), he was no friend of unions. After selling his concern in a great industrial consolidation which created the United States Steel Corporation (1901), he turned to a career of philanthropy. The "Carnegie libraries" which he endowed earned the satire of Finley Peter Dunne (q.v.), but exemplified his philosophy: that society was best administered by those individually most competent, but that they had a duty to serve mankind. He set up influential institutions and trusts, including the Carnegie Endowment for International Peace (q.v.).

CARNEGIE ENDOWMENT FOR INTERNATIONAL PEACE, founded in 1910 as a fact-finding and educational body, it has suggested to reformers the question of whether it has indeed aided the establishment of peace or mitigation of war, or whether it has been no more than a verbal concomitant of active forces making for either one. Its most notable figure was Nicholas Murray Butler (q.v.). During World War I, it took the position that the defeat of Germany was essential to the establishment of peace.

CARPENTER, EDWARD (1844-1929), English socialist and poet, who left the Anglican priesthood to become a writer and lecturer. Influenced by Walt Whitman, whom he visited in the United States, he returned to become famous as an idealist and prophet of love and freedom. His works include: *Civilization, Its Cause and Cure* (1889), and *Love's Coming of Age* (1896).

CARPETBAGGERS, first applied to Kansas emigrants in 1857; following the Civil War identified with unprincipled northerners who hastened, with little more than a carpetbag of personal effects, into the South for self-seeking purposes.

CARTEL, from the German *kartell*, describing trusts and other combinations intended to control a particular market; it became notorious in post-World War II years with revelations that American industrialists had cooperated with cartels engaged in organizing industry in the interests of Nazi Germany.

CARTER, JIMMY (1924-   ), the phenomenon of twentieth century American politics, his rise and decline were instability-indicators of the national process. Of narrow background and artful, ambitious personality, he was candid and winning with friends. His father was not the military figure he claimed, nor was he the nuclear scientist and better than acquaintance of Admiral Hyman Rickover he suggested, for example. He served in the Georgia Senate, 1962-6, was badly defeated for governor in the latter year, and, following a period of psychic depression, followed by "born again" religious confidence, ran a careful, calculated race which made him governor in 1970. His assets were charm, a wooing of press and people, "populist" (q.v.)-style promises of better government, and a hard-headed young team which studied trends and interest groups, working with segregationists on one side and Negro leaders on the other. His placing of Martin Luther King's (q.v.) portrait in the State Capitol was an example of his search for modern gestures, as was his asserted interest in Bob Dylan and Dylan Thomas.

Confusion in Democratic ranks and the crushing of the Nixon (q.v.) Administration persuaded Carter's team that they could profit from bold promises to the electorate. During 1972-1976, they sold their candidate's image as of a decent and competent human being necessary to a distraught time, and, in a bitter campaign against Gerald Ford (q.v.), overcame him by a shade. The coming months tarnished Carter's image. He stood by his financial and political strongarm, Bert Lance, whose business was improper for a director of the Office of Management and Budget. He fired an energetic U.S. attorney investigating corrupt Democratic politicians. He tolerated until they became intolerable the actions and declarations of his ambassador to the United Nations, Andrew Young. Although his "Human Rights" stand and Panama Canal treaty (qq.v.) were defended as legitimate, other of his actions were widely seen as inept or dangerous, even by his apologists. His naming of Red China as having sole title to diplomatic recognition not only ambittered Taiwan; it encouraged China to attack Vietnam, disturbed SALT (q.v.) negotiations with Russia, which went to Vietnam's aid, and deprived the United States of any status in the situation. His bringing together of Israel and Egypt in 1978 seemed a diplomatic triumph, but set no base for continuing action.

Carter's popularity rose and fell, rising when Iran's seizure of American "hostages" (qq.v.) caused Americans to close ranks behind their President. But Carter's fantastic effort to free them made America a tragic laughing stock. Carter then mixed images of patience with images of action, hinting at war, as when Russia undertook to quell Afghanistan patriots; by then, American allies questioned America's capacity for leading the free world. Numerous other misadventures, involving the fled criminal financier Robert Vesco, and Carter's own brother Billy, who profited strangely from Libyan largesse—"Billygate" [see Watergate]—among other unfoldings, were received with varying degrees of media interest and official investigation, some obviously tainted.

Nevertheless, Carter sought re-election, boasting that he would "whip Kennedy's (q.v.) ass," in an unappetizing phrase.

33

Although he did so, his fortunes remained enigmatic, in spite of union, media, Negro, activist female, and anticipated southern support. His landslide defeat raised questions about the competence and objectivity of polling and communicative agencies. Louis Filler, ed., *The President in the 20th Century* (1982); Betty Glad, *Jimmy Carter* (1980); Victor Lasky, *Jimmy Carter: the Man and the Myth* (1979); Clark R. Mollenhoff, *The President who Failed* (1980).

CASTRO, FIDEL, see Cuba.

CASUAL LABOR, see Transient Workers.

CATASTROPHES have probably served reform no more than they have harmed it. Earthquakes have unleashed courage, good-fellowship, and sacrifice; they have also unleashed looters, martial law, and insurance controversies. Catastrophe neither exalted nor embittered Voltaire's *Candide* (*q.v.*). Oliver W. Holmes Sr. (*q.v.*), in his poem, "The Deacon's Masterpiece," credited the Lisbon Earthquake (1755) with destroying Calvinism (*q.v.*), but this is doubtful. The Agadir Earthquake (1960) was soon forgotten. The catastrophes at Galveston and Dayton (*qq.v.*) produced municipal reform plans.

CATCH-22, title of a novel by Joseph Heller (1967), a bitter satire on war; "catch-22" became symbolic of all bureaucracy which created mad distortions of reality through apparently legal and rational operations.

CATHOLIC CHURCH AND REFORM have been related, though not synonymous. Anti-Catholic elements have included both reformer and anti-reformer groups. Thus, in 1960, the president of the Southern Baptist Convention, not a reform body, opposed in principle the nomination of a Catholic for the office of President of the United States. The *Independent* (*q.v.*), a reform publication, believed that the Catholic Church produced more reactionary policies than progressive ones. A major critic of the church was Paul Blanshard. Msg. John A. Ryan (*q.v.*) was an outstanding Catholic and New Dealer (*q.v.*): one of many such personages. The poverty of so many of the Church's constituents gave a portion of its clergy a stake in social melioration and more, though another portion of it emphasized the transient nature of earthly trouble. The Church was, almost wholly, on the Franco side of the Spanish Civil War (*q.v.*). The *Catholic Encyclopedia* (1911) examined the Reformation at length, but not reform; however, it contained articles on socialism and reform subjects. See also *Rerum Novarum*. Equality and life-style agitation touched the Church as well as those outside it; divorce, contraception, priesthood for nuns, abortion divided Catholics in theory and practice. Revolutionary views affected portions of the priesthood in poverty-ridden South American and African nations. E. De Kadt, *Catholic Radicals in Brazil* (1970); Neil Betten, *Catholic Activism and the Industrial Worker* (1976); D. L. Kinzer, *An Episode in Anti-Catholicism* (1964); Y. M. J. Congar, *Catholic Church and the Race Question* (1966).

CATT, CARRIE CHAPMAN (1859-1947), woman suffragist, and, from 1892, a leader of the American Woman Suffrage Association, she organized the League of Women Voters, in 1920, to train women to think and act with respect to public issues. She was also concerned for world peace.

CAUCUS, an Americanism as early as 1724; before 1832 the method by which Presidential nominees were chosen: elected congressmen met together to decide whom they would support for the high offices; in this fashion, only persons with proved success at the polls carried weight in the selection. "King Caucus," as the system was known, was superseded by the party convention, which meant, in effect, that delegates who could not deliver an influential vote could nevertheless help decide who the party candidate was to be. The concept of a caucus—of an in-group, of wire-pullers—continued to influence not merely the major parties, but social reform groups, as well.

CAVALIERS, the Royalists who attacked, and finally overcame, the Puritan Revolution (*q.v.*); enemies of the Roundheads (*q.v.*). Also the name bestowed, ironically, on the leaders of southern secession in the United States, by abolitionists and other antagonistic northerners, who also dubbed them, again ironically, "the chivalry."

C.C.C., see Civilian Conservation Corps.

CENSORSHIP, identified with the printed word, but closely allied to the right to free speech (*q.v.*), and freedom of the press (*q.v.*). The Zenger case (*q.v.*) early established a precedent for the latter, and the First Amendment to the Constitution supported both. Both were challenged by the Alien and Sedition Acts (*q.v.*), and resisted by the Jeffersonians. Censorship was committed by the Jackson Administration against abolitionists whose petitions to Congress were tabled and whose publications given no protection by the Postmaster General. In the post-Civil War Period, Anthony Comstock (*q.v.*) initiated his crusade against what he deemed to be obscene matter, which became a major problem in censorship, involving not merely allegedly lewd material, but information about birth-control, for example. Atheistic and radical publications were also challenged; in 1908, President Theodore Roosevelt sought to exclude the anarchist paper, *La Questione Sociale*, from the mails through his official office. Theodore Schroeder (*q.v.*) was a strong arm of resistance to such attempts. Censorship was exercised under the Sedition Act of 1918, during the War, and the 1920's were an arena within which censorship was exercised and resisted. A book published in that decade printed the Mother Goose rhymes, blacking out innocent words in a fashion to suggest they were obscene. A landmark was the decision on *Ulysses* (*q.v.*) in 1933 which acknowledged that a serious work of art could not be denied the mails on grounds of obscenity. A freer attitude toward the liberties writers was allowed, plus more liberal attitudes toward birth-control information diminished censorship. George Seldes (*q.v.*) helped broaden the area of free political self-expression. "Censorship" became controversial as limits to freedom in order to control harmful excess grew to be a problem. The A.C.L.U. (*q.v.*) was a legal force for maintaining the First Amendment. See Obscenity, Pornography.

CENSUS, BUREAU OF, a basic function of government, since it provides the information for decisions about representation in Congress and relating to taxation. As a patronage (*q.v.*) plum in the post-Civil War period, it employed individuals who were not always capable of providing accurate statistics. Moreover, decisions with respect to information gathered could be significant; wrote Bolton Hall (*q.v.*) in *Free America* (1904), p. 40: "All these census figures are worth noticing, because when the authorities find out the use we are making of them they will cut off the supply from that source—as the figures on mortgage debt demanded in 1890 have been cut off in the last census." Of general use is the annual *Statistical Abstract of the United States*. The 1980 Census was closely watched by city and state officials who stood to lose funds and political representatives because of population flight and uncounted inhabitants, or others in hiding or moving about. In 1980, Detroit sued to have the number of Detroiters who might be missing in the city's diminished census added to the official figure.

CENTRAL AMERICA AND REFORM complemented, on the mainland, the problem in the Caribbean (*q.v.*). Thus, the United States intervened in Nicaraguan affairs in 1909, fearing the possibility of other foreign intervention which might affect plans for a canal; an agreement in 1911 gave the United States the right to intervene in that country. "Dollar diplomacy" (*q.v.*) kept United States Marines in the country, and, in the 1920's, kept them active against native revolutionists led by Augusto Sandino; as late as 1932, elections were supervised by United States troops. Although the presence of American troops gave rebel leaders a reform and revolutionary aura, the key fact about Nicaragua, as with tiny El Salvador, Honduras, Guatemala, Panama, Colombia was not the United States, but a deep poverty which separated the great mass of the people from its leaders. The natural leader of the Central American republics was Mexico (*q.v.*), which however, following its revolutionary decade of the 1910's, failed to develop a moral authority commensurate with its size and apparent destiny. Thus, Americans were more aware of the revolutionary or reform potentials of other nations in the area than of Mexico's, and gave more attention to possibilities in the Organization of American States (q.v.) than to those deriving from United States-Mexican relations. See also United Fruit Company, Charles P. May, *Central America: Lands Seeking Unity* (1966).

CENTRALIA RIOT (1919) culminated a long series of struggles between the I.W.W. (q.v.) and State of Washington business and political interests, and involved the hard, harshly exploited lumber workers of the northwest. Fighting with their usual fearlessness, the I.W.W. suffered persecution and casualties. On November 11, their headquarters being attacked by American Legion elements, they fired shots which killed three of its members. During the ensuing events, Wesley Everett, an I.W.W., was seriously beaten, jailed, then forcibly removed, and after suffering tortures, hanged. Eleven men were charged with murder. Eight of them were sentenced in a courtroom charged with prejudice, to from 25 to 40 years in prison, but a residue of bitterness remains the legacy of the event.

CENTRAL INTELLIGENCE AGENCY (CIA), controversial agency, established as part of the National Security Act (1947), it received special powers in 1949, freeing it of civil service requirements and other restraints. It was expected to emphasize foreign circumstances, the FBI (q.v.) attending to domestic problems. With all but unlimited funds and operatives, the CIA in 1953 organized a coup which overthrew Iranian Prime Minister Mossadegh and put the Shah on the throne. In 1961, the CIA was responsible for the Bay of Pigs (q.v.) adventure; its failure encouraged the Russians to build the Berlin Wall and attempt the set down missile bases in Cuba (qq.v.). In 1973, it interposed to deliver Chile from Allende (q.v.). Involved in Nixon (q.v.) security measures, and shown to have illegally opened mail involving alleged dissidents and spies, but also to have monitored citizens on no direct charges, the CIA found itself under legal and individual pressure. Placed under restraints, officials complained that they were unable to deliver intelligence. Despite liberal protests, Congress and the President acted to help the Agency maintain "covert" operations. The struggle for a strong CIA continued. While a Court of Appeals ordered it to publish the names of its agents, endangering lives and weakening their ability to act, an "Intelligence Act of 1980" was seen as an initial piece of legislation increasing CIA independence. John Marks, *The CIA and the Cult of Intelligence* (1974); John Kelly, *The CIA in America* (1979); Thomas Powers, *The Man Who Kept the Secrets* (1980); E. H. Hunt, *Undercover* (1974); Y. H. Kim, *Central Intelligence Agency: Problems of Secrecy in a Democracy* (1968).

CENTRIST, though technically between the extremes of social reform and revolution, was often used invidiously to designate a vacillator or "confused liberal" (q.v.).

CENTURY OF DISHONOR, A (1881), see Jackson, Helen Hunt.

CHAFEE, ZECHARIAH, JR. (1885-1957), law professor at Harvard University, he was a consultant to the National Committee on Law Observance and Enforcement, and part author of the report on lawlessness in law enforcement (1931). Later, he was a member of the United Nations (q.v.) sub-committee on Freedom of Information and the Press (1947-8). His major contribution was that of a scholar, concerned for the reality of the Bill of Rights (q.v.); see his *Freedom of Speech* (1920), *Free Speech in the United States* (1941), *Government and Mass Communications* (1947), and *The Blessings of Liberty* (1956).

CHAIN GANG, a method of organizing convict labor (q.v.), notoriously in the southern states, for outdoor work; efforts to escape it have produced epics of cruelty and desperation disturbing to humanitarians.

CHAMBERLAIN, JOHN (1903-   ), a once-noted social and cultural critic, whose *Farewell to Reform* (1932) was conceived to be challenging and illuminating. His transformation into

a principled defender of Manchester Liberalism (q.v.) was little noted nor long remembered. However, see Louis Filler, "John Chamberlain and American Liberalism," *Colorado Quarterly*, Autumn, 1957.

CHAMBERLAIN'S UMBRELLA, as a symbol of capitulation to fascism; see Appeasement Policy.

CHAMBERS, WHITTAKER, see Hiss Case.

CHANNING, WILLIAM ELLERY (1780-1842), a leading Unitarian and pacifist, his principles influenced reformers of his generation. He challenged the Calvinist (q.v.) doctrine that mankind was besmirched with "original sin," and that individuals could be saved from hell-fire only by God's grace, which would be granted to no more than a remnant. He emphasized God's love, man's perfectability, and repudiated doctrines of predestination. Channing's *Discourses on War* (1816) and *Second Discourse* (1835) were pioneer productions favoring pacifism (q.v.). His *Slavery* (1835) presented him as an influential convert to anti-slavery. His "Remarks on National Literature" (1823) was a call for original work, a repudiation of slavish imitation. He set down the moral and intellectual foundations for transcendentalism (q.v.).

CHANNING, WILLIAM HENRY (1810-1884), nephew of William Ellery Channing, a Unitarian minister and reformer, he was a friend of Thoreau's (q.v.) and also of the Brook Farm experiment (q.v.). He made an earnest if unsuccessful effort to establish a church among the New York poor. His writings were as varied as his ministry, which took him from Liverpool, in England, to Washington, D.C.

CHAPLIN, RALPH (1888-1961), I.W.W. (q.v.) leader, poet, he was raised in the Chicago slums, became a militant, and edited the Wobbly newspaper, *Solidarity*. He wrote the popular labor and radical song, *Solidarity Forever*. He was responsible for the view which labor and reformers accepted of Joe Hill (q.v.), whom he never saw till Hill was brought to Chicago for ceremonies and cremation. In 1917, he was charged with other I.W.W. leaders for defying the war-time Espionage Act (q.v.), and sent to Leavenworth Prison. His volume of poems, *Bars and Shadows* (1919) reflected his experiences. He was pardoned in 1923, received full pardon in 1933. Though he resumed being a labor editor and a fighter on the side of Harry Bridges (q.v.), he was anti-communist. By 1945, when he published his important autobiography, *Wobbly*, he had reviewed his life, and found it wanting in charity. He became religious, later moved to Tacoma, Washington, where he became curator of the Washington State Historical Society.

CHAPMAN, JOHN JAY (1862-1933), grandson of Maria Weston Chapman, Garrisonian (q.v.) fire-brand, and a descendant of John Jay (q.v.), he developed a sense of *noblesse oblige* (q.v.). As a "goo goo" (q.v.), he took municipal reform with the utmost seriousness, in 1911 performing the unique act of holding a memorial meeting in Coatesville, Pa., for a Negro who had been lynched; his address, delivered to an audience of two (a Negro from Boston, and a stool pigeon [q.v.]) is reproduced in *Memories and Milestones* (1915). His two important books are *Causes and Consequences* (1898) and *Practical Agitation* (1900), analyses of American corruption and the means for coping with it, requiring courage and resourcefulness. Less useful were Chapman's anti-semitism and anti-Catholicism. He was also a critic and scholar of traditional character; see Richard B. Hovey, *John Jay Chapman—an American Mind* (1959).

CHAPPAQUIDICK, in Massachusetts, the 1969 scene of Edward M. Kennedy's (q.v.) automobile mishap in company of a female, in 1980 still a vivid, though muted, symbol of his fitness for the Presidency. It thus confused the question of public attitudes toward the Kennedy program, a mixture of old New Deal attitudes plus the code word "compassion," basically government spending in ways deemed social service. For the classic pro-Kennedy defense intended to repeat his 1960 triumph of a biography of John F. Kennedy, see James McGregor Burns, *Edward M. Kennedy and the Camelot Legacy* (1976).

"CHARACTER ASSASSINATION," see "McCarthy Era."

"CHARCOALS," those who, in Missouri, during the Civil War, were invidiously presumed to be protagonists favoring the Negro; the Black Republicans (q.v.), sometimes even scornfully called Niggers—the German settlers in St. Louis had been dark-complexioned, and their republican sentiments offended their pro-slavery neighbors; see Louis Filler, ed., *The New Stars*, by Manie Morgan (1949), p. 120.

CHARDON STREET CHAPEL CONVENTION (1840), famous gathering of reformers in Boston, to discuss the status of the church in their spiritual and temporal affairs. It drew abolitionists and universal reformers (q.v.) who upbraided the institutional churches for inadequacy. Present were Theodore Parker and George Ripley, among others, and, as observers, Ralph Waldo Emerson and James Russell Lowell (qq.v.). Among other subjects discussed was the Sabbath (q.v.) question, which to them involved questions of freedom, as well as of truth.

CHARITIES AND REFORM have been ill-connected; as Emerson (q.v.) wrote, in "Self Reliance": "Do not tell me . . . of my obligation to put all poor men in good situations. Are they *my* poor? I tell thee, thou foolish philanthropist, that I grudge the dollar, the dime, the cent I give. . . . There is a class of persons to whom by all spiritual affinity I am bought and sold; for them I will go to prison if need be; but your miscellaneous popular charities; the education at college of fools; the building of meeting-houses to the vain end to which many now stand; alms to sots, and the thousand-fold Relief Societies;—though I confess with shame I sometimes succumb and give the dollar, it is a wicked dollar, which by and by I shall have the manhood to withhold." To the extent that charities distinctly aimed at melioration, rather than reform, emphasized that the poor were being preferred something beyond their due, and did not seek for the roots of social trouble, charity-givers seemed hateful, rather than admirable. Such figures as Charles Loring Brace sought more positive approaches. By 1879, the National Conference of Charities and Corrections was developing more promising aspects of fact-finding, the developing of a class of professionals in the field, and other elements, which still kept charities out of the class of such more positive institutions as Hull House (q.v.) symbolized. See also Foundations.

CHARTIST MOVEMENT, 1837-1848, warrants contrast with Jacksonian reform and Loco-focoism (qq.v.). It derived from the People's Charter, drawn up by six members of the Working Men's Association and six radical members of Parliament. The Chartists asked universal manhood suffrage, equal electoral districts, the vote by ballot, annual Parliaments, no property qualifications, and the payment of Members of Parliament. Thus, it was a middle-class movement, but promised to open gates for the poor as well. Notable leaders were William Lovett, Henry Vincent, and the Irish editor of *The North Star*, Fergus O'Connor. The movement stirred great enthusiasm in the cities. It resulted in a monster petition signed by a million and a quarter names which was presented to Parliament in 1839 under conditions of great agitation, and rejected. In November, troops fired upon Chartists at Newport, killing ten and wounding fifty; leaders were arrested and several transported. Nevertheless the movement struggled on through the "Hungry Forties," culminating in 1848—the revolutionary year—when another petition, said to have been signed by over five and a half million people, was once more presented to Parliament. Ridicule was poured over the many false signatures attached; the fact that some two million were set down seriously was ignored. The grim fact that the Duke of Wellington mobilized some two hundred thousand special constables to crush what might turn into an uprising was adequately displayed. Following this defeat, Chartism dwindled to its death in 1855. It mobilized masses for an expanded suffrage, and supplemented the Anti-Corn Law (q.v.) League's economic demands with political demands. It was a great

educational and propaganda vehicle. See Asa Briggs, ed., *Chartist Studies* (1959).

CHASE, SALMON P. (1808-1873), politician and lawyer, raised to reform status by the increasing differences between north and south. He had a notable career as a defender of fugitive slaves, and was an organizer of the Liberty Party and Free Soil Party (qq.v.). As a senator from Ohio, he resisted the Compromise of 1850 and the Kansas-Nebraska Bill (qq.v.). As Secretary of the Treasury during the Civil War, he issued the greenbacks (q.v.) which became a reform issue. Later Chief Justice of the Supreme Court, his determined legalism prevented the rushing through of the impeachment proceedings to which the Radical Republicans had exposed President Johnson (qq.v.).

CHASE, STUART (1888-   ), economist and liberal publicist, whose *A New Deal* (1932), gave the name to Franklin D. Roosevelt's (q.v.) program. He was associated with the Garland Fund, the Rand School (q.v.), and other reform organizations. His works recommended government experiment, expenditure in the interest of the public weal, and similar ideas; see *The Tragedy of Waste* (1925), *Your Money's Worth* (1927), with F. J. Schlink, *Rich Land, Poor Land* (1936). In old age, he wrote in admiration of the Standard Oil Company.

CHAUVINISM, see Patriotism.

CHECKS AND BALANCES, see Separation of Powers.

CHECKWEIGHER, a union man appointed to oversee the process of checking the weight of the coal brought up by the miner. The unions had a long tradition of fighting for an honest weighing of the results of their labor, and the checkweigher was therefore a strategic person from this point of view: one whose probity and reliability would be beyond question. He was thus likely to be a bulwark of unionism and reliable social understanding.

CHEEVER, GEORGE B. (1807-1890), celebrated minister who, in 1835, caused a sensation by publishing a tale, "Inquire at Amos Giles' Distillery," a dream of the Devil's vengeance on a manufacturer of spirits which named an actual distiller; as a result Cheever was assaulted, fined, imprisoned, and made famous. He became a noted New York divine, a writer for the *Independent* (q.v.), with a remarkable, apocalyptical prose which, in due course, served Free Soil (q.v.) and the Union, during the Civil War.

CHEKA, a word made up from the first two initials of the official name of an organization set up by the Bolsheviks, following their victory in October 1917: "Extraordinary Commission to Fight Counter-Revolution." This was a terrorist organization intended to suppress minority opinion. The Cheka was succeeded by the more famous G.P.U. (pronounced *Gay-Pay-OO*) (q.v.).

CHEMICAL WARFARE, one of the weapons developed before World War I, which raised fears that atrocities might be multiplied, difficult to control, and constituting a danger to the agent employing it, it was used much less than anticipated. Its effectiveness was not widely appreciated. Only 10% of the shells fired by German troops contained poison gas, but they accounted for 30% of American casualties. In the post-World War I period, there were great developments in chemical and bacteriological agents. However, their vastly increased effectiveness acted as a built-in deterrent. The control occasioned by the frightfulness of these instruments was offset by the frightfulness of high explosives, flame-throwers, and other instruments of war, topped by the atom-bomb. Research, nevertheless, continued in the area of chemistry and bacteriology. The most impressive products were gases which attacked the nerve centers and could incapacitate whole civilian populations, and biological materials which could destroy food sources and stuffs. In view of the increased effectiveness of explosives and carrying agencies, there seemed no purpose in distinguishing between the frightful nature of chemical, biological, or explosive materials. See Germ Warfare.

CHEROKEE INDIANS, the most notable of the "Civilized Tribes" in the South, who had signed treaties with the United States government securing their tribal lands, notably in Georgia, but also including pieces of other states. The Cherokee were remarkable in that they determined to match the civilization of the white people. They became Christians, and invited missionaries to help them in their work. One of their leaders, Sequoya (q.v.) created an alphabet, with which they published the *Phoenix*. Such measures did not endear them to the Georgians, who determined to rid the state of them. In 1827, the Cherokee constituted themselves a nation, but the State of Georgia denounced all their claims, and threatened missionaries with imprisonment who challenged Georgian sovereignty. The situation was aggravated by the discovery of gold in 1829, which brought ruthless prospectors into Cherokee land. The Rev. Samuel A. Worcester, who cooperated with the Cherokee, was jailed; in the case of *Worcester v. Georgia* (1832), Chief Justice Marshall affirmed the rights of the Cherokee. It was of this case that President Jackson was alleged to have said: "John Marshall has made his decision, now let him enforce it!" Jackson's Administration cooperated with Georgia, found Cherokee with whom to make a treaty removing them, and, under U.S. Army guard, set the Cherokee on the notorious "Trail of Tears" which finally brought them, under difficulties, to Oklahoma. Cherokee removal was the classic case of American injustice toward the Indian: see Jackson, Helen Hunt, Indian, The, and Reform.

CHESSMAN, CARYL, CASE. A petty, if remarkable, criminal, condemned to death in the California gas chamber for atrocious rape, Chessman displayed unexpected gifts in successfully deferring execution for twelve years on various appeals. He always denied his culpability for the acts of which he was accused. While under sentence he wrote four books, one of which was a best-seller. His long ordeal permitted defenders to observe that he had been subjected to cruel and unusual punishment. One of his final appointments with the gas chamber was deferred because of agitation in Latin American countries which might have embarrassed President Eisenhower's tour; this last incident highlighted the doubtful nature of the legal processes involved; see W. M. Kunstler, *Beyond a Reasonable Doubt?* (1961); Caryl Chessman. *Cell 2455* (1954).

CHICAGO *TRIBUNE*, notorious among liberals and radicals as reactionary, committed to "red baiting," and fanatical in its isolationist (q.v.) sentiments. They explain its firm hold on mid-west readers by sardonic references to its superior comic section, and similar features, and associate its methods and program with that of Hearst (q.v.). It was a major supporter of Abraham Lincoln (q.v.) for the Presidency; a photograph of August, 1854, depicts him posed with the Chicago *Press and Tribune*, as it then was. It insists on Negro rights under the Constitution, and runs features about Negroes in Chicago. It moved from a Progressive position, in the pre-World War I era, to one of chauvinism, and emerged from the conflict, under Col. Robert R. McCormick, with a program of extreme isolationism, anti-radicalism, and defense of free enterprise. It bitterly opposed the New Deal (q.v.). Its position made it liable to excessive statements, but sharp on others, such as the subtleties of British policy. In the late 1970s, social changes in Chicago, and the death of Mayor Daley (q.v.) reduced some *Tribune* originalities. See also Patterson, Joseph Medill.

CHIEF JOSEPH (1840?-1904), one of the great Indian chieftains, a leader of the Nez Percé tribe, who resisted an effort of the United States government to evacuate them from their lands in the Northwest, in the interests of white settlers. His subsequent battles with Federal troops were outstanding for their brilliance and daring. His final statement, on laying down his arms, ranks in tragic eloquence with that of Logan (q.v.). R. G. Davis and B. Ashabranner, *Chief Joseph, War Chief of the Nez Percé* (1962).

CHILD, LYDIA MARIA (1802-1880), popular writer who, in 1833, took a public stand as a Garrisonian, publishing *An Appeal in Favor of That Class of Americans Called Africans,* a work which harmed her popularity but influenced such notables as William Ellery Channing and Charles Sumner (qq.v.). She edited the Garrisonian *National Anti-Slavery Standard.* No feminist, her influence-served woman's rights. Although she became embittered by the quarrels among abolitionists, she continued to be a force in anti-slavery opinion. Her husband David L. Child's *The Taking of Naboth's Vineyard,.or History of the Texas Conspiracy* (1845) is an early example of "muckraking" (q.v.).

CHILD LABOR, a major American reform cause in the twentieth century. In the pre-World War I era, all states passed laws intended to regulate the area, but in such general terms as to have little effect. The National Child Labor Committee worked to educate the public and to promulgate progressive legislation. Edwin Markham published in *Cosmopolitan* (1906-7) a great series, "The Hoe-Man in the Making," later augmented and published in book form, 1914, as *Children in Bondage*. The Children's Bureau, set up in the Department of Labor, 1912, began investigations and other services. The Keating-Owen Act (1916) attempted to regulate child labor by forbidding its products in inter-state commerce when made by children under fourteen years of age or other conditions; the act was struck down in the case of Hammer v. Dagenhart (1918). Congress then levied a tax of ten percent on the net profits of employers of child labor; this also was overruled, in 1922, in Bailey v. Drexel Furniture Company. In 1924, Congress passed an amendment to the Constitution giving itself the right to regulate child labor, but could not obtain sufficient ratifications. However, the Cotton Textile Code of 1933 outlawed child labor in the industry, the Walsh-Healey Act of 1936, regulating the operations of government contracts, did not permit the use of youngsters under eighteen. By 1981, with children protected by welfare (q.v.), and young "drop-outs" (q.v.) preferring the pursuit of self-identity to work, the social problem often became not saving the youth from excessive labor, but finding it for them, for their own well-being and that of people who suffered from the malice, vandalism, or loss of character of empty-handed youth (q.v.)

CHILDREN, DEPENDENT, AID TO, see Welfare Legislation.

CHILDREN, GIFTED, AMERICAN ASSOCIATION FOR, organized in 1946, dedicates itself to the discovery and development of the "gifted child." It seeks to determine methods for identifying him or her, and considers alternative types of program which could be offered. These include, a library period a week, an extra subject for study, a core or block program, a period or two with a special teacher, honors programs, rapid advance classes, and special schools. "A combination of these methods—grouping, acceleration, and enrichment—is generally most effective," the AAGC believes.

CHILDREN IN BONDAGE (1914), see Markham. Edwin.

CHILDREN'S BUREAU, created April 9, 1912, in the U.S. Department of Labor; transferred to the Department of Labor when it was organized in 1913. It was given a variety of services to administer under the Social Security Act of 1935 (q.v.), and the Fair Labor Standards Act of 1938 (q.v.). Not the least of its services was fact-finding, valuable in formulating legislation respecting children.

CHINA, long a source of concern for reformers who opposed its exploitation by imperialists, who lacked faith in Chiang Kai Shek's potential as a reformer and democrat, who feared that Japan might make a colony of it, were faced with new problems when, in 1949, the communists under Mao Tse-tung drove Chiang's forces into the sea. The communist regime then undertook a drive to establish itself on the mainland in a fashion reminiscent of the U.S.S.R. following its civil war: it undertook to exterminate its foes, to inaugurate great national building projects, and to create a national communist philosophy, elevating Mao's ideas to those of Marx and Lenin. It threatened Formosa (q.v.), where Chiang was entrenched, protected by the United States fleet. It supported the communist North Korean regime, in its attempt to over-throw the Korean (q.v.) Republic headed in the south by Syngman Rhee, and when United States troops under General Douglas MacArthur pressed the communists back and threatened their land holdings, intervened directly, in November 1950. Problems for Americans, including reformers, were whether to recognize Red China, whether to permit its entrance into the United Nations, whether China constituted a growing threat to western democracy or a check on Soviet communism. With the possibility that China would attain the atom bomb (q.v.) went the necessity for considering terms under which "peaceful coexistence" (q.v.) could be maintained. 1972 was the great turning point with a Nixon-Kissinger arranged detente (qq.v.) which, however, did not reject American-protected Taiwan. Youth-radical infatuation with the person and opinions of "Chairman Mao" (q.v.) declined following his death in 1976, and the increase in Chinese pedestrian concerns for their economy, pressure on neighbors, world relations, peace with Japan, and image. Carter's (q.v.) determination to recognize only mainland China in 1979 was countered by Congress's will to continue to support Formosa-Taiwan. Struggle between Maoists, who had conducted a bloody "Cultural Revolution" in 1974, and a newer, pragmatic leadership culminated in a 1980 trial of a "Gang of Four" Maoists, including Mao's widow Jiang Quing, reminiscent of the Moscow Trials (q.v.), with undetermined results. William L. Tung, *The Chinese in America, 1820-1973* (1974); S. Leys, *Chinese Shadows* (1977); J-c Hsieh, *The Kuomintang...1894-1969* (1970); Ta-ling Lee, *Foundations of the Chinese Revolution, 1905-1912* (1970).

'CHINA LOBBY," name given to elements partisan to Chiang Kai-Shek and Formosa (q.v.), in their battle, ideological and otherwise, with Red China. They worked to persuade the Department of State of the need for supporting Chiang, and were alert to possible pro-communist influences in connection with official American policy. Alfred C. Kohlberg, a business man was especially active with the "China Lobby," which was accused by left-wingers of close relations with right-wingers. The Lobby was active in the Owen Lattimore Case (q.v.).

CHINESE EXCLUSION ACT (1882), see Immigrants and Reform.

CHRISTIAN FRONT, an organization in the late 1930's which attracted aggressive and frustrated elements, notably among the poor Irish, but involving other groups as well, who took the viewpoint of Rev. Charles E. Coughlin (q.v.) as gospel. A distinctly fascist-type group, they sought to rouse sentiment against Jews and other minority groups, and to assert their Americanism and right to power. See *Tommy Gallagher's Crusade.*

CHRISTIAN SCIENTISTS, adherents of the Church of Christ, Scientist, and followers of Mrs. Mary Baker Eddy. A movement of economic conservatives and social conservatives, Christian Scientists were nevertheless products of spiritual unrest, in the post-Civil War decades, and in their capacity of seekers, helped to create the wave of interest which made Edward Bellamy's *Looking Backward* (q.v.) influential.

CHRISTIAN SOCIALISM, first formulated in Great Britain, in the middle of the nineteenth century, and calling a number of vigorous ecclesiastical talents to its program of a revitalized church, concerned for poverty and degradation. Frederick D. Maurice and Charles Kingsley were among many who sought to rouse the public conscience and inaugurate an era of well-being and cooperation; there were similar developments in Germany and France. In the United States, the movement grew in the post-Civil War era, but evolved out of attitudes and ideas implicit in the older transcendentalism and communitarian (qq.v.) experiments. Henry George and Edward Bellamy (qq.v.) were laymen, whose solutions to social trouble included a religious component. W. D. P. Bliss, Walter Rauschenbusch, Washington Gladden were among many who emphasized their feeling of solidarity with the workers, rather than the employers, and who sought to recover the militant spirit of Christ. Charles M. Sheldon's shabby, but phenomenally successful novel, *In His Steps* (1897) was the lowest common denominator of their aspirations. George D. Herron (q.v.) was most forceful in his equation of Christ's principles and those of socialism, and repudiated first one and then the other. See James Dombrowski, *The Early Days of Christian Socialism in America* (1936).

CHRISTIANS, see National Conference of Christians and Jews.

CHURCHES AND REFORM, viewed with skepticism by anti-church reformers, but associated in all eras. Some churches and church elements themselves constituted reforms, Unitarians and Universalists refusing to believe in a God of wrath, Quakers emphasizing their "inner light," and, later, "Progressive Quakers" representing a critical view of conservative trends among their sect. But, in addition, the Congregationalist Church, despite its Calvinist tenets, supported the American Revolution. Later, the churches became large arenas in which the battle over slavery was fought. It is obvious that there could have been no Civil War had the churches remained united. The most momentous struggle was carried on in the great Baptist and Methodist Churches, which split into northern and southern fellowships. The Catholic Church (q.v.) was less swayed by temporal dilemmas. In the post-Civil War period, although much of the church was a bastion of conservatism, it did produce Christian Socialists (q.v.), as well as such variant elements as Christian Science (influential in turning attention to Edward Bellamy's *Looking Backward* [q.v.]) and Ethical Culture (q.v.). Reformers in the twentieth century challenged the churches to prove their sincerity and effectiveness, and none repudiated the aid and comfort of clergymen. Anti-clericalism reached its highest point in the 1930's, when materialists repudiated "pie in the sky." The churches, however, appeared to recover ground in the post-World War II period. Thus, Negroes who had concluded that religion was the opium of the people were confounded by finding themselves mere followers of the militant desegregationists among them, to whom religion and their church were indispensable in conducting their crusade. In the 1970s, strong legal sanctions against school prayer roused religious and family anxieties, and resulted in constant court action and semi-legal efforts. Pro-prayer legislators pondered a constitutional amendment taking the issue out of court hands. Whether large religious waves of people, in 1980 the "Moral Majority," were a significant factor in politics, interested observers of the American scene. Anson Stokes and Leo Pfeffer, *Church and State in the United States* (1964); R. K. Hudnut, *Church Growth Is Not the Point* (1975). See also Spiritual Unrest, The.

CHURCHILL, WINSTON (1871-1947), American novelist, once so popular that the British politician and author of the same name (q.v.) utilized one of his given names, "Spencer," when publishing his books, so as not to be confused with the American. Churchill's fiction contained a deadly touch of sweetness and light which gave him contemporary validity and authority, but ultimately destroyed his effectiveness. However, his *Mr. Crewe's Career* (1908) has some minor usefulness as a novel of politics.

CHURCHILL, WINSTON S. (1874-1965), English statesman and author, whose emergence as the leader of the forces resisting fascist domination during World War II forced a reorganization of liberal and reform perspectives. That an anti-communist and imperialist should have proved to be the necessary chieftain to mobilize a democratic victory compromised much of the thinking of the 1930's. Churchill offered the opinion that Mussolini was a great man. His realistic war program included the view that he was interested in anyone who would kill Germans. He announced that he had not been appointed the first minister of Great Britain in order to preside over the dissolution of the British Empire. Although the British discriminated between his social opinions and his war-time qualities, and overthrew his government, once the Nazis had been overthrown, it was evident that social reformers would have to be less cavalier in their attitude toward conservatives, if they did not wish to offend their constituents.

CIA, see Central Intelligence Agency.

CIGARETTE CONTROVERSY, see Anti-Tobacco Crusade.

CINCINNATI, see ORDER OF THE CINCINNATI.

CINEMA, THE, with television offering the greatest potential among the popular arts (q.v.) for good or ill, at its lowest representing a lost opportunity, rather than a positive evil, since the television could confuse or destroy serious public issues, while the cinema dealt with human and cultural quanties. The American motion-pictures utilized generally greater resources than foreign pictures, and brought a formidable technical equipment to bear on their projects, but the general level of production was low, and the best pictures were less adequate than the best foreign pictures. Cinema fanciers made much of the "classical" era of American comedy of the late 1910's and the 1920's, but it offered little to stand beside Charles Chaplin's best work. Walt Disney's escapist films were sometimes pleasing, but rarely stirring: at peak, they were very good for children. For the rest, the films offered sociological fare: they described American moods, dreams, efforts, from the crude anti-Germanism of the World War I films, through the over-rated *All Quiet on the Western Front* (1930), and a succession of films which were excellent in part, but limited in various ways: *Mr. Smith Goes to Washington* (1939), *The Grapes of Wrath* (1940), *Citizen Kane* (1941), *Gone with the Wind* (1939), *The Ox-Bow Incident* (1943), and films on Woodrow Wilson, *Moby Dick*, and other themes were interesting as much for what they failed to do as for what they accomplished. The masterly *Greed* (1923), by Eric von Stroheim circulated among some film art theaters, but rarely elsewhere. Such films as *Rasputin*, *Ninotchka*, and *Anastasia* did little more than offer indications about shifting American attitudes toward the Russia of Czar and of commissar at different dates. *On the Beach* (1960) was intended to be an impressive warning about a world destroyed by atomic war, but left no residue. Such films as *Susan Lenox, I Am a Fugitive from a Chain Gang, Crossfire, The Treasure of the Sierra Madre, Nanook, The Asphalt Jungle,* some of the work of the Marx Brothers and of W. C. Fields, among much else, could be seen as offering a structure for building, but no great impulse for doing so was evident. Pare Lorentz's *The River* (1937) was a documentary which, it would have seemed, would open floodgates to a torrent of others, but did not. In the post-World War II period, films seemed to grow feebler, the films fearing to offer their torpid spectators any challenge. The changing climate of the 1960s and 1970s made tragic endings to films available, as well as "overt" sex, but rarely memorably. Charles Higham, *The Art of the American Film* (1973); G. Battcock, *The New American Cinema* (1967); Paul Trent, *The Image Makers* (1972).

C.I.O., see Congress of Industrial Organizations.

CITY PLANNING, work offering strategic possibilities, enabling the planners to face the public with the alarming challenge of the urban configuration, the need for bold assaults on slum developments, the concentrations of homogeneous underprivileged people, the fact that movements within cities were not creating a balance of economic and social communities. Instead, the "flight from the cities" of those who could afford flight, the concentration on show-piece projects which did not come to grips with the fundamental problems, the fact that the city parks had become unsafe at night, and that vital statistics were multiplying these problems and others were not emphasized by the city planners, who did not appear interested in attempting to challenge the municipal administrations which employed them, in the traditional fashion of employers. An observer remarked that the first action of a thoughtful city planner was to acquire a home in the suburbs. All this was unlike leaders of the earlier settlement house (q.v.) movement, who had taken pains to live among the people to whom they hoped to minister. Basic was the fact that pre-World War I cities had been in process of growth; later developments saw the cities on the downgrade, a fact legitimate planners would build upon; Urban Problem, The. Lewis Mumford, *City Development* (1945); M. L. Colean, *Renewing Our Cities* (1953); B. J. Frieden and M. Kaplan, *The Politics of Neglect* (1975); Jane Jacobs, *Death and Life of Great American Cities* (1961).

CIVIC FEDERATION, see National Civic Federation.

CIVICS, first developed by Henry Randall Waite, president of the American Institute of Civics, organized 1885, an educational body which worked to instil principles of concern for and understanding of the operations of social and political institutions. Emphasis was placed on educating children to the world in which they were entering, but adults were also instructed in the need for better and more effective laws, political circumstances, and other related topics.

CIVIL DISOBEDIENCE (1849), Thoreau's (q.v.) famous essay on non-cooperation with authority. Its ringing phrases inspire anarchists and passive resistants, its most famous reader was Gandhi (q.v.). Although it is reproduced in numerous textbooks, it scarcely inspires a fraction of change in its hundreds of thousands of readers, or of refutation. Among its phrases are: "This American government,—what is it but a tradition . . . each instant losing some of its integrity? . . . I ask for, not at once no government, but *at once* a better government. . . . Must the citizen ever for a moment, or in the least degree, resign his conscience to the legislator? . . . Can we not count upon some independent votes? . . . Unjust laws exist: shall we be content to obey them . . . ?"

CIVIL LIBERTIES, long a concern of social reformers, but also of others troubled by such questions as the ability of the nation to reconcile the liberties of antagonists—of communists *and* fascists, for example—and the limits of liberty in the presence of a "clear and present danger" (q.v.). The subject has been a perennial with the U.S. Supreme Court. It could have invoked the First Amendment to the Constitution to strike down the Alien and Sedition Acts (q.v.), but chose not to do so. The "Gag Rule," too, should not have survived exposure to the First Amendment, but it did. The Supreme Court was helpless, in 1861, to preserve the writ of habeas corpus (q.v.) against infringement, by its decision in *Ex parte* Merryman, but the case became classic for its findings. (See it, and also *Ex Parte* Milligan.) *In Re* Debs (1895) threatened the security of the writ of habeas corpus, as the "separate but equal" (q.v.) doctrine threatened Negro civil rights, enunciated in 1896. Civil liberties suffered during World War I, and the Court felt duty-bound to defend the Espionage Act and the Sedition Law (see Schenck v. U.S., Abrams v. U.S.). However, Gitlow v. New York (1925) (q.v.) offered another great Holmes dissent favoring free speech. The crisis over communists in America offered numerous challenges, as in De Jonge v. Oregon (1937), which voided an Oregon criminal syndicalist law, and Dennis *et al.* v. U.S. (1951) which upheld the Smith Act (q.v.). West Virginia State Board of Education v. Barnette (1943) overthrew a state law requiring a flag salute. Jehovah's Witnesses (q.v.) fought for civil liberties, though no reformers. But it was the civil liberties of Negroes which haunted the Court until its historic decision of Brown v. Board of Education of Topeka (1954); see also American Civil Liberties Union; Osmond K. Fraenkel, *The Supreme Court and Civil Liberties* (1960). See Bakke Case, Skokie Case.

CIVIL RIGHTS LEGISLATION was intended to implement existing legislation which ensured civil rights by providing machinery which would put teeth into the statutes. The Civil Rights Act of 1957 created a Civil Rights Commission and a division in the U.S. Attorney-General's Office concerned with the subject, and threatened offenders with injunctions and government suits. It was further implemented by the Civil Rights Act of 1960, which permitted the government to make further moves upon states' rights in the interests of aggrieved persons. The Civil Rights Act of 1964 opened public accomodations to Negroes, and another act the following year expanded their voting rights. Under Johnson (*q.v.*) sponsorship still further civil rights legislation materialized. Supreme Court interpretation was vital to its functioning. David Fellman, *The Limitations of Freedom* (1959); Arthur J. Goldberg, *Equal Justice...in the Warren Era* (1971); M. R. Konvitz, ed., *Bill of Rights Reader* (1973 ed.); Stephen L. Wasby, ed., *Civil Liberties* (1977).

CIVIL SERVICE REFORM, an answer to the "spoils system" (*q.v.*), spurred by the Civil War which revealed to the country catastrophes and uncertainties created by simple incompetence. The first Civil Service Commission was set up 1871 under George W. Curtis, but with little power, especially in view of the determination of the Republican Party to maintain its ascendancy over the Democrats, and the use of patronage (*q.v.*) in doing so. Dorman B. Eaton (*q.v.*), who succeeded Curtis, had no more power; in 1874, Congress cut off the Commission's appropriation, and on March 9, 1875, competitive examinations were discontinued entirely, President Grant abandoning the reformers. See Pendleton Law, which established the Civil Service Commission. There were later special campaigns to get officers enforcing Prohibition under civil service regulations, census employees, and others, and still later temporary civil service appointees to enable rapid expansion of personnel to eventuate, to satisfy war emergencies, but the major battle had been won. In due course, the question was raised whether civil service did not fix persons in government and municipal positions who may have been adequate at the time of appointment, but who, being secure in their jobs, felt free to deteriorate in unspectacular but debilitating fashions. See also Patronage.

CIVIL WAR, THE, an instrument of reform—even of revolution, in that it undermined the plantation system of the South —and yet, paradoxically, questionable to elements of social reform antipathetic to the military, mortal conflict, regimentation, the harm done to civil liberties, the corruption which attended the war's financial aspect, and the limited goals pursued by the Federal Administration which kept Negroes in minimum regard. William Lloyd Garrison (*q.v.*) accepted the war, though opposed to the use of "carnal weapons." Wendell Phillips (*q.v.*) denounced the government for not freeing the slaves immediately. Many abolitionists could not resist lending a hand; many women reformers offered moral and practical support. The Negroes served wherever they were permitted.

CIVIL WORKS ADMINISTRATION (1933-1934), hastily set up as a stop-gap measure to put unemployed people to work in the desperate winter months. Under Harry L. Hopkins (*q.v.*), it utilized almost a billion dollars to employ some four million people. Jobs were often make-work, in order not to compete with those who were holding on to tenuous salaries and prospects; hence, the "leaf-raking" projects which, to critics of the relief program became symbolic of the worthlessness of government-sponsored work. C.W.A. ended in March, and its functions were transferred to the F.E.R.A. (*q.v.*); from them emerged, in 1935, the W.P.A. (*q.v.*). See Boondoggle; also, Henry G. Alsberg, *America Fights the Depression...the Civil Works Administration* (1934).

CIVILIAN CONSERVATION CORPS (1933), inspired by the experiences with juvenile delinquents of Los Angeles administrators, who put the youth to work rather than inflict useless punishment on them. The high percentage of poor youth with nothing to do in the midst of depression inspired the creation of the C.C.C., Congress providing for the employment of some two hundred and fifty thousand young men to work on roads, fire-fighting, flood control, reforestation, and similar projects. The fact that this work was carried on under army officers alarmed liberals and radicals, who feared regimentation might become political. In 1935, the C.C.C. came under the W.P.A., and the numbers employed were expanded. In 1961, the Kennedy Administration considered plans for reviving the C.C.C. to take care of youth in depressed areas.

CIVILIZED NATIONS, the Cherokee (*q.v.*), Chickasaw, Choctaw, Creek, and Seminole Tribes of the Indian Territory, now Oklahoma. See Indian, The, and Reform.

CLAFLIN, TENNESSEE, see Woodhull, Victoria.

CLASS ACTION SUITS, a development in law giving outlets to individuals resentful of false or arbitrary corporation or government policy. It permitted suit in behalf of a class, without the cooperation of large numbers of people. Class action has been employed in civil rights (*q.v.*) suits, but also in other matters of public interest. Thus in 1980 an individual sued eight of the largest sugar refining firms for price-fixing, and, winning, forced them to publish coupons entitling any purchasers to a discount on future sugar purchases.

CLASS CONCEPT OF SOCIETY involves the assumption that persons belong to different "levels" of social and economic endeavor. An old epigram had it that in America you could be put in jail for saying that there were classes, in Europe for saying that there weren't. It has been argued that all Americans are, or pretend to be, of the middle classes. Laborers aspire to middle class status, the wealthy assume middle class trappings when seeking office. Marx (*q.v.*) anticipated a "classless society," but gave too little thought to the impact of bureaucracy and the elite (*qq.v.*) on society.

CLASS CONSCIOUSNESS, a more explicit permutation of the class concept of society, intended to indicate that the worker is aware of the strategic "role" his "class" must play in affairs, and that he realizes his duty to his "class." This realization gives him insight into the trend of affairs, and enables him to think, act, and vote, in ways which will benefit his class and all society. Identified with socialist ideology, at the other extreme from the outlook of the *lumpenproletariat* (*q.v.*). See also Class War.

CLASS STRUGGLE, a major tenet of Marxian Socialism which conceives the reactionary elements as unwilling to give up their power and prepared to resist the just demands of the suppressed classes. To overthrow them required organization and discipline, according to Marx and his followers, under the leadership of the "class conscious" revolutionary elements.

CLASS WAR, more identified with communist than socialist ideology; the "class conscious worker" realized the irreconcilable differences between the form of society he required and that defended by the "reactionaries," and did not deceive himself with self-destructive dreams of class "collaboration," but, rather, prepared for the inevitable show-down between his class of the future and that of the obdurate reactionaries.

CLAY, CASSIUS MARCELLUS (1810-1903), southern abolitionist, and kinsman of Henry Clay (*q.v.*). His principles derived from his view that the future belonged to the poor whites. Son of a wealthy Kentucky slaveholder, he had no regard for Negroes, but freed his own slaves. He defended his right to preach abolition with pistols and bowie-knives. His courage misled northern abolitionists to believe that the South might yet abandon slavery voluntarily. He disappointed them by derogating Negroes, fighting in the Mexican War, and by eccentric personal behavior. But he was one of the inspirations for Hinton R. Helper (*q.v.*), helped found Berea College (*q.v.*), and was rewarded with an ambassadorship to Russia by Abraham Lincoln.

CLAYTON ACT, October 15, 1914, an anti-monopolist measure supplementing the Sherman Anti-Trust Act (*q.v.*), but exempting "fraternal, labor, or agricultural organizations" from its provisions. "Labor's Magna Carta (*q.v.*)," as it was termed, failed, however, to live up to its name. Although it was expected to protect labor from the use of the injunction (*q.v.*), Supreme Court interpretations deprived labor of its benefits. See also Monopoly, Anti-Monopoly, N.L.R.B.

"CLEAR AND PRESENT DANGER," famous phrase of Justice Holmes (*q.v.*) in setting a limit to the infringement permitted to government in interfering with freedom of speech and press in order to defend itself. (See Schenck v. United

States.) However, in Dennis v. U.S. (1951), the U.S. Court voted to uphold the Smith Act (*q.v.*) as a curb against communists, even though it involved not so much action in behalf of revolution, but advocacy: "Petitioners intended to overthrow the Government of the United States as speedily as the circumstances would permit." Thus, it was held, they had created "a clear and present danger."

CLEMENS, SAMUEL L. (1835-1910), "Mark Twain," born at the crossroads of the country, in Hannibal, Missouri, he went on to experience much of it personally, and to pick up its feelings and attitudes. He joined the Confederate forces, but left them, entertained hopes of quick riches in the West, but became a reporter for the *Territorial Enterprise,* in Virginia City, Nevada, and, like Bret Harte (*q.v.*), "struck gold" in his writings, which imbedded a critical view of life and American life in broad humor and idealized views of good people. Going East and marrying into gentility (*q.v.*) may have curbed his Rabelaisian impulses, but added art and form to his writings. *The Gilded Age* (1873), which he wrote with Charles Dudley Warner, criticized the crude standards of post-Civil War America, but he himself admired the buccaneer entrepreneurs of the time, and sought, unsuccessfully, to make a fortune in industry. *The Adventures of Huckleberry Finn* (1884), his masterpiece, involves a complex view of American-Negro relations, but he himself took part in no libertarian actions at home, and deserted Maxim Gorki (*q.v.*), when his American visit was undermined by hostile criticism. A number of Twain's fictions, however, serve reform purposes, including *A Connecticut Yankee in King Arthur's Court* (1889); *Personal Recollections of Joan of Arc* (1896); and such other writings as that denouncing King Leopold's rule in the Congo.

CLEVELAND, GROVER (1837-1908), notable for having come rapidly to the political fore, having been no more than Mayor of Buffalo, N.Y., in 1882, but President of the United States in 1884. Between these dates, he was governor of New York state, where he became known as a "reformer." Though his "reforms" were moderate, they seemed refreshing in an age of machine politicians. His integrity was genuine, as shown by his unwillingness, during the Presidential campaign, to repudiate a woman who claimed a child by him, and by his conversion to Free Trade with his re-election looming in 1888. He was both elected and defeated by close margins. Running again in 1892, he was re-elected, and during his second Presidency played the conservative—some would say the reactionary—role into which his Manchester liberalism (*q.v.*) led him.

"CLIMBING BOYS," see Shaftesbury, Earl of.

CLINTON, DE WITT (1769-1828), long-time New York political leader, most famous for his work in building the Erie Canal. He served as mayor of New York and governor of the state, and was defeated for the Presidency in the elections of 1812. During his maneuvers in Democratic and Federalist politics, he was a major figure in originating the spoils system (*q.v.*), yet he worked vigorously against debtors' prisons, the abolition of slavery, and the organization of a public school system.

CLOSED SHOP, see Open Shop.

C.L.U.S.A., see Cooperative League of the United States of America.

COAL STRIKE OF 1902, one of the great strikes, involving some 147,000 men and the desire of the United Mine Workers (*q.v.*) for recognition. The strike was led by John Mitchell (*q.v.*). The employers were obdurate in rejecting arbitration, and the governor of Pennsylvania brought out the entire National Guard of the state, to the number of ten thousand, to parade the mines. Nevertheless, the strike held, the mines could not function, and with winter coming on, President Theodore Roosevelt intervened sufficiently to persuade J. Pierpont Morgan (*qq.v.*) to order a type of arbitration. The concessions did not include union recognition. The president of the Reading Railroad, George F. Baer, strategic in the strike, immortalized himself with the statement that: "The rights and interests of

the laboring man will be protected and cared for, not by the labor agitators, but by the Christian men to whom God in his infinite wisdom has given the control of the property interests of the country." See also Guffey-Snyder Coal Act.

COBBETT, WILLIAM (1762-1835), British journalist and reformer, notable as having exchanged Tory principles for liberal principles, and having been influential in both Great Britain and the United States. Of peasant stock, he was self-educated, served in the British army, and agitating for an increase in soldier's pay, had to leave the country, settling in Philadelphia in 1792. He became a highly controversial defender of Great Britain, as "Peter Porcupine," and wielded a remarkable pen in his criticisms of democracy and Thomas Paine (*q.v.*). In 1800, he returned home, in 1802 began the famous *Cobbett's Weekly Political Register,* and became a defender of the needy and oppressed. For denouncing military flogging, he served two years in prison (1810-12) and suffered a thousand pound fine. Released, he became an unbridled agitator, scorned William Wilberforce (*q.v.*) as a canting moralist, and wrote with such effect as once again to face imprisonment. He returned to America (1817-19), and came home with Thomas Paine's bones, to honor one he now admired. The leading reform writer, he incurred government prosecution for incitement to sedition (1831), but this time won. A constant stream of arresting prose flowed from his pen, ranging from quarrels on immediate themes to pensive thoughts about the countryside. He wrote an idolatrous *Life of Andrew Jackson President of the United States of America* (1834). His own *Autobiography,* pieced together from his writings (1933), offers an introduction to his career.

COBDEN, RICHARD (1804-1865), English free trader and merchant, a leading "Manchester liberal" (*q.v.*). As a major proponent of the Anti-Corn Law League, 1839-46, he fought to repeal the tariff on wheat. As a member of Parliament, he sought to encourage commercial treaties with foreign nations, and to oppose militarism and war. The commercial treaty he negotiated between France and England, 1859-60, was a landmark in the two countries' relations. His support of the Federal cause during the Civil War was gratefully received in the North. See also Bright, John.

"CODES OF FAIR COMPETITION," see National Recovery Administration.

"COERCIVE ACTS, THE," see Intolerable Acts, The.

COEUR D'ALENE STRIKES (1892-1899) were an expression of deep unrest among the silver miners of that Idaho area. Numerous acts of violence forced state and national intervention. The Western Federation of Miners (*q.v.*) was the principal agency acting in behalf of the miners. The disorders ultimately resulted in the assassination of ex-Governor Frank Steunenberg and the great Haywood trial (*q.v.*).

COEXISTENCE, see Peaceful coexistence.

COFFIN, LEVI (1789-1877), notable Quaker abolitionist, who, with co-religionists, left North Carolina when it turned cold toward libertarians, and settled in Indiana. There he developed underground railroad activities and also propagandized, unsuccessfully, for "free produce"—substitutes for the product of slave labor. His *Reminiscences* (1876) includes valuable data and observations about aspects of the anti-slavery movement.

COIN'S FINANCIAL SCHOOL, by William H. Harvey (1894), see Silver Issue, The.

COLD WAR, a massive development following World War II which promised to endure as a feature of life and international affairs. Although Winston Churchill in 1946 announced the falling of an "Iron Curtain" across eastern Europe, it was the Russian detonation of an atom bomb in 1949, destroying American monopoly of the weapon, which began a race between East and West for power and security. The Truman Plan, the Marshall Plan, the Alliance for Progress were instruments for countering Russian expansionism throughout the world. Stalin's death in 1953 permitted a "thaw" in Russian social control and iron domination over satellite nations. But Russia also opposed NATO with the Warsaw Pact, crushed democratic efforts in Poland and Hungary and Czechoslovakia, and worked to make even more awesome the nuclear bomb. China's withdrawal from Russian policies provided some easing of the cold war by complicating it, but the need for security compelled a frightening arms race. Efforts to limit nuclear production by treaty under Eisenhower and succeeding Presidents were clouded by the Cuban missile crisis of 1962, later evidence of Russian industry in the field, and American efforts to counter it. SALT talks were a promise and a danger, since deception could subject the world to slavery or devastation (qq.v. for above). See also Peaceful Coexistence, Nuclear Question, Rosenberg Case. D. F. Fleming, *The Cold War and Its Origins, 1917-1960* (1961); Walter Lippmann, *The Cold War* (1947); N. A. Graebner, ed., *The Cold War* (1976); L. E. Davis, *The Cold War Begins* (1974).

COLD WATER PARTIES, popular with New England abolitionists who were equally earnest in their temperance crusades; they met to discuss matters of high and uplifting moral import, while imbibing plain water, instead of stimulants like tea or coffee.

COLE, G. D. H. (1889-1959), Oxford University professor in social and political theory, and a supporter of Guild Socialism (q.v.). He was a voluminous writer on aspects of labor and society, including a life of William Cobbett (q.v.), *The World of Labor* (1913), *Socialism in Evolution* (1938), and *An Intelligent Man's Guide to the Post-War World* (1947). His detective stories were not major contributions to the genre. His *Politics and Literature* (1929), however, was a valuable aid in helping to clarify the subject in English terms.

COLLECTIVE BARGAINING, the basic function of a union: to organize labor in order to present its needs and demands to employers with a maximum of strength. Such an aim was denounced as a "conspiracy" (q.v.), in early labor cases and held punishable by law. It was resisted by employers, supported by government, during the nineteenth century, and was opposed in the name of the open shop and the "American Plan" (qq.v.), in the twentieth century. Section 7a of the National Industrial Recovery Act (1933) recognized labor's right to "organize and bargain collectively through representatives of their own choosing." Although N.R.A. was struck down by the Supreme Court, the succeeding N.L.R.B. (q.v.) maintained the legality of collective bargaining.

COLLECTIVE SECURITY, a plan among nations to support one another against nations they consider dangerous to their interests, held suspect by isolationists (q.v.) as well as by pacifists who hold the alliance to create a threat of war, and by radicals who criticize the alliance, when it does not support cherished interests. Franklin D. Roosevelt's speech of October 5, 1937, calling for an international "quarantine" (q.v.) against aggressors was also a call for collective security with an eye on Nazi Germany, as the 1949 North Atlantic Treaty Organization was set up as a bastion against communism.

COLLECTIVISM, term invented by Jean Guillaume Colins (1783-1859), in his *Le Pact Social* (1835), in which he advocated Rational Socialism, and a mixture of spiritualism and atheism. He conceived of an aggregate of indisputable reasoning to constitute "impersonal reason": the result of group understanding, and asserted that "immovable property belongs to all." Bakunin (q.v.) used the concept of collectivism to distinguish his ideas from those of Cabet. The Marxists used it to distinguish his ideas from their "scientific socialism." Later, however, it acquired socialist, as opposed to anarchist connotations. Following the Russian Revolution, and with the increase of communist areas, notably Red China, collectivism was associated with strong efforts to overthrow individualist and democratic economies, especially on the farm, in favor of communal ownership and operation. Compare Individualism.

COLLEGES, see Higher Education.

COLLIER'S, one of the most famous of the "muckraking" (q.v.) magazines; under Norman Hapgood, Mark Sullivan (qq.v.) and other editors, it conducted notable campaigns on the patent medicine frauds (see Pure Food and Drugs Act of 1906) and "Tainted News," among others. Early in the 1910's, it passed out of muckraking control and into hands dominated by more conservative tendencies; see George Seldes (q.v.), *One Thousand Americans* (1947), 69-70. It became a magazine of quasi-serious "entertainment," and a first-class "property." Its failure in 1956 was newsworthy because of the great expense which had been incurred to maintain *Collier's* as a "popular" magazine: it raised the question of just what people thought they wanted, and how much money was necessary to provide them with "it."

COLOMBIA, see Panama Canal, The.

COLONIALISM AND ANTI-COLONIALISM, see Anti-Imperialism.

COLONIES, see Labor Colonies, Brook Farm, Fourier, François C. M.

COLONIZATION, see American Colonization Society.

COLOR LINE, the invisible line which marked off the areas in which segregation was practiced against Negroes. *Following the Color Line* (1908) was a famous book by Ray Stannard Baker. Although Margaret Halsey's *Color Blind* (1946), taking off from Harlan's (q.v.) opinion that the Constitution was color blind, was a publishing success, Negro agitation in the 1960s demanded visibility for the color black. See also Affirmative Action, Guilt, Blacks, Minority Groups.

COLORADO INDUSTRIAL COMMISSION LAW (1915), denounced by labor as the "can't strike law," since it put severe impediments in the way of labor contemplating strikes.

COLORADO PLAN, THE, proposed by John D. Rockefeller, Jr., as an Industrial Representation Plan which would have presumably made for industrial peace, since it provided for a body of representatives of workers and management to discuss mutual needs. In effect, this created a company union (q.v.), which could not do the work of a union, and was intended to deprive Colorado mine labor of the services the United Mine Workers offered. These developments capped several of the cruelest strikes, approaching civil war, that the area experienced. See Graham Adams, Jr., *Age of Industrial Violence* (1966); H. Lee Scamehorn, *Pioneer Steelmakers in the West* (1976).

COME-OUTERS was the name assumed by northern religious liberals of the pre-Civil War period, Garrisonians (q.v.) in view, who resented what they thought of as their churches' subservient attitudes toward slaveholders. Their program involved rising during church services, and denouncing those who were willing to recognize slaveholders as fellow-Christians. They would then, often, call upon the congregation to join them in "coming out" of a degenerated church. They sponsored and attended conventions for church reform, and patronized reformed congregations. See also Free Churches.

COMING AGE, THE, see Flower, Benjamin Orange.

COMMISSION GOVERNMENT, see Municipal Reform.

COMMISSION TO STUDY THE ORGANIZATION OF PEACE, a research affiliate of the American Association for the United Nations, was organized in 1939 to clarify the purposes and principles which would be necessary to an international body following the war. Following the organization of the United Nations, it concentrated upon such topics as "Security and Disarmament under the United Nations," and means for strengthening the UN in its work. It has considered the challenge of "Cold War," and the means for attaining "Peaceful Coexistence" (qq.v.).

COMMITTEE FOR NONVIOLENT ACTION, founded in 1959, but grew out of a 1957 protest project at the Las Vegas nuclear bomb testing site, and the sailing of the ketch *The*

Golden Rule into the missile testing area at Eniwetok. Other protest actions took place against bomb sites and bacteriological warfare at Edgewood, Cheyenne and Omaha. The Committee advocated immediate unilateral disarmament, refused to pay taxes to support war preparations, or to work in armaments and related industries. *Polaris Action* was a special project intended to call attention to the deadly purposes of the *Polaris;* actionists swam toward the submarine, or approached it in boats, defying orders to avoid the restricted area and submitting to arrest. A second major project was their San Francisco to Moscow walk, carrying banners bearing such legends as "Defend Freedom with Non-Violence." They solicited contributions to finance such activities. In March 1961, they claimed a mailing list of some 6,000. Their national chairman was A. J. Muste *(q.v.)*.

COMMITTEE ON POLITICAL EDUCATION, set up by the A.F.L.-C.I.O., when merged in 1955, and composed of two previous groups: the A.F.L. Labor's League for Political Education and the C.I.O. Political Action Committee. A more ambitious operation than either previous agency, it issues leaflets and pamphlets, and develops other communication techniques for providing solidarity for its union constituents and influencing the general public in behalf of unions' and workers' demands. It is Democratic in its orientation. It has become somewhat more historical-minded than before. Its major focus is upon elections, though it has attempted to function more actively between them.

COMMITTEE ON PUBLIC EDUCATION, see Creel, George.

COMMITTEE ON RACIAL EQUALITY (C.O.R.E.), a militant organization, set up in 1942 in order to further Negro concerns, especially, since 1954, to hasten the end of segregation and attendant discriminations ordered by the U.S. Supreme Court (see "Separate but Equal"). In 1961, C.O.R.E. claimed 25,000 members mostly Negro in the South, white in the North, and seemed to be increasing in membership. It has considered itself as operating in more vital fashion than the N.A.A.C.P. *(q.v.)*. It sent organizers into the field to train persons to develop effective demonstrations against segregation, emphasizing Gandhi *(q.v.)* techniques of passive resistance. It conducted major campaigns against department store chains, in northern cities, to force them to stop discrimination in their southern stores. It has employed "sit-ins," "stand-ins," and "wait-ins," among other methods of forcing service in restaurants in St. Louis, Baltimore, and Washington, as well as in Atlanta, Georgia. C.O.R.E. was the organizing force in the "Freedom Ride" *(q.v.)*. It later defended violence on casuistic grounds, and still later lost significance as Congressional and other measures created a large number of visible Negroes with favored jobs and status who had no stake in CORE rant and action. A. Meier and E. Rudwick, *CORE* (1973).

COMMITTEES OF CORRESPONDENCE (1772), established throughout the American colonies to strengthen the resistant spirit of those opposed to British policy, and keep them informed of developments from Georgia to Massachusetts. A purely informal body, the Committees were a barometer of colonial unrest and willingness to defy authority; the support they received helped set the measure of the quantity of action so bold a rebel as Samuel Adams *(q.v.)* could undertake.

COMMITTEES OF SAFETY, a revolutionary instrument, developed as the dissident colonists moved toward defiance of constituted government, in 1775. They were agencies for organizing rebellion, seizing military stores, and threatening Tories *(q.v.)*. They were given the recognition of the Continental Congresses *(q.v.)*, and supplemented the work of its armies: see Agnes Hunt, *The Provincial Committees of Safety of the American Revolution* (1904).

COMMODITY THEORY OF LABOR, bitterly denounced by labor leaders and reformers, resentful of having labor treated and handled as a commodity, something which one might wish to buy as cheaply as possible. Labor, the reformers em-

phasized, was composed of human beings with rights, privileges, and expectations which could be ignored only at the expense of society, and which, if ignored, would inevitably result in social unrest and disturbances.

"COMMON," a word used with discrimination by reformers, who identified it in one form with snobbery: "He is a common person." "Common labor" had a more technical meaning, being synonymous with "day labor," that is, of an unskilled type. The "common law" was important to reform, but not peculiar to it. "The Common Man," intended to be a phrase expressing admiration for the masses, employed during the Wallace *(q.v.)* campaign of 1948, was taken by critics to be insulting, equivalent to the faceless people of graphic charts.

COMMON CAUSE, a public interest organization which played a role in persuading Congress to enact spending limits in Federal Elections. A controversial gain, since the Supreme Court in 1976 decided independent funds could not be limited, since that would limit the right of Freedom of Speech. Democrats complained this created a "loophole" to excess expenditures.

COMMON GROUND, publication edited by Louis Adamic (1899-1951), with foundation funds, intended to create a new pride in the antecedents of the "New Immigrants," in particular, and a sympathy among Americans of various nationalities. Thus, Italian leaders of the community reminisced about their grand-parents, Poles, Jews, and others wrote with affection and detail about their youth, in the United States and abroad. The publication, with its aura of good-will, failed to be impressive, being unwilling to come to grips with the hard, and harsh, facts of the lives of its subjects, whether seen as separate groups or as inter-related groups.

COMMON SENSE (1776), see Paine, Thomas.

COMMONER, THE, William Jennings Bryan's *(q.v.)* publication of the 1900's; its similarities to, and differences from, the "muckraking" *(q.v.)* periodicals of the same period help distinguish the Populist from the Progressive.

COMMONWEAL ARMIES, groups of unemployed and rebellious who intended to meet in Washington to put pressure on the government to recognize their demands, following the economic crash of 1893; only the contingent under "General" Coxey *(q.v.)* reached the Capital.

COMMONWEALTH V. HUNT (1842), see Conspiracy Cases.

COMMUNES, See Brook Farm, Utopia, Youth.

COMMUNISM AND REFORM, considered incompatible by reformers who believe that communists maintain a rule or ruin policy and pretend to an interest in reform only in order to engage the cooperation of reformers. Communists argue that they believe in reform, but believe in more than that; that, however, they are the best proponents of "immediate demands," or "day to day demands." Thus, in 1961, they "demanded" peace, an end to American imperialism, nationalization of public utilities, aid to the needy, and other goals often held by reformers. Their record in communist fronts and united fronts *(qq.v.)*, however, dampened reformist enthusiasm for communist cooperation, and suggested the practicality of thinking of communists as revolutionists.

"COMMUNISM IS TWENTIETH CENTURY AMERICANISM," asserted by Earl Browder *(q.v.)* in the *Communist*, September 1937, as part of his Popular Front *(q.v.)* campaign.

COMMUNIST FRONT, widely employed in the 1930's to designate an organization which purported to be a popularly-led and democratically conceived instrument, but which was in reality manipulated by communists and their pawns. Among other groups accused of being "communist fronts" were the American League against War and Fascism, the American Youth Congress, the International Labor Defense, the Workers Alliance *(qq.v.)*, and a wide variety of committees, leagues, action agencies, and others intended to appeal to intellectuals, workers, women, and special-interest elements of every sort. See also Attorney-General's List of Subversive Organizations.

COMMUNIST INTERNATIONAL, see Third International.

COMMUNIST MANIFESTO, THE, prepared by Karl Marx and Friedrich Engels in 1848, at the invitation of the Congress of the Communist League *(q.v.)* in London in 1847. The fundamental document in the history of modern radical thought and organization—and continuing inspiration for radical movements throughout the world—posits an unmitigated war between exploiters and exploited, as seen in all recorded history, and in present circumstances. It is a manual for action, as well as a statement of aims and explanations.

COMMUNIST PARTY, an outgrowth of events which split the Socialist Party *(q.v.),* in 1919 into those holding to the traditional perspectives of socialism, and those disillusioned by the support socialists gave their governments during the Great War, and excited by the Bolshevik Revolution, and the call of its leaders for a new International. Expelled by the Right Wing from the S.P., the dissidents formed the Communist Labor Party, seeking American perspectives, and the Communist Party, heavier with language groups and more ardent in devotion to the Russian leadership. A group of the latter, dissatisfied with their overweaning foreign temper, joined with the Communist Labor Party to form the United Communist Party. Both the C.P. and the U.C.P. suffered government and vigilante persecution, and, under the pressure of the Communist International, united in 1921. The new party continued underground, but a legal party, The Workers Party of America was instituted. A government raid at Bridgman, Mich., during a secret meeting was a blow to the communists. However, it recovered to end the underground apparatus, and to stand before the country as the Workers (Communist) Party of America, officially, as of 1929, the Communist Party, U.S.A. In the 1930's, "Lovestoneites" and "Trotskyites" disturbed communist unity, which had become international as "Stalinism" *(qq.v.).* J. R. Starobin, *American Communism in Crisis* (1972); David Caute, *The Great Fear: the Anti-Communist Purge under Truman and Eisenhower* (1978).

COMMUNISTIC SOCIETIES OF THE UNITED STATES, THE, (1875), by Nordhoff, Charles *(q.v.).*

"COMMUNITARIAN," often employed to describe earlier socialistic and communistic experiments in the United States, in order to distinguish their purposes and methods from modern "communistic" operations. Communitarian ventures were often based on religious principles. John H. Noyes's *(q.v.)* *History of American Socialisms* concluded that only religiously-based communities had the means to survive. Robert Owen's New Harmony community, not concerned for religion, did fall apart readily. More substantial were the Harmonists, founded by George Rapp in 1805, in Pennsylvania; the Zoar Community, founded 1817 by Joseph Bäumler; The Amanda Community, in Iowa; the Shaker *(q.v.)* communities; Hopedale, founded by the Rev. Adin Ballou *(q.v.)* in 1841, dissolved 1857; among others. See also Mormons, Frances Wright, *Icaerie, Voyage en.*

COMPACT, see Mayflower Compact.

COMPACT THEORY, significant in American libertarian thought, and throughout Europe in the eighteenth century, notable in the thinking of John Locke and J. J. Rousseau, as well as in the Declaration of Independence *(qq.v.),* it assumed that government had been instituted by consent of the governed, and for their benefit. When this "compact" had been broken by dissolute or tyrannical rulers, the people were free to disavow them, and replace them with more suitable leaders.

COMPANIONATE MARRIAGE, an experimental form of relationship proposed by Benjamin B. Lindsey *(q.v.)* and Wainwright Evans, in *The Companionate Marriage* (1927) which stirred discussion at the time. In effect, it suggested that persons tentatively try each other's company to determine whether they found fullness and satisfaction in it. If experi-

ence demonstrated that they were better off apart, they could separate without the problems and recriminations which could attend more socially committed alliances.

COMPANY, accumulated invidious connotations among reformers and radicals through being combined with such words as police, spies, unions, town, man, store—in all these cases suggesting the organization of individuals and agencies concerned for the company's welfare, rather than that of the employees. Lowell, Mass., the first "company" town, presented itself as one performing a public service, of which the *Lowell Offering (q.v.)* was an example, but soon resigned philanthropic pretensions. The negative overtones accreted by such phrases as "company police" appear to have been accepted by the companies themselves, which, when seeking programs making for better relations with their employees, sought other phrases, like the "American Plan" *(q.v.),* to describe their propositions. *The Company* (1930), by Edwin Seaver, dealt invidiously not with industrial relations, but with the white collar workers in the office, described as frustrated, empty, crushed, or otherwise less promising than the proletariat.

COMPASSION, a code word among Democrats in the 1960s and 1970s for welfare and giveaway policies intended to service the needy and rehabilitate cities and neighborhoods. The crashing 1980 political defeats of Democrats, suggested to one of them the need for new cliches which might be borrowed from Republicans. He suggested the use of "throwing money at problems," "forced prayer" (instead of "forced busing" *q.v.),* "You can't legislate morality," and "spending us into bankruptcy." "Pro-family" seemed useful for all purposes.

COMPENSATED EMANCIPATION, a major plan for ending slavery in the United States without civil war. Since it was obvious that the North was implicated in the fostering of the slavery system, and since the North had dropped it not so much for moral scruples, but because it was not economical, it seemed best to end slavery by compensating the slaveholders. The simplest way would have been to pay them off with funds acquired from the sale of the public domain. This, however, would have put the financial burden on the North, as well as the South, and northern legislators were averse to offending their constituents by doing so. Abolitionists opposed paying compensation on moral grounds; slavery was a "sin," and one did not pay the sinner for giving up his sin. Emerson said:

> Pay ransom to the owner
> And fill the bag to the brim.
> Who is the owner? The slave is the owner,
> And ever was. Pay *him!*

Abraham Lincoln *(q.v.)* thought constantly of compensated emancipation as a solution to the national dilemma, and linked it with the colonization *(q.v.)* of slaves elsewhere. He succeeded, however, only in attaining it in the District of Columbia, where, for a brief period, there was a "black market" in slaves, brought in to take advantage of the generous government prices; see also Slavery.

COMPETITION, identified with capitalism and free enterprise, and praised by defenders of these systems as a spur to action, a means for eliciting the best from humanity. It is criticized by socialists as resulting in struggles for advantage, to the detriment of social needs, and also as creating false goals and unscrupulous methods in industry and social life.

COMPROMISE OF 1820, see Missouri Compromise.

COMPROMISE OF 1850, Henry Clay's last effort to appease both North and South. It accepted California as a free state; permitted new states to enter the Union with or without slavery from territory gained from the Mexican War (protesting that it was unlikely that slavery would be introduced); abolished the slave trade in the District of Columbia; and included the Fugitive Slave Act *(q.v.),* intended to end once and for all the troubles arising from controversies over runaway slaves. Daniel Webster's "Seventh of March" speech, defending the

Compromise, called down upon him scorn from the North as a traitor to its interests; John Greenleaf Whittier pilloried him in his poem, "Ichabod."

COMPULSORY, a general area of concern to reformers and anti-reformers. Thus, *compulsory military service* was decried by both reformers and radicals before World War I, encouragement coming from the fact that the United States had no tradition in the area, even the draft (*q.v.*) of the Civil War having limited weight. Not until World War II and the subsequent "Cold War" was opposition to compulsory military service limited to principled pacifists. *Compulsory arbitration* to curb strikes developed in New Zealand (*q.v.*) and elsewhere. Voluntary arbitration organizations developed in the United States; see Arbitration. *Compulsory labor* in Russia was developed by the Communists to make certain that none would starve, but that all would work. This developed into "slave labor" (*q.v.*), rarely defended by Americans. *Compulsory medical care* was bitterly opposed by the American Medical Association (*q.v.*) but defended by reformers as necessary to sustain the nation's health. "Health insurance" (*q.v.*) remained controversial in details in 1982. "Compulsory" remained a word of uncertain reform status and dependent on specific contexts.

COMPUTERS, an inevitable feature in operations of official and private matters, they concerned even their advocates because they could make errors harmful to society and individuals. An enormous literature, technical and controversial, sought to stay abreast of their potential. E. A. Tomeski, *Computer Revolution* (1969); Hubert L. Dreyfus, *What Computers Can't Do* (1972).

COMRADE, before World War II fancied as connoting brotherhood by socialists as well as communists, and suggesting the decades of labor and radical struggle for organization and achievement. Since World War II associated with communists and their sympathizers, and avoided by reformers who fear to be misconstrued.

"COMRADE JESUS," a conception of pre-World War I socialism, which saw him as an early revolutionist of compassion. It constituted a bridge from Christian Socialism (*q.v.*) to nonsectarian socialism, and suggested that if Christ were alive in the modern era, he would be a socialist; see Upton Sinclair's (*q.v.*) *They Call Me Carpenter* (1922).

"COMSTOCKERY," name taken from that of Anthony Comstock (1844-1915), best known for his activities as head of the New York Society for the Suppression of Vice. As special agent for the U.S. Post Office, he published the valuable *Frauds Exposed* (1880), which gave the details about bogus bankers, mine developers, counterfeiters, lottery and jewelry swindlers, quacks (*q.v.*), as well as the purveyors of obscene literature. In his capacity as vice-hunter, his services were more debatable, for Comstock made no distinction between art and free speech, on the one hand, and obscenity on the other. Heywood Broun (*q.v.*) and Margaret Leech's *Anthony Comstock: Roundsman of the Lord* (1927) spelled out his services in this respect. In 1905, when the New York Public Library removed Bernard Shaw's *Man and Superman* from its shelves, this author coined the word "Comstockery," to describe such acts of censorship. See Robert W. Haney, *Comstockery in America: Patterns of Censorship and Control* (1960).

CONCENTRATION CAMPS, made especially infamous by the excesses practiced by Nazis during World War II and before, but used by others to hold large numbers of prisoners or others under rude surveillance. Notorious was Andersonville, Georgia, during the Civil War, where great numbers of Federal prisoners were confined and a large percentage died or suffered for lack of adequate attention or regard. The concentration camps maintained by the Spanish during the Cuban insurrections which preceded the Spanish-American War were also notorious. Americans shortly after, maintained inadequate concentration camps for insurgent Filipinos, during their resistance to American occupation of the Philippine Islands.

CONCILIATION, see Arbitration.

CONCORD, Massachusetts, with Lexington (*q.v.*) symbol of the opening hostilities which attended the American Revolution. At North Bridge, on April 19, 1775, in Emerson's (*q.v.*) words, the "embattled farmers . . . fired the shot heard round the world." It often requires underscoring that more than a year passed before independence from Great Britain was proclaimed. The dynamics attending the passage from resistance to repudiation of the British government repay study.

CONCURRENT POWERS, powers which are held by both state and Federal governments, such as the power to tax, borrow money, regulate relations of various types. A type of judicious restraint is involved here, since Congress is theoretically able to regulate the states as seems to it proper. However, the theory of concurrent powers has a reform potential to the extent that the states may defy the government, standing behind the Constitution. Such was the sense of the Kentucky and Virginia Resolutions (*q.v.*). Such was the intention of the Wisconsin Supreme Court, which denounced the Fugitive Slave Law (*q.v.*) and freed from prison Sherman M. Booth, who had flouted it. (See Ableman v. Booth.) The South, before the Civil War, invoked the doctrine of concurrent powers whenever it could not otherwise attain its ends, the doctrine of nullification (*q.v.*) being an extreme form of concurrency. It has employed other tactics, for the most part, in its battle to prevent integration (*q.v.*).

CONFEDERATION, see Articles of Confederation.

CONFERENCE FOR PROGRESSIVE LABOR ACTION, organized in 1929 under the leadership of A. J. Muste (*q.v.*) and including independent trade-union elements which became radicalized under the force of the depression of the 1930's. The C.P.L.A. led several notable strikes, particularly that in Paterson, N.J., and organized the unemployed. In 1933, it projected the American Workers Party. It negotiated with the Trotskyites (*q.v.*) and joined with them in 1934 into a communist Workers Party which was short-lived.

CONFERENCE FOR PROGRESSIVE POLITICAL ACTION, organized 1922 out of a number of liberal elements. It adopted a legislative program calling for repeal of the Esch-Cummins Act (*q.v.*), urged direct election of the President and Vice-President and increased taxation of large incomes and inheritances, a Federal Child Labor Law, amnesty for political prisoners, regulation in the coal mines, and civil liberties aids. The C.P.P.A. opposed give-away schemes for Muscle Shoals (*q.v.*), and imperialism. It denounced the use of injunctions against labor. Its aim was to provide strength in the elections of 1924. It endorsed Robert M. La Follette (*q.v.*), who all but wrote their platform, which received A.F. of L. approval. It concluded its work in February 1925. See also Progressive Party.

CONFESSIONS, like "brainwashing" (*q.v.*) a threat to the integrity of the individual which concerned partisans of democracy. It first became notorious during the Moscow Trials (*q.v.*) of 1936-8, during which a succession of famous Bolsheviks, whose courage and dedication to their cause was presumably long secured, "confessed" to degenerate, anti-communist treachery and crimes in what seemed to observers outside Russia unnatural and incredible terms. Noteworthy was the "confession" of Nicolai Bukharin, an old Bolshevik, who took special cognizance of the fact that outsiders were skeptical of the sincerity of his public statement to assure the world that he was; his final speech contributed to the interpretation of the trials offered in Koestler's *Darkness at Noon* (*q.v.*). Confessions became a part of communist ritual, as Stalinism (*q.v.*) undertook to obliterate opposition in communist ranks, and later was extended to non-communists whose confessions served communist purposes. Confessions as social and religious instruments have been traced back to the Inquisition (*q.v.*) and before. See O. John Rogge, *Why Men Confess* (1959).

CONFORMITY AND REFORM have been related to the extent that reform and reform attitudes have been a la mode, from time to time, persons with a low reform pulse finding it expedient to simulate regard for reform in various circles with status and funds. Thus, numerous shoddy writers leaped on the bandwagon of reform, during the muckraking era (*q.v.*), whose work needs to be distinguished from that of more talented and substantial investigators. Some causes were more vulnerable to the attraction of mere camp-followers and dilettantes than others. Thus, child labor tended to attract persons concerned for the problem, and willing to contribute real interest and effort; the labor movement, too, before World War II, was no mere hostelry for incompetents and trifling opportunists. But progressive education, literary experimentation, religious reform were among causes which attracted energies which could have been more innocuously employed elsewhere. And a sense of indignation which allowed an individual to pass as progressive so long as he could utter such words as the trust, John D., capitalists, rights of labor, freedom, and, in due course, imperialists, red-baiters, oppressors, White Guards, McCarthyites—and any one of a number of epithets (*qq.v.*), could offer an individual social opportunities with a minimum expenditure of effort. See P. Viereck, *The Shame and Glory of the Intellectuals* (1965).

CONGO, once an international reform cause, because of the ruthless administration practiced by the Belgians under Leopold II; concern over Belgium's "trusteeship" reached its height about 1903-1906. For a bitter, imaginative survey of some of the reform literature, including photographs, see Mark Twain's (*q.v.*) *King Leopold's Soliloquy; a Defense of His Congo Rule* (1905). The Belgians then took account of the international scandal and embarked on a policy of rebuilding their administration in terms of a firm program of paternalism and separation of races. In 1960, as a part of the rising African nationalism (*q.v.*), the Congo was freed, and became a pawn in the struggle between communist efforts to spread international influence, and those of the western democracies. Jules Archer, *Congo: the Birth of a New Nation* (1970).

CONGRESS, see House of Representatives, Senate of the United States.

CONGRESS FOR CULTURAL FREEDOM, founded 1950, is an independent world-wide association of scholars, writers, scientists, and artists. It sponsors conferences and seminars in which aspects of freedom and its relationship to culture are treated, publicizes its views of such tragedies as the Hungarian uprising of 1956, and the publication of such books as James Rorty and Moshe Dector, *McCarthy and the Communists*. In addition it publishes magazines in English, French, Spanish, and other languages, and maintains world-wide contacts with related organizations.

CONGRESS OF INDUSTRIAL ORGANIZATIONS, organized in 1935 as the Committee for Industrial Organization under the firm leadership of John L. Lewis (*q.v.*) and others dissatisfied with the unwillingness of the A.F.L. (*q.v.*) to extend itself to organize the great mass industries, organization of which would inevitably infringe upon the power of the craft unions. Organizing committees were set up for steel, textiles, automobiles, rubber, and other industries. Organizers led fierce strikes, in the course of which the "sit-down" (*q.v.*) strike was developed in the face of company (*q.v.*) police and spies, and the police forces of cities and states. Notable strikes took place at Akron, Detroit, Flint, and elsewhere. The Memorial Day Massacre (*q.v.*) in South Chicago was a milestone in the path of organization. By 1938 the C.I.O. was established as its rival A.F.L., and with as adequate control over its local organizations. Under its president, Philip Murray, it consolidated its gains, at the expense of the bold union energy which had established it. The A.F.L. was also galvanized to action, and its membership increased, maintaining a superiority to that of its rival. The war helped membership, since employers were eager not to have lucrative contracts disturbed by strikes. By 1947, year of the Taft-Hartley Act, both organizations totalled about fourteen million members. The C.I.O. Political Action Committee (*q.v.*) maintained, verbally,

a sense of social militancy, and some of its unions, though not the C.I.O. proper, concerned themselves for the third-party Progressive Party (*q.v.*) effort of 1948. Walter Reuther (*q.v.*), C.I.O. spokesman, often employed militant terminology. But by the time C.I.O. and A.F.L. united in 1955, little distinguished their programs or methods. Paul Jacobs, *The State of the Unions* (1963); Fay Calkins, *The CIO and the Democratic Party* (1975).

CONNECTICUT WITS, also known as the "Hartford Wits," a group of intellectuals who took pride in their talents, and also in a Revolutionary America which they hoped to see great; they feared excessive democracy would be demoralizing and disrupt it, and satirized states' rights and atheism. Their shift in emphasis from defense of American nationalism to a demand for a strong central government exemplified the career of conservatives who moved from revolution to federalism. Significant in this respect was John Trumbull's *McFingal*, the first part, written in 1755, lampooning anti-revolutionary Tories, the second part written in 1782, lampooning, among other things, a weak Congress:

> Nor can you boast, this present hour,
> The shadow of the form of power.
> For what's your Congress or its end?
> A power t'advise and recommend:
> To call forth troops, adjust your quotas—
> And yet no soul is bound to notice;
> To pawn your faith to th'utmost limit,
> But cannot bind you to redeem it.
> And, when in want, no more in them lies
> Than begging of your State-Assemblies.

See also Barlow, Joel, *Anarchiad, The*.

CONSCIENTIOUS OBJECTORS, see Pacifism.

CONSCRIPTION ACT OF 1863, see Draft Riots of 1863.

CONSENSUS HISTORY, a phenomenon of the post-World War II affluence, which suggested that differences between elements in American society had been more superficial than real, and that Americans had harbored similar goals and purposes. This interpretation glossed over the vital differences between contending forces which, for example, did not defend their slavery heritage, but demeaned the anti-slavery heritage, did not defend monopoly but scorned the anti-monopoly forces. Neither side disappeared but one gained authority, the other lost it in part or in whole. What suffered was dialogue, ensuring rough victories and rougher defeats, harmful to students with little stake in extremes; see Louis Filler, "Consensus," in J. Waldmeir, *Essays in Honor of Russel B. Nye* (1978).

CONSERVATION, a relatively recent reform cause; through most of their history, Americans were too busy exploiting the country's resources to be concerned for their more adequate use, or the future. The dramatic exhaustion of southern lands through cotton and tobacco and the equally dramatic destruction of forests created an anti-conservation tradition. By the 1900's, the country was willing to close some of the barn-doors, where the horses had been stolen. Gifford Pinchot (*q.v.*) had a reform attitude toward the public domain; the Ballinger affair (*q.v.*) was, in large part, a conservation crusade, as were Muscle Shoals and Teapot Dome (*qq.v.*). The Agricultural Adjustment Administration (*q.v.*) found itself involved in conservation, not only in terms of soil conservation, but in creating lives for farmers which would permit them to use the public domain more adequately. World War II and the subsequent "Cold War" (*qq.v.*) changed the view of conservation from saving to making the best use of national resources for national needs. However, militant conservationists mixed hatred of nuclear power as a force for war with its potential for harming environment; they tried to save dolphins by tearing Japanese fishermen's nets; and they fought legally and illegally in behalf of redwood trees, and to protect forests from oil drillers. A major interest of environmentalists was to work for bills in state legislatures and Congress in furtherance of their causes. A. S. Mossman, *Conservation* (1974); Kai Curry-Lindahl, *Conservation for Survival* (1972); James N. Smith, *Environmental Quality and Social Justice in Urban America* (1974).

CONSERVATISM AND REFORM, sometimes seen as opposed, but needing to be distinguished from reactionary movements which make a principle of opposing change. Conservatives have often sought change, in order to preserve the principles they defended. Thus, Benjamin Franklin (*q.v.*) supported the American Revolution, as did such other conservatives as John Adams (*q.v.*) and George Washington. John Quincy Adams associated with abolitionists, while defending the First Amendment to the Constitution (*qq.v.*). Wendell Phillips (*q.v.*) was a patrician who, fearing tyranny, defended the rights of Negroes and laborers. Theodore Roosevelt (*q.v.*) observed that the capitalists were making it difficult for him to save capitalism; Franklin D. Roosevelt (*q.v.*) was credited with a similar observation. Some neo-conservatives (*q.v.*) argued that they were the best reformers, in a time of totalitarian thinking; see William M. McGovern and David S. Collier, *Radicals and Conservatives* (1957). See also *National Review*; William F. Buckley, Jr., *Four Reforms* (1973); M. W. Miles, *The Odyssey of the American Right* (1980); A. Crawford, *Thunder on the Right; the "New Right" and the Politics of Resentment* (1980). The election of Ronald Reagan (*q.v.*) in 1980 was not seen as a harbinger of "reform"; his campaign seemed rather a fusion of older verities which had been under attack, but been honed into view by liberal and radical catastrophes as well as by criticism of liberal misrule by increasing numbers of competent social analysts; see George H. Nash, *The Conservative Intellectual Movement in America since 1945* (1976).

CONSPICUOUS CONSUMPTION, a durable notion of Thorstein Veblen (*q.v.*), who held that dominant society needed ways to flaunt its privileges and wealth, vulgarly adorning "its" women, prizing useless but expensive articles, and the like. Although the concept did not take into account types who preferred to seek obscurity, or less favored human products of democracy who took advantage of affluent (*q.v.*) eras to flaunt worthless possessions—sports cars, elevator shoes, psychedelic paint jobs, even "pet rocks" (ordinary rocks costing money to buy, and termed pets)—basic elements of social control and democratic vulgarity continued meaningful.

CONSPIRACY, a major theme of rightist and leftist elements, intended to impugn the sincerity and rationality of the foe, by seeing them as subversive of healthy, open dialogue. Birchites (*q.v.*) traced left conspiracy back to the nation's beginnings; leftists, embattled with Dies, Hiss, McCarthy, Lattimore (*qq.v.*) and other cases and revelations, fought for their causes, but also gave some attention to the roots of conspiracy thinking. An ingenious thought was to equate the right with radicalism, it being traditionally identified with the left; see Daniel Bell, *The Radical Right* (1963). See also R. Hofstadter, *The Paranoid Style in American Politics* (1965).

CONSPIRACY CASES (1806ff.), representing a basic challenge to the concept and future of trade unions; strikes were held to be conspiracies, as in the Philadelphia Cordwainers Case of 1806, a cordwainer being a worker in leather, notably a shoemaker. A landmark was Justice Lemuel Shaw's decision, as Chief Justice of Massachusetts, in the case of Commonweal v. Hunt (1842), that trade unions were legitimate organizations, and strikes lawful.

CONSTITUTIONAL CONVENTIONS took place first in the states, for the most part during the American Revolution. Thus, they built up a fund of experience which was brought to bear on more national compacts. Most significant was the Virginia constitution, drawn up in 1776, which provided for a Bill of Rights; its formulator was George Mason, an outstanding slaveholder. The critics of the Articles of Confederation (*q.v.*) who gathered in Philadelphia in 1787 were mainly men of property concerned for a stable government. However, they represented so many diverse interests, that they had to couch their articles in a form general enough to offer all interests the possibility of gains. The Bill of Rights (*q.v.*) *was* not part of the original Constitution which was ratified; it was added in 1791, and southerners and northerners shared the honor of imposing it on the country. But the Constitution also contained provisions dubious from the point of view of reformers, notably in the three-fifths clause (*q.v.*); it did nothing for women, children, education, culture. It was an equation, the content of which would be determined by those who had the strength to force their interpretation of it upon others through Congress, the Courts, and the Executive. See Paul L. Murphy, *The Constitution in Crisis Times, 1918-1969* (1972).

CONSTITUTIONAL GUARANTEES, see Civil Liberties.

CONSUMERS, a social element which can be organized for reform action to protest the quality or price of goods, or to challenge the social politics of businesses. The National Consumers' League gave labels (*q.v.*) bearing their name to companies which did not use "sweated" (*q.v.*) labor." Consumers' Research, under J. B. Matthews, undertook to test and evaluate products. In 1935, its own employees struck for higher wages, and were resisted as radicals. Arthur Kallet led a secession from the organization, and helped form the more intransigent Consumers Union, which mixed bold criticism of capitalism with its analyses of its products. Arthur Kallet and F. J. Schlink, *100,000,000 Guinea Pigs; Dangers in Everyday Foods, Drugs, and Cosmetics* (1933) was a best-seller. War prosperity modified the enthusiasm of their readers, and resulted in a turn toward "best buys" type of analyses, and a dilution of social criticism. See also Nader, Ralph.

CONSUMERS' RESEARCH, an organization resulting from the publication in 1927 of a book by Stuart Chase and F. J. Schlink, *Your Money's Worth,* a study of the waste of consumers' money. Because of requests for further information, Schlink organized a local consumers' club. This was the seed of Consumers' Research which by 1934 had 48,000 members; see introduction to *Skin Deep,* by M. C. Phillips (1934), a book critical of harmful cosmetics. Consumers' Research tested products for value and price and issued an annual *Handbook of Buying* and monthly bulletins. In 1935, an element in the organization headed by Arthur Kallet conducted a strike which the organization denounced as communistic-inspired; for a bitter view of this operation, see J. B. Matthews, *Odyssey of a Fellow Traveler* (1938), pp. 259 ff. As a result, a rival organization, Consumers Union, was organized in 1936. It had a militant, anti-capitalist tone, and was intended to strengthen the buyer in his battle with the mercenaries of industry. It, too, tested products and made recommendations in Consumer Reports. In due course, the emphasis was upon buyers' discrimination, rather than political concerns. A film, "Consumers Want to Know," explained the functions of the Union.

CONTINENTAL CONGRESSES (1774-1775), significant to reformers for the issues which brought them together and their technique of organization. The immediate issue was the Intolerable Acts (*q.v.*) which forced the colonies to consider their program and strength. The malcontents raised delegates in every state but Georgia, organized a boycott against British goods, and took other practical measures. Lexington and Concord (*qq.v.*) marshalled the second Continental Congress, which named George Washington the chief of their armed forces, and, in effect, undertook to direct increasing hostilities. Thereafter, they constituted a *de facto* government, for whom the Declaration of Independence (*q.v.*) was but one milestone, and which wielded power until succeeded by that government created under the Articles of Confederation (*q.v.*).

CONTINENTAL CURRENCY, issued by the Continental Congress, and, due to the fortunes of the Revolutionary War, drastically depreciated in value; hence, "not worth a continental." Resulted in unrest among the soldiers in particular, and later caused resentment when Alexander Hamilton, as

Secretary of the Treasury, undertook to "fund the revolutionary debt," that is, pay off the face value of the currency, in effect to speculators who had bought it up from the needy or careless citizens at trifling prices. Thus, the foot soldier and farmer paid for the currency twice, first in original services, secondly in taxation: a problem for social reformers in the justice of the public policy.

CONTRABAND, a concept originated by Benjamin F. Butler (q.v.) in order to enable him to free Negroes who fell into the Union lines during his movements off South Carolina. He argued that these slaves were "contraband of war," and that he had a right to employ them in order to prosecute the war, especially since southerners claimed that Negroes were property. President Lincoln overrode General Butler's order, which, however, gave him inordinate popularity.

CONTRACT LABOR, a source of bitterness to American labor and reformers, since it created a class of workers who labored at very low wages, to the detriment of free labor. It grew out of the system of indentured servitude (q.v.) created to bring laborers to the American colonies. However, they "worked out" the terms of their indentureship and became themselves free workers or landholders. The mill and factory owners constantly sought cheaper labor, and found it in convict labor (q.v.), in Chinese imported on the west coast and as help during the building of the trans-continental railroads, and in labor contracted for by agents sent abroad, to Italy and other Mediterranean areas. Such labor elements contracted to work at low wages, and thus deprived workers already in the country of jobs, and were a disheartening competitive force. Organized labor, 1885-1917, fought contract labor in every form. A modern and complex form of contract labor involved Mexicans, which organized labor also opposed, on both economic and humanitarian grounds.

"CONTRADICTIONS" OF CAPITALISM, a Marxist concept which assumes the inability of capitalism to feed its poor, because it deprives them of the product of their labor: a concept inspiring to those who look forward to opportunities for work in revolution and reform. Deficit spending (q.v.) has modified the classic contradictions, and given those hopeful of new reform or revolutionary movements less reason to anticipate social crises on a domestic than on an international basis. In 1981, however, it suffered disrepute.

CONTROLLED DEPRECIATION, a theory developed during the 1950's, intended to maintain capitalism and the free enterprise system, while ministering to the needs of the working population. Thus, goods—notably such commodities as automobiles—would not be built to last as long as possible, but would contain materials of a quality which would guarantee their depreciating, and hence require the owner to get rid of it and purchase another car. This would ensure production, and jobs, and keep industry on an even keel. The question was, whether industries would cooperate in manufacturing depreciating goods, and what would happen to workers who were unemployed, or meanly employed, and had nothing but rapidly depreciating homes, refrigerators, clothing, cars, and other basic items. Post-World War II depressions, with attendant unemployment, made this question larger. In 1961, "planned obsolescence" was being criticized as being essentially unplanned, controlled depreciation as being essentially uncontrolled; but a strong core of industrialists held on to the concept as necessary to the American way. The need to save energy and stop waste, and the diminished respect for American products, notably automobiles, made the concept obsolete.

CONVICT LABOR, developed out of systems which saw convicts as excruciating examples of moral delinquency, and therefore as subject to expiation which would have a deterrent effect through the harshest punishment, rather than a rehabilitating effect. Hence convicts were given the most onerous tasks, leased (q.v.) to contractors for money-making purposes, given tasks the results of which redounded to the benefit of the institution rather than the convict, and otherwise set in competition with free labor, which protested that such work

not only took work from it, but lowered its value, and was thus demoralizing to it. In the south, convict labor was also a means of social control, from the post-Civil War period down to modern times, constituting a threat to aggressive poor whites (q.v.), and especially to Negroes: for examples of its workings, see Robert E. Burns, I Am a Fugitive from a Georgia Chain Gang (1932), and Earl Conrad and Haywood Patterson, Scottsboro (q.v.) Boy (1950).

COOKE, MORRIS L. (1872-1960), municipal reformer, significant as concerned for the modernization of the city, and for an interest in scientific management (q.v.), thus constituting a link from the reform movement to the movement toward an elite (q.v.). See his Our Cities Awake: Notes on Municipal Activities and Administration, with a foreword by Newton D. Baker (q.v.) (1918). Cooke became the first administrator of the Rural Electrification Administration (q.v.).

COOLIDGE, CALVIN (1872-1933), as governor of Massachusetts won the attention of the country by his response to the Boston police strike of 1919: "There is no right to strike against the public safety by anybody, anywhere, anytime." The strike raised the question of whether there were areas of labor and social endeavor which reformers ought to discriminate, in creating programs and tactics for social improvement. Although his Administration, as President, did not emulate that of Harding (q.v.) in the production of scandals, it did little to clarify them or to punish their perpetrators, and had no notable accomplishments of its own. Coolidge's grasp of foreign affairs was typified by his view of the war debts (q.v.). Although he may not have precisely said, "They hired the money, didn't they?" his actions exhibit this understanding of the situation. See Louis Filler, ed., The President in the 20th Century (1981).

COOLIE LABOR, used colloquially to refer to underpaid, oppressive labor conditions, but, more specifically to labor which had low status in India, China, and the South Pacific Islands, some of which was used in the United States with little humanitarianism or concern, especially on the west coast.

COOPER, PETER (1791-1883), industrial pioneer and inventor, founder of Cooper Union, in New York (1857-9), which offered democratic instruction in science and art. As Presidential candidate for the Greenback Party (1876) (q.v.), he offered a panacea (q.v.) for hard times. He received 80,000 votes, no electoral votes.

COOPERATION, a watchword of reformers, best conceived in terms of cooperatives and cooperative societies. These, earlier, suggested high ardor and advanced social, and socialist thoughts. In post-World War I decades (and, especially when contrasted with communist programs and actions) they stood forth as meliorative, rather than radical, in their approach: sensible and economical, rather than evangelical. The Co-operative League of America combined to attract some idealists and ardent spirits, but cooperation revealed itself in cooperative dairies, stores, and other businesses, more than it did in terms of social unrest.

COOPERATIVE COMMONWEALTH, THE, commonly used phrase to refer to the ideal of a state which would be based on cooperation; also the title of a book by Laurence Grönlund (q.v.).

CO-OPERATIVE COMMONWEALTH FEDERATION, formed in 1932, a fusion of farmer and labor sentiments and perspectives in Canada. It has a substantially socialist perspective, but concerns itself for meliorative and welfare measures. It has been particularly successful in Saskatchewan, in western Canada. It has held the Social Credit (q.v.) movement to be an impediment to its plans. Its program and experiences have had some interest for American reformers. See Dean E. McHenry, The Third Force (q.v.) in Canada (1950).

COOPERATIVE MOVEMENT, THE, needs to be distinguished from such cooperative enterprises as Brook Farm (q.v.), in that the latter sought to bring the entire personality of the individual into play, where cooperatives emphasized creating controls over economic factors of production, distribution, and consumption. Although there were evangelical aspects to the organization and development of cooperatives, and dedicated individuals, they necessarily emphasized details of administration, the technical problems involved in the handling of specific commodities, and other matters which tended to cool or transmute enthusiasm. In theory, cooperative organizations and cooperative experiments in living should have complemented each other; in practice, they tended to attract different types of individual. Cooperatives were often quite conservative, as with the National Council of Farmer Cooperatives. See Emory S. Bogardus, ed., *Dictionary of Cooperation* (1943).

COOPERATIVES IN THE UNITED STATES, although there were consumers' cooperatives as early as 1844, they deteriorated with the reform movement of which they were part. Consumers' cooperatives developed among the Populist groups. Following World War I, cooperatives proliferated in production, distribution and consumption areas. During the 1930's, they became an aspect of the reform and social impulse. They declined during World War II and after into businesses of a somewhat generous and friendly cast. The Cooperative League of the United States of America, founded 1916, offered leadership and ideas to a wide range of cooperative associations, and published *Consumers' Cooperation*. The United States government provided information and funds, as through its Cooperative Division of the Farm Credit Administration and the bulletins of the U.S. Department of Labor. Aside from consumers' cooperatives, there are credit unions (*q.v.*), the fields of cooperative insurance and medicine, marketing cooperatives, cooperatives which produce goods for sale, and such testing organizations as Consumers Union.

COPPERHEADS, originally a word of hatred and contempt applied to Indians, during the Civil War applied by northerners to northern sympathizers of the southern cause.

C.O.R.E., see Committee on Racial Equality.

COREY, LEWIS (1894-1953), born "Louis C. Fraina," a self-educated radical and founder of the American Communist Party; his *Revolutionary Socialism, a Study in Socialist Reconstruction* (1918) was an early work in this genre. His early ambition to become an American communist leader was dissipated; in 1922, he said, he left the Communist Party. He reorganized his interests in terms of study and social commentary. In 1930, his first book in his new style was published: *The House of Morgan*. His concentration on American essentials produced *The Decline of American Capitalism* (1934) and *The Crisis of the Middle Class* (1935). He was also associated with Alvin Johnson (*q.v.*) on the Encyclopedia of the Social Sciences. With the collapse of the "left" in the period following the Nazi-Soviet Pact (*q.v.*), he joined the staff of Antioch College (*q.v.*), and was Professor of Economics when he departed in 1951. *The Unfinished Task* (1942) marked his total commitment to democratic principles. Benjamin Gitlow's *The Whole of Their Lives* (1948) portrayed him as an opportunist. He was a fighter who neither gave nor asked quarter and whose analyses were stimulating and challenging. He left unfinished a biography of Frances Wright (*q.v.*).

CORN LAWS, a target of humanitarian criticism and economic concern, for Manchester Liberals (*q.v.*) in Great Britain and sympathizers abroad. English wheat growers were accused of keeping bread from the poor by placing duties on competitive wheat from abroad. Americans in the wheat-growing North were divided on whether to sympathize with English efforts to overthrow the Corn Laws, or sponsor a system of protection themselves. Some northern abolitionists feared to lose potential farmers' votes by appearing to be concerned for English interests, but also feared to antagonize an England which had abolished slavery in 1833. The repeal of the corn laws in 1846 served humanitarian purposes in Great Britain, and appeased American farmers, who could now send some of their wheat abroad. See also Free Trade.

CORPORATION, a typical form of industrial organization and symbol of the capitalist system. It was the subject of attack from Populism through the Progressive Era (*qq.v.*) and continued to attract radical criticism and suspicion thereafter. However, it also raised increasingly competent defenders who identified it with free enterprise, democratic control by stockholders, the American standard of living, adventures in science, and other allegedly good things. Various scandals rocked the esteem it enjoyed, its product, the "organization man," was subjected to criticism, its ability to produce in competition with the U.S.S.R. (*qq.v.*) became increasingly an open question. An enigmatic phenomenon in the late 1970s was the "rescue" of troubled corporations by the government, which put it into business, as, leftist academics had once warned, business was intruding on government. However, so much of the new policy was covered by law and subject to news and debate as to indicate a modernizing trend. E. J. Bander, ed., *Corporations in a Democratic Society* (1975); M. V. Nadel, *Corporations and Political Accountability* (1976). See also Berle, A. A.

CORPORATISM, a system developed in Fascist Italy, under Mussolini (*q.v.*), which bound the labor unions to the state, presumably integrating its legitimate affairs with national interests, in actuality destroying the life and purposes of the trade-union and placing the worker at the total will of the bureaucrat. Thus, the "corporate state" was the essence of the fascist system, and intended to maintain a watchful control of the laboring classes. Compare Soviet.

"CORRUPT BARGAIN, THE," a demagogic slogan of the followers of Andrew Jackson (*q.v.*) and his political managers, following the election of 1824. In this election, in which no candidate received a majority of the electoral votes, the House of Representatives was required to pick the President of the United States. Henry Clay cast his influence in favor of John Quincy Adams (*qq.v.*), who thereby assumed the Presidency. Since he chose Clay to be his Secretary of State, he was denounced, with considerable popular success, as having consummated a "corrupt bargain." This became the major tenet of the Jacksonians in Congress, who would allow no legislation to pass which the Administration might profit by it, whether or not the country might profit by it. The Jacksonians prepared for the election of 1828 by forging an agreement between themselves and the followers of John C. Calhoun (*q.v.*), it being understood that he would succeed the Tennessee hero as President.

CORRUPT PRACTICES ACTS, passed by the states in the 1890's and after, were intended to define ethical practices in election proceedings, making illegal bribery, excessive campaign expenditures, undercover support, undue political advertising, and other actions which might give a candidate an unfair advantage. The persistence of corrupt practices, the vague nature of "corruption," at least in legal definition, and other factors continue to constitute a challenge to reform.

CORRUPTION, a favorite target of opposition parties and reformers, an unofficial means of acquiring emoluments for which democracy makes no provision, though it often raises have-nots (*q.v.*) to power without providing direct means for placing them among the haves. Pre-democratic governments, including those in the United States, offered privileges, offices, and monopolies (*q.v.*) directly to the favored classes. Democracy could only offer, with the Jackson revolution (*q.v.*) the spoils system (*q.v.*). In Jackson's administration, it also produced a Samuel Swartwout, Collector of the Port of New York, who stole nearly a million and a quarter dollars before absconding. The two major periods for blatant corruption were those following the Civil War and World War I, both periods of Republican Party ascendancy. They were a response to moral relaxation and prosperity, rather than the particular party; corruption was widespread, and symbolic of it was Tammany Hall (*q.v.*), a Democratic Party stronghold. The scandals of the Truman administration (1945-1952) made less of an impression, and were not remembered during the election campaign of 1960, it being appreciated, perhaps, that in a world of welfare privileges, "swindle sheets," and deficit spending, sin was not readily defined. See also, *Sin and Society* (1907), by Edward A. Ross. Corruption in the 1950s and after involved combinations of politics and individual greed, complicated by social and political stances. Thus Bobby Baker, a Johnson (*q.v.*) loyalist, used his political clout for personal gain. The Watergate (*q.v.*) participants, however, labored, though distortedly, for national security. Less meriting compassion was their excessive fund-raising, at any cost, to re-elect the President in 1972. The Agnew (*q.v.*) catastrophe was notable for how relatively little money was involved. These scandals did not deter other public servants from lining their pockets or risking exposure. Mike Royko in Chicago was one of numerous investigative reporters everywhere who worked incessantly to reveal corrupt judges, politicians, businessmen, most of whom escaped censure even when exposed. Welfare cheats boasted openly of false declarations and connivance with administrators. Government programs took billions of dollars in waste and direct fraud in government services and unpaid student loans. Congressman Charles Diggs of Detroit drew money from his own modestly paid employees, yet was defended as compassionate and loyal to constituents. Jailed for his shoddy crimes he had his sentence shortened, his successor opining that "further detention would serve no useful purpose."

Notable in 1980 were the Abscam (Arab "scam") revelations by FBI undercover agents. They showed with tapes and motion pictures a number of Congressmen accepting bribes to help fictional Arabs receive favors. Two Philadelphia congressmen, Michael Myers and Raymond Lederer, though exposed, won primary elections for re-nomination.

With Congress dragging its feet on "Billygate" (see Watergate), among other social-political issues, and revelations of corporate malfeasance as in John Brooks, *The Games Players* (1980), it seemed likely that an age of integrity was not at hand. As Brooks said: "Two lowdown modern business institutions are the junket and the convention." See R. E. Wraith and E. Simpkins, *Corruption in Developing Countries* (1963); V. W. Peterson, *Barbarians in Our Midst* (1952); Robert G. Baker, *Wheeling and Dealing* (1978).

COSMOPOLITAN MAGAZINE, in the 1890's under John Brisben Walker, a magazine of general interest and lively educational features, under William Randolph Hearst (*q.v.*), in the middle 1900's, it emerged as a powerful muckraking (*q.v.*) organ. It published David Graham Phillips's "The Treason of the Senate" (*qq.v.*) articles, and Edwin Markham's "The Hoe-Man in the Making" (*qq.v.*), among other reform features. It also published less distinguished articles with a sensational tinge. With other reform publications, it deteriorated in the 1910's.

"COSSACKS," see Police.

COTTON GIN, THE, invented in 1793 by Eli Whitney, made slavery profitable in the South, since it permitted the ready cleaning and preparation of cotton for market with such unskilled labor as the Negro provided. Before this invention, it appeared that slavery might deteriorate as a system simply because (as in the North) it would prove less economically sound than free labor. Thus, the cotton gin is a major example of humanitarian and democratic perspectives being directly influenced by technical inventions.

COUGHLIN, REV. CHARLES E. (1891-1979), known in the 1930's as the "radio priest," he commanded an impressive following, from his Royal Oak, Mich., headquarters. He mixed financial panaceas with denunciations of international communism, bankers, and Jews. His eloquence attracted such partisans as Gerald L. K. Smith and followers of the Townsend movement (*qq.v.*). He was the spiritual force behind the Christian Front (*q.v.*) elements, and circulated his views through his newspaper, *Social Justice*. The effect which he had on frustrated listeners caused his superiors to curb him. See Carlson, John Roy; also *Tommy Gallagher's Crusade*, and C. J. Tull, *Father Coughlin and the New Deal* (1965).

COUNTER CULTURE, a concept popularized during the youth (*q.v.*) eruption of the 1960s, suggesting that American ways would have to give way to the new demands of the young; as in T. Roszack, *The Making of a Counter Culture* (1968).

COUNTER-REVOLUTION, groups, parties, or military alliances organized to resist, usually by extra-legal means, the coming to or maintenance of political power by labor and socialist forces; also used as an epithet (*q.v.*).

COUP D'ÉTAT, in French, a blow directed against the state, a political overturn, a concept of greater interest to revolutionaries than to reformers, but containing possibilities for them in "bloodless revolutions," or sharp changes achieved in state policies.

"COURT PACKING ISSUE," THE, raised in 1937 by President Franklin D. Roosevelt, who proposed that the number of justices on the U.S. Supreme Court be raised from nine to no more' than fifteen, as justices over seventy years of age refused to resign their seats. Other provisions were also intended to give the government added opportunity to develop its program, as it encountered resistance due to court decisions. It was evident that the Roosevelt Administration was frustrated by such decisions as those which had struck down N.R.A. and A.A.A. (*qq.v.*). This was the greatest crisis faced by the Supreme Court (*q.v.*) since the Civil War. Roosevelt's effort split the Democratic Party. Whether it influenced Supreme Court thinking is controversial, though the Court did find occasion to sustain such New Deal legislation as the Wagner Act and the Social Security Act (*qq.v.*). Moreover, in the next several years, the President had occasion to appoint no less than seven justices, including Hugo Black, Felix Frankfurter, William O. Douglas, and Frank Murphy (*qq.v.*).

COVENANT OF THE LEAGUE OF NATIONS, adopted at the Plenary Session of the Peace Conference at Paris, April 28, 1919. The famous Article Ten of the Covenant occasioned the greatest amount of opposition among its American foes. It provided that "The Members of the League undertake to respect and preserve as against external aggression the territorial integrity and existing political independence of all Members of the League." This was interpreted in the United States to mean that this country could readily be dragged into another foreign war, and doomed American adherence to the League.

"COVENANT WITH DEATH AND AN AGREEMENT WITH HELL," Garrison's (*q.v.*) bitter description of the Constitution of the United States (*q.v.*), because of its compromises with slavery, which his anti-slavery society maintained from 1843 to the Civil War.

COVENTRY, symbol, during World War II, of the ruthlessness of German airpower, this English city was subjected to "saturation bombing." Of obscure origins, the phrase, "send to Coventry," refers to the isolation of an individual by his peers who are dissatisfied with his actions. A tradition on the part of English labor, going back into the nineteenth century, was its practice of sending to Coventry individuals who did not cooperate with their fellows in labor policies, such as refusing to go out on strike on union orders, or otherwise infringing upon labor solidarity.

COVER UP, a phrase produced conspicuously by the Watergate catastrophe. Presidents had kept their own secrets from earliest times, patently covering up because of loyalty, self-interest, or their interpretation of Executive duty. This was notably the case with Jackson, Martin Van Buren, Grant, Garfield, Harding, and Truman, among others. However, the attack on Nixon matched First Amendment rights of freedom and privacy against Executive Privilege. Due to an unpopular war, the failure of the Pentagon to establish cover up rights in the Supreme Court decision sanctioning Daniel Ellsberg's right to publish restricted government documents, and the uncovering of Nixon's private tapes, which defeated him, cover up became established as a political crime. However, cover ups continued to be selective, not being invoked in connection with "Billy-gate," but being attempted unsuccessfully during Senate questioning of Alexander Haig's fitness to be Secretary of State in view of his relations with Nixon *(qq.v.)* for the above. See also Post-Watergate Morality.

COXEY, JACOB S. (1854-1951), Ohio businessman who sought to solve the economic crisis of 1893 by persuading the government to undertake public works which would employ the needy, and to print paper money for that purpose. He rallied the unemployed to march on Washington, D.C., in order to exert pressure on the Administration. "Coxey's army" drew followers from as far as California, but dwindled to a few hundred by the time it reached the Capital, where they were dispersed by the police. They were a precursor of the "Bonus Marchers" of 1932 *(q.v.)*. Coxey repeated his glamorous effort in 1914.

CRACKER, a poor southern white, used in the north with contempt to designate backward and aggressive elements, in the south more benignly, but without respect.

CRAFT UNIONS, a nineteenth century development in labor organization, leaders in the different crafts seeking to bring together their fellow-workers for common action and clarification of needs, then considering further how they might harmonize with other craft unions for increased strength. Such skilled crafts as that of the printers tended to be more conservative than those of the miners, who were separated from civilized locales, were shadowed by company *(q.v.)* police and aggressive superintendents, and therefore were driven to class *(q.v.)* feeling and bold action. The American Federation of Labor *(q.v.)* developed as a congeries of craft unions, and resisted organizing on an industrial union *(q.v.)* basis.

CRANDALL, PRUDENCE, CASE (1833) resulted from the effort of a young woman in Canterbury, Connecticut, a Garrisonian *(q.v.)* sympathizer, to open a school for young Negro girls. The townspeople took legal and illegal steps to close it. Such abolitionists as Samuel J. May and Arthur Tappan *(q.v.)* gave her moral and material support. A state law passed to close such schools as Prudence Crandall's was defied, and she was ordered arrested. Her refusal to pay bond, and her overnight imprisonment, was sensational and aided the abolitionist cause, as did her subsequent trials, which ended inconclusively, but underscored the fact that the Negro was a question for the North as well as the South. Her brother, *Dr. Reuben Crandall,* was persecuted by Francis Scott Key *(q.v.)*, district attorney in Washington, for allegedly attempting to circulate "incendiary" publications in the Capital. He was kept in jail for eight months in 1835 pending trial, and, though acquitted, suffered infected lungs, as a result of which he died in 1838.

CREDIBILITY GAP, largely a product of the Vietnam War *(q.v.)*, and such other demoralizing or controversial factors as the youth *(q.v.)* eruption, Watergate, the Nixon pardon, and disillusionments attending the Carter regime *(qq.v.)*. Government pronouncements by Johnson and his successors were greeted with skepticism and disbelief, yet more information and access to governmental papers was demanded. In effect, administrators found it difficult to deal with other heads of state who gave out as little information to their people as they chose. See Freedom of Information Act. Congress struggled with legislation which would protect necessary freedom of action by government agents.

CRÉDIT MOBILIER SCANDAL (1872), the first notable revelation among many which made President Grant's second administration notorious as having been incapable of preventing corruption. Crédit Mobilier was a construction company set up to build the Union Pacific Railroad, and which received government and other subsidies. U.S. Representative Oakes Ames, a Republican, was politically denounced by a Congressional investigation for, among other things, having given the Vice-President of the United States, Schuyler Colfax, and Rep-

resentative James A. Garfield stock in the company. See, however, R. W. Fogel, *the Union Pacific Railroad* (1960) and J. B. Crawford, *The Credit Mobilier* (1880), which question historical cliches; see also Corruption.

CREDIT UNION, THE, though an old idea in Europe, did not develop in the United States until the twentieth century. The basic idea was to pool the resources of many people, in order to make easy credit at modest rates available to all: essentially a program in cooperation. Its development was subsidized by E. A. Filene *(q.v.)*, and energetically pursued by Roy F. Bergengren; see his *Crusade: the Fight for Economic Democracy* (1952). Various states passed laws permitting the organization of credit unions; in 1934, a federal law was passed in its behalf. By then, the Credit Union National Association (C.U.N.A.) was in operation. Credit unions are generally established in group situations: to care for the needs of workers in a large industrial plant, or other circumstances permitting individual attention. The funds are insured by a national organization. In addition, since C.U.N.A. is a nonprofit organization, it divides its gains from investments and other operations among its members. The Credit Union operates on principles opposed to those which direct the bank *(q.v.)*. Nevertheless, its resources are small compared with those of a bank, which offers (according to the advertisement of one bank): the word "bank," the security of F.D.I.C. *(q.v.)*, and the use of checks, among other services.

CREEL, GEORGE (1876-1953), controversial head of the Committee on Public Information, set up during World War I to help sell the war to a sharply divided nation, as well as to inform the country of the government's aims. Creel had a legitimate background in reform, having opposed the Pendergast machine in Kansas City, and fought for regulation of utilities, woman suffrage, and other reform causes. Creel made unappreciated efforts to keep what amounted to his propaganda machine one which served the public interest. The paradox lay in the need of such a machine at all, in view of the era of expose and public enlightenment which had just been experienced. The government, and Creel, could not permit a free press when their major premise saw a portion of the population as traitors or dupes who could not be permitted ordinary liberties. For Creel's own defense of his course, *Rebel at Large* (1947).

"CREEPING SOCIALISM," see Free Enterprise.

CREMATION, a reform of the latter part of the nineteenth century, and intended to create a more socially acceptable method of disposing of corpses. However, the different classes of feeling involved in the matter kept the subject from becoming more than a specialized one. The pioneer of cremation in the United States was Dr. Francis J. LeMoyne *(q.v.)*.

CREOLE AFFAIR, THE (1841), an incident in abolitionist history as well as international controversy. The *Creole,* carrying seventeen slaves from Norfolk, Va., to New Orleans, suffered an insurrection, the slaves taking the brig to British-owned Nassau, where they were freed, except for those implicated in the murder of their white masters. The United States demand for the return of the slaves was denounced by antislavery partisans as implicating the government in the proslavery views of one section of the country at the expense of the others. The extradition of the slaves was refused by the British authorities.

CRIME, see Sensational Crimes and Court Actions.

"CRIME AGAINST HUMANITY," a concept developed during the trials of Nazi leaders for war crimes *(q.v.)*, in 1945 and after. Although genocide *(q.v.)* seemed patently culpable, some observers concerned themselves over such other charges as plotting to bring on war, which might enable any nation to accuse the leaders of any other nation of "crimes against humanity." Thus, instead of being an instrument for rendering criminals infamous, this precedent might give any successful nation a means for executing its defeated enemies, with apparent legality.

CRIME AND REFORM are associated as one inspires the other. Reformers see crime as an effect, rather than a cause: given better circumstances, criminals will not proliferate. Reformers like Rev. Charles Loring Brace sought to better conditions; reformers like Rev. Charles Henry Parkhurst (q.v.) sought to stir the public by exposing sin. Socialists like Bernard Shaw (q.v.) thought that only poverty was a crime; poverty ended, crime would disappear. Lincoln Steffens believed "crime waves" could be manufactured, simply by focusing attention on them; that, otherwise, crime was a constant in human affairs. It made famous such New York district attorneys as William Travers Jerome and Thomas E. Dewey. Juvenile delinquency (q.v.) has particularly troubled reformers as suggesting that not only social circumstances, but the family and educational programs are inadequate. Such phenomena as *The Ballad of Reading Gaol*, the Leopold and Loeb case, the Chessman case, (qq.v.) and others, have raised questions respecting the validity of particular attitudes toward crime and punishment. The punishment of political dissidents as though they were criminals has involved civil liberties (q.v.) questions. See also Sacco-Vanzetti Case, and Peter Wyden, *The Hired Killers* (1963); Lois G. Forer, *Criminals and Victims* (1980).

"CRIME OF '73," a view of the Coinage Act of 1873 which saw it as a plot to put debtors in the power of those who controlled gold. Before 1873, federal law had kept silver at parity with gold, that is, made them interchangeable at the ratio of sixteen to one. Since silver sold as a commodity at better than that on the open market, there was no public impulse to exchange silver for gold. However, great silver discoveries at home and abroad in the 1870's drove down the price of silver, and silver miners agitated to reestablish the price of their bullion by forcing a government linkage with gold. Debtors hoped that such a re-establishment of legal parity would drive down the price of gold. Although the backers of the Coinage Act of 1873 could not have known that silver was soon to become a glut on the market, they were concerned to build up the value of the more scarce gold as a standard of finance, and could thus be accused by their Populist critics of policies which would make life more difficult for debtors. See also Silver Question, The.

CRIMINAL SYNDICALISM LAWS (1917-1920), passed by the government and half the states, and intended to deal harshly with those convicted of terrorism and other violence in the interests of social change. The California Act (1919) was sweepingly utilized. Members of the I.W.W. (q.v.) were arrested and convicted, in some cases, simply for having belonged to their organization. Antagonism toward social rebels was aggravated by the war situation. New Mexico law punished employers who could be proved to have hired "anarchists." The State of Washington not only punished sabotage, but also the interference with business.

CRISES, often equated with economic depressions (q.v.), but also evoked with respect to social clashes such as have attended racial difficulties, and international differences which have seemed to make war imminent. Reformers are more prone to see crises than others, since they see human affairs in terms of progress or regression. The Spanish-American War and the two World Wars were not classed as crises, once the country entered into them, American confidence mixing with victory propaganda to give crises talk the suspicious sound of defeatism. However, the rise of international communism, and its patent victories over the democracies, and the rise of African nations, which made various racial problems acutely embarrassing to the United States government, gave the events involved the status of crises. Their internationalization in the 1950s and after suggested Americans would have to live with a state of permanent crisis, and educate themselves to doing so intelligently.

CRISIS, THE, organ of the N.A.A.C.P. (q.v.), from 1910 into the 1930's dominated by the personality and ideas of W. E. B. Du Bois (q.v.), but also reflecting aspects of Negro concern and aspiration. Its influence decreased somewhat as other significant Negro publications grew and expanded.

CRISIS, THE (1776-1783), see Paine, Thomas.

CROLY, HERBERT (1869-1930), a significant figure in the development of the concept of an American elite to dominate American affairs. His *The Promise of American Life* (1909) ridiculed the current reform movement as sentimental, and proposed a program which would unify the nation. It is a seminal work in political thought. It sought "Jeffersonian ends with Hamiltonian means." It advocated satisfying the various classes and groups in American life, in exchange for loyalty and sacrifice which would advance the nation as a whole, in nationalistic competition with other developed nations. Croly exhibited Anglo-Saxon pride, and derogated Negro abilities, but could not see reform as meaningful, if it did not give the United States added status in the world. *The New Republic* (q.v.), which he founded 1914, sought to attract the elite he sought. Although Croly's thinking influenced Theodore Roosevelt (q.v.), Croly also was willing to follow Woodrow Wilson's (q.v.) lead. *The New Republic's* thinking in terms of an international organization which could end war—later crystallized in the League of Nations (q.v.)—helped Woodrow Wilson decide to intervene in World War I. Croly was glad to see muckraking (q.v.) stamped out, since its methods did not appeal to him as sophisticated, but he deplored the decline of American liberalism after the war ended. See Charles Forcey, *The Crossroads of Liberalism* (1961), for a sympathetic view of Croly's achievement.

CROMWELL, OLIVER (1599-1658), see Puritan Revolution.

CROP-LIEN SYSTEM, see Tenant Farmer.

CROPPER, see Share Cropper.

CROSBY, ERNEST HOWARD (1856-1907), a vital figure in reform circles at the turn of the century, he interrupted a conventionally successful career which included a judgeship at the international court at Alexandria, Egypt, to interest himself in the Single Tax, anti-imperialism, settlement work, and other humanitarian and civic causes. He helped to popularize Tolstoi's ideas, as in his *Tolstoi and His Message* (1903). His *Shakespeare's Attitude toward the Working Classes* (1903) was an original achievement which has been inadequately recognized. It established the argument that Shakespeare has been unsympathetic to the poorer elements of society. It inspired Tolstoi to write his remarkable, and controversial essay on *King Lear*.

"CROSS OF GOLD SPEECH, THE," delivered by William Jennings Bryan (q.v.), July 8, 1896, one of the most famous of all political addresses in America.

CROSSER-DILL ACT (1934) advanced labor mediation proceedings in the strategic field of railroads by establishing a National Railway Adjustment Board, supporting the substantial labor unions against the possibility of company unions (q.v.), legislating against yellow dog contracts (q.v.) and otherwise providing against stoppages harmful to the public and social interest.

CRUM, BARTLEY C. (1900-1959), liberal lawyer and Republican, he was influenced in his approach by Clarence Darrow (q.v.), whom he met in 1933. He defended Harry Bridges (q.v.) during Department of Justice efforts to deport him, denounced the proposal in 1947 to outlaw the Communist Party, and served as special counsel on the President's Committee on Fair Employment of Negroes on the Southern Railroads. In 1948 he became the publisher of *PM* (q.v.). He managed Wendell Willkie's (q.v.) campaign in 1940, but later supported Truman and Stevenson (qq.v.).

CRUSADE AGAINST SLAVERY, THE (1960 ff.), by Louis Filler; see also Abolitionism, Slavery, and modern relations in Liberia, Africa, India, and elsewhere.

"CRUSADE FOR DEMOCRACY," applied to American participation in World War I; the phrase suited the Socialists and reformers who had previously denounced war as an instrument of national policy; they argued that they were expanding their work of the Reform Era: having opposed industrial tyranny at home, they were now opposing the tyranny of the German master-class. Those who held the war to be a mere contest between imperialists denounced this reasoning as illogical or mendacious.

"CRY OF THE CHILDREN, THE," (1843), poem by Elizabeth Barrett Browning which expressed sorrow for the plight of the poor; see also "Song of the Shirt, The."

CUBA, in 1961 the most significant single fact in Latin American relations with the United States. Long restless under Spanish rule, the island developed a tradition of revolt followed with some sympathy by Americans during the nineteenth century. In the latter half, American investors interested themselves in its main product, sugar. The demand for *Cuba Libre*, in the 1890's, grew with increasing American feelings favoring extra-continental expansion. The Spanish-American War *(q.v.)* brought Cuba into the American orbit, and permitted periodic interventions, until 1934, when the island received total sovereignty, as well as the dictatorship of Fulgencio Batista. Commercial relations, however, remained close, the United States absorbing some sixty percent of Cuba's products, and other relations being largely limited to tourist trade. The revolutionary movement late in the 1950's under Fidel Castro was followed with traditional regard for libertarian sentiments, especially as it appeared that Batista was losing his grip, and its success in 1959 was hailed with considerable pleasure and a sense of festivity. Castro's unwillingness to cooperate with United States policy, his willingness to tolerate communists and pro-communists in his ranks, and his radical economic program, turned the United States government against him. This made him more friendly toward Soviet overtures, and U.S.-Cuba relations became critical. *Listen, Yankee (q.v.)* was one of the few "respectable" reports on the situation. The abortive American effort (1961) to have Fidel overthrown gave him international prestige, and placed what seemed a communist-type state on the doorsteps of the United States. In 1962 the Russian effort to erect missile bases in Cuba was stopped by American protest, but Cuba undertook to spread her communist message through South America, and, later, to provide a surrogate armed force for Russian interests in Africa. Revelations that there had been CIA *(q.v.)* plans to assassinate Castro harmed American prestige.

Nevertheless Cuban prestige also suffered when Cubans in 1980 made concerted efforts, to permit over 100,000 men, women, and children to abandon Cuba by every manner of conveyance for the United States, creating in Miami, Florida, a refugee and immigration problem *(qq.v.)*: bare evidence of the Cuban revolution's failures. David L. Larson, *The "Cuban Crisis" of 1962* (1963); Lowry Nelson, *Cuba: the Measure of a Revolution* (1972); Jay Mallin, ed., *"Che" Guevara on Revolution* (1969); Lee Chadwick, *Cuba Today* (1976); D. B. Jackson, *Castro, the Kremlin, and Communism in Latin America* (1969).

CULTURE, a benign, often stormy, component of social change, it has involved related and opposed features of high art, "middle brow" expression, and popular culture *(q.v.)*. Thus, proponents of high and popular art united intellectually to protest the intrusion of McDonald chainstore additions into favored urban neighborhoods on grounds that they vulgarized their streets. Yet elements of all these trends, and elsewhere as in America, united to mourn without clarification the death in 1980 of one of the entertainment Beatles, John Lennon, as a catastrophe for art and humanity, though he was also admired by many of the denizens of McDonald's. The Beatles had given vent to a "rock" rhythm, irreverence, and the tenets of sexual freedom and drugs, and were a phenomenon of popular excitement, and they had thus contributed to social change, especially as it affected youth *(q.v.)*.

They contrasted with the "social significance" *(q.v.)* writing in fiction, theater, and music of the 1930s, which lost status

following World War II as dogmatic and unreal, though it had produced such artists as John Steinbeck, Arthur Koestler, and Marc Blitzstein, none indispensable to worshippers at 1920s shrines. The youth erruption of the 1960s highlighted popular music, rather than the art of writing. It repudiated tradition and love of home, and produced, in addition to the songs of the Beatles, the Animals, and other groups such theater sensations as "Oh! Calcutta!" of erotica fame and the nightclub guru *(q.v.)* Lenny Bruce. The *New York Times* among other leading organs, striving for empathy with the critical and discontented, published articles filled with deep hatred for *The Star-Spangled Banner*, but none defensive of its purposes or tradition.

Although the derivative arts flourished in museums and opera houses, original work veered between the suburbs-concerned notions of John Cheever and John Updike and the musings of the "Me" generation (as Tom Wolfe termed it) writers like Norman Mailer and Truman Capote who provided escapes for a people troubled by inflation and loss of national pride—thanks to such protracted traumas as the Watergate investigation, the controversy over Vietnam intervention, and the "hostages" humiliation in Iran *(qq.v.)*. Americans were clearly not "Number One," in their vainglorious boast. A grotesque "rescue attempt" under President Carter to free the "hostages" failed for lack of personnel and decent and sufficient equipment; a cartoon of the time showed the comic Marx Brothers in charge of the operation. This incident capped a long domestic campaign in and out of the schools to degrade American heroes *(q.v.)* from General George Washington, who was scorned as a pompous racist to Sergeant Alvin York, who was not sufficiently recalled for scorn. Major vehicles of communication, such as the *New York Times*, made no attempt to resist the derogation process, and, indeed, aided it by their praise and receptivity toward "anti-heroes" of many sources among youth, minority spokesmen, and female activists, including Joan Baez and Gloria Steinam, who believed they served a larger humanity.

Literature and history studies in the schools notoriously declined, being deemed "racist" and irrelevant by their practitioners as well as students. A turn toward conservatism by such erstwhile liberal critics as Daniel Bell and Norman Podhoretz helped indicate a revaluation of Sixties values, notably in terms of government welfare policies and ethnic agitation, in a nation totally composed of minorities. A species of dialogue was manifested in the contrasting motion-picture successes, both in 1979, of *The Deerhunters*, which implicitly justified the American Vietnam effort, and *Coming Home*, featuring the anti-American actress Jane Fonda, in a picture which demeaned American warriors. Whether the conservative "revolution" of 1980, raising Ronald Reagan *(q.v.)* to the Presidency, could set off a novel trend in cultural work, or reinvigorate an old one, was unclear. See also Patriotism, Conservatism, Reform, Progressive Era, Debunking, Liberalism, and related topics in the arts.

CURRENCY REFORM, see "Money Question, The."

CUSTOMS HOUSE, a favorite locale for political patronage *(q.v.)* and political corruption. Most notable was the stealing of almost a million and a quarter dollars by Samuel Swartwout, an appointee of Andrew Jackson, as Collector for the Port of New York, over a number of years till his exposure in 1838. In 1878, President Hayes *(q.v.)* made war with Roscoe Conkling over control of the Port of New York: a battle which helped split the Republican Party.

C.W.A., see Civil Works Administration.

CYCLES, see Business Cycles.

CZAR, ruler of Russia before the revolutions of 1917; used colloquially about autocrats of any type, e.g., czar of labor, of rackets, of industry. Joseph G. Cannon *(q.v.)*, though spoken of as a "Czar," was better known as "Uncle Joe," because of his unprepossessing appearance and backwoods manners.

CZECHOSLOVAKIA, linked to American perspectives in being

a product of World War I and the break-up of the old Austro-Hungarian Empire, and of the concept of "self-determination" of nations, which Woodrow Wilson (q.v.) pressed upon his fellow-arbiters at Versailles. Masaryk (q.v.), founder of the new nation, sought to draw varied peoples together on constitutional terms he had derived from his study of United States history. Czechoslovakia became an advanced and industrial republic. As such, it was eyed by Hitler, who appealed to its German minority in the Sudeten section. The British Premier, Chamberlain, seeking peace in 1938, decided to accede to Hitler's demands; in the bitter jest of the time, he purchased peace with Czechs; ironically, the Sudeten Germans, too, had demanded "self-determination." Hitler's incorporation of the Sudeten signalled the general break-up of the little state, parts of it going to Hungary and Poland. President Beneš left for the United States. Following the fall of Hitler, Czechoslovakia was reconstituted, with Beneš as President, Masaryk's son, Jan, as Foreign Minister. In 1948, the communists, following careful preparation, threatened civil war, and persuaded Beneš to accept a substantially communist government. Shortly after, Masaryk died from a fall out of his office window, allegedly a suicide; Beneš soon resigned, pleading ill-health, and then died. Czechoslovakia was now securely behind the "iron curtain" (q.v.). In 1968, Russian troops and political power acted to crush any hopes or aspirations toward an increasing democracy. William Zartman, ed., *Czechoslovakia: Intervention and Impact* (1970); V. Mastny, ed., *Czechoslovakia: Crisis in World Communism* (1974); A. G. Mezerik, ed., *Czechoslovakia Invasion* (1968).

D

DACHAU, one of the most memorable of the concentration camps (q.v.). Among other distinctions, here were performed the first "human guinea pig" experiments, February 1942, by Nazi Captain Sigmund Rascher.

DALEY, RICHARD J. (1902-1976), long-time boss (q.v.) of Chicago, condemned as corrupt and dictatorial, yet clung to and even admired by liberals among others as holding together, with payoffs and authority his sick city: a reversal of expectations from the era of the Progressives (q.v.). It was generally conceded that Daley had "delivered" crucial Illinois to John F. Kennedy (q.v.) in 1960 by fair means and otherwise: a fact his well-wishers were able to forget. Mike Royko, *Boss* (1971); Eugene Kennedy, *Himself: the Life and Times of Richard J. Daley* (1978).

DANA, CHARLES A. (1819-1897), notable example of a turn-coat from reform principles; member and treasurer of Brook Farm (q.v.) in the 1840's, he became the bitter and cynical editor of the *New York Sun*, and the enemy of all reformers.

DANA, RICHARD HENRY, JR. (1815-1882), author of the classic *Two Years before the Mast* (1840), which included notable pages about the inhumane treatment accorded seamen, he later became an attorney who sponsored reform legislation, and, though no radical, an outstanding defender of fugitive slaves and an advocate of Free Soil; see Charles F. Adams, *Richard Henry Dana* (1890), Seamen.

DANBURY HATTERS CASE, see Boycott.

D.A.R., see Daughters of the American Revolution.

DARKNESS AT NOON (1941), by Arthur Koestler, one of the famous novels of the twentieth century, it sought to explain the total reversal of attitude which characterized the defendants of the Moscow Trials (q.v.), and their incredible "confessions." As later turned into a play, and widely performed in the United States, it became an anti-communist tract; however, the intention of the original novel was not so much anti-communist as anti-Stalinist (q.v.).

DARROW, CLARENCE (1857-1938), the greatest of American lawyers concerned for labor, radical, and lost causes, he was active in behalf of Debs (1894), of "Big Bill" Haywood (1907), of the McNamaras (1911) (qq.v.), among others; it was significant of changing times and interests, that he should have turned to Loeb and Leopold (q.v.) in 1924, as a case of consequence. The Sweet Case (1925) (q.v.) maintained the Darrow tradition of humanitarianism and of challenge to reaction. The Scopes Trial (q.v.), that same year, was a turning point in both his life and that of William Jennings Bryan, whose candidacy for President he had once supported. See Darrow's *The Story of My Life* (1932). See also Arthur Weinberg, ed., *Attorney for the Damned* (1957). Kevin Tierney, *Darrow* (1979).

DARTMOUTH COLLEGE V. WOODWARD (1819), a decision by Chief Justice John Marshall (q.v.) intended to underscore the inviolability of contracts. A charter granted in colonial times was altered by the State of New Hampshire in the interests of a more modern arrangement. Standing on the "contract clause" of the Constitution, Marshall rejected the State's argument that Dartmouth was a public, not a private, corporation, and that its charter, therefore, was not covered by the clause as intended. The effect of Marshall's decision would have been to curb the efforts of reformers to alter past conditions. The Charles River Bridge v. Warren Bridge (1837) decision of Chief Justice Roger B. Taney, which also involved the permanence and substance of contracts, considerably modified the Dartmouth findings; it emphasized that "the object and end of all government is to promote the happiness and prosperity of the community."

D'ARUSMONT, MADAME FRANCES [WRIGHT], see Wright, Frances.

DARWINISM, derived from the investigations of Charles Darwin, but not identical with them. Darwin was a student and emphasized the collection of data; his theories of natural selection and the descent of man from other forms of animal carried, to him, a minimum of implications. It was Thomas Henry Huxley who spelled out what he thought to be *Man's Place in Nature* (1863), and developed a materialistic, and atheistic, view of the universe. Darwin's *On the Origin of Species by Means of Natural Selection* (1859) was a major challenge to fundamentalism (*q.v.*) in religion. When coupled with the mass deaths of the Civil War, it could create severe doubts as to the meaning of life. In due course, Darwinism could be reconciled with religion; evolution could be the method through which divinity operated; but the first revelation undermined the faith of some people, and created a strain of pessimism, as in major writings by Stephen Crane and Theodore Dreiser (*q.v.*). Darwinism seemed to tally with Marxism (*q.v.*), to the extent that both views of existence posited development and change, one biological, the other institutional. See also Social Darwinism. R. D. Alexander, *Darwinism and Human Affairs* (1979); Rene Dubos, *Beast or Angel?* (1974); Stephen J. Gould, *Since Darwin* (1979).

DARWINISM AND POLITICS (1890), by David G. Ritchie, confronted particular aspects of "Social Darwinism" (*q.v.*), arguing that "the theory of Natural Selection (in the form in which alone it can properly be applied to human society) lends no support to the political dogma of Laissez faire." In effect it argued for men to intervene to modify their processes: that the law of the jungle was an unfit law for human beings.

DAUGHTERS OF THE AMERICAN REVOLUTION, conspicuous, among social reformers, for their sensitiveness to non-American influences, in their definition, and generally more famous than the Sons of the American Revolution. Their unwillingness to open their Washington hall to the singing of Marian Anderson, Negro singer, exposed them to a sharp criticism in 1939, and a concert was arranged elsewhere in the Capital, sponsored by Mrs. Franklin D. Roosevelt, among others. In 1980, the DAR sponsored a major historical exhibition on Jews in early America; their curator called it a major step for the organization. Martha Strayer, *The DAR, an Informal History* (1973).

DAUMIER, HONORÉ (1808-1879), noted for his caricatures of middle-class French society which exposed its pretensions and encouraged reform attitudes and ideas.

DAWES ACT (1887), see Indian, The, and Reform.

DAYTON (OHIO) PLAN, adopted in 1914 for efficiency purposes, following a disastrous flood. A commission elected by general suffrage runs the city, devising ordinances, budgets, and appointing a city manager, with whom it works closely. It constituted an improvement over the Galveston Plan (*q.v.*) which had earlier set up a commission.

DAYTON (TENNESSEE) TRIAL, see Scopes Trial.

DEAF, see Institutional Reform, Gallaudet, Thomas H.

DEARBORN *INDEPENDENT*, a publication subsidized by Henry Ford (*q.v.*) which, in 1920-1, became notorious for its anti-semitic articles on "Jewish Activities in the United States." Liberals denounced Ford; whether those who argued him socially naive, technologically invaluable, were also anti-semitic requires individual analysis. E. A. Filene (*q.v.*), though himself of Jewish birth, was one of those who continued to hold Ford in esteem for his contributions to mass-production (*q.v.*).

DEATH PENALTY, see Anti-Capital Punishment Crusade.

DEBATES, also known as "The Great Debates," the greatest being those between Richard M. Nixon and John F. Kennedy (*qq.v.*) competing for the Presidency in 1960. President Eisenhower (*q.v.*) later commented that he would not have granted Kennedy the visibility the debates afforded. Nixon's Vice-Presidency had given him experience and publicity not available to his rival. The debates enabled Kennedy to exploit his "Charisma" and apparent freshness. A notorious detail of the meetings was Nixon's "five o'clock shadow," which may have detracted further from his not exceptional good-looks. The debates may have made Kennedy the hair-line President. The 1976 Ford-Carter (*qq.v.*) debates were made notable by Ford's apparent *"gaffe"* (French for mistake), exploited by pro-Carter journalists and television commentators, in declaring that the Poles (*q.v.*) were not under the rule of Russia; a view which was almost prophetic of 1980 events, but at the time determinedly turned in Carter's favor. Carter harmed his 1980 candidacy by refusing to debate with third-candidate John Anderson, though Carter had won his Presidency on open-forum principles, and demanded debates in 1976. Sidney Kraus, ed., *The Great Debates* (1962); *The Great Debates, Carter v. Ford* (1976); *The Great Debates, Kennedy v. Nixon* (1977). See also Lincoln-Douglas Debates.

DEBS, EUGENE VICTOR (1855-1926) was the founder, in 1893, of the American Railway Union. As leader of the Pullman Strike (*q.v.*) in 1894, Debs was sentenced to six months in prison. He became a socialist, editor of *The Appeal to Reason*, and a Presidential candidate. In 1912, he received 901,000 votes. In 1920, though in prison for having opposed the participation of the United States in World War I, he received 919,000 votes for President. He was a symbol of socialist aspiration, and of unity, rather than an architect of Socialist Party policy. See also *In Re Debs*.

DEBTORS' PRISONS, a peculiar institution which caused sorrow and catastrophe from Revolutionary times on, and helped bring on Shays's Rebellion (*q.v.*). Debtors were lodged in jail, but being there were prevented from taking steps to liquidate their debts. Thus, unless friends or family intervened and raised money to pay off the sum involved, a debtor might languish in prison indefinitely. By the 1820's, the practice had become an anachronism. Moreover, it afflicted reputable members of the community; the poor were rarely able to incur debts, or underwrite notes which might land them in prison. Thus, the battle against debtors' prisons was a middle-class crusade, offensive to its partisans even when "imprisonment" was legal rather than actual. It was a Jacksonian (*q.v.*) cause. See also Prison Reform.

DEBTS, see War Debts, Funding of the Revolutionary Debt, Keynesian Economics.

DEBUNKING, from "Bunk," a corruption of Buncombe County, North Carolina. Felix Walker of the Sixteenth Congress, from that county, amused the nation by advising fellow-Congressmen that they need not listen to him; that he was only speaking for his constituents of Buncombe. "Bunk" became a cultural impulse which accompanied "disillusionment" with the goals of World War I. It found moral flaws in George Washington and American history generally, and in American life, as in W. E. Woodward's *Bunk* (1923) and Sinclair Lewis's *Babbitt* (1922). Communist dreamers during the 1930s depression sought a "working-class history" of the nation, with meagre results. Anti-patriotism (*q.v.*) generally in the 1960s and 1970s, and the decline of American prestige produced shelves of books and textbooks such as F. Gentles and M. Steinfield, *Dream On, America* (1971) which presumed to find the difference between American "ideals" and harsh American practice. See also Heroes, Anti-Heroes.

DECENCY, see National Legion of Decency, The.

DECLARATION OF INDEPENDENCE, famous manifesto, largely prepared by Thomas Jefferson (*q.v.*) for a committee appointed by the Continental Congress of 1776, which accepted it on July 4. Although sometimes imagined to be a legal instrument, it differs from the much later Constitution of the United States (*q.v.*) as being an assertion of principles, rather than of legal premises. The Declaration appealed to "natural rights," as learned from John Locke (*qq.v.*). It has been observed that the Rosenbergs (*q.v.*) died because they confused the Declaration with the Constitution. Carl L. Becker, *The Declaration of Independence: a Study in the History of Political Ideas* (1958); Garry Wills, *Inventing America* (1978).

DECLARATORY ACT, appended to a Parliamentary act in 1766 which repealed the Stamp Act (*q.v.*). It declared that Parliament was the ultimate authority for the passage of laws, and, with the King, stood superior to any colonial enactments. Although this view had presumably been official in periods past, Parliament felt it necessary to reaffirm the fact. However, taken in connection with Stamp Act repeal, it was a clear sign of weakness. Had Parliament either made determined efforts to enforce the Stamp Act, or gracefully accepted the colonial point of view, empire relations could have been maintained. Under the circumstances, the colonists were encouraged to feel that they had obtained one victory, and could obtain more.

"DEFICIT SPENDING," always necessary during war-time, introduced by the New Deal Administration during the 1930's as a means for combating depression. It gave new powers of taxation to the government, and thus added a socialist component to the American economy. It was defended by reformers and revolutionists, denounced by conservatives and Manchester Liberals (*q.v.*). It was maintained following depression and war for "cold war" purposes, and in order to meet the increasing demands of missile, bomb, and space experimentation. Reformers have criticized government spending less on principled grounds than because of specific fears for peace or of unbridled bureaucracy. Deficit spending developed its own "contradictions," and was in disrepute by the 1980s, having brought on inflation, as well as corruption in welfare, employment, and other expansive policies. An oddity was its use in other parts of the world; see, for example, R. G. Kulkarni, *Deficit Financing...*and *Indian Economic Development* (1966), and N. Ahmad, *Deficit Financing...the Ghanian Experience, 1960-65* (1970).

DEFLATION, see Inflation.

DEGRADATION OF THE DEMOCRATIC DOGMA (1919), see Adams, Henry.

DEISM, a religious view of the late eighteenth century, product of the rationalistic thought of that time, which saw the universe as a product of God, but not subject to his interposition in human affairs. The classic analogy was with a watch, too complex not to have a Maker, but running according to its own laws. Deism rejected Revelation, and its effect on the intellectuals who mostly patronized it varied from a mild faith in the good-will of the Universe to patent agnosticism and atheism. Its significance so far as the American Revolution was concerned was that it freed the minds of such protagonists as John Adams and Thomas Jefferson (*qq.v.*) from any regard for the "divine right of kings." It inspired a former preacher Elihu Palmer, to consider it a proper religion for a democracy, as in his *Principles of Nature* (1797). It was bitterly attacked by orthodox sects, especially during the controversy attending the French Revolution (*q.v.*); see Peter Gay, *Deism: an Anthology* (1968).

DE LEON, DANIEL (1852-1914), born in the Dutch West Indies, came to the United States in 1872. He joined the Knights of Labor, became interested in Bellamy's Nationalist (*qq.v.*) views, in 1890 joined the Socialist Labor Party (*q.v.*). In 1895, founded the Socialist Trade and Labor Alliance. He was hailed by his followers as having added to Marxian theory, but though he intended to influence all aspects of socialist developments, his major influence was on the soviet (*q.v.*) workers councils, which were adapted in part apart from some of his views. See also Socialism and Democracy.

DELINQUENTS, see Juvenile Delinquency.

DEMAGOGUES have been a natural concomitant of democracy (*q.v.*). The greater the number of voters, the greater the number of public figures skilled in appealing to their interests and impressions, often in company with more substantial personages who could contribute competence to popularity. The demagogue typically exploited special issues for political purposes, and was free with promises. One of the earliest demagogic issues was democracy itself, and the Whigs, while protesting the unscrupulous flattery of the mob, as it seemed to them, themselves exploited David Crockett, Tennessee frontiersman, as a critic of the Tennessee Democratic President, Andrew Jackson, and also engaged in the demagogic "Log Cabin" (*q.v.*) Campaign of 1840. The Anti-Masonic and Nativist campaigns (*qq.v.*) bore the marks of demagoguery, but attracted such serious persons as John Quincy Adams (*q.v.*) and the artist and inventor Samuel F. B. Morse. The post-Civil War period developed an increased number of demagogues, especially in the North, where politicians could advance their cause by "waving the bloody shirt" (*q.v.*). David R. Locke ("Petroleum v. Nasby") expressed public awareness of the phenomenon in his political novel, *The Demagogue* (1891). In the twentieth century, demagogues proliferated North and South, producing such figures as James M. ("Boss") Curley, of Boston, who flattered the Irish at the expense of the local "Brahmins"; "I Am the Law" Frank Hague of Jersey City; Gene Talmadge, who exploited Georgian fear of Negroes, and Joseph R. McCarthy, who exploited the country's fear of communism. Most significant was Huey P. Long (*q.v,*), Louisiana demagogue, who bid fair to become a national figure, rather than merely a demagogue; see Reinhard H. Luthin, *American Demagogues* (1954). Ambitious politicians never ceased to emerge, though whether they rated as demagogues was partially in the eyes of beholders. McCarthy (*q.v.*) seemed clearly to have taken advantage of the public's legitimate fears. Agnew's (*q.v.*) indignant prose seemed too studied for sincerity, at least in the light of the revelations which led to his political demise. That demagogues were not indigenous to one party was indicated in the 1968 Democratic Party Convention, in the peroration of Congressman Wayne L. Hays, whose own political career went down in petty intrigue. He denounced demonstrators protesting the convention as those who "would substitute beards for brains, license for liberty. They want pot instead of patriotism, sideburns instead of solutions. They would substitute riots for reason."

DEMAND, see Supply.

DEMOCRACY, see Abstract Terms.

DEMOCRACY (1880), see Adams, Henry.

DEMOCRACY AND FASCISM, at first glance contradictory, yet depending on mass support in both cases. Thus, Adolf Hitler argued he could not stay in power a moment, without the support of his people. It was observed that he had first incapacitated as many of the opposition as he could reach, yet he had required mass support in order to do this. His followers, in addition, continued to fight with extraordinary persistence long after it was clear that they were doomed to defeat; nor did they rise in revolt against him, even when he could clearly offer them nothing more. Much earlier than the twentieth century, democratic uprisings supported dictatorial types of great variety, notably in the course of the French Revolution, from Robespierre to Napoleon (*qq.v.*). Thus, the problem of keeping democracy democratic was built into its very premises; see J. L. Talmon, *The Rise of Totalitarian Democracy* (1952). See also People.

DEMOCRACY AND REFORM have seemed traditionally related. Appeals to democracy accompanied Bacon's Rebellion, the American Revolution, the Jefferson and Jackson political uprisings, the later Populist Revolt (*qq.v.*). A phrase of the reformers of pre-World War I years was that "The cure for the evils of democracy is more democracy." However, it has been noted that democracy, when more than an abstract term (*q.v.*), has involved different camps concerned for different reforms. Thus, John Quincy Adams (*q.v.*) fought for free speech and aided anti-slavery, but was conservative with respect to debtors' prisons and the Second Bank of the United States; his Jacksonian opponents took reverse positions. A popular, "democratic" movement, later hailed Chinese exclusion from the country, a policy which included a reform component only to the extent that it could be argued that the Chinese helped keep down wages. Aristocratic elements throughout the country's history sponsored reforms, sometimes in order to resist democratic pressures. Thus, the fight, late in the nineteenth century, for "clean elections" was sponsored by such anti-Democrats as E. L. Godkin (*q.v.*) who resented the democratic hordes which, in New York, kept Tammany Hall (*q.v.*) affluent. Whether a democratic wave or an elite wave directed the reforms of the New Deal (*q.v.*) is controversial. Whether democratic decisions could adequately provide leadership for the United States in the 1960's was also argued. Vice Adm. Hyman G. Rickover denounced an education too tolerant of incompetents and a policy which enabled Russians to acquire information about American nuclear submarines by purchasing models costing $2.98, "toy kits" prepared by commercial manufacturers after exact government specifications.

DEMOCRACY AND SOCIALISM, see Socialism and Democracy.

DEMOCRACY IN AMERICA (1835), see Tocqueville, Alexis de.

DEMOCRATIC CENTRALISM, a Leninist concept intended to rationalize as well as support the operations of the Dictatorship of the Proletariat. Once the party has agreed on action, individual differences are to be submerged to the will of the party. The fingers of the hand close into a fist, no component of which has the right to weaken the striking power of the whole. In practice, the word "democratic" was superfluous.

DEMOCRATIC PARTY, see Politics and Reform.

DEMOCRATIC-REPUBLICAN PARTY, the party led by Thomas Jefferson (*q.v.*) which resisted the policies of the Federalist Party in the late 1790's, and which took power itself in 1801. It maintained a sympathy for the radical factions of the French Revolution, resisted the Alien and Sedition Acts, was suspicious of Great Britain, as a bastion of royalism and conservatism, and forged an alliance of southern slaveholders and northerners concerned for popular opinions. For Democratic Party, see Politics and Reform.

DEMOCRATIC VISTAS (1871), by Walt Whitman (*q.v.*), a significant title for the students of the realities of democracy. Although Whitman sang its ideal, he was too well trained in journalism and in experience to offer nothing more than pieties. His book is both an asseveration and a criticism; as he says: "Our New World democracy, however great a success in uplifting the masses out of their sloughs . . . and in a certain highly deceptive superficial popular intellectuality, is, so far, an almost complete failure in its social aspects. . . . "

"DEMOCRATS, GOLD," the conservative wing of the party which refused to accept the silver panacea offered in 1896; it included ex-President Grover Cleveland (*q.v.*).

DEMOCRATS, PEACE, see Copperheads.

DEMONETIZATION OF SILVER, see Silver Issue, The.

DEMONSTRATION, a vital element in labor developments and social reform movements, particularly during times of crisis. The demonstration permitted elements to manifest their discontent with the situation or present their demands, while also offering a show of strength which in itself constituted a warning to employers or public authorities. Poorly used, the demonstration could exhibit the weakness of the labor or political elements involved and could result in lock-outs (*q.v.*) or police brutality. See also General Strike. Demonstrations became a vital strategy of dissidents during the youth (*q.v.*) eruptions of the 1960s and 1970s.

DENNIS, LAWRENCE (1893-1977), American intellectual fascist, Harvard '20, served in the diplomatic corps, 1920-27, in Haiti, Nicaragua, Honduras; involved in American intervention proceedings in Nicaragua, 1927. A banker and a broker, early in the 1930's, he emerged as a theoretician of fascism, publishing *Is Capitalism Doomed?* (1932), *The Coming American Fascism* (1936), and *Dynamics of War and Revolution* (1940). Dennis developed a dispassionate approach, seeking to appeal not to the masses but to the elite. Nevertheless, he was indicted under the Smith Act of 1940 (*q.v.*), with such others as William Dudley Pelley, George Sylvester Viereck George Deatherage, and Elizabeth Dilling (*q.v.*), and armed forces. Their sedition trial (*q.v.*) of 1944 was an effort to strike a blow at native fascism, failed, and was dismissed. Dennis analyzed it in his book, prepared with one of the defense attorneys, Maximilian J. St. George, *A Trial on Trial* (1946). He continued to issue a newsletter analyzing international trends.

DENNIS V. U.S., see "Clear and Present Danger."

DEPORTATION, a tactic long latent in American affairs intended to rid the country of undesirables, often identified as radicals, which reached its height of usefulness following passage of the Deportation Act of October 16, 1918, under which some four thousand persons were seized, and expelled from the country. Many were subjected to "third degree" (*q.v.*) methods to force them to make desired admissions. Many had American families from whom they were separated, or were otherwise subjected to harsh inconvenience by deportation. See *The Deportation Delirium of Nineteen-Twenty*, by Louis F. Post (*q.v.*) (1923). See also Bisbee Deportations.

DEPRECIATION, see Controlled Depreciation.

DEPRESSED AREAS, a concept attending increased government power and responsibility. It premised the recognition of economic distress in specific locales, due to the closing down of businesses, loss of government contracts, or a combination of factors. John F. Kennedy, when running for the Presidency in 1960, met the fact of local depressions head-on and was free with promises to give aid if elected. Soon after election, work at acquiring information about "depressed areas," and "depressed area bills" in Congress, gave the phrase currency.

DEPRESSIONS, see Economic Depression.

DESCAMISADOS (the Shirtless Ones), followers of Col. Juan D. Perón. Where other dictators gave their followers striking or imposing garb, the Argentinian (*q.v.*) demagogue emphasized the poverty of his people.

DESEGREGATION, see Education and the Negro, "Resegregation."

DES MOINES (IOWA) PLAN, an improvement over the Galveston Plan (*q.v.*) for city government, by commission, but strengthened to include the referendum and recall (*q.v.*). See also Dayton (Ohio) Plan.

DESMOULINS, CAMILLE (1760-1794), the "tribune" of the French Revolution, who led the march on the Bastille (*q.v.*). A moderate in his approach to revolutionary needs, and a supporter of Danton, he was guillotined with him. His deportment at his trial, and his cry to the jeering crowd which attended him to his death ("Citizens! My only crime is that I have shed tears") are memorable.

DESPOT, an autocrat, a tyrant; though some of those who have found the qualities of a despot patently reprehensible saw no contradiction contributing to the legend of Stalin's (*q.v.*) wisdom, sanity, and universal acceptability.

DETENTE, a hopeful word suggesting peace, and growing peace, between mighty aggressors with dangerous powers, it was initiated at summit meetings during the Nixon Administration and directed by Kissinger (*q.v.*). Critics argued that it encouraged passivity in Americans while failing to deter Russia from, in 1973, providing weapons for Arabs to attack Israel, and, the next year, standing behind the North Vietnam troops as they overran the South. Under Ford and his renewal of detente, it did not prevent Soviet troops, along with Cubans, from intervening in the Angolan civil war, establishing a "Marxist" state near sealanes carrying vital quantities of oil to the West. Defenders of detente ranged from admirers of socialism and friends of the Soviet Union, to realists who saw detente as one step toward necessary international relations which could bring disappointments and even some defeats, but which could bring victories for peace and security as well. Although the apparent Vietnam "defeat," the patent "hostages" humiliation, and the Soviets's rough intervention in Afghanistan lost the United States some of its Allies's confidence—France, for example, seeking a species of separate detente with Russia—friends of detente argued that all was not lost. Carter had indeed appeared absurd declaring that Russian leaders had "lied" to him, but the very revelation suggested a new era, and a more sophisticated one, for American diplomacy. Russian brutality to a degree provided its own antidote. Detente joined such other concepts as "Peaceful Coexistence" (q.v.) and such instruments as NATO and SALT (qq.v.) as means for maintaining the continuing dialogue for peace. M. S. Agwani, ed., *Detente* (1976); Coral Bell, *The Diplomacy of Detente: the Kisssinger Era* (1977); Arthur M. Cox, *The Dynamics of Detente* (1976); Alexandr Solzhenitzyn, *Detente: Prospects for Democracy and Dictatorship* (1979).

"DETROIT PLAN" FOR AIDING THE UNEMPLOYED (1894), an effort directed by Mayor Hazen S. Pingree (q.v.) which involved utilizing vacant lots for gardening purposes. Some 430 acres were so put into use. Although little more than a gesture of good-will during grim economic times, it furnished evidence that municipal government could take the initiative in recognizing need and ministering to it, and that the energies of the unemployed could be employed. Indirectly, the experiment (which was imitated in some measure in other municipalities) furnished evidence favoring Henry George's (q.v.) contention that land gained its value from the presence and labor of people.

DEVALUATION, see Deflation.

DEVIATIONIST, an epithet (q.v.) intended to indicate that an individual or group has fallen away from principles of scientific socialism; usually identified with Marxism, a serious charge in Soviet-aligned areas.

DEWEY, JOHN (1859-1952), philosopher and leader in education, whose linking of thought and action revolutionized educational perspectives. As director of the Experimental School of the University of Chicago, he sought to find means for eliciting the creativity of the children, rather than to inculcate facts and attitudes; such were the basic premises of what came to be called "progressive education" (q.v.). He later became a name and a symbol to "Deweyites" who, in many cases, had not complicated their loyalty to what they conceived to be his ideas by making contact with his writings. As a spokesman for liberalism and free inquiry, he headed the unofficial Dewey Commission to Mexico City which heard testimony from Leon Trotsky in repudiation of the numerous charges which had been brought against him during the Moscow Trials (q.v.); see *The Case of Leon Trotsky* (1937). Dewey's "pragmatism" (q.v.) differed from that of William James (q.v.) in its greater emphasis on results. A disillusioned follower like Randolph Bourne (q.v.) believed Dewey's philosophy was persuasive in peacetime, a weak reed in a crisis; during World War I, Dewey became an advocate of preparedness for war.

DIAL, THE, name of two notable magazines, the first (1840-1844), edited by Margaret Fuller and Ralph Waldo Emerson (qq.v.), printed writings by them, as well as by Thoreau, Parker, Alcott, and other outstanding dissidents (qq.v.), the second, founded in 1880 in Chicago, shed its conservative traits when it moved to New York, where it printed writings by Randolph Bourne, John Dewey, and Veblen (qq.v.), among others, contributing intelligence and energy during the war-period, and after; it ended in 1929.

DIALECTICS, a shibboleth in Marxism (q.v.) which saw mankind operating within a frame of logical necessity. Marx borrowed from Hegel but "stood him on his head"; where Hegel saw each thesis producing its antithesis, and both concluding in a synthesis of reality, Marx undertook to start with reality, which, however, included its own contradictions, or antithesis, which, in struggle, must produce a newer reality. In effect, dialectics posited change, which was neither startling nor remarkable; however, it also posited progress and evolution; Engels saw dialectical philosophy as exposing "the uninterrupted process of becoming and of passing away, of

endless ascendancy from the lower to the higher." Lenin, too, spoke of a "development that repeats . . . the stages already passed . . . in a different way, on a higher plane." Dialectics, then, offered its devotees hope, inspiration, and the certainty of achievement. The materialistic conception of history (q.v.) which accompanied it endorsed their belief that they based their conceptions on reality.

DICKENS, CHARLES (1812-1870), great English novelist, whose popularity and reform attitudes made him a social as as well as literary figure. *Nicholas Nickleby* (1839) contained critical portraits of the "cheap schools" of Yorkshire; *Hard Times* (1854) satirized brutal capitalists and viewed the lot of the poor compassionately; Oliver Twist's hunger, while in the workshop, achieved a special immortality when he asked for "more" (1838). Dickens's sentimentality and talent for caricature have been criticized, but his general services to reform seem securely established. His *American Notes* (1842) raised a storm because of his criticisms of slavery, and other topics; they continue to merit study.

DICTATOR, not too popular an epithet in a land too patently decentralized to be amenable to one-man rule. The rise of dictators in the 1920's and 1930's, however, made the concept more familiar, and created some American admirers of fascist or communist dictators. Moreover, the serious nature of the economic crisis of the 1930's suggested to some the need for a "man on a white horse." However, the most popular use of the word was in *The Great Dictator* (1940), a motion picture starring Charles Chaplin, which ridiculed the German dictator, Adolf Hitler. See also, Butler, Smedley D., Tyranny.

DICTATORSHIP OF THE PROLETARIAT, a theory of socialist rule proposed by Karl Marx (q.v.) and followers, to form a link between the rule of capitalism and the classless society. Defended as a stage necessary for resisting the force of the counter-revolution, and held to sustain social and human relations under a system of "democratic centralism" (q.v.), it nevertheless appeared, especially to forces in the capitalist and non-communist world, to perpetuate terror and authoritarianism (qq.v.), rather than socialist principles. Compare Marx's *Critique of the Gotha Program* (1875). Liebknecht and Kautsky (qq.v.) argued that the dictatorship of a *class* could not be a true dictatorship. Marx called the Paris Commune (q.v.) a dictatorship of the proletariat, though it was based on universal suffrage.

DIE-HARDS, identified with nineteenth century Tories, in Great Britain, who were unwilling to recognize urgent social demand; in the United States, with similar elements during the twentieth century, such as the Republicans of the 1930's who attempted to ignore the facts of depression in their appeal for the preservation of classic free enterprise principles.

DIES, MARTIN (1900-1972), controversial U.S. Representative, son of Texas Progressive of the same name, who, as a U.S. Representative, revealed the reactionary impulses which could be found among aspects of Progressivism (q.v.). As chairman of the Special House Committee for the Investigation of Un-American Activities, formed in 1938, he was expected to expose skulduggery on the "Right" as well as the "Left" (qq.v.). However, he soon emphasized what he termed un-American activities among the communists, welcoming a long line of informers, disillusioned C.P.ers, and others to offer their testimony. The communists and liberals struck back, popularizing the slogan that "Dies Lies!" with considerable success, though he continued to receive his annual appropriations for the continuation of the committee. Dies' own *The Trojan Horse in America: a Report to the Nation* (1940) emphasized the Communist menace. However, the Grand Alliance of World War II made his strictures temporarily unpopular, and his reputation faded, though the committee itself became permanent in 1946. By the time "McCarthyism" (q.v.) emerged, Dies had been remarkably forgotten, even though, following an election defeat, he was able to return to the House of Representatives. See August R. Ogden, *The Dies Committee* (1945), HUAC.

DIETING, a reform in pre-Civil War years, as in Sylvester Graham's (q.v.) emphasis on proper eating, and in vegetarianism (q.v.). Involved in diet, too, was a Puritan principle of self-restraint and anti-epicureanism. Diet was a minor reform during the pre-World War I era, as in Upton Sinclair's (q.v.) *The Fasting Cure* (1911) and Fletcherism (q.v.). Some reformers held that their concern ought to be with an individual's contributions to social reform, more than with his individual preferences in eating. In post-World War II years, some Americans, released from the confines of poverty, but often not from their spiritual dissatisfactions, found themselves involved in "compulsive eating." America found itself the one country in the world troubled with overeating. Dieting became less a reform than a phobia: fads favoring one diet over another swept the country. The older connections between personal programs and social programs having been loosened, when not broken, the question of diet became almost wholly technical, except as it was maintained by religious elements, vegetarians, and a few others.

DIGGERS, see Levelers.

DILLING, ELIZABETH (MRS. ALBERT W.), see *Red Network, The, Roosevelt Red Record and Its Background, The.*

DIPLOMACY, traditionally used invidiously by social reformers as characteristics of conniving, reactionary governments, but held in higher esteem since social reformers have themselves engaged in matters of state; also conceived of as constituting a hope for peace between mighty antagonists who might destroy themselves as well as others in a general catastrophe.

DIRECT ACTION, a concept associated with "working-class" purposes, which, since they were assumed to transgress those of the "ruling classes," scorned parliamentary action and efforts to win bourgeois cooperation. Notable in this connection was the threat made by the British Trades Union Congress (1919) that it would declare a general strike (q.v.), if the government did not cease to interfere with the Russian Revolution; see also Syndicalism, Sabotage.

DIRECT GOVERNMENT, see Referendum, Initiative and Recall.

DIRECT PRIMARIES were an attempt to bring democracy into the process of nominating candidates usually by having party members nominate the candidates, rather than party conventions. It made little difference since the party organization continued to play a major role in the naming of candidates, through endorsements and other means of emphasizing the alleged qualities of particular individuals. However, by 1980, primaries had come in for serious criticism as cumbersome, prolonged, expensive, and failing to respond to the needs of the electorate. P. T. Davis and James W. Ceaser, *Proportional Representation in Presidential Nominating Politics* (1979); Roy Hoppes, *Primaries and Conventions* (1978); D. R. Mathews, ed., *Perspectives on Presidential Selection* (1973).

DIRECTORY, THE, set up in 1795, following the fall of Robespierre (q.v.), and marking another step in the decline of popular spirit and participation which had marked earlier stages of the French Revolution. The Directory was composed of five directors, but little policy; their four-year existence was a period of transition, during which the social elements unleashed by the revolution became stabilized and bureaucratized; Napoleon Buonaparte (q.v.) inherited their labors in 1799. George Lefebre, *The Thermidorians and The Directory* (1964).

DISARMAMENT, used often as in connection with the Hague Peace Conferences (q.v.), Pope Benedict XV's 1918 appeal to the great powers to find a basis for peace in arbitration and disarmament, the essential disarming of Germany under the Versailles Treaty (q.v.), on the theory that this would ensure peace, the Washington Armament (or disarmament) Conference of 1921-2, which was supposed to reduce the danger of war by limiting the tonnage of capital ships—Japan's being more limited than that of the United States and Great Britain —and other "disarmament" conferences, including the Geneva Naval "Disarmament" Conference of 1927, during which the participants failed to agree on who was to disarm the most. It was evident that disarmament was a euphemism. William T. R. Fox et al., *American Arms and a Changing Europe* (1973); L. C. Bloomfield, *Disarmament and the UN* (1978); Trevor N. Dupuy, Comp., *A Documentary History of Arms Control* (1973).

DISCIPLINE, more associated with labor and radical operations than with reform. Labor unions enforce discipline in order to maintain the rules and regulations of the union, to keep morale high during a strike, to prevent union-splitting disagreements. "Party discipline" is intended to sharpen the principles and practice of a radical group. The emphasis on discipline was strong during the 1930's, when the march of Stalin to international power among communist factions resulted in an emphasis on "discipline," and "disciplinary action," which reflected itself in the dissident communist groups as well, which insisted on maintaining discipline even when they were but a few associated "comrades." They believed that firm discipline then would pay them when the "revolutionary situation had matured" and they had become people of power and responsibility. Compare Anarchy.

DISCRIMINATION, a key target for reformers, who oppose it in education, job opportunities, housing, such social circumstances as fraternities and sororities, service in restaurants and on public transportation facilities. Emphasis is upon discrimination where it affects public education, housing, etc., which theoretically should be open to all, but informal situations, involving private schools, real estate, etc., have received perhaps as much attention. Negroes and Jews have been outstanding elements involved in the problem. It was then complicated by the fact that all elements, to one or another extent, discriminate against others, within and without their milieu; the American fascist, Gerald L. K. Smith, seized upon this fact to emphasize that he had early learned (from his mother) that he ought to discriminate—that discrimination was a sign of having standards. The problem has been one of details; thus, "private" schools have been vulnerable to the argument that they had no right to discriminate to the extent that they gained from the taxes of everybody. Some institutions rationalized their position by arguing that they sought to be "representative" in their selection of students, a policy which, in effect, permitted them to choose a few "representative" minority individuals, as well as individuals from the various sections of the country. Medical schools kept up a species of "quota" (q.v.) in selecting their students. Since numbers of persons in various jobs and professions, in various towns and cities, in various schools and government offices, etc., are fairly constant, it follows that a tacit understanding controls much of society's actual operations, which reformists' agitation and propaganda illuminates only to a degree, and which accumulated facts and analyses could illuminate more; see also Integration, Reverse Discrimination.

DISCRIMINATION, STATE COMMISSION AGAINST (New York), set up in 1945 "to eliminate and prevent practices of discrimination in employment because of race, creed, color or national origin." Amendment to the law exempted religious and denominational institutions from the provisions of the act. Penalties for non-compliance, including imprisonment, were provided. Nevertheless, a study by the Commission, published in 1960, revealed "a high incidence of discrimination against middle-class Negro homeseekers," and the many techniques for getting about the law. An amendment to the law which legislated against discrimination because of age was also flouted. From 1945 to 1959, SCAD processed 6,602 complaints of discrimination and conducted 873 informal investigations. It believed it had accomplished educational objectives, and that exclusion of minority groups from hotels and restaurants had been largely stopped.

DISLOYALTY, see Patriotism.

DISPLACED PERSONS, elements tragically uprooted from their homelands by catastrophic international and political events, and condemned to live under unreal and subsistence conditions with no means for rebuilding their lives and personal dignity. World War II was lavish in creating displaced persons who waited in concentration camps for haven. Israel was the major repository for displaced Jews. Arabs displaced from Israel during the effort of the various Arab nations to destroy that nation found themselves living unassimilated in Arab countries, fed through the United Nations, and maintained in misery as a pawn to demonstrate the alleged obduracy of the Israeli, who, for various reasons, refused to permit their return to their country. Hungarians who fled their country following their defeat by Soviet forces also found themselves living in hopeless squalor, as did Cubans (*qq.v.*), among others. Displaced persons constituted a problem largely for the United Nations, which coped with Palestinians who, led by the P.L.O. (*q.v.*) became crucial to world peace, the "boat people" of Vietnam, and other hordes of refugees in Africa and elsewhere. Roger Daniels, *The Decision to Relocate the Japanese Americans* (1975); T. Grygier, *Oppression* (1954); Stanko Guidescu and John Prceles, *Operation Slaughterhouse...Postwar Massacres in Yugoslavia* (1970). See Refugees.

DISPUTED ELECTION OF 1876, a crisis in American history resulting from the Reconstruction (*q.v.*) controls set over the defeated southern states which gave the suffrage to the freed Negroes and took it from the ex-Confederates. The southern states individually resisted Federal rule; by 1876, it only obtained in South Carolina, Florida, and Louisiana. Northern Democratic machines, too, profited from the dissatisfaction with the weak and graft-ridden Grant Administration. The Republicans offered as Presidential candidate the vaguely reformist Rutherford B. Hayes, the Democrats the also dubiously reformistic Samuel J. Tilden (*qq.v.*). First reports gave the latter a sweeping victory; however, questions over Oregon raised the hope that if it and the three doubtful southern states could be claimed for Republicans, Hayes would be President by one electoral vote. The Republicans boldly claimed all four sets of electoral returns, as, more legitimately, did the Democrats. Southern desperation raised the possibility of civil war, and President Grant fortified Washington. Tilden supplied inadequate leadership to his party. Fears that a President could not be named caused the creation of an Electoral Commission, composed of five Congressmen, five Senators, four Supreme Court justices who chose the fifth, who, with the others evenly divided, could, in effect, name the President. Desperate behind-doors work caused a change in the first selection, who would probably have named Tilden; the second, too, was swayed by extra-legal considerations, and chose Hayes. The desperate Democrats might still have refused him their acceptance, but a famous "deal" (based less on southern principles than economic and other considerations) caused the tacit agreement which gave Hayes the Presidency (he promised not to run for a second term) and got him to order the removal of the last Federal troops from the southern states. Thus, the Republicans, who claimed credit for having emancipated the slaves by way of the XIII, XIV, and XV Amendments to the Constitution (*qq.v.*), won the election by permitting the reestablishment of white supremacy (*q.v.*) in the South.

DISSENTERS, historically those who dissented from the Church of England, the Non-Conformists (*q.v.*), mostly identified with the Puritans and Pilgrims, though Presbyterians, too, resisted the tenets of the official church. However, the word was secularized to take in those who resisted authority, especially when it constituted a breach of faith with the Bill of Rights (*q.v.*). Dissenters trace the cause they defend back to the early architects of American liberties, though rarely willing to associate themselves with such episodes as the Salem Witchcraft trials (*q.v.*).

DISSIDENTS, a distinguished chapter in the post-Stalin (*q.v.*) Russian state, they constituted a window on its operations. They included authors, scientists, engineers, and others who suffered for being Jews who wished to emigrate to Israel, for protesting bureaucratic cruelties and stupidities, for writing or expressing views and experiences favoring freer life and attitudes. They were accorded execution, torture, transportation to the infamous Gulag (*q.v.*), degradation of various sorts, and treatment for lunacy. Nevertheless, something of their experiences, and some individuals, reached the West, often in notable form. Solzhenitzyn (*q.v.*) continued his career in the West. The appeals from Russia of Andrei Sakharov, Nobel Prize winner, the writings of A. A. Amalrik (*Involuntary Journey to Siberia* and *Will the Soviet Union Survive until 1984?*), and the work of Tatyana Velikanova, a founder in 1969 of, within Russia, the Initiative Group for the Defense of Human Rights, which won her condemnation in a 1980 Russian court as having systematically and illegally slandered the Soviets, and a sentence of four years in a labor camp and five years of "internal exile." The persistence of dissident effort and opinion, and its publicization in the West, was a softening element in Soviet policy and action, and gave promise of a democratization process, at great human cost, helpful to prospects for world peace and progress. Rudolf L. Tokes, ed., *Dissent in the USSR: Politics, Ideology and People* (1975).

DISTRICT OF COLUMBIA, in 1961 finally received the privilege of voting for President of the United States. The Twenty-Third Amendment to the Constitution ended a notorious situation. However, the southern bloc in Congress, fearing the Negro majority in the Capital, did not give them equality with other areas, but restricted them to a number of electors equal to that of the least populous state, though it had far fewer inhabitants than Washington. Nor was the Capital given home rule, nor voting representation in Congress. Washington was given three members in the electoral college. About two hundred thousand voters were created, who would be able to cast ballots in 1964. An additional forty to fifty thousand voters maintained residence outside of Washington.

DISUNIONIST, those who were prepared to let the Union break up, rather than surrender their principles; thus Garrisonians, on the one hand, preached disunion in order to rid the north of complicity in southern slavery, southern disunionists warned that continued association with the north might cost them their freedom from anti-slavery Supreme Court decisions and Government decrees.

DIVORCE, though somewhat less recent a victory for more liberal attitudes toward the sanctity of marriage than is generally supposed (see Theodore D. Woolsey, *Essay on Divorce* [1869]), it was a reform plank for advocates of woman's rights, who sought better terms for women united to or separated from husbands. By the twentieth century, it had largely become something of a technical question, some efforts being directed at obtaining a uniform divorce law. Easier divorce raised more fundamental questions of proper legal relations between the sexes. The companionate-marriage idea (*q.v.*) was controverted in the 1920's. Radical views of free love and easy separation, as observed in the experiences of the U.S.S.R., seemed to indicate that some form of social control was inevitable, influencing as it did not only the adults involved, but their children. In 1958, his divorce seemed to make the difference between Nelson A. Rockefeller becoming President of the United States, or not. By 1979, when he died in odd circumstances, divorce had become all but a minor detail in the lives and peccadillos of numerous public individuals, and unlikely to be decisive in any of their careers. Much of divorce literature was in the "How To" and "What To" class. David Von Albrecht, *Divorce in the "Liberal" Jurisdictions* (1955); Nelson M. Blake, *The Road to Reno* (1962); Edward Z. Epstein, *Notorious Divorces* (1977).

DIX, DOROTHEA L. (1802-1887), institutional reformer, her eloquent and detailed Memorial to the Legislature of Massachusetts (1843) condemning contemporary attitudes toward and lack of proper care for the insane, began a career which left a trail of new and reorganized hospitals, houses of refuge and prisons, in this country and abroad. Dix was one of the few reformers who emphasized her specialty at the expense of any other reforms; most reformers found it comported with their feelings and was expedient to relate their reforms to others. She made it a point to offer no views on slavery, in order to be able to carry her crusade into the South and to fight for a Federal bill aiding institutional reform. During the Civil War, she was superintendent of women nurses.

DIXON-YATES CONTRACT, see Tennessee Valley Authority.

DOCK WOLLOPERS, slang for casual labor elements among the longshoremen (q.v.).

"DR. WIN-THE-WAR," see New Deal, The.

DOCTRINAIRE MOVEMENTS, those dependent on special bodies of data and material, notably Marxism, from which has sprung a great variety of separate movements involving additional canons of writings by Stalin, Lenin, Trotsky, Kautsky, Bernstein, and many others. De Leon offered essential nourishment to his followers of the Socialist Labor Party. Fascism offered essential writings of its revered leaders including Hitler and Mussolini. Although all movements to one degree or another compile libraries of preferred books and tenets, doctrinaire movements are identifiable by their efforts to bend reality to their premises. Thus, the Bolsheviks were somewhat troubled by their success in Russia, in 1917; their doctrines had prepared them for revolutions first in the more "advanced" countries. It reassured them to believe that Marxism was not confounded by facts, but was vindicated, rather, in that the imperialist chain had broken at its "weakest link." The John Birch Society, in 1961, seemed interested in creating a body of doctrine (qq.v. for all above references).

DOCUMENTARIES, see Lorentz, Pare.

DOLE, an ancient term for funds usually left from bequests for charity, applied in England after World War I and during the depressed 1930's for sums given to the poor; inaccurately, the term did not distinguish between money given, to the accumulation of which the recipient had himself contributed, and money given under the Poor Laws (q.v.). The American equivalent for the dole was relief (q.v.).

DOLLAR DIPLOMACY, a concept developed during President Taft's administration, and associated with the American effort to increase banker's loans to specific governments in order to strengthen United States relations with them, and, in addition, permit intervention to the extent that other nations might attempt to infringe on the sovereignty of such countries. Although a tactic of imperialism, it was intended to involve peaceful influence, as opposed to that which Taft's predecessor, Theodore Roosevelt, had been willing to advocate. "Dollar Diplomacy" was utilized with respect to China, where, in 1909, French, British, and German financiers undertook to supply the money for building railroads. Taft's efforts to involve American bankers in loans to China were unsuccessful. More successful, in one view, was "dollar diplomacy" in Central America and in the Caribbean (qq.v.), where financial arrangements permitted intervention and influence. Disreputable with reformers, "dollar diplomacy" fell into disuse during the 1930's, when the "good neighbor" (q.v.) policy came into being. See Scott Nearing (q.v.) and Joseph Freeman, Dollar Diplomacy: a Study in American Imperialism (1925).

DOMINICAN REPUBLIC, formerly Santo Domingo, early in the nineteenth century viewed with sympathy by reformers because of its apparent efforts to free itself both from Haiti, engrossing the western third of the island, and from France. In 1844, it established its independence, but in conditions of internal weakness which later caused it to be voluntarily annexed to Spain, and in 1868-70 to seek annexation to the United States, thanks to the efforts of adventurers who received President Grant's (q.v.) support. The treaty was rejected, after a sharp struggle, in the United States Senate (q.v.). During much of the early twentieth century, American bankers were involved in the finances of Santo Domingo, and, fearful that foreign nations might use the condition of the government to intervene in its affairs, the United States maintained a watch upon it; in 1916, American forces were landed there to assure order and control the customs. Marines remained there, criticized by reformers, until 1922. After 1930, the history of the "republic" became largely that of Trujillo (q.v.)

In 1965, President Johnson (q.v.) sent troops to the island, fearful that a communist coup was in progress; the action was criticized at home as reminiscent of an old imperialism; it was defended as a realistic action in the world as it was. See A. F. Lowenthal, The Dominican Intervention (1972).

DOMINO THEORY, a concept introduced by President Eisenhower in 1954, which argued that nations vulnerable to Soviet expansionism merited the armed support of the United States, since, left to their fate, other "domino" pieces would fall to the Soviets. Eisenhower failed to make a stand on his own theory in 1956 when Hungarian republicans stood up to the Russians, but were left to die as Soviet tanks rolled into Budapest with guns firing. The powerful argument against the "Domino theory" in the 1960s was that nations had a right to "self determination" (q.v.) or that the proper stance for Americans respecting the world was "isolationism" (q.v.). Evidence of the results of such theories, when the United States troops left southern Vietnam (q.v.), was the extermination process pursued by the "victorious" Viet Cong, at home and in Cambodia.

DOMINION OF NEW ENGLAND, THE, the name given to a plan for organizing the northern British colonies for greater efficiency (1686-9). Power was centralized in the hands of a governor and council, both appointed by the King. The Dominion ultimately included colonies from Maine to New Jersey. The efforts of the governor, Sir Edmund Andros, to carry out his task were resisted by the colonists, who complained of taxes and the lack of a representative assembly. The failure of the Dominion of New England is significant as showing the unwillingness of the English in America to accept rule from abroad. Compare, New England Confederation, The.

DONNELLY, IGNATIUS (1831-1901), "Tribune of the people," a founder of Minnesota, politician, and writer; he served as lieutenant-governor of Minnesota, and in Congress (1863-9). Thereafter he was an eloquent populist and author of the Preamble to the Populist Platform of 1892 (q.v.). His works on the so-called "Lost Continent" (Atlantis: the Antediluvian World [1882]) and the Baconian Theory of the authorship of Shakespeare's plays (The Great Cryptogram [1888]) were very successful. Sensational was his novel, Caesar's Column: a story of the Twentieth Century (1891) a "reverse utopia" of catastrophic times which sold about a million copies. It offers an insight into the Populist mind.

"DOOLEY, MR.," see Dunne, Peter Finley.

DORR, RHETA CHILDE (1866-1948), individualist who aided woman's rights; an outstanding woman muckraker (q.v.). Dissatisfied with conventional marriage and expectations, she left her home to embark on journalism in New York. She made personal investigations into conditions attending women in factories. She was inspired by the suffragettes she met in England. After employment on Everybody's (q.v.), she did her significant book, What Eight Million Women Want (1910). She continued to work for woman suffrage until World War I made a fervent nationalist of her, and separated her from her erstwhile associates. Her autobiography, A Woman of Fifty (1924), though untrustworthy in details, as her birth-date and date of publication indicate, is important for its record of determined self-expression.

DORR'S REBELLION, in Rhode Island, resulted from the unwillingness of property-owners to set aside an outmoded state constitution which limited the franchise to themselves and their eldest sons. As a result, more than half the adult male population could not vote. Thomas W. Dorr led a mass movement to call a popular convention, which, in 1841, framed a "People's Constitution," and submitted it to the citizens of Rhode Island for ratification. Although the conservatives hastened to draw up a more liberal constitution than that which they had been defending, the Dorrites gained the popular suffrage. They proceeded to set up a rival government which was denounced by the officers of the established order. "Governor" Dorr made an attempt to take over the state arsenal at Providence, using cannon, but a famous "flash in the pan"—the failure of his cannon to discharge—frightened his followers, who deserted him. He himself fled, but returned to surrender to the incumbents, and was sentenced to prison. Although the Dorr Rebellion failed, it forced the conservatives to reconsider their stand, and a new constitution established an almost universal manhood suffrage. M. E. Gettleman, *The Dorr Rebellion* (1973).

DOS PASSOS, JOHN (1896-1970), novelist of "social significance" (*q.v.*), whose career divides into liberal-radical and anti-liberal radical phases. The son of a corporation lawyer, he aspired to "lift the gauntlet" thrown down by Walt Whitman (*q.v.*). *Three Soldiers* (1921) was critical of an army and a war which destroyed sensitivity and talent. *Manhattan Transfer* (1925) saw a superficial civilization. *U.S.A.* (*q.v.*) was a trilogy which moved from criticism of that civilization to dissatisfaction with those seeking to change it. *Adventures of a Young Man* (1939), a novel which did not employ techniques associated with Dos Passos's work, recorded him as at cross-roads: disillusioned with communism as it operated during the Spanish Civil War (*q.v.*), and itself an enemy of freedom. His book of essays, *The Ground We Stand On* (1941), showed Dos Passos on the road back, seeking in American history principles which had seemed to him unnecessary before. His career thereafter was one of increasing conservatism; he argued that what held his career together was a consistent concern for freedom. Townsend Ludington, *John Dos Passos: a Twentieth Century Odyssey* (1980).

DOUGHFACE, first used by John Randolph during the debate over Missouri in 1820, and then as later used to designate northerners with southern principles.

DOUGLAS, WILLIAM O. (1898-1980), associate justice of the U.S. Supreme Court since 1939. He served in the Department of Commerce, was chairman of the Securities and Exchange Commission (*q.v.*). He became noted for his efforts to preserve liberal interpretations of constitutional questions; thus, in Dennis v. U.S. (*q.v.*), his dissent distinguished between conspiracies dangerous to the country, and the teaching of Marxist principles. His *An Almanac of Liberty* (1954) is a valuable organization of notable cases, events, and opinions relevant to aspects of American liberties. His 1953 intervention in the Rosenberg (*q.v.*) case, granting them an extension from execution, earned him a Congressional effort at impeachment. He was an outstanding naturalist and conservationist. He retired in 1975. Vern Countryman, ed., *The Douglas Opinions* (1977); E. P. Hoyt, *William O. Douglas* (1979); *The Court Years, 1939-1975: the Autobiography of William O. Douglas* (1980).

DOUGLASS, FREDERICK (1817-1895), outstanding American Negro, a fugitive slave from Maryland who joined the Garrisonians (*q.v.*) to preach abolitionism from the public platform, though himself liable to seizure at any time. His *Narrative of the Life of Frederick Douglass* (1845, and in many later editions) is one of the great American autobiographies. His newspaper the *North Star* (1847-60) was pioneer Negro journalism, as well as a feature of the reform era. During the Civil War and after, he was a spokesman for his people, during passage of the XIII, XIV, and XV Amendments to the Constitution (*qq.v.*) and in crises relating to their needs. He received various positions from the United States government. He was criticized because his second wife was white; his answer was that as a mulatto, he had patronized both races from which he had sprung.

DOW, NEAL (1804-1897), Maine prohibitionist, mayor of Portland (1851), during which time he administered temperance legislation with startling determination. The Maine Law of that year set a precedent for prohibition legislation. He continued his work as a reformer, being the Prohibition Party's candidate for President in 1880.

DOWN-AND-OUTS, see Unemployables.

DRAFT DODGER, a term of scorn used by intolerant patriots during World War I to designate persons who either feared conscription into the armed services, or opposed conscription for anti-militaristic reasons, and so sought to avoid service. See also Yellow Back.

DRAFT REGISTRATION, an effort in 1980 to move toward Preparedness (*q.v.*) while not rousing the anti-war sentiment of the Vietnam War (*q.v.*) years. Spurred by firm Soviet alert and troop movements in several parts of the world, including Cuba, President Carter (*q.v.*) demanded and received Congressional authority to call up young men for registration, though not yet for the draft. The issue was complicated by the question of whether women—for whom Carter had been advocating "Equal Rights" (*q.v.*)—were also subject to registration, especially since military academies were graduating women officers for the Services. The American Civil Liberties Union filed a sex-bias suit against the draft. The Central Committee for Conscientious Objectors announced that it had more than 250 draft counselors ready to advise young men in forty states. The U.S. Student Association in Washington, D.C. called for resistance to the draft as being a first step to military intervention abroad. Partisans of the draft argued that the all-volunteer military force authorized by Congress in 1973 did not suffice for American military exigencies. Renee G. Kasinsky, *Refugees from Militarism: Draft Age Americans in Canada* (1976); R. W. Little, ed., *Selective Service and American Society* (1969); John O'Sullivan and Alan M. Meckler, eds., *The Draft and Its Enemies* (1974); H. A. Marmion, *The Case against a Volunteer Army* (1971).

DRAFT RIOTS OF 1863, a tragic incident of the Civil War, resulting from a combination of factors. New York City's poorer classes, sympathetic to Tammany Hall and the Democratic Party (*qq.v.*), were not sympathetic to the war's purposes and were antagonistic to the Negro. There was a powerful criminal class in the city, and the law enforcement agencies were weakened by the drawing off of soldiers for the engagement which was being prepared at Gettysburg. The Conscription Act passed by the government roused indignation because it permitted persons to buy off service in the forces on payment of three hundred dollars. The attempt to enforce the Act caused enormous riots throughout the city which cost uncounted lives; estimates have gone into the thousands. Negroes were lynched, property destroyed, the lives of civic leaders threatened. After four days of rioting, disorder was controlled. There were riots elsewhere, but none approximating those in New York. Adrian Cook, *The Armies of the Street: the New York City Draft Riots of 1863* (1973).

DRAGO DOCTRINE (1902), formulated by the Foreign Minister of Argentina, a corollary to the Monroe Doctrine (*q.v.*), it stipulated that European nations must not use force to collect debts owed them by nations in the Americas. The Doctrine was accepted by the second Hague Peace Conference of 1907 (*q.v.*).

DRAMA, see Theater.

DRED SCOTT CASE (1847-1857), involved the taking of a Negro slave into territory made free by the Missouri Compromise (*q.v.*), and his subsequent return to Missouri, a slave state. Here he sued for his freedom in trials which ultimately brought the question before the United States Supreme Court. Decision was delayed in order not to affect the Presidential election involving John C. Frémont (*q.v.*) and John Buchanan. On March 6, 1857, Chief Justice Roger B. Taney (*q.v.*) handed down his fateful decision. Although he could have limited it to declaring that Scott had no standing in the courts, he chose to go on and declare that the Missouri Compromise unconstitutionally forbade slavery above 36' 30°. He thus entirely cemented northern opposition to the Fugitive Slave Law of 1850 (*q.v.*). *Dred* (1856), a novel by Harriet Beecher Stowe (*q.v.*), was issued before the historic decision, and dealt with a Negro insurrectionary figure, roughly modeled after Nat Turner (*q.v.*). Charles M. Wilson, *The Dred Scott Decision* (1973).

DREISER, THEODORE (1871-1945), more of a temperament

compounded of revolutionary and reactionary elements, rather than of reformist, he saw people as puppets of their instincts. Nevertheless, the compassion perceived in his novels, including the famous *Sister Carrie* (1900) and *An American Tragedy* (1925), stirred reformers as well as others. His *Tragic America* (1932) was an awkward survey of the country in depression which his admirers approved on principle, as they did not his equally awkward anti-semitic remarks of the same period. His forthright descriptions of illicit sex were defended by them in the name of a free press, notably in 1916, when his *The "Genius"* was banned by the courts as obscene. In 1932, he headed a committee to investigate conditions in the coal-mine area of Kentucky. A local attempt to discredit him by framing him in adulterous circumstances was confounded by his public assertion that he was no longer capable of a sex act. His life-long search for religious and cosmic solutions left him in the end a sympathizer of the Communist Party. He compares strikingly with David Graham Phillips (*q.v.*); see Louis Filler, "A Tale of Two Authors from Indiana," in *New Voices in American Studies*, R. B. Browne et al., eds. (1966).

DRESS REFORM, an adjunct of the battle for woman suffrage, notably in the career of Amelia Bloomer (*q.v.*), and a minor reform of the post-Civil War period which emphasized health and reasonable fashions, pressed by enlightened conservatives rather than reformers. For a typical statement, see "The Reforms Needed in Dress," in Abba Goold Woolson, *Woman in American Society* (1873). It was a woman's cause almost entirely. "Emancipation," when it came after World War I involved modernization rather than reform. See Abba G. Woolson, ed., *Dress Reform: A Series of Lectures Delivered in Boston—Dress as It Affects the Health of Women* (1874).

DREW, DANIEL (1797-1879), one of the principals in the "Erie War," a scandalous episode in railroad history, an associate of Jay Gould and James Fisk (*qq.v.*). His piety attracted the irony of reformers; he endowed Drew Theological Seminary. He is the target of Bouck White's *The Book of Daniel Drew* (1910).

DREYFUS AFFAIR, THE (1894-1906), a symbol of injustice attending military intrigue and presumed capitalistic decay, it had as its victim Alfred Dreyfus, an officer in the French Army and a Jew. Accused of the betrayal of military secrets to German agents, he was convicted by a military tribunal and sentenced to degradation and deportation for life. Revelations of the actual culpability of another officer, Esterhazy, were hastily covered up, but blown to light by the famous letter of Emile Zola (*q.v.*), "J'Accuse," published in Georges Clemenceau's *l'Aurore*. Zola was placed on trial for criminal libel, but fled the country. Renewed efforts in Dreyfus's behalf made the case of international import to social reformers, who did not cease to use it following his full vindication in 1906. Finley P. Dunne's (*q.v.*) famous essay, "On the Dreyfus Case," was less an essay in social reform than in criticism of American indifference to foreign affairs. See Nicholas Halasz, *Captain Dreyfus: the Story of a Mass Hysteria* (1955).

DROP-OUTS, a concept of the 1960s, referring to discontented youth who revealed their displeasure with society by refusing concern for its workings: a class of youth made minimal by the collapse of the youth (*q.v.*) movement, its commune dreams, and the need to work.

DRUG ADDICTION, see Narcotics Problem.

DUAL UNIONISM, the presence of two unions serving the same element of workers, deplored as splitting the strength of the workers in the industry, and as providing the employers with means for keeping them separated, since they could take the position that they could not determine which was the proper bargaining agency, or in other fashions defer or confuse negotiations. The A.F.L. tended to take the position that non-AFL unions were dual unions, especially when it was prepared to undertake an organizational drive in a particular industry. Notable dual unions were created by the Socialist Labor Party, by the Western Federation of Miners, the I.W.W., and the Trade Union Educational League (*q.v.*). The C.I.O. was a major effort in unionism which, based as it was on different principles from the A.F.L., changed the character of the debate over dual unionism, which, however, was negated when the two organizations united.

DU BOIS, W. E. B.(1868-1963), one of the most distinguished of American Negroes, New-England born, Harvard trained, he undertook to teach ideals of intellectual grasp to his race, setting examples with such works as *The Suppression of the African Slave Trade to the United States of America, 1638-1870* (1896), and numerous research projects in Negro life and conditions which he carried on at Atlanta University; see, for example, his *The Negro in Business* (1899). A proud man, he resented circumstances repressive to Negroes in America, and was impatient with Booker T. Washington's (*q.v.*) modest and patient program to advance the status of Negroes. He headed the "Niagara Movement" (*q.v.*) which demanded an equal share of American opportunity, and was the most famous of the Negro and white associates who formed the N.A.A.C.P. (*q.v.*). He edited the *Crisis*, which came to symbolize Negro aspirations. He supported American participation in World War I, and afterwards sought to organize the power of Negroes internationally. Picking up his older idea of an elite which would guide the race to victories, he made himself part of the Negro cultural "renaissance" of the 1920's. He became more and more impatient with the slow pace of Negro acceptance, and after leaving the N.A.A.C.P. in 1934, he became increasingly Marxist in views, as in his *Black Reconstruction* (1935). He received honor from American communists and honors from the U.S.S.R. In 1951, he was indicted by the U.S. government for failing, as a chairman of the Peace Information Center. to register as an agent of a foreign power. See Francis L. Broderick, *W. E. B. Du Bois* (1959). Compare H. Hawkins, ed., *Booker T. Washington and His Critics* (1974).

DUE PROCESS CLAUSE of the U.S. Constitution, found in V and XIV Amendments (*qq.v.*), and guaranteeing that no one can be deprived of life, liberty, or property "without due process of law." Thus, any claim that such an infringement on rights had taken place could be appealed beyond local and state jurisdictions to the highest courts. The effect of due process on the privileges protected by the XIV Amendment was especially notable. See Virginia Wood, *Due Process of Law, 1932-1949* (1951); F. P. Graham, *Due Process Revolution: the Warren Court's Impact on Criminal Law* (1971).

DUELING, see Anti-Dueling.

DUMA, before the Bolshevik Revolution the Czarist version of a parliament. Its impotency, its inability to honor or minister to popular wants or beliefs made it a thing of scorn to the general population, and with no prestige abroad. Its inability to act as a safety valve for discontent helped build up the frustration culminating in explosive social action.

DUMB, see Institutional Reform.

DUNNE, FINLEY PETER (1867-1936), creator of "Mr. Dooley," a philosophical saloon-keeper, whose comments upon the Spanish-American War and, later, events of the Progressive Era (*q.v.*) made him famous to a generation of Americans. Dunne's tolerance and humanitarian sentiments seemed to place him with the reformers, though his hard realism made him skeptical of their programs. Among Dunne's most notable essays were "A Book Review," which poked fun at Theodore Roosevelt's (*q.v.*) egocentric memories of the Cuban War, and "On the Dreyfus Case," which satirized the too-careless attention Americans accorded foreign affairs. See, Louis Filler, ed., *The World of Mr. Dooley* (1962), which also contains essays written in Dunne's own impeccable English.

DUPLEX PRINTING PRESS CASE, see Secondary Boycott.

DURANT, WILL (1885-1981), radical in his youth, he was director of the Labor Temple (*q.v.*) school, 1914-27. His *Transition* (1927) is a vivid record of his change to more conservative perspectives. His career was changed by publication of *The Story of Philosophy* (1926), which was a phenomenal best-seller and freed him for later elaborate studies of the development of civilization. See *Will and Ariel Durant: a Duel Autobiography* (1977).

DYNAMITE: THE STORY OF CLASS VIOLENCE IN AMERICA (1931), by Louis Adamic, written by one "not an active radical, nor a member of any labor union, but my sympathies are with labor." It suggested that terrorism was, in part, a result of infirm social circumstances, and even found a connection between the racketeering which could be discerned in free enterprise, and that associated directly with outlawed operations. Highlighted were the Molly Maguires, the Haymarket Affair, Homestead and Pullman, the Steunenberg assassination, the Wobblies, the McNamaras, Mooney, the Steel Strike of 1919, Centralia, and, somewhat indirectly, Sacco-Vanzetti (*q.v.*).

EARLE, THOMAS (1796-1849), a Philadelphia Quaker of means who was a lawyer and writer, and, thanks to local conditions, supported both Jacksonian and Garrisonian (*q.v.*) principles in the 1830's. He was the Vice-Presidential candidate of the Liberty Party (*q.v.*) in 1840, but after 1845 separated himself from the abolitionist movement, and later still became a conservative on the subject.

EASLEY, RALPH M., see National Civic Federation.

EASTERN PENITENTIARY, see Prison Reform.

EASTMAN, MAX (1883-1969), a leader in the Youth Movement (*q.v.*) who edited the *Masses* (*q.v.*) and the *Liberator*, in the 1910's and early 1920's, and had status among reformers and radicals, as well as among litterateurs. His *Journalism Versus Art* (1916) was a popular statement of the attitude of the younger generation. His own verse was conventional, and his *Enjoyment of Poetry* (1913) was derogated by more subtle practitioners of later vintage. He tried to see "the science of revolution" in "commonsense" terms, and in his *Marx and Lenin* (1926) argued that Lenin's greatness lay in meeting the facts rather than following "Marxian dialectics." As an admirer of Leon Trotsky (*q.v.*), he dissapproved of the Stalinist campaigns of the 1930's. He wrote *Artists in Uniform* (1943) in criticism of communist regimentation in the arts; due to the spirit of the time, it was a publishing failure. The Moscow Trials (*q.v.*) wholly disillusioned him, as his *The End of Socialism in Russia* (1937) indicated. Throwing light on his frame of reference was *Enjoyment of Laughter* (1936) and *Enjoyment of Living* (1947), which were unshadowed by his other concerns. He translated Trotsky's *History of the Russian Revolution* (1932-3). He became an editor for the *Reader's Digest*.

EATON, DORMAN B. (1823-1899), "the father of American Civil service (*q.v.*) reform," began as municipal reformer in New York, drafting a number of basic laws establishing departments for health, police, and other services, was chairman of the ineffective Civil Service Commission of the Grant administration, author of the important *Civil Service in Great Britain: a History of Abuses and Reforms and Their Bearing upon American Politics* (1880). He drafted the Pendleton Act (*q.v.*), and served as chairman of the reinvigorated Civil Service Commission.

EBERT, FRIEDRICH W. (1861-1925), German Socialist who became head of the Provisional government of Germany in November 1918, and subsequently President of the Republic. Identified with the killing of Karl Liebknecht and Rosa Luxembourg (*qq.v.*) and thus with the great rift between German socialist and communist movements, through which Hitler came to power.

ECONOMIC DEPRESSION, a term used to define periods of economic trouble, characterized by business failures, marked unemployment, and attendant social and individual turmoil. Years notable for depression have included 1837 and 1857, in pre-Civil War decades, 1873, 1883, and 1893, in post-Civil War decades (*cf.*, Panic of 1907). Such dates were high points in depressions which wore on for longer periods of time. In addition, sections, industries, and groups have been in depression even during periods of prosperity. Thus, miners in Illinois and mill-workers in North Carolina did not share in much of the prosperity of the 1920's. The economic depression of the 1930's has been held different in kind, in that natural processes of industrial expansion were not sufficient to overcome it in time-honored, free-enterprise fashion, but that government intervention was instituted on a permanent basis. Reformers have held the term "depression" to be inaccurate, a euphemism for "crisis" (q.v.). Such "classic" economic conditions were overthrown by new extremes of international embroilment, inflation, under-production, and the costs of world security operations, oil, and space probe costs. In 1981, Americans were stunned to learn that, for example, Japan was "Number One" in automobile production, once replete with proud insignia of American superiority. Contradictions appeared in the "savings" to industry by way of close-downs and unemployment being balanced by the futile costs of welfare payments. It was evident that American expectations and social organization would have to be readjusted to novel circumstances. See Oil, Inflation, Production, Welfare, and other related topics. Raymond Vernon, *Economic and Political Consequences of Multinational Enterprise* (1972); David Mermelstein, *Economic Crisis Reader* (1975); Harry D. Hutchinson, *Economics and Social Goals* (1973); Robert Ghelardi, *Economics, Culture and Society* (1976).

ECONOMIC DETERMINISM, see Materialistic Conception of History.

ECONOMIC INTERPRETATION OF THE CONSTITUTION, AN, see Beard, Charles A.

ECONOMICS, the supposed science governing the production and distribution of wealth. Distinctions have been made by reformers between conservative economics, presumed prejudiced in favor of the existing order, and scientific or progressive views of the same. The "Sun Spot Theory" (q.v.) has become the symbol of the ineffectiveness of older conservative economic fancies. The "Law of Supply and Demand" has been rendered doubtful by government interventions. "Deficit spending" (q.v.) has been defended and opposed. Strategic areas have been taxation policies, agricultural policies, the definitions of prosperity and depression, and budget and production analyses. "Mathematical economists" have separated themselves from the social content of economics, and, in effect have become efficient keepers of the books. As more critical times unfolded in the 1970s, they were relegated to accountant status, and gave way to such economic prophets as John K. Galbraith, an advocate of social spending, as in *Economics and the Public Purpose* (1973), and Milton Friedman, whose free market economics, emphasizing "monetarism" was admired by conservatives; see his *Capitalism and Freedom* (1962). See also Misery Index.

ECONOMICS AND REFORM have been related to the extent that questions of equity could be discerned in economic operations. Thus, Adam Smith's *The Wealth of Nations* (1776) advocated free enterprise (q.v.), as opposed to an economic system of government controls, which was the essence of mercantilism, on moral grounds of justice to the poor. Yet free enterprise was itself attacked by reformers as creating the worst of tyrannies. Labor reformers demanded higher wages, unions, shorter hours and other reforms. Free trade reformers thought the lower prices they would achieve would lift the burden of want from the poor. The better distribution of money which they demanded was attacked by defenders of the status quo as interfering with the free flow of money, with supply and demand, and with liberty. New Deal reforms required heavy financing and received justification in the so-called Keynesian economics, derived from the name of its major theoretician, John M. Keynes. Essentially he argued that a great public debt did not endanger the economy, since the public simply owed the money to itself. The implications of his system involved a limited form of socialized money. The inflation of money, heavy taxes, and a remarkable public debt horrified conservatives who saw not only an improper financial system, but moral and social decay. Henry Hazlitt, a former liberal turned rigid anti-state economist edited *The Critics of Keynesian Economics* (1960); (qq.v.) for above topics. See also Mixed Economy.

EDDY, THOMAS (1758-1827), a former Philadelphian and Tory, who became a wealthy insurance broker in New York. A converted Quaker (q.v.), he was interested in the ideas of Beccaria, William Penn, and John Howard (qq.v.); after examining the famous Philadelphia prison, he persuaded the

New York legislature to authorize the building of a prison. He helped supervise its operations, using the single-cell, or "solitary," system. Known as the "American Howard," he helped reform the penal code. His *Account of the State Prison or Penitentiary House in the City of New York* (1801), and *Hints for Introducing an Improved Method of Treating the Insane in the Asylum* (1815) were pioneer documents. He helped found the Bloomingdale Asylum for the Insane, opposed imprisonment for debt (q.v.) and slavery, and aided Quaker work with the Indians.

EDUCATION has, since its assumption by democratic elements, begun in reform and ended in mere vocational or entertainment techniques. Puritan education of its young "vipers" deteriorated into charity schools which spirited youth often preferred to avoid. Education developed in several directions. In the pre-Civil War period, the public school system was developed. Mechanics' institutes (q.v.) gave opportunities for knowledge, practical and otherwise. Phrenologists (q.v.) and other popular writers and speakers imparted information of more or less validity. The Lyceum (q.v.) offered sometimes distinguished speakers. In the post-Civil War period, education was further democratized by the development of the high school, the vocational school, and, in the 1890's, progressive education (q.v.). The fight against child labor (q.v.) was, in part, a fight for more schooling. Adult education (q.v.) and "Americanization" classes broadened the field further. With World War II, the field exploded into innumerable technical and non-technical classes, much of it sponsored by the government. Oddly, labor (q.v.), which had once urged education as a glorious entrance into the realm of the spirit, and which had published innumerable pamphlets and books in order to strengthen its membership, lagged beyond its budget in this field. Laborers were not interested in extra-curricular classes, and the few "institutes," and the like, which labor sponsored, pointed up its colossal failure in this area. The colleges and universities increased their student enrollments; whether they increased quality of their student bodies, and just what the criteria were for improvement, were not the first-line questions of admissions departments. A national propaganda urged students not to quit school, because additional years in school would increase their annual income.

The youth uprising of the 1960s and 1970s had its center in schools, higher and lower, and disrupted them in goals and the special problems of female roles, drugs, sex relations, and homosexuals. The liberal arts declined in quality and quantity; they no longer offered jobs, and were not needed to avoid military service. Sports, always a scandal of excessiveness and low-literacy athletes, were rendered more malignant in results. A grotesque phenomenon of 1980 was a ditty, delivered by young rock singers to international acclaim which went: "We Don't Want No Education." A New York black received his Ph.D. and entree into higher levels of the educational system with a thesis and publication by an elite publishing firm which the critic John Simon, in the *New York Times*, showed to be filled with ghastly errors and misapprehensions. A Mobile, Alabama teacher with a Master's degree sent the following note to a child's parent: "Scott is [sic] dropping in his studies he acts as if he don't Care. Scott wont pass in his assignment at all, he a [sic] had a poem to learn and he fell to do it."

Regard for the handicapped in schools was the one bright spot in the national picture. Although Scholastic Aptitude Tests (SAT) increased in popularity, this signalled no new concern for standards. They saved, when passed, parents's money in tight and inflated times, enabling high school students to waive introductory—often merely remedial— courses in college. Even more somber was the emergence of the National Education Association (NEA) as a major interest group in politics, less concerned for the quality of its teacher-members, recognized as a disgrace, than for their tenure and wages; a number of states, mainly in the South, but multiplying beyond, passed laws requiring teachers to pass examinations in the 3Rs—Reading, Writing, and Arithmetic—to demonstrate they had the skills to pass on to pupils. Teachers's strikes, as well as parents's and students's strikes, were a feature of the educational year. The need for quality education to meet the domestic and international exigencies of the nation was emphasized by the diminished budgets within which those responsible for education would have to work. The president of Johns Hopkins University spoke for many in deploring the lack of the teaching of values; universities, he said, were turning out highly skilled barbarians. Harold D. Love, *Educating Exceptional Children in Regular Classrooms* (1975); Robert M. Anderson and John G. Green, eds., *Educating the Severely and Profoundly Handicapped* (1976); Russell G. Davis and Gary M. Lewis, *Education and Employment* (1975); Frances Fitzgerald, *America Revised* (1980); G. D. Spindler, *Education and the Cultural Process* (1974); B. C. Wallace, *Education and the Drug Scene* (1974); Dean T. Jamison et al., *Education as an Industry* (1976); Robert J. Havighurst, ed., *Education for the Gifted* (1958); Michael Katz, *Education in American History* (1973); G. M. Inlow, *Education: Mirror and Agent of Change* (1970). See also, Progressive Education, Affirmative Action, Dewey, John, Mann, Horace, Morgan, Arthur M.

EDUCATION AND THE NEGRO, long a moral reform (*q.v.*), abolitionists often opening schools for Negroes. Negroes in the North, especially those of somewhat higher economic or other qualifications, opened schools for themselves. In the post-Civil War period "Negro schools" proliferated, and "Negro colleges" grew in number, several with distinction, as in the cases of Fisk, Hampton, and Howard. Tuskegee Institute (*q.v.*) was outstanding as a sample of Negro enterprise and achievement which attracted special attention. The Slater Fund, established by John Fox Slater, a northern philanthropist, in 1882, left a million dollars to help in the education of southern freedmen. The schools were almost totally Negro in enrollment. In the North, a relatively few Negroes attained graduation from notable northern institutions, but the number increased, as the Negro population and its attendant elite increased. The "separate but equal" (*q.v.*) doctrine made progress difficult, though the N.A.A.C.P. (*q.v.*) tested laws and regulations at every point. Better education for most Negroes was limited by their poverty and necessary neighborhoods. The desegregation decision of 1954 touched off not only demands for desegregation of pre-college schools, but for desegregation of those on the higher levels. Little Rock, Arkansas (*q.v.*) became one symbol of southern resistance. Louisville, Kentucky, schools were integrated thanks to the efforts of the local superintendent of schools; see Omer Carmichael and Weldon James, *The Louisville Story* (1957). The danger to Negro ambitions was that "token integration" might be achieved—a few Negroes granted entree to "white" schools—and the heart taken out of the drive for desegregation. Busing and Affirmative Action (*qq.v.*) became vehicles for liberal aspirations toward Negro equality in education. The glaring problem which emerged was one of quality; not only were black and white students kept from study, confused by politics and theory remote from education, and given ambitions having nothing to do with social needs, but teachers and administrators were eroded by the same forces. The one good hope, pending a national educational revival, involved honorable and intelligent individuals who might be able to save some of the talented students from being submerged; see Erwin Flaxman, *Educating the Disadvantaged* (1976); Thomas Sowell, *Black Education: Myths and Tragedies* (1972); William Moore, Jr. and Lonnie H. Wagstaff, *Black Educators in White Colleges* (1974).

EDUCATIONAL REFORM has involved techniques alleged to give better educational results. Thus, Horace Mann's (*q.v.*) organization of the first normal school, his report on teaching methods which he had observed in Europe, and other efforts all constituted aspects of educational reform. Bronson Alcott's (*q.v.*) work with children, though wholly unsuccessful in a temporal sense, helped create the foundations for later educational developments. Reform in the post-Civil War period centered on the question of how to care for the educational needs of a growing and complex population, including the children of isolated farmers and friendless immigrants. Moreover, there was a question of what constituted education in a nation composed of unstable and constantly shifting groups. A. J. Nock, later, in *The Theory of Education in the United States* (1932), argued that education—as distinguished from vocational training—could only consist of an understanding of past experience, by way of ancient languages, literature, history, and other humanistic studies. Progressive education (*q.v.*), on the other hand, argued for a creative approach to the child, and for relevant instruction. The "Gary School system," developed in Indiana, concentrated on a full use of the "educational plant." The ideal of "universal education" disturbed few educational thinkers; it appeared to them that it would ensure universal literacy. The possibility that dullards might impede the progress of quick learners little troubled educationalists before World War II. (See Children, Gifted.) Disillusionments with liberalism, produced in part by cases of subversion (see Hiss Case), and revelations that in key cases Russian "know-how" was apparently better than "Yankee know-how" gave a forum to grim opponents of progressive education, who advocated emphasis on "basic disciplines" of reading, writing, and facts. At that point, it was unclear who were the educational reformers: the advocates of a return to principles which produced results, or those who defended progressive education as maligned, and insisted that the traditionalists were romanticizing the tradition. In general, too, those who maintained regard for "the whole person," "individual needs," and other tenets of progressivism, tended to favor Federal aid to education, its opponents suspecting that the government might force its views on the local community, along with its funds. Progressives argued that there was an urgent need for classrooms, and that government money would in no way infringe upon local autonomy. A special problem was that of parochial schools, which desired government money but met resistance in those who felt a principle in church and state separation was in danger; see Non-Public Schools.

EDWARDS, JONATHAN (1703-1757), "hell-fire" preacher and philosopher of free will, he took it to be his task to restore the Puritan faith to its early rigor. Though a subtle logician, he considered it as proper to frighten his congregation into a fear for its salvation, as to appeal to its reasoning powers. Hence such a famous sermon as "Sinners in the Hands of an Angry God." As a philosopher, he strove to square predestination (*q.v.*) with free will, showing that those who would suffer eternal damnation ought to agree that they deserved to do so. He was an almost exact contemporary of Benjamin Franklin (*q.v.*), though earlier deceased. See also Calvinism and Reform.

E. E. C., see European Economic Community.

EFFICIENCY, see Taylorization, Veblen, Thorstein.

"EGGHEADS," see Intellectuals and Reform.

EGYPT, see Arabs, Fellahim, Sadat, Anwar.

EICHMANN, KARL ADOLF (1906-1962), key Nazi delegated to exterminate the Jews of Europe. His famous boast was that "he would leap into his grave laughing because the feeling that he had five million people on his conscience would be for him a source of extraordinary satisfaction." His estimate is disputed by Gerald Reitlinger, in his *The Final Solution* (1953), who argues that "the murders in which Eichmann had a direct hand numbered less than a million, for his connection with the massacres in Poland and Russia seems rather remote" (p. 27).

EIGHT-HOUR DAY, THE, a major slogan of labor in the post-Civil War Period, especially urgent because of the great industrial advance and the coming of a horde of new immigrants in desperate need and competition, who could be worked, in some industries, to almost any extent. The slogan of an eight-hour work day was vigorously proposed by the American Federation of Labor (*q.v.*). Although deemed an advance over conditions of labor in previously dominant societies, the eight-hour day had obtained, for example in the sixteenth century.

Specific trades required special approaches. Thus, in 1907, Congress decreed that train employees could not be kept on duty more than sixteen hours per day; not until 1916 did the Adamson Act set the eight-hour day for railway employees involved in interstate commerce. The forty-hour week and the six-hour day (qq.v.) represented further advances in labor aspirations, see also Automation, Ten-Hour Day.

(1800), see "Revolution of 1800."

1812, WAR OF, a study in national interests and developments, rather than reform, though sometimes called "the second American revolution," because it presumably once more "freed" the United States, this time from Great Britain's command of the sea. There was little more reason for war against Great Britain than against France, since both harassed American shipping. The former did impress some American seamen (q.v.), but since they were a despised caste, it was ironic that this should have touched national honor. The war was humiliating, Detroit being surrendered and the Capital being burned, though largely saved by a "miraculous" storm. (Americans had earlier burned the capital of Upper Canada, York.) Andrew Jackson's victory at New Orleans solaced national pride, though it took place after the signing of the peace treaty at Ghent. The most remarkable result of the war was its effect on sectional attitudes. Thus, John C. Calhoun (q.v.), representing southern opinion, had been an ardent nationalist, interested in internal improvements (q.v.), an advocate of strong central government, and hopeful that a policy of protection (q.v.) would bring industry to the South. Daniel Webster (q.v.), speaking for New England, feared the "Virginia dynasty" which had dominated national politics and defended state rights, was suspicious of internal improvements which might build up the West to compete with the East and draw away its populations, proposed free trade (q.v.) as an aid to New England shipping. It was, however, New England which profited from the War of 1812, and blossomed out with industries which Webster yearned to defend with protection tariffs. He became an ardent nationalist, and eager for roads which would bring New England goods into the interior. Calhoun, on his side, was disillusioned. The war had brought little industry to his South. He turned to free trade, which might enable the South to pit New England prices for manufactured goods against those from Great Britain and elsewhere. He became suspicious of a central government which might infringe upon states-rights prerogatives, opposed to internal improvements, since a government which could build roads, might enforce anti-southern policy. Thus, the two great antagonists stood opposed once more, denouncing the arguments of the other, which they had themselves once maintained. John K. Mahon, War of 1812 (1972).

(1828), see "Revolution of 1828."

1837, PANIC OF, a product of over-speculation and the "good times" so adequately portrayed, for one section of the country, in Joseph G. Baldwin's The Flush Times of Alabama and Mississippi, published in 1853, but dealing with the period preceding the panic. This first national crisis resulted partly because of the increased interrelatedness of business institutions. Thus, the post-Revolutionary depression seems to have affected western Massachusetts much more than it did Philadelphia. The Panic of 1837 caused bread riots (q.v.), among other signs of disorder. It wiped out a promising movement for organizing trade unions on a national basis, but gave a new incentive to cooperatives, notably the Fourierist (q.v.) movement. R. C. McGrane, Panic of 1837: Some Financial Problems of the Jacksonian Era (1965).

1846, called The Year of Decision (1943), by Bernard DeVoto because of the trek of Mormons and adventurers westward, the seizure of California, and the declaration of war on Mexico. The book argued that the tide of events had made the later Civil War inevitable.

1848, revolutionary year, involving the June uprising in Paris, following the promulgation on February 25, 1848, of a decree for the organization of the Ateliers Nationaux (national workshops) (q.v.), which would guarantee "the right to work." These being dissolved, the workingmen of Paris rebelled, and were quickly suppressed at the cost of some 15,000 dead; see also Germany, Hungary, Forty-Eighters, The.

1873, see "Crime of '73."

1873, PANIC OF, precipitated by the failure of Jay Cooke & Company, which had become involved in the disastrous business operations of the Northern Pacific Railroad. The drawn-out depression which followed impressed the country with the inter-related nature of business, and strengthened the argument of reformers who believed that so responsible a power as economic security should not be in the hands of individuals who were essentially concerned for self-serving purposes. See also Economic Depression.

1876, see Disputed Election of.

1877, RAILROAD RIOTS OF, capped a long series of difficulties between management and the railroad brotherhoods (q.v.), growing from the depression of 1873 which had caused the railroads to reduce wages and personnel. A new ten percent wage cut caused the brotherhoods to plan a massive strike for fall, but so desperate were the workers that they broke into action during the summer. Working along the line forced them to develop novel strike tactics; thus trainmen took their trains out of the station, and left them idle along the road. Laws were passed in several states making such actions illegal. To Martinsburg, West Virginia, a great railroad center, President Rutherford B. Hayes sent troops to maintain order. Violence took place in several centers, notably in Pittsburgh, where strikers fought troops sent from Philadelphia. The strike spread through the west. Some two hundred persons were estimated to have died in the proceedings. The strike inspired the first labor novel, John Hay's (q.v.) The Breadwinners (1884), a poor novel and anti-labor, which was well received by the reading public. R. V. Bruce, 1877: Year of Violence (1959).

EIGHTEENTH AMENDMENT, see Prohibition.

EISENHOWER, DWIGHT D. (1890-1969). His steady, unassuming Army career was capped with the fearful responsibility given him in 1942 as U.S. commander of the European Theater of Operations and his subsequent, 1943, designation as supreme commander of the Allied Expeditionary Forces. As such, he made the ultimate decisions leading to the assault on the Europe-dominated Nazi armies; see his Crusade in Europe (1948). His record and personality made him of interest to public and political leaders in post-War developments and worrisome to American liberals; a liberal canard of the time was that he was appointed president of Columbia University in 1948 because its trustees confused him with his brother Milton Eisenhower, a university president. Eisenhower organized NATO (q.v.), then ran successfully for President in 1952. Although he was responsible for ending the Korean War (1953), arranging the Southeast Asia Treaty Organization (1954) to resist communist expansion, and initiating with Russia an "Atoms for Peace" beginning (1955), liberal unease continued to follow him through his Administration, expressing itself in whispered questioning of his intelligence, scorn of his golfing, and of his English which was precise in military phrasing, but less graceful than that of his political rival Adlai E. Stevenson (q.v.). At home he pressed for economy, though not in the military sector, and civil rights which opened the way for later developments. He maintained a good relationship in this area with the Democratic leader in Congress Lyndon B. Johnson (q.v.). His Mandate for Change (1963) and Waging Peace (1965) are durable records of Eisenhower's achievements. Though dimmed by later Democratic and radical efforts at social change, Eisenhower's credibility as a leader in peace as well as in war increased with disillusionment over the results of the liberal administration. Peter Lyon, Eisenhower (1974); Dean Albertson, ed., Eisenhower as President (1963); Herbert S. Parmet, Eisenhower and the American Crusades (1974); L. H. Larsen and Robert L. Branyan, eds., The Eisenhower Administration (1971).

ELDERLY, see Old Age Dependency, Senior Citizens, Nursing Homes.

ELECTION CAMPAIGNS have always provided deep insights into the state of the Union. Notable ones to reformers have been those in which were elected Thomas Jefferson (1800), Andrew Jackson (1828), Abraham Lincoln (1860), Grover Cleveland (1884), Theodore Roosevelt (1904), Woodrow Wilson (1912), and Franklin D. Roosevelt (1932) (qq.v.). The election of 1840 was notable for the "Hard Cider" campaign which successfully accompanied Whig demagogy, the election campaign of 1872 for the efforts of the Liberal Republicans to overcome President Grant's (q.v.) hold on popular northern feelings. Most notable was the great effort of the Populists in 1896 to elect William Jennings Bryan (q.v.). Election campaign slogans have provided insight into political strategy. The 1980 elections seemed critical because of the adjustments Americans had to make to crises in Iran (q.v.), where American "hostages" were held, and at home where inflation (q.v.), humiliation, and lack of direction lost the nation a good deal of the world's respect. See also Caucus. D. A. Leuthold, *Electioneering in a Democracy* (1968); Kevin P. Phillips and Paul H. Blackman, *Electoral Reform and Voter Participation* (1975).

ELECTION REFORMS have included numerous crusades against corruption at the polls, but also the more positive reforms involved in the Australian ballot (q.v.) (first adopted by cities in 1888), the short ballot idea which came a little later, suffrage reforms, and the various refinements of proportional representation, the initiative and referendum, and recall (qq.v.).

ELECTORAL COMMISSION (1877), see Disputed Election of 1876.

ELIOT, JOHN (1604-1690), early minister and reformer, who sought peace between white men and Indians. In seeking to convert them, he studied their language and instructed them in Christian principles. His success in establishing "praying Indians" near white communities helped to inspire the organization in London of the Society for Propagating the Gospel in New England. King Philip's War (q.v.) (1675) left little more than a memory of his efforts.

ELITE, THE, see Intellectuals and Reform.

ELKINS ACT, THE (1903), an example of legislation which had the appearance of reform, but was little more than an exercise in efficiency. It outlawed rebates (q.v.) long after such an act would have constituted a curb on discriminating railroads. Its sponsor, U.S. Senator Stephen B. Elkins, was himself a railroad promoter, and anxious to cut down disastrous competition between railroad lines, now in a monopoly stage, as well as to protect them from the demands for rebates on the part of great industries.

ELLIS ISLAND, a symbol now imbedded in history, its role as an immigration (q.v.) station having ended in 1954. It processed some twenty million immigrants, mostly from Europe, the majority of whom had become assimilated into one or another aspect of the American social complex. Its loss of vitality as a measure of American openness and mobility reflected Americans's new need to look outward, sometimes to the meaning in their lives of old homelands. See David M. Brownstone et al., *Island of Hope, Island of Tears* (1979).

ELLISON, RALPH, see *Invisible Man* (1952).

ELLSBERG, DANIEL (1931-   ), Harvard University economics student and Fellow, whose expertise enabled him to work with the Department of Defense to analyze policy in Vietnam. Persuaded that it was a "criminal war" being criminally conducted—he subsequently compared toleration of it with the Nazi Albert Speer's toleration of Hitler (see Speer's *Inside the Third Reich*)—he determined to release confidential and classified American military files for publication in the *New York Times*. This expose, useful to all American military foes, sparked a sense of outrage in the White House which, with other "leaks" (q.v.), led to Watergate (q.v.). Ellsberg defended his course in *Papers on the War* (1972). He received a species of

endorsement by having dismissed in 1973 charges against him of conspiracy, theft, and violation under the Espionage Act. He became associated with the Center for International Studies at Massachusetts Institute of Technology. See also Pentagon Papers. Peter Schrag, *Test of Loyalty: Daniel Ellsberg and the Rituals of Secret Government* (1974).

ELMER GANTRY (1927), by Sinclair Lewis (q.v.), the tale of a religious hypocrite and of the shallow audiences he was able to influence; it reflected upon the shabbier aspects of fundamentalism (q.v.) in the post-World War I era.

ELOQUENCE, THE, of revolutionary and social reform figures and martyrs has been part of the heritage of protest. Socrates' phrases in support of freedom of inquiry, famous last words, from Desmoulins to Joe Hill (q.v.), and the courtroom speeches of Albert B. Parsons, Vanzetti, and Clarence Darrow (qq.v.) have all furnished ammunition for the arguments and turns of phrase of social reformers, during active periods.

ELY, RICHARD T. (1854-1943), professor and Christian Socialist (q.v.), whose writings furnished materials for persons like himself who sought a program of good will and class collaboration. His works included *French and German Socialism in Modern Times* (1883), *The Labor Movement in America* (1886), and *Ground under Our Feet; an Autobiography* (1938).

EMANCIPATION, see Compensated Emancipation, British Emancipation, Abolitionism.

EMANCIPATION PROCLAMATION (1863), see Slavery.

EMBALMED BEEF SCANDAL, part of the poor record of the War Department during the Spanish-American War (q.v.). A commission appointed by the President, late in 1898, brought out facts which shocked the country. Large amounts of beef purchased from the Beef Trust (q.v.) had been refrigerated and sent to Cuba. It had been treated with chemicals which made it a danger to health. General Nelson A. Miles, employing a current Army phrase, called it "embalmed beef." The difference between a country in and out of a reform movement was shown by the fact that though patriotism and health were involved in this investigation, no formidable demand for a clean-up of the Beef Trust developed, and the incident passed over. A few years later, the concerted efforts of the muckrakers (q.v.) resulted in passage of the Beef Inspection Act.

EMBARGO, see Arms Embargo.

EMBARGO ACT (1807-1809) President Jefferson's (q.v.) effort to avoid American involvement in the war raging between France and Great Britain by keeping American ships at home. The Embargo Act thus constituted a great experiment in neutrality (q.v.). Its failure was due to several causes. American shipping was overwhelmingly in New England; it thus appeared to the antagonistic Federalists of that region that the Administration was striking a malicious blow at them. It became almost a matter of honor for shippers to subvert the law by continuing their trade, while others smuggled goods across the border to Canada, and thence to Great Britain. The Embargo, too, as an instrument for peace was deficient in that it was a negative program, calling Americans, in effect, to the work of avoiding the conflict: a program, it appeared, which stirred little enthusiasm. Louis M. Sears, *Jefferson and the Embargo* (1967). See also Oil.

EMERGENCY PEACE FEDERATION, an effort, in 1914-5, to rouse and organize pacifist sentiment following the outbreak of war in Europe. Led by Jane Addams and Rosika Schwimmer, among others, it exhibited great energy and apparent influence. In 1917, in the face of impending American intervention, an effort was made to revive it, but to no effect.

EMERGENCY PEACE MOBILIZATION (1940), see American Youth Congress.

EMERGING NATION, see Newly Emerging Nation.

EMERSON, RALPH WALDO (1803-1882) transcendentalist (q.v.) and spokesman for individualism at a time when the assertion of the individual represented a protest against anti-democratic forces. He left the Unitarian pulpit because he felt he needed a new approach to God and man; his *Nature* (1836) sounded a trumpet to his generation. Thoreau (*q.v.*) did what Emerson preached; Whitman (*q.v.*) was an indirect offspring of his intentions. His oration on "The American Scholar," again, called for a fresh, individual approach, and his "Divinity School Address," delivered at Harvard and critical of conventional interpretations of Christianity, debarred him from the University for many years. He helped edit the *Dial* (*q.v.*). As a professional lecturer, he carried his message of self-reliance and faith in nature to the country. No professional reformer, he had cordial relations which extended as far as John Brown (*q.v.*) though he was not aware of his desperate program. Although an associate of reformers and an inspiration to them, in the post-Civil War era, his optimism, contempt for charity, and other traits were used by opponents of humanitarianism, labor and radical movements, and reformers, who were accused of undermining "individualism" by their demand for respect for the underprivileged.

EMINENT DOMAIN, the right of the government to take over private properties when the public good so requires. Although this right is strictly circumscribed by the duty of the government to provide just compensation, it constitutes good official recognition of the principle that the public weal stands before the private.

EMPIRE, a variant version of imperialism (*q.v.*) which has been utilized by critics of aspects of American foreign policy; see Scott Nearing, *The American Empire* (1921), and Paul Blanshard, *Democracy and Empire in the Caribbean* (1947).

EMPLOYERS AND WORKMEN ACT (1875), passed by the British Parliament, which placed employees and employers on an equal footing before the law, thus recognizing the operations of organized labor as permissible as those of organized capital; thus, peaceful picketing (*q.v.*) was given status in law.

EMPLOYMENT ACT OF 1946, see Full Employment Act (1946).

ENCYCLOPEDIA OF SOCIAL REFORM, ed., W.D.P. Bliss (*q.v.*), first issued in 1897, and revised in later editions of 1908 and 1910. An invaluable compilation of data and opinion with reference to its subject.

ENCYCLOPEDIA OF THE SOCIAL SCIENCES, THE, see Johnson, Alvin.

ENCYCLOPÉDIE NOUVELLE, L' (1834-1841), edited by Pierre Leroux and Jean Reybaud, eight volumes, unfinished; a pioneer encyclopedia which first used the term "socialism" significantly.

ENCYCLOPÉDIE OU DICTIONNAIRE RAISONNÉ DES SCIENCES, DES ARTS, ET DES MÉTIERS (1751-65), see Enlightenment.

ENERGY, a key concept of the 1970s, and promising to be a perennial. Once assumed as given by nature, through forests, coal, gas, and oil, it became subject to the fears of conservationists (*q.v.*), and the needs of people and industry. Inflation and oil (*qq.v.*) combined to raise questions as to the best approach to the "energy crunch." Paradoxes included Alaskan oil which somehow entered into international sales while domestic prices mounted. The need to "save energy" and cut the passenger-car use of oil linked the problem to the vital automobile industry, directly and indirectly affecting millions of employees and customers. "De-regulation" of oil prices promised to confront Americans with learning what was necessary to their lives as automobile users. "Alternative" forms of energy, including nuclear power, solar energy, and "synthetic fuels," such as gas and alcohol mixtures, stirred quarrels over industry responsibility and the disposal of toxic wastes, as well as the willingness of citizens to change their styles of life. The Federal Regulatory Commission and the new U.S. Federal Energy Administration had no clear mandate for action in these areas. Their future was subject to international events and the decisions of government. See also Environment, the Nuclear Question. Barry Commoner, *The Politics of Energy* (1979); Robert Stobaugh and Daniel Yergin, *Energy Future: Report of the Energy*

Project at the Harvard Business School (1979); Melvin Laird et al., *Energy Policy* (1976).

ENGELS, FRIEDRICH (1820-1895), born of well-to-do Germans, he became a collaborator of Karl Marx (*q.v.*) and with him prepared the *Communist Manifesto* of 1848 (*q.v.*). He became one of the founders and theoreticians of the First International (*q.v.*), and, with Marx, prepared numerous works which set the ground for socialist thinking and action all over the world. Among his more popular works are: *The Condition of the Working-Class in England in 1844* (1845), *Socialism: Utopian and Scientific* (*q.v.*), *The Origin of the Family* (1884).

ENGINEERS AND THE PRICE SYSTEM, THE (1921), by Thorstein Veblen; see Technocracy.

ENLIGHTENMENT, associated with a new interest in the laws of the physical world and universe, in reason, in rationalism, especially in France, in the decades preceding the French Revolution (*q.v.*). Such notables as Denis Diderot, whose monument was the great Encyclopedia, repository of the scientific studies and researches of the era, and François Marie Arouet (Voltaire) inspired libertarians and individualists. Deism (*q.v.*) was a significant by-product of their efforts. Their thinking affected Americans of the Revolutionary Era. *The Age of Reason*, by Thomas Paine (*q.v.*), derives from them, The Illuminati, another by-product of the Enlightenment, were made scandalous by American conservatives.

"ENTANGLING ALLIANCES," usually imagined to be part of President George Washington's "Farewell Address" of September 17, 1796, which did, indeed, warn the nation against permanent foreign alliances; it was Jefferson, in his Inaugural Address of March 4, 1801, who pleaded for friendship with all nations, "entangling alliances with none." The odd imputing of his phrase to Washington appears to have expressed the nation's desire for a less embattled source for the benign counsel than Jefferson. His own practical effort to avoid "entangling alliances," by way of his Embargo Act (*q.v.*) drew a storm upon his head.

"ENTERPRISE ZONES," see Private Enterprise

ENTERTAINMENT, a striking development in the 1970s, mainly in reaction to the catastrophic use made of rock music, mime, and "guerrilla theater" by youth (*q.v.*) agitators of the 1960s who made of entertainment a social challenge. The former communist and later sports writer and conservative Murray Kempton called the dangerous antics of the black actionists Rap Brown and Huey Newton a form of entertainment to the general public watching television. Society had, however, during that time, though in debate over movie stars, "boob tube" nonsense generally, and violence and licentiousness on "family" programs maintained a sense of what constituted standards in social behavior. In the 1970s, interest or support of the radical rant declined; the Yippie Abbie Hoffman complained that television had been agog with excitement when he and his abettors had loosed pigs in Chicago streets during the 1968 Democratic Convention, but that the television circuits had failed him in 1972 when he brought an elephant to the Republican Convention in Miami.

In the 1970s, the line between entertainment and reality broke down significantly. Television was outstanding in providing endless hours of senseless "soap operas," the plots of which were regularly reported in newspapers as a duty to readers who might have missed an episode. Other bizarre programs vied with one another in exploiting violence, empty challenges, and "adult" scenes discouraging even to hardened television and motion-picture critics. A phenomenon of 1980 was the television shooting of a character, "J. R."—"the man you love to hate"—in a continuing feature "Dallas," which was reported as though news. "Who shot J. R.?" was a question which received international concern as worth serious attention. As striking was the world-wide mourning for the former Beatle singer and composer of songs John Lennon, whose killing by a fantasy-ridden acolyte was seen as a blow to civilization by hundreds of thousands and perhaps millions of his adorers. Notable also was the breakdown in differences between fantasy and reality in estimates of the careers of the playwrite and radical sympathizer Lillian Hellman and her longtime companion Dashiell Hammett, among others whose values as entertainers and as thinkers were confused by public appreciation. The singer Frank Sinatra was outstanding as having been tainted by association with criminals, yet sought after and admired by the Kennedys (qq.v.), yet having been able to raise money among those moved by his style, for use by political candidates. Former Vice-President Spiro T. Agnew (q.v.) dedicated his apologia to Sinatra. Entertainment became one touchstone of American democracy's capacity to discriminate among its conspicuous figures, with respect to standards of deportment and roles in society. See also Popular Arts.

ENTREPRENEURS, adapted from the French, especially applied to capitalists of the post-Civil War generation. Unlike John Jacob Astor, of an earlier period, they depended less on governmental prerogatives, preferring to make their fortunes by appealing to public willingness to support their ventures, through purchase of stocks and bonds. Unlike financiers of later vintage, they acted with high individuality in projecting and organizing the building of railroads, factories, mining enterprises, and towns; they were originators, rather than inheritors; the difference would be between John Pierpont Morgan (q.v.) and John Pierpont Morgan, Jr., between John D. Rockefeller (q.v.) and, John D. Rockefeller, Jr. Still later would come the "Managerial Revolution" (q.v.), when power would be wielded not so much by persons with money, as, it was claimed, by persons with authority.

ENVIRONMENT, held responsible for social ills; thus, Bernard Shaw's (q.v.) epigram that the one crime is poverty, implying that its eradication would eradicate crime: a view strongly associated with social reform theories and distinguished from the thinking of psychoanalysts (q.v.) who hold that man's actions are determined by more basic and largely unconscious motives and compulsions. Although the latter concepts are held in disesteem by Marxist thinkers, it is not held contradictory by social reformers to believe that the sub-conscious can be coped with by competent and socially-minded mental health (q.v.) specialists. In the 1970's, this concept gave way to that of environmentalists, especially as supported by the U.S. Environmental Protection Agency, which, for example, exercised its power by in 1980 assessing three Washington State pulp mills civil penalties of $785,000 for pollution. Differences between private environmentalists and government, however, were seen in the protests of the Society for Animal Protective Legislation and the Interior Department's Fish and Wildlife Service, when the latter lifted a six-year ban on imports of kangaroos and kangaroo products, on grounds that kangaroos were more numerous than had been previously believed. Both agencies were more concerned for the survival aspect of conservation than for the benefits to human kind by a better social environment, as in the earlier definition of environment: a goal which had been preempted by the welfare state ideal (q.v.) which often patently had not produced improved environments. Robert Cahn, Footprints on the Planet: a Search for an Environmental Ethic (1978); M. Stalley, ed., Patrick Geddes: Spokesman for the Environment (1972); James Ridgeway, Who Owns the Earth (1980); Roderick Nash, ed., Environment and Americans (1979);R. Kelley et al., The Economic Superpowers and the Environment (1976).

EPIC, see Sinclair, Upton.

EPITHETS, a means of social control intended to separate the "ins" from the "outs" (q.v.), to express individual egos, to develop personal advantages. Epithets can be thought, or suggested with confidential smiles. They need not even pretend to reflect negative group characteristics. "Shmoe," "nit-wit," even "fool," will do though they be patently inaccurate, if they represent a group judgement or propaganda. Humanitarians can be inhumane, and liberals illiberal, if they fall in with inappropriate clichés, slipping easily into "fat-bellied capitalists," "labor rat," "labor faker" (q.v.), and the like. World War I produced many wounding epithets, including "slacker" and "yellow-back" (q.v.), Negroes have been pelted with epithets, being termed "buck," to suggest animalism, and "darkey," to emphasize color; their friends have been scorned as "niggerworshippers." Liberals have fought tolerance of the word "nigger," and taught their youngsters to recite a popular verse as "catch a tiger by the toe." A long series of epithets, sometimes pronounced good-naturedly, but resented by liberals as inhibiting mutual self-respect, include: Hunky (labor of Slavic origin; also Bohunk); Dago (Spaniards; from Diego); Guinny (from Guinea; an Italian; also Wop); Yids (from Yiddish; Jews); Spik (Spaniard); Frog or Frenchie, for Frenchman; Mex or Greaser, for Mexican; and, in a return compliment, Gringo, for Americans. Even colors carry invidious connotation, when invidiousness is sought: yellow, white, pale-face. C. P. Flynn, Insult and Society: Patterns of Comparative Interaction (1976); Insult Dictionary: How to Snarl Back in Five Languages (1970).

EQUAL RIGHTS AMENDMENT, a project of Women's Lib (q.v.) partisans in the 1970s, more specifically of NOW, intended to ensure constitutional privileges. Supported by President Carter (q.v.) and his wife, the Amendment was resisted by women of the Stop ERA Committee who feared its social and legal effects, and by legislators who doubted its usefulness. Although failing of victory in the constitutional time alloted, the Amendment was granted a controversial Congressional time extension. In May of 1980 it failed a crucial Illinois legislative ratification, where it was also disgraced by a NOW partisan, a Chicago business woman who attempted to bribe a legislator with $1,000 to vote in its favor. It continued to have Presidential support, though from a "lame duck" (q.v.) Executive.

EQUAL RIGHTS PARTY, the name for several minor parties. The Loco-Focos (q.v.) also carried the name. In 1872, Victoria Woodhull (q.v.) was nominated for President of the United States by a group bearing the name, with Frederick Douglass (q.v.) for Vice-President. The effort scarcely had symbolic significance, because of the character of the woman. More consequential was the nomination of Belva A. Lockwood (q.v.) for President in 1884 and 1888, by the Equal Rights Party of California. Lockwood conducted a sensible and educational campaign in both instances, and merited the title of the first woman who had run for the Presidency.

EQUALITY, a controversial concept stated in classic terms in the opening passages of the Declaration of Independence (q.v.). It has been held that Jefferson (q.v.) did not believe all people were in fact equal, but only in law, which would, however, take their inequality of conditions and capacities into account. Reformers have been generally sanguine about the ability of people to improve, given adequate opportunities, have held, therefore, that equality could be pursued as an ideal goal. Radicals have been more sweeping in demands for equality, accusing a reactionary civilization of repressing deserving elements of the lower classes, and preventing them from coming into their own. George Orwell (q.v.) was ironic about the capacity of the radicals to do better than the civilization they wished to supersede; he believed they would tyrannize over their followers; he gave it as a guiding principle of his nightmare utopia (q.v.) that in it all people were equal, but some people were more equal than others; see also Abstract Terms.

ERA, see Equal Rights Amendment.

ERA OF GOOD FEELING (1816-1824), used to designate the Administrations of President James Monroe, though highlighted by crises over the entrance of Missouri into the Union, a duel between John Randolph and Henry Clay, economic unrest and other problems; it better described the political exhaustion of the political contestants than their goodwill.

ERDMAN ACT (1898), Congress established machinery for mediating industrial disputes between employees and employers of railroads involved in interstate commerce. It was superseded in 1913 by the Newlands Act, which established the U.S. Board of Mediation and Conciliation, which, however, proved incapable of providing satisfaction; this resulted in the agitation which caused passage of the Adamson Act (q.v.). In 1934, the U.S. Board was superseded by the National Mediation Board, whose major purpose was to concern itself for differences between employers and employees which might threaten to stop traffic or in any other way interrupt the commercial purpose of the railroads.

"ERIE WAR, THE," a battle in the stock-market which used the Erie Railroad as pawn (1866-8), it pitted Cornelius Vanderbilt against a combination of buccaneering entrepreneurs. The sordid maneuvers involved were detailed in Charles Francis Adams, Jr.'s, *Chapters of Erie* (1871).

ERNST, MORRIS L. (1888-   ), lawyer in liberal cases, among others, particularly concerned for censorship (q.v.). He worked with the American Civil Liberties Union, served as arbiter in the great New York taxicab strike of 1934, was counsel for the American Newspaper Guild when it organized that year and after, and was adviser to other unions. He acted in behalf of the C.I.O. (q.v.) in 1938 to prevent Mayor Frank Hague of Jersey City from interfering with such of its activities as picketing and distributing leaflets. President Truman later appointed him to his Civil Rights Commission. Among his works were (with Pare Lorentz [q.v.]) *Censored* (1930), (with A. Lindey) *Hold Your Tongue* (1932) and *The Censor Marches On* (1939), and *The First Freedom* (1946). See also his reminiscent *The Best is Yet . . .* (1945).

ESCAPISM, preferred by cultural figures interested in reform in describing other figures in culture who are less so; thus, Upton Sinclair often reproved talented scribes for failing to strike a blow for truth as he saw it. Reformers themselves have often been less austere; Charles Edward Russell (q.v.), in *An Hour of American Poetry* (1929), enjoyed sometimes debatably good verse, having nothing to do with society's needs, on the grounds that it was "art." To what extent abstract art (q.v.) was escapist is debatable. See also, Art and Society, Literature and Social Reform. In general, escapism needs to be distinguished from individualism (q.v.).

ESCH-CUMMINS RAILROAD BILL, the Transportation Act of 1920, the U.S. government's grand effort to return the railroads to private industry, following the experience of government-ownership during the World War recently concluded. The government treated the railroads generously, guaranteeing them from five and one-half to six percent profit on the book value of the property, which included billions of dollars in over-valued stock. It set down any strike by railroad employees as constituting a conspiracy, with heavy reprisals threatened. A Railway Labor Board was set up to fix wages, hours, and conditions. The railroads were organized, through the Interstate Commerce Commission, into a number of gigantic systems, and efforts made to have them pool excess profits for the benefit of weaker lines. This program in voluntary cooperation was a failure, and the feeble sums contributed were returned. See also Railroad Shopmen's Strike (1922).

ESPERANTO, a universal language invented in the late nineteenth century, by Professor L. Zamenhof, a Russian scholar. Although intended to facilitate communication and thus provide added encouragement to peace and understanding, it, and similarly-directed systems, attracts the support of small groups of theoretists and enthusiasts.

ESPIONAGE, see Hiss Case.

ESPIONAGE ACT (1917), a war-time measure intended to discourage traffic with the enemy or efforts to impede the conduct of the war by inciting others to refuse cooperation with the military services. The Act also permitted the exclusion from the mails of matter deemed harmful to the conduct of the war. The Act was sustained by the U.S. Supreme Court; see Schenck v. United States; see also Sedition Act of 1918.

ESTABLISHMENT, borrowed from the British tradition of Church and State ties, but in America referring to the central powers in government, and their interrelations with media and popular tribunes. Harvard University loomed large during the

Kennedy (q.v.) Administration; later Establishments were less taken with "Harvards." Brookings Institution, influential in Democratic eras, expected not to be influential with Reagan (q.v.) in control; the Heritage Foundation expected to be. The "Eastern Establishment" was seen as a New York-based conglomeration of liberal-minded Republicans which exercised strength in large political decisions; see A. M. Ducovny, *The Establishment Dictionary, from Agnew to Zsa Zsa* (1971); Art Buchwald, *The Establishment Is Alive and Well in Washington* (1969); Leonard Silk and Mark Silk, *The American Establishment* (1980).

ETHICS AND SOCIAL REFORM have been associated, protagonists for new viewpoints and programs striving to overcome skeptical suggestions that they are merely seeking new ways to assert themselves, or that their programs will upset established social gains and demoralize society. See Florence Kelley (q.v.), *Some Ethical Gains Through Legislation* (1905), which discusses children's "right" to childhood, women's "right" to the ballot, the "right" of people to leisure (q.v.), and other "rights." (See Right.) Howard Selsam, *Socialism and Ethics* (1943) offered a communist interpretation of ethical standards. In 1961, the Adlai E. Stevenson (q.v.) Foundation was set up by Stevenson's admirers to "undertake a searching study of ethical traditions and . . . seek to discover how these concepts can help us cope with the urgent problems of our day." Problems in science and government created dilemmas of ethics and loyalty. To whom did a nuclear physicist owe his first duty, to the government or industry, or to his view of what served the general public? Investigation of genes seemed likely to influence the formation of human beings; how ought it to be pursued? Journalists were found to have acted as agents to the FBI; were they thus being untrue to their newspaper obligations? It was believed by concerned scientists and others that codes of conduct needed to be refined and given official sanction which would create controls within society for clarifying and implementing such issues. A strange work by a well-known "behaviorist," B. F. Skinner, *Beyond Freedom and Dignity* (1971) in effect judged that freedom and dignity were outmoded concepts, which needed to be replaced by efficient social modes and procedures. K. E. Boulding, *Beyond Economics: Essays on Society, Religion, and Ethics* (1968); Stephen D. Ross, *In pursuit of Moral Value* (1974).

ETHNICS, an old topic in America, composed as it has been of minority groups, mixing and intermixing. The struggle against slavery highlighted Negroes, and the coming of the "New" Immigration (q.v.) highlighted southern Europeans. The rage whipped up in behalf of Negroes in the 1960s dimmed the fact of their being one of many ethnic elements in the community, but the mounting anger of dissatisfied Indians, then Italians, Poles, and others, and the excessive and incompetent attention paid to Negroes diminished interest in them, and required their leaders to broaden their demand for consideration as due all needy elements. An odd element was the poor white people of the region designated as Appalachia, who were patently in need of regard, but who were passed over as "white," and thus of a favored class. Hispanics, by sheer number, as pouring into the United States from Puerto Rico, the Caribbean, and Mexico promised to become a major force in the American ethnic configuration. See also Racism. Philip Rosen, *The Neglected Dimension: Ethnicity in American Life (1979)*; (1979); Thomas Sowell, ed., *American Ethnic Groups* (1978); Andrew Greeley, *Ethnicity, Denomination, and Inequality* (1976); W. J. Wilson, *The Declining Significance of Race* (1978); S. Thernstrom, ed., *Harvard Encyclopedia of American Ethnic Groups* (1980).

ETHIOPIAN WAR, prosecuted by Benito Mussolini (q.v.) in 1935; an example of imperialism and fascist aggression, also of the impotence of the League of Nations (q.v.), to which the Emperor Haile Selassie futilely appealed for aid. A prelude to World War II, it instructed western nations in fascist morals and attitudes.

ETIQUETTE in social relations and expression changed as

democracy advanced, affecting even the discourse of drug users and "life style" experimenters. However, the demeaning of "genteel" (*q.v.*) standards of etiquette in no way diminished its necessity, affecting social tendencies and politics. Thus, sexual experimenters moved from 1960s unqualified demands for freedom, to "commitment" to sex partners in the late 1970s. Forthright atheists (*q.v.*) found themselves defining terms of agreement and disagreement with "existentialist" friends who had become "seekers," or Unitarians. Republicans during the 1980 elections avoided identification with Richard M. Nixon (*q.v.*), and Democrats, sensing shifts in public feeling, hesitated how best to exploit him as an issue, some holding to the concept of the "disgraced" former President, others more tentatively making do with the "flawed" former President format.

EUGENICS, the study for improving the breed of human beings by crossing the best elements of male and female, first used by Sir Francis Galton in 1883. Although an aristocratic concept, and as such anathema to democratic social reformers concerned for the rights and distinctions of the "masses," it has attracted the regard of some earlier social reformers; *cf.* Wright, Henry C., and Noyes, John Humphrey. The Eugenics Committee of the United States is a national body affiliated with the International Commission on Eugenics. The subject is also the concern of the National Eugenics Society. See also Euthanasia. D. J. Ingle, *Who Should Have Children?* (1973); J. Robitscher, ed., *Eugenic Sterilization* (1973).

EUROCOMMUNISM, a 1979 idea, promising Marxist action in western capitalist circumstances. Italian communists, seeking elections in Italy's demoralized state, were critical of the Soviet's harsh treatment of dissidents (*q.v.*) and of its invasion of Afghanistan (*q.v.*). French communists split, some claiming an independence of Moscow policy, others identifying with it. Spanish and British communists, though orthodox on Marxist tenets and antagonism to the United States, agreed that the Afghanistan adventure was deplorable. Overall, however, the parties showed little original thinking giving promise of concern for national and European interests, and other communist parties followed docilely the Moscow line. "Eurocommunism" was less evocative in 1980 than it had appeared the year before.

EUROPEAN ECONOMIC COMMUNITY, an effort to create unity of purpose among western European nations. It offered a forum for many problems other than economic, including human rights, sex equality in wages and individual treatment, famine relief as in Uganda, and questions of attitude toward the PLO (*q.v.*). At its European Parliament in Strasbourg, the nine associated nations discussed and ruled upon a wide variety of issues. Most urgent were the Common Market relations, to which farmers of the associated nations were acutely sensitive. Great Britain and France were at particular loggerheads, so much so that Great Britain, a latecomer into the EEC, and aggravated by a painful burden of $9 billion contribution to EEC's workings, was under Labour pressure to secede from the Common Market. Among other problems was that of Turkey, which sought entree into the EEC—granted its foe Greece in 1981—and which had more than half a million Turks laboring in European countries: with families, over two million, mostly in West Germany. Although the ideals of European unity were much higher than their achievement, there were palpable gains, in ending customs duties, in limiting monetary confusions, and ironing out some of the troubles attending agricultural exchange. The EEC in 1981 was far from an impotent agency. Paul Armitage, *The Common Market* (1978); Max Kohnstamm, *The European Community and Its Role in the World* (1964); J. W. Markham et al., *The Common Market: Friend or Competitor?* (1964); Charles Ransom, *The European Community and Eastern Europe* (1973).

EUTHANASIA, a controversial method of putting wrecked, subnormal, or otherwise "unfit" human beings out of their misery or unrelatedness to human society by painless extermination. As identified with arbitrary power over life and death, it is challenged by humanitarians. It is a technique, rather than a social reform program. Its possibilities have probably been retarded by being identified with the mass murders, carried out with advanced technological means in some cases, by medical men under the Hitler regime. J. A. Behnke and Sissela Bok, eds., *The Dilemmas of Euthanasia* (1975); Joseph and Julia Quinlan, *Karen Ann* (1977).

EVANGELICISM, see Revivalism and Reform.

EVANS, GEORGE HENRY (1805-1855), labor editor, came to the United States in 1820. He edited what were among the first labor papers in America: *The Man* (c. 1822), *The Working Man's Advocate* (1829-45), *The Daily Sentinel* (1837), and *Young America* (1837 ff.). His agrarian (*q.v.*) views were similar to Henry George's (*q.v.*). He was a freethinker and equalitarian, and though less concerned for the Negro than the white man, denounced all slavery, chattel or wage. He favored an anti-monopoly program, free land for willing workers, abolition of imprisonment for debt, and delivery of mails on Sunday (*qq.v.*). In 1840, he published *A History of the Origin and Program of the Working Man's Party* (*q.v.*). He opposed associationism (*q.v.*) as inadequate for working men's needs. His brother, *Frederick Williams Evans* (1808-1893), as a youth was enthusiastic over Robert Owen's (*q.v.*) program, and joined a colony in Massillon, Ohio. He then worked with Frances Wright, Robert D. Owen, and his brother in New York, and helped edit the latter's papers. A visit to a Shaker (*q.v.*) community converted him; his later *Autobiography of a Shaker* (1869) explained his views. For over sixty years, he was a Shaker elder, noted for his leadership abilities, eloquence, and literary talents; see his *Tests of Divine Inspiration* (1853), *Ann Lee, a Biography* (1858), *Celibacy from the Shaker Standpoint* (1866), and *Shaker Communism* (1871).

"EVER-NORMAL GRANARY," a concept provided for in the Agricultural Adjustment Act of 1938. Instead of forcing the farmer to dump his surplus crops on the market, thus depressing their price, it permitted him to borrow money from the Commodity Credit Corporation on the surpluses (*q.v.*), and store them through government arrangements, selling the crops during drought and other periods when the prices of the commodities rose to "parity" (*q.v.*), or higher. Thus, excess crops would not be a burden, but a social asset, ready for use when needed. Nevertheless, surpluses continued to be more embarrassing than gratifying.

EVERETT, WESLEY, see Centralia Riot.

"EVERY MAN A KING," see Long, Huey P.

EVERYBODY'S, one of the great muckraking (*q.v.*) magazines, it published Charles Edward Russell's expose of the Beef Trust, "The Greatest Trust in the World," and Upton Sinclair on the same subject, it published Tom Lawson's epochal *Frenzied Finance,* Russell's round-the-world inquiry into cooperative experiments, Judge Ben Lindsey's "The Beast and the Jungle," his story of privileged interests as he knew them, and other major sensations (*qq.v.* for the above). Following the failure of the popular magazines, it deteriorated, finally becoming *Romance Magazine.*

EVOLUTION AND REVOLUTION (1898), by Élisée Reclus, which seeks to find the two concepts as complementary, rather than in opposition; a concept seen with greater approval by evolutionists than by revolutionists.

EVOLUTIONARY SOCIALISM, see Socialism and Democracy, Revisionism.

EWBANK, THOMAS (1792-1870), manufacturer and inventor who became U.S. Commissioner of Patents. His Report of 1850 was famous for its effort to see in inventions the cure for human ills, slavery included, and contained other, controversial views intended to advance reform.

EX PARTE MERRYMAN, *EX PARTE* MILLIGAN, see Merryman, *Ex Parte,* Milligan, *Ex Parte.*

EXCESS PROFITS TAX, one of the steps developed under a free economy which its friends hoped would enable it to curb the excesses of capitalism without espousing socialism. (See also Mixed Economy.) An excess profits tax was in effect during World War I, but was repealed in 1921. The New Deal (*q.v.*)

undertook to create equity of income and tax responsibilities, and reintroduced an excess profit tax which continued, with augmented measures, as a permanent feature of the national economy. World War II and the cold war, thereafter, created dramatic charges on profits, but though "I'm working for the government" became a popular byword, resourceful citizens in the upper categories, with the aid of their lawyers, found numerous ways and means for developing a substantial relationship with their profits.

EXECUTIVE PRIVILEGE, a momentous factor in Watergate (*q.v.*), President Nixon arguing to the end that his private intercourse was necessarily secret, if government was to procede effectively. He was undermined by the unprecedented preemption of his taped conversations, which exposed his privacy to his enemies. That the issue was basically political, rather than constitutional, was shown by contrasting "executive privilege" under President Eisenhower (*q.v.*), who prevented Department of Defense employees from cooperating with Senator McCarthy (*q.v.*), to the satisfaction of liberals, with their rejection of Nixon's claim to the same privilege. The key to executive privilege, then, was the status of the President and the power structure in Congress. Thus, "Billygate" (*q.v.*) could readily have forced President Carter into a difficult legal entanglement. Congressional complacency, however, relieved him of his problems. G. Perrett, *Executive Privilege* (1974); R. Berger, *Executive Privilege: a Constitutional Myth* (1974); Adam C. Breckenridge, *Executive Privilege: Presidential Control over Information* (1974).

EXILES OF FLORIDA, THE (1858), by Joshua Reed Giddings (*q.v.*), a sympathetic account of the sorrows of fugitive slaves to West Florida in 1816, who had made fellowship with Seminole Indians. They had taken refuge in a fort near Pensacola. An American gunboat landed a red-hot shot in the fort's magazine and blew it to bits, killing almost all of its inhabitants.

EXISTENTIALISM, see Sartre, Jean-Paul.

EXPANSIONISM, see Anti-Imperialism.

EXPANSIONISTS, a general term for imperialists, first used popularly to designate those who, in 1899, favored President McKinley's decision, on January 5, 1899, "to extend the military rule of the United States over the whole of the Philippine Islands"; see also Anti-Expansionists.

EXPATRIATES, notably to England, France, and Italy were famous in the post-Civil War period, and also following World War I. The first wave was composed of well-to-do and leisure-class personages; their most distinguished product was Henry James, Jr. The second was more representative of the whole American culture. Both were critical of its insularity, unsophisticated quality, gauche outlook; the first emphasized Old World artistic achievements, the second, adventurous living and experimentation, though art as well. Both emphasized individuality, rather than social reform, though their critical attitude toward America implied reform. The second being more democratically composed, entertained vague views favoring equality with the rich, for geniuses, a sympathy toward some socialist tenets, and other muddled and sporadic impulses, as in the writings of Ernest Hemingway. T.S. Eliot became less an expatriate than an Englishman. Ezra Pound's (*q.v.*) *Exile* (1927) expressed something of the mood of a professional expatriate. Gertrude Stein, Malcolm Cowley, Glenway Wescott, Samuel Putnam, Henry Miller, and Harold Stearns were several of those who maintained the expatriate establishment, until the depression of the 1930's made them less welcome abroad. Alan Holder, *Three Voyagers in Search of Europe: a Study of Henry James, Ezra Pound, T. S. Eliot* (1976); Ernest Earnest, *Expatriates and Patriots* (1968).

EXPLOITATION, a word in bad odor among reformers, expressing for them the desire of people to draw sustenance from others, especially in an industrial situation, without giving a comparable return. Capitalism was traditionally denounced as a system of exploitation, willing to "exhaust" human beings as miners might exhaust a lode. Intellectuals have been some-what less sensitive than labor reformers, thinking it no shame to "pick somebody's brains." See also Welfare State.

EXPOSE, originally exposé, from the French, meaning a revelation of hidden facts, now often printed without the accent; usually connoting sensational matter, of personal, lurid moment, or involving the public interest. Most significantly identified with the literature of "exposure," notably muckraking (*q.v.*), less significantly with sensationalism for its own sake. See also *Independent, The.*

EXPROPRIATION, a program of socialists who conceive that since large estates and industrial holdings have been stolen from the masses of the people, it will be proper for a socialist government to take them back in the name of the people, without compensation; a basic aspect of a nationalization (*q.v.*) program.

EXTRADITION, the demand of a nation upon another nation for the return of a fugitive who had sought asylum; used in connection with criminals, but also with reformers who have found themselves threatened at home. During the nineteenth century, numerous fugitives from Russia, Italy, Germany, and elsewhere sought asylum elsewhere, because of deeds of terror they had committed or plotted, because of publications which put the police on their trails, and for other circumstances which seemed to make them a threat to the governments of their native lands. Great Britain was a popular haven for fugitives, though Paris also attracted them; there, however, they could sometimes be more easily reached for assassination by agents of their government. Much the same tradition of asylum obtained in the twentieth century. In the United States, the problem was best known in terms of the "rendition" of fugitive slaves to their masters, the term extradition being confined to white people being demanded by other states. In the twentieth century, Negro escapees, as from the chain gangs composed of convict labor (*q.v.*), achieved the status of persons demanded for extradition, which was often granted. During World War II, the movement of armies across great areas of the world broke down ordinary national sovereignty, and raised questions of the rights of great masses of displaced Chinese, Russians, Poles, Germans, and others. The operation of the Grand Alliance (*q.v.*), for example, compelled the return of many Russians to Russia who had not given loyalty to that country; it is likely that many of them were punished or executed for their actions. In the 1970s the problem of extradition was complicated by the rise of terrorism (*q.v.*), of the highjacking of planes, and other results of modern despair, weak social control, and the temptations created by instant fame offered by television. Efforts to create uniform policies were limited by national self-interest.

F

FABIANISM, developed by the Fabian Society, first organized in London, 1884, by Sidney and Beatrice Webb, George Bernard Shaw, Edward R. Pease, and many others. It looked toward full socialism, but emphasized reason, education, and the half-measures of immediate demands, municipal ownership, factory and other work ordinances, and the like. It attracted a knowledgeable body of journalists, professors, and others, including laborers, who, along with trade unionists, helped build up the body of the British parliamentary labor movement. For a list of Fabian publications, see Anne Fremantle, *This Little Band of Prophets: the British Fabians* (1960). Most famous were the *Fabian Essays* (1889), edited by Bernard Shaw *(q.v.)*, and published in an American edition (1894), with an introduction by Edward Bellamy *(q.v.)*. "Fabianism" derived from Quintus Fabjus Maximus, a Roman general noted for his cautious policy of "making haste slowly." A. M. McBriar, *Fabian Socialism and English Politics* (1962).

FACTIONALISM, identified with doctrinaire movements *(q.v.)*, identified with elements critical of the leadership of the group, or the principles of the majority; usually evoked to curb debate.

FACTORY AND WORKSHOP ACT (1875), a milepost in British legislation on the subject which summed up the experience of the century to create a labor code dealing with standards for factory operation, the labor of women and children, and other matters, including inspection for violations. Although it left many areas unregulated, it provided the basis for criticism and change.

FACTORY LEGISLATION was a late development, arising out of increased numbers of workers, the rise of unions, and the development of reform movements able to educate the public and influence legislation. Problems arising out of factory conditions included woman and child labor, sanitary facilities, occupational hazards, compensation for injuries, as well as wages, hours and security. The cigar workers of New York, in the 1880's led a fight to end work at home; which created extreme hazards to health, as well as family life. The Fourteenth Amendment was invoked against legislation ending this evil. The battle for unions which workers maintained was a battle for strength to influence employers and law-makers. Such cases as Lochner v. New York asserted the inability of legislation to set up minimum safeguards for workers. Nevertheless, the "Brandeis brief," among other social achievements, declared that the facts of life were more important them abstract theories of freedom, and such horrors as the Triangle Fire forced society to face up, to a degree, to a few of its obligations. Minimum laws—though inadequate and often debatable in principle—were erected to set some limit to the shameful possibilities in factory work; they made possible such careers as that of Frances Perkins. Though they were fought by the employer class in the name of freedom and the American Way, the increasingly complex nature of society forced the creation of a skein of laws which would help give some stability to labor. The National Labor Relations Board was an agency to give labor a practiced and directed consideration of its wants. See also American Association for Labor Legislation. *(Qq.v., for the above.)*

FAGIN, a controversial character in Charles Dickens's *Oliver Twist:* a Jewish scoundrel who made thieves of children. The character has concerned social reformers as a problem in esthetics. Had Dickens the right to portray as disreputable a personage as Jewish? In mass-media, like the films, the pres-

entation of Fagin as a Jew has been opposed by groups fearful of its effect on audiences.

FAIR DEAL, THE, President Truman's *(q.v.)* effort at adapting the New Deal *(q.v.)* to a new time. War prosperity and patriotism had produced a new conservatism. He sought to maintain price controls *(q.v.)*, but was largely defeated. The Internal Security Act of 1951 *(q.v.)*, passed over his veto. The Full Employment Act of 1946 *(q.v.)* was intended to expunge memories of the late depression but failed to do so. Truman projected a long list of bills for ensuring democracy at the polls, coping with housing needs, and with civil rights. Fair employment practices fared little better under him than it had under his predecessor. But the Marshall Plan, the Point Four Program *(qq.v.)*, and possibly the Korean *(q.v.)* no-win program which cost General MacArthur his command, and Truman's manifest desire to serve America promised well for his reputation.

FAIR EMPLOYMENT PRACTICES COMMITTEE, created in 1941 by President Franklin D. Roosevelt's Executive Order 8802; the agitation of A. Philip Randolph *(q.v.)*, and the imminence of war, forced this governmental action. The Committee was empowered to investigate complaints of discrimination, especially against Negroes. The coming of war and the need for labor inspired some action of this Committee, but by 1943 it had weakened in effectiveness. A conference of Negro leaders that year inspired a new Executive Order setting up a new committee in the Office of Emergency Management, and emphasizing the need for equal treatment, especially under government contracts. Continued difficulties caused Negroes to fight for a "permanent FEPC." Bills offered in Congress were killed, and in 1946, Congress refused funds for its work. A number of states, notably New York, enacted F.E.P.C. legislation, as did a number of cities. Although the movement for a "permanent FEPC" did not achieve its aim, the efforts expended had influenced employment practices, clarified issues respecting the relations between free enterprise and the rights of citizens, and given the latter a permanent slogan: F.E.P.C.; see Louis Ruchames, *Race, Jobs & Politics* (1953).

FAIR LABOR STANDARDS ACT (1938), also known as the Wages and Hours Law, set a minimum wage *(q.v.)* which by 1961 had risen to one dollar and twenty-five cents for large categories of workers, though others remained to be reached. It also established a ceiling on hours of forty per week, to be reached by stages from forty-four hours, with time and a half overtime. In addition, it outlawed labor for children under sixteen years of age (see Child Labor), and stipulated safety for those up to eighteen years of age, a law which was upheld in United States v. Darby Lumber Company *(q.v.)*. See also Leisure and the Work-Day.

FAIRBANK, CALVIN (1816-1898), an aide to Negro fugitives from slavery, who made several trips into Kentucky and Missouri for underground railroad purposes. Seized, he served long in a Kentucky prison, and was a symbol of abolitionist martyrdom. See his *Rev. Calvin Fairbank during Slavery Times. How He "Fought the Good Fight" to Prepare "the Way"* (1890).

FAMILY, THE, came conspicuously into question during the 1970s, due to heightened and official issues of women's and men's roles, the abortion controversy, turmoil created by youth, and two-job families which, in effect, disrupted the basic family. Polls of 1980 showed Americans as desirous of family life, but believing it had deteriorated badly in the past fifteen years. The National Commission on Working Women—a majority of women—showed no more than seven percent of American households in the older pattern of father working, mother caring for the home. Other polls revealed fathers as ambivalent in their concept of fatherhood duties. Laws governing juveniles were often not synchronized with social attitudes calculated to rebuild a family structure. Day care center activists, absorbed in their cause, assumed that the traditional" home was obsolete. Although finances were one of the bases of family life—a family of four needed, it was estimated, $20,187 to live as well as it had in 1970 on $10,000—many questions revolving around family were unresolved. President Carter's (q.v.) White House Conference on Families, critics believed, was "loaded" with ERA and other feminist activists, and concluded with pro-abortion and "life-style" recommendations, including free "sexual preferences or biological ties," identified as endorsing homosexual relations. Their further recommendations were protested as merely demanding more government aids, rather than family build-up: an approach which, in the nature of the 1980 conservative backlash, seemed unrealistic (qq.v. for above). G. G. Fein and K. A. Clarke-Stewart, *Day Care in Context* (1973); T. D. Yawkey and Carol Seefeldt, *Day Care: Planning and Implementing* (1972 ed.); William M. Kephart, *Family, Society, and the Individual* (1972); Gerald H. Zuk and Ivan Boszormenyi-Nagy, eds., *Family Therapy and Disturbed Families* (1967); J. Farago and S. Farago, *Family: Vital Force or Outworn Institution?* (1975).

FAMINE, a classic type of social catastrophe, the result of drought, war, siege, poverty, and other natural or man-made conditions. Europe suffered many famines over the centuries; China was a land of famines. Russia suffered a devastating famine as a result of World War I and the civil war which followed the Bolshevik Revolution. The United States sent food under the auspices of a relief commission headed by Herbert Hoover (q.v.). Radicals later maintained the charge that he had used his powers as an instrument for harming the Bolshevik government, a charge which he vigorously denied. There was famine in the United States, in the 1930's, because of depressed conditions coupled with crop failures and drought, and emergency aid became necessary. Henry A. Wallace (q.v.) in 1961 proposed an "ever-normal granary" (q.v.) for world use against famine. The United Nations World Food Council twenty years later had to cope with politics, revolutions, and disrupted primitive conditions to reach the hungry.

FANATICISM, identified with intemperate concern for a principle or deed, a social or religious obsession; once readily applied by upholders of the *status quo* to persons who, like socialists, made appeals to reason. Conservatives who persisted in seeking desperate solutions in competing with the world communist offensives were viewed less as conservatives than as fanatics; the Presidential candidacy of Barry Goldwater in 1964 was seen in that light. Reagan (q.v.) in 1980 denied he was a Goldwater conservative, whom foes could depict as a "radical," that is, of the "radical right."

FANEUIL HALL, market-place and meeting hall in Boston, identified with democratic assemblies on matters of social concern; often called "the Cradle of Liberty," because of its use during the era of the American revolution.

FARMER-LABOR PARTY, THE, grew out of the National Labor Party, organized in 1919; its name was changed in 1920. It had Presidential electors in seventeen states. In some of these, it approved Nonpartisan League (q.v.) candidates. In South Dakota, it was identical with the League.

FARMERS AND REFORM have been largely related in connection with measures intended to augment free enterprise. They were necessarily involved in most major reform actions before the Civil War since they represented an overwhelming majority of the population. In the post-Civil War era, they protested railroad monopoly, the disparity between prices for farm products and the price of manufactured goods, and organized the Granger Movement, the Farmers' Alliances, and the Populist offensive (qq.v.). They had a limited concern for the efforts of labor (q.v.). Their representatives and sons were strong in the muckraking movement and the Progressive Era (qq.v.) as a whole. They fought for plans which would give them an equitable portion of the national income. The Federal Farm Loan Act (1916) activated the government in their behalf, though in limited fashion. Following wartime prosperity, they demanded government aid in supporting farm prices. The McNary-Haugen Bills (q.v.) were defeated. Farm consolidations in the 1920's increased the number of tenant farmers (q.v.), but they, as well as the direct farm laboring class, received little regard. The Agricultural Adjustment Administration (q.v.) was a major government effort in reform. The National Farmers Union, generally known as the Farmers Union, (q.v.) led the fight for government support of agriculture. In 1949, Secretary of Agriculture Charles F. Brannan presented a plan which was heatedly debated; in effect, he sought to put the government behind a program of subsidies to farmers which would have assured them of a high return on their investments. The "Brannan Plan" failed in Congress. Brannan became general counsel for the Farmers Union. As in the beginning, the farmer's efforts continued to center on the independent farmer; migratory agricultural labor (q.v.) found no leaders among farmers. See Rural America.

FARMERS' HOLIDAY, THE, took place from August to October, 1932, when farmers of Illinois, Wisconsin, Iowa, Nebraska, the Dakotas, and Minnesota withheld their goods from market in order to raise their price. The farmers' revolt was influential in some twenty midwestern states and was a further step toward their organization as a special interest.

FARRELL, JAMES T. (1904-1979), Chicago-born novelist whose Studs Lonigan trilogy (1932-5) contributed to naturalist writing. His long short-story, *Tommy Gallagher's Crusade* (1939) offered vignettes of Irish life in the depression, including its Christian Front (q.v.) aspects. His Marxism found expression in numerous essays, as well as in his defiance of changing intellectual currents under pressure of World War II conditions; see hi. *The League of Frightened Philistines* (1945).

FASCISM, the original doctrine from which derived the more deadly Nazism (q.v.). It was the creation of Benito Mussolini (q.v.), a renegade socialist who in 1919 took as his symbol the *fasces,* rods and axe, carried by the Roman *lictor,* or officer given authority to command obedience to magistrates, and to suppress crime. Thus, *fasces* and *lictor* symbolized authority. In 1922, Mussolini seized power and became *Il Duce,* leader and dictator. He preached Italian nationalism, unity, scorn for weakness, hatred of independent trade unionism, radical politics. He offered, instead, dreams of ancient Roman glory, the corporate state in the form of "syndicates" in which, theoretically, labor and capital worked for common goals, but in which labor took instruction from the state. Mussolini labored to win the women and children to his cause, and had the latter wearing the Fascist blackshirts and carrying daggers at an early age. He massed Italians to listen to his bragging speeches, and posed his jutting jaw for their admiration. He began as Hitler's (q.v.) mentor, the latter taking the title of *Fuehrer* (leader) and promising much of Mussolini's program. During World War II, he ended as Hitler's vassal, upheld by German troops, rescued from vengeful Italians by German agents, and finally abandoned to die. But whereas Nazism was indigenous to Germany, Fascism became the core for similar movements everywhere in the world. Fascist Italy produced a great literary antagonist, Ignazio Silone, whose fiction and insight heartened opponents of fascism; see his *Fontamara, Bread and Wine, The Seed beneath the Snow;* also W. Laquer, ed., *Fascism: a Reader's Guide* (1976).

FASCISM AND REFORM are at least related to the extent that unrest and need did provide fascists with a field for operations. They appealed to restless and frustrated middle-class elements—retail merchants, clerks, and others oppressed by a sense of inferiority and humiliation: elements known by Marxists contemptuously as the *petty-bourgeoisie.* They appealed to demobilized soldiers with situations, to demoralized workers, the *lumpenproletariat* (q.v.). Fascists who hoped to emulate Hitler (q.v.) were not interested in reform, but in revolution — or counter-revolution, as the Marxists had it. George Deatherage, who headed the Knights of the White

Camelia, William D. Pelley, leader of the Silver Shirts, and Gerald B. Winrod of the Ku Klux Klan (q.v.) anticipated war with reformers. But Father Coughlin (q.v.) demanded "social justice," and Huey P. Long (q.v.) promised that every man would be a king, and did undertake social reform measures, among others harmful to Democracy, Dr. Townsend (q.v.) distinctly a reformer, found himself in political association with Coughlin and others of similar tendency. The Nazis (q.v.) themselves had after all, been the National *Socialist* German Workers' Party, and had undoubtedly attracted persons who fancied that it would achieve "national" socialism. See also Birch Society, Butler, Smedley D., Carlson, John Roy.

FATHERS AND SONS (1862), see Nihilism.

F.B.I., see Federal Bureau of Investigation.

F.C.C., see Federal Communications Commission.

F.D.I.C., see Federal Deposit Insurance Corporation.

F.D.R., see Roosevelt, Franklin D.

FEATHERBEDDING, union work rules which limit output or forbid the use of labor-saving devices.

FEBRUARY REVOLUTION (1917), the first, democratic Russian Revolution, which unseated the Czar and was expected to open the way, either for a constitutional monarchy or for a republic. It raised Alexander F. Kerensky (q.v.) to power, and was hailed with pleasure in the United States; it embarrassed Americans interested in intervening in the great war then raging to join in as an ally of the despised Romanoff autocracy. The Provisional Government sought to hold their defeatist troops in the war on the side of the Western Allies, it was dilatory in calling a constitutional assembly, it undertook no steps to consider peasant wants, it negotiated with counter-revolutionists. It drove the revolutionary elements underground. As a result it built up quickly an unpromising reputation with soldiers, sailors, and workers and prepared the way for the October Revolution (q.v.).

FEDERAL AID TO EDUCATION, see Educational Reform.

FEDERAL ART PROJECT, most successful of the Federal Arts Projects (q.v.), being composed in largest part of trained personnel not hampered by bureaucracy. Its director, Holger Cahill, was a competent art museum official interested in folk art, who could deal with temperamental artists as well as with politicians. The F.A.P. developed a program of creative art, exhibitions, and services which made it unique. It had a poster painting project which treated its work artistically. It built up a nation-wide chain of community art centers which brought more Americans into art galleries than ever before, and developed art class adjuncts to the centers. It circulated Project and non-project art for exhibitions. Its creative artists included such names as Joseph Hirsh, Jack Levine, Dong Kingman, and numerous others in oils, etchings, sculpture, and other media. Its Index of American Design collected artifacts for copying from one end of the country to another; much of the best of it was later collected and housed in the Mellon Art Gallery, in Washington, D. C. Its mural project completed such distinguished work as that in the favored spot in the New York Public Library outside the Catalogue Room. Its research project developed the silk-screen process, among other improvements in art media and materials. Nevertheless, the F.A.P. was held in contempt by later advocates of "non-representational" art who held their work worthless, thus concurring in opinion with that of the anti-New Deal partisans. Greta Berman, *The Lost Years: Mural Painting in New York City...Federal Art Project* (1978); F. V. O'Connor, ed., *The New Deal Art Projects* (1972).

FEDERAL ARTS PROJECTS, set up under the W.P.A. (q.v.), and including the Federal Art Project, the Federal Music Project, the Federal Theater Project, and the Federal Writers Project, as well as the Historical Records Survey which involved itself in courthouse records, old plans of public buildings, and other work only nominally related to artistic endeavor.

The Projects were part of the relief operations for white-collar workers, and took in only a small percentage of them. Because "Federal One," as it was sometimes technically called, represented a trifling amount of political patronage, the politicians gave it little attention; this permitted the Projects directors to develop their own standards. Though an insignificant portion of the W.P.A. budget the Projects received an amount of attention totally out of proportion to their number or financial consequence. The Hearst (q.v.) press led the field with accusations of communist control, Projects' receptivity to incompetents, criticism of the price which Projects accomplishments required. Since the aim of the Projects was technically relief, their accomplishments were clear gain. All the projects were permitted a percentage of supervisory aid; the rest of the personnel, whatever their skill were certified for relief. The projects were directly administered from Washington, through state organizations; in 1939, control was turned over to the states, with the Washington office acting in an advisory capacity. With World War II, the project dissolved into war work. Milton Meltzer, *Violins and Shovels* (1976).

FEDERAL BUREAU OF INVESTIGATION (FBI), one of the sensitive agencies of government, made famous by its long-time chief, J. Edgar Hoover (q.v.) by his exploits in catching dangerous criminals, and made controversial by its alertness to the presence and danger to national security of communists. It gathered files on potential (as it judged) transgressors in this respect; see Hoover's *Masters of Deceit* (1958). Like the CIA (q.v.) in foreign matters, the FBI suffered criticism for domestic surveillance from radicals and liberal sympathizers, for example, for entering private houses in its search for Weather Underground (q.v.) fugitives, and for telephone surveillance of political suspects without warrant. The Watergate (q.v.) crisis raised new protests against FBI operations which, in 1976, were outlawed by FBI and Department of Justice guidelines. In 1978, Hoover's successor, L. Patrick Gray, was indicted for violating the civil rights of the Weather Underground, along with two other officials. Nixon (q.v.), testifying in their behalf, argued that "black bag" break-ins were justified because America was at war. Although charges against Gray were dropped, his two associates were given fines, though not jail sentences. Since FBI activities involved overseeing terrorists and domestic desperadoes, Congressional efforts were directed at augmenting FBI powers, with assurances of regard for civil rights. W. W. Turner, *Hoover's F.B.I.* (1970); Nelson Blackstock, ed., *Cointelpro: The FBI's Secret War on Political Freedom* (1976); John T. Ebliff, *The Reform of the FBI Intelligence Activities* (1979); James Munves, *The FBI and the CIA* (1975); W. Mark Felt, *The FBI Pyramid from the Inside* (1979). See also John Ehrlichman, *The Company* (1976).

FEDERAL COMMUNICATIONS COMMISSION, one of the regulatory agencies (q.v.) set up in 1934, and once treated with concern to ensure that it did not interfere with freedom of speech. The F.C.C. manifested no tendency to do so, and was, on the contrary, eager to give the major radio and later television networks as much freedom of operation as they deemed necessary. Whether the F.C.C. had any duties to the public to improve the dignity and service offered received decreasing attention. The networks argued that they served the public, that they often offered "cultural fare" at financial losses, and that such phenomena as "payola" (q.v.) could be best handled by themselves. Discussions over equitable allotments of time to political parties were settled along similar lines. Thus, the networks argued for "education of the public," rather than regulation: a process which seemed unlikely to bring reform of any kind during non-catastrophic eras.

FEDERAL CORRUPT PRACTICES ACT (1939), see Corrupt Practices Act.

FEDERAL DEPOSIT INSURANCE CORPORATION, created in 1933 by the Glass-Steagall Act, and intended to ensure the security of a large percentage of savings, thus avoiding the tragedy of losses such as were incurred with the failure of banks in the preceding years. Banks effected by the Act could ensure their depositors' funds, originally up to five thousand dollars; the amount was doubled by legal amendment in 1951.

FEDERAL EMERGENCY RELIEF ADMINISTRATION, precursor of W.P.A. (*q.v.*), set up in May 1933 to dispense government funds to the states for relief purposes. It began with half a billion dollars; by 1935 had spent three billion dollars. Under Harry L. Hopkins (*q.v.*), it began with direct relief, asking the states to match their expenditures according to their ability; New York contributed much more than any southern state. However, F.E.R.A. began to look beyond the dole (*q.v.*) to work programs which would help relief recipients maintain their sense of self-respect. Some of the work was frankly "make work" so that it would not compete with the work of those who were totally dependent on their own incomes. The operations of the Civil Works Administration (*q.v.*), which used about half the workers on F.E.R.A., helped create a program of work which was later stabilized under W.P.A. The C.W.A. project was a stop-gap measure, and when completed, left its incomplete projects and operations with F.E.R.A. to administer.

FEDERAL FAIR LABOR STANDARDS ACT, see Fair Labor Standards Act.

FEDERAL HIGHWAY ACT, 1955-1956, an act which helped transform the nation by proliferating roads. It hastened the rise of suburbia (*q.v.*), drained the cities of traditional inhabitants, and raised the consumption of motor fuel from forty million gallons in 1950 to 105 million gallons in 1972, thus increasing dependence on foreign oil (*q.v.*).

FEDERAL HOUSING ADMINISTRATION, see Housing Problem, The.

FEDERAL MUSIC PROJECT, one of the Federal Arts Projects (*q.v.*), it provided bands and other ensemble groups for public entertainment. Although it was theoretically capable of the varied operations which characterized the Federal Art Project (*q.v.*), it was mainly an outlet for the Musicians Union. It attracted the least criticism and the least enthusiasm.

FEDERAL SECURITY AGENCY, established in 1939, and coordinating the activities of the Food and Drug Administration, the Public Health Service, the Children's Bureau (*qq.v.*), among other offices. In 1953, its functions were largely taken over by the new U.S. Department of Health, Education, and Welfare, its secretary having Cabinet status.

FEDERAL THEATER PROJECT, the most spectacular of the Federal Arts Projects (*q.v.*), it was the most vulnerable to anti-New Deal (*q.v.*) criticism as hiring incompetents and being a tool in the hands of members of the Communist Party. It produced a number of original plays, the phenomenon of Orson Welles (*q.v.*), and a large number of experimental and traditional plays and entertainments, including a dance project. Its weakness lay in being centered in a few great cities, notably New York, Chicago, and Los Angeles, which lost it its potential support among the run of Americans. Although it sponsored a few "caravans" to bring theater to the hinterland, these were mostly window-dressing to prove the Project's "national" character. Its most original creation was "The Living Newspaper": plays built around such public issues as power, housing, agriculture. These plays employed great numbers of personnel, some of whom had a modicum of dramatic technique and training; others had simply managed to get themselves certified by the welfare authorities for jobs on the project. Such plays as *Triple-A Plowed Under* (*q.v.*) angered conservatives and bored would-be theater people who longed for plays which would permit them better opportunities for exhibitionism. The radical nature of some of the F.T.P.'s enterprises, plus their lack of grassroots support, weakened the Project's ability to resist its critics. The *New York Times* asked: "They need not starve, but must they act?" The F.T.P. brought Hollywood stars to Washington to plead for the Project, but it was the first ended, being "killed" in 1939. See *Federal Theater Plays* (1938).

FEDERAL TRADE COMMISSION, set up in 1914, and charg-ed with the responsibility of preventing unfair competition, deceptive advertising, price discrimination, and the prevention of monopolies. A victory of the Reform Era of the pre-World War I years, it theoretically accomplished with efficiency what the reformers had managed to do by stirring public opinion to demand changes. Now, it appeared, the public was secure. However, that public was composed of business people as well as consumers. In time, the agency was affected by bureaucratic symptoms which could harm as well as help; in 1980, its 1,700 employees and $71 million budget required the same surveillance it gave business people. Pricilla LaBarbera, *Consumers and the Federal Trade Commission* (1977).

FEDERAL WRITERS PROJECT, the most eccentric of the Federal Arts Projects (*q.v.*). Musicians, theater people, and artists presumably had a modicum of training in their crafts; it was difficult to prove that a person was a writer, especially if he had nothing published. Assembly lines — from social workers who certified individuals for relief to particular individuals who set up "residence" in a neighborhood which was administered by a particular social worker — helped staff the Project. It was run by Henry G. Alsberg, who had been interested in cooperatives, and had a considerable patience with varied types of person. A former administrator of the Project observed that no one but Alsberg could have handled so mixed a variety of crack-pots and "odd-balls." Although there was a bit of creative writing sponsored by the project, there was not enough possible to employ the personnel. They were put to work at compiling an "American Guide" to the states, cities, locales. Their work was to differ from matter put out by Chambers of Commerce in accurately reporting history, tours, and relevant information, and in avoiding an advertising approach. The humbler levels of "writers" gathered data out of numerous sources; their superiors put the material into clear, accurate, and readable order. "Trouble-shooters" were brought into specific projects to discover why work lagged or was inadequate. Persons of reputation headed projects, including Lyle Saxon, Vardis Fisher, Harlan Hatcher, Ben A. Botkin, Merle Colby, among many others. The volumes of the American Guide were put out by private publishers, who made various arrangements for use of this public material. Seen together, they made a distinguished set, which could not otherwise have been prepared but by a national project. As with the F.A.P. (*q.v.*), it had to be noted that it had been accomplished essentially on work-relief; that the dole (*q.v.*) could have been given without giving dignity and activity to the Project personnel, and no works resulted. See Botkin, B. A., *American Stuff: an Anthology of Prose and Verse by Members of the Federal Writers' Project* (1937).

FEDERALIST PAPERS (1787-8), one of the most remarkable groups of papers in American political history, probing the question of whether the states should or should not ratify the Constitution of the United States. Composed by Alexander Hamilton, who wrote almost two-thirds of them, James Madison, and John Jay (*qq.v.*), they were essentially conservative documents, and appealed to conservatives to realize them that the Constitution would ensure them of stability and checks and balances necessary to conservative security. Thus, they observed that the Constitution would protect minority groups, of which conservatives were one, from domination by majorities. They posed the need for a "republic," as opposed to a "democracy," which was bound to produce "turbulence and contention." People with property and people without were bound to be opposed. A minority could be controlled by the majority. The task of "Publius" (as the authors styled themselves) was to see that the majority did not turn into a faction which overwhelmed the minority, "and at the same time to preserve the spirit and the form of popular government" (Number 10, by Madison). The learning, logic, and clarity of style of the Papers helped turn the strategic states of Virginia and New York toward ratification. G. Dietze, *The Federalist: a Classic of Federalism and Free Government* (1960).

FEDERALISTS, those who advocated acceptance of the Constitution of the United States, in general elements which represented property-owners and conservatives who looked forward to a government which would curb the "excesses" of democracy, as it had manifested itself under the Articles of Confederation *(q.v.)*. They were opposed by farmers suspicious of a government implemented in powers to tax them and dictate policy to the states, by southern agrarians like Thomas Jefferson *(q.v.)*, who feared northern industry, and by others who had taken seriously some of the more libertarian slogans of the American Revolution *(q.v.)*. In the 1790's, Federalists divided sharply from Jeffersonians in antagonism to the French Revolution *(q.v.)*, in cordiality toward Great Britain, in vengeful feelings over the Whisky Rebellion *(q.v.)* and other democratic attitudes and deeds, and in support of their candidate for the Presidency, John Adams, in 1796 and 1800. He won in the earlier year, was drastically defeated in 1800. The Federalists continued strong in New England, but were broken as a national party. Much of their attitude and program reappeared in a developed form in the Whig Party *(q.v.)*.

FEDERATED PRESS, an outgrowth of the International Labor News Service; it was built up by Louis P. Lochner and by Carl Haessler, and aimed to supplement the reports of the Associated Press. In the 1930's, elements with communist and anti-communist tendencies struggled for influence in its affairs. During World War II, these struggles were resolved by the fact that, following the Nazi attack on their erstwhile ally, the U.S.S.R. and the "people's war" could enlist the support of both elements. The Federated Press went out of existence in the 1950's.

FELLAHIM, the poor peasants of Egypt: the critical caste in any social reform movements in that country, subject to demagogic appeals, and in drastic need of bodily and cultural aid.

FELLOW TRAVELER, applied especially to persons who were not ready or willing to join the Communist Party, in the 1930's, but were sympathetic to its aims, patronized its functions and its press, and defended its policies. See also, "Sympathizer."

FELLOWSHIP OF RECONCILIATION, organized in 1914, in England, an American branch was formed in the United States in 1915. It held its first international conference in 1919, delegates from ten nations being present. The Fellowship has sought to set an example of peaceful attitudes and ideas, and has undertaken symbolic actions intended to dramatize its cause. It holds conferences, distributes literature, and makes efforts to demonstrate its indifference to nationalistic projects and antipathies.

FELS BROTHERS, soap manufacturers and reformers; Joseph (1854-1914), was born in Virginia of Forty-Eighters *(q.v.)*, the family moving to Philadelphia in 1873. In the 1890's, the naphtha process made their soap famous and them wealthy. Fels visited England, where he was influenced by humanitarians. He bought thirteen hundred acres for the unemployed to work, and founded vacant-lot farming in London and Philadelphia. He became an outstanding advocate of the Single Tax *(q.v.)*, and was influential in obtaining the land-tax feature in the famous Lloyd George *(q.v.)* budget of 1909. He spent some hundred thousand dollars a year for advancing understanding of the Single Tax, in all parts of the world; thus, he had Henry George's work translated into Chinese. Mary Fels, his wife, wrote a biography of him (1916) and organized the Joseph Fels Foundation. His brother *Samuel S. Fels* (1860-1950), continued some of his interests, and in addition developed his own. He founded in 1908 in Philadelphia, the Bureau of Municipal Research and also established the Crime Prevention Association (1932), as well as the Samuel S. Fels Fund (1935); see his *This Changing World* (1933).

FEMINISM, see Women's Rights.

F.E.P.C., see Fair Employment Practices Committee.

F.E.R.A., see Federal Emergency Relief Administration.

FERRER, FRANCISCO (1859-1909), Spanish idealist, philosophical anarchist, founder of the Escuela Moderna in Barcelona where he made efforts to develop reform principles in education. Treated with antagonism and suspicion by governmental authorities, they found reason to try him, first for attempted assassination, later for complicity in insurrection. Tried on unsubstantial evidence he was convicted and shot. His life and death stirred world sympathy, as well as augmented Spanish republican and anarchist feelings.

FEUDAL DUES AND FORMS were brought over to the colonies by the English and (in New York) the Dutch, but were not highly regarded. Quitrents, entails, and primogeniture *(qq.v.)* were resented and resisted; the Dutch system of patroonship *(q.v.)* persisted but as an anachronism in a surrounding democracy. Land reform *(q.v.)* as a program of social reform was heightened by efforts to maintain the vestigial remains of feudalism.

F.H.A., see Federal Housing Administration.

FIAT MONEY, see Continental Currency, Greenback Issue, The.

FIFTEENTH AMENDMENT (1870), see Negro Suffrage.

FIFTH AMENDMENT (1791), made famous in the 1950's, by reason of various persons who refused to answer questions before investigating committees with respect to their communist associations on grounds that their Constitutional rights were being denied them, the Fifth Amendment stipulating that no one "shall be compelled in any criminal case to be a witness against himself." The usual formula employed was that the individuals refused to answer on the ground that an answer "might tend to incriminate" them. Their friends insisted that this did not prove they were communists, but only that they were resisting an attack on the Constitution. Their foes held that they feared to tell the truth, which was that they were communists, feared to lie because they might then be prosecuted for falsehood under oath; and that persons unwilling to cooperate with official government agencies must have something to hide. The principled nature of the argument was disturbed by the fact that notorious gangsters took to resorting to the Fifth Amendment, in order to impede prosecution. See also First Amendment, House Un-American Activities Committee, "McCarthy Era."

FIFTH COLUMN, THE, secret revolutionary elements within the city or area; from the Madrid friends of the Franco forces fighting the incumbent Republican regime, during the Spanish Civil War *(q.v.)*. Four columns of fascists were converging on Madrid in 1936 under General Emilio Mola, the "fifth" waited for their arrival and operated in subversive fashions.

"FIFTH" ESTATE, see Fourth Estate.

FIFTIES, THE, by P. Lewis (1980), offers a round-up of conspicuous phenomena and events, ranging from the detonation of the H-Bomb to the advent of Elvis Presley. The era saw the visible decline of the British Empire, the rise and fall of Senator Joseph McCarthy, the presence of the Russian leader Khrushchev. Although *McCall's Magazine* smugly preached "Togetherness" for the American family, Jack Kerouac's novel, *On The Road*, ominously prefigured the coming youth uprising.

FILENE, EDWARD ALBERT (1860-1937), social planner and capitalist. His innovations as department-store owner included the bargain basement. His "Boston 1915" project, which involved Lincoln Steffens and Louis D. Brandeis *(qq.v.)*, among others, was a pioneer effort in civic development. Theoretician of progressive capitalism, Filene advocated mass production and distribution, high wages, and efficiency. Filene founded the credit union in America, subsidized the cooperative movement, and established the Twentieth Century Fund *(qq.v.)*. One of the most distinguished of wealthy defenders of the New Deal *(q.v.)*, Filene broke openly in 1936 with the United States Chamber of Commerce, which he had helped build. See his selection of speeches and articles, *Speaking of Change* (1939).

FILIBUSTER, a free-booter, as in the case of the notorious

General William Walker (*q.v.*), who attempted to make himself master of Nicaragua, identified with imperialist tendencies and pro-slavery policies in the United States, before the Civil War; in politics, a program of impeding the passage of legislation by continuing to hold the floor so that no legislation can come to a vote; used notably by southern blocs to prevent the passage of civil liberties legislation, as in 1960.

FILIPINOS, see Philippines and American Reform.

FILMS, see Popular Arts.

FINAL SOLUTION, THE (1953), by Gerald Reitlinger, a master-work dealing with "The Attempt to Exterminate the Jews of Europe 1939-1945." The title was the key phrase adopted by the administrators of the Nazi program. See also Concentration Camps, Eichmann, Karl Adolf.

FINLAND, see Russo-Finnish War.

FINNEY, CHARLES GRANDISON (1792-1875), noted revivalist (see Revivalism and Reform), who made his reputation in the "Burned-Over District" (*q.v.*) of western New York, building up an impressive number of conversions among its agitated people. Although his own emphasis was on theology, he stirred numerous reformers to action, especially in the field of anti-slavery. His influence was felt in the great Lane Debate (*q.v.*). He became associated with Oberlin College (*q.v.*) as professor and later president. His *Memoirs* (1876) throw light on the qualities which gave him distinction.

FIRST AMENDMENT, part of the Bill of Rights (*q.v.*) to the Constitution, it guarantees religious freedom, freedom of speech and press, the right to assemble peaceably, and to petition the government for a redress of grievances. Many acts and actions of government have been denounced on the grounds that they transgressed the First Amendment. See Alien and Sedition Acts, the Gag Rule, Jehovah's Witnesses. In the 1950's, the First Amendment came into the news again, being invoked by alleged communists and communist cooperators, in defiance of HUAC (*q.v.*). In 1961, the Supreme Court declared that the First Amendment did not empower individuals to defy HUAC.

FIRST INTERNATIONAL, see International Workingmen's Association.

FISH, HAMILTON (1808-1893), Grant's Secretary of State (1869-1877), and one of the few competent persons in his Cabinet. Fish exercised a restraining influence upon the Administration, helping to temper dangerous controversies with Great Britain and Spain. His most notable achievement was the Treaty of Washington of 1871 (*q.v.*). His grandson, bearing the same name, a United States Representative from New York, became notorious for his intemperate opposition to radicals. See Allan Nevins, *Hamilton Fish* (1936).

FISK, JAMES (1834-1872), more familiarly known as "Jim Fisk," a financial adventurer and libertine, one of the symbols of post-Civil War social and industrial disorder. Allied with Jay Gould (*q.v.*), he helped precipitate "Black Friday" (*q.v.*).

FLAG DAY, June 14, commemorating the day in 1777 when the Stars and Stripes were proclaimed by Congress to make up the nation's banner. See also July 4.

"FLAPPER AGE," took its name from F. Scott Fitzgerald's *Flappers and Philosophers* (1920); "flappers" was a word applied in pre-World War 1 England to prostitutes; it was popularized by young girls who made themselves friendly to soldiers. The word was brought back to America by soldiers of the American Expeditionary Forces. Flappers and their consorts were consciously light-headed, rather than philosophers, and their search for "freedom" had no social or political overtones. As such, they inspired the criticism, rather than the respect of reformers. See also Twenties.

"FLASH IN THE PAN," see Dorr Rebellion.

FLETCHER *V.* PECK (1810), a milestone in U. S. Supreme Court (*q.v.*) operations, it involved the allotment of Georgia lands in the west to speculators by state legislators who had been bribed. An indignant electorate expelled them from the legislature and put in men who reversed their acts, thus attempting to recover title to the lands on the Yazoo River. Chief Justice John Marshall (*q.v.*), for the Court, ruled that the original grants had been legal, whether executed for venal purposes or not. Although Marshall's decision served the sanctity of contract, a generally conservative cause, it in this case was approved by common people who had acquired the lands through the speculators and were reluctant to give them up; it was thus a popular decision. Compare with Worcester *v.* Georgia, under Cherokee Indians.

FLETCHERISM, a minor health reform (*q.v.*), advocated by Horace Fletcher, who believed that health and digestion would be aided by an individual chewing his food to pulp. Carried to an extreme, properly chewed food would descend into the interior without swallowing at all.

FLOOD CONTROL, see Tennessee Valley Authority.

FLOWER, BENJAMIN ORANGE (1858-1918), reform editor and writer, a precursor of the muckrakers (*q.v.*), born in Illinois. He edited the *American Sentinel* in Boston, and subsequently merged it into the *Arena*, founded in 1889. A Christian Socialist (*q.v.*), he exhorted the age in such works as *Civilization's Inferno, or, Studies in the Social Cellar* (1893). He left the *Arena* in 1896 to edit *The New Time*, "a magazine of social progress," in Chicago, with Frederick U. Adams, then co-edited *The Coming Age* with Anna C.E. Reifsnider; it was merged with the *Arena*, in 1900. (See *Arena*.) When this publication was undermined by the advertising boycott in 1909 (it was merged with *Christian Work*), he began *Twentieth Century*, which lasted two years. It is possible that the Christian Science principles he had acquired did not help his business or editorial acumen. His *Progressive Men, Women and Movements of the Past Twenty-five Years* (1914) is a valuable work.

FLUORIDATION, a measure intended to secure the health of the teeth which has enlisted reform enthusiasm for and against it. Involved in the question are the facts of fluoridation with respect to teeth, its effect on the general health of the body, and the question of public health policy: Are dangerous experiments in progress? Are they being foisted on people against their will, or without their knowledge? For a partisan survey, which, however, covers the various topics involved, see F.B. Exner and G.L. Waldbott, *The American Fluoridation Experiment*, ed., James Rorty (1957).

FLYNT, JOSIAH (1869-1907), pseudonym for Josiah Flynt Willard, a young man of good family and education, which included a long attendance at the University of Berlin, who had developed an extended association with the world of outcasts, among whom he was known as "Cigarette." His travels among hoboes (*q.v.*) took in Europe as well as the United States. His *Tramping with Tramps* (1899) was pioneer sociology; his *The World of Graft* (*q.v.*) (1901) gave that word respectable currency and constituted the first muckraking (*q.v.*) work; see "Cigarette," in Filler, *The Muckrakers*.

FOLK, JOSEPH W. (1869-1923), the hero of Lincoln Steffens's pioneer article, "Tweed Days in St. Louis," which helped usher in the muckraking (*q.v.*) movement. Folk had been elected circuit attorney by the local political machine, which expected that he would be an innocent front for their operations. His determined indictments of influential local politicians and businessmen roused consternation. The ring closed upon him to discredit him; Steffens's article, written with a local newspaperman, focused national attention on St. Louis and Folk, and aided him in his work. He was elected governor of Missouri, when he could not have been re-elected to his post of attorney. He later served the U.S. Department of State and the Interstate Commerce Commission as a lawyer.

FOLK ARTS AND REFORM have been capable of association, though not always associated. Folk tales can help give a sense of the mother wit, the range of interest and situation, of which "the pee-pul" are capable. An appreciation of folk art and folk dances can add a grassroots strength to reform. It can also aid internationalism, as one perceives the essential unity in dances from everywhere in the world. The Federal Arts Projects (q.v.) sent investigators into the field to collect slave narratives and folk stories, and record folk songs. Folk heroes range from Sergeant York (q.v.) to the bandit Jesse James, but include the legendary John Henry, Negro giant and inspiring folk figure, and Johnny Appleseed, who labored for the future. Folk singers have been especially effective in reform. The Hutchinson Family (q.v.) adorned the Free Soil movement; the Wobblies (q.v.) were a singing band. The socialists were significantly weak in singers, and the communists commonplace in the 1930's, except for their more earthy adaptations from the Russian folk literature. In the 1940's, however, they made a turn toward "Americanizing" their crusade, and attracted talented folksingers whose repertoire included the music of the hills and the mills, as well as importations from the folk literature of the world. The movement reached its highpoint in the Henry A. Wallace (q.v.) campaign for the Presidency in 1948, which was weak in understanding of the American scene but strong in hymns and battle-songs for farmer and worker. During the 1960s and early 1970s, it joined the more euphoric crusade of The Beatles and The Animals with songs decrying war in Vietnam (q.v.), and, with Bob Dylan, Joan Baez, Jimi Hendrix, and Jan Joplin orating musically in praise of various freedoms.

FOLK SCHULE, first developed in Denmark and based on the ideas of Bishop Nicolai Grundtvig. The emphasis was on learning, rather than pecuniary advances.

FOLLEN, CHARLES T.C. (1796-1840), German scholar and republican who was dismissed from the University of Jena, and then from the University of Basle, because of his outspoken libertarian views and interests. He came to the United States, where, in 1830, he was made Harvard professor of German literature. He married into the distinguished Cabot family, but, having become a Garrisonian (q.v.), he was dismissed in 1835. He continued to speak and write, as minister and lecturer, his valued services ending abruptly with his death in the sinking of the steamboat Lexington. His wife, Eliza Lee Follen wrote his life and collected his works in five volumes (1841-2).

FOLLOWING THE COLOR LINE (1908), see Baker, Ray Stannard.

FOOD AND DRUG ADMINISTRATION, one of the most famous victories of the Reform Era (q.v.), it was established in 1906. Amendments in succeeding years helped indicate how intricate the subject was with respect to what constituted harmful preparation and false advertising. The subject became more complicated, rather than less, with the years. The fact that the Tugwell Bill of 1934 — intended to bring controls in the field up-to-date — could, in effect, meet defeat in terms of its intentions, and during the period of the New Deal (q.v.), helped indicate that food had lost ground as a target for reform; the public was not interested and preferred to let others shoulder responsibility for it. See also Anti-Tobacco Crusade, Meat Inspection Act, Patent Medicines, Sinclair, Upton, Wiley, Harvey W., Scott Lucas, The FDA (1978); James S. Turner, Chemical Feast: Report on the FDA (1970).

FOOD STAMPS, a controversial element in the welfare (q.v.) system, intended to ensure that none could starve in America, but complicated by myopic administration and fraud. In 1965 an estimated 442,000 persons were given food stamps; by 1980 the figure had approached 21 million, the cost to the government being ten billion dollars. The enormous percentage of fraud and error was notorious, aided, during more prosperous years, with the vague sense that everyone was entitled to food stamps who wanted them, including students—needy or not—and strikers: a policy which, in effect, endorsed all strikes without discrimination. In harder times, the concept of neediness put a larger umbrella over frauds. How to reverse this drain upon the productive in favor of the unproductive, without

harming the genuinely needy and deserving was a problem confronting the nation in the 1980s.

FORAKER, JOSEPH B. (1846-1917), governor of Ohio, one of the flamboyant Republican orators of the post-Civil War period, who profited from the stylish patriotism of that time. When President Grover Cleveland (q.v.) ordered the return of captured Confederate flags to the southern states, Foraker took occasion to defy the Democratic President: "No rebel flags," he declared, "will be surrendered while I am governor." "Fireworks" Foraker, "Fire-alarm" Foraker, "Bloody Shirt" (q.v.) Foraker served as a good example of pseudo-Patriotism.

FORCE BILL (1833) asked of Congress and received by President Andrew Jackson during the contest over nullification (q.v.), as attempted by South Carolina. Jackson had no stomach for making war on his own southern people, and worked for, and attained, the compromise on the tariff, which was the bone of contention. The Force Bill was thus an assertion of Executive power, without the demonstration. In 1890, another Force Bill was passed by the House of Representatives. The southern states had reestablished "white supremacy" over their Negro citizens, in spite of the Fifteenth Amendment (q.v.). The Republican majority in Congress hoped a Force Bill could revive the Negroes's right to vote in the South. The Bill passed the House, but was rejected by the Senate.

FORCED LABOR, see Slave Labor.

FORD, GERALD R. (1913-   ), Republican leader in Congress, made Vice President of the United States following the resignation of Spiro T. Agnew (q.v.), and, on August 9, 1974, President on the resignation of Richard M. Nixon (q.v.). Ford came with good repute as a patriotic conservative; a month later he shocked the nation by pardoning Nixon for any illegalities committed during his tenure. Denying a "deal" between himself and Nixon, he asserted that efforts to charge his predecessor with crimes would have torn the country further apart. Republicans lost control of Congress in November 1974 elections, a result of Watergate (q.v.) rather than the pardon, but depriving Ford of Congressional strength for his anti-inflation, economy program, from which he exempted defense expenditures. He kept on Kissinger (q.v.), named Alexander Haig head of NATO (q.v.), sought detente (q.v.) with the Soviets, confirmed Nelson A. Rockefeller his Vice President, and maneuvered to get American troops out of Vietnam as expeditiously as possible. He lacked Congressional aid to maintain anticommunist support in Southeast Asia. An uncooperative press labored at an image of Ford as stupid and accident-prone, succeeding to a degree. In May, 1975 Cambodians seized the U.S. merchant ship Mayaguez in international waters, an "act of piracy" which Ford answered with prompt Marine action his critics saw as "over-reaction," but which the nation supported. Ford dismayed his conservative supporters by refusing to see the distinguished Russian dissident Solzhenitzyn (q.v.), in the interests of good relations with Russia, with which SALT II (q.v.) negotiations were continuing. He survived two potential assassination efforts. Opposing forced busing, and resisting extreme demands of Negro interests, union chiefs, and female activists, though he approved ERA (q.v.), he fought for the 1976 Republican nomination and overcame the difficult Reagan (q.v.) challenge. Making Carter (q.v.) the issue of his election campaign, as an opportunist with no record or experience, Ford appeared to have won their first debate (q.v.) as a serious incumbent. Their second debate, October 6, featured Ford's famous "gaffe" (q.v.)—French for mistake—as journalists established it, in which Ford declared that there "is no Soviet domination of Eastern Europe and never will be under a Ford administration." Although 1980 Polish events were to vindicate Ford, the immediate result was to wound his credibility as a realistic American interpreter of world affairs. His public support helped keep his candidacy valid to the end; in fourteen states, the candidates were no farther than two percent apart. Ford remained an active President till his term concluded. His memoirs, A Time to Heal (1979), reflected his well-known character and views. John Hersey, *The President* (1975); J. F. ter Horst, *Gerald Ford and the Future of the Presidency* (1974); Malcolm D. MacDougall, *We Almost Made It* (1977); Clark R. Mollenhoff, *The Man Who Pardoned Nixon* (1976); John J. Casserly, *The Ford White House* (1977); Filler, ed., *The Crisis of the Presidency* (1981).

FORD, HENRY (1863-1947), developer of the automobile, who, in the 1910's set a major example in mass production *(q.v.)* by applying assembly-line techniques to his "Model T" Ford: the "flivver." His work was a major manifestation of "Taylorization" *(q.v.)* in action. He pioneered again by introducing a five-dollar minimum wage and the eight-hour day, though these achievements, and profit-sharing *(qq.v.)*, were rendered doubtful in practice by the fact that they were administered arbitrarily by Ford and his minions, by their lack of regard for unions. Ford's sincere desire to be helpful in social matters was shown by his sponsorship of a "peace ship," the Oskar II, in 1915; it carried pacifists to Europe to attempt to initiate steps to end the European War. The ridicule this venture received did not prevent Ford from subsidizing a Conference of Neutral Internationalists and Pacifists in Stockholm, in 1917. Ford's courage and paternalism kept him only moderately responsible; in 1920-1, he sponsored the antisemitic Dearborn *Independent (q.v.)*. Nevertheless, he seemed to so unconditional a liberal as E.A. Filene *(q.v.)* a legitimate possibility for the Presidency. An unfortunate feature of his later organization was the Harry Bennett-led combination of strong-arm men whose task it was to oppose "trouble-makers," and keep the Ford plants from being organized. It was against this agency that the auto workers had to fight to survive, in order to build the United Automobile Workers of America *(q.v.)*. Ford's alleged phrase, "History is bunk," needed qualification. In his 1919 suit against the *Chicago Tribune*, he declared on the stand, "History is mostly bunk." His own services to history, by creating Greenfield Village in Dearborn, Michigan, were inestimable. Allan Nevins and F. E. Hill, *Ford* (1954-62); B. Herndon, *Ford* (1969); R. M. Wik, *Henry Ford and Grassroots America* (1970).

FORD FOUNDATION, most formidable of foundations *(q.v.)*, it has been sensationally in the news because of the large sums it has disbursed or because of the nature of its grants. Its Fund for the Advancement of Education, Fund for Adult Education, Fund for the Republic, and international programs have offered regular items for the press to announce. Its "Omnibus" program on television has attempted to be a force for good in that medium. Its Center for the Study of Democratic Institutions has resulted in a variety of conferences. D. Macdonald, *The Ford Foundation* (1956); Foundations.

FOREIGN AID, an accompaniment of America's increasing involvement in world developments. The Lend Lease Act (1941) set the tone of operations by specifying aid to war-time Allies. The United Nations Relief and Rehabilitation Administration (1943), to which the United States contributed 70% of funds specified revival as a goal. The Marshall Plan (1947) was intended to retard Soviet expansionism, as was NATO. With the revival of Europe, aid was expanded to new and needy nations in Africa, Asia, and Latin America, in loans (1946-68) topping $100 billion. Farmers more clearly than urbanites learned that their surplus went abroad and profited them. Anti-Americans propagandized continuously that the United States was concerned for profits, rather than humanity, emphasized—what could have usefully been explained at home—that much of the loans did return to America, at low or no interest rates, to be sure, and aided American industry as well as agriculture. It was true that rehabilitation of war-torn foreign nations created economic competitors, and that much foreign aid went to governments which professed Marxist or communist principles; at this point, the economic principle was transformed, in part, into a political principle. Were we arming our foes?—or were we preventing them from receiving aid from the Soviets, and falling into their orbit? Since there was no simple formula for answering these queries, they could

only be kept in view and dealt with pragmatically. Lloyd D. Black, *The Strategy of Foreign Aid* (1968); John Cole, *The Poor of the Earth* (1976); Steve Weissman et al., *The Trojan Horse: a Radical Look at Foreign Aid* (1974); John W. Sewell, *The United States and World Development* (1977).

FOREIGN OBSERVERS have often been among the most earnest and substantial critics of American affairs, inspired by their fresh views of its ways and issues, anxious to see them bettered. Though some have been offensive to patriots, and motivated by subjective feelings, they have contributed to the substance and argument of native social reformers. Foreign studies have been among the best of American life and prospects, notably those by de Tocqueville and Bryce *(qq.v.); see* Allan Nevins, ed., *America Through British Eyes* (1948 ed.), Frank Monaghan, *French Travellers in the United States, 1876-1932* (1933). Peter Conrad, *Imagining America* (1980).

FOREIGN POLICY ASSOCIATION, founded 1918, in order to study American relations with the world, as the League of Free Nations; it took its better-known name in 1921. It cooperated with the American Civil Liberties Union *(q.v.)*, and in 1921 organized the National Council for the Prevention of War. Its 1932 pamphlet series was highly estimated, using the services of such publicists and public figures as Morris Hillquit, John A. Ryan, Max Eastman, and John Dewey *(qq.v.)*. It favored recognition of the Soviet Union. Later more pedestrian in its operations, it continued to prepare useful materials.

"FORGOTTEN MAN, THE," phrase coined by William Graham Sumner *(q.v.)*; it referred to the self-supporting citizen who asked no favors of government and sought only to be let alone in his work and efforts. Ironically, the phrase was borrowed by Franklin D. Roosevelt *(q.v.)* but turned upside down in meaning; the "forgotten man," in the second version, was the person blighted by the Great Depression of the 1930's, but passed over and ignored, though in mortal need.

FORMOSA, the island off the coast of China to which the anticommunist leader, Chiang Kai Shek, and his forces, fled, following their defeat in 1949 by the communists. The protection of the United States fleet has been Chiang's major defense against invasion. Social reformers who deplored Chiang's inability to institute a substantial reform program on the mainland, or to curb corruption, noted his limited ability to report substantial progress on Formosa. The tiny islands held by Chiang, close to the mainland, Quemoy and Matsu, threatened to precipitate a war between the United States and Red China, if attacked, and was a major issue in the Presidential election campaign of 1960. Formosa was known as Taiwan to the communists, and became so to Americans, following detente *(q.v.)*. In 1979, the United States broke off diplomatic relations with Taiwan, while establishing full relations with mainland China.

FORTIES, THE: Profile of a Nation in Crisis (1969), an anthology, by C. E. Eisinger, featuring sections on the war, including atom bombs and concentration camps; culture and society; conservatism and anti-communism; and the struggle for One World.

FORTUNE, see Luce, Henry Robinson.

FORTY-HOUR WEEK, the most notable slogan of labor in the area after the eight-hour day. A middle program called for the *forty-eight hour week*, which gained strength from the fact that it could be linked with a regard for the Sabbath *(q.v.)*. Industrialists who insisted upon keeping their plants in operation seven days a week opened themselves to criticism as hypocrites, so far as their denunciations of "atheistic radicals" were concerned; in addition, many of their workers were bitter over the desecration of the Sabbath. The *forty-four hour week* added a component of leisure *(q.v.)* to the above arguments which the forty-hour slogan amplified. See also Six-Hour Day.

FOSTER, WILLIAM Z. (1881-1961), communist leader and one-time labor symbol, emerged from laboring circumstances to socialism; expelled from Socialist Party in 1909 and joined the I.W.W. (q.v.). He announced his opposition to dual unionism, and apparently did not expect that the International Trade Union Educational League, which he helped found in 1916, would operate as a dual union (qq.v.). He helped organize the packinghouse workers and the steel workers; in 1919, he led the great Steel Strike of that year. He joined the Communist Party, and was its presidential candidate in 1924. As head of the T.U.E.L., he led it into the organization of dual unions. He continued to function as a communist leader, though increasingly in figure-head capacities.

FOULKE, WILLIAM DUDLEY (1848-1935), a lawyer and litterateur who served a term in the Indiana State Senate (1883-5), championing unsuccessfully such libertarian causes as equal rights for married women. He was president of the American Woman's Suffrage Association (1885-90) (q.v.). A humanitarian, he pressed successfully for a new state hospital for the insane. He labored to take state correctional and charitable institutions out of politics. His major cause was civil service (q.v.) reform. He joined the National Civil Service Reform League in 1885, and was its president, 1923-4. He was a U.S. civil service commissioner, 1901-3, and president of the National Municipal League (1910-15). His numerous works included literary studies, biographies, and translations. See his *Fighting the Spoilsman* (1919) and *A Hoosier Autobiography* (1922).

FOUNDATIONS, a controversial by-product of American capitalistic enterprise, increasingly so as they have become semi-public agencies, capable of influencing public views. Such great foundations as the Rockefeller and Carnegie Foundations concerned themselves for medicine, peace, and other interests, useful without representing a serious danger to democratic operations. The Russell Sage Foundation concerned itself for social work. E.A. Filene's (q.v.) Twentieth Century Fund conducted valuable studies. The Guggenheim Foundation dispensed grant to artists, writers, and the like. The organization of the Ford Foundation (q.v.), with about half the funds available to all other foundations put together, raised the subject of foundations to national attention. Hearings before a committee of the House of Representatives underscored the fact that such foundations were only in part philanthropic; were the funds not put into foundations, they would, under the inheritance laws, largely revert to the government. Put into a foundation, of which the donors were in large part directors, it enabled them to maintain their hold on the business and securities involved. The problem was whether their administration of the foundations redounded to the public benefit. The Congressional Committee feared that foundation funds were subsidizing radicals and radical projects; see *Tax-Exempt Foundations. Hearings before the Select Committee . . . on H. Res. 561* (1953), and a similar publication, published the next year, continued the inquiry. The role of wealthy scions in radical programs was reminiscent of Lenin's (q.v.) prediction that when capitalism fell, it would be because the collapse had been aided and abetted by capitalist elements. A "Vanguard" group of such in the San Francisco area, heirs of Levi Strauss, Sears Roebuck, J. C. Penney, Union Carbide, and other fortunes subsidized such groups as the Northern California Public Practices Project, the Chinese Youth Alternatives, a "Black Panther"—run school in Oakland, and prison reform, "counter culture," and ethnic self-help enterprises. A similar group in Cambridge, Massachusetts, the Haymarket Foundation, started by an heir to the Pillsbury baking fortune, also subsidized "social activists." Particularly famous was a General Motors heir, Stewart Mott, who had made large donations to the Presidential campaigns of Eugene McCarthy (q.v.), George McGovern, and, in 1980, John B. Anderson. His money supported such projects as Campaign for Peace, Americans for SALT, Women's Campaign Fund, Common Cause, and the National Organization for Non-Parents. A counter-tendency showed many former communists like Murray Kempton, Whittaker Chambers, James Burnham, though rarely moneyed, turning

to conservative principles, in America fairly well implemented by corporation funds.

"FOUR FREEDOMS, THE," named by President Franklin D. Roosevelt (q.v.), in his annual message for 1941; they were freedom of speech and expression, freedom of worship, freedom from want, and freedom from fear; compare with the Bill of Rights (q.v.).

"FOUR HUNDRED," a term applied amiably by those diverted by the activities of "high society," bitterly by those who believed it to be a parasite on the body politic. The original reference was to a party given by Mrs. William Astor in 1892 which was restricted to four hundred guests, presumably the very elite of exclusive New York. O. Henry (q.v.) later saluted the less exclusive masses of the city in his *The Four Million* (1906).

"FOUR MINUTE MEN," a feature of the work of the Committee on Public Information, during World War I (q.v.). Some seventy-five thousand people were sent about the country to deliver short, hard-hitting talks to explain why the war was being fought, and to provide the people with strong, simple, unifying slogans. This propaganda effort put a premium on unquestioning enthusiasm and contrasted markedly with the preceding period of reform which had placed a premium on questions, controversy, and realistic data. The new emphasis was on conformity and acceptance; see also Creel, George, Minute Men.

FOURIER, FRANÇOIS CHARLES MARIE (1772-1837), influential utopian thinker, whose plans for social organization, though based on a priori assumptions of human wants and capacities, inspired thought and notable efforts to materialize them. His basic concept was the Phalanx (q.v.), around which the social order would grow. His followers included Albert Brisbane, Horace Greeley, Victor de Considérat (qq.v.). J.S. Mill (q.v.) gave his ideas earnest consideration in Mill's own *Political Economy* (II, chapt. 1, sec. 4). Among significant colonies incorporating Fourierite principles may be mentioned Brook Farm and Hopedale (qq.v.). However, there were also Fourierite societies in New York, New Jersey, Pennsylvania, Ohio, Illinois, Indiana, Wisconsin, and Michigan.

FOURTEEN POINTS, Woodrow Wilson's (q.v.) program for peace, put before Congress early in 1918; it asked for "open covenants," freedom of the seas, a league of nations, and other basic tenets presumed to ensure equity and amicable relations among nations. The French Premier Clemenceau was unimpressed by Wilson's crusade. Wilson, he observed ironically had required fourteen points, whereas God Himself had been satisfied with ten.

FOURTEENTH AMENDMENT (1868), one of the most potent of all the Constitutional Amendments, its apparent purpose was to seal the victories of the Civil War (q.v.). It denounced the Confederate debt, deprived insurrectionists of their right to hold public office, and gave the vote to male Negroes. In its most controversial passage, it deprived states of the authority to make or enforce laws "which shall abridge the privileges or immunities of citizens of the United States; nor shall any State deprive any person of life, liberty, or property, without due process of law; nor deny to any person within its jurisdiction the equal protection of the laws." The apparent purpose of the Amendment was to secure the rights of Negroes. Ku Klux Klan (q.v.) terror and the withdrawal of Federal troops from the South made it impossible to enforce the Amendment in this connection, despite Civil Rights laws passed in 1870-1. (See also Force Bill.) In 1882, in San Mateo Co. v. Southern Pacific Railroad Company, Roscoe Conkling, the railroad attorney and former Republican Party leader, only surviving member of the committee which had reported the Fourteenth Amendment to the Congress, asserted that by "person," his committee had also in mind corporations, as meriting the protection of the due process clause (q.v.). This interpretation was accepted by the U.S. Supreme Court in 1886, in Santa Clara Co. v. Southern Pacific Railroad Company. In effect, state curbs on monopoly could not stand by themselves, but could be challenged in higher courts, and were. The Supreme Court set itself up as a protector of property against state regulation. See also Munn v. Illinois, Interstate Commerce Commission.

FOURTH ESTATE, a socialist designation of the "proletariat," from the analogy with the bourgeoisie, which constituted the "third estate," and demanded during the French Revolution (q.v.) equal rights and opportunities with nobility and clergy. A bitter wit suggested, during the economic crisis of the 1930's, that the relief (q.v.) clients were the "fifth estate," whose "business" was to get as much aid and comfort as possible through their social workers.

FOURTH INTERNATIONAL, slogan proposed by the Trotskyites (q.v.). Viewing historical developments, they held that the First International (qq.v., for this and following references) had given the workers of the world a banner, that the Second International had raised the working-class to its feet, that the Third International had risen over the ashes of a Second International compromised by the fact that its national sections had supported their national, bourgeois governments. The Third International, too, had been able to boast the U.S.S.R. as a section. It had, however, turned nationalistic itself, and subverted the International in its interest. The Third International had thus outlived its usefulness. It remained for the "Fourth International" to bring the final victory. Although the Third International actually disappeared during World War II (q.v.), the U.S.S.R. was more than ready to dispute the significance of the Trotskyites on any national arena.

FRAINA, LOUIS C., see Corey, Lewis.

FRANCE, see Enlightenment, French Revolution and the United States, 1848, Paris Commune, The, Dreyfus Case, The.

FRANCHISES, a major issue in the development of municipal reform. The granting of street-car, gas-dispensing, and other franchises by city legislators created problems in bribery, poor service, and high rates. Municipal reformers like Tom Johnson and Samuel M. Jones (qq.v.) campaigned on these issues, and organized parties which welcomed energetic and resourceful aides. Notorious among franchise-seizers was Charles T. Yerkes, who was ruthless in his methods for acquiring Chicago's street-car system; he was the original for Frank Cowperwood, in Theodore Dreiser's (q.v.) The Financier (1912) and The Titan (1914).

FRANCO, FRANCISCO (1892-1975), victor in the Spanish Civil War (q.v.), his regime helped indicate a world in flux, not to be subsumed by dogmatic formulas. Although firm in repressing his foes, Franco held himself to be a regent for a revived royalty, which materialized in the Bourbon prince, Juan Carlos. His air bases aided American logistics during the Cold War (q.v.). His death opened the way for further permutations of Spanish life and politics. J. W. Trythall, Franco (1970); George Hills, Franco (1968).

FRANK, ANNE, see Anne Frank.

FRANK CASE, see Leo M. Frank Case.

FRANKFURTER, FELIX (1882-1965), Austrian-born lawyer and jurist, he served in various official capacities, and became a professor at the Harvard Law School in 1914. He became noted for his liberal outlook and authority on matters relating to wages, hours, and the labor injunction, and identified with the Sacco and Vanzetti (qq.v.) case. In 1939, he was appointed an Associate Justice of the U.S. Supreme Court. His testimony for the defense, during Alger Hiss' (q.v.) trial in 1949, and the latter's subsequent conviction for perjury and, in effect, treason, stimulated thoughtful reconsideration about the gullibility of liberals.

FRANKLIN, BENJAMIN (1706-1790), often conceived of as a revolutionist, actually the last American Tory (q.v.) who was practical enough to know that his destiny was with the colonies, that the most active and creative forces favored revolution, and that his place was with them rather than with the loyal stipendiaries of the Crown. When Franklin approved the revolution, the revolution was ready to begin. Franklin's talents and prestige — like those of such other conservatives as John Jay, John Adams (qq.v.), and George Washington — were necessary to a revolution which could hope for success.

FRATERNIZATION, a gambit of socialists and social reformers who hoped to break down the differences between soldiers on opposite sides of an embattled area, or between workers on strike and police, or in other situations to undermine the status quo (q.v.) in the interests of a reform or revolutionary program. Fraternization was attempted between Russian soldiers and Germans during World War I, though to little purpose, and in many other circumstances resulting from World War I. During strikes, workers have often sent their women among the police to urge them to be men and not to harass their own people. Fraternization has appeared to work best when opposing troops were losing faith in victory, and seeking excuses for becoming disaffected.

FRAUDS EXPOSED, OR, HOW THE PEOPLE ARE DECEIVED AND ROBBED, AND YOUTH CORRUPTED (1880), by Anthony Comstock (see "Comstockery").

FRAZIER, LYNN J. (1874-1947), North Dakota farmer statesman, Nonpartisan League (q.v.) governor, 1916-21; in the latter year, the "recall" (q.v.) defeated him. However, the League was still strong enough, despite a coalition of Republicans, Democrats, and anti-Leaguers to send him to the U.S. Senate. In 1924, he was read out of the Republican Party, to which he had adhered, but he was among those who held the balance of power in the chamber. With Senator Lemke (q.v.), he offered bills intended to aid farmers troubled by mortgages. In 1930, he for the third time introduced a constitutional amendment which would have outlawed the preparation for war even if the United States were invaded; his bill was backed by the Women's International League for Peace and Freedom, the Fellowship of Reconciliation, and the War Resisters International, among other organizations.

FREE, compared with slave, in pre-Civil War years, in such combinations as Free North, Free States, Free Produce. So employed in the North, concerned factions comparing such phrases with Slave South, Slave State, Slave Produce. Southern partisans used the word "slave" less often, though they would employ it when necessary, and they were unwilling to identify the North with freedom, preferring such phrases as the slaveless North, which they also identified with hypocrisy, the anarchy caused by reformers, and the presumed contrariety of Bostonians. Southerners also used freedom in their own behalf, when possible, as in defending Free Trade; some urged free trade in slaves. The Free West and the Free World were later juxtaposed with the alleged "slavery" practiced by the communists, who were likewise averse to being identified with slavery, and felt it more desirable to see their opponents as constituting capitalist countries, imperialist nations, or in the toils of Wall Street, McCarthy, or more generally, fascists.

FREE COINAGE OF SILVER, see Silver Issue, The.

FREE ENTERPRISE, a major slogan of pro-capitalist advocates, and intended to contrast with the inadequacies and delinquencies of cooperative or socialist operations, which are usually viewed as leading inevitably to the excesses of communism. Viewed with suspicion, too, are any steps leading to expanded governmental functions in the fields of production, health, education, and other fields, steps usually characterized as "creeping socialism." Principled advocates of free enterprise have sought evidence that it produced better results than cooperative techniques and have taken heart from the turn of the British from the Labour Party to the Conservative Party, following the former's post-World War II victories, and the industrial triumphs of Western Germany in the same period. They have been less impressed by the need for understanding the role of communism abroad than in "Selling America," in the phrase of the National Management Association, which in 1930 launched an educational program directed at employees in industrial plants and at high school students; the program emphasized American Freedoms, American Abundance, and the dangers of inflation. Among many strategic arms of free enterprise were the National Association of Manufacturers (q.v.), and the Saturday Evening Post. Humiliation and economic trouble suffered by the democracies due to inflation, lowered prestige, Soviet expansionism, and loss of prospects raised the Conservatitive Party in Great Britain, following a Labour interregnum, under Margaret Thatcher (q.v.), and the Republican Party in America under Ronald Reagan (q.v.), leaders in the international western effort at anti-inflation measures and patriotic stances. In opposition were forthright socialists who asked a mandate for manipulating the economy without regard to "free enterprise" principles: Anthony Benn in England, and the "liberal Democrat" Edward M. Kennedy in America. Unions reluctantly sought accomodation with often desperate industry. J. D. Forman, Capitalism, Economic Individualism to Today's Welfare State (1973).

FREE LOVE, advocated by idealists and socialist theoreticians, including the poet Shelley and the utopian Fourier (qq.v.), postulates the desirability of free sexual union over the exigencies of family life and social duty. Although encouraged by some species of anarchist and socialists without government power, it has been repudiated by others, and by all successful reform groups. Reformers have, on the other hand, denounced the condemnation of illegitimate children as cruel and harmful to society, as well as hypocritical, and worked to foster a more sophisticated sense of social realities. The changing status of women, the need to legitimatize children born out of wedlock, family variations and legal challenges as in "Palimony" (q.v.) cases largely rendered the "free love" phrase obsolete. See Oneida Community, Warren, Josiah. David G. Croly, The Truth about Love (1972); J. W. and L. F. Bird, Freedom of Sexual Love (1970); Taylor Stoehi, Free Love in America (1979).

FREE NEGROES, a significant factor in the Negro question of pre-Civil War decades. By 1850, there were approximately eight slaves to one free Negro, with most Negroes in the North free. Thus, there was a very substantial body of free Negroes to acclimate slaves to freedom, if the free Negroes were given an opportunity to exercise their competence in the arts of freedom. Free Negroes were, however, treated with the utmost contempt in the South, and were themselves under constant threat of a return to slavery. Such a condition was not inconceivable, or difficult to explain. What was striking was that free Negroes were held under rigid restraints in the North, as well as treated with repugnance and contempt. Thus, the argument that slavery could not be ended for lack of a plan for acclimating the bondsmen to freedom was hypocritical; a program was not only not sought — it was impeded. The remarkable fact was that it was impeded in the North as well as in the South. Filler, ed., The Rise and Fall of Slavery in America (1981).

FREE PRESS ANTHOLOGY (1909), compiled by Theodore Schroeder (q.v.), and published by the Free Speech League and the Truth Seeker Publishing Company. It contains historical defenses of free speech, and, in later selections emphasized toleration of alleged obscenities, free sex-discussion, and liberty of speech for anarchists.

FREE PRODUCE, a slogan especially emphasized by Quaker abolitionists, like Levi Coffin (q.v.), who hoped that northerners would prefer to buy the products of the labor of free men, rather than that manufactured under a slave system. Thus, southern cotton would not have been used by queasy purchasers. Coffin and others hoped this would encourage southerners to turn away from the slavery system. Free Produce was more a slogan than an accomplishment; it affected commerce very little.

FREE SILVER, see Silver Issue, The.

FREE SOIL PARTY (1848), the first Northern amalgam of Free Soilers (q.v.), who found their least common denominator in the candidacy of ex-President Martin Van Buren, frustrated by southern politicians from carrying his Democratic Party's standard in the 1848 election. Although most abolitionists other than the anti-political intransigents felt it necessary to vote for him, he received no more than 291,678 votes, in contrast with Zachary Taylor's (Whig) 1,360,101 votes, and Lewis Cass's (Democratic) 1,220,544. However, the Free Soil Party broke ground for the organization of the Republican Party. Frederick J. Blue, The Free Soilers (1973).

FREE SOILERS, northerners who with increasing ardor maintained that the western lands must come into the Union as free states; along with this conviction went an increasing sensitivity to the encroachment of southern legislators and defenders upon civil liberties and northern states' rights with respect to runaway slaves and slave-catchers. Free Soilers like Dr. Samuel G. Howe and Rev. Thomas Wentworth Higginson (q.v.) took on increasingly the tone and appearance of intransigent abolitionists. Western Free Soilers like Abraham Lincoln were more moderate in their deportment though they became increasingly firm on the right of the government to administer its lands as it democratically preferred.

FREE SPEECH, see Freedom of Speech.

FREE SPEECH LEAGUE, founded in 1902, and concerned for clarifying the privileges and immunities of citizens with respect to their Constitutional rights. Before 1920, the outstanding partisan in behalf of free speech was Theodore Schroeder (q.v.). The League's role was mainly educational, but it also raised legal questions with respect to police brutality at public meetings and similar circumstances. The League was incorporated in 1911 with Leonard D. Abbott as president, and with Brand Whitlock, Lincoln Steffens, and Bolton Hall (qq.v.) as vice-presidents, and Schroeder as secretary. It participated in a notable battle for free speech in San Diego, California, in 1914. It published Schroeder's Free Speech for Radicals, including the striking essay on "Liberal Opponents and Conservative Friends of Unabridged Free Speech," published earlier in the anarchist Mother Earth. The War, and the activities of the A.C.L.U. (q.v.) deprived the League of its function.

FREE TRADE, a major political issue of the nineteenth century, it was defended by southern leaders of the pre-Civil War decades as necessary to their well-being. Since they exchanged their raw materials for the manufactured goods of New York and New England, they argued that they needed goods, in competition with those of their northern neighbors, permitted ready entree into the country, so that prices of manufactured goods would descend to a reasonable level. The defeat of the Confederacy was, in fact, a victory for protectionism (q.v.). In the post-Civil War period, however, two main branches of free traders emerged: those who equated free trade with free enterprise (q.v.) demanded that industry be freed of protection; they had little in common with humanitarians (q.v.) who saw in free trade a means of helping the needy. The principled free traders were not so much concerned for the health of the victims of protection, required to pay for its maintenance in higher prices, as for the health of businesses which were being supported by government favors, of which principled free traders were suspicious. A government aiding business would ultimately be required to aid labor, and bring on what they saw as the evils of socialism (q.v.). Humanitarian free traders sought means for bringing down the high cost of living (q.v.), especially on such essential items as food, clothing, and shelter. The need to do so was acute for city workers, kept at a minimum wage by fierce competitive conditions and impersonal relations. Yet, during the later post-Civil War decades, city and eastern workers were persuaded by protectionists that their jobs depended upon foreign goods being kept to a minimum by high protective tariffs. The battle for free trade was pressed by some southerners (though wealthy southern entrepreneurs were as averse to competition as their northern counterparts), by such principled free traders as Carl Schurz and the converted Grover Cleveland, as well as humanitarian free traders like Henry George (qq.v.). The battle for free enterprise in the west was led by harassed farmers who sought means for maintaining high prices on farm commodities. Their reformers often approved free trade in principle, but demanded protection for their particular farm products. The Sherman Silver Purchase Act of 1890 was the result of a deal; the farmer's representatives received it in exchange for supporting the McKinley tariff of 1890: the highest overall tariff adopted in the United States to that time. Some of the most distinguished western reformers, including La Follette, Borah, and Norris (qq.v.) were protectionists. The Trade Agreements Act of 1934 reversed the long-established policy of putting tariff decisions into the hands of special interest groups by permitting the President to alter Congress-established rates, through negotiation with foreign governments, up to fifty-percent. In effect, tariff scheduling was linked to foreign policy. The key to such agreements was the principle of "reciprocity," especially pressed by U.S. Secretary of State Cordell Hull: nations which offered trade concessions to the United States took status as among the most-favored nations, in United States tariff listings; see also Manchester Liberalism. Low American productivity, fealty to unions, and the sleepless efforts of German and Japanese businessmen and workers made their products attractive to American buyers. In 1981, it appeared that a form of Protectionism (q.v.) might be necessary to enable a sagging American industry to compete with a dominant foreign market. Douglas Evans and Richard Body, *Freedom and Stability in the World Economy* (1976); Barry Turner, *Free Trade and Protection* (1971).

FREEDMEN, a major problem for reformers, faced by an army of some four million Negroes who had been freed from slavery by the Thirteenth Amendment to the Constitution, and who needed to be adjusted to their new circumstances. The southern program for them was incorporated in "Black Codes" (q.v.) which administered them under rigid laws, holding them under conditions not very far from slavery. These were overthrown by Reconstruction measures (q.v.) which enforced their civil rights at bayonet point, and by organization of the Freedmen's Bureau, under General O. O. Howard, intended to help the freedmen in meeting their individual problems. Unfortunately for the freedmen, both the army of occupation in the South and the Bureau became agencies largely for ensuring the right of Negroes to vote for the Republican Party. Philanthropic individuals and agencies sought to be of aid to the Negroes by opening schools for them, but these were relatively few and inadequate. The *Nation* (q.v.) was founded as a medium for discussing the problems of freedmen, but quickly lost this function. The freedmen drifted rapidly into a master and tenant-farmer (q.v.) relationship with the southern white population, once they had overcome Reconstruction and re-established "white supremacy" (q.v.).

FREEDOM, see Abstract Terms.

FREEDOM HOUSE, organized 1941, to act as a clearing house for agencies interested in maintaining ideals of freedom. It offers an annual Freedom Award, assists radio and television forums to develop programs relevant to its interests, compiles lists of books, publishes pamphlets. It established the Willkie (q.v.) Memorial Building, in New York, which houses it, as well as the following organizations: American Council of Voluntary Agencies for Foreign Service, Anti-Defamation League (and Metropolitan Council of B'nai B'rith), Citizens Housing and Planning Council of New York, American Council for Nationalities Service, International Confederation of Free Trade Unions, National Association for the Advancement of Colored People (q.v.), Public Education Association, World University Service.

FREEDOM OF CONTRACT, from the point of view of labor,

the right to collective bargaining (q.v.), from the point of view of industry, the "right to work" (q.v.).

FREEDOM OF INFORMATION ACT (1974), a response to Watergate (q.v.) which caused numerous people to wonder what might be in official files about themselves, many recalling their "radical" years, and others fearful of malice and stupidity operating against themselves in official files. The act permitted access to such files, by private citizens. The F.B.I. (q.v.) complained that it was overwhelmed by frivolous requests which drained their personnel resources. Convicted loan sharks used the files to get the names of informers, whom they executed. The children of the Rosenbergs (q.v.) were awarded almost $200,000 as partial payment for legal work done by their attorneys since filing a Freedom of Information suit in 1975. An oddity of this phenomenon was the persistent refusal of journalists to reveal their sources in murder cases, while propagandizing for "freedom of information." Although Alger Hiss (q.v.) was granted entree to restricted materials about his case, so also was an independent investigator, whose researches turned public opinion against him. L. G. Sherick, *How to Use the Freedom of Information Act* (1978).

FREEDOM OF SPEECH, "guaranteed" by the First Amendment (q.v.) to the Constitution of the United States, but like other guaranteed measures altered by the times and conditions, and requiring specific campaigns to maintain. Freedom of speech was challenged by the Sedition Act, by the Gag Rule, by conditions attending the Civil War, by antagonistic attitudes of the police toward radicals, in the post-Civil War era, by repressive actions toward pacifists and dissenters during World War I, during the Red Raids following it (qq.v.). The I.W.W. (q.v.) conducted notable fights in favor of free speech. The American Civil Liberties Union (q.v.) dedicated itself to the defense of those persecuted for attempting to use this freedom. The phenomena of subversives in behalf of the Soviet Union who sought to protect themselves under the First Amendment raised perplexing questions of tactics and strategies which would best preserve it; see also National Liberal League, Free Speech League.

FREEDOM OF THE PRESS, see Press, Freedom of the.

FREEDOM OF THE SEAS, a major slogan of the Woodrow Wilson Administration, before American entrance in 1917 into the European War, as it then was. The policy of Wilson may be contrasted with that of an earlier Democrat, Jefferson, who attempted to meet the international crisis of his own time by imposing an embargo (q.v.) upon American shipping. Since Great Britain had closed off the Continent to American shipping, freedom of the seas in fact meant the right of Americans to trade with Great Britain and France, but not with Germany. The latter had only the submarine to oppose the dominant British navy. A continuous quarrel with the United States over her right to ship commodities to the English left both unsatisfied: the U.S. government with such sea tragedies as the sinking of the *Lusitania* and the *Sussex*, involving questions of whether they did or did not relate to military needs, and the German government which perceived that, after all, food was as essential to the English effort as guns. Germany resolved her own dilemma by deciding that American aid was helping to sustain the Allies, and that she would gain more by frankly acknowledging the non-neutrality of the American government and by trying for a knockout blow at the Allies before the United States could enter actively into the war. Hence, Germany, January 31, 1917, announced a policy of unrestricted submarine warfare: a policy which soon brought the United States into the war on the side of the Allies. Freedom of the seas was one of Wilson's Fourteen Points (q.v.), and as effectively implemented as most of the others.

"FREEDOM RIDE," a major effort in 1961 on the part of white and Negro partisans, intent on breaking down discrimination on transportation facilities in the South. They were met by riot and non-cooperation on the part of southern state officials.

Riots in Alabama and Mississippi brought Federal marshals to the scene, in the latter state, and focused attention on the Democratic Kennedy Administration's policies and techniques for implementing desegregation.

FREEMAN, THE, founded in 1920, under A. J. Nock *(q.v.)* was one of the best-edited of American magazines: incisive, varied, and thoroughly educational. It ceased publication in 1924, was revived by Suzanne La Follette in 1930 as the New Freeman, but closed the next year, being unable to minister to the spirit of the new time.

FREEMASONS, see Anti-Masonry.

FRÉMONT, JOHN CHARLES (1813-1890), first standard-bearer for the Republican Party, in 1856, he helped indicate how much more eager it was for power, rather than principle. Frémont had no record or standing among reformers, and had made his reputation as a western explorer and expansionist. His acceptance of the anti-slavery Republican Platform of 1856 no more than highlighted the fact that the Republicans needed a national hero, and that he, like his father-in-law, Thomas Hart Benton *(q.v.),* was a nationalist first, and only secondly a southerner. In 1861, as commander of the Federal army in Missouri, Frémont issued an order declaring the slaves of rebels free, but Lincoln *(q.v.),* fearing that this would turn Union sympathizers against it, countermanded the order. R. J. Bartlett, *John C. Fremont and the Republican Party* (1930).

FRENCH REVOLUTION AND THE UNITED STATES, related through the aid which France had rendered to the colonies during their revolution, which provided the inspiration for the later uprising, both lands thus leading in the formulation of libertarian slogans and examples. Aid to the embattled colonists, to the extent that it required official French sanction, was not dictated by love of democracy, the French Court being among the most reactionary in Europe, but by malicious desire to harm the British Empire, which had recently wrested Canada from French control. However, to the extent that France permitted such republicans as Lafayette *(q.v.)* to join forces with the rebellious Americans, it not only contributed to the American victory but inadvertently permitted its own would-be libertarians to think in terms of expanded democracy back home. The French Revolution began with a demand for a constitutional monarchy. The fierce resentment this stirred in other reactionary European capitols, the French King's effort to flee the country and to stir up counter-revolution, roused the revolutionary forces and resulted in a movement to save their gains. The abolition of the monarchy, the execution of the King, the organization of the first coalition of Austria and Prussia to overthrow the National Convention, administrative arm of the revolution, the appeal of its leaders to the people to save it from its enemies was all watched with grave concern by the American Federalists *(q.v.)* and the Administration of George Washington. As the revolution deepened, resulting in the guillotining, first, of great numbers of royalist and other suspected forces, then, of the moderate republicans, official disapproval of the course of the French Revolution increased. It became a major point of disagreement between Federalists and Jeffersonians *(q.v.).* When the French sent as envoy to the United States Citizen Genêt, he was received formally by the Administration, with warmth and enthusiasm by the Jeffersonians. Genêt was of the moderates: a measure of the conservative quality of the Administration. His defiance of its official neutrality stirred resentment not only among the Administration supporters, but even of some of its critics. When the Jacobins *(q.v.)* came into power, they sent a minister of their own, Joseph Fauchet, who sought to arrest Genêt. American neutrality maintained itself by refusing the extradition of Genêt, who became an American citizen. In addition, although Thomas Paine *(q.v.)* had defended the French Revolution, in his *The Rights of Man,* and been made a French citizen, his Girondist *(q.v.)* sympathies put

him in prison after the Jacobins came to power; and though the U.S. Government had no sympathy with his views or attitude, it did secure his release. The dissolution of the Convention, its succession by a Directory and its aggressive military policies, led by Buonaparte *(q.v.)* created still further sympathy between Federalists and France's enemies in Europe. An unofficial war on sea developed between France and the United States, in 1798, as a result of the XYZ Affair *(q.v.).* By then, the Revolution had been reduced to phrases.

FRENEAU, PHILIP (1752-1832), "the poet of the American Revolution," he wrote vigorous verse in its behalf, mostly of an ephemeral sort, aside from its association value, and later edited the *National Gazette* in furtherance of Jeffersonian principles, which matched Federalist scurrility with scurrility. As the first national poet, he later became of interest to academic literary specialists. Several of his poems, notably "The Wild Honey Suckle," which carries no social significance *(q.v.),* are among the true American poems.

FRENZIED FINANCE (1904-5), see Lawson, Thomas W.

FREUD, SIGMUND (1856-1939), one of the greatest of twentieth century pioneers, he opened the door to hidden worlds of human feeling and intention. His revelations of the power of childhood impressions, sexual impulses, repressive influences, compulsions, symbolic acts, and inhibitions impressed the experimental generation of the 1910's, and was further popularized in the 1920's. Although Freud's analyses were more an art than a method, psychoanalysis *(q.v.)* grew into a medical adjunct with time. It added a dimension to art, and complicated perspectives for social reform.

FRIENDS, see Society of Friends.

FRIENDS OF THE SOVIET UNION, an organization of the 1930's which published *Soviet Russia Today* and claimed two million members. It encouraged trips to the U.S.S.R., enlisted the interest, endorsement, and cooperation of numerous well-known intellectuals and others, and constituted a socio-cultural link between the U.S. and U.S.S.R. Since it wholly endorsed the dominant regime and had no independent line of any sort, it was a valuable adjunct to the Communist Party, creating layers of respectability for it among the elite classes of the country.

FRIES' "REBELLION" (1798-9), the result of property taxes laid on lands, houses, and slaves by the Federalist Administration, which anticipated the need for money with which to fight the French (see XYZ Affair). John Fries raised troops in eastern Pennsylvania counties with which to resist tax collectors. President John Adams issued a proclamation for the use of armed force with which to put down the rebellion, and Fries and two others were seized and tried and convicted of treason, but were pardoned by the President.

FRINGE BENEFITS, particular gains which come to a worker from a specific job, which augment his satisfactions without necessarily increasing his salary, though often representing solid economic gain. From the workers' point of view, involving rest periods, vacations, sick benefits, and other gain; on the managerial level, it could include a secretary. During periods of competition for particular services, fringe benefits could tempt a worker or manager to a particular plant, since he could enjoy gains which would not affect his income tax. See Benefits. Stanley M. Babson, Jr., *Fringe Benefits* (1974).

FRONT, see Labor Front, United Front, Red Front.

FRONTIER AND SOCIAL REFORM: The American Frontier differed traditionally from the European in that the former represented an opportunity, the latter a restriction on opportunity. Frederick Jackson Turner's *(q.v.)* theory of the frontier saw it as a "basin of democracy," a "safety-valve" for the more repressive east. The frontier inspired reform efforts, from Bacon's Rebellion of 1676 to the Populist Revolt of the 1890's *(qq.v.),* yet it also encouraged anti-reform and anti-humanitarian actions. Thus, theoretically, slavery should have stopped at the first frontier, as an offense to individualism and democracy. On the contrary, the frontier states in the south became at least as rabid on the subject of slavery as the more established eastern states. Thus, also, the Paxton Boys of Pennsylvania (q.v.) not only demanded better representation in the colonial legislature, but also the continuation of a bounty on Indian scalps. The frontier tended to produce the conditions sought by those who conquered it. Yet the *idea* of frontier democracy continued to inspire reform action and ideals. The "passing of the frontier," late in the nineteenth century, raised the question of whether America must become increasingly European in social structure and expectations. See People; also Richard A. Bartlett, *The New Country* (1976).

F.T.C., see Federal Trade Commission.

FUGITIVE SLAVES, a key factor in the abolitionist (q.v.) crusade, since the willingness of slaves to contrive escapes contradicted the proslavery argument that they were happy creatures who could not do without their masters's protection. In addition, the slave escapes created a complex series of problems in law, North and South relations, relations between Negroes and white people in the North. Laws which touched Negroes could touch white persons. The law which gave the Negro no status in court might deprive a white person accused of being an escaped slave. Federal law overseeing slaves might deprive Northerners of their states' rights. Hence, Personal Liberty Laws (q.v.) were passed in the North which challenged national prerogatives. Northerners were found who were ready to close ranks with abolitionists, whom they otherwise despised for their unconventional attitudes and activities. The Fugitive Slave Act of 1793 and the Fugitive Slave Act of 1850, part of the Compromise (q.v.) of that year, were landmarks. The first was readily accepted by the majority of the population North and South, the second was treated with scorn in the North. The heroine of Harriet Beecher Stowe's *Uncle Tom's Cabin* (q.v.), over whom the North wept, was a fugitive slave. A fugitive slave like Harriet Tubman (q.v.), though of a despised race, was able to function boldly in the North. In the 1960s and 1970s, despite a library of heroic deeds done in behalf of fugitive slaves, academic efforts demeaned the underground railroad (q.v.) and its partisans; see, e.g., Larry Gara, *The Liberty Line: the Legend of the Underground Railroad* (1961). See also *Exiles of Florida, The.*

FULL EMPLOYMENT ACT (1946) was intended to set up machinery which would enable the government to maintain employment. A council of economic advisers was set up to estimate the status of the American economy and to advise the President, enabling him to prepare specific recommendations to Congress looking to alleviations of unemployment. In practice, it was not found possible to arrive at formulas which expunged unemployment.

FULLER, MARGARET, See Ossoli, Sarah Margaret (Fuller), Marchioness d'.

FUNDAMENTALISM, the religious approach of those who took the Bible as the literal word of God, and therefore their guide to action and ideas. They opposed the Freethinkers (q.v.), who took the evidence of their own minds as a primary instrument for understanding. Calvinists (q.v.) in general, notably Methodists and Baptists, appealed to the feelings of those who yearned to be saved, and who saw their salvation in the Bible. Even the Congregationalists, though they were a fundamentalist denomination, to the extent that they represented an established civilization and an established authority, seemed to interpose worldly opinion between the individual and God. Methodists and Baptists outstripped the Congregationalists in their appeal to the humbler rural classes. The Congregationalists, in turn, were critical of the Anglican Church, which they saw as a permutation of the hated Catholic Church, dedicated to ritual and "trappings" which directed attention from true religion. Fundamentalists were essentially anti-reformist, since their interest lay in conforming to God's will, rather than discovering individual

purposes, but they incubated reformers in protest against what seemed to them mere feeling and mere words. Emerson and Garrison were fundamentalists turned inside out; John Quincy Adams, Orestes Brownson, Bronson Alcott (qq.v.), in their several ways, sought to make the Word of God flesh. See also Revivalism and Reform. Fundamentalism received odd converts when the collapse of the youth (q.v.) uprising of the 1960s left some of its "drop outs" from education and family without human base. Some found "gurus" (q.v.) who claimed spiritual powers and administered their lives and finances, rarely for long. A repulsive phenomenon was the emergence of "Rev." Jim Jones, who led his followers to Guyana and mass suicide in 1978.

"FUNDING THE PUBLIC DEBT," see Continental Currency.

FURUSETH, ANDREW (1854-1938), labor leader, of Norwegian stock, he became a seaman who took up residence in San Francisco in 1880. He was the organizer and leading spirit of the Sailors' Union of the Pacific, and as such involved in the development of the labor movement in his times. The poor organization and temperament of sailors made them liable to social and economic distress; Furuseth worked to obtain laws in their favor. Like Samuel Gompers (q.v.), too, he developed a philosophy of the labor movement, in terms of its national organization, tactics, and goals. His main concern was for the seamen — as distinguished from the longshoremen — and for permanent accomplishments. A major target of his work was to resist use of the injunction (q.v.) against labor. His monument was the Seamen's Act (q.v.), for which he fought, and which he defended in the courts. Aside from his cause, he was, like Gompers, conservative in his social aspirations for labor; see Hyman Weintraub, *Andrew Furuseth* (1959).

FUTURISM, an effort to forecast coming developments, presumably on the basis of data and scientific insight. Ronald L. Hunt, San Jose State University, offered the first graduate course in the field. Charles Reich's *The Greening of America* (1970) had the sole virtue of proving people were interested in the topic. Alvin Toffler's *Future Shock* (1970) was a somewhat similar success. Economic, social, and other government and private agencies, including polls (q.v.), studied projections more responsibly, but popular concern about the future continued to be ill-served. A 3-year study by the President's Council on Environmental Quality (1980), prepared with help of other government agencies, urged action to prevent "alarming global problems." A magazine, *Next*, claming 400,000 subscribers conjectured about the future. A World Future Society functioned in Washington, D.C.

G

GADFLY, a fly which hovers over cattle and bites or otherwise disturbs it; used to characterize such a reformer or quasi-reformer as John Jay Chapman (*q.v.*): an individualist, rather than a person operating through normal channels of politics or like-minded groups. Also the title of a novel by Ethel L. Voynich, English writer, whose *The Gadfly* (1897) merits study by social reformers because of its outstanding and continuous popularity and success. Others who might rate as gadflies, though vaguely or clearly associated with more conventional people or groups, include Josiah Warren, Albert J. Nock, Theodore Schroeder, and, among women, the immortal Anne Royall (*qq.v.*).

GAFFE, though exotic in American speech, established by concerted journalism during the Ford-Carter debates (*q.v.*) as indicating Ford's "tendency" toward blundering, and thus dangerous statement. In fact, the Ford assertion inspiring use of the word was an appropriate Presidential statement. The particular reference lost credibility in 1980 because of the strength of Polish resistance to the Russians, but it was given new strength in journalistic attacks on Ronald Reagan (*q.v.*). It appeared to have a future as a pro-Democrat political instrument.

GAG LAW, first applied in 1798 to the Sedition Act of that year (*q.v.*); most notoriously to the act, introduced December 11, 1838, into the House of Representatives by the Hon. Charles G. Atherton of New Hampshire, and intended to prevent bills pertaining to slavery from being debated in the House. Since this was in direct defiance of the First Amendment to the Constitution (*q.v.*), permitting the people "to petition the government for a redress of grievances," it provided abolitionists (*q.v.*) with a first-class issue which could be agitated throughout the North. It also started John Quincy Adams (*q.v.*) on his greatest campaign: to end the "Gag Rule," which became a standing rule in 1840. In the Senate, the Rule was not established, thanks to the efforts of Thomas Morris (*q.v.*), among others. The Gag was repealed in 1844.

GALLAUDET, THOMAS H. (1787-1851), pioneer in organizing educational schools for the deaf, he studied methods of caring for them abroad before opening his own free school in Hartford, Connecticut, in 1817. His work thus complemented that of Dr. Samuel G. Howe (*q.v.*). Gallaudet was a minister and mildly abolitionist, and thus constituted a link between reforms. His tract, *Jacob and His Sons*, aided abolitionists because it was removed from the list of publications of the American Sunday School Union, the reason being that it had been critical of the selling of Joseph by his brothers. The abolitionists made an issue of the event.

GALLUP POLL, a popular name for the American Institute of Public Opinion, organized in 1935 by Dr. George Gallup. Its successful prediction of the election results of 1936, and the catastrophic failure of the *Literary Digest* to come within sight of reality, through its polling of opinion, gave the Gallup Poll substantial prestige. It became the best-known of a number of such agencies. Reformers were concerned that it might now be creating public opinion, as well as reflecting it. By 1948, it was so well established, that when it failed to offer adequate predictions on the results of that year's Presidential elections, it could solicit money to determine where it had made mistakes. A field had been created which involved "pollsters," which required a *Public Opinion Quarterly*, and special training for best results. In addition, polling public opinion had become an international operation. Reformers continued to fear that it influenced sentiment, but also won-

dered whether persons being polled necessarily said what they thought or what they thought they ought to say. The Presidential Elections of 1960 suggested doubtful areas in the value of polls, but for many topics and social circumstances they seemed a useful adjunct to journalism. Michael Edison and S. Heiman, *Public Opinion Polls* (1972); C. W. Roll, Jr. and A. H. Cantril, *Polls: Their Use and Misuse in Politics* (1972); George H. Gallup, ed., *The Gallup Poll* (1978).

GALSWORTHY, JOHN (1867-1933), English writer and chronicler of upperclass life and aspirations. Although concerned for the tone and temper of his people, more than for social implications, his plays and tales help illuminate class attitudes, as in his play *Justice* (1910), and his story, "Quality," the latter deploring the shoddiness of capitalist industrial production.

GALVESTON PLAN, THE, see Municipal Reform.

GANDHI, MOHANDAS K. (1869-1948), leader of the Indian nationalists opposing British rule and spiritual head of the new Indian state. His methods of passive resistance and love of his enemies were highly respected by Americans of all classes and suggested techniques to some American social reformers. He was influenced by Thoreau's *Essay on Civil Disobedience* (*q.v.*). P. C. Roy-Chaudhury, *Gandhi and His Contemporaries* (1974); *Gandhi's Autobiography* (1948); Homer Jack, ed., *Gandhi Reader* (1965).

GANG, THE, refers to several related but not always associated concepts. Thus, a "gang" in pre-Civil War years, referred to groups of city desperados, who prided themselves on their brutality, and who were a force in municipal affairs and politics; see, for example, Herbert Asbury, *The Gangs of New York* (1928). Later, it was taken to refer more directly to a group of outlaws and developed this particular connotation in "gangster." It was also used to suggest, invidiously, an opposition group or party which represented no legitimate principle, but which had been brought together solely for gain, thus being comparable to an *ad hoc* assemblage of criminals; see Ohio Gang. The interrelations of these several meanings are found in Frederic M. Thrasher, *The Gang: a Study of 1,313 Gangs in Chicago* (1927), a classic in sociology which, moreover, precipitates the major challenge in the word, as representing the matrix of juvenile deliquency (*q.v.*): product of the city, the ineffective home, inadequate social controls, uninspiring social leadership, bad examples set by asocial but successful gangsters. James Haskins, *Street Gangs: Yesterday and Today* (1977); Barry A. Krisberg, *The Gang and the Community* (1975); Elliot Liebow, *Tally's Corner* (1967).

GARFIELD, JAMES A. (1831-1881), an educator and Civil War general, who became a Republican Party regular (*q.v.*), and tarred with suspicion because of his association with Crédit Mobilier (*q.v.*). Garfield was elected President in 1880, and promised to fill the office with dignity and responsibility. His repudiation of the Stalwarts inspired one of them, a disappointed office-seeker, to shoot him, and to announce that the Stalwart Vice-President, Chester A. Arthur, would now be President. The tragedy helped the cause of civil service reform (*q.v.*).

GARIBALDI, GIUSEPPE (1807-1882), Italian republican leader, who had to flee his country in 1834 because of his complicity in libertarian plottings; he returned in 1848 and was prominent in the revolutionary efforts of that year. With their failure, he left once more, this time coming to the United States. In 1854, he was home again, and deep in the politics of that divided country. He was a leader in the war against Austria, in 1859, and returned with his "Red Shirts" to battle with the forces of the Two Sicilies which, conquered, increased the unity of Italians. His attempt to add the Papal States to the union caused international controversy and a division of Italian opinion. Nevertheless, he bore the uncontested title of "The Liberator."

GARLAND, HAMLIN (1860-1940), the story-teller of Populism (*q.v.*), son of a frustrated and disillusioned pioneer, whose efforts to attain an education and whose desire for self-expression somewhat tallied with Edwin Markham's (q.v.). Garland's *Main-Travelled Roads* (1891) was a landmark in American realism as well as an expression of Populist embitterment. His *Crumbling Idols* (1894) was a pioneer statement of literary goals. In succeeding years he found himself unable to sustain his campaign; by the coming of the Progressive Era, he was an exploded meteor. Nevertheless, he wrote *A Son of the Middle Border* (1917), one of the great American volumes of reminiscence, throwing light on Populist strength and limitations.

GARLAND FUND, THE, see American Fund for Public Service, Inc.

GARRISON, WILLIAM LLOYD (1805-1879), one of the most remarkable figures in American social reform, he was the first to make an active creed of "immediatist" abolitionism, holding that slavery could not be undermined before it had been covered with moral obloquy. *The Liberator*, issued from January 1, 1831 to the end of 1865, held to this contention without deviation. He thus differed fundamentally with Benjamin Lundy (q.v.), on whose paper he had begun his abolitionist career. In 1832, Garrison founded, with a few persons, the first immediatist society in the United States, the New England Anti-Slavery Society. In 1832, he delivered a wounding blow to the American Colonization Society with his pamphlet, *Thoughts on African Colonization*. The next year, he visited Great Britain, where he helped disillusion its abolitionists with colonization. On his return, he helped found the American Anti-Slavery Society. Some of its leaders thought that a more moderate approach in presenting their program would attract more followers. Garrison disagreed, becoming, instead, more vehement in his denunciations of slavery. In 1835, he was the subject of the most famous anti-abolitionist mob, in Boston, when his life was endangered. His increasing radicalism—his denunciation of the churches, his espousal of woman's rights—seemed to conservative abolitionists to make him a burden to their cause. They missed, however, the significance of his work. The North was increasingly receptive to the antislavery argument because it was economically and politically in competition with the South, especially for control of the West. It had, however, no regard for the Negroes in the North, and kept them closely restricted through "Black Codes." It could thus be legitimately accused of hypocrisy in its criticism of the slavery system. Garrison, by maintaining the moral argument, by refusing to compromise it in the interests of political gains drew the fires of southern opinion and revealed its unswerving pro-slavery character. He also set up a standard of social responsibility toward which northerners increasingly moved, at least to the extent of resisting the efforts of southern leaders to nationalize slavery. Garrison, too, by his demand for free speech, prevented compromisers from burying the slavery issue in the interests of national peace. Yet it would be unfair to blame Garrison for the Civil War, or to make a scapegoat of a person who had no political power, nor funds, nor a mass following. In 1840, his determination that women would be given equal rights with men in abolitionist affairs, split the American Anti-Slavery Society, driving off those who denied that women had a place in public affairs, or who sought political action. In 1848, some of them supported Martin Van Buren (q.v.), who had been a pro-slavery President, as candidate of the Free Soil Party (q.v.). The Compromise of 1850 (q.v.) would have been a staggering blow to Negro hopes had not the North become increasingly "Garrisonian" and refused to obey the law. When Garrison, on July 4, 1854, burned the Constitution of the United States as a pro-slavery document, he symbolized resistance to law which countenanced slavery. Others carried the battle against slavery expansion into law, politics, western settlement, and, ultimately, into the military crisis of the Civil War. In the 1960s, he was vilified by historians; see Filler, "Garrison, Again, and Again," *Civil War History*, March 1965.

"GARVEYISM," the creation of Marcus Garvey (1887-1940), a Jamaican Negro who came to New York and preached Negro nationalism. His "Back to Africa" campaign inspired some feeling among American Negroes and brought him support and funds which he handled irresponsibly. He was convicted of fraud and deported. Elton C. Fox, *Garvey...a Black Nationalist* (1972).

GASTONIA (N.C.) STRIKE (1929), resulted from an effort by the communist-dominated National Textile Workers Union to organize the southern mills, and raise the workers' living standards. The Loray Mills of the Manville Jenkes Co. went on strike April 2, 1929, under the leadership of Fred Beal, an ex-service man, who had organized textile workers in Lawrence and New Bedford, Mass. There were bitter actions between the strikers on the one hand, police and anti-labor civilians, on the other. Several policemen died during one riot, and a group of workers, including Beal, were indicted for murder, and in drawn-out proceedings given jail sentences. They were defended by the A.C.L.U. (q.v.). Meanwhile, agitation and conflict continued in the town. The murder of a woman strike leader resulted in full acquittal of the defendants. The inability to expect justice persuaded the convicted strikers to jump bail. Beal fled to Russia, where he became disillusioned with communism, as he tells in his *Proletarian Journey* (1937).

GAYS, see Homosexuals.

GENERAL STRIKE, THE, labor's most momentous weapon, used in order to gain political ends, as a prelude to revolutionary situations, and as an economic weapon. It involves a rousing of all available labor forces for a distinct end. Its philosophy was formalized in William Benbow's *Grand National Holiday* (1832?), which, avoiding advocating direct violence, did attempt to instil in labor a sense of its united power. George Sorel's *Reflections on Violence* (1908) concerned itself less with the reality of a stoppage of work than with "the myth of the general strike," intended to bind workers in a sense of common effort. The Russian Revolution of 1905 involved general strike efforts. The Belgian General Strike of 1913 had the aim of attaining universal suffrage; that in Germany in 1920 was intended to discourage counter-revolutionary elements from attempting to seize power. American efforts have been largely localized, notably in Seattle, 1919, which resulted in great bitterness on both sides of the struggle. See Wilfred Harris Crook, *The General Strike: A Study of Labor's Tragic Weapon in Theory and Practice* (1931). One of the most noted efforts in the United States was the San Francisco General Strike of 1934, which brought Harry Bridges (q.v.) to the fore.

GENERAL WELFARE CLAUSE, see Welfare Legislation.

"GENÊT, CITIZEN," Edmond Charles Genêt, see French Revolution and the United States.

GENETIC ENGINEERING, a controversial aspect in the ethics (q.v.) of scientific research, in having the capacity to alter the characteristics of human beings, and human growth generally, thus creating a dangerous and evil weapon in irreverent hands. Scientists seemed able literally to transfer genes, the chemical units of heredity, from one organism to another. Their methods and resources showed possibilities of benign service, as in being able to screen diseased and defective fetuses, but large areas remained which raised quarrels among lay people and scientists.

GENEVA CONVENTION (1864-1865), endorsed by leading European powers, provided for civilized treatment of the sick and wounded during war.

GENOCIDE, a word coined at the Nuremburg Trials (q.v.), meaning race-murder, and having particular reference to the efforts of the German Nazis to exterminate the entire Jewish people. Although other peoples suffered severely, due to the Nazi program, including Poles and Gipsies, it was at the Jews that the so-called "final solution" (q.v.) was directed. The subject became one of concern to the United Nations. In December 1948, it adopted a Convention on the Prevention and Punishment of Genocide. Francis Neilson, *The Crime of*

Genocide (1979); I. L. Horowitz, *Genocide: State Power and Mass Murder* (1976).

GENTILITY, associated with persons of noted birth, "good family," and distinguished heredity. Although taken to be anti-democratic, in post-Civil War America, and effete, by realists and naturalists (*qq.v.*), its concern for standards, dignity, and ideals produced an unbroken tradition of public servants and *littérateurs.* Its reformers tended to be in the tradition of "goo-goos," and to act in the spirit of *noblesse oblige* (*qq.v.*); although its literary figures included Henry James, they also included William Dean Howells (*q.v.*). World War I, the succeeding "Flapper Age," and the Depression of the 1930's seemed like death-blows to gentility, but it survived in the respect accorded such writers as T. S. Eliot and Ezra Pound (*qq.v.*), by persons who often prided themselves on their progressive attitudes and ideas. Gentility was scorned in such a la mode books as J. G. Sproat, *"The Best Men"* (1965); John Tomsich, *A Genteel Endeavor* (1971); S. Persons, *The Decline of American Gentility* (1973); P. Schrag, *The Decline of the WASP* (1971). See also George Santayana, *The Genteel Tradition at Bay* (1931).

"GENTLEMEN'S AGREEMENT" (1907), made between the United States government and the Japanese government which, in effect, stopped the bulk of immigration to the United States. The agreement especially discriminated against poor Japanese. A peculiar feature enabled women to come to the United States who were joining their husbands; this permitted a class of women, chosen by pictures and joined in a special rite, to enter the country: they were known as "picture brides." The agreement did not increase the popularity of Americans in Japan, even though the Japanese were able to "save face" by voluntarily restraining her nationals from emigration. See Japan. Y. Ichihashi, *Japanese in the United States* (1932); Eleanor Tupper and G. E. McReynolds, *Japan in American Public Opinion* (1973).

GEORGE, DAVID LLOYD (1863-1945), Welsh statesman, raised in poverty, he became the "people's lawyer," Liberal Member of Parliament, opponent of the Boer War (*q.v.*), and advocate of improved conditions for the poor. As a Cabinet minister, his 1909 Budget was a notable challenge to the propertied classes. As Prime Minister during World War I, he appeared to his admirers to have taken his place among the immortals. His subsequent program, which included "hanging the Kaiser," and foisting the Versailles Treaty (*q.v.*) on Germany, among other measures, seemed less than Olympian. His later career belonged to England, rather than the world.

GEORGE, HENRY, (1839-1897), with Edward Bellamy (*q.v.*), the most notable of post-Civil War creators of panaceas (*q.v.*). Born in Philadelphia, and largely self-educated, he was a sailor and a printer who experienced hard times and considered their source, while struggling in San Francisco to support a wife and child. *Progress and Poverty* (1879), after a slow beginning, became one of the best-read books in political economy. It argued that the land belonged to society, which created its value and properly taxed that value, not improvements on the land. Thus, George hoped to end poverty, without destroying the individual's incentives to work. George's work included a religious component which attracted many followers. Although the "Single Tax" did not conquer governments, as George expected it to do, it affected tax schedules, influenced the famous Lloyd George (*q.v.*) budget of 1909, and inspired numerous social reformers, especially on a municipal level in the United States, and in higher governmental circles, for example in New Zealand. The city being the classic example of high land values, manifestly affected by the coming together of ordinary people, George's ideas motivated such municipal reformers as Tom L. Johnson, Bolton Hall, and Hazen S. Pingree (*qq.v.*). George's works included *Social Problems* (1883) and *Protection or Free Trade* (1886). His son, Henry George, Jr., followed in his footsteps, to no great effect, save that his biography of his father (1904) told an important story in American

reform. George's ideas are sustained by the Robert Schalkenbach Foundation, New York; see also its *American Journal of Economics and Sociology.*

GERM WARFARE, a charge made by the Chinese Communists, during the Korean War: that American troops were dropping germ-laden bombs on the civil population; the charge was echoed by communist sympathizers everywhere. The purpose of the charge was evidently to create propaganda against the United States, as well as to explain epidemics in communist-dominated areas. "Brainwashing" (*q.v.*) techniques permitted communists to persuade American Prisoners of War to "confess" that they had engaged in germ warfare.

GERMAN-AMERICANS, one of the most important of the national groups to help develop the United States and contribute to its social reform traditions. Germans (as in Germantown, Pennsylvania) helped to develop the physical terrain, and such a family as the Mühlenbergs contributed to the independency of the Lutheran Church, to the Revolutionary actions, and to the organization of the new nation. On the other hand, the fundamentalist (*q.v.*) groups of Germany sent over such elements as created the communitarian enterprises of Amana and Zoar, (*q.v.*), among others. Refugee groups fleeing the defeated revolution of 1848 (*q.v.*) helped build Cincinnati, Milwaukee, and St. Louis, among other centers. In St. Louis, they became a bastion of anti-slavery feeling, and ultimately helped save Missouri for the Union, and thus, possibly, the Union itself. Yet they were not generous in their feelings toward Negroes. Conformity in Germany helped produce its opposite, and German anarchists, including Johann Most and some of the defendants of the Haymarket Affair (*qq.v.*) contributed to American radical thought and action, as well as to the development of socialist theory and organization. During World War I, their thoughts were either neutralist or sympathetic toward the German cause, and it became the task of Allied sympathizers to subdue them; this was done, leaving a residue of bitterness from which the country still suffers. In the 1930's, the rise of Hitlerism produced some sympathizers in the United States, and some effort at emulation, notoriously in the organization of the German-American Bund, which was, however, wholly discredited. The Germans as a minority group posed no threat to democracy, but had powers which could contribute to it. Carl Wittke, *German-Americans and the World War* (1936); Richard O'Connor, *German-Americans* (1968).

GERMANY seemed to American reformers more a source of useful ideas and inspiring dissidents than an example of a nation progressive as a whole. Thus, it was Kantian thought which influenced Transcendentalism (*q.v.*), the Hegelian Dialectic which contributed to Marxism (*q.v.*). It was German techniques in education and in science which attracted American visitors, rather than the results in terms of German civilization. Such famed personalities and creators as Ludwig van Beethoven and Heinrich Heine (*q.v.*), it was noted, were dissidents and expatriates (*q.v.*). Germany produced would-be reformers, whose efforts, however, were often permitted to bend before nationalism; see William O. Shanahan, *German Protestants Face the Social Question, 1815-1871* (1954). The defeat of the German Revolution of 1848 (*q.v.*) sent many more questioning spirits abroad. In the latter part of the century, however, Germany became the center of the Second International, and such names as Bebel, Bernstein, Liebknecht, Lassalle (*qq.v.*) became internationally famous. Thanks to the powerful party —and Bismarck (*q.v.*), who hoped to divide socialist and republican forces—Germany set an example of welfare services. When the Socialists voted war credits to the Kaiser in 1914, their prestige was deeply wounded. The murder of Karl Liebknecht and Rosa Luxemburg (*qq.v.*) harmed them still further. The rickety German Republic seemed more a problem in possible revolution or counter-revolution, in the 1920's, than a reform hope. It continued to be a problem, for all its varied achievements in cinema, art, fiction, and other areas, as well as in aspects of science. Berlin was a divided city, its eastern half sealed off by the "Berlin Wall." Turkish migrant workers made it the third largest "Turkish" city, its hundred thousand persons behind Ankara and Istanbul in numbers; some one and a quarter Turks lived in all of West Germany. Germans were haunted by a fear of a revived Nazi movement, clung to "The Fixer," Helmut Schmidt and demonized the Bavarian nationalist Franz Josef Strauss, and endured the presence of some 200,000 American troops, the shadow of East Germany and Russian troops on their border. F. Meinecke, *The German Catastrophe* (1963); Peter C. Lutz, *The German Democratic Republic from the Sixties to the Seventies* (1970); William D. Graf, *The German Left since 1945* (1976); Martin Broszat, *German National Socialism* (1966); G. Goldman, *The German Political System* (1974); A. and E. Homze, *Germany: the Divided Nation* (1970).

GERRYMANDERING, named for Elbridge Gerry (1744-1814), a Massachusetts political leader, whose plan for changing the geographic limits of state districts in order to increase the power of Republican votes during elections for state and national legislative posts, inspired similar political moves elsewhere. A "Gerrymander," about 1812, connoted a deception; it has since taken on a purely political meaning. G. A. Billias, *Elbridge Gerry* (1976).

GESTAPO, the secret police of Nazi Germany (*Geheim-Staats-Polizei*), a symbol of totalitarian cruelty and repression. See also G.P.U.

GHENT, WILLIAM J. (1866-1942), first a compositor, then a reporter, he joined the Socialist Party in 1904, and became one of its notable theoreticians. His *Our Benevolent Feudalism* (1902) was a pioneer analysis of the negative features of the American industrial system, as was his *Mass and Class* (1904).

GHETTO, from the Italian, Jews' quarters in European cities to which they were confined by law, most onerously in Poland and Russia, but in many other nations; in the United States, the term was applied to less legal, but effective segregation of various minority peoples who found themselves living in "Ghetto-like" circumstances. Although violence in the urban "black Ghettoes" of the 1960s was "credited" by pro-Black partisans with having "forced" the vast dollar and personnel expenditures made in the areas, no effort was made to explain the lack of positive residues, the continuing erosion. No important leaders or institutions emerged. Nor was any effort made to force Negro elements in industry, politics, and society to dedicate themselves in behalf of ghetto needs in the fashion of Jane Addams (*q.v.*) and others like her. The Reagan promises of 1980 were for the creation of "enterprise zones" which would rehabilitate the viable portions of the demoralized neighborhoods, such as the South Bronx in New York. Louis Wirth, *The Ghetto* (1956); J. A. MacVicar, *The Ghetto Family* (1969); David P. Demarest and Lois S. Landin, eds., *The Ghetto Reader* (1970); Joe R. Feagin and Harlan Hahn, *Ghetto Revolts* (1973); K. L. Kusmer, *The Ghetto Takes Shape: Black Cleveland 1870-1930* (1976).

GIDDINGS, JOSHUA REED (1795-1864), pioneer political abolitionist (*q.v.*) from the Western Reserve in Ohio, most intransigent anti-slavery area in the land. He joined the House of Representatives in 1838, where he became conspicuous for his rugged and fearless defiance of the pro-slavery bloc, and aided John Quincy Adams (*q.v.*) in his battle against the "Gag Law" (*q.v.*). For his defense of a shipload of slaves being transported on the brig *Creole*, who had revolted and escaped to the British Bahama Islands, he was censured by the House, resigned, and was returned by his spirited constituency. He persisted in holding on to his Whig (*q.v.*) affiliation, feeling that he could be most effective in that way, and acceded, probably willingly, in Ohio laws which deprived the Negro of the vote. He was, however, an organizer of the Republican Party (*q.v.*) who sought to commit it to the rights of men. He wrote *The Exiles of Florida* (1858) (*q.v.*) and *The Rebellion: Its Authors and Causes* (1864).

GILDED AGE, THE, see Clemens, Samuel L.

GILMAN, MRS. CHARLOTTE [PERKINS] [STETSON] (1860-1935), influential woman suffragist and reformer: an active individualist whose personality and writings both exerted influence. Her *Women and Economics* (1898) was her first and greatest success. She edited *The Forerunner*, 1909-16. Other works included *Concerning Children* (1900); *The Man-Made World* (1910); *The Living of Charlotte Perkins Gilman: an Autobiography* (1935).

GIOVANNITTI, ARTURO (1884-1959), poet and labor figure, came to the United States in 1900, and later joined the I.W.W. (*q.v.*). As one of the two major leaders of the Lawrence, Massachusetts, textile mill strike (*q.v.*) in 1912 he became famous for his courage and ability in the face of cruel tactics utilized by the mill-owners and the local police. When a woman was fatally shot in a riot during the strike, he and Joseph Ettor were arrested and charged with being accessories to murder. An I.W.W. campaign raised $60,000 for the defense and helped win acquittal. While in prison, he wrote a poem in irregular unrhymed verse which maintained his fame, "The Walker," which expressed his humanistic feelings. The strike and poem were the high points of his career, though he often appeared at labor rallies during the 1920's, and 1930's.

GIRARD COLLEGE, opened 1848, under the will of the financier Stephen Girard (1750-1831), an institution for orphan boys. Its philanthropy was defined by its inhospitableness to ministers of any denomination, and to Negro children. In 1968, its segregation policy prescribed in Girard's will was overthrown by court action.

GIRONDISTS, the moderate party of the French Revolution, so named because notable leaders among them came from the department of the Gironde. It claimed such distinguished personalities as the mathematician Condorcet and the orator Brissot. The rise of the radical wing, the Jacobins (*q.v.*) or, in political terms, the Mountain, raised a crisis which was sharpened by the fact that France was surrounded by enemies and fighting for existence. The assassination of the Jacobin Marat by the young Girondiste, Charlotte Corday, touched off a "Reign of Terror" (*q.v.*) which dissolved the Girondists, leaving Robespierre (*q.v.*) and his followers in full control of the government.

GISSING, GEORGE (1857-1903), English novelist, whose generous and sensitive efforts at human association were rebuffed, producing, in his fiction an astringent realism, with pessimistic overtones, as distinguished from that of his friend H. G. Wells (*q.v.*), whose socialist vision encouraged humor and optimism. Gissing's novels include *Workers of the Dawn* (1880), *Demos* (1886), and *The Nether World* (1889). His *New Grub Street* (1891) ruthlessly exposed the dreary lot of London writers, talented and untalented, and contrasts with *The Private Papers of Henry Ryecroft* (1903): Gissing's rationale for escaping from a harsh and unfriendly world.

GITLOW V. PEOPLE OF NEW YORK (1925), involving charges of "criminal anarchy," famous for one of Justice Holmes's (*q.v.*) dissents, in which, though recognizing the right of a government to defend itself, he made a ringing defense of freedom of speech: "Every idea is an incitement. . . . But whatever may be thought of the redundant discourse before us, it had no chance of starting a present conflagration. If, in the long run, the beliefs expressed in proletarian dictatorship are destined to be accepted by the dominant forces of the community, the only meaning of free speech is that they should be given their chance and have their way." See also Abrams v. United States, Schenck v. United States.

GLADDEN, WASHINGTON (1836-1918), an outstanding Christian Socialist (*q.v.*) who was long established as a Congregationalist minister in Columbus, Ohio, and who set an example of speaking in terms of the workingman from the pulpit. His denunciation of "tainted money" (*q.v.*) was a subject of controversy in 1905. His writings included *Applied Christianity* (1887), *Social Salvation* (1902), and his particularly useful *Recollections* (1909).

GLADSTONE, WILLIAM E. (1809-1898), noted English statesman, whose turn from Toryism to Liberalism profoundly affected British politics. He sponsored many reforms, including the disestablishment of the Irish Church, denunciation of the Turkish atrocities in Bulgaria, Irish land reform, the secret ballot, and others. His life was also representative of Victorian dilemmas of spirit and democracy; Joyce Marlow, *The Oak and the Ivy* (1977); Peter Stansky, *Gladstone: a Progress in Politics* (1979).

GLOBALISM, a concept on the path of America's increased commitment to participation in world affairs. Clare Booth Luce, a playwrite turned political figure and wife of Henry Luce (*q.v.*), in Congress derogated the concept as "Globaloney," arguing that concern for world conditions was evasion of problems at home, but the word persisted as useful; see Stephen E. Ambrose, *Rise to Globalism* (1971).

GOD, a factor in all social reform movements, though with differing weights. "God's will" could, indeed, serve those who defended miserable or intolerable conditions, but it added strength to the argument of reformers for them to be able to assert that this was a false view of Deity. Anne Hutchinson, Roger Williams, and William Penn (*qq.v.*) were among many who were impelled toward libertarian and philanthropic causes by equating God with justice and human dignity. Deists (*q.v.*) later did the same, though emphasizing an impersonal God, to the scorn of the orthodox. All American Presidents found it necessary or desirable, especially during national crises, to invoke God in behalf of their cause. Frances Wright's and Robert Owen's (*qq.v.*) social usefulness was distinctly limited by their "freethinking" (*q.v.*) proclivities. The national reform movement of the pre-Civil War decades was in part aimed at revitalizing religion in the North; the South closed ranks behind a conviction that true religion lay in supporting the *status quo* (*q.v.*) at whatever cost. Henry George and Edward Bellamy (*qq.v.*) were motivated in large part by religious needs to devising their great reform programs. Robert G. Ingersoll (*q.v.*), in challenging religion, fought for free speech, yet his career largely served the reactionary wing of the Republican Party. The Populist Party Platform (*q.v.*) invoked "the blessing of Almighty God." The Reform Movement which followed it was less fundamentalist; Ray Stannard Baker (*q.v.*) examined *The Spiritual Unrest* (1910) of the time, and was himself a skeptic. The then influential Socialist Party took the position that religion was largely what Marx (*q.v.*) had termed it: an opiate. World War I and the spectacle of religious establishments helping on all sides of the holocaust to maintain its fires, helped further to disillusion many sensitive minds with the reality of God. Christian Socialism (*q.v.*), which had earlier sought to align religion with what appeared to skeptics a universe of matter with no purpose, lost standing and influence. *Elmer Gantry* (1927), by Sinclair Lewis (*q.v.*), seemed to many of its readers an accurate portrait of a religious leader who was not merely a hypocrite, but essentially typical. Pacifists continued to attract some sincerely God-seeking persons. The U.S.S.R. was a militant agency opposed to religion. Its leader, Stalin, however, on one occasion during World War II startled auditors by invoking God's aid to Russia. Some commentators recalled that he had studied at a theological school, in his youth. Kermit Eby was almost unique in his career as a union organizer and ordained minister, before he became a University of Chicago professor; his *The God In You* (1954) offered such chapters as "The Devil Is a Hoodlum" and "Creation Is a Big-Time Job." See also Churches and Reform. The existentialism of the influential Sartre (*q.v.*) posited atheism, though numerous would-be radical leaders found it useful to identify themselves as ministers. A popular educated audience was in 1980 made acquainted with the "Big-Bang" theory in astronomy which, in effect, found the beginning of the universe reminiscent of the account given in Genesis. Robert Jastrow, director of the National Aeronautics and Space Administration's (NASA) Goddard Institute for Space Studies and author of *God and the Astronomers*, reported scientists as curiously upset by evidence of the "Big-Bang" theory's validity; it conflicted with their urge to *know*: an urge the theory could not satisfy.

"GOD IN HIS INFINITE WISDOM . . . ," see Coal Strike of 1902.

GODKIN, EDWIN LAWRENCE (1831-1902), Manchester Liberal and first editor of the *Nation* (*qq.v.*), an Englishman of Irish upbringing who emigrated to the United States in 1856, bringing with him rigid principles of free trade, civil service reform, and anti-imperialism. His reform tenets were mixed with distaste for labor union, socialism, and expanded opportunities for the masses. He made the *Nation* which he edited 1865-1900, and the New York *Evening Post*, which he also headed 1883-1900, journalistic models of good English and forthright statement of principles; for an approach to Godkin, see W. M. Armstrong, *E. L. Godkin* (1978).

GODWIN, WILLIAM (1756-1836), British social philosopher, whose works influenced reformers in a number of countries. In 1796, he married Mary Wollstonecraft, a pioneer of women's emancipation. His *Enquiry Concerning Political Justice and Its Influence on Morals and Happiness* (1793) was anarchist in tendency, emphasizing freedom rather than cooperation, and equality rather than organization. He inspired the poet Shelley's libertarian thought, and stimulated Malthus (*q.v.*) to his epochal work on population.

GOGOL, NIKOLAI V. (1809-1852), noted among social reformers as well as students of literature for his *The Inspector-General* (1836), which satirized the Russian bureaucracy of his time.

GOLD CORNER, THE, see Black Friday.

GOLD STANDARD, THE, see Silver Issue, The.

GOLDEN FLEECE AWARD, see Proxmire, William.

"GOLDEN RULE" JONES, see Jones, Samuel M.

GOLDMAN, EMMA (1869-1940), Russian-born anarchist who came with her family to the United States in 1886. The execution of the Haymarket (*q.v.*) defendants turned her to anarchy and she became a well-known propagandist for her cause. She was associated with Alexander Berkman, who, in 1892, attempted to assassinate Henry C. Frick, in the course of the Homestead Strike (*q.v.*). She herself became notorious to the police. She served a prison sentence in 1894 for contributing to a riot in support of the Pullman Strike (*q.v.*), and was arrested again for having inadvertently influenced the thinking of Leon F. Czolgosz, who assassinated President McKinley. She was, however, released. She founded *Mother Earth* in 1906. Much of her program involved libertarian ideals and feminism, as expressed in *Anarchism and Other Essays* (1910), and the somewhat thin *Social Significance of the Modern Drama* (1914). She was among those deported in 1919 on the *Buford* (*q.v.*). Her *Living My Life* (1931) is an important autobiography.

GOMPERS, SAMUEL (1850-1924), founder and long-time leader of the American Federation of Labor (*q.v.*). He not only eschewed radicalism and idealistic approaches to the purpose of organized labor; he was quick to denounce such labor elements as the Chinese, which represented a threat to labor because of its willingness to work for more humble wages; in addition, Gompers's denunciations of them were on racial and personal grounds, as well as economic. During World War I, his War Committee on Labor emphasized national unity over labor's wants. His point of view reflected some of the prejudices and short-term values of some of his constituents. His Federation was meant to endure, no matter whether prosperity or depression prevailed, as distinguished from more high-minded labor organizations which were unable to continue in hard times. Thus, he can be seen as a labor statesman, or, for those who idealize labor, as a "labor faker" (*q.v.*); see Bernard Mandel, *Samuel Gompers* (1963).

"GOO GOOS," see Municipal Reform.

"GOOD NEIGHBOR POLICY," proposed for the United States by Franklin D. Roosevelt (*q.v.*) at his first Inaugural as President, in 1933; at the Pan-American Conference of that year at Montevideo, the U.S. Secretary of State, Cordell Hull, underscored it, and the "Good Neighbor Policy" became especially identified with U.S.-Latin American relations, in opposition to earlier "Big Stick" and Dollar Diplomacy (*qq.v.*) policy. Accordingly, direct intervention was ended in such Central American and Caribbean countries as Cuba and Nicaragua (*qq.v.*), and efforts made to develop their friendship with the United States. The "Good Neighbor Policy" became increasingly more necessary in order to counter German, Russian, Japanese, and other influences below the Mexican Border, during World War II and after. Increasingly, the use of American force became impossible, serving only to lose the United States further prestige in world opinion. Negotiations, operation through the Organization of American States, and other diplomatic processes took over, retarded by such events as the Cuban (*q.v.*) catastrophe of 1961. A problem with building a firmer "Good Neighbor Policy" lay in the fact that Latin Americans better remembered the painful aspects of their relations with the United States than did the North Americans, and could exploit those aspects for demagogic or sincere purposes; the North American attitude of "Let's forget it" was not useful. Dr. Juan José Arévalo's *The Shark and the Sardines* was by a former president of Guatemala, recounted every bitter detail of American imperialism practiced on Latin Americans, and sold over a million copies in Latin American countries. Irwin F. Gellman, *Good Neighbor Diplomacy: U.S. Policies in Latin America 1933-1945* (1979); Lloyd Gardner, *Economic Aspects of New Deal Diplomacy* (1964).

GOODMAN, PAUL (1911-1972), a guru (*q.v.*) of the 1960s, whose complaints about American life and education, expressed in *Growing Up Absurd* (196), took the "kids" he idealized by storm, and had him talking to massed student audiences across the country. He juxtaposed to life as it was the co-authored life as it ought to be, *communitas* (1947), and expressed it further in his collection of comments, *The Society I Live in Is Mine* (1963), in which, as a sample of his thought, he protested against barring homosexuals from parks on grounds that they needed them to meet, and against light in dark city enclaves, asking where then youth without money to rent motel rooms would have sex.

GORKI, MAXIM (1868-1936), pseud.; originally Aleksei M. Pyeshkov, world-famous for his tales which show sympathy for the feelings and sufferings of the poor and oppressed. He is officially set down in Soviet sources as having been poisoned by Trotskyites, as "revealed" in the Moscow Trials (*q.v.*).

GOTHA, CONGRESS AND PROGRAM OF (1875), a landmark in socialist thinking and planning, it developed a full-bodied program ranging from recommendations for education to specifications for voting requirements. It enabled Karl Marx to consolidate his thinking and forces, in terms of his *Critique of the Gotha Program* of that year, in which he states his controversial advocacy of a "Dictatorship of the Proletariat" (*q.v.*).

GOULD, JAY (1836-1892), with James Fisk and Daniel Drew (*qq.v.*) a classic symbol of the ruthless behavior of free enterprise entrepreneurs of the post-Civil War period. Their business wars were at the expense of the public welfare; they are pilloried in Charles Francis Adams, Jr.'s, *Chapters of Erie* (1871). The attempt by Gould and Fisk to corner gold brought on "Black Friday" (*q.v.*). They, and persons like themselves, earned the invidious name of "Robber Barons" (*q.v.*), in reform lore. A financier like Gould needs to be distinguished from one like John D. Rockefeller, Sr. (*q.v.*); the former was a manipulator and wrecker, the latter however controversial his achievement, a builder.

"GOVERNMENT BY INJUNCTION," a bitter phrase employed by labor, which felt itself undermined by the injunc-

tion (*q.v.*), and, as in the Pullman Strike (*q.v.*), saw the government arrayed against it.

GOVERNMENT OWNERSHIP, see Public Ownership.

G.P.U., secret police of the Soviet Union, whose use of terror to suppress dissident opinion was somewhat more notable than that of the preceding *Cheka,* since the G.P.U. operated for the most part during years of internal peace (1922-34). It was less publicized by friends of the Soviet Union than was the German Gestapo (*q.v.*). It was succeeded by several permutations of initials: N.K.V.D., M.V.D., M.G.B.; in 1953, it became K.G.B. ("Committee for State Security").

GRACCHUS BROTHERS, Gaius Sempronius (159?-121 B.C) and Tiberius Sempronius (168?-122 B.C.), Roman reformers who sought to curb the spread of great estates and to develop other democratic measures in opposition to the *optimates,* the party of the nobility, and in behalf of the proletariat. Gaius developed a particularly ambitious program, following his brother's assassination, demanding a fair price on grain and an extension of the franchise beyond Rome, among other measures. He, too, died in the ensuing struggle.

GRADUALISM, inseparable from social reform, and a distinguishing factor between social reform and revolution. However, conservatives have often refused to distinguish between "gradualists" and "immediatists," at least during the period when they were holding the line against all innovation. Thus, "gradualist" abolitionists were critical of such "immediatists" as Garrison (*q.v.*), holding that he was offending people who might yet be won over to their cause, with patience and an appeal to reason. Yet intemperate southerners put a price on the head of Arthur Tappan (*q.v.*), as well as on that of Garrison. Indeed, there was no essential difference in the practical program of either, since Garrison did not expect "immediate" abolition; he held, simply, that slavery should be treated as an institution which *ought* to be immediately abolished. A healthy reform situation usually finds both gradualists and immediatists in the field acting as curbs upon each other's laxness or irresponsibility.

GRAFT, a term once specialized among criminals, applied by Josiah Flynt (*q.v.*) to his description of the relations between criminals and the law-enforcement authorities, and demonstrating to his startled readers the fact that they were not separate components of society, but in no small measure associated. "Graft" was a means of livelihood, and thus distinguished the enterprising anti-social individual from the hobo (*q.v.*). Many readers perceived that not much necessarily separated the thief from highly respected citizens, at least with respect to graft. See also Municipal Reform.

GRAHAM, A. B. (1868-1960), founded the 4-H Clubs (*q.v.*) in Springfield, Ohio, 1902. He was also a pioneer in the development of extension teaching for the United States Department of Agriculture.

GRAHAM, SYLVESTER (1794-1851), health reformer who advocated vegetarianism as an aid to bodily "symmetry," that is, the avoidance of excess fat; immortalized in the "Graham cracker," though his views on health took in fresh air, sexual circumspection, and other bodily details. His ideas appealed to reformers, to Garrisonians (*q.v.*) almost as a group; see Richard H. Shryock, "Sylvester Graham and the Popular Health Movement, 1830-1870," *Mississippi Valley Historical Review,* XVIII (1931), 172-183. See also S. Nissenbaum, *Sex, Diet, and Debility...Graham* and *Health Reform* (1980).

GRAHAM, WILLIAM ("BILLY"), see Evangelicism.

GRAND ALLIANCE, THE, instituted June 22, 1941, when Hitler made his fateful decision and attacked his erstwhile partner, the U.S.S.R. Winston S. Churchill (*q.v.*) welcomed the diversion of German troops to their eastern front. The United States, which had already developed considerable benignity toward the Russians, for various reasons including the "Popular Front" (*q.v.*), increased her positive view of them, not only in terms of money and materials, but in terms of a tolerant view of the communist system, at least for Russians. Various conferences, at Casablanca, at Cairo, at Teheran, at

Yalta assumed a unity of purpose between the anti-Nazi Allies which deteriorated rapidly under the influence of "Cold War" (*q.v.*).

GRAND NATIONAL CONSOLIDATED TRADES UNION, Robert Owen's ambitious effort in 1834 to mobilize British labor in a great federation. Although it quickly brought together more than half a million workers into what was to have been a powerful organization of crafts, internal confusion and the antagonism of employers and the government soon caused it to dissolve.

GRANDFATHER CLAUSE, THE, a subterfuge developed in the southern states in the 1890's and the 1900's to deprive the Negro of the suffrage, despite the guarantees given him by the Fifteenth Amendment to the Constitution (*qq.v.*). Voters who were unable to prove that they were descendants of persons who voted prior to the Civil War, thus including the bulk of southern Negroes, were made subject to tax, property, and educational provisions which were practically insurmountable by most Negroes. This particular maneuver was struck down by the U.S. Supreme Court; see also Negro Suffrage.

GRANDISSIMES, The (1884), see Cable, George W.

GRANGER MOVEMENT, THE, see Munn v. Illinois, National Grange of the Patrons of Husbandry, Populist Revolt, The.

GRANT, ULYSSES SIMPSON (1822-1885), before Warren G. Harding (*q.v.*) holding the distinction of having been the worst American President; the merits of their successors are disputed. Honored for having helped save the Union, he brought to the high office an incompetence backed by the stubborn qualities which had made him formidable in war; yet he was not only elected but re-elected, and all but given a third nomination in 1880. Not only does he merit study of himself, therefore, but study in relation to the expectations of the voting population. "Black Friday," "Crédit Mobilier," and the unscrupulous effort to annex Santo Domingo (*qq.v.*) could all be traced to inadequate understanding (Grant was personally honest) in the White House. Grant's *Memoirs* (1885-6) have been estimated as among the best of all military recollections.

GRAPES OF WRATH, THE (1939), by John Steinbeck (*q.v.*), one of the great American novels, it tells the tale of the dispossessed tenant farmers of Oklahoma (the "Okies"), and their troubles in California where they sought to begin life again. Its complexity escaped critics and teachers of Steinbeck's time who, infatuated with the values in Ernest Hemingway's and F. Scott Fitzgerald's work, and unable to cope with the several levels of metaphor and reality in *The Grapes of Wrath*, derogated it as mere Thirties (*q.v.*) writing. Like Herman Melville's *Moby Dick*, however, Steinbeck's novel is timeless.

GRASS, GUNTER (1927-   ), influential author of *The Tin Drum* (1962), a metaphoric repudiation of pre-World War II Europe, and of both fascist and communist philosophies and deeds. Notable was his prediction that Poland, though under the weight of the Russians, would rise again: a prediction fulfilled in the shipyard workers's strike in Gdansk (Dansig) in 1980, and revealing widespread Polish pride and energy.

GRASSROOTS, a basic challenge to American social reformers, since it involves midwestern and western population, therefore farm owners as well as farm tenants, and thus a complex mixture of conservative and progressive impulses. Grassroots have spawned the inflexible Republicanism of Iowa, and also the Progressivism of Wisconsin, and in addition the utopian formulas of California, as well as variations on all three. Most important, they have involved the challenge of isolationism (*q.v.*). Grassroots conservatism has been as deceptive as grassroots radicalism, as seen in such figures as Borah, La Follette, Norris, Hiram Johnson, and, more recently, Nye, Lemke, and Burton K. Wheeler (*qq.v.*). See Harold F. Gosnell, *Grass Roots Politics, National Voting Behavior of Typical States* (1942).

GREAT, a word in Shakespeare's time defining a person of high rank and social standing. Romantics subsequently emphasized the individual, and added a mystic connotation, implying quality in the person, and "immortality" in his works. Reformers set up similar measuring-rods for individuals as social integers, sometimes treating artistic types as special cases, but refusing, for example to discern "greatness" in John D. Rockefeller's (*q.v.*) career, or editing out of the career of Abraham Lincoln (*q.v.*) deeds which embarrassed their view of him as "great." By the middle of the twentieth century, the concept of "greatness" had become so much equated with immediate visibility as to appear to require reconsideration.

GREAT AWAKENING, THE, see Revivalism and Reform.

"GREAT BARBECUE, THE," one of V. L. Parrington's (*q.v.*) happy phrases, this one for the post-Civil War era, characterized by a moral let-down in the victorious North, an emphasis upon materialistic advance, and a shallow admiration for wealth and success however obtained; roughly equivalent to *The Gilded Age*, as seen by Mark Twain (*q.v.*).

GREAT BRITAIN, in 1981, under the Tory Prime Minister Margaret Thatcher (*q.v.*), seeking to avoid national bankruptcy threatened by low productivity (*q.v.*), nationalized, unprofitable industry, heavy welfare payments, low sales as of British motors, defense burdens, inflation, EEC (*q.v.*) payments, and labor costs. The Tories, accusing the Labour Party of having heaped these miseries on the country, put their faith in resistance to high wages and low services, and reduced government spending generally: a program termed "monetarism," and opposed to "Keynesian" economics (*q.v.*). Labour termed the program an attack on trade unions and a crucifixion of the needy; its left wing, headed by Anthony Benn, scorned its own "welfare capitalism" as inadequate, and proposed direct socialism, withdrawal from EEC, a mediating role in the arms race, especially curbing the most deadly and expensive weapons. All this would enable Great Britain, Labour thought, to shift about with British resources, including rich North Sea oil fields, satisfying workers and meeting national needs. The Liberal Party, long short on direct power, hoped to have a role as mediating between extreme Labour and Tory policy makers. Richard Rose, *Politics in England* (1980); Denis Barnes and Eileen Reid, *Government and Trade Unions* (1980); Harold Wilson, *The Labour Government* (1971); J. D. Hoffman, *The Conservative Party in Opposition* (1964).

"GREAT COMMONER, THE," see Pitt, William, the Elder, Earl of Chatham; see also Bryan, William Jennings.

GREAT DEPRESSION, THE, see Economic Depression.

GREAT DICTATOR, THE (1940), starring Charles Chaplin; see Dictator.

"GREAT SOCIETY, THE," President Lyndon B. Johnson's (*q.v.*) grand design for "closing the books" on old problems of voting rights, medicare, inequity in schools, city erosion, consumer needs, crime, highway safety and transportation, and environment (*q.v.*). Ruling from affluence (*q.v.*), in control of Congress, Johnson launched what was to be a greater New Deal (*q.v.*) in July of 1965. He saw no contradiction between his domestic program and the Vietnam (*q.v.*) war; in January of 1966, he declared the nation could handle both. An unprecedented number of laws, affecting all parts of American life with direct government intervention, were passed and implemented. It is usually held that Vietnam defeated Johnson and drove him to retirement. It is, however, as true to say that he could not, with lavish funds, acquire the talent and dedication to make his domestic program produce results, and thus build a unified front for the world. The campuses seethed with everything but education. Welfare dispensaries, despite affluence, multiplied in a stew of fraud and inefficiency. "Giveaways" became a communicative word which created no counter-concept. Johnson's "War on Poverty" did not advance for lack of funds, but for lack of effective leaders among or outside the poverty regions. By 1968, when Johnson despaired and gave up, it was evident that "the Great Society," as he had conceived it, moved mechanically, and was directionless. The radical criticism of the great effort was summed up in M. E. Gettleman and D. Mermelstein, *The Great Society Reader: the*

Failure of American Liberalism (1967), which saw good only in the enemies of capitalism. Although Johnson's civil rights and voting rights acts, his medicare enterprise, his equal opportunity legislation, and numerous other actions were later seen as landmarks to be refined or reorganized, they did nothing for "The Great Society" program as such. For Johnson's own view, *The Vantage Point* (1971).

"GREEK DEMOCRACY," a shibboleth of the pre-bellum, slave-holding South, which held that it was a civilization similar to that which had existed in Greece during the centuries of its imperial greatness. The southern apologists held that, like earlier Greek civilization, theirs was built on slavery, but that for the elite there was an unparalleled democracy; with pride, they pointed to Jefferson, Patrick Henry, George Mason, John C. Calhoun, Andrew Jackson (*qq.v.*), and numerous others as bearing out their contention. They contrasted this with what seemed to them the sordid mediocrity and equalitarianism in the North.

GREEK INDEPENDENCE, WAR FOR, the result of a renaissance of national feeling which drew sympathy and support from abroad, including that of the poet Byron, who died at Missolonghi in 1824, and Dr. Samuel Gridley Howe (*q.v.*), who rendered the Greeks valuable services. Americans sentimentalized the Greek struggle, and were enraptured by the sculptor Hiram Powers's inadequate statue of *The Greek Slave*. Southern slaveholders praised the Greek battle for "liberty," which was achieved in 1832.

GREELEY, HORACE (1811-1872), editor of the *New York Tribune* and a prominent Whig and early Republican. He was a late-comer to abolition and an advocate of protectionism (*qq.v.*), but patronized many reforms. See his *Hints toward Reforms* (1850).

GREEN CORN REBELLION, an incident of 1917 when an anti-war, anti-draft march on Washington was planned by Oklahoma farmers; there was some rioting and the movement died down; it was the subject of a novel by William Cunningham, *Green Corn Rebellion* (1935).

GREEN POWER, a slogan of Negro spokesmen of the 1960s who argued for the power of money to enhance their communities's affairs, if necessary, it was inferred, at the expense of ethnic cooperation with others, forcing attention, for example, with boycotts. The slogan dovetailed with that of other "militants" who argued for hatred of "whites" as a force in Negro power. The failure of the "green power" approach was dramatically revealed in 1980 when a gruesome series of disappearances and deaths of Negro children in Atlanta, Georgia brought out numerous volunteers seeking clues. They were expected to be encouraged to ferret out information respecting the criminals by vivid displays of paper money which would be given them for uncovering information. None materialized in months of protracted searches and inquiries, despite the "green power" incentive.

GREENBACK PARTY, THE, organized by Peter Cooper (*q.v.*) in 1875, and advocating increased issues of paper currency in order to make it more readily available for better circulation, payments of debts, and raising of prices. Although it polled only 80,000 votes in the Presidential elections of 1876, it reorganized in 1878 as the Greenback-Labor Party (*q.v.*), with a broader and more effective program.

GREENBACK-LABOR PARTY, THE, represented an effort at an alliance of labor and Greenback partisans, spurred by the long depression of the 1870's; in addition to a variety of currency reforms, it demanded state boards of labor statistics, reduced hours of labor, the abolition of convict labor (*q.v.*) contracts, and restrictions on immigrant (*q.v.*) labor. This last item in particular foreshadowed their almost inevitable dissolution. However, in 1878, they polled more than a million votes, in the East and West, as well as in the mid-West, and elected fourteen congressmen. By 1880, however, when they nominated James B. Weaver (*q.v.*) for President, the Green-back-Labor partisans were largely from the farms, and Weaver

polled a little over three hundred thousand votes. See also Anti-Monopoly Party, Union Labor Party.

GREENBACK ISSUE, THE, see Specie Payment.

GREENBELT TOWNS, model villages erected by the Federal government, as part of its program to transform the countryside with modern services and enriched living. Greenbelt, Maryland, was a planned city near Washington, D.C., in which businesses were conducted by the Greenbelt Consumer Services on a cooperative basis. Other planned towns by the Resettlement Administration (*q.v.*) were Green Hills, in Ohio, and Greendale, in Wisconsin. Each was a village of six hundred and fifty homes owned by the government, for which rent was paid. The projects were transferred to the Farm Security Administration (*q.v.*).

"GRESHAM'S LAW," named for Sir Thomas Gresham (1519-1579), English adviser to royalty, and usually formulated as: "Bad money drives out good"; of two circulating currencies, the one having the greater value will be hoarded. Thus, during the Civil War, with depreciated "fiat money" (*q.v.*) on the market, those who had gold and silver kept it out of circulation, thus depreciating the fiat money further and encouraging inflation (*q.v.*).

GRIEVANCE COMMITTEE, the core element of organizing labor, which takes it upon itself to present to management a statement of dissatisfactions in a shop or plant with conditions of one type or another. It is usually composed of hardier elements, less afraid than others of the possible wrath of management, and more articulate in formulating labor's point of view; since the advent of "Big Labor," it has been less prominent in social and economic operations.

GRIMKÉ, Sarah Moore (1792-1873), one of the two famous "Grimké Sisters"; see Weld, Mrs. Angelina Emily (Grimké). Of distinguished South Carolina family, they became Quakers, and came North in 1836 to give their testimony against the institution of slavery. The interest of anti-slavery partisans and of people curious to see the ladies raised a problem, since women did not then readily exhibit themselves as speakers. They were taken in hand by the Garrisonians (*q.v.*), and though they offended the conservative clergy, broke ground for the woman suffrage (*q.v.*) movement. Angelina's *Appeal to the Christian Women of the South* (1836) was one of the influential pamphlets of the time. They largely retired from the field at the time of Angelina's marriage; see Catherine H. Birney, *The Grimké Sisters* (1885).

GRINGO, Spanish-American epithet (*q.v.*), contemptuously intended, for United States Americans or others of British descent. Often reflects resentment of what can be interpreted as exploitative or otherwise imperialistic deeds or attitudes.

GRÖNLUND, LAURENCE (1846-1899), a pioneer socialist theoretician who emigrated from Denmark to the United States in 1867 and was a schoolteacher and lawyer. He advocated an evolutionary type of socialism. His *The Co-operative Commonwealth* (1884) influenced the writing of Edward Bellamy's (*q.v.*) *Looking Backward;* see Arthur E. Morgan, *Plagiarism in Utopia* (1944). Other of Grönlund's writings included *Dialogue on the Coming Revolution* (1880); *Ca Ira! or, Danton in the French Revolution* (1887); *Our Destiny* (1891); and *The New Economy* (1898). He helped found the Fabian Society (*q.v.*).

GROSZ, GEORGE (1893-1959), great satirist of post-World War I Germany, his caricatures exposed the sickness of its people and social order, and forevisioned the coming fascism; he came to the United States in 1932 and became an American citizen and art teacher. He changed his style of drawing completely, and asserted a new-found "bourgeois" character; some of his work continued to have, however, a horrendous quality of its own. Returning to Germany, he died a few weeks after his landing.

GROWTH, see Productivity.

GUATEMALA, see Central America and American Reform.

GUERRILLA WARFARE, maintained by irregular troops,

usually against superior forces which they attack unexpectedly, from positions difficult to trace. It is usually considered in terms of political dissidence, held by an outlawed minority against an established power, by "partisans" who believe they have been deprived of liberties and speak for a suppressed majority of the population. Social reformers have condoned guerrilla fighting, when they approved the cause it supports: during the insurrection in the Philippines, during the Russian Revolution, in Cuba, Spain, Nicaragua (*qq.v.*), and elsewhere. Aided with arms and training by contending major or contriving powers, guerrilla warriors operated throughout Africa. They took power in former Rhodesia, in 1980, now named Zimbabwe (*q.v.*), and obtained English and American sympathy in their war against the Union of South Africa. Palestine Liberation Organization (*q.v.*) guerrillas committed atrocities (*q.v.*) in order to call attention to their demands, and won regard from mediating agencies. There seemed little prospect of limiting such activists as a force in political adjustments. See also Terrorists. L. H. Gann, *Guerrillas in History* (1971); V. S. Naipaul, *Guerrillas* (1976); O. Heilbrunn, *Partisan Warfare* (1962); *General Grivas on Guerrilla Warfare* (1965).

GUFFEY-SNYDER COAL ACT (1935), sometimes known as the "little N.R.A." (*q.v.*), was a major effort to put order into an industry torn by labor strife. It provided a "code" (*q.v.*) for the production of bituminous soft coal, price adjustments, and labor conditions. Held unconstitutional by the U.S. Supreme Court in Carter v. Carter Coal Company (1936), the way was opened for further industrial crises involving John L. Lewis and the United Mine Workers (*qq.v.*).

GUILD SOCIALISM, originated about 1900 in England, its best-known advocate being G. D. H. Cole (*q.v.*). It asked for self-government by workers, operating through National Guilds; in effect, it united state ownership and guild management. It was a compromise between syndicalism (*q.v.*), which emphasized the trades unions at the expense of the state, and state socialism (*q.v.*). It envisioned the state as an administrative body acting in behalf of the people in their role of consumers; see Cole's *Guild Socialism Restated* (1920).

GUILT, see White Guilt.

GUINEA PIGS, used in experiments, made famous by a work critical of American manufacturers of consumers goods (see Consumers) which charged that they used the general public as their guinea pigs. In June 1961, the Kansas head of food and drug controls told the Association of Food and Drug Officials that new drugs were being tested on the general public: that they were required only to reassure the Food and Drug Administration that their product was safe, not that it was effective. Thus, for two years, manufacturers had sold at drug prices ground-up fruit rinds as "cold curing," on little evidence.

GULAG, Russian labor camps, made infamous by Solzhenitzyn's (*q.v.*) *The Gulag Archipelago* (1974). It detailed at painful length the Soviet system of torture and repression, disturbing to those who sought differences between Nazi barbarism and that associated with heirs of the Russian Revolution.

GULLIVER'S TRAVELS (1726), Jonathan Swift's masterpiece, in which his hero, Lemuel Gulliver finds himself in Lilliput, subsequently in Brobdingnag and Laputa, and finally in the Houyhnms, inhabited by horses. One of the great social and political satires of the world, its bitterness and idealism, hidden in bland and deceptive phrases, offer fare for reformers and anti-reformers.

GURU, Hindu for teacher, a venerable one. Youth (*q.v.*) activists of the 1960s, seeking words and direction among American and foreign Indians, experimenting with drugs and sex, and fighting American life and history, sought aid of such individuals as might legitimatize their cause. These included Paul Goodman, Norman O. Brown, Herbert Marcuse (*qq.v.*), Naom Chomsky, and such lesser though not necessarily less affluent gurus as Philip Slater (*The Pursuit of Loneliness* 1970), Timothy Leary, the drug experimenter, Charles Reich (*The Greening of*

America 1970), and Leslie Fiedler, whose *Being Busted* (1969) described his prosecution on drug violation charges. An oddity of much of their work was the distance between their alleged expertise and their guru usefulness. Thus Slater had been chairman of the sociology department at Brandeis University before his saleability made him independent of his alleged discipline. Reich had taught law at Yale University. Students at such institutions had been accurate in taking their academic work lightly. Chomsky was a linguist before presenting himself as a political guru in *At War with Asia* (1970) and *Peace in the Middle East* (1974). With the collapse of the youth movement, and even before the revelations of the Charles Manson murder and depravity group, with its ramifications in quasi-decent society, some of the survivers sought new gurus, often illiterate, "charismatic" adventurers, who offered the consolations of a hastily rigged fundamentalist (*q.v.*) idea centered in a "commune" and accompanied by rock music, sex, and attempted cooperative living. Filler, *Vanguards and Followers* (1978).

GUTHRIE, WOODY (1912-1967), American folk-singer and song writer, whose career as a wandering minstrel of labor and the people, of sympathy for the poor and deserving became an American saga. Of a more earthy tradition than Pete Seeger, whose father was a collector and student of folk songs and whose uncle was the poet Alan Seeger, Guthrie wandered among working people and unionists, writing songs expressing their hopes and needs, among them the all but national anthem, *This Land Is Your Land*. He became, though inadvertently when laid low with disease, one of the inspirations for the synthetic folksinger Bob Dylan. See Guthrie's autobiography, *Bound for Glory* (1943).

H

HABEAS CORPUS, WRIT OF (Latin translation: you may have the body), a writ ordering someone who holds an individual in his keeping to show cause for the detention, the purpose of the writ being to curb illegal and improper imprisonments. Its suspension during the critical period which preceded the American Revolution was one significant reason for that event. Article I, Section 9 of the Constitution specified that "The Privilege of the Writ of Habeas Corpus shall not be suspended, unless when in Cases of Rebellion or Invasion the public Safety may require it."

HAGUE PEACE CONFERENCES, of 1899 and 1907; the first was called by the Czar of Russia and sought to curb the growing military establishments, without success. It did achieve some declarations presumably making for more "civilized" warfare; for example, dum-dum bullets were held undesirable for combat purposes, since they expanded on contact within the body afflicted, creating an aggravated wound. A Permanent Court of Arbitration (q.v.), mediating international differences was set up. The 1907 conference pressed these subjects further, but though a sense of action was fostered, helped by the activities of the Arbitration Court, and a third conference projected, little of a crucial character was accomplished. See also Internationalism and Reform.

HAITI, stormy western third of the island which also bears the Dominican Republic (q.v.). Its slave revolts stirred the sympathy of American reformers, and the heroic battles of Toussaint L'Ouverture (q.v.) to free the island, first from the English and Spanish, then from the French, thrilled them. The Haitian victory over Napoleon's troops — troops which had conquered Europe — discouraged the French chieftain, and directly led to his sale of the great Louisiana Territory to the United States. But internecine struggles between Haitian factions kept the island in a state of insurrection and undeveloped civilization. Mulatto and Negro vied for control. Voodoo remained potent among the masses. The workers on the coffee, cotton, sugar and other plantations suffered severe exploitation which was shared by foreign capital, including that from the United States. Marines sent in 1915 to maintain order while Haiti's finances were put in shape satisfactory to American creditors roused protests from American liberals disturbed over these manifestations of imperialism. By 1934, when the American troops were finally withdrawn, the dynamics of our Haitian relations had become vague; American liberals had no program for that nation. Desperate efforts in 1980 by Haitians to enter the United States as refugees (q.v.) bared their hopeless prospects. O. E. Moore, *Haiti: Its Stagnant Society and Shackled Economy* (1972).

HALE, JOHN P. (1806-1873), abolitionist statesman, who entered the House of Representatives in 1843 from New Hampshire, and helped John Quincy Adams fight the Gag Rule (qq.v.). In 1847 he beat the Democratic Party in his state to become an anti-slavery senator. Read out of the Democratic Party, he opposed the Mexican War and denounced northern "dough-faces" (q.v.). In 1852, he was the Free Democrats candidate for President, and maintained the argument for Free Soil against a pro-slavery Democratic Party and a disintegrating Whig Party, thus helping to build the Republican Party.

HALE, NATHAN (1755-1776), Revolutionary patriot, hanged by the British as a spy. He was remembered in 1960, when a highly-paid American pilot, flying over the Soviet Union on an observation mission, was forced down, and proceeded to confess all details of his assignment. Arguments mounted

as to whether he was a coward or a wise man. For his cooperativeness, he was given a relatively light prison term, his Army pay continuing back home. The argument continued that relating to American prisoners in China, who had preferred to cooperate, rather than suffer abuse. One argument in their favor was that the Chinese knew much more American history than did they, and that they could therefore easily be confused and misled.

"HALF-BREEDS," see Stalwarts.

HALL, BOLTON (1854-1938), one of Henry George's (q.v.) most active followers. A successful real-estate operator and businessman, he was a life-long critic of unfair taxation and of monopoly. His most successful book was *Three Acres and Liberty* (1907), issued in numerous editions, which began a "back-to-the-land" movement, and inspired many readers to undertake practical farming. In 1909, Hall began Free Acres, a cooperative colony in New Jersey.

HAM'N EGGS PLAN, one of the panaceas (q.v.) proposed for the troubles of the 1930's. It asked for "Thirty Dollars Every Thursday" for the deserving, in California. Unemployed citizens over fifty years of age were to be pensioned. Money for the purpose was to be raised by circulating one dollar warrants on which every one possessing them had to place a two-cent stamp each week before it was spent. "Ham'n Eggs" was a serious threat in the 1938 state elections, and, as directed by astute and not particularly scrupulous agitators, collected a million signatures for a special referendum on the subject, but failed to achieve its objective. This was the highpoint of one of many such plans to end the depression.

"HAMILTONIAN IDEALS," a staple in American politics and generally opposed to reform aims and outlooks. It posits a free enterprise system, and an elite to administer it, with the aid and encouragement of the government, which has the power to offer both. In its concern for the well-to-do, for patriotism, and for industry, it left little thought for the needy or the ambitious, and preferred stability to experiment. It maintained a "realistic" view of human nature as requiring curbs, rather than avenues for expression and stood in flat opposition to Jefferson and the "agrarian democracy" (qq.v.) for which he stood. J. E. Cooke, ed., *Alexander Hamilton: a Profile* (1967); G. Stourgh, *Alexander Hamilton and the Idea of Republican Government* (1969).

HAMMER V. DAGENHART, see Child Labor.

HAMPTON'S (1907-1911), one of the later and perhaps the greatest of the muckraking (q.v.) magazines, created by Benjamin B. Hampton, who intended not merely to expose evil conditions in civic affairs, but also to prescribe remedies for them. He congregated such writers as Charles Edward Russell, Rheta Childe Dorr, and Frederic C. Howe (qq.v.) for this purpose. Their biting articles brought down upon them vengeful retaliation, at a time when all the muckraking publications were under attack. *Hampton's* disappeared from the stands in a matter of months, despite its hundreds of thousands of readers.

HANDICAPPED, one of the better records in American modern social history. Though lacking the inspired and religious motivation of a Dorothea Dix (q.v.), numerous societies were concerned for the mentally retarded, the blind, deaf, spastic, and the crippled. Especially among government agencies and in hospitals, they worked to further legislation favoring the disadvantaged, and find funds enabling them to move in society, and receive treatment, training, and disability aids and support. Such organizations as the Child Welfare League and the Joseph P. Kennedy, Jr. Foundation did work which ranged from publicity opposing crude prejudices and insults to research into causes and cures. The U.S. Department of Health, Education, and Welfare (become, under Carter (q.v.), Health and Human Services) gave direction and funds to states, which set up their own agencies for making easier for the handicapped access to libraries and other public buildings and places. Progress was slowed by employers reluctant to hire the disabled, and a public unwilling to have them in neighborhood buildings, though they gave each other hope and comfort. In 1980, the World Congress for the Disabled met in Winnipeg, Canada, chaired by Alfred Morris, the one man in the world who, under the ousted Labour Government of Great Britain had held the post of Minister for the Disabled. He observed there should be such a Minister in every country in the world. Certainly one would have been appropriate in India, which had more disabled than Great Britain had people. The United Nations designated 1981 as The International Year of Disabled People. See also Old Age. M. Adams, *Mental Retardation and Its Social Dimensions* (1971); Elias Katz, *The Retarded Adult at Home* (1970); John Money, ed., *The Disabled Reader* (1966); M. D. Fantini and G. Weinstein, *The Disadvantaged: Challenge to Education* (1968); Verda Heisler, *The Handicapped Child in the Family: a Guide for Parents* (1972).

HANDICRAFT SYSTEM, a "stage" in the development of industry which produced the artisan who took pride in his work, and the guild; idealized by such artists as William Morris, and by Guild Socialists *(qq.v.)* in general, who sought to revive what they deemed its beneficent features; derogated as utopian by Marxists *(q.v.)*: as unable to produce the necessities of modern life, and impossible to retrieve, in any case. Nevertheless, handicrafts have been encouraged, for example by Berea College *(q.v.)*, as a worthy occupation and a civilizing force among mountain people, and as producing useful and pleasing objects.

HANNA, MARCUS A. (1837-1904), Cleveland, Ohio traction magnate, put the Republican Party on a modern footing, in the campaign of 1896, demanding strong financial support from the industrialists in order to ward off the threat of William Jennings Bryan's victory. Though a manifest conservative, he earned a biography by Herbert Croly *(q.v.)*, published in 1912, and expressing this founder of the *New Republic's (q.v.)* admiration for Hanna's skill as a politician.

HANSON, JOHN (1721-1783), "first President of the United States," that is, under the Articles of Confederation, and so recognized in his time by many people, including George Washington. His loss of all subsequent recognition in this respect is a case-study in propaganda, involving attitudes toward the era of the Confederation and a lack of appreciation of its achievements, which included the passage of the Northwest Ordinance of 1787 *(q.v.)*. It was obviously in the interests of the Federal Constitution makers to denigrate the government which it was superseding, and, with it, its Presidents, including John Hanson.

HAPGOOD, HUTCHINS (1869-1944) pioneer journalist-sociologist; his *The Spirit of the Ghetto* (1902) was illustrated by Jacob Epstein; *The Autobiography of a Thief* (1903), *The Spirit of Labor* (1907), *An Anarchist Woman* (1909) were vivid panels out of the times. See also his autobiography *A Victorian in the Modern World* (1939).

HAPGOOD, NORMAN (1868-1937), brother of Hutchins Hapgood *(q.v.)* and editor of *Collier's Magazine* during the Progressive Era *(q.v.)*. Although Hapgood rejected "sensationalism" employed by William Randolph Hearst and Thomas W. Lawson *(qq.v.)*, his magazine played a strategic role in a number of reform battles, notably those over pure food and drug legislation and the Ballinger Affair *(q.v.)*. Hapgood sought to help preserve free speech during World War I and after, as in such a work as *The Advancing Hour* (1920). As editor of *Hearst's International Magazine* from 1923 to 1925, he exposed the Ku Klux Klan and the anti-semitism sponsored by Henry Ford *(qq.v.)*. See his autobiography, *The Changing Years* (1930).

HARBINGER, THE, see Brook Farm.

HARD TIMES (1854), by Charles Dickens, a humanitarian novel, deploring the lot of the poor and the cruelty of their industrial masters. Though sentimental and too personal to be perceptive, it contains vivid details which evoke the period.

HARDING, WARREN GAMALIEL (1865-1923), notoriously the least competent President of the United States after Ulysses S. Grant *(q.v.)*. He added the neologism "normalcy" to the language, and offered many speeches remarkable for their lack of content. Although not personally corrupt, his good-fellow philosophy opened opportunities in the government to unscrupulous personages, and brought on the "Harding scandals." It was a sign of the vitiating force of prosperity that the Democratic Party was not able to take advantage of this failure of the Republican Administration to win the election of 1924. Reformers could only weather the "Harding Era," and use it to point up the incapacities of the reigning social and economic system. Francis Russell, *The Shadow of Blooming Grove* (1968); R. C. Downes, *The Rise of Warren Gamaliel Harding* (1970).

HARLAN, JOHN MARSHALL (1833-1911), associate justice of the U.S. Supreme Court, noted for his rugged honesty of mind, his numerous dissents, and his fear of government by judiciary. He was a liberal voice on a Court which was, in his time, committed to defending private property at the expense of the public weal. Thus, he dissented from the majority view, in Pollock v. Farmers' Loan and Trust Company (1894) *(q.v.)* that an income tax was a direct tax and therefore unconstitutional. Frank Latham, *The Great Dissenter* (1970).

HARLAN COUNTY, KENTUCKY, center for the mining of bituminous coal, notorious in the 1930's for the ruthless anti-labor practices of the mineowners and the courage and desperation with which the embattled miners resisted them.

HARRIS, FRANK (1854-1931), buccaneer Irish-born editor and litterateur, famous for his services as editor of the *Saturday Review*, in London, during the 1890's, notorious for the lewd and scabrous aspects of his autobiography, *My Life and Loves* (1923-7). In between, he wrote famous short stories, notably those in *Elder Conklin* (1894) and *Montes the Matador* (1900), set down views in *The Man Shakespeare* (1909) provoking to scholars, stimulating to lay people, and produced an original series of *Contemporary Portraits* (1915-23) which, though unreliable as history, contained vivid and useful materials. Untrustworthy and a blackguard, he had a romantic view of literature which made him a friend and encourager of individual writers; his *Oscar Wilde* (1916) was a product of this phase of his personality.

HARRIS, JOEL CHANDLER (1848-1908), Georgia journalist and story-teller, though no reformer, created in the "Uncle Remus" tales a complex vision of Negro thought which is helpful in understanding the realities of southern Negro-white relations. Thus, "Br'er Rabbit" is manifestly a subconscious image of the Negro: though physically weak, he lives freely and victoriously thanks to his native wit. It is also obvious that two stories go on during a telling of an "Uncle Remus" story: the overt relationship between Remus and his associates, white and black, and the story Remus is telling. The stories, as told in Walt Disney's *Way Down South in Dixie*, stirred up resentment, and inspired picket lines, as presenting a stereotyped view of Negroes. Harris also collected Negro folk sayings and stories.

HARRIS, THOMAS LAKE (1823-1906), a transitional figure between pre-Civil War religio-communistic experiments and religious feeling and social dissatisfaction of the post-Civil War era. Harris probed spiritual possibilities and inner feelings in order to attempt to strike an immediate relationship to God; he set up a number of communities where his followers sought to live on a higher plane than others; best known was his "Fountain Grove" community in California. Its most notorious feature was that it probably practiced, in some measure, irregular sex relations. His writings were a combination of individual probings on an intuitive level plus quasi-social criticisms of society including such immediate events as wars and depressions; his best-known disciple in America was Edwin Markham *(q.v.)*.

HARRISON, WILLIAM HENRY (1773-1841), see "Log-Cabin" Campaign.

HART, SCHAFFNER & MARX LABOR AGREEMENT (1911), a model agreement reached with the Amalgamated Clothing Workers of America which set a standard for peaceful clarification of differences between labor and management; the essential feature of the agreement was the setting up of an arbitration board which passed on issues and relevant data and reached conclusions which were respected by the major elements involved.

HARTE, (FRANCIS) BRET (1839-1902), Albany-born writer, who went west, and "struck gold" in a vein of stories which were a sensational success. His half-Jewish background augmented his touch of irony and tolerance which made him critical of self-righteousness (as in "The Outcasts of Poker Flat") and indignant over California treatment of its Chinese citizens. "Plain Language from Truthful James" (1870) was a curious sensation, in that it was taken by many Americans to be an expose of the insidious nature of "the Heathen Chinee," though it plainly satirized those who sought to cheat him and were confounded by his superior strategy. Margaret Duckett, *Mark Twain and Bret Harte* (1964).

HARTFORD CONVENTION (1814), dramatic example of the lack of unity and the critical differences between sections which attended the early years of the Federal Government, following the "Critical Period" (*q.v.*). New England Federalists were bitter about the policies of the Jefferson and Madison Administrations — the "Virginia Dynasty" — and resented "Mr. Madison's War" of 1812. They met in convention at Hartford, Connecticut, and there drew up a series of Resolutions accusing the Administration of highhanded and irresponsible policies, and appearing to threaten to leave the Union. Their action constituted the northern equivalent of the Kentucky and Virginia Resolutions (*q.v.*).

HARTFORD WITS, see Connecticut Wits.

HARVEY, WILLIAM H. (1851-1936), see Silver Issue, The.

HATCH ACT, THE (1939), see Civil Service Reform, Corrupt Practices Act.

HAUPTMANN, GERHART (1862-1946), famous German dramatist, noted for the social content of his works, the best known of which is *The Weavers* (1892). It was a pioneer example of drama in which the masses, rather than personalities, were treated as the major dramatic element. Hauptmann disappointed admirers by accepting the homage of the Nazis in old age.

"HAVE-NOTS," used to designate "under-privileged nations," (*q.v.*) but also to define elements of society which are deprived of adequate food, housing, and other tangibles of well-being. Moral reformers have often sought to distinguish between the helpless and the improvident, for example, in the pre-Civil War period, between the slave and the poor white. Socialists later denounced a capitalist system which, they believed, fostered poverty. The New Deal (*q.v.*), asserted principles of deservingness over the protests of conservatives who warned that individual incentive and freedom were being destroyed.

HAWAII, subject of a *coup d'état* (*q.v.*) by American businessmen, aided by American Marines, in 1893. A treaty of annexation was rejected by President Grover Cleveland (*q.v.*) in a speech notable for his views on the duties of great nations to small nations. The treaty was neither accepted nor wholly repudiated, and Hawaii was annexed during the Spanish-American War without further ado. It was incorporated as a state, in 1959: a problem in the distinction between imperialism and annexation. Its varied population and governmental habits, and position between Asia and the United States, make it a challenge to proper administration. James Michener, *Hawaii* (1959); E. G. Burroughs, *Hawaiian Americans* (1947); George Chaplin and Glenn D. Paige, eds., *Hawaii 2000: Continuing Experiment in Anticipatory Democracy* (1973).

HAWTHORNE, NATHANIEL (1804-1864), great American story-teller, who both served and did not serve reform. Some of his *Twice-Told Tales* (1837) were critical of the intolerance of his Puritan forebears, but he had no regard for reformers in his own time, was a Democratic Party "regular," and a firm friend of the "dough-face" President Franklin Pierce. Although Hawthorne remembered his stay at Brook Farm (*q.v.*) as a romantic episode in his life, his *The Blithedale Romance* (1852) treated it with scorn. Essentially a Puritan himself, he treated Transcendentalism (*q.v.*) with irony.

HAY, JOHN (1838-1905), although not associated with reform, either as secretary to Abraham Lincoln, or, as Secretary of State, his *Pike County Ballads* (1871) took a democratic tone toward Americans in the West. His *The Breadwinners,* published anonymously in 1883, was inspired by the railroad riots of 1877 (*q.v.*), and was bitterly anti-labor. A comparison between Hay and William Dean Howells (*q.v.*), also a westerner gone East, is instructive. See also Open-Door Policy.

HAYES, RUTHERFORD B. (1822-1893), President of the United States as a result of the Disputed Election of 1876 (*q.v.*). Although nominated as a "reform" candidate, and though interested in anti-capital punishment ideas and Negro education, his actual achievements in reform were meager. His major significance to reformers was in his unwillingness to cooperate with the "Stalwarts" (*q.v.*) of the Republican Party, splitting it and permitting the election in 1884 of Grover Cleveland (*q.v.*). Hayes sent Federal troops against strikers during the 1877 (*q.v.*) riots. H. Barnard, *Rutherford B. Hayes and His America* (1954).

HAYMARKET AFFAIR, THE, resulting from the explosion of a dynamite bomb in the midst of a squadron of police attempting to disperse a labor meeting in Chicago, on May 4, 1886. Seven police were killed and some sixty were wounded. During a wave of hysteria, a number of anarchists and alleged anarchists were indicted, almost all of German birth, but the most notable, Albert R. Parsons (*q.v.*), of native stock. Though no sound evidence proved their connection with the actual bomb-throwing, they were tried freely for their opinions and condemned to death. Parsons's speech in defense of labor highlighted the proceedings, and a young defendent, Louis Lingg, created a sensation by committing suicide in prison, using a bomb, on November 10, a day before the execution of four of his fellow prisoners. The sentences of three of them were commuted, and they occasioned the famous pardoning seven years after by Governor Altgeld (*q.v.*) The Bomb (1908). H. David, *History of the Haymarket Affair* (1936).

HAYS, ARTHUR GARFIELD (1881-1954), civil liberties advocate, concerned in the Scopes trial, the Sweet case, the Sacco-Vanzetti case, and civil liberties in Puerto Rico (1937) (*qq.v.*), among other affairs. He was general counsel for the A.C.L.U. (*q.v.*). His writings included *Let Freedom Ring* (1928) and *Trial by Prejudice* (1933). See his autobiography, *City Lawyer* (1942).

HAYWOOD, WILLIAM D., "BIG BILL" (1869-1928), a revolutionary, rather than a reformer, and a descendant of early English settlers. He was a founder of the Western Federation of Miners (*q.v.*) and led them in bitter strikes. He was implicated by Harry Orchard (*q.v.*) in the murder of ex-governor Frank R. Steunenberg of Idaho, who had been accused of breaking promises to the miners of the state. Haywood was successfully defended by Clarence Darrow (*q.v.*). Haywood was a founder and leader of the I.W.W. (*q.v.*). During World War I he was indicted for sedition, and fled to Russia in 1921, where he died. *Bill Haywood's Book* (1929) is a major work in labor lore.

H-BOMB, more devastating than the atom bomb (*q.v.*), it struck the popular imagination as being another step forward in man's ability to destroy himself: a fact which was soon underscored by the production of still more incredible weapons. See also Nuclear Question.

H.C.L., see High Cost of Living.

"HE KEPT US OUT OF THE WAR," Democratic slogan during Woodrow Wilson's *(q.v.)* campaign for re-election in 1916. It was later claimed that he could have, had he wished, taken us into the war earlier: a doubtful assertion, since there were so many anti-intervention elements still to be neutralized. It was also claimed that the slogan had not promised that he could continue to keep us out of the war; this is contradicted by the actual fashion in which the slogan was exploited. The entire emphasis upon what Woodrow Wilson could or could not do demonstrated that Americans were tiring of the "We, the People" shibboleth.

HEALTH, EDUCATION, AND WELFARE, U.S. DEPARTMENT OF (under Carter *(q.v.)* Health and Human Services, with Education becoming a separate department and its secretary a Cabinet post); see Federal Security Agency.

HEALTH INSURANCE, a reform issue rendered more acute in the 1950's by higher expectations of state aid (in view of the state's increasing expectations from its citizens), the high cost of living, and the mounting percentage of indigent aged people. Although organized labor, by 1916, opposed health insurance, fearing bureaucracy, many states introduced it. Many categories of need continued unattended to. The American Medical Association *(q.v.)* became the foremost antagonist to "socialized medicine," and worked tirelessly to prove that need for such insurance was vastly less than was claimed, that it would be a burden on the taxpayer, that it would produce bureaucracy, corruption, demoralization of the medical profession, new classes of cheats and parasites, and other evils. Early efforts of the Kennedy *(q.v.)* Administration to introduce health insurance were repulsed. Significant in this connection was Great Britain's experiences with socialized medicine, which were controverted as successful and unsuccessful. Patricia Scheidemandel et al., *Health Insurance for Mental Illness* (1968); R. W. Hetherington et al., *Health Insurance Plans* (1975); Melvin R. Laird et al., *Health Insurance: What Should Be the Federal Role?* (1975); Paul M. Insel and W. R. Roth, *Health in a Changing Society* (1976).

HEALTH REFORM, often associated with dissident elements or groups in society; a species of perfectionism, and so relating mental and spiritual health with bodily health. Dieting *(q.v.)* has been a staple of health reform, but fresh air, the virtues of walking, the dangers of spraying fruit with anti-insect preparations, the avoidance of tobacco and the embracing of temperance are among tenets of health reform. "Health stores" have traded on this interest, run, in many cases, by mere tradesmen. Printed matter usually accompanies "health" products in this connection, for education or advertising purposes. Perplexing was whether government helped or hindered more in the search for better health care. Thus, pharmaceutical firms complained that many drugs could serve patients which they could not prepare because of unrealistic HEW standards. Doctors wrote painfully of numerous terminal cases who were kept artificially alive to no purpose at the expense of needy patients with a future to themselves and humanity to preserve. With only one doctor available to every 715 people (among poor, one to 3500), their expertise and facilities needed rational allocation. For a while, acupuncture anesthetic techniques raged as a patient demand; China in 1980 admitted it had lied for years about its effectiveness—patients had secretly been given pain-killing drugs. Abortion *(q.v.)* continued to range "pro-life" advocates against "give-women-a-choice" advocates, in interest-groups which besieged doctors and legislators. See also Fletcherism, Fluoridation. John P. Dolan and William N. Adams-Smith, *Health and Society* (1978); Moos Insel, *Health and the Social Environment* (1974); Lester A. Sobel, ed., *Health Care: an American Crisis* (1976).

HEARD, GERALD (1890-1971), born Henry Fitz Gerald Heard, social philosopher and author who began as a reformer, working with Sir Horace Plunkett in Ireland to start agricultural cooperatives. The bombing of Plunkett's house by Irish "freedoms" persuaded Heard that a moral and religious approach was necessary to desired social change, and he studied history, science, religion, and psychology for a working philosophy. His mental adventures took him into social dynamics and catastrophe, as in *These Hurrying Years* (1934), into the extraordinary *Gabriel and the Creatures* (1952), which interpreted the condition of life as human from sub-human development, in direct comparison with religious and scientific phenomena, as in his *The Ascent of Humanity* (1928) and *A Preface to Prayer* (1944), and in a series of science fiction and even "detective" tales which probed human possibilities and psychology; one of the most popular was *A Taste of Honey* (1941). Heard accounted mysticism a legitimate avenue into the complexity of man, and won converts, the most famous being Aldous Huxley. See Filler, "The New Time," in *Appointment at Armageddon.*

HEARST, PATRICIA CASE, somewhat comparable to that of Joseph Medill Patterson *(q.v.)* as involving a scion of journalistic wealth experiencing a "radical" period. A daughter of William Randolph Hearst's son, Patricia Hearst was in 1974 kidnapped by a terrorist *(q.v.)* gang styling itself the Symbionese Liberation Army. She was "brainwashed" *(q.v.)* and probably tortured to become "Tania," a gun-carrying guerrilla *(q.v.)*. After the police killing by fire and bullets of some of her companions in Los Angeles, she was finally captured and charged with bank robbery. She was given probation on mitigating circumstances, and finally discharged from probation. Shana Alexander, *Anyone's Daughter* (1977).

HEARST, WILLIAM RANDOLPH (1863-1951), one of the most controversial of all elements associated with reform, he conducted powerful campaigns against such monopolistic agencies as the Southern Pacific Railroad, but showed no scruples in his own techniques for getting his own way. He gave a forum to reformers, sympathized with labor, exposed municipal corruption, and developed sensationalist methods for bringing issues before the public, but he manipulated public sentiment, as in his distortions which helped bring on the Spanish-American War, he exploited low-grade tastes for shallow sensations and sex, he identified his personal interests with the public interest, and used patriotism as a weapon rather than a dedication. His associate, Arthur Brisbane *(q.v.)* worked from a similar premise of contempt for the public upon which they fattened. Thus, reform elements were generally correct in holding them to have been a catalyst for ill, but inadequately studied the components which made them forces in American journalism and life. See "Hearst," in Filler, *The Muckrakers.*

HEINE, HEINRICH (1797-1856), German-Jewish poet, wit, and radical, whose verses and comments serve various humanitarian and libertarian ideas. An expatriate *(q.v.)* who lived much of his life in Paris, he conceived many varied criticisms of his fatherland which furthered astringent purposes, in connection with Germany, but also other civilizations. His poem, *The Weavers,* offered revolutionary inspiration, and gave title to Gerhart Hauptmann's *(q.v.)* play, *The Weavers.*

HELICON HALL was the main building of a cooperative colony in Englewood, New Jersey. Founded by Upton Sinclair *(q.v.)* in 1906, it was destroyed by fire, March 16, 1907.

HELP, see Self-Help.

HELPER, HINTON R. (1829-1909), a North Carolina "poor white," whose *The Impending Crisis* (1857) was a violent attack on slavery as detrimental to the prosperity of the South and the hopes of his class. Helper was thus a southern abolitionist, who, however, despised Negroes, and was totally concerned for his own class. His book was declared outlaw in the South, and was distributed by millions as a Republican political document. Its implications for social reformers have not been probed.

HELVERING *ET AL. V.* DAVIS (1937), see Welfare Legislation.

HENRY, O., see Porter, (William) Sydney.

HENRY, PATRICK (1736-1799), revolutionary patriot and

orator, Virginia's equivalent of Samuel Adams of Massachusetts (q.v.). He rose from modest circumstances and by means of great eloquence and a feeling for popular interests won a position among the most influential Virginians. Henry was neither a deep thinker nor profound student, but he reflected the ambitions of frontiersmen, small traders, and other Americans who resented being held down by British economic and political policies. Like Adams, he did not fear to counsel boldness, leading the fight against the Stamp Act and defying Lord Dunmore's dissolution of the Virginia assembly. His speech of March 23, 1775, advocating armed resistance to the British is one of the highpoints of all American oratory. He served the Revolution as delegate to the Continental Congress and as governor of Virginia. In the post-Revolutionary period, he exhibited increasingly conservative qualities, and was a Federalist in his last years.

HENRY STREET SETTLEMENT, see Settlement Movement, The.

HEPBURN ACT (1906), an achievement of the pre-World War I Reform Era which capped the efforts of the western farmers to achieve equity in their dealings with the railroads. The Interstate Commerce Commission (q.v.) had proved impotent; in the meantime railroad consolidations had made competitive techniques a danger not only to their customers but their own stability. La Follette (q.v.) led the fight to give more power to the I.C.C., in the face of a solid core of Senators committed to reaction; the muckrakers (q.v.) put increasing pressures favoring reform on both Houses of Congress, with their criticisms of railroad inefficiency and corruption. The Hepburn Act was a measure sponsored by President Roosevelt, and intended to undermine the agitation for government ownership of railroads, which William Jennings Bryan (q.v.), among others, demanded. The strategy succeeded, and the experiment of government ownership (q.v.) of railroads was put off until World War I.

HERESY, as associated with dogmatic religion, criticized by social reformers as a concept stifling thought, and a weapon in the hands of bigots; historically, invoking memories of excommunication, the Massacre of St. Bartholomew, and the Inquisition (qq.v.). However, those subscribing to Marxian tenets, and other social dogmas, have not conceived of themselves as bigots, and have defended the use of repression in the Soviet Union and elsewhere. Since World War II, with direct liberal support largely withdrawn from them, the communists have argued that they were themselves heretics, who were being persecuted, for example by the House Committee on Un-American Activities (q.v.). In considering the rights of communists under American law, Sidney Hook has argued that heresy was justifiable, but treason not. See also Brown, William Montgomery. Reo M. Christenson, Heresies Right and Left...Reexamined (1973).

HERNDON CASE (1932), involved a young Negro leader in the Unemployment Councils (q.v.), Angelo Herndon, who attempted to act in behalf of the unemployed in Atlanta, Georgia. He was sentenced to eighteen to twenty years imprisonment under an 1861 statute which would have permitted a sentence of death for "incitements to insurrection."

HEROES of social reform have included such relevant personages as Eugene V. Debs, John P. Altgeld, William Lloyd Garrison, Thomas Paine (qq.v.), and others in past and more recent America, as well as martyrs (q.v.) of labor and social struggle. Social reformers have also tended to increase their prestige by finding elements which identified their cause with that of less distinctively reformer types who achieved fame. During the Thirties, a widely-used phrase among reformers and revolutionists was: "They belong to us." That is, they asserted that the great people of history belong to the forces of progress, whether technically in their ranks, or not. They were thus able to claim Christ, Goethe, Shakespeare, Andrew Jackson, and other disparate figures. During the Stalin era, a Russian motion-picture placed Ivan the Terrible among reformers. See also Anti-Heroes, Debunking.

HERRIN MASSACRE (1922), a tragic incident in labor and coal mining history. During a severe strike in the Illinois coal mining area, during which coal miners were flouted and one finally killed, a savage retaliation occurred: some twenty strike-breakers and guards were brutally slain. Over two hundred labor union men were indicted, but all acquitted thanks to the firm pro-union sentiment in the area. An ironic Terre Haute newspaper wrote: "One more acquittal in the Herrin cases and the rumors that someone was killed down there will be permanently set at rest."

HERRON, GEORGE D. (1862-1925), a clergyman who made his reputation in the 1890's as a Christian Socialist (q.v.). His writings in that period included such works as A Plea for the Gospel (1892). He increased in radical outlook, and left Grinnell College, where he was a professor, in 1899. His unorthodox marriage to a wealthy woman, and his emergence as a full-fledged socialist, kept him in the public eye. He was a co-founder of the Rand School of Social Sciences (q.v.), and became increasingly skeptical about the content of religions. President Woodrow Wilson sent him as a personal representative to Germany. He had developed an intense anti-Germanism, and developed an enthusiastic faith in the possibilities of fascist Italy. The content of his thought and purposes has wanted analysis.

HERVÉ, GUSTAVE (1871-1944), French historian and lawyer, he became a socialist and a symbol of anti-militarism, his newspaper La Guerre Sociale maintaining an intransigent position on the subject. Hervéism was an international symbol. In 1914 he totally abandoned his program in favor of patriotism, renaming his newspaper La Victoire, and with the fall of France in 1940 became an advocate of French-German cooperation, a defender of Pétain's Vichy regime.

HESSIANS, soldiers from Hesse, Germany, mercenaries employed by the British in prosecuting their war against the American revolutionaries. The use of mercenaries was standard procedure in wars as waged in the eighteenth century and before, but revolutionary propaganda backed by libertarian concepts bred by the revolutionary effort, successfully identified the Hessians with venality and brutal suppression.

HEWITT, ABRAM S. (1822-1903), industrialist and "goo goo" reformer (q.v.), he was of the wing in the Democratic Party which opposed Tweed (q.v.), was a manager of Tilden's (q.v.) campaign in 1876, and served in the House of Representatives. In 1886, he defeated both Theodore Roosevelt and Henry George (qq.v.) for the office of New York mayor. Allan Nevins, Abram S. Hewitt (1935).

"HEY! YELLOWBACK!" (1930), by Ernest L. Meyer, an account of the author's experiences while a war-resister confined in an army camp, during World War I; foreword by William Ellery Leonard.

HIBBEN, PAXTON (1880-1928), an American diplomat and soldier, who topped a conventional career by becoming disillusioned with the possibilities in American capitalism and espousing radical sentiments and associates. His biographies of Henry Ward Beecher (q.v.) (1927) and, published posthumously, of William Jennings Bryan (q.v.) (1929) were couched in irony. He was honored with a portrait in Dos Passos's U.S.A. (q.v.) and abuse in Dilling's Red Network (q.v.).

HICKS, ELIAS (1748-1830), Quaker leader, founder of the Hicksite Quaker set, reform branch of the Society of Friends, and influential anti-slavery spokesman; see his Observations on Slavery (1814).

HIGGINSON, THOMAS W. (1823-1911), a leader in the fight against the Fugitive Slave Act, in Massachusetts, and in favor of a Free Soil Kansas; colonel of the first colored regiment in the Civil War; and a woman suffrage advocate. See his Travellers and Outlaws (1889); Women and Men (1888); and Cheerful Yesterdays (1898).

HIGH COST OF LIVING, a concern of reformers, especially as respects the incomes of lower-paid workers. Students of the subject offer statistics as to the relationship of wages to real wages in terms of the prices of basic commodities. They have studied the distribution of wealth in order to observe the disparity of income as between the wealthy and the poor. Before World War II, they criticized the Department of War budget as a burden on the poor as well as a threat to their well-being. The international gyrations of the dollar, inflation (q.v.), and foreign threats to American industry have made HCL an obsolete concept.

HIGHBROW, see Lowbrow.

HIGHER CONSCIOUSNESS, a concept of women activists (q.v.), intended to suggest that women who were not activists had been "brainwashed" (q.v.) by society to accept their painful lot, and needed to have their consciousness "raised" to an awareness of their condition and its cure. This process, often carried out in men-excluded circles, added up to brainwashing in its own right.

"HIGHER LAW, THE," see Seward, William Henry.

HIGHLANDER FOLK SCHOOL, organized in 1932 by a native Tennessean, Myles Horton, near Monteagle in the Tennessee mountains. It dedicated itself to democratic ideals, accord between Negroes and white people, emphasizing poor whites, and a clarification of society's needs. Its emphasis on integration kept it under attack, but its grassroots leadership, and the support and encouragement of liberals and labor unions, enabled it to survive crises. During the 1930's, the Great Depression gave it substantial support from energetic reformers; the post-World War II weakening of liberal and radical ties required it to reforge its program and techniques. It worked with rural leaders, and provided leadership for organizing and educating farmers, and instructing them in their identity of interests with workers, white or black.

HIGHWAYS, see Federal Highway Act.

HILDRETH, RICHARD (1807-1865), historian, utilitarian (q.v.) and anti-slavery advocate. His Federalist rationalism limited his influence, as seen in the contrasting receptions given Uncle Tom's Cabin (q.v.) and his own The Slave; or, Memoirs of Archy Moore (1836), which went into a number of editions in the United States, England, and France, but made a qualified impression; it survives mainly as having been the first anti-slavery novel. See also his Despotism in America (1840).

HILL, JOE (1882-1915), born "Hillstrom" in Sweden, he became a mariner who was in the United States about 1902. He became an ardent I.W.W. (q.v.) and union organizer, and known in labor circles for the popular songs he composed for use by the "singing Wobblies." The most noted of these was Solidarity, but others included Casey Jones, the Union Scab, Rebel Girl, and Pie in the Sky. While he was in Salt Lake City, Utah, helping organize a construction workers union, he was arrested on the charge of holding up a grocery store and killing the owner. The state supreme court upheld a verdict of guilty. Mass protests failed to stop his execution for murder. Ralph Chaplin (q.v.) helped create the picture of his personality and martyrdom. Wallace Stegner (New Republic, Jan. 5, 1948) cast doubt on his innocence. Barrie Stavis's The Man Who Never Died (1954), a play about Hill, was sympathetically received by off-Broadway audiences. His last words before execution, "Don't mourn for me — organize," was once part of the inspiring lore of the labor movement.

HILLMAN, SIDNEY (1887-1946), organizer and long-time president of the Amalgamated Clothing Workers of America, and an organizer of the C.I.O. (qq.v.). During World II, he was one of the strong-arms of the government charged with synchronizing the operations of labor with war-time necessities. As chairman of the C.I.O. Political Action Committee, he helped mobilize the labor and liberal vote in favor of President Roosevelt's re-election in 1944. Roosevelt's quip, "Clear it with Sidney" was made as notorious as possible by anti-Roosevelt forces, striving to suggest undercover alliances between government and labor elements.

HIPPIES, a transitional but related phase of the youth (q.v.) uprising of the 1960s, they featured drugs, promiscuity, repugnance toward the general society, rock music, and an amorphous idealism. A limited vocabulary featured code words: "far out, man," "groovy," "spaced out." Long hair, rock music, and primitive styles and gestures were trimmed and assimilated into the general culture. Mass rock festivals, notably at Woodstock, New York, were part of the hippie heritage. Such stage and film successes as Hair, Oh! Calcutta!, Lenny Bruce, and Jesus Christ, Superstar were part of their visual bequest.

HIRABAYASHI V. UNITED STATES (1943), see Japanese Relocation Order.

HIROSHIMA, important Japanese city which received the first atomic explosion, August 6, 1945, with devastating effects to city and people, of whom some 80,000 died, immediately or from later effects of the blast. Although Nagasaki soon after received the second atomic bomb, with almost equally devastating effects, thus precipitating the war's end, Hiroshima became the symbol of this radical change in human warfare. A museum in Hiroshima memorializes the event. A French motion picture, Hiroshima, Mon Amour, was credited with having caught the meaning of the catastrophe in human terms. John Hersey, Hiroshima (1946); Michihiko Hachiya, Hiroshima Diary (1955).

HISPANICS, an American strain destined to grow in power and affect American life and thought nationally. Strong in the Southwest, where Spanish was all but a first language, they were augmented by growing populations of Puerto Ricans, multiplying in New York City, but increasingly visible in numerous other cities in the East, and also in the Midwest and beyond. The Cuban strain was unmistakeable in Florida, but extended elsewhere; and the sensational influx of Cubans as refugees in 1980 revealed that immigration authorities, long lax, would have to create policy and help formulate understanding of these permanent Americans, their problems, their duties, and their prospects.

HISS CASE, one of the significant episodes of the twentieth century, it revealed to the light American tendencies nurtured in the 1930's, and lost them social prestige. In 1948, Whittaker Chambers, a left-wing writer who had become a Time editor, testified before the House Committee on Un-American Activities as to subversive work he had carried out for the Soviet Union, and implicated Alger Hiss, president of the Carnegie Endowment for International Peace, and formerly a trusted official in the Department of State, with a record of responsible governmental missions. A dramatic confrontation between Chambers and Hiss raised the direct question of which one was lying. First opinion was sympathetic to Hiss. When, however, he instituted a libel suit against Chambers, the latter produced copies of official government documents copied, it was later demonstrated, on a typewriter Hiss had possessed. He was indicted by a Federal grand jury in New York, and his trial followed with intense interest. The government effort to prove his guilt involved efforts to prove his communist associations. He brought to the witness stand character witnesses including Associate Justice of the Supreme Court Felix Frankfurter; and Secretary of State Dean Acheson offered the remarkable statement that he would not turn his back on his friend Hiss: the latter following his second trial and conviction. He was sentenced to serve a five year term in prison. Chambers's book, Witness (1952), was recognized as one of the extraordinary accounts of his time; Hiss' own account, written after his release from prison, disappointed his friends and foes because of its curious one-dimensional quality and lack of illuminating data. A curious work was Lionel Trilling's novel, The Middle of the Journey, (1947) written before the case broke and possibly involving both Hiss and Chambers: the one behind-the-scenes view of the affair. The case took an unexpected turn in 1978 with publication of Allen Weinstein, Perjury: the Hiss-Chambers Case, written, paradoxically by one who had begun with a prejudice favoring Hiss. His intensive research persuaded him of Hiss's culpability. Ironically, his conclusion was furthered by materials released under the Freedom of Information Act (*q.v.*), which Hiss-advocates had assumed contained data helpful to him. Although die-hard partisans continued to declare their faith, larger public moral support fell away.

HISTORICAL DETERMINISM, see Materialistic Conception of History.

HISTORY, AMERICAN, always controversial, absorbed learned arguments for and against the Revolution, the pros and cons of democracy versus the need for an elite, of states rights as compared to Federal power, the role of government, of workers, of dissidents from mugwumps to communists (*qq.v.*). In the 1960s, an attack was mounted not on interpretations, but on history itself, in terms of "relevance," bias, and need. Agitators in and out of the history profession argued against "white" (*q.v.*) history, partisans of youth (*q.v.*) for no history at all, and discontented historians for an "alternative" history. Following stormy sessions and intrigues, the history profession bent to their agitation, absorbing them with benefits and prestige. A broad history gave way to a monographic history, building on its own premises. Also accepted as stimulating and just as good by a more general public was a fictional history which featured the impressions of Norman Mailer respecting subjects from the moon probes to Marilyn Monroe, and the made-up scenes of an E. L. Doctorow manipulating actual historical personages. Typical of the situation at the top level of history study was the reception given to *The Progressive Presidents* (1980), written by one of the best known Presidential scholars, J. M. Blum. The volume was downgraded as giving "little concession to the demands for less government [the conservative view] or for the more radical socioeconomic order [that is, socialism, the influential "New Left" goal and interpretation]." (John D. Buenker, in *American Historical Review*, February, 1981). There was no discussion of Blum's evidence, his accuracy or inaccuracy. The rebuilding of a responsible history remained imponderable. Frances Fitzgerald, *America Revisited: History Schoolbooks in the Twentieth Century* (1979); R. J. Maddox, *The New Left and the Origins of the Cold War* (1973).

HISTORY OF AMERICAN SOCIALISMS, see John Humphrey Noyes.

HISTORY OF THE PEOPLE OF THE UNITED STATES, see McMaster, John Bach.

HISTORY OF THE STANDARD OIL COMPANY, THE (1904), see Tarbell, Ida M.

HITLERISM, identified with the rise of Adolf Hitler (1889-1945) to power in Germany, as leader of the National Socialist Party. His program for returning his country to first-class status was made easier by his identifying it with anti-communism, and his effort to exterminate the Jews was disapproved, but not vigorously opposed. However, the Nazi-Soviet Pact of 1939 freed him for an attack on the western democracies, and his subsequent attack on the Soviet Union (1941), paved the way for a military agreement between the democracies and Russia. Hitlerism now stood thoroughly condemned, but the opposing Stalinism (*q.v.*) enjoyed a period of benign interpretation, even among non-social reformers. Norman Stone, *Hitler* (1980); Werner Maser, *Hitler: Legend, Myth and Reality* (1973); J. P. Stern, *Hitler: the Fuhrer and the People* (1975).

HOBO, the tramp's name for himself; Josiah Flynt (*q.v.*) demonstrated that the denizens of "Hobohemia" constituted a way of life, rather than a type of person merely meriting moral judgment. Hoboes, or, more familiarly, "bos," are homeless men, largely equivalent to the inhabitants of Skid Row, but more mobile, and including restless and individual elements, as well as degenerate or degenerating types. Some hoboes have been seen as part of the last frontier of individualism. The I.W.W. (*q.v.*) were hobo almost by definition during the high point of their career, in pre-World War I years. The spectrum of hobo types included intellectuals and striking personalities, and resulted in a literature of songs and ballads. See Nels Anderson, *The Hobo* (1923). The high mobilization demanded during World War II infringed upon the hobo's privacy and freedom of choice, but post-War conditions enabled him to revive, to a degree.

HOFFA, JAMES (1913-1975?),president of the International Brotherhood of Teamsters, Chauffeurs, Warehousemen and Helpers of America, generally known as the Teamsters Union (*q.v.*), and a phenomenon of labor. His career went back to the 1930's, when he fought union battles fearlessly and ruthlessly, being committed to prison many times for battles on the picket line, assault and battery charges, and other stormy encounters. In his rise, he defeated the radicals of the Minneapolis Teamsters union, and centralized wages, hours, and working conditions problems and programs in his hands. Nevertheless, *Who's Who in Labor* (1946) found no reason to mark his presence. Unlike Dave Beck, whom he succeeded as president, Hoffa took a personal interest in unionists, who, in return, gave him their loyalty. The earnest efforts of the McClellan Committee (*q.v.*) proved that the union was crawling with gangsters, petty and substantial, that there was probably extortion of money from employers by union insiders, who employed terror and probably did not hesitate at murder; but the Committee failed to pin any of these matters on Hoffa. He explained the large sums he received by luck at gambling, loans, and other means, in addition to his fifty thousand dollar a year salary and limitless expenses. His union appeared to agree with him that he was being "persecuted" for being a good union man. Although he boasted of increasing power and indifference to having been dropped by the A.F.L.-C.I.O., he appeared, in 1961, to wish his union could return to the fold. His subsequent murky career, in and out of prison for crimes while yet president of his union—he resigned in 1971 evidently as part of high level political deals—ended in 1975 with his disappearance and presumed death as part of union power struggles. They raised questions of relations between crime and society, and the latter's power to control crime in so crucial an area as labor. Walter Sheridan, *The Fall and Rise of Jimmy Hoffa* (1972).

HOFFER, ERIC (1902-   ), self-educated social philosopher, born in New York, a wanderer who settled in San Francisco as a longshoreman. He read widely in history and the human condition, and took readers by storm in 1951 with his *The True Believer*, which probed the appeal of mass movements involving such factors as desire for change, potential converts, and "factors promoting self-sacrifice." He indirectly refuted the presumptions of "inevitability" touted by Marxists and believers in progress, spoke for the individual, and rejected sentimentality toward the poor. Middleclass readers were impressed by his identification of boredom as a source of revolutionary urges. Later works, including *The Ordeal of Change* (1963) and *The Passionate State of Mind* (1955), underscored the trend of his thought. Hoffer's unwillingness to accept youth and minority group cliches lost him some public interest, and he tired of and retired from talk shows which exploited his worker's manners and weathered appearance. See his *Writing and Thinking on the Waterfront* (1969).

HOFFMAN, ABBIE, see Yippies.

H.O.L.C., see Home Owners' Loan Corporation.

HOLLEY, MYRON (1779-1841), pioneer political abolitionist (*q.v.*), one of the organizers of the Erie Canal, in New York, and an outstanding Anti-Mason (*q.v.*); his *Address... to the People of the United States* (1830) was a notable statement of its principles. At the anti-slavery convention in Cleveland in 1839, he moved the nomination of an anti-slavery candidate for President in 1840; rebuffed, he moved the same at a county anti-slavery convention in New York. Soon after, at Warsaw, New York, James G. Birney (*q.v.*) was given the nomination. Although the Liberty Party (*q.v.*) received no more than 7,100 votes nationally, in that campaign, political abolitionism had been set under way. Holley edited the *Rochester Freeman* in 1839-40.

HOLLYWOOD, a symbol of popular art and mass appeal, a villain in the piece featuring the great American "sell out": the talented writer, or actor, or director, who might have been able to illuminate American purposes and ideals, who is beaten down by brutal commercial interests, rendered impotent, blind, or diabolic. A considerable canon of writings has grown up about this theme, though no major work has resulted. The question can be asked, whether the writers involved were, in fact, as talented as believed. On the other hand, the quality of the Hollywood product requires more careful consideration than it sometimes receives; see Cinema *(q.v.)*. A striking development was the investigation by the Congressional Committee on Un-American Activities of radicalism in Hollywood, which reached its high point in the legal prosecution of the so-called "Hollywood Ten," in 1947. Those protesting these proceedings argued that the Hollywood writers involved were no more than earning a living, and that there was no evidence that they had infected the motion-pictures they helped create with subversive messages. A turning point in the receding "hysteria" was the actor Kirk Douglas's decision to give the best known of the "Hollywood Ten," Dalton Trumbo, screen credit for having prepared the script of the motion-picture *Spartacus (q.v.)*. Vibrant with clichés, this production seemed calculated to make the democratic ideals portrayed seem insufferable, though this may not have been the intention of its creators.

HOLMES, OLIVER WENDELL (1809-1894), once a national figure, as a distinguished professor of anatomy and physiology at the Harvard University medical school, a poet, essayist, contributor to the *Atlantic Monthly*. Relatively little of his work maintains its vitality, though his verse, "The Deacon's Masterpiece" remains a brilliant comment on Calvinism, and some of his scientific work and his novel, *Elsie Venner* (1861) have pioneer status. Some of his other work carries the aura of the imperial New Engand tradition. His work is, however, entirely overshadowed by that of his son, Oliver Wendell Holmes, Jr. (1841-1935), whose view of the function of law, and many of whose decisions as Associate Justice of the U.S. Supreme Court became foundation stones of liberal thinking and legal philosophy. His *The Common Law* (1881) expressed his sense of law as a living and growing thing, responsive to reality. His great dissents, as in Abrams *v.* United States (1919) *(q.v.)* became precedents for law, while the dominent majority views were all but forgotten. His many famous phrases accreted commentary in the fashion of classic statements, their appeal being not so much to ideals as to reason and experience. See Max Lerner, ed., *The Mind and Faith of Justice Holmes* (1943).

HOLT, HAMILTON (1872-1951), editor of the *Independent* (q.v.), and an internationalist whose ideas created the Carnegie Endowment for International Peace and the World Peace Foundation. He was a founder of the League to Enforce Peace *(q.v.)*, and accepted American intervention in World War I. A mild but consistent progressive, with causes including the founding of the N.A.A.C.P. *(q.v.)*, his acumen was shown by his support of Taft over Theodore Roosevelt for President, in 1912, on the ground that Taft was the better Progressive; he approved Taft's legal approach to international harmony. He served as president of Rollins College. Warren F. Kuehl, *Hamilton Holt* (1960).

HOME OWNERS' LOAN CORPORATION (H.O.L.C.), a New Deal *(q.v.)* measure, in operation from 1933 to 1936, it refinanced home mortgage debts for non-farm owners and provided money for taxes and repairs under stipulated conditions. A measure intended to sustain the individual in the maintenance of his property, it emphasized the concern of the Administration for the human aspect of survival during the depression.

HOME RELIEF, see Relief.

HOME RULE, a tenet of municipal administration intended to protect a local government from unwarranted interference by state authorities. See also Municipal Reform.

HOMESTEAD ACT (1862), result of long agitation for the opening of the West to free settlement, within particular regulations; it had reform implications to the extent that it offered a way out to some discontented elements in the east, but served free enterprise *(q.v.)*, more than it did reform, to the extent that poor, gregarious elements found it difficult to go west, and continued to require humanitarian and reform consideration in the east: see also Land Reform, Public Domain.

HOMESTEAD STRIKE (1892), one of the industrial tragedies of the post-Civil War era. Henry C. Frick, manager of the Carnegie *(q.v.)* Works near Pittsburgh, on the Monongahela River, determined to break the union and incited a strike; he then requisitioned several hundred strikebreakers, through the Pinkerton *(q.v.)* Detective Agency. These were brought up the river on barges; a gun battle between strikers and strike-breakers resulted in seven dead. State troops seized some two hundred strikers and held them on murder and other charges. The attempt of the young anarchist Alexander Berkman to assassinate Frick helped the company to identify, unfairly, this individualistic action and the strike effort, to its detriment. The strike was broken. See also Steel Strike of 1919.

HOMOSEXUALS, considered a libertarian cause in some restricted circles, a disease in others. Radclyffe Hall's *The Well of Loneliness* (1928) argued sensitively for a live-and-let-live philosophy, but by its nature the cause has had a limited social appeal. Government has feared homosexuals as being liable to blackmail, and hence useful for subversive purposes. In post-World War II years, some centers for radical-bohemian thought attracted persons of this persuasion. About 1950, a strain of broad-mindedness on the subject appeared in literary circles. During the 1960s and 1970s, however, spurred by the youth *(q.v.)* revolt and woman activist *(q.v.)* demands, homosexuals worked strenuously to "come out of the closet." They claimed ten percent of the population, and a successful New York magazine, *Christopher Street*. They went to court to seek entree into the United States services, and received court orders overthrowing Service regulations which barred them from the military. The National Security Agency agreed to allow a known homosexual employee to keep his job and access to highly classified material. A Federal judge granted a male high school student's request to bring a male date to his senior prom, on First Amendment *(q.v.)* grounds, and ordered the school official to provide security for the couple: a decision a National Gay Task Force took to be a victory for its cause. The Carter *(q.v.)* White House endorsed a proposal to repeal a section of the immigration law which prohibited entry of homosexual aliens into the United States. In San Francisco, a homosexual capital, the Mayor, Dianne Feinstein, solicited "gay" support, and endorsed homosexuals, male and lesbian, for jobs in the police department. Nevertheless, the homosexual path was neither straight nor smooth. Lesbian misconduct in the Navy resulted in discharges which the American Civil Liberties Union *(q.v.)* determined to fight, but which did little for their tendency's public reputation. Anita Bryant, beauty queen, singer, and Florida Citrus Commission's spokeswoman on television, fought the homosexual drive for status in Dade County as an attack on the family *(q.v.)*, and, though she won the campaign, drew so much satire and derogation on television shows and in the press, that she lost her contract, the Commission having a distaste for controversy. The homosexual interests counted this a victory for their cause. Of equal importance was the exposure of a famous art historian, Professor Anthony Blunt, in England, as having been a Soviet agent and part of a university clique of such agents who were also homosexuals. The novelist John Le Carre believed that their sense of being different from others, and above their values, prepared them for their treason. In America, there were a number of impressive incidents and exposures of personalities. One involved a Maryland Congressman, Robert Bauman, esteemed among conservatives, as having "homosexual tendencies." Although he lost a bid for re-election, he drew compassion from his social and political friends, and appeared likely to continue his career. The concept of illness which appeared in many friendly statements, with the implicit suggestion of a cure, tipped judgment toward the desirability of more "normal" sexual impulses and controls, especially as related to youth. It appeared that some accomodation between affirming of the family, and a regard for private, unmilitant preferences might be in the making. Jonathan Katz, ed., *Gay American History* (1976); C. Weiss and D. J. Friar, *Terror in the Prisons: Homosexual Rape and Why Society Condones It* (1976); Rictor H. Norton, *The Homosexual Literary Tradition* (1974); Parker Tyler, *Homosexuality in the Movies* (1972); Leonard Barnett, *Homosexuality: Time to Tell the Truth to Young People, Their Families and Friends* (1975).

HOOKER, THOMAS (1586-1647), early liberal Congregationalist minister who emigrated to Massachusetts in 1633. Dissatisfied with the rigidity of Puritan government, he left the colony with his entire congregation to set up a colony in Connecticut. His congregationalism was wholly democratic; he believed authority must rest in the will of the people. His teachings found expression in the "Fundamental Orders of Connecticut" (1639): the first written constitution in America.

HOOVER, HERBERT (1874-1964), President of the United States, 1929-33, and theoretician of Republicanism and free enterprise, his career illustrated the changes which had overtaken Manchester Liberalism (q.v.). A much-traveled mining engineer in backward countries, he was a sincere administrator of relief to the needy, during World War I. In 1921, when he was appointed Secretary of Commerce in Harding's cabinet, "Hooverize" meant to be saving, philanthropic. He encouraged businesses to organize their interests, in effect fostering monopolies. As President, he resisted pressures to aid the most needy victims of the depression of 1929, holding that this was a municipal responsibility. He refused to countenance the Bonus Army (q.v.), sacrificing further popularity. He set up the Reconstruction Finance Corporation (1932) (q.v.) to aid needy banks and other substantial concerns, hoping that their improved conditions would create work for the unemployed. A brilliant Democratic Party campaign identified shacks and other flimsy housing put together by homeless people as "Hoovervilles." Hoover campaigned for reelection in 1932 on his record, and was severely beaten. During the New Deal (q.v.) era, he was a scapegoat for the failure of free enterprise. His defenders were confident that these would ultimately seem less reprehensible than the failures of communism, of which he was a foe. They were correct; his *Hoover Commission Report on Organization of the Executive Branch of the Government* (1949), drawn up under the Democrat Truman (q.v.) became the source for other "Hoover Commission"-style reports. The Hoover Institution on War, Revolution and Peace, at Stanford University became seminal in its field. Hoover's death began an elaborate intellectual process in revaluation. W. S. Myers and W. H. Newton, *The Hoover Administration: a Documented Narrative* (1936; reprinted 1971); M. L. Fausold and G. T. Mazuzan, eds., *The Hoover Presidency: a Reappraisal* (1974); Jordan A. Schwarz, *Interregnum of Despair: Hoover, Congress, and the Depression* (1970); David Burner, *Herbert Hoover* (1979).

HOOVER, J. EDGAR (1895-1972), controversial long-time head of the F.B.I., who began his career as director of the Palmer Raids (q.v.). His exploits against gangsters in the 1930s netted him much public approval, his campaign against communists caused continuous debate. His rigid control of Bureau operations, and accumulation of dossiers against high officials in government, disturbed even many conservatives who feared Hoover might inhibit necessary work involving communists and their friends. There was protest against naming the new F.B.I. building in Washington for the deceased chief. William W. Turner, *Hoover's F.B.I.* (1971); Ralph De Toledano, *J. Edgar Hoover: the Man in His Time* (1973).

HOPKINS, HARRY L. (1890-1946), social worker and aide to Franklin D. Roosevelt, he had a varied experience in administrating pensions and relief before Roosevelt, as governor of New York State, appointed him head of the New York State Temporary Emergency Relief Administration. His essential trait was that he had no fear of expanding the areas in which aid to the needy could be offered. When Roosevelt (q.v.) became President in 1933, Hopkins became Federal Emergency Relief Administrator and was receptive to suggestions for multiplying opportunities for service. As head of the Works Progress Administration, he allocated money for building roads, dams, bridges, schools, postoffices, and numerous other structures and services. The white collar workers were not scorned, or even the artists. This work was maintained in the face of constant criticism and ridicule. It represented the highpoint of Hopkins's career. His subsequent services as Roosevelt's emissary to Great Britain and Moscow, his work on several wartime committees, and his association with Roosevelt at various international conferences, and in connection with the organization of the United Nations (q.v.) were competent, rather than creative. Henry H. Adams, *Harry Hopkins* (1977).

HOPKINSON, FRANCIS (1737-1791), Philadelphia lawyer and political writer, best known for his satirical poem written during the Revolution; *The Battle of the Kegs* (1777).

HOPPER, ISAAC T. (1771-1852), abolitionist and humanitarian, a Hicksite (q.v.) Quaker, who, in Philadelphia, aided the poor, concerned himself for Negro education, and for prisoners and other unfortunates. Moving to New York, he and his son-in-law, James S. Gibbons were so vigorously abolitionist in word and deed that they were disowned by their Quaker congregation. For a sympathetic review of his many sided career, see L. Maria Child (q.v.), *Isaac T. Hopper: a True Life* (1853).

HORIZONTAL UNIONISM, see Craft Unions.

HOSTAGES, see Iran.

HOT-WATER REBELLION, THE, in July 1798, Congress passed a law to assess a direct tax of two million dollars; Pennsylvania was to raise $237,000 by taxing Negro slaves, houses, lands. In January 1799, assessors went about assessing property. Their counting and measuring the windows for assessing houses roused resentment, and the scalding water thrown on some gave the name to the incident.

HOUSE, EDWARD M. (1858-1938), famous for the unofficial influence he wielded in the Woodrow Wilson (q.v.) administration, having been helpful in securing his nomination for the Presidency in 1912. "Col." House — the title was purely honorary — had never held any public office; yet Wilson trusted him with delicate missions relative to America's status with the European belligerents of World War I. House was an early elitist, who believed that a class of persons was necessary to run affairs for the masses; see his anonymously published novel, *Philip Dru: Administrator: a Story of Tomorrow, 1920-1935* (1912). It included dubious "reforms" which, however, do not seem to have disturbed his "other self," Wilson. Charles Seymour, ed., *The Intimate Papers of Colonel House* (1928); A. L. and J. George, *Woodrow Wilson and Colonel House* (1956).

HOUSE OF BURGESSES (1619), established in Virginia: "the first representative assembly in the New World." That year, the first cargo of "slaves" (see Slavery) was brought to Virginia. Thus, a fateful paradox was instituted: of democracy and slavery persisting and developing side by side. See also Massachusetts and Virginia.

HOUSE OF REPRESENTATIVES, though the more popular branch of Congress, not necessarily the more distinguished body of legislators. In the pre-Civil War decades, the Senate prided itself on its possession of Clay, Webster, and Calhoun; but the House, though without pride until his dramatic death, had John Quincy Adams (qq.v.). In the post Civil War era, concerned conservatives like Henry Adams *(q.v.)* deplored the fall of Congress from dignity and greatness, and reformers had no more reason to admire a body which more clearly seemed to reflect pecuniary interests, rather than principles. From "Czar" Reed in the House to "Czar" Cannon *(q.v.)* seemed an even greater fall, but the Reform Era of the pre-World War I period interposed public pressure and debate to produce reforms, and the deposition of Cannon, in a House revolt. See also Lobby.

HOUSE UN-AMERICAN ACTIVITIES COMMITTEE, long the object of scorn and hatred by liberals and radicals, it went underway in 1938, headed by Martin Dies *(q.v.)*. Theoretically opposed to fascism as well as communism, it emphasized the latter. Jerry Voorhis *(q.v.)*, a distinct liberal, served with the Committee, 1939-43, when he resigned in protest over the irregularities it practiced. J.B. Matthews, a former fellow-traveller *(q.v.)*, who had been head of the American League for Peace and Democracy, was research director for the Dies Committee, which became the "Thomas" Committee, and took over Committee chairmens' names. Its record of achievements, as compared with its failures, is rarely balanced. It was Chambers's testimony before the Committee which broke the Hiss Case *(q.v.)*. Other testimony has been presumed to add to public knowledge of matters affecting the public interest. On the other hand, the Committee has been accused of character assassination, the harassment of defenseless individuals, offense offered to American intellectual leaders, and inquisitorial methods. Hence, it was taken to constitute part of the "McCarthy Era," *(q.v.)* even though it preceded his appearance on the public stage, and survived his leaving it; being able to acquire from the House the annual funds necessary to continuance. Its work was augmented by similar state committees, as in California and Connecticut. However, the apparent decline of "hysteria" prompted critics of HUAC (as they preferred to have it) to hope that they could agitate successfully for its discontinuance. Although the invoking of the First and the Fifth Amendments to the Constitution *(qq.v.)* had lost its force, because others, including gangsters, had become adept at utilizing it manifestly for non-libertarian purposes, and because increasingly public opinion thought that persons with nothing to hide ought to cooperate with a search for knowledge serving the public interest, critics of HUAC massed opinion from such respectable sources as the *New York Times,* the *Christian Science Monitor,* and the American Jewish Congress, such Democratic stalwarts as Eleanor Roosevelt and former President Truman, among many others, and launched a campaign to have HUAC abolished. They suffered a defeat in February 1961, when the U.S. Supreme Court ruled by a 5-4 vote that a contempt conviction against Frank Wilkinson, a critic of HUAC, for refusing to tell the Committee whether he was a communist party member in 1958 was affirmed. In a similar decision involving another individual, the Court, in effect, ruled that the First Amendment did not protect persons from legitimate inquiries intended to determine Communist infiltration and propaganda, which Congress had authorized. See also National Committee to Abolish HUAC, "Operation Abolition."

HOUSING PROBLEM, THE, one of the most strategic challenges to reformers, involving the healthy growth of cities, the dignity of the family unit, the relationship of races as affected by free opportunities or discrimination. The great growth of the cities from the middle of the nineteenth century onward went along with the building of tenements which housed the greatest number of poor at the least cost. "Old law" tenements were fire-traps, vermin-infested, with meager light, sanitary facilities, and other human wants. They were a target of reformers; the Tenement House Bill of 1901, in New York was typical of reform legislation in the area, which sought to set down minimum specifications for new housing. What those who applauded reform in housing did not realize was that this far from obliterated old housing,

which continued to be home, for better or worse, to great numbers of people; moreover, that the newer housing, built as economically as possible, within the law as it could be parsimoniously interpreted, grew older: that almost as important as the building of a house was the law seeing to its maintenance. The state of housing tended to be judged by its convenience to the better-to-do classes in society. Thus, there was, indeed, a housing "boom" in the 1920's, but it affected the affluent and advancing elements, rather than the poor, who continued to live in squalor. The 1930's stopped housing as well as other businesses, and brought the New Deal *(q.v.)* into action. The Federal Housing Administration (established 1934) helped maintain already existing housing and was intended to encourage private building. The Wagner-Steagall Act of 1937 set up the U.S. Housing Authority to lend money to local housing agencies to clear slums and create housing units under federal supervision. Once again handsome neighborhoods began to appear where there had been slums, and it was noted that about one-third of the units went to Negroes. Less examination was given to the question of where those who had inhabited the obliterated slums had gone. For the most part, they had no choice but to double up in other slums, or, for lack of money and training to make new slums of such housing as they found. Overall, the new housing once more benefited elements of the middle-class, though under difficult conditions, rather than those who were solidly on rock-bottom. The increasing population, augmented by Negroes streaming North, and Puerto Ricans coming in an ever-augmented stream, created new housing needs. Ambitious white people, their fortunes improved by war-time jobs, streamed into the countryside; cities began manifestly to deteriorate. The Urban Problem *(q.v.)* made its unmistakable appearance. The Housing Act of 1949 created an immediate challenge in terms of discrimination. The National Committee against Discrimination in Housing was organized in 1950. Although all great cities had showcases which revealed healthy and happy neighborhoods of Negroes, these represented only a small percentage of the Negro people. Southerners argued for equal but separate housing developments, and accused northerners of hypocrisy: of offering Negroes as a whole neither equal nor adequate housing. Although the South was held in contempt by northern liberals, it remained a fact that most northern house-owners feared to have their property lose value by admitting Negroes into the area in significant numbers, on equal terms. In 1961 there were still old law tenements being inhabited in New York. See also Discrimination. Edith Abbott, *The Tenements of Chicago, 1908-1935* (1936); M. J. Reynolds, *Housing of the Poor in American Cities* (1893); M. Kaufman, *Housing of the Working Classes and of the Poor* (1907); Chester Hartman, *Housing and Social Policy* (1975); G. Sternlieb and J. W. Hughes, *Housing and Economic Reality: New York City 1976* (1976); Michael Stegman, *Housing and Economics: the American Dilemma* (1971); *Housing in Retirement* (1974).

HOW THE OTHER HALF LIVES, (1890), see Riis, Jacob A.

HOWARD, JOHN (1726-1790), pioneer of prison reform *(q.v.)*. As high sheriff of Bedfordshire, he was impressed by the evil state of the prisons he observed, and sought successfully to establish a system of salaries for jailers and end the venal fee system. He made careful inspections of English, Scottish and Irish prisons, and also examined them on the Continent. His *The State of the Prisons in England and Wales* (1777) was an influential work. His concern for plagues also caused him to study the pesthouses, which he reported in *Account of the Principal Lazarettos in Europe* (1789). His influence was present in the organization of the Philadelphia Society for Alleviating the Miseries of Public Prisons, as well as in the development of prison reform throughout the states.

HOWE, FREDERIC C. (1867-1940), reform writer and student of municipal government, he updated and deepened the work of Albert Shaw *(q.v.)*. In 1905 he was sent officially to investigate municipal ownership as it operated in Great Britain. See his *The City, The Hope of Democracy* (1905), and *The British City, the Beginnings of Democracy* (1907). He was director of the People's Institute, in New York, 1911-4, and commissioner of immigration at the Port of New York, 1914-9. See his *The Confessions of a Reformer* (1925).

HOWE, JULIA WARD (1819-1910), best known for her "Battle Hymn of the Republic" (1861), and wife of Dr. Samuel G. Howe (*q.v.*), in old age became an influential advocate of woman's rights, and associate of Rev. James Freeman Clarke and Lucy Stone (*q.v.*). She helped form the New England Woman Suffrage Association in 1868, and became its long-time president. She also gave her name and time to other women's organizations. For a selection of her speeches and essays, see Florence H. Hall, ed., *Julia Ward Howe and the Woman Suffrage Movement* (1913).

HOWE, SAMUEL GRIDLEY (1801-1876), philanthropist and reformer, he received his medical degree from Harvard University, then went to Greece to serve it in its battles with the Turks. On his return, having been offered the direction of a school for the blind, he went abroad to study methods of dealing with the problem: on his return in 1832, he opened what became the Perkins Institute. He contributed also to related reforms, and became an ardent Free Soiler, at one time editing with his wife Julia *The Commonwealth*, and even becoming implicated in the plots of John Brown (*q.v.*). He served on the Sanitary Commission during the Civil War, and after it returned to Greece to minister to distressed Cretans.

HOWELLS, WILLIAM DEAN, (1837-1920), American novelist and "Dean of American Letters." He made a moderate contribution to the development of realism in fiction, most notably in *The Rise of Silas Lapham* (1885) and *A Hazard of New Fortunes* (1890). His social conscience was touched by the execution of the Haymarket defendants (see Haymarket Affair), which he denounced as judicial murder, and by Edward Bellamy's *Looking Backward* (*q.v.*), which inspired his own *A Traveller From Altruria* (1894). He encouraged such pioneer realists and naturalists as Stephen Crane, Frank Norris, and Harold Frederic.

HUAC, see House Un-American Activities Committee.

HULL HOUSE (1889), see Settlement Movement, The.

HUMAN RIGHTS, a modern variation on the older ideal expressed in "the rights of man," intended to take into account new pressures in America and elsewhere to include equal rights for women. In America, *civil* rights expressed better the demands of concerned persons. Elsewhere, "human rights" literally involved resisting enslavement, torture, and death. President Ford's Helsinki Charter, drawn up with the Soviet Union in 1975, which pledged itself to honor human rights was criticized at home by putting Russia on the side of virtue verbally, while ignoring her desperate flouting of decency in administering gulag (*q.v.*) and other atrocious systems of repression. Ford approved UN Ambassador Moynihan's denunciation of the Ugandan dictator as a "racist murderer," but refused to name others who merited that stigma; suggesting that "human rights" was fated to be subject to political pressures and alliances. See also United Nations Human Rights Commission. A. I. Melden, *Human Rights* (1970); W. J. Butler and G. Lavasseur, *Human Rights and the Legal System in Iran* (1976); Aileen Fisher and Olive Rabe, *Human Rights Day* (1966). See also S. Vogelgesang, *American Dream Global Nightmare: the Dilemma of U.S. Human Rights Policy* (1980).

HUMANE SLAUGHTER, the cause of those who were not so much disturbed by the eating of meat, as in the case of vegetarians (*q.v.*), but by what seemed to them cruel means for slaughtering livestock. Since August, 1960, by Federal laws, beasts were required to be made insensible before being shocked, hoisted, cast, thrown, or cut. However, the law applied only to animals involved in interstate commerce; some twenty-percent of them, or an estimated twenty-five million animals were still processed by less considerate means: a fact which continued to provide a cause in numerous states.

HUMANITARIANISM, a general category taking in such causes as better regard for the young, the old, the sick and poor, for animals, for orphans, for abandoned women and women who have been abandoned, for idiots and criminals, for the handicapped, for slaves and freedmen, for the needy abroad, for mass victims of catastrophes. Humanitarianism can be distinguished from charity (*q.v.*) — enterprises which involve patronage rather than concern — and from revolutionary movements determined to overthrow the conditions presumed to create human distress. Revolutionary movements can even be anti-humanitarian, holding that it is a sop intended to blind the needy to basic injustice. In pursuing their goals, revolutionists may even shoot, torture, and starve, in the interests of the beneficent world they promise, or because they have been made to suffer such punishments. Reform tends to appeal to humanitarian sentiments, charity to the guilty conscience, revolution to the angry and impatient.

HUMPHREY, HUBERT H. (1911-1978), an ardent New Dealer (*q.v.*), he served as mayor of Minneapolis, the first Democrat from Minnesota elected to the U.S. Senate (1948), and aspirant to the Presidency. As Vice President to Lyndon B. Johnson (1965-1969), he followed the Johnson line, defending the Vietnam War, and seeking to propitiate Governor George Wallace (*q.v.*) of Alabama, whose "populism" threatened the Johnson political drive. Humphrey's civil rights record gave him liberal support which all but made him President in 1968. He was remembered as a decent man who could not believe that civil rights and rhetoric favoring the poor could be manipulated by self-seeking politicians. See his own *The War on Poverty* (1964), and *The Cause Is Mankind* (1964).

"HUN," epithet used to describe the Germans during World War I, reference being to an Asiatic nation of barbarians which moved into Europe by way of the sword, ultimately, under Attila (445-453 A.D.), "the Scourge of God," exacting great tributes, and penetrating Italy almost to Rome. Although the Vandals would have made for a more relevant epithet, since they were a Germanic tribe which sacked Rome, it was "the Hun" that caught on with the common people.

100,000,000 GUINEA PIGS, see Consumers.

"100%", a concept developed during World War I, which complements Theodore Roosevelt's fear of "hyphenated Americans" (*q.v.*). It assumed a uniform concept of the American, and, like the "Americanization" drive (*q.v.*), limited the potentialities of the term. See also Upton Sinclair's bitter novel, *100%, the Story of a Patriot* (1920).

HUNGARY, remembered for its republican effort in 1848, under Kossuth (*q.v.*), and its abortive Bolshevik revolution, under Bela Kun, in 1919, reappeared in the post-World War II era as a republic, which was gradually liquidated by the communists. The resistance of the Catholic Church came to a head in the arrest of Josef Cardinal Mindszenty (*q.v.*), December 27, 1948, for treason. In 1950, the last remnants of democratic government were expunged. The Hungarian uprising against what was essentially rule from abroad was crushed by Soviet troops in November 1956. The inability of the "free world" to help created a sense of scandal in the west. America quietly assimilated some 50,000 Hungarian fighter-refugees. The departure of Cardinal Mindszenty later helped ease some of the after-revolution tensions. The government rid itself of some of the more fanatical Stalinists in its folds, and, helping the Russians to destroy incipient democracy in Czechoslovakia in 1968 (*q.v.*), lost some of its own aura of martyrdom; N. M. Nagy-Talavera, *The Green Shirts and Others* (1970); Paul Ignotus, *Hungary* (1972); G. Kurland, *The Hungarian Rebellion of 1956* (1974); Janos Radvanyi, *Hungary and the Superpowers* (1972).

HUNGER, a massive problem at all times; some analysts saw starvation as one of "nature's" ways of controlling population. It was complicated by factors of human relations. The introduction of technology into rural and primitive areas, for example: land which fed African people was unattended while administrators sought industrial enterprises, making food imports urgent, and millions of natives liable to starvation. Wars and government eruptions, stealing of supplies, and supplies siphoned off for bureaucratic gain, drought and abnormal heat complicated the simplest processes of aid or rebuilding of food production. Nigeria, though oil-rich, could not prevent suffering from starvation. Bangladesh, with sparse resources to begin with, when torn apart from Pakistan, endured agonies of deprivation. India's food shortages were long endured. The United Nations World Food Council mediated desperate efforts to prevent mass starvation. The politics of national budgets, priority areas, and international relations retarded mercy shipments while civilian masses starved around the world. C. S. Russell et al., *Drought and Water Supply* (1970); P. A. Sorokin, *Hunger as a Factor in Human Affairs* (1975); Harold A. Boner, *Hungry Generations: the Nineteenth Century Case against Malthusianism* (1971); Georg Borgstrom, *Hungry Planet: the Modern World at the Edge of Famine* (1972).

HUNGER MEETINGS, held in New York, notably, but elsewhere in the North as well, during the depression of 1852, to protest the lack of work and food.

HUNGER STRIKES, a weapon in the hands of prisoners who claim to be suffering injustice, or who wish to call attention to a cause. The effectiveness of this weapon depends in part upon the support which they have, or can inspire. In modern times, the woman suffragists of England employed it effectively, despite forced feeding. "The Cat and Mouse Act" of 1914 permitted the authorities to release prisoners in ill health temporarily, thus giving them leeway in the discharge of their duties. The best publicized hunger strike in America was by Alice Paul, a suffragist, in 1917. The Lord Mayor of Cork, Ireland, Terence MacSwiney, an Irish nationalist, died after a hunger strike of seventy-four days; a curious byproduct of the tragedy was its educational value with respect to the human need for food; many people had imagined that a few days without food would suffice to kill a person. Gandhi (*q.v.*) employed the hunger strike, but not against imprisonment.

HUNKERS, conservative faction of the Democratic Party, especially in New York State, about 1842 and in following years, supporters of Polk, and political opponents of Van Buren and the Barnburners (*qq.v.*), whom they compared, in the old adage, with the farmer who burned down his barn to kill the rats.

HUNTER, ROBERT (1874-1942), pioneer social worker and student of social conditions, who conducted investigations in Chicago and in New York. A socialist, he provided his party with data which it employed in its criticisms of municipal administrations. See his *Tenement Conditions in Chicago* (1901), *Poverty* (1904), and *Socialists at Work* (1908). Hunter was one of the "millionaire socialists" of the period whose serious purposes encouraged the view that socialism might become respectable without becoming corrupt.

HURD, JOHN C. (1816-1892), although no reformer, his *The Law of Freedom and Bondage in the United States* (1858-62) was of use to pro-slavery and anti-slavery advocates.

HUTCHINSON, ANNE (1591-1643), pioneer religious liberal and woman's rights advocate, though she couched her cause in the language of the time. She accused the Puritan leaders of Boston of substituting their will for that of God, whose will she believed herself able to read by inspired understanding of the Bible. Thus, she emphasized not only an individual interpretation of Holy Writ, but her equality as a woman. She persuaded other women to assert themselves. Condemned in 1637 by an ecclesiastical synod and excommunicated, she was shortly after banished, and with her family became a founder of Rhode Island. She later died at the hands of Indians. E. J. Battis, *Saints and Secteries* (1962); W. K. Rugg, *Unafraid: a Life of Anna Hutchinson* (1930).

HUTCHINSON FAMILY, a group of singers from New Hampshire who, during the abolitionist era, became extremely popular in the North, with sentimental, religious, and patriotic songs, and who therefore created a forum from which their songs favoring Free Soil could be offered. Thus, they helped decrease the distance which separated abolitionists and the general public; see Charles E. Mann, ed. and comp., *A Story of the Hutchinsons . . . , by John Wallace Hutchinson* (1896).

HYNDMAN, HENRY M. (1842-1921), English socialist leader; in 1881, he founded the Social Democratic Federation, and was the chairman of the British Socialist Party which succeeded it (1911). He was a critic of British imperialism. A student of Marxism, he helped explain its principles to the nation; see his *The Historical Basis of Socialism in England* (1883), *The Economics of Socialism* (1896); *The Commercial Crises of the Nineteenth Century* (1908); and *A Record of an Adventurous Life* (1911).

"HYPHENATED AMERICANS," Theodore Roosevelt's (*q.v.*) famous epithet for those he feared entertained divided loyalties. Although he was sophisticated enough to include in his denunciation all persons who would consider themselves anything more than Americans, there can be little doubt he had most clearly in view those who thought of themselves as German-Americans. Those who exalted Anglo-American ties, who praised the "English heritage," and who otherwise put themselves down as English-Americans were not accorded the same suspicions of loyalty.

I

"I TOOK THE CANAL ZONE," notorious phrase employed by Theodore Roosevelt (q.v.) in speeches delivered in 1908 and 1911, in order to underscore the difference between action and irresolution, and to put himself in a hero role. It is sometimes quoted as "I took the Panama Canal." Roosevelt added: "...and let Congress debate." The subsequent Woodrow Wilson Administration expressed "sincere regret" for the American intervention of 1903, and committed the nation to paying offended Colombia twenty-five million dollars, to Roosevelt's chagrin. In due course, the Roosevelt diplomacy became obsolete.

"I WAS A NEGRO IN THE SOUTH FOR 30 DAYS," (1948), by Ray Springle, a striking piece of journalistic enterprise, intended to reveal that southern prejudice was not a matter of race—since Springle was a white man—but of reputation. Subsequent experiments by others (such as the turbaned Negro who claimed to be from India, and thus of the "white" race) underscored this finding. Although it tended to make the accepted southern viewpoint seem ludicrous, as well as contemptible, to unsympathetic observers, it may have underscored for others the tenacious and conventional quality of the South's approach to the problem.

IBSEN, HENRIK (1828-1906), great Norwegian dramatist, whose writings inspired and aided reformers: critical of social standards and expectations were *The League of Youth* (1869), *Pillars of Society* (1877), *A Doll's House* (1879), *An Enemy of the People* (1882), *Hedda Gabler* (1890), among others. His works excited controversy as well as the emulation of such figures as Bernard Shaw (q.v.); see his *The Quintessence of Ibsenism* (1891). Though some of Ibsen's works were alleged to be argument rather than art, his dramatic and poetic understanding survived his critics. Michael Meyer, *Ibsen* (1971).

I.C.A., see International Cooperative Alliance.

I.C.C., see Interstate Commerce Commission.

ICKES, HAROLD L. (1874-1952), picturesque New Deal (q.v.) administrator, came from a background of progressive politics in Chicago and Illinois, concerned for good government and especially for resistance to special business interests which sought to influence contracts and the allocation of franchises. As Secretary of the Interior, he made a reputation for vigor in administration and forthrightness in the expression of his opinions. As chairman of the Public Works Administration (q.v.), his presence gave assurance that contracts were being distributed equitably and supervised with competence. Ickes was responsible for the spending of four and a quarter billion dollars on over thirty thousand projects. More controversial was his effort to move the Bureau of Forestry into his Department, which occasioned a duel with Gifford Pinchot (q.v.). Ickes vehemently opposed President Truman's effort to appoint a wealthy oil man as Under Secretary of the Navy, and resigned when the President persisted in his recommendation. As a columnist and author he was stimulating and informative; see his *Autobiography of a Curmudgeon* (1943).

IDEOLOGY, a concept in America of the 1930s, which ranged communists who saw comparable aggregates of "workers and farmers" everywhere in the world, against anti-communists who stipulated a unique "American way of life." Post-World War II conditions juxtaposed sympathizers of "Marxism" against defenders of capitalism, with appropriate attention given to imperialism, "emerging nations," and other topics deemed within the spectrum of "Marxist" and anti-"Marxist" tenets. A rationalization of the sharp antagonism between the two seemed to be the "mixed economy" (q.v.), borrowing ideas from both capitalism *and* communism. But this approach tended to lead to pragmatic results, rather than the fulfillment of a theory. The declaration of a former left-winger turned academic, Daniel Bell, in *The End of Ideology: on the Exhaustion of Political Ideas in the Fifties* (1960) signally for many like him the need for following events, rather than trying to impose a theory upon them. The youth (q.v.) uprising of the Sixties, based on emotion and rejecting reason as a guide, gave unexpected substance to the end-of-ideology approach. However, the persistence of the discipline of "Marxism" in the major communist nations, and their disciples, and the rise of a new academic impulse at home, made up partially of "drop outs" who had dropped back, and which termed itself "Marxist," resulted in a quasi-"ideological" approach somewhat comparable to that of the earlier era.

IDI AMIN (1925-   ), a symbol of the barbaric aspects of African liberation movements, the former British soldier in 1971 led an army revolt against Ugandan president Milton Obote to make himself commander in chief and president for life. He sought popularity by glittering appearances, mass expulsion of Ugandan Asians, and humiliation of foreigners, and secured his place with the murder of dissenters, by well-paid troops. His overthrow in 1980 was accompanied by ruin which brought in Tanzanian troops to help preserve a semblance of order. Amin received sanctuary from the somewhat comparable Libyan dictator, Colonel Gadaffi, made notorious the same year by having murdered Libyan exiles as far away as England and Italy. Amin's presence, however, proving embarrassing, the Ugandan transferred his presence to Saudi Arabia, where he was temperately welcomed as being a "devoted Moslem," and so of some relevance to Arab ambitions in Africa. P. M. Gukiina, *Uganda: a Case Study in African Political Development* (1972).

IDIOTS, CARE OF, see Institutional Reform, Retarded Children, Care of.

I.L.A., see International Longshoremen's Association.

I.L.D., see International Labor Defense.

I.L.G.W.U., see International Ladies Garment Workers Union.

ILLUMINATI, THE, a movement of rationalists in Europe of the Eighteenth Century, offensive to the church establishments, rumor of which disturbed conservatives in the United States after the Revolution, fearful of its effect on democratic thinking; see John Robison (1739-1805), *Proofs of a Conspiracy against all the Religions and Governments of Europe...* (1797); Vernon Stauffer, *New England and the Bavarian Illuminati* (1918).

I.L.O., see International Labor Organization.

"IMMEDIATIST" ABOLITIONIST, see Abolitionism.

"IMMEDIATE DEMANDS," see Communism and Reform.

IMMIGRANTS AND REFORM have been associated from the beginning of colonization, immigration itself being (at least in the intentions of the immigrants) a species of reform, an opportunity to get away from undesirable conditions. Three strains of immigrants can be discerned: colonial immigration, "old" immigration—most noticeably Irish, but including the important German strains, and "new" immigration, from the 1880's on, involving peoples from the Mediterranean countries: peasant types who were called upon to work in mine and mill, and, in the cities, to face exploitation in the infamous sweat shops (q.v.). The Democratic Party was conspicuous in currying favor with these people; Whigs were in the forefront of the Know-Nothings (q.v.) of the pre-Civil War Era, Republicans manned the American Protective Association (q.v.) of the post-Civil War period. Russian Jews, fleeing persecution, brought with them an outstanding intellectual class. All the immigrant groups produced powerful reactionary elements, as well as labor leaders, reformers, and radicals. The Immigration Restriction League of the 1890's led to the 1917 Literacy Test Law. Henry Cabot Lodge (q.v.) was the outstanding proponent of immigration restriction; Emma Lazarus (q.v.) wrote a sonnet made immortal by its sentiments. The Reform Era of pre-World War I times made much of the needs of minority groups, and especially immigrants, as in Upton Sinclair's (q.v.) The Jungle. The Immigration Law of 1921 limited aliens to three percent of the number of a given nationality, as determined by the 1910 Census; in practice the law operated largely against the laboring classes; the 1924 law all but closed the "golden gates." Reformers took this to be a defeat of American principles and needs. See also McCarran-Walter Act of 1952. A somewhat specialized problem in immigration was that of orientals, special in that it attracted antagonism not only from the "established" groups with high self-esteem and expectations, but from the "interlopers," as well; the "whites" closed ranks on the issue. Chinese immigration was solicited in the 1850's by those in California seeking cheap labor and interested in employing Chinese for such service functions as washing and cooking, as well as a general weapon for keeping salaries as low as possible. The building of the railroads added a reason for soliciting Chinese immigration. Hence, such a demagogue as Dennis Kearney (q.v.) could make political capital of the antipathy of workers for the Chinese, and labor generally led the fight for the Chinese Exclusion Act of 1882. The difficulty with the anti-Chinese campaign was that it did not focus on the mercenary intentions of those who sought to transport Chinese to the United States, but derogated them as human beings and encouraged malicious and lying rumors about their outlook and habits. Bret Harte's (q.v.) verses on the Chinese, though intended satirically, were read as true by prejudiced Americans. Such spokesmen against organized labor as E.L. Godkin (q.v.), though doubtless idealistic on the subject, wrote more rationally about it than their labor antagonists. In general, Americans built up a record in this field of foreign relations, as in others, for which they were bound to pay in due course. The day came unheralded. Puerto Ricans, brought in by box-car planes during World War II to New York to implement low-paid jobs passed over by Negroes employed in shipyards and elsewhere, and who stayed and multiplied; Mexicans who were encouraged by mine-owners and farmers in the Southwest illegally to cross over in hordes to labor at minimum wages, and who found their way as far north as Chicago; Cubans who fled Castro (q.v.) Cuba to populate Florida; and refugees (q.v.) from Asia, as well as further refugees from the Caribbean—all these faced the nation with problems of immigration policy and assimilation. Paradoxes abounded. The Mexican government, unable to feed its own people or to give promise of improved conditions, was affronted by the United States interest in controlling illegal Mexican immigration, estimated at twelve million and growing, who considered themselves "economic refugees." Cuban refugees, come by private boat and including criminal and other questionable types deliberately included by order of Castro, were indignant at being processed by immigration authorities and deprived of immediate access to American bounty. They rioted in compounds. Illegal Mexican aliens in California struck for better wages, due to inflation (q.v.), while fearing deportation, which did not materialize though their names and places were known and printed in the press. Haitians joined the exodus from that land of misery, and, faced with deportation, roused journalistic, indignation, since they faced torture by the dread Haitian police, the Tonton Macoutes, if returned. One control suggestion was a national registration system of work cards, which would wipe out of the labor market illegally-entered immigrants. This horrified some commentators as opposed to American traditions. But since it inspired the suggestion by then President-elect Reagan (q.v.) that there be work cards for unnaturalized immigrants seeking work in the United States, it

seemed likely to enter into the process of reorganizing immigration procedures and goals. But with refugee hordes everywhere on earth, and few other nations ready to adopt assimilation policies, it was evident that America would have to do so, for the poorer elements which no nation welcomed with open arms. There were bright spots in a dark picture. The Southwest, already populated with Hispanics (q.v.), could treat comparable peoples with some understanding and efficiency. The first wave of Cubans from Castro's land were thoroughly assimilated in Florida, with an educated and competent leadership, and could help in necessary readjustments. Los Angeles was a congeries of "whites," Chinese, Negroes, and Spanish-speaking men, women, and children who could be accorded municipal power in accordance with their numbers and organization. Official data was accumulating which could resist harmful prejudiced impressions, that immigrants took away low-paying jobs and social services from Americans, without returns in productive work and taxes. The growth of immigrants who had become executives gave promise of new leadership for assimilated groups. W. D. Borrie, Cultural Integration of Immigrants (1960); M. A. Jones, American Immigration (1960); John Thomas, Planned International Migration and Multilateral Cooperation (1971); William Peterson, The Politics of Population (1965); A. T. Bouscaren, International Migration since 1945 (1963); Paul Tabori, The Anatomy of Exile (1972).

IMPEACHMENT, a drastic legislative move which threatened the integrity of the Supreme Court (q.v.) during Jefferson's Administration, and the Presidency (q.v.) when the Radical Republicans jeopardized Andrew Johnson's tenure. His resistance to their Reconstruction measures (q.v.) caused them to seek his removal, so that their own man, Benjamin F. Wade, would succeed him. Johnson's unwillingness to carry out the Tenure of Office Act, which took from him his right to remove unwanted Cabinet members, gave them their opportunity. He was impeached and brought to trial (1868) on various grounds, but mainly 'for having failed to carry out an act of Congress. Radical Republican control of the Senate, before which he was arraigned, gave Thaddeus Stevens (q.v.) confidence that Johnson would be convicted. Seven Republican Senators ruined their political careers by refusing to vote for conviction, thus depriving their party leaders of a Senate majority, by one vote. An equally partisan Congress was backed by a public opinion spearheaded by the liberal press, and implemented by revelations during Watergate (q.v.) hearings. More important, it had at its command tapes (q.v.) implicating the President. It therefore drove toward impeachment. Although Nixon (q.v.) could have defied it on grounds of "Executive Privilege" in a trial which would have torn the country still further apart, his Republican colleagues in Congress persuaded him that he did not have their votes, and must suffer indictment and condemnation in impeachment proceedings. He therefore accepted the alternative of resignation. John F. Kennedy, Profiles in Courage (1956); D. M. Dewitt, Impeachment and Trial of Andrew Johnson (1902); Raoul Berger, Impeachment: the Constitutional Problems (1973); New York Times Staff, Impeachment of Richard M. Nixon . . .The Final Report of the Committee of the Judiciary [H.R.] (1975).

IMPENDING CRISIS, THE (1857), see Helper, Hinton R.

IMPERIALISM AND REFORM have been less appreciated, by social reformers, in conjunction than has imperialism alone. The former has been discerned in British and American assaults upon Indian sovereignty, from earliest colonization days, in the policy of "manifest destiny" (q.v.), in the program behind the Mexican War (q.v.), the Ostend Manifesto, the Spanish-American War, the Open Door Policy, the politics which attended building of the Panama Canal, Caribbean policy (qq.v.), and other elements of foreign policy; see Albert K. Weinberg, Manifest Destiny (1935) and Victor Perlo, American Imperialism (1951). The American Fund for Public Service (q.v.) sponsored a group of studies in American imperialism. Less adequately realized has been the fact that imperialism has served reform purposes, thanks to its emphasis on national unity, and the need for satisfying and paying off those who have contributed to nationalist policies. Thus, soldiers have always been given generous allotments of western lands, in national gratitude for their services. The Jackson (q.v.) Administration professed a concern for the lot of the common man, and peremptorily sacrificed the Indians to his demand for their lands. The contempt which laborers developed for the Negro, the Chinese, and elements of the "New Immigration" (q.v.) rested partly in their fear that these despised minorities would depress their standard of living by agreeing to work for "slave" wages; nevertheless, their malicious views of these people encouraged nationalistic pride, and aided imperialist thought. The Spanish-American War was fought in part, with the energy provided by such figures as Theodore Roosevelt and Albert J. Beveridge (qq.v.). The Woodrow Wilson Administration, though dedicated to domestic reform, was dedicated to more aggressive purposes, so far as the Caribbean nations (q.v.) were concerned. American intervention in World War I could not have been accomplished without the cooperation of such figures as Herbert Croly and Charles Edward Russell (q.v.); see also Anti-Imperialism. The rise of Soviet (q.v.) imperialism was made evident by its take-over before and during World War II of Latvia, Lithuania, and Estonia. It became blatant in the physical repression which accompanied take-overs in Czechoslovakia, Hungary, Poland (qq.v.), and elsewhere. This did not interfere with abuse in communist countries, but also at home, of American "imperialism"; such authors as W. A. Williams (see his Americans in a Changing World) were hailed as penetrating historians for their critiques of America. Their basic bias lay in failing to compare American operations abroad with those of other nations, including the allegedly imperialized leaders. Thus, Aguinaldo, hero of the Filipino insurrection against American imperialism (1899-1901), lived to express gratitude that American "expansionists" had won: "For the alternative to annexing the Philippines entirely might have been partition. The Philippines might have become another Poland...and we should have lost all chance of becoming a free and independent nation." (Quoted in Filler, Appointment at Armageddon, p. 196.) The United States promised the Filipinos independence in 1916, and granted it in 1935. Geoffrey Bocca, The Philippines: America's Forgotten Friends (1974); T. Mukerjee, Economic Imperialism (1972); George Lichtheim, Imperialism (1970); Philip D. Curtin, ed., Imperialism (1972); W. Gurian, ed., Soviet Imperialism (1951); H. Hanak, Soviet Foreign Policy since the Death of Stalin (1972); Alan Lawrence, ed., China's Foreign Relations since 1949 (1975).

IMPLIED POWERS, traditionally a legal and political argument, involving the question of whether the Federal government has, or has not, the right, under the Constitution, to extend its operations, under the clause permitting it to "make all Laws which shall be necessary and proper for carrying into Execution the foregoing Powers" (Article I, Section 8). This provides reformers with an argument for pressing the government to satisfy their particular wants in legislation.

IMPRESSMENT OF SEAMEN, an ironic issue which led to war between the United States and Great Britain, involving the boarding of American ships by Britishers who claimed to recognize fugitives from His Majesty's Fleet among the Americans and removed them for service in it. The sentimental indignation of Americans over the treatment accorded their nationals conflicted with the actual contempt and indifference with which they treated this class of Americans; see seamen.

IMPRISONMENT FOR DEBT, see Debtors' Prisons.

INCENTIVE, see Productivity.

IN FACT, a news-letter published by George Seldes (q.v.), 1940-50, which emphasized information which he felt was improperly omitted or treated lightly, or distorted, in the general press.

IN RE DEBS (q.v.) (1895), decision of the U.S. Supreme Court in the appeal from the decision of the Circuit Court which found Debs in contempt of court for refusing to heed the injunction (q.v.) commanding him to cease from interfering with interstate commerce, under the Sherman Anti-Trust Act (q.v.). Although the Supreme Court passed over the question of whether the Sherman Act applied, its refusal to grant Debs a writ of habeas corpus was taken by labor to constitute an anti-labor decision.

IN RE JACOBS (1885), a reversal for labor and an example of the narrow thinking of the U.S. Supreme Court in the post-Civil War era, in its refusal to outlaw cigar-making in the home: a practice which corrupted the family life of the poor as well as turned the tenements into sties of filth and disease. The Court could not perceive how the cigar maker was to be improved in health or morals "by forcing him from his home and its hallowed associations and beneficent influences, to ply his trade elsewhere." The Court held that it was thus protecting the cigar workers' civil rights.

INCOME TAX, see Taxation.

INCOMES, see High Cost of Living.

INCREASING MISERY THEORY, controversial Marxian theory: that the maturing of monopoly capitalism must result in the increasing misery of the masses; critics argued that this, in fact, did not happen, that capitalism made concessions, and, under the pressure of reform movements, better than concessions. The changing terms of controversy in the post-World War II period, seemed to detract from the effectiveness or usefulness of this theory.

INDENTURED SERVITUDE, a primary method of acquiring labor in the English colonies; individuals signed papers committing themselves to labor for a stipulated period under specified conditions. For all general purposes, they were the slaves of their masters. In exchange, they received passage to America, and other perquisites. The success of "white slavery," as in Pennsylvania, was held the reason for the inability of Negro slavery to get a foothold in that Province, and it ultimately produced a large body of freedmen who were intent on acquiring further rights. J. B. McMaster, The Acquisition of Political, Social, and Industrial Rights of Man in America (1961 ed.); C. A. Herrick, White Servitude in Pennsylvania (1926); M. W. Jernegan, Laboring and Dependent Classes in Colonial America, 1607-1783 (1931); A. E. Smith, Colonists in Bondage: White Servitude and Convict Labor in America (1947); Louis Filler, ed., The Rise and Fall of Slavery in America (1980).

INDEPENDENCE, see Declaration of Independence.

INDEPENDENCY, see Congregationalism.

INDEPENDENT, THE, founded in 1848 as an organ of Congregationalist ministers concerned for church policy and progress. Since Congregationalism was a wholly northern product, its social outlook was northern. It therefore emerged as an influential Free Soil (q.v.) organ which, though wholly respectable, could reflect increasing anti-slavery sentiment without being deemed irresponsible. In effect, it was a forum for cautious northerners who were unwilling to associate with abolitionists, but who increasingly sought means for expressing their anti-slavery sentiments. Its most conspicuous figure was Henry Ward Beecher (q.v.), but it attracted others of influence, including his sister, Harriet Beecher Stowe (q.v.). After the Civil War, under Theodore Tilton, it engaged in such radicalism as advocating woman's rights. It later turned into an organ which preached the idealistic liberalism of Hamilton Holt (q.v.). See also Leavitt, Joshua.

INDEPENDENT, see Dearborn Independent.

INDEPENDENT LABOUR PARTY, founded 1893 on socialist principles by such trade unions and labor stalwarts as Tom Mann and Keir Hardie. It began as a federation of local groups seeking to gain labor representation in Parliament, and concerned for such issues as the eight-hour day, and other immediate goals. It was a major force in organizing the

British Labour Party *(q.v.)*, with which it cooperated. The I.L.P. was pacifistic during World War I and increasingly anti-capitalistic after; the Labour Party, on the other hand, mixed an acceptance of nationalistic goals with socialistic aims, and gained strength at the expense of the I.L.P. The latter maintained some strength among hard-core laborers, especially in Scotland and Wales. Its membership was further diminished by the Communist Party, while it repudiated the Labour Party of J.R. MacDonald *(q.v.)*. By 1948, with a membership of some three thousand, it was little more than a propaganda agency for a position somewhere between socialism and communism.

INDEPENDENT REGULATORY AGENCIES, see Regulatory Agencies.

INDEPENDENT UNIONS, an element of labor which ranges from more conservative associations to others which are radical or communist-controlled. The unions include the Railroad Brotherhoods *(q.v.)*, the National Federation of Telephone Unions, the Foreman's Association of America, the Farm Equipment Union, among others.

INDEPENDENT VOTER, theoretically the balance wheel of the two-party system, forcing both parties to vie for his vote with promises and facts. His strength was not markedly noted during the critical 1930's and the ensuing war era, but the return of "good times" and a relative peace reinvigorated the two-party system, and seemed to add significance to the "independent voter." His ability to judge issues and capacity for learning disturbed some elite analysts. The extreme closeness of the 1960 election, and the increasing interest manifested by the public gave hope that the independent might have a promising future; the hope was augmented by the remarkable elections held in New York City, in 1961. Mayor Robert F. Wagner, Jr., after long connection with Tammany Hall *(q.v.)*, broke with the organization, and, defeating it in the primary elections, went on to win a third term. Certainly, there had been an independent factor in this victory. The independent vote was not easily traced in Truman's *(q.v.)* hairline triumph in 1948, or in Nixon's *(q.v.)* loss of 1960 or win of 1968. It could not be readily discerned in Carter's gain over Ford *(qq.v.)* in 1976. However, Reagan's *(q.v.)* landslide of 1980 so far deviated from commentator and pollsters's predictions of a close race as to suggest that independency had cut through routine techniques and efforts at manipulation. Gerald M. Pomper, *Voters' Choice: Varieties of American Electoral Behavior* (1975). See also Silent Majority.

INDETERMINATE SENTENCE, an element in prison reform, developed by Zebulon R. Brockway in the post-Civil War period; it stipulated a maximum and minimum period during which a convicted individual might serve, leaving the actual time served to be determined later following an analysis of his record and potentialities.

INDIA, a great sub-continent, its affairs inevitably touched those of Pakistan, China, and, though at some distance, the Soviets and the world. Its malignant problems of poverty, drought, inter-caste violence, and uneven education limited the direct influence of its great traditions, philosophy, and beauty. With more than half of its 660 million people living below the poverty line, India had great potential for breeding demagogues and fanatics. However, traditions of the great Indian National Congress, and despite deep divisions, held the teeming nation together. Its role in the larger affairs of developing nations and superpower adjustments was indeterminate. See Gandhi, Nehru, Untouchables. B. K. Chatterjee, *Congress Splits* (1970); D. H. Butani, *India of the 1970s* (1972); Arthur Stein, *India and the Soviet Union* (1969); Sampooran Singh, *India and the Nuclear Bomb* (1971); V. B. Kulkarni, *India and Pakistan* (1974); P. Talbot and S. L. Poplai, *India and America* (1958); V. S. Maipaul, *India: a Wounded Civilization* (1977).

INDIAN, THE, AND REFORM, a significant barometer of American humanitarianism, ability to live with other people, and the status of a minority group. The earliest reform lay in the English willingness to Christianize the Indian, presumably for his own advancement. In general, the English were less concerned for doing this than were the French; to the English, the only good Indian was a dead one. However, such persons as John Eliot *(q.v.)* manifested regard for Indians, and, as he was driven farther west, sentimentalized him as the Noble Savage. The Indians in the southeast attracted northern sympathy when they were persecuted by the state governments and the federal administrations, partly for sectional reasons, but partly for reform purposes. The Cherokee *(q.v.)* attracted reform efforts. In the post-Civil War period, with the Indian destroyed as a competitor to the white people, reform interests multiplied, Helen Hunt Jackson's *(q.v.)* efforts in his behalf being typical and outstanding. The Dawes Act of 1887, making the Indian a ward of the state was a step forward, interposing the government between the Indian and his persecutors, to a degree. Francis E. Leupp, *The Indian and His Problem* (1910) expressed the attitudes of friends of the Indian. His circumstances varied with locations; he enjoyed a quantity of status in Oklahoma, he was treated with contempt and antagonism in New Mexico. The Carlisle Indian School in Pennsylvania educated their wards; the Navajo of the southwest, decade after decade, were unable to learn English. Although Friends of the Indian wrote and spoke in their behalf, the nation as a whole evinced little interest in him or his circumstances. It appeared that Indian reform would be largely a product of the Indian himself, if it materialized at all. In the 1960s, however, the Indian cause accelerated thanks to the perturbations begun by youth and woman activist agitators. Although Indians proved less adept in public rhetoric than other activist minority and dissident media exploiters, they found a cause in the Wounded Knee, South Dakota episode of 1890, in which Sioux confronted Army units and suffered deaths and injuries. Dee Brown's *Bury My Heart at Wounded Knee* (1971), a best-seller, among other such works, helped push public sentimentality in Indian behalf, as did the youth activist fancy for "Indian"-style headbands, primitive gestures, and other identity signals. More basic was a consolidation of Indian tribal units, with headquarters in Washington, which, pressing a long tradition of claims and adjudication going back to colonial days, was able to work with renewed vigor for money covering redress, education, government services, and other tribal and reservation issues. The U.S. Claims Commission, created by Congress in 1946, proved helpful and sympathetic to Indian claims, some going back a hundred years, though not always approved by Department of Interior or the Supreme Court. Claims in Maine, for example, would have given Indians a major part of the state, but settlement of the claim was substantial, if not revolutionary. Equally important was a realistic movement which had Indian leaders working for education which prepared their 29,000 college students for civic responsibility, reached agreements on national law as related to tribal law (Martinez v. Santa Clara) and rejected doctored presentations of Indian life intended to feed images of Indians which did not comport with facts. Wounded Knee remained controversial, an Army study which rejected the popular impression of a massacre being in turn rejected by Indian spokesmen, and Col. George A. Custer, though demeaned by Indians, continuing to attract sympathetic interest. More positive for the status of Indians in the American groove was a vigorous program in the Office of Indian Affairs favoring Indian enterprise, and the enlightening work of such writers as N. Scott Momaday, whose *House Made of Dawn* (1968) won a Pulitzer Prize, and James Welch's sensitive fiction, including *Winter in the Blood* (1974). Murray L. Wax, *Indian-Americans* (1971); W. A. Brophy and S. D. Aberle, *The Indian: America's Unfinished Business* (1972); Charles Brill, *Indian and Free...Life on a Chippewa Reservation* (1974); J. E. Levy and Stephen J. Kunitz, *Indian Drinking* (1974); W. E. Washburn, *The Indian in America* (1975); F. P. Prucha, *The Indian in American History* (1971); A. W. Lauber, *Indian Slavery in Colonial Times* (1913); R. W. Mardock, *The Reformers and the American Indian* (1971); Louis Filler and Allan Guttmann, *The Removal of the Cherokee Nation* (1977 ed.); C. C. Royce, *Indian Land Cessions in the United States* (1900).

INDIAN CAPTIVITY NARRATIVES, from earliest colonial times, were calculated to help justify, to Americans, their right to end the rule of barbaric and unprogressive tribes, and preempt their hunting grounds; see for example Samuel G. Drake, *Indian Captivities, or Life in the Wigwam* . . . (Auburn, New York, 1851).

INDIAN REMOVAL, a tragic episode in the long history of Indian-white associations and wars in the United States southeast, which reached its climax in the 1830's when large elements of the so-called Five Civilized Tribes (Choctaws, Chickasaws, Seminoles, Cherokee, and Creeks) were removed from their tribal lands in Florida, Georgia, Tennessee, and adjacent areas and resettled in Oklahoma. Most tragic was the fate of the Cherokee (q.v.).

INDIVIDUAL AND REFORM have been related to the extent that outraged individuality has opposed conditions which affronted it. The Declaration of Independence (q.v.) emphasized the rights of the individual. Imprisonment for debt affected substantial classes more than they did persons without the means to accumulate debts; and it was the former that demanded reform; northerners who denounced slavery were as much—perhaps more—disturbed by the competition slave labor provided to free labor, the challenge slave soil provided to free soil, as by the sorrows of the slave. The Populist Revolt was primarily a revolt of landed farmers who feared to be stripped of their property and power by giant corporations; the farmers aimed to preserve competition, not outlaw it. Reformers have distinguished between their individualism and that of Rockefeller (q.v.), whom they saw as putting his own individualistic (or anarchistic) wants above society's. Emerson's (q.v.) essay, "Self-Reliance," was the voice of an earlier individualism. The economic crisis of the 1930's raised the question of whether individualism any longer had meaning to an inter-related community. Communists found the concept of the individual futile and "bourgeois." Those who disagreed found some relationship to persist between the individual and freedom (q.v.). Diminished resources, notably in oil (q.v.), caused would-be reformers and liberals in the Carter (q.v.) White House and beyond to preach the need for austerity and planning, so that the wealthy and powerful would be controlled in their relations with the poor. The election of Reagan (q.v.) in 1980 seemed to be, in part, a vote for optimism and a belief in individual energy and ideas as creating new wealth and opportunity. This was also the message of George Gilder, *Wealth and Poverty* (1980): "Because no one knows which venture will succeed, which number will win the lottery, a society ruled by risk and freedom rather than by rational calculus...can call forth an endless stream of invention, enterprise, and art."

INDOOR RELIEF, see Workhouse, Outdoor Work.

INDUSTRIAL RELATIONS, a large and proliferating area in management intended to insure smooth-running operations in the plant; it concerns itself with worker problems and dissatisfactions, taking in material and psychological factors. It employs technicians acquainted with facts and figures of various types, but also consultants who often appear to have no information of any sort, but who are thought to smooth difficulties and soothe industrial nerves; the latter were, in part, a creation of prosperity when worker and manager sought mediation which would enable them to get on with the filling of the government contract. Whether they would survive more rigorous times was uncertain. John H. Crispo, ed., *Industrial Relations: Challenges and Responses* (1966), M. Beesley, ed., *Industrial Relations in a Changing World* (1975).

INDUSTRIAL REVOLUTION, refers to that change in technical advance which outmoded the small producer as a major factor in industry. Such mechanical inventions as James Hargreaves' spinning jenny (1763), Samuel Crampton's mule spinner (1774), James Watt's steam engine (1782), and James Cartwright's power loom (1785), made handworkers unable to compete, and congregated laborers in mills, increasingly with nothing to offer factory owners but the labor of their hands. Although *craftsmen* could continue to offer services, to a degree, most workers fell into one or another category of unskilled workers or specialists, and dependent upon their strength as an aggregate to receive respect and a minimum of security, rather than upon their skill and irreplaceability. With the advent of a mechanized, "push-button" assembly, and a beleaguered industry with problems of production (q.v.) and survival, only "Big Labor" unions stood between such workers and worklessness. Cuts in wages and perquisites, retraining, self help, and other solutions suggested the imminence of another industrial revolution. C. S. Doty, ed., *The Industrial Revolution* (1976).

"INDUSTRIAL UNIONISM," opposed to craft unions (q.v.), and concerned for organizing all workers and emphasizing a community of interests, rather than the interests of individual crafts. The Knights of Labor tended toward a species of industrial unionism; the A.F. of L. (qq.v.) felt that greater union strength was generated by maintaining the integrity of individual crafts. The American Railway Union (q.v.) was an earlier effort at industrial unionism. The socialists fought the A.F. of L. leadership on that issue. The C.I.O. (q.v.), in the 1930's, represented a triumph of industrial unionism.

INDUSTRIAL WORKERS OF THE WORLD, THE, began in 1905 as a reform movement, intended to unite skilled and unskilled workers into "one big union." Sponsors included William D. Haywood, Daniel De Leon, and Eugene V. Debs (qq.v.). The I.W.W. quickly turned into a revolutionary organization, led by Haywood, and repudiated by the reformers. It attracted fearless fighters and individualists, including Ralph Chaplin, Arturo Giovannitti, and Joe Hill (qq.v.), as well as a picturesque variety of transient workers. The "Wobblies" emphasized strikes "at the point of production." Their strength lay in their brilliant maneuvers and appeals for public sympathy, their weakness in their opposition to political action. They led sensational strikes at Paterson, New Jersey, 1913, and Seattle, Washington, 1919, among others. During World War I, a combination of mob action and legal prosecutions as well as newer labor perspectives created by the Russian Revolution of 1917 (q.v.), caused their swift decline. Ralph Chaplin, *Wobbly* (1948).

INDUSTRY, given a satiric connotation in the 1970s, by conservatives in their criticism of the welfare state (qq.v.). Conservatives made reference to the social work industry, the Third World industry, the statistics, protest, regulation and other industries. Basic was their ironic contrast with true industry, their conviction that such "industries" were not productive (q.v.) and created more social evils than they legitimately ministered to.

INFANT INDUSTRIES, see Protectionism.

INFLATION, in the Greenback and Free Silver (qq.v.) crusades, a form of liberal thinking; their purpose was to make money easier to obtain. (However, compare Specie Circular [q.v.]). By the 1930's, money and general social needs were so interwoven that inflation could not be a major cause; whether money was inflated or deflated in value made little difference to a person with no money. However, with the increase in civil servants and social stipendiaries of every kind, the inflation of the currency—revealed in an increasing high cost of living (q.v.)—served no class, and caused complaints from all. People living on annuities suffered acute hardship in many cases, as their fixed incomes decreased in value. For others, inflation had become part of a social contradiction. Since money purchased less, workers demanded more pay. When they received it, industry passed on the cost to the consumer through higher prices. Inflation, then, required a reformer with a good head, as well as a good heart, including a head for mathematics. Although inflation was a problem in the 1960s, its malignancy was overshadowed by President Johnson's (q.v.) belief that America could carry on war in Vietnam and social services at the same time. The fierce attack on government at home for waging war abroad, and with no visible results, and on Nixon (q.v.) following Johnson's retirement, obscured the unresisted increase in commodity and other prices. The dramatic jump in oil prices instigated by OPEC (q.v.) raised inflation warnings which were not made a priority till late in the decade. Then, the decline in the dollar, uncontrolled inflation, Cleveland's bankruptcy and the threat of New York City's insolvency, a clear recession, unemployment, and America's evident lack of a plan to combat these factors forced a consideration of their roots. President Ford's (q.v.) program of limited social services drew abuse from liberals who preferred a cutting of the Defense budget. Liberal belief in a soak-the-rich program clashed with the government's tax reduction incentive strategy. The fall of the British Labour Government brought in an austerity Tory administration which demanded less government spending and more and better work from its labor force. President Carter (q.v.) was hurt in prestige by seeming to want to do everything: cut Defense and increase it; cut social services, but permit them to grow; meet labor's demands for more, while urging restraint upon them. *Time* (April 28, 1980) offered a headline which would have stirred incredulity a few years back: "For an Overwrought Economy, the Recession Comes Better Late than Never." That industry, meaning labor, must have more productivity (q.v.) to bring down prices, and better products, was hard for Americans to accept. They did, however, elect Reagan (q.v.) in 1980, in part because of his devout feeling that energy alternatives could be created, and that Americans were able to, and should, sacrifice by not squandering oil, by holding up work standards, and by scrupulous industrial programs. They would thus beat back inflation, regain foreign confidence, and move forward in the world. M. Bruce Johnson, ed., *The Attack on Corporate America* (1978); Martin Mayer. *The Fate of the Dollar* (1980); I. S. Friedman, *Inflation: a World-Wide Disaster* (1973); Brian Griffiths, *Inflation: the Price of Prosperity* (1976).

INGERSOLL, ROBERT G. (1833-1899), lawyer, Civil War soldier, attorney-general of Illinois, he was famous as a major defender of the Republican Party and notorious as "the great Agnostic," who believed the Bible a tissue of palpable falsehoods. His conservative Republicanism permitted him to make a career which his atheism would have frustrated. He defended those implicated in the "Star Route" frauds, and gave the name of "Plumed Knight" to James G. Blaine (qq.v.), at the Presidential convention which nominated him in 1884, despite the "Mulligan Letters" (q.v.). Ingersoll's major service to reform lay in his fight for free speech and free press. Eva Ingersoll Wakefield, ed., *Letters of . . . Ingersoll* (1951); C. H. Cramer, *Royal Bob* (1952).

INITIATIVE AND REFERENDUM, means for attaining direct legislation, in the event that the elected legislatures are not responsive to the popular will. The initiative permits the submission of a law which the legislature has refused to act upon directly to the people; if passed it becomes a law. The referendum provides for a popular election to determine whether a law which has been passed should, or should not, become law. See also Recall, The, as a method for applying direct government to elected officials. A striking use of the initiative and referendum has been in the administration of labor unions, in order to augment the power of the individual member to maintain democracy within them. J. G. Palombara, *The Initiative and Referendum in Oregon* (1950).

INJUNCTION, a serious weapon employed against labor by way of the courts, since a simple order that labor desist from striking could hold back or demoralize a large movement intended to organize a union or maintain living standards. The Pullman Strike (q.v.) was harmed by the "blanket injunction" then issued. The injunction has been effective against labor boycotts (q.v.). It has been used against labor sometimes in defiance of state laws permitting strikes. The Clayton Act (q.v.) specifically forbade the use of injunctions against strikers, except to prevent property damage. However, see Norris-La Guardia Anti-Injunction Act.

INQUISITION, traditionally despised by social reformers as a subversion of liberty and humanity. Although there was an *inquisitio* in the early ninth century, it was an inquiry of neighbors; from it has been said to have grown the jury system. It is distinguished from the later Inquisition sponsored by the Catholic Church, which was an inquiry by officials, by a separate class, free to conduct their inquiry as it suited them. Most notorious of the Inquisitors was Torquemada, Spanish monk, who became a world symbol of fanaticism and cruelty, in his zeal for purifying the Church of "Judaizers," that is Christians of Jewish extraction (in most cases forced by persecution to repudiate their original creed) who were accused of practicing Jewish rites in secret. Although the sincerity of Torquemada and his associates has been noted, it has also been noted that the tortures they inflicted on suspects, theoretically for the good of their souls, they did not inflict on themselves. The Inquisition reached its height in the late fifteenth century; Torquemada himself died in 1498. Comparison with the Inquisition was made by those dissatisfied with the operations of communist justice, as in the Moscow Trials (q.v.), which, however were also defended, not only by communists, but by the American Ambassador to the Soviet Union, Joseph E. Davies, in his *Mission to Moscow* (1941). For a judicious account of the earlier Inquisition, see Rafael Sabatini, *Torquemada* (1924 ed.).

INSANE, see Institutional Reform.

INSPECTOR-GENERAL, THE, (1836) see Gogol, Nikolai V.

INSTITUTE OF PACIFIC RELATIONS, organized in 1925 as an agency for studying the Pacific nations and especially the Far East. Charges and revelations deriving from the Owen Lattimore Case (q.v.) made it a subject of controversy.

INSTITUTIONAL REFORM, a humanitarian movement of the nineteenth century, intended to do away with the demeaning of human life which accompanied contemptuous and indifferent treatment of idiots, lunatics, the blind, the deaf, and the dumb. There were few institutions concerned for these classes of people, many of them lived in infinite degradation in families and on the town. The giant of institutional reform was Dorothea Dix (q.v.), but the pioneer work of Samuel Gridley Howe and Thomas H. Gallaudet (qq.v.) in behalf of the blind and the deaf and dumb is immortal. Among others who contributed to the work were Edouard Seguin (1812-1880), a French physician who came to the United States and specialized in the training of idiots (see his *Idiocy* 1866) and William Swett (1825-1884), a deaf mute, who founded the Deaf Mute Industrial School at Beverly, Massachusetts. In terms of reform, such work has suffered from the factors which have impinged upon social work (q.v.).

INSULAR CASES, involved the responsibility of the United States for the territories it had acquired, as a result of the Spanish-American War (q.v.), and otherwise. In several cases, the U.S. Supreme Court concluded that the "Constitution follows the flag." In Downes v. Bidwell (1901), however, the Court found subordinated areas under the jurisdiction of the United States could be given less than equal status in law. In his essay. "The Supreme Court's Decisions," Finley Peter Dunne satirized its findings, and added the immortal opinion that "no matther whether the constitution follows th' flag or not, th' supreme coort follows th' iliction returns"; see Filler, ed., *Mr. Dooley: Now and Forever,* p. 162.

INSULL, SAMUEL (1859-1938), a symbol of irresponsible business enterprise in the 1920's, he capped a long association in the utilities business with a gigantic network of interests in the middle west, unscrupulously administered, and, thanks to the free hand given such enterprise, unregulated. The economic crash of 1929 forced him into a series of desperate and grossly illegal manipulations to save his fortune, but they collapsed in 1932, and he left the country to avoid indictment. A series of efforts to bring him back for trial kept him in the news before unsympathetic readers, but, brought back finally for trial, he was acquitted, and died abroad. Probably less a machiavellian than Ivar Kreuger *(q.v.)*, he no better served society. Forrest McDonald, *Insull* (1962).

INSURANCE INVESTIGATION OF 1905-6, an unforeseen product of Thomas W. Lawson's *(q.v.)* exposes of "frenzied finance." Americans were alarmed to learn that their insurance moneys were being irresponsibly administered. The result was the Armstrong Committee investigation of insurance, in Albany, New York, which utilized the services of Louis D. Brandeis and brought Charles Evans Hughes before the country *(qq.v.)*. The highly publicized findings brought a sharp public demand for reforms, which the legislature satisfied so adequately that relatively little needed to be added in order to modernize it, a later investigation, in Washington, in 1939, discovered.

INSURGENTS, identified with the Progressive movement of pre-World War I years.

INSURRECTION, the exception, rather than the rule in American social and political crises, since they in most cases burned themselves out in heated debate and compromise. This was partly the case because the classes were not isolated from one another, but shared interests. Bacon's Rebellion, Shays's Rebellion, the Whisky Rebellion, Dorr's Rebellion *(qq.v.)* contained elements within them which kept their protagonists part of the disturbed body politic. The Civil War *(q.v.)* was remarkable in that it left no residue of secessionists; southerners re-entered the Union and elected a President in Woodrow Wilson *(q.v.)*. The Disputed Election of 1876 *(q.v.)* would have caused an insurrection anywhere else in the world. The Railroad Riots of 1877, Coxey's Army *(qq.v.)* and similar phenomena were byproducts of a search for justice, rather than a change in government. Foreigners, and domestic analysts, often failed to understand the difference. During the San Francisco General Strike of 1934, streets were being fixed for ordinary maintenance purposes. *Pravda*, official Soviet newspaper, published a photograph of one such street, with the caption that a workers's insurrection was beginning: the streets were being torn up for barricades. See also Slave Revolts.

INTEGRATION, the most conspicuous reform issue in American domestic affairs, in 1961, receiving more attention than municipal reform, the unemployed, labor, the crisis in education and other social needs. The reason lay in a number of factors: the rise of African nationalism, the impatience with conditions of a frustrated Negro elite in collision with united southern white supremacists, criticism of the south by northerners who, however, did not trouble to encourage integration in the north, among other factors. The great integration decision of the U.S. Supreme Court, May 17, 1954, unleashed Negro demands for action, through the N.A.A.C.P. *(q.v.)*, which spurred legal actions, through such tacticians as the Rev. Martin Luther King *(q.v.)*, whose weapon was nonviolent action, through C.O.R.E. *(q.v.)*, which marshalled earnest hordes of enthusiasts to create situations in bus terminals and elsewhere, and through groups of parents and children who resisted pressures to maintain separate living and educational facilities. A survey by the American Jewish Committee and the Anti-Defamation League, early in 1961, showed that 28 northern, western, and border southern states had laws banning racial and religious discrimination, that 19 had set up F.E.P.C. *(q.v.)* commissions, and that five states had laws barring discrimination in private housing.

Twenty years later, with many more victories to show, questions as to their significance abounded. Polls indicated that the idea of integration was widely accepted. Public facilities were integrated. "Salt and pepper" personnel could be found working side by side everywhere. The poor, however, gained little from their elites's advancement. Busing *(q.v.)* and affirmative action *(q.v.)* had not achieved their primary objective, a heightening of the quality of life. In 1981, it appeared that a new dialogue was necessary which would meet the questions of achievement and freedom of choice. See also Education and the Negro, Sit-ins, "Resegregation." N. Harris et al., *Integration of American Schools* (1975); M. R. Konvitz, *A Century of Civil Rights* (1961); R. C. Angell, *Integration of American Society: a Study of Groups and Institutions* (1941).

INTELLECTUALS AND REFORM had an early, natural association in the limited suffrage and educational range of opportunities of colonial America. The Revolution required them in order to justify the break with the British Empire, and persuade provincial Americans to lend support for the effort. Thomas Jefferson's *(q.v.)* political rise was a victory for the intellectuals; his inventions and ideas were derogated by the opposition, his religious views treated as suspect. Such abolitionists as Garrison and Theodore Parker *(qq.v.)* were influential, even though they appealed to abstract views of justice and civil rights; their cerebrations filled needs for elements less capable than themselves in formulating ideas. Liberal Republican *(q.v.)* leaders were newspaper editors and theoreticians, but their protest against regular Republicanism filled a need in 1872. The ideas of Henry George and Edward Bellamy *(qq.v.)* filled more fundamental needs and generated storms of protest. Such socialists and muckrakers as Upton Sinclair and Lincoln Steffens *(qq.v.)* were in the forefront of pre-World War I reform, and such others as Oswald Garrison Villard and A.J. Nock *(qq.v.)* kept it alive in the difficult years of war and reaction. The New Deal *(q.v.)* demanded ideas to save the country, and the Brains Trust *(q.v.)* helped to provide it. In the 1950's, the presence of "eggheads" became notorious to those who suspected them of subversion or other irresponsibility; the defeat of Adlai E. Stevenson *(q.v.)* in 1952 and 1956 seemed setbacks for them, but they were thought to have been active in the nomination and election of John F. Kennedy *(q.v.)*. The 1970s were striking in their production of an impressive number of conservative intellectuals, alert to current affairs, and determined to influence them. Many of them appeared in the *National Review*. How they might influence the Reagan *(q.v.)* White House was a theme for conjecture. Norman Podhoretz, *Making It* (1968); Julien Benda, *The Treason of the Intellectuals* (1969); William F. Buckley, *Up from Liberalism* (1959).

"INTERESTS, THE," a term invented by David Graham Phillips *(q.v.)* to describe the financial and industrial forces which made their influence felt in Congress, and thus contributed to "the treason of the Senate."

INTERNAL IMPROVEMENTS, an issue of the early nineteenth century, it lacked reform potential, since the issue was not whether the building of roads and canals would improve society, but whether it was more properly a state or a federal function. In modern decades, such improvements have involved the health and comfort of the nation, yet only patchwork plans have materialized. Since it seems unlikely that road-building is susceptible to a moral approach, it is unlikely that reformers can become strategic in its development.

INTERNAL SECURITY ACT (1950), see McCarran-Wood Act.

INTERNATIONAL, see First, Second, Third, Fourth International.

INTERNATIONAL ASSOCIATIONS have helped to create possibilities for international communication and understanding. Though often disappointing to reformers, and the objects of scorn to radicals, because they were unable to forestall international catastrophes, they have constituted a network for the creation of common vocabularies and some accomplishment. Among significant groups less famous and less strategic than the League of Nations and the United Nations *(qq.v.)*, have been: the International Association for Labor Legislation, the International Congress of Working Women, the International Cooperative Alliance, the International Council of Trade and Industrial Unions, the International Federation of Trade Unions, the International Labor Organization.

INTERNATIONAL COOPERATIVE ALLIANCE, founded in 1895, a central office for cooperative societies all over the world; it held regular congresses, and published the *Review of International Cooperation.* In 1943 it represented some seventy million persons.

INTERNATIONAL COURT OF JUSTICE, see Permanent Court of International Justice.

INTERNATIONAL LABOR DEFENSE, the legal arm of the Communist Party, U.S.A., section of MOPR or Red International of Labor Defense, or Red International Aid. In 1946, it merged with the National Federation for Constitutional Liberties to form the Civil Rights Congress.

INTERNATIONAL LABOR ORGANIZATION, founded in 1919 as an autonomous associate of the League of Nations. It studied types and conditions of labor, and sought to create standards of practical significance to students and negotiators of labor's problems in all parts of the world. In 1946, the United Nations recognized the I.L.O. as the specialized agency competent to speak authoritatively on labor conditions, industrial relations, employment organizations, social security, and other aspects of labor. It maintained committees to work on specific problems, prepared documents for the use of its International Labor Conferences, and issued a wide variety of publications.

INTERNATIONAL LADIES GARMENT WORKERS UNION, one of the "model" unions, with a long record of democratic concern for its constituency, educational and recreational services, and social goals. The "uprising of the 20,000," in 1909 resulted in a strike which won the workers various benefits and inspired action among the cloakmakers. The "Protocol of Peace" which concluded the ILGWU strike set up labor-capitalist arbitrational relations which, though defective, constituted a landmark in labor organization. See also Amalgamated Clothing Workers of America.

INTERNATIONAL SOCIALIST BUREAU, see Second International.

INTERNATIONAL WORKINGMEN'S ASSOCIATION, the "First International," held its first conference in London in September 1865, where it adopted, in more moderate form than the Communist Manifesto *(q.v.)* had declared, the ideas of program and organization which Karl Marx sponsored. It held a number of conferences in subsequent years, a struggle for control going on between followers of Marx and the anarchist adherents of Bakunin *(q.v.)*. In the last Congress at The Hague in 1872, the latter were expelled; by then, the role of the First International was deemed completed and its General Council transferred to New York. Anarchist and socialist elements continued to oppose each other in fragments of organizations, both in Europe and the United States, but the First International was essentially defunct. See also Second International, Third International, Fourth International.

"INTERNATIONALE, THE," anthem of the socialists and, later, of the communists of the Second and Third Internationals, composed by Eugene Pottier (1816-1887), a French designer of materials and a member of the Working Men's Association. He was a member of the Paris Commune, and following its collapse escaped to England and then to America. His *Chants Revolutionnaires* appeared in 1887. The first verse and refrain of *L'Internationale* are:

> Debout! Les Damnés de la terre!
> Debout, les forçats de la faim!
> Le raison tonné en son cratère
> C'est l'eruption de la fin.
> Du passé faisons table rase,
> Foule esclave, debout! debout!
> Le monde va changer de base;
> Nous ne sommes rien, soyons tout!
>
> C'est la lutte finale,
> Groupons nous et demain,
> L'Internationale
> Sera la Genre humain.

INTERNATIONALISM AND REFORM have gone together in vast quantities of high-minded sentiment, as well as in some practical results. Governments have sent commissions to observe schools, industrial operations, the workings of municipal planning boards, and other institutions and systems and report methods which could be adapted to conditions at home. The League of Nations *(q.v.)* sponsored conventions for international curbs on prostitution, the opium trade, and slave-selling systems. In the 1920's, it was thought that the sending of technical experts from the United States to the Soviet Union would help modify some of the differences between the two systems. The United Nations *(q.v.)* made more determined efforts to further reform as a part of its program, acting as a clearing house for sending aid to underdeveloped countries, in the form of doctors, teachers, medicine, food, and encouraging cultural exchanges calculated to raise international appreciation of other people's virtues and talents. Whether the UN accomplished more than did the League is a matter of judgment. The UN's problems were more desperate and neither attained dramatic victories. It seemed clear that, on the international stage, reform was in competition with revolution.

INTERNATIONALS, see First, Second, Third, Fourth.

INTERVENTION, originally seen as the state's participation in the management of industry; since, indicates the entering of one nation into wars or crises of other nations. The "cold war" made the problem of intervention a constant in the affairs of Formosa, Guatemala, Korea, Laos, and other debated areas.

INTOLERABLE ACTS, THE, (1774), known to the British as the "Coercive" Acts, were an imperial revenge for the Boston Tea Party *(q.v.)*: an effort to prove to the colonists that defiance of the Empire would only bring trouble and discomfort. The "Boston Port Bill" closed that port to shipping. The "Administration of Justice Act" would have permitted capital crimes to be tried in England. The "Massachusetts Government Act" in effect ended charter government. The "Quartering Act" could have set British troops in private houses. And painful to the colonists was an act which they lumped with the "Coercive" acts: The "Quebec Act," which offended them by its tolerance of Catholics, and outraged them because it expanded Canada to include land down to the Ohio River: land claimed by Massachusetts, as well as Virginia and Connecticut. Had these acts been enforced, independency would have been defunct in America.

INTOLERANCE, a shibboleth of reformers, necessarily, since their reforms require tolerance in order to advance. Its definition varies, but rarely includes tolerance for views defending the *status quo (q.v.)*. Thomas Jefferson *(q.v., for this and following references)* was extremely impatient of Federalists, abolitionists of all non-abolitionists, whether proslavery or not, Progressives of non-Progressives, pacifists of non-pacifists, New Dealers of non-New Dealers. Marxists became notorious for their dogmatism (see Deviationist), but were not alone in their capacity for firmness in the right. By 1981, the grounds for tolerance had become shaky, because of problems in what pressure of insult and fear society could bear. Could it endure Ku Klux Klan parades in Negro communities? —Nazi-style Storm Troopers in Jewish-tenanted areas? Such demonstrations were especially difficult to endure when they also had international reverberations, involving the feelings of Negroes in Africa and Germans both in America and in Germany, where neo-Nazism stirred tragic memories and tensions. Oliver Wendell Holmes, Jr.'s *(q.v.)* dictum against crying "Fire!" in a crowded theater gave some direction, but was not sufficient to meet all exigencies.

"INVISIBLE GOVERNMENT," used, as a result of reform movements, always invidiously to refer to the powers behind the apparent network of municipal, state, or other group of officials, to boss *(q.v.)* rule; see also Municipal Reform.

INVISIBLE MAN (1952), by Ralph Ellison, an outstanding novel which used symbolism and satire to depict the loneness of the individual, made doubly lone by his being a Negro.

The novel argued obliquely against such clichés as the reputed high sexuality of the Negro, was critical of radical solutions for his troubles, and sought to treat challenges in Negro life as no more or less formidable than challenges anywhere. John Hersey, ed., *Ralph Ellison: a Collection of Critical Essays* (1974).

IPR, see Institute of Pacific Relations.

IRAN, a "trouble-spot" which came to American attention in 1946 when it protested the presence of Soviet troops on its territory before the Security Council of the U.N. *(q.v.)*. The troops were withdrawn, but communist designs on Iran did not disappear. Early in the 1950's, Iranian communists, aided by the neighboring Soviet Republics, threatened to take over that Near-Eastern territory, but the close concern of American central intelligence managed to repel the threat. As in Korea *(q.v.)*, however, American aid and comfort did not appear able to build democratic structures and programs, and U.S.S.R. dissatisfaction with Iran persisted. Iran, at this point seemed to be an area, under Shah Muhammad Reza Pahlevi, which not only merited military aid and help in modernization, but would know how to use it. The Shah worked to create cooperatives, small land owners, and capitalist entrepreneurs. In 1963 he gave the vote to women. 1971 was a proud year of celebration of 2500 years of continuity since the reign of Cyrus the Great. Less attention was paid to the burning resentment against the contents of motion-pictures, modern clothes, and foreign manners by religious leaders, notably the Ayatollah Khomeini, and the fundamentalists who followed his preachments and despised the Shah. He and his harsh security staff had so far fallen away from contact with the people of tradition that neither their efforts at strict punishment and authority or of democratic tolerance could appease them. In January of 1979, the Shah, made conscious of his loss of a power base and anticipating overthrow, left the country. He stayed in several lands before, made aware that he suffered a form of cancer, he received admission to the United States for special treatment. In his absence, long repressed resentment burst forth against him in Iran, fanned by the now triumphant Ayatollah, who demanded that he be returned to Iran to answer for his "crimes." In November of 1979, the United States Embassy in Teheran was stormed by "students" who undoubtedly included many political activists. They took over the Embassy and declared its American employees, numbering fifty-three, would be held as "hostages" till the Shah and all his criminally-gathered funds were returned. Thereafter, American policy veered between attempting to reach a "civilized" settlement through negotiation and considering how American power could be more directly employed in the "hostages's" behalf. Grotesque aspects included the International World Court of Justice decision that the "hostages" must be released and damages paid for this transgression of international law; but neither the "students" nor the Iranian government, which patently worked through them, paid any attention to this decision. As grotesque was an unauthorized visit to Iran by former U.S. Attorney General Ramsey Clark, who took it upon himself to plead for the "hostages" as not responsible for "thirty years of wrongful United States intervention in Iran." Another of Clark's views had him attempting to use the Freedom of Information Act *(q.v.)* to acquire documents in government coffers proving its criminality in Iran. By then, the Shah was dead in Egypt, and his funeral unattended by official American dignitaries. Richard M. Nixon *(q.v.)* went in his own person in tribute to an American ally. Substantial scorn accrued toward America in Europe and elsewhere as no ally a nation could trust. A conference of over 300 delegates from 54 countries convened in Tehran to mull over the charges of "hostage" espionage and malfeasance which the Iranians threw about and mixed with their demands for the Shah's assets, "frozen" in American banks: large enough to lose him and his surviving family much of the sympathy of the world community. But by then the American government had lost all credibility, having attempted in April of 1980 to send out a rescue mission of eight helicopters from an aircraft carrier in the Gulf of Oman to a desert landing point, there to rendezvous with eight transport planes sent from an Egyptian base. The mission was called off after three of the helicopters failed. Before the men and equipment could be evacuated from the desert, one of the transport planes collided with a helicopter, killing eight soldiers. The sense of diplomatic and military duty available was shown by American newspapers keeping score on the possibility that casualties might have reached thirty commandos and at least fifteen hostages; thus, thirty eight hostages might have been rescued at the cost of forty-five lives. The gross ineptitude of the American operation, though officially made an occasion for pleading old equipment and the need for more money for new equipment, lost the United States vast respect in the world. Efforts were made thereafter to admire President Carter *(q.v.)* for his patience in difficult times, even though a secret report, revealed by the muckraker Jack Anderson *(q.v.)*, had warned that "patience without pressure is often perceived as paralysis." Although the Iranian government was a hodgepodge of contrary declarations, it was bolstered by confidence that the United States lacked the courage and capacity for action. Negotiations were mainly suspended while the American election campaign came down to its conclusion. With Reagan *(q.v.)* elected, negotiations moved swiftly, the Iranians fearing what the new Executive might do. Iran was granted all that it was in Carter's power to give, and the "hostages" were released one hour before his term ended. Reagan spoke of them as "war prisoners"—it had been earlier suggested that declaring a state of war would have given them that status. It seemed likely that the world had not yet heard the end of that drama. See also Oil. Amin Saikal, *The Rise and Fall of the Shah* (1980); M. M. J. Fischer, *Iran: from Religious Dispute to Revolution* (1980); Barry Rubin, *Paved with Good Intentions: the American Experience and Iran* (1980).

IRISH-AMERICAN REFORM resulted from their poor and Catholic circumstances which inspired a species of sympathy and tolerance, especially from Democratic politicians. The Irish in America entertained libertarian feelings for their compatriots in Ireland. They despised the American Negroes with whom they competed in humble vocations. Notable in this respect was John Mitchel (1815-1875), Irish revolutionary hero, who manifested heroism and eloquence in Ireland and in prison, and in the United States proved a Negrophobe who, in the Civil War, was on the Confederate side. Although Irish served on the Federal side, others engaged in the Draft Riots of 1863 *(q.v.)*, and had a cause in the discriminatory terms of the Conscription Act. In 1866, some of them crossed the Canadian border and sought to capture the country and hold it as a hostage till Ireland was freed by Great Britain. There were numerous "labor priests" and liberal laymen, such as Father McGlynn, Monsigneur Ryan, and Frank Murphy *(qq.v.)*, and numerous deviants from the church, as in the case of James T. Farrell *(q.v.)*. Irish-American voters played a role in lifting the Kennedys *(q.v.)* to power, and thus to impact on liberal legislation, and they took pride in such leaders as Speaker of the House of Representatives Tip O'Neill, Governor of New York Hugh Carey, and U.S. Senator Daniel Moynihan, who were of a generally liberal persuasion. They resisted, too, the activities of the Irish National Caucus, which responded with funds and support to Irish Republican Army (IRA) visitors and condoned their terrorist campaigns in North Ireland. The Dublin government, though dreaming of union with the northern counties, looked to American moderates among the Irish to help them toward a peaceful solution to the tragedy which took lives and offended decency in the six counties. John B. Duff, *The Irish in the United States* (1971); Morris Fraser, *Children in Conflict: Growing Up in Northern Ireland* (1973); T. Q Steward, *The Ulster Crisis* (1967); A. Bailey, *Acts of Union: Reports on Ireland, 1973-79* (1979).

"IRON CURTAIN," Winston Churchill's *(q.v.)* designation for the domination which the U.S.S.R. had established over eastern Europe, following World War II, separating it from the western democracies. The phrase was employed in a speech delivered at Fulton, Mo., on March 5, 1946. Other curtains were later noted, particularly the "bamboo curtain" erected by Red China.

IRON-CLAD AGREEMENT, pledge of an employee not to join a trade-union; a form of the "yellow dog contract" (*q.v.*).

IRON LAW OF WAGES, a discredited economic theory which would, in effect, have made futile the battle of laborers to raise their wages, for it argued a direct relationship between the level of wages (*q.v.*) and the rate of population: a lower level of wages kept the population in check to the limit of subsistence. With each rise in wages, the families increased in number, using up the addition. See also Malthusianism.

"IRREPRESSIBLE CONFLICT, THE," see Seward, William Henry.

IRRESPONSIBLES, THE (1940), by Archibald MacLeish (*q.v.*), an attack on American writers who had inadequately concerned themselves for their responsibility as American citizens, by one who had consorted with them.

ISOLATIONISM AND REFORM, though sometimes conceived of as opposed, have had traditional associations. The apparent security of the United States between two oceans and two weak neighbors seemed to make international affairs secondary to domestic concerns. Thus, Thomas Jefferson's effort at isolationism, as practiced in the Embargo (*q.v.*), was an effort at reform. American applause for democratic revolutions, in Latin America and in Europe, suggested no intervention to them. The abolitionists sought Kossuth's (*q.v.*) approval of emancipation, but evinced no interest in Hungarian democratic aspirations. Embattled workers, farmers, and others with reform impulses in the post-Civil War period focused their attention on American sorrows, American dilemmas, rather than those elsewhere. Reform spoke through imperialists (*q.v.*) as well as isolationists, during the Spanish-American War, in the person of Theodore Roosevelt, on the one hand, William Jennings Bryan, on the other (*qq.v.*). Isolationism plus pacifism (*q.v.*) offered one formula for reform. Albert J. Beveridge (*q.v.*) sought *domestic* reforms which would unite the nation—for imperialist purposes. Robert M. La Follette (*q.v.*) also emphasized domestic reforms, but, speaking for the isolationist midwest (which included German constituents) denounced American intervention in World War I. Isolationism in the 1920's emphasized a retreat from world problems; reformers sought world understanding, through the League of Nations (*q.v.*) or more sympathetic regard for the U.S.S.R. (*q.v.*). In the 1930's, the New Deal retreated from world affairs in the interests of domestic reform. In succeeding years, the threats of fascism and communism left isolationism in the hands of cautious, nationalistic, and otherwise non-reformist elements, which, however, also included such personages as Charles A. Beard. See Selig Adler, *The Isolationist Impulse* (1957). A curious chance brought together opposites, at least in intellectual configuration: individuals who had opposed action on the international scene because of pacifist, capitalist, and even fascist convictions, and others who had admired socialism and labor, including its radical aspects. This made for a new isolationism, based on a rejection of globalism (*q.v.*), at least as it has manifested itself in Southeast Asia; see Ronald Radosh, *Prophets of the Right* (1975).

ISRAEL, established in 1948, as a fulfilment of Zionist (*q.v.*) hopes and a survival of the war launched by Arab states to prevent its being born. Its reform features included a quasi-socialist administration and mode of life, its cooperatives, its heterogeneous population for which it sought to prescribe in fashions respecting their differences, its aid to and assimilation of the survivors of Nazi (*q.v.*) terror, its combination of regard for its ancient features as well as for the most advanced technology. In effect, Israel was a center of civilization in a backward area. Although it expressed its eagerness to be of service to its Arab neighbors, their **extreme hatred** of Israel and readiness to use it as a scapegoat to explain their own backwardness limited the use they could make of the Israelis. An example of their attitude was their use of Arab refugees from Israel as a result of the 1948 war; they were kept in camps in destitution and uselessness, to be fed by United Nations units and permitted to grow up in squalor and desuetude, as propaganda to demonstrate Israel's cruelty toward them. Thanks to their own refugees, Israel accumulated a remarkable number of varied talents, which, however, were employed on farms as well as in universities. Crisis in the Middle East involved civil war in Lebanon and unrest throughout the Middle East. It made the entire area potentially liable to major and possibly nuclear war. Israel, surrounded by foes, in June of 1967 attacked Egypt, Jordan, and Syria in a "Six Day War" which gained it buffer areas on three sides. The Arabs, in response, vowed war to the death with Israel. In 1973, on Israel's holy day of Yom Kippur (Day of Atonement), Egypt and Syria struck at an unprepared Israel, an attack which was repulsed, but at home cost. That year, too, the Arab refugees, organized as the Palestine Liberation Organization (P.L.O.) (*q.v.*), undertook their campaign of atrocities against individual Israelis which put them among the terrorists (*q.v.*) of their time. The Arab oil nations, too, made their dramatic jump in oil prices, which helped face the United States with a challenge to their economy and way of life. Several years of "shuttle diplomacy" by United States negotiators, notably Kissinger (*q.v.*), between Cairo and Jerusalem culminated in 1977 with President Sadat of Egypt's flying trip to Jerusalem to plead for peace and settlement: a trip which won him and the Israeli Prime Minister Begin the Nobel Peace Prize. Although other Arab nations raged in protest at Sadat's action, his initiative was revolutionary in the Middle East, and offered hope for diminishing threats to basic stability, even though an untiring P.L.O. continued to gain respectability among world agencies and unsettled nations. K. Carr, ed., *Israelis and Palestinians* (1974); W. Laquer, *Israel-Arab Reader* (1976).

IT CAN'T HAPPEN HERE (1935), by Sinclair Lewis (*q.v.*), a famous title which took off from the cliché that fascism couldn't happen in the United States, and undertook to portray its having happened. Useful was Lewis's keen ear for Americanisms, which enabled him to give a sense of reality to the events narrated, and the personalities described.

I.W.W., see Industrial Workers of the World.

J

J'ACCUSE! (1898), Emile Zola's (*q.v.*) famous headline to his article, published in *L'Aurore*, which broke through the haze of secrecy and rumor which had permitted the plot against the French officer Dreyfus (*q.v.*) to succeed; a highpoint in humanitarian concern and expose. A. and P. Dreyfus, *The Dreyfus Case* (1937); F. W. I. Hemmings, *Emile Zola* (1953).

JACKSON, HELEN HUNT (1830-1885), poet and writer, whose concern with justice for the Indian (*q.v.*) resulted in two distinguished writings: *A Century of Dishonor* (1881), which discussed the many treaties, made by the United States in their dealings with Indians, and the novel *Ramona* (1884), which offers a more personalized version of an Indian tragedy. See Ruth Odell, *Helen Hunt Jackson* (1939).

"JACKSONIAN REFORM," identified with President Andrew Jackson (1829-1837), whose vigorous individualism added strength to his office and appeared to advance American democratic ideals. Unadmirers of his own time took him to be no more than a successful spokesman of the slaveholding class. The ardent partisans he attracted saw him as a voice of the developing democracy, especially in his increasing opposition to monopoly, as signalized by his battle with the Second Bank of the United States (*q.v.*). The Jackson Administration opposed imprisonment of debtors, asserted the right of the common man (*q.v.*) to the vote—largely achieved by 1828, year of Jackson's apotheosis—and quarrelled with Whigs on various issues, from Peggy Eaton's purity to a proper policy on public lands in the west. Jackson's nationalism kept him hungry for Mexico's Texas, aggressive toward France, and grimly determined that South Carolina should not defy his government in the interests of free trade (*q.v.*). To the extent that national administrations must represent compromises between the sections, Jackson's obviously represented one which respected the humbler voters, whether they were northerners or southerners. His contempt for Negroes and Indians (*qq.v.*) distinguishes him from moral reformers (*q.v.*). See Alfred A. Cave, *Jacksonian Democracy and the Historians* (1964). A curiosity of scholarship was A. M. Schlesinger, *The Age of Jackson* (1945), a brief for the Democratic Party, which ignored both slavery and Jackson's anti-Indian drive, yet was received with liberal acclaim as implicitly endorsing Franklin D. Roosevelt (*q.v.*). (The author later reversed his method to find a Jackson in Roosevelt.) In the 1960s, the civil rights, anti-history drive scorned Jackson, and lost the book its readership.

JACOBINS, in America, used as an epithet to describe alleged sympathizers with the radical wing of the French revolutionary movement; identified with the rule of Maximilien Robespierre; an extremist. See also, Leveller, Democrat, Radical, Republican.

JAMES, WILLIAM (1842-1910), though no social or political reformer, his studies in psychology and his development of pragmatic (*q.v.*) tenets, were relevant to reform. Thus, his relativistic view of truth and reality suggested that *a priori* assumptions respecting either were bound to bring the reformer (as well as anyone else) into difficulties: conditions would not adjust to his expectations. Moreover, human psychology was not wholly "logical," but in part the result of a human response to conditions, in part a problem in human need. Thus, a truly reasonable program would respect both facts. His most important essay in reform attempted to do this; *The Moral Equivalent of War* (1910), respecting the human desire to do battle, suggested that people battle adverse nature, rather than each other. Among his relevant works were *The*

Meaning of Truth (1909) and *Essays in Radical Empiricism* (1912). See Henry James his son, ed., *The Letters of William James* (1920).

JAPAN AND SOCIAL REFORM, one of the enigmas facing American reformers and non-reformers in 1961. Japan, opened to world intercourse in 1854 by Commodore Perry, developed a modern culture upon feudalistic premises which, in 1894-5, enabled her to defeat China, and, in 1904-5, to humble Russia. Her gigantic effort during World War II was defeated, and her royal and militaristic classes discredited. The classes which took over ranged from extreme democrats to communists. Their deep trauma, caused by defeat, but also by a shattering of their national unity, created relationships which were probably as little understood in Japan as abroad. Japan was as receptive to reform as to the deepest reactionaryism. In 1981, Americans were shocked to be told that Japan was "Number One" in the production of automobiles. It was possible that such a stark fact could turn attention to Japan's larger substance than many profound analyses and revelations. Bernice Goldstein and Kyoko Tamura, *Japan and America...Language and Culture* (1975); R. E. Osgood et al., *Japan and the United States in Asia* (1969); Frank Gibney, *Japan: the Fragile Super-power* (1975); *Japanese Americans: the Untold Story* (1971); Donald C. Hellmann, *Japanese-American Relations* (1975).

JAPANESE RELOCATION ORDER (1942), issued by President Franklin D. Roosevelt, permitted the "relocation" of over 100,000 Japanese, most of them American citizens, and, in effect, uprooted them and subjected them to military authority, presumably for security purposes. It was a disturbing blow to the self-respect and social outlook of many of them, as individuals and family units. Little reform energy was mobilized to offset these effects. The Supreme Court, in Hirabayashi v. United States (1943), sustained the government; in a follow-up case, with the same conclusion, Korematsu v. United States (1944), Associate Justice Black (*q.v.*) led the majority opinion. See Michi Weglyn, *Years of Infamy* (1976).

JAURÈS, JEAN L. (1859-1914), French socialist leader and founder of the famous *L'Humanité*; he was active in the Dreyfus case (*q.v.*); central to all socialist activities in his country, very active as speaker, writer, organizer, and legislator; his assassination on the eve of World War I was once remembered as part of reformist and socialist lore.

JAY, JOHN (1745-1829), Revolutionary statesman and first Chief Justice of the Supreme Court of the United States. The Treaty which he made with Great Britain in 1794 outraged ardent democrats, who believed that he had propitiated the late enemy because of his sympathy with their social and political system. He was an anti-slavery advocate and first president of the New York Manumission Society. His son and biographer, *William* (1789-1858), was a noted abolitionist and advocate of peace.

JEAN CHRISTOPHE, see Rolland, Romain.

JEFFERSON, THOMAS (1743-1826), one of the most famous of all Americans, as spokesman, libertarian, President, and all-around genius and public figure; vulgarly known as "Tom" Jefferson by persons who know nothing about him. His democracy was largely idealistic, as in his immortal Declaration of Independence (*q.v.*), which asserted the equality of men: a view which his actual attitudes do not bear out. To aspiring indentured servants, would-be free Negroes, and others, his view of humanity's rights offered as much hope as anything. As President, he conducted a savage war on the Supreme Court, which he saw as a bastion of conservatism, which it was, though its destruction—which he hoped for—would have created new dangers. His nationalism was more real than his fear of a strong executive, and he purchased the Louisiana Territory, even though he doubted his right to do so, under the Constitution. His Embargo Act (*q.v.*) was sincerely intended, in the interests of peace, though bitterly suspect in New England. The supreme verbalist, his catch words offer to humanity as much hope as any. The attack on the Founding Fathers during the 1960s and 1970s as racist and imperialist did not spare Jefferson, despite his monumental achievements as father of the Northwest Ordinance (q.v.), resister of the Alien and Sedition Acts (q.v.), author, architect, and molder of the nation. Detractors seized on rumors respecting his private life, emphasizing an alleged affair with a Negro servant, of some interest had there been actual materials to exploit. It was drawn out in fiction by a scribbler, but also laboriously constructed by a quasi-historian; see Fawn M. Brodie, *Thomas Jefferson: an Intimate History* (1974). More persuasive and circumstantial is *Jefferson at Monticello*, ed. James A. Bear, Jr., including *Memoirs of a Monticello Slave* (1967). See also L. W. Levy, *Jefferson and Civil Liberties: the Darker Side* (1973); and J. C. Miller, *The Wolf by the Ears: Thomas Jefferson and Slavery* (1977), V. Dabney, *The Jefferson Scandals: a Rebuttal* (1981).

JEHOVAH'S WITNESSES, like the Mormons (q.v.), one of the vigorous religious sects, in an age, the faith of which had been shaken. Fundamentalist in views, it had little regard for reform issues. Its connection with them lay in its right to approach individuals and attempt to influence them as it wished: a right which court tests established. Its vitality was shown in the fact that, between 1940 and 1960, it increased in number from some 60,000 to more than 950,000; that it developed a spectacular affluence; and that Catholics were warned by their church not to discuss the Bible with members of Jehovah's Witnesses, because "unprepared Catholics will accomplish little and may endanger their faith." A. A. Hoekema, *Jehovah's Witnesses* (1974); Tony Hodges, *Jehovah's Witnesses in Central Africa* (1976).

JESUS, see "Comrade Jesus."

JEWS, famous everywhere for their monotheism, their persistence, and their status as scapegoat (q.v.) whenever trouble required one. Some of their most challenging figures, like Marx and Freud (qq.v.) have been unorthodox figures, and even antagonistic to the Jewish community. Their crucifixion under the Nazis of Germany made their fate identical with that of humanity at large. The creation of Israel (q.v.) made them a primary force in the Middle East. The hatred of Arabs for Jews created the paradox of semites entertaining malevolent feelings for semites. Anti-semitism (q.v.) has been justified on various grounds, such as that people have a right to like or dislike individuals or groups; the holocaust built up by the Nazis did the argument no good. Levelage, *Le Socialisme Contemporain*, argued that Jews everywhere were the initiators of socialism: that they had a stake, in other words, in stirring up equalitarian sentiments, presumably to the detriment of legitimately exclusive groups; in short, that they were "pushers." The argument is most sympathetically received behind closed doors, by the groups affected. See also National Conference of Christians and Jews. Marshall Sklare, ed., *The Jew in American Society* (1974); Leon Harris, *Merchant Princes* (1979); Samuel Joseph, *Jewish Immigration to the United States* (1914); J. N. Porter and Peter Dreier, ed., *Jewish Radicalism* (1973); Allen Guttmann, *The Jewish Writer in America* (1971); O. I. Janowsky, *Jews and Minority Rights* (1933); Schneir Levenberg, *Jews and Palestine: a Study in Labour Zionism* (1945).

JIM CROW, identified as originally a Negro slave and stable hand in Louisville, Kentucky, whose song and dance was mimicked by the minstrel Thomas D. Rice; came to designate Negroes in general and to be associated with all policies for excluding Negroes from contact on an equal plane with white people. Hence, Jim Crow laws, Jim Crow cars, Jim Crow department stores, and other places theoretically open to the general public.

JINGO, a word of invidious connotations applied to persons with aggressive patriotic and imperialistic attitudes. (See Patriotism.) Of uncertain origin, possibly a corruption of the Basque *Jincoa*, meaning *God*, possibly an indirect echo of *By Jove*. First direct reference was to Lord Beaconsfield's sending of a British fleet to Turkey to forestall Russia in 1878. The words

of a popular music-hall song in England ran: "We don't want to fight, but by jingo if we do, / We've got the ships, We've got the men, we've got the money too."

JOHN REED CLUBS, see Reed, John.

JOHNSON, ALVIN S. (1874-1971), notable American liberal, especially significant because of his grassroots (q.v.) origins. He was a founder of the New School for Social Research (q.v.). How much its quarterly, *Social Research*, advanced social reform is a matter for conjecture. His co-editorship of the *Encyclopedia of the Social Sciences* (1930-5) is less controversial: it is a manifest storehouse of liberal and social reform thought and history. See his *Progress: an Autobiography* (1952).

JOHNSON, ANDREW (1808-1875), a self-made "poor white" of Tennessee, who rose to be its political leader, to resist efforts to secede from the Union, and to become President of the United States. Like Abraham Lincoln, he did not favor equality for Negroes, and did for white people. His major reform involved a land policy which would make it possible for poor people to become land owners. His resistance to the Radical Republicans (q.v.), and the failure of their impeachment proceedings (q.v.) intended to remove him from the Presidency (May 1868) helped re-establish the authority of that office. D. M. Dewitt, *The Impeachment and Trial of Andrew Johnson* (1903); L. P. Stryker, *Andrew Johnson, a Study in Courage* (1929); E. L. McKitrick, *Andrew Johnson, a Profile* (1969).

JOHNSON, JAMES WELDON (1871-1938), one of the great Negroes of the Twentieth Century, he was the first Negro to be admitted to the bar in Florida, and practiced law before becoming a writer of light operas and songs in New York with his brother Rosamond. He served as U.S. consul in Venezuela and Nicaragua, was a founder and secretary of the N.A.A.C.P. (q.v.), and wrote and taught to great effect. His own autobiography, *Along This Way* (1933) compares interestingly with his fictional *The Autobiography of an Ex-Colored Man* (1912), a seminal work. Also famous is his volume of poems, *God's Trombones* (1927).

JOHNSON, LYNDON BAINES (1908-1973), whose Presidency (1963-1968) ended in a haze of doubt and controversy. Johnson early learned the politics of friendly persuasion and power in the south Texas farm area in which he was raised. A staff member to a Texas congressman at the New Deal's (q.v.) inception, he learned the ways of Washington politics so well that he was sacked. Following a turn as Texas director of the National Youth Administration, he was elected to Congress, where he worked under the tutelage of Texas Sam Rayburn, soon to be Speaker of the House of Representatives. Johnson served with the Navy during World War II. In 1948 he won the Texas primary for U.S. Senator—equivalent to victory in the election —by 87 debated votes out of almost a million. Democratic majority whip after 1955, he worked with Republican President Eisenhower (q.v.) while with light fingers, charm, inside knowledge, flattery, and a firm grip on his party's leadership, and hoped for the Presidential call himself in 1960. His charm, however, could not match Kennedy's (q.v.) charisma, and, in his most extraordinary move, he astonished his followers and the Kennedys by accepting their reluctant offer of a Vice Presidential candidacy. Johnson probably made his rival President by lending him his influence and political resources. Johnson's glum place in the younger man's shadow ended November 22, 1963 with Kennedy's assassination. As President, Johnson made a graceful transition, maintaining a facade of reverence for his predecessor. In a stormy age of civil rights agitation, he seemed to stand better than in control, meeting demands with laws: the Civil Rights Act of 1964, the tax reduction Kennedy had projected. In the 1964 Elections, Johnson overwhelmed the Goldwater forces and went on to propose a "Great Society" program, most of which, on the surface, he achieved: the great Voting Act of 1965, Medicare, a new department of Housing and Urban Development, equal opportunity in the schools and employment, training and retraining, transportation, loans to students and building programs for schools and colleges, a black Supreme Court Justice and long lists of black officials and aides everywhere. None of this stirred so much as a glimmer of appreciation or patriotism in the youth and disaffected of the time. Fateful was the alleged report of North Vietnam units, August 1964, attacking U.S. Navy ships, which elicited from Congress the "Gulf of Tonkin Resolution." This seemed to give Johnson authority to use American forces wherever he deemed necessary in support of American policy and "advisors" in Vietnam. Johnson's rapid build up of troops to half a million and materiel in billions of dollars in South Vietnam expanded in bloody and frustrating actions in the area, with increasing loss of life and credibility at home, implemented by powerful and continuous anti-government demonstrations in the streets, reported on television. The "Great Society" flagged. Johnson was subjected to a ceaseless barrage of concerted abuse. His pride hurt, the sound of the demonstrators's "Hey, hey, LBJ/ how many kids did you kill today?" ringing in the White House, he felt less humiliated by his raffish haters than by the heartland Democratic voters of New Hampshire who, March 1968, all but rejected him in favor of Senator Eugene J. McCarthy. In response, he announced with restrained irony his unwillingness to seek another term in the coming elections. He returned dejectedly to Texas, where he indited a defense of his Administration, *The Vantage Point* (1971). His key error had been in believing that money and opportunity would grow talent. In Roosevelt's time, necessity had produced a New Deal. Affluence had not gained for Johnson a "Great Society." Doris Kearns, *Lyndon Johnson and the American Dream* (1976); Alfred Steinberg, *Sam Johnson's Boy* (1968); Louis Filler, ed., *The President in the 20th Century* (1981); J. M. Burns, ed., *To Heal and Build: the Programs of . . . Johnson* (1968).

JOHNSON, TOM L. (1854-1911), inventor and organizer of streetcar systems, his career was a personification of the contentions of Henry George *(q.v.)*, since the basis of his fortune was not his manifest wit and executive ability, but the bribes to city officials which gained him his franchises to land and city routes which had to be patronized by the city masses, and whom he could therefore tax by way of fares to his own benefit. His reading of George's *Progress and Poverty* shocked him with the revelation that his class of entrepreneurs was a danger to freedom. As a convert to the Single Tax, he became, first, a congressman, then mayor of Cleveland where he attracted a notable number of civil talents to his banner. He fought for public ownership of necessary civic services, opposed Mark Hanna *(q.v.)*, and sought a three-cent fare on street-cars. The history of the fare since his administrations furnishes a thought-provoking approach to the meaning and value of reform movements in the area. See his *My Story* (1911).

JONES, JIM, a phenomenon of American Fundamentalism *(q.v.)* and democratic politics. He was an adventurer in evangelism and neo-Marxism who organized as The People's Temple, a power base in San Francisco composed mainly of blacks—Jones himself was a white from Indiana—and with passionate rhetoric persuaded them to follow him first in his personal plottings for influence, which reached as far as Washington. The key to his success was his ability to deliver a solid bloc of voters at the polls. His ambitions outriding his status, he transferred his entire colony of some one thousand men, women, and children to tiny Guyana, east of Venezuela, where he ruled in "Jonestown." Information respecting its bizarre activities, and Jones's, called U.S. Representative Leo J. Ryan of California, to visit the place with three newsmen as investigators. The young drug-ridden patriarch ordered them killed, November 18, 1978, and then persuaded his followers to join him in death, rather than face trial by law. Some 911 persons died by being given or imbibing poisoned Kool-Aid, a soft drink, or by murder, for those who sought to escape. The Jones "Charisma" was somewhat similar, minus its drastic elements, to that of "Father Divine," who won numerous followers in New York and vicinity to believing him God; see Sara Harris, *Father Divine* (1971). Most impressive, aside from the dimensions of mass-suicide, was the fact that Jones had been appointed Director of Housing, thanks to his vote-delivering abilities in San Francisco. P. Kerus and D. Wead, *Peoples Temple, Peoples Tomb* (1979); J. P. Nugent, *White Night* (1979); Shiva Naipul, *Black and White* (1980).

JONES, SAMUEL MILTON (1846-1904), immortal as the "Golden Rule" mayor of Toledo, who believed that tolerance and humanity were not only just but practical. Like Tom Johnson *(q.v.)*, he was a successful man of business who turned to politics, though, unlike Johnson, he did not depend upon corrupt politics as an aid to financial advancement. Though opposed by the self-righteous elements of the community, he appealed successfully in 1897 to the electorate of Toledo, Ohio, and continued its mayor until his death, passing his ideals of democratic government on to his successor, Brand Whitlock *(q.v.)*. Jones' *Letters of Love and Labor* (1900) reflect his rare personality.

JONES ACT (1916), see Philippines and American Reform.

JONES ACT (1917), a landmark in American policy toward its possessions, it made the citizens of Puerto Rico *(q.v.)* citizens of the United States.

JOSEPH, see Chief Joseph.

JOURNALISM AND REFORM have been associated from earliest times. Pamphleteering *(q.v.,* for this and all subsequent items) has been an aspect of journalism. The trial of John Peter Zenger was a landmark in journalism and reform. Philip Freneau warred with the Federalists in the interest of Jefferson; the Sedition Act was aimed at journalists like himself. William Cobbett was a journalistic force in himself. Theodore Dwight and Arthur Tappan were political conservatives who sponsored notable reforms. The Penny Press broadened the base of journalism, with James Gordon Bennett introduced sensationalism, and, in its concern for an increased reading public, sponsored, as with Horace Greeley, numerous reforms. The *National Philanthropist* (temperance), the *Liberator* (abolitionism), the *Lily* (woman suffrage), the *Non-Resistant* (pacifism), and the *Hangman* (anti-capital punishment) were examples of reform journalism. Magazines of the pre-Civil War period were not associated with reform, for the most part. In the post-Civil War period, popular magazines were created. The penny press publications had become conservative, and a new popular journalism had to be created; the labors of E.W. Scripps, Joseph Pulitzer, and especially William Randolph Hearst resulted in the creation of "yellow journalism," the adjective referring to a popular Hearst cartoon, "The Yellow Kid," which became a symbol for a means for arresting attention. Among the great entrepreneurs of the popular magazine were S.S. McClure, Frank Munsey, Edward W. Bok, and, less popular, but as significant to reform, B.O. Flower. The reform-minded writers of the newspapers became the leading writers for the reform magazines, during the Muckraking Era. Now, too, and for the first time, literary opinion began to distinguish, invidiously, between journalism and literature, as in the writings of David Graham Phillips. Gentility contributed to journalism and reform in the work of E.L. Godkin and Oswald Garrison Villard. Herbert Croly distrusted democratic reform journalism, and sought, rather, with his *New Republic* to create a sophisticated elite which would direct the masses toward reform. World War I erased the last traces of popular reform journalism, and also revealed the relative impotence of the elitists. Twenties journalists publicized Harding scandals, municipal corruption, and such evils as syphilus, juvenile delinquency, and ghettos. They seemed unable to reflect a reformist will in their readers. The rise of columnists—Drew Pearson, Walter Lippmann, Westbrook Pelger, Heywood Broun—raised a type of guru *(q.v.)* who influenced thought immoderately. Consolidations of newspapers created concentrated centers of journalistic power which made the *New York Times* a "national" organ. Its policies, and those of the *Washington Post*, the *Chicago*

Tribune, and the *Los Angeles Times* were influenced by city transformations which gave exaggerated importance to their city problems and populations, at the expense of a national spectrum of feeling and opinion. Nothing like the old *Literary Digest* was about conscientiously to report week by week newspaper opinion across the nation. Howard Smith and L. Norris, *Newsmakers: the Press and the Presidents* (1974); John E. Drewry, ed., *Journalism Enters a New Half-Century* (1976); T. E. Berry, *Journalism in America* (1976); James Aronson, *The Press and the Cold War* (1973); A. K. MacDougall, ed., *The Press* (1972); R. A. Rutland, *The Newsmongers* (1973).

JOYCE, JAMES, see *Ulysses.*

JUAREZ, BENITO PABLO (1806-1872), Mexican revolutionist and patriot, executor of the French-sponsored Emperor Maximilian; generally approved, by reformers and non-reformers, as an acceptable example of popular leader and innovator abroad. Ronald Syme, *Juarez, the Founder of Modern Mexico* (1972).

JUDICIARY ACT (1789), see Marbury v. Madison.

JUKES, THE, A STUDY IN CRIME, PAUPERISM DISEASE, AND HEREDITY (1877), by Richard L. Dugdale, which traced descendants of a family, and appeared to indicate that an inferior line produced inferior descendants. It thus supported the tenets of Social Darwinism *(q.v.),* in its belief in inferior and superior racial stocks.

JURISDICTIONAL DISPUTES were a source of strife among labor unions and of weakness in the development of a labor movement, when rival organizations claimed the right to organize the workers in a plant or to control the affairs of an organized local. Such strife often occurred when a craft union *(q.v.)* claimed authority over that section for workers in an industrial plant which was performing its duties. The rise of the C.I.O. *(q.v.)* caused many jurisdictional disputes with the A.F. of L. *(q.v.),* in the 1930's, when the organization of labor was accelerated. The N.L.R.B. *(q.v)* settled many of them, the union of both organizations, in 1955, cut down many jurisdictional disputes, but individual unions continued to be alert to their claims among organized workers. G. W. Foster, Jr., *Jurisdiction, Rights and Remedies...*(1975).

JUSTICE, the *sine qua non* of social reformers, though its precise content tends to be debatable. What is a "fair" profit? What is "reasonable" punishment for offenses? What is "decent" behavior toward minority groups? Bernard Shaw once suggested that one ought not to do unto others as he would have them do unto him; tastes may differ. In practice, reformers have refused to see that there was anything controversial about the values of slavery, imprisonment for debt, harsh treatment of lunatics, democratic standards for voting, woman's suffrage, and education. The question of a "fair" profit they have left with representative and informed commissions. They have often appeared, to non-reformers, obsessed by their crusades to the exclusion of a larger view of human nature and its need to be reconciled to half-measures. On the other hand, competent reformers have often shown themselves as remarkably aware of the details of their opponents's lives and points of view, and subtle in their understanding of the implications of the situation they want reformed, and how to dramatize these nuances to the public. The abolitionists and the muckrakers *(qq.v.)* were particularly expert from this point of view. See also Abstract Terms, Permanent Court of International Justice.

JUVENILE DELINQUENCY, a major social problem which once concerned such major reformers as Jane Addams *(q.v.)* as a part of the general problem of poverty, lack of public attention to the relationship of crime to home and social inadequacies, the need for assimilating immigrants into American patterns; now largely in the hands of routine social institutions such as the police, social work stipendiaries, settlement house personnel, and others interested in keeping the social fabric of relationship whole. Scandals which have attended juvenile delinquency have included gang wars of large proportions, cruel and unusual assaults on persons which have suggested that no individual, however comfortably placed, was secure from violence, the fact that city parks can no longer be safely used at night, and other phenomena attending the capture of cities by minority groups. (See Urban Problem, The.) Citizen groups have sought to temper the situation as in the creation in 1956, in New York, of Interfaith Neighbors, representing the cooperation of churches and synagogues. Such organizations as the Chicago Boys' Clubs have sought to develop new techniques in their approach to juveniles. They have sometimes given a reformist tone to their operations. However, they tend, for the most part, to work within their program rather than in terms of the larger social questions, of which juvenile delinquency is a symptom. In the last decades, the problem was complicated by the condition of the cities, adult delinquency as well as juvenile, "white collar" crime, and the spreading of "drug culture" to the high schools and below. Abortion, prostitution *(qq.v.),* and teenage parents also challenged society's capacities. Thomas R. Phelps, *Juvenile Delinquency: a Contemporary View* (1976); James E. Teele, *Juvenile Delinquency: a Reader* (1970).

K

KANSAS-NEBRASKA ACT, a fatal turning point in North-South relations, as introduced in Congress in 1854 by Stephen A. Douglas, it was intended to settle the question of whether the west would be slave or free by leaving it to "squatter sovereignty" (q.v.). This meant, in practice that slavery could legally be voted into northern territory. The battle by slavery and anti-slavery partisans to capture control of Kansas roused the entire country and created free soilers (q.v.) and pro-slavery die-hards in mass. It gave status to John Brown (q.v.) whose point of view had heretofore been considered disreputable in the North. Although "Bleeding Kansas" is something of a misnomer, since all frontier areas provided avenues for violence, Kansas was something of a dress-rehearsal for the Civil War. Samuel A. Johnson, *The Battle Cry of Freedom* (1954); Filler, ed., *The New Stars: Life and Labor in Old Missouri*, by Manie Kendley Morgan (1951).

KAPITAL, DAS, (1867-94), by Karl Marx, honored in the name more than in the reading, but presumed to provide a scientific statement of the rise and content of capitalism, and of its inner contradictions both to the well-being of humanity and its own continuance. At second-hand, and, occasionally, at first-hand, it inspired some classes of social reformer to efforts intended to hasten the demise of capitalism.

KATYN FOREST MURDERS, discovery by the Nazis in 1943 of thousands of Polish officers's graves in Russia's Katyn Forest; the Russian government objected to Polish demands for an investigation by the International Red Cross, and broke diplomatic relations with the Polish government-in-exile. The atrocity confounded admirers of the Soviet legend of brotherhood. J. K. Zawodny, *Death in the Forest* (1972).

KAUTSKY, KARL (1854-1938), Austrian socialist of international influence as organizer and theoretician. Though ardent in his socialist principles; he vigorously opposed the implications of the dicatorship of the proletariat (q.v.). Among his influential works were; *Thomas More and His Utopia* (1887), *The Road to Power* (1909), *Origins of Christianity,* (1914). He was a pacifist during World War I, and opposed to the program of Lenin and Trotsky (qq.v.).

KEATING-OWEN BILL, passed 1916 by Congress, it declared illegal the transportation among states of products involving the labor of children under fourteen years of age, or children between the ages of fourteen and sixteen who worked more than eight hours per day, who worked at night, or who labored six days per week, or who, under the age of sixteen, were employed in mines. The act was struck down by the U.S. Supreme Court in 1918 as unconstitutional. See also Child Labor.

KEFAUVER, ESTES (1903-1963), Tennessee statesman who sought a balanced, national perspective on American social and political affairs. A member of the House of Representatives from 1939, he became a Senator in 1948; in 1951, as chairman of a committee investigating crime, he brought out vivid and arresting testimony which, on television, made arresting news. His bid for the Democratic nomination in 1952 was frustrated; the party leaders found his vigor and independence disturbing; they did again in 1956, when, however, he won the vice-presidential nomination over John F. Kennedy (q.v.), and was part of a defeated ticket. Although he maintained his Senate seat against bitter opposition, and although his campaigns for equity and public responsibility, for example, in the manufacture and merchandising of drugs, gave him a certain status in the news, it was not clear that he would at any time be called to larger duties by public or party. William H. Moore, *The Kefauver Committee and the Politics of Crime 1950-1952* (1974); C. L. Fontenay, *Estes Kefauver* (1980).

KELLEY, FLORENCE (1859-1932), a significant figure in the reform movement of her era, both in terms of her causes and the evidence her career provided of the capacity of women to operate in public affairs. She was an inspector of factories in Illinois, during the 1890's, is best remembered for her labors as secretary of the National Consumers League (q.v.). She was also a pioneer in the organization of settlements and their programs. Josephine Goldmark, *Impatient Crusader* (1953); D. R. Blumberg, *Florence Kelley* (1966).

KELLOGG-BRIAND PACT, THE (1928), as signed, ultimately, by sixty-three nations, became, to social reformers, a symbol of the impotence of capitalist states to plan a substantial program making for peace. No machinery implementing this pact outlawing war was set up. The nations involved maintained and developed their military establishments. The pact ignored social, economic, and other factors which created war situations. Kellogg was awarded the Nobel Peace Prize in 1929. R. H. Ferrell, *Peace in Their Time* (1952).

KENNEDY, JOHN F. (1917-1963), elected President of the United States by a combination of traditional Democratic Party elements plus an articulate palace guard which promised reform, and harked back to New Dealism (q.v.) in a world setting. It thus promised to be reminiscent in some respects of Jacksonianism (q.v.). Whether it would create original features remained to be seen. The catastrophic intervention of the Kennedy Administration in Cuba (q.v.) sobered it, and took some of the wind out of its slogans. The national fear of an atomic war with Russia caused the people to close ranks, to a degree, behind the Administration, and created the possibility that it might improve in substance, and even gain color from a reform movement of genuine stamp, if it should appear. The nation was grateful for Kennedy's firm stand against the establishment of Soviet missile bases in Cuba in 1962. Kennedy's assassination, November 22, 1963 raised so large a storm of horror and argument, as to make difficult a thorough and dispassionate assessment of his work and potential. Raised to visibility was Kennedy's creation of the Peace Corps and the Alliance for Progress (qq.v.). Kennedy was slow to challenge Congress on civil rights issues, though his successor Johnson (q.v.) depicted him as about to put a program into motion. Kennedy's other achievements were entirely overshadowed by Johnson's patent legal victories in the several urgent fields. Unqualified admiration for Kennedy as the visionary of "New Frontiers" cooled over the years, as his wife Jacqueline went on to private enterprises not bearing on public ones, and as evidence of his own peccadilloes came to light. Nevertheless, his good humor and wit, and sincere regard for the nation seemed to ensure him of a measure of public godwill; see T. C. Sorenson, *Kennedy* (1965); Victor Lasky, *JFK: the Man and the Myth* (1963); Earl Latham, ed., *J. F. Kennedy and Presidential Power* (1972); Tom Wicker, *Kennedy without Tears* (1964); H. S. Parmet, *Jack* (1980). Even his immediate presence continued to be seen as living in the continuing career of his brother *Robert Francis Kennedy* (1925-1968), who had helped guide him to the Presidency, and who served as his Attorney General. A pragmatist, he had served Senator Joseph R. McCarthy (q.v.) as counsel, and a Senate committee investigating labor racketeering, and notably Jimmy Hoffa (q.v.). He left Johnson's Cabinet to run successfully for the Senate, as from New York. In a time of demonstrations and apparent radical, anti-Vietnam War power, he bided his time, and held back from opposing Johnson until the New Hampshire primaries revealed Johnson as vulnerable; he then announced his candidacy for President. Though manifestly an opportunist, he roused enthusiasm among minority elements whom Johnson reached less empathetically despite his manifest achievements in law and expenditures in their behalf. It was Kennedy's promise of action in ending American commitment in Vietnam which made it likely he would be the Democratic challenger for Johnson's relinquished leadership. Following a crucial primary victory in California, he was assassinated in Los Angeles, June 6, 1968, and after protracted ceremonies laid beside his brother in Arlington National Cemetery. As with his brother, numerous books were issued in respect to his public image or in retrospect; pros and cons appeared in David Halberstam, *The Unfinished Odyssey of Robert Kennedy* (1968); Douglas Ross, ed., *Robert Kennedy: Apostle of Change* (1968); Victor Lasky, *Robert F. Kennedy: the Myth and the Man* (1971). This left among the brothers only *Edward Moore Kennedy* (1932-), whom the Kennedy charisma had made Senator in 1962. Despite fears that the blight of violence might reach him, and his serious misadventure at Chappaquidick (*q.v.*) in 1969, the political force of Democrats held him in view as of long experience and proved minority concern, and as one matured by tragedy. He sat out the 1972 election, presumably because bemused by problems of family, of which he was now the head. Nevertheless even though he had announced in 1974 that he would not be available for the 1976 race, his followers's view that, in addition to the Kennedy name, he carried traditional Democratic programs better than any other Presidential contender, kept their hopes for him alive. Books defending and explaining him were capped by one by James Macgregor Burns, who had made his larger reputation with a serious study of John F. Kennedy in the year of his triumph over Nixon. Now Burns issued *Edward Kennedy and the Camelot Legacy* (1976), timed, he wrote, for the 1976 or later elections. Jimmy Carter's campaign that year took the field away from the Kennedy loyalists; but Carter's manifest gaffes (*q.v.*) and failures, and the apparent need for him caused Kennedy to fight fervently for the Democratic nomination in 1980. He was unable to break Carter's grip on the party machinery, but he concluded the Democratic convention which renominated Carter with an emotional appeal which enthralled his party listeners. Unsympathetic listeners outside judged it to be the rant of an obsolete liberalism.

KENTUCKY AND VIRGINIA RESOLUTIONS (1798), see Alien and Sedition Acts.

KENT STATE TRAGEDY, one of the notable events of the youth eruptions of the 1960s and 1970s. It involved a confrontation between radicals who had led anti-war agitation on the Ohio campus. Their burning of its ROTC building and other threatening displays brought a unit of the National Guard which, May 4, 1970, faced with a mixture of rock-throwing and other students, and through nervousness and poor organization, fired upon them. Four students died, and nine were injured. The action's most famous relic was a photograph showing a girl kneeling over a body in apparent anguish. Evidence that she was no student, and that her rock-throwing had no intelligent purpose did not, for some time, prevent its exploitation as a symbol of harassed virtue. The event was used for annual memorial meetings, featuring new causes, with slogans such as: "Hell, no, we won't go,/ We won't fight for Texaco!" and "No Nukes! (*q.v.*) Shut 'em [nuclear plants] down!" For the most responsible account, James A. Michener, *Kent State: What Happened and Why* (1971).

KERENSKY, ALEXANDER F. (1881-1970), Russian lawyer, he represented the Labor Party in the Duma (*q.v.*). Following the February Revolution (*q.v.*), he became Prime Minister of the Provisional Government, in which capacity, he made an effort to hold Russia in the war against Germany, but was overthrown by the Bolsheviks (*q.v.*). He fled to Paris, and came to the United States, in 1940, where he was well received by anti-Bolsheviks. Although his writings emphasized liberty and freedom—as in *The Crucifixion of Liberty* (1934)— the growing invocation of such conceptions during international crises involving Russia did not seem to add to his stature; he was generally seen as out of step with history.

KEY, FRANCIS SCOTT (1779-1843), though generally identified with nationalistic ideals, thanks to his anthem, *The Star-Spangled Banner* (1814), he was the district attorney in Washington, D.C., an ardent Jacksonian with pro-slavery convictions, who persecuted alleged abolitionists, as in the Crandall (*q.v.*) case.

KEYNES, JOHN MAYNARD (1883-1946), whose *Economic Consequences of the Peace* (1919) threw light on World War I propaganda, and helped understanding of the dilemmas it entailed. His turn to active governmental intervention in economic crises, like Darwinism, reached numerous people who could not read in his chief work, *The General Theory of Employment, Interest and Money* (1936), but who were satisfied that government spending created no difficulties. This concept rooted itself in democratic thinking, and maintained its authority during economic ups and downs of the 1940s and after, until the full paradox of full employment based on military and other government expenditure failed to prevent inflation and unemployment. A turn to monetarism spelled a decline in "Keynesian" thinking, and a need to emphasize character, honest workmanship, restraint in wages and social services, and other qualities and practices which had been dimmed in affluent decades. Sidney Weintraub, *Keynes and the Monetarists* (1973); N. J. Marshall, ed., *Keynes: Updated or Outdated?* (1970); D. E. Moggridge, *Keynes: Aspects of the Man and His Work* (1974). (*qq.v.*) for above.

KHAMA, SIR SERETSE (1921-1980), one of the most respected African Negro leaders of the twentieth century, a grandson of the chief of the Ngwato tribe, Khama was the chief designate of the Bamagwato people, in 1966 elected first president of independent Botswana. A graduate of South Africa schools, he attended Balliol and the Middle Temple in England. In 1948 he shocked friendly South Africans and the English, as well as his own people, by marrying a white British Air Force veteran and Lloyd's secretary. His dignity and will finally accepted, he administered in created Botswana a firm, compromise program of internal development and realistic relations with both the Union of South Africa on one side, and Rhodesia (later Zimbabwe (*q.v.*) on the other. He unlocked vital resources in his arid land, including copper, nickel, and diamonds, using foreign experts, and labored for free universal education and tolerance which guerrillas elsewhere criticized, but which left a legacy of promise. Isaac Schpera, *The Tswana* (1953); Anthony Sillery, *Botswana* (1974).

KINDERGARTENS, an aspect of progressive education (*q.v.*) first developed in Germany early in the 19th century by Friedrich Froebel, its essentially progressive quality lying in the fact that it took into account the nature of the child, in attempting to instil principles of learning and understanding in him. It was introduced into the United States by the most notable of the Peabody sisters (*qq.v.*), Elizabeth, in 1860, and later gained from the innovations of Maria Montessori, who sought to influence even younger children. John Dewey (*q.v.*) also introduced principles and philosophy into the training of young children. The proliferation of kindergartens watered down its reform principles, since many kindergartens became mere places to leave children: a kind of baby-sitting substitute. The kindergarten, however, continued to constitute a challenge to reformers, since so much of the child was formed within its confines.

KING, MARTIN LUTHER, JR. (1929-1968), made his reputation as pastor in a Montgomery, Alabama church, by heading the Montgomery Improvement Association boycott of "Jim Crow" (*q.v.*) bus laws, after Rosa Parks, a black woman, was arrested, December 1, 1955, for refusing to move to the rear of a bus. King's tactic of Gandhian (*q.v.*) non-violence set off a series of actions, including the bombing of his home, which ended in November of 1956, when the Supreme Court ruled against Jim Crow laws. King helped organize the Southern Christian Leadership Conference in 1957 and became its president. His book *Stride toward Freedom* (1958), his influence in "sit in" (*q.v.*) actions against segregation, and, in 1963, his effort to break down segregation in Birmingham, which captured national attention, making the police chief "Bull"

Connor's police dogs and water cannons notorious on television added to King's prominence, as did his March on Washington for Jobs and Freedom the same year. It featured his speech, which attained classic reference for its phrase "I have a dream." The next year he received among many other signs of regard and encouragement the Nobel Peace Prize. Although his voter-registration drive and Selma-to-Montgomery protest march sustained his dominance on national television and in high political circles, King was resented by the revolutionary minded and advertised self-styled Negro commanders, who also drew liberal homage. There were serious plans among them to rebuff King as a compromiser and misleader. These plans disintegrated when King was assassinated on April 4, 1968 in Memphis, Tennessee, where he had gone to aid sanitation workers, mainly Negroes, in their fight for improved wages and conditions. King's death, his last speech featuring the words "Free at last!" made him a legend around the world; at home, national leaders convened in Atlanta, Georgia to attend his obsequies. Subsequent Negro memorials to King, and their labors to create a Martin Luther King Day, kept his memory alive, though, in an anti-patriotic era, they could not persuade Congress to proclaim his birthday a national holiday. Flip Schulke, ed., *Martin Luther King, Jr.: a Documentary* (1976); Stephen Goode, *Assassination! Kennedy, King, Kennedy* (1979); D. L. Lewis, *King, a Critical Biography* (1970).

KING PHILIP'S WAR (1675-6), a major clash between English settlers in New England and a number of Indian tribes. It culminated long resentment over continued English encroachments upon Indian tribal land. Bitterly fought, and involving massacres as well as harsh battle tactics, the war concluded in the total defeat of the Indian allies. A casualty of the war were "praying Indians," on the one hand, friends of the Indian, on the other, who had hoped to live in peace and to gain from association.

KINGSLEY, CHARLES (1819-1875), Christian Socialist *(q.v.)* and author, his works included *Yeast, a Problem* (1848) and *Alton Locke, Tailor and Poet* (1850), among other once famous works. Although Chartist *(q.v.)* in his sympathies, and associated with "muscular Christianity," there was a strain of sentimentality in his writing which produced his children's classic, *The Water Babies* (1863).

KIRK, RUSSELL (1918-   ), social philosopher and litterateur, a son of Michigan pioneers, who formed his philosophy in study at St. Andrews University in Scotland. His *The Conservative Mind* (1953) had a strong influence on a revived conservatism, and was implemented by his numerous public appearances and such writings as *Enemies of Permanent Things* (1969) and *The Roots of American Order* (1974), which juxtaposed religious, moral, and cultural tenets to the liberal outlook of his time. A long-term contributor to the *National Review* *(q.v.)*, Kirk also founded *The Modern Age* and *University Bookman*. He was a critic of American education, as in *Academic Freedom* (1955), having left Michigan State University in protest against its tolerance of mediocrity. Culture formed an important adjunct to his philosophy, expressed in such an extended study as *Eliot and His Age* (1972), Eliot having been a close friend. Fiction was another aspect of Kirk's writing and concern, displayed in such Gothic writings as *The Surly, Sullen Bell* (1962) and *Lord of the Hollow Dark* (1974). See his *Confessions of a Bohemian Tory* (1963), and George H. Nash, *The Conservative Intellectual Movement in America since 1945* (1976).

KISHENEV MASSACRE (1903), one of the most notorious pogroms *(q.v.)* inflicted upon the Jews in Russia, under the Czar. Its spectacular cruelty and peasant stupidity shocked the western countries and provoked official protests. It encouraged the migration of the Jews to other countries and lost Russia the uses of a remarkable intelligentsia. It also helped discredit a regime notorious for its corruptness and reduced in world opinion because of its disgraceful failures in the Russo-Japanese War.

KISSINGER, HENRY A. (1923-   ), architect of detente *(q.v.)*,

he was a German emigre who rose rapidly in Harvard University's government department, making his mark with two brilliant books, *Nuclear Weapons and Foreign Policy* and *A World Restored: Metternich, Castlereagh and the Problems of Peace*, both issued in 1957. Sponsored by Nelson A. Rockefeller *(q.v.)*, he became a consultant in Kennedy's and Johnson's administrations, but came into his own when he joined Nixon's staff as Presidential Assistant for National Security Affairs. So influential was his role as negotiator that he later assumed the Secretary of State position. His great coup was discussions which led to Nixon's 1972 visit to Mainland China and the admission of China to the United Nations. Although these actions stunned American conservatives who would have preferred to see China kept out of the company of nations, China's hostility to the Soviets, which kept power parcelled out and diffuse, the Metternich *(q.v.)* policy of balancing nations was persuasive. It seemed more promising to many unsympathetic to communism than attempting to separate a billion armed people from the debates of others. Kissinger continued his "shuttle diplomacy" between Israel and Egypt, among others. He also was outraged by "leaks" *(q.v.)* which endangered his work, and approved the wiretaps which made vehement liberal critics of the Nixon Administration. Kissinger's work attracted its share of anger and sneers from those he termed "unpacifiable Doves," but it was too vital to bring him down. He served the Ford Administration and concentrated on his autobiography, *White House Years* (1979). Uncalled by Carter, he made an unauthorized trip to the Middle East, late in 1980, which observers thought might be a prelude to further service in a Reagan White House. (*Qq.v.*) for above. Roger Morris, *Uncertain Greatness* (1977); L. A. Sobel, ed., *Kissinger and Detente* (1975); S. A. Graubard, *Kissinger: Portrait of a Mind* (1974); *Kissinger Study of Southern Africa: National Security Study Memorandum 39 (Secret)* (1976).

"KITCHEN CABINET," a creation of the Jackson Administration, it was informally composed of Andrew Jackson's confidants and advisers, and included such personalities as the Postmaster General Amos Kendall, the journalist Francis Preston Blair, and Martin Van Buren: politically astute men with a sense of what their public wanted to hear. The "Kitchen Cabinet" had no reform potential whatsoever; compare Brain Trust.

K.K.K., see Ku Klux Klan.

KNEELAND, ABNER (1774-1844), a Universalist and civil rights advocate, he turned atheist and was arraigned in court for blasphemy and jailed, rousing the sympathy and fellowship of such reformers as Bronson Alcott, Theodore Parker, and Emerson *(qq.v.)*. The next year, 1839, he turned pioneer and moved to Iowa, where he attempted, but did not succeed, in setting up what he termed the First Society of Free Enquirers.

KNICKERBOCKER TRUST COMPANY, FAILURE, OF (1907), a turning point in bank administration; heretofore banks had been totally dependent upon their own resources, hence a "run on a bank" could bankrupt it if the "run" continued until its liquid resources were exhausted. This was true even when a bank had manifestly large holdings in real estate, non-convertible bonds, etc. The run on the Knickerbocker—one of the largest financial institutions in the country—was obviously the result of quarrels among bankers, rather than a product of doubt respecting the company's stability. Once it failed, it was "reorganized" to the greater satisfaction of interested elements. In the meantime, the failure had caused many other companies to fail, and lost depositors their savings. As a result, the Aldrich-Vreeland Currency Act *(q.v.)* was passed, intended to offer a measure of relief to harassed bankers. This Act has no status in reform; only in reform history. See "The Panic of 1907," in Filler, *The Muckrakers*.

KNIGHTS OF LABOR, THE, organized 1869, under the leadership of Uriah S. Stephens, it succeeded the National

Labor Union *(q.v.)* as a rallying point for workers. The title it assumed in 1871, "The Noble Order of the Knights of Labor," emphasized its interest in adding dignity to the concept of the workman. It was generous in its view of what constituted labor, admitting employers, and was interested in political influence and panaceas *(q.v.)*, as well as "pure and simple unionism" *(q.v.)*. Under Terence V. Powderly *(q.v.)*, it grew in strength, and by 1880 was a formidable social element, emphasizing the fraternity of secret meetings and ritual and counting some 700,000 members. Following the organization of the American Federation of Labor *(q.v.)*, it rapidly declined. The Knights were criticized by students of the labor movement for inadequate "class consciousness" *(q.v.)*, for failing to keep their ranks "clean" of non-workers, and for recklessly proliferating strikes for which they had inadequately prepared themselves. The Knights were first viewed askance by the Catholic Church, but were ultimately granted tolerance. The Knights were in principle an early version of the C.I.O. *(q.v.)*, in their effort to cut down the distinctions between skilled and unskilled workers *(qq.v.)*.

KNIGHTS OF ST. CRISPIN, org. 1869, with ritual and other means of dignifying the shoemaker's trade. Its program was reactionary, intending to oppose the introduction of machinery. It declined after the depression of 1873, though for a period it had been the best organized labor union in the country, counting some forty to fifty thousand members.

KNIGHTS OF THE GOLDEN CIRCLE, the most notorious of the pro-southern, anti-war northern organizations, secretly organized and derived from earlier sympathetic movements and ideas. Active in the border states, as well as Indiana and Ohio, its influence died with the war. Its major figure was Clement L. Vallandigham, of Ohio *(q.v.)*. It sported a variety of names, including Mutual Protection Society, Circle of Honor, and Knights of the Mighty Host. As reorganized in 1864, it became the Order of the Sons of Liberty.

KNOW-NOTHINGS, the most famous or notorious of parties which called themselves American *(q.v.)*, it had its genesis in the fear and suspicion which the mounting tide of Irish immigrants in the 1840's roused, especially in the cities, among those offended by their Catholic religion or their Democratic vote. As the Native American Party, they held a convention in 1845, but the Mexican War and attendant agitation over slavery issues put them into temporary eclipse. The accelerated disintegration of the Whig Party into pro-slavery and anti-slavery elements gave the nativists a new role: a halfway house in which homeless Whigs could rest while the Republican Party *(q.v.)* was being built. Samuel F.B. Morse was a dedicated partisan of nativism. Henry Wilson *(q.v.)* worked strenuously to turn it into an arm of free soil politics, but failed; it was seized in 1855 by the pro-slavery forces, and their opponents left it to help build the new anti-slavery alliances. The Know-Nothings ran Millard Fillmore for President in 1856 and continued influential through the 1860 elections. See also American Protective Association. R. A. Billington, *The Protestant Crusade* (1938); see also American Protective Association.

KOESTLER, ARTHUR, see Darkness at Noon.

KOREA, an American crisis in foreign affairs of the late 1940's and early 1950's, arising from the fact that northern Korea was in the hands of communists, South Korea occupied by United States troops. In 1948, a "People's Republic" was established in the north, a republic in the south, the northerners claiming title to all Korea. In June, 1950, North Korean forces invaded the south, which was given prompt support by U.N. *(q.v.)* forces, largely American, under the command of General Douglas MacArthur, which fought back from positions of largely over-run South Korea. Painful duels rewon the southern capital, Seoul, and offensives into 1951 finally resulted in the capture of the northern capital, Pyongyang. In October, the Chinese communists entered the war directly, and drove U. S. forces back to the thirty-eighth par-

allel, dividing north and south Korea. General MacArthur was relieved of his command by President Truman when he threatened to attack communist China itself. South Korea took up domestic life with U. S. subsidies, under Syngman Rhee as president; his major program was denouncing communists. It sufficed until May 1961, at the expense of substantial rebuilding of the nation and the economy, when a military junta took over and promised, with financial aid, to do better. There was no pause between communist efforts to shake the South Korea regime, encouraged by the American Vietnam *(q.v.)* catastrophe; communist "discipline" in North Korea left no leeway for such discomforts there. Rhee's successors worked between quasi-democratic procedures, and the dangers of basic government disruption. A "deal" the northern, and southern, communists could exploit in 1980 was between former Prime Minister Kim Jong Pil and other officials who had amassed, on report, more than $143 million through corrupt practices, which they had agreed to give up, along with all public office, to avoid prosecution. E. Traverso, *Korea and the Limits of Limited War* (1970); K. C. Chung, *Korea: The Third Republic* (1971); Edward R. Wright, ed., *Korean Politics in Transition* (1975); H-C Kim, *Koreans in America* (1974).

KOREMATSU V. UNITED STATES (1944), see Japanese Relocation Order.

KOSCIUSKO, THADDEUS (1746-1817), a Polish patriot in the American Revolution, like other idealistic Europeans, notably Lafayette *(q.v.)*, drawn to its defense by its democratic premises. He returned to Poland to become a major hope for leadership by its revolutionary elements. They made their great effort to overthrow Russian rule in 1794; it failed, and Kosciusko was kept in prison until 1796. The remainder of his life was spent seeking aid for renewing the struggle to free Poland *(q.v.)*.

KOSSUTH, LOUIS (1802-1891), a Hungarian revolutionist who led the unsuccessful attempt to end Russian rule in 1848. He was received with acclaim in the United States, 1852, but though he attempted to avoid being implicated in the slavery controversy he became an uneasy symbol of liberty.

KREUGER, IVAR (1880-1932), Swedish industrialist and "Match King," whose cynical financial frauds, when contrasted with the social honors he received almost up to time of his suicide, furnished evidence for social reformers of the inadequacy of capitalism. See also Insull, Samuel.

KROPOTKIN, PRINCE PETER ALEXEIVITCH (1842-1921), a Russian philosophical anarchist, whose idealistic views were welcomed by American reformers and not held offensive by conservatives. He was a geologist and geographer, who made notable exploratory trips to Finland, Manchuria, and Siberia. Nevertheless, having become a revolutionary, he suffered arrest in Russia in 1874, escaping from the country two years later, served a prison term in France, 1883-6, and then settled in England. He published memoirs and discussions of social issues, but was world famous for his *Mutual Aid, a Factor in Evolution* (1902), an effort to find revolutionary principles in nature. He returned to Russia in 1917, but was unsympathetic to Bolshevist rule. Martin A. Miller, *Kropotkin* (1976).

KU KLUX KLAN, a movement of southerners originally created to resist, in the post-Civil War period, the efforts of the Federal government to foist Negro equality upon them, chiefly for political reasons but backed by emotional recollections of wartime propaganda. The Klan was a secret organization which aimed to terrorize Negroes, preventing them from using their voting privileges. A Congressional inquiry and court actions broke up the organization, though it had taught the South how to resist, and the increasing indifference of the North and the removal of Federal troops restored "white supremacy" *(q.v.)*. During the 1920's, a new movement began which borrowed the Klan's name, and some of its methods. It was, however, not confined to the South, nor was it solely concerned for the Negro. It claimed several million members, who functioned actively in Indiana and

Vermont, as well as below the Mason-Dixon Line. It deteriorated in influence, thanks to proved corruption by its leaders. In the 1930's, the Klan cooperated with other fascist-type groups. It was diminished by the pro-black drive of the 1960s and the government implementation of equality laws in that time and after. However, the pressure of busing, anti-discrimination and anti-segregation laws, and the futile expenditure of vast sums of money for urban "renewal" left a residue of frustration which would-be Klan "commandos" hoped to exploit. They "trained" for class war. They were gratified by new volunteers north and south, watched the Skokie (q.v.) controversy with interest. In Arizona, they made news as seeking to become an "equal opportunity" employer, for hiring workers to sew 500 sheets for wearing; they were refused by the State's Department of Economic Security as "inadequate" in their request. More adequate, from Klan perspectives, was a California Klan leader's nomination for a Democratic Congressional seat from the nation's most populous district despite opposition from party leaders and from the U.S. President's wife, Rosalynn Carter. The Klan's new "emphasis" was on obedience to the laws, and also on guerrilla training, details of which they kept secret. "The nation," wrote the *Detroit Free Press*, responsive to its black constituency, "has been hard-hit by recession, and tough economic times do not always bring out the best in people." Don Whitehead, *Attack on Terror: the FBI against the Ku Klux Klan in Mississippi* (1970); D. M. Chalmers, *Hooded Americans* (1968); A. S. Rice, *The Ku Klux Klan in American Politics* (1962); D. Lowes, *Ku Klux Klan: the Invisible Empire* (1967).

KULAK, see Peasant.

KUOMINTANG, Chinese nationalist party created by Sun Yat Sen (q.v.), it embodied republican aspirations; under Chiang Kai Shek it became a dictatorship. Since the latter's retreat to Formosa (q.v.), its significance to social reformers has diminished. Milton J. Shieh, *Kuomintang* (1969).

L

LABEL, the "union label" is a sign of the status of a union in the industry, and its use by a company a sign of its acceptance of the union as a proper bargaining agent, of harmonious labor-capital relations. It can act to the company's interest, as the boycott (q.v.) can act against it. See also Buttons.

LABOR is most usefully viewed as organized and unorganized labor, and also as unemployed labor. All three categories influence the overall picture of the status of labor. The traditional view of labor was that of the trade-union and radical which saw him as the most worthy or needy element in society. The Marxian view saw him as the sole producer of the world's goods. The official A.F.L. (q.v.) view was that labor, like capital, competed for its share of the world's goods. The more radical saw him as heir to a world based on more cooperative tenets than those offered by capitalism. The rise of the C.I.O. and unions in general during the 1930's and after changed the position of labor in the industrial picture. Scandals in trade-unions raised the question of whether additional power had corrupted labor organizations beyond the power of laborers to control them, and whether the traditional approach to labor through labor organization would not have to be revised. Featherbedding (q.v.), especially where it might help endanger national security, was only one among other problems which interested otherwise indifferent citizens. Unemployment (q.v.) was no more urgent for labor than it was for others. Philip Selznick, *Law, Society, and Industrial Justice* (1969); D. Bok and John Dunlap, *Labor and the American Community* (1970); P. Foner, *American Labor Songs in the Nineteenth Century* (1975); S. Cohen, *Labor in the United States* (1975); see Productivity.

LABOR, DEPARTMENT OF, evolved out of the United States Bureau of Labor, provided for in law, 1884. Never reformist in any aspect, it confined itself to gathering data and evaluating trends. It was considered a forward step for its Secretary, under Woodrow Wilson (q.v.), to have been a working man: William B. Wilson, a moderate functionary of the United Mine Workers, whose major achievements was to keep labor in line for the war effort of 1917-8. The Department's most significant feature became its Bureau of Labor Statistics, which issued a monthly labor review, of value to reformers and anti-reformers. Frances Perkins (q.v.), as Franklin D. Roosevelt's Secretary of Labor, drew from a social work experience to aid the passage of New Deal (q.v.) legislation. President Kennedy's Secretary, Arthur Goldberg, came to his office from the most actively militant pro-labor background of all, but showed no signal achievement. Despite labor-wooing under Presidents Johnson and Carter, the Department manifested no creativity or strength.

LABOR, SLAVE, see Slave Labor.

LABOR AND CHILDREN, see Child Labor.

LABOR AND REFORM have been a function of the struggle between business unionism and social unionism (q.v.). When unorganized, without security, and underpaid, it has responded to reform slogans. In "good times," enjoying war prosperity, rendered confident by a strong union, it has permitted its affairs to fall into conservative hands, intent on maintaining their control. Thus Samuel Gompers (q.v.) expressed concern for unorganized workers, while the A.F.L. was being built; by 1901, he was an exclusionist in policy, and opposed to organizing women laborers; their place was in the home, he thought. Labor racketeers (q.v.) were, by nature, opposed to reform. A significant index of labor's reformism was education; pioneers of labor urged study and thought as a means for improving labor's lot. Except for some showcase unions, like the I.L.G.W.U. *(q.v.)*, labor education did not advance in "good times." The problem was not whether labor was willing to hold on to sentimental, outmoded attitudes; reformers agreed that laborers not in need were preferable to laborers in need. The question was whether labor, needy or otherwise, maintained social attitudes, whether it was pulling its freight. Laborers whiling away inordinate amounts of time at the pinball machines had no discernible relationship to George Henry Evans, Josiah Warren, Brook Farm, Terence V. Powderly, Debs, De Leon, William Z. Foster *(qq.v.)*, or to Gompers. Just what the relationship was between them and Walter Reuther *(q.v.)*, or of him to them, was a moot question. The general public, by 1981, had lost a sense of identity with, let alone responsibility for, labor; it was everybody for himself. However, there was genuine alarm that too much business unionism might destroy everybody; there was resentment that union officials forced Air Force officials at Cape Canaveral to reject materials made elsewhere for capsule production, and ready for use, in order that they be produced by union workers at the field. They thus slowed up preparations and permitted the Russians to get their man in space before the United States could. An electrical union which picketed a Roman Catholic shrine because a monk had installed electrical wiring for the stations of the cross seemed less than delicate in its public relations. There was alarm, too, over such unions as the Teamsters which was large enough to slow down or demoralize operations, if it chose to do so, and might do so inadvertently, since unionists were not trained to assume or understand responsibility. Although union leaders lobbied for minimum wages, medical aid for the aged, housing and unemployment compensation, unsympathetic observers felt that this had the effect of diverting attention from their own achievements as unionists. See also C.I.O.

LABOR AND WOMEN have been long associated, if only because women toiled as slaves as well as men. The expectation that they would marry and keep house distinguished their careers as workers, the *Lowell Offering (q.v.)*, which symbolized awareness of the fact that they were workers as well as women taking a tone which recognized that they were women as well as workers. Impersonal factory conditions of the post-Civil War era did not increase public awareness of the mass nature of their commitment to work; they were unfit for the ruthless wars which broke out between labor and capital. A pioneer work was that by Marie and Mrs. John Van Vorst, of aristocratic family, *The Woman Who Toils, Being the Experiences of Two Ladies as Factory Girls* (1902). Rheta Childe Dorr *(q.v.)*, a woman of high individuality, expanded and deepened their experiences, and her *What Eight Million Women Want* (1910) spelled out some of the complex story involved. Although the U.S. Supreme Court had struck down laws intended to recognize that women in factories could not endure conditions which men might without danger to their roles of mother and wife, Louis D. Brandeis defended an Oregon law which prohibited the employment of a woman in a factory or laundry for more than ten hours a day by presenting a mass of data bearing on the subject which swept away the abstract arguments defending the "freedom" of women to so labor (see Muller v. Oregon 1908). Thereafter laws in women's behalf multiplied. As late as 1923, however, the Supreme Court nullified a law establishing a minimum wage for women working in the District of Columbia. The multiplication of service jobs, such as typing, and the need for women workers during World War I expanded their place in industry; the depression of the 1930's forced them to seek work to feed dependents, in many cases (see *Why Women Work* 1938, a Public Affairs Pamphlet). As teachers, social workers, typists, and laborers, they engaged in sitdown strikes *(q.v.)* and other

tactics of the era. They grew in number during the all-out effort of World War II. However, they still preferred marriage, when possible. But whether workers or wives, their contribution to reform tended to be no better, if no worse, than that of the men with whom they associated. See also Women and Reform.

LABOR CAMPS, see Gulag.

LABOR FORCE, a term having relative significance, referring to the number of persons available for work in the categories of skilled and unskilled, but varying in number with specific circumstances. Thus, the labor force increased during the Great Depression of the 1930's, because persons who did not belong to it by reason of their status in society as housewives, children, and others, were "thrown upon the labor market" by necessity. The demand for labor during World War II also affected the definition. The increase in population *(q.v.)* during the 1950's affected the size of the labor force. Nevertheless, the Department of Labor predicted that the increase in the labor force would exceed the increase in population by the end of the 1960's. It predicted a 41% increase in technicians and professionals; 18% increase in semi-skilled labor, no increase in the number of unskilled, and a 17% decrease among farm workers.

LABOR JOURNALISM developed in the pre-Civil War period out of the efforts of such a partisan as George Henry Evans *(q.v.)*, and reflected the needs and desires of the craftsman more than of the unskilled laborer. In the post-Civil War period, the coming of the "new immigration" *(q.v.)*, the flow of labor into mill, mine, and factory, economic crises, and the crises in labor-capital relations created a new journalism veering between radicalism and trade union agitation, intended to appeal to workers and speak their needs. The new popular journalism *(q.v.)*, too, tended to be pro-labor. The establishment of the trades unions, as symbolized by the American Federation of Labor *(q.v.)* created a large number of house-organs which retailed shop gossip, details of labor business, and references to general affairs which were told more competently in non-labor organs. Although famous publications considered themselves close to labor, or even at one with it, as in the cases of the *Appeal to Reason*, the *Masses*, and the *Daily Worker (qq.v.)*, they were not mouthpieces of labor, which seemed unable to produce an outstanding publication. The rise of the C.I.O., and the creation of a labor elite of education and social standing seemed unable to change this situation, though house-organs proliferated. During the 1950's, there were some sixty million copies of labor papers produced to cover labor's clientele, but there is little evidence that it had much binding or educational influence, or even that it was seriously read. In many cases, the union members preferred to peruse the employer's personnel messages, printed on better paper, and containing more items of interest to them.

LABOR PARTY, a dream of many decades, opposed by the A.F.L. *(q.v.)*, which held that labor could only advance itself through economic measures, politicians being untrustworthy. In 1919, the Indiana State Federation of Labor workers demanded it, and formed the Indiana Labor Party. The Chicago Federation of Labor approved the idea. The next year, a Farmer-Labor convention met in Chicago, in cooperation with the Nonpartisan League *(q.v.)*. The idea failed of fulfillment, but in 1921-2, sixteen railroad unions, the United Mine Workers, the Typographical Union, the Amalgamated Clothing Workers, and others organized the Conference for Progressive Political Action *(q.v.)*, but would not organize a third party. See also American Labor Party.

LABOR QUESTION, THE, recognized by reform elements as of crucial significance in the post-Civil War decades. It involved recognition of the desperate need of labor to receive regard and consideration in a civilization which was placing a premium on individualism and "free enterprise."

Since the mills, mines, and factories were not environments which encouraged individualism, and since the state and society responded with force to the efforts of labor to gain strength by union, ways and means had to be investigated which would gain labor the dignity and sustenance it required. All society had a stake in labor achieving them.

LABOR RACKETEERING, the bane of reformers, and a major argument employed by those who, sincerely or otherwise, seek curbs on unions. It increased as the growth of unions provided opportunities for careerists aligned with thugs. In the 1890's, the president of the waiters and bartenders union, W. C. Pomeroy, mishandled its funds. In the building trades, "Skinny" Madden became notorious. "Umbrella" Mike Boyle, who headed the electrical workers union in Chicago gained power. In 1911, he achieved the closed shop by excluding all switchboards not manufactured in Chicago. He was later sentenced to prison under the Sherman Anti-Trust Act (q.v.), but his sentence was commuted. Similar types operated in other unions. The drive, often heroic, to build unions during the 1930's, coupled with subsequent hot and cold war labor prosperity created a stabilized unionism which attracted skillful organizers, sometimes of a racketeer nature. Their arrogance and sense of power was revealed when Victor Riesel, a labor columnist who had been exposing rackets in unions, had acid flung into his eyes by a young thug, Abe Telvi, who was himself soon after murdered. The shocking incident turned attention to rackets in unions, in 1956. A special committee of the U.S. Senate, headed by John McClellan (q.v.), was set up to investigate the subject, and many unsavory situations and personages were exposed. In 1959, the Landrum-Griffin Bill was passed, intended to prevent corruption in labor unions and protect democracy within them. The career of a Jimmy Hoffa (q.v.) suggested that labor required the same public monitoring as capital.

LABOR RELATIONS have involved management, the public, and government. Labor traditionally appealed to the public for sympathy and support during its bouts with management; it appealed to city, state, or federal authorities not to help in harming its strikes, it made efforts to organize and show strength at the polls, in order to elicit respect or neutrality from conservative politicians. Its major effort was to define its needs with respect to union recognition, scales of wages, standards of work conditions. It took "Section 7 (a)" of the NRA (q.v.) to put the government behind its demands, and, through the 1930's, multiplied its unions and membership. The urgent demands of World War II enabled it to gain unprecedentedly satisfying contracts, aided by the NLRB (q.v.). The Taft-Hartley Act (1947) was an effort to curb "Big Labor," by permitting the hiring of non-union workers, requiring a cooling-off period before permitting strikes, forcing union officials to swear they did not belong to the Communist Party, and otherwise curbing the power of unions. Repeal of the Taft-Hartley Act became a major aim of unionists, and of reformers who were not dismayed by labor racketeering (q.v.).

LABOR TIME, a socialist theory which emphasized the quantity of time spent on production, rather than the quality of the work done. John Bellers, Robert Owen (q.v.), and others advocated the issuance of notes which paid labor for time spent. The theory did not take into account the value of the time spent, or the possibility of having stipendiaries who had accomplished little with their time: "time servers." Later developments, including "coffee breaks," which could eat up much of available time, suggested the need for a reconsideration of the question. See Productivity. See also Warren, Josiah.

LABOR'S MAGNA CARTA, see Magna Carta.

LABOUR EXCHANGES, first suggested by Robert Owen (q.v.), to enable producers to exchange their goods for that of others. They grew in France, Italy and other countries,

the most famous being the Bourse de Travail in Paris, founded in 1887.

LABOUR PARTY OF GREAT BRITAIN, see British Labour Party.

LADD, WILLIAM (1778-1841), peace advocate and organizer of the American Peace Society (1828), the first such society in history. He developed ideas relating to the technique of achieving peace which influenced the Hague Peace Conferences (q.v.) and the League of Nations (q.v.). He sought to keep his crusade unadulterated by other reforms of his time, and to avoid the extremism of the Non-Resistant Society (q.v.). See his An Essay on a Congress of Nations, for the Adjustment of International Disputes without Resort to Arms (1840).

LAFAYETTE, MARQUIS DE (1757-1834), French nobleman and idealist, who, at his own expense and on his own initiative, equipped troops and brought them (1777) to fight in the American Revolution. Though a young man, he fought with talent in important engagements, and earned the friendship of General Washington. He took part in the French Revolution, where, as commander-in-chief of the national guard, he assisted in the destruction of the Bastille (qq.v.). He was moderate in his political aims, and not esteemed by the extreme radicals. His visit to the United States (1824-5) was a triumphal tour. As with Kossuth (q.v.), he seemed a spirit of social aspiration binding reformers everywhere.

LA FOLLETTE, ROBERT M. (1855-1925), governor of Wisconsin (1901-6), thereafter U.S. Senator; his Autobiography (1913) records the classic tale of grassroots origins, awareness of the oppression suffered by the farmer at the hands of special interests, the appeal to the people, the outrageous offer of a bribe, and, in 1900, victory. Two major planks in his program were the regulation of railroads and the use of experts, in this instance, from the University of Wisconsin. "The Wisconsin Idea" was the first development in a governmental technique which ultimately produced the "Brain Trust" (q.v.). The standard image of La Follette as the paladin knight requires qualification: he had a political machine and paid off his constituents, notably in opposing free trade with Canada, in the farm products which concerned Wisconsin voters. Lincoln Steffens (q.v.) described him as a boss who was dictating democracy. He fought for the Hepburn Bill (q.v.) and other reform legislation. Though the natural leader of the Progressive Party (q.v.), he was deprived of its nomination in 1912. He cooperated with the progressive legislation of the Wilson Administration, but fought it bitterly in his unpopular attempt to stop American intervention in the Great War. Afterwards, he fought ratification of the Covenant of the League of Nations. In 1924, he was the candidate of the Progressive Party, and received the electoral votes of his state, as well as a total of some five million votes. His son, Robert, "Young Bob" (1895-1953) also served in the Senate, and headed the notable La Follette Civil Liberties Committee (q.v.). He was defeated by Joseph McCarthy in 1946. His brother, Philip (1897-1965), served as governor of Wisconsin in the 1930's.

LA FOLLETTE CIVIL LIBERTIES COMMITTEE, set up in 1936, took extended testimony on the curbs on free speech and assembly and anti-union tactics employed by corporation leaders, police, and others. It exposed the harsh measures utilized in the "Little Steel" or Memorial Day Massacre (q.v.). It failed to achieve the legislative safeguards against repression which it recommended to Congress. One aspect of the Committee's findings was publicized in Leo Huberman's The Labor Spy Racket (1937).

LA FOLLETTE SEAMEN'S ACT OF 1915, See Seamen.

LA GUARDIA, FIORELLO H. (1882-1947), mayor of New York (1934-46), and an outstanding example of practical reform politics. Following a career of law, he became a congressman, who interrupted his career to serve with distinction in the Air Force, during World War I. His most notable achievement in Congress was the Norris-La Guardia Anti-Injunction Act (1932). As candidate of the Fusion ticket, he began his career as mayor of New York, winning adherents by his warm and unpredictable personality, by his shrewd ability to pay political debts and maintain his political alliance, and, most substantially, by demanding returns in the form of city improvements. His program of slum clearance and park and highway development, and his attack on bureaucratic organization which served old-line politicians were real and tangible. He attracted such substantial public servants as Robert Moses. His peccadilloes—running to fires, wearing wide-brimmed black sombreros, directing traffic, reading the comics on radio during a newspaper strike—were freely enjoyed because his admirers knew that they were not a cover for inadequacy, but an expression of genuine neighborliness. His delegation of an all-Jewish squad of policemen to guard a delegation of Nazi visitors was an example of his confidence in New York. The musical comedy, *Fiorello!* captured the *décor* of the man; his techniques are more difficult to master. See Charles Garrett, *The La Guardia Years: Machine and Reform Politics in New York City* (1961).

LAISSEZ-FAIRE PRINCIPLES, see Free Enterprise.

LAMONT, THOMAS W. (1870-1948), a partner in J.P. Morgan *(q.v.)* & Company from 1911 on, and concerned for its public relations. For years, he was a director of the Crowell Publishing Company. He was involved in the transmutation of muckraking *(q.v.)* publications into organs more gracious to the business point of view. On the other hand, he became a major supporter of the *Saturday Review of Literature*. He was influential in the floating of Allied bonds while the United States was still supposed to be neutral, during World War I, and was later criticized by the Nye *(q.v.)* Committee. In 1918, he acquired the *New York Evening Post* from Oswald Garrison Villard *(q.v.)* and thus put an end to Villard's criticisms of the Wilson Administration. His money built the Lamont Library at Harvard University. His relationship to American communication merits study. His son, *Corliss*, wrote *The Illusion of Immortality* (1935) and believed in the reality of *Soviet Civilization* (1952), including its constitution.

"LAND, BREAD, AND PEACE," Lenin's famous slogan upon his return to Russia in April, 1917, intending to mobilize opinion favoring the breakup of the great estates, a guarantee of subsistence, and disassociation from what he saw as a struggle among imperialist powers.

LAND REFORM, one of the oldest and most characteristic American reforms, involving the basic concept that Americans in trouble had the right to correct their affairs by making a new beginning out of the public lands. The Proclamation of 1763 *(q.v.)*, stirred up what were essentially reform protests, and was one grievance leading to the American Revolution. The patroon system of land-holding led to the Anti-Rent War *(q.v.)*. Squatters settled on government land without paying fees; later put pressure on their representatives in Congress to legalize their claims retroactively. The demand for free land in the west was a major plank in the program of the workingmen's parties in the 1830's, and mingled with the aspirations of Free Soil *(qq.v.)*. Andrew Johnson *(q.v.)* gained fame in fighting for a homestead act for poor whites, speaking for the south as Horace Greeley's *(q.v.)* "Go West, young man" spoke for the north. The passage of the Homestead Act of 1862 *(q.v.)* was a victory for the free enterprise of the little man. However, *land grants* to the railroads were a victory for corporative free enterprise; overall, the government gave them some 158,293,377 acres of land to administer and sell, and a strategic position in a west which needed their services. Thus, the railroad problem and the farmers' problem *(qq.v.)* were closely connected, and called up new reform movements. Henry George's Single Tax scheme *(q.v.)* was the last major effort at reform based on the land question. The closing of the frontier *(q.v.)* made land reform, for the most part, an obsolete issue.

LANDRUM-GRIFFIN BILL, see Labor Racketeering.

LANE DEBATE (1834), an incident in the developing anti-slavery crusade. Lane Seminary, in Cincinnati, had been organized to produce domestic missionaries to combat Catholicism in the west. It attracted a brilliant and talented student body. Theodore D. Weld *(q.v.)* organized a nine-day discussion on the comparative virtues of colonization and abolition for ridding the country of slavery. The students agreed that they preferred abolition, and began to organize on that basis. When the Lane trustees attempted to halt their activities, a large number of them resigned, and moved north to enroll in the recently organized Oberlin College *(q.v.)*. The Lane Debate attracted the interest of the country, converted many people to abolition, and impressed upon them its relationship to civil liberties, which the trustees had attempted to suppress; see Filler, *Crusade against Slavery*

LANGUAGE CHANGES have drawn the strength from some words, and put new, first-level meaning into others. They have been affected not merely by language evolution (reflected in books on "American English") but by direct social upset and international pressure. "Camp" had been related to homosexual ways in the 1920s; in the 1950s it spread to mean tasteless things which were somehow interesting, or art; Andy Warhol made his reputation by presenting cans of tomato juice as art. The camp fad seemed to diminish by the 1970s. However, homosexual agitation, and tolerance or sympathy for their cause, appeared to lose "gay" its traditional meaning, and associate it with homosexuals. "Negro" lost much of its identity as descriptive of Negro people; the concept of "black," once a bigot's word since most Negroes were not black, gave it priority over Negro, at least as a word used in rhetoric and propaganda. (See Black English.) Activist woman protest—"activist" itself assuming a radical connotation—demeaned some words, such as "mankind" as well as "chairman," which were claimed, sometimes with etymological inaccuracy, to give males priority over females. Other words under duress in this area included "mailman" (which became "mailcarrier") and fireman (which became "firefighter"). "Girl" was intensely impugned as condescending even when applied to teen-agers; "woman" was preferred, and not "young woman," even when young. The shifting role of the family raised possibilities of language change, involving such concepts as "constant companion," "singles bar," and "commitment," which were, however, in flux in 1980. "Bachelor" had a doubtful future. International etiquette and relations put out of use "backward countries," in behalf of "emerging" or "underdeveloped" nations. Euphemisms and code words overlapped with genuine, descriptive words to overlap, in turn, with hypocritical phrases and blatant lies. Other fields affected by changing relations and propaganda included youth, which gave new and recognized meanings to many words, including "high," and politics which identified "compassion" with liberal spending, or, recognizably as Democratic, "give-aways." or, in Democratic use, as Republican largesse to big corporations. "Bureaucratese" and "Pentagonese" flourished in sentences which evaded understanding, and slopped over into ordinary living and even, it was learned, in school teaching and English classes. However, they attracted ridicule and even laws, when their intention was not only to confuse, but lose customers money in the confusion. The journalist William Safire discussed new meanings and accuracy of expression in his newspaper column, and political phrases in his *Political Dictionary* (1978). See also Clifford Adelman, *No loaves, No Parables; Liberal Politics and the American Language* (1974).

LASKI, HAROLD (1893-1950), English professor, socialist, and economist, student of public affairs, he was well-known among American liberals of various tendencies, visited Harvard University and other institutions. He wrote *The Strategy of Freedom* (1941), and *Reflections on the Revolution of Our Time* (1943), among other works. He was influential in the Labour Party and took broad views of the possibilities of cooperating with communists which exasperated anti-communists. His writings decreased in influence, following his death.

LASALLE, FERDINAND (1825-1864), one of the founders of modern socialism born of wealthy Jewish parents in Breslau, Germany. His meteoric career took him through personal and social causes in great number. He took part in the Revolution of 1848, and served a year in prison. Only in the last two years of his life did he embrace socialist politics, advocating his program with a brilliance and ardor which ultimately created the Democratic Socialist Party in Germany. His plan emphasized political action rather than working class force, as a weapon, and avoided Marxian internationalism. His love affair with the daughter of a German aristocrat ended when he felt compelled to challenge Count von Racowitza to a duel, in which he died. The tragedy was treated in George Meredith's *The Tragic Comedians* (1880).

LATIN AMERICA AND REFORM have only recently been recognized in official American policy as urgent to its own survival. Although Americans maintained their traditional approval of "democratic" revolutions, and hailed the overthrow of Spanish rule in Central and South America early in the nineteenth century, they gave relatively little regard to its details. As governments were established which emphasized power cliques at the expense of democratic perspectives, Americans concerned themselves for the security of their investments, rather than the content of the governments with which they dealt. American policy in Central America and the Caribbean (*qq.v.*) was not an advance over this attitude. Between World War I and World War II, it became clear that the Monroe Doctrine (*q.v.*) would not ensure American influence below the Mexican border, and that the "good neighbor policy" (*q.v.*) would not alone secure good neighbors. Yet social reformers were quicker than Department of State officials to speak sharply of such figures as Trujillo (*q.v.*) of the Dominican Republic, and the dictator Perón of Argentina. The growing power of the Soviet Union in international affairs, and its ability to speak the language of depressed peasants and frustrated intellectuals raised the question of whether reform could be opposed to revolution. "Democratic" victories in Argentina, Peru, Colombia, Honduras, and Venezuela left enigmatic residues. There was no enigma in the tyrannies resident in the Dominican Republic, Paraguay, Haiti, and Nicaragua. The case of Cuba (*q.v.*) was a constant reminder that the United States required a crash program of vast proportions to do its part in creating worthwhile friends. See Charles O. Porter and Robert J. Alexander, *The Struggle for Democracy in Latin America* (1961). Salvador De Madariaga, *Latin America between the Eagle and the Bear* (1962); J. S. Tulchin, ed., *Latin America in the Year 2000* (1975); F. Parkinson, *Latin America, the Cold War and the World Powers* (1974); John Rothchild, ed., *Latin America Yesterday and Today* (1974). See also Allende, Salvador, Panama Canal, Mexico, Brazil, Argentina.

LATTIMORE CASE, see Owen Lattimore Case, The.

LAW, vital to American change. A "plague of lawyers" defined the issues leading to the Revolution. States rights versus national law created dangerous situations during the War of 1812, the Cherokee issue, the protracted slavery controversy (*qq.v.*), and during succeeding eras of war and peace, The Supreme Court (*q.v.*) increasingly adjudicated critical problems, drawing bitter criticism that it had assumed "legislative functions." However, in the deepening domestic crisis of the 1970s, involving Negro, Indian, female, children, and almost all fields of human endeavor, law became the major instrument for offering decisions which slowed the road to chaos. Whether the society could reconstruct enough consensus (*q.v.*), tradition, and majority opinion to limit the endless suits which cluttered the courts was a question for the 1980s. Tom Dove, ed., *Law and Political Protest: A Handbook to Your Political Rights under the Law* (1970); M. Summers and T. Barth, *Law and Order in a Democratic Society* (1970); Samuel I. Shuman, ed., *Law and Disorder: the Legitimation of Direct Action as an Instrument of Social Policy* (1971); Jeffrey Jowell, *Law and Bureaucracy* (1975); H. R. Rodgers and Charles S. Bullock, *Law and Social Change* (1972); G. Drewry, *Law, Justice and Politics* (1975).

LAWES, LEWIS E. (1883-1947), prison reformer, superintendent of the New York City Reformatory (1915-20), and famous as warden of Sing Sing Prison (1920-41). His work pleaded for an understanding of criminals and a more reasonable and humane program for them; see *Man's Judgment of Death* (1923), the widely-read *20,000 Years in Sing Sing* (1932), and *Meet the Murderer* (1940).

LAWRENCE (MASS.) TEXTILE STRIKE (1912), led by the militant Wobblies, Arturo Giovannitti, (*q.v.*) New York labor editor and poet and Joseph Ettor. The harsh treatment meted out by the police included indiscriminate arrests and beatings, and the clubbing of children who were being sent out of town by their elders so that the strike could be prosecuted more freely. The effort ended in victory for the strikers, and acquittal for their leaders, who had been arrested in an attempt to weaken strike morale.

LAWSON, THOMAS W. (1857-1925), multimillionaire and financial independent, whose revelations of stockmarket and industrial chicanery performed by his associates was one of the muckraking sensations of the 1900's. His exposes brought on the insurance investigations of 1905 and led ultimately to the work of the Pujo Committee (*qq.v.*). See "Frenzied Finance," in Filler, *The Muckrakers.*

"LAY-OFF," dreaded by workers habituated to a specific job or location; the separation of a worker from his job, due to a "slow" season, cancelled contracts, falling profits, or other circumstances. Sometimes the "lay off" is thought to be temporary, and the worker able to live on benefits (*q.v.*) pending re-employment. Lay-offs can affect so many workers as to affect the strength of the local union or even community. It can affect individual seniority on the job, so a fancied economic security disappears with the lay-off.

LAZARUS, EMMA (1849-1887), best known for her sonnet, "The New Colossus," carved on the base of the Statue of Liberty: a signal honor which expressed the esteem she had won for the ardor and idealism of her verses. Although of Jewish birth, she had sought more universal modes of expression; the Russian persecutions of Jews, 1879-1883, sharpened her sense of identity with them. Her 1882 volume of verse was entitled *Songs of a Semite*. As important was her eloquent denunciation of a defense of Russian antisemitism, in "Russian Christianity *versus* Modern Judaism," which appeared in *Century Magazine*, April 1882. Her fame as poet and Jewish spokesman reflected, in part, the liberalism of the period.

"LEAF-RAKING," see Civil Works Administration.

LEAGUE OF NATIONS, a creation of the Versailles (*q.v.*) Conference and intended to produce a world force which would make war impossible. The requirement that its Council agree unanimously on action insured that it would be a do-nothing organization. Although its Assembly produced much eloquence, it was evident that its disassociation from power would vitiate most of it. Its critics used the League to demonstrate that an international body was impossible of achievement. Its sponsors and friends believed that it constituted a banner for men of good will, who would rally around it in time of trouble. Its impotence in the Manchurian and Ethiopian (*qq.v.*) crises seemed to demonstrate that their faith was without foundation. Nevertheless, World War II created a similar need, which was met by the call for a United Nations (*q.v.*) organization, to which the League deferred, being dissolved in 1946. See also Internationalism and Reform. Ruth Henig, ed., *The League of Nations* (1973).

LEAGUE OF WOMEN VOTERS OF THE UNITED STATES, established by Mrs. Carrie Chapman Catt (*q.v.*) in 1920, under the name of the National League of Women

Voters: an organization intended to help women to use the vote granted them by the Nineteenth Amendment to the Constitution (q.v.). Entirely an educational body it has attracted liberals among the women who make efforts to lay their views before the general public. In 1980, during the Presidential campaign, it sponsored a debate which brought together Reagan (q.v.) and third-party candidate John B. Anderson. The President, Carter, refused to appear with him present, probably harming his own cause by his absence.

LEAGUE TO ENFORCE PEACE, organized in 1915 by such persons as Hamilton Holt and William Howard Taft (qq.v.). Although sincerely intended, it became a halfway house for those who needed a reason for joining in the war. The two stages of their transformation were the condemnation of Germany as the aggressor in the war, and the formulation of the League of Nations (q.v.) idea.

LEAKS, an increasing problem in domestic and world adjustments, which hounded authoritarian governments to a lesser degree. Leaks involved a respect for freedom of the press and the democratic "right to know"; but also a need for privacy in government, as well as individual privacy. In the 1970s, government security suffered in creating a foreign policy. The Pentagon Papers (q.v.) were one of a massive number of leaks which not only retarded war, but negotiations for ending war. White House frustration turned members of the President's staff to illegal schemes for stopping leaks, including wire tapping, until curbed by the Supreme Court in 1972. Leaks continued, to the satisfaction of the foes of American policy, encouraged by major news media which thus became a species of government with none of its responsibilities.

LEASE SYSTEM OF CONVICT LABOR, involves the leasing of convicts to contractors, who feed and clothe the prisoners, and pay stipulated sums to the institution for the use of this labor. The system was bitterly criticized by labor spokesmen and organized labor, as they emerged from systems of convict servitude and indentured servitude. (q.v.). It continued in malignant form into modern times, and was protested as harmful to the prisoners as well as to the standards and opportunities of free labor. See also Convict Labor.

LEAVITT, JOSHUA (1794-1873), influential reformer of pre-Civil War period, he aimed at moderate formulations which would mobilize the widest range of public opinion; his program, therefore, led directly to the organization of the Republican Party (q.v.). A moral reformer, he served the Seamen's Friend Society and was earnest in furthering the work of the American Seventh Commandment Society. In the 1830's, he edited the *Evangelist*, which, in its success, helped revolutionize religious journalism. In 1837, he became editor of the New York *Emancipator*, and an influential moderate abolitionist, as well as concerned for free trade, cheap postage, and other liberalizing causes. In 1848, he began his significant work as managing editor of the *Independent* (q.v.). That year he was a leading figure in organizing the Free Soil Party, with its candidate Martin Van Buren, even though he did not respect the ex-President's politics.

LEFT WING, general designation for militant reformers, dissidents, and revolutionists, a concept borrowed from Europe, where their counterparts in legislatures occupied the left wing of the chamber. The use of "the left," "leftist," and other variations was especially strong during the 1930's, which made careful distinctions between "right of center" and "left of center" (see also Centrist), in the course of which a "rightist" could be made to seem extremely conservative, though held to be an extreme radical by conservatives. See also *Waiting for Lefty* (1935), by Clifford Odets. A headline in 1961 read: "Leftists Stilled by Prosperity," and blamed this phenomenon on New Deal reforms, general prosperity, and the discrediting of the Communist Party. Since a scandalous unemployment existed, and since marked distress was admitted among transient workers, and in slums, and af-

fecting old, abandoned children, minority groups, among others, it raised the question of whom the "leftists" had represented in less prosperous times. "Leftist" assumed being a part of a spectrum of left, right, and center. The youth uprising of the 1960s involved radical alienation and a type of chaos, consciously induced. However, a "New Left" of university persons, historians included, undertook to rewrite American life and tradition, and gained some credence in the process; see Harold Jaffe and John Tytell, *The American Experience: a Radical Reader* (1970); see also R. J. Maddox, *The New Left and the Origins of the Cold War* (1973).

LEGAL TENDER, see Greenback Issue, The.

LEGGETT, WILLIAM (1801-1839), one of the most sincere of the Jacksonians (q.v.), an equalitarian frustrated by the opportunism which corroded the causes he hoped to advance. An editor of the New York *Post* under William Cullen Bryant (q.v.), he sought to make the Democrats a cause, as well as a party. *The Plaindealer*, which he edited in 1837 continued his campaign. See *A Collection of the Political Writings of William Leggett* (1840), and Loco-Focos, The.

LEISLER, JACOB (1640-1691), seventeenth century liberal and victim of judicial injustice, he was a German who became a soldier and came to New York in 1660. He became wealthy in the Indian trade, and also captained a New York military force. The "Glorious Revolution" of 1688 in England, representing a Protestant victory, in the ascension of William and Mary, caused perturbation in the New York colony. Leisler took the part of the new sovereigns, with the approval of the soldiery, and the middle classes. The aristocrats supported the incumbent administration of Francis Nicholson, the lieutenant governor whom Leisler deposed and whose title he assumed, there being no formal successor. Leisler aroused the further hostility of the aristocrats by his vigorous measures to suppress them. Troops and a new governor sent to take over power found a community of interests with the anti-Leisler faction, and though he laid down his arms, he was hanged as a traitor. Parliament later passed a bill reversing the judgment upon which this deed had been committed. Compare with Bacon's Rebellion. Jerome Reich, *Leisler's Rebellion* (1953).

LEISURE AND THE WORK-DAY, touted, since the 1950's, as a coming problem and challenge, thanks to the shorter work-week, labor-saving devices, and automation (q.v.). It has been taken seriously by such middle-class theoreticians as David Riesman, and by their middle-class readers. Implying more time which can be profitably used, it fails to appreciate that this can be no more than an extension of less time which has been profitably used. It emphasizes the need for educating people to the better use of leisure, but does not offend its readers by noticing that they are the "educated," for the most part. It is quite meaningless to great classes of the poor and the unemployed, and can have no meaning to a reformer who is concerned for an intelligible and a vital society, rather than one which can rationalize its inadequacy; see Max Kaplan, *Leisure in America: a Social Inquiry* (1960). See also Kenneth Roberts, *Leisure* (1970); American Alliance for Health, Physical Education and Recreation, *Leisure and the Quality of Life* (1972); R. and R. N. Rapoport, *Leisure and the Family Life Cycle* (1975).

LEISURE CLASS, see Parasite, Veblen, Thorstein.

LEMKE, WILLIAM (1878-1950), a leader of the Nonpartisan League and, in Congress, a representative of the farmers' interest. In 1936, he received the backing of Father Coughlin, Francis E. Townsend, and the heirs of Huey P. Long (qq.v.) as candidate of the Union Party. The 900,000 votes he received alarmed some liberals with the possibility that agrarian, utopian, and fascist-type followings might be united to give birth to an American version of fascism. The alliance, however, rapidly disintegrated.

LEMOYNE, DR. FRANCIS J. (1798-1879), leading advocate

of antislavery in western Pennsylvania and opponent of the American Colonization Society. He was offered the Vice-Presidential candidacy of the Liberty Party *(q.v.)*, in 1840, but declined it; however, he was later its candidate for the governorship of Pennsylvania several times. He was one of the operators of the "underground railroad" *(q.v.)*. Among his philanthropies was the gift of $20,000 to the American Missionary Association *(q.v.)* to build what became the LeMoyne Normal Institute for colored people. He became the first prominent advocate in the United States of cremating *(q.v.)* the dead. In 1876, he built the first crematorium in the United States in his hometown, Washington, Pa.: an event which caused much public controversy.

LENINISM, presumably Marxism *(q.v.)* brought up to date, allowing the principles of the inevitable debacle of capitalism to be brought up to date: to take into account the appearance of the U.S.S.R., to provide official explanations of programs and events, and to oppose those brought up by others outside the official communist fold who also claimed Marx as a guide. Leninism amounted to a canonization of the dead Bolshevik leader. Its principles were unclear, since he had acted boldly to seize power in Russia, but also, later, denounced "infantile leftism"; had instituted war communism, but also retreated to the New Economic Policy (NEP), which amounted to a more moderate program of socialization, and otherwise played the role of a tactician as well as an intransigent. In general, he had emphasized an international perspective, but partly, perhaps, for lack of a strong communist stronghold; it is impossible to guess how he would have coped with a rising nationalism at home. Stalin exalted Leninism for his own purposes; it became whatever it pleased him to think it; and his followers soon added Stalinism *(q.v.)*.

LEO M. FRANK CASE (1913-1915). The murder of a fourteen-year old Atlanta, Georgia, girl, employed by the National Pencil Company, called attention to the factory superintendent, Leo M. Frank, and several Negroes there employed. Although the circumstantial evidence was based on the testimony of one of them, a person of weak character and reputation, Frank was indicted for murder and became the victim of anti-Semitic feeling and propaganda, led by Thomas B. Watson *(q.v.)*. Condemned three times, and despite national protest, Frank's sentence was commuted by Governor John M. Slaton, who was politically ruined by the act. August 16, 1915, a lynching mob of respectable citizens took Frank forcibly from prison and hanged him; see Leonard Dinnerstein, *The Leo Frank Case* (1968).

LERNER, MAX (1902-   ), liberal figure of the 1930s, he edited the *Nation (q.v.)* and *PM*, and gave the era two contemporary titles: *It is Later than You Think* (1938), and *Ideas Are Weapons* (1939), which reflected the times's left-wing liberal premises, as did also Lerner's edited *The Mind and Faith of Justice Holmes (q.v.)* (1943). Later writings made no impact.

LEUPP, FRANCIS E. (1849-1918), friend of the Indian, an American journalist who studied the problem at first hand, and who became Commissioner of Indian Affairs in 1903. He made efforts to educate Americans to the meaning of his office and to Indian needs; see *The Indian and His Problem* (1910), *In Red Man's Land* (1914).

LEVELERS MOVEMENT, THE, an equalitarian movement which developed during the distraught social circumstances attending the Puritan Revolution *(q.v.)* in England. It was the product of a millenarian movement, related to, but not the same as the Fifth Monarchy movement, which anticipated the return of Christ. Some of the levelers were agrarian in tendency, but their overall appeal was not to the peasants. They were influential among the soldiery of Oliver Cromwell, whom they incited against an arrogant clergy and church, as well as against aristocrats. Leaders among the Levelers were Richard Overton, John and Richard Lilburne, and Gerrard Winstanley, some emphasizing individual rights,

especially during the troubles which attended the Long Parliament, others seeing beyond constitutional issues to communitarian goals. They were active throughout the 1640's, but Cromwell's rise to dictatorial powers ended what had been a species of romanticism in the Puritan psychology; and the Leveler impulse passed. "Leveler" survived long as an epithet, especially employed by aristocrats and elitists. G. E. Aylmer, ed., *Levelers in the English Revolution* (1975).

LEVIN, MEYER (1905-1981), Chicago-born novelist, who employed naturalism in an effort to capture the meaning of his times. *The Old Bunch* (1935) gives an exhaustive portrait of the development of a group of Jewish youth. *Citizens* (1940) is a tale of the Memorial Day Massacre *(q.v.)*. *Compulsion* (1956) was, perhaps, his masterpiece, though it had no more than the status of a best-seller. He helped introduce Anne Frank's *(q.v.)* diary to the American public. Disillusioned with the United States, he asserted his departure from it. Israel *(q.v.)* concerned him deeply; see his *My Father's House* (1947), and his autobiography, *In Search* (1950).

LEVINE, JACK (1915-   ) painter of social content and satire, he made his start in the Federal Art Project *(q.v.)*. His mordant portrait of American generals, exhibited in Moscow at an official American show, roused conservative protest at home that it insulted the American military. President Eisenhower, himself a painter, opined that it was poor art. The American arranger of the show gave her view that the President was no judge. Frank Getlein, ed., *Jack Levine* (1966).

LEWIS, DIO (1823-1886), Boston physician and health reformer. He founded the Boston Normal Institute for Physical Education, invented the first wooden dumbbell, and the game of "bean bag," and phrased the slogan: "a clean tooth never decays." See his *New Gymnastics* (1862); *Our Girls* (1871); *Our Digestion* (1872).

LEWIS, JOHN L. (1880-1969), tempestuous figure in the labor movement, he became chief of the United Mine Workers, their grim conditions of existence giving play to his harsh and peremptory character. (See, for example, Herrin Massacre.) Though long affiliated with the A.F.L., he disagreed with its policy of craft unions *(q.v.)*, demanding an overall organization of the miners. In 1935, he led the movement to form the C.I.O. *(q.v.)*, and supported the Roosevelt Administration. Later, he rejoined the A.F.L., and later still the U.M.W. became an independent union *(q.v.)*. He did not hesitate to take his union out on strike in the midst of World War II: a policy which brought him much criticism. This was the highpoint of his fame and notoriety. Following the war, he became less conspicuous. The rising use of oil created trouble in the coal mining industry, and the U.M.W. on occasions aided the mine-owners in order to keep them in business. A phenomenon of labor, rather than a reformer, Lewis helped dramatize the role of labor in public affairs, for better or worse; see also Guffey-Snyder Coal Act. Saul Alinsky, *John L. Lewis* (1949); David F. Selvin, *The Thundering Voice of John L. Lewis* (1969).

LEWIS, SINCLAIR (1885-1951), realist and satirist from Sauk Center, Minn., who attended Yale University and also Helicon Hall *(q.v.)*. He was briefly a member of the Socialist Party, but found its members too dogmatic for his taste. His best fiction displayed an understanding of his shallow protagonists which was very close to sympathy; a remarkable photograph of Lewis attending a Yale football game long after he attained success shows him wearing a "beanie" and carrying a pennant with evident satisfaction. Several of his writings were plainly in defense of traditional values, as in *The Prodigal Parents* (1938). However, *It Can't Happen Here (q.v.)* was taken to serve reform purposes. *Kingsblood Royal* (1947) was extremely unsuccessful in attempting to contribute to the clarification of the Negro problem.

LEXINGTON, BATTLE OF, an example of propaganda over

facts, it being generally and patriotically supposed by Americans that the British had been repulsed on I xington Green (April 19, 1775). It was the Americans who were repulsed on that place; only later in the day did they counterattack with effect at Concord (q.v.).

LEXOW COMMITTEE (1894), appointed by the Senate of the State of New York to investigate conditions in the New York City Police Department. The Committee's investigations revealed corrupt ties between the underworld and police officials, and resulted in the election of a municipal reform administration. The investigation also taught methods and approaches in dealing with civic problems to numerous reformers and agitators who were subsequently leaders during the Progressive Era (q.v.). See also, Parkhurst, Rev. Charles Henry, Municipal Reform, Crime.

LIBERAL CAPITALISM, see Capitalism and Reform, Jacksonian Reform.

LIBERAL PARTY, a pressure group in New York City politics and state issues, which offered informed opinion on varied subjects, and endorsements which were prized by candidates for office in city and state. Its special committees on such topics as proposals for aiding colleges and universities were staffed by experts who gave a semi-official character to their pronouncements; see also American Labor Party.

LIBERAL RELIGION, identified with such organizations as Unitarianism, the Society for Ethical Culture, the American Humanist Society, reform Judaism, and others which do not observe a hard and fast ritual, or place their religious duties above their social and personal concerns. Whether they constitute religion in a tangible sense is questionable; some repudiate supernaturalism, revelation, and religious traditions. The "religion of humanity" professed in some instances add up to a mild good will or social reform, usually in a middle-class context. Pacifism, cooperative efforts, and mediation between belligerents inspires some younger elements of liberal churches or fellowships. Liberal religion in the suburbs is an instrument of sociality.

LIBERAL REPUBLICANISM, a reaction to the degeneration which Republican leaders perceived to have affected their party under President Grant. The movement attracted such brilliant journalists as E.L. Godkin (q.v.), as well as public figures of the stamp of Carl Schurz, Charles Francis Adams, and Horace Greeley (qq.v.). They met in convention in Cincinnati, in 1872, to nominate a candidate pledged to civil service, responsible politics, and a more positive policy toward the defeated South than was signalled by levies of troops to put down disorders. Their choice of Horace Greeley was ill-advised, since his personal eccentricities, the fact that he had raised bail for the defeated Confederate President, Jefferson Davis, following the Civil War, and other facts, made him a doubtful choice. For that election, however, most Democrats had no alternative to voting for Greeley. Although he made a reasonable campaign, he could not overcome the personal abuse, the waving of the "bloody shirt" (q.v.), and other tactics in which the regular Republicans indulged. The Liberal Republican-Democratic Party was buried in defeat: an abortive third party.

LIBERALISM, a particularly difficult concept in the United States where no tradition of a liberal party has existed to provide a norm for liberal opinion. Both major political parties have liberal phases, and liberalism permeates all avenues of social operation where opportunity is a condition of affairs. It can easily be confused with liberality. In general, it emphasizes the rights of the individual; the Bill of Rights (q.v.) is a liberal document. But the famous "freedom from want" (see Four Freedoms, The) suggested that an economic base was necessary to give meaning to other freedoms. Different situations provided different emphases for liberals; thus, a liberal in Spain emphasized religious liberalism. Communists scorned liberals as unwilling to face the fact that without state power and the crushing of freedom's enemies, there could be no freedom. The collapse of communist

pretensions in America permitted an expansion of liberalism to include liberal conservatives, liberal Republicans, and so forth. Most enigmatic was the southern liberal, which meant, according to the Mississippi journalist, Hodding Carter, that one was called no southerner in the South, and no liberal in the North. In a cold war (q.v.) situation such as Americans endured in 1961, the liberal's prime quality, flexibility, promised to serve him well. However, the youth attack on society—it is doubtful that the embattled dissidents could have described an administration they would have preferred in place of those they challenged—constituted an attack on liberalism as well; see, for example, M. E. Gettleman and D. Mermelstein, eds., The Great Society Reader: the Failure of American Liberalism (1967). From the other end of the socio-political spectrum liberalism was viewed as opening doors which put traditional America at risk, as in Willmoore Kendall and G. W. Carey, Liberalism versus Conservatism (1966). In effect, liberalism, having come far from the circumstances which had produced the key movers of the nation, was seen as a brake on a new world, or a degradation of the old. Liberalism still served some identifying purpose, as for example distinguishing a George Wallace from a Hubert Humphrey, among Democrats, or a Barry Goldwater from a Nelson A. Rockefeller, among Republicans. It had, however, little vibrancy and promise in its own right. Quasi-liberals referred to the "Radical Right." Spiro T. Agnew upbraided "radic-libs" as using their liberal pretentions as a shield to hide their basic pro-communist sympathies. The 1980 elections produced a candidate who proclaimed himself a Libertarian; Ed Clark wanted the state out of government, not interfering with abortion, drugs, or homsexuality, but also doing away with welfare programs, farm subsidies, public education, and whatever else took away from the individual and gave it to the state. Although Clark's program was too drastic for a society interwoven with government, he received a respectable hearing, some votes, and gave evidence that many people wanted less government on their backs. How much they would want, or would get depended on their reading of history; see J. Salwyn Shapiro, Liberalism: Its Meaning and History (1958).

LIBERATOR, THE, a name given to various persons, usually, embodying national aspirations and the hope of social reforms; see Bolivar, Simon; Garibaldi, Giuseppe; O'Connell, Daniel. Also the name of William Lloyd Garrison's (q.v.) newspaper.

LIBERATOR, THE, see Masses, The.

LIBERIA, an American creation, intended to serve as a home for freed American Negroes, where they could demonstrate their abilities, thus encouraging slave-holders to emancipate their slaves in increasingly great numbers. The American Colonization Society (q.v.) was to administer this great enterprise. Progress in building Liberia was disappointingly slow, despite the gifts of Congress and of philanthropists. Slaveholders were reluctant to free their slave property, shiploads of settlers were slow to fill up: most Negroes preferred to stay in the United States. Organization and purpose lagged in Liberia. Power, such as it was, lay in the hands of small, self-serving settler groups. Some reverted to the bush. Though population grew, it showed no striking qualities. Liberia's rubber, oil, and ore were exploited by foreign capitalists, notably American. Resentment against the leaders exploded early in 1980, and, amid blood, promised a more democratic regime, but left open the question of direction. See American Colonization Society. See also C. Clapham, Liberia and Sierra Leone (1976).

LIBERTY, see Abstract Terms.

LIBERTY LEAGUE, organized 1934 to protest against the operations of the New Deal (q.v.), attracted such elements as corporation executives, conservatives among Republicans and Democrats, and others, fearful of the effects upon established ideas which they deemed peculiarly American by such innovations as the National Labor Relations Act (q.v.). Although it did not last long, it did reveal the attitudes of its sponsors. See also America First Committee.

LIBERTY PARTY, significant as a third party *(q.v.)* and because of its striking effect upon the political scene, though it was a small party. Organized by impatient abolitionists, eager to mobilize northern opinion about slavery at the polls, in 1840. The party received only 7,100 votes, and its candidate James G. Birney *(q.v.)* was not even in the country at the time. The Liberty Party was not only ridiculed by major party spokesmen, but by moral abolitionists, too; they argued that it was the duty of abolitionists to ·exert moral pressure on candidates of the mass parties. However, in 1844, the Liberty Party offered Birney again, and his 15,812 votes in New York State, taken away from the Whig ticket of Henry Clay, in a close election, were sufficient to sink the Whig Party in the state and elect James K. Polk over Clay. Thus, it was argued that the Liberty Party had achieved the opposite of its intentions, electing a vigorous pro-slavery Democrat over a middle-of-the-road Whig. Defiant Liberty Party adherents rejected the impeachment, denying that Clay represented an improvement. It was just as well, they thought, to have an unequivocal southern representative in office, and let the North mobilize against him. See also Free Soil Party.

L.I.D., see League for Industrial Democracy.

LIEBKNECHT, WILHELM (1826-1900), an associate of Marx and Engels *(qq.v.)*, leader of the German Social Democratic Party, and editor of its major newspaper, *Vorwarts*. An opponent of the Franco-Prussian War, he was imprisoned for treason in 1872. His son, *Karl* (1871-1919), was a vigorous opponent of war, whose *Militarism and Anti-Militarism* (1907) caused him to be sentenced to eighteen months of imprisonment for high treason. As a member of the Reichstag, he fought to prevent the granting of war credits to the Kaiser. He defied Socialist Party discipline, continued to criticize the government and was sentenced to prison. Liebknecht was liberated following the collapse of the German Empire, in November 1918, and organized the Spartacans *(q.v.)*, who hoped to emulate the Bolsheviks and overthrow the provisional republican regime set up by Friedrich Ebert and other conservative socialists. Arrested with Rosa Luxemburg *(q.v.)*, Liebknecht was with her murdered by police operating under state directions, if not orders. This deed helped embitter relations between communists and socialists in succeeding years.

LILIENTHAL, DAVID E. (1899-1981.), a public servant who was appointed to be one of the three directors of the T.V.A. *(q.v.)*. In this capacity he opposed the nominal chairmanship of Arthur E. Morgan *(q.v.)* and survived him on the board of directors, becoming himself the chairman in 1941. His services in this capacity are controversial, since T.V.A. declined from being a seminal force in the transmutation of the Tennessee Valley into no more than a flood control and power-producing agency. His services as chairman of the Atomic Energy Commission were responsible but not reformistic. He became a convert to the benign and dependable aspects of American business; compare his *TVA: Democracy on the March* (1944), and *Big Business: a New Era* (1953).

LINCOLN BRIGADE, see Abraham Lincoln Brigade.

LINCOLN, ABRAHAM (1809-1865), prime figure in American life, he could be claimed by reformers and anti-reformers. He did not drink hard liquor, but would not associate with temperance societies; he praised labor, but himself acquired a substantial fortune; he favored free soil and expressed distaste for slavery, but was anti-abolitionist and with no regard for the Negroes as individuals; he held on to the Whig Party while others deserted it as a crumbling edifice, but joined them in due course; he sought to avert civil war, offering to carry out the Fugitive Slave Law *(q.v.)*, if the South would remain in the Union, but prosecuted the war with energy. Seeking to be in accord with public opinion, he nevertheless earned its ire by his stubborn unwillingness to agree with its popular and irresponsible views, as in its adulation of General Benjamin F. Butler *(q.v.)*. His Emancipation Proclamation *(q.v.)* freed no slaves of itself, but acted to do so in

some degree; see John H. Franklin, ed., *Emancipation Proclamation* (1963). In the 1970s, he was subjected to "debunking" as a "racist," but was too soundly based for more than trifling challenge. John S. Wright, *Lincoln and the Politics of Slavery* (1970); B. Quarles, *Lincoln and the Negro* (1962); L. Minear, *Lincoln and Slavery: Ideals and the Politics of Change* (1972).

LINCOLN-DOUGLAS DEBATES (1858), attended their competition for a seat in the United States Senate; extraordinary for their refinement of logic and argument, and their democratic appeal to reason, directed not at an élite *(q.v.)*, but at the most ordinary citizen. Though both contestants were essentially conservative, and little separated their viewpoints, their strong respect for democratic processes offered lessons to reformers. R. Z. Kelly, *Lincoln and Douglas* (1954); R. W. Johannsen, ed., *The Lincoln-Douglas Debates* (1965).

LINDBERGH, CHARLES A. (1859-1924) and Charles A., Jr. (1902-1974), a tale in itself of reform and its deterioration; the father was a Progressive, an opponent of intervention in World War I, and a pillar of the Nonpartisan League *(q.v.)*. The rough treatment which pacifist reformers were accorded during the war embittered him. His son became an aviator, his "lone eagle" flight across the Atlantic Ocean, in 1927, made him a national hero at a time when his father had become totally forgotten, apparently by his son as well as his countrymen. He married the daughter of the wealthy American ambassador to Mexico, and engaged in non-political personal and scientific interests. The murder of his son and the vulgar interest attending the event appears to have embittered him, and he moved abroad. He engaged in influential and enigmatic interest in Nazi power, which has been interpreted as reflecting pro-Nazi feeling, on the one hand, undercover work in behalf of the United States, on the other; the facts are not presently known. In 1939, he returned to the United States and lent his name to the America First Committee, *(q.v.)*, and once more a Lindbergh opposed intervention in a war abroad. A motion-picture about him emphasized his contribution as helping to expand the uses of airplanes. It was totally apolitical. See his *The Wartime Journals* (1970).

LINDEMAN, EDUARD C. (1885-1953), liberal educator, began his career as a laborer and social worker, and became associated with the New York School of Social Work, then with the New School for Social Research *(q.v.)*. He helped develop adult education *(q.v.)*. He served as director of the Department of Community Organization for Leisure, a branch of the W.P.A. *(q.v.)*, and was influential in many social work and planning operations of private and governmental agencies. His works included *Social Discovery* (1924), *The Meaning of Adult Education* (1926), and *Leisure: a National Issue* (1939).

LINDSAY, VACHEL (1879-1931), major poet of the Progressive tradition, he put his faith into intuitive understanding of rhythms fitting earthy and loving themes, which, however, he set down with conscious art. His "naivete" respecting religion, idealized sex, and admiration for primitive and rural values undid him in the end, but in his youth gave him the joy and responsiveness which produced such masterpieces as "The Congo," "The Chinese Nightingale," "Bryan, Bryan, Bryan," among others. Lindsay's spontaneity and energy made him a favorite in recitals, which entertained his audiences, as he whispered, sing-songed, and shouted, but his populist effort to rouse them to a purifying excitement, and his failure to do so, increasingly discouraged him. Following art studies, he had begun his career in 1906 by walking the countryside, exchanging poems for food. His great era was the 1910s, when he broke sensationally into fame with his poem "General William Booth Enters into Heaven" (1913). The next year, he published his *Adventures While Preaching the Gospel of Beauty*. By the middle 1920s, a world war and post-war sophistication had made his public appearances more theatrical than inspiring, and though he wrote excellent poems, he felt increasingly insecure and feared for his talent. The coming of the

Depression, and the change in public taste it caused, made Lindsay paranoid and despairing. He died December 5, 1931, having swallowed poison. See Peter Viereck, "Vachel Lindsay: the Dante of the Fundamentalists," in Filler, ed., *A Question of Quality: Popularity and Value in Modern Creative Writing* (1976).

LINDSEY, BENJAMIN BARR (1869-1943), Denver judge, and reformer in the treatment of children brought before the bar. He established a juvenile court, and in 1902 organized the Juvenile Protection Association for the Protection and Betterment of Children. He participated in the concerns of the Progressive Era *(q.v.)*; see his *Problems of the Children* (1903) and *The Beast and the Jungle* (1910), his denunciation of plutocracy. He later developed controversial views of youth and marriage, expressed in *The Revolt of Modern Youth* (1925), and *The Companionate Marriage* (1927). See his autobiographical *The Dangerous Life* (1931).

LINE, especially applied, during the 1930's, to the political program of communist groups. Of particular interest was the "Party line," or line of "the Party," as the Communist Party was known to its adherents and "sympathizers." *(q.v.)*. The sometimes drastic changes in the official line were notorious, most drastic confusion being caused by the Nazi-Soviet Pact. Opponents waxed satiric over variations in the Communist Party's policies, as in parody of a Negro spiritual:

"Ah knows it, Browder, *(q.v.)*,
Ah knows it, Browder,
Ah knows it, Browder,
The Line's been changed again."

LIPPMANN, WALTER (1889-1974), wonder-boy of the youth movement of the 1910's, he came from Harvard University to New York to become a journalist and political commentator. He quickly abandoned a radical viewpoint to assume one positing an elite competent to administer affairs in the interests of people and nation. *A Preface to Politics* (1913) and *Drift and Mastery* (1914) were less significant for their depth or weight of learning than for the hard line of argument contained. As an editor of the *New Republic* (q.v.), he was able to put his ideas into practice. The war seemed to offer him a practical opportunity. As an adviser in the Wilson Administration, he could help contribute to the grand strategy of war, victory, and reconstruction. However, the public which Lippmann and other intellectuals were able to persuade to accept death, following the Armistice turned out to be unwilling to accept the victors's plans for the millennium. Disillusionment provided Lippmann with his deepest insight; in *Public Opinion* (1922) he recognized that there was not one public, but many publics. Increasingly, it became clear that he had no more mastery over them than did those who merely drifted. Although he never ended his search for a master plan, as in *The Good Society* (1937) and *U.S. Foreign Policy: Shield of the Republic* (1943), he failed to persuade his readers that his views had the pragmatic base which had once seemed their primary characteristic. His reputation took an upswing in 1980 by publication of *Walter Lippmann and the American Century*, by Ronald Steel.

LIQUIDATION, popularized by the Russian Revolution, which conceived of itself as righting the wrongs of the ages while concluding, or liquidating, the last remnants of previous, bankrupt, regimes. Liquidation proceeded not only in terms of institutions and agencies, but of individuals, who were "liquidated" as occasion seemed to demand, and who continue to be.

LISTEN, YANKEE: THE REVOLUTION IN CUBA (1960), by C. Wright Mills, *(q.v.)*, report by a sociologist seeking to present the Cuban point of view with respect to Fidel Castro *(q.v.)* and the United States. It was praised by persons fearing that American prestige had been harmed by its efforts at intervention in Cuban developments, praised also by the communists, and criticized by others who believed that Cuban developments demanded reprobation.

LITERACY Test Law, see Immigration and Reform.

LITERATURE AND SOCIAL REFORM. Literature has served conservatism as well as it has reform; this is worth emphasis in view of the belief of some radicals and reformers that distinguished men and women of letters of the past "belong to us." The essay by Ernest Crosby *(q.v.)*, *Shakespeare's Attitude toward the Working Classes* (1903), which inspired Leo Tolstoi's more famous diatribe on *King Lear*, argued that Shakespeare was conventional and unfair in his treatment of the lower classes. It illustrated the proposition that there is no necessary connection between literary stature and reform attitudes. In America, antireform can claim such distinguished names as Washington Irving, James Fenimore Cooper, Edgar Allan Poe, Henry James, Paul Elmer More, Willa Cather, and John P. Marquand, among many others. Moreover, few reform writers were "universal reformers," but mixed particular reform interests with conservative, and even anti-reform, convictions.

Nevertheless, American literature includes one line of writing distinctly sympathetic to social reform. Bacon's Rebellion *(q.v.)* inspired the anonymous "Bacon's Epitaph, by His Man," one of the earliest of fine American poems. The American Revolution *(q.v.)* resulted in many nobly-expressed sentiments, including some by Benjamin Franklin, Thomas Paine, Thomas Jefferson, and Philip Freneau *(q.v.)*. The reform era of 1830-1850 was prolific in producing gifted reform writers, though their qualities required careful discrimination. Thus, Nathaniel Hawthorne *(q.v.)*, in *The Scarlet Letter* (1850), was critical of the intolerance of his Puritan ancestors, but he was also critical of contemporary reform, as in his *The Blithedale Romance* (1852), which satirized Brook Farm *(q.v.)*. Walt Whitman's *(q.v.)* generous Jacksonian principles were limited by his practical indifference to the problems and point of view of Negroes.

Others were more categorical in their dedication to reform causes. Henry D. Thoreau advocated civil disobedience to evil laws. Richard Henry Dana, Jr., in his *Two Years before the Mast* (1840), exposed the cruel treatment of seamen by ship's officers. Wendell Phillips uttered immortal apostrophes to freedom. John Greenleaf Whittier, James Russell Lowell *(qq.v.)*, and others, in verse and prose, took their places with the reformers.

During the post-Civil War decades, a tradition of reform writing was developed which included, as high-water marks, Henry George's *Progress and Poverty* (1877), Edward Bellamy's *Looking Backward* (1887), Henry Demarest Lloyd's *Wealth against Commonwealth* (1894), Hamlin Garland's *Main-Travelled Roads* (1891), and Edwin Markham's "The Man with the Hoe" (1897) *(qq.v.)*. The muckraking period *(q.v.)* which followed built upon their foundations, and produced numerous authors whose prose especially presented a vision of society requiring changes of every kind. Although major reform writers abandoned reform, for the most part, during World War I, a few, like Upton Sinclair and Charles Edward Russell *(qq.v.)*, continued to campaign against an unjust society, as they saw it, in fiction or essay.

Post-World War I decades produced no major poet, storyteller, or essayist of social reform. The social antagonisms created by militant patriots opposing militant internationalists created a tradition of writers whose work contained revolutionary implications much more than it did social reform. Such writers as John Dos Passos, James T. Farrell, Michael Gold, Kenneth Fearing, and Albert Halper sought to expose what they thought of as infirm civilization, rather than to rescue it. Their movements and point of view was a casualty of World War II. Typical efforts to defend their achievements are James T. Farrell's, *The League of Frightened Philistines, and Other Papers* (1945), Granville Hicks's, *Where We Came Out* (1954), and John Dos Passos's *The Theme Is Freedom* (1956). Dos Passos later wrote unanalyzed fiction which reversed his earlier psychological view of American life, but which did not achieve the fame and study of the *U.S.A.* series.

Post-World War II literature produced no distinguishable current of authors, reform or otherwise, other than the youth (*q.v.*) eruption which did not, however, feature words as art. Works by J. D. Salinger, Jack Kerouac, John Cheever, Sylvia Plath, Larry McMurtry, William Burroughs, Joyce Carol Oates, Ken Kesey, among others tended toward "drug culture" or unrelated but equally nationally-undirected themes. The gurus (*q.v.*) of writing were Saul Bellow and Norman Mailer, one making panoramas of insignificant people, the other the bad boy of current events who fancied himself, and perhaps was, the successor of Ernest Hemingway, though without his achievement in the short story.

LITTLE, FRANK H., CASE, like that of Wesley Everett at Centralia (*q.v.*), was a product of vigilante (*q.v.*) enterprise. Little, a one-eyed I.W.W. organizer of Indian ancestry, was fearless in his work among the unorganized, that labor element in which the Wobblies (*q.v.*) specialized. He was one of their leaders in the 1909 battle for free speech; in Spokane, Washington, he was badly handled by the police for having attempted to read the Declaration of Independence from a soapbox. He was also bitter in his opposition to war. This combination of traits aroused ire which came to a peak when, in 1917, he went to Butte, Montana, to help the embattled miners there conduct a strike. Seized by anonymous persons, he was dragged behind a car to a railroad trestle, on July 31, and hanged. The atrocity was one of a number carried out as part of creating a war-time unity. Patrick Renshaw, *Wobblies* (1967).

LITTLE MAGAZINES in the 1890's and 1900's, like Michael Monahan's *The Phoenix*, considered themselves harbors for individualism. In the 1910's, they emerged as the organs of the Youth Movement (*q.v.*). Magazines like *Poetry*, the *Masses*, the *Little Review*, the *Seven Arts* depended on sponsors, rather than advertisers, they believed themselves concerned for quality, rather than, as with the "popular magazines," popularity. They were concerned for experiment, and, as with the oddly-named *Masses*, individualist and also socialist principles. In the 1920's, they emphasized individualism often to the point of deliberate obscurity, as in the *Fugitive*, *Broom*, and *Secession*, though the *New Masses* held up the banner for communism. They declined during the 1930's, though the John Reed Clubs (*q.v.*) sponsored little magazines for their writers. With the end of World War II, and a new generation of introvert writers and escapists, little magazines proliferated without distinction on the open market, but augmented by subsidized little magazines on college campuses, in neither case marked by notable individualism, experimentation, or social concern.

"LITTLE N.R.A.," see Guffey-Snyder Coal Act.

LITTLE ROCK, ARKANSAS, one of a number of key cases in the South's "massive resistance" (*q.v.*) to integration. Involved was the question of policy on admission to public schools. Governor Orval E. Faubus set himself up as a defender of traditional segregation. A relatively liberal Arkansas congressman, Brooks Hays, was unseated by a write-in candidate who had been firm on segregation as a member of the school board. In 1957-8, Central High School included nine Negro students, thanks to the presence of Federal troops. In August 1958, Faubus closed the four high schools, and in the fall a private all-white high school was incorporated. Through the following year, the city struggled to reach a solution satisfactory to them, and satisfying the law, the school board and its membership being a major scene of controversy. In August, 1959, it was announced that the schools were being opened. Rabid segregationists sought to stop the entrance of the three Negroes assigned to Central High and three to a second high school, but order was maintained. By May 1960, seven Negroes were attending Central, four the other high school. There was no evidence that Little Rock had softened in its attitude toward Negroes.

"LITTLE STEEL," popular name for the Bethlehem, Republic, Inland, and Youngstown Sheet and Tube steel corporations. Republic Steel was its leader, and, under Tom M. Girdler, resisted the organization of the steelworkers: a policy leading to the Memorial Day Massacre (*q.v.*).

"LIVING NEWSPAPER, THE," see Federal Theater Project.

LLOYD, HENRY DEMAREST (1847-1903), famous for his *Wealth against Commonwealth* (1894), a classic and eloquent expose of monopoly, concentrating on the Standard Oil Company (*q.v.*). Significant was Lloyd's own development, from free trade to socialist principles, which, as in the case of Eugene V. Debs (*q.v.*), revealed a dissatisfaction with older liberal principles. In his trips to New Zealand, Switzerland, and elsewhere, he sought new social techniques which could be utilized on the American scene. Among his important works, some issued posthumously, were: *Labor Copartnership* (1898); *A Country without Strikes* (1900); *Man, the Social Creator* (1906); *The Swiss Democracy* (1908).

LOBBY, LOBBYING, LOBBYISTS, the latter sometimes said to constitute a "Third House." Persons representing special interests, including particular industries, organizations, sectional concerns such as farming, mining, fishing, are present in state capitals, as well as in Washington, to concern themselves with legislation which might affect the interests of their clients. Early lobbyists were often patent corruptionists, intent upon influencing legislators to pass particular laws. Lobbyists have since become a complex tribe which claims to perform a public service, in providing the legislators with detailed information which they could not readily come by in ordinary ways. Laws requiring lobbyists to register their presence has cut to a minimum common bribery and pressure, since it has focused public attention upon them. Nevertheless, the line separating friendly concern and legitimate persuasion from devious purposes and illegal operations has continued to be hazy and to attract the concentrated analysis of reform journalists. "Lobbying" has continued to connote questionable meddling with legislative operations; see, however, People's Lobby, The; Marsh, Benjamin C.

LOCHNER V. NEW YORK (1905) struck down a minimum-wage law; Justice Holmes (*q.v.*), in celebrated language, argued, in his dissent, that the Fourteenth Amendment (*q.v.*), in the name of which the decision was made, "does not enact Mr. Herbert Spencer's Social Statistics"; that is, that liberty is not the liberty to oppress people.

LOCKE, JOHN (1632-1704), English philosopher, whose works offered American leaders of resistance to British policy, during the era of revolution, intellectual grounds for defiance of law. His own practice was conservative; the constitution which he drew up (1669) for the proprietors of the Carolinas was feudal in structure. However, his "Essay Concerning Toleration" (1666), his "Essay on the Human Understanding" (1690), and his "Two Treatises on Government" (1690), among other works, offered aid to new ideas. Locke rejected a priori reasoning, appealing to experience for truth. He upheld natural rights, and asserted that a sovereign who defied them lost his privileges. Locke did not favor all revolutions; he was apologizing for the Glorious Revolution of 1688. The colonists, however, found him useful for their own purposes. S. P. Lamprecht, *Locke: Selections* (1971).

LOCKOUT, a "strike on the part of the employer," who finds labor demands unsatisfying, opposes unionization proceedings, or otherwise seeks to preserve his plant by closing it to his employees. The Taft-Hartley Act (*q.v.*) and the National Labor Relations Board (*q.v.*) provided the frame of reference to determine the validity of a particular lockout.

LOCKWOOD, BELVA A. (1830-1917), a former teacher and school-mistress who was early widowed and later remarried, she became a lawyer, lobbied energetically for laws giving women Federal employees equal rights with others, among other such legislation, and became the first woman admitted to practice before the U.S. Supreme Court. She was nominated for President by the Equal Rights Party of California *(q.v.)* and prepared reasonable programs for it, herself making good appearances before audiences. She handled claims in law, notably for Indian tribes, and put her training at the service of the woman's rights strategists. She wrote much and spoke at many conferences in favor of peace among nations.

LOCOFOCOS, the radical wing of the New York Democratic Party in the 1830's, which took seriously the equal rights asseverations of the Jacksonian leaders. The designation was given in 1835, at a meeting in Tammany Hall, the regular Democrats sought to stifle the radicals by turning off the gaslights and dissolving the meeting. The radicals struck friction matches, called locofocos, to keep the room lit. Although they soon dissipated their energies, they left a tradition of reformist zeal; compare Barnburners. F. Byrdsall, *The History of the Loco-Foco or Equal Rights Party* (1842).

LODGE, HENRY CABOT (1850-1924), historian, conservative Republican Senator from Massachusetts, leader of the fight for immigration restrictions, friend of Theodore Roosevelt; best known for his leadership in the Senate fight for rejection of the League of Nations, and scapegoat to those who held rejection a blow to the possibilities of world peace, though he was supported by major progressives. See also Isolationism and Reform. *Henry Cabot Lodge, Jr.* (1902-), his grandson also a Senator from Massachusetts, became United States Ambassador to the United Nations (1953-1960). J. A. Garraty, *Henry Cabot Lodge* (1953); H. C. Lodge, Jr., *The Stream Has Many Eyes* (1973).

LOEB-LEOPOLD CASE (1924), involved the premeditated murder of fourteen-year old Bobby Franks, May 21, 1924. Richard A. Loeb and Nathan Leopold *(q.v.)* were the eighteen and nineteen-year old sons of rich Chicago parents. Loeb was the youngest graduate of the University of Chicago, Leopold had mastered thirteen languages and seemed destined for a phenomenal career. Loeb, a reader of pulp-paper murder tales, aspired to being a master-criminal; Leopold was then imbued with a superman philosophy. Although they planned murder, Loeb casually and Leopold not at all were acquainted with the young neighbor whom they murdered, and who happened accidentally into their hands. When apprehended, following the failure of their "perfect crime," the death penalty was asked for them. Clarence Darrow defended them solely on an anti-capital punishment argument, his plea for mitigation of sentence being based upon their personalities rather than their sanity, which he conceded. By strong implication, he indicted the society which had produced them. The extraordinary interest in the case shown by the public indicated a respect for his arguments; the anti-capital punishment movement was given a strong push, which it had lost during World War I. Loeb and Leopold were sentenced to life imprisonment. Loeb was murdered under savage circumstances, in 1936, by a fellow-prisoner for reasons which continue obscure, despite the claim of his friend Leopold that the murder had no warrant. Nathan F. Leopold, Jr., *Life Plus 99 Years* (1958); Meyer Levin, *Compulsion* (1956); Louis Filler, "Meyer Levin's *Compulsion*," in *A Question of Quality* (1976).

LOG CABIN AND HARD CIDER CAMPAIGN (1840), conducted by the Whigs *(q.v.)*: evidence that elections have symbolic significance for Americans, as well as practical relationship to their problems. The Democrats inadvertently gave the Whigs the theme for their campaign by derogating their candidate, William Henry Harrison, as a shabby old soldier who too much enjoyed his jug of cider. Although Harrison was a Virginia aristocrat, Whigs seized upon this to portray their candidate as an honest frontier patriot, serene before his log cabin, and featured log cabins during parades and rallies, in the course of which they distributed free hard

cider. They contrasted their candidate, too, with his opponent, Martin Van Buren *(q.v.)*, whom they depicted as an aristocrat; actually, he was the son of an upstate New York farmer. Whig demagogy won over Democratic demagogy, in this campaign; and though the Whigs gained little from their victory, Harrison dying soon after assuming office, the campaign signalled a new concern for the lower-class voter. H. R. Shurtleff, *The Log Cabin Myth* (1939); R. G. Gunderson, *The Log-Cabin Campaign* (1957).

LOGAN (1725-1780), an Indian chief of the Mingo tribe, led them in waging war against the Virginians (1774), in retaliation for an attack by settlers upon his family. During subsequent negotiations, he delivered himself of sentiments which were made famous by reproduction in Thomas Jefferson's *Notes on the State of Virginia*: one of the notable statements by Indians on their circumstances and qualities. He had been a friend of the white men, he said, and had rejected war. Nevertheless, all his family had been wiped out by the interlopers: "This called on me for revenge. I have sought it. I have killed many. For my country I rejoice at the beams of peace; but do not harbor a thought that mine is the joy of fear. Logan never felt fear. He will not turn on his heel to save his life. Who is there to mourn for Logan? Not one."

LONDON, JACK (1876-1916), writer and spokesman for both socialist and social Darwinian *(qq.v.)* ideas; born out of wedlock, he had a hectic and adventurous youth in the Bay Area of the west coast, engaged in fishing and gold mining, as well as joining Coxey's Army *(q.v.)*. A rather short adventure in the Klondike, during the Gold Rush, also netted him material which he later exploited in stories. He became famous for adventurous tales emphasizing the struggle between men and nature, notably in *The Call of the Wild* (1903) and *The Sea-Wolf* (1904). At the same time, he asserted his socialist principles, as in *The War of the Classes* (1905), and helped to establish the Intercollegiate Socialist Society *(q.v.)*. Other significant works included *The People of the Abyss* (1903), describing the tragic life of London's East Side, *The Iron Heel* (1907), describing a fascist-type revolution, once admired by socialists who were unaware of London's racist compulsions, and his greatest novel, the autobiographical *Martin Eden* (1909). *John Barleycorn* (1913) described his career as a drinker. He varied socialist views with living in grand style, charm and simplicity with arrogance and indifference to others, dedicated prose with hastily-produced screeds intended only to make money. In one of his moods of confusion and depression, he committed suicide. See Richard O'Connor, *Jack London* (1964).

LONDON ECONOMIC CONFERENCE (1933), called by the League of Nations and intended to create a currency stabilization program helpful in curbing the international depression and creating cooperation between the western nations. Franklin D. Roosevelt, concentrating on domestic problems, was reluctant to commit himself to any program which would limit his freedom of action in the area, and therefore set conditions which essentially undermined the Conference, thus signalling a retreat to nationalism in Europe, isolationism in the United States.

LONDON SCHOOL OF ECONOMICS, founded by a grant from the Fabian *(q.v.)*, Henry H. Hutchinson, it has attracted many liberals and radicals who came to study under such instructors as Harold Laski *(q.v.)*, returning to such far points as India and the United States to involve themselves in contemporary events. William H. Beveridge, *London School of Economics and Its Problems* (1960).

LONG, HUEY P. (1893-1935), the individual who showed the greatest capacity for making an effective tool of fascism in the United States, he came legitimately by his radical perceptions, coming from a parish in Louisiana which had a radical tradition. However, he became a lawyer, a party leader, and an effective demagogue who was able to draw upon literate English for national audiences, and upon homely backwoods language for his humbler constituents. As governor of Louisiana and U.S. Senator, he not only fastened his hold entirely upon his home state, but was increasingly influential throughout the South, and with sympathizers in the North as well. He instituted genuine reforms in Louisiana, in terms of roads, educational facilities, and other social wants, but did so by paying his supporters and punishing his foes. In addition, he permitted a high incidence of corruption. His "Share-Our-Wealth" (q.v.) program, casuistically developed under the general slogan "Every Man a King," borrowed from an inspirational writer, Orison Swett Marden, was flexible and intended to attract power to his organization and self. His national associations included Dr. Townsend and Father Coughlin (qq.v.), as well as patent and conscious fascists. Having been influential in securing the Democratic nomination for Franklin D. Roosevelt, he was outraged at having been ignored by him after he became President, and made him a target for virulent appeals to dissatisfaction. His career ended by assassination, and he became a legend of unfulfilled power, as well as the subject of numerous studies and many novels, the most famous being Robert Penn Warren's *All the King's Men* (1946).

LONGSHOREMEN, like the teamsters (q.v.), a key element of labor which could be decisive in national crises and which is formidable at all times. Though generally distinguishable from seamen (q.v.), they are intertwined with them in a complex of unions, and, for that matter, with unions in such other labor areas as railway transport. In addition, the considerable amount of autonomy existing in the West Coast, East Coast, and Gulf shipping areas makes for problems in cooperation, union rivalries, corruption, and, occasionally, heroic struggles. Such unions as the International Longshoreman's Association, the National Maritime Union, counting some 37,000 members in 1961, the Seafarers International Union, with its Atlantic, Gulf, and Lakes sections counting 22,000, and such others as the Sailors Union of the Pacific and the Marine Cooks and Stewards on the West Coast, quarreled and cooperated as separate units and within district and international councils. Famous among the leaders were Harry Bridges (q.v.), organizer of the general strike (q.v.) in San Francisco in 1934, and Joseph E. Curran, who led a desperate strike in 1936 out of which grew the National Maritime Union. Both of these leaders freely used communist cooperation in building their organization against desperate opposition. The unions produced idealists in their early stages of organization. Better times, coupled with valuable union funds, made the longshoreman organizations targets of gangsters and other criminal elements, who found aid among unionists for various reasons. Thus, legislation intended to make ex-convicts ineligible to hold union offices was protested as preventing reformed convicts from making an honest living, causing organizational difficulties, and raising constitutional questions.

LOOKING BACKWARD (1887), see Bellamy, Edward.

LORENTZ, PARE (1905-   ), pioneer in motion-pictures of social significance: the famous "documentaries." *The Plow that Broke the Plains* (1936) and *The River* (1937) were, following the 1930's, ignored by those who contrasted "art" with "mere" photography, but appeared to receive the status of classics in the late 1950's and early 1960's. *The River* and commentary were made into a book (1938). Robert L. Snyder, *Pare Lorentz and the Documentary Film* (1968).

LOS ANGELES BOMBING, see McNamara Case.

LOTTERY, a reform of the nineteenth century, it was attacked in the 1830's and 1840's as immoral, as depriving the poor, and as serving cheats of various types. Banned is most eastern states, it flourished in the western territories, and received a renewed and definitive attack, from the states and Federal government, in the 1890's. Arguments in its favor reappeared from time to time, and in the 1960s it was completely rehabilitated, furnishing revenues for states.

LOVE, ALFRED HENRY (1830-1913), American pacifist and Friend who refused to accept the Civil War despite the libertarian principles alleged to be at stake, and explained his stand in *An Appeal in Vindication of Peace Principles* (1862). He was a spokesman for the Universal Peace Union, and was later held as notorious because of his opposition to the Spanish-American War. He was also an earnest advocate of abolition of capital punishment, and sought to turn his organization, the Pennsylvania Prison Society, to his viewpoint.

LOVE, see Free Love.

LOVEJOY, ELIJAH PARISH (1802-1838), editor and abolitionist, became a symbol of free speech (q.v.). Ordained a Presbyterian minister in 1833, he went west as a domestic missionary. As editor of the *St. Louis Observer*, he denounced "popery" and slavery. His latter cause aroused protest. After his office was gutted by a mob, he moved across the Mississippi River to Alton, Illinois. There, three presses were destroyed by mobs opposed to his abolitionist principles. Lovejoy's fourth press was placed in a warehouse which was besieged by armed rioters. During its defense by a group led by Lovejoy, he was struck down by a bullet. His death, wrote John Quincy Adams (q.v), sent a "shock as of an earthquake throughout this continent." His brother *Owen* (1811-1864), a clergyman in Illinois who became a congressman, was ardently anti-slavery but supported Abraham Lincoln in his rise to the Presidency.

LOVEJOY, OWEN R. (1866-1961) social worker and child labor reformer, who left the ministry to form the National Child Labor Committee, which he served as secretary till 1926. He continued his work in behalf of children through the Children's Aid Society, and was assistant director of the American Youth Commission.

LOVESTONITES, followers, in the 1930's, of Jay Lovestone, a leader of the Communist Party, U.S.A., who sought a moderate approach which would enable his party to be influential in the nation's affairs during its "prosperous" 1920's period. Utilized by the Stalinist leadership in the Communist International to expel the Trotskyites, his faction was then itself expelled, though it contained a majority of the membership. Known as the "Right Opposition," that is, to the official Communist Party, it maintained some influence in the labor movement. It later met in convention and declared itself bankrupt in political ideas, and dissolved as an organization. Lovestone continued to consult with labor officials, and, later, to offer information to government officers concerned with labor and related problems. Best known of the Lovestonites was Bertram D. Wolfe who became a noted authority on communism.

LOVETT, ROBERT MORSS (1870-1956), University of Chicago literature professor who became a noted liberal, turned active and unequivocal by the execution of Sacco and Vanzetti (q.v.). He contributed to the work of the League for Industrial Democracy, the American Civil Liberties Union (qq.v.) and other such organizations, and in the 1930's did not hesitate to work with communists in communist front (q.v.) organizations in which he believed. He became a civil liberties case when, accused of holding communist ideas, he was dismissed from his post as government secretary of the Virgin Islands, and his salary withheld by act of Congress—a deed which was overthrown by decision of the Supreme Court. See his autobiography, *All Our Years* (1948).

LOWBROW, a cultural illiterate, to be distinguished from "highbrow." Lowbrows are not necessarily under-educated persons: college graduates often admit to being lowbrow, meaning that they read little and do not concern themselves with social and intellectual affairs. They often despise "highbrows" for being "intellectuals," that is, cut off from earthy, "human" responses. "Highbrows" and "intellectuals" (q.v.) have often been criticized by reformers as being remote from vital concerns and activities, and self-centered and irrelevant in their thinking. Van Wyck Brooks was critical of a nation separated into highbrows and lowbrows, but increasingly appeared to be no more than one of the former himself.

LOWELL, JAMES RUSSELL (1819-1891), in his youth a poet and wit, he added gaiety and insight to criticism, in his *A Fable for Critics* (1848), and in his *Biglow Papers* (1848 volume) used the vernacular to satirize conservatism, and to denounce the Mexican War *(q.v.)*. He turned conventional as he grew older, and though his *Commemoration Ode* (1865) praised Lincoln, it did so with rhetoric rather than the highest art. Still later he was U.S. minister to Spain and to Great Britain. His conservative criticism and essays have a strength of their own, but none of the vitality of his earlier work.

LOWELL, JOSEPHINE SHAW (1843-1905), one of the greatest social reformers of the late nineteenth century, she suffered the tragedy of early widowhood to the Civil War hero, Col. Charles Russell Lowell. She absorbed herself in social work, wrote durable reports for the New York State Board of Charities designed to improve attention to women, the handicapped, and the criminal, and founded the influential Consumers' League of New York and the Women's Municipal League, and issued her pioneer *Industrial Arbitration and Conciliation* (1893). See Filler, "Josephine Shaw Lowell," in *Appointment at Armageddon.*

LOWELL OFFERING, THE (1839-1845), a literary by-product of the experiment in labor-capitalist relations, in Lowell, Massachusetts, the first company town set up in the country. The mill-girls, mostly from the country, were supposed to be uplifted and raised in status by their employment. Visitors were shown their living quarters and work areas, and invited to appreciate their pleasing aspects. *The Lowell Offering* printed the literary effusions of the girls. However, it soon became clear that the purpose of the mill was to make money, and the idealistic frills were abandoned. See Hannah Josephson, *The Golden Threads* (1945).

LOYALISTS, those who, during the American Revolution, supported the British cause, opposing the patriots, as they styled themselves. Loyalists in America were also known by their foes as Tories, though Whigs in Great Britain also supported the war against the colonies. However, during the Spanish Civil War (1936-9) *(q.v.)*, the Loyalists were those who supported the Madrid government of liberals and radicals against the attacks of the fascist columns of Generalissimo Francisco Franco.

LOYALTY DAY, see May Day.

LOYALTY OATH, a byproduct of national alarm and indignation over the implications of the Hiss Case *(q.v.)*, and similar affairs. A number of states required teachers to sign avowals of loyalty to the nation, and the National Defense Education Act required disclaimers. Liberal and other teachers and administrations were indignant, asserting that the oath accomplished nothing not already accomplished by other legislation, and represented no more than a bullying gesture. They made efforts to have loyalty oaths removed from among the statutes. John H. Schaar, *Loyalty in America* (1957). See also Patriot.

LOYALTY ORDER, issued by President Truman, March 22, 1947, was in response to dissatisfaction with the excesses of liberalism, as it seemed to its critics, especially in such groups as the House Un-American Activities Committee *(q.v.)*, and was intended to provide authority for determining possible disloyalty within the Federal service, and dispensing with that of persons proved to be of doubtful or subversive tendencies.

LUCE, HENRY ROBINSON (1898-1967), magazine tycoon, eternally associated with *Life, Time,* and *Fortune,* and often held to have harmed American culture by making stipendiaries of sensitive and talented writers and artists. He believed that they were not very talented, and were being paid properly for what they were doing. W. A. Swanberg, *Luce and His Empire* (1972).

LUDDITES, named for a leader, a man named Lud, of the rioters at Nottingham and other English towns who opposed the introduction of machinery into industry as a threat to labor (1811-12, 1816).

LUDLOW AMENDMENT (1938), sponsored by Representative Louis Ludlow, of Indiana, which demanded that, except in the course of a national emergency, Congress would be constrained from declaring war except by authority of a national referendum. A poll of the time indicated that a majority of Americans then believed that a referendum was desirable. President Roosevelt put his authority against the movement for a constitutional amendment on the subject, and it failed to advance in the House of Representatives.

"LUDLOW MASSACRE" (1914), a tragic incident in the battle between miners and mine-owners in Colorado. The miners had organized a tent colony which included women and children. The state militia sought to evacuate them, and, in accordance with this aim, burned their tents, in the course of which two women and eleven children died, as well as a number of miners. On the site is a memorial to the dead; the mines have long since been abandoned.

LUMPENPROLETARIAT, German for demoralized workers; a concept especially known among communists of the 1930's, for whom it explained the rise of fascism. Elements of labor, soured from perpetual unemployment, remembering with regret the days of their war service, during which they had enjoyed a sense of power and dignity, envious of others in better circumstances, eager to accept explanations for their lack of consequence: such persons were ready candidates for fascist military units. A term employed in the *Communist Manifesto.*

"LUNATIC FRINGE," one of Theodore Roosevelt's *(q.v.)* striking phrases, apparently intended to distinguish sane reformers from crackpots, but actually including a solid bulk or reformers in its purview, as his letters to such non- or anti-reformers as Henry Cabot Lodge *(q.v.)* and Sir George Otto Trevelyan make plain.

LUNDEEN, ERNEST (1878-1940), midwestern statesman who served in the Spanish-American War *(q.v.)*, but who became a sharp partisan against war. In the House of Representatives (1917-9), he voted against entering the war and against conscription. In the 1930's, he conducted the first Congressional referendum on war. He opposed American participation in the League of Nations. *(q.v.)*. He had been a La Follette *(q.v.)* Republican in his Minnesota district, 1910-4, and became a Farmer-Laborite. He entered the U.S. Senate in 1936. An associate of Lynn J. Frazier and William Lemke *(qq.v.)*, he was wooed by fascists; see *Under Cover (q.v.)*, by John Roy Carlson. He died in a plane crash.

LUNDY, BENJAMIN (1789-1839), a pioneer abolitionist, he organized the Union Humane Society in Ohio, in 1815, and began publication of the *Genius of Universal Emancipation,* in 1821, both landmarks in a career of "gradual" abolitionism. He sought to develop colonization enterprises in Canada, Texas, and elsewhere, not, however, in order to rid the United States of Negroes, but to help them organize their resources and hasten emancipation. In 1836, he was active in the campaign to prevent Texas from being brought into the Union on a pro-slavery basis, and that year established the *National Enquirer* as an aid in the work. He helped bring William Lloyd Garrison into the antislavery crusade.

LUSK COMMITTEE REPORT, named for Senator Clayton R. Lusk, of New York State, who headed a joint legislative committee which investigated "seditious" activities and published a four-volume report calculated to reveal a network of "Reds," up to the year 1920.

LUXEMBURG, ROSA (1870-1919), German socialist and theoretician; she was imprisoned (1915-18) during World War I for her anti-militaristic stand. She joined Karl Liebknecht *(q.v.)* in organizing the communist-style Spartacus Party, and with him was arrested by police of the moderate Socialist government, and murdered. This action helped build up the antagonism between communists and socialists.

LYCEUM, a movement of the 1820's and after, intended to provide people with interesting or famous speakers, offering information or eloquence; the movement became popular and resulted in organization of the National American Lyceum which attracted famous and interesting speakers who spoke on set circuits; Emerson *(q.v.)* made much of his living addressing Lyceum audiences, presenting his set speeches which later appeared in book form as essays. The Lyceum movement was both a means for extending popular education and for binding the North together in terms of the material presented by its most admired speakers. It was succeeded, in post-Civil War decades, in its essential functions, by Chautauqua which, however, played a less strategic role in reform.

LYNCH LAW, equated with the operations of a "mob"; *cf.* Vigilantes. Lynching often took place throughout the West, especially during the era of the cowboy, there being a minimum of law-enforcing agencies available. However, it was there perceived mainly in terms of justice or injustice; see Walter Van Tilburg, *The Oxbow Incident* (1940) for a literary narrative of a western tragedy. Lynching was also prevalent in the Old South before the Civil War, affecting many more white people deemed malefactors than blacks, though lynching of Negroes related directly to support of the slavery system. In the post-Civil War era, lynchings rose proportionately to the effort of white southerners to recapture political control of their section particularly in the 1890s. When this goal was achieved, the percentage of lynchings diminished. The work of the N.A.A.C.P. *(q.v.)* was crucial to giving publicity to these atrocities and educating the public to its purposes and recurrence. Measures developed during the New Deal and World War II years *(qq.v.)*, in the 1930s and 1940s, and mounting civil rights agitation which gave augmented power to Negroes throughout the South, all but put an end to lynching as a social measure, and made accounts of them historical; See NAACP, *Thirty Years of Lynching in the United States* (1919); Walter White, *Rope and Faggot* (1929).

LYON, MATTHEW (1750-1822), ardent Jeffersonian who became a national issue for having written critically of President Adams and been sentenced to prison under the Sedition Act *(q.v.)*. His party re-elected him to Congress while he was still in jail. His life continued to reflect his democratic impulses; he moved to Kentucky, where he continued to be a factor in society and politics.

MACDONALD, JAMES RAMSEY (1866-1937), Scottish labor leader, known for his rise from poverty to leadership of the British Labour Party in 1911, and his Parliamentary career which, in 1924, made him first Labour Premier of the British Government. After that known for his "renegacy" from labor and social principles.

MACHIAVELLI, NICCOLO DI (1469-1527), Italian historian and student of political science, whose *The Prince* (1513), based on the career of Caesar Borgia (1475-1507), has been taken to be a masterpiece of cynicism, a realistic view of political exigencies for the society involved, or a satirical expose intended to create its own antidote. "Machiavellian" tactics seemed to reformers inseparable from feudal and capitalistic societies, and to be distinguished from those employed by democrats and socialists. Their experiences in the twentieth century made famous the epigram of Lord Acton (1834-1902), English historian: "Power corrupts, and absolute power corrupts absolutely." For its relevance to American affairs, see Louis Filler, "Machiavelli for the Millions," in D. Madden, ed., *American Dreams, American Nightmares* (1970). See also, Orwell, George.

MACKENZIE, WILLIAM LYON (1795-1861), Scottish-born Canadian, journalist, and Queentown (later Toronto) agitator for Canadian reforms, he made an armed effort (1837) to seize Toronto, but was forced to flee across the border to the United States, where he served eighteen months in prison for breaking the neutrality laws. Released, and before he was granted amnesty to return as a distinguished patriot to Canada, he became a pioneer American muckraker *(q.v.)*, exposing great masses of secret corrupt correspondence related to the Jackson and Van Buren *(qq.v.)* Administrations; see Mackenzie's *The Lives and Opinions of Benj'n Franklin Butler...Van Buren...and Their Friends and Political Associates* (1845), of which 50,000 copies were printed. Mackenzie's *Life and Times of Martin Van Buren* (1846) added materials to the previous revelations, announcing, indirectly, the advent of a new, democratic politics. Mackenzie's epic career in America was lost between Canadian indifference and American acceptance of the new politics, as well as a conspiracy of silence among Democratic Party historians. See also Royall, Anne, and Filler, "William Lyon Mackenzie," in *Appointment at Armageddon.* Stephen Leacock, *Mackenzie* [et al] (1926), E. C. Guillet, *The Lives and Times of the Patriots* (1938).

MACLEISH, ARCHIBALD (1892-   ), poet and publicist, who filled among other roles, including government posts, that of Librarian of the Library of Congress and Harvard University professor. Following a "pure art" period, he turned out poems deemed significant in the 1930's and constituting his claim to "social significance" *(q.v.)*, including *Frescoes for Mr. Rockefeller's City* (1933), *Panic* (1935), and *America Was Promises* (1939). He later spoke in behalf of Ezra Pound *(q.v.)*.

MADISON, JAMES (1751-1836), "Father of the Constitution" and a member of the Virginia planter aristocracy. He prepared many of the *Federalist* (q.v.) papers, presenting essentially conservative arguments in favor of ratification of the Constitution, working in concert with Alexander Hamilton and John Jay. His subsequent career in support of Jeffersonian principles, varied with Hamiltonian sympathies, helps to explain that the differences between Virginia and New York were a matter of time and circumstances, rather than principles. M. D. Peterson, ed., *James Madison: a Biography in His Own Words* (1974).

MADISON SQUARE GARDEN PAGEANT (1913), a brilliant conception prepared by John Reed (q.v.) with the aid of other talented artists and intellectuals, dramatizing a great strike then going on in Paterson, New Jersey, silk mills. The event attracted a great crowd, and some twelve hundred strikers whose lives were being sketched in scenes and music. A giant electric sign outside Madison Square Garden flashed the letters "I.W.W." (q.v.), leaders of which organization were heading the strike which ultimately took in Passaic and Hoboken, New Jersey, and other cities. The Pageant represented a union of the efforts of intellectuals and workers and "focused the attention of millions of Americans on the intolerable conditions and labor relations existing in the textile industry" (Ralph Chaplin (q.v.), Wobbly).

MAFIA, a Sicilian secret society of criminals, which affected Italian elements in the United States, as soon as their immigration went under way in the 1880's. A high point was the killing of the Chief of Police of New Orleans in 1890, which resulted in the lynching of 11 Italians by local citizenry who broke into prison. This occasioned an international incident, the U. S. paying the families of the slain Italians "in comity" (friendship). The interlinking of the Mafia organizations with routine American affairs was a discouraging factor during the post-World War II period, though respectable Italians protested against having one American strain of criminals singled out from others. Disturbing was the Mafia being accepted by the public as just being engaged in business, as was any business; such was the message, read and viewed on screen by a substantial percentage of citizens, in Mario Puzo's The Godfather (1969). Even more disturbing were revelations that a President had shared the friendship of a female with a Mafia figure (see Judith Exner, My Story 1977), who had also trafficked with the CIA (q.v.) on doubtful missions. See G. Selvaggi, The Rise of the Mafia in New York (1978); Joseph Albini, The American Mafia (1971); N. Gage, Mafia U.S.A. (1972); Peter Maas, The Valachi Papers (1969).

MAGNA CARTA (1215), "Great Charter," a landmark in the development of constitutional guarantees, result of a struggle for power between the English King John (though supported by the Pope) and his feudal barons. Though a totally feudal document, concerned for established privileges, it stipulated that "No freeman shall be arrested and imprisoned... unless by the lawful judgment of his peers and by the law of the land." Reformers have used Magna Carta to designate acts which seemed to advance their causes, thus referring to the Clayton Act (q.v.) as the Magna Carta of Labor, and the Seamen's (q.v.) Act of 1915 as the Magna Carta of the American Seamen.

MAHAN, ALFRED THAYER (1840-1914), United States naval officer and historian of the significance of the navy in world affairs; see, for example, his The Influence of Sea Power upon History 1660-1783, (1890). His views had a great influence on American expansionists, notably Theodore Roosevelt (q.v.). He was an American delegate to the first Hague Peace Conference (q.v.).

MAILER, NORMAN (1923-   ), whose The Naked and the Dead (1948) painted an authentic picture of men in war. Mailer's first response to civilian life following army service was left-wing sympathy, expressed in the symbolic Barbary Shore (1951). He resisted publishers's authoritarianism in Advertisements for Myself (1959), but, made free, embarked on a personal safari of drugs, egocentric impressions of serious events, including The Armies of the Night (1968), which won him wide attention but was unenlightening respecting the clash of dissidents and the Pentagon (q.v.). Similarly, Of a Fire on the Moon (1970) added nothing to knowledge, psychological or otherwise, of space probes. Mailer sometimes perceived that he had basically become an entertainer, but had no time or occasion to question a large reading public which permitted him to toy with substantial questions.

MAIN-TRAVELLED ROADS (1891), see Garland, Hamlin.

"MAKE WORK," see Federal Emergency Relief Administration.

MAILS, see Sunday Mails.

"MAINE LAW" (1851), see Prohibition.

MALCOLM X (1925-1965), born Malcolm Little, a phenomenon of the 1960s, who, following a career of crime, was converted to the "Nation of Islam," a sect which resisted American ways. An energetic and magnetic "Black Muslim," Malcolm X as he became emerged as a personality who attracted followers so successfully as to rouse the jealousy of his coworkers, who suspended him from the organization late in 1963. Early the next year he formed a rival group in New York, The Muslim Mosque, Inc., spoke with the militancy of the time, and made trips to the Near East to create a wider base. Differences with the original organization led to his assassination in February 1965. The Autobiography of Malcolm X, done with the Negro writer Alex Haley, and issued after Malcolm X's death, gave him a place in the lore of protest, emotional attitudes obscuring the fact that he had died by the hands of those in his own larger community; Peter Goldman, Malcolm X (1972); C. E. Lincoln, The Black Muslims in America (1973).

"MALEFACTORS OF GREAT WEALTH," Theodore Roosevelt's famous denunciatory phrase for irresponsible industrial and financial leaders. A typical Rooseveltian phrase, it exhibited great vigor and offered no detail; it could thus appease public dissatisfaction without presenting any particular threat to capitalists, malefactors or otherwise.

MALTHUSIANISM, in the principal work of Thomas R. Malthus (1766-1834), Essay on the Principles of Population (1798), maintains that the production of food cannot keep up with the increase in population, and thus causes hunger and poverty. He advocates restriction of marriages and the curbing of family growth. Socialists repudiated his doctrine as an apology for exploitation practices, and asserted that there was enough for all under a reasonable social order. Malthus was denounced and ridiculed by a wide variety of reformers and revolutionists, including William Godwin, Henry George, Karl Marx, and Karl Kautsky (qq.v.). However, modern reform has countenanced the usefulness of birth control (q.v.), and the classic case of China as illustrating Malthusianism in practice has been borne out by the drive of China's communist leaders to enforce birth control. Oddly, the Malthus hypothesis entered into later liberal thinking, in its assumption that the world was one of scarcity, requiring controls and an equitable parcelling out of available goods. This view was protested by those advocating the benefits of free enterprise and private creativity and initiative.

"MAN WITH THE HOE, THE," (1899), see Markham, Edwin.

MANAGERIAL REVOLUTION, THE (1941), by James Burnham, a study by a former Trotskyite (q.v.) which held, pessimistically, that democracy was being pulverized by authoritarian forces. Socialism was an impossibility; the author took the U.S.S.R. (q.v.) to be proof that it must fall to dictators. Capitalism, with attendant free enterprise, he saw as having failed. In its place was rising a race of managers with a totalitarian capacity. Compare, Croly, Herbert.

MANCHESTER LIBERALISM derived from the activities of a notable group of English businessmen who fought for repeal of the Corn Laws, which, discriminating against wheat brought into England from the outside, in the interests of English wheat-growers, kept the price of bread high. John Bright, Richard Cobden, and others, were denounced by the landed aristocracy as hypocrites, who sought to undermine "English corn" while themselves maintaining an inhumane factory system. But the Manchester Liberals maintained they were supporting free enterprise, while supporting free trade (q.v.), and implemented their program with an interest in international peace, immigration—which would relieve unemployment and build up new areas—and other tenets. E. L. Godkin (q.v.) brought them over from Great

Britain, and made the *Nation* a repository of them; with William Graham Sumner *(q.v.)*, he was their most notable exponent. Grover Cleveland *(q.v.)*, was a less learned but influential Manchester Liberal; his conversion to free trade, in 1887, was a courageous act and cost him a second term as President. His fight against free silver *(q.v.)* emphasized his commitment to free enterprise, as, during his second term as President, did his aid in breaking the Pullman Strike *(q.v.)*. His anti-imperialism was confused: he rejected the treaty of annexation with Hawaii (1893), but supported Secretary of State Richard Olney's aggressive challenge to Great Britain (1895), during the Venezuelan Dispute *(qq.v.)*. Herbert Hoover's *(q.v.)* Manchester Liberalism emphasized free enterprise and peaceful aid to international friends, but laid aside free trade in the interests of nationalism. Manchester Liberals have tended to emphasize principles; cf. Humanitarianism.

MANCHURIA, one of the great way-stations to World War II, signalled Japan's abrogations of its treaties with the United States and the League of Nations signatories; on September 18, 1931, its army units invested key Manchurian cities, and followed further invasion measures by establishing a puppet state. The League of Nations revealed its impotence to halt the development of Japan's imperialistic designs. See also Ethiopian War.

MANIFEST DESTINY, a slogan identified with "Young America" *(q.v.)*, the Democratic Party, and, especially, the southern states, which hoped to divert attention from the slavery issue by leading the nation in an expansionist program which would patently give it more than enough land to satisfy pro-slavery plantation owners and anti-slavery free soilers. The first known use of the phrase was by John L. O'Sullivan, editor of the *United States Magazine and Democratic Review*, in 1845, having the acquisition of Texas *(q.v.)* in view. However, Oregon, to the north, also concerned the expansionists, certainly those who were northerners. (See Wilmot Proviso.) The mystic note in "Manifest Destiny"—that God had manifestly intended Americans to spread over the continent—continued to influence American thought, and even thoughts of reformers, as with Albert J. Beveridge *(q.v.)*, but it was resisted, successively, by northerners fearful of slavery's expansion, by such Manchester Liberals as E. L. Godkin *(q.v.)*, by anti-imperialists of the stamp of Moorfield Storey *(q.v.)*. By World War I, "Manifest Destiny" was not being used even by ardent imperialists, in a world of major powers and stirring underdeveloped countries, it was too arrogant and truculent to be useful in foreign diplomacy. F. Merk, *Manifest Destiny and Mission in American History* (1966).

MANN, HORACE (1796-1859), noted educational reformer; as a Massachusetts legislator, he aided Dorothea Dix *(q.v.)* in her crusade for institutional improvements. As first secretary of the Massachusetts Board of Education (1837-48), he renovated the decayed public school system of his state, created the first normal school in the United States, and issued annual reports which were landmarks in American educational theory. He was John Quincy Adams's *(q.v.)* successor in the United States House of Representatives and an outstanding political abolitionist *(q.v.)*. As first president of Antioch College *(q.v.)*, he developed memorable principles of educational accomplishment. Jonathan Messerli, *Horace Mann* (1972); Louis Filler, ed., *Horace Mann on the Crisis in Education* (1965).

MANN ACT, THE (1910), a product of sensational exposes during the reform era, it made the transportation of women and girls across state lines for immoral purposes a legal offense, and perpetrators subject to fines and imprisonment. Though reflecting Puritan tenets, this Congressional Act provided legal agents with a weapon which helped them combat criminals engaged in interstate commerce, and has attracted no substantial criticism from reformers.

MAO TSE-TUNG (1893-1966), Chinese revolutionary leader and theoretician, who, on taking power over mainland China *(q.v.)* in 1949 became "Chairman Mao" at home and to admirers abroad, including the United States. His stand as leader of a world power offended Soviet Leaders, as did his criticism of them as seeking "peaceful coexistence" with the West. Mao's leadership of the "Proletarian Cultural Revolution" in the later 1960s was intended to cleanse the Chinese Communist Party of his competing and ideological opponents. It was a drive which cost many lives and reputations. Conspicuously raised was Jiang Qing, Mao's wife, who led the young fanatical Red Guards in their terror campaign against moderates, in power struggles and pitched battles all over the country. By 1968, compromises had been reached on all levels of party and provincial leadership, the Red Guards diminished, and Mao's position as first among the foremost at least technically maintained. Meanwhile the China-Soviet schism intensified, the several million troops stationed on both sides of their border a constant reminder of issues between them. An extraordinary turn-about in 1972 saw the anti-communist President Nixon in China for conversations on detente *(q.v.)*, precisely the policy Mao had denounced in United States-Russian relations. In 1974, Mao, beset by high functionaries who continued to attract elements dissatisfied with the Chinese economy or prospects, announced a new Cultural Revolution, but lacking the power he had still wielded a few years back. He died in 1976. His wife tried to help maintain his apparatus with herself in a favored role. In 1980 her pretentions collapsed with her arrest as part of a "Gang of Four" charged with crimes against the revolution. At her trial she defied her accusers, taking refuge behind her dead husband's prestige. Though Mao had been subtlely demeaned, there was no such drastic attack as had taken place during the "thaw" which followed Stalin's *(q.v.)* death. Accusations of murder and misrule were permitted to stand against Jiang, and proved mainly accurate. However, she was not executed, but given two years to reform. E. E. Rice, *Mao's Way* (1972); E. Stuart Kirby, ed., *Contemporary China* (1958); Klaus Mehnert, *Peking and Moscow* (1963); Tai-Sung, *Mao Tse-Tung's Cultural Revolution* (1972); Stephen Uhalley, Jr., *Mao Tse-Tung: a Critical Biography* (1975).

MARBURY V. MADISON (1803), foundation stone of Supreme Court authority, a *coup d'état* by John Marshall *(q.v.)*. Aware that the administration of Thomas Jefferson *(q.v.)* was determined to undermine the Court, Marshall sought a case which would permit him to assert the right of the Court to review the laws of Congress, without being defied and discredited. Section 13 of the Judiciary Act of 1789 had empowered the Supreme Court to issue writs of mandamus, that is, to order something done, in cases of differences between citizens and the government. William Marbury, appointed a justice of the peace of the District of Columbia by outgoing President John Adams, was refused his commission by Secretary of State James Madison *(qq.v.)*, and sued for a writ. Marshall agreed that Marbury deserved his commission, but denied that he had power to grant the writ on the grounds that the Constitution did not give him that power. Thus, Marshall gave up this privilege, in exchange for the greater privilege of interpreting the Constitution and being able to overthrow an act of Congress. W. M. Jones, *Chief Justice John Marshall: a Reappraisal* (1956).

MARCANTONIO, VITO (1902-1954), controversial New York politician, who began his career as La Guardia's *(q.v.)* secretary and manager. He proved to be a skillful manipulator who won nomination of the Republican and City Fusion parties and served in Congress, 1934-6. Defeated in the latter year, he returned to Congress in 1938. In 1940, he was read out of the American Labor Party; he had been read out of the Republican Party in 1938, but continued to enjoy the loyalty of his constituents of both parties. He was re-elected in that year. He continued to find support among the major parties, and to play politics with them successfully. His enemies declared him to be a fellow-traveler *(q.v.)* and to remark that his program never departed far from that of the

Communist Party. Nevertheless, he achieved state chairmanship of the American Labor Party *(q.v.)*, and put his influence in the scales for the candidacy of Henry A. Wallace *(q.v.)*, in 1948. This was a turning point: his try for the office of mayor of New York City, in 1949, netted him small return, and, in the 1950 congressional race, the Democrats and Republicans united to defeat him; see Annette T. Rubinstein *et al.*, *I Vote My Conscience; Debates, Speeches and Writings of Vito Marcantonio, 1935-1950* (1956).

MARCUSE, HERBERT (1898-1979), philosopher of the youth *(q.v.)* revolt, he was a legitimate student of Freud and society whose conjectures took him beyond conjecture in the need of disruptionists to find civilized endorsement of their random actions, before Vietnam *(q.v.)* gave them a cause. (See also Guru.) Marcuse's love of the socialist ideal and hatred of whatever inhibited its coming took the form of hating the well-being of workers in America, and calling for violence to combat affluence and stability. Accordingly, he received unexampled popularity on campuses for his *Eros and Civilization* (1955), which scorned the repression and sublimation principles in Freud *(q.v.)* as rejecting the values in violence; and especially *One-Dimensional Man* (1964), which preached violence and derogated Gandhiesque, and Martin Luther King's *(qq.v.)* passive resistance as mere submissiveness. Such counsel, plus that in *An Essay on Liberation* (1969) and *Counter-Revolution and Revolt* (1969) made him a major force in the turmoil of the time, though his unattractive prose style and inability to see the results of his hypotheses ensured that much of his work would become period pieces rather than seminal, certainly in socialist-style countries. See Alasdair MacIntyre, *Herbert Marcuse* (1970).

MARIJUANA, significant as being a drug capable of inducing euphoria and even hallucination, yet relatively mild in its effects, and so a relatively persuasive argument for the loosening of laws governing its use. Opponents of such decontrol protested that it was a first step toward the use of more exciting and habit-forming—"heavier"—drugs, and particularly harmful to younger people who could be brought into the "drug culture" at the expense of their more responsible growth. Advocates of decontrol argued that marijuana was far less harmful than alcohol use, alcohol being less subject to regulation. See also Narcotics Problem. J. Kaplan, *Marijuana—the New Prohibition* (1970); J. S. Hochman, *Marijuana and Social Evolution* (1972).

MARKHAM, EDWIN (1852-1940), author of "The Man with the Hoe" (1899), most famous of all poems of reform. During the 1900's, Markham was accepted popularly as the poet and conscience of American democracy. His series on "The Hoe-man in the Making" *(Cosmopolitan*, 1906-1907; published in book-form, 1914) is a landmark in the campaign against child labor *(q.v.)*. Louis Filler, *The Unknown Edwin Markham* (1966).

MARRIAGE, see Companionate Marriage, Divorce.

MARSH, BENJAMIN C. (1877-1952), reformer, whose causes included work for the A.S.P.C.A. *(q.v.)*, for numerous social work organizations, for city planning programs, and others involving civic standards and needs. As a lobbyist *(q.v.)*, he was signally successful in fighting the effort of Henry Ford to acquire Muscle Shoals *(q.v.)* in the early 1920's. His most distinguished achievement was the People's Lobby, organized in 1931, through which he fought for public enlightenment, and in the public interest. He was a critic of the New Deal *(q.v.)*, which he accused of "passing the buck to Providence and the bill to posterity." See his posthumously-published *Lobbyist for the People* (1953).

MARSHALL, JOHN (1755-1835), one of the greatest of Americans, in thirty-five years on the U.S. Supreme Court he set his seal on all American law. He was essentially a conservative, who was determined to set up precedents against intemperate experimentation, to encourage capitalism by defending the permanence of contracts, and to help create a strong central government. That his views found some response in the body politic there can be no doubt. Had the country not been willing to accept his findings in Marbury v. Madison, he had no power to enforce it. (See Marbury v. Madison.) His work sometimes aided specifically reactionary, sometimes manifestly reform situations. Thus, Fletcher v. Peck *(q.v.)* permitted scoundrels to preserve their booty; Worcester v. Georgia *(q.v.)* on the other hand, gave support to persecuted Indians. See also Supreme Court and Reform.

MARSHALL PLAN (1947), essentially a plan to bolster the economy of nations so that they could resist agitation from within which might make them liable to revolutions and be strong enough to meet communist threats from abroad. A Committee for European Economic Cooperation sought to determine Europe's needs, and the Foreign Aid Act of that year, providing funds for several nations was followed by a European Recovery Program. The Marshall Plan was no more than an economic support for the earlier enunciated Truman Doctrine, which expressed American determination not to permit Russian power to spread, but, rather, to support its potential victims with arms and the sinews of peace. Isolationists and critics generally of government spending observed the flow of goods abroad and protested that it made us no friends, was draining our resources, and that the nations which received our foreign aid were not being strengthened by it. Less recalcitrant Americans interpreted the aid as a sign of American "generosity," and could not understand why we did not attract friendship and admiration; see also Point Four Program, Foreign Aid. H B. Price, *The Marshall Plan and Its Meaning* (1955).

MARTÍ, JOSÉ (1853-1895), Cuban literary figure and revolutionary leader, whose ardor for freedom forced him into exile. He traveled to Spain, to Mexico and Guatemala, and lived for fifteen years in New York. He died during the revolutionary effort against Spanish rule. His writings are relevant not only to Cuban and Spanish American life, but to the United States; see the selections in *The America of José Martí* (1953).

MARX, KARL (1818-1883), founder of "scientific socialism," and one of the most influential thinkers of all time. The son of a converted German Jewish lawyer, he studied law and philosophy and interested himself in journalism. In 1844, he accepted socialism, and, having examined the theories of Proudhon, Saint-Simon *(qq.v.)* and others, concluded that only a materialistic base to socialist conceptions could ensure their validity. He studied history and political economy, and, with Friedrich Engels *(q.v.)* entered upon studies which culminated in their publication of the *Communist Manifesto* *(q.v.)*. His major work in the organization and direction of the First International *(q.v.)* is matched, in the field of action, with his major work in the field of theory: *Das Kapital* *(q.v.)*. However, his steady flow of polemical writings and correspondence were more influential in the last analysis than either bulking achievement, and have been given at least as much attention by students and activists, from Moscow around the world, possibly the least attention being accorded in the United States. David McLellan, *Marx before Marxism* (1970); David Childs, *Marx and the Marxists* (1973); Paul Mattick, *Marx and Keynes: the Limits of the Mixed Economy* (1971).

MARXISM, the Bible of scientific socialism *(q.v.)*, and believed by its adherents to open to them an understanding of the basic principles underlying human life and its social development. It involves dialectics, the materialist conception of history, the dictatorship of the proletariat *(qq.v.)*, among other tenets. Its dependability is a matter of interpretation. Thus, the U.S.S.R. suffered one desperate defeat after the other in the 1930's, in the fall of Germany to Hitler, the fall of Spain to Franco, the failure of the Third International *(q.v.)* to produce internationalism, the shameful record of the U.S.S.R. in the Russo-Finnish War, and the powerful thrust of the Nazis against Russia, which reduced the Ukraine, threatened Moscow and Leningrad, and threatened the Soviet regime entirely. Yet it came back, not only to win its great share of the spoils, following the defeat of Germany, but to become leader of the undisillusioned international communist movement, including China, as well as numerous underdeveloped countries and highly developed Czechoslovakia. In the United States, survivors of the youth uprising worked into the establishment as government employees and educators, maintaining as remnants of their past their status as "Marxists," a presumably legitimate analysis of American ways and operations. Such adjustments took odd turns; see Ronald Radosh, *Prophets on the Right: Profiles of Conservative Critics of American Globalism* (1975), which looked afar for its critics of American "imperialism," from the liberal Charles Beard to the fascist Lawrence Dennis (*qq.v.*), and Todd Gitlin, *The Whole World Is Watching: Mass Media in the Making and Unmaking of the New Left* (1980), by a former "activist" become a "Marxist" sociologist. See also, I. Deutscher, *Marxism in Our Time* (1971); R. Aaron, *Marxism and the Existentialists* (1970); Clinton Rossiter, *Marxism: the View from America* (1965).

MASARYK, THOMAS GARRIGUE (1850-1937), founder of Czechoslovakia (*q.v.*), out of some of the most valuable lands of the old Austro-Hungarian Empire. During World War I, he traveled, seeking support for his plans, and was influenced by his study of the American Revolution and the subsequent history of the United States under the Constitution. With Eduard Beneš (*q.v.*), among other Czech patriots, he in 1918 set up a provisional government; in 1920, the new republic went under way. Masaryk was president during most of the period till his death. Z. Zeman, *Masaryks: The Making of Czechoslovakia* (1976).

MASON, GEORGE (1725-1792), "father of the Bill of Rights"; Virginia aristocrat whose regard for states' rights and the rights of the individual (within the context of his class bias) caused him to emphasize their establishment in law. At the Virginia convention in 1776 to draft a constitution, he did much of the work, and his Declaration of Rights found expression, in considerable degree, in the Declaration of Independence and the later Bill of Rights (*qq.v.*).

MASONRY, see Anti-Masonry.

"MASS ACTION," see Mob. "Mass" has been a favorite word with those tending toward revolutionary attitudes, more so than with reformers. Mass meeting, mass following, the *Masses*, massed might: such phrases have reflected idealized views of the people *en masse*. Reformers tend to suggest the individual, to whose heart and mind they can appeal. See, however, Terrorists.

MASS MEDIA, see Popular Arts.

MASS PRODUCTION, to the reformer an opportunity or a threat, depending on the uses to which it is put. E. A. Filene's (*q.v.*) outlook made it the inevitable solvent of the world's troubles. Friends of the Soviet Union cheered her efforts, advertised in the 1930's, to achieve mass production. The theory of "controlled depreciation" (*q.v.*) was based upon ever increasing mass production. Another type of reformer has feared the effects of mass production on the individual, and on the quality of the product. *1984* (q.v.) warned, in part, against a tepid and mediocre civilization coming. Such theorists as Arthur E. Morgan (*q.v.*) have sought to build up the potential of small business. Compare Morris, William.

MASSACHUSETTS AND VIRGINIA, for reformers constituting a study in contrasts and similarities. Although "the Old Bay State" prided itself on its democratic history, the Puritan fathers sought freedom for themselves; they were bigots respecting others, driving Roger Williams and Anne Hutchinson (*q.v.*) out of their colonies—to be sure, they founded other Puritan colonies. The democratic heart of their system was congregationalism (*q.v.*), which produced Emerson as well as the Salem Witchcraft trials (*qq.v.*). Virginia, in its turn, produced the House of Burgesses (*q.v.*), a democratic

body, though limited to an élite, and bringing on Bacon's Rebellion (*q.v.*) and a tradition of dissidence which could claim such giants as Thomas Jefferson and George Mason (*qq.v.*). Yet Virginia also fostered slavery (*q.v.*).

MASSACRE, a propaganda word, as in the Boston Massacre (*q.v.*), but often used in the history of industrial warfare, as with the Memorial Day Massacre (*q.v.*). The most noted massacre in western history is that of St. Bartholomew (*q.v.*), though Tamerlane put some 100,000 Hindu prisoners to the sword in 1398, and many other mass-slaughters have been consummated, in successive eras. See, for example, Katyn Forest Murders, *Final Solution, The.*

MASSES, THE, a creation of the New York intellectuals, an element of the "Youth Movement" (*q.v.*), in 1911. They included Max Eastman, John Reed, and Randolph Bourne (*qq.v.*). Its art was superior to its verse, and that to its fiction: the youth was more concerned for itself than for reality. Most curious was its title, in view of their temperament; the famous jingle went:

> They draw nude women for the *Masses*,
> Thick, fat, ungainly lasses,
> How does that help the working classes?

Nevertheless, there was a fresh, perceptive note, for example in Art Young's (*q.v.*) cartoon showing two young lovers in the moonlight, the boy remarking: "Gee, Mag, look at all them stars. Thick as bedbugs." More grim was the fight of the *Masses*, in 1917-8, with the government, on the issue of the magazine's pacifism; its publication was suspended that year. Soon after, Eastman began to issue *The Liberator*, which continued until 1924, becoming firmer as time passed in its communist views. In 1926, the *New Masses*, headed by communist party members and their sympathizers began to appear.

"MASSIVE RESISTANCE," concept proposed by Senator Harry F. Byrd of Virginia to oppose integration (*q.v.*) in the South. In this campaign, school children were locked out of schools to prevent integration. The educational routine for white children suffered, though perhaps not quite so seriously as that for Negroes. See Benjamin Muse, *Virginia's Massive Resistance* (1961).

"MASSIVE RETALIATION," policy of the U.S. Department of State announced in 1954: there was to be a new emphasis on atomic instruments of war as a deterrant to would-be attackers. The announcement gave concern to those who sought peaceful solutions to the duel being waged between communists and anti-communists, since it seemed to them to encourage a build-up of retaliatory devices which could be touched off by any accident.

MASTER RACE, a concept identified with the German people, by their enemies, who traced it to Friedrich Nietzsche, and its effect on Kaiser Wilhelm, whom they blamed for World War I. Nietzsche dreamed of supermen, rather than of a master race, and he despised the mob. If a German warrior class was, in fact, influenced by Nietzsche—which is doubtful; a monograph should establish whether they read his poetic prose—it was to limited ends. Jews died in the German trenches for the Fatherland, during World War I. Germany was allied with the somewhat earthy Bulgarians. There was a distinct contrast between the Germans of World War I, and those who accepted the atrocities perpetrated by Nazis with the equanimity appropriate to a master race. The deeds of the latter held the concept up to hatred and contempt which was not abated by the fiery failure of Nazism, its arraignment at Nuremburg (*q.v.*), and the Eichmann trial (*q.v.*).

MATERIALIST CONCEPTION OF HISTORY, also known as *historical determinism* and *economic determinism*, promulgated by Marx and Engels and postulating the realities of history as deriving from class structures based upon control of the means of production and the methods of distribution. Thus, ideals of justice and human purposes became rationalizations of these fundamental realities, no more than culture "superstructures" created on the more substantial bases of economic relations.

MATSU, see Formosa.

MAY, SAMUEL JOSEPH (1797-1871), noted antislavery figure of Syracuse, New York. He also vigorously favored woman's rights and educational reform, at one time heading the normal school which Horace Mann (*q.v.*) established. See his *Revival of Education* (1855), and *Some Recollections of Our Antislavery Conflict* (1869).

MAY DAY (May 1), once universally celebrated as a day for showing working class solidarity throughout the world. Derives from a proposal offered at the International Socialist Congress, held in Paris in 1889 that a day be set aside for publicizing the 8-hour day (*q.v.*) program. May 1 had already been fixed by the A.F.L. (*q.v.*) for a demonstration to be held in 1890, and was accepted. As of 1891, May Day was given broader meaning in the labor and radical movements. May Day is a major celebration in the Communist world. Since World War II, it has almost disappeared in the United States. In 1948, New York City proclaimed May 1 as Loyalty Day, and in succeeding years the state and other cities followed the practice, on occasion with rites and parades. In 1955, President Eisenhower first proclaimed it to be Loyalty Day.

MAYFLOWER COMPACT, suggesting reform, to those who have not troubled to read it; in reality a means for instituting law and order, since some of the *Mayflower* passengers had voiced individualistic sentiments, and alarmed their more responsible or conservative companions.

MAYHEW, THOMAS (1592-1662), a founder and governor of Martha's Vineyard in Massachusetts, who aided and Christianized the Indians of that island; known as the patriarch of the Indians. His grandson, *Experience Mayhew* (1673-1758), translated portions of the Bible into the Indian tongue, and carried on further civilized associations with the Indians; see his *Indian Converts* (1727). His son, *Jonathan* (1720-1766), was an influential Congregationalist minister of Boston, noted for his eloquence, and for views which helped create justifications for revolutionary action. See his *Discourse Concerning Unlimited Submission and Non-Resistance to the Higher Powers* (1750), and *The Snare Broken* (1766), which coped with the Stamp Act (*q.v.*).

MBOYA, TOM (1930-1969), Kenya leader and agitator for the freedom of Africans from the domination of the white people. A labor leader and a scholarship student at Oxford University, he proved to be adroit and persuasive so far as his own people were concerned and a liaison figure between them and their anti-colonial sympathizers abroad. For Kenya, he demanded total self-rule. Admired by other African peoples as representing the kind of leadership they desired, he was elected chairman of the All-Africa People's conference held in 1958 in Accra, Ghana. In 1960, when Kenya became independent, he was made Minister of Economic Planning and Development. A spokesman for himself as well as Africans, he issued his autobiography in 1963, *Freedom and After*. He died by assassination in 1969, at the hands of a political oppositionist. President Jomo Kenyatta prepared the foreword to a volume of Mboya's speeches and writings, *The Challenge of Nationhood* (1970). See also Mohamed Amin, *Tom Mboya: a photograph Tribute* (1969).

MCCARRAN-WALTER ACT (1952), a major change in the immigration-restriction system set up in 1924. In addition to preserving the quota (*q.v.*) system based on national origins and curbing the number of immigrants who could be admitted into the country, it raised criteria of subversion or possible subversion which made it difficult for suspected aliens to be admitted, and easy for suspected aliens to be deported. In

his veto of the bill, which Congress nevertheless made law, President Truman wrote: "These provisions are worse than the infamous Alien Act of 1798 (*q.v.*), passed in a time of national fear and distrust of foreigners, which gave the President power to deport any alien deemed 'dangerous to the peace and safety of the United States.'"

MCCARRAN-WOOD ACT OF 1950, passed over the veto of President Truman, was aimed directly at the Communist Party and affiliated organizations, and intended to augment national security by depriving its adherents of entree to government work and by making them liable to internment during periods of national emergency. It also deprived aliens of access to the United States who were shown to have been members of related organizations.

MCCARTHY, CHARLES (1873-1921), originator of the first reference library for the use of legislators and others concerned in law-making affairs, in the state capital, Madison, Wisconsin; he was also first director of the U.S. Commission on Industrial Relations. He thus helped to develop, within his state, what became later known on a national level as "The Brain Trust." See his *The Wisconsin Idea* (1912) (*qq.v.*).

MCCARTHY, EUGENE (1916-   ), a phenomenon of the 1968 elections, he played an uneventful Senate role, where he questioned CIA (*q.v.*) foreign activities, but voted for the "Gulf of Tonkin Resolution" which gave President Johnson (*q.v.*) the mandate for conducting war in Vietnam. Having lost confidence in the conduct and purpose of the war, McCarthy urged withdrawal, but without recognizing the difficulties therein. However, his announcement of candidacy for the Presidency drew the dissatisfied to his side, and, March 1968, enabled him to astound the political world by winning twenty of the 24 convention seats in the New Hampshire primaries. "Clean Gene," as his enthusiasts termed him, to ensure his distinction from another McCarthy (see "McCarthy Era"), thereafter proved irresolute and directionless; and though he lost a major opponent in the assassination of Robert F. Kennedy, he was soundly defeated at the Democratic Convention by Hubert Humphrey (*qq.v.*) Thereafter, the McCarthy forces dissolved, as did his political career: a vagary of the time. See his *A Liberal Answer to the Conservative Challenge* (1965), and *The Year of the People* (1969).

"MCCARTHY ERA," so designated by liberals and others who believed that the activities of Senator Joseph R. McCarthy constituted an irresponsible low in American political life and a threat to democracy. Exploiting a national disillusion with the good faith of communists and their friends and fellow-travelers (*q.v.*), thanks to revelations of espionage, of communist groups in government, and, most sensationally, the Hiss Case (*q.v.*), the junior Senator from Wisconsin made news with sweeping charges of the existence of communist groups in the higher echelons of the government. As chairman of the Senate Committee on Government Operations, he dealt harshly with people summoned before it for questions, and was arbitrary in his definitions of what constituted communism, suspicious behavior, or civil rights. The heavy pall of accusations which he laid about himself was created with little plan or direction. McCarthy did not hesitate to open fire at the most respectable elements in government because they did not sufficiently cooperate with him. Yet his career of stirring up suspicions continued for four years. In 1954, he was himself in position of having to defend himself from a disturbed Department of the Army, at a Senate investigation. The hearings were unprecedented in the national interest they attracted, considering that he was but one person who had accomplished relatively little from the great forum on which he had found himself. The hearings were inconclusive, but attention to McCarthy subsided rapidly, though his supporters insisted he had done a great work of agitating for attention to the communist problem. Compare William F. Buckley, Jr., and L. Brent Bozell, *McCarthy and His Enemies*

(1954) and Robert Griffith, *The Politics of Fear* (1970). See also Earl Latham, ed., *The Meaning of McCarthyism* (1965).

MCCLELLAN COMMITTEE, set up in 1957 in the U.S. Senate, to investigate corruption in labor unions exposed shocking cases of gangsterism and fraud, notably among the longshoremen on both the east coast and the west coast, and in the great Teamsters Union. Public sensibilities were particularly touched by the fact that both areas of labor were strategic in the national economy, and that both had produced heroic labor action in their time: in the San Francisco General Strike of 1934, led by the longshoremen, and in the general strike of truckers, that same year, organized with bloody and powerful effect in Minneapolis. The parade of uncooperative witnesses and of criminal types, the revelations which put the wealthy head of the teamsters in prison for embezzlement, harmed the public image of labor. Labor held that there was a component of persecution in the McClellan hearings: that it ought to be investigating industry as well. (Industry was investigated; see Price Fixing.) But the pot calling the kettle black did not impress the general public. Labor's reputation continued to suffer, and the McClellan Committee to be influential in this connection. Bewildering statistics about salaries drawn by workers at Cape Canaveral, while their union insisted on policies which prevented adequate prosecution of the program to conquer space by rockets appalled readers, in 1961.

MCCLURE, SAMUEL S. (1857-1949), one of the greatest of American editors, he pioneered in establishing the McClure's Syndicate, in 1884: a service which supplied stories and other material to many publications, rather than to one: a democratic idea which helped to disseminate cultural materials. With his syndicate a success, he established his individualistically-named *McClure's Magazine* which was supported by the Syndicate until Ida M. Tarbell's (*q.v.*) popular life of Abraham Lincoln changed the trend and established *McClure's* as self-sustaining. It became a vehicle for Lincoln Steffens, Ray Stannard Baker (*qq.v.*) and other reform writers. *McClure's* was a middle-of-the-road publication, and McClure himself distinctly conservative; he soon drove his more energetic reform writers to taking up the *American Magazine* (*q.v.*), to give themselves a better forum. *McClure's* continued to be a magazine to conjure with, using such other strong writers as George Kibbe Turner. In 1912, McClure lost control of his famous publication. His *My Autobiography* (1914), prepared with the aid of his editor, Willa Cather, is a folk classic.

MCMASTER, JOHN BACH (1852-1932), professor of American history at the University of Pennsylvania, whose *History of the People of the United States* in eight volumes (1883-1913) pioneered social history, emphasized the use of newspapers and ephemera, and was sharp and detailed in pointing out evils of poverty, injustice, and other backward social conditions during early years of the Republic. McMaster believed in progress, and ignored onerous conditions in his own time; but these facts did not impugn the value of his method and findings; see introduction by Louis Filler to McMaster, *The Acquisition of Political, Social and Industrial Rights of Man in America* (1961 ed.).

MCNAMARA CASE (1911), a turning point in the public's attitude toward trade-unions; violent anti-unionism in Los Angeles turned labor elements toward terrorism. On October 1, 1910, an explosion of dynamite shook the Los Angeles *Times* Building, resulting in 21 casualties. Indicted for murder were J. J. McNamara, secretary of the International Association of Bridge and Structural Iron Workers, and his brother, J. B. McNamara. Organized labor supported them on the grounds that this was a frame-up, and Clarence Darrow (*q.v.*) defended them. Lincoln Steffens (*q.v.*) naively sought to attain a settlement above law, and was used by Darrow to support a crumbling case. The McNamaras confessed and were sentenced to prison; J. B. became a prison mate of Tom Mooney (*q.v.*). The case was a blow to public confidence in labor.

MCNARY-HAUGEN BILLS (1924-8), intended to help farmers receive a better return on their crops, with the cooperation of the government. These bills, defeated by Congress or vetoed by President Coolidge, recognized that the low price of key products, notably wheat, but later including cotton and tobacco, was due to high production. Accordingly, a government agency was to purchase as much of the annual yield as was responsible for reducing the price; the agency would sell its goods on the world market, losing money in the process, since the world price was much lower than a fair domestic price would be. The government's loss would be covered by a special equalization fee levied on producers of each staple. The bills were struck down as socialistic or aiding special groups of farmers rather than all farmers. See Farmers and Reform.

MEAT INSPECTION ACT (1906), result of one of the most dramatic legislative battles in American history, it helped indicate how high was the individualism of Americans that so minimal a measure for public health should have required as much pressure as it did. The muckrakers, especially Upton Sinclair and Charles Russell (*qq.v.*) made vivid social, sanitary, and economic aspects of the question. It tied in with the revelations of Samuel Hopkins Adams (*q.v.*)with respect to poisonous patent medicines. It forced President Roosevelt to release part of a report calculated to stir public indignation. The bill which achieved passage no more than set up a basic structure of sanitary control, but was subject to improvements which ultimately had the government more concerned for health control than was the public. See also Wiley, Harvey Washington.

MECHANICS' INSTITUTES, like the Lyceum (*q.v.*) a movement for self-improvement of the 1830's and after; however, the Lyceum appealed to middle-class interest, curiosity, and ambition; the mechanics' institute, wholly self-supported, was intended to help the worker learn information which would aid him in more directly material fashions: the more practical subjects were emphasized, even though intelligent workers were sometimes attracted to humanistic aspects as well. The Lyceum emphasized style, eloquence, idealism in its speakers.

MEDICAL INSURANCE, see Health Insurance. See also Social Security Legislation.

MEIN KAMPF, by Adolf Hitler, written while he served a prison term, following the failure of his attempt to seize the German government in 1923. This work (*My Battle*) projected a blueprint of his program for gaining power, detailing his view of a Germany betrayed, and needing to be fused under his leadership. Hitler employed a powerful, emotional prose, mixing feelings, attitudes, and impressions into a lurid picture of German affairs, deliberately mixing falsehoods with facts, and promises with threats. His book won the admiration of those who sought action, feared communism, and hated Jews. For the most part ridiculed outside Germany, before Hitler took power, it was later studied carefully by those who sought to emulate him and to master his demagogic skills, and still later, when his military machine was being opposed, denounced as an expose of his demoniac purposes.

MELTING POT, THE, a conception which saw America as a land which brought various peoples together, offered them a haven and a home, and an opportunity to become something other and better than they had been: Americans. The difficulty lay in the Anglo-Saxon presumptions of some theoreticians of the "melting pot," that Anglo-Saxon backgrounds included freedom and intelligence, but that Europeans were "slaveminded," and needed to throw off their heritage and "learn" new methods of thought and action. Such presumptions complicated the task of "Americanization" (*q.v.*). However, the melting pot as an equalitarian aspiration did prove stimulating to many immigrants, more so than to reformers or to nativists who rejected assimilation processes.

MEMORIAL DAY MASSACRE (May 30, 1937), took place when

union demonstrators at the Republic Steel plant in south Chicago were fired upon by police. Four workers were killed, over eighty injured. The event was made notorious by motion pictures released by the La Follette Senatorial committee investigating anti-labor activities of corporations and citizens groups. It was memorialized in Meyer Levin's *Citizens* (1940).

MENTAL HEALTH, a major American problem, because of the many conflicts presented by an "affluent" society in which shabby cities offend expectations, by an impulse toward "togetherness" amid shattered families and mobility, and by a need for squaring competition with conformity. It was said that one American in ten would have to spend time in a mental institution, and many more required psychiatric aid; accordingly there was a movement to improve institutions and services. It was more palliative in purpose than reformistic; compare Social Work. Henry Samuels, *Mental Health* (1975); L. E. Martin, *Mental Health—Mental Illness: Revolution in Progress* (1970); David Mechanic, *Mental Health and Social Policy* (1969).

MERCANTILISM, a pre-capitalist, national view of international exchange. It posited a national developed center—London, Paris, Amsterdam—which hoarded gold, an international currency, sought colonies for expansion, cheap labor, and raw materials, as well as for unloading manufactured goods. It welcomed war as a means for furthering national pride and gaining further colonies. It built navies for sea battles and commerce. The American Revolution (*q.v.*) came in part from resistance to British mercantile policy. W. E. Minchinton, *Mercantilism: System or Expediency* (1969); Leonard Silk, ed., *Mercantilist Views of Trade and Monopoly* (1972).

MERIT SYSTEM, see Civil Service Reform.

MERRYMAN, *EX PARTE* (1861), involved the case of a Baltimore sympathizer of the Confederacy, seized by Federal troops and imprisoned in Fort McHenry. A writ of habeas corpus (*q.v.*) served upon the commanding officer was refused, on the grounds that the public safety superseded the rights implied. Chief Justice Taney, of the United States Supreme Court, reaffirmed the validity of the writ, declaring that it could be suspended only by act of Congress. See also, Milligan, *Ex Parte.*

MERRY-MOUNT, an episode in Puritan New England, resulting from a settlement of colonists in 1623, near Boston. Under Thomas Morton, the colony undertook maypole dancing and informal relations with the Indians, to the indignation of the Puritans. Morton later denounced the Puritans in his *New English Canaan* (1637). He has been admired as a liberal spirit among illiberal people, though he does not seem to have had notable character. Nathaniel Hawthorne (*q.v.*) treated the incident as a delightful interlude in the Puritan way of life.

METROPOLITAN, THE, in 1912, and supported by funds from the millionaire Payne Whitney, was reorganized as a magazine proposing a socialist program. A popular magazine, it was intended to symbolize the permanent status of the Socialist party in the United States, but lost this quality.

METTERNICH, CLEMENS (1773-1859), Austrian statesman, identified with efforts to secure a balance of power favorable to his country and the dominant powers, and resistant to popular and liberal unrest. His best-known triumph was the forging of a "Holy Alliance," intended to range the conservative governments against uprisings in their own and neighboring lands, especially after the fall of Buonaparte (*q.v.*), which had made them more vulnerable to democratic aspirations. Metternich was accorded the approval of Peter Viereck in *Metapolitics: from the Romantics to Hitler* (1941) as part of a new conservatism disillusioned with products of the romantic dream. Metternich's most effective follower in modern times was Henry Kissinger (*q.v.*), who saw the balance of power as necessary to a world loaded with death dealing missiles; see his *A World Restored: Metternich, Castlereagh and the Problems of Peace* (1957). For Metternich, see Enno E. Kraehe, ed., *The Metternich Controversy* (1977); H. F. Schwartz, ed., *Metternich:*

The Coachman of Europe of Evil Genius (1962); Barbara Cartland, *Metternich: the Passionate Diplomat* (1974).

MEXICAN WAR, THE, resulted from a combination of American expansionism, southern ambitions to extend slavery, the machinations of the imperialist wing of the Democratic Party (*q.v.*), and other factors involved in the program of Manifest Destiny (*q.v.*). The adventure was opposed by New Englanders fearful of a much expanded South, the representation of which in Congress could upset the balance of power in that body, moral opponents of war, Whigs (*q.v.*), and anti-slavery partisans. The Mexican War presents a problem to those who find it offensive to their ideals but who cannot see how the past can be undone. James Russell Lowell's *Biglow Papers* (1848) endure as a poetic protest against war and imperialism. A. H. Bill, *Rehearsal for Conflict: the War with Mexico* (1945); O. B. Faulk and J. A. Stout, eds., *The Mexican War: Changing Interpretations* (1973).

MEXICO-UNITED STATES RELATIONS have been meager, so far as reform has been involved. Mexico's early nineteenth century revolt from Spain was applauded, on general, anti-royalist principles. The Texan revolution (*q.v.*) against Mexico was in the name of freedom, but, behind it, was the imperialist will to separate Mexican territory from Mexico, a will which was adequately satisfied by the Mexican War (*q.v.*) settlements. The revolutionary intentions of Benito Juarez (*q.v.*) were sentimentally applauded, but United States developers of Mexican mines worked comfortably with the Mexican dictator Díaz, and did not welcome the revolution which began in 1910. Hearst (*q.v.*), who owned Mexican mines, led American industrialists who insisted that their property be protected through the influence of the United States government; the *A.F. of L.* (*q.v.*) maintained a broader vision of the revolution, cooperating in degree with the plans of the Mexican labor federations, then and later. The United States appreciated stability, rather than efforts tending to advance democratic possibilities, but it did avoid the temptation to try to make political capital of the internecine wars among Mexicans. The nationalization drive of the 1920's was bitterly protested by American church and business representatives, but Americans, suffering from the famous "disillusionment" with World War I aims, had no stomach for further crusades for "democracy," and, gradually, better relations obtained between the two countries. However, though American reformers and radicals appreciated such Mexican art as Diego Rivera's, they gave decreasing amounts of thought to Mexico's social needs, or its disappointing role as a leader of Central America. Although tourism increased, dynamic relations between the two countries ground to a standstill. Despite deep and apparently unbreakable poverty among its 65 million inhabitants, Mexico's potential for achievement was increased by new factors in the post-World War II years. One was the drive for change signalled by the Cuban Castro revolution and break-up of the British Empire, affecting Caribbean nations. Another was the discovery of great oil deposits in Mexico. Although it displayed no arresting plans for profiting democratically from either of these factors, they were likely to enter into Mexico's hemispheric contributions, especially as her former nationals in the United States grew better organized and articulate in American and Latin American affairs. See also Immigration. Charles M. Flandrau, *Viva Mexico!* (1908); Dan Hofstadter, ed., *Mexico, 1946-1973* (1974); Karl M. Schmitt, *Mexico and the United States* (1974); Manuel P. Servin, *Mexican Americans* (1974).

MIDDLE CLASSES AND REFORM, the key to American reform, since middle-class aspirations on the part of the working classes, and the need for sounding democratic on the part of the upper classes has enabled the middle classes to produce or attract spokesmen or active leaders who have found words or programs which could excite elements from all groups in behalf of a reform, which might otherwise have been stifled for lack of popular support. Thus, the issues of the American

Revolution (q.v.) most directly affected the interests of American businessmen and other elements of property or enterprise; on the face of it, it offered nothing to slaves and indentured servants, who constituted a great percentage of the population. However, the nationalistic and abstract appeals to Freedom and Justice (see Abstract Terms) helped curb the slaves' tendencies to gain from what was, in effect, a civil war and in other ways helped forge a basic unity favoring the anti-British effort. Much the same equation operated during the two Reform Eras, the Civil War, and the Fair and New Deals (qq.v.). The middle classes, as liaison agencies between the classes, and symbolizing the fluidity of American life, continued to be the basic ingredient in reform, for better or worse. Cf. Lewis Corey (q.v.), *The Crisis of the Middle Class* (1935); Arthur N. Holcombe, *The Middle Classes in American Politics* (1940); M. Helms, *Middle America* (1975); Robert Coles and Jon Erikson, *Middle Americans* (1971).

MIDDLE EAST, see Arabs, and related topics.

MIDDLETOWN (1929), by Robert S. and Helen M. Lynd, a study of a typical American community—Muncie, Indiana—and intended to trace its major characteristics. Based on intensive investigations, conducted in 1924-5, it ventured to offer a base for discussing the Americans in general, and their potential. Although sectional differences obviously affected the specific analyses which could be made—even in Muncie itself—and though world and domestic experiences, and refined sociological techniques, made *Middletown* obsolete in a particular sense, it continued to have useful comparative data to offer. See also *Middletown in Transition* (1937).

MIDDLE WAY, SWEDEN, THE (1938), by Marquis W. Childs, popularized in America the concept of cooperatives as a form of government between capitalism and communism. Its relevance was threatened, however, by such market forces as inflation (q.v.), which diminished its effectiveness. See also Mixed Economy.

MIDNIGHT APPOINTMENTS, see Marbury v. Madison (q.v.).

MIGRATORY AGRICULTURAL LABOR, the most significant single element of labor to help indicate the militant and dynamic quality of reform in the field. Unable to build strong ties among themselves, because of their migratory nature, less rugged and resourceful than the lumberjacks, in many cases immigrants, especially from Mexico, without public sympathy or associations, and further hampered by illiteracy, lack of leadership, and family encumbrances, they have been exposed to the harshest exploitation, in Florida and California, in New Mexico, in New Jersey and New York, and, less conspicuously, in such states as Ohio. In fact, a national problem, efforts to help them have varied from revolutionary to legislative. The I.W.W. (q.v.) made the most determined voluntary effort to organize the transient workers; their program was totally destroyed by the vigilante (q.v.) excesses of World War I. The communists floated bold schemes to organize a transient population which, in 1930's, was augmented by dispossessed landholders and tenant farmers with native American expectations; John Steinbeck's (q.v.) two novels, the communist-oriented and unsuccessfully conceived *In Dubious Battle* (1936) and the great *The Grapes of Wrath* (1939) reveal aspects of the problem. The New Deal (q.v.) failed to provide for the migrant workers, and the World War II period made them unavailable. They reappeared after the war as degraded a form as before, and although the "affluent society" heard of them in congressional and state investigations, and on occasions of tragic accidents incident to degraded conditions, only the communists maintained a steady propaganda on the subject, and they were accused of seeking to exploit it for their own ends. In the 1960s, a charismatic migratory worker, Cesar Chavez (1927-   ) worked to organize wine-grape workers, and by 1966 had formed his Agricultural Workers Organizing Committee within the AFL-CIO. Made nationally famous by the news media and consumers organizations, he in 1968 launched a boycott of the table grape growers. By 1972 he was president of the United Farm Workers, and required to fight both employers and Teamsters for authority. The nature of the migrant and his family made them a problem within labor. Marion Hathway, *The Migratory Worker and Family Life* (1934); Jan Young, *Migrant Workers and Cesar Chavez* (1974); R. B. Taylor, *Chavez and the Farm Worker* (1975). See also Steinbeck, John.

MILITARISM, see Imperialism and Reform.

"MILITARY-INDUSTRIAL COMPLEX," a concept of President Eisenhower (q.v.) recognizing the responsible nature of arms manufacture, but taken by those fearing war as making capitalists a dangerous factor in an "arms race." It thus tied with earlier fears brought out in the Munitions Investigation (q.v.) of 1934. It recognized, rather, problems, for example, involved in sales of arms abroad, and in decisions of what arms manufacture required priority attention. The abortive "rescue" attempt in the Carter Administration of "hostages" in Iran (q.v.) brought out apologies that the Armed Services were operating with worn-out equipment, and needed increased defense funds for carrying out their missions properly. Fritz Sternberg, *The Military and Industrial Revolution of Our Time* (1959); Sam C. Sarkesian, ed., *The Military-Industrial Complex: a Reassessment* (1972).

MILITARY DUTY, see Draft Registration.

MILITARY SLANG contains no element of reform, perhaps by definition; irony, "griping," vulgarisms serve to "let off steam," rather than to open the way for change. Thus, "Jim Crow" (q.v.) means to a soldier no more than a watcher for planes, a look-out; left, right, and center have no political connotation. See Eric Partridge, *et al., Forces Slang, 1939-1945.*

MILL, JOHN STUART (1806-1873), son of the utilitarian (q.v.) philosopher and reformer, James Mill, he was a child prodigy, a writer on social and political questions, whose writings on political economy and the principle of liberty established his reputation. The philosopher of a responsible elite, he showed powers of growth, though on a philosophic level, rather than the level of action. His *Subjugation of Women* (1869) disappointed his more conservative admirers, as did his interest in land nationalization, which in 1870 led him to help found the Land Tenure Reform Association. In his later years he took a socialist position; his essays on the subject were collected by W.D.P. Bliss (q.v.) in 1891. Too coldly logical and intellectual, for many tastes, his *Autobiography* (1873) nonetheless found many readers who were absorbed in his intellectual development.

MILLENARIANS, a Judaeo-Christian sect which believed that the coming of Christ would usher in a thousand years of peace and happiness of humanity, to be followed by the Last Judgment. Millenarian views inspired reformist thought in the pre-Civil War decades, though it produced no major reformers.

MILLIGAN, *EX PARTE* (1865-1866), a legal milestone in American civil rights. It involved the arrest of a sympathizer of the Confederate cause in Indiana, not through civil, but military process, even though Indiana was not actively involved in martial proceedings. In addition, in opposition to Article I of the United States Constitution (q.v.), he was denied the writ of habeas corpus (q.v.), and first sentenced to death, later to life imprisonment. The decision of the United States Supreme Court, April 3, 1866, that civil proceedings held, except under conditions requiring martial rule reaffirmed the validity of habeas corpus, earlier weakened in the case of John Merryman (q.v.).

"MILLIONAIRE SOCIALIST," a phenomenon of the Reform Era, it included Robert Hunter, Gaylord Wilshire, William English Walling (qq.v.), among others.

"MILLIONS FOR DEFENSE, BUT NOT ONE CENT FOR TRIBUTE!", a felicitous phrase sometimes associated with the American war with the Barbary pirates, but more accurately a by-product of the XYZ Affair (*q.v.*), which gave the Federalists an opportunity to display themselves before the public as proud and dependable leaders who would brook no insults from foreign powers. The words, attributed to C. C. Pinckney, U. S. Minister to France, were more likely: "No, no, not a sixpence." Strangely, recollection of neither the Barbary pirates (*q.v.*) nor the XYZ Affair came to the surface during the protracted Iran (*q.v.*) "hostages" affair of 1979-1981, possibly because the heroism of the American Navy and the firmness of American legislators contrasted too painfully with that displayed by later Americans.

MILLS, C. WRIGHT (1916-1962), most challenging of sociologists of his time, he came from Texas to be director of the labor research division, the Bureau of Applied Social Research, Columbia University, where he became a professor. He was also (1945) a special consultant to the Smaller War Plants Corporation, War Production Board. *The New Men of Power* (1948) analyzed "left" and "right" tendencies among labor leaders. Mills was co-author of *The Puerto Rican Journey: New York's Newest Migrants* (1950) and *The Psychology of Social Institutions* (1953). *White Collar* (1951) made his reputation, and saw the new middle-classes as up for sale, that is, ready to follow a powerful leadership. *The Power Elite* (1956), in effect, saw the shibboleths of democracy as less consequential than the actual social forces and their manipulators. *The Causes of World War Three* (1958), critical of "crackpot realists" who prepared for, and thus prepared, the catastrophe of war, was chiefly notable as coming from so conventionally-established a source as Mills, as was *Listen, Yankee* (*q.v.*). His position as a left-wing critic of society could be observed in Herbert Aptheker's *The World of C. Wright Mills* (1960).

MINDSZENTY, JOSEF CARDINAL (1892-1975), Hungarian Catholic prelate, and chief figure in a Budapest communist-controlled trial, in 1949, during which he "confessed" to crimes of treason against the state, joining the numerous personages whose "confessions" (*q.v.*) had become a feature of communist social regulation. In 1956, during the Hungarian revolt against communist rule, Mindszenty was released from prison; with the return of the communists, he found asylum in the American Legation. The trial made him a world-figure, and resulted in wide circulation of details respecting his life and services. His most famous remarks were written on the back of an envelope before his arrest: "I have taken no part in any conspiracy of any kind. . . . [I]f despite what I now say you should read that I have confessed or resigned, and even see it authenticated by my signature, bear in mind that it will have been only the result of human frailty." He was generally considered to have become a victim of what became known as "brain-washing" (*q.v.*). See *Cardinal Mindzenty Speaks* (1949).

MINERS IN THE WEST offered peculiar problems, since many of them were individualistic, frustrated capitalists and used to the free ways of western warfare. Notable strikes took place at Coeur d'Alene, Idaho (*q.v.*), Telluride, Colo. (1903), Goldfield, Nevada (1907), and at Ludlow, Colo., (1913-15) (*q.v.*); see Western Federation of Miners.

MINIMUM HOURS OF LABOR see Eight-Hour Day.

MINIMUM WAGE, first suggested as a principle in 1874 by Lloyd Jones. Beginning in 1912, states began to enact laws providing minimums for women and children. The Fair Labor Standards Act (1938), known also as the Wages and Hours Law, pegged the minimum originally at forty cents an hour, to be reached by stages. This followed on the heels of a U. S. Supreme Court decision, the year before, in the case of West Coast Hotel Company *v.* Parrish, which overthrew earlier decisions that minimum wage laws were unconstitutional. Beginning at twenty-five cents per hour, the minimum wage was advanced to thirty cents in 1939, forty cents in 1945, seventy-five cents in 1950, one dollar in 1955. By 1974 the wage was geared to become two dollars and thirty cents, including some 7 to 8 million workers not earlier covered, and including, among others, domestic workers. See also Servants, Migratory Agricultural Labor.

MINISTRY AT LARGE, organized after the Depression of 1819, and involving such famous clergymen as William Ellery Channing (*q.v.*) and Joseph Tuckerman. It premised a sense of the relevance of religion to human need such as later expressed itself in Christian Socialism (*q.v.*).

MINORITY GROUPS, a basic problem in American life, since the nation is composed of minority groups, some of which, however, are powerful on local or regional bases and have a sense of deserving more than others deserve. Minority groups are not all under-privileged. One of the reasons for creating a senate in the government of the United States was to ensure that the minority group of aristocrats would not be overwhelmed by increasing American democracy. The concept of minority groups as a field for social controversy and reform grew during the twentieth century and accreted a list of rights and privileges allegedly due them, many of which were openly or secretly resisted. Minority groups were not necessarily minorities in a given area; thus, there were areas in the South which had more Negroes than white people—a fact which only multiplied southern efforts to curb their social effectiveness. Although exclusivist groups emphasized their right to seek association with their own kind, equalitarians argued that, first, this was patently improper where their "own kind" gained from the tax-money contributed by minority groups. They protested, too, against the inhumaneness of the exclusivists. Thirdly, they observed that malicious attitudes toward minorities harmed the nation in its international dealings; thus, Negroes in Africa, and their representatives in the United States, resented the treatment American Negroes received from white Americans, and the attitudes they themselves had to cope with. The same was true of Chinese, Japanese, Mexicans, Arabs, any many others; see also Immigrants and Reform. Wayne Charles Miller, *A Handbook of American Minorities* (1976).

MINUTE MEN, first formed in 1774 by a congress of patriots who met and decided to organize a number of themselves who would be ready at a moment's notice to act in their behalf, spread as a revolutionary institution; later popularized as a symbol of ready patriotism; used by the Confederates in the early days of what they deemed to be their "second" American Revolution. During World War I, the Committee on Public Information (*q.v.*) employed seventy-five thousand "Four Minute Men" to make a whirlwind tour of the country in order to apprize it of the presumed reasons for American intervention in the war. See Creel, George.

MIRANDA DECISION (1966), decision of the Supreme Court, one of the most controversial of the era. It was intended to protect the rights of a defendent to counsel and not to be "compelled" to testify against himself. Although police officials had been caught brutalizing arrested persons and maliciously deceiving them as to their rights, mounting crime everywhere —New York police were said to have "given up" trying to control it—raised questions as to the limits for protecting known and confessed criminals. The Supreme Court itself seemed unable to define controls on Miranda interpretations.

MISCEGENATION, a mixing of the races, notable especially when involving Negroes. D. G. Croly, father of the founder of the *New Republic*, Herbert Croly (*q.v.*), coined the word for his book *Miscegenation* (1864), approving the process as producing a finer race. Such mixture was forbidden by law as early as 1663 in Maryland, and increasingly outlawed particularly in the South. Most such unions were between black men and white women. Marriage between white men and Indian women was not uncommon on the frontier. Freedom to make such alliances increased with agitation and civil rights laws in post-World War I years. The percentage of successes in such unions has been controversial. E. B. Reuter, *Race Mixture* (1931); S. J. Holmes, *The Negro's Struggle for Survival* (1937); James H. Johnson, *Miscegenation in the Ante-Bellum South* (1939).

MISERY INDEX, a concept developed by the chairman of President Johnson's (*q.v.*) Council of Economic Advisers, Arthur

Okun, which simply added the unemployment rate to the inflation rate to measure the condition of the economy. It recorded 7.4 percent in 1960, as compared with 17.5 percent in 1980. It was this which enabled President Reagan (*q.v.*) to inform the public that it was "very much worse off" than it had been earlier. However, personal income after taxes and inflation suggested it was much better off, in money terms. Other factors helped explain why the public mood was "pessimistic." Unemployment should have modified the inflation rise, but both rose. Interest rates rose to record highs and economic growth the reverse. The "misery index" was one means of judging the value of Reagan's turn against "deficit spending" (*q.v.*)

MISSISSIPPI PLAN, applied to several programs and tactics employed in many parts of the South, but either originated or developed in Mississippi. In post-Reconstruction (*q.v.*) years, white citizens developed the practice of carrying guns and rifles on election day as a means of warning Negroes to stay away from the polls. The constitutional convention of 1890, in that state, prescribed conditions for voting which were also intended to strike hardest at the Negroes; these included the poll tax (*q.v.*), proofs of literacy (which could be arbitrarily determined by officials), and freedom from specified crimes, including wife-beating and theft.

MISSOURI COMPROMISE, resulted from the request that Missouri Territory be admitted by Congress into the Union as a state with slavery: the first such challenge presented by the Louisiana Purchase. It aroused, to Americans, an alarming amount of debate; they had not realized there was so much feeling about whether western territories would or would not tolerate the slave system. Henry Clay's compromise stipulated that although Missouri would be admitted with her slaves, no further such concessions would be granted by the North, above 36° 30'. Maine was admitted as a free state to balance Missouri's influence in Congress. Thus Americans thought they had devised a formula for ensuring peace, between slavery and anti-slavery interest; see Compromise of 1850. Glover Moore, *Missouri Controversy* (1953); Manie Morgan, *The New Stars: Life and Labor in Old Missouri* (1951).

MISSOURI VALLEY AUTHORITY, intended to do for the Missouri River Valley what T.V.A. (*q.v.*) had done for the Tennessee Valley. Plans were submitted by the Bureau of Reclamation, of the Department of the Interior, and by the Corps of Engineers, of the Department of the Army. The so-called Pick-Sloan Plan which resulted was not actually a plan, since the Engineers and the Bureau had not resolved differences in their points of view, and did not do so. Essentially, neither agency was willing to embark on the kind of overall planning which had characterized T.V.A. Thus, piece-meal construction became the order of the day: a policy which gave no promise of ultimate synchronization of program or facilities. Indeed, it was argued by critics of the piece-meal policy that the presence of inadequate construction increased the force of the flood when it got out of hand. Although there was building on the Missouri River, and others, tragic floods, including devastation of property and ruin of top soil, as well as loss of lives, was predictable for the foreseeable future. Thus, in 1959, following the spring thaws, in the Missouri area alone, some 220,000 acres of land were inundated, with an estimated loss of about five million dollars in damage. In the West, the battle to make the Hell's Canyon project a public project was entirely lost. Other valley authorities which seemed to have no possibility of development, let alone attainment, included: the Savannah Valley Authority, the Connecticut Valley Authority, the Central Valley of California Authority. Arthur E. Morgan, *Dams and Other Disasters* (1971).

"MR. DOOLEY," see Dunne, Finley Peter.

MITCHELL, JOHN (1870-1919), coal miner and a founder of the United Mine Workers. His high-point of significance was as leader of the miners in a fight for better wages and union recognition (1900-2). Recognition was not attained, but some betterment of conditions was; the lengthy negotiations established Mitchell as one of the moderates, who was honored by the A.F. of L. (*q.v.*), regarded with some impatience by the more aggressive branch of reformers. See his *Organized Labor* (1903), *The Wage Earner and His Problems* (1913).

MIXED ECONOMY, concept urged by liberals and socialists dissatisfied with what they see as the short-sightedness of capitalism, the authoritarianism and threat to human personality of communism. They see some areas of human endeavor as amenable to planning and organization, others which can be safely left to individual choice and social competition. Thus, they argue, the operation of railroads is too basic to national requirements to be handled with half-measures; best nationalize them, and remove them from the private domain. Steel production, too, could probably profit from a greater degree of regulation. Farmers and nation would gain from firm controls of production and distribution of crops, without "collectivizing" the farms. Many fields of light industry could be left to private enterprise, experimentation, speculation without harming the national economy. Thus, the nation would reap the benefits of socialistic techniques, without losing the benefits of free enterprise. Great Britain seemed the best example of the "mixed economy" available, in the middle of the twentieth century. The break-up of the British Empire, however, and desperate problems in production, inflation, and union operations brought in a Tory government which, under Margaret Thatcher (*q.v.*), fought the nationalization and other measures which, she declared, had brought them to this pass. The ousted Labour Party, on the other hand, had moved away from the "mixed economy" concept to outright socialist hopes and perspectives.

MOLLY MAGUIRES, THE, a secret society of workers, named for a legendary Irish revolutionary, which operated in the mining regions of Pennsylvania from the early 1850's until exposed by the famous Pinkerton (*q.v.*) agent, James McParland in 1877. The Mollies were accused of plotting the assassination of mine superintendents and others whose policies they resented; and ten were hanged as ring-leaders in the conspiracy. Although some labor partisans have denied that Mollies existed at all, and put the accusations down to labor provocation and other anti-labor plots, there appears little reason to doubt that these workers, under the repressive conditions then existing throughout the mining regions, did plot and plan to give themselves a measure of power by subversive actions. See Wayne G. Broehl, Jr., *The Molly Maguires* (1964).

MONETARISM, see Great Britain, Supply Side Economics.

MONEY ISSUES, see Continental Currency, Greenbacks, Sub-Treasury Plan, Silver Issue, "Old Bullion" Benton.

"MONEY PANIC," see 1907, Panic of.

MONEY TRUST INVESTIGATION, see Pujo Committee.

MONOPOLY, legally outlaw and offensive to American expectations of opportunity for all. Efforts to "end" monopolies culminated in the reorganization of the American Tobacco Company and the dissolution of the Standard Oil Company of New Jersey, in 1911. The U. S. Supreme Court utilized the "rule of reason" with respect to the dangers presented by the activities of these companies. Associate Justice John M. Harlan protested against the decision of his colleagues, accusing them of "judicial legislation." It was their business, he insisted, to find the Sherman Anti-Trust Act unconstitutional, or else to abide by it. Thereafter, businesses avoided monopoly status, when they could, and developed understandings among large units in the several industries, for example to avoid price wars. Herbert Hoover (*q.v.*), as U. S. Secretary of Commerce, helped this process along by encouraging the formation of trade associations. Practical monopolies were thus permitted during the 1920's; they were even made official in the 1930's, since the industries were asked by the National Recovery Administration (*q.v.*) to reach understandings, presumably in the public interest. Certain industries, like the telephone and telegraph, and the automobile, were unequivocally monopolistic in character, and accepted without question by Americans. See also Anti-Monopoly. Dean A. Worcester, Jr., *Monopoly, Big Business, and Welfare in Postwar United States* (1967); Mark J. Green, *Monopoly Makers: The Report on Regulation and Competition* (1973).

MONROE DOCTRINE (1823), the result of intrigue, intended by Great Britain to warn European nations away from Central and South America, which were breaking away from their Spanish overlords, intended by the United States, in addition, to hold Great Britain at a distance from the American mainlands. The Doctrine was a declaration of policy, rather than a program. It could be utilized by the United States as an imperialist weapon, or as an aid to reform. For the most part it furthered neither for many years. The purposes of the Ostend Manifesto (*q.v.*) were defeated; the Pan-American Union (*q.v.*) projected more promising objectives. The Roosevelt Corollary (1904) (*q.v.*) assumed the right and power of the United States to intervene in affairs south or west of the border when she deemed it proper to do so, as she did on a number of occasions. The increasing strength of the American states other than the United States, however, made it necessary for the latter to turn to a good neighbor policy (*q.v.*). However, when it appeared, in the 1950's, that Guatemala might embrace communism, the Monroe Doctrine was boldly enunciated by the United States. However, the state of the world had become such by 1960, that it could not be evoked readily against Cuba. Armin Rappaport, ed., *The Monroe Doctrine* (1976); Charles M. Wilson, *The Monroe Doctrine: an American Frame of Mind* (1971).

MONTESQUIEU, CHARLES LOUIS DE SECONDAT, BARON DE (1689-1755), a social analyst and philosopher, whose works influenced libertarian thought. *Lettres Persanes* (1721) satirized the French society of his time. His masterpiece, *L'Esprit des Lois* (1748), discussing the relationship between human and natural law, was reprinted numerous times, and elicited admiration for the felicity of its prose as well as the challenging nature of its ideas.

MONTEVIDEO CONFERENCE (1933), see Good Neighbor Policy.

MOONEY-BILLINGS CASE (1916), resulted from the explosion of a bomb, July 22, 1916, during a Preparedness parade in San Francisco, killing nine persons and wounding at least 40 more. Indicted were Thomas J. Mooney and Warren K. Billings. The former was a union organizer, the latter was a member of the Shoemakers' union, who had, in 1913, at the age of nineteen, been "framed," he declared, by detectives into carrying a suitcase containing dynamite. For this offense he had served two years in the penitentiary. Evidence favoring the defendants (a photograph showed Mooney a mile from the scene of the explosion at the time indicated) and evidence that witnesses had been tampered with by the prosecution was passed over in the heated atmosphere, and the defendants were sentenced to death. However, labor protest which extended to Russia, then in the throes of revolution, persuaded President Woodrow Wilson to intervene and urge that execution be suspended. Although the conviction was affirmed by the Supreme Court, continued protest, the work of the journalist Fremont Older (*q.v.*), and the findings of the Densmore investigation brought forth sufficient proof of the faithless behavior of the prosecution, resulted in the commutation of the sentence to life imprisonment, November 29, 1918. Agitation in behalf of the prisoners continued through the 1920's, and added evidence of malice and conspiracy by the prosecution revealed. The case, a labor classic, came to a conclusion in the 1930's, thanks to the continuing and strengthened work of radicals and reformers, which even enlisted, in 1931, the personal plea of Mayor "Jimmy" Walker, of New York. In 1933, the International Labor Defense (*q.v.*) organized the National Mooney Council of Action. In 1939, Mooney was pardoned and Billings's sentence was commuted. Mooney, who had become sympathetic to

the Communist Party, spoke in its behalf; he died in 1942. See Lillian Symes, *Our American Dreyfus Case* (1935), and *The Mooney Billings Report, Suppressed by the Wickersham Commission* (1932). See also Richard H. Frost, *The Mooney Case* (1968).

MORAL EQUIVALENT OF WAR, (1910), see James, William.

MORAL RE-ARMAMENT, a movement launched in 1938 by Frank Buchman (*q.v.*), intended to revitalize world society with "God's Mind" operating through human nature. Revivalist without the limiting component of specific secular tenets, it has juxtaposed its concepts with those of communism, and believes Moral Re-armament can overcome communist tenets by converting communists. It has provided a means through which civic and political leaders were able to express general sentiments of good-will without offering specific political suggestions. It has thus been able to make impressive displays of apparent strength, at world conferences and assemblies in great number. MRA (Moral Re-armament in Action) "teams" have been sent to or requested from troubled spots in the world, and have appeared to contribute to their well-being, if not their solution. A typical writing of MRA has been *Ideology and Co-existence* (1959), eighty-six million copies of which were in print in twenty-five languages, in 1961. Buchman died in 1961. See his speeches, *Remaking the World* (1961), and G. Ekman, *Experiment with God: Frank Buchman Reconsidered* (1972).

MORAL REFORM, may be distinguished from reform sponsored by political parties, often symbolic or demagogic, as with much Jacksonian (*q.v.*) reform, often a mixture of compromise and a ministering to specific needs, as with the New Deal (*q.v.*) program. Reform (*q.v.*) is usually, in considerable degree, a process of adjusting outmoded circumstances to more modern wants. *Moral* reform adds a component of principle to reform, and involves a search for more permanent values, as well as a regard for the possibility of eternal principles of justice. Moral reform often is the dynamo behind practical reform. Thus, the abolitionists contributed the eloquence and courage without which the Free Soilers (*qq.v.*) would have been mere competitors with pro-slavery partisans for western land. The muckrakers did the same for the Progressives (*qq.v.*). The leftwingers (*q.v.*) of the 1930's thought of themselves as exponents of scientific principles, but they also exploited the indignation, aspirations, and other feelings of sufferers from depression. They helped formulate the wants to which the New Deal responded with an eye to political exigencies. Thus, it gave relief to the Negroes, but it also respected the South's desire to maintain segregation. Moral *issues* have appealed to anti-reformers, opposed to birth control, homosexuality, euthanasia (*q.v.*) and sterilization, artificial insemination, and suicide; advocates and apologists in these areas have appealed to their civil rights and human prerogatives, rather than to moral or Christian principles.

MORE, SIR THOMAS, see Utopias.

MORGAN, ARTHUR E. (1878-1975), engineer, educator, and social engineer, made his reputation as creator of the Miami Conservancy District, following the disastrous Dayton, Ohio, flood of 1913: a first draft of the later T.V.A. (*q.v.*). As re-creator of Antioch College (*q.v.*), he added significant ideas to education. He became the first chairman of the Tennessee Valley Authority, but proved too idealistic for the work, which he hoped would develop an overall social as well as flood-control and power-producing capacity; only the latter was made permanent, Morgan himself being separated from the agency. He became concerned for small business as a brake on big business, and sought means for making the development of small business practical. As a consultant, he advised the government of India on educational policy, and made contributions in other countries. His work on Edward Bellamy (*q.v.*), a byproduct of his studies in the methodology of social progress, helps explain Bellamy as well as himself. His study, *Nowhere Was Somewhere* (1946) argues for an original view of "utopias" (*q.v.*). See also Pilot Plants. His work continued almost to the time of his death. In 1971 he published his shocking technical and social study of the Army Corps of Engineers, *Dams and Other Disasters*, defining a national view of civil works. See Missouri Valley Authority, and Walter Kahoe, *Arthur Morgan* (1977).

MORGAN, JOHN PIERPONT (1837-1913), American financier, a grandson of John Pierpont (*q.v.*), and, to reformers, personifying the dangers in American capitalism to democracy. His organization of the United States Steel Corporation, in 1901, acquainted the public with his power. The Reform Era, ranking him with John D. Rockefeller, made "old J.P." as familiar a nickname as "old John D." Morgan's role during the Panic of 1907 (*q.v.*) is controversial. However, the Money Trust Investigation (*q.v.*) gave him new notoriety as a financial tycoon. Upton Sinclair (*q.v.*) lampooned him in *The Money-changers* (1908). His public gifts emphasized art, rather than philanthropy. A particularly nagging charge, that Morgan had profited unduly and unpatriotically from Civil War needs in rifles was rigorously examined by R. Gordon Wasson, in The *Hall-Carbine Affair: a Study in Contemporary Folklore* (1941, 1971), and found Morgan entirely innocent; see, however, George Wheeler, *Pierpont Morgan and Friends* (1973).

MORGAN, LEWIS HENRY (1818-1881), pioneer student of the Indians, "father of American anthropology," who, as an early friend of the Indians, helped mitigate some of the trouble and disorder which accompanied their supercession by white men. He was later adopted into the tribes of the Senecas and the Iroquois.

MORGAN CASE (1826), involved the disappearance and probably murder of a former Mason who had decided to reveal the "secrets" of that Order. For social and political reasons, it became a celebrated case, and resulted in the fomenting of much sentiment for and against Masonry, being an issue in a number of elections, and creating the first major third party (*q.v.*) in American political history; see Anti-Masonry. The realistic uses made of the issue are exemplified by the remark of Thurlow Weed, leader of the New York Whigs, who was exploiting anti-Masonry, and, apropos of a body which his party was insisting was that of Morgan, remarked that it would be *a good enough Morgan* till after the elections. See Lorman Ratner, *Antimasonry* (1969).

"MORGANHEIMS," see Ballinger Affair, The.

MORMONS, a product of the religious and social unrest of the 1830's, they persisted under persecution, moving west, from New York to Ohio, to Illinois, and, following the murder of their "prophet," Joseph Smith, to Utah, under the strong leadership of Brigham Young. There they developed a strong social system under a centralized government, which practiced polygamy and resisted the authority of the United States government. It suffered a major schism from the followers of Joseph Smith, and troubles with fundamentalist groups which defied its official orders to abandon polygamy. But it grew in strength and maintained a vital church which depended on the voluntary efforts of its younger people to carry its evangel abroad. Although a dissident group in its inception, it became the major, and essentially conservative, force in its region. "Jack Mormons," that is, Mormons who did not keep the faith, held liberal or radical ideas, but could not leaven Mormon opinion. Joe Hill's (*q.v.*) death focused attention on the antilabor policy practiced in Utah. In 1960, there were perhaps a million official Mormons, some 200,000 Joseph Smith Mormons; with tabernacles set up in Los Angeles, and in Hawaii and England. See W. J. Whalen, *The Latter-Day Saints in the Modern World* (1966); P. D. Bailey, *The Armies of God* (1968); Fawn Brodie, *No Man Knows My History* (1971).

MORRIS, THOMAS (1776-1844), Ohio legislator and U.S. Senator, 1833-9, a pioneer proponent of anti-slavery principles who fought the Gag Rule (*q.v.*) in the Senate, thus encouraging John Quincy Adams's (*q.v.*) battle in the House. Morris's speech in the Senate of February 9, 1839, denouncing slavery, was kept famous by anti-slavery partisans. Morris was read out of the Democratic Party for his stand. He was the vice-presidential candidate of the Liberty Party (*q.v.*), in 1844.

MORRIS, WILLIAM (1834-1896), English poet and guild-socialist (*q.v.*), whose vision of a peaceful and cooperative world contributed to social reform and socialist thinking; see his *Art and Socialism* (1884), *True and False Society* (1885), *Signs of Change* (1889), *Monopoly* (1893), *Useful Work and Useless Toil* (1893). He was essentially an individualist, in protest against centralized industrial power, with a nostalgia for what he saw as the beauties of the Middle Ages. Hence, he became a craftsman, noted for his artistic products, who found no beauty in Edward Bellamy's (*q.v.*) *Looking Backward*; he wrote *News from Nowhere* (1891) in rebuttal, in which he depicted what seemed to him a more desirable future. See also his *A Dream of John Ball (q.v.)* (1888).

MORSE, SAMUEL F.B. (1791-1872), better known as the inventor of the telegraph, but famous in his time for his ardent Know-Nothing (*q.v.*) views. C. Mabee, *American Leonardo* (1943).

MORTON, THOMAS (c.1575-1646), see Merry-Mount.

MOSCOW TRIALS (1936), the first mortal assault of the Stalinists (*q.v.*) on the opposition to their regime in the U.S.S.R. Previously, Trotskyites (*q.v.*) and others had been shunted into obscurity, ridiculed, exiled. Stalin took advantage of the assassination of the communist chieftain, S.M. Kirov—which he may have himself engineered, in order to dispose of this popular figure—to round up "Old Bolsheviks," including G.E. Zinoviev, L.B. Kamenev, and I.N. Smirnov, and accuse them of having created a terroristic "center," under the direction of the exiled Trotsky. Here first appeared the communist technique for persuading defendants to deliver unnatural and improbable "evidence," in which they "voluntarily" covered themselves with vilification; Arthur Koestler's *Darkness at Noon* (1941) (*qq.v.*) was, in part, an explanation of this phenomenon. See *Report of Court Proceedings. The Case of the Trotskyite-Zinoviev Terrorist Centre* (1936). An informal commission, headed by John Dewey (*q.v.*), examined Leon Trotsky in Mexico, and published *Not Guilty. Report of the Commission of Inquiry* (1938). These were the first of a series of trials, intended to exterminate the opposition, and unite world communism behind the Stalinist leadership. The naive or contrived aspects of American foreign policy were revealed in the memoirs of U.S. Ambassador to Russia, *Mission to Moscow* (1941), as well as *New York Times* dispatches, which accepted the travesty at face value. See also Francis Heisler, *The Moscow Trials* (1976), and Robert Conquest, *The Great Terror* (1968).

MOST, JOHANN (1846-1906), German anarchist who crowned a long career as an agitator in Europe by emigrating to the United States in 1882. He became a notorious proponent of violence which distinguished him from a more idealistic branch of anarchism which no more than resisted conventional principles of behavior and the authority of a machine civilization, and which could claim relationship to Thoreau (*q.v.*). Most's ideas appealed to a small segment of workers who, oppressed by harsh employers, and with no faith that socialist principles were immediately practical, resorted to terrorism in the hope that it would chasten their masters. An "anarchist of the deed" was probably present at the Haymarket Affair (*q.v.*). Emma Goldman (*q.v.*) was influenced by Most's principles, the European origin of which can be contrasted with those which inspired the murder of Steunenberg (*q.v.*). See George Woodcock, *Anarchism* (1962); Paul Elzbacher, *Anarchism: Exponents of the Anarchist Philosophy* (1960).

"MOST-FAVORED-NATION" CLAUSE, see Free Trade.

MOTION PICTURES, see Cinema.

MOTT, JOHN R. (1865-1955), co-winner, with Emily G. Balch (q.v.), of the Nobel Prize for Peace, 1946; world-famous evangelist and president of the World's Alliance of Young Men's Christian Associations. He emphasized an efficient approach to missionary work, and organized conferences which pooled the experiences of missionaries around the world. This work culminated in the establishment, 1921, of the International Missionary Council, Cf., Buchman, Frank.

MOTT, LUCRETIA COFFIN (1793-1880), pioneer woman's rights advocate and reformer. She was early a minister of the Society of Friends, and, with the cooperation of her husband, James Mott, helped establish the right of women to make public appearances and speeches. With Elizabeth Cady Stanton, she helped initiate the Seneca Falls Convention of 1848 (qq.v.). Mrs. Mott was influential in movements advocating abolitionism, temperance, and liberal religion (qq.v.). A. D. Hallowell, ed., *James and Lucretia Mott* (1884).

MS, a "woman activist" magazine of the 1970s, and possibly of the 1980s.

MUCKRAKERS, THE, a loosely-formed band of journalists with varied backgrounds who became leaders in a movement to expose conditions in the country which harmed its citizenry and democratic potential. The movement was begun accidentally by Josiah Flynt (q.v.), was taken up by *McClure's* writers, notably Lincoln Steffens, Ida M. Tarbell, and Ray Stannard Baker (qq.v.), and soon involved such others as David Graham Phillips, Charles Edward Russell, and Thomas W. Lawson (qq.v.). The movement began with exposures of fraud in municipal politics and soon took in trusts, land frauds, and frauds in patent medicines and meats. From these resulted the Pure Food and Drug Act of 1906 and the Meat Inspection Act. Upton Sinclair's (q.v.) services in the latter area, Lawson's exposures of financial chicanery, which brought on the Insurance Investigation of 1905-6 (q.v.), and Phillips's "Treason of the Senate" articles were highpoints of muckraking in its exposure period. Methods of muckraking varied from those of *Collier's,* which sought a responsible tone, to *Everybody's,* which saw virtues in direct sensationalism. Hearst's (q.v.) publications were related to muckraking, but not identical with them in all phases. From 1906 onward, the most responsible muckrakers sought to develop a positive program, rather than mere exposures, however illuminating. *Hampton's* (q.v.) was particularly active in this connection. The Ballinger Affair (q.v.) seemed to show muckraking in all its strength. At the same time, forces were operating to undermine it; see chapter "Armageddon," in Filler, *The Muckrakers* (formerly, *Crusaders for American Liberalism*). "Muckraking" has been used angrily by offended people as meaning false or sensational statements. George Seldes (q.v.) considered himself a muckraker.

MUGWUMPS, an Indian word meaning chieftain; used to designate an independent Republican in the Presidential campaign of 1884: a Republican who would not accept James G. Blaine (q.v.) as his standard bearer; used with contempt by the Party regulars, with pride by the dissidents.

MULATTO, not preferred by reformers to describe a light-complected Negro, since it appears to set up hierarchies of color for purposes of discrimination of a social or otherwise harmful type. Shadings of racial "mixture," for those who concern themselves with them, are detailed, under "Mulatto," in John S. Farmer, comp. and ed., *Americanisms Old and New* (1889). The Negro and associated agitation of the 1960s wiped the word out of normal intercourse, "black" being preferred and only "Negro" providing a variant as having been the long established preference of the Negroes themselves. Edward B. Reuter, *The Mulatto in the United States* (1918).

MULLER V. OREGON (1908), see Brandeis, Louis D.

"MULLIGAN LETTERS," an incident in the career of the Republican Party in the post-Civil War decades: its descent into affluence and corruption. It involved the use by James G. Blaine, Speaker of the House of Representatives, of his influence in the interests of the Little Rock and Fort Smith Railroad, whose bonds he sold for personal profit. Incriminating letters he managed to get into his own hands, and to answer accusations by a dramatic defense of his actions, with partial readings from the letters. Between James Mulligan's charges and Blaine's apologetics, the country received a lesson in political morality.

MUMFORD, LEWIS (1895-   ), author of numerous studies, some of them stronger for sensibility than for depth, but also of *Technics and Civilization* (1934) and *The Culture of Cities* (1938), among other writings, which offer experimental and reformist views of America based on technical knowledge and experience.

MUNICH, as a symbol of capitulation to fascism; see Appeasement Policy.

MUNICIPAL GOVERNMENT IN GREAT BRITAIN (1895), see Shaw, Albert.

MUNICIPAL REFORM, a primary field for opposition to corruption in administration; battles against slums and for parks, better streets and other civic improvements; technical advances, as in sanitary engineering; civil service (q.v.) reform; efficiency in municipal government; and concern for the processes of democracy, helped by free nominations, unfettered voting, minority representation, and ballot reform. Concern for the government of cities went along with the growth of cities in the post-Civil War decades. Charles A. Dana (q.v.) sardonically termed "Goo Goos" the partisans of the Good Government Clubs: city organizations intended to speed municipal reform. The Lexow Committee (q.v.) investigation in New York publicized corruption among police, theoretically pillars of the community. Thomas C. Devlin's *Municipal Reform in the United States* (1896) summed up efforts to understand the municipal organization as a technical problem in efficient controls. The muckraking movement (q.v.) brought the inadequacy of current municipal organization and reform to public attention in vivid hues. Tom L. Johnson's (q.v.) fight for good government in Cleveland was one of many battles intended to *modernize* city government by doing away with the evils of boss rule (q.v.). For a summary of the problem of franchises (q.v.), see Delos F. Wilcox, *Municipal Franchises* (1910-1). The idea of commissions, essentially adding experts and democratic controls to city government entered into the conception of the Galveston and Dayton Plans, and the Des Moines Idea (qq.v.). The drastic deterioration of the major cities, the "white flight" to the suburbs, Negro mayors in Atlanta, Georgia, Newark, New Jersey, Cleveland, Ohio, Detroit, Michigan, and elsewhere, and threats of bankruptcy and repudiation of municipal debts separated cities from older reform traditions. Whether they could be revived depended on whether the deteriorated cities could create reform cadres and publications, and could spawn politicians with character who could handle with social effectiveness whatever holdings and populations they had in hand. See John J. Jackson, *The Urban Future: a Choice between Alternatives* (1972); L. I Ruchelman, *Big City Mayors* (1969); C. R. Adran. *Governing Urban America* (1972).

MUNITIONS INVESTIGATION (1934), conducted by a special Senate committee under the chairmanship of Senator Gerald P. Nye (q.v.). Its findings disclosed that munitions manufacturers had been assiduous in selling their products during World War I, and might thus have influenced American opinion in moving toward intervention; tied in with these findings was the inquiry intended to determine the truth of a popular cliché: that the United States had entered the war "in order to rescue J.P. Morgan's loans to the Allies," the Morgan interests having indeed acted in behalf of Great Britain and France. Robert E. Sherwood's play, *Idiot's Delight* (1936), lampooned munitions manufacturers and was awarded the Pulitzer Prize. Popular feeling was reflected in the passage of the Neutrality Act (q.v.), in 1935.

MUNN V. ILLINOIS (1876), one of the key decisions of the U.S. Supreme Court, which decided that the so-called "Granger Laws"—laws passed in midwestern states under pressure of their farmer-constituents regulating rates for grain storage, and thereby for all carrying and distributing services, were constitutional. This seemed to partisans of free enterprise (q.v.) a tremendous blow and a step toward socialism. The Court, however, was conservative and had no desire to harm private property. The farmers, too, represented private property. The Court's intention was, in view of the power the Federal government had wielded during the Civil War, to help strengthen states' rights, in this case by respecting their right to regulate industry. But the Court emphasized that such regulation must be in the "public interest," and hastened to underscore that private property must not be taken away without due process (q.v.). The Court went on in later cases, notably the Wabash Case (1886) and the Chicago, Milwaukee & St. Paul R.R. Co. v. Minnesota Case (1890) to weaken the effect of Munn v. Illinois, and, finally to take on itself the right to decide whether a railroad rate was just. In effect, the great decision was deprived of teeth; but it continued as a milestone in the effort to attain regulation of business, in the public interest. See Hepburn Act. Also, B. R. Trimble, *Chief Justice Waite, Defender of the Public Interest* (1938); S. J. Buck, *The Granger Movement* (1913).

MUNSEY, FRANK A. (1854-1925), magazine and newspaper publisher who had no purpose but to make money and whose only claim to remembrance among reformers is that he inadvertently aided their cause by fighting the American News Company, a monopoly which was refusing, in the 1890's, to help distribute the new popular magazines. Munsey's fight helped establish the popular magazine, which became the vehicles of the muckrakers (q.v.). He varied his total dedication to pecuniary ends, next, by becoming one of the sponsors of the Progressive Party in 1912, and, in helping to curb its anti-trust program, undermining its purposes. His own notorious consolidations of newspapers raised questions of whether democratic communication might not be sacrificed in behalf of efficiency. See George Britt, *Forty Years—Forty Million* (1935).

MURPHY, FRANK (1893-1949), outstanding New Deal (q.v.) figure; as mayor of Detroit (1930-3) and as Governor General and U.S. High Commissioner of the Philippine Islands (q.v.) he made a reputation for humaneness and justice; as governor of Michigan (1936-9) he was famous for his firm pro-labor attitude, especially during the strike troubles of 1937. He was U.S. Attorney General in 1939, and investigated corruption without equivocation. His work overthrew the Pendergast machine in Kansas City, and put its leader in prison. Murphy became an associate justice of the U.S. Supreme Court in 1940, and was usually aligned with Justices Hugo Black and William O. Douglas (qq.v.) and Wiley Rutledge in liberal interpretations. He was especially alert to the rights of defendants in criminal cases. See J. W. Howard, Jr., *Mr. Justice Murphy* (1968).

MUSCLE SHOALS, in Alabama, on the Tennessee River, where, during World War I, the Federal government built a large hydroelectric plant and anticipated manufacturing nitrates. Early in the 1920's, an effort was made by Henry Ford to acquire the properties and improvements; this was successfully resisted by reformers. Senator George W. Norris (q.v.) led the fight for public power at Muscle Shoals, but bills passed in 1928 and 1931 were vetoed as socialistic by Presidents Coolidge and Hoover. Muscle Shoals became the central point for a plan envisioning the harnessing of the Tennessee River and the use of power to develop the entire Tennessee Valley; in 1933, the Muscle Shoals Act began a new era; see Tennessee Valley Authority.

MUSSOLINI, BENITO (1883-1945), long-time socialist, who became founder of fascism (q.v.) and dictator of Italy; like Buonaparte (q.v.), a notable example of anti-democratic and inhumane ambitions deriving from social reform circumstances.

MUTUAL AID SOCIETIES, voluntary associations of workers which pool economic resources to give the needy among them a cushion of security against catastrophe; they have also been a means for increasing the sense of community among workers, and educating them to their cooperative strength, even when the worker has been too individualistic to endorse militant unions or reformist perspectives.

MUTUAL WELFARE LEAGUE, see Osborne, Thomas Mott.

MUTUALISM, concept of French socialist and anarchist thinker Pierre Joseph Proudhon (1809-1865) (q.v.), who praised justice and cooperation at the expense of oppressively powerful individuals and states. His famous dictum: "Property is theft" has been misconstrued. He defended private property as an individual right, in the context of social responsibility. Also used to describe a society in which cooperation (q.v.) would be a basic tenet.

M.V.A., see Missouri Valley Authority.

MY LAI MASSACRE or INCIDENT (March 16, 1968), depending on the politics being pursued. It involved an American Army unit entering a South Vietnam hamlet reputed to be a Viet Cong bastion, in battle array. In subsequent action, women and children, and men of all ages, were killed by the Americans. News of the event was kept secret or distorted in home reports, at a time when Americans at home had become totally habituated to being taken by television to the front lines, and assumed their right to know all: a luxury not provided by their enemies, who rigidly screened and controlled their operations. News of the My Lai atrocity remained hidden until late 1969, when letters to government officials from veterans opened the case, which was further publicized by Seymour Hersh, a journalist and author of a book on chemical and bacteriological warfare. His *My Lai 4: a Report on the Massacre and Its Aftermath* (1970) gave ammunition to the opponents of United States intervention in Southeast Asia, and those who believed, like Daniel Ellsberg (q.v.) (see *Papers on the War*), that America was engaged in "murder" generally, not only in My Lai. Special Army and House of Representatives investigations culminated in a courtmartial trial for five participants, and pushed to the fore Lieutenant William Calley, accused of having killed 22 civilians. Under the lights of television and the press, there was no way a beset Armed Services could avoid sentencing him to life imprisonment, though later court actions resulted in Calley's total release. The My Lai issue helped turn a surfeited public away from concern for the fate of Southeast Asia. Subsequent events made a mockery of the apparently intense social concern displayed in America during depiction of the My Lai horrors. The victorious Viet Cong driving the Vietnam-Chinese, men, women, and children into the sea to starve or drown, and Vietnam slaughter of Cambodians in horrendous numbers gave some hint of what the masters of North Vietnam had been about at the time of the My Lai tragedy. A later film, *The Deerhunter* (1979), presented a point of view in this connection which the masses of American motion picture viewers appeared to accept. These genocidal (q.v.) actions drove erstwhile American critics of United States Vietnam policy first to an emphasis on "Self-Determination" (q.v.) with which American intervention had presumably interfered, and then to isolationism (q.v.) as the best American foreign policy. It was evident that this could be changed again whenever occasion suggested, as in the case of policy toward the Union of South Africa (q.v.). See also Cover Up, Domino Theory. Gerald Kurland, *The My Lai Massacre* (1973); Joseph Goldstein et al., *The My Lai Massacre and Its Cover Up* (1976).

N

N.A.A.C.P., see National Association for the Advancement of Colored People.

NADER, RALPH (1934-   ), consumer advocate who, interested in auto safety in Connecticut, moved to Washington to move action at the national level. In 1965 he wrote *Unsafe at any Speed*, which attacked auto manufacturers safety standards. Working with a Senate committee which highlighted the problem on television, he was made famous by revelations that he had been secretly investigated by General Motors, which sought evidence to disgrace him. Nader's criticisms put the model Corvair out of production. His safety standards for cars were put into law. Nader then emerged as a crusader for safety in such fields as meat, insecticides, coal mining, pollution; and even such regulatory bodies as the Federal Trade Commission fell subject to his criticism and effective change. "Nader's Raiders," a core of young lawyers and researchers with reform perspectives expanded their view of the American scene to take in all manufacture and administration. An established institution, Nader continued to develop his technique of mixing analysis with publicity, directed at regulation. He attracted funds and public support. Criticism grew respecting his arbitrary sense of what was, and what ought to be. His tactless expressed view that West Australian laws of public assembly would be unconstitutional in America, during a brief visit caused the Police Minister to dub him a "multinational troublemaker." His reference, at a Senate hearing, to the death in an auto accident of a senator's wife caused widespread comment as in doubtful taste; also questioned was Nader's effort to influence the auto manufacturer's banking as well as production. Most noticed was Nader's triumph in foisting seatbelts on cars. Evidence that drivers did not want them, and the expense, trouble, and bureaucracy involved in change-overs, raised questions of over-regulation. In 1981, evidence that Japan had overtaken the United States in car production lost Nader some of his support. Nevertheless, he had raised to eye-level questions of public interest, class-action in legal affairs, "whistle-blowing" on consumer problems, and regulation generally. Charles McCarey, *Citizen Nader* (1972); James T. Olsen, *Ralph Nader* (1974); Hays Gorey, *Nader* (1975); *Ralph Nader's Conference on Corporate Accountability* (1971); Nader and Mark J. Green, eds., *Corporate Power in America* (1973).

N.A.M., see National Association of Manufacturers.

NAPOLEON, see Buonaparte, Napoleon.

NARCOTICS PROBLEM, THE, was one which patently demanded reform energies. It has, however, experienced several stages of attention. Before 1909, the use of opium was largely restricted to Chinese and those persons, frequently depraved, who fell into their ways and byways. Reformers met them, when at all, in the police courts or social service organizations, and sought to fit them for respectable lives. An act by Congress of February 9, 1909, prohibited the importation of smoking opium or opium prepared for smoking. This created a relatively small class of criminals. The Harrison Narcotics Law of December 17, 1914, however, required all persons handling narcotics to register and pay an occupational tax, and render account of all narcotics. This, in effect, made criminals of all addicts whose systems craved drugs, however respectable their circumstances. Users of heroin were especially placed in desperate circumstances, and rendered capable of the most anti-social behavior. The effect of drugs was such that no unsupported appeal to moral attitudes could suffice to help addicts resist their compulsions. So drastic an act of Congress, therefore, should

have been supported by the most adequate social work system possible; this was not, however, provided. Although international conferences in 1912, 1913, 1914, and after helped clarify the problem of international traffic in drugs, and methods of controlling it, and though prison reformers developed programs for the treatment of addicts, actual programs lagged behind need. Relaxed controls over youth in the 1920's, the increasing popularization of marijuana—a milder, but effective drug, and easily obtainable, and a rash of juvenile delinquency accompanied by the use of drugs in the post-World II period brought home to reformers the inadequacy of a moral approach. Narcotics became a staple of the youth (*q.v.*) uprising of the 1960s and 1970s; the "Weatherwoman" Bernardine Dohrn claimed, in a letter to the *New York Times* sent from her underground, that law prohibiting drug use was creating millions of revolutionaries who would overthrow the government. Although such rant affected few and little, legal and social arguments kept interest in the narcotics question active. Doctors argued for the use of the "hardest" drugs, for terminal patients. Pain-killers could often not be distinguished from drugs, in the addictive sense. A government study showing 68% of young adults as having tried marijuana (*q.v.*) and one-third of them as having experimented with "harder" drugs raised questions of controls. The campaign for legal "pot" swayed many who saw little harm in marijuana—less so than alcohol—and wished it rated as a malfeasance rather than a crime. An education campaign, at least, seemed in order to stop children from sniffing glue, causing brain damage or death. Research gave mixed results. One study showed marijuana, far from being an innocent diversion, as harmful to the antibacterial system of the human body. "Bumper" crops of narcotics, from Colombia, Thailand, and elsewhere made controls difficult. Heroin was a particularly vicious substance which dehumanized its slaves and threatened bystanders and homes. James Berry, *Heroin Was My Best Friend* (1974); Robert Coles et al., *Drugs and Youth* (1971); Ursula Etons, *Angel Dusted: a Family's Nightmare* (1979); Kenneth Leach, *Youthquake* (1977); C. Kirsch, *Birth Defects and Drugs* (1979).

NASHOBA COMMUNITY, see Wright, Frances.

NAST, THOMAS (1840-1902), German-born political cartoonist, noted for his creation of the Democratic, Republican, and Tammany (*qq.v.*) symbols of donkey, elephant, and tiger. His powerful cartoons in denunciation of the Tweed Ring (*q.v.*) contributed to its fall. However, he also turned his skill and satire on Horace Greeley, during that candidate's race for the Presidency under the Liberal Republican (*qq.v.*) banner. Like the *New York Times* (*q.v.*) of his era, Nast exemplified reform accomplished under partisan auspices. See J. Chal Vinson, *Thomas Nast* (1967).

NAT TURNER'S REBELLION (1831), one of the most significant of the slave revolts (*q.v.*) because it came at a time of mounting anti- and pro-slavery feeling and precipitated critical debates and decisions. The leader of the revolt was a slave of masterly qualities, who gathered some seventy Negroes in Southampton County. in southeast Virginia. They slaughtered fifty-seven white persons before meeting an overwhelming force and being cut down without mercy. The effort inspired intense debates in the state legislature, members of which were alarmed by the presence of slaves and eager to rid the state of them; their defeat put an end to all anti-slavery effort in the South; the pro-slavery forces took over. In the 1960s, Turner was raised into a folk hero of rebellion, William Styron's conjectural fiction, *The Confessions of Nat Turner* (1967) gaining him a Pulitzer Prize, amid angry criticism by Negro writers who possessed no more information. Henry I. Tragle's *Nat Turner's Slave Revolt 1831* (1971) carefully gathered such evidence as was actually available.

NATION, CARRY A. (1846-1911), prohibitionist, whose personal life was embittered by drunkenness, and whose religious convictions and vigorous physique enabled her to undertake a direct-action crusade against saloons. She became famous for the disorder she created in such establishments, and for the axe which she brandished in her destruction of liquor. Her fame was a product of her Kansas campaigns; her assault upon New York City was abortive. Although a symbol of intolerance and fanaticism, she added the component of deeds to the propaganda of other prohibitionists, and inspired some of them; she undoubtedly influenced the developments which resulted in passage of the Volstead Amendment (q.v.). See her autobiography, *The Use and Need of the Life of Carry Nation* (1904); also Herbert Asbury, *The Life of Carry Nation* (1929).

NATION, THE, founded 1865, with E.L. Godkin (q.v.) as editor, intended to aid new Negro freedmen adjust to their novel status. This aim was quickly forgotten; the magazine became outstanding as an organ of Manchester Liberalism *(q.v.)* and cultural and scientific comment. It favored free trade and honest government, and opposed militant labor and radicals. Under Paul Elmer More (1909-14) its essential conservatism was more marked by reason of the surrounding muckraking and Progressivism *(qq.v.)*. Under Oswald Garrison Villard *(q.v.)*, it turned out-going toward labor, the U.S.S.R., civil liberties, and other tenets of a widening and more experimental democracy. During the 1930's, it made few efforts to distinguish between liberalism and Marxism. Throughout this time, it had functioned as a serious organ of attitude and opinion, which was read by elite and responsible members of society. Increasingly, in the post-World War II years, it lost consequence. See also *New Republic, The.*

NATIONAL ASSOCIATION FOR THE ADVANCEMENT OF COLORED PEOPLE, formed in 1909 by a number of concerned Negroes and white persons, including William E. Walling, Oswald Garrison Villard, and such others as Jane Addams, John Dewey, Charles Edward Russell, Hamilton Holt, and W.E.B. Du Bois *(qq.v.)*. It undertook many legal and educational campaigns in behalf of Negroes, in both North and South, especially under the resourceful leadership of Walter White *(q.v.)*. When the great drive for integration went underway in the 1950's, some Negroes concluded that the N.A.A.C.P. acted with technical rather than reformist zeal, and found more inspiration in the leadership of Martin Luther King *(q.v.)*. It published *The Crisis (q.v.)*. The 1960s explosion of "protest" featured many young black pretenders, encouraged by such endorsement as Norman Mailer's *(q.v.)* essay, "The White Negro" (1959) and a teacher, Jerry Farber's, essay on "The Student as Nigger" (1969), circulated on campuses. Veteran Negro leaders like John C. Dancy of Detroit lost place on television and in the press to such bold activists as Rap Brown, Eldridge Cleaver, and Stokely Carmichael. Although they lost credibility, they hindered the more patient work of the NAACP. In the 1980s it became visible again as a special interest group. B. J. Ross, *J. E. Spingarn and the Rise of the NAACP* (1972); John C. Dancy, *Sand against the Wind* (1966); Rap Brown, *Die, Nigger, Die* (1969); Robert Scheer, ed., *Eldridge Cleaver: Post-Prison Writings and Speeches* (1969); Ethel N. Minor, ed., *Stokely Speaks* (1971).

NATIONAL ASSOCIATION OF MANUFACTURERS, founded in Cincinnati in 1895, became a symbol of capitalist intransigence with respect to augmented labor rights or augmented government prerogatives infringing upon private property rights. Under early presidents David Parry and T.W. Van Cleave it undertook anti-union drives. Van Cleave's Buck Stove and Range Company, of St. Louis, was particularly aggressive in defense of what it conceived to be its rights. In the 1920's, which were amenable to anti-labor action, the N.A.M. sponsored the "American Plan" *(q.v.)*, and in the 1930's protested against what it deemed to be the excesses of the New Deal *(q.v.)*. However, it developed a modern approach to its problem of preserving free enterprise amidst tendencies inimical to it; its affiliated National Industrial

Conference Board concerned itself with labor and industrial problems, employing a highly efficient research and technical service.

NATIONAL CHILD LABOR COMMITTEE, see Child Labor.

NATIONAL CIVIC FEDERATION, founded in Chicago in 1893 by Ralph M. Easley, took on the name by which it became famous in 1900. It sought to find means for mediating differences between labor and capital, and persuaded so important an employer as Mark Hanna and so important a labor leader as Samuel Gompers *(qq.v.)* to cooperate with its program. It was bitterly criticized by reformers as obfuscating labor's needs and seeking to undermine reform programs. Gompers was held to have been duped by his affluent associates. The Federation increasingly emphasized its distaste for radicals. It played the part of super-patriotism during World War I, and joined the anti-red hunt afterwards. By then, its role of mediator had all but disappeared. See Marguerite Green, *The National Civic Federation and the American Labor Movement* (1956).

NATIONAL CONFERENCE ON SOCIAL WELFARE, an organization made up of some 6500 individual and agency members concerned for health and welfare in the United States. It began in 1874 as the Conference of Boards of Public Charities. Its major function is to hold an annual meeting for discussions of important social issues. In early years, it discussed aid to children, lunatics, immigrants; more recently it has emphasized the phenomenon of suburbia, integration *(q.v.)*, the recruitment of social work personnel. Associated agencies include the AFL-CIO Community Activities, American Immigration and Citizenship Conference, Muscular Dystrophy Associations of America, National Urban League *(q.v.)*, and the Planned Parenthood Federation of America.

NATIONAL CONGRESS OF AMERICAN INDIANS, founded 1944, a major effort to develop strength through numbers, in the interest of legislation beneficial to Indians, in order to educate the general public to understand Indian problems, and to diminish the distance between Indians and other Americans, socially, economically, and in other ways. Not a reform organization, its program furthered causes which concerned reformers, including Indian land rights, the repeal of discriminatory legislation, the improvement of Indian education, the furthering of accuracy in recounting the history of Indian tribes in their dealings with the United States. Over seventy tribes subscribed to the Congress. See also Indian, The, and Reform.

NATIONAL ENDOWMENT FOR THE ARTS, established 1965, one of President Johnson's *(q.v.)* efforts to give something to every branch of American society. The Endowment was a large attempt to foster creativity in all avenues of the arts and life. Grants ranged from outright gifts to individuals for experimenting or finishing projects, to institutions claiming to attempt enterprises of use to other institutions. Groups were subsidized to attempt stage, television, or other presentations enlightening to audiences. In the nature of things, relevance or creativity took some shape from contemporary interests—minority problems, women's claimed interests, the individual attitude. The Endowment faced awesome problems in determining what constituted a legitimate project, and, as everywhere, recommendations tended to move in predictable channels. Nevertheless, it was observed that they did not seem to create a sense of a national purpose of direction, or to add up in any definable way. Unsympathetic critics argued that it was not the government's business to tell anyone what to create. But why ought he or she to be subsidized? Was the government not, in effect, defining priorities by judging one project superior, or meriting subsidy, over another? The public was paying for the grants, but had no voice in their selectivity. Compared to the Federal Arts Projects *(q.v.)* of thirty and more years earlier, the National Endowment neither sought public-serving enterprises, nor presented coherent programs with national implications. The Endowment, it was estimated, would be spending some $300 million by 1985. With much criticism of its policies and achievement about in 1981, it remained to be seen what judgment might be made of them in that period. M. M. Mooney, *The Ministry of Culture* (1980).

NATIONAL ERA, outstanding anti-slavery periodical, set up in Washington, D.C., it was edited by Gamaliel Bailey and featured the work of John Greenleaf Whittier *(qq.v.)*. It informed and influenced northern congressmen. *Uncle Tom's Cabin*, by Harriet Beecher Stowe *(q.v.)* first appeared in its pages.

NATIONAL FARMERS' ALLIANCE, also known as the Northern or Northwestern Alliance, organized 1880 as a non-secretarian farmers' organization, and built upon the principles and efforts of the National Grange of the Patrons of Husbandry *(q.v.)*. The Alliance was the northern counterpart of the National Farmers' Alliance and Industrial Union *(q.v.)*. Following years of growth and concern for political possibilities, the Alliance leaders helped formulate the Ocala Demands (1890) which led to the organization of the National People's Party, in Omaha, Nebraska, in 1892. By then, the Alliance had largely spent its force.

NATIONAL FARMERS' ALLIANCE AND INDUSTRIAL UNION, also known as the Southern Alliance, organized in the 1880's, notably under C.W. Macune, who brought together elements from a number of separate organizations, including the Texas State Alliance and the Farmers Mutual Benefit Association. It pressed for a number of measures, including curbs on railroads and other monopolies, and joined in the movement which created the People's Party; see Populist Revolt, The.

NATIONAL GRANGE OF THE PATRONS OF HUS-BANDRY, an element in farmers's thought and organization, was founded at Fredonia, New York, in 1867, its first secretary being Oliver Hudson Kelley. A social and fraternal organization, roughly modeled on the Masons, it inevitably concerned itself with the farmers's troubles. It grew rapidly, in the 1870's, in 1875 claiming some 21,000 granges, with a membership of over three-quarters of a million. It entered into, and survived the populist revolt *(q.v.)*. At its height, it captured several state legislatures, and was influential in others, being responsible for the famous "Granger Laws" which established state commissions to determine fair rates for transporting farm goods by rail and for storing them in grain elevators. The Grange was especially powerful in Wisconsin, Illinois, Minnesota, and Iowa. It still maintains offices in Washington, D.C.

NATIONAL GREENBACK PARTY, THE, see Greenback Party, The.

NATIONAL LABOR RELATIONS ACT, created an era in the history of capital-labor relations, since it guaranteed the right of workers to organize and bargain collectively, and thus put the government into the business of determining that this right was being respected. It created the National Labor Relations Board to direct inquiries into the operation of the Act, thus creating a machinery which the defunct Section 7 (a) of N.I.R.A. *(q.v.)* had not. The N.L.R.B. was active and efficient, and, for the most part, to the profit of labor. A major reason was that World War II needed labor, and the government was eager to defer to its wants and to have labor organizations which would expedite the mobilization of labor. War-time strikes, and the rising anti-radical tide caused some reaction against labor, and the passage of legislation which qualified its rights; see Labor Relations. But the N.L.R.B. had become established as a mediating agency necessary to keep industry functioning. See Frank W. McCulloch and Tim Bornstein, *The National Labor Relations Board* (1974).

NATIONAL LABOR UNION, organized 1866, the first national effort at trade union organization, it rallied some 600,000 workers, under such leaders as Ira Stewart and William Sylvis. It sought to attain the eight-hour day *(q.v.)*, encouraged the organization of cooperatives, attracted universal reformers and idealists of the pre-Civil War period, as well as firm trade unionists. Although it failed to achieve the eight-hour day for the country, it did achieve it for government-sponsored projects, and got repealed the reactionary Contract Labor Law of 1864. Turning to politics, it projected the National Labor Reform Party. The Panic of 1873 *(q.v.)* and the rise of the Knights of Labor *(q.v.)*, completed its pioneer labors.

NATIONAL LEAGUE OF WOMEN VOTERS, see League of Women Voters of the United States.

NATIONAL LEGION OF DECENCY, THE, was established in 1934 under the authority of the Hierarchy of the United States to protect Catholics against moral dangers created by motion pictures and to influence producers "against the production of bad films and towards the production of good films." It offers the following classifications: Morally unobjectionable for general patronage; morally unobjectionable for adults and adolescents; morally unobjectionable for adults; morally unobjectionable in part for all; and condemned. In addition, there is a separate classification for films which, "while not morally offensive, require some analysis and explanation as a protection to the uninformed against wrong interpretations and false conclusions."

NATIONAL MUNICIPAL LEAGUE, organized in 1894, following the development of various local organizations concerned for good government. It considered techniques for more efficient city government, sponsored writings in the area, and sought to coordinate efforts in the field. It has been largely concerned with program-making and models for administration, notably the City-manager plan *(q.v.)*. It has drawn its adherents from among civic-minded elements of the wealthier classes and academicians; see also Municipal Reform.

NATIONAL ORIGINS ACT (1924), see Immigrants and Reform.

NATIONAL POPULAR GOVERNMENT LEAGUE, organized 1913, and in the next several decades attracted the sympathy and cooperation of noted liberals. An educational organization, it circulated pamphlets and other matter in favor of public ownership, and was alert to civil liberties issues. In the 1930's, it was respectful of the more intensive causes of the period. It was a recipient of the Garland Fund *(q.v.)*. It conducted a Forum in the Capital, as part of its educational activities.

NATIONAL RECOVERY ADMINISTRATION, a major effort under the New Deal *(q.v.)* to give the government authority to foist such measures upon labor and industry as would revive the cycle of production and distribution. Created by act of Congress in 1933, it placed its emphasis upon business, seeking to establish "Codes" which would ensure prices for products which would help move goods into the hands of consumers. Businessmen drawn to Washington for this work consulted the views of the industries they served. Whether their decisions helped bankrupt retail merchants is a moot question. Labor was thrown the famous sop of Section 7 (a), which stated the right of labor to organize, but no machinery was established to protect this right. However Section 7 (a) did provide a propaganda tool for labor organizers, who inspired strikers with such slogans as "F.D.R. wants you to organize." Attempted minimum wage and hour regulations were less successful; minima became maxima. Labor and the radicals distrusted N.R.A. Under the administration of General Hugh S. Johnson, they feared it might lead to the corporate state *(q.v.)*. Struck down in 1935, by decision of the U.S. Supreme Court, the agricultural aspect of N.R.A. revived as A.A.A. *(q.v.)*. The effort to control business was abandoned. The Wagner Act (*q.v.*) gave labor the fighting change it wanted, and which Section 7 (a) had not provided.

NATIONAL RESOURCES BOARD, created in 1934, changed its name several times before it became the National Resources Planning Board, and, as such, ended in 1943. It was intended to organize the information and ideas which would enable the nation best to employ its natural and industrial resources; as such, its work was an aspect of conservation (*q.v.*). However, the competitive nature of the American economy, and the fact that the nation had to deal with international problems which kept planning for peace in a secondary position, rendered much of its work academic.

NATIONAL REVIEW, THE, founded 1955 by William F. Buckley, Jr., a militant organ of conservatism, it attracted the writings of well-seasoned conservatives, as well as of such formerly outstanding non-conservatives as James Burnham, John Chamberlain, Will Herberg, Suzanne La Follette, J. B. Matthews. It was the other side of the coin of the *New Leader* (*q.v.*), deploring progressive education, Sacco-Vanzetti, peace with the U.S.S.R., the welfare state, the Peace Corps, and desegregation. Buckley's personal fame, and the national readership of such contributors as John Simon, James Jackson Kilpatrick, Russell Kirk (*q.v.*), and Jeffrey Hart attracted increased attention and regard. The *Review* fed on liberal errors and fixations respecting Hiss, Castro, Solzhenitzen, Vietnam (*qq.v.*), and other issues, and, though doctrinaire to a degree, drew together a free-wheeling wit, memory, and expertise which served less committed readers. Reagan's (*q.v.*) victory in 1980 gave a new urgency to its outlook and particular opinions. Its Twenty-Fifth Anniversary issue was edited on a note of triumph.

NATIONAL TRADES UNION, the first effort to organize labor on a national basis, it was created in New York in 1834, and served as an advisory and informational unit to local and central trade union bodies in a number of cities. The Depression of 1837, far from causing the beset unions to draw closer together, impelled individuals to seek their own survival; many of them emigrated to the west, and the National Trades Union disappeared.

NATIONAL UNION FOR SOCIAL JUSTICE, see Coughlin, Rev. Charles E.

NATIONAL URBAN LEAGUE, see Negro and Reform.

NATIONAL WOMEN'S TRADE UNION LEAGUE OF AMERICA, set up in 1905, with the aid of a number of socialists and others, including William English Walling (*q.v.*). It aimed to advance the cause of equality for women on the job. It attracted intellectuals concerned for women's rights, as well as working women, and received the endorsement of the A.F.L. (*q.v.*) and other workers' organizations. It established locals and maintained a majority of trade unionists on its executive board. The League called the first International Congress of Working Women in 1919, and was represented at the International Federation of Working Women's congresses. It maintained a Washington lobby, collected data, and held conferences.

NATIONAL WORKSHOPS, see Blanc, Jean.

NATIONAL YOUTH ADMINISTRATION, see Youth Movement, The.

NATIONALISM, Edward Bellamy's (*q.v.*) effort to "Americanize" the principles of nationalization (*q.v.*), which, in effect, sought to "sell" socialist principles to Americans suspicious of socialism as a "foreign" concept. His publication, *The New Nation* (1891-1894) preached his principles.

NATIONALISM AND REFORM have been almost fatally related, from the viewpoint of reformers who believed their work advanced the brotherhood and weakened the hand of those who approved wars. Major American wars advanced reform. The American Revolution augmented democratic right. World War I brought on the Eighteenth and Nine-

teenth Amendments (*qq.v.*). World War II consolidated the gains of organized labor. Anti-slavery opponents of the Mexican War, and anti-imperialist opponents of the Spanish-American War were anti-nationalist reformers, who, in these instances, were overwhelmed by the nationalists. Nationalists have sponsored reform when doing so has strengthened their cause; in effect, they have undertaken to take care of their own people. There was no contradiction between A. J. Beveridge's (*q.v.*) concern for child-labor and pure food laws and his desire for American expansionism (*q.v.*). Theodore Roosevelt's New Nationalism (*q.v.*), too, mixed paternalistic regard for Americans with an interest in expansionism. Such humanitarian feelings tended to stop at the American borders. Thus, reformers dissatisfied with reform as a concomitant of war had first to recognize that relationships had developed between nationalism and reform, and then to find means for preventing the relationship from becoming malignant. E. H Carr, *Nationalism and After* (1945); Edward M. Earle, ed., *Nationalism and Internationalism* (1951); Karl W. Deutsch, *Nationalism and Its Alternatives* (1969); Hans Kohn, *Nationalism* (1965).

NATIONALIZATION, the principle of having the state take over a service, economic area, or institution, on the grounds that society cannot afford to leave it in private hands. Railroads, gas and electric power, radio and television, and land, are examples. Germany led the way by nationalizing the railroads in the time of Bismarck; his purpose was not to spread democracy but to control it. Great Britain's post-World War II nationalization of railroads was part of a Labour Party drive to spread equality in the nation. Tories argued it would create a state which lacked incentive for workers to perform properly. Partly because of the dissolution of the British Empire, partly because of a loss of national responsibility in unions, labor appeared to lose much of its character, and voters turned to Tories for new answers. These included "Privatization": an effort to sell off nationalized industries to private firms which would have profit incentives to make their businesses pay. Bankruptcies in the private sector did not promptly bear out these hopes and predictions, but other factors, like wages, could be cited to explain why de-nationalization was working, but slowly. See Public Ownership. E. Eldon Barry, *Nationalization in British Politics: the Historical Background* (1965).

"NATIONALIZATION OF WOMEN," a canard directed at the Bolsheviks, at the height of fears and antipathies which followed their revolution in Russia. It derived from their sweeping anti-capitalist offensive, what was understood to be their loose morality, their nationalization of industry, and similar factors.

NATIVE AMERICAN PARTY, see Know-Nothings.

NATIVE SON (1940), see Wright, Richard.

NATIVISM, see Know-Nothings.

NATO, popular name for North Atlantic Treaty organization, set up in 1949 to combat the Cold War (*q.v.*) offensive of the Soviet Union and its satellites, which threatened Europe in particular. Organized under the aegis of the United Nations (*q.v.*), it basically posited a military force, headed by the United States, which would oppose Soviet aggression upon independent nations. Russian actions, especially in Berlin (*q.v.*), but involving *Hungary* (*q.v.*) and other lands raised questions about NATO's actual power. The Soviet invasion of Czechoslovakia (*q.v.*) raised questions about American leadership. The Iranian (*q.v.*) fiasco made thoughtful the leadership of West Germany and France, which saw itself as possibly invaded, with America engaged in nothing but futile protests. NATO troops engaged in "war games" and NATO officials met, but their effectiveness, and that of American nuclear warheads as deterrants remained unproved. Lord Hastings Ismay, NATO (1954); P. H. Spaak, *Why NATO?* (1959); James Hutley, *The NATO Story* (1969).

NATURAL RESOURCES, see Conservation.

NATURAL RIGHTS AND REFORM have been associated since the American and French Revolutions (qq.v.). They have opposed conservative philosophies which assumed the necessity for a stable society, the inevitability of inequality, and the duty of persons of whatever degree to attend to their duties and not yearn for increased opportunities. Jean Jacques Rousseau (q.v.) wrote eloquently and influentially on natural rights; both he and John Locke (q.v.), for different reasons, made much of the "compact theory" (q.v.), which justified not reform alone, but even revolution. Humanitarianism assumed that natural rights had been desecrated in situations demanding reform. Leo Strauss, *Natural Rights and History* (1953).

NATURALISM, a literary genre, identified with Zola (q.v.) abroad, with Theodore Dreiser and James T. Farrell (qq.v.), among others, in the United States. It was deterministic, assuming an indifferent universe and persons caught in their own instincts; it was also tragic in its view of man's inevitable defeat. It encouraged compassion for man's fate, and, in telling the "truth" about his circumstances, encouraged some reform and some revolutionary attitudes. However, some genteel (q.v.) reformers found the sordid detail naturalists often employed distasteful, and some revolutionists opposed the tragic vision, which they saw as debilitating to the militant spirit. Naturalists tended to act differently from the way they wrote. Thus, Norman Mailer's *The Naked and the Dead* (1948) did not much distinguish between men and maggots; but its author sought to further the candidacy of Henry A. Wallace (q.v.) for the Presidency. By 1981, naturalism seemed to have done its work of presenting the reading public with "facts" which were now the clichés of every shoddy "sex" writer.

NAZIS, masters of Germany under Hitler (q.v.), rendered themselves infamous by the premium they put upon power, however attained, their cowardly persecution of minority people, notably the Jews (q.v.), their brutal contempt for civilized methods and ideas. Their record as warriors comported with their domestic record, and, by contrast, did much to rehabilitate that of their predecessors of World War I. They appealed to some delinquents who aspired to their toughness, but generally became symbols in America of brutal action. Nazi-type groups formed as early as the 1930s—see John Roy Carlson (q.v.), *Undercover* (1943)—and appeared from time to time in response to civil rights legislation and unsettled conditions. In 1979 the Skokie (q.v.) case presented dilemmas. Anticommunists claimed to see no difference between Nazis and communists especially in the regimes of Hitler and Stalin (qq.v.).

NAZI-SOVIET PACT (1939), an astounding betrayal of professed communist principles by Soviet dictator Stalin (q.v.), who had denounced socialists as "social fascists" (q.v.), and now, having delivered communists and their friends to the mercies of anticommunist regimes in China, Spain, and Germany, sought partnership with fascism itself. His foreign minister Molotov's remark that "fascism is a matter of taste" achieved a certain immortality, but also put an end to many sentimentalities.

NEARING, SCOTT (1883-   ), critic of United States government and civilization, he was, in 1915, an academic freedom case, being dismissed from the University of Pennsylvania for his lack of sympathy with capitalism. Following several years of activity in education at the University of Toledo and the socialistic Rand School of Social Science, he settled into the career of a lecturer and writer of analyses of social and economic conditions. His works included *Social Adjustment* (1911), *Solution of the Child Labor Problem* (1911), *Wages in the United States* (1911), *Woman and Social Progress* (1912), *Social Religion* (1913), *Reducing the Cost of Living* (1914), *Income* (1915), *Poverty and Riches* (1916), *The American Empire* (1921), *Dollar Diplomacy* (1925), *The British General Strike* (1926), *Education in Soviet Russia* (1926), *War* (1931), *Soviet Union as a World Power* (1945), among

many other books and other writings. His remarkable productivity was not matched by increasing influence; his sharp independence, coupled with his persistent radicalism and perhaps increasing bitterness toward a country which had withheld honors from him, apparently separated him from mainstreams of liberalism or radicalism. A final judgment of the sum total of his work seemed in doubt. In old age he became a back-to-the-land symbol and author, forgotten by "left wing" poseurs, but noticed by some people interested in the land.

NEGRO, ABROAD, has radically changed his role from the viewpoint of social reformers. In the nineteenth century, they conceived of him as requiring instruction and improvement. Liberia (q.v.) was to be an outpost of civilization from which light emanated to the well-being of "Darkest Africa." Negroes in the Caribbean, and in Central and South America, too, were thought of in terms of sympathy and meliorative measures. Negroes in the United States, for the most part, feared to be identified with African Negroes; "Garveyism" (q.v.) inspired a few Negroes who were embittered by their lack of status and opportunity, but "Back to Africa" was not a mass movement. An anti-reformer, Lothrop Stoddard, called attention to *The Rising Tide of Color against White World-Supremacy* (1920). The white leaders of the Union of South Africa took the lead in resisting this tide in enforcing their principle of "Apartheid," writing into law social, political, and economic rules calculated to keep the Negroes and whites apart, and the latter in command. Nationalistic movements throughout Africa and successful separations from European rule created large classes of Negro aristocracies, having talents and authority. In the latter part of the twentieth century, American Negroes and social reformers were required to reconsider their attitudes toward Africans, and also Jamaicans and other island people who had acquired new status. J. W. Bowen, ed., *Africa and the American Negro* (1896); Alex Crummel. ed., *Africa and America* (1891); Hollis Read, *The Negro Problem Solved: or, Africa as She Was, as She Is, and as She Will Be* (1864); Joseph A. Tillinghast, *The Negro in Africa and America* (1902); Willis D. Weatherford, *The Negro from Africa to America* (1924); Eric Williams, *The Negro in the Caribbean* (1942); L. A. Williams, ed., *Africa and the Afro-American Experience* (1977); E. U. Essien-Udom, *Black Nationalism; a Search for an Identity in America* (1962).

NEGRO AND REFORM, THE, have been related by definition, due to the long and unmitigated injustice to which the Negro has been subjected. However, the condition of Negroes as individuals and groups has varied, from those on the lowest social and economic rungs of society to the "Sugar Hill" section of Manhattan where exclusive Negroes have lived. Their wants have differed, from those who desired the right to join a golf club to those who desired a job of whatever kind. Moreover, although most Negroes have had a sense of having been despised and oppressed, they have had different thresholds of rebelliousness or idealistic concern for their race; many of them have been less evangelical on the subject than sympathizers of other races. Various elements among Negroes have been averse to reform. Thus, desegregation in housing would harm the business of important Negro real estate interests. Hence, Negroes could be served in two categories of reform: that of civil rights and political rights, permitting them to vote and attend unsegregated schools; and that of human rights, maintaining an active sense of the plight of poor and uninteresting Negroes, whose high incidence of disease, delinquency, and squalor made them a threat to themselves and to the general community. The National Urban League, organized 1910, concerned itself for reforms in both categories, and developed a program which was pragmatic, rather than radical. The civil rights (q.v.) upsurge of the 1960s resulted in laws, agencies, and expenditures, and made more visible Negro politicians, long there. Their lack of a reform program, however, prevented them from building a community establishment of the Jane Addams-Florence Kelley (qq.v.) pattern. Riots, as in Miami (1980), continued to be one indicator of inadequate community, despite vast sums poured into cities and neighborhoods.

NEGRO CHURCH IN AMERICA, an important instrument for both reform and anti-reform efforts among the Negroes. The African Methodist Episcopal Church, founded 1794, was a gathering place for Negroes and Negro discussion. As such, it was able to function mainly in the North, where it was of some aid to anti-slavery advocates, and received aid from philanthropists. For a general survey of the subject, see W.E.B. Du Bois, ed., *The Negro Church...* (1903). Militant Negroes came to distrust its conservative tendencies, and to believe that it dissipated Negro energies in religious raptures, being an opiate. In the 1930's, it produced such a phenomenon as Father Divine, whose millenarian presumptions probably served him better than it did his "children." Intellectuals among the Negroes who aspired to regard as artists, radicals, and professionals sought associations which found satisfaction in less homely catharsis. The 1954 decision of U.S. Supreme Court denouncing segregation roused sensitive elements of the Negro community, particularly in the South, and the Church became a vital center for their debates and development of strategy; see Integration, King, Martin Luther. E. Franklin Frazier and C. Eric Lincoln, *The Negro Church in America* (1973).

NEGRO COLONIZATION, see American Colonization Society.

NEGRO EDUCATION, see Education and the Negro.

NEGRO, FREE, see Free Negroes.

NEGRO GENIUS, THE (1940), by Benjamin Brawley, an evaluation which emphasized achievement, rather than effort alone, and which sought to be comprehensive. Thus, it did not emphasize rebels in the arts, but, by the nature of its subject-matter, necessarily included them. The date precluded concern for Richard Wright, Ralph Ellison (qq.v.), and others who stirred readers and auditors with their art.

NEGRO LABOR was a significant factor in American society from its earliest decades. The slavery system set up a standard for labor which affected nonslave labor. Free Negroes were kept in a status of contempt and mean opportunity, North and South, and drew the hatred of poor white people who competed with them for jobs. This was notably true, in the nineteenth century in New York, where the free Negroes and Irish came in collision. Nevertheless, Negroes struggled for opportunities, and found them at sea, where the degraded position of the sailor opened some places for Negroes; indeed, it has been claimed that as high as one-half the number of American seamen were Negroes in 1850. They also worked as scavengers, cooks, and in other fields. In the post-Civil War period, when white laborers worked to create unions, they resisted accepting Negroes into them, and the A.F.L. (q.v.) adopted the policy of not organizing them. Nevertheless, organized labor was bitter because industrialists used Negroes in order to break strikes. In 1902, W.E.B. Du Bois estimated that forty-three national labor organizations had no Negroes, and that sixteen of these had direct discriminating policies; twenty-seven included a few Negroes; in all, the A.F.L. counted only 40,000 Negroes in its ranks. There was little improvement in succeeding decades. Southern labor held the line against Negroes. In the North, a notable achievement was A. Philip Randolph's (q.v.) organization of the Brotherhood of Sleeping Car Porters. The organization of the C.I.O. (q.v.) helped bring into organized labor Negroes in industrial operations; but following its initial drive, it slowed up its pace of organization, especially where it would have involved Negroes. Despite improved Federal and state regulations, F.E.P.C. (q.v.), gains through social security (q.v.), and

other factors, Negroes continued to suffer from the old policy: Last hired, first fired. Ray Marshall, *The Negro Worker* (1967); Louis A. Forman et al., eds., *Negroes and Jobs* (1968).

NEGRO MOBILITY, a factor in American society and social relations. Negroes found themselves rejected in the north, following the Civil War, and established themselves as sharecroppers in the south, in Negro sections of southern cities. World War I took many of them abroad with the Army Expeditionary Forces, and others to northern cities to work in the factories of Chicago, Detroit, and elsewhere. One fruit of this movement was the Jackson Park riot of 1919, in Chicago, with attendant clashes and assaults elsewhere in the city. Southern response to this movement, in the War and post-War period was to attempt to retain Negroes for agricultural purposes; warrants were issued to bring back Negroes from the North, on various grounds. In the 1930's, Negroes continued to explore possibilities for living in various cities, fighting the various forms of "gentlemen's agreement" between realtors and white property-holders to keep them out. A major effort was to find a haven on the West Coast; for this and other details, Arna Bontemps and Jack Conroy, *They Seek a City* (1945). World War II offered new opportunities to Negroes, and encouraged new strategies aiming toward equality; new riots, notably in Detroit, attended these efforts. They culminated in the great desegregation (q.v.) U.S. Supreme Court decision of 1954. The new strategy of the south was to defend its customs and program, and to suggest that Negroes dissatisfied with them go north, where they had a right to expect different treatment. Some southern elements dreamed of an industrialization which would not require Negro labor. Others seized on radical tendencies and slogans of the Kennedy-Johnson (qq.v.) era to expand equality principles. With Atlanta, Birmingham, and other centers building Negro power structures, it appeared that Negro communities must fare well in the South. A phenomenon, not well explained, of the 1970s was a reverse movement from the old, with Negroes leaving northern cities to seek southern roots and places, despite the heavy panoply of northern "affirmative action" (q.v.) and opportunity laws. Eli Ginzberg, *The Negro Challenge to the Business Community* (1964); L. B. De Graaf, *Negro Migration to Los Angeles* (1962).

NEGRO SPIRITUALS, see Folk Arts and Reform.

NEGRO SUFFRAGE, a strategic force, in American political life, since the three-fifths clause (q.v.) in the Constitution made the Negro a factor in the voting power of the slaveholder, and his own vote during Reconstruction (q.v.) made him a weapon in the hands of the Republican Party. In the decades following, his voting power was severely curbed in the South, because of laws intended to discourage or impede its use. Such laws also harmed the voting power of poor whites, as in the case of literacy laws which they, too, could not cope with. In the North, they were able to derive bits of political advantage from their vote. The New Deal (q.v.) won them from the Republican Party, in considerable degree. In the 1960s, agitation wiped out limitations on Negro voting (q.v.) in southern elections. Negro politicians sought to expand their influence by voting "their" constituency nationally as they often did locally. It was no new goal; they had long claimed to have elected Woodrow Wilson (q.v.) in 1912. Nixon's (q.v.) 1968 campaign wrote off the Negro vote as not winable. The Negro vote may have elected Jimmy Carter (q.v.) in the razor-thin 1976 national election. However, it failed of effect in 1980. Donald S. Strong, *Negroes, Ballots, and Judges* (1968); Alex Poinsett, *Black Power Gary Style...Mayor Richard Gordon Hatcher* (1970); J. Q. Wilson, *Negro Politics* (1960); see also Black Caucus.

NEGRO WOMEN, see Women, Negro.

NEHRU, JAWAHARLAL (1889-1964), co-leader with Gandhi (q.v.) of the Free-India movement against British rule. Nehru lacked Gandhi's dedication to non-violence and non-materialistic life which made Gandhi a world legend. As Prime Minister of India, however, Nehru pressed for democratic advances which won him respect in America, as elsewhere. He tried to right injustices in the Indian caste system, notably though the Untouchability (q.v.) Act of 1955, and found resistance to it deep in his country's traditions. Nehru's effort at "non-alignment" between the democracies and communists was not consistent, but persisted as a slogan. His daughter Indira Gandhi's (1917-   ) role as party leader and warrior marked the distance from Gandhi-Nehru idealism to Indian-style machine politics. See Nehru's autobiography, *Toward Freedom* (1941); B. R. Nanda, *The Nehrus* (1962); G. W. Tyson, *Nehru: the Years of Power* (1966).

NEP, see New Economic Policy.

NEUTRALITY has theoretically served pacifists, but in practice has been a tool in the hands of partisans. The Embargo (q.v.) instituted by Jefferson in 1807 did not accomplish its neutral purpose. During World War I, German-Americans who agitated for American neutrality were often insincere; knowing it was not possible to enlist the United States on the side of Germany, they sought to prevent the nation aiding the Allies. When the Spanish Civil War broke out in 1936, a Neutrality Act was intended to separate the United States from the event. In practice, the Act operated against the Loyalist government in Madrid, which was deprived of aid which their fascist rivals obtained from Germany and Italy. See Nils Orvik, *The Decline of Neutrality, 1914-1941* (1971).

"NEW COLOSSUS, THE," see Lazarus, Emma.

NEW DEAL, THE, major effort of the Franklin D. Roosevelt Administration to meet the economic crisis he had inherited from Herbert Hoover (q.v.). The New Deal had several parts. A currency manipulation program was turned into a domestic effort, thanks to the failure of the London Economic Conference (q.v.), and was essentially ineffective. The National Recovery Administration (q.v.) sought to gear industry and labor to an organized assault on industrial stagnation. The U.S. Supreme Court struck down N.R.A. in 1935. More significant were acts designed to minister to specific problems. The C.C.C., the F.E.R.A., the A.A.A., the T.V.A., the H.O.L.C., the S.E.C., the F.H.A., and, most famous, the W.P.A., were major agencies set up to deal with unemployed youth, the unemployed, the farmer's problems, the need for power and flood-control, stock market control, the housing problem (qq.v.). In 1935, the Social Security Act (q.v.) was passed. N.Y.A. and the National Labor Relations Act (qq.v.) were instituted. The National Housing Act, in 1937, marked an epoch. Roosevelt's battle with the U.S. Supreme Court seemed a drastic attack on established ways of life. Thus, reformers tended to approve the New Deal, as conservatives to scorn it. Radicals saw it as a series of stop-gap and compromise measures, and observed that unemployment —the core of the depression— did not materially decline. That the New Deal changed rules could not be denied; whether it did more than the minimum required by the drastic conditions of human suffering was the question. With the coming of war (which ended the depression), Roosevelt remarked that he was substituting Dr. Win-The-War for Dr. New Deal; he did not explain the difference between these two. W. E. Leuchtenburg, eds., *The New Deal* (1969); Frank A. Warren and M. Wreszin, eds., *The New Deal: an Anthology* (1969).

NEW ECONOMIC POLICY, adopted in 1921 by the Soviet Union in order to placate the farmers who had suffered by and been rendered rebellious by the "war communism" maintained by the embattled Soviets, in the course of the civil war. The food levy which had been enforced was abolished, and a more limited tax on grain substituted; this gave the peasants more of a stake in the surplus produced, and possibilities for free enterprise in limited degree. The implications in NEP

were spelled out in related ordinances. NEP seemed to observers a retreat from the communist tenets maintained by the regime; some hoped that it foretold bankruptcy of communist expectations.

NEW ENGLAND CONFEDERATION, THE (1643-84), an early example of colonial cooperation, it was set up to ensure unity between its members, in the event of war with the Indians or the Dutch. It was composed of Massachusetts, Connecticut, New Haven, and Plymouth; the antagonism of Massachusetts kept out liberal Rhode Island. An important reason for the existence of the confederation was to encourage cooperation in the remanding of criminals, and fugitive servants. Although the league functioned with only moderate effectiveness, it was remembered by those who sought precedents for joint action during the later revolutionary crisis. See also Dominion of New England, The.

NEW FREEDOM, Woodrow Wilson's (q.v.) slogan in the Presidential campaign of 1912, juxtaposed to Theodore Roosevelt's "New Nationalism" (q.v.). William Allen White's (q.v.) remark that it was the difference between Tweedle-dee-dum and Tweedle-dee-dee is still relevant. The difference was in their background; Roosevelt seeking to take up power where he had last left it in Washington; Wilson prepared to wield power, but (thanks to his states'-rights upbringing) in the name of the People. His southern youth had taught him a respect for farmers, a suspicion of industrialists, a belief in free trade as a Democratic principle.

"NEW FRONTIERS," a slogan of the new Kennedy Administration (1961); Americans were to attack their problems with the spirit of pioneers. By the end of the year, commentators were agreed that the Administration had apparently shelved the slogan and intended to deal with its domestic and international dilemmas pragmatically.

NEW HARMONY COMMUNITY, a major effort initiated in 1825 by Robert Owen (q.v.) to set up a colony on rational principles. Owen's prestige, derived from his having made a fortune in industry, turned respectful attention on New Harmony, Indiana, where people were to work with maximum satisfaction and efficiency. In practical terms, the experiment was a failure. However, its immortality was guaranteed by the fact that, as a "pilot plant" (q.v.), analysts could study its principles and practice to determine their relationship and the possible uses in the future of elements of the experiment. See W. E. Wilson, *The Angel and the Serpent: the Story of New Harmony* (1964); John S. Duss, *The Harmonists* (1943).

"NEW IMMIGRATION," see Immigration and Reform.

NEW LEADER, THE, conservative socialist periodical which attracted the somewhat dull prose of old-time socialists, disillusioned communists, and various species of liberals, who used its pages as a sounding board. Although the publication should theoretically have resounded with helpful controversy, it seemed unable to get beyond general principles of virtue to an understanding of principles of human behavior.

NEW NATIONALISM, THE, Theodore Roosevelt's (q.v.) program as candidate of the Progressive Party in 1912; he called for strong central government, in the interests of the people, and recall of judical decisions—the latter in response to bitter criticism of the U.S. Supreme Court which had accumulated a record of indifference to public need. Roosevelt was influenced by Croly's *The Promise of American Life* (q.v.), but he was also responsive to wealthy supporters who wanted a strong government which would support their belief that their multiple business interests were in the public interest. The previous Taft Administration had proved itself a weak reed for this purpose, though devoutly conservative. Although Roosevelt endorsed child labor laws, the initiative, referendum, and recall, and anti-trust laws, they had a considerably different connotation to him and to La Follette (q.v.), whom he superseded in the Progressive Party; also compare with New Freedom.

NEW REPUBLIC, THE, founded by Herbert Croly (q.v.) in 1914, with Walter Lippmann among its editors, and Randolph Bourne (qq.v.) less firmly as contributing editor. Its purpose was to create a program for a ruling elite. It helped create the idea of a league of nations which provided a reason for American entrance into World War I, which it accepted. Although it had patronized the liberalism of the muckrakers as naive and inadequate, it deplored its passing in the 1920's, and endorsed labor, the U.S.S.R., civil liberties, and other tenets of a widening and more experimental democracy. During the 1930's, it made few efforts to distinguish between liberalism and marxism. Throughout this time, it had functioned as a serious organ of attitude and opinion, which was read by elite and responsible members of society. Increasingly, in the post-World War II years, which were punctuated with the editorship of Henry A. Wallace (q.v.), it lost consequence. See also Nation, The.

NEW SCHOOL FOR SOCIAL RESEARCH, a liberal institution which attracted a great number of liberal and reform intellectuals who lectured and experimented with educational devices, for the benefit of an avant-garde clientele. Its major figure was Alvin Johnson. It sponsored a Labor Research Bureau which attracted interest. Following the rise of Hitlerism (q.v.) in Germany, it performed a service by bringing over distinguished scholars who constituted a University in Exile, and who devoted themselves to graduate instruction. It also sponsored the publication Social Research.

"NEW SOUTH, THE," a concept popularized by the Georgia journalist Henry W. Grady (1850-89) who envisioned a South of industry and progress, in which, however, the Negro would be retained in a secondary capacity.

NEW YORK TIMES, became a semi-official national newspaper partly because of its conscientious verbatim reports of basic governmental and international speeches and statements, partly because of newspaper consolidations and bankruptcies which defeated other newspapers of substance and distinction, such as the New York Herald-Tribune. The Times began as a Republican paper which helped overthrow the corrupt Tammany Democrat William Marcy Tweed (q.v.) but also glided over the corruption within the Republican Grant (q.v.) Administration. It became a Democratic paper. Responding to urban forces which tolerated corruption and decay, the Times developed a defensive posture which, in effect, subordinated news to interpretation which manipulated the news. It was approved by numerous readers inside and out of New York who agreed with the Times's partisan program. Its dividing line was, first, publication of the unauthorized Pentagon Papers (q.v.), which committed it to an anti-Administration freedom of information (q.v.) program; and, secondly, its protracted probing of the Watergate (q.v.) break-in as the major crime in American political annals. It thus led the attack which unseated Nixon (q.v.). Although other papers, notably the Washington Post and the Los Angeles Times took somewhat similar positions in defense of their deteriorated cities, the Times had status as the most influential newspaper name in politics and news presentation, and culture administration. Elmer Davis, History of the New York Times (1951); Gay Talese, The Kingdom and the Power (1969); H. H. Dinsmore, All the News that Fits (1969); Harrison E. Salisbury, Without Fear or Favor (1980).

NEW YORK EVENING POST, see Post, New York Evening.

NEW ZEALAND, famous among reformers for its pioneer legislation, including the Land Act of 1892 which was directed against land monopolies, early boards of arbitration, which enabled Henry Demarest Lloyd (q.v.) to term it "a country without strikes" (although it did attain them), nationalization and welfare legislation of various kinds, and general programs looking forward to social cooperation, rather than competi-

tion. These were products of special conditions: the island character of the country, its dependence on such basic industries as sheepraising and dairy-products, the need for unity among the white people in their struggle to dominate the native Maoris and to resist the incursions of orientals; thus in 1899, at the height of passage of advanced legislation, was also passed an educational test intended to keep out orientals. During the 1910's and 1920's, reform was at a low ebb; the depression of the 1930's, however, revitalized the movement toward social reform, which continued to be better-known than the progress of New Zealand's relationship to native populations. M. P. Lissington, New Zealand and the United States (1972).

NEWLANDS ACT (1913), see Erdman Act.

NEWLANDS RECLAMATION ACT (1902), a significant milestone in conservation (q.v.), it designated the proceeds of public lands in the West for the construction and maintenance of irrigation projects in territories which needed them, thus setting a precedent for further measures in the field by the Federal government.

NEWLY EMERGING NATION, another euphemism for "underdeveloped" (q.v.) country or nation, and intended to be more pleasing to its statesmen. More significant as revealing the attitudes and hopes of the statesmen of the developed nations, than of a deeper understanding of the people they hoped to influence.

NEWSPAPERS, see Journalism and Reform.

NIAGARA MOVEMENT, THE, headed by W.E.B. Du Bois (q.v.), developed in 1905 in protest to the policies of Booker T. Washington (q.v.), as leader of the Negro people, who asked for moderate policies with respect to the white people, and for the right to work and prove their qualities. Du Bois and his followers, on the other hand, in their declaration of principles, demanded the right to be heard in Negro conclaves, and on the score of their belief that more in the way of opportunity and respect was due them than Washington demanded. The Niagara Movement—named for the meeting which took place at Fort Erie, Ontario—was a critical, and soul-searching effort, which Washington opposed as divisive and harmful. It created much of the thought and organization which ultimately resulted in the founding of the N.A.A.C.P. (q.v.).

NICARAGUA, one of the Central American (q.v.) republics which, subject to American intervention, stirred the sympathies of reformers. From 1912 to 1933, intervention was direct, though less direct intervention went back to the middle of the nineteenth century, due to the machinations of William Walker (q.v.) and United States concern for a canal route. In 1912, the fear that the canal route might slip into foreign hands and threaten United States control of the area brought American troops into the little country. In 1926, renewed concern over revolutionary disturbances brought fresh troops to support the presidential pretensions of Adolfo Díaz, a conservative. Their presence was resented by General Augustino César Sandino, who undertook guerrilla warfare which continued till 1933. Sandino was assassinated the next year. Nicaragua continued in the shadow of American foreign policy which was, however, unable to raise the level of democracy in that country, or lower the tragedy of want. The latter continued to produce revolutionary disturbances which gave hope to the Castro government of Cuba (q.v.) that Nicaragua might be brought into an anti-United States alliance. Neill Macaulay, The Sandino Affair (1967); Isaac J. Cox, Nicaragua and the United States (1976).

NIGERIA, one of the leading African lands, with a population of seventy-nine million—one-fifth of the continent's 460 million—and an oil-rich economy. It came out of a slave-trading and agricultural economy to profit from English missionaries and administrators. Made independent in 1960, a republic in 1963, it fell heir to tribal and sectional leaders and soldiers who employed assassination and messacre to fend off secessions, notably during the Nigerian-Biafran war in 1970. Its petroleum wealth enabled it to recover quickly from civil disorder and get on with education, trade relations, including the United States, and a subsistence agriculture which would feed its people. S. K. Painter-Brick, *Nigerian Politics and Military Rule: Prelude to Civil War* (1970); Sir Alan Burns, *History of Nigeria* (1972).

"NIGGER," see Epithets.

NIGHT RIDERS, see Ku Klux Klan.

NIHILIST, a term first used in the novel by Ivan S. Turgenieff, *Fathers and Sons* (1862). Although best identified with anarchist and terrorist thought in Russia, it was used sympathetically by American liberals, as well as revolutionists, who felt that much could be forgiven those who suffered under the Czar's rule.

"NINE OLD MEN," bitter phrase employed against a U.S. Supreme Court *(q.v.)* which seemed to the Franklin D. Roosevelt *(q.v.)* Administration bent on frustrating a legislative program which the public patently needed and had demanded; see "Court Packing Issue," The.

1900, see Edward R. Tannenbaum, *1900: the Generation before the War* (1977).

1905 REVOLUTION, in Russia, although crushed, created the concept of soviets *(q.v)* which in 1917 enabled the Bolsheviks to develop the extra-legal organization with which they overthrew the Provisional Government.

1907, see Panic of 1907.

1910, see "Revolution of 1910".

1912, a year of unexplored significance in American history: both a highpoint and a turning point. On the surface, it appeared that Americans have never been in greater control of their destiny; in the Presidential elections of that year, the candidates vied with one another to plunder progressive programs, and, in the cases of Roosevelt and Wilson *(qq.v.)*, even socialistic planks. Debs, the Socialist Party *(q.v.)* candidate, polled nearly a million votes. The power of public opinion had recently been shown in the Ballinger Affair *(q.v.)* and the great public interest displayed in the findings of the Pujo Committee *(q.v.)*. Yet the muckraking publications had been quietly destroyed, for the most part, and an offensive against labor and minority elements was underway which would produce the Ludlow Massacre, the Leo Frank Case, the Mooney conspiracy, and other such tragedies *(qq.v.)*. Roosevelt's candidacy was substantially directed by such anti-democrats as Frank A. Munsey *(q.v.)*. The imminence of war was not appreciated, and a casual pacifism assumed a relationship between peace and good business. The country was moving toward stronger central government, and taking it for granted that the battle for free speech and necessary information had been permanently secured.

1913, see Alan Valentine, *1913: America between Two Wars* (1962).

1914, see James Cameron, *1914* (1959).

1919, STEEL STRIKE OF, see Steel Strike of 1919. See also John Dos Passos, *Nineteen-Nineteen* (1932), and David Mitchell, *1919: Red Mirage, Elegy for a Lost Cause* (1970).

1920s, see Twenties.

1929, year of the Wall Street panic which ushered in the depression of the 1930's; notable to reformers as a major year of crisis for free enterprise principles and the capitalist system in general.

1930s, see Thirties.

1934, GENERAL STRIKE OF, see General Strike.

1940s: Decade of Triumph and Trouble, by Cabell Phillips (1975).

1946, STRIKES DURING, a drastic concomitant or reconversion from the labor conditions of World War II. Labor,

which had more than tripled its union membership in ten years to fourteen and a half million, feared the loss of wartime pay and bonuses, and other conditions, and entered upon mass strikes in the auto industry, in steel, and in mining, as well as in railroads: a situation which tied up the nation's economy. There was comparatively little violence; this was a struggle of Big Labor against Big Business, with the Federal government in the middle and sensitive to public responsiveness. The nation, seeking to construct a postwar economy, debating a full employment bill, came up with the Maximum Employment Act, which guaranteed nothing, and was a mere endorsement of the idea. The battle to control prices by maintaining the O.P.A. *(q.v.)* was lost. Finally, the Taft-Hartley Labor-Management Relations Act *(q.v.)* of 1947 was enacted.

1949, a momentous year, featuring Russia's achievement of the atom-bomb, and the victory of Mao *(q.v.)* in China.

1950s, see I. F. Stone, *The Haunted Fifties* (1963).

1960s, see W. L. O'Neill, *Coming Apart...America in the 1960s* (1971); Andrew Kopkind and James Ridgeway, eds., *Decade of Crisis* (1972).

1974, President Nixon's *(q.v.)* resignation creates a crisis in the Presidency.

1980s, see Howard Baker, *No Margin for Error: America in the Eighties* (1980).

1984 (1949), by George Orwell *(q.v.)*, one of the most important fictional works of the twentieth century, it depicted a world divided into major warring factions, for whom war was a way of life and social control, and whose program was based on propaganda techniques to which the masses were forced to conform, either through ignorance and persuasion, or, in the case of rebels, through techniques which manipulated their character. *1984* popularized a wide variety of concepts, most famous being "Big Brother." It was seen as a satire on dictatorship, and also as a bitter comment upon the faded hopes of socialism and especially the U.S.S.R. Others, however, believed that much of the psychology depicted could be applied to western civilization, which, they alleged, had descended into dull conformity, was satisfied with tepid and synthetic living, which spoke and thought in clichés, and did honor to cynics and manipulators. F. H. Kuelman, *1984 and all That: Modern Science, Social Change and Human Values* (1971); Frank Thompson, Jr., *1984 Notes* (1967); Robert D. Wolff, *1984 Revisited* (1973).

NINETEENTH AMENDMENT, see Woman Suffrage.

N.I.R.A., see National Recovery Administration.

NIXON, RICHARD M. (1913-   ), a major political figure, he confounded friends and foes with his rises and falls, as Congressman and Senator (1947-1952), Vice-President (1952-1960), and then, following defeats for the Presidency and Governorship of California, President (1969-1974). He was re-elected to that office in 1972 by the greatest majority in history. His *Six Crises* (1961) detailed his dangerous commitment in pressing the Hiss Case *(q.v.)*; charges of misuse of funds, which threatened his Vice-President candidacy in 1952; efforts to "dump" him in 1956; and others. Although intensely hated by liberals and radicals, he received striking popular endorsements, as when a Howard K. Smith television special following his California defeat, entitled "The Political Obituary of Richard M. Nixon" brought 80,000 telegrams and letters of protest. Smith had brought Hiss on the program as a commentator. As President, Nixon sought to wind down the Vietnam War *(q.v.)* amid protest and demonstrations demanding that he end American involvement unilaterally. He astounded friends and foes alike by breaking through American-Red China antagonisms in 1972 by visiting China in order to establish detente *(q.v.)*, which would create a balance between Russia, China, and America. In 1974, Watergate *(q.v.)*—related tape *(q.v.)* disclosures brought him down, forcing his resignation from office. But, following a serious operation for phlebitis and a period of retirement from public view, he returned with a resounding best-seller, his *RN: the Memoirs of Richard Nixon* (1978), which enemy efforts and protests could not lower from domestic and international attention. Apprehensive that he could return to public attention, his foes were required to note the rise in national conservative feeling, the damage done to Hiss die-hards by Weinstein's *Perjury* (1978), and to note that Nixon was well-regarded and consulted by such Republican leaders as Ronald Reagan (*q.v.*). Nixon achieved still another best-seller in 1980, with his *The Real War*. It demanded recognition of the Soviet Union as a determined competitor on the world scene in arms and action. Reagan's Presidential victory in 1980 left open the question of whether events would make it politic for him or his Secretary of State Alexander Haig to call Nixon to service again. Louis Filler, ed., *The Presidency in Crisis* (1982); William Safire, *Before the Fall* (1975); T. H. White, *The Making of the President* (1960); White, *Breach of Faith* (1975); Jules Witcover, *The Resurrection of Richard Nixon* (1970); Carl Bernstein, et al., *The Presidential Transcripts* (1974); Earl Mayo, *Richard Nixon* (1959); Rowland Evans, Jr. and Robert D. Novak, *Nixon in the White House* (1971).

N.L.R.B. see National Labor Relations Act.

NOBEL PEACE PRIZE, a presumed incentive to thought and action which makes for peace; it was won by Theodore Roosevelt in 1906 for his negotiation of peace between Russia and Japan; other American recipients of the award included Elihu Root, Woodrow Wilson, Jane Addams and Nicholas Murray Butler together, and Emily G. Balch and John R. Mott together (*qq.v.*), among still others.

NOBLESSE OBLIGE, literally, "nobility obliges," that is, being of noble family places a duty upon the individual to serve his people and his country. Reformers have, when sensitive to democratic slogans, been unimpressed by what they have seen as an arrogant and paternalistic motto. However, many reformers and quasi-reformers have, in effect, been inspired by it. Much of "goo goo" (*q.v.*) reform obviously reflected the spirit of *noblesse oblige*. Such patricians as Theodore and Franklin D. Roosevelt acted according to its tenets.

NOCK, ALBERT J. (1873-1945), writer of aristocratic tastes who held most of humanity to be sub-human and ineducable, and who believed that a viable society could only be based on a sound grounding in classics. He mixed a distaste for naturalistic (*q.v.*) fiction with an admiration for Rabelais, contempt for those who appealed to the masses with a respect for Robert M. La Follette. His relation to reform lay in his advocacy of the Single Tax (*q.v.*) and his opposition to American intervention in the two World Wars, which he believed proceeded from demagogy and led to a further deterioration of American civilization. As editor of the *Freeman* (*q.v.*), he helped give a forum to fresh and creative minds; see his *The Myth of a Guilty Nation* (1922); *The Theory of Education in the United States* (1932); *Henry George* (1939); and *Memoirs of a Superfluous Man* (1943).

NON-CONFORMITY, see Conformity and Reform.

NONPARTISAN LEAGUE, THE, a major reform movement in the midwest, organized in 1915 by A.C. Townley (*q.v.*), it grew sensationally while the Progressive Era (*q.v.*) waned. The League emphasized state ownership of storage facilities, state inspection of grain, state hail insurance, and other aids for farmers. In 1916, it elected Lynn J. Frazier governor of North Dakota. It also organized in other western states, which it sought to unite as a national Nonpartisan League. Townley's "autocratic" rule was exploited by the Republican-Democratic coalition and aided by others who fought for cooperation rather than state ownership. The war provided the League's enemies with an opportunity to challenge the League's "patriotism." Their opposition, plus post-War reaction, caused the League's decline in the early 1920's. R. L. Morlan, *Political Prairie Fire* (1955).

NON-RESISTANT SOCIETY, formed in 1838 by Garrisonian

perfectionists, led by Henry C. Wright (*q.v.*), in protest against what seemed to them the too-moderate program of the American Peace Society. The non-resistants repudiated the use of all "carnal" weapons. Though apparently fanatical extremists whose tactics could have no conceivable use, they affected the later thinking of Gandhi (*q.v.*) and the Negro anti-segregation movements at home and abroad.

NORDHOFF, CHARLES (1830-1901), New York journalist whose *The Communistic Societies of the United States* (1875) is a primary work in the literature of Socialism in America.

"NORMALCY," see Harding, Warren Gamaliel.

NORRIS, GEORGE W. (1861-1944), distinguished midwestern liberal from Nebraska, who led the coalition which carried out the "revolution of 1910" to loosen the grip of "Czar" Cannon on House of Representatives procedure. He was intensely opposed to Woodrow Wilson's (*q.v.*) foreign policy, which he saw as calculated to implicate the United States in the European War, and he fought to the end to prevent American intervention. Although an opponent of trusts, he found himself at the war's end cooperating with such defenders of big business as Henry Cabot Lodge (*q.v.*) to prevent the entrance of the United States into the League of Nations (*q.v.*), which he saw as no more than another step toward repeating the tragedy of World War I. A friend of public power, he sponsored legislation to establish a government facility at Muscle Shoals, and, in 1933, offered the bill which created T.V.A. (*q.v.*). For his support of Al Smith in 1928, and his approval of New Deal legislation (*qq.v.*), he was, in 1936, excluded from the Republican Party. He was defeated during his campaign for a sixth term in the Senate. R. Lowitt, *George W. Norris* (1965).

NORRIS-LA GUARDIA ANTI-INJUNCTION ACT (1932), culmination of the battle, more than a quarter of a century old, to prevent the use of the injunction (*q.v.*) against labor preventing it from action intended to protect its union and other rights. In effect, a single judge had the power to break a strike by the simple expedient of issuing a restraining order preventing strike action on grounds having more or less validity. The Pullman Strike (*q.v.*) had been so broken. The Clayton Anti-Trust Act (*q.v.*) had been intended as an anti-injunction law, but had not operated effectively in behalf of labor. The Norris-La Guardia Act was more detailed and explicit in its specification of grounds on which it would be illegal to invoke injuctions against labor's free associations and deeds.

NORTH IRELAND, the six counties, tragic in its war between half a million Catholics who looked south to the Irish Republic, and a million Protestants holding grimly to their British connection. Efforts at home rule and coalition breaking down, Belfast and vicinity were paraded by British troops who shot and were shot as incidents occurred. Several thousand men, women, and children were cut down, often atrociously, by terrorists and counter-terrorists (*q.v.*), in troubles which challenged decency, but also solution. Although North Ireland was unlike Israel, where the P.L.O. (*q.v.*) was a constant threat to world peace, the terrorism was similar in that it struck at people whether they were committed or unembroiled, and nurtured children to be murderers. Efforts at peaceful solutions, and noble human efforts to inject mercy and rationality into Ulster living did not progress. G. MacEoin, *Northern Ireland: Captive of History* (1974); Simon Winchester, *Northern Ireland in Crisis* (1975); Richard Rose, *Northern Ireland: a Time of Choice* (1976).

NORTHWEST ORDINANCE OF 1787, generally appreciated as a momentous achievement of Congress, since it barred slavery from the American West, provided for freedom of worship, right of jury trial, and public education, and specified that states made from the territories north of the Ohio River would enter the Union on terms equal to those of the original states. It is generally unappreciated that this was an achievement of Congress operating under the Articles of Confederation *(q.v.),* rather than under the Constitution of the United States; and that this fact qualifies, in degree, the reputation of the earlier Congress as weak and ineffective.

"NOT WORTH A CONTINENTAL," see Continental Currency.

NOYES, JOHN HUMPHREY (1811-1886), notorious as the founder of the "free love" Oneida Community *(q.v.),* he was an earnest seeker who collected others who sought an immediate contact with eternal values, whose patent sincerity confounded conventional public opinion. Noyes argued that monogamous love was selfish, that multiple love could be enjoyed, so long as it was freely given and received. The community developed rituals of public self-examination intended to curb vanity, egotism, malice, and other undesirable traits. Noyes and other leaders had a free hand in leadership which they used successfully to build up their community. He developed theories of sexual relations explained in *Male Continence* (1848), and of a eugenical *(q.v.)* nature, as in his pioneer *Scientific Propagation* (1873). His *History of American Socialisms* (1870) is an important work of analysis, as well as of data.

N.R.A., see National Recovery Administration, "Little N.R.A."

NUCLEAR QUESTION, THE, most momentous of all questions facing governments and people toward the close of the century. It involved control of plans to employ *nuclear energy* for civil purposes, priorities in building plants for nuclear production, problems in the disposal of *nuclear waste,* and realism and desired results from *nuclear weapons* as part of the national defense system. "Anti-Nuke" protesters opposed any work in this field as causing pollution of earth and sky, and creating such dangers as occurred in September 1980, in Arkansas, where a nuclear missile silo exploded after a workman dropped a wrench socket that punctured the missile's fuel tank. Although no radiation was said to have escaped, the accident underscored the dangers which nuclear manufacture involved. Leakages from drums of radioactive waste dumped at sea thirty-five miles off San Francisco over twenty-four years also created unease, especially when the drums were said to have been second-hand and carelessly handled.

Such events kept the most optimistic of citizens tense, persuaded though they might be of the need for nuclear energy. Nuclear reactors were developed world-wide, with protests tirelessly alive, and side issues and effects constant. Thus, an accident at Three Mile Island in Pennsylvania not only roused radiation fears, but citizens suffered from their increased smoking and use of tranquilizers, as well as health costs and moving expenses for those whose nerves could no longer endure fear. Although *Time* Magazine termed fears "irrational," observing that in twenty years, the seventy-one nuclear reactors had killed no one, and would not, fear of the reactors continued.

The use of *nuclear weapons* as defense armaments added the component of fear of the ultimate catastrophe. Some critics, like Richard J. Barnet *(The Economy of Death* [1969]) were consistently against American defense, having nothing to say about Russian, Chinese, or Cuban arms. Others, like T. H. White *(The Making of a President* [1964]) were smug about American "probably superfluous" strategic arms superiority, though later counts showed Russia ahead of American defense. The Carter *(q.v.)* fiasco in attempting to free American "hostages" in Iran *(q.v.)* raised questions of American capability. The problem of universal catastrophe in case of war was complicated by arguments over how to limit nuclear strikes, for example, to military targets rather than cities teeming with people. SALT *(q.v.)* talks, whether continued or interrupted between the United States and Russia, gave no certainty that they might not be smoke screens for more refined nuclear production. False alarms at nuclear installations heartened some military spokesmen as proving American alertness, but frightened others despite reassurances that war might not be induced by computer errors and triggered firing responses. *Nuclear materials,* notably uranium, were major items in international negotiations, involving Canada, France, Italy, China, Australia, and other nations, with the transformation of materials into strategic war uses, though international barter, haunting observers.

The greatest hope lay in the universal diplomatic, commercial, and moral dialogue engendered, creating masses of experts in all nations who were abreast of technical, but also human factors. Although this could result in instances of sabotage and even murder, as in the case of Israel's apparent effort to retard Iraqui efforts to obtain an atom bomb, plans continued to maintain a nuclear defense while also furthering mass transit and other benign goals, using the same substances. Arthur I. Waskow, ed., *The Debate over Thermonuclear Strategy* (1965); Edward Teller, et al., *Power and Security* (1976); Gar Alperovitz, *Atomic Diplomacy* (1965); E. Gluekauf, ed., *Atomic Energy Waste* (1961); H. Peter Metzger, *The Atomic Establishment* (1972); Michael Mandelbaum, *The Nuclear Question* (1980); Richard C. Lewis, *The Nuclear Power Rebellion* (1972).

NULLIFIER, NULLIFICATION, associated with the theories of John C. Calhoun *(q.v.),* whose "South Carolina Exposition" (1828) preached states' rights and the right of a state to nullify an unjust Federal law, the state itself being the judge of what constituted injustice. The force of this theory was felt in the passage by the legislature of South Carolina (November 24, 1832) of an Ordinance of Nullification, defining the tariff acts of 1828 and 1832, as passed by the Congress of the United States, illegal in South Carolina. President Jackson had small interest in the tariff, but was determined that the laws of the United States must be obeyed. Although he received Congressional authority to carry out the revenue acts involved, in the "Force Bill" of March 2, 1833, he had no interest in subjugating the militant state. A compromise tariff was contrived, and both he and South Carolina could claim to have had their way. Nullification represented a half-way stand between that implicit in the Kentucky and Virginia Resolutions *(q.v.)* and the secession from the Union by the southern states.

NUREMBERG LAWS (September 15, 1935), passed by the German Nazi Government, as a major blow at Jewish citizens. They deprived all Jews, including those having one-fourth Jewish blood, of citizenship. Intermarriage between Germans and Jews was forbidden. The Nuremberg Laws represented a new level of Jewish persecution by the Nazi regime, prior to their campaign to exterminate the Jewish people entirely. See also, Genocide.

NUREMBERG TRIALS, see War Crimes.

NURSING HOMES, a scandal of American treatment of the old. People who professed disgust with nineteenth century treatment of the sick and infirm produced no such crusader as Dorothea Dix *(q.v.).* They shunted their elderly off to cold and meagre places run for nothing but profit, where such unfortunates could wait for death to relieve them. How Americans had worked themselves into such an untenable position was yet to be determined. U. A. and G. Falk, *The Nursing Home Dilemma* (1976); Linda Horn and Elma Griesel, *Nursing Homes: Citizens' Actions Guide* (1977).

N.Y.A., see National Youth Administration.

NYE, GERALD P. (1892-   ), newspaperman and Republican Senator from North Dakota, famous as chairman of the special committee investigating munitions sales during World War I (1934-1936). His committee sought to discover whether financial powers, notably the Morgan interests, had been a force in bringing the United States into the war. The investigation stirred fears of "war profiteers" *(q.v.)* and inspired the Neutrality Acts of 1935, 1936, and 1937, the last of which aimed to prevent America's being implicated in the Spanish Civil War *(q.v.).* In the same period, Nye was discovered to have sympathy and relations with would-be American fascists; see John Roy Carlson, *Under Cover* (1943). An extreme isolationist, and pillar of the America First Committee, he was defeated in the election of 1944.

O

O.A.A., see Old Age Assistance.

O.A.S., see Organization of American States.

OBERLIN COLLEGE, projected in 1833 by the Rev. John J. Shipherd, a disciple of Finney (q.v.), it received the seceded students of Lane (q.v.) Seminary and in 1834 went under way as technically coeducational and with a strong anti-slavery attitude among its administrators and students. From Oberlin graduated Lucy Stone (q.v.) and John M. Langston, among many noted reformers and persons of distinction. Oberlin was a center of abolitionism, and a station on the underground railroad (q.v.). Oberlin leaders were involved in one of the notable incidents attending defiance of the Fugitive Slave Act of 1850 (q.v.): the "Oberlin-Wellington Rescue," during which a fugitive was, in 1858, forcibly removed from custody and transported to Canada and freedom.

OBSCENITY, in the 1960s a cause, begun on the University of California Berkeley campus and featuring "students" carrying signs declaring the importance of foul words. They became all but the complete vocabulary of mindless "militants" and infected intelligent conversation and dialogue as well. The return of followers of the trend to the Establishment (q.v.) and its emoluments diminished the use of what one commentator called the "fuck and shit school." The reluctant revelations in the Presidential tapes (q.v.) further encouraged a general desire for privacy. It was thus a long way from the arguments which had pled "social relevance" in behalf of James Joyce (q.v.), D. H. Lawrence and others. See Pornography. Charles Rembar, *The End of Obscenity* (1970); M. L. Ernst and W. Seagle, *To the Pure* (1928); L. A. Zurcher, Jr. and R. G. Kirkpatrick, *Citizens for Decency* (1976); Ray C. Rist, ed., *Pornography Controversy* (1974).

OBSOLESCENCE, see Controlled Depreciation.

O.B.U., see One Big Union.

OCCUPATIONAL HAZARDS, see Factory Legislation.

O'CONNELL, DANIEL (1775-1847), nationalist leader of Ireland, who personified its aspirations in the first part of the nineteenth century. A reformer, rather than a revolutionist, he agitated for Catholic emancipation, which, under conditions of the island's investiture by Protestants, was a powerful instrument for Irish unity. O'Connell's efforts were aided by his election to Parliament in 1828 and his inability under its rules debarring Roman Catholics, to take his seat. The rules were revised, but he persisted in non-cooperation until the Catholic Emancipation Act opened all public offices but two to members of his faith. As a member of Parliament, he advocated a number of reform measures. He also persisted in his agitation to end the Act of Union (1801) which bound Ireland to Great Britain. Famous among the Irish in America, he earned their wrath because of his opposition to slavery. (See Irish-American Reform.) Nevertheless, he deprecated radical action intended to gain Ireland her independence, and was criticized by supporters of the Young Ireland movement. O'Connell's total dedication to his people, however, won him their universal regard. M. R. O'Connell, *Correspondence of Daniel O'Connell* (1973).

OCTOBER REVOLUTION, see Russian Revolution, The, of 1917.

OCTOPUS, The (1901), by Frank Norris, one of the great American novels, which embodied the ideals and attitudes of the Populists (q.v.). Other features included an idealized poet, suggested by Edwin Markham (q.v.), strong symbolism, as with the sheep being cut down by the railroad, a touch of anti-semitism in his unnecessary depiction of the railroad's agent as a Jew, some strong naturalistic (q.v.) passages, and a controversial supernaturalism.

OFFICE OF PRICE ADMINISTRATION, set up in 1941 as a war measure, undertook to exercise price controls and prevent runaway inflation, such as had overtaken the nation during World War I, destroying many of the wage gains during that period. It set ceilings on many commodities, and maintained a system of rational goods. Its significance lay in its firm efforts to control national economic processes in the interests of the total economy. Though it was resisted by such special interests as farmers, and challenged by "black market" transactions, as well as by simply inadequate enforcement facilities, the O.P.A. helped to hold the line on prices, notably on rents. It was, however, unable to resist pressures for raising prices, once the war had ended, and after a year of struggle came to an end in 1947. See Regulation.

OFFICE-SEEKERS, used invidiously by their opponents, with a considerable amount of self-righteousness by the seekers: "What are we here for except for the offices?" asked Webster Flanagan, a Texas delegate to the Republican Convention of 1880, during a debate on a civil-service reform plank.

OGLETHORPE, JAMES (1696-1785), a combination of soldier and reformer, he was concerned for the well-being of prisoners, and conceived the idea of aiding those in debtor's prison (see Prisons) by sending them to America. Many of them helped to establish the colony of Georgia, in 1733. He also instituted a policy of religious toleration which attracted dissident Protestants. He conducted a war with the Spaniards to the south of Georgia, and did not extend his reformist zeal to the Cherokee Indians. Christian Priber, a German who did, was made a prisoner by Oglethorpe, and died while incarcerated.

"O. HENRY," see Porter, (William) Sydney.

"OHIO GANG, THE," name given to a group of politicians who helped lift Warren G. Harding (q.v.) into the Presidency. They symbolized the socially indifferent office seekers and manipulators, to whom public office was no more than a means for personal enrichment. Most notorious was Harry M. Daugherty of Washington Court House, Ohio, whom Harding made Attorney-General in his Administration. In 1927, he was tried for malfeasance in office, on charges involving the Alien Property Office, but escaped conviction because of jury disagreements. His *The Inside Story of the Harding Tragedy* (1932) is a study in the logic of a politician.

OIL, once an inspiring tale of domestic discovery, war between producers and refiners, notably John D. Rockefeller (q.v.), the battle against monopoly, expansion in foreign lands and underwater probes, and problems in government control; see Henry Demarest Lloyd, Ida M. Tarbell, E. Kilman and T. Wright, *Hugh Roy Cullen* (1954). In the 1960s, warnings were issued that oil was not a reproducible substance, and must disappear. The warnings made no public impression. Prices for car and furnace fuel continued low, until the OPEC (q.v.) nations in 1973, sensing opportunity in the world competition between the United States and Soviet Russia, and frustrated by U.S. support of Israel, raised oil prices to unheard of heights. Billions of new dollars poured into their coffers causing international monetary problems and questions of the uses to which Arab masters would put their augmented resources. The rise in United States prices was far less dramatic than elsewhere but shocked American car-users. Prices continued to rise, though not yet to the *New York Times* 1980 demand for two dollars per gallon, nor the European three dollars per gallon. Demands for smaller cars affected the automobile industry. Fear of being at the mercy of Arab oil producers turned attention to "alternative fuels"—solar and nuclear (q.v.) power, gas, coal, electricity-powered cars, "gasohol"—as well as Alaskan oil and new probes on and off-shore. Suspicion of the good faith of such giant firms as Mobil Oil, which continued to show astonishing profits though harassed by OPEC and government regulations, mixed with a hope that "individual enterprise" in oil would produce new sources of oil and energy. This hope won Senate approval in 1980 of a twenty billion dollar plan for uncovering synthetic fuel. This hope, too, helped bring on the overwhelming Reagan (q.v.) victory of 1980. Questions remained of oil and gas price controls, which, removed, might put the national economy at risk, or change the "American way of life." Also in doubt were United States-OPEC-Russia relations, possibilities for war and peace, American relations with other oil-producing lands like Nigeria and Venezuela, and, these shadows laid, what would happen to the Arab states when their oil ran out. A. P. Blaustein and J. J. Paust, *The Arab Oil Weapon* (1977); John Blair, *The Control of Oil* (1978); Peter R. Odell, *Oil and World Power* (1970); Luis Vallenilla, *Oil, the Making of a New Economic Order* (1975); Tim Niblock, ed., *Social and Economic Development in the Arab Gulf* (1980); J. B. Kelly, *Arabia, the Gulf, and the West* (1980).

OLD AGE ASSISTANCE, see Social Security Act, Welfare Legislation.

OLD AGE DEPENDENCY, recognized as increasingly demanding a problem because of the longer life-span which raised the percentage of persons over sixty-five years of age from less than five percent in 1890 to over fifteen percent in 1960. Yet the percentage of persons over sixty-five in the labor force dropped from over forty percent in 1890 to a little over twenty percent in 1960. Efforts to persuade employers to use the wisdom and experience of the aging were not encouraging in results. This meant that increasing numbers of old people were dependent on savings, social security, children. Health insurance (q.v.) could be for them a matter of life or death. Social security (q.v.) had, indeed, created a principle not available earlier in a time of labor union benefits, fraternal benefits, and meagre pension systems; see L. W. Squirer, *Old Age Dependency in the United States* (1912). New Problems of old age included extreme loosening of family ties, which left many of the old in limbo, subject to the anguish of inflation (q.v.) as well as the dark tragedy of nursing homes (q.v.). Unlike old civilizations, and, indeed, much of older America, age did not accumulate reverence or prestige. The deterioration of the cities put many of the old at the mercies of young sadists and older thieves and cheats. The erosion of the family unit made for callous and abusive treatment not only by strangers but relatives. Senility drew ridicule, rather than loving care. The mock respect paid "senior citizens" shallowly overlaid brazen competitiveness and contempt for the old by the younger, whose malice and cold-heartedness drove increasing percentages of the aged to suicide (q.v.). A grotesque feature of the 1980 elections had been shameless arguments in the press, by way of satire and bold pronouncement, that Ronald Reagan (q.v.) was unfit to be President because he was too old, though his physiology was patently superior to that of many younger people. With Reagan now President, the nation had a person in the White House of promise to older citizens.

A notable figure in this social crisis was Representative Claude Pepper, distinguished Florida Democrat, who at age seventy-nine was chairman of the House Select Committee on Aging. He estimated up to two and one-half million cases a year of abuse of the old. Although some fifteen states offered protective services for them, such services did not suffice for the condition of society. White House Conferences on Aging were held in 1961, 1971, and (scheduled) 1981 which produced and were expected to produce further recommendations resulting in legislation helpful to the situation. Basic was Medicare, created under President Johnson (q.v.) in 1965 as a Social Security (q.v.) amendment, and providing hospital care and supplementary benefits which soon paid some 40% of the health care bill for the aged. Social equality was harder to acquire. Youth sought with unseemly eagerness to supplant its elders, and employers sought youth despite evidence that the older employee was more conscientious, interested, and dependable. Most formidable operating in the older people's favor was their numbers. The average age of Americans went up to thirty years, thanks to the drop in child birth and the longer American life span. Between 1970 and 1979 the under-fourteen population (q.v.) decreased by 14%, while that of over-sixty-five rose 24%.

This raised a political fact, as their very numbers promised the elderly increased political power at local and national levels. The Gray Panthers, a national organization a decade old in 1980, were producing leaders who were formulating demands ranging from lower street-car fares to changes in Medicare regulations providing better and more equitable service, involving not only shelter and long-term care, but spiritual well-being. The Older Americans Act (1965) promised to have a larger future than a past. Jessica Mitford, *The American Way of Death* (1978); D. D. Van Tassel, ed., *Aging, Death, and the Completion of Being* (1980); Ronald Gross et al., *The New Old: Struggling for Decent Aging* (1978); Christine L. Fry, ed., *Aging in Culture and Society* (1980).

"OLD IMMIGRATION" see Immigration and Reform.

OLD LAW TENEMENTS, see Housing Problem, The.

OLDER, FREMONT (1856-1935), Progressive editor of the San Francisco *Bulletin, Call,* and combined *Call-Bulletin,* notable for his services in combatting corruption in his city, and also for his efforts in behalf of Tom Mooney (q.v.), whom he sought to have freed; see Older's autobiography, *My Own Story* (1926).

OLMSTEAD, FREDERICK LAW (1822-1903), American landscape architect and traveler. He designed Central Park in New York City as well as other parks in Boston, Buffalo, and elsewhere. His attempt to develop a disinterested view of slavery influenced Northern opinion on the subject; see his *A Journey in the Sea-Board Slave States* (1856); *A Journey Through Texas* (1857); *A Journey in the Back Country* (1860).

OLNEY, RICHARD (1835-1917), a qualifying figure in the liberal picture of Grover Cleveland (q.v. for this and following topics); as his Attorney General, he was unsuccessful in drawing up cases curbing unfair business practices under the Sherman Anti-Trust Law; however, he was successful in acquiring a "blanket injunction" against the American Railway Union (q.v.) which was presumably acting as a trust. As Secretary of State (1895-7), his declaration on the Venezuelan Dispute (q.v.) was a classic of imperialist utterance. Gerald G. Eggert, *Richard Olney: Evolution of a Statesman* (1974).

OLYMPICS, though "just a game," reminded neutrals that there was little in the world which did not descend into combat and potential combat. The London Olympics of 1948 had excluded Israeli athletes in order to appease Arab opinion. The 1968 Mexico City Olympics had featured American Negro athletes who refused to honor the playing of the *Stars Spangled Banner* and had raised clenched fists, black-gloved, to symbolize their sense of Negro oppression in "racist" America. The shocking P.L.O. (q.v.) murders of eleven Jewish athletes in 1972 were doubly shocking to a German city, Munich, which would have been happy to forget a past which included the nearby city of Dachau (q.v.). An irony of this event was Rhodesia's (Zimbabwe) (q.v.) exclusion from these Olympics at the demand of leaders of black-led nations. The P.L.O. murders were substantially forgotten.

The controversy over boycotting the Olympics of 1980, in Moscow, stood out among such debasements of sport and politics because it followed Russia's military adventure in Afghanistan (q.v.), an event which threatened world peace, and so underscored the critical nature of U.S.-Soviet relations. Although a major goal of diplomacy was to create as many avenues of dialogue as possible, the Olympics—presumably dedicated to goodwill—helped little in this direction. It was in no sense "just a game," being taken with deadly seriousness by great masses of soccer, boxing, running, and other sport fans. The partial boycott of the Moscow Olympics, notably by the United States, highlighted the problem, but offered no solution. See Sport. M. I. Finley and H. W. Picket, *Olympic Games: the First Thousand Years* (1976); Lord Killanin and John Rodds, eds., *Olympic Games: Eighty Years of People, Events, and Records* (1976); Julian May, *Olympics* (1975).

OMBUDSMAN, a governmental official, long found in Sweden, but since employed by many other nations, who mediated between dissatisfied individuals or groups. His emphasis was on injustice rather than compromise such as the NLRB (q.v.)

considered. Government agencies, such as the Federal Trade Commission, were intended to provide such services, but, being laced with bureaucracy and regulations, often failed to reach the point of injustice, at least in time to be of particular service. Ombudsmen in America were less the product of misunderstandings than of general disruption of civil life. Hawaii first established an Ombudsman's office in 1969, and other states followed. Results seemed meagre, especially for the funds spent on individual cases, but they often found patent injustice, and set up precedents for similar cases. Above all, they helped defuse centers of potential violence and bring paranoid situations to light. Roy V. Peel and T. Sellin, *Ombudsmen or Citizen's Defender: a Modern Institution* (1968); Walter Gellhorn, *Ombudsmen and Others: Citizen Protectors in Nine Countries* (1966).

"ONE THIRD OF A NATION ILL-HOUSED, ILL-CLAD, ILL-NOURISHED," noted passage from the second Inaugural Address by President Franklin D. Roosevelt, January 20, 1937; it gave the title to the Federal Theater Project play, *One Third of a Nation* (1938).

ONE WORLD (1943), see Willkie, Wendell.

ONEIDA COMMUNITY, established in 1847 in western New York State, by John Humphrey Noyes (*q.v.*) and notorious as a "free love" colony which gained some measure of acceptance for being in the "Burned-Over District" (*q.v.*), which received various brands of dissident, but also because of the decorum with which these "Perfectionists" pursued their system of "complex" marriages. Their economic security was secured by their manufacture of a successful steel-trap; by 1881 a combination of neighborly dissatisfaction with their community and lack of enthusiasm for unconventional living on the part of the younger generation broke up the community into traditional units, bound together only by stock in their manufacturing establishments. Oneida became famous once more as the producer of "community silver," advertised as joyfully in the possession of newly-weds who would be able to use it together forever.

O.P.A., see Office of Price Administration.

OPEC, a phenomenon of the economic wars and adjustments centered around oil, in which was embroiled the Organization of Petroleum Exporting Countries, in the Arabian Gulf, but also in Nigeria and Venezuela. In 1973, OPEC quadrupled its price for crude oil, sending a shock among American auto users, who accounted for some 41% of the world's automobiles. Difficult to understand was the role of American oil giants who carried most of the crude for the OPEC nations, thus giving them a stable distributing and merchandizing mechanism. Industry and government used savings in oil use, and pointed out that American oil prices had been kept artifically low by regulation. As Americans adjusted to the new pressures on their inflation-troubled incomes, and wondered at the flow of unprecedented billions into Arab hands, they were told that new technology and alternative energy systems would in time free them from dependency on world energy resources, but that meanwhile they must pay the price of careless fuel use and low productivity in higher prices. Although suspicion of giant fuel company veracity persisted, the oil crisis and OPEC taught world economics to the ordinary motorist and home owner faster than did conventional economics. Mana S. Al-Otaiba, *OPEC and the Petroleum Industry* (1975); Dankwart A. Rustow and John R. Mugno, *OPEC: Success and Prospects* (1976).

"OPEN COVENANTS OPENLY ARRIVED AT," one of President Woodrow Wilson's Fourteen Points, later embodied in the Covenant of the League of Nations (*qq.v.*). Proposed in opposition to secret treaties, it was taken by its friends as a noble ideal, by disillusioned reformers as a mockery of Allied goals, in view of the secret treaties exposed by the Bolsheviks, following their coup, and Allied dismemberment of the German empire, as a result of the Versailles Treaty (*qq.v.*).

"OPEN DOOR POLICY," see Imperialism and Reform.

OPEN SHOP, the right to hire workers in a particular plant or industry, independently of whether or not they belong to a union. Historically, the open shop policy was an anti-union policy; it enabled plant managers and owners to keep the union weak, or, during a strike, to hire strike-breakers (*q.v.*). Thus, the fight for a "closed" shop was a fight for union organization. Labor racketeering has always strengthened the demand for an open shop. The Open Shop was initiated in Dayton, Ohio, in 1900, when thirty-eight firms united and maintained an open shop for two years. With N.A.M. (*q.v.*) encouragement, others emulated the Dayton employers, boycotting union goods, utilizing strike-breakers, and other means for discouraging union organization. See also American Plan, The, and Right to Work, The.

OPPENHEIMER CASE (1954), involved the question of the loyalty (*q.v.*) to the United States of Dr. J. Robert Oppenheimer, physicist, who was instrumental in developing the atom bomb. After World War II, he was a consultant for the Atomic Energy Commission. Charges that he had consorted with persons associated with communism raised the question, not so much of Oppenheimer's loyalty as of his responsibility. A special government commission ruled that he was a security risk and was not to be given access to restricted materials, though it emphasized its view of his positive services to the country. John Major, *The Oppenheimer Hearing* (1971); Philip M. Stern and H. P. Green, *The Oppenheimer Case* (1969).

ORCHARD, HARRY (1866-1954), born Albert E. Horsley, in Ontario, Canada, principal in the assassination of former Governor of Idaho Frank Steunenberg, on December 30, 1905. The subsequent trial centered less on Orchard, who confessed this and other crimes under the influence of religious conversion, than on William D. Haywood (*q.v.*) and others of the Western Federation of Miners, whom he implicated in his crimes. His *The Confessions and Autobiography of Harry Orchard* (1907) comprise a major document of the era. He served the remainder of his life in the state penitentiary, devoting his life to religious writing and to being a model prisoner.

ORDER OF THE CINCINNATI, organized by officers of the Revolutionary War before separation, May 13, 1783, at Steuben's headquarters on the Hudson. Membership was hereditary. In 1787, Washington was elected President-general and re-elected till his death. It was denounced as a secret organization threatening to democratic liberties. It languished, but was revived in 1893 as the Society of the Cincinnati.

ORDINANCE OF NULLIFICATION, see Nullifier.

ORGANIZATION OF AMERICAN STATES (O.A.S.), a step in the direction of hemispheric cooperation. Argentina's (*q.v.*) course under Péron, and anxieties during World War II suggested the need for better understanding between the United States and her Central and South American neighbors. The Treaty of Rio de Janeiro (September 2, 1947) pledged the nations to consider an attack on any one of them an attack on all. In the spring of 1948, an Inter-American Conference was held at Bogotá, Colombia, which created the O.A.S., and provided for conferences and an exchange of information, with the Pan-American Union operating as a general secretariat. The crisis created by Cuba in 1960-61 raised to new significance the role of the O.A.S. It did not, however, impede Cuba's progress. A. V. and A. J. Thomas, Jr., *The Organization of American States* (1963).

ORGANIZATION MAN, THE, (1956), by William H. Whyte, Jr., a significant study of a phenomenon of business civilization: a cog in the wheel wholly dependent for personality and significance on the machine which utilizes him. The study was intended as a description and a criticism, but revealed a bankruptcy of social purposes and resources more shocking than radical denunciations could be; for an analysis, see Louis Filler, "The Critic of Business and the Organization Man," in *Crusaders for American Liberalism* (1961 ed.).

ORIENTALS, see Immigration.

ORWELL, GEORGE (1903-1950), a seminal figure in libertarian thought in his time, he came of fringe elements of the British upper classes, attended Eton College, which did not impress him, served in the Burmese constabulary, where he learned to despise British imperialism, and then undertook to become a writer. *Down and Out in Paris and London* (1933) as unswervingly as the title suggested attempted to tell the truth about his experiences and observations, as did *Burmese Days* (1934), in fictional form. *A Clergyman's Daughter* (1935) and *Keep the Aspidistra Flying* (1936) broadened his canvas, and included (his least appreciated trait) memorable pages of wit and humor. *The Road to Wigan Pier* (1937) showed him as involved in radical political thought. He served in the Republican Army during the Spanish Civil War; his *Homage to Catalonia* (1938) had the distinction of failing on both sides of the water; the radical groups had no interest in his merciless honesty; ironically, the book was later republished with an introduction by Lionel Trilling. He published valuable essays in several collections, but scored sensational successes with his brief *Animal Farm* (1946), a satire on Soviet "socialism," but also on casuistic "socialist" thought anywhere, and *1984* (*q.v.*). Although he was persuaded by hypotheses (such as that luxuriant eating was necessarily filthy) and suffered touches of antisemitism, no writer of his time made a more determined effort to tell the truth than did Orwell. Peter Stansky and William Abrahams, *Orwell: the Transformation* (1980).

OSBORNE, THOMAS M. (1859-1926), one of the most attractive figures in prison reform (*q.v.*). Of wealthy family, he concerned himself with the problem of prison techniques which would aid reform, and in 1913 was appointed chairman of the New York State Commission on Prison Reform. In a famous episode, he had himself incarcerated in the Auburn Penitentiary in order to acquire some of the sense of what it meant to be a prisoner. As warden of Sing Sing (1914-16) he began his campaign for reform, to such effect that he was tried for misconduct, but acquitted. He served also as commandant of the Portsmouth Naval Prison (1917-20). His most remarkable innovation was the Mutual Welfare League which brought prisoners into action to accomplish their own rehabilitation, with spectacular results in many cases. See his *Within Prison Walls* (1914), *Society and Prisons* (1916).

OSCEOLA (1804-1838), though not a chief of the Seminoles, he gathered forces who determined to resist being expelled from their tribal lands, according to treaties requiring their removal west. In 1835 they killed an American agent sent to lead them away, then prepared to resist troops sent to enforce the order. Osceola led resourceful engagements; the pride of the tribe was that he was never defeated by General Thomas S. Jesup's force. The Seminoles took refuge in the Everglades, but actions continued. In one of the more shameful episodes of American-Indian relations, Jesup offered to discuss terms of peace, and, Osceola, coming forth, he was seized and imprisoned in Fort Moultrie, where he died. Ronald Syme, *Osceola, Seminole Leader* (1976); W. Hartley and E. Hartley, *Osceola, the Unconquered Indian* (1973).

OSSOLI, SARAH MARGARET [FULLER], MARCHIONESS D' (1810-1850), a figure in Transcendentalism (*q.v.*), whose personality inspired woman's rights advocates as much as did her writings. *Woman in the Nineteenth Century* (1845) was a pioneer contribution to the cause.

OTIS, JAMES (1725-1783), an early formulator of principles which colonists were able to use in order to resist British efforts to integrate them into Empire policies. Acting as counsellor for Boston merchants, he denied the validity of Writs of Assistance (*q.v.*), in 1761, and in doing so struck deeper principles of independency. According to notes taken of his speech, he argued that: "An act against the Constitution is void; an act against natural equity is void; and if an act of Parliament should be made, in the very words of this petition it would be void. The executive Court must pass such acts

into disuse." His pamphlets were influential; see *A Vindication of the Conduct of the House of Representatives of the Province of the Massachusetts-Bay* (1762), and *The Rights of the British Colonies Asserted and Proved* (1764), among others. He was active in the Committee of Correspondence of Massachusetts, and was influential in calling the Stamp Act Congress (*qq.v.*) before he suffered an assault by a customs official which incapacitated him.

OVERPRODUCTION, a concept intended to explain recurrent depressions, unemployment, and business cycles (*qq.v.*). It assumes a limited capacity on the part of the business market to assimilate the products of manufacturers. Thus, a certain amount of social disorder was "inevitable," until the backlog of finished goods had been disposed of. Reformers ridiculed this economic concept, arguing that the problem was with underconsumption, rather than overproduction, and that if society would pay its laboring force just wages, there would be no problem of "overproduction." See also Productivity.

OWEN, ROBERT (1771-1858), self-made British industrialist who, at his New Lanark, Scotland, mills instituted reforms intended to raise the moral, social, and intellectual conditions of his employees, and of the town. He was particularly interested in education which he believed could be developed in such wise as to form the character of the children involved. Essentially a paternalist, he hoped to persuade leaders in society to institute communities in which labor and social relations would be rationally organized; but though he drew considerable interest, in part because of disturbed social relations and attendant misery among the poor, in part because his ideas had not prevented him from amassing a fortune, he was unable to attain laws underwriting social experiments. He purchased the property of a communistic-religious sect in Indiana, and came to the United States amidst interest and expectancy. The people he assembled in New Harmony disappointed him, and his cause was not helped by his atheism of the period. The great experiment failed, and he returned to England, where he continued to be significant among labor and cooperative elements. His "Equitable Labor Exchange," intended to organize labor's resources for its mutual benefit, and though it, too, collapsed, it was the seed for the later cooperative movement. His Grand National Consolidated Trades Union (*q.v.*), too, found later fulfillment. Active to the end, he became converted to spiritualism; there is a large literature about his experiments, ideas, and experiences. R. H. Harvey, *Robert Owen: Social Idealist* (1949); J. Butt, ed., *Robert Owen: Aspects of His Life and Work* (1971).

OWEN, ROBERT DALE (1801-1877), a son of Robert Owen (*q.v.*) and his associate at New Harmony. With Frances Wright, he propagandized in favor of atheism and labor and woman's rights. They published the *Free Enquirer* in 1829, and helped to form the Workingmen's Party in New York. After a period in England, where he helped his father to promote his plans, he returned to Indiana, and went on to become an influential politician and several years before the Civil War, an ardent emancipationist. In his last years, he was, like his father, a spiritualist. R. W. Leopold, *Robert Dale Owen* (1940).

OWEN LATTIMORE CASE, THE, broke into the open when U.S. Senator Joseph McCarthy, in 1950, accused Lattimore of being a "top Russian espionage agent." Lattimore (1900-   ) had formerly been a businessman and writer about Japan, who had become director of the Walter Hines Page School of International Relations, Johns Hopkins University, in 1939, political adviser to Chiang Kai Shek, and later deputy director of Pacific Relations, Office of War Information, 1942-4. During this period and after he was accorded many distinctions in and out of academic life. He also served as editor of the Institute of Pacific Relations organ, *Pacific Affairs*, and was one of the Institute's most influential personages. The Institute itself was one of the most influential agencies in the field, heavily subsidized by foundations. Following the expression of charges against Lattimore, he defended himself at a Senate hearing, denied that he was influential or pro-communist, and brought the testimony of important public figures to bear upon the proceedings, they holding him to be a positive factor in American understanding of the Far East. A key question became whether he had, by urging a coalition Chinese communist-non-communist government been working for the communists, and whether he had been playing their game by urging that the United States stop supporting Formosa *(q.v.)*. He was directly accused by a former communist, Louis Budenz, of having been under "communist discipline": charges which he ridiculed and denounced as irresponsible. He conceived of himself as exonerated by the proceedings, and detailed them in *Ordeal by Slander* (1950). However, the discovery of a large quantity of Institute records kept the case open and resulted in further hearings, which could no longer be laid to the machinations of the so-called "China Lobby" *(q.v.)*. Students were disturbed by Lattimore communications which seemed to point to no innocent search for academic truth. Thus, an IPR study, subsidized by the Rockefeller Foundation resulted in the appointment of personages who were the reverse of impartial; as Lattimore wrote to the head of the IPR: "I think you were pretty cagey to turn over so much of the China section to Asiaticus, Han-seng and Chi. They will bring out the essential radical aspects, but can be depended on to do so with the right touch." He recommended that "it would pay to keep behind the official Chinese Communist position." As to Russia: "[Back] up their international policy in general, but without using their slogans, and above all without giving them or anyone else the impression of subservience." Although to anti-communists, the problem seemed to be one of communism versus anti-communism, it is probable that to many readers the problem was, at least in part, also one of candor versus lack of candor, despite the *Ordeal's* tone of intimacy. See John T. Flynn, *The Lattimore Story* (1953), for an unfriendly version. Lattimore appears to have ceased being director of the Page School in 1953, and the school itself was transformed. The Institute ceased being a tax-exempt agency, but fought this decision in the courts. However, its foundation funds declined so drastically that in 1960, it left New York for Canada. He went on to England, where he was welcomed in academic circles.

PACs, originally a labor-election branch (see Political Action Committee), expanded to refer to any special interest which set up a PAC to further its preferences in elections. PACs included organizations favoring businesses, unions, environmentalists, the American Medical Association, and others. It was estimated that, 1978-1980, PACs had contributed \$55-60 million in U.S. House and Senate races. A House-passed bill would have stipulated that no candidate would accept more than \$70,000 from all PACs for a primary and general election combined; the bill was stopped by filibuster *(q.v.)* in the Senate.

PACIFIC AFFAIRS, see Institute of Pacific Relations.

PACIFISM, see Peace Crusade, The.

PAINE, THOMAS (1737-1809), one of the great American journalists and liberals, an Englishman of indifferent upbringing and self-educated who adopted America as his home in 1774; in January 1776, he issued the immortal *Common Sense* which stirred great numbers of Americans into favoring the patriot cause: a prime example of the influence of polemical writing on public opinion. His *Crisis* papers, that same year, continued to hearten Americans confused and rendered insecure by events. Paine's pamphleteering methods, which continued to aid the American cause, deserve analysis. At the end of the war, his prestige was at its height. In 1789, while in England, he became a supporter of the French Revolution; his papers on *The Rights of Man* (1791-2) were suppressed, and prosecution proceedings instituted against him. He fled to Paris, where he was made a French citizen and elected to the Convention. A friend of the moderate Girondists *(q.v.)*, their fall led him to prison, from which he obtained freedom with the not over-enthusiastic aid of American representatives. In 1794 and 1796, he prepared *The Age of Reason* which detailed his deistic *(q.v.)* beliefs, but which earned him an unfair reputation as an atheist among the orthodox. By the time he returned to the United States, in 1802, his services to the country had been thoroughly forgotten, and he lived his last years in obscurity. Theodore Roosevelt's *(q.v.)* view that he was a "filthy little atheist" has the distinction of being wholly wrong, since he was neither filthy, nor little, nor an atheist. Audrey Williamson, *Thomas Paine* (1973).

PALESTINE LIBERATION ORGANIZATION, representative of the one million Arabs debarred from Israel *(q.v.)*, once part of the terrain they inhabited, but unassimilated by Arab nations and living in compound areas outside Israel. The refugees were a bargaining point for Arabs in their original plan to destroy Israel. However, its success in war against them created guerrilla groups determined to call their cause to the world's attention. the P.L.O., formed in 1964, and under its leading spirit Yasser Arafat of the El Fatah group, engaged in random atrocities which inspired emulation and acts of terrorism throughout the world. In 1974 the P.L.O. received United Nations *(q.v.)* recognition, and thereafter worked between guerrilla actions and efforts to have an area determined which would be independently administered by them, Israel's right to existence not being conceded. Various "peace initiatives" included one by the European Economic Community *(q.v.)*, by which time it appeared that the P.L.O. had achieved international recognition, and even respectability, with the London *Times* asserting that "the only realistic and valid representative of the Palestinian cause is the Palestine Liberation Organization." The highly political nature of the issue was seen in 1980 when American Indians, petitioning the United Nations for redress of grievances against the United

States, "recognized" the P.L.O. as representing a similar cause. Henry Catton, *Palestine and International Law* (1976); Mehmood Hussain, *The Palestine Liberation Organization: a Study in Ideology, Strategy and Tactics* (1975); Yasser Arafat, *Palestine Lives* (1975); Frank C. Sakran, *Palestine: Still a Dilemma* (1976); Yehoshafat Harkabi, *Palestinians in Israel* (1974); Frank H. Epp, *Palestinians* (1976).

PALIMONY, see Singles.

PALMER, ELIHU (1764-1806), a New York writer and Congregationalist minister who became a Deist (*q.v.*). He believed Deism a proper religion for Americans and sought, unsuccessfully, to popularize it. See his *Principles of Nature* (1802).

PALMER RAIDS (1919-20), a notorious attack upon civil rights conducted by the U.S. Attorney-General, A. Mitchell Palmer, as a byproduct of alien and sedition acts passed by Congress. Palmer utilized information gathered by agents of the Department of Justice to carry out a wide series of simultaneous raids on alleged radical headquarters, bringing into his net anyone who happened to have been on the scene during the raid. Liberals, radicals, aliens, and acquaintances were arrested to the number of about four thousand and tried without regard for their legal, and often human, rights. Although most of them were ultimately set free, they had suffered painful experiences, and many of those deported had been treated in peremptory fashion. Although rabid anti-reds applauded Palmer's energy, many citizens, some of them conservatives, feared that such enthusiasm might destroy liberty in America. R. K. Murray, *Red Scare* (1955).

PAMPHLETEERING has been a major instrument of reform during several periods of American history. During the seventeenth century, Roger Williams (*q.v.*) warred with the Puritans through pamphlets, in behalf of religious liberty. The Revolutionary crisis loosed a "pamphlet war," as malcontents and loyalists sought to win, or, at least, neutralize, sections of the population. Thomas Paine's (*q.v.*) *Common Sense* and *Crisis* were sensationally successful in making friends for the patriot cause. During the antislavery crusade, pamphlets were the major weapon for conducting arguments on the numerous aspects of the problem; there were an endless number of famous pamphlets. Pamphlets declined in importance in the post-Civil War period, though special topics, like Free Silver and the Tariff Question created pamphlet literatures. The magazine, rather than the pamphlet, was the major weapon during the Muckraking Era (*q.v.*). The decline of reform in the 1920's affected the use of pamphlets and magazines, which required an alert and interested audience. This was achieved in the next decade, with pamphlets being termed "literature," but revolutionary propaganda exploited the medium more than did reform.

PAN-AMERICAN UNION, the result of long interest in building up United States-Latin American relations. Henry Clay sought to further them, while Secretary of State; but the unwillingness of the Jacksonians to cooperate with the Administration of John Quincy Adams (*q.v.*) stymied Clay's plans. James G. Blaine, as Secretary of State under Garfield, sought to make the United States an arbiter in Latin American disputes, without success, and planned a Pan-American Conference. As Secretary of State under Benjamin Harrison, he achieved it, in 1889. Although it failed to organize a means for arbitrating Latin American disputes, it set up an International Bureau of American Republics, precursor of the Pan-American Union. The latter sponsored a series of conferences, during the next several decades, which helped to establish educational and informational relations; it offered a vehicle through which the United States could express its aims and interests, with respect to the nations south of the border. Headquarters of the Pan-American Union are in Washington, D.C. S. G. Inman, *Problems in Pan-Americanism* (1925); Arthur P. Whitaker, *The Western Hemisphere Idea; Its Rise and Decline* (1954); R. B. Gray, ed., *Latin America and the United States in the 1970s* (1971).

PANACEA, a social "cure-all," which finds the source of human ills in a single cause, usually economic, and seeks to end it with a single remedy. Although associated with "cranks" and fanatics, panaceas have often exposed social inequities and contributed to social solutions. See also, Silver Issue, Single Tax, Greenback Issue, Townsend Plan, Utopia, Warren, Josiah, Ham'n Eggs Plan.

PANAMA CANAL, THE, fulfilled an old American dream of more rapid sea connections from the Atlantic to the Pacific Oceans. Nicaragua (*q.v.*) and Colombia both offered strategic possibilities, which were investigated by Congress and private financial and construction interests. In a welter of intrigue and negotiation, attention focused on Colombia, then exercising sovereign rights over Panama. Its leaders, seeking larger profits and assurances, stood in the way of American plans. Thereupon, interested persons let it be known to Panamanian politicians that the United States would support their revolutionary effort; in November 1903, with American ships in attendant waters, Panama revolted and declared her freedom from Colombia. A treaty between the new nation and the United States gave the latter a permanent lease to the canal zone, ten miles wide, and the epic of building was then begun; the Panama Canal opened officially in 1914. Roosevelt's notorious phrase, "I took the Canal Zone," shadowed the achievement, but had no immediate effects. Not until the Cuban (*q.v.*) crisis stirred the entire area to a revaluation of its relations to the United States would the Panamanian nationalists add their note of unfriendliness and self-assertion. These were fulfilled in 1978 when President Carter (*q.v.*) and Panama's government head signed a treaty giving Panama control over the Canal at the end of 1999. The Canal would be open to all nations thereafter. Present at the signing were former President Ford (*q.v.*) and others of previous administrations. Important, too, were the sums the treaty granted to Panama for maintaining the Canal, plus pledges and loans not included in the treaty which were expected to be in the hundreds of millions of dollars. All Americans were not satisfied with the treaty, which impugned retrospectively the heroism and enterprise which had gone into the Canal's making. Howard Baker, influential Republican, was thought to have lost his chance to be Vice Presidential running mate to Reagan (*q.v.*) in part because he had given support to the treaty. Whether it signalled a new relationship with Latin America, or merely a weakening of the old one was unclear. H. Arias, *Panama Canal: a Study in International Law and Diplomacy* (1911); Jon P. Speller, *The Panama Canal: Heart of America's Security* (1972).

PANIC OF 1873, 1907 (*qq.v.*), among others; panics differ from depressions (see Economic Depression) in emphasizing the catastrophe in business dealings and conditions, as distinguished from the social and individual difficulties created by the lengthier depression. Panics have usually heralded a depression; however, the Panic of 1907, a "money panic," severely damaged savings without, at the same time, undermining the business community.

PANKHURST, EMMELINE (1858-1928), militant leader of the English suffragettes, whose desperate strategies for gaining attention to her cause gained world attention, and inspired American fighters for woman suffrage. She organized the National Women's Social and Political Union with the aid of brilliant lieutenants, including her own daughters. Her party forced attention by demonstrations in the House of Commons, by making "Votes for Women!" an unforgettable slogan, by striking policemen in the face, by defacing and destroying public property, and by producing martyrs, one of whom threw herself under the feet of horses at the racetrack. Mrs. Pankhurst urged the hunger strike (*q.v.*) to good effect. During World War I, she laid down her cause to cooperate with the government. Her daughters were Adela, Christabel, and Sylvia, the last probably the most famous, due to her activities as a writer; see her *The Suffragette* (1912) and *The Life of Emmeline Pankhurst* (1935).

PAPER MONEY, a means for financing government and conducting society's business; offering the reformer a weapon for criticizing government operations in this area, and suggesting improvements. Continental currency and Greenbacks (*qq.v.*) have been major problems in the field, in the United States, and challenged reformers with their inflationary (*q.v.*) qualities. See also Monetarism.

PARIS COMMUNE, THE (1871), an uprising of the working-class people and parties of Paris against the regime of Napoleon III, following the defeat of his army during the Franco-Prussian War. The event shocked or thrilled all social and political tendencies, and the ruthless suppression of the Commune by domestic republican forces did not obliterate the fear, or hope, that it no more than presaged further workingclass and socialist convulsions. Stewart Edwards, *The Paris Commune 1871* (1973).

PARITY, a concept in government programs for farmers, intended to help him attain a price for his commodity equal to the purchasing power he had enjoyed during a period set up as a base period; this was defined for all commodities except tobacco as the period from August 1909 to July 1914. For tobacco, the base period was August 1919 to July of 1929.

PARKER, JOEL (1799-1873), noted minister, significant as a liberal who turned conservative under the pressure of events. In New Orleans, he had dared to question the validity of slavery, with riotous results. Returned North, he became disillusioned with radicals, took a patriotic stand on the Mexican War, and, when quoted by Harriet Beecher Stowe in criticism of slavery, threatened suit for false quotation; see *The Discussion between Rev. Joel Parker, and Rev. A. Rood, on the Question, "What Are the Evils Inseparable from Slavery,"*... (1852).

PARKER, THEODORE (1810-1860), religious liberal and scholar, he advanced from traditional Unitarianism to a congregation at the Music Hall in Boston which attracted varied people from among the dissidents of the city. His interpretation of Christianity, and his broad view of other religions, caused critics to label him an atheist. He became extreme in his detestation of slavery, and his resistance to cooperation with the law in respect to fugitive slaves. He was particularly active in such cases as that of Anthony Burns (*q.v.*). His writings have a literary quality; see his *Additional Speeches, Addresses, and Occasional Sermons* (1855).

PARKHURST, REV. CHARLES HENRY (1842-1933), principal in one of the most sensational episodes involving a clergyman: a conducted tour in 1892 in the vice area of New York for the purpose of obtaining evidence of police corruption and protected vice. Details of the several-day long tour, subsequent legal actions, and the revelations of the Lexow Committee (*q.v.*) combined to scandalize, entertain, and outrage those who followed accounts in the press, and inspired later reform crusades in municipalities; Chas. W. Gardner, *The Doctor and the Devil* (1894), Pankhurst, *Our Fight with Tammany* (1895); M.R. Werner, *It Happened in New York* (1957).

PARKINSON'S LAW (1957), as expounded by C. Northcote Parkinson, an historian, was a combination of satire and analysis which struck a public response: "Work expands so as to fill the time available for its completion. . . . [A]dministrators are more or less bound to multiply." He expressed this view in mathematical terms, and exemplified it with various real and typical situations. His next book, however, *The Law and the Profits* (1961), argued that government spending automatically rises to eat up all available income, and suggested that taxation be limited to twenty-percent of the national income. This "law" was denounced as dangerous by a variety of political scientists.

"PARLIAMENT OF MAN, THE FEDERATION OF THE WORLD, THE," one of the distinguished lines in the poem by Alfred Lord Tennyson, "Locksley Hall," which foresaw battles in the air, but also an end of war. The above phrases have often been used by advocates of international peace and cooperation.

PARRINGTON, VERNON L. (1871-1929), English professor at the University of Washington, whose *Main Currents in American Thought* (1927-30) was a major effort to cover the field from colonial decades to the present. Parrington's third volume was left in fragments at his death, but contains striking materials. His firm Jeffersonian liberalism was shadowed by disillusionment, in later pages. Although he claimed to be interested in ideas, rather than literature, his work is distinctly relevant to both; see Louis Filler, "Parrington and Carlyle: Cross-Currents in History and Belles-Lettres," *Antioch Review*, June, 1952.

PARSONS, ALBERT R. (1848-1887), leading figure among the defendants of the Haymarket Affair (*q.v.*), he was of notable lineage—Parsons was among the oldest names in New England, and his brother served in high office during the Civil War—and a member of the Typographical Union. An idealist and a self-taught intellectual, he interested himself in labor, and, in his travels was concerned for its organization. The difficult conditions of the period turned him to anarchism, and he edited *The Alarm*. He spoke at the meeting in the Haymarket where the bomb was exploded, but had already left when the event took place. Recognized in court, where suspects were being processed, he was seized and placed among them. Although he could have repudiated them, and appealed successfully for separate consideration, he refused to do so. As a native American among immigrants and as an eloquent speaker, he became their leading figure. His last words before hanging, "Let the voice of the people be heard," were once famous; see his *Anarchism, Its Philosophy and Scientific Basis* (1887).

PARSONS, FRANK (1854-1908), reformer and railroad authority, he was a teacher and lecturer who was concerned for adequate regulation of responsible government facilities. His *The Telegraph Monopoly* (1899) was a pioneer work. His travels through the United States and Europe, during which he studied railroad systems and cooperative ventures gave him perspective on the American railroad problem. His testimony in 1901-2 before the U.S. Industrial Committee on Public Ownership of Railroads, Telegraph, and Telephone, was informed, though ineffective. His *The Heart of the Railroad Problem* (1906)—emphasizing discrimination—sought to persuade its readers that only regulation in the public interest could satisfy public need. See his *The Story of New Zealand* (*q.v.*) (1904) and *The Railways, the Trusts and the People* (1906). Parsons is recalled as "father of vocational education"; he is better remembered as, like Sylvester Graham (*q.v.*) of a race of American heroes (*q.v.*) who worked to serve their fellowman; see Filler, *Appointment at Armageddon*.

PARTY, THE, in the 1930's, universally understood to refer to the Communist Party, U.S.A.

PARTY LINE, see Line.

"PASSING," the act by a Negro of light complexion of disassociating himself from Negroes, and "passing" in society as a white person. Although the word is associated with Negroes, in a land of minorities, almost any person might wish to try to "pass" into the society of others: a Jew as non-Jew, for example; see Laura Z. Hobson, *Gentleman's Agreement* (1947), for the issue. Propaganda in favor of "Black" for "Negro" in the 1960s caused many all but white Negroes to be called, or to call themselves "Blacks."

"PASSING OF THE FRONTIER, THE," see Turner, Frederick Jackson.

PASSIVE RESISTANCE, see Gandhi, Mohandas K., King, Martin Luther.

PASTERNAK, BORIS (1890-1960), Russian poet, translator, and *littérateur*, whose novel, *Dr. Zhivago* (1958) became a world-wide symbol of the need for free expression. Of Jewish birth, but concerned for Christian principles, he depicted in his novel an individualist. Unpublished in Russia, the book fell into foreign publishers's hands during the "thaw" in international relations which followed Stalin's death. The effort to stop its publication, the abuse in Russia to which Pasternak was subjected, his rejection of the Nobel Prize in literature all focussed criticism on Russia's interference with creativity.

PATERSON STRIKE (1913), see Madison Square Garden Pageant.

PATON, ALAN (1903-   ), South Africa writer and public conscience, who dreamed of a rapprochement between his country's Negroes and white people. He was a teacher who became (1936-48) principal of the Diepkloof Reformatory for Africa Juvenile Delinquents, in Johannesburg, and president of the Liberal Party. His *Cry, the Beloved Country* (1948) made him famous in the West, and was an appeal, in moving prose, for mutual understanding. *Too Late the Phalarope* (1953) and *Hope for South Africa* (1958), among other works, sustained his reputation in the West, but did not increase his influence at home. Paton, *Towards The Mountain* (1981).

PATRIOT, often repudiated in the twentieth century by social reformers as opposed to an international viewpoint or as having been preempted by crass and reactionary elements, often used ironically, as in connection with the Chicago *Tribune*. However, reformers under duress tended to emphasize that they were better patriots than their persecutors, more concerned for the reality of American freedom. The unity produced by World War II and the drive against "commies" drove repudiation and irony underground, for the most part. See also "100%," Loyalty Oath, Anti-American feeling.

PATRIOTISM PREPAID (1936), by Lewis J. Gorin, "National Commander, Veterans of Future Wars," a pacifist effort reflecting the strong anti-war feeling of the time, as well as its inadequate sense of the dynamics of war and society.

PATRONAGE, a constant concern of reformers who hold that patronage—the technique of paying off political debts with jobs—results in corrupt appointments and inefficient employees. The patronage was held responsible for the poor quality of the census-gathering machinery in the post-Civil War period. The post office was a notorious target for patronage, as was the customs office. The operation of the patronage was the major source of argument for the advocates of civil service reform (*q.v.*). A modern argument developed that the expanded government bureaucracy on all levels ensured a mediocre average of civil service employees, no better than what the old patronage system had given. Also, that diminishing the existing patronage system would drain the power from executives from the President down, thus undermining the major parties. Carl R. Fish, *Civil Service and the Patronage* (1904); Alan Gartner et al., ed., *Public Service Employment* (1973),.; Paul Van Riper, *History of the United States Civil Service* (1958).

PATRONS OF HUSBANDRY, see National Grange of the Patrons of Husbandry.

"PATTER-ROLLERS," immortal in Negro and abolitionist lore as being the slaves' designation for the "patrols" which southern communities organized throughout the south as a control feature of their society. The patrols were intended to be ready to follow after runaway slaves, to intercept Negroes who were accused of crimes or other deviations from their expected doings, and, above all, to be ready to curb any possibility of a Negro uprising against their masters, with or without the aid of free Negroes or white people.

PATTERSON, JOSEPH MEDILL (1879-1946), a curious American career, in elements comparable with that of William Randolph Hearst (*q.v.*), he was born into a wealthy family of journalists, in 1906 asserted his socialist convictions, and wrote a novel, *A Little Brother of the Rich* (1908) which presumably exemplified his principles. With the collapse of Progressivism, he discovered patriotism (*q.v.*), which he thereafter exploited sensationally with his cousin, Robert Rutherford McCormick of the Chicago *Tribune* (*q.v.*). In 1919, Patterson instituted the New York *Daily News*, which, in its powerful appeal to the lowest common denominator of readers was a remarkable compound of democracy and totalitarian thinking. See John W. Tebbel, *An American Dynasty* (1947).

PAULING, LINUS (1901-   ), distinguished chemist and physicist, winner of two Nobel prizes in his fields. He determined to be relevant to public issues, opposed nuclear (*q.v.*) testing as an invitation to catastrophe, and was critical of the space program. Unlike Robert Oppenheimer (*q.v.*), another scientist of stature, Pauling did not operate furtively with respect to his views on public affairs, but expressed himself boldly and in public. He drew narrow "patriotic" suspicions, and enraged medical authorities with his faith that Vitamin C was a cure for colds. He was patently an invaluable public servant, in whom Americans could take pride. Robert Gilpin, *American Scientists and Nuclear Weapons Policy* (1962).

PAXTON BOYS (1763), an incident in frontier unrest and the democratic struggle for more equitable representation. Western Pennsylvanians being inadequately protected from Indian raids, during the French and Indian War, undertook their own defence, and carried out a raid in Lancaster County. For this act, they were ordered arrested and to be tried in Philadelphia. They intended to threaten the state legislature, but were dissuaded from creating further disorder, and attained better representation in that body. Their status as maintaining the battle for democratic rights is complicated by the fact that they had attacked peaceful Indians, and their complaints included the fact that a late bounty on Indian scalps had been revoked.

PAYNE, DANIEL A. (1811-1893), one of the greatest of nineteenth century Negroes, he was a Charleston, South Carolina child of free parents who was such an inspiration to other free Negroes with his precocious teaching and learning that a local ordinance (1834) forbade him to teach. Going north as a teacher and minister, he gathered materials for his invaluable *History of the African Methodist Episcopal Church* (1891). In 1863, as a founder of Wilberforce University in Ohio he helped produce the leaders of the post-Civil War Negro community. His *Recollections of Seventy Years* (1888) is a seminal work.

"PAYOLA," a development in the exposure of corruption on television programs and in other fields of entertainment. They seemed to reveal a failure in maintaining social standards of honesty and public regard for reality. Thus, when the first revelations came that the "quiz" programs which supposedly featured brilliant and retentive intellects no more than displayed foolish actors who had been told the answers they presumably knew, there was a casual surprise that anyone would be annoyed. Why the excitement? asked one journalistic pillar of the community, in Dayton, Ohio. "Who worries when a fight is fixed or a wrestling match goes into extra rehearsal?" Quizzes were entertainment, and their only "moral guilt" was that they were "$64,000 Bores." Later, a certain amount of moral indignation was generated because the television frauds had tampered with public credulity. "Payola" proper referred to sums paid "disc jockeys" who played records on radio for "pushing" records issued by particular companies. Favorite "jockeys" were implicated, shabby testimony given before congressional committees and ultimately in the courts. The Federal Communications Commission took up questions of renewing the licenses of stations involved in the frauds. The amount of sympathy extended to the cheats suggested an empathetic regard for them on the part of the public. Drew Pearson (q.v.) asked whether payola was confined to disc jockeys. He observed that an admiral of the United States received a $12,000 a year pension, and $90,000 from five corporations for vaguely defined services.

P.C.A., see Progressive Citizens of America.

PEABODY, ELIZABETH P. (1804-1894), associated in her youth with A.B. Alcott (q.v.); see her *Record of a School* (1836). Later, she was a pioneer in organizing kindergartens. She was the most noteworthy of the "Peabody sisters"; the others married Horace Mann and Nathaniel Hawthorne (qq.v.).

PEACE CORPS, one of the most successful of the Kennedy (q.v.) proposals, during his campaign for the Presidency in 1960. It struck the imagination: the idea of an army of Americans going abroad to aid backward nations to advance, a living testimony to American vitality and camaraderie. There was an eager response from students and persons fearful of world catastrophe and of the world's opinion of the United States. The "peace corps" idea stimulated imaginations; Sen. Hubert H. Humphrey of Minnesota proposed the creation of a national peace agency. The United Presbyterian Church planned a peace corps of its own of youth to be sent abroad. Inquiries poured into Washington, D.C., requesting information on the subject. With a Peace Corps approved by Congress—though with relatively meagre funds—recruiting and training of recruits were undertaken. A number of projects in South America and Africa were certified. Skepticism was expressed by Congressmen and others who thought members of the Peace Corps were naive, and had little understanding of the task they had undertaken. Some critics feared Peace Corps participants might do more harm than good by inadvertent errors and misunderstandings. An excellent campaign slogan and ideal, it did little evident harm. R. A. Liston, *Sargent Shriver* (1964); M. Windmiller, *The Peace Corps and Pax America* (1970); Pauline Madow, ed., *The Peace Corps* (1964).

PEACE CRUSADE, THE, one of the older reform movements, it had its roots in New England dissatisfaction with the War of 1812 (q.v.), interpreted as improperly directed at Great Britain, which the Federalists (q.v.) saw as a bastion of conservatism. The American Peace Society was an example of pioneer reform organization in the United States. It attracted conservatives who, for whatever reason, sincerely abhorred war. Different in temperament and social relations were Elihu Burritt and William Ladd (qq.v.), but both were strong supporters for pacifist thought. The Non-Resistant Society, as directed by Henry C. Wright (qq.v.) took an "extreme" view of war, but was no more a failure than the American Peace Society, so far as stopping the Mexican War was concerned. Much of New England became pacifist in its fear that Mexico's defeat might open all but endless acres to slavery. During the Civil War, the peace cause became insignificant, though such a person as Alfred Henry Love (q.v.) held on to his principles. The increasingly powerful war instruments encouraged hope that mankind would no longer tolerate devastating wars; the Carnegie Endowment for International Peace (q.v.) secmed a powerful organization. World War I changed perspectives. Lenin's (q.v.) anti-patriotic stand was not popular in the west. Peace, as preached by communists who advocated class war, seemed contradictory to anti-communists. Communists argued, on the other hand, that the "contradictions in capitalism" required nations based on free enterprise to engage in war. Many pacifists feared that the rank and file who were dependent for a livelihood on "defense jobs" would prefer war to unemployment. The Carnegie Endowment, the World Peace Foundation, Promoting World Peace and other organizations continued to issue materials on their subject. The conscientious objectors had stirred some sympathy for the humiliations they had endured during World War I; see Norman Thomas, *The Conscientious Objector in America*

(1923), with an introduction by Robert M. La Follette (q.v.). They were made insignificant, for the most part, during World War II by the widely-held opinion that Hitlerism wanted crushing, and by the Armed Services's business-like processing of them, which reduced their potential for martyrdom. With the advent of the atomic bomb, they gained in consequence, as a sobered world watched the mounting series of tests, which threatened inconceivable damage, as well as a fouling of the atmosphere. See also, Commission to Study the Organization of Peace, Committee for Nonviolent Action. See also Appeasement, Hague Peace Conferences, Emergency Peace Federation, Anti-War; Charles DeBenedetti, *The Peace Reform in American History* (1980).

PEACE DEMOCRATS, see Copperheads.

"PEACE IN OUR TIME," see Appeasement Policy.

"PEACE IS INDIVISIBLE," famous phrase employed by Maxim Litvinov, as U.S.S.R. representative to the League of Nations where he sought to persuade the capitalist powers of the need for "collective security" against the fascist bloc. The slogan attracted liberals as well as communists to the Popular Front (q.v.).

"PEACE WITH HONOR," phrase associated with Prime Minister Benjamin Disraeli at the Congress of Berlin in 1878; often used in connection with differences between the western democracies and the Soviet Union. It has suggested intransigence to some pacifists, and thus containing the possibility of war. Some have proposed: "Better Red than Dead."

PEACEFUL COEXISTENCE between the U.S. and the U.S.-S.R. presented itself as urgent to human survival, after the Soviets exploded their first atomic bomb in 1949, and the United States almost immediately after began work on creating the more powerful hydrogen bomb. Plans for inspection of bomb-making installations were formulated, discussed, and criticized. The role of the United Nations seemed to grow. The "Third Force" (q.v.) concept was presented as an influence in curbing irresponsible actions by the great nations. Walter Lippmann, *The Cold War* (1947); James P. Warburg, *Germany: Bridge or Battle Ground* (1947); George F. Kennan, *On Dealing with the Communist World* (1964). See Detente.

PEACETIME MILITARY CONSCRIPTION, see Conscription.

PEANUTS, an Americanism for trifles, usually applied to expenses, and often to government expenses, in affluent times. Since the latter usually ranged in the millions of dollars, it took a partisan view to see expenses in welfare, corruption, foreign aid (qq.v.) and other moral and financial charges in such terms.

PEARL HARBOR, ATTACK ON (December, 7, 1941), a key issue in the arguments of the revisionist (q.v.) historians of the beginnings of World War II (q.v.).

PEARSON, DREW (1897-1969), newspaper columnist with a background in journalism and work for relief missions; his *The Washington Merry-Go-Round* (1931), written with Robert Allen, established his reputation as a sharp commentator with varied and "inside" information. He developed these qualities, maintaining a watch for signs of chicanery or bad faith in individual political figures and Administrations. He also ventured bold predictions of things to come which his followers admired. Although he attracted the ire of numerous persons, including Presidents, he constituted a latter-day link with muckraking (q.v.). See Oliver Pilat, *Drew Pearson* (1973).

PEASANTS, PEASANTRY, the country people of Europe, popularized by the Russian Revolution to refer more specifically to the poor of the countryside, distinguished from the Kulak class of rich farmers. Americans became familiar with the association of "workers and peasants" as forming the core of a reform or revolutionary development, and tended to apply it somewhat mechanically to all situations abroad. "Peasants" has never been appropriate to American social circumstances, the native equivalent being "workers and farmers," or, more usually, "a farmer-labor alliance." Mexican labor has suited the description of peasant, to a degree, but has been referred to in terms of "migrant labor" (*q.v.*). The rise of "third world" nations, with attendant leaders and protocol, tended to limit the concept. See, however, Peonage, and Eric R. Wolf, *Peasant Wars of the Twentieth Century* (1969); Philip K. Bock, ed., *Peasants in the Modern World* (1969); David Lehman, ed., *Peasants, Landlords and Governments: Agrarian Reform in the Third World* (1974).

"PECULIAR INSTITUTION," a phrase descriptive of the slavery system in the south, used by southerners, but without a sense of apology, rather with pride, or with overtones indicating that criticism of the system resulted from ignorance and a lack of understanding of its virtues; used sarcastically by northern critics of the system.

PENN, WILLIAM (1644-1718), son of an English naval hero, who became a leading Friend (*q.v.*), endured imprisonment in behalf of his faith, founded Pennsylvania, which became a haven not only for other Friends, but for other dissident religious groups. His proprietorship created a more decorous race of "Quakers" than had previously evangelized adherents of major sects; they increasingly practiced frugality, quietude, and administration. Penn was exemplary in his peaceful and honest dealings with Indians, and in his concern for peace and plans leading to peace. His tracts constitute a Quaker heritage, and included *No Cross, No Crown* (1669), *Some Fruits of Solitude* (1693), and *Essay towards the Present and Future Peace of Europe* (1693).

"PENNY PRESS," a revolution in popular communication, not only in that it put more printed material into more hands, but forced a change in editorial attitudes, requiring writers to probe the journalistic desires of a democratic readership. The genius of the penny press, and prototype of the "yellow journalist" (*q.v.*) was James Gordon Bennett, who mixed sex and scandal with other sensational ingredients, and appealed to the conservative, rather than the reformistic, impulses of his readers in his *New York Morning Herald*. Benjamin H. Day's *New York Sun* preceded the *Herald*, and took a less cynical approach. Other notable papers appeared in major cities, and the system of "exchanges," whereby newspapers were scanned by editors for striking or significant items and reprinted, gave the readers a substantial view of what was going on and being thought elsewhere in the nation. See also Journalism and Reform.

PENSION GRABS, a post-Civil War development deplored by reformers. Republican Party deference to veterans caused them to be generous to their demands for pensions. In addition, congressmen made a practice of submitting bills giving pensions to individual members of their constituency, in many cases, obvious frauds. Grover Cleveland (*q.v.*), by vetoing some of them, made himself further unpopular with Republicans, who pretended that as a Democrat he was averse to honoring northern heroes. Pensions also helped to spend the Treasury surplus, which embarrassed Protectionists (*q.v.*) who claimed that customs duties helped supply revenue; when the new Commissioner of Pensions was sworn in, in 1890, a Republican year, he voiced the immortal program: "God help the surplus!" Thanks to increased outlay for pensions, they rose from fifty-six million in 1885 to one hundred and thirty-five million in 1893.

PENTAGON, the largest office building in the world, a symbol of American military planning and operations, suspect in a world which, in its "free" component, looks to it for defense against Soviet tanks and agents. Routinely, a whipping boy for nations which and leaders who practice a minimum of democracy; see Juan Bosch, *Pentagonism: a Substitute for Imperialism* (1968). The concept *Pentagonese* covers the military's tendency toward bumbling prose and evasion of facts, though often by commentators who practice forthright selec-

tivity of partial truths, markedly by avoiding comparison of Pentagon operations with those of America's foes. Most notable product of the Pentagon was the *Pentagon Papers*, illegally released to the *New York Times* by Daniel Ellsberg (*q.v.*). They fed the foes at home and abroad of American intervention in Vietnam (*q.v.*), and helped discredit the American effort. Although wounding to American intelligence and operations, the exposure of American military bureaucracy to enemy eyes probably accomplished as much good as harm, by forcing the military to be alert to dissent at home. The demoralization created may have been roughly balanced by a more sophisticated sense of propriety and action in the modern world. J. W. Fulbright, *The Pentagon Propaganda* (1970); Clark R. Mollenhoff, *The Pentagon Politics, Profits, and Plunder* (1967); W. McGaffin and E. Knoll, *Scandal in the Pentagon* (1969).

PEONAGE, a form of servitude especially identified with labor in Central and South America, where workers are so far committed in debts to their employers as to have little hope of emerging into independence. "Peons" have also crossed the border to labor in United States fields, and though their circumstances have not been worse than those suffered at home, they have acted to downgrade opportunities and perspectives for native Americans engaged in "transient labor." Peonage is used as a synonym for what is close to slavery.

PEOPLE, an American shibboleth, implying active, democratic energy being expended in order to maintain the best possible government, criticized by radicals as being deceptive and false, since the "people" are of all types, including capitalists, workers, transient labor, and other categories representing interests, rather than a common interest; but used as though real by all candidates for public office, whether sincerely or insincerely. Uttered sardonically by cynics, who caricature it as "Pee-pul" (pronounced so reverently by Carl Sandburg). A subject for manipulation by elitists (*q.v.*), sometimes disillusioning to democrats of large "D" or small "d." See Ferdinand Lundberg, *The Treason of the People* (1954). Also see Vox Populi.

PEOPLE OF THE UNITED STATES, HISTORY OF THE, see McMaster, John Bach.

PEOPLE'S FRONT, see Popular Front.

PEOPLE'S LOBBY, THE, an informally-organized group of reformers and reformer journalists which undertook to exert pressure on Congress for the passage of necessary legislation, and to inform the general public of developments in this field. It was instituted in 1906, and inspired a number of distinguished persons in the field, notably Mark Sullivan and Lincoln Steffens (*qq.v.*) to think and write in terms of overall social programs. *Success Magazine* was the unofficial organ of the Lobby, and published inside news on developments in Congress. The Lobby did not function long. Its most significant achievement was to crystallize antagonism to the autocratic rule of "Czar" Cannon (*q.v.*), in the House of Representatives. The People's Lobby, begun in 1931 by Benjamin C. Marsh (*q.v.*) was inspired by this earlier example.

PEOPLE'S PARTY, THE, see Populism.

PEOPLES TEMPLE, see JONES, JIM

PERFECTIONISTS, name applied to John Humphrey Noyes's followers; see Oneida Community.

PERKINS, FRANCES (1882-1965), social worker and labor investigator, she directed investigations (1912-3) for the N.Y. State Factory Commission, and later headed the N.Y. State Industrial Commission. From 1921 to 1923, she directed the Council on Immigrant Education. She served on the N.Y. State Industrial Board until she was called, 1933, to be Secretary of Labor under President Roosevelt, the first woman cabinet member. See her *Life Hazards from Fire in New York Factories* (1912), *A Plan for Maternity Care* (1918), *Women as Employers* (1919), and *People at Work* (1934).

PERMANENT COURT OF INTERNATIONAL ARBITRA-
TION, see Internationalism and Reform.

PERMANENT COURT OF INTERNATIONAL JUSTICE,
a creation of the League of Nations *(q.v.)*, and intended to
arbitrate international differences as they arose from different interpretations of law. Since "World Court" membership did not require adherence to the League, the United
States Presidents of the era approved membership, but were
unable to win the sanction of the Senate. It is doubtful that
much was gained or lost by the attendant debates. With the
liquidation of the League, the Court concluded its deliberations, being succeeded by the United Nations's *(q.v.)* International Court of Justice.

"PERMANENT REVOLUTION, THE," concept proposed
by Leon Trotsky *(q.v.)* which opposed the Stalinist slogan
of "Socialism in one country" *(qq.v.)*. Trotsky held that the
differences between capitalism and socialism were irreconcilable; that, therefore, it was not possible for partisans of
socialism—as in the Soviet Union—to rest upon their victories.
Their circumstances required them to maintain an internationalism which kept active and advancing revolutionary
movements throughout the world, for their own local purposes, and as a necessary international support to the
"Workers's Fatherland," Russia. In due course, stipendiaries
of *Fortune Magazine,* some of whom might have learned
their idealism during less affluent days, proposed that the
United States of America represented a "permanent revolution," in the course of which more and more affluence was
disseminated among its citizens, some of whom were not
employed by *Fortune.*

PERSONAL LIBERTY LAWS, a powerful grass-roots movement which cut down the differences between "radical"
abolitionists and the great mass of northerners who disliked
Negroes and disturbers of the peace, but were anxious to
preserve their own rights. The Fugitive Slave Law of 1793,
the Prigg decision *(q.v.)*, and, finally, the Compromise of
1850 *(q.v.)* all had the effect of increasing the rights of slave-
catchers to make claims upon individuals alleged to be
runaway slaves. These great decisions not only threatened
runaways; they threatened free Negroes alleged to be slaves
and even white persons alleged to be Negroes. Above all,
they weakened the power of the state in matters of freedom
and legality, as compared with that of Federal authority.
Hence, "personal liberty laws" were passed in northern
states intended to ensure that individuals could not be
peremptorily accused of being runaway slaves and returned
or sent into slavery before evidence had been fully established. Such brakes upon rapid action often gave time for
rescuing runaways. The battle for personal liberty laws in
effect weakened respect for the priority of Federal law and
Supreme Court decisions and gave encouragement to the
bolder and manifestly illegal actions of abolitionists, especially in so defiant a state as Massachusetts, but also in Wisconsin, Ohio, and elsewhere, and hastened the unification of
northern opinion against slavery as well as slave-catching.

"PET BANKS," those in which the Democratic Administration,
under Jackson, placed the government funds, which had been
removed from the Second Bank of the United States, in
1836, as a climax of Jackson's war on Nicholas Biddle. The
pet banks were run by Administration Democrats.

PETERLOO MASSACRE (August 16, 1819), tragic incident in
the development of industry in England, which broke up
older and more personal social and economic relations, and
created the need for legal defenses to prevent mass starvation
and degradation. Workers met outside Manchester, in
St. Peters Field, to agitate in favor of Parliamentary action
and in opposition to the Corn Laws *(q.v.)*. Mounted troops
dispersed them without mercy, leaving dead and wounded.
The embittered workers "congratulated" the Tory Government which had administered the war against Napoleon
which had ended at Waterloo on another victory, at
"Peterloo."

PETERS, MRS. PHILLIS (WHEATLEY) (1754-1784), African-
born Boston slave, whose early production of verse was often
cited as evidence of the capacity of Negroes to engage in
intellectual pursuits; see her *Poems on Various Occasions,
Religious and Moral* (1772). Abolitionists circulated the
*Memoir and Poems of Phillis Wheatley, a Native African and
a Slave* (1834).

PETITION, RIGHT OF, see Gag Rule.

PHALANSTERY, basic organization unit in Fourier's *(q.v.)*
plan, an association of about 1800 persons divided into groups
for necessary and organized labor.

PHILANTHROPY, see Charities and Reform.

*PHILIP DRU: ADMINISTRATOR: A STORY OF TO-
MORROW, 1920-1935*
(1912), see House, Edward M.

PHILIP, KING, see King Philip's War.

PHILIPPINES AND AMERICAN REFORM, a record of
movement from blunt imperialism to preparations for independence and collaboration. Reformers protested the military
operations, during the Spanish-American War, which began
against the Spanish and concluded against Filipino patriots,
notably Aguinaldo *(qq.v.)*. They approved the Jones Act
(1916), which promised independence to the Islands when
they should have established firm conditions permitting the
withdrawal of a resident American governor. They received
curious support from American beet sugar and other American interests, eager to have the Philippine Islands outside
American protection, and thus subject to tariff restrictions.
Independence was achieved in 1935, though radical critics
insisted this was an accommodation between American and
Filipino interests. World War II made a battle ground of
the Islands; the ejection of the Japanese by American forces
returned them to a relationship closely similar to what they
had been earlier. Americans had little interest in the de-
tails of Filipino domestic problems. G. A. Grundey and W. E.
Livezey, *The Philippines and the United States* (1951); David J.
Steinberg, *Philippine Collaboration in World War II* (1967);
Grayson L. Kirk, *Philippine Independence* (1974); J. E. Walsh,
Philippine Insurrection (1973); Gerard Drummond, ed.,
Philippine Martial Law, 1972-1976 (1976).

PHILISTINE, a term intended to describe a smug, unad-
venturous person, insensitive to the ways of art and the needs
of society; more contemptible when pretending to literacy
and social perspective, including even "parlor pinks" *(q.v.)*;
derived from Matthew Arnold's use of the word, but more ex-
pansively to include the individual's general role in society, as
well as his cultural role; see James T. Farrell's title essay
in *The League of the Frightened Philistines* (1945).

PHILLIPS, DAVID GRAHAM (1867-1911), muckraker *(q.v.)*
and novelist, he brought Indiana Republican ideals to bear
upon the Democratic line of Pulitzer's *World (qq.v.)*. During
the 1900's, he became a legend of hard-working production
and sharp criticism of self-flattering American ideas. *The
Plum Tree* (1905) dealt with the depressing realities of politics; *Light-Fingered Gentry* (1907) in part reflected the insurance scandals of the time. But Phillips was mostly concerned
with man-woman relations, as in *Old Wives for New* (1908)
and *The Hungry Heart* (1909). He is best remembered for
"The Treason of the Senate" series in *Cosmopolitan* (1906),
which evoked from Theodore Roosevelt the epithet "muckraker," and for *Susan Lenox: Her Fall and Rise* (1917),
which was attacked successfully in the courts by the Society
for the Prevention of Vice; see Louis Filler, *Voice of the
Democracy: a Critical Biography of David Graham Phillips*
(1978).

PHILLIPS, ULRICH B. (1877-1934), historian and defender of
the old regime in the Old South, who won national regard for

its viewpoint, and survived the youth uprising of the 1960s to retain his prestige as an unchallenged authority on its workings. His *Life and Labor in the Old South* (1929) is perceived as a classic. See Louis Filler, introductions to Phillips's *Plantation and Frontier* (1958 ed.) and *Georgia and State Rights* (1967 ed.). See also W. H. Stephenson, *The South Lives in History* (1955).

PHILLIPS, WENDELL (1811-1884), one of the great Garrisonian *(q.v.)* abolitionists, a peerless orator, whose causes included temperance and woman's rights, as well as an anti-slavery position which demanded disunion from a slave South, and an uncompromising attack on the U.S. Constitution as a defender of slavery. The apparent impracticality of such a program was explained by the fact that Phillips held a moral position necessary to maintaining a campaign to change the nature of the Union and Constitution. His extemporaneous speech on the occasion of a meeting memorializing the martyred Elijah P. Lovejoy *(q.v.)* is a highpoint in American oratory; see his *Speeches, Lectures, and Letters* (1864). He was a bitter critic of Abraham Lincoln's course during the Civil War. Following Negro Emancipation, he interested himself in the labor question; see Charles Edward Russell's *(q.v.) The Story of Wendell Phillips* (1915). See also Louis Filler, ed., *Wendell Phillips on Civil Rights and Freedom* (1965).

PHONETIC SPELLING, see Spelling Reform.

PHRENOLOGY, a pseudo-science of the nineteenth century which presumed to read people's characters by reference to alleged divisions of the brain, commonly understood in terms of "bumps." In practice, successful phrenologists were simply shrewd readers of character. However, such distinguished reformers as Horace Mann and Dr. Samuel Gridley Howe *(qq.v.)* were encouraged by phrenology to believe in the improvement of humanity, and popular interest in the "science" also stimulated interest in ways and means to "develop the mind," maintain health, and other goals which survived after phrenology lost status. J. D. Davies, *Phrenology: Fad and Science* (1955).

PICK-SLOAN PLAN, see Missouri Valley Authority.

PICKETING, a major action during a strike, the strikers placing guards upon the industrial plant who attempt to persuade other workers to join them in the strike, to prevent strike-breakers *(q.v.)* from entering into the plant, and to win the sympathy of the public with placards which announce their grievances. Picketing has also been employed by reformers to influence the public in the interests of their cause. Thus, women seeking the vote, in the 1910's, picketed the White House; many picket-lines were set up in protest to the various decisions attending the Sacco and Vanzetti case *(q.v.)*; women picketed establishments during the 1930's in protest against the high cost of living; embassies were picketed in protest against policies developed at home or abroad by Germany, Italy, Russia, and other nations; in the post-World War II era, pacifists picketed government offices in protest against the production of armaments.

"PICTURE BRIDES", see "Gentlemen's Agreement".

PIECE WORK, a method of production in which payment is by the completed piece, as compared with *time work* in which payment is by the unit of time. Piece work is associated with operations which do not require workers to produce in company. Thus women could finish blouses at home, rather than in a factory. However, since they did not work together with other blouse finishers, they could be paid meagre wages, and have no means for enforcing a protest. Labor strategists, therefore, sought ways and means for developing collective bargaining *(q.v.)* techniques to ensure that individual workers were not at the mercy of the employer. *Time work* took place under circumstances which usually ensured the employer of control of the production schedule, thanks to the assembly line or the taskmaster *(qq.v.)*. However, the fact that workers

were congregated gave them a basis for organizing in order to better their conditions.

PIERPONT, JOHN (1785-1866), Boston Unitarian clergyman and poet, who challenged conservative elements among his denomination, and contributed to reform movements of his time. His *Anti-Slavery Poems of John Pierpont* (1843) was highly esteemed by his reform contemporaries. His grandson was John Pierpont Morgan *(q.v.)*.

PIGS, see Police.

PILL, THE, a key factor in the sexual *(q.v.)* turmoil of the 1960s and 1970s. It made sexual contact of whatever sort more readily available to all classes of male and female, who may or may not have known of the rhythm method of birth control *(q.v.)*, foams, interuterine devices, premature withdrawals, and other means for avoiding impregnation. Dr. John Rock, gynecologist, who refined the pill had no intention of increasing licentiousness; as a Catholic, he hoped to aid Family *(q.v.)* Planning; see his *The Time Has Come: a Catholic Doctor's Proposals to End the Battle over Birth Control*. As with so many other discoveries, the invention no more than opened up the field beyond his conception of it. Variant pills, male pills, sniffing devices, injections, once-a-month pills were convenient, though not always safe. What was certain was that moral and religious controversies were multiplied by the pill, rather than diminished. A remarkable development was the multiplication of illegitimate births, rather than their diminution; from 89.5 thousand reported cases in 1940 to about half a million in 1976, covering all ages, from under fifteen years of age (about 10,000 in 1976, up from two thousand since 1940), to 40 years and over, a modest doubling of one to 2,000, but an increase nevertheless. Perhaps a good percentage of such cases could adjust in society; teen-age mothers attended schools; but the untold anguish of the unreported was less probed by social workers *(q.v.)* than it would have been by compassionate scribes and reformers in the 1900s. Most positive and yet disturbing was the use of the pill in "underdeveloped countries," where traditionally unrestrained birth except by social sanctions resulted in long histories of infanticide, cruelty toward female children, and countless harrowing deaths by starvation, disease, and the ravages of war. The pill fought habit, superstition, theft, and simple, limited supplies in attempting to hold back harmful overpopulation. Stabilizing the use of the pill, in primitive or advances civilizations, appeared to have a difficult future. Marie C. Stopes, *Contraception* (1949 ed.); John Rock and Doris Loth, *Voluntary Parenthood* (1949); E. Draper, *Birth Control in the Modern World* (1965); B. R. Berelson, *Family Planning Programs* (1969); G. J. Hardin, *Birth Control*; H. and H. Silverman, *The Pill Book* (1979).

PILOT PLANTS, a concept in the thinking of Arthur E. Morgan *(q.v.)*: as the engineer builds in small-scale a machine which may cost great sums ultimately to erect, in order to test the principles of its construction, so the "social engineer" can try a social experiment on a small scale in order to analyse it for possible defects. Thus, a cooperative store, a school, a project may be a pilot plant from which may spring whole movements; see Louis Filler, "Pilot Plants, Utopias, and Social Reform," *Community Service News*, April-June, 1954.

PINCHOT, GIFFORD (1865-1946), pioneer conservationist *(q.v.)*, chief of the U.S. Bureau of Forestry, 1898-1910. His views and dedication influenced Theodore Roosevelt's policies in the field. He was a principal in the Ballinger Affair *(q.v.)*, and maintained his concern for American natural resources throughout his life. During the 1930's, he quarreled with Harold Ickes *(q.v.)* because the latter sought to transfer the Bureau of Forestry to his Department of the Interior. Pinchot's successful campaign to prevent the transfer called forth Ickes's vengeful article in a May 1940 article in the *Saturday Evening Post* denouncing Pinchot's role in the Ballinger Affair. Pinchot was also governor of Pennsylvania, 1923-27. M. L. Fausold, *Gifford Pinchot: Bull Moose Progressive* (1961).

PINGREE, HAZEN S. (1842-1901), one of the great American

mayors, ranking with Tom Johnson and "Golden Rule" Jones (*qq.v.*). A self-made, wealthy manufacturer, he was elected mayor of Detroit in 1889 on an anti-corruption platform. He developed a populist set of ideas which included a battle for municipal ownership of street-railways, quarrels with the gas companies for lower rates, a demand for free water, democratic election procedures, and other legislation. He inspired reformers elsewhere to emulate him. In 1896, he was elected governor of Michigan, and, as such, continued his humanistic services. See also "Detroit Plan." M. G. Holli, *Reform in Detroit* (1969).

PINK, PINKO, used by radical-minded persons to designate radical-minded persons who are deemed less firm or effective in their views than themselves; by conservatives as a synonym for "Red," with the implication that the individual is a shade less candid in his expression of radical opinion than the forthright radical (*q.v.*). "Parlor pink" carried an overtone of condescension when employed by more active elements against presumably less active elements. However, revelations that a parlor could be the stage for undercover communist machinations, and even treason, took much of the sting out of the phrases.

PINKERTON, ALLAN (1819-1884), a Chartist (*q.v.*) who came to America in 1842 and settled in Chicago where he set up a famous detective agency. Although associated with antislavery in the pre-Civil War period, he later became associated in the public mind with anti-labor and anti-union activities. See his *Thirty Years a Detective* (1884); *Strikers, Communists, Tramps, and Detectives* (1878). "The Pinkerton Agency," "Pinkerton Police," and "Pinkerton strike-breakers" called up memories of their operations among the Molly Maguires, during the Homestead Strike, and the Harry Orchard case (*qq.v.*), among other crises which tried labor's resources. J. D. Horan, *The Pinkertons* (1967).

PIONEERS, see Frontier and Social Reform.

"PITCHFORK BEN" TILLMAN, see Tillman, Benjamin R.

PITT, WILLIAM, THE ELDER (1708-1778), the "Great Commoner," defender of Parliamentary prerogatives, who, during the earlier phases of the Revolutionary crisis, rejoiced "that three million Englishmen were unwilling to be slaves." Pittsburgh, Pennsylvania, was named for him. However, his insistence upon the rights of Parliament to pass whatever laws it deemed proper, and to have them enforced, cost him his popularity in America, where dissatisfied elements were unwilling to be taxed by any agency including, in Patrick Henry's phrase, "the tyrannical hands of Parliament."

PLANNED OBSOLESCENCE, see Controlled Depreciation.

PLANNING AGENCIES, although possessing little power and undetermined influence, as in the case of the National Resources Planning Board (*q.v.*), they gave some prestige to the idea of social planning—as contrasted with the alleged values of decentralized and competitive social operations—and thus constituted an endorsement of reformers' efforts to work from a plan for society. Compare Regulatory Agencies; see also City Planning.

PLATT AMENDMENT, a result of the Spanish-American War, which placed American troops in Cuba, and the United States government in position to determine its relationship to Cuba. Although the Teller Amendment of 1898 avowed the government's unwillingness to exercise power in Cuba, it had no intention of letting the little country do so in any fashion detrimental to American interests. The Platt Amendment stipulated that Cuba was not to permit any other foreign power to wield influence in Cuba's affairs, and that Cuba was to permit American bases on her shores. Thus, the United States assumed a protectorate (*q.v.*) position which continued until 1934.

PLESSY *V.* FERGUSON (1896), see "Separate but Equal."

P.L.O., see Palestine Liberation Organization.

PLUM TREE, THE, notorious expression employed by the Pennsylvania political boss Matthew (Matt) S. Quay (1833-

1904), who organized a system of corrupt payments, in exchange for political favors; on their delivery, he wrote, in a letter which came to public view, he would shake the plum tree. David Graham Phillips's novel, *The Plum Tree* (1905) probed the methods and implications of boss rule (*q.v.*).

PLUMB PLAN, suggested (1919) by Glenn E. Plumb, counsel for the Railroad Brotherhoods, which would have had the government purchase the railroads through a corporation composed of railway employees, managers, and Presidential appointees. Opposed by railroad owners, who had seen the railroads run by the government during the late war, and who, with others, feared the coming of socialism, it was rejected. See also Railroad Problem.

"PLUMED KNIGHT, THE," see Blaine, James G.

"PLUTOCRACY'S BASTILLES," so called by labor leaders disturbed by the building of armories during the 1890's to house national guard units, reorganized out of the older state militia units; and obviously intended to give greater striking force to the guards, operating in coordination with the United States Army proper, to be able to help break strikes, as during the Pullman Strike.

PM (1940-1948), a brilliant journalistic episode intended to consolidate the liberal gains of the 1930's, and resist drives against welfare legislation, communists, liberals, and those favoring rapport with Soviet Russia. It developed a style of its own, compounded of tabloid and *Time* characteristics, and attracted entertaining, as well as arresting scribes, including the erratic Ben Hecht. The increasingly conservative tolerance of American readers made more difficult *PM*'s work, and in 1948 its Chicago publisher, Marshall Field (*q.v.*) sold it to Bartley C. Crum (*q.v.*); as *The Star,* it continued for another six months, but with a circulation of 140,000 had to close for lack of adequate financing. Its functions were assumed, to a degree, by the New York *Evening Post* (*q.v.*), in its very latest phase.

POETRY AND SOCIAL REFORM have not always cooperated, though social reformers have always esteemed themselves the best patrons of culture, as intending it for wider and more democratic audiences. Philip Freneau (*q.v.*) sought to serve both. William Cullen Bryant (*q.v.*) sought to serve both, but separately. The reformers of pre-Civil War days tended to use exhortatory verses in their periodicals, rather than poems; however, they could also claim James Russell Lowell and John Greenleaf Whittier (*qq.v.*), among others. Social reform produced the most famous American poem: Edwin Markham's (*q.v.*) *The Man with the Hoe.* Although famous poets indited poems of social reform, including William Ellery Leonard, and Archibald MacLeish (*q.v.*), others like Edwin Arlington Robinson and Robert Frost did not; and those who did wrote other, and usually more famous poems. The poets of social protest proper were almost uniformly minor poets. Thus, it appeared that poetry and social reform could inter-relate, rather than unite. The poetry of "social significance" (*q.v.*) tended to be revolutionary in implications, rather than reformistic, as in the verse of Kenneth Fearing.

POGROMS, a notorious type of informal social control employed in Czarist Russia against the Jews, who, restricted by law in ghettoes and social opportunities, were subject to jealousy, superstition, and the need of bureaucrats and priests for a convenient scapegoat. Especially active were the so-called "Black Hundreds," disorderly groups which roused the village louts to conduct raids on the Jewish communities. Often inspired priests would leave their churches bearing before them great crosses and call upon the peasants to join them in exterminating the Jews. Especially offensive to western opinion were the excesses attending the Kishinev Massacre of 1903. The increasing irresponsibility of the pogromists caused the Jews to despair of Russia, and, since the Czarist laws did not permit them officially to emigrate, to redouble their efforts to "steal across the river": leaving Russia clandestinely. These efforts were aided by the corruption of the border troops. Emigrants found their way to Germany, and from there crossed to England or to the United States. See N. W. Ackerman and M. Jahoda, *Anti-Semitism and Emotional Disorder* (1950).

POINT FOUR PROGRAM, proposed by President Truman, on the occasion of his own inauguration in January, 1949; it provided for aiding "underdeveloped countries" to attain economic stability. Although, like the earlier "Truman Doctrine," its purpose was to keep susceptible areas from falling to the communists, it seemed more distinctly to contain an altruistic principle, and thus to bear some relationship to reform; see also Marshall Plan. U.S. Dept. of State, *Point Four, Near East and Africa* (1951); J. B. Bingham, *Shirt-Sleeve Diplomacy* (1954).

POLAND, remembered by American social reformers, for its revolutionary effort against the Czar's rule, in 1830-1, the emergence of the famous pianist, Ignace Jan Paderewski, as its Premier, following proclamation of a republic in 1918, its resistance to the Red Army, under Marshal Josef Pilsudski, in 1920, its persecution of the Jews within its borders, the bombing of Warsaw by Germans, and the division of Poland by Germany and the U.S.S.R.: a product of the Nazi-Soviet Pact *(q.v.)*. The October 2, 1944, uprising in Poland against German occupation troops, under General Bor (Tadeo Komorowski) was crushed because the Russians held back aid to the insurgents, unwilling to have them receive credit for the victory. The Soviets promised free elections to liberated Poland, at the Yalta Conference *(q.v.)*, but began immediate interference in its affairs. The anti-communist forces of Stanislaw Mikolajczyk suffered persecution, he himself fleeing Poland to avoid execution. De-Stalinization of Russia in 1956 (see Stalin) encouraged democratic hopes behind the Iron Curtain *(q.v.)*, and inspired anti-Soviet riots in Poland. Although these were put down, and reaffirmations of loyalty to the U.S.S.R. given by Polish leaders, they also saw fit to permit elements of free speech and action not tolerated in Hungary *(q.v.)*. In 1959, when Vice-President Richard M. Nixon *(q.v.)* visited Poland, he was accorded public ovations. *Ashes and Diamonds* (1958), a Polish motion-picture, sensitively interpreted the Polish mood, for those alert to its complexities and manifest intentions. In 1981, President Ford's press-contrived "gaffe" *(qq.v.)* of denying that Poland was dominated by Russia, which had perhaps lost him the 1976 election, lost its last shred of credibility. For months, trade unionists, plagued by overwork and a low standard of living, had defied their communist overseers by pressing their demands for union autonomy under the leadership of Lesh Walesa. Their militancy frightened the West into anticipating Russian tanks patrolling Polish streets. Instead, there appeared to be concessions to the workers, operating under union banners of Solidarity. It forced shifts in official policy and communist leadership, with Walesa taking on the appearance of an uncrowned chieftain. The unionist demands shaped up into a program of Human Rights *(q.v.)*, and, specifically, a five-day week of forty hours. In January of 1981, the world was startled by Walesa's visit to the Pope, also of Polish birth and offensive to communism's official atheistic line. Thus, a tentative union was created, even though Walesa emphasized that Solidarity was not and never would be a political group, and the Pope urged caution. The situation seemed comparable to earlier ones in Hungary and Czechoslovakia *(qq.v.)*. In the United States, Polish-Americans took pride in their homeland's courage and dignity, having been long stereotyped as backward and clumsy in "Polish jokes." With Russians watching events in Poland ominously, the new Reagan *(q.v.)* Administration warned the Soviets that intervention in Poland could have severe repercussions on U.S.-Soviet relations. Frank Renkiewicz, *The Poles in America 1608-1972* (1973); A. Bromke and J. W. Strong, eds., *Gierek's Poland* (1973).

POLICE, an element in municipal reform *(q.v.)*. Police practices have often given cause for concern, as with the use of the third degree, a method of torture or torment intended to elicit confessions, sometimes false ones. Police scandals have been weather-warnings suggesting the need for reform. They have precipitated notable individuals to the fore, among others, Theodore Roosevelt in New York, Smedley D. Butler in Philadelphia *(qq.v.)*. For a typical reform pamphlet in the field, see Dorman B. Eaton, *The Problem of Police Legislation* (1895). Landmarks in the area were the Parkhurst and Seabury *(qq.v.)* investigations. See also Coolidge, Calvin. In the 1960s, ghetto youth *(qq.v.)* taught their sympathizers to term the police "pigs," but modified this publicly as the police expanded their Negro personnel, and were led by them in strategic cities. David W. Abbott et al., *Police, Politics and Race* (1969); Harlan Hahn, ed., *Police in Urban Society* (1971).

POLITICAL ABOLITIONISM, an extension of abolitionism *(q.v.)*, but distinguishable from it. Abolitionists emphasized the moral aspects of the anti-slavery program, and tied it in with a perfectionist *(q.v.)* view of life in general. Political abolitionists sought practical results in legislation, and hoped to unite voters on this issue without confusing it with others in the moral spectrum. The Liberty Party *(q.v.)* was sponsored by individuals no less ardently opposed to slavery than the moral abolitionists. The Free Soil Party *(q.v.)*, however, represented a joining of political abolitionists with such total opportunists as Martin Van Buren *(q.v.)*, who had been anti-abolitionist, and would be the same after the Free Soil campaign, but who had a temporary political purpose in accepting the support of the political abolitionists. Increasing North-South differences, the emotional effect of *Uncle Tom's Cabin (q.v.)*, northern resentment because of the Fugitive Slave Law *(q.v.)*, and other factors seemed to increase anti-slavery and abolitionist sentiment, which the rising Republican Party *(q.v.)* reflected, thus appearing to increase the number of political abolitionists. Many of them, however, Abraham Lincoln *(q.v.)* included, had no program for emancipation; they no more than hoped to confine slavery to the South. For contrasting views of the crisis, see A. C. Cole, *The Irrepressible Conflict* (1934); Avery Craven, *The Repressible Conflict* (1939).

POLITICAL ACTION COMMITTEE, set up in 1943 by the C.I.O., in President Philip Murray's words: "to conduct a broad and intensive program of education for the purpose of mobilizing 5 million members of CIO and enlisting the active support of all other trade unions, AFL railroad brotherhoods and unaffiliated, for effective labor action on the political front." Better known than A.F.L.'s Labor's League for Political Education, set up in 1947, the PAC was especially active during election time, and had a Democratic orientation. The PAC and LLPE merged to become the Committee on Political Education, at the time when the A.F.L. and C.I.O., merged in 1955. See Fay Calkins, *The CIO and the Democratic Party* (1952). See also PACs.

POLITICAL ACTIVITIES ACT (1939), see Hatch Act, The.

POLITICAL MACHINE, often a target for reformers for whom it has the connotation of an instrument serving special interests and stipendiaries, rather than the public. Defenders of the machine have argued for political realism, and pointed out the futility of expecting politicians to work without remuneration. They have defended patronage *(q.v.)* on grounds that loyal workers deserve rewards for having come to the aid of their party. They have protested against the "Throw the rascals out" attitude as demagogic; their opponents have retorted that it is only accurate.

POLITICS AND LITERATURE (1929), see Cole, G.D.H.

POLITICS AND REFORM are necessarily associated, since the opposition to the party in power is required to find issues to justify its demand for support. It strives to suggest that the dreadful policies and mistakes being committed by the incumbents could not be present under its aegis. Jeffersonian *(q.v.*, for this and following references) criticism of the Federalist Alien and Sedition Acts and defense of the French Revolution had a reform component. The problem is to distinguish reform criticism from a "smear" campaign. Jacksonian criticism of the Adams Administration because it had allegedly been born in a "corrupt bargain" was an invention of fraud, rather than reform. The battle against the Democratic "Gag Rule" was clearly in the area of reform, intended to preserve civil rights. Yet the Jacksonian drive against the Second Bank of the United States probably helped build the anti-monopoly tradition. Similarly, the Republican Party attracted anti-slavery (though not necessarily pro-Negro) sentiment; yet it was also the pillar of protectionism, which, whatever its virtues, was scarcely in the category of reform. In the twentieth century, the Democrats could claim the New Freedom and the New Deal, and the Republicans the Square Deal. Republican identification of the Democratic Party with war seemed unfair, and with economic depression, impudent. Corruption seemed as happy with Democrats as with Republicans.

POLK, JAMES K. (1795-1849), "dark horse" Democratic candidate for President from Tennessee in 1844. The Whigs jeered, "Who is James K. Polk?" He confounded their expectations by defeating Henry Clay, thanks to the votes of the Liberty Party. During his Administration, Texas came into the Union, the Mexican War (q.v.) was fought and won, the Oregon question settled, California made part of the Union, and New Mexico. On this record, it has been argued that Polk was a great President: that others would not have his single-minded desire to expand the American borders. In rebuttal it has been argued that Polk was no more than a function of expansionist sentiments, and that he voiced no single memorable principle.

POLK, LEONIDAS L., org. of National Farmers' Alliance (q.v.) in the South.

POLL TAX, like the Grandfather Clause (q.v.), intended to keep Negroes from the polls, though differing from the former in that it affected Negroes and also non-Negroes, and had been used in all periods of American history, and in the North as well as the South, and continued so to be used. See also Mississippi Plan. The poll tax was struck down by Congress in 1965. See Frederic D. Ogden, *The Poll Tax in the South* (1958).

POLLOCK V. FARMERS' LOAN AND TRUST COMPANY (1894), struck down the proviso in the tariff bill of that year creating an income tax, on grounds that it conflicted with the Constitution in being a direct tax which was not apportioned between the states in accordance to population. This finding was reversed by the Sixteenth Amendment to the Constitution; see Taxation.

POLLS have aspired to be scientific, and have attained some triumphs. They have, however, been made vagarious by special factors, including the will of the pollsters. The 1980 Presidential polls were phenomenal as indicating a dead heat as voting began. The poll-takers were abashed by Reagan's (q.v.) overwhelming victory. Whether it would have helped Carter (q.v.) to have freed the "hostages" in Iran (q.v.) before the elections raised questions about the dependability of American voters to make long-range decisions. See also Gallup Poll.

POLLUTION, mainly a concern of environmentalists, as distinguished from pacifists alarmed for the human destructiveness of nuclear weapons, and others dismayed by toxic wastes which might threaten their lives or the normality of unborn children. It has technical aspects, such as the *pollution control* necessary for particular industries or conditions; see, for example: Clifford R. Bragdon, *Noise Pollution* (1979). See also Arthur Bourne, *Pollute and Be Damned* (1973); E. H. Rabin and M. D. Schwartz, *Pollution Crisis* (1975); D. F. Paulsen and R. B. Denhardt, eds., *Pollution and Public Policy* (1973).

POLYGAMY, see Mormons.

POOR LAWS OF GREAT BRITAIN, originated in the Elizabethan Act of 1601, which culminated a long series of particular measures intended to regularize employment, need, the treatment of vagrants, and other conditions. Under the Poor Law, the parishes were given the responsibility for taking care of those in want. Amendments in the eighteenth century were intended to bring the Act up to date, but the Industrial Revolution (q.v.) required some new instrument of legislation. This was provided in 1834, when a new Poor Law set up workhouses (q.v.) for the needy. These created an institution to which reformers, and revolutionists, could address themselves.

POOR RELIEF, see Relief.

"POOR WHITES," see South, The, and Reform.

POPULAR ARTS, THE, including the motion-pictures, radio, television, cartoons, song-writing and rendition, and popular aspects of the theater, have provided many avenues for expressing social reform attitudes, as well as tests for principles of social reform. "John Brown's Body," *Uncle Tom's Cabin*, "I Didn't Raise My Boy to Be a Soldier," and *Li'l Abner* were among songs, plays, and cartoons which contributed light and life to notable causes. *The Birth of a Nation*, the drawings of Art Young, Robert Minor, and William Gropper, the cartoon *Barnaby*, by Crockett Johnson, "Brother, Can You Spare a Dime," some of the work of Charles Chaplin, and such entertainments as *The Cradle Will Rock* have encouraged or projected social reform attitudes. During and shortly after World War II, the motion-pictures permitted the portrayal of generous attitudes toward Negroes and other minority groups, as in *Cross-Fire* and *Pinky*. The television, though maintaining a mediocre average, has presented notable documentaries. Moreover, there have been efforts intended to encourage the use of dissident and unconventional talents, and to curb Negro and other caricatures in the popular arts. Open to question is the weight of such accomplishments: whether they no more than underscore the success of a few talents rather than the rise in standards generally; whether they encourage self-satisfaction and patronage. A notable popular feature of the 1970s was the "Doonesbury" cartoon by Gary Trudeau (1948-   ). It not only entertained a wide audience, but entered into serious concerns. John B. Anderson, running for President in 1980 and given a chance to influence the results was known as the "Doonesbury candidate," thanks to his treatment in the comic strip. Jane Fonda's social attitudes, which included sympathy for the North Vietnam (q.v.) cause, reflected themselves in motion pictures which evoked public response. See also Cinema, Art and Society, Hollywood, the publications of the Popular Culture Association.

POPULAR ELECTION, see Senators, Popular Election of.

POPULAR FRONT, a political program launched by the communists in the late 1930's which represented a change from that held earlier. The Communist International had maintained that the world economic crisis represented capitalism *in extremis*; hence, revolution was the order of the day, and those who opposed it were conscious or unconscious tools of capitalism. The crashing failure of communism in Germany, however, set the communists to reconsidering their resources and to raise the cry for an anti-fascist front, which, however, they intended to dominate, and did, in the case of the Spanish Republic, during the Spanish Civil War (q.v.). Meanwhile the idea of a Popular Front enabled great numbers of avowed liberals to feel free to cooperate with communists on grounds that they were aiding in the battle against fascists; for a chart of the communist cosmos, in this period, see Earl Browder, *The People's Front* (1938).

POPULAR MAGAZINES, a product of the expanded suffrage and democracy of the post-Civil War decades, the need for a clarification of social aims and programs. Magazines differed from newspapers in that they provided an opportunity for second thought and more deliberated expression. They also helped create a common vocabulary for social statements. Such pioneers as S.S. McClure, Frank Munsey, John Brisben Walker, and P.F. Collier did not intend reform, but popularization; moreover, they did not intend cheapened prose, but the best prose, equal to that of the distinguished *Harper's*, *Atlantic*, and *Century*, but cheaper to purchase. To sell to a wider public, they had to widen their horizons of interest. Thus, they could create an instrument for communication which the public could employ as they chose. The public, early in the 1900's, chose reform, making a sensational best-seller of an issue of *McClure's* which contained articles on labor, trusts, and municipal problems. Thereafter, popular magazines dedicated to reform multiplied, including *Collier's, Success, Everybody's*, the *American, Hampton's, Cosmopolitan* among others. They were central to muckraking (*q.v.*) and when stamped out, muckraking disappeared, too. Thus, "popular" magazines, which had meant reform magazines came to mean magazines for light entertainment. They were derogated by "little" magazines (*q.v.*), which often did not distinguish between earlier and later "popular" magazines. It is likely that television (*q.v.*) as information-plus-entertainment in time diminished interest in magazines as popular vehicles for furthering or reflecting change in society. Herbert J. Gans, *Popular Culture and High Culture* (1975); Henry N. Smith, ed., *Popular Culture and Industrialism* (1967).

POPULAR SOVEREIGNTY, see Squatter Sovereignty.

POPULATION PROBLEM, a reform issue for those who hold that the growth of population represents a threat to humanity, raising basic difficulties in food supply, as well as in literacy, disease, and social controls. The "population explosion" has given new energy to birth control advocates. Their major opponent has been the Catholic Church which has minimized the food shortage and other dangers, and has recommended its own birth control measure: the so-called "rhythm" system —dubbed "Vatican roulette" by Bishop James A. Pike. Views of the population crisis vary from that of Garrett Hardin, professor of biology, University of California, who believes there is no solution for it, and that not facing it heaps up further anguish for those who suffer. Others have faced the unswerving growth in population without fear, holding that growth runs in cycles and is thus self-controlling. A White House-sponsored report in 1980 saw a world population of 6,350 million within twenty years, with further increases beyond—a growth which "will imperil the world." D. Callahan et al., *Population Control* (1973); Jack Parsons, *Population Fallacies* (1976); H. M. Bahr et al., *Population Resources and the Future* (1972); C. B. Nam and S. O. Gustavus, *Population: the Dynamics of Change* (1976).

POPULIST REVOLT, THE, fulfillment of a quarter-century of western farmers's unrest, which had expressed itself in efforts to regulate the railroads, to exercise influence through the National Grange, and through such efforts as the Greenback-Labor Party (qq.v.). In 1890, farmers's representatives meeting in Ocala, Florida, formulated a list of demands which became the basis for a later platform, adopted in Omaha, Nebraska, after the People's Party had been officially organized. The Populist Platform was the greatest political platform ever drawn up, notable for the Preamble which was written by Ignatius Donnelly (*q.v.*), as well as for its demands. These included the famous Populist stand on silver (see Silver Issue, The), but also the nationalization of railroads, a graduated income tax, postal savings banks, direct election of Senators, and other provisions. Although the Platform was condemned by conservatives as insane or anarchistic, almost every recommendation was ultimately expressed in law, by either Republican or Democratic Administrations. The Populists nominated James B. Weaver (*q.v.*) for President in 1892; he received over a million popular votes and twenty-two electoral votes. The Populists, in addition, made great gains in legislatures and among executives in the west. Encouraged, they drove toward greater gains in 1896. In that year, the radical wing of the Democratic Party captured a party which had four years before elected Grover Cleveland. William Jennings Bryan (*q.v.*) became their standard-bearer and won the support of the Populists, who put all their hopes on the Silver Issue. A frightened Republican Party received generous corporation

financial support and labored to stem the Populist tide. The great eastern vote—that is, the vote of laborers—won the Republicans victory, though frustrated Populists compared the popular vote with the electoral vote: 7,035,638 for McKinley, 6,467,946 for Bryan; 271 for McKinley, 176 for Bryan. In effect, the Populists had failed to win the workers, despite their "cordial" sympathy with labor's wants. The Populist Revolt was an effort on the part of the farmers to resume their authority as the primary factor in the nation's economy. Although this effort "failed," it reappeared in new guise during the ensuing Reform Era (*q.v.*); an impressive percentage of Progressives and muckrakers were from the midwest and west. For decades, Populism was forgotten by the general public, subject to malice by such academics as Richard Hofstadter, who found mean-mindedness and bigotry in its traditions. The 1960s social turbulence produced, first, praise of "the people" in Eugene McCarthy's 1968 campaign, then praise of a "new populism" by ignorant urban adventurers who seized the Democratic party in 1972, denouncing "corporate America"; see Jack Newfield and Jeff Greenfield, *A Populist Manifesto* (1972), Simon Lazarus, *The Genteel Populists* (1974). Carter's vague "populism" tied in unnoticed with that of the white racist Tom Watson; it was acceptable to his supporters, including *Time* and the *New York Times*, in 1976; it failed him in 1980. (*Qq.v.* for the above.) J. D. Hicks, *The Populsit Revolt* (1931); R. F. Durden, *The Climax of Populism* (1965); Louis Filler, ed., *From Populism to Progressivism* (1978).

PORNOGRAPHY, to be distinguished as a cause from obscenity (*q.v.*), though pornographic images are often seen as obscene. "Adult" bookstores have been defended by enterprising lawyers as justifiable under the Constitution. Refuge has been taken behind the Bible, Shakespeare, and others up to and beyond James Joyce (*q.v.*). Henry Miller's death in 1980 was memorialized as that of a talented man who opened doors to freedom. "Hard core" pornography was deemed less respectable than more devious or "artistic" appeals to interest and curiosity. A formidable section of "porn" disciples, mixing excrement with lubricity were of the "heartland" working and middle classes, who made wealthy purveyors of such publications as *The Hustler*. By 1980, the cause had lost status, and examples of pornography could be purchased easily and at low cost. Ray C. Rist, ed., *The Pornography Controversy: Changing Moral Standards in American Life* (1974).

PORTER, (WILLIAM) SYDNEY (1862-1910), "O. Henry," American short story writer of southern birth and upbringing; although with conventional social ideas and attitudes, his use of colloquialisms and democratic persons and situations served some of the intentions of social reform; moreover, his troubles as a bank clerk accused of mishandling funds, his flight from the law, and the time spent in prison sharpened his sense of humanity and tolerance, and resulted in impressions critical of social injustice as in his story, "The Unfinished Story," which was rejected by several publications before being printed in *McClure's* (*q.v.*), because it imaginatively wondered how a girl working for six dollars a week in a department store might respond to her confining circumstances.

PORTUGAL, a somewhat blank space in the map of social reform: since 1910 with no distinct trend signifying augmented democracy and encouragement to individuality. Its willingness to work with whatever forces would support its continuance has deflected international interest in its affairs. In 1932, it became a dictatorship under Oliveira Salazar. It acquired new distinction in 1961 as being, with the Union of South Africa, outstanding in its intransigent attitude toward the nationalists of its African Angola colony. As its delegate to the United Nations announced: "Our laws have not changed, our fundamental aspirations have not changed, since the 17th Century." Nevertheless, Portugal elected to free Angola, which entered upon a quasi-"Marxist" career, nurturing terrorists its neighbor, the Union of South Africa, deemed dangerous to its internal peace. Its security forces, therefore, did not hesitate to cross over into Angola in raids intended to capture arms and disperse guerrilla units. Although the *New York Times* Third World spokesman Anthony Lewis urged recognition of Angola, it appeared likely that events would yet unfold which would define possibilities between the Union of South Africa and those connected with SWAPO (South West Africa Peoples Organization). A. De Figueirdo, *Portugal and Its Empire: Angola* (1969); Alvaro Cunhal, *Portugal: The Democratic and National Revolution* (1974); E. Harsch and Tony Thomas, *Angola* (1976); T. M. Okuna, *Angola in Ferment* (1974).

POSITIVISM, a philosophic effort by Auguste Comte (1798-1857), French philosopher, who attempted a synthesis of scientific principles with social science and religion in the interests of an understanding of human affairs which would remake society. He argued that earlier syntheses had made God the sole creative force, that later ones had left God out of their calculations, but that a large view of man and the universe would put them in harmony. Although Positivism influenced the thinking of American and British, as well as Continental thinkers, it was more in terms of impulse than as a guide to mastering the details of civilization's dilemmas; for a striking product of Positivist thinking, "intended to illustrate the general theory of historical development put forth in various works" by Comte, see, Frederic Harrison, S.H. Swinny and F.S. Marvin, eds, *The New Calendar of Great Men; Biographies of the 559 Worthies of All Ages & Nations in the Positivist Calendar of Auguste Comte,* first issued in 1892, revised 1920. It offered an historical sequence of personalities, rather than an alphabetical one, and sought those who were deemed to have advanced civilization.

POST, LOUIS F. (1849-1928), Single-Taxer *(q.v.)* and lawyer, he became a publicist for his cause, running for office, editing (1886) Henry George's campaign paper, *The Daily Leader,* contributing to and editing the Single Tax *Standard* (1886-92), and, later, *The Public* (1898-1913). He was U.S. Assistant Secretary of Labor (1913-21). His books included *The George-Hewitt Campaign* (1887), *The Prophet of San Francisco* (1905), *Social Service* (1915), and *The Deportations Delirium of 1920* (1923).

POST, NEW YORK EVENING, founded in 1801 by Alexander Hamilton *(q.v.)* and others, it became one of the most distinguished American newspapers under the editorship of William Cullen Bryant *(q.v.)* (1829-78), setting high standards for literate journalism and supporting reform Democratic politics. It later enjoyed the editorial services of E.L. Godkin, Lincoln Steffens, Oswald Garrison Villard, among others *(q.v.),* and still later continued in liberal esteem as a Scripps-Howard paper. Still later it became a liberal tabloid, employing such liberals as Joseph Wechsler, Max Lerner, Murray Kempton, and Joseph Lash. Allan Nevins, *The Evening Post* (1922).

POST, NEW YORK MORNING, founded by Horace Greeley *(q.v.)* in 1833; the first daily penny *(q.v.)* newspaper.

POSTAL REFORM addressed itself to several questions: organizing a postal system which would be more uniform in its operations, which would be cheaper, which would not be misused, which would promote moral purposes. In 1848, the New York Cheap Postage Association was formed which ultimately achieved a three-cent letter rate for three thousand miles. Four years earlier, Lysander Spooner *(q.v.)* had opened up a mail service between Boston and New York in competition with the United States Post Office, and helped force down rates. Under Elihu Burritt, "Ocean Penny Postage" was agitated, as an aid to international peace. Free-thinkers and libertarians fought, unsuccessfully, for mail delivery on Sundays. Protests against the overliberal use of the mails by congressmen, under government franchise, were largely defeated. Other elements of postal reform, as seen in pre-

Civil War years are noted in Pliny Miles, *Postal Reform: Its Urgent Necessity and Practicality* (1855). The increased use of the mails, and expansion of the mails by the government, in large measure, shifted responsibility for aspects of the mail service from the post office to other branches of government, and reduced its reform questions to questions of technique and expediency. The cumbersome bureaucracy, and other problems, created the United Parcel Service, which helped take the edge off public frustration. Problems, however, clung on. See John Haldi, *The Postal Monopoly: an Assessment of the Private Express Statutes* (1974).

POST-WATERGATE MORALITY, a notion of Spiro T. Agnew *(q.v.),* who felt he had been victimized by a public attitude which did not take into account expectations of conduct widely practiced in pre-Watergate days. Gratuities were then, in his view, distinguishable from friendship. With Watergate came a new view of old routines. According to Nixon, Agnew had, in their last pre-resignation talk, stated that he was embittered by the hypocricy of members of Congress who had formerly been governors. He believed "that most of the governors in other states had followed practices such as those common in Maryland. He emphasized that he had always awarded contracts on the basis of merit, and he felt that the amounts he had received had been so small that no reasonable critic could claim that they could have influenced him to make a decision that contravened the public interest." (Nixon, *RN* [1978], 923.) What he did not explain was why he had taken them at all, or, taking them, was unwilling to fight for his point of view in the courts, in behalf of those who had given him their passionate allegiance. The evidence that "post-Watergate morality" had no working future as a point in time was seen in the Abscam *(q.v.)* cases, which victimized congressmen even more oddly than Agnew had been victimized, if he had been at all. Spiro T. Agnew, *Go Quietly, or Else* (1980).

POTEMKIN VILLAGES, so dubbed for a powerful Russian nobleman of the eighteenth century, who, in 1787 organized Czarina Catherine's tour of the Crimea. His reputation for tidying up homes and conveniences along her route of travel became the symbol of all such facades. American officials may have done something similar in some places in South Vietnam visited by cameramen and reporters, before the situation got out of hand and permitted shocking scenes to enter into American homes via television *(q.v.).* In 1980 the Russians were accused of having set up false fronts of good will and comfort for visitors to the Olympic *(q.v.)* games to experience, in order to hide wretched shortages and abuse of human rights *(q.v.),* thus creating a modern version of Potemkin villages.

POTTAWATOMIE MASSACRE (May 24, 1856), John Brown's *(q.v.)* desperate act in Kansas; with a small band he visited a group of persons who lived by Pottawatomie Creek and murdered five. Significant were the fashions in which the deed was defended by Free Soilers *(q.v.),* who held that Brown was in a frenzy of grief because of cruelties inflicted upon members of his family by pro-slavery fighters; that he was visiting retaliation on them for murders inflicted on Free Soilers; that the "executions" were a mere incident in territory-wide conflicts. The fact appears to be that Brown's victims were connected with the district court, which was about to try him and his few followers for lawless operations; see James C. Malin, *John Brown and the Legend of Fifty-Six* (1942). Thus, the justifications concocted for Brown illustrated the tendency of reformers, among others, to close ranks in defense of their own, whether on legitimate or illegitimate grounds.

POUND, EZRA (1885-1972), Iowa-born American expatriate, made famous by his long dedication to poetry and influence upon such poets as T.S. Eliot and Hart Crane, and even more by the controversy which followed after he had been arrested for treason (1945), having broadcast speeches in Italy on behalf of the fascist cause. His friends cited his services as editor, critic, and poet, and argued that his misdemeanors ought to be ignored in view of his distinctions. Others pointed to his unbridled anti-American viewpoint, his equally unbridled anti-semitism, his ingratitude (thus, he had been received with honor in America, in 1939), and were critical of his verse. The deep schism between traditionalists and *avant-garde* was demonstrated in the willingness of the former to see him executed, in effect because they could not endure his writings, while, on the other hand, his devout admirers reprinted his fascist writings, as examples of his prose. Pound was not brought to trial; he was incarcerated as insane in St. Elizabeth Hospital, Washington, D.C. It was observed that he had not said anything on the Rome radio that many of his friends had not also been writing in American periodicals. He was released in 1960, and left the country. Eric Hamberger, ed., *Ezra Pound: The Critical Heritage* (1973).

POVERTY, considered irrational and intolerable by evangelical reformers, who point to poverty in the midst of plenty. Bernard Shaw *(q.v.)* considered it the one crime. Reformers repudiate the contention of conservative critics that the workings of human nature bring one person into security and comfort, another to poverty. They denounce it as injustice, and also as creating social hazards. George Orwell *(q.v.)* felt compelled to probe its workings in his own person, as recounted in *Down and Out in Paris and London* (1933). Socialism has claimed to provide a system which would obliterate poverty; social reformers have sought welfare measures which would diminish it. A definition of poverty is not readily agreed upon, but it lies somewhere between subsistence and the opportunity for growth. Charles Booth was the great student of the subject in England, in 1885 beginning the labors intended to ascertain the "numerical relations which poverty, misery, and depravity bear to regular earnings and comparative comfort." Employing a large corps of helpers, he published his results in the sixteen volumes of *The Life and Labor of the People of London*. Robert Hunter's *(q.v.) Poverty* (1904) was an American effort. Because of the welfare nature of the modern state, the subject has required reconsideration. See also Henry George, *Progress and Poverty*. A curious statement appeared in Andrew Shonfield, *The Attack on World Poverty* (1960), which cited the operations of the United Nations *(q.v.)* in this area, observed that they were insignificant, but made reference to the man who was arraigned in court for having sold "earthquake pills," during the Lisbon Earthquake (see Catastrophes); he "silenced his accusers thus: 'What,' he asked, 'would you put in their place?'" For American views of poverty during the Reform Era, see Robert Hunter, *Poverty* (1904), Isado Ladoff, *American Pauperism and the Abolition of Poverty* (1904), Scott Nearing, *Poverty and Riches* (1916). Since welfare state *(q.v.)* funds and administration had been in operation since the New Deal *(q.v.)*, and poverty had been on display in good times and ill, it appeared time to reconsider its nature and experiences. George L. Wilber, ed., *Poverty: a New Perspective* (1975); Pamela Roby, ed., *Poverty Establishment* (1974). See also M. Ui Haq, *Poverty Curtain: Choices for the Third World* (1976).

POWDERLY, TERENCE V. (1849-1924), figure in labor history, head of the Knights of Labor *(q.v.)*. A moderate in his view of Labor-capitalist relations, he helped to create such machinery as arbitration boards to help cut down the incidence of violent labor conflicts. His books *Thirty Years of Labor* (1889) and *The Path I Trod* (1940) help clarify aspects of the development of the labor movement.

POWELL, ADAM CLAYTON (1908-1972), a human incident in the minority affairs of the Negro people, he made his reputation in New York municipal affairs demanding jobs for his people, and was conspicuous in the 1941 demonstrations calling for non-discrimination in war-related industries. Elected to Congress in 1944 he was conspicuous in pressing for bills in furtherance of Negro interests, and, lasting into President Johnson's *(q.v.)* Administration, busied himself with anti-poverty programs. He was demagogic in presenting a personal image of arrogance which would appeal to the less sophisticated of his constituents. His corrupt financial dealings were so blatant that he was expelled from Congress in 1967, but was nevertheless re-elected from his district and seated the next year. His defense, made famous on television, was: "I paid my dues, baby." In 1970 his district, tired of his embarrassing public gestures, unseated him, retiring him affluent to a Caribbean island. See his *Keep the Faith, Baby* (1967) and *Adam by Adam* (1971).

POWER, see Federal Power Commission.

PRAGMATISM, an intellectual development of the post-Civil War era, intended to provide Americans with a more viable sense of reality. In William James's *(q.v.)* formulations, it struck a more pertinent relationship between human psychology and needs and the "objective" world; this could be distinguished from earlier idealisms which stipulated how the world *ought* to be viewed. It observed that an object could be seen a number of ways, depending on the purpose involved. John Dewey *(q.v.)* added a heavier emphasis on education as a preparation for real life, as it developed and was molded, and a concern for *experiment*, which would presumably reveal the best methods, techniques, and results. Pragmatism was intended to be a self-correcting philosophy, since further education for life, further experiment would reveal errors and failures in previous efforts. Pragmatism was essentially optimistic. It assumed that children given the opportunity to express themselves, would express good and desirable traits and ideas. It assumed that pragmatists would welcome criticism of their results. It failed to notice that if one desired a result that "worked," then the status quo *(q.v.)* could claim to be pragmatic, or at least "practical": a vulgarization of the hopes and aspirations of the great pragmatic philosophers. In the education controversy of the 1950's, pragmatism was made the scapegoat of American education, which had not only failed to produce a regard for culture, but had failed to produce scientific results to match those of the competing Russians: a failure of the highly-touted "Yankee know-how." Pragmatists could only protest that education was a function of society, not of their philosophy; and that a "return" to "discipline" would not produce creative personages, but parrots. Nevertheless, pragmatism seemed to have lost its force as an inspiring approach to reality, with reform alternatives not clearly defined.

PRAVDA official newspaper of the Soviet Union, in translation: "Truth."

PREEMPTION ACTS, Congressional measures which provided for the distribution of the public domain, and were seen by popular leaders as democratic and reformistic, since they offered hope and opportunity to oppressed victims of economic crises and other conditions. Thus, the Preemption Act of 1830 permitted settlers to acquire one hundred and sixty acres at a dollar and a quarter an acre. The Preemption Act of 1841 contained the significant feature that land which had been settled before it had been purchased was legally held; thus, *illegal* settlement was not denounced or discountenanced, but given status in law. The Homestead Act of 1862 *(q.v.)* opened the still available public domain to citizens who would work it for five years for no more than the registration fee. The great land grants to the railroads *(q.v.)*, coupled with the fact that settlers were often casual in their regard for the land they easily acquired, qualified what should have been great democratic victories.

PREJUDICE, a quantity sometimes difficult to distinguish from preconceptions—as that New Yorkers are "pushers," or that all Negroes enjoy "spirituals"—and in a formal sense common to all "in-groups," liberal as well as conservative. Most significantly identified with attitudes harming minority group status or economic opportunity, and feeding on subtle as well as patently malicious social and psychological fare. Whether Stephen C. Foster's (1826-1864) immortal pseudo-folk songs (*My Old Kentucky Home, Massa's In de Cold, Cold Ground, Old Black Joe*) have aided prejudice may be doubted, though reform-minded individuals are prone to sing them without dialect. They have also firmly insisted on the words of a popular jingle reading: "Eenie-Meenie-Minie-Moe, Catch a tiger by the toe..." The campaign against *prejudice*, as such, is largely middle-class, concerned with creating "nicer" attitudes. Reformers think more fundamentally of economic considerations, legal rights, constitutional guarantees, social and political alliances. See also Minority Groups, Discrimination, Epithets, F.E.P.C.

"PREMATURE ANTI-FASCISM," a concept intended to excuse the unqualified support given to communists by persons in conventional social circumstances who before World War II created an alliance between the United States and the U.S.S.R., and who afterwards came under fire from the House Un-American Activities Committee. It was argued that they had not been so much pro-communist as anti-fascist, and had foreseen the threat to democracy posed by fascism before their countrymen had.

PRESIDENCY, THE, has inspired numerous reform sentiments from aspirants to the post, numerous warnings against the harm they might do. They have tended to embody democratic ideals, rather than reformist deeds. Thus, Jefferson was presented as a reformer; the actual measures of his Administration did not embody reforms, and its attack on the Supreme Court was of doubtful reformist quality. Andrew Jackson took office as a friend of the people but actual measures in their behalf are few. His assault on the Second Bank of the United States must be balanced by his assault on abolitionists. The impeachment of Andrew Johnson was presumably in the interests of a popular program headed by Radical Republicans, but whether the impeachment of Johnson served reform or democracy may be doubted. Yet the Presidency as a symbol can serve reform. Though Theodore Roosevelt was no muckraker and scarcely a Progressive, muckrakers and Progressives claimed fellowship with him. Franklin D. Roosevelt's N.R.A. emphasized the wants of business, but labor cited the unimplemented Section 7 (a) as evidence that he desired labor's organization. Thus, the Presidency, dependent as it is on moderate as well as more energetic support, can be only as reformist as given times allow, but it has often taken on color from the activities of reformers (*qq.v.* for all above references). Since 1960, the Presidency's prestige has been in decline, thanks to bad luck and disillusionment which has followed every President since Eisenhower. From fears in Johnson's and Nixon's terms of an "imperial president," there have been new fears of a President who might be too weak, leading a disunited people, and unable to gain the respect of foreign statesmen. See also Activist President. Ann E. Weiss, *The American presidency* (1976); Herman Finer, *The Presidency: Crisis and Regeneration* (1960); R. E. Neustadt, *Presidential Power* (1960); David Goldman, *Presidential Losers* (1970); Filler, *The Presidency in Crisis* (1982).

PRESS, FREEDOM OF THE, guaranteed by the First Amendment of the Bill of Rights, it was not firm enough to withstand the force of the Sedition Acts of 1798 and 1918, both of which were violently attacked by their opponents. Expressions of opinion were also employed against dissidents in the Haymarket case and in later cases involving radicals. Justice Holmes sought to defend the freedoms stipulated in the First Amendment, though in Schenck v. United States he qualified this in a classic phrase. The latter-day *Independent* was firm on the need for freedom of the Press, as was George Seldes. The fact that communists had lost public sympathy, because of revelations of their unpatriotic spying activities for Russia, lost them much of their support from the Bill of Rights in general, which, they insisted, was thereby enfeebled for everybody; (*qq.v.*) for the above. Since

publication of the *Pentagon Papers (q.v.)*, on one side, and prosecution of journalists unwilling to give sources for information damaging to individuals, on the other, the limits of press freedom have been bruited, but to no satisfactory constitutional conclusion. William Ruckelshaus et al., *Freedom of the Press* (1976); Benno C. Schmidt, Jr., *Freedom of the Press Vs. Public Access* (1976); J. A. Barron, *Freedom of the Press for Whom?* (1973).

PRIBER, CHRISTIAN, see Oglethorpe, James.

PRICE CONTROL, see Office of Price Administration.

PRIESTLEY, JOSEPH (1733-1804), noted English philosopher, chemist, and controversialist, best known for his discovery of oxygen, which he termed "dephlogisticated air," but significant for a wide variety of other discoveries in the field, as well as for an increasingly libertarian viewpoint in religion and on social questions. Such works as his *History of the Corruptions of Christianity* (1782), which was burned by the public hangman, and his constant polemics and challenges to public opinion, culminated in a sympathetic attitude toward the French Revolution *(q.v.)* which so outraged the conservatives of Birmingham that they burned his home in 1791, destroying his library and scientific equipment. He removed to the United States in 1794, and was a target for Federalist abuse there, though well regarded by scientists and Democratic-Republicans.

PRIGG V. PENNSYLVANIA (1842), a key case in growing North and South antagonism over slavery. The United States Supreme Court, in an effort to settle the problem of fugitive slaves *(q.v.)*, decreed that they were a matter for Federal legislation, and that "personal liberty laws" intended to stop slave-catchers from seizing alleged fugitives and taking them out of the state were unconstitutional. Both North and South resented this decision, the South because it was reluctant to have the government claim authority to deal with its "peculiar institution," the North because it wished to administer the problem of runaways itself. If slave-catchers could arbitrarily decide that individuals were runaway Negroes, they could nab free Negroes and remand them to slavery, or even bring away white persons on false accusations. If northern states were not permitted to legislate on the problem, they could refuse to cooperate with federal authorities. A new series of "personal liberty laws" *(q.v.)* throughout the North signalled an increased unwillingness to cooperate with slaveholders and to tolerate Federal action in their behalf.

PRIMARIES, see Direct Primaries.

PRISON LABOR, see Convict Labor.

PRISON REFORM had its start in the desire of William Penn *(q.v.)* to develop a humane program of punishment in his new American colony. The Quaker interest continued to be strong in the field; in Pennsylvania; in 1787, the Philadelphia Society for Alleviating the Miseries of Public Prisons began its work. The problem in America was augmented by the meagerness of prison facilities, which made mutilation and death a major instrument of crime-deterrence. Benjamin Rush *(q.v.)* was one among many who sought to build up the prison as a reformatory, rather than a place which could breed further crime. The Eastern Penitentiary which the prison reformers obtained instituted the system of solitary confinement, which, in their theory, preserved prisoners from evil influences. The Auburn Prison in New York State, by contrast, utilized group work, conducted in silence, and cell blocks. The era of reform, of pre-Civil War years, called up many reformers, such as Dorothea Dix *(q.v.)*, to concern themselves for separating sick people from law-breakers, and for other improvements in prison facilities and administration. In 1870, thanks to the efforts of the Rev. Enoch C. Wines *(q.v.)* and others, a congress in Cincinnati organized the National Prison Association which thereafter dealt with humane efforts to improve prison purposes. It considered the experiences of the New York State Reformatory at Elmira. It pondered the possibilities of the "indeterminate sentence," which set maximum and minimum years, but left for future determination how soon a prisoner could be released. (The important point was that the prisoner would have to be evaluated as an individual.) Massachusetts was the pioneer in experimenting with probation: under specific regulations giving the prisoner a chance to prove that he could utilize freedom properly. Thomas M. Osborne (q.v.) was a major crusader for building up the character of prisoners by giving them substantial responsibilities. Alternatives to imprisonment were suggested: a system of fines and restitution; qualified freedom within the context of family, neighborhood, or community; and others. A problem difficult to handle was the irregular quality of sentences and prison service—a person might be executed in one state and imprisoned in the next, might have one attitude in a "model" prison and another in a shabby and indifferently-run prison. See also Debtors' Prisons, Anti-Capital Punishment Crusade.

PRIVATE ENTERPRISE, distinct from capitalism (q.v.), which requires capital, yet related to it. Reformers criticized it as not very private, as seeking government grants and favors, yet pleading self-interest when challenged. Advocates of private enterprise responded with criticism of government administrators who did not produce anything, and with a record of failure, as in urban renewal. The 1980 Elections brought out the Republican faith in "enterprise zones"—eroded districts such as, notoriously, the South Bronx in New York—to which they would invite energetic and intelligent businessmen to provide employment, rebuild the area, aided by tax and other credits: a step toward full-bodied private enterprise, based on the profit motive, in a modern context.

"PROCESSING TAX," see Agricultural Adjustment Administration.

PRODUCTIVITY, earlier a topic in industrial planning and relations. In the late 1970s, it became a watchword in government, notably in Great Britain, but increasingly in the United States, and stirred bureaucrats and union members looking for public support. Samuel Gompers (q.v.) had denounced excessive demands for worker-production as making slaves of them. Veblen (q.v.) had praised the "instinct for workmanship." Since their time, a time of Big Business, labor had become Big Labor, with time, salary, and benefit guarantees, augmented by welfare supports. Yet the economy did not flourish. "Quality control" did not produce quality. With the coming of inflation and acute unemployment (qq.v.) old rationalizations did not suffice. The superior productivity of once prostrate West Germany and Japan made for a direct criticism of the American business and industrial system. What, then, could revive a dull and dwindling economy? Not mere productivity, otherwise farmers would not receive subsidies to produce less, in order to keep farm prices up. Not mere productivity, when American automobiles sat in auto sales windows unbought, buyers preferring a foreign make. The answer lay in more production of superior make, handled intelligently by producers and distributors, troubled by a minimum of incompetent workers and destructive capital-labor relations. These would require government and legal policies which created an incentive for better work; it was irrational to expect quality production from a shoddy society. P. E. Haggerty, The Productive Society (1974); Michael Beseley, ed., Productivity and Amenity (1974); E. M. Glaser, Productivity Gains through Worklife Improvement (1976); Mildred E. Katzell, Productivity: the Measure and the Myth (1975).

PROFIT SHARING, an element in cooperative production and distribution, a middle ground between free enterprise and socialism. Although encouraged by elements of free enterprise and touted as capitalism's answer to socialism, it is criticized by the latter as too little, and as constituting a sop rather than a solution to social ills. Although Samuel Gompers (q.v.) denounced it as a strategy for resisting unionism, it was proposed by industrialists as a factor in union negotiations under secured union conditions.

PROGRESS AND POVERTY (1879), see George, Henry.

PROGRESSIVE EDUCATION, a reformist strain in education, seeking not only more education for more people, but experimental methods of educating and a concern for the individual child. Thomas Jefferson sought universal education, but only in its initial stages; the "rubbish" was soon to be weeded out. A. B. Alcott, H. D. Thoreau, and the teachers of Brook Farm (qq.v.) satisfied tenets of progressive education, though in the age of the "common man," the emphasis was on attaining universal education. In the post-Civil War period, the great developments were in acquiring more education at the high school level and in building into the school system such new ideas as vocational education. John Dewey (q.v.) was a leader among the experimentalists who sought not merely to inculcate knowledge into children, but to evoke from them their individual talents. The 1910's were an era of experimentalism, but the growing atomization of the American family placed new burdens on the teacher, required to maintain a discipline lacking at home. Progressive education expanded not because Americans were receptive to experimentation, but because the growing numbers of children, and the lagging numbers of teachers demanded teacher training and the creation of "educationalists." In the 1950's, parents and public figures feared that the schools were not teaching basic disciplines, and made a scapegoat of Progressive Education. It was, however, no more than a function of society, which shared responsibility. See Education, Children, Gifted, Rugg, Harold.

PROGRESSIVE ERA, THE, one of the highpoints in American reform, it sought to cope with the problems which had accumulated in the post-Civil War era. Muckraking (q.v.) was the exposure and educational arm of Progressivism, and mobilized public opinion in favor of legislative enactments. Examination of the Progressive achievements reveals priorities as they recommended themselves to the age. They were essentially middle-class (q.v.), and concerned for securing freedom from want. Hence outstanding sensations were produced in municipal government, the question of pure food and drugs, insurance, railroad regulation, and, as in the Ballinger Affair, the public domain (qq.v.). The Progressive Party (q.v.) challenged the major parties. The Wilsonian reforms emphasized regulation (qq.v.), especially of business. Yet the age permitted so drastic a blow against union as the Danbury Hatters case (q.v.). The Triangle Fire (q.v.) was necessary to reveal the intolerable nature of lax factory controls. The advent and handling of World War I (q.v.) revealed the positive and negative features which Progressivism had incubated. Progressivism continued in memory as a great era meriting emulation until the post-World War II era, when Beats, Hippies, and other features of social disintegration protruded themselves upon the social consciousness, and demeaned the ideal, not only in the public forum but in the schools. Academics found racism, bigotry, subservience to "corporate America," imperialism, and bad art in icons of Progressive personalities and achievement. Leading academics including Richard Hofstadter, the southern successor to Ulrich B. Phillips (q.v.) C. Van Woodward, among others, led the attack on Progressives. Although some lip-service was still given Robert M. La Follette, Louis D. Brandeis, and Lincoln Steffens (qq.v.), Jane Addams (q.v.) was demeaned as giving too little to the poor of Hull House too late, and suspected of homosexual tendencies (D. Levine, Jane Addams and the Liberal Tradition [1971], and Theodore Roosevelt (q.v.) was set down as an insane imperialist (Hofstadter, The American Political Tradition [1948]). Although Roosevelt was somewhat rehabilitated in a 1979 best-seller (E. Morris, The Rise of Theodore Roosevelt), the general status of the movement continued low. One Hofstadter academic, Robert Schneider, in British American Studies thought Progressivism had nothing to offer to the study of American Studies; another representative teacher in the area, Luther Spoehr, in Reviews in American History (1977), pronounced Progressivism a bore; still another, Peter Filene, pronounced on "Obituary" for Progressivism in line with such reason and non-material. Populism (q.v.) came erratically back at Progressivism's expense. It seemed likely that a new historical survey by competent researchers conscientiously motivated would be in order for both to be given fresh focus in a larger, changing world—one which gave regard to "Marxists," "people's" movements, "popular" regimes, and other political groupings ranging from dictatorships to quasi-democracies. R. Hofstadter, *Progressive Historians* (1970); David Noble, *The Progressive Mind* (1969); J. Burnham, et al., *Progressivism* (1977); Arthur X. Ekirch, *Progressivism in America* (1974); David M. Kennedy, ed., *Progressivism: the Critical Issues* (1971).

PROGRESSIVE PARTY, THE, existed in three manifestations: the most important was that of 1912 (*q.v.*), and represented a summation of social and Populist (*q.v.*) and other middle-class (*q.v.*) efforts. Although Roosevelt ran far ahead of the official standard-bearer, Taft (*q.v.*), of the Republican Party, the unscrupulous nature of the Progressive alliance, which permitted the undermining of La Follette's (*q.v.*) candidacy and the influence of Frank A. Munsey (*q.v.*) permitted the new party to decay and disappear. The Conference for Progressive Political Action (*q.v.*) which in 1924 created another Progressive Party, represented farmer and labor elements, and offered La Follette, but though he polled over four million, eight hundred thousand votes, the Party could not establish itself on a permanent basis. The Progressive Party which offered Henry A. Wallace (*q.v.*) in 1948 sought grassroots phraseology, but was encumbered by communist and quasi-liberal influence of a politically unsubstantial type. Representing neither the farmer nor labor interest, it failed catastrophically to make an impression on the elections of that year. It appeared possible that "progressivism" as a slogan was securely in history. W. E. Walling, *Progressivism and After* (1914); H. M. Hooker, ed., *History of the Progressive Party*, by Amos R. E. Pinchot (1958); R. B. Nye, *Midwestern Progressive Politics* (1951).

PROHIBITION, a problem in reform, since it was a distinct cause with such notable reformers as Susan B. Anthony, Wendell Phillips, Horace Mann, and others (*qq.v.*) who held drinking immoral and debilitating. The cause also produced such zealots as Neal Dow (*q.v.*), who were influential, but whether in a fashion which promoted individual or social health is debatable. Frances Willard's (*q.v.*) services to education and women's rights were manifest social gains, and freely linked by her with prohibition sentiments. The Prohibition Party produced a succession of minor-party candidates at national elections; in the close elections of 1884 and 1888 it was a factor in the decisions. It appeared to prohibition advocates that Americans were about to accept the results of their long battle for a constitutional amendment, which resulted in passage of the Eighteenth Amendment to the Constitution (January 29, 1919). Liquor was spilled in the streets, citizens took their "last" drinks. The "Roaring Twenties" appalled observers, as the rank and file of citizens worked in harmony to undermine the Constitution by patronizing bootleggers, and thereby vast syndicates of lawlessness and crime. Such a book as Rheta Childe Dorr's *Drink—Coercion or Control?* (1929) sought, ineffectually, to treat the problem sensibly. The choice was, rather, coercion or non-control. The abandonment of prohibition, through passage of the Twenty-First Amendment, in 1933, opened the sluices to drink, which subsequent war, cold war, and despair widened into a flood. The Prohibition Party continued to offer candidates, even during the Prohibition Era, and to receive votes, which did not, however, increase after abandonment of the Great Experiment. There was evidently little faith in the return of prohibition, or even the value of a protest vote. "Repeal after Twenty Years," by Charles M. Crowe (*Christian Century*, February 14, 1951), observed that bootlegging had not diminished as a result of repeal, that drinking had increased spectacularly, influencing crime, accidents, and mental and physical health, and that women and young people were major social victims of drink. "Most temperance advocates," the

article said, "are now working to educate people in the effects of drink. They want people to be as free not to drink as they are to drink." It thus appeared that prohibitionists were seeking realistically to influence the incidence of drink, rather than to prohibit it. *Alert*, a digest organ of the International Temperance Association offered facts and figures. See also Temperance. Herbert Asbury, *The Great Illusion* (1950); A. Sinclair, *Prohibition* (1962); John Kobler, *Ardent Spirits* (1973).

"PROLETARIAN ART," see "Social Significance."

PROLETARIAT, in Karl Marx's view, the "grave-digger" of capitalism, that element in society having, increasingly, nothing to offer but its hands for labor. As increasing technology and the inexorable operation of the "value theory" increased unemployment, and created a standing army of unemployed, they would finally have no alternative but to rise and overthrow their oppressors, taking from the latter what had been wrongly withheld from them. The term "Proletariat" was popular abroad, and used freely by revolutionists; it had some vogue in the United States in the 1930's, but was ultimately without prestige.

PRO-LIFERS, represented anti-abortion (*q.v.*) on the offensive, not only resisting such organizations as National Organization for Women (NOW), with its call for abortion on demand and freedom of choice, but petitioning for an amendment to the Constitution reversing the Supreme Court's decision sanctioning abortion and, instead, banning it. The new Reagan (*q.v.*) Administration came in, in 1981, with a President who approved such an amendment. The Pro-Lifers staged a "March for Life" in the Capital which convened 50,000 marchers, many carrying roses, and received from the new Secretary of Health and Human Services a promise that his department would "implement a pro-life policy." In response, the National Abortion Rights Action League promised to fight for its cause in all the states.

PROMISE OF AMERICAN LIFE, THE (1909), by Herbert Croly (*q.v.*).

PROPAGANDA, deemed increasingly important as agencies for "creating" public opinion and "influencing the masses" raised catastrophic possibilities for society. "Propaganda" was made invidious by the "disillusionment" which followed World War I, and the release of evidence that British propagandists had lied many Americans into hating Germans. Communists saw no harm in withholding truth from the "masses," as from "confused liberals." Nevertheless, they joined liberals in denouncing the "Big Lie" as employed by Hitler. *Semantics*, a fad of the 1930's, was supposed to enable the analytical student to penetrate falsehood. Historians who believed that truth was relative, in effect condoned partial statements of reality, and honored works which were based upon such. (See Saint Bartholomew Massacre.) Propaganda was a basic weapon for social control in Orwell's *1984 (qq.v.)*. A. Rhodes, *Propaganda: The Art of Persuasion in World War II* (1976); Richard A. Maynard, *Propaganda on Film: a Nation at War* (1975); S. Kalisher, *Propaganda and Other Photographs* (1976); *Propaganda and Public Opinion* (1973).

"PROPERTY IS THEFT," see Mutualism.

PROPERTY RIGHTS, see Private Enterprise.

PROPOSITION THIRTEEN, historic proposal submitted in California in 1978, supported by voters and emulated elsewhere with "Proposition Thirteen"-type proposals and amendments. It cut property taxes which property owners considered onerous, and deprived the state of money used to subsidize welfare state (*q.v.*) and other activities. It was denounced as harming education and the poor. In California, its effects were buffered by a surplus, which, however, was bound to be depleted. Elsewhere, there were victories, and variations on victories. Thus in Corpus Christi, Texas, a tax cut and ceiling was successful at the polls, but faced court action since it seemed to transgress the state constitution. In Michigan, the education union revealed itself as a special interest power by spending lavishly to defeat a Jarvis-type tax plan which would have cut assessed property valuation 50%. The "Tisch" Plan did so well, however, that its threat continued to hang over the state's services. That the public was thinking as never before was seen in the fact that another Jarvis initiative in California, asking drastic income tax cuts, was turned back in 1980. Tax cuts, then, had become part of government and anti-government strategy in determining the priorities of the nation. George E. Peterson, ed., *Property Tax Reform* (1973); R. W. Lundholm, *Property Taxation and the Finance of Education* (1974); Walter Rybeck, *Property...Tax Reform and Assessment Modernization* (1970).

PRO-SLAVERY, in the pre-Civil War period, an increasingly positive point of view developed by its defenders, who argued that their "peculiar institution" was preferable in its workings to those of free labor systems, and, in any event, their own. *The Pro-Slavery Argument* (1853) was a major collection of arguments and discussion by outstanding southerners intended to persuade the reader. See also Slavery.

PROSTITUTION, taken by "goo goos" (*q.v.*) to be a moral question involving evil persons, notably "bad women", and to be best combatted by direct action. Indignant committees were wont to make efforts to close brothels; where the towns were small enough, to drive the women out of town. Social reformers protested against the inequity, observing that prostitutes could not subsist without clients. They argued, too, that the evil was a function of wrong economics, that prostitutes were driven to their trade by want. Brand Whitlock (*q.v.*) in his antagonism to socialism, criticized its inadequate view of human nature; though a reformer, he believed that there were, in fact, "daughters of joy," to whom the economics of light living were secondary. The pre-World War I reform movement did expose rings dedicated to fostering prostitution, and succeeded in erecting some laws and social controls, including the Mann Act (1910), (*q.v.*). The loosening up of the family, the "flapper age" (*q.v.*), emancipated thought attending the 1930's, and further tears in the social fabric during World War II blurred the dividing lines between sordid sex and liberated standards. Social work became the most significant field for reformers facing the continuing fact of prostitution. The freedom drives of the 1960s included demands for freedom of sex choices, with Stanford University females asserting their right to use their bodies as they pleased, and San Francisco prostitutes attempting to organize a union. The Internal Revenue Service being interested only in receiving tax money from business transactions, it was at odds, to a degree, with moral societies and police who discerned problems in prostitutes and brothel operators. See Family, The, Singles.

PROTECTIONISM, a major political issue through most of the nation's history, fancied by professionals because its complexities offered infinite opportunities for political adepts, easier to handle than such elemental problems as slavery, poverty, and peace. Protectionism was *nationalistic* in essence. Alexander Hamilton, as Secretary of the Treasury, advocated a system protecting home industry from foreign competition by placing a heavy duty upon the latter. Before the War of 1812, southerners hoped to develop their own industry, and approved a high tariff. Disappointed by their failure to achieve industry, and envious of New England which did, southerners became earnest advocates of free trade (*q.v.*), and critics of protective tariffs. The Tariff of Abominations (*q.v.*) and that of 1832 outraged southern opinion and brought on the Nullification (*q.v.*) crisis, foreshadowing secession. Horace Greeley (*q.v.*) was a protectionist and a reformer; he opposed labor unions and other radical measures, and he favored aid to home industries; for the poor he advocated education, cooperative living, free land in the west. The Republican Party was supported by advocates of free enterprise, who raised the tariff through the Civil War, and made it a Republican institution thereafter. It was supported by workers who believed that

their jobs depended on manufacturers being free of competition from abroad, which was said to employ labor which existed on standards far below that of Americans. In effect, industry was subsidized by the high tariff, which enabled it to ask higher prices than it could otherwise have expected; yet it criticized the farmer (*q.v.*) for asking government aid in keeping up farm prices. The Tariff Commission which was set up in 1916 was intended to invest the subject with the public interest, but it had little effect in the 1920's. The New Deal Administration sought reciprocity agreements. In 1980, with foreign cars outselling American cars, there was a clamor from laborers, made unemployed by the foreign competition, for protection of home manufactures; but other political and social needs limited such actions. See Free Trade.

PROTECTORATE, in English history, the rule of Oliver Cromwell following the Puritan Revolution (*q.v.*); more generally, the system of interference and control practiced by large nations in their dealings with small ones. Theoretically for their own good, the protectorate aims to secure political and economic advantages for the dominant power. The United States held on to its control over Cuba (*q.v.*), in large measure, and Nicaragua and Haiti (*qq.v.*), among other territories. The concept of a protectorate dwindled in prestige as the rise of backward and under-developed nations made imperialism impractical as well as unpopular in its blunter terms.

PROTEST VOTE, see Third Parties.

PROTOCOLS OF ZION, notorious canards against Jews (*q.v.*) of undetermined authorship, promulgated since early in the twentieth century, but with earlier progenitors, and treated with respect wherever anti-semites convene. The forgeries were featured in the Dearborn *Independent* (*q.v.*).

PROUDHON, PIERRE JOSEPH (1809-1865), the "Father of Anarchism," whose concern for individual freedom opposed him to socialism as conceived by Marx (*q.v.*). Proudhon's *Philosophy of Misery* (1846) was criticized at length by Marx in *The Misery of Philosophy* (1847). Proudhon's most famous phrase was "Property is theft." See also Mutualism.

PROXMIRE, WILLIAM (1915-   ), Senator from Wisconsin since 1957, prominent for his battles against government waste, who made himself conspicuous after 1975 with his monthly "Golden Fleece Awards" for wasteful and foolish expenditures. His very first went to the National Science Foundation "for squandering $84,000 to try to find out why people fall in love." Other awards went to the Department of Agriculture which put out $46,000 to determine how long it took to cook breakfast; a more modest sum of $1,718 went to a California zoo to send two animal keepers to a workshop on caring for elephants. Proxmire blew the whistle on larger game, joining environmentalists (*q.v.*) in 1970 to strike down a subsidy for supersonic transport. Proxmire, *Report from Wasteland* (1970); Jay G. Sykes, *Proxmire* (1972). See Waste.

PSYCHOANALYSIS AND REFORM seemed related, in the 1910's: the revelations of psychoanalysis would reveal the patient to himself, emancipate him from harmful and unnecessary guilt complexes, inhibitions to normal living, childish distortions and fears. Moreover, psychoanalysis would leaven merely moral judgments with insight, explaining, for example, so monstrous a crime as that committed by Leopold and Loeb (*qq.v.*). Thus, it would act as an aid to crime control and prison reform. Psychoanalysis was reserved, before World War II, for a limited clientele. The mass demands of the crisis forced an expansion of psychoanalytical services, in order to keep key personnel "functioning," so that, for example, a pilot, whose training perhaps cost fifty thousand dollars and more, would not be lost because of mental upset. Therapeutic treatment became more popular, its purpose being not so much to provide the patient with mental challenges as to reconcile him to himself; the "brain mechanic" had a minimum of social goals. Psychoanalysis was condemned by communist theoreticians as representing a sign of American decadence and indulgence: a pampering of individual weakness, at the expense of social needs. How psychoanalysis could be geared with social responsibility was a challenge to social reformers. R. A. Koenigsberg, *Psychoanalysis of Racism, Revolution, and Nationalism* (1976); I. Pilowsky, ed., *Psychiatry and the Community* (1969); Wolf Wallace, *Psychiatrists* (1976); Thomas Szasz, *Psychiatric Slavery* (1977).

PUBLIC DOMAIN, see Frontier and Social Reform, Land Reform, Preemption Acts.

PUBLIC HEALTH, a matter of social reform when it has inspired consideration of factors and groups in society which are debilitating to society. Thus, the embalmed beef scandal, Harvey W. Wiley's work, the fight for a pure food and drug act *(qq.v.)* fell into the realm of social reform. The U.S. Public Health Service, on the other hand, represented an agency of social control, intended to prevent epidemics and similar catastrophes. The importance of public health in social reform seemed unclear, in 1980; see Anti-Tobacco Crusade.

PUBLIC INTEREST, see Munn v. Illinois.

PUBLIC INVESTIGATIONS, an important force in stirring public interest and action in numerous fields and in many eras, as in the insurance investigations, the work of the Pujo Committee, and the findings of Nye, La Follette, McClellan, and Kefauver *(qq.v.)*. The published records of these investigations were a vast storehouse of fact and experience which were inadequately used by later reformers.

PUBLIC OPINION POLLS, see Gallup Poll.

PUBLIC OWNERSHIP, a major field of conflict between social reformers and private enterprise *(q.v.)*. The fear of the latter that public ownership could become a habit, that given an inch advocates of public ownership would demand a yard stick *(q.v.)* has kept them restless in the presence of any vestige of public ownership. Thus, they tolerated the government ownership of the railroads during World War I; but as soon as it was over, they hastened to demand and force their return to private hands. They could not stop the creation of T.V.A. *(q.v.)*, but it was no secret that they fought its extension and sought to make the principles it embodied unpopular. Proponents of public ownership liked to point to the postoffice as a type of public ownership which did not undermine American initiative. Edward Bellamy and Henry George *(qq.v.)* proposed famous programs in the field. Samuel Insull *(q.v.)* seemed a strong argument against the private operations of public utilities. Others placed their faith in regulatory *(q.v.)* agencies.

PUBLIC RELATIONS, a development primarily in the business community, intended to give the public a desired view of a particular firm, or personality. During the pre-World War I reform era, public relations principles were developed by such workers in publicity as Ivy Lee, bitterly nicknamed "Poison Ivy" Lee, by such critics as Upton Sinclair. The publicity methods of such entrepreneurs were augmented by the development of advertising in the post-World War I period, and studied seriously, and perhaps more disinterestedly by such innovators as E.L. Bernays, who had been interested in poetry, and served on the Creel Committee on Public Information before entering ambitiously into public relations. In the meantime, reformers had made less artful and contrived appeals to public interest, seeking to tap humanitarian and civic feelings in the public. With the advent of "Big Labor" in the 1940's, it felt bound to create public relations offices through which to influence the general public, in competition with "Big Business." Although an academic praised Ivy Lee for having opened up the public relations field (see Eric Goldman, *Two-Way Street: the Emergence of the Public Relations Counsel* [1948]), most concerned students of society felt that, like advertising, public relations needed close supervision to keep it in line with truth and reality.

PUBLIC WORKS ADMINISTRATION (P.W.A.) had to be distinguished from the Works Progress Administration (W.P.A.), the former being an augmented program of contracts to private building and construction companies whose work, it was hoped, would employ increasing numbers of people, putting salaries in their hands for purchases which would help overcome the depressed conditions in the 1930's. W.P.A. *(q.v)*, on the other hand, was a relief project run under government auspices.

PUERTO RICO, acquired from Spain following the Spanish-American War, had status as a dependency. Heavily over-populated, it suffered from extremes of poverty. In 1917, Puerto Ricans were made citizens of the United States, though still subject to rule from Washington. Nationalists and communists created dangers of revolutionary conspiracies which the New Deal *(q.v.)* helped modify. In the 1930's, the bringing of Puerto Ricans to the mainland, in order to provide cheap labor stimulated a migration which added to the immigration problem, one complicated by the fact that these were not "foreigners." The second World War, and the need for strengthening United States outposts increased interest in Puerto Rico; in 1947, an act of Congress made the governorship subject to popular election, and raised Luis Muñoz Marín to leadership. Rexford Tugwell *(q.v.)* had already made significant efforts, as governor, to set down bases for increased democracy and economic advance; see his *The Stricken Land* (1947). The attempted assassination of President Truman in 1950 by two Puerto Rican nationalists raised the question of the islanders' real desires. A report by the Inter-American Association for Democracy and Freedom, signed by a group which included Roger Baldwin and Norman Thomas *(qq.v.)*, and published in the *New Leader*, January 24, 1955, asserted that the island had advanced notably; the drive for industries and improvements, termed "Operation Bootstrap," was succeeding. It was certain that the general American public was inadequately informed with respect to Puerto Ricans, on the island and on the mainland. The mainland migration became a flood, reaching two million in 1977, with needy and harassed families—lowest paid of all minorities—uncertain whether they would suffer less in the United States or back home in Puerto Rico. Despite "Operation Bootstrap," over-population (three and a quarter million) and distress teemed in Puerto Rico; as Bootstrap's director grimly said: "There's just no way. The unemployed of twenty years from now were born yesterday." As the Island contemplated asking for statehood, it did so in the face of pro-independence groups which in 1980 claimed responsibility for bombing eleven Air National Guard fighter jets. It appeared off-shore developments might finally reach public debate. See also Thomas, Piri. F. Cordasco and E. Bucchioni, *The Puerto Ricans* (1973); K. and O. J. de Wagenheim, *Puerto Ricans: a Documentary History* (1975); Byron Williams, *Puerto Rico: Commonwealth, State, or Nation?* (1972).

PUJO COMMITTEE (1912), concerned for banking and currency conditions, investigated the charge that there was a "money trust," and heard testimony which revealed the manner in which financial tycoons, and first of all J.P. Morgan, were able to control the assets of numerous financial houses by strategic representation on their boards. They were thus able to lend money to themselves and withhold it from others in a fashion which amounted to a trust. The revelations helped encourage legislation which created the Federal Reserve System *(q.v.)*. Louis D. Brandeis *(q.v.)* helped the public to understand the issues involved with his *Other People's Money* (1914).

PULITZER, JOSEPH (1847-1911), brilliant Hungarian-born newspaper editor and owner, he is identified with the growth and influence of the St. Louis *Post-Dispatch,* and especially the New York *World.* He employed resourceful editors and reporters with democratic aspirations, some of whom went on to have careers during the muckraking *(q.v.)* period and after. Although he exploited sensationalism, Pulitzer was more scrupulous than Hearst, and his campaigns kept closer to ideals of public service. An autocrat who became more and more peremptory in his demands on his employees as his sight failed him, he nevertheless poured an energy and creativity into his papers which gave them a place in reform history. W. A. Swanberg, *Pulitzer* (1967).

PULLMAN STRIKE, THE, one of the great tests of labor in post-Civil War decades, it took place in 1894 when dissatisfied workers of the Pullman Parlor Car Company found their employer, George M. Pullman, unwilling to arbitrate their differences, or even to honor their grievances. The American Railway Union (*q.v.*) supported them, and the railway superintendents supported Pullman. A general strike took place in the town of Pullman, a suburb of Chicago at the time. Eugene V. Debs (*q.v.*), as leader of the strikers, urged them to refrain from violence, but the Pullman managers were not averse to employing agent provocateurs (*q.v.*), since violence could justify police intervention. Governor Altgeld engaged in a controversy with President Cleveland (*qq.v.*) over the latter's desire to send Federal troops; Altgeld averred he could keep order with state militia. A blanket injunction was obtained from the U.S. Circuit Court ordering Debs and others to cease from interfering with interstate commerce, and, it being defied, the strike leaders were jailed. Government troops moved in to prevent strikers from interfering with the mails, though their critics were ironic in asking how much mail normally traveled in Pullman luxury cars. That the Sherman Anti-Trust Act (*q.v.*), which had been found ineffective against industrial combinations, should have been used successfully against labor, as it now was, was a blow to labor. The failure of the Pullman Strike, and of the American Railway Union caused intense concern among strategists of organized labor and among reformers. A Lindsey, *The Pullman Strike* (1964).

"PURE AND SIMPLE UNIONISM," formulated by Samuel Gompers (*q.v.*) as the sole program for successful labor organization: the unionist should abjure far-reaching goals, should work to build the union, in numbers, in funds, should press "day to day" demands and ignore side-issues; compare Social Unionism.

PURE FOOD AND DRUG ACT OF 1906, culminated a series of exposures of unclean and inadequate processing of food and dangerous claims for and preparations of patent medicine. Exposures centering about the meat-packers of Chicago were fired into demands for public action by the sensation caused by Upton Sinclair's *The Jungle* (*q.v.*). The result was passage of the Meat Inspection Act and the creation of the Food and Drug Administration (*q.v.*). See also Wiley, Harvey W., Adams, Samuel Hopkins, Russell, Charles Edward. The events attending passage of the Act in 1906 and those attending passage of the Wheeler-Lea Act of 1938, which sought to erect new controls over food and drugs, were revealing of the difference between a reform movement and one for adjustment of social checks and balances in the area. The Nader (*q.v.*) activities touched upon the work of the FDA, as did concern over insecticides, toxic wastes, and other results of chemical and other adulteration; see Beatrice T. Hunter, *Consumer Beware* (1971).

PURITANISM, a major force in American settlement and reform. The Puritans were somewhat less radical in their beginnings than the Separatists; the latter separated from the Anglican Church, the former intended only to purify it, though this aim did create an element of asperity in their outlook. The Separatists settled Plymouth, the Puritans Boston. Both groups, however, were Calvinists (*q.v.*), and both gained and lost reform potential by this fact.

PUTSCH, German, an unsuccessful revolutionary effort, or counter-revolutionary effort; e.g., the Kapp Putsch in Berlin of 1920, a monarchical effort, Hitler's Munich Putsch of 1923, both dispersed by government troops.

P.W.A., see Public Works Administration.

QUADRAGESIMO ANNO, see *Rerum Novarum.*

QUACKS, more associated with nineteenth century itinerant sellers of nostrums than with modern medicine and politicians. It is, however, relevant to numerous diet, beauty, cancer, aging, virility, and other nostrums. Some are doubtfully in this category, requiring as they do the cooperation of the "victim," such as cigarettes for "women" (You've Come a Long Way, Baby) and "consciousness-raising sessions" intended to "free" people from their preconceptions: essentially a propaganda device for winning adherents. Political and religious quacks multiply by the score, including patent quacks like Jim Jones (*q.v.*), wooed for his vote-getting capacities, and "Scientologists" having neither a science nor a discipline to offer. Authors flourished among such quack nostrums, submitting conjectures as insight into the "future" and conversation as education, warranting degrees. The author of *I'm O.K., You're O.K.* was evidently not himself O. K. President Johnson's (*q.v.*) grants-giving machine produced quack projects by the thousands, requiring a government publication advising grants-wishers on how to present their proposals and to which bureaucratic office. S. Weir Mitchell, *The Autobiography of a Quack* (1900); Phil R. Russell, *Quack Doctor* (1974).

QUAKERS, see Society of Friends.

QUALITY OF LIFE, a generalized view of the American condition in the area of the maintenance of manners, social relations, standards of behavior and choice, and their effect on American lives and work. *Quality Control* was an industrial idea, developed in the 1950s, and believed capable of holding up work standards by means of industrial relations counseling such as was practiced by Douglas MacGregor of Massachusetts Institute of Technology, or by computer measurements. (See, for example, N. L. Enrick, *Quality Control and Reliability* 1969.) The evident erosion, despite computers, of cities, and of means of control, raised questions about education, family life, work, and public behavior. Problems involving the quality of life reached climaxes in the confrontations of the 1960s. These included quarrels over Vietnam, street demonstrations, drug use, sexual exhibitions, the forms of crime and crime control, pornography, Watergate (*qq.v.*) and others. Visible was shoddy workmanship and deportment, which made decent public and private services hard to find. One fire department not only went on strike, but was thought to have indulged in arson as an effective instrument of protest. A "sanitation workers" strike took place in New York, not because of a growing issue requiring resolution, but simply because a fire department strike had gained it a rise in wages. A related problem was the era's downgrading and blatant scorn of heroes. Thus George Washington was a strategic target for the malicious canards of the debunkers (*q.v.*); this seemed to one academic evidence "that a critical spirit could flourish" in America. (Howard Moscowitz, in *Icons of America,* Browne and Fishwick, eds., 1977.) As a result, however, bad feeling about gross scandals on television and in sports, vicious pollution of lakes and wooded areas was blunted. Automobiles recalled by the tens of thousands for engineering failures in gears, motors and steering wheels kept drivers uneasy or fatalistic. The crisis in education went deep into the failures of instructors and educators, and of standards of achievement which, in startling cases, gave doctorates to illiterates and masters degrees to almost anyone. The problem was present in the 1980 fiasco of trying to rescue the "hostages" in Iran, which cost lives. It was a failure in planning and equipment which shocked the world and called into question what had once been famous as "Yankee know-how." It raised open discussions about America's capacities in the world, let alone its ability to help lead it. Positive was the recognition that a change in thinking and judging performance was overdue, if life was once more to attain quality. Carnegie Commission on Higher Education, *Quality and Equality: Revised Recommendations* (1970); Angus Campbell, *The Quality of American Life* (1976); James A. Michener, *The Quality of Life* (1972); A. Pollis, *The Quality of Living: Environmental Viewpoints* (1973).

QUARTERING ACTS, 1765 and following, were intended to provide quarters for British troops in the American colonies: theoretically hospitality for their own people. The act of 1765 stipulated barracks, alehouses, inns and unoccupied buildings; by 1774, conditions had become such that quartering was sanctioned for occupied buildings as well: a colonist might have to "entertain" troops in his own house. The fashion in which the Acts was received helped reveal the increasing schism between Great Britain and its American colonists: a schism which the Empire chieftains lacked insight and experience for understanding.

QUEBEC ACT (1774) indicated that the British government in London had no understanding of American ambitions: a misconstruance of the sort always worth study for modern equivalents. The Act extended Canadian territory down to the Ohio River; thus administrators deprived the American colonists of their West. The Act also, by declaring a tolerant policy toward the Catholic Church, offended the Protestant feelings of the majority of Americans. The myopia behind such policies entered into Benjamin Franklin's (*q.v.*) satiric "Rules by which a Great Empire may be reduced to a Small One."

QUEMOY, see Formosa.

QUISLING, term applied to puppet heads of German-occupied lands during World War II; from the name of Vidkun Quisling, kept in power by the Germans, 1942-5, when he was executed by the Norwegians.

QUITRENT, a system of continuous obligation to pay rents to the giver or seller of land, on the part of its tenants, inherited from feudal eras. It conflicted with the desire of colonists to have full title to their land, never functioned adequately, and was a source of aggravation: a factor in creating revolutionary feeling, though relatively small sums of from two to four shillings on a hundred acres were involved. The revolutionary state assemblies struck down quitrents.

QUOTAS, a strategic aspect of the immigration problem (*q.v.*), and the McCarran-Walter Act (*q.v.*). Critics have pointed out the difficulties embodied in the Act: It maintained the system established in the restrictive immigration act of 1924, omitting Negroes, American Indians, and other white peoples. It therefore required the special licensing of groups by Congress, including G.I. brides, Free Poles, orphans, anti-communists seeking asylum, and others. The "quotas" have, thanks to the dilemmas of various people everywhere, become increasingly embarrassing in their confusions, as well as in their nonhumanitarianism. Thus, they theoretically expressed appreciation of Anglo-Saxon people; yet Australians and New Zealanders were given only trifling entree. Each year gave less hope to a Latvian who sought entry to the United States. One obvious adjustment was to distribute to other people quota opportunities not used, for example by Britishers. Another was to adopt a more generous policy which reestablished a link with earlier American attitudes, as expressed in Emma Lazarus's "The New Colossus" (*q.v.*). The system of quotas was disrupted by world upsets and changes, which permitted the United States, after the crushing of the Hungarian Revolt of 1956 (*q.v.*) against its Soviet masters, to let in some 50,000 Hungarian freedom fighters who were assimilated brilliantly into the general American population. Quotas, too, had no relation to visas and processing in respect to illegal Mexican entry into the United States, which rose to the millions. In 1980 the in-pouring of Cubans and Haitians became enormous. See Immigration. "Quotas" were also disrupted in connection with

ethnic and racial discrimination in colleges and universities in the 1960s and 1970s, and were even furthered through "affirmative action" (*qq.v.*).

RACISM, a basic target in social reform, which has, however, not been totally dissociated from it. Abolitionists (q.v.) were plagued by anti-Negro attitudes and presumptions in their own following. A few radical Populists (q.v.) saw that distinguishing between Negro farmers and white farmers weakened Populist ranks, but they were in the extreme minority. Organized labor, in its battle for recognition, discriminated against the Negro; A. Philip Randolph (q.v.) was almost uniquely successful as a labor leader, and that on a discriminated basis. The Socialist Party, preaching brotherhood, included strong racist elements, certainly among its southern and southwestern membership. The increasing influence of Negroes abroad (q.v.) complicated the problem of racists required to adjust their attitudes and their expression on practical grounds. Anti-racists could be divided into sentimentalists, who experienced glows of self-righteousness by avowing themselves against racism, and those who sought to buttress their own opinions with tangible and intelligent deeds. The communists placed much of their hope for increasing influence on a program for principles and techniques in the field. A phenomenon of "Racism" was that it could be used as the equivalent of "white racism," thus evading the dangerous fact of "black racism," permitting the mindless use of the word as an epithet. Its overuse, and a public tiring of endless self-serving agitation gave some surcease, but not so much as peace and intelligence required. Kelly Miller, *Race Adjustment* (1924); Franz Boas, *Race and Democratic Society* (1945); William Barclay, ed., *Racial Conflict, Discrimination, and Power* (1976); J. Stone, *Race, Ethnicity and Social Change* (1976); R. A. Goldsby, *Race and Races* (1971); R. M. Burkey, *Racial Discrimination and Public Policy* (1975); D. M. Reimers, *Racism in the United States: an American Dilemma?* (1972).

RACKETS, big business in the United States, hence, extremely competitive. Since they depended in large measure on the cooperation of ordinary citizens, who put up the money for illegal betting games, drugs, and other rackets, their entrepreneurs (q.v.) had a quasi-respectable status, and, where they were outstandingly successful, could attract interest and even admiration. Al Capone, notorious racketeer of the 1920's, was given more space in some reference works than many poets, public officials, and other responsible citizens. Radicals (q.v.) made notorious his view that communism represented a threat to the American way. They argued, controversially, that racketeering was inseparable from free enterprise (q.v.). Gangsters preyed impartially on industry and labor, and could be used as a terror agency by one against the other. Labor racketeering (q.v.) was different in that racketeers built themselves into the sinews of labor, and sometimes became amalgamated with it. Thus, some unions protested against laws making it illegal for ex-convicts to hold labor union offices, and otherwise seeking to keep unions clean of notorious criminals. Public fatalism permitted it to accept the idea implicit in Mario Puzo's *The Godfather* (1969), that criminal rings engaged in "just business." See Crime, Daley, Richard J.; Kefauver, Estes; also Raymond Clapper, *Racketeering in Washington* (1974 ed.)

RADICAL REPUBLICANS, a faction of the Republican Party which became extremely powerful in the course of the Civil War under the leadership of Thaddeus Stevens, Charles Sumner, and Benjamin F. Wade (qq.v.), among others. It demanded firm prosecution of the war against the Confederate States of America, early emancipation of the Negroes, and a vengeful policy against the rebels. It dominated the congres-

sional Joint Committee on the Conduct of the War, and, following the conclusion of hostilities, sought to forge a program which would ensure continued Republican power. Its major effort was to overthrow Andrew Johnson (q.v.) as President of the United States, in 1868, the year of Stevens's death. By 1874, when Sumner died, the Radical Republican tide had spent its force, See also Black Republicans. Hans L. Trefousse, *Radical Republicans* (1975).

RADICALS, employed variously, but intended to connote an extreme political position calculated to disturb, and more than disturb, the *status quo*. In England and France, the word was directed at vigorous liberal elements, as well as at Marxists and others of the "extreme left." The latter were relatively few in pre-Civil War decades, in America, and the preferred word was "incendiary." "Radical Republicans" (q.v.) of the Civil War and post-Civil War Era were at the head of government, unlike European radicals who were often proscribed by government. "Radical" came into increased use as social and industrial disorder grew in the latter part of the nineteenth century. It maintained its popularity in the twentieth century, until the rise of communist power raised the question of whether followers of a monolithic organization could be properly termed radicals, and whether various classes of union official, socialist discussion leaders, and peace advocates were in fact radical. For a thought-provoking discussion of social psychology under pressure, see the lead article in Walter Weyl, *Tired Radicals and Other Papers* (1921). A novel development was the *Radical Right*, first noted in the 1955 edition of the book by Daniel Bell, a former socialist turned sociologist. It hoisted the conservative on his own petard, presenting him as a "pseudo"-conservative wildly denouncing decent people as being radicals. The reason given for their behavior, according to Richard Hofstadter and others was that some conservatives had lost their priority in life because of the "status" (q.v.) revolution which had brought liberals to the fore. In 1980, the conservative search for moderates with which to build their power rendered much of this analysis obsolete. Saul Alinsky, *Rules for Radicals* (1972); R. Hofstadter, *The Paranoid Style in American Politics* (1967); Arnold Kaufman, *The Radical Liberal* (1970); Donald I. Warren, *The Radical Center* (1976); Tom Wolfe, *Radical Chic and Mau-Mauing the Flake Catchers* (1970).

RADIO, once a phenomenon apparently superseded by television (q.v.), it had, in fact, an active life with potential for more when needed. It accompanied motorists in quantities of time which challenged television. If offered news, entertainment, and special features as did television. To a degree it had similar problems of quality (q.v.). However, it also reached into homes, to housewives too busy to watch television, and elderly and blind who lacked television or could not see its offerings. Richard M. Nixon (q.v.) believed his campaigns received more on radio from the advertising dollar than on television. CB (Citizens Bands) had vast potential for good on the roads, though there were complaints that much of the potential was wasted on trivial conversation. Radio Free Europe received the greatest acclaim as providing an outlet for Iron Curtain (q.v.) habitants. In 1980 there were 4,575 AM Stations at home and 4,358 FM stations. Regulations which had controlled station output in entertainment and non-entertainment programs were modified to permit choice of programming according to local need: a triumph over excessive regulation (q.v.). Radio divided with television funds made available by the government Corporation for Public Broadcasting (CPB), intended to control and contribute to the quality of public features. Dissatisfaction with CPB's operations made it possible that it might be abolished. Leo G. Sands, *CB Radio* (1976); Donald Shanor, *The New Voice of Radio Free Europe* (1968); Julian Hale, *Radio Power: Propaganda and International Broadcasting* (1975); UNESCO, *Radio and Television in the Service of Education and Development in Asia* (1967); A. and L. Kirschner, *Radio and Television: Readings in the Mass Media* (1971); Harry W. Lowe, *Radio Church of God* (1970).

"RADIO PRIEST," see Coughlin, Rev. Charles E.

RAGGED-TROUSERED PHILANTHROPISTS, THE (1914), by Robert Tressall, an important novel written by an English artisan in bitter condemnation of his fellow-workers: "philanthropists" who gave their labor and health to their social betters, and resisted the efforts of reformers to organize them in behalf of themselves, their families, their future. Written with great and intimate detail, on the eve of World War I, it resisted the optimism which clouded the efforts of reformers, the vague belief that "things" were getting better, that there could be no major catastrophe because civilization had advanced too far.

RAILWAY BROTHERHOODS, though there are a number of employee organizations serving railroad workers, some of whom call themselves "brotherhoods," four major ones are known as "The Brotherhoods": the Brotherhood of Locomotive Firemen and Enginemen, the Brotherhood of Railroad Trainmen, the Grand International Brotherhood of Locomotive Engineers, and the Order of Railway Conductors of America. Except for the Locomotive Engineers and the Railroad Trainmen, the unions attempt some united action by way of the Railway Labor Executives Association, which includes A.F.L. unions. Aside from other labor and reform problems, they have shared the basic problem of unions: their policy of discrimination against Negro workers. The significant development was the organization, by A. Philip Randolph *(q.v.)* of the Brotherhood of Sleeping Car Porters in 1925. Year in year out action and argument got the Brotherhood an international charter in 1936, but its efforts to open other unions to Negroes, and to expand its own influence, for example, among other train porters, met opposition. The Brotherhoods were an outstanding example of "craft" *(q.v.)* unions in operation.

RAILROAD PROBLEM, THE, was a development of the post-Civil War period, during which the great trans-continental systems were built. Because they involved great sums of money and government, state, and local subsidies, they created gigantic scandals of corruption, of which Crédit Mobilier *(q.v.)* became a symbol. But, in addition, they accumulated excessive power. In the east, they had competition in waterways, roads, conveyances, and relatively short distances between towns. In the West, they were able to make or break entire towns, to discriminate in the prices they charged farmers, notably through the rebate *(q.v.)* and an unfair rate differential between long hauls and short hauls *(q.v.)*. With farmers being traditionally the most individualistic element in American society, with high expectations, and a sense of worthiness, being the providers of food, their frustrations and sense of outrage was high. They demanded regulation of the railroads, and won the "Granger Laws," which the Supreme Court endorsed in Munn v. Illinois *(q.v.)*. Thus, it appeared to conservatives that the farmers were "socialistic." They were, in fact, anti-socialist, wanting no more than the security of their property and opportunities. The railroad thus became to them the symbol of unbridled power, especially as the Supreme Court receded from its position on the right of a state to regulate business in the public interest. Thus, the railroad fostered Populism *(q.v.)*, as such industrial combinations as Standard Oil fostered unionism *(q.v.)*. The Hepburn Act *(q.v.)* began a process of controlling railroads which was augmented by the competition provided by automobiles, trucking companies, great national highways, aeroplanes. The question of railroad-employee relations was dealt with by the Erdman Act, the Adamson Act, the Crosser-Dill Act *(qq.v.)*, in succeeding periods. Despite some brave efforts and subsidies to make the railroad system a great adjunct of automobile and air travel, it furnished a dramatic example of lag in quality of service and upkeep. Although a few elite lines provided a modicum of usefulness, though rarely esthetic satisfaction, the overall system was retarded by prideless workers, routine union negotiators, and management without incentive or vision. A few magnificent railroad terminals, and some small terminals with charm, stood as reminders of better days. Bruce Mazlish,

The Railroad and the Space Program (1965); Paul Hastings, *Railroads: an International History* (1972); G. Kolko, *Railroads and Regulation* (1965); George H. Miller, *Railroads and the Granger Laws* (1971); L. E. Decker, *Railroads, Land and Politics* (1964); Carroll Meeks, *Railroad Station: an Architectural History* (1975).

RAILROAD RIOTS OF 1877, see 1877, Railroad Riots of.

RAILROAD SHOPMEN'S STRIKE (1922), because of an effort to reduce wages, brought out some four hundred thousand workers in the repair shops. President Harding threw his influence behind the railroads, as did the U.S. Railroad Labor Board. This was the largest such effort in the post-World War I period to hold the line for railroad labor organization and a living wage.

RANDOLPH, A. PHILIP (1889-1979), Negro leader and organizer, in the 1920's, of the Brotherhood of Sleeping Car Porters. A former editor of a Negro socialist magazine, *The Messenger*, Randolph organized his union without the aid or cooperation of the American Federation of Labor, of which it ultimately became part. As an active and functioning union, it represented a forum from which Randolph could persistently denounce discrimination against Negroes in labor ranks, and demand attention to their needs. In 1941, Randolph forced the creation of the FEPC by threatening to bring fifty thousand Negroes to Washington to demonstrate against discrimination in employment in defense and war industries. Jervis Anderson, *A. Philip Randolph* (1973).

RANTOUL, ROBERT (1778-1858) was a Massachusetts pioneer in liberal religion, temperance, pacifism, and anti-capital punishment movements. First a follower of John Quincy Adams *(q.v.)*, he joined the Jacksonians in his opposition to monopoly; his *Personal Reminiscences* were published in 1916. His son, *Robert* (1805-1852), became a lawyer and a Democrat, supporting Jackson's war against the Second Bank of the United States *(q.v.)* and other causes. His fight against capital punishment resulted in papers prized by reformers. In 1842, the state supreme court upheld his contentions favoring collective bargaining *(q.v.)*. His arguments opposing monopoly, anti-Catholic prejudice, favoring an expanded public school system and temperance were famous; see Luther Hamilton, ed., *Memoirs, Speeches, and Writings of Robert Rantoul, Jr.* (1854).

RAPP-COUDERT COMMITTEE (1940-2), a New York State investigating committee conducted hearings on communism among teachers in the New York City schools and colleges, in the face of protests from the Teachers Union, the American Student Union *(q.v.)*, and many other organizations, including the American Civil Liberties Union *(q.v.)*. The investigation was taken to be, by the beset teachers, a kind of little House Un-American Activities Committee *(q.v.)* operation. A number of teachers were expelled for communist activities, or for failure to cooperate. A notable event was the jailing of Morris U. Schappes for perjury. *Winter Soldiers* (1941), by Louis Lerman, foreword by Franz Boas *(q.v.)*, memorializes the investigation as a "Conspiracy against the Schools." It contains a notable collection of drawings supporting this viewpoint. A preface by Bella V. Dodd, for the Committee for Defense of Public Education, thanks the contributors. Miss Dodd later turned upon her associates and denounced them as cooperating with the Communist Party.

RATIONALISM, see Enlightenment.

REACTIONARIES, freely applied by all partisans against one another, it may be properly applied to persons and groups which not only hold positions which defy reality, but demand that others do the same. Hence, it is not clear that "utopians" must perforce be reactionaries, since they may be making a contribution from which society gains. ("Utopians" are, to be sure, liable to be called reactionaries by urgent reformers who believe that everyone is either helping or hindering.) The Liberty League *(q.v.)*, however, would probably rate as reactionary, since it took a principled position against the New Deal without offering any tangible program which took into account the problems facing the latter; similar considerations might warrant terming the America First Committee reactionary. *Under Cover,* by John Roy Carlson (*q.v.*), was a compendium of reactionaries. Compare Conservatism and Reform, Fascism and Reform. In the late 1970s, the shift from "social action" to the need to cope with inflation, unemployment, rise in student tuition and fall in student opportunities, and other economic complexities to which would-be "radicals" (*q.v.*) could not accomodate themselves, caused some who fancied themselves as liberals to terms radicals "reactionaries."

REAGAN, RONALD (1911-   ), President of the United States, whose rise, however, was far from "meteoric," as those taken aback by it believed. Like Gerald Ford (*q.v.*), a poor boy from the Midwest, he was constrained to make a career. He attended a small college where he interested himself in campus affairs including athletics, gained his public spurs as a radio sports announcer, and became a successful Hollywood actor. He played modest roles which comported with his self-image, on occasion refusing roles he could not endorse. Reagan was especially noticeable in *Knute Rockne-All-American* (1940) and *King's Row* (1941). He was for many years a leader and president in the A.F.L. Screen Actors Guild, where he met racketeers and communist pressures which turned him from a New Deal Democrat to an advocate of free enterprise, though he asserted his title to what he saw as the best of the New Deal's program. In 1947 he testified before the House Un-American Activities Committee (*q.v.*) on communist infiltration in his union. In 1954, recognized as a fluent and intelligent speaker with an attractive personality, he began his long service with General Electric Theater, speaking in behalf of free enterprise principles and becoming nationally known for his opinions. He augmented his reputation by innumerable personal appearances before social and political gatherings which took him deeper into practical conservative politics. In 1964 he co-chaired Citizens for Goldwater-Miller in the Presidential race of that year, and came out of its catastrophic conclusion as a viable alternative to the dedicated Goldwaterites. Reagan continued to speak for conservatism to such effect as to make him a creditable candidate for governor of California, and even, if he won, for the Presidency later on. Meanwhile he issued his unpretentious and attractive autobiography, *Where's the Rest of Me?* (1965), which marked his transition from union executive to political figure. The governor's race of 1966 was bitterly fought, his opponents passing over his long years in public life to reach him as a person. A malicious article in the *New York Times,* for example, partisan to Reagan's opponent Edmund G. Brown, who had defeated Nixon (*q.v.*) in 1962, conjectured that Reagan, having been an actor, might mix fantasy with reality and endanger the state. Nevertheless Reagan won with a million-vote margin on a platform of curbing campus unrest, cutting taxes and unwarranted welfare services, and encouraging industry. Reagan quickly disappointed devout Goldwaterites, making place for Nixon and Rockefeller-style Republicans, and Democrats with whom he could work. Although he conducted no vendetta against the more extreme campus radicals, he did quell student unrest. His tax cuts were no more drastic than his welfare cuts, but he defended both in following years as part of a program to reverse the Brown giveaway years which had harmed the state's solvency. Reagan's approach outraged part of his following; see Kent Steffgen, *Here's the Rest of Him* (1968), which correctly saw that he looked past them to a larger alignment of moderate conservatives. Reagan was formidable in the 1968 Republican convention, as was his optimistic dream of a *Creative Society* (1968), but not sufficiently so to overcome the Nixon campaign. Reagan's general drive against Federal over-regulation, unbridled welfare, and tolerance of crime held, and gave him the governorship again in 1970. Reagan forces made another attempt at the Republican nomination in 1976, he himself offering "idealistic democracy" (see *Ronald Reagan's Call to Action,* by Charles D. Hobbs [1976]). It did not suffice to shake Gerald Ford's hold on the Republican nomination. In the

following four Carter (*q.v.*) years, numerous Republicans claimed to have greater political charisma and authority than Reagan. However, with his easy, persuasive presentation on television and radio (*qq.v.*), which snide references to "actor" could not damage, his optimistic call for a positive approach to American problems, and with manifest energy crude references to his age could not diminish and may have helped with the increasing older population, Reagan's campaign rolled to give him the Republican nomination. Despite a blurred pro-Carter drive in which pollsters combined with pro-Carter media operators to claim the result was in doubt, Reagan won a landslide victory. It served notice that a new era was on the way. See also Bill Boyarsky, *The Rise of Ronald Reagan* (1968); Gladwin Hill, *Dancing Bear* (1968).

REASON, see Enlightenment, Deism, Paine, Thomas.

REBELLION, see Insurrection.

REBELS, connoting southern resistance to northern policy, in the Civil War by means of "Rebs," or "Johnny Rebs," and, in the north, connoting labor activists of the "Wobbly" (*q.v.*) stamp; in post-World War II years indicating dissidents of a more general type: "rebels without a cause." A motion picture with that name in 1955 depicted young people who played the game of "chicken" (coward), and who proved their courage by racing in a car toward a cliff, coming as close to it as possible before stopping the car. It starred James Dean, whose sullen confusion and death that year in a car accident, made him the center of a cult of young people who sought a mystic identity with him.

RECALL, THE, a means for democratic control of political processes; citizens dissatisfied with the actions of executive or judicial officers may circulate a petition demanding a recall; upon receiving the signatures of a percentage of the population, they can, in effect, obtain a reversal of the election; see also initiative and referendum.

RECESSION, the jest ran in the post-World War II period that it was a recession if the other person had lost his job, a depression if one was himself jobless; see Economic Depression. The economic downturn of the 1970s caused a realization that it was not merely a time for "pump-priming" (short-term government expenditure) but, being the result of multiple factors, a time for "enhancing the quality of the recovery," as a Joint Economic Committee of Congress phrased it, by attending to taxes and savings in ways which built the overall economy.

RECIPROCAL TRADE AGREEMENTS, see Free Trade.

RECLAMATION, see Newlands Reclamation Act.

RECONSTRUCTION FINANCE CORPORATION, initiated under President Herbert Hoover in July, 1932, to spur business activities of large financial organizations, and thus fight the economic crisis, was criticized by opponents as having emphasized the former, rather than the latter. Under New Deal policies, R.F.C. powers were expanded to permit loans which affected wider areas of the population. Jesse H. Jones, *Fifty Billion Dollars* (1951).

RECONSTRUCTION MEASURES, as formulated by the Radical Republicans (*q.v.*), were intended to prevent the defeated South from influencing national legislation through its representatives in Congress and from reviving white supremacy (*q.v.*) in southern states; in effect, they were intended to maintain the Radical Republicans in power. Since it was the South's intention to return to pre-war conditions, except for the ending of legal slavery, as its "Black Laws" (*q.v.*) indicated, it is difficult to see how this could have been prevented without an abrogation of states' rights (*q.v.*). Hence, the First Reconstruction Act (March 2, 1867) placed the South under military rule, permitted military tribunals in peacetime, disqualified from voting former Confederates, and gave the vote to former slaves. Later laws made firmer the rule of Federal troops, carpetbaggers, scalawags, and Negroes. The Tenure of Office Act took from President Johnson his right to dismiss Cabinet members he did not wish to retain, and the Command of the Army Act took from him the powers vested in him as Commander-in-Chief of the Army and Navy. The impeachment of Johnson (q.v.), and the failure to convict him by one vote, represented the highpoint of Reconstruction, under the Radical Republicans. Their breaking of the Ku Klux Klan (q.v.) did not affect southern unity, and their winning of the Disputed Election of 1876 (q.v.) did not prevent a final removal of Federal troops from the last southern states which still were affected by their presence. S. M. Scheiner, *Reconstruction: a Tragic Era?* (1968).

RED, used invidiously by the enemies of socialism, as associated with its encouragement to anarchists and other instigators of social irresponsibility. To those who despised "reds," it suggested the blood-letting attending revolution, and the alleged satisfaction which they took in chaos and violent death. The red flag was raised during the French Revolution, and in succeeding revolutionary efforts like the Paris Commune, which can be distinguished from nationalistic uprisings in which national symbols were exploited. To the friends of revolution, red symbolized the suffering and sacrifices which had attended mutinies against oppression, and also the new dawn which awaited the embattled fighters. The Bolshevik Revolution gave new dignity to the appellation "red," especially as applied to the Red Army. Enigmatic developments in the U.S.S.R. and among its associated parties and states added fury to the use made of "red" by their foes.

RED CHANNELS: THE REPORT OF COMMUNIST INFLUENCE IN RADIO AND TELEVISION (1950), like *The Red Network* (q.v.), intended to expose communist infiltration in normal American avenues. It was published by *Counterattack: the Newsletter of Facts to Combat Communism*, and consisted of a list of alleged communists and communist sympathizers, with the "evidence" of their "red" connections: for the most part a list of organizations or events with which it was claimed they were associated. The difficulty with learning that an individual had signed a petition said to have been sponsored by a communist-front (q.v.) organization, had his name on the letterhead of a second organization, perhaps sung or played at a meeting co-sponsored by a third, and so on, was that these revelations did not distinguish the individual from others who might also have done so. In practice, *Red Channels* accomplished little more than to deprive Americans of, for example, the splendid harmonica performances of Larry Adler, who, for several years, became an exile from the United States. The volume also contained an interesting list of organizations alleged to be communist fronts.

RED FRONT, an agitational slogan intended to unite the working forces, but, during the 1930's, serving the communist tactical program most effectively.

RED NETWORK, THE (1934), by Elizabeth Dilling, sub-titled *A "Who's Who" and Handbook of Radicalism for Patriots*: notorious "labor-baiting" and "red-baiting" compilation. She included Eleanor Roosevelt among the radicals, opposed the entrance of Albert Einstein into the United States, and recorded the actress Alla Nazimova among the "Reds," because she had contributed to the publication *Soviet Russia Today*. Her measure of "Reds" was their deviation from her views. Thus Sigmund Freud (q.v.) was a radical in her eyes because he believed religious ideas illusory, and because he had supported the World Congress against War. Although eccentrically compiled, *The Red Network* contained much information, luridly and irresponsibly collected. Mrs. Dilling was a defendant in the Sedition Trial of 1944 (q.v.). See also *Roosevelt Red Record . . . , The.*

"RED SCARE," a mood of hysteria which affected Americans in 1919, following the conclusion of World War I. A wave of strikes, the result of organized labor's effort to maintain its position won under war conditions, was denounced as a result of Soviet (q.v.) intrigue. The newly-born American Communist Party was seen as a dark conspiracy against the American way

of life. *Red Friday* (1919), a novel by George Kibbe Turner, formerly a reform writer, depicted an alien plot to seize power in America. The result was the Palmer Raids (q.v.), in the course of which constitutional rights were abrogated by government agents.

RED SHIRTS, worn by the followers of Garibaldi (q.v.), thus, at one time, identified with vital republicanism; compare Black Shirts, Descamisados.

REED, JOHN (1887-1920), the son of a notable Oregon Progressive (q.v.), he attended Harvard University and came to New York to be a poet. Lincoln Steffens (q.v.) introduced him to journalism and he wrote for the *American* and *Metropolitan*, as well as the *Masses* (qq.v.). He was one of the organizers of the Madison Square Garden Pageant (q.v.), and reported the Ludlow, Colorado, strike (q.v.). Such experiences made him receptive to radical thought, at the expense of his bohemian associates. He reported *Insurgent Mexico* (1914) sympathetically, and returned from eastern battle-fronts, about which he wrote in *The War in Eastern Europe* (1916) to say: "This is not our war." The Bolshevik Revolution inspired his most famous work, *Ten Days That Shook the World* (1919). He helped organize the American Communist Party, and died in Russia, being under indictment for sedition back home. Not a reformer, he represented the schism between Progressivism (q.v.), as represented by his father, and the Youth Movement (q.v.). He became a legend to radical intellectuals of the 1930's, some of whom joined John Reed clubs composed of communist litterateurs; they disappeared with the era.

REFERENDUM, THE, long employed for refurbishing entire state constitutions which had become outmoded, and changing particular aspects of local government, as well as dealing with such questions as liquor laws. The Referendum became a matter of urgency with the rise of municipal reform (q.v.) in the 1890's and 1900's. It is associated with the Initiative and Recall (q.v.). For precedents leading back through American history, see Ellis P. Oberholtzer, *The Referendum in America* (1912 ed.).

REFORM, a concept which has inspired or depressed individuals and generations, suggesting hope and fresh approaches to some, half-measures to others; it has differed from revolution in its concern for existing conditions, rather than new principles. Reform is not necessarily bloodless, as witness the drive for unions in post-Civil War America, though the industrial revolution which forced that drive had been bloodless in principle. The United States have been subject to reform movements because of the fluidity of classes, high social expectations, and rapid social and economic changes which forced adjustments. The American Revolution began as a reform movement. Reform in pre-Civil War America divided into political reform, led by the Jacksonians (q.v.), and the moral reform of abolitionists, temperance, woman's rights, and other advocates. It was the latter which helped bring on the Civil War. The Reform Era (q.v.) of pre-World War I years capped an accumulation of needs and resentments. That it should have blended into the military "crusade for democracy" seemed to some a limitation on its value. The New Deal (q.v.) was a reform effort, but, taking place in the midst of revolutionary social and international conditions, seemed to some, too little, to others, too undefined. The permanent cold war, with its attendant bureaucracy, suggested that reform alone could help keep society flexible and responsive to its own needs. Anti-reform has often been a species of reform, concerned for the state of society, urgent in its demand for a return to allegedly better conditions. The neo-conservatives (q.v.) have been notable in modern times for their evangelical anti-reformism. Reform tends toward hypocrisy when it pretends to more than it has to offer. Unless the reformer aspires actively toward what great reformers have accomplished, they are likely to come nowhere near Jane Addams, William Lloyd Garrison, Booker T. Washington, Benjamin Marsh (qq.v.), are likely to know little about them, or, knowing, be critics of them as having done much less than what they would do, if their own private business did not limit their public activities. See also Corruption, Demagogues, W. F. Buckley, Jr., *Four Reforms* (1973).

REFORM ABROAD, see British Reform, Mexico-United States Relations, Greek Revolution, Turkey and Reform, Czechoslovakia, 1848, Russian Revolution (February, 1917), Formosa, Garibaldi, Giuseppe, Sun Yat Sen, O'Connell, Daniel, Caribbean Nations and American Reform, Central America and Reform, Southeast Asia and Reform, Latin America and Reform, African Nationalism.

REFUGEES, a problem in world adjustments as nations asserted their independence, but showed no talent or compassion for caring for their own, or others. An irony was Vietnam (*q.v.*), Laos and Cambodia, which pridefully threw off the *Indochina* label of the French, but in the horrors of war and ethnic hatred, permitted millions to starve or be ravaged in all three countries, but made the task of succoring victims the task of others to care as best they could for "Indochinese refugees." The primary force to help was the United States, and without the aid of former dissidents and demonstrators in the country who had accused their own government of "genocide" in Vietnam. One of them calmly stated that his cause had been withdrawal from Vietnam, not humanitarianism. With Travis Air Force Base near San Francisco becoming the Ellis Island (*q.v.*) of the West, America was processing Indochinese early in 1981 to the number of 99,276 refugees, with more due monthly. Many of them quickly established themselves in work and family routine; a major worry was that the native American poor might hate them on ethnic and economic grounds and cause suffering, such as had happened earlier with Chinese and Japanese. On the east coast similar conditions prevailed, as Cuba (*q.v.*) dropped its mask of "Marxist" strength and self-sufficiency, and frankly sought to rid itself of its "overpopulation," throwing in for the road its criminals and degenerates. First welcomed with thoughtless generosity by the Carter (*q.v.*) administration, efforts were then made to control the influx, which included Haitians and Dominicans. The Immigration authorities were ill-prepared to find jobs, housing, welcoming locales, health controls, and language solutions to the inpouring hordes, especially with a Federal judge insisting that a single Cuban criminal be accorded all "human rights" of legal process, or be released on the streets. Public opinion ranged from the sentimental to the prejudiced on the issue. The problem was complicated further by being part of an international problem of refugees in such enormous situations as involved Ethiopia-Somali, Afghans, Palestinians, Biafrans, Ugandans, and Angolans, among others, where not only resettlement, but simple hunger and disease were overwhelming to the World Food Program, the UN High Commission for Refugees, and volunteer organizations. It was anticipated that the United States would have to help significantly here, too. H. C. Brooks and Y. El-Ayouty, eds., *Refugees South of the Sahara* (1970); L. W. Holborn, *The International Refugee Organization* (1956); *Refugees, a Problem for Our Time, the UN High Commission for Refugees* (1974).

REGIONALISM, see Sectionalism and Reform.

REGULATORS, identified with North Carolina, an extra-legal group of men, concerned for taxing and other inequities which troubled them, who banded together to stop the onerous actions of constituted authorities; they arose in the Revolutionary era, and developed a tradition which involved patriotic operations, but also moved over into a species of Lynch Law (*q.v.*). They are remembered in both connections. William S. Powell et al., eds., *The Regulators in North Carolina* (1971).

REGULATORY AGENCIES have seemed to have a reform potential, in that they could be appealed to for redress. Such agencies as the Federal Trade Commission, the Federal Power Commission, and the Federal Communications Commission (*qq.v.*) have had the authority to curb monopoly, satisfy public needs, and combat offensive practices which corrupt the general taste. Although the agencies have been reluctant to assume programs which would offend private business, they have reflected public suspicions and alarms, and been a springboard for reform controversies. Regulatory agencies proliferated under the aegis of James M. Landis (see Donald A. Ritchie, *James M. Landis, Dean of the Regulators* 1980), and their functions multiplied thanks to the work of Nader (*q.v.*). The agencies came under increased criticism as bureaucratic, an inhibiting force on industry and normal operation, inordinately expensive and self-serving. In 1980, there were 57 major agencies. One, the Department of Energy, issued a handbook of 400 pages of regulation, with over a thousand more of documentation. Although, obviously, much, like nuclear power, needed sharp regulation, all government spokesmen agreed that regulation needed to be controlled. William L. Cary, *Politics and the Regulatory Agencies* (1967); R. E. Cushman, *The Independent Regulatory Commissions* (1941); Elizabeth Rolph, *Regulation of Nuclear Power* (1977); R. E. Caves and M. J. Roberts, *Regulating the Product* (1974); Frances Fox Piven, *Regulating the Poor: the Function of Public Welfare* (1971).

REIGN OF TERROR, THE, the most famous being that unleashed by the Jacobins under Robespierre (*qq.v.*), 1793-4, against the alleged enemies of the state. Since the monarchists had already been dispersed or decimated, the King himself going to the guillotine January 21, 1793, the Terror was principally directed against the moderates, especially the Girondists, in Paris, and in various centers throughout France. It left Robespierre and his Committee of Public Safety in total control of the country, and continued until the slaying of Robespierre himself. Since then, various crises have been designated as constituting a reign of terror, notably the crushing of the moderate opposition following the Bolshevik Revolution in 1917, and subsequent episodes which attended the civil war which followed; and the attack on Jews throughout Germany, after a German diplomat had been assassinated by a Jewish person in Paris, in November 1938. See also Saint Bartholomew Massacre, Terrorists.

RELIEF, originally conceived as charity or temporary aid, to tide the unfortunate person over until his crisis had been overcome: a job found, a family united, or whatever the case may be. The long and devastating economic depression (*q.v.*) of the 1930's, was of such proportions that "relief" went on indefinitely. Some persons were aged or demoralized, and their receipt of "relief" became a permanent part of their lives. Relief was further institutionalized by greater welfare expectations, by the fact that some poor or degraded people had little more to gain by working than by drawing relief, by the growth of social work stipendiaries who, in a real sense, needed relief clients as much as they were needed, and by other factors. Conservatives denounced relief as demoralizing to society and unnecessary, reformers tended to defend it without qualification. "Relief" tended to fall out of use, since it suggested temporary aid, rather than the institutionalized industry which welfare administered. With welfare, as functioning, under attack as a growth operation rather than a social aid for the deserving, it was possible that "relief" might come back in use, to a degree. Michael E. Rose, *Relief of Poverty, 1834-1914* (1972).

RELIGIOUS LIBERTIES, see Churches and Reform.

RENEGADE, employed against reformers and quasi-revolutionaries who have abandoned their principles; the suggestion is always that they did this for sordid and pecuniary reasons, the faithful being unwilling to concede that there might be virtues of loyalty, disinterestedness, and the like on the other side. George Sokolsky, conservative newspaper columnist, was denounced by former associates as a renegade from socialism, in the 1930's. Other notable "renegades" included Benjamin Gitlow (*q.v.*), Louis F. Budenz, and J. B. Mathews. Hundreds and doubtless thousands, particularly on less conspicuous levels, "switched" their allegiances with little notice except in their own circles, though their feelings and rationalizations influenced public opinion; see also "Sell Out," Epithets.

RENT, see Anti-Rent War.

REPARATIONS, identified with post-World War I arrangements, which held Germany responsible for the war and liable to pay for the damage brought upon the Allies. A commission assessed Germany over thirty billion dollars, which, however, could not be readily seized for fear that an already weak and chaotic Germany might fall into communism. Although German industry made energetic efforts to revive, and would have been able to pay some of the reparations in goods, it was frustrated by the protectionist (*q.v.*) tariffs which the United States Congress erected to prevent German goods from competing with American goods. Such policies seemed to some reformers, as well as Marxists, to expose "contradictions" (*q.v.*) in the operations of American capitalism. Theoretically, reparations should not have been demanded; Woodrow Wilson (*q.v.*) in his War Message had declared that the battle was not against the German people, but their "irresponsible" government, which had since been overthrown; see also War Debts. In the late 1970s, the *New York Times* and other agencies sought to identify "reparations" with the duty of Americans to pay back Negroes for the group wrongs to which they had been historically subjected, by "affirmative action" (*q.v.*) in connection with educational, job, and other opportunities. Not spelled out were the contours of "reparations": to whom, how much, and the like; and whether "reparations" would also be allowed to others who could show unfair to evil handling: Irish, Chinese, Jews, Poles, and many others. Although vague conceptions respecting slavery (*q.v.*) continued to circulate in support of the "reparations" idea, it did not appear to gain strength or currency.

REPUBLICAN PARTY, see Politics and Reform.

RERUM NOVARUM (1891), epochal Encyclical of Pope Leo XIII; "Of New Things," popularly known as "On the Condition of the Working Classes," which, on the one hand, denounced socialism, on the other the excesses of free enterprise principles of the nineteenth century which absolved employers of any responsibility for the conditions of their workers. It offered encouragement for Catholics concerned for the problems of the poor, warning for those who might be tempted to drift from regard for religious considerations. Pope Pius XI's Encyclical, *Quadragesimo Anno* (On the Fortieth Year), in 1931 restated the principles enunciated by Leo.

"RESEGREGATION," an ironic word intended to indicate that segregation was a normal state in society, that efforts to desegregate schools and neighborhoods simply resulted in white people leaving a given neighborhood and reconstituting themselves elsewhere, leaving the Negroes as segregated as before. David Lawrence, a conservative columnist took satisfaction in assembling data which revealed this process of "resegregation," and wondered whether legal efforts would be made to force people to remain in neighborhoods they chose to leave.

RESETTLEMENT ADMINISTRATION, one of the most idealistic of the New Deal (*q.v.*) agencies, as formulated and led by Rexford G. Tugwell (*q.v.*). Its essential purpose was to put out of production low-grade farm areas, and to resettle the uprooted farmers in more promising terrain. Along with this purpose, which involved loans to farmers for purchase of farms and homes went plans for remaking the countryside, purifying streams, preventing erosion, landscaping deteriorated locales, and unifying services for community development, cooperative enterprises, and utilizing total human resources. "Greenbelt towns" (*q.v.*), intended as pilot plants (*q.v.*) for the nation, were projected in number, but fulfilled sparsely. The Resettlement Administration was rich in plans, poor in money. It became the Farm Security Administration (*q.v.*) in 1937, after no more than two years of activity.

RETARDED CHILDREN, CARE OF, like modern social work (*q.v.*), more a function of society than a reform, but one which has increasingly attracted conservative humanitarian and technical talents concerned for saving what they could of undeveloped human powers. Turning away from traditional practices of merely segregating the retarded and according them neither compassion nor interest, they have studied ways and means for using and improving their capacities, and for increasing their productivity and happiness. In 1950, the National Association of Parents and Friends of Mentally Retarded Children was formed; it became in 1952 the National Association for Retarded Children. It promotes research, education, the collection of funds, and related activities calculated to promote understanding of the problem and minister to it. See Gunnar Dybwad, "Mental Retardation," in *Social Work Yearbook for 1960*. By 1980, social attitudes toward the retarded and their families had become a touchstone of social concern, and separated those inordinately concerned for the upkeep of their neighborhoods and others who saw it necessary to rehabilitate social decency and ethics. Philip L. Browning, *Rehabilitation and the Retarded Offender* (1976); Elias Katz, *The Retarded Adult in the Community* (1972); Robert Isaacson, *The Retarded Child* (1974).

REUTHER, WALTER (1907-1970), capped a rich labor and union background by helping to organize the auto workers, and becoming their president in 1946. He became president of the C.I.O. (*q.v.*) in 1952. He fought obscure administrative battles with communists and anti-communists, in order to attain his position. Although a labor spokesman and offensive to labor racketeers (*q.v.*), and although an advocate of world peace, aid to underdeveloped peoples, and other worthy goals, he appeared too securely rooted in partisan labor politics to rate as a reformer. J. Gould and H. Lorena, *Walter Reuther* (1972).

REVENUE REFORM, see Wells, David A.

REVERSE DISCRIMINATION, a by-product of "affirmative action," which, in seeking to augment opportunities for Negroes, was prone to do so at the expense of valid applicants of other ethnic groups. The Bakke Case (*q.v.*) represented an effort to reverse discrimination. Involved in the question was also the capacity of education and industry to provide quality (*q.v.*) products. Nathan Glazer, *Affirmative Discrimination* (1976); Barry R. Gross, *Discrimination in Reverse: Is Turnabout Fair Play?* (1978).

REVISIONISM, developed by the German, Eduard Bernstein (*q.v.*), who advocated socialist aims, but rejected the Marxist (*q.v.*) views of class-war, arguing that no sharp differentiation from capitalism was required, no program of violence or doctrinaire expectations. Socialism, he felt, needed only to be the fulfillment of the efforts of reformers of various types who would introduce cooperative measures into the structure of society until it had evolved into socialism. Among revisionists were James Ramsey MacDonald, in Great Britain, and John Spargo, in the United States (*qq.v.*).

"REVISIONIST" HISTORIANS, a group of critics of the New Deal or of Franklin D. Roosevelt (*qq.v.*), personally; from various points of view and in behalf of various assumptions, they questioned the integrity of the United States Government, and accused it of deliberately maneuvering the country into war. Roosevelt they held to have uttered false or insincere statements. The ultimate accusation was that he had needed the catastrophe of Pearl Harbor to enable him to wage war on Japan. Charles A. Beard and Harry Elmer Barnes (*qq.v.*) were among many historians who levelled the most serious charges at the President; others included William Henry Chamberlin, George Morganstern, and Charles C. Tansill. For the pros and cons of the revisionist argument, see G. M. Waller, ed., *Pearl Harbor: Roosevelt and the Coming of the War* (1953). See also Warren I. Cohen, *The American Revisionists* (1967); Manfred Jonas, *Isolationism in America* (1966); Charles A. Beard, *Giddy Minds and Foreign Quarrels* (1939).

REVIVALISM AND REFORM have been related in several eras, but not in all. The revivalist spirit did not serve reformers in the era of the American Revolution, which was dominated by an intellectual elite. The era of reform, 1830-60, on the other hand, stirred many revivalist spirits, including

Charles G. Finney (q.v.). The "Come-outers" (q.v.) were evangelists in protest against a non-reformist church. Evangelicism entered into some of the oratory of the Populist Revolt (q.v.) and was echoed in such famous political calls to arms as Theodore Roosevelt's: "We stand at Armageddon, and we battle for the Lord." Nevertheless, it has been argued that revivalism was largely an escape from the problems of reform, and burned up energies which could have been more profitably employed in social action; see Whitney R. Cross, *The Burned-Over District* (1950). In 1980, a "Moral Majority" alarmed liberals and some moderate conservative elements by mounting political campaigns against targetted Congressmen, and defeating them at the polls. It was feared they heralded a drive oppressive to the broad electorate. Some alarmists saw a connection between "Big Money" and the evangelical Right Wing. Since other special interests, including unions and the National Education Association, also supported preferred candidates, it little became them to criticize others for doing the same. A more persuasive approach might have been to underscore principles, augmenting them with sufficient funds to broadcast them to the voters.

REVOLTS, see Slave Revolts, Weavers, Revolt of the.

REVOLUTION AND REFORM have been both associated and opposed. To reactionaries (q.v.), they have appeared to be the same thing. The American Revolution (q.v.) began as an effort at reform, and involved patent conservatives like George Washington, as well as determined revolutionists like Samuel Adams (q.v.). Circumstances have often given a more violent revolutionary force to moderately-intended changes. Thus, the French reformers intended to set up a constitutional monarchy after the British model. The royalist determination to destroy the reformers first destroyed the monarchy, then, as the revolutionary wave developed momentum, the reformers as well. The overthrow of slavery in the United States, as achieved in Lincoln's Administration (q.v.), began as an effort to halt slavery extension into the West. The Russian revolutionists thought, before they achieved their revolution, that they would have to support a "bourgeois" revolution, because Russia had to pass through a capitalist era. After they had set up the "Dictatorship of the Proletariat" (q.v.), some American reformers thought it proper to defend the Soviet Union as an effort beneficial to humanity. The evolution of the Soviet state tended to disillusion reformers with respect to the initial promise it offered. Events in China, in the Chile of Allende, and elsewhere suggested the need for a more pragmatic approach to revolutions in general, some promising greater stability and bargaining capacity than others.

"REVOLUTION OF 1800," the victory of the Democratic-Republicans, headed by Thomas Jefferson (qq.v.), over the Federalists (q.v.), who warned that their opponents would institute a reign of anarchy. Much of this demagogy resulted from the quarrel between the two parties over the French Revolution (q.v.), which the Jeffersonians defended, the Federalists condemned. Jefferson, in his Inaugural Address, tried to quiet Federalist fears: "We are all Republicans, we are all Federalists." He had no social program, and hoped for a quiet Administration: a sign to him that the country was in health and busy with its private affairs. Nevertheless, his effort to undermine the U.S. Supreme Court (q.v.) did have almost revolutionary implications.

"REVOLUTION OF 1828," like the "Revolution of 1800" strictly limited in its perspectives. It praised the "common man," but did little to augment his significance. Its position on internal improvements (q.v.), tariffs, and other issues was purely political. The Jackson Administration was essentially pro-slavery. It took a humanitarian position on "debtors' prisons" (q.v.) and an anti-monopolistic position on the Second Bank of the United States (q.v.).

"REVOLUTION OF 1910," an uprising against "Czar" Cannon (q.v.) of the House of Representatives which loosened his control of the strategic Rules Committee, and permitted more democratic procedure in that body and in the House.

"REVOLUTION OF 1912," conceived as having occurred as a result of the Ballinger Affair, the findings of the Pujo Committee (qq.v.), and other dramatic events, culminating in the Presidential election of that year, in which the candidates vied with one another to promise reforms; see, however, 1912.

RHODESIA, see Zimbabwe

"RIGHT TO LIFE," see Abortion.

"RIGHT TO WORK" LAWS have become a means of resisting what has been thought of as unwarranted power of labor leaders who can, it is argued, foist their will, and often the will of racketeers, upon laborers, forcing them into unwanted unions and penalizing them with onerous dues. Right to work laws have also been seen as an attack on labor unions. In 1959, they existed in 19 states. Right to work was originally a socialist slogan, signally society's duty to provide a willing person with the means for earning his living. Fourier (q.v.) formulated it as a principle of moral society. See also Nels Anderson, *The Right to Work* (1938), Anderson being, then, Director, Section on Labor Relations, Works Progress Administration. Compare, Rev. Edward A. Keller, *The Case for Right to Work Laws: a Defense of Voluntary Unionism* (1956). In 1981, the National Right to Work Legal Defense Foundation was under attack by unions and a U.S. District Court order to disclose its list of contributors: a decision, if fulfilled, which would destroy the foundation.

"RIGHT WING," see Conservatism and Reform, Fascism and Reform.

RIGHTS OF MAN, THE (1791-1792), see Paine, Thomas.

RIIS, JACOB A. (1849-1914), immigrant from Denmark and *New York Evening Sun* journalist, whose exposes of slum conditions in New York pioneered such work and helped improve conditions in his time. His most famous title was *How the Other Half Lives* (1890), but his autobiography, *The Making of an American* (1901) also repays study.

RIOTS have been notable as expressions of public unrest, prejudice, political sympathy, and other manifestations of group psychology. Notable riots have included the Negro riots in New York City (1741); the Stamp Act Riots (1765) which took place in various colonies; the Doctors' riot in New York (1788), in protest against their use of corpses for dissection; the riots against abolitionists in New York, Utica, Boston, and elsewhere (1834, 1835); the Flour Riots of New York (1837); the Astor Place riots (1849), an expression of anti-British feeling; the riot between police and gangs in New York (1857); the Draft Riots of 1863 (q.v.); the riot between Catholic and Protestant Irish (1870,1871); and the Railroad Riots of 1877 (q.v.); see J. T. Headley, *Pen and Pencil Sketches of the Great Riots* (1882). The riots accompanying Negro unrest in the 1960s, notably in Watts, Los Angeles, and Detroit, Michigan merited analysis rather than appeasement; compare Peace Corps, C.C.C., "Moral Equivalent of War, A." In 1980, destructive riots in Liberty City, near Miami, Florida raised fears that the earlier wave of riots might be repeated; it remained to be seen what had been learned from earlier experiences. A. Deane-Drummond, *Riot Control* (1975); Barbara Ritchie, ed., *Riot Report...the National Advisory Commission on Civil Disorders* (1969); L. H. Masoti and D. R. Bowen, eds., *Riots and Rebellion...in the Urban Community* (1968).

RIVER, THE, see Lorentz, Pare.

RN, autobiography of Richard M. Nixon (q.v.), issued in 1978. Notable for the effort by anti-Nixon partisans to curb its sale with the slogan: Don't Buy a Book from a Crook. Nevertheless, a world-wide best seller. Curiously, partisans to this offensive were not disturbed by Abbie Hoffman's 1971 title, *Steal This Book*, a handbook on theft.

"ROBBER BARONS, THE" a phrase descriptive of the entrepreneurs (q.v.) of post-Civil War decades. Indifferent to law and the public interest, they competed for control of giant monopolies. The phrase was utilized successfully in 1934 as the title of a study of big business in that era, by Matthew Josephson. General acceptance of the phrase as accurately describing the qualities and significance of big business constituted a victory for the reform point of view. The rise of "business history" in the post-World War II years, much of it subsidized by business, brought with it criticisms of the implications and adequacy of the phrase. The vindication of John D. Rockefeller *(q.v.)* as a philanthropist and industrial statesman broke ground for the vindication of the businessmen of the era as a whole. See Thomas B. Brewer, ed., *The Robber Barons: Saints or Sinners?* (1976).

ROBESPIERRE, MAXIMILIEN ISIDORE (1758-1794), identified with the French Revolution *(q.v.)* in its extreme, Jacobin phase. Although it has been realized that he was personally a young man of incorruptible principles and social ideals, he has been scorned by those who hold him to have been a self-righteous bigot. He was a leader in the movement to execute Louis XVI as a traitor to the nation, and afterward in that to destroy the Girondist party of moderate revolutionists. This left his Jacobin group in sole control and compelled to multiply terror and the activities at the guillotine in order to combat the increased number of dissidents. His death was mourned by few, but his program (which involved worship of a Supreme Being) has been studied by revolutionaries anxious to emulate his political purposes and avoid his errors. Jean Matrat, *Robespierre: the Tyranny of the Majority* (1975).

ROBIN HOOD, thought to be a legendary figure of Medieval England and Sherwood Forest, but a person who in fact lived in the thirteenth century. He is noted for having taken from the rich and given to the poor, and his "merry band" has symbolized freedom, justice, and humanity. In American cartoons and films, he is too vaguely delineated to serve tangible social purposes.

ROBINSON-PATMAN ACT (1936), an implementation of the Clayton Anti-Trust Act *(q.v.)* and aimed against practices which aided chain stores to compete with unwarranted success against independent and small merchants, especially through mass purchases and lower prices.

ROBOTS, since 1920, when the term was invented by the Czechoslovakian author Karel Capek, in his play *R.U.R.* (Rossum's Universal Robots). The concept has haunted fiction and films exploiting the fear that human beings were becoming machine-like; see, for example, *Modern Times* (1936), with Charlie Chaplin. The proliferation of controlled machines in industry caused worries that they might supplant workers. "Robertics" research looked beyond simple, assembly-like robots performing more complex operations, on earth and in space. The United States was behind Japan in robot-production in 1981, 3,500 industrial robots to 17,000. Clerical and household robots were not yet in demand. F.H. George and J.D. Humphries, *Robots Are Coming* (1974); M. Allaby and Floyd Allen, *Robots behind the Plow* (1974); Don Dwiggins, *Robots in the Sky* (1972).

ROCHDALE COOPERATIVES, root organization of the co-operative idea, organized at Rochdale, England, in 1844, by twenty-eight persons who aimed to advance social organization while avoiding the principles of class war. All cooperatives owe their ideas to the principles of democracy and economic practice which they put into motion. The "Rochdale Plan," still utilized by cooperatives, involved the purchase by members of shares of stock, which brought interest; goods were sold for cash, and at the end of stipulated periods, the "profits" were divided among the members according to a prepared system.

ROCKEFELLER, JOHN D., SR. (1839-1937), once a symbol of ruthless and unscrupulous business dealings, to reformers who did not cope with the question of how he was able to weather the numerous attacks made upon him and the Standard Oil Company *(q.v.)* and to grow in the process. Though pilloried as a man without moral sensibilities, a miser, the possessor of "tainted money" *(q.v.)*, he no more than more competently administered the ideals and aspirations of his less successful

business contemporaries. His overwhelming success forced upon them the necessity for advocating the regulation *(q.v.)* of business in the interests of continued free enterprise *(q.v.)*. His career as a philanthropist, involving as it did such institutions as the University of Chicago and the Rockefeller Foundation, underscored his status as an industrial statesman as well as a "robber baron" *(q.v.)*. Henry Demarest Lloyd, *Wealth against Commonwealth* (1894); Ida M. Tarbell, *History of the Standard Oil Company* (1904); William Manchester, *A Rockefeller Family Portrait* (1959); Allan Nevins, *John D. Rockefeller, a Study in Power* (1953).

ROCKEFELLER, NELSON A. (1908-1979), most famous of five powerful brothers, sons of John D. Rockefeller, Jr., and upholders of the family fortunes. Rockefeller marked the distance the Rockefellers had come since their grandfather had been burned in effigy in the Pennsylvania oil fields. Rockefeller's public career was impressive, from 1940 when he acted as coordinator of the Office of Inter-American Affairs, a long-time commitment which went on in various offices; see his *Rockefeller Report on the Americas* (1969). His career gained breadth in the planning of the United Nations, and the reorganization of the government structure, reflected in his *The Future of Federalism* (1962), among other reports. He was involved, too, with Health, Education and Welfare *(q.v.)*, and with President Eisenhower himself, as special assistant. In addition, Rockefeller's public presence did not offend ethic and other minority folk; partaking of ethnic foods with potential voters and addressing a variety of people as "fella" became a trademark in his public relations. He overcame another aristocrat, Averell Harriman, at the polls in 1958, and occupied his governor's chair in New York easily till he chose to resign in 1973. His program of civil rights, and largesse with state money for urban renewal and the building up of the state university gained him a liberal reputation, balanced by his concern for national defense and strong anti-crime measures intended to reassure conservatives. Rockefeller's divorce in 1962 and remarriage in 1963 included details which retarded his Presidential ambitions in 1964, but, in the loosening social fabric of the youth revolt of the time, harmed him little in 1968; Nixon's Republican appeal was simply too great. Rockefeller accepted the Vice-Presidential post under Gerald Ford, but wrote himself out of the same nomination for 1976. His death in the apartment of a protege caused a several days stir, and evoked tales, kept politely before from the papers by journalists selectively respectful of personal peccadillos. His grandfather would not have approved. James Desmond, *Nelson Rockefeller* (1964); R. H. Connery and G. Benjan, eds., *Governing New York State* (1974); Peter Collier and David Horowitz, *The Rockefellers* (1976); Ferdinand Lundberg, *The Rockefeller Syndrome* (1975); Frank Gervasi, *The Real Rockefeller* (1964); M. Kramer and S. Roberts, *I Never Wanted to Be Vice President of Anything* (1976).

ROCKEFELLER PLAN, see Colorado Plan, The.

ROLLAND, ROMAIN (1866-1944), French novelist and humanitarian, world-famous for his *Jean Christophe* (1904-12), an extended novel based generally upon the spirit which Rolland perceived in Beethoven; democratic and inspired. Rolland sought to play a positive role in social affairs, and became a contemporary conscience. His *Above the Battle* (1916) avoided the easy chauvinism *(q.v.)* of other writers of his time. His drama, *Danton* (1936) sought to recapture the idealism which informed the French Revolution. He maintained a sympathy toward the apparent aims of the Soviet Union, and, more freely a whole-hearted admiration of Gandhi, about whom he wrote a study (1924). His writings on music and his second series of novels, entitled *The Enchanted Soul* (1922-34), were read by reformers as well as persons concerned with the arts. William T. Starr, *Romain Rolland, One against All* (1971).

ROOSEVELT, FRANKLIN D. (1882-1945), architect of the New Deal *(q.v.)* and administrator of American policy during World War II, he was a politician rather than a reformer, whose activities, before attaining the Presidency, included service with a law firm, with the New York Senate, as assistant secretary of the Navy, and as candidate for the Vice-Presidency of the United States (1920), when he was defeated. He was a member of the Hudson-Fulton Celebration Commission (1909), an overseer of Harvard University (1918-24), president of the Boy Scout Foundation of New York, and a trustee of the Woodrow Wilson Foundation, among others. As President, he operated within a spectrum of experimentation of which his predecessor, Herbert Hoover (q.v.), was incapable. As such, he became a magnet for a wide variety of reformers and even, for special purposes, revolutionists. Thus, the communists, in the early days of his Administration, portrayed him as a potential fascist, but later deemed him preferable to his more conservative opponents, found him more than tolerable during the Grand Alliance (q.v.), and were able to offer him more or less unstinted praise after his death. Reflecting, as well as directing, public opinion, a judgment of him could not be separated from a judgment of it. Although Roosevelt's unprecedented four-term election victories established the welfare state (q.v.), they did so on premises and expectations which did not anticipate permanent governmental structures antagonistic to self-help, individual preferences, and free enterprise. Even T.V.A. and Social Security (qq.v.) were thought to put these areas outside of the larger field of incentive and competition, not to supersede them. The expansion of bureaucracy and regulation (q.v.), of non-incentive welfare, grants, and loans which reached their height in President Johnson's (q.v.). administration derived from the New Deal, but was not identical to it. Rexford G. Tugwell, Roosevelt's Revolution (1977); C. K. McFarland, Roosevelt, Lewis, and the New Deal; F. Friedel, Franklin D. Roosevelt (1952-1973); E. E. Robinson, The Roosevelt Leadership (1955); F. Lowenheim and H. D. Langley, Roosevelt and Churchill [correspondence] (1975). See also New Deal, Works Progress Administration, Supreme Court, Welfare Legislation, Yalta, "Revisionist" Historians, Hopkins, Harry L., and related personalities and topics. Roosevelt's wife, Eleanor Roosevelt (1884-1962), was a manifest aid in his entire career, and furnished a striking contrast with First Ladies before and after. In her own time, she became a symbol of women concerned for public issues. Although much of her work and understanding was superficial, it represented good will and directed attention to the numerous places and situations she visited, and to the needs of working people and people in the world. See her On My Own (1958); Autobiography (1961).

ROOSEVELT, THEODORE (1858-1919), at his death there was but one Roosevelt in the public eye, identified with the events of the Reform era, numerous individual quarrels and issues, from phonetic spelling (q.v.) to "race suicide"—Roosevelt evidently feared that the immigrant people were not reproducing fast enough—the issues and campaigns of 1912 and 1916, the "Preparedness" campaign which was intended to make the United States strong for any emergency evolving out of the European War begun in 1914, and such special matters as big game hunting. In the 1920's, all these topics dwindled in public importance, and Henry F. Pringle's biography of Roosevelt (1931), which won the Pulitzer Prize, treated him ironically. By the time Franklin D. Roosevelt had assumed the Presidency, there was but one Roosevelt in the public eye. "Teddy" was known familiarly, and somewhat contemptuously, as the man who had shaken a big stick at some vaguely-defined antagonist. A major project in collecting his letters produced no public impression. As his kinsman, Franklin, receded into history, however, the light both emanated became somewhat more comparable; mention of "Roosevelt" brought the question: "Which?" Both were seen as strong conservatives speaking for a responsible elite. See Roosevelt's Autobiography (1913); John M. Blum, The Republican Roosevelt (1954); Filler, "Theo," in Appointment at Armageddon; Morton Keller, ed., Theodore Roosevelt: a Profile (1967); W. H. Harbaugh, Power and Responsibility: the Life and Times of Theodore Roosevelt (1961); E. Morris, The Rise of Theodore Roosevelt (1979).

ROOSEVELT COROLLARY, pronounced in 1904, an episode in American imperialism (q.v.); it supplemented the Monroe Doctrine (q.v.) in asserting that the United States would interfere in the internal affairs of other American nations when they were guilty of "wrong doing or impotence," and thus liable to investiture by other foreign powers. Under the Roosevelt Corollary, American troops entered the Dominican Republic, Haiti, and other areas. The Corollary was directly repudiated at the eighth Pan-American Conference in 1938.

ROOSEVELT RED RECORD AND ITS BACKGROUND, THE (1936), by Elizabeth Dilling, a follow-up volume on *The Red Network* (q.v.); like the other, a lurid work, informed, but without focus. It saw the Rockefellers, the American Telephone and Telegraph Company, the Swift Packing Company, "even the 'House of Morgan'," as helping the communists, in a devious line through Thomas W. Lamont, its "radical" partner, to his son Corliss Lamont, national head of the Friends of the Soviet Union. As an example of her method, she found socialists opposed to unemployment, and Roosevelt also; accordingly, he could be set down as socialistic, Marxian, and the like.

ROSENBERG CASE, THE, an incident in the outbreak of atom-bomb spy cases (q.v.), it captured world-wide attention because of the court's decision that they were to die for their crimes of treason. Exploited by communists and their sympathizers as a latter-day "Sacco-Vanzetti" case (q.v.), it contributed to a wave of anti-American feeling abroad, though not to pro-communist feeling at home. See Leslie Fiedler, "Afterthoughts on the Rosenbergs," in *An End to Innocence*; for a dissident view, John Wexley, *The Judgment of Julius and Ethel Rosenberg* (1955). Efforts to obtain new evidence in the FBI files, under the Freedom of Information Act (q.v.), do not appear to have been fruitful.

R.O.T.C. (Reserve Officers Training Corps), which operated on campuses, and was a factor in the Kent State (q.v.) tragedy, agitators having burned the R.O.T.C. building as a prelude to the fatal confrontation. During the anti-Vietnam War demonstrations, the R.O.T.C. lost credit and supporters on campuses as a war-related activity. A sign of changing times was its comeback as a student interest and activity. Observers saw it not as a renewed military concern of participants; "each individual is motivated for a different reason." Scholarships helped, in a time of dwindling student opportunities. It appeared, however, that students were bringing a spectrum of attitudes toward possible individual goals.

ROUSSEAU, JEAN JACQUES (1712-1778), turbulent apostle of nature, individualism, and the social contract, he has been credited with formulating the thought and feeling which entered into the French Revolution (q.v.), and for its excesses. His placing of his five children in a foundling home has received the scorn of critics. His famous thought: that man was born free, and is everywhere in chains, has been an inspiration to radicals. See Irving Babbitt, *Rousseau and Romanticism* (1919).

ROYALL, ANNE (1769-1854), "Grandmother of the muckrakers (q.v.)," she lived a pioneer youth, a wealthy middle age which was ruined by malicious court action. She turned desperately to writing as a means of support. Her pen-portraits of living great men and conditions, in such books as *Sketches of History, Life, and Manners in the United States* (1826) and *Letters from Alabama* (1830) are a national heritage. Her turn to criticism of the government in her newspapers *Paul Pry* (1831-1836) and *The Huntress* (1836-1854) were an epic of courage. She suffered sentence in court in 1829 as a "common scold," a sentence since reversed by time. See Bessie Rowland James, *Anne Royall's U.S.A.* (1972); Filler, "Common Scold," in *Appointment at Armageddon*.

RUGG, HAROLD O. (1775-1960), Columbia University professor and a leading exponent of Progressive Education (q.v.). He was author of successful textbooks in the field, including *Changing Governments and Changing Cultures* (1932) and

Citizenship and Civic Affairs (1940). He came under severe attack from such agencies as the American Legion (*q.v.*), which held that he was unwarrantedly receptive to the positive features of the Soviet regime. The concerted attacks harmed his prestige with the less liberal boards of education. See his *That Men May Understand* (1941). Driven from education, he made a last, brilliant attempt to save Progressive principles from being watered down into mindless permissiveness with his *Imagination*, published posthumously in 1963. It sought and found evidence that vital work was not found in docile study, but required creative thinking and independence.

"RUGGED INDIVIDUALISM," praised by Herbert Hoover (*q.v.*), as Republican Party candidate for President, October 22, 1928, in a speech in New York; he upheld what he saw as American individualism and independence, in opposition to state aid. The phrase became one which was treated with bitterness and irony by victims of the ensuing depression.

"RUM, ROMANISM, AND REBELLION," a phrase used by a supporter of James G. Blaine's candidacy for President, during the election of 1884. The race was exceedingly close, and the phrase stirred enough resentment in Irish Catholics of New York to tip the balance in the state, and give it, and the victory, to Grover Cleveland.

RURAL AMERICA, including farmers, but others as well. Farmers were identified with Truman (*q.v.*). subsidies which swung the 1948 election to him, and with subsidies generally. However, the rural *poor*, passed over in favor of the urban poor, were in 1981 among the poorest of all. With 30% of Americans living in rural areas, they harbored 40% of the recognized poor in the nation, the figure including women, Negroes, and Hispanics. The Rural Development Act (1972), the Housing and Community Development Act (1974) and the Rural Development Act (1980) sought to redress those wrongs, but were meagrely funded. Rural America, founded in 1975, sought to speak for this interest group. See *Poverty Dimension of Rural . . . America: New Perspectives* (1976).

RURAL ELECTRIFICATION ADMINISTRATION, like the Resettlement Administration (*q.v.*), one of New Deal (*q.v.*) projects intended to modernize the country, and bring electricity to the more than eight million farm homes which were without such service. Set up in 1936, the Administration made loans permitting the building and operating of electric generating plants, and advised borrowers on engineering, management and legal problems. The bulk of such loans were to cooperatives, and the encouragement of their formation necessarily involved criticism of private enterprise (*q.v.*); as a government pamphlet put it: "Commercial companies are in the power business for profit. They usually cannot make as much profit from rural lines as from urban lines." The co-operatives were run on democratic principles, and may have influenced rural attitudes toward reform in some small degree.

"RURAL IDIOCY," a concept in early Marxism (*q.v.*) which saw the farmer as incompetent in larger understandings and requiring the direction of the sophisticated city workers for the attainment of a socialistic state. The Populist Revolt (*q.v.*) revealed considerable brain power among the farmers, and the Bolshevik Revolution (*q.v.*) confounded the revolutionists who had imagined that their first successful uprising must take place in a more "advanced" country. They more modestly projected peasant-worker revolts, thereafter. Moreover, it dawned upon some students of sociological phenomena that not only were farmers improving their awareness of the world, thanks to 4-H and other social organizations, better roads, radios, and other aids to communication, but that there was also a species of *urban idiocy* which could be observed among the patrons of the pinball machines, bowling alleys, and those with "TV eyes."

RUSH, BENJAMIN (1745-1813), the outstanding American reformer of his time, concerned for anti-slavery, institutional reform, progress in education, woman's rights, and other causes. Although fearless in his efforts to help victims of yellow fever, during the epidemic of 1793, in Philadelphia, he proba-

bly helped numerous patients to their graves by his excessive bleeding methods. N. G. Goodman, *Benjamin Rush* (1934); J. H. Powell, *Bring Out Your Dead* (1949).

RUSSELL, CHARLES EDWARD (1860-1941), leader of the muckrakers (*q.v.*), mixed a populist (*q.v.*) background with service for William Randolph Hearst (*q.v.*). The result, in 1902, was *Such Stuff as Dreams*, a book of verse. Russell esteemed himself an authority on English and American poetry, but his contribution was that of a critic of American monopoly. No other muckraker touched so many areas of American affairs, including the Beef Trust, the problem of government ownership, prison reform, the pitifully cheap policies of Trinity Church in New York, the careers of financial tycoons, and of business leaders, and (what was close to his heart) the railroads. *The Greatest Trust in the World* (1905), *The Uprising of the Many* (1907), *Lawless Wealth* (1908), and *Business: the Heart of the Nation* (1911) were several byproducts of his labors in the field. His basic change of view was explained in *Why I Am a Socialist* (1910). His support of American intervention in World War I embittered many admirers, but he felt it justified, as he justified his detestation of communism; see his *Bolshevism and the United States* (1919). He continued his career as a litterateur and a "right-wing" socialist to the end; see his *These Shifting Scenes* (1914) and *Bare Hands and Stone Walls* (1933), the latter one of the outstanding memoirs of Populist and muckraking thought.

RUSSIA, AMERICAN ATTITUDES TOWARD, have varied with the times, and with official relations. Thus, Russia was, before the Civil War, a largely legendary land to Americans. During that conflict, the northerners believed that Russian officialdom had maintained a positive attitude toward the Federal government, on somewhat tenuous evidence. Shortly after, some official concern in America respecting the intentions of Russia inspired, in part, the purchase from her of Alaska. In succeeding decades, an American sense of Russia as a land of serfs and tyrants permitted a sentimental sympathy for anarchists and socialists. The "pogroms" (*q.v.*) against Jews were deemed reprehensible. American sympathy during the Russo-Japanese War (1904) was with the Japanese. Maxim Gorky was received with honor as a great novelist and humanitarian in America (1905), though a socialist and without honor in Russia. (The revelation that he was not married to Madame Gorky, because of principled opposition to the Greek Orthodox Church, lost him American regard.) The ruthless suppression of the 1905 Russian Revolution added to popular antipathy to Czarist rule. Although pro-Allied feeling, at the beginning of World War I, enabled many American elements to look more positively at a land which had produced distinguished writers, musicians, scientists, and which had repelled Napoleon in 1812, its catastrophic collapse before the German war-machine, and other evidence of decay and corruption, enabled Americans, officially and unofficially, to hail the February, 1917, overthrow of Czarist rule. However, the second, Bolshevik revolution, in October, and the new rulers' determination to abandon the Allies, divided America. Socialists praised the communist regime, liberals were willing to give it a chance to prove its worth. The government and anti-socialist opinion portrayed it as crueler and more irresponsible than that of the late Czar. During the 1920's, the Union of Socialist Soviet Republics had many visitors, including admirers and skeptics. It conducted business relations with Americans; the witticism went that a Russian communist was *persona non grata* in the United States, unless he came to purchase goods or machinery. Officially, the United states refused U.S.S.R. recognition, and criticized her unwillingness to pay debts incurred by the Czar, and other policies. Recognition of Russia (1933) encouraged the possibility of better relations, economic and political, which did not materialize. The Moscow Trials (*q.v.*) disillusioned many "friends" of the Soviet Union, but permitted other Americans to imagine that it was "liquidating" extreme revolutionary elements, and thus bringing the United States and itself closer together in fact. The anti-Hitler alliance during World War II encouraged this view, and made sympathetic attitudes toward Russians and their policies feasible. However, sharp post-war differences reversed this trend. American attitudes toward Russia have since been a close combination of official policies and hopes, immediate circumstances, and public opinion respecting measures and attitudes which might be calculated to strengthen American security. V. Bukovsky, *To Build a Castle: My Life as a Dissenter* (1979); M. T. Florinsky, *Russia* (1969); L. J. Oliva, ed., *Russia and the West...to Khrushchev* (1965); Ronald Hingley, *The Russian Mind* (1977); S. Block and P. Reddaway, *Psychiatric Power: How Soviet Psychiatry is Used to Suppress Dissent* (1977); Wayne Vucinich, *Russia and Asia* (1972); Don C. Price, *Russia and the Roots of the Chinese Revolution* (1974); Victor Serge, *Russia, Twenty Years After* (1937); A. Yarmolinsky, *Russians, Then and Now* (1963); D. Tschizewsky, *Russian Intellectual History* (1976); Peter Kropotkin, *Russian Literature* (1905); L. H. Haimson, *Russian Marxists and the Origins of Bolshevism* (1966); R. P. Browder and A. F. Kerensky, *The Russian Provisional Government* (1961).

RUSSIAN BEAR, once a symbol of Czarist force and terror, now often symbolizing the force exercised by the U.S.S.R.

RUSSIAN REVOLUTION, THE, OF 1917, one of the two major events of the twentieth century, the other being the fall of Germany to the followers of Adolf Hitler (*q.v.*). The revolution was completed in two stages: the February revolution unseated the Czar; it should have resulted in a republican government, with the extremists acting as a militant opposition, and with worker, peasant, and the intellectual elements represented in a constituent assembly. The fact that Russia was a congeries of nationalities should have complicated the problem of government. However, the Provisional Government chose to make a first task of the continuation of the war against Germany. The fact that Russia had suffered cruel and discouraging defeats at the hands of German troops did not deter the would-be republicans, who were encouraged in their delusion by Allied representatives. The troops were defeatist in temper and eager for peace; so were the workers, in such industrial centers as Russia possessed; so were the Russian sailors. The peasants wanted land. The broken-down economy left hordes of Russians hungry. V. I. Lenin's slogan, "Land, Bread, and Peace" attracted the enthusiasm of strong socialist elements which infiltrated the army, the navy, the industrial workers. The result was the October uprising, which overthrew the rickety government. Its leader, Alexander Kerensky, fled. Some elements were jailed. The constituent assembly, which the Bolsheviks had demanded, was never convened. The Bolshevik government made its peace with Germany at Brest-Litovsk; Lenin had declared it necessary, if no alternative presented itself, to retreat to the Ural Mountains, and there keep the flag of proletarian revolution flying until the industrial west rose in revolution. Leon Trotsky (*q.v.*) proved a master of organization and created the Red Army, while Bolsheviks and guerrillas fought off White Guard (*q.v.*). armies aided by the Allies, determined to reestablish the Czar upon his throne. "Bolsheviks" was made a word of infamy in America, by the general press and also by the outraged socialists. They were accused of "nationalizing women," destroying the churches, indiscriminate murder, as well as having "deserted" the Allies in their struggle against the Central Powers. The Russian Revolution divided the West into sympathizers and antagonists, and thus changed the character of social reform. W. H. Chamberlin, *The Russian Revolution* (1935); M. K. Dziewenowski, *The Russian Revolution: an Anthology* (1970); L. Trotsky, *The Russian Revolution* (1932); E. H. Carr, *The Bolshevik Revolution* (1950-1953).

RUSSO-FINNISH WAR (1939-40), a turning point in world sympathy toward Russia as a "worker's state" and leader of the Third International (*qq.v.*). Russia's attack on Finland placed her on a level with other "imperialist" nations. Thereafter, her appeal to other people could only be in terms of

their own national (rather than their "international") interests. Alan L. Paley, *The Russo-Finish War* (1973).

RYAN, MSG. JOHN A. (1869-1945), Roman Catholic leader and a professor at several of its universities; an outstanding defender of the New Deal (*q.v.*) and an authority on labor. He helped bring to fruition minimum wage laws and collective bargaining (*qq.v.*); see his *A Living Wage* (1906), *Distributive Justice* (1916), and *A Better Economic Order* (1935), as well as *Seven Troubled Years* (1937). He was director of the Social Action Department of the National Catholic Welfare Conference. Nevertheless his liberalism had distinct limits; his *Francisco Ferrer* (*q.v.*) (1910) treated that liberal without regard, and he was an opponent of Morris Hillquit (*q.v.*) in their debate on socialism, in 1914. Francis L. Broderick, *Right Reverend New Dealer* (1963).

S

SACCO-VANZETTI CASE, the most important of all cases involving American justice to radicals. Nicola Sacco and Bartolomeo Vanzetti, "a good shoemaker and a poor fish-peddler," in Vanzetti's famous phrase, were in 1921 arrested and charged with the murder of two employees of a shoe factory in South Braintree more than a year before. The anti-radical feeling of the time was said to enable the prosecutor to develop circumstantial evidence beyond legitimate limits. Sacco and Vanzetti were charged with displaying "consciousness of guilt" at the time of arrest, and ballistic experts testified that the bullets in Vanzetti's pistol were "consistent with" those in the bodies of the murdered men. Judge Webster Thayer harbored prejudiced views of the defendants but did not separate himself from the case. Witnesses who testified against the defendants were criticized on many counts. Sacco and Vanzetti were sentenced to electrocution. The confession of a convicted murderer, that the robbery and murder had been by the Joe Morelli gang, among other evidence, was passed over by Thayer, who, under Massachusetts law of the time, was able to rule on the appeal from sentence. The state supreme court and the U.S. Supreme Court, saw no legal reason to intervene. An appeal to the governor for commutation of sentence caused him to appoint an advisory committee made up of President Abbott L. Lowell, of Harvard University, President Samuel W. Stratton, of Massachusetts Institute of Technology, and Judge Robert Grant. They found no cause for commutation. World protests were unavailing. Vanzetti's remarkable literary gifts no more than aggravated public opinion which was impressed by the inability of American justice to stop the executions, which took place August 22, 1927. John Dos Passos spoke for much of his generation in pronouncing the words: "all right then we are two nations" (U.S.A.). C. Louis Joughin and Edmund M. Morgan, The Legacy of Sacco and Vanzetti (1948) was a monument to the literary and technical evidence in behalf of their subject. A shock was delivered to those who, in 1960, still cherished the case as a twentieth century landmark by the publication of Robert H. Montgomery's Sacco-Vanzetti: the Murder and the Myth, which after exhaustive study of the official record concluded the defendants had been guilty as charged. At least a few Sacco-Vanzetti partisans concluded they had been deceived. See also Francis Russell, Tragedy in Dedham (1962); D. Felix, Protest: Sacco and Vanzetti and the Intellectuals (1965). On July 19, 1968, the Governor of Massachusetts ruled that all stigma be removed from the record of the defendants.

SADE, MARQUIS DE, a curious "anti-hero" (q.v.) of the 1960s and 1970s, read for his lubricity and "sadism" and justified as a presumed comment on the inadequacies of society. Simone de Beauvoir's essay, "Should We Burn Sade?" (1953) answered the question in the negative, while heroes (q.v.) were being "burned," at least in terms of respect, and forgotten as irrelevant. Peter Weiss's The Persecution and Assassination of Jean Paul Marat...under the Direction of Marquis de Sade (1964), staged as in a lunatic asylum, suggested that it was a mad world. An effective play, it came ill from a disillusioned author who had thought communism was sane. See Sade's Justine (1797).

SADAT, ANWAR AL- (1918-1981), president of Egypt since 1970, part of the Arab bloc, who acted in its behalf in waging war against Israel in 1973. Most stable and advanced of all the Arab states, with some 43 million people and a distinguished history, Egypt nevertheless had a delicate economy, with wealth badly distributed. In addition it had much to fear from the Soviet Union. Such factors helped explain Sadat's stunning turnabout, from long established anti-Israeli hatred to his 1977 visit to Israel to plead for peace. He swept aside Arab protest and threats to isolate Egypt; they cannot do without Egypt, he said. His continuation of the peace initiative, at Camp David in America, during which he, Carter, and the Israeli Prime Minister Begin exchanged the most extreme compliments and avowals still left open the question of the Palestinians (q.v.). Concessions and promises could not hide that unsettled problem. Nevertheless, in 1981, Sadat remained the best hope for building peace in the Middle East. Anwar Sadat, Revolt on the Nile, foreword by President Nasser (1957), and In Search of Identity, an Autobiography (1978); R. W. Baker, Egypt's Uncertain Revolution under Nasser and Sadat (1978); Uri Ra'Anan, the USSR Arms the Third World (1969); A. Z. Rubenstein, Red Star on the Nile (1977).

SAINT BARTHOLOMEW MASSACRE (1572), an outstanding atrocity (q.v.), this one involving Catholic French slaughtering Protestants at home. The capacity of people to dim lights on embarrassing events is illustrated in D. R. Kelley, "Martyrs, Myths, and the Massacre, the Background of St. Bartholomew," American Historical Review, December 1972; cf. N. M. Sutherland, The Massacre of St. Bartholomew and the European Conflict (1973). See also Filler, "Machiavelli for the Millions," in D. Madden, American Dreams, American Nightmares (1970).

SAINT SIMON, CLAUDE H. DE R., COMTE DE (1760-1825), pioneer French socialist and humanitarian theoretician, who dreamed of an ideal state, but aided the American Revolution. He was not a violent revolutionist, but advocated cooperation between industrialists and workers, both of which classes he saw as productive. He opposed regimentation. Though considered a utopian, his thought reflected the unfulfilled state of industrial development of his time, see F.M.H. Markham, ed., Henri Comte de Saint-Simon... Selected Writings (1952).

SAKHAROV, ANDREI, notable Soviet dissident, Nobel Peace Prize winner (1975) and nuclear physicist, whose effort at free speech and non-nationalistic humanity earned him the fear and anger of Soviet leaders. In 1980 he was stripped of his honors and consigned to house arrest in Gorky. Most promising was the fact that information respecting the abuse he was accorded could circulate in the world.

SALARIES, a basic index of American values and needs, they varied curiously, nationally and by field. Thus New York professors, though their institutions were shambles (see Geoffrey Wagner, The End of Education 1976), earned astronomical amounts compared with professors nationally, as did trash people ("sanitary engineers") compared with garbage collectors elsewhere. A practical nurse earned half what the laundry manager in the same hospital received. Entertainers were paid from well to fabulous. The President of the United States, though having vast abilities to dispose of public money, was himself far from the rarefied areas inhabited by others in private industry or enterprise. Doctors, lawyers, and educators, once fairly even in financial possibilities, had come apart, doctors attaining more money than the others. Curiously, radiologists, internists, and pathologists, because of their technical monopolies, earned more than the doctors. The status (q.v.) of professions remained a problem in the quality (q.v.) of American life. David Harrop, America's Paychecks (1980); see also Jacqueline Thompson, The Very Rich Book (1981).

"SALARY GRAB, THE," voted by Congress in 1873, and stipulating that the salaries of Members of Congress be raised from five thousand to seven thousand five hundred dollars, and made retroactive to permit the payment of five thousand dollars each in back pay. This was widely protested and repeal of the law forced the next year. A generous doubling of the President's salary to $50,000, which had been part of the Act, was permitted to remain. The "Salary Grab" was notable as having been attempted without furtiveness, congressmen apparently believing that the public temper would not be outraged; see "Great Barbecue, The."

SALEM WITCHCRAFT TRIALS, the highpoint of witchcraft persecutions in the American colonies, took place in 1692, arising from the hysterical and exhibitionistic accusations made by some young girls. Before the hysteria had worked its way out, bringing accusations against the very select of the town, nineteen persons had been hanged and one pressed to death. Although opinion favored the belief that witches existed, and although witchcraft persecutions took place after the Salem episodes, the excesses they unleashed sobered public opinion, which was unwilling to see them repeated in this form. Judge Sewall *(q.v.)* later made public acknowledgement of his errors in the case, and one of the girls publicly confessed the falseness of her charges. A later analogy with radical persecutions was reflected in books entitled *Witch Hunt (q.v.)*. Arthur Miller's *The Crucible* (1953), exploiting such an analogy, and endowing its protagonists with twentieth century psychology, was taken seriously by its viewers.

SALOMON, HAYM (c. 1740-1785), born in Poland, and a republican whose opinions required him to flee from home in 1772. He came to New York, where he opened a brokerage business. He was an ardent patriot, in 1776 arrested as a spy and imprisoned. He set himself to disaffecting Hessian soldiers. Paroled, he continued his business and underground activities. In 1778, he was again arrested, and this time condemned to death. By bribery, he escaped and came to Philadelphia, where an appeal to Congress for restitution produced no results, though he was without means and his family abandoned in New York. He opened an office as a dealer in bills of exchange and other securities and prospered, becoming the leading broker in the city. He was paymaster for the French forces in America and handled the funds provided for the American cause by France and Holland. His excellent business sense helped maintain the revolutionary government's credit. The amount of money he advanced it was amazing, mounting to over half a million dollars. After the war, his fortunes declined, and at his unexpected death, he left about forty-five thousand dollars. Over a century's efforts failed to recover the funds due him and his descendants. He received, however, a considerable amount of post-humous admiration. See C. E. Russell, *Haym Salomon* (1930).

SALOON, see Anti-Saloon League, Prohibition, Temperance, Volstead Amendment.

SALT (Strategic Arms Limitation Talks), of seemingly momentous concern to all mankind, SALT I summed up U.S.-Soviet discussions going back to 1967. They were intended to begin a long process of disarmament agreements which would reassure the world of its basic security. Nixon *(q.v.)* and the Soviet leader Brezhnev signed an accord in 1972 limiting the number of strategic weapons and launchers for intercontinental ballistic missiles which could carry nuclear warheads. The agreement was viewed with suspicion by those fearful of Soviet treachery, and its ability to use the more indefinite terms of the treaty for a rapid advance in nuclear power, for example by stockpiling materials which could be readily converted into war weapons in overwhelming number. SALT II represented a "second round" of talks consummated by signature in 1979 by Carter *(q.v.)* and Brezhnev. It alarmed critics further as providing loopholes by which the United States, honoring the limitations, could be straightjacketed, while the Soviet Union built still further its massive ability to destroy strategic parts of the United States and its people. Carter's agreement was shelved in the Senate; his successor-to-be Reagan *(q.v.)* said he opposed it in principle. The Afghanistan *(q.v.)* crisis suggested the Soviets would abrogate any treaty they chose. Friends of SALT II, including the *New York Times*, felt the Russians needed an "incentive" to restraint arms production, and that serious SALT II talks should go on, looking forward to still further

SALT III disarmament talks. Meanwhile, SALT I, monitored to some extent, held the field, the Carter initiative lying dormant while government agencies determined whether disarmament was progressing at all. Mason Wilrich and J. B. Rhinelander, eds., *SALT* (1974).

SAN FRANCISCO, known as the "Paris of America," famous for its high incidence of vice, and also its receptivity to generous and experimental types, including reformers, among them Fremont Older *(q.v.)*. Still others who gave the city distinction were Edwin Markham, Ambrose Bierce, Jack London and George Sterling, most of them individualists at least as much as reformers. In the 1950's, the city played host to the "Beatniks," *(q.v.)* who involved a reform principle, though not a reform accomplishment. The city continued to offer dramatic leadership in vice, with 1300 bars, and an estimated alcoholic population of one person in ten, and a vigorous peace movement. See also Bridges, Harry. By 1980, the city had become the "homosexual capital of the country," with "gays" a substantial voting population and political force.

"SAND, GEORGE" (1804-1876), pseud. for Amantine L.A. Dudevant, whose emancipated love life and humanitarian fiction influenced reformers and their aspirations, including Margaret Fuller and Walt Whitman *(qq.v.)*. Such novels as *Lélia* (1833) and *Consuelo* (1844) were in the romantic tradition, mixing exaggerated fancies with strong sensibility.

SANDINO, GEN. AUGUSTINO, see Nicaragua.

SANGER, MRS. MARGARET (HIGGINS) (1883-1966), birth control advocate, whose distressing experiences as a nurse caused her to enter into a struggle for the right to disseminate birth control information. She was indicted in 1915 for sending such information through the mail, and arrested the next year for opening a birth-control clinic. She founded the American Birth Control League in 1917, and in 1923, the first permanent clinic. Her lecturing and organizing activities continued for many years, resulting in formidable agencies, associates, and publications. Among her own were *Woman and the New Race* (1920), *Happiness in Marriage* (1926), and *My Fight for Birth Control* (1931).

SANITARY CONDITIONS, a slogan in the fight for better housing and better working conditions. A social critic argues that "Rome grew with sanitation and declined with its decline"; see Reginald Reynolds, *Cleanliness and Godliness* (1946), 5-6. A jest during the Russian Revolution *(q.v.)* told of a workers' committee demanding better toilet facilities and the world revolution. Reformers never went astray who came to grips with the realities of unsanitary conditions, and who publicized their findings.

SANTO DOMINGO, see Dominican Republic.

SARTRE, JEAN PAUL (1905-1980), French philosopher and litterateur, who became a guru *(q.v.)* of the western world. His combination of despair and mystical conjecture enabled him to mix ego with social thinking, which he termed *existentialism* in ways differing from the "existentialism" of other philosophers. He served in the French Resistance of World War II, and afterwards found justifications for communist betrayals which were not available to those more loyal to democratic tenets, but whose plays, fiction, and essays were less influential. Sartre's constant companion, *Simone de Beauvoir*, though sharing his egotistical tenets, was more socially relevant with researches into women and old age; see her *All Men Are Mortal* (1946), and *The Second Sex* (1949). For Sartre's atheistic existentialism, *Being and Nothingness* (1943). See also Max Charlesworth, *The Existentialists and Jean Paul Sartre* (1976).

SASKATCHEWAN, a central province of Canada *(q.v.)*, largely agricultural in interest, and a stronghold of the Co-operative Commonwealth Federation *(q.v.)*, which was of interest to reformers.

SATYAGRAHA, the powerful weapon of passive resistance which Mohandas Gandhi *(q.v.)* developed in order to force the British government to retreat from its policies.

SAVONAROLA, FRA GIROLAMO (1452-1498), Florentine reformer of the Dominican Order, he attacked social corruption, raising forces which helped undermine the Medici, and also denounced Pope Alexander VI. A fanatic whose death at the stake stirred Italian society, his role as reformer has been a matter for controversy.

SCALAWAGS, southern white people who cooperated with Federal troops, freed Negroes, and carpetbaggers *(q.v.)*, as a result of Reconstruction measures *(q.v.)* in the post-Civil War period. The epithet entered into northern idiom as well, as a term of contempt.

SCAPEGOAT, understood, in social reform circles, to refer to groups which are treated as responsible for social ills by elements in society having a stake in hiding problems in social inequality. Although many social groups have been persecuted, to the satisfaction of frustrated dissolute, military, bureaucratic, and other social components, Jews *(q.v.)* have constituted the classic scapegoat, from the Pharaohs of Egypt to Hitler.

SCHENCK *V.* UNITED STATES (1919), involving the constitutionality of the Espionage Act of 1917 *(q.v.)*, notable for one of Justice Holmes's *(q.v.)* famous passages, though he affirmed the judgment against the Socialist defendant. Nevertheless, he underscored that only such an emergency as the current war could excuse the government's violation of the First Amendment *(q.v.)* to the Constitution: "The most stringent protection of free speech would not protect a man in falsely shouting fire in a theatre and causing a panic... The question in every case is whether the words used... are of such a nature as to create a clear and present danger..." Compare Abrams v. United States.

SCHOOL AND SOCIETY (1899), see Dewey, John.

SCHROEDER, THEODORE A. (1864-1953), lawyer and libertarian from Wisconsin, founder of the Free Speech League *(q.v.)*, with Lincoln Steffens and Brand Whitlock *(qq.v.)*. He prided himself on having published more controversial matter than any other polemicist of his generation. Logical in his crusade, he defended the publication of matter deemed obscene, an incitement to riot, or otherwise anti-social. He entered into psychology and became a specialist in evolutionary psychology and psychoanalysis. Schroeder advocated psychoanalysis of judges and teachers to free them of prejudices; see his *Last Will*, published with a memoir in 1958.

SCHURZ, CARL (1829-1906), a refugee from Germany following the defeat of the German Revolution, and a leader of German-Americans. He served as a general for the Union Army during the Civil War and was an editor of the New York *Evening Post*. As Secretary of the Interior under President Rutherford B. Hayes *(q.v.)* he pressed for civil service reform. He was also a leader of the Liberal Republican Party *(q.v.)*.

SCHWIMMER, ROSIKA (1877-1948), outstanding pacifist, born in Budapest, who, during World War I, traveled to various capitals urging peace. In the United States, she won the confidence of Henry Ford *(q.v.)* with the program of getting "the boys out of the trenches by Christmas." He put at the disposal of Mme. Schwimmer, Louis P. Lochner and other pacifists the *Oskar II*, a ship which carried them to Europe, where they were to persuade the war-makers to cease their activities. Ford left them at Christiania, and Mme. Schwimmer found herself attacked as an adventuress. She returned to Hungary, where, during the revolution of 1918, she was appointed ambassador to Switzerland. With the fall of the revolutionary government of Bela Kun, she was warned that she was in danger, and left Hungary. She became a woman without a country. She sought United States citizenship, but, in 1929, was barred from citizenship because she would not swear to bear arms in the country's defense. Brandeis and Holmes *(q.v.)* dissented from the majority verdict.

SCIENTIFIC MANAGEMENT, see "Taylorization".

SCOPES TRIAL (1925), a trial resulting from the passage, in the State Legislature of Tennessee, on March 21, 1925, of a bill making it a misdemeanor, punishable by fine, to teach the theory of evolution in the public schools. A test case was therefore set up, involving a high school instructor of Dayton, Tennessee. It was supported by the American Civil Liberties Union *(q.v.)*, which sent to Dayton as counsel also Clarence Darrow, Dudley Field Malone, and Arthur Garfield Hays *(qq.v.)*. Major counsel opposing Scopes included William Jennings Bryan *(q.v.)*. The trial assumed classic proportions, as arguments favoring and opposing the rights of teachers, as well as the validity of the Darwinian hypothesis, were brought forth. The highpoint of the trial was Darrow's cross-examination of Bryan. Although Scopes was found guilty, the sentence was revoked on a technicality. The William Jennings Bryan University opened its doors in Dayton in 1930. M. L. Settle, *The Scopes Trial* (1972).

SCOTTSBORO CASE (1931), involved the alleged rape of two white girls, "hoboing" out of Alabama and into Tennessee, by nine Negro youths and children, and the effort of the State to sentence the latter to death. The N.A.A.C.P., the I.L.D., the A.C.L.U. *(qq.v.)*, the communists and others rallied national and world opinion to the slogan, "The Scottsboro Boys Shall Not Die." The famous New York lawyer, Samuel Leibowitz, was assigned to the defense. He fought anti-Negro and anti-Semitic prejudice to prevent summary sentences of death from being consummated. In the course of appeals, Ruby Bates, one of the girls, repudiated her earlier testimony. Evidences of connivance and fraud in the prosecution were widely publicized. Although the communist tactics jeopardized the case, the furor which was raised permitted the completion of a deal between the State and the defense whereby the Negroes escaped execution, but were remanded to prison. The most famous of them, Haywood Patterson, escaped and wrote a significant memoir, *Scottsboro Boy* (1950), while in hiding in the north, where he later died. Another notable relic of the event is John Wexley's *They Shall Not Die* (1934). See also the biography of Samuel Leibowitz, by Quentin Reynolds, *Courtroom* (1950). Dan T. Carter, *Scottsboro: a Tragedy of the American South* (1979).

SCRIPPS, E.W. (1854-1926), with William Randolph Hearst and Joseph Pulitzer *(qq.v.)* among the newspaper entrepreneurs of the late nineteenth century who modernized the press and made it an instrument of democratic causes. He organized the first chain of newspapers: a step which helped create a national perspective on social needs. He was a philosopher of human nature and needs and helped clarify journalistic techniques for reaching the masses without condescension. The Scripps-McRae newspaper chain later became the Scripps-Howard chain, and, in the course of affairs lost considerable liberal energies. O. Knight, ed., *I Protest: Selected Disquisitions of E. W. Scripps* (1966).

SEABURY INVESTIGATION (1931-2), the result of charges that corruption was rife in New York, it was instituted under an order by Governor Franklin D. Roosevelt *(q.v.)* and resulted in lurid revelations which helped to overthrow the rule of Tammany Hall in 1933, and to elect the La Guardia *(qq.v.)* administration.

SEAMEN, an element of labor long held in onerous conditions, due to the individualism of sailors and conditions which made it difficult for them to organize. They were humiliated, overworked, and subject to cruel and unusual punishments. Richard Henry Dana, Jr. *(q.v.)* reviewed some of their troubles in *Two Years before the Mast* (1840). The Seamen's Act of 1915, sponsored by Robert M. La Follette *(q.v.)*, put some of the harshest measures outside the law, but lack of organization continued to make the sailor's lot difficult. During the 1930's, longshoremen, especially embittered over discriminatory hiring policies which kept them needy and divided, organized under Joseph Curran on the Atlantic and Gulf coasts, and under Harry Bridges (q.v.) on the Pacific coast. *Waterfront* (1955), a novel by Budd Schulberg, which was popular also in the motion-pictures, though shoddy in texture, reminded the public that all was not wholly resolved in the industry. See also Furuseth, Andrew.

SECESSION, most notably attempted by the Confederate States of America, but considered in several eras, and in the interests of reform as well as anti-reform. Thus, westerners who were suspicious of the good faith and policies of the new Federal government (1788) tolerated the concepts of secession. The Kentucky and Virginia Resolutions (q.v.), if they did not threaten secession, implied defiance of the central government, and the Hartford Resolutions (q.v.) may have implied more; they capped a long discontent with the "Virginia Dynasty" (q.v.). Mayor Fernando Wood's recommendation (1861) that New York City secede from the Union was a pro-slavery move. More hysterical than treasonable were similar proposals by New York scribblers who felt abused by President Ford's (q.v.) reluctance to help the city avoid bankruptcy, and ruminated the pros and cons of leaving the Union. In a gloomy time needing genuine entertainment, the experiment merited serious consideration.

SECOND BANK OF THE UNITED STATES, chartered in 1816 by Congress and subject to its authority, though otherwise enjoying a quasi-independent status. It was the respository for government funds. Nicholas Biddle, who became a director of the Bank in 1819, became its president in 1822. Although the Bank developed an efficient system of currency controls, it roused resentment from debtors who preferred an inflated currency, and jealousy among state bankers. Biddle developed substantial power as one of the country's financial leaders and did not hesitate to support it by building up influence among conservative political figures. Although the Bank's charter did not expire until 1836, he made its recharter an issue in the Presidential election campaign of 1832, when his cause was maintained by the Whig candidate, Henry Clay, running against the incumbent, Andrew Jackson. The result was a resounding defeat for Clay, and Jackson's increased belief that the Bank represented a monopolistic threat to free enterprise. To the extent that conservative opinion closed ranks behind Biddle, and more adventurous and indebted elements approved Jackson's stand, he was correct. His removal in 1833 of the government deposits from the Bank, and their distribution among twenty three "pet" banks stirred national excitement on the issues of policy and Jackson's arrogation of authority. Whether Jackson had halted a malignant monopoly or merely augmented the funds available for Democratic supporters, and whether his strengthening of the power of the Executive had strengthened reform were problems for the social reformer. J. A. Wilburn, *Biddle's Bank* (1967).

"SECOND CLASS CITIZENSHIP," a concept borrowed from the problem of the status of persons living in territories acquired by the United States, most regularly applied to Negroes who have been denied the protection of the laws, as guaranteed by the Constitution, but also applied to any minority group which has suffered discrimination.

SECOND INTERNATIONAL, formed in 1889, at Paris, reorganized from remnants of the First International (q.v.). An International Socialist Bureau, maintained at Brussels, kept the several national affiliates in communication. During World War I, this was drastically curtailed, though informal conferences were held. A Congress in 1917 at Stockholm was attempted, but not fulfilled. At the Conference of Lucerne, 1919, a plan for the renewal of the International was accepted and a Congress met at Geneva in February 1920. The New Labour and Socialist International was organized in 1923,

at Hamburg, but declared a dead letter by the Third International (q.v.), organized in 1919. See James Joll, *The Second International, 1889-1914* (1956).

SECONDARY BOYCOTT, a problem in union tactics. Thus, the unwillingness of the Duplex Printing Press Company, in Battle Creek, Mich., to cooperate with the International Association of Machinists caused them not only to strike the plant, but to refuse to install presses in New York City which had come from the company. The union argued that it had instituted a "sympathetic" strike (q.v.), the company that it had been subjected to a secondary boycott. An injunction ordering the union to desist from this type of strike was upheld by the U.S. Supreme Court in 1921: a decision which qualified the value of the Clayton Act (q.v.) to labor. See also Boycott. The Taft-Hartley Act (q.v.) emphasized the illegality of the secondary boycott. By 1952, fourteen states had prohibited it by specific enactment.

SECRET SOCIETIES, See Patriotic and Political Secret Societies.

SECRET TREATIES, usually disturbing to reformers, as suggesting skulduggery, as well as mistrust of public opinion. President John Tyler's undercover negotiations to acquire Texas incited one U.S. Senator, Benjamin Tappan, of Ohio, to publish documents which the President had submitted to the Senate in confidence in the New York *Post*. The Ostend Manifesto, submitted as a secret memorandum to the U.S. Cabinet, became public and excited anti-imperialist sentiment. The most notorious secret treaties were those which the Allies of World War I had prepared for dividing the anticipated territorial gains. These the Bolsheviks found in the Czarist Archives, following their successful revolution. Published to the world, they embarrassed the Allies as evidence of their gross imperialistic designs.

SECTION SEVEN (A), see National Recovery Administration.

SECTIONALISM AND REFORM have been related when reformers have opposed national policy as harmful or reactionary. Thus, the Kentucky and Virginia Resolutions challenged the Federalist Alien and Sedition Acts (q.v.), and, on the other hand, abolitionists appealed to northern pride and interests in order to turn them against slavery. "No slave-hunting in the old Bay State!" was Wendell Phillips's appeal to one part of the North, and was echoed in one form or another in other states, notably the Western Reserve in Ohio, and in Wisconsin. Troubled western farmers made a sinister symbol of Wall Street, in New York and saw their West as united in its need for justice in the face of railroad depredations. Sections, and even states, continued to influence the nation. Proposition XIII (q.v.) in California caught the mood and attention of the country. The auto industry, centered in Michigan, became one of the nation's barometers of good times and depression. Texas (q.v.) was all but a section in itself.

SECURITIES AND EXCHANGE COMMISSION, created in 1934, as part of the New Deal (q.v.) program, it aimed to curb unfair and fraudulent practices which had resulted in scandals and helped undermine the national economy. It thus, finally, dealt with the problem which the Pujo Committee (q.v.) had exposed. Although the S.E.C. theoretically had the power to control unwarranted speculative pursuits, it was reluctant to interfere with free trading operations. P. Tyler, ed., *Securities, Exchanges, and the SEC* (1965).

SEDITION ACT OF 1798, an enactment of the Federalist Congress and President John Adams (q.v.), directed against the followers of Thomas Jefferson (q.v.); it provided for a maximum penalty of five years' imprisonment and $5,000 fine for publicizing false or malicious statements against the United States government, Congress, or the President. A notable case resulting from it was that of J. Thompson Callender; see also Alien and Sedition Acts.

SEDITION ACT OF 1918, supplementing the Espionage Act of the year before (q.v.); it was a war-time measure which severely restricted freedoms guaranteed under the First Amendment *(q.v.)*. It was especially intended to impede the operations of socialists and others who took principled positions in opposition to the war. Numerous persons were peremptorily arrested and prosecuted under the act; see Berger, Victor L., Debs, Eugene V., Abrams v. United States.

SEDITION TRIAL OF 1944, a governmental effort to prosecute persons variously associated with fascist sympathies and concerns under the Smith Act of 1940 *(q.v.)*. As developed by O. John Rogge, acting for the Department of Justice, the case was thought to have been inadequately prepared. It failed to strike a persuasive equation between the anti-communist and pro-fascist feelings of the defendants, on the one hand, and their varied interests, on the other. The defendants made a major point of their constitutional prerogatives. See Maximilian J. St. George and Lawrence Dennis *(q.v.)*, *A Trial on Trial* (1946).

SEGREGATION, see Desegregation.

SELDES, GEORGE (1890-   ), latter-day muckraker *(q.v.)* concerned himself with the problem of a free press, involving in his analyses forces making for war, anti-labor activities, anti-radical and anti-liberal groups and individuals; among his works were *You Can't Print That* (1929), *Iron, Blood and Profits: an Exposure of the World-Wide Munitions Racket* (1934); *Freedom of the Press* (1935) grew directly out of muckraking materials, brought up-to-date; *Lords of the Press* (1938); *Witch Hunt: the Technique and Profits of Redbaiting* (1940); *Tell the Truth and Run* (1953), contained more consistently autobiographical materials, including his libertarian background. His newsletter, *In Fact,* was one of the more illuminating of such publications of the 1940's and early Fifties. His brother *Gilbert* (1893-1970), was mostly interested in the popular arts *(q.v.)*; his *The Seven Lively Arts* (1924) struck the rich vein of Charles Chaplin, "Krazy Kat," a cartoon, and other phenomena treated as art; *The Stammering Century* (1928) treated reformers and utopians of the nineteenth century with Freudian skepticism; he became a television executive, and author of various rationales for things as they were.

SELF-CRITICISM, a mode of communication and control within the individual communist parties and the parent Third International under Stalin *(qq.v.)*, in the 1930's. Communists were encouraged to admit their ideological "errors," their "deviations" from Marxian truth and the party "line," and to detail such errors at great length and in a total spirit of abasement. The feudal ritual of self-criticism, as practiced directly under Stalin, was parodied in other lands with grim or amusing results, depending on the point of view of the beholder.

"SELF-DETERMINATION OF NATIONS," sometimes known as the "Principle of self-determination," pressed by Woodrow Wilson *(q.v.)*, appeared one calculated to ensure peace. Thus, instead of permitting questions about national sovereignty to be settled by the sword, a peaceful vote could inform the world how a particular people chose to be ruled. Self-determination failed to take into account the fact that many nations could lay claim to the same territories, that propaganda *(q.v.)* could sway multitudes one way or another. In addition, a multiplicity of nations multiplied the number of clashes which multiplied borders rendered possible. Observers, fearful over differences between Czechs and Slovaks, between Slovaks and Hungarians and Poles, between Austrians and Hungarians, and so on, often longed for the great simplicities engrossed, for example, in the old Austro-Hungarian Empire. Hitler *(q.v.)* did not hesitate to appeal to self-determination, for example in "behalf" of the Sudeten Germans, "oppressed" by Czechoslovakia, and "longing" to return to the German "Homeland." The problem became so acute in the following era of de-colonization, with hordes of refugees *(q.v.)* drifting agonizedly about all over the world, as to make the "Self

Determination" slogan a mockery, and obsolete. Rupert Emerson, *Self-Determination Revisited in the era of Decolonization* (1964).

SELF-HELP, a concept in labor important in the history of the building up of trade unions *(q.v.)*. It argued that only workers best understood their needs, and could alone take steps to satisfy them. Thus, it was their duty to join for purposes of clarifying those needs, developing an adequate leadership, and forming associations to minister to particular requirements. Thus, self-help was both altruistic and practical. For a valuable review of the place of self-help in labor developments, see Herbert N. Casson, *Organized Self-Help: a History and Defence of the American Labor Movement* (1901).

SENATE OF THE UNITED STATES, once considered the American equivalent of the British House of Lords, and, as such, the object of reform criticism which reached its climax in David Graham Phillips's *Treason of the Senate* (qq.v.). The passage of the Seventeenth Amendment to the Constitution made it a popular body, elected by general vote, rather than through state assemblies, and thus as liable to produce a McCarthy as it was likely to produce a Kefauver *(qq.v.)*. R. and L. T. Rienow, *Of Snuff, Sin and the Senate* (1965).

SENECA FALLS CONVENTION (1848), historical woman's rights meeting in New York which was attended by Lucretia Mott and Elizabeth Cady Stanton *(qq.v.)*, among others, and which issued a declaration favoring equal treatment for women. It was a hastily organized affair, bringing together a number of people who represented only themselves. In addition, a man chaired the proceedings. More important was the first national woman's convention which was brought together on a call headed by Lucy Stone *(q.v.)* at Worcester, Massachusetts, in 1850: it brought together delegates from the east and west, and featured a woman in the chair. Nevertheless, the Seneca Falls Convention maintains its standing as the pioneer convocation.

SENIOR CITIZENS, a phrase intended to give dignity to older persons and to suggest their usefulness to the community. Senior Citizens centers sprang up in many places in the United States in the post-World War II years; but whether they would become mere recreation centers, or centers for creative thinking about the uses of age and experience remained undetermined. See Old Age; C. C. Osterbind, ed., *Independent Living for Older People* (1972).

"SEPARATE BUT EQUAL" DOCTRINE (1896), enunciated in the case of Plessy v. Ferguson; the U. S. Supreme Court ruled that segregated railroad facilities were not an infringement of the Fourteenth Amendment to the Constitution *(q.v.)*, so long as equal facilities were provided. This dictum was overthrown by the historical decision of Brown v. Board of Education of Topeka (1954) which ruled that separate facilities were "inherently unequal." The U. S. Court followed this with a separate ruling that equal conditions must be established "with all deliberate speed." The N.A.A.C.P. *(q.v.)* then undertook a campaign intended to force desegregation, especially in the schools: a campaign which quickly expanded in many directions. See Desegregation.

SEPARATION OF CHURCH AND STATE, see Church and State.

SEPARATISTS, see Puritanism.

SEQUOYA (1770?-1843), tribal name of George Gest, Cherokee half-breed, who invented the Cherokee alphabet, a major step toward civilizing them; a leader of his people, and a notable figure among all Indian statesmen and creative geniuses. See Cherokee Indians.

"SERGEANT YORK," see York, Alvin C.

SERVITUDE, see Indentured Servitude.

SETTLEMENT HOUSE MOVEMENT, THE, a development of the late nineteenth century, it inspired social workers and reformers. Hull House, opened in 1889 by Jane Addams (q.v.) pioneered in the field, offering dedicated workers eager to understand the problems of bewildered and needy immigrants among whom they found themselves in Chicago, offering them instruction, counsel, a place to meet, a haven for their children. In addition, Hull House attracted men and women interested to study and observe the conditions in the neighborhood, who went out to write and report, to influence social legislation, and to set up settlements of their own in other cities. Also a source of original experiments and dynamic leadership was the Henry Street Settlement, set up by Lillian D. Wald (q.v.). The settlement reached its apogee of energy and usefulness in the pre-World War I period, afterwards becoming defined as a useful type of agency which attracted efficient, but not especially notable administrators, who provided opportunities for artistically inclined youth, and a variety of educational services which supplemented the work of playgrounds and neighborhood houses. An unfortunate development, derived from the demeaning impulse toward Progressives (q.v.) was the scorn of pioneer settlement workers as having been Anglo-Saxon in heritage, and therefore indirectly "patronizing" of immigrants by having helped them adjust to American conditions, for example by teaching them English. It is not clear what a reasonable alternative would have been, or whether the pro-"ethnic" critics gave any time at all to immigrants; the great settlement pioneers had given their lives to them; see Sam Bass Warner, Jr.'s strange preface to Robert A. Woods's and Albert J. Kennedy's pioneer work, drafted earlier, *The Zone of Emergence: Observations of the Lower Middle and Upper Working Class Communities of Boston 1905-1914* (1962). See also R. A. Woods and A. J. Kennedy, *Settlement Houses: a National Estimate* (1970); J. A. Trolander, *Settlement Houses and the Great Depression* (1975); A. F. Davis, *Spearheads for Reform* (1967).

SEVENTEENTH AMENDMENT (1913), see Senate of the United States.

SEVENTH OF MARCH SPEECH (1850), see Compromise of 1850, Webster, Daniel.

SEWALL, SAMUEL (1652-1730), a Boston jurist who, though notorious for his connection with the Salem witchcraft trials (q.v.) (which he later repented), was early opposed to slavery, and favored good relations with the Indians. See his *The Selling of Joseph* (1700); *A Memorial Relating to the Kennebeck Indians* (1721). His diary is a piece of valuable Americana.

SEWARD, WILLIAM HENRY (1801-1872), American lawyer and statesman, whose combination of issues and political needs gave him associations in reform. As a lawyer, he developed the plea of insanity to prevent capital punishment (q.v.). He opposed imprisonment for debt, and approved Andrew Jackson's stand on nullification (q.v.). His opposition to Masonry (q.v.), however, was largely political. Elected governor of New York, in 1838, he was a firm Whig with a keen sense of public opinion. By 1848, when he entered the U. S. Senate, he had a good deal of approval among anti-slavery forces, and also strong influence on President-elect Zachary Taylor, a southern slave-holder. Seward found himself a spokesman of the non-slavery North, and, as such felt free to denounce the Fugitive Slave Act (q.v.) and declare that there was a "Higher Law" than the Constitution: a phrase which had an astounding success in the North, and seemed to conservatives to be an invitation to lawlessness. Seward had no radical intentions; nor had he any when, in 1858, he asserted that there was an "irrepressible conflict" between North and South. These political assertions cost Seward the Republican nomination in 1860, the party managers preferring the apparently more conservative Abraham Lincoln (q.v.). G. M. Van Deusen, *William Henry Seward* (1967).

SEX, traditionally more democratic in America than elsewhere, women having shared responsibilities on the frontier (q.v.) and in settled places. They shared with men work, politics, and influence progressively augmented from Abigail Adams and Ann Royall (q.v.) to editors of *Ms* magazine. From Lucy

Stone's demand for the suffrage and for retaining her birth name to Charlotte Gilman's and Rheta Childe Dorr's hunger for independence and public careers, Progressive campaigns differed in kind from Victoria Woodull's (qq.v.) tattered crusade for (as she said) disposing of her sexual parts as she preferred. Margaret Sanger's (q.v.) plea for birth control emphasized women hampered and harmed by ignorance of means for restricting conception. Communist females of the 1930s underscored their commitment to dogma, rather than to sex; women and men broke over differences between Stalin and Trotsky (qq.v.). A more "sexual" line ran from Flappers of the 1920s to the drug and sex "Beats" of the 1950s and the "Hippies' 1960s, and such blunt topics for technical discussion as the role of the orgasm in males and females. "Adult" books and movies won prestige, overlapping into the "family (q.v.) programs" of television (q.v.). Although "femininity" sought to stay abreast of simple lust, it fought social confusion. In 1980 the Pope, John Paul II, denounced lust when directed at wives, beginning a world-wide debate over its meaning. The columnist and sociologist Joseph Sobran upset readers by declaring he did not wish to "see" more of a current "sex symbol," Bo Derek, believing that the "flesh peddlers" sought to "legitimize assaults on decency." See also Women, Abortion, Pill, The, Family. B. J. Sadock, et al., *The Sexual Experience* (1976); Fraser Harrison, *The Dark Angel: Aspects of Victorian Sexuality* (1977); E. Adelson, ed., *Sexuality and Psychoanalysis* (1975); Frank Beach, ed., *Human Sexuality in Four Perspectives* (1976); Thomas Szasz, *Psychiatric Slavery* (1977).

SHAFTESBURY, EARL OF (1801-1885), Lord Ashley until 1851, one of the greatest English philanthropists of the nineteenth century; his work constituted a one-man attack on the evils of the factory system. Like William Wilberforce (q.v.), he was an Evangelical Christian, but closer to the conditions he wished to reform. His major work lay in opposing poverty and slums, child labor and the hardships which attended female employment. In 1847, he achieved the Ten Hours Bill, a landmark in British factory legislation, and he wiped out the institution of "climbing boys," whose task was to clean out chimneys. He abandoned his own class to join in the fight to repeal the Corn Laws (q.v.). He sponsored the famous "Stafford House Address," signed by thousands of Englishwomen, and directed at American women, pleading with them to do something for the slave: an address which stirred much indignation in the South. G. Battiscombe, *Shaftesbury* (1975).

SHAKERS, an offshoot of the Quakers (q.v.) in the eighteenth century, "Mother" Ann Lee, their leader, who came to America in 1774, developed tenets of regeneration, the most famous of which was celibacy. The Shaker communities were very well organized, removed from ordinary worldly concerns, communitarian so far as property-holding was concerned, and productive of zestful living. The celibacy which appalled unthinking observers was no more than the obverse of the "free love" practiced by the Oneida Community (q.v.); the purpose of both types of community was to attain a sense of contact with divinity. The Shaker dances, spirituals, and furniture were too manifestly basic in nature and creative to prove that non-sexual living had withered the psyches of the sectarians. Their continuity into the twentieth century, without natural reproduction, was proof that they satisfied the needs of part of the overall society; see Edward D. Andrews, *The People Called Shakers* (1953).

SHAKESPEARE PRODUCTIONS have often included anti-reform elements, even though their producers might have considered themselves progressives or more. Thus, whatever the content of Shakespeare's plays, and their royalist assumptions, it is difficult to believe that those of humble birth who paid to attend his plays did so to be insulted. Yet in modern versions, the mobs of *Coriolanus,* and respectable craftsmen in *A Midsummer Night's Dream,* have been portrayed not merely as slow of mind, or intemperate, but as apparently epileptic and idiotic. It has been assumed, and with some justice, that democratic audiences would be amused by such portrayals, as they imagined the nobility which attended Shakespeare's plays originally did; for Shakespeare's attitude toward the working classes, see, also, Crosby, Ernest H.

SHAME OF THE CITIES, THE (1904), by Lincoln Steffens (*q.v.*), a key work in the literature of the muckrakers (*q.v.*), it exposed the relationships of political machines not only with organized crime, but with "respectable" businessmen and other pillars of the community. The originality in Steffens's work lay in his discovering patterns of corruption which were the same in different communities, whatever differences there might be in details. Thus, an individual concerned for Minneapolis, or St. Louis, or Chicago, or Philadelphia ("Corrupt and Content") could explore the dark recesses of the political alliances in his town with some idea of what he would find, and with some information about how other reformers had dealt with that situation elsewhere. For qualifying details respecting *Shame of the Cities*, see Steffens's *Autobiography* (1931), and *Letters* (1938).

SHARE CROPPER, see Tenant Farmer.

"SHARE-OUR-WEALTH" MOVEMENT, a grass-root effort projected by Huey P. Long (*q.v.*) which promised a five thousand dollar minimum income to every family. Following Long's assassination, the "Share-our-Wealth" clubs fell into the control of the militant reactionary, Gerald L. K. Smith. He took advantage of the general similarity of purposes implied in their programs to organize relationships with Francis E. Townsend and Father Coughlin (qq.v.). Their joint efforts created William Lemke's (*q.v.*) candidacy for President in 1936. Smith lacked the organizational ability to sustain his movement.

SHAW, ALBERT (1857-1947), a genteel (*q.v.*) student of municipal affairs, rather than a reformer; his studies, however, pioneered the way for such writings. Among his most useful works were *Icaria* (*q.v.*)—a *Chapter in the History of Communism* (1884); *Municipal Government of Great Britain* (1894); *The Outlook for the Average Man* (1907).

SHAW, ANNA HOWARD (1847-1919), one of the leaders of the last drive to attain woman suffrage, she was English-born, became a minister and a medical practitioner, and, having been inspired by Susan B. Anthony (*q.v.*), she became a fighter for woman's rights, rising to the presidency of the National American Woman Suffrage Association (1904-15). She was one of the movement's best orators; see her *The Story of a Pioneer* (1915).

SHAW, GEORGE BERNARD (1856-1950), one of the most notable of all literary proponents of social reform, he held that the only crime was poverty. Early influenced by Marxian analyses of capitalist society, he became one of the theoreticians of Fabianism (q.v.). He began as a literary man and wrote a series of novels, of which the most relevant to social reform was *An Unsocial Socialist*. He became a well-known art, dramatic, and music critic. His resourcefulness was shown in popularizing his initials, "G.B.S.," which happened to be the name of a popular whisky. Nevertheless, his plays appeared in print before they could reach the stage. *Widowers' Houses*, concerned for landlords and slums, *Mrs. Warren's Profession*, the profession being prostitution, and *Arms and the Man*, regarding war without respect, were included in *Plays Pleasant and Unpleasant* (1898), and ultimately broke through conventional expectations to become a public force. The famous prefaces, some longer than the plays, carried social messages with wit, sting, and data. The plays varied from those which emphasized situations to those which emphasized character, as in the case of the famous *Candida*. His prose included *The Quintessence of Ibsenism* (1891) and *The Intelligent Woman's Guide to Socialism* (1928), among a steady stream of letters, articles, debates, and comment on contemporary affairs, much of which was published in one form or another. Although revolutionaries professed impatience with his work, his views of western policy and of the U.S.S.R. were

exploited by them whenever they comported with their own. The literature by and about Shaw is one of the largest of his time which is concerned for the relationship between art and society.

SHAYS'S REBELLION (1786-7), an incident on the road to organization of a Federal union. It resulted from disappointment with the results of the recent Revolution, depressed economic conditions, foreclosures on property due to inability to pay taxes, the imprisonment for debt (*q.v.*) of formerly substantial farmers, the conservatism of the Massachusetts government, among other complaints. There were actions throughout the state, but unrest was particularly acute in the western part of the state. Captain Daniel Shays, who had an excellent record in the Revolution, led an angry multitude to Springfield to prevent the convening of court. Similar actions took place at Northampton and Worcester, among other places. Shays's followers decided to implement their strength with weapons and proposed to capture the arsenal in Springfield. Met by state militia, the rebels were put to flight. Although heavy penalties were threatened, the general leadership, and later even the ringleaders were ultimately pardoned. Shays's Rebellion was considered an argument proving the ineffectuality of government under the Articles of Confederation (*q.v.*). The Rebellion was the subject of Edward Bellamy's (*q.v.*) *The Duke of Stockbridge* (1900).

SHERMAN ANTI-TRUST ACT (1890), the result of twenty years of resentment and fear that big business might grow to proportions which could not be controlled: an invisible government which would destroy the meaning of freedom in the United States. That the Republican Party should have been the instrument ʌor formulating the Act was a measure of the wide-spread nature of this fear. The act stipulated that combinations in the form of a trust "or otherwise," acting in restraint of interstate commerce, were illegal. The trust action against E. C. Knight Company, the sugar refining trust, failed before the U.S. Supreme Court; the Court was unable to perceive a monopoly, or restraint of trade. It saw it clearly in the operations of the American Railway Union, and permitted Eugene V. Debs (*q.v.*) to go to prison. Organized labor was acutely upset that it should have been singled out as liable under the Sherman Act. But some twenty years passed before the Clayton Act (*q.v.*) sought to remedy this situation. See also Monopoly, Anti-Monopoly.

SHIRTS, see Red Shirts, Black Shirts, Descamisados, Fascism and Reform.

SILENT MAJORITY, THE, invoked by Richard M. Nixon (*q.v.*) in a 1969 speech as the vital element in the nation, sometimes outshouted by transient opportunists. However, "it" tired of Watergate (*q.v.*) and abandoned him. He knew it also as the "Heartland." See Grassroots. Independent Voter.

SILENT SOUTH, THE (1885), see Cable, George W.

SILVER ISSUE, THE, major panacea (*q.v.*, for this and following references) of the post-Civil War period. As a result of the resumption of specie payment, which deprived greenbacks of much of their power to provide a cheap currency for more ready payment of debts, and because the "Crime of '73" had demonetized silver, farmers seized on it as a political issue. If they could force silver into association with gold, silver would cease to fall in value, as it was doing on the open market, and it would curb the price of gold. This program for making money more readily available created common ground for harassed farmers and for the silver kings of the west. Although this program struck conservatives as interference with "natural processes," and socialistic, the farmers, not to say the miners, were far from socialists. They merely sought a means which would protect them from monopolies while continuing the competitive free enterprise system. The unwillingness of the Republicans to honor this demand, drove members of the Grand Army of the Republic into the Democratic Party. The Bland-

Allison Act of 1878 required that the government purchase at least two million dollars worth of silver each month, but since it was purchased at the market price, which was lower than the sixteen to one ratio the farmers demanded, such purchases did not affect the price of silver. Agitation finally produced the Sherman Silver Purchase Act—a Republican measure; to an extent, a corrupt bargain, since the silver advocates conceded, in exchange, the protectionist McKinley Tariff—an Act which provided for almost all the silver mined in the country; however, since the government was to purchase it at market prices, the measure continued to frustrate the demands of the silverites. Their feelings were aggravated by its repeal in 1893. The Democratic Platform of 1896, Populist-inspired, asked "the free and unlimited coinage of both silver and gold at the present legal ratio of 16 to 1": a demand which drove conservatives out of the Party during the election, though it attracted a few Silver Republicans. An indication of the feeling of the time on the issue is provided by the phenomenon of *Coin's Financial School* (1894), by William H. Harvey, which circulated in the hundreds of thousands; numerous people believed there was such a school, where the "principles" of the silver issue were taught. Gold was associated with evil, miserliness, and other emotional concepts. It is difficult to be sure what might have been the result of a victory by William Jennings Bryan, so far as the silver-gold controversy is concerned. Certainly, the victory of Bryan would have precipitated a reform era. The defeat of Bryan was a mortal defeat for silver. The return of prosperity, following the long depression begun in 1893, the discoveries of gold, in the Yukon and elsewhere, and the Spanish-American War, all these contributed to diminishing the silver panacea; it exercised what remained of its strength in the election of 1900, when once more it went down to final defeat. A. B. Hepburn, *The History of Coinage and Currency in the United States* (1903); James L. Laughlin, *The History of Bimetallism in the United States* (1897).

SIMONS, ALGIE M. (1870-1950), a founder of the Socialist Party, an editor of socialist papers, and author of such books as *The American Farmer* (1902), and books on the class struggle in American life and history which went into a number of editions. He enlisted whole-heartedly in World War I, breaking with the socialists, whom he vilified. Afterwards, he wrote *The Vision for Which We Fought* (1919). Later productions were *Personnel Relations in Industry* (1921) and *Production Management* (1922).

SIMPSON, JERRY (1842-1905), Kansas Populist statesman who was swept into politics during the crash which came in 1883. The Farmers Alliance (q.v.) organized desperate farmers faced with bankruptcy, and, in 1890, the People's Party elected Simpson to Congress. Unsuccessful campaigns for state legislature had given him a varied and vigorous style of speaking. A statement intended to say that he did not wear silk stockings was twisted to mean that he wore none at all, and gave him the immortal name of "Sockless Jerry." He was elected to Congress again in 1894, but lost two years later. While in Congress, he preached Populism, the Single Tax, and free silver (qq.v.). He later published *Jerry Simpson's Bayonet* (1899-1900).

SIN AND SOCIETY (1907), by Edward A. Ross, published in the midst of the exposes of the muckrakers (q.v.), who denounced individual corruption, argued that sin was now difficult to isolate: that the rise of the corporations had created a species of corporate sin; the individual was a mere, and often an innocent, element in something much larger than himself. The problem of individual responsibility grew still more complicated, involving the individual who pressed a button which released death upon numerous persons he did not see, scientists who contributed to dangerous purposes of which they were not even often aware, citizens who were inactive in civic affairs which they were unable to fathom.

SINCLAIR, UPTON (1878-1968), outstanding reform writer,

his southern progenitors helped give him an undimmed view of the confused nature of northern life, the hectic poverty of his youth a sense of inequality. He aspired to be a poet; *The Journal of Arthur Stirling* (1903), professing to be the writing of a poet of genius who committed suicide gave Sinclair his first success. *The Jungle* (1906) was one of the famous novels of the twentieth century: a vivid account of tragedy and brutality in Packingtown (q.v.), it stirred pity, but even more, fright, for it depicted shockingly unsanitary conditions of meat preparation in the Chicago stockyards. It was the largest single factor in securing passage of the Meat Inspection Act of that year. With his financial gains, Sinclair sponsored Helicon Hall, a cooperative colony in New Jersey which, however, was destroyed by fire. *The Industrial Republic* (1907) described the coming social democracy. *The Money-Changers* (1908) muckraked (q.v.) financial tycoons. *The Fasting Cure* (1911) added a facet to his views of healthful living. *The Cry for Justice* (1915) was a valuable anthology. He was one of the socialists who supported American intervention in World War I, a step he later regretted. He produced a number of muckraking analyses of American life: *The Profits of Religion* (1918), *The Brass Check* (1919), a study of American journalism, and *The Goose-step* (1923) and *The Goslings* (1924), studies in education, as well as *Mammonart* (1925) and *Money Writes!* (1927) which saw art as serving money or humanity. Among other of his accomplishments were helping to organize the Intercollegiate Socialist Society, (in 1905) (q.v.) and *Singing Jailbirds* (1924), a notable expressionistic drama. *Upton Sinclair Presents William Fox* (1933) threw revealing light on the chicanery which attended Hollywood (q.v.) affairs. In 1934, his End Poverty in California (EPIC) Party frightened both Democratic and Republican Parties by threatening to give him the governorship of the state. Sinclair was an uncompromising prohibitionist, credited mental telepathy, and had other views and attitudes which complicated his work and associations. His Lanny Budd series of novels (1940 ff.) were best-sellers which reminded some readers of his pulp-paper novels, written in youth, and on a more sophisticated and knowledgeable level, but one of them was granted the Pulitzer prize.

SINGLE TAX, THE, see George, Henry.

SINGLES, a concept of the 1970s said by some to constitute a pattern for the 1980s as well, of divorced or unmarried persons, with the potential or reality of children and problems formerly shared by the nuclear family (q.v.). Maswick and Bane, *The Nation's Families, 1960-1990* (1980) predicted many varieties of household, with males and females operating according to individual will or necessity. "Palimony" couples—long time male-female "pals"—established essentially married conditions, or sought to establish them in the courts, when money was involved, with mixed judicial results.

SIT-DOWN STRIKES developed rapidly as a method of industrial warfare during 1936 due to the new courage given the workers by the passage of the Wagner Act (q.v.) and the unwillingness of employers to honor its provisions. The sitdown took various forms: work-stoppage for a few moments or a few hours till a dispute was settled; stoppage by a group of workers which developed into a general walk-out; a sit-down resulting in the workers being ejected from the plant, thus causing a lock-out; a procedure in which employees reported for work each day, but performed no services; and a stay-in strike, when they did not leave for home at all. The sit-down resulted in a sweep of successful strikes, from which the C.I.O. (q.v.) particularly profited. In 1937, it fell into disuse, because local courts treated it with sharp disapproval, and because union leaders themselves feared that it played too easily into the hands of adventurers; the United Automobile Workers of America threatened to punish members who resorted to it. S. Fine, *Sit-Down: the General Motors Strike of 1936-1937* (1969).

"SIT-INS," a major technique for protesting segregation of

Negroes, especially in such public services as department stores, restaurants, train stations and bus terminals. C.O.R.E. (q.v.) was the most active force in organizing Negro and white enthusiasts in the work of creating situations within the limitation of non-violent action. It filled prisons with singing protestants, in a fashion reminiscent of the Wobblies (q.v.). It was significant that the movement should have been most active in the South, rather than the relatively more "emancipated" North, but one which practiced segregation on a wide scale. In 1961, the results of the movement were obscure, C.O.R.E. and its supporters being in some practical difficulties, in terms of finances and adequate publicity. For an interim report, see *A Survey of the Southern Student Sit-In Movement and Nationwide Student Activity*, printed for the U.S. National Student Association for the National Student Conference on the Sit-In Movement, April 22 and 23 (1960). See also, Integration, Education and the Negro, King, Martin Luther, Negro Mobility.

SIX-HOUR DAY, deemed by labor a further advance in the destiny of its constituency, and an answer to the challenge of automation (q.v.). The uses of leisure (q.v.) under such circumstances has been controversial. Whether the United States could cope with the challenge of the U.S.S.R., and attain "New Frontiers" (q.v.), utilizing a six-hour work day, has brought different answers from labor and industrial spokesmen.

SIXTEEN-HOUR WORK DAY, see Eight-Hour Day.

SIXTEENTH AMENDMENT (1913), see Taxation.

SKIDMORE, THOMAS (d. 1832), a mechanic and an early New York radical who was far in advance in his views of the rights of men. In 1829, in alliance with Frances Wright and Robert D. Owen (qq.v.), he spoke for the wage-earners in the Working Men's Party, which was largely led by skilled "workers" who were in fact labor entrepreneurs. Skidmore propagandized boldly for the redistribution of wealth. Although the Party did well in the elections of that year, it was unwilling to follow his lead. His Poor Man's Party and his newspaper, *Friend of Equal Rights*, equally failed to attract supporters. *The Rights of Man to Property, Being a Proposition to Make It Equal among the Adults of the Present Generation* (1829) was his unappreciated monument. See also "Agrarian Democracy."

SKILLED WORKERS, one of the natural divisions among workers, also including semi-skilled workers and unskilled workers; such divisions kept to a minimum the possible unity in labor ranks, and accounted for the "craft union" nature of the labor movement. In effect, the worker's skill represented his capital, which he was unwilling to share with workers of lesser status. Only the exigencies of circumstances in the industrial plant, where the machines represented maximum efficiency, requiring a minimum knowledge on the part of the "skilled worker," and the need for powerful organization, forced the creation of the industrial union (q.v.).

SKOKIE (Illinois), an incident of 1978, American-style "Nazis" seeking to attract public attention by marching through a section of town inhabited by Jewish people, some survivors of European persecution. Though protested as an incitement to riot, the American Civil Liberties Union (q.v.), the head of which was of Jewish birth, created a sensation by declaring the Nazi march legal, if deplorable. The Union lost substantial membership by this statement of principles, but gained some prestige. An example of public-private feeling overcoming technical "rights."

SLAVE LABOR, a concept identified with post-World II communism, though also employed in mass quantities in Nazi Germany, in Africa colonies, and elsewhere. The system, devised in communist Russia differed from the others in being better systematized and with emotional factors of humanitarianism or vengefulness kept at a minimum. In 1951, the United Nations Economic and Social Council set up a commission to investigate forced labor. It had been pressed to this step, despite protests from the Soviet Union and the communist governments of Poland and Czechoslavakia, by the International Confederation of Free Trade Unions, which, in 1952 issued a report on *Stalin's Slave Camps: an Indictment of Modern Slavery*. In 1960, a North Atlantic Treaty publication estimated that there were still an estimated million persons in forced labor camps in the Soviet Union. The report continued that there were three types of camps: "strict" ones of the slave labor stamp; "normal" camps, where they received adequate treatment, and "mild" camps, where prisoners could be visited. Nevertheless, Solzhenitzyn's (q.v.) *The Gulag Archipelago* stunned the West with its "revelations" of communist tyranny.

SLAVE REVOLTS, a significant topic in the consideration of the weight and meaning of the slave system in the South. Were the slaves docile and as a whole willing to accept their status and content themselves with various situations in a hierarchy of house and field hands? Herbert Aptheker, *American Negro Slave Revolts* (1943), the work of an American communist, denies this, and offers the evidence of research to portray Negroes as rebellious under slavery. Efforts such as those by Denmark Vesey and Nat Turner (q.v.) are cited to reveal Negroes as irrepressible in their search for freedom, worthy of claiming kinship with a Toussaint L'Ouverture (q.v.).

SLAVE TRADE, an aspect of slavery (q.v.) with features of its own. Thus, northern ships brought the bulk of the Negro slaves to America, and continued to do so, even while northern states were taking pride in having ended slavery. Southern slaveholders were willing to stop the foreign slave-trade, especially when they had slaves of their own to breed and sell, and received competition from imported slaves. Some opposed "protectionism" in slaves, on the grounds that slave-restrictions reflected on what they insisted was a wholesome traffic. Nevertheless, the congressional debate to end the foreign slave trade concluded in victory for the abolitionists, and it became illegal in 1808. Nevertheless, too, the African slave trade quietly continued, outside the law, Yankee shippers bringing in cargoes as of yore. The Federal government developed no energetic policy to extirpate it. In the 1850's, southern fire-eaters agitated for "free trade" in slaves. P. S. Foner, *Business and Slavery* (1941); G. F. Dow, *Slave Ships and Slaving* (1927); W. S. Howard, *American Slavers and the Federal Law* (1963); D. P. Mannix, *Black Cargoes* (1962); F. Bancroft, *Slave Trading in the Old South* (1931).

SLAVERY technically refers to the ownership of human beings as property. In practice, it involved gradations of property rights and prerogatives, which depended on the times and circumstances. Thus, indentured servitude (q.v.) had the force of slavery, the servant having few rights beyond the terms of his contract. The first Negroes, brought to America in 1619, differed little (aside from the stigma of color) from indentured servants. There were no laws binding them to slavery, and not a few were freed and amalgamated through marriage into white society. Not until the 1660's were laws first instituted which defined slaves and restrained them in their opportunities. Slavery seemed no hardy labor system. With one Negro in four free, and no threat to white supremacy posed, many Americans imagined slavery would die out due to its inadequacy. In Pennsylvania, the success of indentured servitude has been held responsible for the weakness of slavery and its abolition, undertaken in 1780. The increasing number of laborers with few rights and little social status or security created, in pre-Civil War decades, the concept of "white slavery," it being argued by such a partisan as George Henry Evans (q.v.) that the plantation slave was in better circumstances than the white toiler. Abraham Lincoln's (q.v.) Emancipation Proclamation (1863) was a war measure intended not so much to free the slaves as to demoralize the Confederacy. It freed slaves only where

Federal troops were not in control to enforce the order, and specifically ruled out of the terms of emancipation all slave areas where Federal troops were present, in Louisiana, Virginia, and the Border States. Slavery was legally ended by the Thirteenth Amendment to the Constitution (1865). Social, economic, and constitutional questions continued to involve "wage slavery" of post-Civil War years, Negro, Puerto Rican, and other civil rights, and suffrage *(qq.v.)*. Slavery continued as a world problem, under its own or other names, in Arab countries, in Africa, in Yucatan, in South America. The International Labor Organization in 1980 estimated 50 million *child* slaves alone in the world, notoriously in India *(qq.v.)*. The 105 year old British Anti-Slavery Society was almost alone in its persistent monitoring of the problem. M. I. Finley, *Ancient Slavery and Modern Ideology* (1980); Louis Filler, *The Rise and Fall of Slavery in America* (1981).

SLAVES, WAR OF THE, refers to three uprisings against Rome. The first revolt took place 135-133 B.C., and was led by the Syrian Tussus, the second occurred 105-102 B.C. Both arose in Sicily. A million slaves are said to have been destroyed in these efforts. The more famous uprising, that under Spartacus *(q.v.)* continued from 73 to 71 B.C. and involved most of Italy. It became a symbol for all uprisings of suppressed classes.

S.L.P., see Socialist Labor Party.

SLUMS, see Housing Problem, The.

SLURS, a means of expressing personal, local, sectional, racial, or national attitudes in ways derogatory to others. Slurs are often taken as a front-line of offense by social reformers, who hold that to pass over slurs is to encourage their use. Whether jokes which employ dialect and stereotyped characteristics (the beer-drinking German, the phlegmatic American Indian) are necessarily harmful to social and international relations can be argued; see A.A. Roback, *A Dictionary of International Slurs* (1944), see especially its essay on "Aspects of Ethnic Prejudice"; see also Prejudice, Epithets.

SMALL BUSINESS, once a reform cause, contrasted with "monster" business; to curb it, the Sherman Anti-Trust Act *(q.v.)* was passed. Thanks to government and U.S. Supreme Court policy, it was found difficult to enforce with respect to industry; it was first used effectively against organized labor, in the Pullman Strike *(q.v.)*. The aim became, rather to regulate big business in the public interest, as through the Federal Trade Commission. William Jennings Bryan, in his "Cross of Gold" *(qq.v.)* speech, had praised a "broader class of business men," which included "the merchant at the cross-roads store," but Americans wanted the results of mass-production, and received it gladly in the 1920's. The N.R.A. *(q.v.)* was mainly intended to work through big business, and probably aided it during the economic depression of the 1930's more than it did small business. By then, much of small business was composed of service personnel, dispensing already manufactured and packaged articles. During World War II, a Smaller War Plants Corporation was operated by the government, in order to mobilize as much production as possible, and after the war a Small Business Administration presumably functioned in the interests of small business. Major contracts were dispensed by the government to major corporations, which sublet them to their small business satellites. Arthur E. Morgan *(q.v.)* made efforts to forge a philosophy for upbuilding small business in the interests of a healthy and balanced economy. However, the potential of small business as a lever for reform seemed small. S. W. Bruchey, ed., *Small Business in American Life* (1980); Center for Environmental Studies [London], *The Job Generation Process in Britain* (1980); E. F. Schumacher, *Small Is Beautiful* (1973); and Schumacher, *Good Work* (1980).

SMALL NATIONS, see Assembly of Captive European Nations.

SMITH, ALFRED E. (1873-1944), the "Abraham Lincoln of the Tenements," a poor New York boy who worked his way up through the Tammany organization to become governor of New York, and Democratic Party candidate for President in 1928. He had a generally "liberal" outlook, favoring welfare legislation for workers, and votes for women; after 1920, he favored repeal of prohibition. In a year of deep social regression, he seemed to old progressives a promise of better times; see Norman Hapgood *(q.v.)* and Henry Moskowitz, *Up from the City Streets* (1927), a campaign biography of Smith. A powerful campaign of bigotry *(q.v.)*, aimed at the fact that he was a Roman Catholic, contributed to his drastic defeat at the polls. "Al" Smith's liberalism was thin. In the 1930's, he adhered to the Liberty League *(q.v.)*.

SMITH, GERRIT (1797-1874), New York philanthropist and reformer. He deeply concerned himself for colonization, abolition, temperance, and other moral causes. A notable deed was his gift of a large tract of land in New York State to settlers whom a group he appointed judged to be deserving. Smith ran for President on a fractional abolitionist platform, and served a term in the House of Representatives. He helped subsidize John Brown's *(q.v.)* plots, and suffered temporary insanity following the Harpers Ferry affair; see *Speeches of Gerrit Smith in Congress* (1855).

SMITH, LILLIAN (1897-1966), a teacher who was born in Florida, taught in Virginia and in China, and took up residence in Georgia. A manifest "lady," she was not open to insults possible toward some types of person who defied southern attitudes. Her *Strange Fruit* (1944), a novel which boldly challenged segregationist attitudes, was a phenomenal best-seller. *Killers of the Dream* (1949), a non-fictional writing, appealed for humane and equalitarian treatment of the Negroes. Whether her writings influenced southern opinions, and whether they represented the views of any substantial body of citizens were moot questions. She was a member of the national board of the American Civil Liberties Union *(q.v.)*. L. Blackwell and F. Clay, *Lillian Smith* (1971).

SMITH ACT (1940), otherwise known as the Alien Registration Act, was intended to check subversive activities in the United States. Although it was principally intended to curb communist activities, it was employed in a major attempt to strike at fascists and fascist sympathizers, in the sedition trial of 1944 *(q.v.)*. In 1949, it was invoked in a major effort to undermine the communist party. Eleven of its leaders were tried and convicted, and sentenced to prison, the first of a number of such group trials. See also McCarran Act.

SOCIAL CREDIT, a reform program undertaken in Alberta, Canada, which promised every adult citizen of the Province twenty-five dollars a month, the money to be gained from a tax of about ten percent on domestic goods. The depression of the 1930's won support, and the Social Credit Party was swept into office in 1935. However, legal duels prevented full experimentation for the program, and though the party remained in power it was on the basis of general welfare legislation. J. A. Irving, *The Social Credit Movement in Alberta* (1959).

SOCIAL DARWINISM, the creation of Herbert Spencer, a large-scaled effort to apply Darwinism *(q.v.)* to society; essentially an analogy which pretended to be science. Spencer assumed that because animals engaged in a struggle for existence, societies needed to do so as well. He saw the Anglo-Saxon civilization as a superior development out of previous civilizations, and the result of competition. He reversed himself from earlier, more generous views of the human potential, to put his trust in progress in the law of the jungle, and to become an unequivocal foe of the state, whose interposition might aid the weak at the expense of the strong. His "synthetic" philosophy attempted to synthesize all knowledge, including the "Unknowable," in a series of volumes which were inordinately popular in the United States, which seemed an outstanding example of free enterprise and competition, and where major proponents of

Social Darwinism included E. L. Youmans and William Graham Sumner (*qq.v.*). Social Darwinism, like Darwinism, inspired pessimism based on doubts of human capacity to control its less amiable qualities. It inspired such refutations as that by Prince Peter Kropotkin (*q.v.*), who emphasized the cooperative qualities of nature, rather than its combativeness. It also inspired reformist optimism; David Graham Phillips (*q.v.*) argued that man was not a fallen angel, but a rising animal. See also *Jukes, The.* Brian Tierney et al., *Social Darwinism: Law of Nature or Justification for Repression?* (1977).

SOCIAL DEMOCRATIC PARTY OF GERMANY became the symbol of successful organization toward achieving socialism. Its decision to support the Kaiser during World War I was a major blow to socialist expectations. The disillusionment which created the communist movement in Germany split the laboring and middle classes and prepared the way for Hitler's rise. The Social Democratic Party has become the bulwark of West Germany, and thus a major element in the cold war between the democracies, on the one hand, and the communist alliance under the U.S.S.R. on the other.

"SOCIAL DISEASES," see Prostitution.

"SOCIAL ENGINEER," see Morgan, A.E.

"SOCIAL FASCISM," one of Joseph Stalin's (*q.v.*) theories, calculated to divide the ranks of the left (*q.v.*); it was employed by Stalinists everywhere, but nowhere with more fateful results than in Germany. Stalin asserted that it was inaccurate to believe that the socialists and the fascists were different or antagonistic. They were parts of the same reactionary force, like two sides of the same coin. Thus, the socialists were, in reality, "social fascists," and, as such, to be "exposed" and denounced by the followers of the one party of proletarian integrity: the Communist Party. A slogan of the German Communist Party, intended to maintain the purity of its membership was: "Kick the little social fascists out of the kindergarten." See also, United Front from Below.

"SOCIAL GOSPEL," see Christian Socialism.

SOCIAL QUESTION, THE, was the name given to the manifest problem, in the post-Civil War decades, for offering a minimum of security and expectation to the great armies of workers, plagued by poverty and haunted by the spectre of unemployment. The question involved not merely poverty, but all the related questions of housing, sanitation, prostitution, drink, and others including the ultimate catastrophe of war.

SOCIAL SECURITY LEGISLATION, long desired by workers beset by insecurity and lack of resources for crises and contingencies. The American Federation of Labor opposed government old age pensions, in its early period; it wished to develop its own systems, and thus bind the workers closer to its organization. By 1907, it had been won to agitate for Federal legislation. Industry, too, resisted such ideas. The 1930's crisis revealed the need for action in the field, and such plans as those proposed by Francis E. Townsend and Huey P. Long (*qq.v.*) rallied such impressive numbers of supporters that the government was moved to action. The Social Security Act of 1935 set up a system of unemployment compensation, another for old age and survivors's insurance, and still another for grants to states to finance programs for the needy aged, blind, orphaned, and disabled. The sums available were meager, and had basic limitations, notoriously for not providing for domestic workers, migratory workers, and others in need, but additional clauses were added which strengthened the Social Security Act. It still left great areas of workers unprotected, or recipients of trifling sums of money. As of 1953, the Social Security Administration was part of the newly-created Department of Health, Education, and Welfare. Medicare was added in 1965. Whether all should receive Federal benefits, or some, was pondered in Milton Friedman and Wilbur J. Cohen, *Social Security: Universal or Selective.* The economy, tangled by international factors as well as easy spending of the post-War prosperity, put federal benefits in question. In 1981, half the families in the nation paid more social security taxes than income taxes. There were changes instituted to buttress and equalize benefits, as well as battle inflation. Nevertheless, waves of alarm were generated by hints that social security was in trouble, and might be unable to make payments at some unspecified time. The new 1981 Administration affirmed that social security would be a first responsibility. Warren Shore, *Social Security: the Fraud in Your Future* (1975); Paul H. Douglas, *Social Security in the United States* (1936); Rita Ricardo Campbell, *Social Security: Promise and Reality* (1977); G.M.J. Veldkamp, *Social Security and Medical Care* (1978); Robert M. Ball, *Social Security: Today and Tomorrow* (1978).

"SOCIAL SIGNIFICANCE," a cultural concept developed in the 1930's, but found earlier, as in Upton Sinclair's (*q.v.*) analysis of *Mammonart.* It advocated writing and art and theater which reflected a sense of society and society's needs. It agreed that an artist had to have a personal vision, but denied that this ought to interfere with his awareness of the real issues of life. It was critical of "bourgeois" art and narcissism, found virtues in the "collective novel," and approved work which showed a knowledge of objective conditions. "Proletarian art" was excessive in its regard for social significance, treating stories and poems as though they were articles and editorials, and treating the politics of artists as seriously as their art. The 1940's saw a violent reaction away from "Proletarian art," which was equated with social significance; see Louis Filler, "The Question of Social Significance," *Union Review,* January, 1962.

SOCIAL WORK, a field arising out of the charity organizations of the pre-Civil War period; these were moral in temper, emphasized "doing good," asked gratitude and humility from those patronized, and were clearly intended to maintain existing social conditions. The drastic depressions of the post-Civil War period, the cruel toll exacted of the poor by winters, strikes, unemployment, and patent exploitation raised questions with respect to the adequacy of existing charity conceptions. Such pioneers as Henry Bergh, Jane Addams, the Christian Socialists (*qq.v.*), among others experimented with new approaches to needy people, distraught families, bewildered immigrants, adult criminals and juvenile delinquents, the problems of women workers and children. By the 1920's, the professional social worker was in the field, emphasizing "individual case-work." The depression of the 1930's posed the problem of mass need, which was met by innovations in old age assistance, child care, social security legislation, rehabilitation techniques, and permanent relief giving agencies. The social worker of the 1930's was "socially conscious"; following the war, he tended to become "professional" in ways which removed him from the root questions of social disorder. A specialized jargon, set means for "disposing" of cases, distinctions between case workers, psychiatric workers, medical workers, and others, made him part of a machine, rather than a motivating force. Social work had ceased to be a reform, and had become a function of the *status quo.* Tony Tripondi et al., *The Social Worker at Work* (1977); S.B. Kamerman and A. J. Kahn, *Social Services in the United States* (1976); National Association of Social Workers, *Social Services in the Seventies* (1974); Colin Pritchard and Richard Taylor, *Social Work, Reform or Revolution?* (1978).

SOCIALISM: UTOPIAN (*q.v.*) *AND SCIENTIFIC* (1880), by F. Engels (*q.v.*), a key work in Marxist (*q.v.*) thought, it undertook to analyze previous tendencies and movements in socialism, and found them idealistic and infirmly grounded in the relationship of classes. Only a movement based on the working class and intent upon seizing the means of production could hope to establish socialism. Some movements had been incapacitated for lack of an adequate economic development of capitalist conditions in their country, some, like "socialist" thought among royalists, had been mere rationalizations for continued royalist ambitions.

SOCIALISM AND DEMOCRACY, their relationship was debated; World War I resulted in decisive and opposed conclusions. "For us," wrote Kautsky (q.v.), "Socialism without Democracy is unthinkable." Nevertheless, the concept of the Dictatorship of the Proletariat (q.v.) divided evolutionary, revisionist socialists from revolutionary Marxists (qq.v.). The De Leonites (q.v.) in America were a bit apart, in that they seemed more revolutionary than the revolutionaries, disdaining reform and thereby problems in democracy. Their impotence in real affairs, however, removed them from problems in socialism. See also Scientific Socialism, Democratic Centralism.

SOCIALISM IN ONE COUNTRY, one of Joseph Stalin's significant slogans, in support of the Soviet "Five Year" Plans, instituted in 1928. In opposition to the defeated Leon Trotsky, who advocated a Permanent Revolution (q.v.), Stalin held that socialism could be achieved within the Soviet Union, even before proletarian rule had spread to other countries. This meant that he believed the classless society would be attained while Russia existed encircled by capitalist and other societies. To the extent that the slogan was maintained by believers, it affected the definition of "socialism."

SOCIALIST LABOR PARTY, began in 1877 as the Workingmen's Party of America, and maintained principles during a period which saw the rise of labor unions under onerous conditions. In the 1890's, it fell under the influence of Daniel De Leon, becoming critical of the A.F.L. (q.v.) for its lack of revolutionary principles, took the position of intransigent trade unionism aimed at revolutionary objectives. In practice this made the S.L.P. neither effective economically nor politically. The De Leonites had a moment of significance during the organization of the I.W.W. (q.v.), which presumably also stressed militant unionism, but their differing tactics and objectives soon removed the S.L.P. faction from the organization. It continued to display its analysis of events and of competing radical and reform factions, but with little effectiveness.

SOCIALIST PARTY OF AMERICA, formed in 1900 out of elements of the Social Democratic Party and a group withdrawn from the Socialist Labor Party (qq.v.). Its leader was Eugene Debs, but it quickly attracted an array of brilliant and varied talents. These included Morris Hillquit, Victor L. Berger, Charles Edward Russell, Upton Sinclair, William J. Ghent, George D. Herron, J. A. Wayland, among many others: journalists, political figures, educators, and others. Debs was their Presidential candidate, and polled increasing votes: almost a million in 1912. The Great War shook all socialist perspectives; many observers had thought the United States was moving toward social democracy. But the war effort unleashed a bitter anti-socialist offensive, and the successful Bolshevik revolution attracted some elements which had previously esteemed itself socialist but were disillusioned by the national support given the various governments by their socialist parties. At the St. Louis convention of 1917, the S.P. voted against intervention and conscription. Pro-war elements withdrew to form the American Social Democratic League, which did not grow. Others, like Russell, supported the war, but emphasized its alleged gains to socialism. Still others repudiated the S.P., organizing splinter communist groups. With the war over, the S.P. took up its affairs again; Debs, from prison, in 1920 again polled almost a million votes; but most of them were protest votes against the weak Democratic and Republican candidates. Norman Thomas's (q.v.) votes, as Debs's successor at the polls, were far fewer and less consequential. The New Leader, organ of the old-time socialists, surveyed the news and criticized communists, but had no dynamic program, during the 1930's. However, the catastrophic collapse of the communist

elements, at the end of that decade, left a vacuum which the New Leader filled for "disillusioned," New Dealish, reformist and other loose elements, who used its pages to express views and opinions. As significant a symbol as any of the decay of socialism was the fate of the invaluable Party records which had accumulated over the decades. Early in the 1940's, the Party decided to move its national headquarters to smaller offices, and called in a wastepaper dealer to take away their accumulated documents. Even the dealer realized that they were valuable, sold the 95,000 items to a book-dealer, who, in turn, sold them to the Duke University Library; see David A. Shannon, The Socialist Party of America (1955), p. 271.

SOCIALIZED MEDICINE, a more institutionalized form of health insurance (q.v.), and more sweeping in the implied controls over the medical profession, over planning and prescribing for society's needs, and for administering the area.

SOCIETY OF FRIENDS, arose in England as a dissident religious group which abjured religious rites, emphasized simplicity of speech and deportment, and invoked the "inner light" for religious guidance. Individuals who came over to New England were persecuted by the Puritan regime. This sensitized them to the need for religious liberties, which they advocated especially in New Jersey, when it came under their control, and Pennsylvania. (See Penn, William.) The name of "Quakers" derived from their original nonconformist behavior. However, under the affluent Penn, and other influences, they tended toward a severity of demeanor and deportment, rather than radicalism. They withheld fellowship from such reformers as Benjamin Lay, who, early in the eighteenth century, denounced them for condoning slaveholding. Although they finally stopped the practice, and became principled pacifists, as a result of the challenge of the French and Indian War, they opposed active abolitionists in their ranks, and reproved active reformers in other fields. Thus, like other denominations, they produced such reformers as John Woolman and Isaac T. Hopper (qq.v.), but were not a reform denomination except in their connection with the more energetic followers of Elias Hicks (q.v.) and in such variant groups as the "Progressive Friends": composed of more or less Quaker reformers and their associates. Friends like to think of themselves as a mediating group, as in the operations of the American Friends Service Committee (q.v.).

SOIL CONSERVATION AND DOMESTIC ALLOTMENT ACT OF 1936, see Agricultural Adjustment Administration.

SOLZHENITZYN, ALEKSANDR (1918-   ), a product of the "thaw" in Russia which followed the death of the dictator Stalin (q.v.) and the campaign to discredit his personality cult. Solzhenitzyn, mathematician, honor student, soldier in the anti-Nazi war criticized Stalin in correspondence and endured acute suffering in Soviet slave labor camps (q.v.), and afterwards exile and humble teaching opportunities. He was made famous by his penetrating One Day in the Live of Ivan Denisovich (1961). Quarrels with Soviet literary conformists placed him among the dissidents (q.v.). His subtle and symbolic The Cancer Ward and The First Circle, both 1968, built his reputation in the West, made firm by the award of the Nobel Prize in 1970. Thereafter Solzhenitzyn's days were numbered at home. Publication of Gulag Archipeligo (1973) was followed by expulsion from the Soviet Union. He became an international symbol of freedom. His full embrace of Christianity and forthrightness soured westerners who were soft on Russia; see his Detente (q.v.): Prospects for Democracy and Dictatorship (1976) and Warning to the West (1972). A New York Times stipendiary skirted his career to derogate his writing as heavy-handed. Solzhenitzyn's The Oak and the Calf (1980) maintained in autobiography the quality of his work, as well as his status as a figure of conscience. See Leopold Labedz, ed., Solzhenitzyn: a Documentary Record (1973).

"SONG OF THE SHIRT, THE" (1843), famous poem by

Thomas Hood, which expressed his indignation for the inhumanity which attended the rise of industry in Great Britain; see also "Cry of the Children, The."

SONS OF LIBERTY (1765), a democratic-revolutionary development, resulting from the Stamp Act (q.v.), and intended to discourage Stamp Act agencies from operating to enforce the measure. Offices were rifled, Stamp Act collectors threatened and occasionally mishandled. Respectable merchants united with colonists of humbler status to carry out such acts, which helped create a disregard for law and order. The phrase, "Sons of Liberty," itself, entered into the lore of American reform thought.

SOREL, GEORGES (1847-1922), a theoretician of anarchism, and especially of the General Strike (q.v.), his most important work was Réflexions sur la violence (1908).

SOUTH, THE, AND REFORM, a key problem for reformers, usually avoided. Southerners produced a proportionate quota of reformers, from Nathaniel Bacon to Thomas Jefferson (qq.v.), interested in civil rights, the rights of frontiersmen as compared with those in eastern and aristocratic circles, and including anti-slavery. Their turn to a defense of slavery as a "positive good" went along with a reaffirmation of the South as comparable to Greece, in her democracy, based on slavery, and to the England of west country squires. The development of a middle class was not encouraged. The South before the Civil War opposed reform, identified with northern abolitionism. Poor white southerners, even more than some classes of more elite stock, despised the Negroes who, in slavery, deprived them of jobs or involuntarily helped keep their wages low, despised, too, the free Negroes. They joined the aristocratic class in seeking to establish the Confederacy, and, following its failure, in resisting Reconstruction measures (q.v.). Following the withdrawal of Federal troops, they led the terroristic offensive which put the Negro in a humbled status. Poor white leaders like Tillman and Watson (qq.v.) denounced capitalists and aristocrats, but in a "solid South" of Democrats united in suppressing the Negro could develop no tradition of vital non-conformity and regard for individual rights necessary to reform. So outstanding a southern product as Woodrow Wilson (q.v.) had a program for the nation and the world, but not for the South. The argument that southern racism (q.v.) was a product of poverty fell before the fact that New Deal funds and World War II (qq.v.) affluence made little difference in the South's attitudes. Although it produced such a determined liberal as Lillian Smith (q.v.), its compulsion to defend racism shadowed all hopes of producing a varied liberalism. Its leading spokesmen emphasized northern hypocrisy, the noisome aspects of northern city life, the malefactions of northern industry in the South, the tyranny of "Wall Street," in the tradition of the pot and the kettle. Such attitudes did not foresee the revolution, at least on the surface, which would be caused in 1954 by the historic decision of the Supreme Court in Brown v. Board of Education in Topeka, and later by the Civil Rights and Voting legislation of Johnson's (q.v.) Administration, as well as by Negro political activity throughout the South. Such developments created similarities between North and South in Negro-white relations. Grady McWhiney, Southerners and Other Americans (1973); N. V. Bartley and Hugh D. Graham, Southern Politics and the Second Reconstruction (1976); I. A. Newby, The South (1978); M. L. Billington, The South: a Central Theme? (1976); L. M. Seagull, Southern Republicanism 1940-1972 (1974). See also Negro Suffrage, Carter, Jimmy, Phillips, Ulrich B., Racism.

SOUTH AMERICA, see Latin America and Reform.

SOUTHEAST ASIA AND REFORM presented themselves as enigmatic quantities in the post-World War II period, which saw the emancipation of such great territories as Burma, Thailand, Viet Nam, and Indonesia from the western powers of Great Britain, France, and The Netherlands. Their major emancipation slogan derived from nationalism (q.v.): Bur-

ma for the Burmese, etc. Along with this, however, went appeals for democratic and socialist goals. The crucial challenge to the possibilities of reform lay in the role of communism in these lands; thus, the rise of the communist dictatorship in China, in 1949, was the greatest fact in Southeast Asia following independence. Communism established in any one of these countries could lead to the rise of communism in the rest of them. A major effort to establish communism in Viet Nam was supported by Communist China, resisted with the help of the United States. In 1954, a truce established communist North Viet Nam, and anti-communist South Viet Nam, divided at the seventeenth parallel. Marxism was less important in Burma than was nationalism; but an overthrow of neutral Thailand could have repercussions in Burma. Indonesia, too, was a great, restless combination of backward peasants, and warring elite. In 1960, President Sukarno suspended parliamentary government on the grounds that it was endangering the well-being of the country. In 1961, Laos, delicately situated between Viet Nam and Thailand, became the scene for communist-anti-communist hostilities which raised the possibility of United States intervention imminent. The succeeding build-up exploded into a U.S.-U.S.S.R.-China intervention which shook America as well as the embattled areas; see Vietnam. Although China and the U.S.S.R. were less directly shaken, not being democracies, they were required to follow events and scheme with regimes in terms of their own dynamics. W. A. Withington and Margaret Fisher, eds., Southeast Asia (1979); Wayne Raymond and K. Mulliner, eds., Southeast Asia, an Emerging Center of World Influence? (1977); Edwin Martin, Southeast Asia and China (1977); R. M. Smith, ed., Southeast Asia: Documents of Political Development and Change (1974).

SOUTHERN CHRISTIAN LEADERSHIP CONFERENCE, originally established as a result of a meeting in 1957 which sought to combat segregation. Inspired by the Montgomery (Alabama) Bus Boycott led by Martin Luther King, Jr. (q.v.), various protest groups began to spring up in emulation and sought advice, especially when their protests resulted in such retaliations as legal and personal harassment, and even the dynamiting of homes. The setting up of the Conference resulted.

SOUTHERN TENANT FARMERS' UNION, an effort in the 1930's to organize the tenant farmers (q.v.) and influence legislation. At its second annual convention at Little Rock, Arkansas, January 7, 1936, the Union called for a National Agricultural Authority "for the acquisition, regulation and control of agricultural lands."

SOVEREIGNTY, see Popular Sovereignty, Squatters.

SOVIET, in Russian, "Council"; the 1905 workers's councils in Petrograd (later Leningrad) were a first draft of the soviets set up by the Bolsheviks (q.v.) in 1917, which, functioning independently of the official government, challenged it in October of that year and overthrew it. (See Russian Revolution.) A symbol of democratic operations, the paradox of Russia was revealed in such a title as Charles G. Haines, The Threat of Soviet Imperialism (1954).

SPANISH-AMERICAN WAR, a challenge to reform thought, since it began with a quantity of distaste for Spanish rule in Cuba and sympathy with Cuban guerrilla action, and ended in an American protectorate there and persecution of guerrillas in the Philippine Islands. The United States had a long tradition of concern that Cuba not fall into the hands of a powerful nation (see Monroe Doctrine, Ostend Manifesto), and such imperialists as Captain Mahan and Theodore Roosevelt (qq.v.) envisioned American expansion which might well include Cuba, but the public which read the provocative articles in the Hearst and Pulitzer (qq.v.) press chose their reading matter freely. It could have patronized the anti-imperialist New York Evening Post. It seems evident that it was the general public which felt imperialist urges, and filled the ranks of the volunteer regiments; there was no conscription between 1863 and 1917. Indeed, conservative opinion was against war, fearing that it was a dangerous adventure. Spain's deep weakness was not known. The United States might suffer a catastrophic defeat. Mark Hanna (q.v.) did not want war, but though he had "bought" the election of McKinley in 1896, he could not buy peace. The war was an incredible triumph. Despite inept organization and provisioning which killed more American soldiers through dysentery and other ailments than did bullets, the Spanish were in far worse straits. Cuba was invested by American troops, so was Manila. In the latter outpost steps were taken to make sure that a native government under Aguinaldo (q.v.) did not take root. Spain was peremptorily stripped of her possessions. The Platt Amendment (q.v.) gave the United States control of Cuba's destinies and a two year war ended with the Filipino guerrillas resigning themselves to American rule. See also Cuba, Philippines and American Reform. Walter Millis, *The Martial Spirit* (1931); Frank Friedel, *The Splendid Little War* (1958).

SPANISH CIVIL WAR (1936-9), a drawn-out episode on the road to World War II (q.v.). The bulwark against nationalistic wars were the labor, socialist, and communist alliances. The triumph of Hitlerism (q.v.) overthrew these, and did the same wherever it advanced. With the rise of the Spanish Republic, and the challenge presented to it by the fascist alliance under Generalissimo Franco, Spain became a testing ground. German and Italian military aid came to the fascists; Russia sent aid to the Loyalists in Madrid. International brigades were mobilized in many countries, including the United States, in support of the Republic. The communists adopted their usual rule or ruin policy, directing their bullets with more effect against anarchists and Trotskyites than against fascists. The fascists fought with redoubtable courage, as in their famous defense of the Alcazar in Toledo, in 1936. The American Neutrality (q.v.) Acts of 1937 hindered the Loyalist cause. Although radicals denounced democratic do-nothingism, "non-intervention," which had contributed to the defeat of the Republicans, this was an admission that the radicals had been inadequate to handle the affair themselves. George Orwell's (q.v.) honest account of the proceedings, in *Homage to Catalonia*, was unappreciated by the left (q.v.).

SPARGO, JOHN (1876-1966), English-born contributor to American socialism, he opposed the Boer War, and came to America in 1900. He founded the *Comrade*, and joined the Socialist Party. He expounded revisionist Marxism (q.v.) in a number of books, urged humanitarianism in *The Bitter Cry of the Children* (1906), and repudiated violence in his *Syndicalism, Industrial Unionism and Socialism* (1913). His hatred of Bolshevism expressed itself in a series of books. In 1917, he left the Socialist Party, and began a new career as a student and citizen of Vermont.

SPARTACUS (died 71 B.C.), a native of Thrace who became a Roman gladiator, but escaped in 72 B.C. and rallied slaves to revolutionary action. The next year his troops defeated two Roman consuls sent against them, in the south of Italy. Spartacus enjoyed other triumphs before he and his followers were overwhelmed by Roman legions. He was slain with some forty thousand others near Strongoli, in Calabria. Some six thousand of his captured men were crucified along the way from Capua to Rome. Despite the malicious accounts of Spartacus which the Romans sponsored, democratic opinion idealized him and his cause. (See Hollywood.) During World War I, Karl Liebknecht (q.v.) organized the *Spartacus* group, which fomented strikes and mutinies against the regime. Early in 1919, it was suppressed. In October 1920, the majority decided to join the Third International (q.v.).

SPEAKER OF THE HOUSE, see "Revolution of 1910."

SPECIE CIRCULAR (July 11, 1836), President Jackson's act to stop the inflation of the currency which was resulting from speculation in western lands and paper money being issued on the basis of land values. His circular stipulated that

after August 15, only specie (q.v.) would, for the most part, be accepted by the government in payment for lands in the public domain. The effect of this act was to force the speculators to produce hard money which they did not have. The result was a financial panic (q.v.), which Jackson left as a legacy to his successor, Martin Van Buren (q.v.). The striking fact about the Specie Circular was that a "people's" party of the pre-Civil War period should have advocated a deflated currency. Following the War, popular causes were attracted by Greenbacks and silver (qq.v.) programs, both of which were calculated to cause inflation (q.v.).

SPECIE PAYMENT, a condition of government finance which created opportunities for reformers. Specie (gold and silver) was the base for government payments in pre-Civil War times. Gold and silver were officially exchangeable at a ratio of sixteen to one. During the war, Greenbacks (q.v.) were issued, to finance the war, and specie payment was stopped. Unsupported by specie, Greenbacks fluctuated in value, having a purchasing power of only thirty-nine cents on the dollar in July 1864. The Federal victory sent the value of Greenbacks up, but they were still able to purchase less than specie. Farmers preferred them for paying off debts, and demanded that more be issued, since the greater the number of unsupported Greenbacks, the lower would be their value. Bankers agitated for the government to resume specie payment and to take Greenbacks out of circulation. President Grant (q.v.) was unwilling to end Greenback currency but willing to restrict its issuance. Early in 1875, the resumption of specie payment was decreed, as of 1879, thus frustrating debtors's hopes for an unsupported paper currency. Although Greenbacks continued to have reform possibilities, major attention swung to the Silver Issue (q.v.); see also Greenback Party, The.

SPECULATION AND FREE ENTERPRISE have been associated as inevitable in a capitalist economy, private gain requiring operations which entailed risk. Reformers have criticized the combination as making for insecure economics, and for tempting the speculator to chance not only his own holdings but those of other people which he controls. To the argument that risk operations were necessary to develop the economy, critics have replied that social incentive could be substituted for private incentive, that speculation created false values which could put society in jeopardy, and that it prevented social planning: that speculators could not control the effects of their experiments. A book by R.H. Mottram, *A History of Financial Speculation* included these observations about the speculative "boom" of the 1920's: "The long sustained boom in financial values remains a breath-taking spectacle to the European. True, it is very widespread. It is said that every bell boy and hotel porter participates... Physical disaster seems powerless against a country so immense, and with such developed means of communication. . . . Is financial disaster possible? At the moment, it seems very remote." The book was published in 1929 (q.v.); see also Internal Improvements.

SPEED UP, sharply opposed by labor and reformers: the act of speeding up production in an industrial plant to unnatural heights, detrimental to the interests of the worker, especially his health. This can be accomplished by threats, or, more subtly, by setting unusually skilled workers in strategic places in an assembly-line (q.v.) operation. The rapidity of this worker forces those before him and those ahead of him to speed up their work in order to keep up with him. Compare Stakhanovism. See also Productivity.

SPENCER, ANNA GARLIN (1851-1931), minister, feminist, and educator, as pastor of the Bell Street Chapel, in Providence, R.I., a liberal congregation, she preached woman's rights and deplored such social evils as prostitution (q.v.). She became a leader in the New York Society for Ethical Culture (q.v.) and a director of the New York School of Philanthropy. Although she essentially advocated traditional virtues and social forms, her efforts to modernize them and make them attractive to the newer generations produced a species of marriage counseling techniques; and though her campaign against prostitution did not end it, it did help produce the American Social Hygiene Association (q.v.). Her *Woman's Share in Social Culture* (1913) was a pioneer production; see also her *The Family and Its Members* (1922).

SPENCER, HERBERT (1820-1903), formulator of "social Darwinism" (q.v.), a byproduct of his "synthetic philosophy": a dubious attempt to bring together all human knowledge. His work was a compound of utilitarianism (q.v.), emphasis upon alleged scientific principles, and concern for the individual and the superior race, as necessary to maintain and advance civilization. *The Man versus the State* (1884) expressed a greater fear of socialism than of anarchy. His turn-about on the land question, from radicalism to extreme conservatism, was dissected by Henry George (q.v.) in *A Perplexed Philosopher; Being an Examination of Mr. Herbert Spencer's Various Utterances on the Land Question* (1892).

SPIRITUAL UNREST, THE, a concept in Ray Stannard Baker's (q.v.) *The Spiritual Unrest* (1910), in his report on the state of the churches, old and new, in the Progressive era, but applicable to various eras, from the Revolutionary era, which featured Deists, through the reform-antislavery era which nurtured such phenomena as Mormonism and Christian Science; see Filler, "Schisms and Debates" in *The Crusade against Slavery.* It reappeared in successive eras. It has been held that communism was a form of religion, and as such could enable "adherents" to endure its atrocities for their faith's sake. The youth uprising of the 1960s was too confused to permit a consistent development of spiritual support, though drugs provided some; with the movement's collapse, many bereft followers turned to various novel forms of Fundamentalism, which required little instruction and much resignation of self to charismatic leaders and groups. It undoubtedly entered into the drive and triumph of Jimmy Carter; see Wesley G. Pippert, comp., *The Spiritual Journey of Jimmy Carter: in His Own Words* (1978). See also P. Carter, *The Spiritual Crisis of the Gilded Age* (1971); G. K. Nelson, *Spiritualism and Society;* Filler, "The Spiritual Unrest," in *The Muckrakers.* (Qq.v.) for the above. See also Churches and Reform, and related topics.

SPOILS SYSTEM, see "To the Victor Belongs the Spoils".

SPOILSMEN, used to describe "machine politicians" (q.v.) who utilized public offices as bribes and incentives for maintaining their political organizations; see William D. Foulke (q.v.), *Fighting the Spoilsmen: Reminiscences of the Civil Service Reform Movement* (1919), and *Roosevelt and the Spoilsmen* (1925).

SPOONER, LYSANDER (1808-1887), a Boston lawyer who held extreme individualist views. He opened a mail route in competition with the U.S. government, and forced Congress to institute various postal reforms. He wrote effectively on *The Unconstitutionality of Slavery* (1845), thanks to northern sympathy with his thesis. He was less effective in his challenge to government right to tax citizens. See also his *Poverty: Its Illegal Causes and Legal Cure* (1846).

SPORTS, though no more relevant to social reformers than to conservatives, have often provided personalities who, and situations which, could be used to give emotional expression to a social point of view, or, demagogically to cater to mass feelings. Thus, the exploits of Jesse Owens, an American Negro, at the Olympic games held in Berlin in 1936 were given signal attention because he was displaying his prowess before the world in a fascist stronghold. Thus, too, various Negro athletes, including Joe Louis, the prizefighter, Jackie Robinson the baseball player, and Althea Gibson, the tennis-player, among others, have been taken as symbols of Negro quality and acceptance in elite circles, and also as examples of the social deportment of which Negroes were capable, given the opportunity to develop it. They have also been targets for popularity, among white persons as well as Ne-

groes. Sports shared with business, labor, and other staples of American life the susceptibility to fraud and corruption which accompanied a pecuniary civilization. With academic administrations eager to acquire oxes and kangaroos who could adorn gridirons and basketball courts, it was hardly surprising that some of these "students" would think it no harm to acquire some gratifying sums from gamblers in order to interfere with the natural development of what were after all no more than "games." The moral indignation which accompanied revelations that players had fixed games was warm rather than weighty. See Olympics.

"SQUARE DEAL, THE," Theodore Roosevelt's (q.v.) program on assuming the Presidency. He intended neither to harass industry nor to pamper it, but to carry out the law. This became the famous "On the one hand . . . on the other hand" policy which enabled him to maintain supporters in both radical and conservative camps. *Square* then suggested firmly-placed, sound. The word's career in the 1960s was peculiar, *square* standing with agitators and others of the time for immovability, dullness, archaic attitudes. By the late 1970s, the new definition had lost its impact and stamped its user as an ex-hippie (q.v.).

SQUATTER SOVEREIGNTY, applied to the doctrine enunciated by Stephen A. Douglas in connection with his Kansas-Nebraska Bill: let the settlers themselves decide whether they wished to have slaves in their territories, or not. This doctrine, in fact, overthrew the premise of the Missouri Compromise.

STAKHANOVISM, STAKHANOVITE, a curious Russian development in 1935 which revealed its supporters's mentality. A Russian coal-miner, Alexei Stakhanov, was said to have produced wonders of achievement, his output of coal being a number of times that of ordinary workers. The key to his record was said to be socialist efficiency. His techniques were recommended to other workers, and he himself was feted as a hero of socialism. Other Russian coal-miners were said to have become enthusiastic emulators of his feats. Communists elsewhere in the world hailed Stakhanov as a product of socialism. Skeptics wondered whether the "speed up" (q.v.) was not being made a part of socialist lore.

STALINISM, a phenomenon which arose in the 1920's, and held the stage till the death of the dictator, Joseph Stalin, in 1953. A former divinity student and terrorist, Stalin organized a political machine while his colleagues, V. I. Lenin and Leon Trotsky (q.v.) held the world's attention. He made the post of secretary a weapon of patronage and organization in the U.S.S.R. With Lenin's death, he conducted a campaign against "personalities," intended to undermine Trotsky's popularity and influence, with great success. While holding on to the international apparatus of the Third International (q.v.) he declared his intention of establishing "socialism in one country," namely, the U.S.-S.R. In the 1930's, he moved aggressively against all competition, preaching the doctrine of "social fascism" and of "the united front below" (qq.v.), and executing the competition at home, beginning with the Moscow Trials (q.v.). Opposition victories, however, from Chiang Kai Shek to Hitler (qq.v.) increased his longing for associates. He cooperated with the League of Nations, then perpetrated the Nazi-Soviet Pact, and finally joined the Grand Alliance (qq.v.). The Third International, long a dead letter, vanished. Americans were persuaded that he was a kindly Russian equivalent of a Bronx political boss, but the rapid movement of Russian troops into occupied territories and Stalin's continued policy of executing dissidents cooled off enthusiasm for him; when he died in 1953, little seemed to remain of him but the empire he had left. Set down beside Lenin in Red Square, his corpse was pondered by the endless parade of visitors. A startling attack upon his memory by his successor, Khrushchev, began a process of revaluation painful to the faithful, confusing to observers. In 1961, long preparations culminated in the removal of Stalin's corpse from Lenin's tomb and insignificant burial outside it near the graves of some communist dignitaries. R. C. Tucker, *Stalin as Revolutionary* (1973); L. Trotsky, *Stalin* (1946); Isaac Deutscher, *Stalin* (1966); B. D. Wolfe, *Three Who Made a Revolution* (1948); G. F. Kennan, *Russia and the West under Lenin and Stalin* (1961); R. A. Medvedev, *Let History Judge* (1971).

STALWARTS, a low-point in Republican Party politics, the term was originally used by James G. Blaine (*q.v.*) to refer to a continuing antisouthern Republican. It was used by Roscoe Conkling, political boss of the New York Republican Party, to mean a person loyal to the Party. Conkling equated this with loyalty to himself. With no political program but patronage, he was frustrated by President Hayes' (*q.v.*) efforts favoring civil service (*q.v.*), and termed sympathizers with such cause "Half-Breeds." The quarrel between the two factions suddenly culminated in the assassination of President Garfield, and the killer's statement that he was a "Stalwart" who preferred that Chester A. Arthur, a Conkling man, be President. The fact that he was a disappointed office-seeker helped educate the public to the limited virtues of Stalwartism.

STAMP ACT CONGRESS (1765), a first step toward colonial organization, inspired by indignation over passage of an act which struck hard at the most articulate and intellectual elements in the colonies: an act of remarkable obtuseness on the part of the British. Sons of Liberty (*q.v.*) organized to hold the Act and its agents in contempt. The congress in New York convened a group from eight of the twelve colonies which was remarkable for its high level of statesmanship. Its resolutions were moderate in tone, and gave no hint of its potentiality for eloquence and extraordinary action.

STANDARD OF LIVING, earlier conceived of as the elements of food, clothing and shelter necessary to life; more recently interpreted in terms of quality and appurtenances, the *American* standard of living being held to be the highest in the world. The problem has been to determine how many must be affected by an alleged standard of living for it to be held characteristic of society. In 1980, there was no consensus on what constituted a valid standard of living, inflation and other urgent factors having dimmed the question of satisfaction, pride in production, and other basics once assumed in food, clothing and shelter. See, however, Kenneth E. Boulding, *The Economy of Love and Fear* (1973). Americans were no longer held to have the highest "standard of living," even in material terms; and its rehabilitation was evidently no mere matter of curbing inflation. See Urban Problem, The, Rural America, Middle Classes and Reform.

STANDARD OIL COMPANY, a major example of monopoly (*q.v.*) calculated to drive free enterprise (*q.v.*) out as an American system. Emphasizing the *refining* of oil, rather than the *production* of oil, it became the industrial equivalent of the processor of dairy products who kept for himself the major part of the profit for bottled milk and wrapped cheese. Henry Demarest Lloyd's (*q.v.*) *Wealth against Commonwealth* (1894) detailed the numerous ways in which Standard had developed and expanded its monopoly; these had included legal and illegal chicanery, rebates (*q.v.*), threats, and the employment of strong-arm personnel. Ida M. Tarbell's *The History of the Standard Oil Company* (1904) sought to explain its "greatness," as well as the dangers it presented. Its leader, Rockefeller (*q.v.*) held that he had given stability and order to an industry which had been in chaos; critics held that he had given the industry the stability of death. The "dissolution" of Standard by order of the U.S. Supreme Court, in 1911, theoretically created competition in the industry. Those unwilling to give unqualified endorsement to business noted that prices of gasoline seemed to be the same everywhere. They wondered too, how competent was the oil industry to handle its

relations in foreign countries: how much its agents strengthened or weakened the American position abroad. P. H. Giddens, *Standard Oil Company (Indiana) Oil Pioneer of the Middle West* (1955).

STANTON, ELIZABETH CADY (1815-1902), suffrage leader of wealthy family; she married Henry B. Stanton (1805-1887) in 1840. He was then a notable abolitionist, and with her attended the World Anti-Slavery Convention in London, from which women were excluded. She was one of the organizers of the Seneca Falls Convention in 1848 (*q.v.*), and several years later became associated with Susan B. Anthony (*q.v.*) in woman's rights agitation. Becoming increasingly radical in her view of woman's rights, she opposed the Fifteenth Amendment (*q.v.*), since it did not grant the vote to women. With Miss Anthony and Parker Pillsbury (*q.v.*) she edited *The Revolution*, subsidized by the eccentric George Francis Train, 1868-70. Her National Woman Suffrage Association competed with Lucy Stone's (*q.v.*) American Woman Suffrage Association. She helped prepare the *History of Woman Suffrage* (1881-7), a compendium of materials, and wrote an autobiography, *Eighty Years and More* (1898). Her relationship with her husband wants study. He became a conservative journalist.

STAR ROUTE FRAUDS resulted from the government practice of dispensing contracts to private firms to distribute mail in western areas not accessible to regular mail service. Revelations in 1881 showed that figures in government had contrived with mail contracters to cheat the Post Office through padded contracts and other devices. The Republican Party found it desirable to support the defendants in order to prevent loss of prestige, and though numerous frauds were demonstrated, succeeded in preventing convictions. See also Corruption.

STATE, THE, a formal view of the administrative arm of society, usually examined in terms of its role, duties, and expectations. Philosophic opponents of socialism like Herbert Spencer, (*q.v.*) held it in suspicion as a challenge to freedom and the individual. Socialists maintained that, as administered by the "capitalist class," it was a repressive agency upon those who might wish to transform it into an arm of "working class" democracy. Communists have denied that the state plays a comparable role in their political structures as in those of "bourgeois governments": that communist governments are servants of the "rank and file," and that remnants of older state forms will progressively wither away under their administration.

STATE SOCIALISM, the initiation by non-socialist governments of policies which could be identified as socialist policies, but which serve purposes intended as palliatives, or which otherwise look to a strengthening of the capitalist or other regime, rather than its dissolution. Thus the nationalization of railroads, the institution of government insurance, the intervention of the state into matters involving conditions of labor, may be related to state socialism. Revisionists, Fabians (*qq.v.*), and other reformers have welcomed such means as steps toward the cooperative state; doctrinaire socialists have resented them as half-means, intended to deceive the working classes as to their real interests.

STATES' RIGHTS, see Sectionalism and Reform.

STATUS, not unrelated to salaries (*q.v.*), yet part of the lore of civilized living. It was made a means for distorting history for partisan purposes. Cases were made for seeing Progressives (*q.v.*) as elite people pushed out of power by upwardly mobile elements, the erstwhile elite attempting to reassert their priority by moral, half-measure reforms; for example G. Mowery, *California Progressives* (1963), Rich. Hofstadter, *Anti-Intellectualism in America* (1963). More generally, status was asserted variously: by "green power," fancied by upwardly mobile Negroes; status vacations ("I don't want to see other Americans while I'm on vacation"); status drinks: gin was once the drink of degenerates; its popularity demanded advertisements which "distinguished" one gin from another. In 1980, partly due to inflation, partly oil prices, cars had lost their status importance to consumers. Richard Murphy, *Status and Conformity* (1976); Gary Blake and Nicky Zane, *Status Book* (1978); Vance Packard, *The Status Seekers* (1961).

STEEL STRIKE OF 1919, a major effort in labor organization, the greatest in steel after the Homestead Strike (*q.v.*), and the greatest strike effort in the nation till that time. Its leader was William Z. Foster (*q.v.*) who organized the strike against the reluctance and apathy of the A.F.L. (*q.v.*). As a result of World War I, some one hundred thousand workers had been organized, and a vigorous campaign organized some two hundred and fifty thousand more. They demanded collective bargaining, union security, the eight-hour day and the six-day week, a living wage, and an end of company unionism among other points. The mill-owners fought the strike with firm determination, and aided by U.S. government troops, among other agencies. There were many casualties. The breaking of the strike marked the end of significant organization until the economic depression of the 1930's presented the steel workers with another crisis and opportunity. See also United States Steel Corporation. William Z. Foster, *The Great Steel Strike* (1920); David Brody, *Steelworkers in America: the Nonunion Era* (1960); Grant McConnell, *Steel and the Presidency* (1963).

STEEL WORKERS ORGANIZING COMMITTEE, set up by the C.I.O. in 1936, led a series of strikes which by the next year gained them the recognition of the United States Steel Corporation as a bargaining agency, a ten-percent raise in wages, and the forty-hour week. Its differences with "Little Steel" (q.v.) culminated in the Memorial Day Massacre (q.v.). S.W.O.C. became the United Steelworkers of America.

STEFFENS, LINCOLN (1866-1936), journalist and reformer. A distinguished student of municipal corruption and reform for *McClure's* Magazine, he published *The Shame of the Cities* (1904) (*q.v.*), *The Struggle for Self-Government* (1906), and *Upbuilders* (1909). In 1910, he intervened in the battle between the owners of the *Los Angeles Times* and labor organizers. Steffens's attempt to persuade them to abide by the "Golden Rule" disgraced him with labor and capital. Although less influential in subsequent years, he contracted many striking friendships and made numerous trips to such troubled areas as Mexico, Russia, and Italy. His classic *Autobiography* (1931) contains numerous reflections on the significance of reforms and reformers.

STEINBECK, JOHN (1902-1968), author of *The Grapes of Wrath* (*q.v.*), a novel of such power it raised the question of why he had been unable to repeat the performance. He was fascinated by natural processes, elemental creatures, as in *Of Mice and Men* (1937) and *Sea of Cortez* (1941). He was concerned for, though not persuaded by the idea of divinity, as in his unsuccessful *To a God Unknown* (1933). He had a regard for low-grade people, as in *Tortilla Flat* (1935), at least because they lacked pretentiousness and self-righteousness. His "communist" novel, *In Dubious Battle* (1936), was unconvincing. *The Grapes of Wrath* synthesized a Christ figure, Jim Casy (J.C.), among numerous other symbols, a fierce humanity, a trip west which covered aspects of America, and other features which gave weight to the words and images, many of which required a knowledge of the Bible to be fully grasped. War and prosperity did not appear to inspire Steinbeck. His best writings included *The Red Pony* (1937) and *The Pearl* (1947). His 1962 winning of the Nobel Prize for Literature confounded the literature industry which had bypassed him as a "popular writer," so much so as to have humbled him in his own opinion.

STEREOTYPES, deplored by reformers as giving false pictures of individuals whose minority status, recent arrival (as with immigrants), or low financial rating gives them high visibility unaccompanied by respect. Thus, "Jewish" characteristics could be perceived by prejudiced persons without concern for the individual involved; see Edgar Rosenberg, *From Shylock to Svengali: Jewish Stereotypes in English Fiction* (1960). Reformers repudiated all stereotypes, but notably those involving the Negro. However, they often created stereotypes of their own, as in their idealization of the "worker," "the common man," and, on the other side, the "fat-bellied capitalist," the "confused liberal," and similar stereotypes. In addition, their idealizations of minority personages sometimes took their individuality no more into account than the stereotypes they were intended to combat. By 1981, stereotyping had shifted some of its components, but produced as dreary a string of electronic responses involving white male, energy-wasting, racism-supportive, corporative, capitalistic, oppressive, repressive, religious emptiness.

STERILIZATION, a special cause for persons concerned over the health of the community, the need for maintaining standards of the quality of humans by not permitting degenerates and low-grade mentalities to procreate. It is related to problems in eugenics and euthanasia (*qq.v.*), as well as social planning; see Leon F. Whitney, *The Case for Sterilization* (1934). Its potentialities were seriously damaged by the "experiments" carried out by the Hitler Regime in Germany in its concentration camps (*q.v.*). Among free people, the subject was complicated by other considerations; see J. P. Boyle, *The Sterilization Controversy: a New Crisis for Catholic Hospitals* (1977); W. W. Williams, *Sterility: the Diagnostic Survey of the Infertile Couple* (1964).

STETSON, MRS. CHARLOTTE, see Gilman, Mrs. Charlotte Perkins Stetson.

STEUNENBERG MURDER TRIAL (1907), a crisis in labor's relationship to public opinion. The embattled Western Federation of Miners (*q.v.*) kept a sharp eye on their rights and possibilities in the several states. They believed that Frank Steunenberg, governor of Idaho had betrayed them during a strike in 1899. On December 30, 1905, he was fatally wounded by a bomb. Arrested was Harry Orchard (*q.v.*), an enigmatic figure who testified against "Big Bill" Haywood (*q.v.*) and other officers of the W.F.M. as having directed him in terroristic acts. Clarence Darrow (*q.v.*) was main counsel in their defense. In his cross-examination and summary, he emphasized the desperate position of the miners, in their struggle with the employers, compared their lives with Orchard's dissolute life, and asked in effect that his clients be given the confidence of court and public. His defense was social, rather than technical, and in this case he received the benefit of the doubt; the defendants were freed. Compare, however, with the Los Angeles Bombing Case.

STEVENS, THADDEUS (1792-1868), leader of Reconstruction (*q.v.*), following the Civil War, he was a Pennsylvania lawyer whose most notable cause had been public education. Though a hard-headed Whig politician, he developed firm anti-slavery principles, helped, to some extent, by his militant protectionism (*q.v.*) and anti-southern views. As a leading Radical Republican, he advocated uncompromisingly harsh treatment of the secessionist southern states. Leader of the House of Representatives and of the Joint Committee on Reconstruction, he in large measure directed the military occupation of the South. His great effort was the impeachment of President Johnson (*q.v.*), and he directed the prosecution. Whether he was more reformer or politician is a matter of controversy. His equalitarianism appears to have been sincere. He directed that he be buried in Negro ground. T. H. Williams, *Lincoln and the Radicals* (1942).

STEVENSON, ADLAI (1900-1965), a favorite of eggheads (*q.v.*), son of a Vice-President of the United States (1893-1897) bearing the same name, he was a New Deal (*q.v.*) functionary, and active in the early organization of the United Nations (*q.v.*). He was governor of Illinois (1948-1952), and in the latter year nominated as Presidential candidate by the Democratic Party. Whether his nomination was, in fact, a grassroots upsurge which overthrew the plans of the master politicians is a matter of controversy. Stevenson's literate speeches pleased literate Democrats and foreigners. His wit was thought to affront the less cerebral. Whether he had a genuine sense of social processes and movements is problematic; he was, in any event, drastically defeated in 1952 and again in 1956. See his *Major Campaign Speeches* (1953); also J. B. Martin, *Adlai Stevenson of Illinois* (1976); Kenneth S. Davis, *The Politics of Honor* (1967).

STEWARD MACHINE CO. *V.* DAVIS (1937), see Welfare Legislation.

STILL, WILLIAM (1821-1902) Philadelphia Negro abolitionist and underground worker who became a clerk in the office of the Pennsylvania Society for the Abolition of Slavery of kept records which he later used in his valuable *The Underground Railroad* (1872). In 1859, he began a struggle to desegregate streetcars in Philadelphia, in defiance of Negro opinion. He defended his course in *A Brief Narrative of the struggle for the rights of Colored people in Philadelphia in the City Railway Cars* (1867). Victory was achieved in 1867. He also was criticized by Negroes for voting Democrat in 1874: a course he defended in his *An Address on Voting and Laboring.* He worked to give aid to orphans, aged people, and others in need among the Negroes. He became a member of the Philadelphia Board of Trade.

STOKES, ROSE PASTOR (1879-1933), a picturesque episode in American reform, an immigrant girl who married into one of the wealthy and old New York families, James G.P. Stokes having interested himself in settlement and socialist causes. She continued her interest in radical causes, in 1912 leading a New York hotel workers's strike, and being active in other strikes as well. She wrote considerably, and published a play, *The Woman Who Wouldn't* (1916) which had no merit. She was opposed to America's entrance into the war, and separated from her husband on the issue. The first case under the Espionage Act of 1917 *(q.v.)*, she was indicted for saying, "I am for the people and the government is for the profiteers." She later became an active communist.

STONE, LUCY (1818-1893), one of the most important of the woman's rights advocates, she was the first woman to lecture regularly on the subject, as well as on anti-slavery and related topics. In 1850, she helped convene the first national woman's convention. (Compare Seneca Falls Convention.) She lectured extensively, and with success. In 1855, she married Henry B. Blackwell, retaining her own name; persons who did the same or sympathized with the deed, were called "Lucy Stoners." In 1858, while living in New Jersey, she permitted her household goods to be sold for taxes in protest against her lack of a vote. She helped organize a number of woman's rights associations, notably (1869), the American Woman Suffrage Association, which pressed for the vote, but did not sympathize with the radical tactics employed by Susan B. Anthony and Elizabeth Cady Stanton, through their National Woman Suffrage Association. The schism was healed in 1889, Stanton being president, Anthony vice-president, and Stone chairman of the executive committee of the National American Woman Suffrage Association. She also edited the *Woman's Journal.* A. A. Blackwell, *Lucy Stone* (1930).

STOWE, HARRIET BEECHER (1811-1896), daughter of Lyman Beecher, one of the most influential ministers of his time, touted as a reformer, though his "reforms" emphasized distaste for Catholics and liquor. Her presence at Lane *(q.v.)* Seminary, which her father headed in Cincinnati, gave her some sense of abolitionist arguments, though she avoided them, and her marriage to the Rev. Calvin E. Stowe kept her busy with house and children. Nevertheless, she wrote easily and often. *Uncle Tom's Cabin, or Life among the Lowly* (1851-2) was published in the *National Era (q.v.).* Its success as a book and as a play became historical, influencing feeling in the North and in the South, as well as abroad.

Its success was due to the fact that it did not offend the prejudices of its readers; thus, it was colonizationist rather than abolitionist *(qq.v.).* But it fed the emotional estrangement of northerners and southerners. Stowe's second novel in the area, *Dred; a Tale of the Great Dismal Swamp* (1856) contributed further to this achievement. Better as literature were her tales of the people, as in *Oldtown Folks* (1869). Forrest Wilson, *Crusader in Crinoline* (1941); Constance M. Rourke, *Trumpets of Jubilee* (1927).

STRESS, a tension by-product of activities which shifting social standards left no sure defenses or support. Hence, teachers were unclear about their prerogatives for keeping order in classrooms where students might vengefully claim discrimination, sex harassment, or malice. Boredom at monotonous work produced its own variants of stress, as could housework, where a woman's or man's "role" was put in question. Doctors, lawyers, government workers were also subject to stress. G. Kerry Smith, *Stress and Campus Response* (1968); A. Monat and R. S. Lazarus, eds., *Stress and Coping* (1977); C. R. Figley, ed., *Stress Disorders among Vietnam Veterans* (1978); J. L. Kearns, *Stress in Industry* (1977); W. D. Haynes, *Stress Related Disorders in Policemen* (1978).

STRIKE, a cessation of work on the part of organized labor, or labor congregated in one plant or on one job, for the purpose of enforcing demands relating to job conditions, wages, or the right to organize. Strikes have sometimes had political purposes to protest against conditions of government, as during 1905 in Russia, when the strike was an instrument of attempted revolution; the Socialist Labor Party *(q.v.)* has opposed strikes as taking workers *out of the factory*, while their place was in it, and because strikes are usually confined to partial demands, rather than to demanding full ownership of the factory itself; the S.L.P. has been itself scourged as a do-nothing organization; see also General Strike, Akron Rubber Strike, Homestead Strike, Pullman Strike, Railroad Riots of 1877, Steel Strike of 1919, Paterson Strike, Strike Tactics.

STRIKE-BREAKERS, developed in post-Civil War decades and were brought from various points for temporary work while the strike was being combatted. Pinkerton Police *(q.v.)* made a specialty of providing strike-breakers, who often also doubled as company police intended to help break down strikers' organizations. Negroes were sometimes brought in: a technique which served the dual purpose of providing strike-breakers and harming the fraternity of white and black workers. Since the institutionalization of mediation boards and the rise of powerful unions, the problem has been raised as to the difference between strike-breaking and right to work *(q.v.).*

STRIKE TACTICS, see General Strike, Boycott, Sympathy Strikes, Industrial Workers of the World, Sit-Down Strike.

STUDENT MOVEMENTS have been taken seriously by all reform groups. Lenin's remark, that he who had the youth had the future made reformers, as it did revolutionaries, eager to spur and organize youth. The legend, too, that young people were more idealistic than old, more prompt to sacrifice, less corrupted by routine and comfort aided the formation of youth groups. The nineteenth century saw no American equivalent of European republican idealism among the youth. However, the Intercollegiate Socialist Society, founded in 1905, was a step in the direction of organizing students, and fed the Youth Movement *(q.v.).* After World War I, Young Socialists vied with Young Communists, on campuses as well as off. Conscription in 1940 largely demolished their organizations, but with the return of peace, neo-socialist and neo-communist groups sprouted again. There was energetic student support for Henry A. Wallace's candidacy for President on the Progressive *(q.v.)* ticket in 1948. During the 1950's, though secondary to student apathy and panty-raiders, groups on campus were concerned for racial equality, peace, socialism (which was sometimes a euphemism for communism), and McCarthyism (q.v.). The drive against segregation in the South gave them added energy and coworkers, and the increased threat to civilization because of the dangerous differences between the U.S. and U.S.S.R. gave them increased status. The loosening of family (q.v.) ties created an army of undirected youth whose energy flowed into "Beatle-mania," drugs, undifferentiated sex, and anti-war (qq.v.) attitudes which stirred the nation. The phenomenon of the late 1970s was students turning to credit-bearing course work leading to jobs.

SUBSISTENCE THEORY, see Iron Law of Wages.

SUB-TREASURY PLAN, a byproduct of Andrew Jackson's fight against the Second Bank of the United States (q.v.). Government funds were to be kept in an "independent treasury." Jackson's chosen successor, Martin Van Buren (q.v.) made an issue of the sub-treasury and had a law passed creating it in 1840. This was repealed in 1841, and continued to be a matter for debate until 1846 when the subtreasury system was finally established. The subtreasury furnished an example of a political issue, touted as a reform issue, but which had little more than administrative and tendentious significance.

SUBURBIA, description of the great stretches of terrain outside the cities, occupied by middle-class and well-to-do white populations which have fled the urban centers in order to enjoy country living and quieter environs, or to avoid contact with burgeoning Negro, Puerto Rican, or other minority elements which had grown up. Because of the growth of the suburbs, they were becoming, in effect, new cities, though without vital centers of purpose or tradition. Thus, reformers could observe that the original cities continued to challenge the nation, and were receiving inadequate support from those inhabiting the suburbs; for such reformers, "suburbia" could be pronounced with irony and disapproval. John E. Ullman, The Suburban Economic Network (1977); Robert Goldston, Suburbia: Civic Denial (1970); L. H. Masotti and J. K. Hadden, Suburbia in Transition (1974). See Urban Problem, The.

SUBVERSIVES, a term not preferred by reformers, who equate it with persecution, "100%ism" (q.v.), and other conformist tendencies. See also McCarran-Wood Act of 1950 (also known as the Subversive Activities Control Act), Patriot.

SUFFRAGE, THE, next to fair legislative representation (q.v.) the earliest democratic reform. Although largely limited to property owners in pre-Revolutionary decades, it spread rapidly for white males; by 1830, most of them could vote. Dorr's Rebellion (q.v.) in Rhode Island overthrew the last major stronghold of limited suffrage in the north. A problem of democracy has been that qualified voters do not use their votes fully. See also Negro Suffrage, Woman Suffrage. Compare, Chilton Williamson, American Suffrage, from Property to Democracy, 1760-1860 (1960).

"SUGAR HILL," see Negro and Reform, The.

SUGAR TRUST, see United States v. E. C. Knight Company (1895).

SUICIDE, an increasing phenomenon as justified by elements of society. Though still sustained legally as a crime, lowered human expectations created cause for suicide in irreparable loss or philosophical despair. One doctor developed a "three-second" pill for use by the old and chronically ill. A group of Americans formed a society to campaign for "voluntary euthanasia" and information on the subject. A group in England sponsored publication of a manual on self-destruction, but, amusingly, since it broke the law, were dissuaded from publishing it. The American group vowed to break United States law by issuing the work. Arnold Madison, Suicide and Young People (1978); David Lester, Why People Kill Themselves (1972); M. L. Farber, The Theory of Suicide (1968); Erwin Stengel, Suicide and Attempted Suicide (1965).

SUMMIT CONFERENCES, began in 1943, in the Teheran meeting of Roosevelt, Churchill, and Stalin (qq.v.) on war plans against the Axis (q.v.) powers. They continued in meetings at Yalta and Potsdam in 1945, and were resumed in 1955 by United States, France, British and Russian heads of state. By 1961, seven "summit" conferences had been held. They symbolized for many people the increasingly narrow range of responsible individuals who were in position to make or break persons or pacts; as such they created problems of efficiency as contrasts to problems of reform.

SUMNER, CHARLES (1811-1874), a distinguished name in nineteenth century reform, there was a question of what he had ever accomplished. He developed an ornate style of speaking, and, when elected to the U.S. Senate, was deemed to be the "scholar in politics." His fierce but rhetorical attack on the slavery system, in his speech on "The Crime against Kansas," in 1856, called forth a physical assault from a pro-slavery partisan on the Senate floor, and created an issue between North and South. During his long convalescence, Massachusetts kept his seat vacant for him. Sumner returned to active life a rabid Radical Republican, endorsed the military occupation of the South, following the Civil War, and the impeachment of President Johnson (qq.v.). As chairman of the Foreign Affairs Committee, he fought President Grant's effort to annex the Dominican Republic (q.v.), and lost his chairmanship. Though esteemed a living immortal, his works are rarely read. He is often confused with Fort Sumter, named for Thomas Sumter, a Revolutionary general.

SUMNER, WILLIAM GRAHAM (1840-1910), the outstanding American Manchester Liberal and advocate of Social Darwinism (qq.v.). Though trained for the ministry, he became professor of political and social science at Yale College. He opposed trade unions, benevolence, and socialism (qq.v.). His concern for freedom disturbed conservatives who disliked his free-trade principles. A pioneer in sociology, he created the concept of mores. His many works included What Social Classes Owe to Each Other (1883), and Folkways (1907).

"SUN SPOT THEORY," a phenomenon of economics (q.v.), anticipated in 1843 by Heinrich Schwabe's discovery that "sun spots" moved in cycles. The British economist W. S. Jevons, in 1878, presented a paper intending to show that the cycles of economic prosperity and depression correlated with those of sun-spots. His view was that the sun spots affected agricultural production negatively, and that this inaugurated a cycle of depressed economy. Professor H. L. Moore, in Economic Cycles, Their Law and Cause (1914) equated rainfall with wholesale prices. The key article in the field—and in the midst of a catastrophic depression—was that by Carlos Garcia-Mata, of the Argentina Embassy, and Felix I. Shaffner, of Harvard University, "Solar and Economic Relationships," Quarterly Journal of Economics, November, 1934, which showed the high correlation between the sun spot cycle and the business "cycle", but cast doubt on the relationship of agricultural production and sun spots. They found, however, a startling correlation between sun spots and other business production. They conjectured that sun spots might affect men psychologically, producing depression psychology. They noted evidence that they definitely affected the thickness of skins of fur-bearing animals, the timing of magnetic storms, and other phenomena. Why would they not affect business cycles? It this was true, Marxism (q.v.) was a dream, economic, idealistic, political, moralistic, and other interpretations of the phenomena of business and industry were inadequate. It would be necessary to gear man's activities to the sun-spot phenomena for best results. Economists were kept so confident by the now famous correlations that many of them contributed to adding to the evidence or to their interpretation. All works on business cycles treated sun spots as relevant to the subject, some more gingerly than others. Harlan True Stetson,

Research Associate, Massachusetts Institute of Technology, and director of the Cosmic Terrestrial Research Laboratory, published *Sunspots in Action* (1947), the chapter on "Sunspots and the Economic Cycle" presumably being a part of the action.

SUN YAT SEN (1866-1925), organizer of the Chinese forces which sought to overthrow the Manchu dynasty and set up a republic, achieved in 1911. Elected provisional president of the United Provinces of China, he resigned in order to work for the unification of the country. He became a symbol of Chinese democratic aspirations, though his desire to build up Chinese strength to resist aggressions against her and his desire for agrarian reform kept him friendly to Russia. Upon his death, his Kuomintang Party fell into the hands of Chiang Kai Shek. His wife lived to endorse the communist regime in China. Charles R. Hensman, *Sun Yat Sen* (1971).

SUPPLY AND DEMAND, a theory associated with capitalist economics, held in suspicion or contempt by reformers or radicals; it argues that supply follows demand, and that the price of a commodity rises as the demand increases without a proportionate increase in the supply. Applied to labor as a commodity (*q.v.*), it has been especially challenged by friends of labor. In addition, they have argued that supply and demand do not explain social wants: that there is much unsatisfied demand and unused supply which the theory fails to take into account. See Economics, Keynes, John Maynard, Productivity.

SUPERHIGHWAYS, see Federal Highway Act of 1955-1956.

SUPPLY SIDE ECONOMICS, influential in the late 1970s and the new Reagan (*q.v.*) Administration. It was conceived by Arthur Laffer, an economist, who argued that "demand" was not sufficient to inspire a healthy productivity (*q.v.*) and growth. Only encouraging businessmen to make money would do this. Accordingly, it was desirable that government, rather than taxing business to subsidize social programs, inviting inflation (*q.v.*), should be cutting taxes to stimulate production and a legitimate demand. The theory was the reverse of Keynesian economics and associated with "monetarism" (*qq.v.*). Arthur Laffer, *Private Short-Term Capital Flows* (1975); D. Meiselman and Laffer, *The Phenomenon of World Wide Inflation* (1975); Richard Jones, *Supply in a Market Economy* (1976).

SUPREME COURT AND REFORM, never actively related, but brought into association under varying circumstances. Thus, the Supreme Court was by its nature conservative, being composed of propertied personnel whose training circled about property interests. Jefferson's (*q.v.*) attack on the Supreme Court, however, threatened to deprive the nation of one of its agencies for check-and-balance purposes, and its preservation helped maintain democracy, if not reform. Again, Marshall's (*q.v.*) defense of Cherokee (*q.v.*) property rights, though emphasizing the property rather than the Cherokee, did give support to an oppressed minority. Prigg *v.* Pennsylvania (*q.v.*) showed the Court as seeking to mediate between North and South on slavery, and satisfying neither, but the Dred Scott and the Merryman cases (*qq.v.*) showed how a pro-slavery Democratic justice could manipulate the language of democracy for demagogic purposes. In post-Civil War days, the Court set itself up increasingly as a defender of private property at the expense of human rights, though in Munn *v.* Illinois, (*q.v.*) the "public interest" was affirmed, at least, to transcend private interests. The Court continued, in the twentieth century, to maintain its conservative tradition, though great dissents by Justices Holmes, Brandeis, and Harlan (*qq.v.*) leavened their effect, and received the support of such a justice as Benjamin N. Cardoza. Once again under attack in 1937 (see Court Packing Issue), the Court soon after received infusions of new blood. Brown v. Board of Education of Topeka (*q.v.*) opened the battle for integration, and won the Court liberal

enthusiasm. However, its 1961 decision upholding the Smith Act clause condemning membership in a party sanctioning violence brought mixed responses. See O. K. Fraenkel, *The Supreme Court and Civil Liberties* (1960). *The Brethren* (1979) by Bob Woodward of Watergate (*q.v.*) fame and Scott Armstrong was a behind-the-scenes expose which brought more profit than honor. See also Arthur S. Miller, *The Supreme Court, Myth and Reality* (1978); Joel Seligman, *The High Citadel: the Influence of the Harvard Law School* (1978); Philip B. Kurland, *The Supreme Court and Judicial Function* (1975); A. M. Bickel, *The Supreme Court and the Idea of Progress* (1978).

SURPLUS VALUE, defined by Marx as "congealed labor," for which workers have not been paid. He argued that the profit system not only deprived its real creators of their just due, but made it impossible for them to effect a just distribution of the goods, since its makers had not been given the means for purchasing it. Thus, the capitalist seizure of surplus value not only robbed its armies of laborers, but forced the search for foreign purchasers: a process ultimately resulting in war (see Imperialism). The claims of communists that the U.S.S.R. and sister and satellite states had abolished the system of profit involved in surplus value has been challenged.

SURPLUSES, a problem in production, notoriously in food, which social reformers took to be a criticism of the operations of free enterprise. The defense that what was wrong was overproduction (*q.v.*) was condemned; in a needy world, it was asserted, the problem was one of underconsumption. The problem fed the propaganda of radicals, in the 1930's. The Federal Surplus Relief Corporation, set up to distribute food to Americans in want, in 1933, became in 1935 the Federal Surplus Commodities Corporation, with the broader function of directing the marketing of agricultural products. Farm surpluses were more acute than other commodities because they were more difficult to control, involved perishables, and carried a moral overtone. They were a major problem to the A.A.A. (*q.v.*), none at all during World War II (*q.v.*), and reappeared in the post-War situation. Plans to cope with it included putting land out of production, subsidies for not utilizing land, foreign sales, loans, and aid. (Americans were often unable to understand why foreign people did not appreciate the help they received from the United States.) Nevertheless, surpluses mounted, and created a storage problem. Storage facilities were also set up overseas. In 1982, the surplus problem was as acute as before. However, see Productivity.

SURVIVAL OF THE FIT, see Darwinism.

SWASTIKA, an ancient symbol, the "hooked cross," found among the designs of ancient Greece, India, China, and Japan, and in many other areas and times, including those of North and South America. It was often of religious significance, or a symbol of good luck. It was rendered infamous by the Nazis (*q.v.*), who made it a symbol of their cause. Donald M. McKale, *The Swastika outside Germany* (1977).

SWEATING SYSTEM, especially identified with "piece work" (*q.v.*), since workers who did their sewing, or cutting, or ironing, at home were in weaker position to organize in order to attempt to raise the price they could ask for their work. However, *sweat shops* brought together accumulations of workers, at low wages and in onerous working conditions, and defied them to attempt to improve their lot while employed there.

SWEDEN, developed socialist principles and cooperative associations which seemed to many reformers to make it outstanding in what it had to offer workers and reformers. Its Socialist Party, its cooperatives, and its generally high standard of living (*q.v.*) attracted attention to its operations and principles; see *Middle Way, Sweden, The.*

SWEET CASE (1925), was a product of local anti-Negro prejudice in Detroit. Dr. Ossian H. Sweet and his family having moved into a white neighborhood, they attracted threatening crowds. When they shot in self-defense, a white man was killed. Sweet, his wife and nine other Negroes were charged with murder. Clarence Darrow (*q.v.*) served with the defense. After several weeks of trial the jury disagreed. In a second trial of one defendant, he was acquitted.

SWISSHELM, MRS. JANE GREY (1815-1884), a pioneer woman journalist and abolitionist from western Pennsylvania, later of St. Cloud, Minnesota, editor of the famous *Visiter* (*sic*, on the authority of Dr. Johnson, the lexicographer). Despite an unhappy married life, she had no regard for the woman's rights movement. She hated Indians and despised drunkards. She was an example of a political abolitionist (*q.v.*). See her autobiography, *Half a Century* (1880), and Arthur J. Larsen, *Crusader and Feminist: Letters of Jane Grey Swisshelm, 1858-1865* (1934).

SYLVIS, WILLIAM H. (1828-1869), pioneer labor organizer, an iron moulder who helped organize the Iron-Moulders International Union in 1859. As a Union Democrat, he was instrumental in convening a national gathering of workingmen opposed to prosecuting the Civil War. In 1863, he became president of the iron moulders, and his efforts not only put their affairs on a stable footing but went beyond to convening the "Labor Congress" at Baltimore in 1866 which was an important step toward arranging the first meeting of the National Labor Union (*q.v.*), that same year. Sylvis became president of that body of some six hundred thousand organized workers. He appointed a permanent lobby to press its point of view on congressmen in Washington. His program included the eight-hour day, cooperatives, monetary reforms, and other tenets. Although Sylvis did not favor strikes, his organization broke important ground in this area. When he died, he was the best-known labor leader of his time; see J. C. Sylvis, *The Life, Speeches, Labors, and Essays of William H. Sylvis* (1872); compare Powderly, T. V., and Gompers, Samuel.

SYNDICALISM, see Industrial Workers of the World.

TAFT, WILLIAM HOWARD (1857-1930), a significant feature of the Progressive (*q.v.*) Era, since, though he was a conservative of unequivocal pattern, legalistic, and imperceptive respecting social needs he was nevertheless uncritically accepted by a substantial portion of the Progressives, solely because he was Theodore Roosevelt's (*q.v.*) choice. He thus illustrated the fact that Progressivism inadequately evaluated the role of national government, and was satisfied with lip-service from the central authority. It concentrated on municipal affairs, congressional commitments, and the conscience of the individual citizen. Hence, Taft's record as a judge who did not hesitate to apply the injunction (*q.v.*) against labor, as a bureaucratic governor of the Philippine Islands, as Secretary of the Department of War was passed over, merely because he promised to continue the policies of his friend. The revelation that he was no more than a Republican Party functionary with a legal mechanism built in, his role in the Ballinger Affair (*q.v.*) disillusioned reformers who had had no cause for illusions. A curiosity of historical writing was that Henry F. Pringle, whose biography of Roosevelt (1931) was written with critical and skeptical tones, wrote one of Taft (1939) with warmth and admiration impudently crediting him with the achievements of the period, though they had nothing to do with the Executive, who lost his control of Congress in 1910. Taft's son, Robert A. (1889-1953) became "Mr. Republican" on somewhat better grounds than his father. The elder Taft's touted internationalism, though a contrast to the isolationism (*q.v.*) of some of the Progressives, had no more depth than the Carnegie Endowment for International Peace, and the League to Enforce Peace (*qq.v.*). See Robert Taft's *Foreign Policy for America* (1951). An irony of the late 1970s was his becoming a hero to academic socialists who ran from clamor against the war in Vietnam to isolationism which relieved them of responsibility for what had been abandoned. Taft would not have appreciated their appreciation. See R. Radosh, *Prophets of the Right* (1975), which praised Taft for opposing "the urge to imperialism...which could not be removed without fundamental structural change." See also J. T. Patterson, *Mr. Republican* (1972).

TAFT-HARTLEY ACT (1947), see Labor Relations.

TAGORE, RABINDRANATH (1861-1941), Hindu poet and reformer, winner of the Nobel Prize for literature (1913). His personality and work served the cause of Indian nationalism, as did his work in advancing educational methods and institutions.

"TAINTED MONEY," a term applied in 1905 by the Rev. Dr. Washington Gladden (*q.v.*) to the gift of $100,000 by John D. Rockefeller, Sr., to the American Board of Foreign Missions. The success of the phrase reflected current public fear or suspicion of trusts and monopoly (*qq.v.*).

TAIWAN, see Formosa.

TAMMANY HALL, the political headquarters of the New York City Democratic Party, originally incorporated as a beneficial society in 1805 after some sixteen years of existence; it became a major symbol of political corruption, as a result, in part, of the operations of the "Tweed Ring" (*q.v.*), and for related reasons in years following. As a symbol of bad government, it attracted the ire of reformers; one notable examination is that by Gustavus Myers, *The History of Tammany Hall* (1901). The "new" Tammany, subsequently organized under Alfred E. Smith (*q.v.*), was also rendered notorious in a series of scandals causing the resignation of Mayor James J. Walker in 1932.

TAPES, the momentous factor in the Watergate (q.v.) investigation and Nixon (q.v.) resignation. Testimony earlier had involved assertions and views which might or might not implicate the President. The statement, July 13, 1973, by Alexander Butterfield of the White House staff that there were tapes of Presidential conversations began legal demands for access to the tapes which changed the character of Presidential immunity. The most relevant previous analogy was to the place of President U. S. Grant in the Whisky Ring scandals (qq.v.). There were evidently documents which could have devulged the truth of White House complicity, which were destroyed; see Filler, *Appointment at Armageddon*, pp. 86 ff. Had Nixon destroyed his tapes, his Administration would have proceded, under a fire which would probably have diminished. His decision to stand on Executive Privilege (q.v.) was the major reason for the generally agreed statement that he was himself responsible for his own defeat. The official tapes were made public in 1980, and created little interest. It seemed unlikely any future President would permit himself to be similarly victimized. An effort in 1981 by Senate Democrats to acquire unavailable tapes to buttress them in their investigation of General Alexander Haig's fitness for the Secretary of State post, he having been close to Nixon in his last White House days, was rebuffed, there being no legal process involved.

TAPPAN BROTHERS, THE, famous among reformers, especially in the 1830's. Arthur (1786-1865) became famous first, but Lewis (1788-1873) plowed deeper furrows of reform. In the 1930's, witless historians, reading his loyal *Life of Arthur Tappan* (1870), probed no further, and permitted his achievements to remain in the shadows. They were New Englanders who became wealthy merchants in New York. Arthur, a rigid, humorless reformer, patronized the American Sunday School Union, the American Tract Society, and similar organizations, helped build churches, pressed sabbath observance, temperance, anti-tobacco crusades (qq.v.). In 1827, he founded the *New York Journal of Commerce* to combat "immoral" advertisements, and in 1831 was president of the New York Magdalen Society, which hoped to end prostitution and issued a notorious report exposing conditions and possibly advertising them. He favored free churches, which would welcome Negroes, and contributed to Lane Seminary and Oberlin (qq.v.), among other institutions. He was one of the founders of the American Anti-Slavery Society (q.v.), and was helpful in the Prudence Crandall (q.v.) case. However, he lost his money in 1842, and became of less practical influence. Lewis was a personality, as well as a purse, author of pamphlets and reports which contributed to the era's affairs. In 1841, he founded "The Mercantile Agency," the first commercial credit-rating agency, and became wealthy, retiring in 1849 to attend to reform interests. He had been with his brother in all the above interests; in 1834, his house was wrecked by an anti-abolitionist mob. In 1839, he led the movement to free the Amistad captives (q.v.). When the American Anti-Slavery Society split, in 1840, he practically became the American and Foreign Anti-Slavery Society, which preached moderate abolitionism. He practically led the American Missionary Association (q.v.), influenced political abolitionists (q.v.), subsidized Alexander M. Ross who led fugitive slaves to freedom, sought to win the English over to annex Texas (q.v.) and thus prevent it coming into the Union with slavery, helped found the *Independent* and the *National Era* (qq.v.), and was a liaison agent between American and English abolitionists. His pamphlet, *Is It Right to Be Rich?* (1869) answered the question in the negative. The one study of him unfortunately, and inaccurately, traced his achievements to neurosis; B. Wyatt-Brown, *Lewis Tappan and the Evangelical War against Slavery* (1969).

TARBELL, IDA M. (1857-1944), one of the most famous figures among the reform writers of the pre-World War I period; a product of the western Pennsylvania oil fields which had felt oppressed by John D. Rockefeller's monopolistic proclivities, she became a biographer and editor of *McClure's*. Her *History of the Standard Oil Company* (1904) was intended to be a disinterested study, but, appearing when it did, fed the public's wrath. (Compare with Lloyd, Henry Demarest.) As an editor of the *American Magazine* (q.v.), she continued her moderate reformist services. During World War I, she served on the Council of National Defense, and was a member of President Wilson's Industrial Conference (1919). Her biography of Judge Elbert H. Gary, head of the U.S. Steel Corporation (1925), brought her conservative traits into stronger relief. Ida M. Tarbell, *All in the Day's Work* (1939).

TARIFF AND REFORM, see Free Trade, Protectionism.

TARIFF OF ABOMINATIONS (1828), a study in political maneuvering, it was the result of a plot by those managing Andrew Jackson's (q.v.) campaign for the Presidency to satisfy both southern and midwestern states, and such interests as those of Pennsylvania. They reasoned that New England would vote for John Quincy Adams in any event, and so could be ignored. They planned an excessively high tariff, which would please their protectionist (q.v.) voters, but which would be defeated, being so very high—a result which would please the Free Trade South. The Virginia gadfly, John Randolph, quipped that the tariff bill was intended not to refer to manufactured goods, but only to "the manufacture of a President of the United States." Although the bill surprisingly passed, the Jackson managers saw to it that it redounded to their political benefit. It prepared the way for the nullification (q.v.) controversy.

TAXATION, a reform issue mainly of interest to the middle and upper classes. American colonists endured Empire taxation with equanimity mainly because they bypassed it, whenever possible; when, at the conclusion of the French and Indian War, the British attempted to enforce their system of taxes, in order to help pay off their heavy debts, the colonists resisted. They denounced taxation without representation in the British Parliament (see American Revolution). They distinguished between internal taxes and external taxes (see Stamp Act and Townshend Acts). It is probable that they simply did not care to be taxed. They were unhappy over the taxation policies which attended the continental currency (q.v. for this and following references). Shays's Rebellion and the Whisky Rebellion both resulted from taxing policies deemed unjust. The search for an equitable tax continued; also for one which would take cognizance of ability to pay. Thus, a general sales tax was not necessarily equitable; a poor man might require more medicine than a rich man. M'Culloch v. Maryland (1819) recognized "That the power to tax involves the power to destroy." A major argument favoring protectionism was that it lightened the tax burden of Americans; the foreigner would pay it through customs duties. The income tax during the Civil War taxed the patriotism of those affected. The attempt to write an income tax into law was struck down by the U.S. Supreme Court in Pollack v. Farmers's Loan and Trust Company (1894), on grounds that it was unconstitutional. The Sixteenth Amendment (1913) made it constitutional. Henry George's Single Tax would have substituted for all other taxation. Enormously increased taxes during the 1930's and the ensuing war and cold war eras created numerous techniques for getting around taxes, including drastic views on the part of some right-wing groups for getting rid of all taxes. The solution of lotteries was even suggested, for meeting governmental requirements. High death duties created foundations which constituted a social problem in themselves. Lotteries came back. Tax protests on constitutional and other grounds increased, to the consternation of the Internal Revenue Service. In 1981, taxation was one of the major components in the government problem of reorganizing society; see also Ford Foundation, Excess Profits Tax, Proposition Thirteen. Walter W. Heller, et al., *Taxation: Dollars and Sense* (1971); Sidney Ratner, *American Taxation* (1942).

"TAYLORIZATION," the invention of Frederick W. Taylor (1856-1915), who proposed that studies of the time and motion (q.v.) employed by workers to carry out various aspects of production would enable managers to set up standards for efficient activity on the job, as well as reasonable quotas of production. His own experiments were of pioneer significance in the field; see his *The Principles of Scientific Management* (1911). Labor leaders observed the movement he had inaugurated with skepticism and fear; it seemed to them no more than the "speed up" (q.v.). Compare Stakhanovism. See Productivity.

"TEACH-INS," initiated in 1965 at the University of Michigan, and intended to raise the level of student debate over American intervention in Vietnam. It quickly became a lever for building agitation against the war; see Filler, *Vanguards and Followers;* R. Radosh, with L. Menashe, eds., *Teach-ins, U.S.A.* The concept crossed the seas, "Teach-Ins" being exploited by malcontents among West German students.

TEAMSTERS, in the late 1950's, emerged as a symbol of the power of labor and of its inadequate sense of responsibility, which lost it much public sympathy. Once, in the 1930's, a leader in the battle for organization, treated "reverently" in John Steinbeck's (q.v.) *The Grapes of Wrath,* it had become a union of a million and a half-membership rendered strategic by the fact that it could support other unions by withholding trucking. It was later observed that it could, indeed, immobilize the nation's economy, if not regulated. It therefore became a matter of social concern that it was racket (q.v.) ridden. Some radicals took the attitude that the McClellan Committee (q.v.) which exposed these facts was being anti-labor. They even were unwilling to join the non-labor interests in condemning the rule of the president of the International Brotherhood of Teamsters, Dave Beck, though he was convicted in court of embezzlement. The new president, Jimmy Hoffa (q.v.), became news, for his bold disdain of public opinion, for his defiance of the A.F.L. (q.v.), which had dropped his union from affiliation for unwillingness to drive out the criminal and corrupt elements among the teamsters, and for the manner in which he flaunted his power. He capped large projects for expansion with a declaration that he would organize any group which wanted organization, and would thus make a species of federation of his union. The A.F.L. chieftains were content to treat his boasts as impotent. McClellan, referring specifically to his plan for uniting with such powerful unions, also infected with corruption, as the International Longshoremen's Association, stated: "All of our lives are too intricately interwoven . . . [for us] to sit passively by and allow the Teamsters to create such a super-power in this country ...greater than the people and greater than the Government." Robert D. Leiter, *Teamsters Union* (1973); Steven Brill, *Teamsters* (1978).

TEAPOT DOME SCANDAL, associated with the Harding (q.v.) Administration, an indicator of the moral let-down which followed World War I. Secretary of the Interior Albert B. Fall, whose office administered the Navy oil reserves in Wyoming which bore the name Teapot Dome, leased it and a California oil reserve to individuals who were not required to engage in competitive bidding. Revelations that Fall had suddenly attained wealth opened lurid investigations which exposed the values by which Administration leaders lived. In the atmosphere of the time, they affected adversely few Republican fortunes; see also Corruption. Burl Noggle, *Teapot Dome: Oil and Politics in the 1920's* (1965).

TECHNICS AND CIVILIZATION (1934), by Lewis Mumford (q.v.), a seminal work in architecture and city planning.

TECHNOCRACY, a concept which had a brief period of popularity early in the great depression of the 1930's. Under Howard Scott, the technocrats developed the concept of the erg as a basic unit of social energy and production, which was intended to revolutionize social production, planning, and compensations; see Frank Arkright, *The ABC Of Technocracy* (1933). Technocracy was part of a social idea, foreshadowed in Thorstein Veblen's (q.v.) *The Engineers and the Price System* (1921) which anticipated the leadership of the American system falling into the hands of experts, rather than entrepreneurs (q.v.), and which was later announced as having arrived, in Burnham's *The Managerial Revolution* (q.v.).

TELEVISION, a momentous feature of American life, perhaps more so than journalism, magazines, cinema, or radio (qq.v.) earlier, because of the more cohesive audience. Television's hordes of reporters, camera people, directors, producers, entertainers have turned attention off and on of events of high significance, by treatment of details, or by ignoring them. Television channels have indeed respected Nielson poll ratings and cut and changed programs according to popularity. Also, events have taken power away from apparent masters of the medium, and placed it elsewhere. Thus, television coverage in the beginning of the Vietnam (q.v.) war escalation was used by the Johnson Administration to "educate" the public to the necessity for escalation. It soon became an expose of South Vietnamese corruption and American military incapacity. "Armchair generals" at home before "the tube" made judgments which ultimately led to Johnson's fall in 1968. The Watergate (q.v.) hearings, held interminably on television, brought out revelations which destroyed the Nixon Presidency. Whether soap operas, canned laughter, aimless violence, entertainment, and debasement of history and culture did harm which distinguished programs could not neutralize challenged observers. Although Ronald Reagan (q.v.) was an acknowledged master of television presence, it had not gained him the Presidency in previous trys before 1980. One study argued that voters learned more from paid political commercials than from evening news coverage (T. E. Patterson and R. D. McClure, *The Unseeing Eye* [1976]). Another study, sponsored by the American Association of Advertising Agencies and conducted by Purdue University psychologists, found that more than 10% of the TV-watching audience misunderstood some part of the simplest programs. The incredible interest in 1980 respecting the shooting of a "soap opera" character in *Dallas,* at the expense of serious concepts or news of any sort confounded analysis. Indeed, soap opera plots and continuity were synopsized daily for those who might have missed a ridiculous episode. There was, however, the possibility that those indulging such fantasy could control their escapist impulses when survival impulses surfaced. See also Popular Arts. G. Blumler and D. McQuail, *Television Politics* (1969); W. P. Dizzard, *Television: a World View* (1966); Martin Mayer, *About Television* (1972); R. E. Gilbert, *Television and Presidential Politics* (1972); Harry J. Skornia, *Television and the News* (1974); Anthony Piepe, *Television and the Working Class* (1975); Douglas Cater and Richard Adler, *Television as a Social Force* (1975); G. J. Goodhardt et al., *The Television Audience; Patterns of Viewing* (1975); J. Frank, *Television: How to Use It Wisely with Children* (1976). See also Debates.

TELLER AMENDMENT, see Platt Amendment.

TEMPERANCE, a relatively modern movement, intemperance rather than temperance being the rule, historically considered; but associated with the problem of reform since the beginning of the national period. Whether the temperance work of Lyman Beecher (q.v.) served reform or merely exploited unease on the subject, to no purpose, is uncertain. The Washingtonians, formed in 1840, are of interest as being a temperance movement which emphasized moral support, rather than religious fears; thus, they were similar to Alcoholics Anonymous (q.v.), of later vintage. Temperance was one of the reforms which helped give anti-slavery agitators some social status; later, it helped give northern Whigs and northern Democrats something in common, as they maneuvered to dissociate themselves from their southern counterparts. Women concerned for the suffrage found it advantageous to blend their concern for temperance and woman's rights, in order to give themselves a forum. In 1874, the Woman's Christian Temperance Union undertook its drive against drink, its program now being substantially one favoring prohibition, and leading to the tactics of Carry A. Nation *(q.v.)*. Socialists tended toward temperance, emphasizing that drunkenness incapacitated the oppressed classes, and made them unable to fight for their rights. However, various elements among the reformers saw no contradiction between drink and reform. Local option and state regulation acted to have a temperance effect. Prohibitionists, after their defeat in 1933, became students of the liquor problem, and assembled valuable data on the subject, becoming, in effect, critics of intemperance, rather than authoritarian advocates of total abstinence.

TENANT FARMER, a product of Reconstruction conditions in the South *(q.v.)*, when many of the great slave plantations had been broken up and an economic system was being forged to control the Negroes and accommodate the poor whites *(qq.v.)*. The tenant farm was subject to the ultimate control of the owner. A sharecropper was subject to a division of a harvest which roughly took one third of the returns for the use of the land, one third for feed, tools, provisions, and other necessities; he received what was left. The crop-lien system emphasized the merchant, who advanced the farmer his requirements for the season's work, and administered the sale and division of the crop. The increasing troubles of northern farmers made tenancy an economic system in their section as well, especially in the west; later great consolidations of farms increased the number of tenants, ultimately producing the tragic characters of *The Grapes of Wrath* *(q.v.)*.

TENDENZ WRITING, writing from a particular viewpoint. The English "partisan" and "prejudiced" does not convey the meaning of the French, emphasizing as the former do the personal attitude of the writer; the French underscores the social and political interest for which he speaks, the party he serves. Thus identified, the writer is prevented from pretending an impartiality he does not feel or attempt to attain; for better or worse, the source roots of his opinions and attitudes can be traced.

TENEMENTS, see Housing Problem, The.

TEN-HOUR DAY, a major demand of labor in the pre-Civil War era; the government in 1840, under President Van Buren *(q.v.)*, extended the ten-hour ceiling on labor performed by government workers, thus setting an example to the nation. Although large numbers of laborers continued to have to give much more of their time to private employers, the ten-hour day spread; by the time the Civil War created great needs for workers, the ten-hour day was generally established, among organized workers; see also Eight-Hour Day, Sabbath.

"TEN-PERCENT PLAN," see Reconstruction Plans.

TENNESSEE VALLEY AUTHORITY, a major achievement of the New Deal *(q.v.)*, it acquired its vision from Arthur E. Morgan *(q.v.)*, who saw it not merely a series of dams and electricity-producing units, but a key agency, for transforming the valley by educating the farmers, reinvigorating the soil and cooperating with programs which would reshape the countryside. A significant feature of the T.V.A. program was to be its use as a "yardstick" for privately held utilities rates to power-users. Morgan was squeezed out of the chairmanship, thanks to his associates on the Board of T.V.A. The larger plan for the Authority was scrapped. Although the "yardstick" was under constant attack as unfair, since T.V.A. did not pay taxes, and could absorb its deficits, it was established as successful. An effort in 1954 by President Eisenhower to have the Atomic Energy Commission draw up a twenty-five year contract with the entrepreneurs Dixon and Yates to erect a private facility in Arkansas to supply power for the T.V.A., for use by the A.E.C. was taken as a first-line attack

on T.V.A. The intention was evidently to limit the expansion possibilities of T.V.A., mix its operations with private industry, and perhaps expand the trend. A year-long battle ended with the withdrawal of the contract. The weight of the protest, however, came not from national reform elements but from the conservative groups in the Valley itself. In addition there appeared no immediate prospect that the T.V.A. idea, even as limited to power and flood control, would be notably extended elsewhere. See also, Missouri Valley Authority. T. K. McCraw, *TVA and the Power Fight* (1971).

TERRORISM, a growth in the 1970s, developing out of a loosening of social sanctions and a breakdown of national and international consensus against terrorism. Thus, highjackers of planes were often given sanctuary by governments at odds with the highjacked governments. Hatred of the United States made American terrorists a means for expressing such hatred. Palestinian atrocities *(q.v.)*, endured by Arabs and others fearful of uncontainable Middle East war gave inspiration to terrorists everywhere, notably in Northern Ireland and in Italy, where nationalism and poverty raged. West Germany, a "miracle" of economic recovery, produced some of the most desperate terrorists, seeking to "reach" the nation's materialistic leaders. Terrorism in Libya was official, and reached dissident Libyans, who were killed on foreign soil. Africa's "freedom fighters" practiced terrorism, sternly resisted by the Union of South Africa, but justified elsewhere. A remarkable fact, passed over by United Nations committees and others concerned for terrorism, was that many terrorists were solicited, armed, and trained by Soviet agencies working to expand Soviet influence from Uganda to El Salvador, and involving assaults in the European nations with which the Soviets dealt diplomatically. Although world terrorism made much of life close to unbearable in the areas most acutely affected, it was hard to fashion cooperation for diminishing it, though security forces became more adept at snaring unprotected desperadoes. Modern terrorism was the opposite of the Reign of Terror *(q.v.)*, where the dominant forces terrorized the weak and few. Paul Wilkinson, *Terrorism and the Liberal State* (1979); G. McKnight, *The Terrorist Mind* (1975); M. Hussain, *The Palestine Liberation Organization* (1975); Murray C. Havens et al., *Assassination and Terrorism* (1975); A. M. Burton, *Urban Terrorism* (1976); J. B. Bell, *Terror out of Zion: the Irgun, 1929-1949* (1977); Lillian Becker, *Hitler's Children: the...Baader-Meinhof Terrorist Gang* (1977).

TEXAS, a problem for social reformers, being born of a "fifth column" operation and, by the nature of its terrain and industries, being especially receptive to extremes of individualism. Walter P. Webb, a Texas professor, author of the distinguished *The Great Plains* (1931), which saw the subject it discussed as one of a civilization, was also author of *Divided We Stand* (1936), an odd little book which saw his section as under the heel of eastern monopoly. Apparently, the Texas point of view distinguished between eastern tycoons and western tycoons. It was difficult to think of social reform movements in connection with Texas, except in cases of temperance *(q.v.)* and some other special areas. More typical seemed such a personality as Hugh Roy Cullen; see Oil. However, Dallas was the publication locale for the *Southwest Review*, a liberal quarterly, though extremely limited in circulation.

THATCHER, MARGARET (1925-   ), first woman Prime Minister of Great Britain, until 1979 known, when at all, as the first woman in Great Britain to head a political party, which she had done since 1975. Her role in Parliament, following studies and degrees in chemistry and law, went back to 1959 when, as Conservative MP from North London she became joint parliamentary secretary to the Ministry of Pensions and national insurance. In 1970 she became Secretary of State for education and science. As Prime Minister she inherited a difficult condition of lagging economy in both private and nationalized sectors, inflation, doubtful education policies, and a struggle among competing nations. She determined on a curb on government spending, diminishing the socialist features of the economy, demanding higher and better productivity from both industry and unions, minimum rises in cost of living wage increases, and avoidance of a "U Turn" which would drain the program of its solvency goals. For cutting back on aid to Third World nations, the *Observer* called the government report on aid "mean, callous, short-sighted, pompous, mealy-mouthed." Her reluctant aid to "lame duck" industries provoked scorn and hope that the "Iron Lady" was breaking. Inflation coming down, attention centered on unemployment, which rose to over three million—12½% of the working population—and increased Labour hopes of a return to power. An attempt to down tools by unionists, to help bring the government down, failed badly. The slogan "Ditch the Bitch" disturbed feminists as well as others. Mrs. Thatcher stood firm on "monetary" economics *(q.v.)* with their complex unemployment-dole, interest rates, and pound-value components. Mrs. Thatcher's hope of success was aided by the separations in Labour of socialists and non-socialist elements, weakening both. A "shrewd suspicion" even developed, as Reagan *(q.v.)* took office that "President Thatcher" was in charge in Washington, and raising the value of the beset dollar by "her" policies. Whatever the fate of her administration, it was evident that the Thatcher Prime Ministry marked an era. Hugh Stephenson, *Mrs. Thatcher's First Year* (1980). See also Great Britain, and *(qq.v.)* for above.

THEATER, a medium for the transmission of social reform ideas or feelings, effectively or otherwise. *Uncle Tom's Cabin* *(q.v.)*, though muddled in understanding, probably did help crystallize northern views about the wrong of slavery. Ibsen and Shaw *(qq.v.)* were strong forces for stimulation in the area. Rose Pastor Stokes's *(q.v.)* *The Woman Who Wouldn't*, however, furnished a poor contrast with her more consequential deeds. John Howard Lawson, **Elmer Rice, and** Eugene O'Neill on occasion furnished sharp social criticism, in the 1920's. Robert E. Sherwood's *Idiot's Delight* parasitized on current interest in munitions *(q.v.)*, rather than helped clarify their meaning. The Federal Theater Project *(q.v.)* came the closest to being by its nature a social, if not a social reform, theater movement. After its close, it was scorned by intellectuals as mere documentation and relief work. The theater brought from abroad the work of Hauptmann, Rolland, Gorki *(qq.v.)*, and others of depth and social profundity. The Moscow Art Theater displayed technique as well as subject matter in the United States. Valentine Katayev's comedy, *Squaring the Circle*, encouraged a human view of the Soviets. A play on Joe Hill *(q.v.)* as late as 1954, sought a public response to the portrayal of the life and death of a social rebel. A phenomenon of the youth *(q.v.)* movement was the rise of *Guerrilla theater*, often given in the streets, an agitational means for expressing "militancy" and sympathy with militancy, anti-establishment attitudes, and assertions of freedom to present nakedness, rock music, and approval of drug and body use. It produced no art. Walter Laqueur, *Guerrilla Reader* (1977); Michael Shamberg, *Guerrilla Television* (1971).

THEORY OF THE LEISURE CLASS, THE (1899), see Veblen, Thorstein.

THEOCRACY, see Calvinism and Reform.

THEOSOPHICAL SOCIETY, organized in 1875 by Madame Helena Petrouna Blavatsky, a woman of uncertain origins; it attracted middle class and otherwise respectable elements. It embraced mystical doctrines comprehending the search for Universal Brotherhood, the unity of existence, the relations of all religions, and other tenets suggesting, if remotely, cooperative principles. It reflected the spiritual unrest, though with less social concreteness than did Christian Socialism *(q.v.)*. However, members of the Boston chapter were impressed by Edward Bellamy's *Looking Backward* *(q.v.)*, being as much arrested by its religious overtones as

by its mechanical ingenuities, and helped stir up interest in the book. M. Heindel and M. P. Hall, *Blavatsky and the Secret Doctrine* (1972).

THERMIDOR, the eleventh month in the calendar of the first French Republic; period of its overthrow by Napoleon Buonaparte *(q.v.)*. Leon Trotsky *(q.v.)* and his followers termed the rise of Stalinism *(q.v.)* as constituting a similar "Thermidor" for the Russian revolution *(q.v.)* .

THIRD ESTATE, see Fourth Estate.

THIRD FORCE, the concept that lesser military nations, and even those of the smallest size, could, by their appeal to the conscience of the world, rather than its fear of armaments, offset the fear and authority which the United States and the U.S.S.R. could employ. France, under De Gaulle, became a symbol of the ability of a "second-rate" nation to return to respectability in international councils, though its own Algerian difficulties dramatized the fact that no nationalist group was too backward to create trouble and command attention and respect; see also Cold War.

THIRD INTERNATIONAL, or Communist International, organized in Moscow in March 1919 under the auspices of the triumphant Bolsheviks. A manifesto, drafted by Lenin, Trotsky *(qq.v.)*, Zinoviev, among others, was issued, which declared for the Dictatorship of the Proletariat and denounced the Second International as bankrupt. In the view of the Communists, the First International had given the working classes a banner, the Second had raised the working masses to their feet. The Third International would bring the final victory. During the struggle of Stalin and Trotsky for power, the Third International became a pawn. Following Stalin's ascendancy, annual meetings were dispensed with. The International was a victim of World War II, being officially disbanded in 1943. It was succeeded by a Communist Information Bureau (Cominform) which maintained one type of liaison with its national units. In 1933, when the German Communist Party fell before the Nazis, the "Trotskyites" *(q.v.)* declared the Third International bankrupt, and raised the slogan favoring a Fourth International *(q.v.)*. W. S. Sworakowski, *The Communist International and Its Front Organizations* (1965); D. E. Albright, *Communism and Political Systems in Western Europe* (1978); F. Claudin, *The Communist Movement: from Comintern to Cominform* (1977); Earl Latham, ed., *The Communist Controversy in Washington: from the New Deal to McCarthy* (1969); C. A. Johnson, *Communist Policies toward the Intellectual Class* (1970); Harry G. Shaffer, ed., *The Communist World: Marxist and Non-Marxist Views* (1967).

THIRD PARTIES have been dissident groups by their nature, though their dissidence has been of the extreme right and left *(q.v.)*, as well as of a social reform character. For third parties of the latter category, see Anti-Masonry, Liberty Party, Free Soil Party, Liberal Republican Party, Greenback-Labor Party, People's Party, Progressive Party. The Republican Party was not a third party, though often set down as such; it superseded the Whig Party. See also Fred E. Haynes, *Third Party Movements Since the Civil War with Special Reference to Iowa* (1916). The major parties have not been threatened seriously more recently, though there have been alarmist signs. Strom Thurman's 1948 States Rights Democratic Party hoped to create a deadlock in the Truman-Dewey race, but though Thurman received 39 electoral votes, failed to do so. George Wallace's American Independent Party ruined its momentum in 1968 when Wallace announced his running mate to be General Curtis LeMay. John B. Anderson's 1980 candidacy was touted as darkhorse and imponderable, but was revealed to be an empty shrine. Howard P. Nash, *Third Parties in American Politics* (1958); D. A. Mazmanian, *Third Parties in Presidential Elections* (1974).

THIRD WORLD, a synonym for "underdeveloped nations" and other euphemisms. The quest of great powers for influence or actual holdings in such lands led them to grant power and courtesy even to patent tyrants and murderers like Idi Amin and Libya's Gaddafi. Soviet Russia provided veneers of "socialist" jargon for them, and, generally, gained from direct shows of power in "third world" nations.

THIRTEENTH AMENDMENT (1865), see Slavery.

THIRTIES, THE, as compared with Twenties (q.v.), drab, receptive to communist legends, willingness toward regimentation, and despairing of American traditions; yet featuring the New Deal (q.v.), and a sense of purpose, to "change the world"; see Filler, ed., The Anxious Years (1964); Frank Gloversmith, ed., Class, Culture and Social Change (1980).

THOMAS, NORMAN (1884-1968), former clergyman, editor of the World Tomorrow (1918-1921), and successor to Eugene V. Debs (q.v.) as Socialist Party standard-bearer; indicative of the relative fall from consequence of the cause he represented. Unlike Debs, he could muster no strategic words or deeds, though his writings often contained useful information; see The Conscientious Objector in America (1923), Is Conscience a Crime? (1927), and Prosperity? (1927), among others. A wit dubbed him "Normal Times." See Murray B. Seidler, Norman Thomas, Respectable Rebel (1961).

THOMAS, PIRI (1928-   ), Puerto Rican-American author, born in New York City, whose Down These Mean Streets (1967) expressed his rage and triumph over poverty and ethnic humiliation, the life of a heroin addict and thief, and inmate of Sing Sing, and his emergence as a person of pride and philosophy. His confessional writing and good reception was comparable to that accorded a variety of black and American Indian writers, some of whom were, like Piri, sent abroad to read from their works under Department of State auspices.

THOREAU, HENRY D. (1817-1862), social rebel who, in Parrington's (q.v.) words, spent his life considering how one could live without committing his time to futile labor. Best known is his refusal in 1848 to pay a poll tax because the money went to a government which was waging war on Mexico, and his essay, Resistance to Civil Government (1849), which influenced Gandhi (q.v.). The key to his life was his art, and his interest in creating symbols of meaning. Thus, he spent no more than one day in prison for refusing to pay the tax, but it sufficed to indicate his views and his method. Again, he lived but two years in the location which gave the material for and the name to his masterpiece, Walden (1854); but, again, it sufficed to accomplish a cycle of effort. The work itself was filled with symbols and indirect references usually missed by the careless reader. For the rest, he sought personal identity with nature and reality, and thought that others might profitably do the same. In the last few years before the Civil War, he became perturbed over the reality of fugitive slaves, and when John Brown (q.v.) made his own symbolic gesture at Harpers Ferry, he felt it necessary to offer lectures in which he pleaded not so much for Brown's life as for his character. Thoreau's fame was entirely posthumous and misconstrued; readers thought he was a fresh-air fiend. Later they sentimentalized his desire to live the "higher" life, and get away from the hurly-burly of life. A publisher who made a great deal of money from a selection of Thoreau's work wondered, privately, what readers saw in him. The answer was that the many purchasers of the work were students, and most of them saw no more in Thoreau than did the publisher.

THOUGHT REFORM, ssu-hsiang kai-tsao, a project of the communist Chinese regime, which has impressed reformers because it seems to attack the basic qualities of the individual and democracy. Unlike "brain-washing" (q.v.), identified with American prisoners and with torture as well as blandishments, thought control probes at the roots of the individual, and seeks to persuade him to become a critic of his entire mental outlook, viewing it from Communist Party perspectives. He becomes a function of the party, viewing

his personal and private values as "bourgeois" and "decadent." The process is similar to "self criticism," as practiced under the auspices of Stalin. "Self criticism" (q.v.), however, was a less intensive method of thought control. The notorious confessions (q.v.) elicited at the Soviet trials of former comrades were more a police than a social measure. See Theodore H. E. Chen, Thought Reform of the Chinese Intellectuals (1960).

THREE-FIFTHS CLAUSE of the U.S. Constitution, Article I, Section 2, stipulates that "Representatives and direct Taxes shall be apportioned among the several States which may be included within this Union, according to their respective Numbers, which shall be determined by adding to the whole Number of free Persons, including those bound to Service for a Term of Years, and excluding Indians not taxed, three fifths of all other Persons." Thus, the Negro was considered a "Person": a fact which social reformers held on to tenaciously, even when they protested that slave-holders ought not to have the political benefit of having slaves.

TILDEN, SAMUEL J. (1814-1886), elected President of the United States, but not able to assume the office in the dangerous complexities of the "Disputed Election of 1876" (q.v.). He was a lawyer and party regular among the Democrats, and their governor of New York, in which capacity he helped prosecute the "Tweed Ring" (q.v.). Essentially a conservative, he was put up by the Democrats as one who could promise that the noisome scenes of Grant's Administration would not be repeated, but that nothing radically useful to farmers or laborers would be instituted. Had he been decisive, it is probable that he would have received the Presidency, for there was much public feeling against the tainted Republicans and a realization that the election had been clearly Tilden's. Choosing to become legalistic, in a situation for which no legal instrument was available, he revealed himself as weak and dispensable. His words under his statue in New York, "Let the People Judge," are misleading. Paul L. Haworth, The Hayes-Tilden Disputed Presidential Election of 1876 (1906).

TILLMAN, BENJAMIN R. (1847-1918), South Carolina's spokesman for the common white man, United States Senator from his state from 1895 to the end of his life; an ardent proponent of experimental farms, and other means, direct and indirect, of improving the fortunes of farmers; "Pitchfork Ben," one of his pieces of oratorical violence caused him to be called. Like Tom Watson (q.v.), he was a Negrophobe. F. B. Simkins, Pitchfork Ben Tillman (1944).

TILTON, THEODORE (1835-1907), editor of the Independent (q.v.) and of the Golden Age. He became liberal in religion, a vigorous abolitionist, and an advocate of woman's rights (qq.v.), and famous in the 1860's and early 1870's for his public views, being notable in the campaign to impeach President Johnson (q.v.). He was most famous, however, as a principal in the suit against Henry Ward Beecher (q.v.) for adultery: a noisome affair which involved woman suffragists and orthodox personages of Beecher's congregation, and dragged on from 1870 until it became the topic of all conversation in 1875. Tilton wrote verses and pamphlets which were esteemed in their time, including a life of Victoria Woodhull (q.v.). He left the country in 1883 and died abroad.

TIME, see Luce, Henry Robinson.

TIME AND MOTION, concepts in Taylorization (q.v.), involving the use of stop-watches in order to determine by repeated actions how long it takes to accomplish a specific operation in an industrial plant. The average thus defined can be utilized to discover defects in an overall project: to learn what or who is "holding up the works," impeding completion of the work, being a "bottle-neck." Improperly employed, time and motion studies can result in an undesired "speed up." (q.v.).

TIME WORK, see Piece Work.

TIPPING, long despised by labor and social reform theoreticians as degrading, but persisting in custom and necessity. It has affected such labor groups as waitresses, taxi drivers, newspaper carriers, check-room girls, and barbers. The lack of definitions in the area, maintained by interested elements, such as employers who kept wages low on the understanding that tips would provide a living wage, has kept the topic in the realm of snobbish fears, bad conscience, misunderstanding, and cynicism. Crusades against tipping have been met with crusades against heartlessness. It has been noted that many areas involve not so much service as special service: a waitress's smile, prompt production of matches when wanted, and other individualizing features. It appeared difficult to regularize such matters under the Fair Labor Standards Act (q.v.), despite the fact that many persons affected were obviously laborers in the most onerous sense of the word. The fact that the Government prepared a manual for the use of participants in a White House Conference on Children and Youth in 1960, suggesting proper tips to taxi drivers, porters and hotel employees did not help to combat the practice of tipping. The gross inflation of the 1970s and plummeting in service did not appreciably affect it. If anything, the diminished coin and dollar, when mixed with fear and hope, appeared to augment it.

TITO, MARSHAL (1892-1980), originally Josip Broz, Yugoslavian communist and underground fighter during the Nazi interregnum, he emerged in the post-World War II period as dictator of a Yugoslavia which had exterminated the opposition. He shattered the communist pattern by refusing to conform to Moscow dictation, and was expelled from its Cominform. As such, he became of interest to the U.S. government, which put him on the list for foreign aid, despite the protests of principled conservatives. Tito exemplified the dilemmas of the time, being himself a ruthless killer and jailer of oppositionists, yet respected by the democracies for his stand against the greater danger of an unleashed Russia. Ernst Halperin, *The Triumphant Heretic: Tito's Struggle against Stalin* (1958); J. Roucek, *Tito* (1973); H.M. Christman, ed., *Tito Speaks* (1978).

"TO THE VICTOR BELONGS THE SPOILS" (1831), notorious phrase voiced by William L. Marcy, Democratic Party politician from New York, which was seized upon as embodying the philosophy of the party which had crystallized about Andrew Jackson (q.v.). Although their opponents also rewarded their friends and punished their foes, the Democratic Party, thanks to its more ready contact with the city poor, was prone to greater directness in recognizing the power of favors and perquisites.

TOBACCO, see Anti-Tobacco Crusade.

TOCQUEVILLE, ALEXIS DE (1805-1859), brilliant French traveler in the United States (1831), sent there by the French government to study the country's penal system; on his return he published a report on its possibilities for France. Several years later, however, he published the work which became famous in America as *Democracy in America*, more vital and evocative than the later classic study by James Bryce (q.v.), *The American Commonwealth*.

TOKENISM, long established in politics, social and practical, to create liaison personalities between minority groups and the dominant leadership, as well as to pay off helpful figures for services rendered. As a result of the minority and youth unrest of the post-World War II period, tokenism took on new aspects and reached into higher and more numerous areas. President Johnson was lavish in token appointments, especially to Negroes. His appointment of Thurgood Marshall to the Supreme Court was more than token, but raised discussion about the first woman who would receive such an appointment. President Carter's appointment of his political ally Andrew Young as UN representative was, again, more than token, but provoked debate respecting his qualifications,

considering his declared view, among others, that America jailed many political prisoners. By 1980, the media were alert to political appointments, hastily headlining Reagan's (q.v.) early lack of Negro or woman Cabinet appointments. He was, however, evidently seeking to broaden the range of minority agency and aide appointments to include Hispanics. The media were generally more alert to the possibility of bigotry among "token" appointees than of incompetence.

TOLERATION ACT of 1649, a landmark in official recognition of just religious differences before the law. It resulted from the fact that Maryland had been founded by Catholics, under Lord Baltimore, but that Protestants had quickly joined the colony and competed for authority. The quarrels and battles finally suggested to a deputy-governor, William Stone, a Protestant, the need for pacifying deeds; the Toleration Act granted religious freedom in Maryland, though it limited it to Christians. The act was later revoked (1654). See Intolerance.

TORIES, a party in England, crystallized under George III, which opposed extended Parliamentary privileges. It attracted the sympathy of American "Loyalists," who, however, were not far from the radical faction among Americans who also were suspicious of Parliament, to the extent that it felt free to tax patriotic Americans. Once American revolutionary sentiment had crystallized to make a scapegoat of the Crown, the politics of the Tories in America and Tories in Great Britain became one. Tories, early in the nineteenth century, became Conservatives in Great Britain, as their opponent Whigs became Liberals. In the United States, Whigs became the more conservative faction, on some issues (qq.v.). In slang, "Tory" retained the connotation of reactionary, and defender of the *status quo* (q.v.).

TOTALITARIAN LIBERALS, a curious permutation of liberal produced by excessive sympathy with communist goals and rationalizations, in the 1930's and after. Such "liberals" felt that anything less than total endorsement of Soviet policy was "reactionary," and used epithets (q.v.) freely in defense of their attitude. The less permissive atmosphere of the 1940's and after caused most of them to abandon their totalitarian liberalism, though maintaining elements of their approach, as in applying epithets in uncompromising fashion to General Douglas MacArthur, President Dwight D. Eisenhower, and others.

TOUSSAINT L'OUVERTURE (1743-1803), Haitian liberator, a Negro slave who rose through revolts and differences between English, Spanish, and French elements on the island of Hispaniola, in the Caribbean Sea, to become master of the western third of the island, Haiti. He sought to organize a program which would raise the opportunities of the slave caste and create a stable government for all. Having accepted a nominal relationship to France, he now proclaimed himself president; in retaliation, Napoleon (q.v.) sent a force to subjugate him. Following desperate conflicts, Toussaint was tricked into visiting France for negotiations; there he was killed. The poet Wordsworth honored him in a noble sonnet; Wendell Phillips (q.v.) in an eloquent oration. G. F. Tyson, Jr., ed., *Toussaint L'Ouverture* (1973); Ronald Syme, *Toussaint, the Black Liberator* (1971).

TOWN MEETING, a colonial institution deriving from the congregational form of Puritanism (q.v.) in New England, and a major contribution to American democratic techniques. Meetings were called which all citizens could attend, and where they could directly affect basic town policy. Though it is now administered by duly elected officers, the town meeting still persists in much of New England, and encourages individual opinion as well as civic conscience.

TOWNLEY, ARTHUR C. (1880-1959), organizer and leading spirit of the Nonpartisan League (q.v.), a former socialist who manifested extraordinary ability to win the confidence and support of middle-western and northwestern farmers in behalf of a program intended to minister to farmer's needs. He created the League in 1915, and led it, developing its state ownership principles, until its decline early in the 1920's. Since the movement was in no small measure the result of his personality and individual abilities, both merit study and understanding.

TOWNSEND PLAN, devised by Dr. Francis E. Townsend, and intended to take the United States out of the Great Depression, while also providing for their needy old people. All Americans over sixty years of age were to be given a pension of two hundred dollars each month, the money to be acquired by taxing commercial enterprises two-percent. Recipients of these funds were to spend them within five days, thus keeping the money in circulation. The organization of "Townsend Clubs," and their effect on legislators, were an important factor in the institution of social security (q.v.). Even following the depression, and the ensuing "war prosperity," Townsend Clubs continued in existence, for social purposes, and because inflation (q.v.), and meagre returns from social security, kept old people conscious of their troubles as a class.

TOWNSHEND ACTS (1767), an effort on the part of Great Britain to maintain a taxing policy with respect to the American colonies, in view of the failure of the Stamp Act (q.v.). Colonists had averred that they were opposed to "internal taxation"; the Townshend Acts placed a duty on commodities being imported from Great Britain, including glass, red and white lead, painters' colors, paper, and tea. The dissatisfaction created in the colonies ultimately resulted in the Boston Tea Party (q.v.).

TOXIC WASTES, POISONING, a problem of the 1980s, thanks to the proliferation of chemical compounds and nuclear waste. Although Congress acted in 1976 to require companies to keep "cradle to grave" records of toxic substances and their disposal, companies hastened to rid themselves of their toxic holdings before the deadline, in order to save money. Many of the tales unearthed by correspondents proved horrendous: companies putting their enduring, harmful waste almost anywhere, including public car lots, employing gangsters to help them get their waste off the premises, and permitting the waste to sink into areas including "ground water" which affected up to 100 million people by estimate. The Environment Protection Agency followed these developments as best it could, considering that many of the industrial centers they monitored, and the Chemical Manufacturers Association which looked out for their interests, were reluctant to cooperate with what they felt were oppressive regulations. The military, too, handling radioactive wastes, nerve gas, and other highly toxic chemicals dumped its waste on old principles of the land being able to absorb waste without harm to those using water containing residues of waste. Although federal, state, and municipal agencies spent substantial sums on air and water pollution— $11.9 billion in 1978—it required a major tragedy to focus the attention of the nation. Toxic wastes dumped into the Love Canal in New York so severely contaminated the neighborhood over the years as to require emergency action for the 710 families living in the area. Chromosome defects had been caused by the chemicals, buried as early as 1950 in the region. Although one particular company was found culpable in the matter, the harm it had done to a community called attention to numerous other potential tragedies elsewhere. In Michigan, a giant toxic waste pit was being erected at a cost of 15 to 20 million dollars, lined with chemically impregnable clay, to hold 1.2 million cubic yards of toxic chemical wastes. The result of a "consent" agreement between the company and the state, the pit was expected to serve as a model for cleanup operations throughout the United States. Marshall S. Shapo, *A Nation of Guinea Pigs: the Unknown Risks of Chemical Technology* (1979).

TRACTORS FOR FREEDOM, a humiliating episode among many attending the ineffective American effort to aid in the overthrow of the Castro government in Cuba (q.v.), in 1961.

Castro offered to trade the Cuban invasion prisoners he had on hand for tractors, and a committee under distinguished auspices took steps to raise the necessary money to purchase the necessary tractors. Castro however, became pertinacious about the kind of tractors he desired in return for some twelve hundred prisoners, and the negotiations were finally broken off, the sixty to seventy thousand letters containing money being returned to the donors by the American committee without having been opened.

TRADE AGREEMENTS ACT (1934), see Free Trade.

TRADE UNION UNITY LEAGUE, a phase of the communist ultra-leftist policy, it developed out of the Trade Union Education League (T.U.E.L.), run by William Z. Foster (q.v.) in the 1920's, and influential among clothing workers and miners dissatisfied with the conservative leadership of the A.F.L. (q.v.). The T.U.U.L., organized in 1928, took the attitude that workers were becoming ripe for mass organization under militant, revolutionary leaders. As such, it functioned as a dual union (q.v.), and was held by both A.F.L. leaders and communists at odds with the official Communist Party to be a strike-breaking organization. Nevertheless, the T.U.U.L. continued to function, in many cases with paper organizations, until 1934, when the increasing militancy of labor made it more practical for communists to work within the mass organization movements which soon crystallized into the C.I.O. (q.v.).

TRADES UNIONS, the overall designation for workingmen associations before the challenge of mass-production industries. Workers organized by crafts on local, district, and national bases and sought representation in central bodies which convened to consider common interests. The American Federation of Labor (q.v.) committed itself to a trade union form of labor organization, and resisted the demands for organization or aid of unskilled or weak labor elements. Mass production machinery increasingly infringed upon the integrity and significance of the trades. The C.I.O. (q.v.) met the challenge with its program of vertical unionism (q.v.), in the 1930's, but not with a vigor which rendered the A.F.L. obsolete; when they joined in 1955, it was as equals who needed one another for strength.

TRANSCENDENTALISM, a movement among intellectuals in New England in the 1830-60 period, it drew from older religious unrest and idealism, and newer wants for a more satisfactory relationship with the world and the universe. Influences included German idealistic philosophy, Platonic thought and such English literary influences as Carlyle (q.v.) the poet Samuel Taylor Coleridge, as well as Oriental and Indian mysticism. In such essays as Emerson's (q.v.) "The Over-Soul" and "Self-Reliance" Transcendentalists voiced their desire for a spontaneous sense of life, and for self-expression. They had in common with the reformers of the era an individual responsibility for private or public affairs, and an impatience with ritual and the mere letter of the law. Thus, even Emerson, though concerned for persons rather than society, found himself speaking in behalf of reformers; and such others as Theodore Parker, A. Bronson Alcott, and Margaret Fuller (qq.v.) were energetic in contributing to education, woman's self-expression, and anti-slavery, among other fields, as well as furnishing some of the spirit as well as the substance of Brook Farm (q.v.). Perry Miller, *Transcendentalism: an Anthology* (1950).

TRANSMISSION BELT, in the radical jargon of the 1930's, a "communist front" organization intended to enlist the interest and support of persons who were not members of the Communist Party, but could be persuaded to aid causes of interest to the C.P., and do better work because they could not be accused of being communists. In some cases, persons so employed became sufficiently absorbed in the cause to join "the Party." Thus, the organization was a transmission belt bringing new recruits to the cause. The American League for Peace and Democracy was one such transmission belt.

TRANSPORTATION ACT OF 1920, see Esch-Cummins Railroad Bill.

TREASON, an unexpected problem to social reformers who believed there were developing higher concepts than those involved in patriotism (q.v.): an international attitude which would ensure peace among nations and quell the chauvinists (q.v.) at home. William Lloyd Garrison asserted that his country was the world, but he emphasized domestic affairs and associations almost to the exclusion of those abroad. However, the rise of international socialism, and its breakdown during World War I, resulted in a more militant internationalism dominated by the U.S.S.R. (q.v.). Its admirers believed they were helping all mankind by, first, "defending the Soviet Union," and, later, cooperating with its agents. Though this seemed a form of friendship during the 1930's and during World War II, it seemed less so once the "cold war" (q.v.) began. Fear of Russia gave a new meaning to treason, and ultimately brought the Rosenbergs (q.v.) to the electric chair. See Nathaniel Weyl, *Treason* (1950), which develops the history of its subject from Benedict Arnold to Alger Hiss (q.v.). A number of subsequent revelations indicated treasonable sentiments were shared by elements of the public and government. Thus, Kim Philby, a highly placed British traitor, long absconded to Russia, believed he had served "his" English people as well as his Soviet hosts. An Oxford group of traitors, aired in 1980 in Andrew Boyle's *The Climate of Treason*, featured Sir Anthony Blunt, an esteemed art critic. Oddly, his treason had been long known to government, but the fact hidden, presumably because of his expertise in art. The historian A.J.P. Taylor praised the British Academy not expelling Blunt as a victory for decency and commonsense. Although Blunt was stripped of his honors, it was evident that he had substantial sympathy in his country. After all, wrote one correspondent, he had transmitted secret information to Britain's ally in World War II, Russia. See R. B. Fowler, *Believing Skeptics: American Political Intellectuals, 1945-1964* (1978). A famous title by the French novelist Julien Benda continued in recollection: *The Treason of the Intellectuals* (1927). It argued that intellectuals had abandoned their search for truth in the interests of dogma. See also Ferdinand Lundberg, *The Treason of the People* (1954).

TREASON OF THE SENATE, THE (1906), by David Graham Phillips the highpoint of muckraking in its expose phase, a series of articles which ran in *Cosmopolitan* from March to November. It indicted the Senate as a self-conscious brake on public wants and demands, and marshalled arguments and data in support of its thesis which reverberated throughout the west in particular, and began the movement which resulted in the passage of the seventeenth amendment to the Constitution, providing for popular election of senators, rather than, as formerly, by the state assemblies. It also evoked from Theodore Roosevelt his speech indicting the muckrakers (q.v.). G. L. Mawry and J. A. Grenier, eds., *The Treason of the Senate* (1964).

TREATY OF WASHINGTON (1871), of interest to social reformers as an historical example of an amicable solution to a complex international situation, involving "national honor" and powerful, as well as sensitive, nations. The "Alabama Claims" involved a British-built ship, among others of British make, which had been sold to the Confederate government and which had done damage to Federal shipping, in serious quantity. The Radical Republicans headed by Charles Sumner (qq.v.) pressed inordinate demands for restitution upon Great Britain. Both governments were angry and belligerent. Grant's Secretary of State, the responsible and conservative Hamilton Fish (q.v.), by careful and deliberate diplomacy, managed to get Senate agreement to an impartial commission, composed of Swiss, Brazilians, and Italians, as well as Americans and British which decided, the next year, that although Great Britain bore financial responsibility for the damage, it was nowhere near the massive sum Sumner would have received. (He offered to accept Canada in satisfaction of United States claims.) The United States received fifteen and a half millions of dollars, but, more important, the danger of war was averted.

TRENDIES, a word of the late 1970s, indicating shallow liberalism, especially in New York City; not always stated with scorn, since it assumed funds and social acceptability inspiring to the upwardly mobile in urban areas. The opposite of "Squares" (q.v.), and, like it, emphasizing social gestures as well as politics.

TRIANGLE FIRE, THE (1911), a fire which occurred March 25 in a New York building housing the Triangle Shirtwaist Company, which employed over six hundred immigrant girls, mostly Jewish and Italian. For lack of adequate fire prevention and fire-fighting facilities, 146 girls died. The event roused demands which created the New York State Factory Investigation Commission and the initiation of reform measures. A Fiftieth Anniversary Memorial Meeting was held at the site of the fire, sponsored by the I.L.G.W.U. (q.v.). Leon Stein, *The Triangle Fire* (1962).

TRIANGULAR TRADE, THE, a system of shipping routes in colonial decades, which involved, in its most famous phase, the shipping of rum to Africa, where it was exchanged for slaves, who were then carried through the notorious "Middle Passage" to the French West Indies, or to the southern colonies; in the former, they were exchanged for molasses, which was then carried to New England, to be made into rum. In this way New England, though its soil and circumstances did not permit slavery to flourish, became wholly implicated in the fixing of slavery as an institution in the western world and the American South.

TRIBUNE, NEW YORK, founded 1841 by Horace Greeley (q.v.), the most influential northern newspaper of the pre-Civil War era, and remarkable for the number of reforms and reformers it sponsored. These included Fourierism and its American advocate Albert Brisbane, Margaret Fuller, and Karl Marx (qq.v.).

TROJAN HORSE TECHNIQUE, derived from the Homeric tale, in which the Greeks win their way into Troy by erecting a gigantic horse which they fill with soldiers. The horse is dragged inside the gates by the Trojans; during the night, the Greeks descend from the horse, open the gates to their comrades and attack the Trojans. In 1935, Georgi Dimitroff, communist hero of the Nazi trial of persons alleged to be responsible for burning the Reichstag (q.v.), urged the "Trojan horse" technique upon communists for developing the world revolution by infiltrating the institutions of the countries they intended to overthrow with their personnel and ideas. The technique was also termed "boring from within" (q.v.). The Fifth Column (q.v.) was a fascist variation of the tactic. Martin Dies' (q.v.) *The Trojan Horse in America* (1940) was received without enthusiasm, especially by communists.

TROTSKY, LEON (1879-1940), Bolshevik leader, proponent of the world revolution. His opposition to Stalinism (q.v.) resulted in his exile and ultimate assassination in Mexico. As the theorist of the "permanent revolution" (q.v.), he was the opponent of social reform, but as the leader of a minority faction, he appealed for and to democratic processes, and his steady criticism of the ruling Soviet government and its Third International (q.v.) persuaded them of his treachery, social reformers of his usefulness. See also Moscow Trials. Rendered politically weak in his last phase, the disgrace of Stalin gave him a posthumous parity. New searchers for radical ideas and solutions found Trotsky's eloquence and mind more inspiring than Stalin's ponderous dullness and evil reputation, and created "Trotskyite" enclaves in some countries, with most significant impact on the Labour Party in Great Britain.

TRUDEAU, PIERRE ELLIOT (1919-), Canadian leader. He served in the Liberal government and, in 1968, was overwhelmingly elected Prime Minister. His intention was to build Canada, and make it an independent force in the world. These were goals which enabled him to survive hard times, a serious separatist movement in Quebec, and marital problems. Trudeau recognized Mainland China, and, himself French-Canadian, pursued a steady, anti-separation line, aided by business people and the non-French speaking minority in Quebec. Its harsh Language Act of 1974 created difficulties for English-speaking children and immigrants by making French the province's official language. Continuing economic troubles and unemployment, as well as embarrassments caused by publication of Trudeau's separated wife's autobiography, caused him to be turned out of office by the Conservatives. However, only six months later, their government fell on the budget they presented to Parliament. On the same day, the Canadian Supreme Court ruled that Quebec's language act was unconstitutional. It was evident that for the time Canadians needed Trudeau, as one to hold the separatists at bay, and also to negotiate for a greater degree of freedom from the British mandate. See his *Conversations with Canadians* (1972); also, Bruce Thordaison, *Trudeau and Foreign Policy* (1972), and Walter Stewart, *Trudeau in Power* (1971).

TRUJILLO, GEN. RAFAEL (1891-1961), dictator of the Dominican Republic (*q.v.*), and a symbol of anti-democratic forces in the poverty-stricken nations in the Caribbean, as well as Central and South America. Reformers were critical of American foreign policy which seemed unable to develop an approach which would build democracy in this and related areas. Earlier experiences with dollar diplomacy (*q.v.*), military intervention, the Roosevelt Corollary (*q.v.*), and other principles and events made difficult a change in approach. Trujillo received a mixture of early cooperation —his rule began in 1930—because of his efforts to gain status with the United States, especially in financial affairs, with increasing criticism. In 1937, his slaughter of some 15,000 Haitians within his country's borders stirred anger and dismay, and focused attention on his ruthless proscription of dissidents. Evidence that his agents in New York murdered a former resident of the Dominican Republic, in 1956, while he taught at Columbia University, helped undermine Trujillo's reputation. His complicity in the attempted assassination of the Venezuelan president, Romulo Betancourt, brought criticism to a height which in 1960, caused the Organization of American States to recommend economic sanctions until there was evidence that Trujillo would undertake democratic reforms. His death by assassination was unmourned, survivors promising evidence of improved conditions. R. D. Crassweller, *Trujillo* (1966).

TRUMAN, HARRY S. (1884-1972), advanced in politics by the Pendergast machine of Kansas City and Missouri, he entered the U.S. Senate in 1936. He was a man of personal probity who, however, did not question the practical work of the political machines. He became Vice-President when the Democratic wheelhorses concluded that they wanted no more of Henry A. Wallace (*q.v.*) in that post, and President when Franklin D. Roosevelt (*q.v.*) died. He dealt with momentous matters, including the discharge of the first atom bomb and relations with Russia (*qq.v.*) with courage, patriotism and dispatch, within the range of his understanding. For the New Deal (*q.v.*), he sought to substitute the "Fair Deal." Relative prosperity, the break up of the Grand Alliance into cold war (*qq.v.*), and revelations of betrayal of American interests, as in the Hiss case (*q.v.*), gave strength to conservatives. Truman did not aid matters by dubbing investigations into communism a "red herring." Party loyalty and farm subsidies maintained him, but the McCarran-Walter Act and the McCarran-Wood Act (*qq.v.*) survived his vetoes. The Taft-Hartley Act (*q.v.*) would not down. His Full Employment Act (*q.v.*) was reduced to a gesture. His Civil Rights Act (*q.v.*) was words, rather than deeds. He responded to revelations of scandal in his political household as a politician. Nevertheless, he continued to aspire to be a statesman. Alfred Steinberg, *The Man from Mis-*

souri (1962); Louis W. Koenig, ed., *The Truman Administration* (1956); John W. Spanier, *The Truman-MacArthur Controversy* (1959); *Truman Speaks: On the Presidency, the Constitution, and Statecraft* (1975); Filler, *The President Speaks* (1982).

TRUST, see Monopoly, Anti-Monopoly.

TRUST-BUSTING, identified with Theodore Roosevelt (*q.v.*) and his prosecution of the Northern Securities Company. It has often been noted, however, that relatively few trusts were "busted" during his Administration, the most notable prosecutions, those against the Standard Oil Trust and the Tobacco Trust, occurring during the following Taft (*q.v.*) Administration. Although the dissolution of the trusts was essentially a failure—Americans preferred efficiency—the anti-trust campaign did expose their nature, and result in a canon of laws administered by the Anti-Trust Division in the Department of Justice which could permit Americans to control trusts if they wished.

TUBMAN, HARRIET (1821-1913), Negro leader of fugitive slaves who herself escaped from slavery in Maryland and returned often to lead bold flights into free soil and Canada. Her nineteen forays into the South, including the Deep South, involved careful planning and use of the Underground Railroad (*q.v.*). She became a legend of defiance of Negro stereotypes of docility, cowardice, and stupidity.

TUGWELL, REXFORD G. (1891-1979), New Deal (*q.v.*) theoretician and "brain-truster" (*q.v.*), he to some extent anticipated its attitude in such works as *Industry's Coming of Age* (1927) and *The Industrial Discipline* (1933). He was made Undersecretary of Agriculture in 1934, and director of the Resettlement Administration (*q.v.*). As governor of Puerto Rico, he gave it the idealistic attention he had accorded his other government assignments; see his *The Stricken Land* (1946). See his autobiography, *The Light of Other Days* (1962).

TURKEY AND REFORM was largely the design of Mustafa Kemal Pasha, whose family name was Ataturk (1881-1938): a nationalist and dictator who labored to overthrow medieval Turkish traditions, to emancipate Turkish women, introduce universal education, and establish democratic procedures. Turkey received economic aid from the United States, eager to help support it against its neighbor, the U.S.S.R. The Turkish rulers prided themselves on their modernity. How deep Turkish reform went, how well-founded in its society, Americans were unwilling or unable to ask. Lord Kinross, *Ataturk ...Father of Modern Turkey* (1965); E. J. Cohn, *Turkey: Economic, Social, and Political Change* (1970).

TURNER, NAT, see Nat Turner's Rebellion.

TURNER THESIS, THE, conception of Frederick Jackson Turner (1861-1932), a professor of American history at the University of Wisconsin, whose theory of the frontier (see Frontier and Social Reform) has a permanent place in American historiography, but the immortality of which is assured by the fact that individuals who have never heard of Turner nevertheless recapitulate its thesis without hesitation. Individuals who have had no contact with each other, to say nothing of Turner, will repeat as though by rote: "Whenever Americans grew tired of the repressive conditions in the East, they would pick themselves up"—they always pick themselves up—"and cross the mountains to begin a new life in the West." Thus, the Turner Thesis reflected American expectations. Its status toward the end of the twentieth century was unclear; see G. R. Taylor, ed., *The Turner Thesis* (1972).

TUSKEGEE INSTITUTE, outstanding Negro facility of higher education, founded by Booker T. Washington (*q.v.*) in 1881, and committed to combining vocational understanding with humanistic and other study; its full name is Tuskegee Normal and Industrial Institute. A Negro island in the sea of poor whites, non-elite Negroes, and other southern social elements, Tuskegee is no militant reform agency, though it has provided knowledgeable persons for aspects of Negro-white relations tending toward reform. It has been observed that Tuskegee does not, in fact, emphasize the production of vocational leaders for Negro communities, but produces intellectuals and other components of the ordinary university.

T.U.U.L., see Trade Union Unity League.

T.V.A., see Tennessee Valley Authority.

TWAIN, MARK, see Clemens, Samuel L.

TWEED RING, an outstanding example of post-Civil War municipal corruption, under the aegis of Tammany Hall (*q.v.*). Key city officials, under the leadership of William Marcy Tweed plundered New York City, largely through the sale of city property and the purchase of supplies, all transactions requiring payments to the Ring and its stipendiaries. Tweed's influence in the state legislature aided their machinations. The most spectacular transaction was the sale by the Ring of the area which became Central Park to the city. Non-reformers have argued that it was worth the graft (*q.v.*) which the city fathers took to themselves: a piece of muddled logic with which social reformers must cope. Thomas Nast's (*q.v.*) cartoons and the *New York Times's* (*q.v.*) exposures helped to crystallize the indignation of middle and upper-class reformers who, by acquiring strength at the polls and through successful legal suits, managed the fall of the Tweed Ring in 1872, though Tammany Hall itself reorganized to continue its work. An extraordinary academic disrespect for reformers, though not clearly stated in the interests of what, produced nothing less than a grave appreciation of Tweed and persons like him; S. J. Mandelbaum, *Boss Tweed's New York* (1965); John G. Sprout, *"The Best Men": Liberal Reformers in the Gilded Age* (1965).

TWENTIES, THE institutionalized as an era of cultural internationalism, experiment, and emancipation, in literature featuring Ernest Hemingway, Gertrude Stein, James Joyce, T. S. Eliot; in art, Picasso; in music, Schoenberg, Prokofief, Bartok; among others in cinema, theater, and the popular arts (*qq.v.*). Women have been seen as moving in the Twenties toward "emancipation," though its dimensions remain unclear, especially in the light of later programs and perspectives. Helpful would have been a gearing of the attitudes and desires expressed in some of the above with those dominating life at the same time outside the arts; they tended to be seen separately from those connotatively termed "the Twenties." See also "Flapper Age," Sex. Bill Severn, *The End of the Roaring Twenties: Prohibition and Repeal* (1969); P. Carter, *The Twenties in America* (1975); Joan H. Wilson, ed., *The Twenties: the Critical Issues* (1972).

TWENTIETH CENTURY FUND, set up by E.A. Filene (*q.v.*) as a fact finding body, especially in economic aspects of social operations, it broadened its investigations to take in whatever investigations seemed to its directors useful. Filene's view was that reform needed data as much as it needed social goals. The Fund, however, developed into a function of the existent society, rather than a force capable of turning it from its preconceptions.

TWENTY-FIRST AMENDMENT, see Prohibition.

TWENTY-THIRD AMENDMENT, see District of Columbia.

"TWO AND A HALF INTERNATIONAL," the International Working Union of Socialist Parties, an effort of socialist groups unwilling to be committed either to the Second or the Third Internationals (*qq.v.*), in the 1920's, to give one another unity and strength. In 1921, they met in Vienna and set up a working union intended to attract dissidents to their standard. A strong-arm of this "international" was the British Independent Labour Party (*q.v.*).

TYLER, WAT (d. 1381), English leader of a peasant uprising, who aspired to be, in Shakespeare's sarcastic and antagonistic phrase, "the mouth of England," and to express its social woes. He suffered martyrdom.

U

ULTRAIST, one who holds extreme opinions, widely used in pre-Civil War decades to describe the evangelical type of reformer who often held extreme opinions not only on one or another topic, but, as with the perfectionists, held extreme opinions on most topics. Conservatives, however, did not always distinguish between the abolitionist, for example, and such an ultraist as John Humphrey Noyes (q.v.); to the conservative they were both ultraists.

ULYSSES (1922), by James Joyce, noted novel by expatriate Irish writer, utilizing stream of consciousness technique, and other literary devices intended to present the realities of life and spirit. It became a key civil liberties case, intended to define the differences between literature and obscenity, and as such was defended by the A.C.L.U. (q.v.). Its vindication in 1933, by decision of Federal Judge John M. Woolsey represented a major break-through against Comstockery and censorship (qq.v.).

UN-AMERICAN ACTIVITIES COMMITTEE, see House Un-American Activities Committee.

"UNCLE REMUS" TALES, see Harris, Joel Chandler.

UNCLE SHYLOCK, a term used with bitterness by the Allies of World War I who resented United States efforts to receive payments for debts incurred in the course of the war. The argument was that the Allies had suffered in blood and treasure in defense of the common cause; and that this effort to exact payment at a time when they were attempting to rebuild their economies was cruel and brutal; an effort, as in the case of Shylock, in Shakespeare's The Merchant of Venice, to exact a pound of flesh. See also Khalid L. Gauba, Uncle Sham; being the strange tale of a civilization run amok (Lahore, 1929).

UNCLE TOM'S CABIN (1852), see Harriet Beecher Stowe. "Uncle Tom" was a scornful epithet (q.v.) employed by militant Negroes and social reformers to describe a Negro who was humble and servile toward white people, and thus a negative quantity in social reform movements. Overlooked and ignored was "Uncle Tom's" dignity and unbreakable spirit, which could have made the novel interesting to students of literature: a casualty of the social war. Cf. Richard Wright, Uncle Tom's Children (1938). See also Forrest Wilson, Crusader in Crinoline (1941); J. C. Furnas, Goodbye to Uncle Tom (1956).

"UNCONDITIONAL SURRENDER" General Grant's (q.v.) famous terms to the Confederates besieged at Vicksburg; also employed by President Franklin D. Roosevelt (q.v.) in connection with the Nazis (q.v.), engaged in World War II.

"UNDEFENDED FRONTIER," see Canadian-American Relations.

UNDER COVER, see Carlson, John Roy.

UNDERCONSUMPTION, see Overproduction.

"UNDERDEVELOPED NATIONS," see Third World.

UNDERGROUND RAILROAD, an informal system of friends and sympathizers along distinct routes calculated to help fugitive slaves out of zones of danger. They usually extended from the borders, including the Maryland, Pennsylvania borders and the Ohio River, northward to Canada. Delaware was a good state for fugitive slaves in transit because, though slave, it was in northern terrain and so offered availability plus such determined underground workers as Thomas Garrett. John Rankin's (q.v.) station at Ripley, on the Ohio River, was famous; it attracted the real Eliza of Stowe's (q.v.) Uncle Tom's Cabin. Levi Coffin's (q.v.) labors in Indiana made him

outstanding in the work. Calvin Fairbank (q.v.) was one of a number of laborers in the U.G.R.R. who received prison terms when nabbed. See also Torrey, Charles T. An odd impulse in the academic history profession has sought to institutionalize the idea that there was in reality no underground railroad, that it was a figment of the abolitionist imagination. The purpose of this fantasy is apparently to endorse a strong impulse in southern historiography that Negroes were docile and abolitionists inconsequential. Larry Gara, The Liberty Line: the Legend of the Underground Railroad (1961) added the further figment that Negro runaways had been responsible for their own emancipation; compare W. H. Siebert, The Underground Railroad from Slavery to Freedom (1899 ed.); William Still, Underground Rail Road Records (1883); M. G. McDougall, Fugitive Slaves (1891).

UNDER-PRIVILEGED, a word carrying democratic overtones, and applied to elements at home as well as abroad. Although criticized by conservatives who argued that it took attention away from duties, the need for unity in the face of dangerous challenges from abroad forced politicians to give thought to the question of privileges; involved in the problem were Negroes, Indians, transient workers, unemployables, victims of old age and disease, among others. Rising nationalism in Africa, the fear that Middle Eastern peoples might be successfully wooed by communism, and even fear that underprivileged elements among the democracies might lose their enthusiasm for freedom kept concern for them alive. The Democratic Party, in its 1960 campaign, successfully emphasized this theme. Johnson's (q.v.) Administration represented the high point of the "compassion" program, sharply criticized for its weakly administered "giveaways," with which later programs had to cope, in order to fight inflation, corruption, and other undesirable by-products. The new Reagan Administration in 1981 sought to popularize the concept of aiding the "Truly Needy."

UNEMPLOYABLES, used less effectively as a sense of community and inter-relationship has increased, especially in post-World War II years. Originally intended to refer to types of persons who could not be utilized in the industrial process, and including abnormal types, dissolute and degenerate elements, as well as persons who had been worn out and harmed during their service to industry. The increase in the number of old people, and realization that all of these people together constituted a burden on the community turned attention to the possibility of utilizing them, rather than merely maintaining them in uselessness. Thus, "senior citizens," older persons who had been passed over in favor of youth, and mentally and physically handicapped were considered in terms of their employability, rather than their unemployability. Whether the propaganda favoring a positive approach would overcome prejudices among Americans, remained an open question in 1981.

UNEMPLOYED, THE, acquired a peculiar consequence in the 1930's because they included so large a proportion of persons who were not eccentric, unambitious, without family, or in some fashion infirm, but normally workers who had been deprived of status and necessities by the economic crisis. They therefore became a serious target of attention from the communists and social reformers. The communists early organized the Unemployed Councils, in 1930, as a section of the T.U.U.L. (q.v.). But Workers Leagues, Unemployed Unions, Unemployed Citizens Leagues, Associates of Unemployed, and Workers Committees on Unemployment proliferated under the auspices of various socialist and communist elements. They demanded legislation to care for their plight, produced by their numbers some influential spokesmen, and were a force in New Deal (q.v.) legislation. They provided evidence that every social element is a power element when organized; unemployed leaders were in some cases more consequential than leaders of employed and even elite groups. See also Labor. Conditions changed drastically by the 1980s. Two-job families had provided more income than family: a condition which changed the job market as to men and women employees. Established welfare supports created more recession than depression; a laid-off worker with welfare and union benefits might take home more "pay" than he had on the job. The recognized decline in pride in and quality of work created economic weaknesses in American competitiveness in the world, cutting jobs. World inflation and unemployment conditions made re-employment policies difficult to define. Education, the largest industry, was in trauma, as potential students sought work rather than the inferior instruction available, causing unemployment among teachers, rather than a resurgence of quality education. The decline in American automobile production touched many industries. Strikes, and an appeal to labor's heroic past became irrelevant, so much of "labor" now being *service labor*, rather than material production. The unemployed were attached to unions and government offices, rather than to each other. Propaganda, statistics, and negotiations became the weapons of labor and capital, with mediators central to the battle to revive the economy. *(Qq.v. for above.)* See also Full Employment Act (1946). Studs Terkel, *Working* (1975); Harry Maurer, *Not Working: an Oral History of the Unemployed* (1980); Roger L. Miller and R. M. Williams, *Unemployment and Inflation: the New Economics of the Wage Price Spiral* (1974); John A. Garraty, *Unemployment in History: Economic Thought and Public Policy* (1978); Milton Friedman, *Unemployment versus Inflation* (1975); Richard A. Easterlin, *Birth and Fortune* (1981).

UNEMPLOYMENT COMPENSATION was denounced as a "dream" by Samuel Gompers (q.v.) in 1914. His cure for unemployment was an eight-hour *(q.v.)* day and no overtime work. Unemployment insurance began in 1938. See also Social Security Legislation.

UNESCO, see United Nations Educational, Scientific, and Cultural Organization.

"UNFAIR METHODS OF COMPETITION," see Federal Trade Commission.

UNFAIR LABOR PRACTICES, defined under the National Labor Relations Act, emphasizing practices of employers directed against labor, and the Taft-Hartley Act, emphasizing practices of labor directed against employers (qq.v.). The former include coercion and restraints which discourage union organization or create company unions, the latter techniques for forcing workers into unions they do not prefer, under union organizers for whose services they do not care. Both Acts emphasize the priority of collective bargaining *(qv.).*

UNION LABOR PARTY, a party influenced by the program of the Knights of Labor (q.v.) which sought to revitalize the Greenback Labor Party (q.v.) by implementing its relationship to workers, with little success; they preferred the major parties. It emphasized such farmers (q.v.) issues as railroad regulation and currency reform (qq.v.), and, in the election of 1888 received some 147,000 votes, or one and one-third percent of the vote. It differed from the United Labor Party (q.v.) on the Single Tax (q.v.), labor legislation, and other points. The United Labor Party, in that election polled no more than two thousand, eight hundred votes.

"UNION NOW," like World Federation (q.v.), an interim effort to draw up a plan which would end the possibility of war, developed by Clarence K. Streit. *Union Now* (1939) demanded a Federation—finding an analogy with the course of affairs which created the American Confederation—with a world parliament and world citizenship.

UNION OF SOUTH AFRICA, see Africa, Union of South.

UNION OF SOVIET SOCIALIST REPUBLICS, see Soviet, Russia, American Attitudes toward, Russian Revolution, The, of 1917.

UNIONISM, see Labor, Industrial Unionism, Craft Unions, Business Unionism, Social Unionism, Independent Unions, Dual Unions.

UNITARIANISM, a sectarian viewpoint which involved both dogma and social outlook. In New England, in the eighteenth century it challenged the view of the Trinity, conceiving of God as one. Under William Ellery Channing (q.v.), it cut loose from Congregationalism, denied the depravity of man, and the truth of predestination. However, it quickly developed conformists who opposed agitators; as a result Ralph Waldo Emerson (q.v.) left his Unitarian pulpit to seek a more vital approach to life. Theodore Parker (q.v.) preached a radical gospel which raised the question of whether he believed in God at all. By the twentieth century, Unitarianism attracted every variety of religious liberal, some of whom could be classified as seekers, but others who explicitly repudiated supernaturalism, and manifestly had no concern for the question of the trinitarian or the unitarian nature of Deity. See also Universalism.

UNITED AUTOMOBILE WORKERS OF AMERICA, strategic in Labor (q.v.) not only because of its large membership, over a million in the 1950's, but because the automobile industry, a practical monopoly (q.v.) affected some seven million additional workers in related occupations. Thus, the fortunes of the Auto Workers were bound to affect practically all American industry and society. In general, their main object was to get more money. Although their officials adopted "statesmanlike" attitudes, proposing plans intended to cut down the industry's profits in the interests of the consumer, they had no practical program for curbing inflation (q.v.) or for contributing to any other aspects of labor-industry relations. Their most manifest lack was of an educational program calculated to add cubits to the stature of the auto worker. Their "research" was almost entirely in dollars and cents matters intended to furnish argumentative materials for negotiation purposes. The auto workers were no more, if no less, than any other "common man" available in the city streets and bowling alleys. See also Walter Reuther.

UNITED FRONT, like "Red Front," intended to bring the working and anti-fascist forces together for strength. It failed most catastrophically in Germany, where the communists attempted to enforce what they termed the "united front from below." They argued that their socialist opponents were not sincere anti-fascist fighters, but, in fact "social fascists" who were misleading their rank and file following. They would not "sit down at the table" with such scoundrels. Instead, they appealed to the rank and file to leave their traitorous leaders and join them, the communists, in a "united front from below." It did not materialize.

UNITED FRUIT COMPANY, industrial American giant in Central America, with vast resources and influence in Costa Rica, Honduras, Colombia, Nicaragua, Guatemala, and elsewhere, based on the banana. Armed with a powerful fleet of ships and an army of agents, it continues to be a strategic factor in United States-Central American relations; see Charles D. Kepner, Jr., and Jay H. Soothill, *The Banana Empire: a Case Study of Economic Imperialism* (1935). S. and E. Bruchey, *The United Fruit Company in Latin America* (1958).

UNITED MINE WORKERS, drawing together almost all coal miners in the anthracite and bituminous regions. Founded in 1890, it passed through difficult stages on the way to becoming one of the most powerful unions, with some 600,000 members in 1953. Once militant and engaged in desperate strikes, it reached its peak of significance during World War II, soon after the war began to feel the pinch of American conversion to oil. Hard times in the coal regions lost it members and consequence. See Mitchell, John; Lewis, John L.

UNITED NATIONS, successor to the League of Nations (q.v.), and of interest to social reformers who wondered whether it was likely to have a more distinguished career. Its early career, during which its deliberations took second place to such realities as the erection of the Iron Curtain, the expulsion of Chiang Kai Shek from the Chinese mainland, and the Korean

War (qq.v.) created a reminiscent sense of the post World War I situation. However, the atomic arms build-up in the East and in the West, creating dangers of the actual destruction of human life, gave the U.N. increased importance. Although it could not be effective in the Algerian crisis which rent France, or mitigate the Hungarian tragedy, or help make the Arab refugee situation less malignant, it still constituted a mediating factor in a situation which desperately required mediating factors. Its most doubtful feature, then, was not that it was failing to perform miracles in resolving East-West difficulties, but that it was setting both no sparkling example in its operation of such subsidiaries as UNESCO and UNRRA (qq.v.). The accretion of numerous small, authoritarian, and unsteady nations created in the UN a Third World (q.v.) attitude toward the United States which caused Americans angry at many of the UN's demagogic decisions to wonder what the nation gained by its heavy subsidy to the organization, whether there might be some gain in separating from it. It seemed unlikely that such a step would take place. Leland M. Goodrich, *The United Nations in a Changing World* (1976); E. Berkley Tompkins, *The United Nations in Perspective* (1972 ed.); James Barros, ed., *United Nations: Past, Present and Future* (1973).

UNITED NATIONS EDUCATIONAL, SCIENTIFIC, AND CULTURAL ORGANIZATON, intended to close gaps between the nations through humanistic concerns, including liaison in educational, cultural, and scientific problems and projects. Although UNESCO had occasions to call on distinguished personages from all parts of the world, and to conduct inquiries on such topics as world illiteracy, it seemed unable to develop any force or momentum which would make it a potent factor in UN operations: it was a pious aspiration, rather than an achievement.

UNITED NATIONS HUMAN RIGHTS COMMISSION, in 1948 drafted a "Universal Declaration of Human Rights," intended to clarify them and set them up as a standard toward which people and groups could work. Its thirty articles refined a wide variety of rights, from the right to be born free to the right not to have those freedoms taken away. The Commission publishes a *Yearbook on Human Rights*. It does not tread on sensitive, powerful toes, such as those of the Soviet Union, with its notorious labor camps, or take significant stands on atrocities, slavery, and other formidable problems. *(Qq.v.) for above.)* J. Buncher, ed., *Human Rights and American Diplomacy* (1977); Ann F. Ginger, ed., *Human Rights Docket, 1977-1978* (1978); T. Buergenthal, ed., *Human Rights, International Law and the Helsinki Accord* (1978); George W. Forell and W. H. Lazareth, *Human Rights: Rhetoric or Reality* (1978).

UNITED NATIONS RELIEF AND REHABILITATION ADMINISTRATION, probably most impressive in its beginnings, when launched in 1943 as an agency intended to bring relief to the victims of the war, particularly those under Axis (q.v.) control. It gave the members of the Grand Alliance (q.v.) a great and benign project in common and offered a promise of what the coming United Nations (q.v.) was expected to be. Since there were numerous relief organizations operating in every area and capacity—some seven hundred—it was the rehabilitation aspects of UNRRA which might have been most significant. UNRRA was dominated by the United States and Great Britain, but cooperated with others of the United Nations. Its greatest emphasis was on relief, though it also fought epidemics, aided in the reconstruction of utility services, and in the handling of displaced persons (q.v.). It was administered first by the well-regarded Governor Herbert H. Lehman, of New York, then by Fiorello La Guardia (q.v.). Dissolved in 1947, its functions were presumably taken over by a variety of UN agencies.

UNITED STATES HOUSING AUTHORITY, see Housing Problem, The.

UNITED STATES STEEL CORPORATION, one of the great industrial combinations, organized in 1901, and the owner of railroads, coal mines, ship building plants, as well as steel mills. Although overcapitalized, its development was so steady, that the stock issued rapidly rose outstandingly in value. It was a major impediment to organization of the steel workers (q.v.), and only reluctantly abandoned the twelve-hour day and the seven-day week. Julian Szekely, *The Steel Industry and the Energy Crises* (1975); Robert Hessen, *Steel Titan: the Life of Charles M. Schwab* (1975).

UNITED STATES *V.* BUTLER *ET AL.*, see Agricultural Adjustment Administration.

UNITED STATES *V.* DARBY LUMBER COMPANY (1941) upheld the Fair Labor Standards Act of 1938 (q.v.), but went further in upholding the right of Congress to legislate without inhibition with respect to interstate commerce, overthrowing premises which had prevented the regulation of child labor (q.v.) in earlier decades.

UNITED STATES *V.* DEBS (q.v.) *ET AL.* (1894), resulted from the unwillingness of the leaders of the Pullman Strike (q.v.) to honor the injunction (q.v.) issued by the Circuit Court, ordering them to cease interfering with interstate commerce. They were found in contempt and sentenced to prison, under the Sherman Anti-Trust Act. It struck liberals as outrageous that an Act which was impotent to curb trusts could be so employed against labor. See also *In Re Debs.*

UNITED STATES *V.* E. C. KNIGHT COMPANY (1895), see Sherman Anti-Trust Act.

UNIVERSAL EDUCATION, see Education and Reform.

UNIVERSAL MILITARY TRAINING, a government project of the 1950's which would have made all able-bodied young men liable to such training, thus, theoretically creating a nation ready for all emergencies. It was retarded more by practical and financial considerations than by moral ones. It would have instituted a system more familiar in European terrain than American. Social reform protest was less loud and articulate than at any other time in the twentieth century. Nor did it stir memories of the visions of Edward Bellamy and William James (qq.v.) for an army of youth in combat with nature, in behalf of mankind.

"UNIVERSAL REFORMERS," proliferated in the pre-Civil War era; such persons as Henry C. Wright, Theodore Parker, John Humphrey Noyes (qq.v.) were not concerned solely for one or another reform; they were attracted by millenarian visions, and determined to see heaven on earth in their time, or, at least, to act in its interests. Thus, Wright was energetic in the cause of peace, temperance, anti-slavery, bodily health, high-thinking, and other areas of human purpose. Parker delved into all religions and maintained a wide perspective in his sermons and strictures; Noyes sought in his Oneida community to create a way of life "perfect" in its premises, though little concerned for the sinful world outside.

UNIVERSAL SUFFRAGE, a democratic goal which first overcame property restrictions, then sex and race restrictions, in large measure, though frustrated by southern recalcitrance with respect to the Negro. It was not literally intended to be "universal," since children, mental incompetents, persons incarcerated for crime, and other categories did not receive the suffrage. In addition the question was unresolved whether a person who did not employ his suffrage deserved to have it. Such questions were aggressively explored by people who saw harm to society in the expanded suffrage, as in expanded education (q.v.), and made the phrase an idealistic aspiration in any event.

UNIVERSALISM, a liberal religion akin, at least in ultimate expectation, to Unitarianism. The latter, it was said, believed that God was too good to damn people, whereas the Universalists believed that people were too good to be damned. Universalists were more numerous than Unitarians, but had fewer distinguished ministers. They were stronger among rural elements; the Unitarians flourished in the New England towns.

UNKNOWN SOLDIER, THE, a sentimental memory to patriots,

often treated bitterly or ironically by anti-militarists, as in the final chapter of John Dos Passos's *(q.v.) Nineteen Nineteen.* "The Body of an American."

UNRESTRICTED SUBMARINE WARFARE, see Freedom of the Seas.

UNRRA, see United Nations Relief and Rehabilitation Administration.

UNTOUCHABLES, a humiliated social class among the Indians, the eradication of untouchability was one of Gandhi's *(q.v.)* major battles. In the United States, the word was best identified by the overwhelming majority of Americans with a shabby television show, featuring government knights who slew underworld "punks" and would-be "big shots" in such number that it remained a mystery why the word did not get around to the rest that crime did not pay. Eliot Ness and Oscar Fraley, *The Untouchables* (1957); J. Michael Mahar, *Untouchables in Contemporary India* (1972).

UPHAM, THOMAS C. (1799-1872), professor of Mental and Moral Philosophy at Bowdoin College and a notable reformer, especially memorable for his work on the theory and practice of pacifism; see his *The Manual of Peace, Embracing I. Evils and Remedies of War, II. Suggestions on the Law of Nations, III. Consideration of a Congress of Nations* (1836).

UPHAUS CASE, THE, a *cause célèbre* in 1960, when Dr. Willard Uphaus, a Christian pacifist, completed a year in prison for having refused to give the names of persons who had attended a World Fellowship of Faith camp in 1941 to the attorney general of New Hampshire in 1954. In 1959, the U.S. Supreme Court held that the state law requiring the divulgence of such information did not abridge his constitutional rights. Dr. Uphaus therefore served a year in prison for his refusal of cooperation with the state. Released, he appeared to receive respect from responsible people who felt that he had committed no crime by honoring his own conscience, but he soon disappeared from the news.

URBAN LEAGUE, THE NATIONAL, see Negro and Reform.

URBAN PROBLEM, THE, key to American domestic affairs since its rise to dominance over the countryside. Essentially, the problem remained the same: of developing its services, of controlling its inevitable depreciation and deterioration, of caring for and offering opportunities for its youth, maintaining an alert system of communication and education, continuing the endless battle against corruption and crime, and otherwise sustaining civilization. At the beginning of the twentieth century, reformers made efforts to assimilate the immigrants into the city structure. Settlements, housing regulation, factory inspection, civil service reform, and municipal reform *(qq.v.)* in general were some of their vehicles for controlling and improving city developments. Adult education *(q.v.)* was intended to implement other civilizing devices. Efforts of Negroes in particular to find a place in the northern cities were resisted, but offered a field for reformers. Continued deterioration of the cities combined with a number of factors to create an unprecedented situation. World War II scattered great numbers of Americans out of their urban environments. The advent of the great atomic bomb, a search for new areas for factories, and a general decentralization movement drew great numbers of elite workers out of the cities. The more determined effort and need for housing on the part of minority groups and poor people generally caused a "flight from the city" into the suburbs. The minority groups, in large measure, took over. In New York, the striking phenomenon was the Puerto Ricans who rose in some twenty years from a handful to two million. Moreover, the poverty of such groups multiplied the rate of urban deterioration, threatening to turn the city into a jungle. Essentially, the same process took place in all the major cities. Alarmed property holders made the same efforts everywhere: to create "lungs" for traffic in the city centers, to tear down the most frightful slums, to erect showplaces: new civic buildings, a few superhighways, some model housing. It did not appear to concern them what happened to the evacuated tenants, who had no choice but to double up in other slum areas and multiply the rate of deterioration. Settlements, social work agencies *(qq.v.)*, and civic groups did not appear to be able to create a *national* understanding of the urban problem, so that concerned persons in St. Louis, Philadelphia, Detroit, and Los Angeles could know each other's problems and compare solutions. Functionaries, rather than reformers, despite their college degrees and completed theses, put in their eight hours each day, but were neither inspired nor inspiring. In 1981, a government report recommended that people living in discomfort and bad prospects in eastern cities move to the "Sunbelt States"; at least that government funds would be best expended there, since the drift of population was in that direction. However, the government was also pledged to encourage the creation of "enterprise zones" in the deteriorated cities: zones which would receive tax relief and other encouragements to attract enterprising builders and businessmen, to rehabilitate troubled or destroyed neighborhoods. See Private Enterprise, City Planning. G. F. Mott and R. D. Lambert, *Urban Change and the Planning Syndrome* (1973); Bennet Harrison, *Urban Economic Development* (1974); Alan Booth, *Urban Crowding and Its Consequences* (1976); J. V. Lindsay et al., *The Urban Crisis* (1969); Susan E. Clarke and Jeffrey L. Obler, *Urban Ethnic Conflict* (1976); John N. Jackson, *The Urban Future* (1972); Alan Shank and Ralph Conant, *Urban Perspectives* (1975); J. F. Blumstein and Eddie J. Martin, *The Urban Scene in the Seventies* (1974).

U.S.-U.S.S.R., see American-Soviet Relations, Union of Soviet Socialist Republics.

U.S.A. (1930-36), by John Dos Passos *(q.v.)*, appeared to be a classic statement of much of the confusion, false ambition, deceived altruism, and operations of sensitive, articulate, or influential and representative American types. The novel concerned itself little with the "common people," either of farm or city, though in such a character as Joe Williams it attempted to portray a sound "working-class" type. The trilogy's most extraordinary feature was its change in tone, in succeeding volumes. It appeared, in volume one, to be assaying the nation's spiritual resources with irony, recognizing its essential lack of substance and dignity: a whited sepulchre. Promising persons included an I.W.W. *(q.v.)* and a sincere, if not too effective girl. But others of the personnel included an empty-hearted executive and his female counterpart, a furtive labor leader, and other mediocre types. World War I was depicted as a vain charade which misused human energies, and the 1920's, the time of the "Big Money," as one of futile ambitions and associations. Opposed to this was the revolutionary movement, building up in terms of resistance to the henchmen of big business. Prose poems honored rebels and dissidents. Yet by volume three, the revolutionaries were revealed as cold, impersonal, doctrinaire, and, in their own ways as harmful or reprehensible as those they combatted. Dos Passos had an excellent ear for the cliches and word-contours of his time, but little for their content. His equation had almost no meaning when separated from other U.S.A. factors which he had not taken into account, such as had produced Emily G. Balch, Tom L. Johnson, Lincoln Steffens, Lillian Wald, Anna Garlin Spencer, and E. A. Filene *(qq.v.)*, among many others.

UTILITARIANISM, formulated in Great Britain, but influential in the thinking of Americans, notably Benjamin Franklin *(q.v.)*. Its influence on reform is less clear. Its famous tenet of "the greatest happiness of the greatest number" had a democratic component built into it; and, indeed, Jeremy Bentham, the philosopher of utilitarianism, was a reformer, as was Franklin, in contemporary terms. But the "pleasure" principle by which the good could be discerned had obvious dangers, even though its expounders sought to derive the highest morality from it. In essence, utilitarianism preached "enlightened self-interest." Moral reformers *(q.v.)* did not find it sufficient for their need. Utilitarianism has been seen as a precursor to Pragmatism *(q.v.)*.

UTILITIES, see Public Utilities, Privately-Held Utilities.

UTOPIA, the title of Sir Thomas More's famous work, published in 1516. It describes an ideal commonwealth. "Utopian" has been popularly understood to refer to plans for reorganizing society which, though well-meaning and ingenious, ignore practical conditions and human nature. However, Arthur E. Morgan's *Nowhere Was Somewhere* (1946) undertakes to prove that More was not writing fiction, but recounting fact, and that "social engineers" cannot function without "utopias." See also Brook Farm, Helicon Hall, Bellamy, Edward, and related topics. Pessimism produced "anti-utopias," notably Aldous Huxley's *Brave New World* (1932), as well as the hopelessness of Orwell's *(q.v.)* 1984 (1949).

UTOPIAN SOCIALISM, defined by Engels as that which various individuals and groups attempted to achieve without deriving it from actual historical and social process; see his *Socialism, Utopian and Scientific*. In effect, he defined all systems other than his own as utopian, though his would also be so evaluated. Thus, the dreams of socialism, as foreseen by Marx and Engels, and crystallized in the operations of the Soviet Union could be so interpreted. From this point of view, "utopian socialism" could be set aside as a definition of earlier cooperative efforts, and these seen as *contributions* to the history of socialist effort, rather than merely as successes or failures. "Utopian" and "socialism" seem to impress unsympathetic minds as synonyms, at least in the democracies.

V

VACCINATION, less a crusade than a problem in medical certainty and public confidence. Evidence of its efficacy in smallpox control won over suspicions and fears. However, the public agencies involved had to win over such groups as the London Society for the Abolition of Compulsory Vaccination, operating in the post-Civil War period. The increased power of the government to institute health measures made the use of the Salk Vaccine to control polio less formidable, in the 1950's. See also Fluoridation.

VAN BUREN, MARTIN (1782-1862), eighth President of the United States and a prominent Jacksonian (q.v.) whose suaveness of manner earned him his chief's confidence. Jackson left him a legacy of economic depression; his Specie Circular (q.v.) brought on the Depression of 1837. Van Buren cooperated wholeheartedly with the pro-slavery forces, notoriously in the *Amistad* (q.v.) affair. Defeated in the election of 1840, and deprived of the nomination in 1844, he was receptive to third party (q.v.) pressures, and took the Barnburners (q.v.), whom he led, into the Free Soil Party (q.v.), which offered him as Presidential candidate in 1848. Although many abolitionists were indignant that a doughface (q.v.) should be holding the banner for Free Soil, it underscored for others that voting Free Soil did not commit them to abolitionism. By 1852, Van Buren was back in the Democratic fold, voting for another doughface, Franklin Pierce. His endorsement of Abraham Lincoln (q.v.) helped indicate the complex nature of the Republican following. See his long unpublished *Autobiography* (1920), patently self-serving, but giving some sense of the smoothness of personality which earned him his success.

"VANITY PUBLISHING," that is, publishing done not in recognition of the quality of an author's work, but in order to abstract from him or her the expenses for publication, with part of the sum pocketed as a profit. The "publisher" has feeble distribution facilities, and ordinarily prints the book as cheaply as possible, in order to save as much of the sum for himself as possible. Viewed by some as harming literary and publishing standards, and therefore requiring exposure and reform, by others as the result of the author's vanity, and so meriting ridicule and contempt. See Edward Uhlan, *The Rogue of Publishers' Row: Confessions of a Publisher*. (1956).

VANZETTI, BARTOLOMEO (1888-1927), see Sacco-Vanzetti Case.

VAUX, ROBERTS (1786-1836), Philadelphia Quaker and citizen, more concerned for benevolence than reform (qq.v.), but influential in both areas; he helped organize homes for juveniles and infirm people, as well as the Eastern Penitentiary (see Prison Reform). Although he wrote *Memoirs of the Lives of Benjamin Lay and Ralph Sandiford* (1815), and of Anthony Benezet (q.v.), all energetic abolitionists, he refused to preside at the meeting organizing the American Anti-Slavery Society (q.v.).

VEBLEN, THORSTEIN (1857-1929), American social and economic critic, whose ambivalent place in society, between immigrant and "native" cultures, kept him in the status of failure till the age of thirty-five; it was not until 1900, following the success of *The Theory of the Leisure Class* (1899), that he was given the rank of assistant professor at the University of Chicago. This masterpiece can be too readily taken to be merely a "satire"; Veblen had suffered too deeply to afford such easy attitudes. He sought to understand the reality of American civilization, to understand the potential of a pecuniary civilization and to minister to it. Later works maintained his equivocal, quasiacademic style, but moved toward socialist perspectives in the context of a capitalistic economy. Thus, *The Engineers and the Price System* (1921) foreshadowed Technocracy *(q.v.)*. His personal life is necessary for an understanding of his books; see Joseph Dorfman, *Thorstein Veblen and His America* (1934). Economics *(q.v.)* in the post-World War II era found almost no use for Veblen.

VEGETARIANISM, a facet of health reform *(q.v.)*; it holds that the eating of animals, or such animal products as eggs and milk, is undesirable, for moral, religious, or hygienic reasons. Various vegetables are preferred by those advocating their use because of the particular minerals, salts, liquids, or other materials in their composition. An experiment of the 1850's sought to establish a city of settlers in Kansas devoted to this reform. The Vegetarian Settlement Company, led by Henry Stephen Clubb, stirred interest and acquired funds for the enterprise, but rapidly fell apart.

VENEREAL DISEASE, see Prostitution.

VENEZUELAN DISPUTE, of long standing, between Great Britain and Venezuela over the boundary line between that country and British Guiana; brought to a head when Secretary of State Richard Olney demanded that Great Britain arbitrate the matter. His sensational invocation of the Monroe Doctrine included the view that "The United States is practically sovereign on this continent, and its fiat is law upon the subjects to which it confines its interposition. Why? . . . It is because, in addition to all other grounds, its infinite resources combined with its isolated position render it master of the situation and practically invulnerable as against any or all other powers." President Cleveland supported Olney, and war was feared, with Great Britain fearing her prestige was at stake. However, her troubles with the Boer Republic *(q.v.)*, and the sympathy expressed with it by the German government decided the English against a quarrel with Americans. She accepted a tribunal of arbitration, which ruled in her favor.

VERSAILLES TREATY, (June, 1919), to reformers, a symbol of harsh terms calculated to create new threats to world peace and cooperation, exploited by German nationalists as an act of bad faith. This Allied statement forced Germany to assume the entire burden of "war guilt," onerous reparations *(q.v.)*, and to be stripped of colonies and pieces of territory, notably the Saar, the latter pending a plebiscite in fifteen years. The Treaty of Brest-Litovsk, imposed by Germany on the new Bolshevik regime in Russia (March 3, 1918) had put her at the mercy of the German overlords, and provided the democratic powers in the west evidence that their opponents had been a threat to the peace of the world. Reformers, some of them "disillusioned," concluded there had been no justice on either side of the conflict, during World War I. H. C. Vaughan, *The Versailles Treaty* (1975).

VESEY, DENMARK (1767-1822), a free Negro who planned a slave insurrection in Charleston, S.C., which was exposed by an informer. Thirty-seven persons were executed. The careful planning manifested in the conspiracy alarmed southerners, and resulted in rigid rulings intended to prevent free Negroes from infecting slaves with ideas of freedom. The significance of this action has been controverted. R. Wade, *Slavery in the Cities* (1964) held it involved no more than Negro unrest and white hysteria; R. Starobin, ed., *Denmark Vesey* (1970) questioned this account.

VETERANS, see American Legion, American Veterans Committee, Pension Grabs, Bonus Marchers.

VICE PRESIDENTS have varied in quality and effect, from Jefferson *(q.v.)*, to whom it was a step toward the Presidency, to Walter F. Mondale, whose pallid Vice Presidency, in Carter's *(q.v.)* Administration left no residue. Having been Vice President won the Presidency for John Tyler, who later chose Virginia's side during the Civil War, Millard Fillmore, and Chester Arthur, as well as Andrew Johnson, Theodore Roose-

velt, Calvin Coolidge, Harry S. Truman, Lyndon B. Johnson, and Gerald Ford *(qq.v.)* were made President by their Vice-Presidency. Many others served their term to no end. Had Nixon been impeached and convicted, and had Spiro T. Agnew *(q.v.)* managed to ride out his own indictment, he would have succeeded to the Presidency; but Congress would probably have been reluctant to impeach, with Agnew waiting. Several of the Presidents had been forceful and significant as Vice Presidents. The turmoil of the Nixon era underscored the urgency of having a Vice President who could fill the President's seat adequately, if necessary. Donald Young, *American Roulette: the History and Dilemma of the Vice Presidency* (1965).

VIETNAM WAR, a vital contrast in intervention with that prosecuted under President Truman in South Korea *(qq.v.)*, which was threatened with a communist take-over. Truman undertook to resist the engulfment of an ally without opening a wider war with China. Johnson *(q.v.)*, having inherited a similar situation in South Vietnam, but backed technically by the Southeast Asia Treaty Organization (SEATO), an alliance organized in 1954 by representatives of Australia, France, Great Britain, New Zealand, Pakistan, the Philippines, and Thailand to stop communist expansion in the area. Although elements of the alliance withdrew, the principle seemed in good standing. In 1964, South Vietnam seemed hard pressed by North Vietnamese operating tandem with South Vietnamese communists, the Viet Cong. Using the "Ho Chi Minh Trail" in Laos, northern troops pressed upon the southern nation in ways threatening to its survival. A bombing of two American destroyers in the Gulf of Tonkin resulted in a Congressional resolution in effect giving the President a free hand in resisting North Vietnam's assaults. Johnson's escalation of the war involved a careful discrimination, unknown in other wars, between curbing North Vietnamese infiltration and attacks from Laos and maintaining the separation barriers between the two Vietnams by bombing North Vietnam military installations. All this was done under the eyes of the television cameras which became the decisive factor in the war, ceasing to become an instrument of American war policy and becoming instead an independent instrument of correspondents and cameramen, mainly anti-war partisans. Never was the point under-scored in any fashion that this powerful instrument was not matched by free access to the contrivings of the North Vietnam government which profited from the American civil war. American-based protests and demonstrations, a flow of supportive anti-war correspondents, and the constant monitoring of the war by television broke the Johnson Administration despite its endless largesse for his "Great Society" program *(q.v.)*, and Nixon *(q.v.)* took office determined to end the futile engagements while bringing the troops home in good order and inhibiting a North Vietnamese offensive upon a prostrate people. Although peace talks, disengagements, and troop withdrawals matured, the unceasing demonstrations, implemented by My Lai, the *Pentagon Papers (qq.v.)*, and newspaper-sparked outrage at allegedly "secret" and inhumane bombings demoralized the Nixon-Kissinger *(q.v.)* initiatives, and kept the North Vietnamese military strokes strong. Nixon having been brought down, it was left to President Ford to end American relations with the Vietnam situation. The final troops were brought home in ragged formation. The verdict that America had "lost" the war was established world-wide, though the concept of a "free world" opposing international communist offensives necessarily persisted among the non-communist and "non-aligned" nations which had accepted a version of affairs which affected their own destinies. Obviously, had the United States elected to carry through as the Soviet Union had from Hungary to Afghanistan *(qq.v.)*, and China in Tibet, the North Vietnam offensive would have been short-lived in 1964 or 1965. But from the Truman program to Ford—who had been scorned for "over-reacting" to the *Mayaguez* assault, the gross journalist point even being made that it had cost 15 killed and 3 missing to save "only" 39 crew lives—the United States had embarked on a "no-win" war at the expense of the American military establishment and the national position in the world. Almost amusing was the complaint of the North Vietnamese that the

United States had transgressed promises to help reconstruct "the country it had laid waste." Also significant was the turn of anti-war American academic historians from approval or involvement in demonstrations and domestic assaults to isolationism *(q.v.)*, in order not to be inculpated in the monstrous slaughter which accompanied North Vietnam's take over in Saigon, and assaults on their own people and neighboring Laos and Cambodia. Their isolationism did not include isolationism from the affairs of the Union of South Africa or of Central American governments which displeased them. Following the fantastic "heroes welcome" given for the released "Hostages" from Iran *(q.v.)*, complaints surfaced in behalf of the Vietnam veterans, who had been sneered at, insulted, or ignored on their return home. New-President Reagan *(q.v.)* spoke out in their behalf while awarding a Medal of Honor to one retired Army Master Sergeant, stating they had come home without a victory only "because they have been denied permission to win." The father of one dead soldier spent eleven years building his Vietnam Veterans Peace and Brotherhood Chapel near Eagle Nest, New Mexico, mostly with his own money. E. S. Herman and R. B. Du Boff, *America's Vietnam Policy— the Strategy of Deception* (1966); J. W. Fulbright, *The Vietnam Hearings* (1966); F. Schurrmann, P. Dale Scott, R. Zelnik, *The Politics of Escalation* (1966); D. Halberstam, *The Making of a Quagmire* (1965); Robert Shaplen, *The Road from War: Vietnam 1965-1970* (1970); C. A. Stevenson, *The End of Nowhere* (1972); Ernest Gruening, *Many Battles* (1973); Frances Fitzgerald, *Fire in the Lake* (1972); Alan Dawson, *55 Days: The Fall of South Vietnam* (1977); Gareth Porter, *Peace Denied* (1976); G. Lewy, *America in Vietnam* (1978); Leslie Gelb and Richard Betts, *The Irony of Vietnam* (1979); G. C. Herring, *America's Longest War* (1979); Prince N. Sihanouk, *War and Hope* (1980).

VIGILANTES, an informal citizens's agency intended to express public sentiment where law enforcement agencies were unable or unwilling to do so. Famous among Vigilance Committees was that of San Francisco in 1856, organized to combat criminal elements, at a time when Federal authorities were reluctant to commit themselves to action. Other such committees were closer to a lynching mob than to a law enforcing instrument. Vigilantes operated freely and with little regard for human rights during World War I, when they deemed it necessary to suppress persons unenthusiastic about the Great Crusade of the time, as in the case of Wesley Everett *(q.v.)*. They developed a substantial tradition in quieting radicals in the decades following. John Steinbeck *(q.v.)* developed a notable antipathy toward Vigilantes; see his *In Dubious Battle* (1936), chapter nine, and "The Vigilante," in *The Long Valley* (1938).

VILLARD, OSWALD GARRISON (1872-1949), liberal journalist and owner of the New York *Evening Post* (1897-1918) and the *Nation* (1908-1932). He opposed American imperialist operations in the Philippines, opposed the excesses which accompanied World War I, advocated peace, civil rights, and an alert public and press. A grandson of William Lloyd Garrison *(q.v.)*, he wrote a classic life of John Brown (1910), and a notable liberal autobiography, *Fighting Years* (1939). See also D. J. Humes, *Oswald Garrison Villard* (1960).

VIOLENCE, a controversial fact of social movements; reformers have sought formulas which could ensure necessary social change without violence; revolutionists have argued that violence was inevitable. They have quoted Thomas Jefferson *(q.v.)* on Shays's Rebellion *(q.v.)* to the effect that the tree of liberty must from time to time be watered with the blood of tyrants. One approach has seen violence as a deplorable concomitant of earlier, ruder social organization, but no longer necessary or feasible; thus, one could sympathize with the needs of railroad, steel, mine, and other workers and excuse the violence which accompanied their strikes without condoning violence in a present which includes such adjustment agencies as the N.L.R.B. *(q.v.)*. An associated thought noted that the violence was precipitated by short-sighted policies of business executives. Revolutionists, too, have

argued it would not be they making a revolution, so much as their enemies seeking to defend a counter-revolution in the face of necessary change. 1960s and 1970s violence accompanying the youth and anti-Vietnam *(qq.v.)* war actions was deplored, but also justified by responsible people. The August 1970 explosion on the University of Wisconsin campus destroyed a mathematics research center and killed a young researcher. The action brought as witnesses in court for the defendents the unofficial discloser of the *Pentagon Papers* *(q.v.)*, Daniel Ellsberg, and former U. S. Senator Ernest Gruening, on grounds that the bombing, though wrong, "pales in comparison with the calculated deaths of thousands in the Vietnam war." Similar defenses appeared in numerous other confrontations. In the Kent State tragedy *(q.v.)* the argument was turned, the violence of students being passed over in focusing on the responsive violence of the National Guardsmen. See also Terrorists. Numerous works treat violence as individual, urban, ethnic, psychological, mob, and social; among those with a larger approach: R. Jeffreys-Jones, *Violence and Reform in American History* (1978); E. A. Duff and J. F. McCamant, *Violence and Repression in Latin America* (1976); R. L. Sadoff, *Violence and Responsibility* (1978); R. A. Liston, *Violence in America: a Search for Perspective* (1974); Feliks Gross, *Violence in Politics...Eastern Europe and Russia* (1973); R. T. Takaki, *Violence in the Black Imagination* (1973); H. D. Graham et al., ed., *Violence: the Crisis of American Confidence* (1972); Edgar Stanton, *Violence, U.S.A.* (1976).

VIRGINIA, see Massachusetts and Virginia.

VIRGINIA DYNASTY, so termed by exasperated Federalists *(q.v.)*, frustrated by a government which seemed to them concerned only for southern interests, and willing to sacrifice the interests of New England. Thus, the Presidency of Jefferson, with its attacks on the Supreme Court and Embargo Act *(qq.v.)*, the Administration of Madison, with its War of 1812 *(q.v.)*, and of Monroe, which, though more manifestly national, seemed to continue an endless line of Virginians, took on, to rabid Federalists, almost the air of a conspiracy.

VIVISECTION, the use of living animals for experimental purposes, especially of interest to scientific personnel associated in such organizations as the National Society for Medical Research. They consider themselves humanitarians, in that their experiments can help discover methods which will ease the pain and mitigate the physical troubles of human beings. They are opposed by animal lovers, and others, who deplore their cruelty and what they consider to be their disrespect for living creatures. The vivisectionists argue, in response, that they do not conduct irresponsible experiments, that all states have laws curbing cruelty to animals, and that they constantly seek ways and means of keeping pain at a minimum; indeed, that this is one of their goals. It has been observed that anti-vivisectionists are not only easily aroused to action, but that they rarely have alternative suggestions to offer. They not only maintain close vigil over the operations in the medical schools, but have protested the use of animals in moon-rocket experiments. In addition, they are able to appeal to formidable numbers of animal-lovers, who are quick to flood legislators with their protests and advice. Legislation has been offered in Congress intended to withhold federal funds from researchers using animals until they received the approval of the U.S. Department of Health, Education and Welfare; researchers protest this would involve them in endless red-tape, and deter workers in the field.

VOLSTEAD AMENDMENT (1919), see Prohibition.

VOORHIS, JERRY (1901-), California congressman elected in 1936, he served in the House of Representatives until 1946, when he was defeated by Richard M. Nixon *(q.v.)*. His main interest was cooperatives *(q.v.)*, but he also fought for much New Deal legislation, including the Fair Labor Standards Act *(qq.v.)*. He served on the Dies Committee on Un-American Activities *(q.v.)* and sought to keep it an honest instrument for uncovering the facts; in 1943, he resigned in protest against the demagogic operations of its chairman. He was much concerned with post-War planning. Defeated in 1946, he entered into a new career as a spokesman for cooperatives; see his *Confessions of a Congressman* (1947). He later offered a more elaborate account of his liberal viewpoint in *The Strange Case of Richard Milhous Nixon* (1972). P. Bullock, *Jerry Voorhis: the Idealist as Politician* (1978).

VOTING, of greater interest to social reformers, who appeal to reason and to voluntary endorsement, than to revolutionaries, who find the suffrage (*q.v.*) to be only one measure of the popular will or need. Reformers have been concerned for "voting strength," "getting out the vote," "a vote-getter," and for stirring the conscience of citizens to "get out and vote." They have also worried about whether they would "waste their vote," for example by voting for a reformer and thus depriving a person deemed the lesser of two evils of a necessary vote. They have been concerned for "educating the voter": a particular goal of the League of Women Voters (*q.v.*). The Voting Rights Act of 1965, one of President Johnson's "Great Society" measures, was intended to help protect minority rights at the polls, especially those of Negroes in the South, by requiring states or other jurisdictions covered by it to get prior federal approval for any political changes (such as the redrawing of legislative districts) that could affect minority voting rights. Several realities qualified its effect, one being the perennial problem of getting Americans to go to the polls. In elections from 1928 to 1980, an average of about 57% of the eligible voters had voted, with highs of 64% electing John F. Kennedy and lows of 54.4% electing Carter (*qq.v.*). In the extremely close election race of 1976, the Negro bloc vote for Carter had made a difference. Four years later it had done nothing for the same candidate. In 1981, the Voting Rights Act was under attack from Strom Thurman of South Carolina, now chairman of the Republican Senate's Judiciary Committee, who argued that federal control was unnecessary in local affairs; dissatisfied citizens could appeal to the courts. Gerald Pomper, *Voter's Choice* (1975); G. Allen Foster, *Votes for Women* (1966); Robert D. Cantor, *Voting Behavior and Presidential Elections* (1975); W. S. Sayre and J. H. Parris, *Voting for President: the Electoral College* (1970); R. J. Dinkin: *Voting in Provincial America* (1977).

WABASH, ST. LOUIS, AND PACIFIC RAILWAY *V.* ILLINOIS (1886), see Munn *v.* Illinois.

WAGE-FUND THEORY, first suggested by Adam Smith, held that there was only so much money available for the payment of wages, that, therefore, demands upon employers were limited in their possibilities. In effect, the theory encouraged employers to resist demands for pay-rises on the ground that they were unlawful in fact, as well as in law. The theory no longer has status, except to help illuminate historical frames of reference; see also Iron Law of Wages.

WAGE SLAVERY, a labor slogan intended to suggest the lowly status of workers under capitalism, somewhat weakened in effectiveness since the rise of "Big Labor."

WAGES, a major concept in socialist thinking, "the iron law of wages," formulated by Lassalle, declaring that they were inevitably forced down by employers to the point of subsistence. The increase of government mandate everywhere to affect wages according to the political or social needs of the moment and the operation of mediation boards in the U.S. has rendered much of the traditional socialist thinking on the subject obsolete. However, the need to contain market forces to avoid inflation (*q.v.*) and other evils, raised the concept of *wage control* as one element in fighting onerous social conditions. See also Salaries. R. Perlman, *Wage Determination* (1964).

WAGES AND HOURS LAW, see Fair Labor Standards Act (1938).

WAGNER, ROBERT F. (1877-1949), associated with a number of distinguished and fundamental laws affecting the public welfare, including social security, housing, and labor relations (*qq.v.*). In 1961, his son, following a mediocre career as a Tammany Hall (*q.v.*) appointee to the office of mayor, was driven into an anti-Tammany position and, as such, into becoming the banner-bearer of reform in New York City. His victory at the polls raised imponderables for reformers in that city, in the Democratic Party, and elsewhere in the nation. J. J. Hutmacher, *Sen. Robert F. Wagner and the Rise of Urban Liberalism* (1968).

WAGNER ACT (1935), see National Labor Relations Act.

WAGNER-STEAGALL ACT of 1937, see Housing Problem, The.

WALD, LILLIAN (1867-1940), with Jane Addams (*q.v.*) among the most notable of those who headed the Settlement House Movement (*q.v.*). She pioneered organization of nursing work in the schools, and led the campaign for a governmental Children's Bureau, which was created in 1908. For her most personal achievement, see her *The House on Henry Street* (1915).

WALKER, MARY EDWARDS (1832-1919), an individualist among feminists, she became a medical practitioner who wrote, sometimes with more feeling than scientific detachment, about female wants in the socio-sexual relationship. She served with distinction as a surgeon during the Civil War and, in the post-Civil War era created the idea which gave her a special place among immortals: of wearing men's clothes. Women did not admire her for it, nor was she honored for her crusade by the ladies who demanded the suffrage. C. M. Snyder, *Mary Walker: the Little Lady in Pants* (1962).

WALKER, WILLIAM (1824-1860), outstanding filibuster, who hoped to make himself a Central American leader, and whose adventures linked him with southern hopes for an expansion of slave territory to the South. In 1855, he took advantage of warfare in Nicaragua to establish himself as its President. In 1857, his regime was overthrown. In 1860, during an effort to establish himself in British Honduras, he was seized and shot. See his *War in Nicaragua* (1860); also W. O. Scroggs, *Filibusters and Financiers* (1969 ed.).

WALKING DELEGATE, a trade-unionist sent to labor areas or groups to encourage organization of and cooperation with other workers and worker organizations; for a fictional treatment, see Leroy Scott, *The Walking Delegate* (1905).

"WALL STREET," long a symbol of American financial and industrial manipulations, and thus of capitalism; as such employed by its critics and also by the critics of the United States. Also taken as a symbol of the "East," which presumably kept other sections of the country in financial toils; hence criticized demagogically by spokesmen for the "West," "South," and "Southwest"; see Texas, as an example. Populists *(q.v.)* held that the West was in fealty to Wall Street and the East, and were inadequate in their perception of non-Wall Street inhabitants of the East, as well as of the centers of power elsewhere in the country to which easterners paid tribute. A striking change in the 1970s was a swell of liberalism in the *Wall Street Journal* which gave it added respect among its more liberal readers and did not interfere with its faithful reports on profits and losses. Such deviation from stereotype required critics of "corporative" government to hunt machiavellian programs under friendly or generous social analyses. See Donald Moffitt, ed., *The Wall Street Journal Views America Tomorrow* (1977).

WALLACE, GEORGE C. (1919-   ), a phenomenon of the social turbulence of the 1960s, he promised, like Huey Long *(q.v.),* to make a place for himself as a quasi-"populist" spokesman. Elected governor of Alabama on a segregationist platform in 1962 he uttered much-repeated words: "I draw a line in the dust and toss the gauntlet before the feet of tyranny. And I say, Segregation now! Segregation tomorrow! Segregation forever!" The collapse of this program did not halt his popularity. Prevented by law from running for governor in 1966, he had his wife run and win. His run for President in 1968 showed increasing strength, not only in the South but in the North. He now employed code words for expressing anti-Negro sentiments, and, in addition, appealed to anti-liberal feeling, most famously in his scorn for "pointy-headed intellectuals," but also for bureaucrats, socialists, and left-wingers. His gathering crusade was halted during the 1972 race, when he was shot by a disturbed person and paralyzed. Although he was re-elected governor in 1974, it appeared that his national crusade had reached a dead end. Marshall Frady, *Wallace* (1968).

WALLACE, HENRY A. (1888-1965), Iowa farmer and influential editor of *Wallace's Farmer*, appointed Secretary of Agriculture under President Roosevelt (1933-40), and, as such, noted for the experimental A.A.A. policies, and his apparently liberal vistas of thought. He was Vice-President of the United States, 1941-5. He resigned as editor of the *New Republic* to run for President on the Progressive Party *(q.v.)* ticket, in 1948. His candidacy was embarrassed by the revelation that he evidently credited spiritualist investigations of a bizarre type. He polled over a million votes, but they were an end, rather than a beginning. See Karl M. Schmidt, *Henry A. Wallace: Quixotic Crusade 1948* (1960). See also N. D. Markowitz, *Rise and Fall of the People's Century: Henry A. Wallace and American Liberalism* (1973).

WALLAS, GRAHAM (1858-1932), seminal thinker on the nature of society. He was a founder of the London School of Economics and a Fabian socialist. His most important work was *Human Nature in Politics* (1908) which argued, inspiringly to the intellectuals of his time, such as Walter Lippmann *(q.v.)* that it did not suffice for a social scientist to have a program; he needed to keep in mind that people responded emotionally as well as rationally. An optimist, Wallas failed to recognize that their irrationality might bring people to what were to evolve into communism and fascism, as well as to socialism. Nevertheless, his original thinking directed readers away from mere dogma to consideration of what people were. He did encourage the growth of elitist *(q.v.)* thinking. His title, *The Great Society* (1914), provided President Johnson *(q.v.)* with the slogan for his Administration.

WALLING, WILLIAM ENGLISH, (1877-1936), one of the "millionaire socialists," who contributed serious studies during the Progressive Era *(q.v.)*. He was one of the organizers of the Intercollegiate Socialist Society and the N.A.A.C.P. *(qq.v.)*. *Russia's Message* (1908), *Socialism as It Is* (1912), and *Progressivism and After* (1914) were valuable accumulations of data and ideas. As a bitter enemy of the Bolsheviks and an ardent supporter of American intervention in World War I, he expressed himself energetically on the related subjects. Interest in his work and personality disappeared in the post-war period.

WALSH, THOMAS J. (1859-1933), Montana progressive Democrat, served in the U.S. Senate 1912-33, as such represented the most principled elements in support of the Woodrow Wilson *(q.v.)* Administration. He helped formulate and pass both the Eighteenth and Nineteenth Amendments *(qq.v.)* to the Constitution, and fought for the Child Labor *(q.v.)* Amendment, as well as for the American entrance into the League of Nations *(q.v.)*. Exposure of the Teapot Dome *(q.v.)* scandal and its prosecution was almost a personal triumph. Walsh was one of the outstanding transitional figures from the Progressive Era to the New Deal *(qq.v.)*. J. L. Bates, ed., *Tom Walsh in Dakota Territory* (1966).

WAR, a momentous topic for social reformers and revolutionists, both of whom profess a distaste for it. Before World War I, various arguments defended it. Imperialists, elitists, Malthusians *(qq.v.)* believed that a virile nation needed to fight, to advance if it did not wish to fail, to weed out its incompetents. World War I was devastating enough to cause them to moderate their tones, if not their thesis. Mussolini's *(q.v.)* brag that it was better to live briefly like a lion than to spend a life-time as a sheep did not inspire non-fascists. The view that war was caused by munitions merchants (popular in the 1930's) was not borne out by facts; thus, the Spanish-American War was a popular war. The view that war brought progress—as World War I resulted in industrial advances and woman suffrage—was denied by John U. Nef, in *War and Human Progress* (1950). "The war to end war"—the American rationale for intervening in World War I—was subjected to ridicule in the post-War period. Revolutionaries denounced war as the responsibility of capitalists; they sanctioned war to end or resist capitalist machinations. The American communist stands on war were instructive. During the period of the Nazi-Soviet Pact *(q.v.)*, they denounced "war-mongers" in the United States who wished to concern themselves for the struggle going on between Germany and Great Britain; they affirmed no more was involved than a battle between imperialisms. When, however, the Nazis attacked the Soviet Union, they demanded immediate intervention in the name of civilization opposing barbarism. The advent of the atom bomb, and its attainment by the U.S.S.R., created new dangers, and a sense of alarm respecting the new possibilities of war and destruction. Pacifists redoubled their activities, and with a fresh sense of meriting respect and cooperation. "Realists" felt it necessary to maintain military supremacy, even though this created dangers of a military outbreak, and infection of the atmosphere which would certainly affect some unborn children and might destroy life and civilization. Two slogans about war in 1960 were "Better Red than Dead" and "Peace with Honor"—the latter a phrase of Disraeli. By 1970 it was evident that more wars than ever were being carried on involving mighty powers either through surrogates or directly. The U.S.-U.S.S.R. engaged in heavy peace talks mixed with connections and disconnections involving China, Taiwan, and others, but war was naked in Vietnam and related nations, in South America, Africa, and between India and Pakistan. The goal appeared to limit wars to surrogates, as the United States withdrew its forces from Vietnam. See Detente, Geneva Convention, Nuclear Question, The, World War, "Military-Industrial Complex," Cold War. (Qq.v. for above.) Richard Nixon, *The Real War* (1980); Stuart H. Loory, *Defeated: Inside America's Military Machine* (1973); J. E. Mueller, *War, Presidents, and Public Opinion* (1973); J. M. Winter, ed., *War and Economic Development* (1975); M. S. Stohl, *War and Domestic Violence* (1976); E. and E. Huberman, *War: an Anthology* (1969); George Liska, *War and Order: Reflections on Vietnam and History* (1968); T. A. Taracousia, *War and Peace in Soviet Diplomacy* (1975); Michael Howard, *War and the Liberal Conscience* (1978); War Games Research Group, *War Games* (1977).

WAR, see "He Kept Us Out of the War."

"WAR BETWEEN THE STATES," name given to the Civil War in the South; it preserves the idea that the Union was no more than a compact that, therefore, the individual states were justified in seceding from a "confederation" which no longer gave due regard to their individual rights, especially those relating to their slave property. Thus, the new Confederate States of America held that they were fighting for freedom, resisting a federal tyranny, as during the American Revolution. See, also, Sectionalism and Reform, Union.

WAR CRIMES, a concept developed after World War II, through the United Nations (q.v.), which established a Commission for the Investigation of War Crimes. Ultimately, a Tribunal was set up at Nuremburg to try a number of notorious Nazi leaders for "crimes against humanity" (q.v.); these included Hermann Goering, Julius Streicher, Joachim von Ribbentrop, Franz von Papen, among others. Such Nazi organizations as the Gestapo (q.v.) were found to be criminal organizations, others like the German General Staff were acquitted as having done no more than their duty. Goering committed suicide, others were sentenced to hang or serve prison sentences. Somewhat similar fates resulted from trials in Tokyo, which brought former Premier Hideki Tojo to the gallows. Although some thousands of German and Japanese leaders were executed, for the most part by their own courts, the trials were criticized, by some for resulting in too many deaths, by others for opposite reasons. See also Eichmann, Karl Adolf. In effect, American dissidents in the 1960 and 1970s created their own unofficial American "war crimes" operation, as with the My Lai (q.v.) incident. S. Shiroyawa, *War Criminal, the Life and Death of Hirota Koki* (1977); S. S. Glueck, *War Criminals: Their Prosecution and Punishment* (1944).

WAR DEBTS, general term applied to those debts incurred by various nations, but notably Great Britain, France, and Italy, to American financiers during World War I. They became associated with Reparations (q.v.); the Allied governments and others argued that they would be glad to pay their debts to Americans as fast as they could recover the amounts they claimed due them from defeated Germany. Subsequent efforts to scale down war debts and reparations accomplished little more than to create bitterness on both sides of the Atlantic Ocean, and to elicit such nicknames as "Uncle Sap," on the part of Americans who conceived of themselves as cheated, and "Uncle Shylock" (q.v.) on the part of discontented former Allies of the United States. War debts became a symbol, to reformers, of the short-sightedness and commercialism which had attended World War I, and persisted in its liquidation. Notorious became the perhaps apocryphal phrase attributed to President Coolidge: "They hired the money, didn't they?" The war debts amounted to about twelve billion dollars; the later "lend lease" funds of World War II amounted to some fifty billion dollars, for which little repayment was expected due to the change in American attitude and expectations. Harold G. Moulton and Leo Pasvolsky, *War Debts and World Prosperity* (1932).

WAR FOR INDEPENDENCE, see American Revolution.

WAR HAWKS, first used to refer to the pro-war party of Federalists who, in 1798, wished to have a full-scale war against France; but more widely identified with the pro-war party of 1812, composed of ambitious young men, largely from the south and the west, and headed by Henry Clay and John C. Calhoun (q.v.) who hoped not only to defeat the British, but to capture Canada.

WAR-LABOR DISPUTES ACT, see Smith-Connally Anti-Strike Act.

"WAR PROFITEERS," a phrase made popular by the Nye Committee (q.v.) investigating the traffic in munitions maintained by "merchants of death." Such phrases tended to make scapegoats of businessmen, and divert attention from other components involved in the creation of wars, including the interest of common people in jobs, whether related to war production or not, the interest in war of revolutionists, and the desire of people to fight, which William James recognized in his *The Moral Equivalent of War* (q.v.). Robert Sherwood's *Idiot's Delight* (1936), a Pulitzer Prize-winning play exploited the theme of war profiteers.

WAR PROSPERITY, one of the most serious threats to reform, it has qualified the potential values of war, from the American Revolution to World War II, and nourished great nests of demagogues (qq.v.). It has weakened popular morale through the temptations of easy and often manifestly undeserved emoluments, through the black market, and through the fact that technological improvements cut down war "sacrifices" to lip-service, and permitted the proliferation of hypocrisy. Much of this deterioration of national character continued in peace time, helped by "cold war" prosperity, and found expression in such phenomena as "payola" (q.v.), an effort at stabilizing corruption.

WARING, GEORGE E. (1833-1898), a pioneer in sanitary engineering for cities, developer of the "Waring System" of sewer construction which revolutionized the field, most famous as the commissioner of the street-cleaning department in New York City (1895-7), where he had been brought to bring the metropolis's problem under control. He died of yellow fever in Havana, to which he had come for similar, but more urgent, reasons; see his *Sanitary Conditions of City and Country Dwelling Houses* (1877); *Modern Methods of Sewage Disposal for Towns* (1894).

WARREN, JOSIAH (1799-1874), social experimenter and a founder of philosophic anarchism, he pondered social principles while living in Robert Owen's New Harmony colony (qq.v.), in Indiana. In 1827, he set up his "Time Store" in Cincinnati, Ohio, where he attempted to transact business in terms of equity rather than profit. He probably earned more regard because he was a brilliant inventor, who made distinct contributions to the development of the printing press. He moved to New York in the 1830's, and organized the village of Modern Times on Long Island, which became notorious as a "free love" community, but persisted into the 1860's, being a haven for other substantial experimenters, as well as for erratic personalities. See his *Equitable Commerce* (1846), and William Bailie, *Josiah Warren, the First American Anarchist* (1906).

WARSAW PACT (1955), the "Iron Curtain" (q.v.) answer to NATO (q.v.); the Soviets's combination of nations intended to marshall communist powers against western powers. It included East Germany, Rumania, and Bulgaria, as well as Hungary, Czechoslovakia, and Poland (qq.v.). Robin Remington, *Warsaw Pact: Case Studies in Communist Conflict Resolution* (1971).

WASHINGTON, BOOKER T. (1859-1915), the greatest Negro figure in succession to Frederick Douglass (q.v.), whose life he wrote. Born a slave, Washington graduated from Hampton Institute, 1875. He became the founder of Tuskegee Institute, Alabama (q.v.), in 1881, and the outstanding spokesman for American Negroes. His famous Atlanta Exposition Address, in 1895, enunciated a policy for his race: to learn the dignity of work, to work separately from the white people, but in cooperation, and with mutual respect. This program was increasingly criticized by rebellious elements among the Negroes, who considered it an Uncle Tom (*q.v.*) policy, and opposed to it the program of the N.A.A.C.P. (*q.v.*). Washington's autobiography, *Up from Slavery* (1901), is a classic among the writings of Negroes.

WASHINGTON, see District of Columbia.

WASHINGTON, TREATY OF, see Treaty of Washington.

WASHINGTONIANS, see Temperance.

WASTE, a major charge against the capitalist system by reformers, who argue that by definition it is concerned for individual profits rather than social need. E.A. Filene (*q.v.*) expected saving from waste to multiply abundance. Strikes, crime, unemployment, a "leisure class," and the production of nonsense (including advertisements, "junk mail," and various commercial fads and fancies) have been characteristic of "free enterprise." Much of the above has been set down as the legitimate vagaries of democracy. However, the ability of less affluent Russia to defeat the United States in crucial military and scientific races, suggested even to proponents of freedom the need for controlling production at least to a degree which would enable the United States to compete with her more single-minded antagonist. Jack Anderson and Ralph Nader (*qq.v.*) were "watchdogs" against waste. It was a sign of the built-in resistance to reform in the area that their clear cut revelations of public waste, naming names and situations, accomplished little in long campaigns. See Vance Packard, *Waste Makers* (1960); R. F. Detweiler, *Wastes Can Produce Cheap Energy* (1978); V. S. Kimball, *Waste Oil Recovery and Disposal* (1975). See also Proxmire, William.

WATERGATE, the major social trauma of the 1970s, it brought to temporary prominence numerous persons who might in reasonable times have been footnotes or less in history. It astonished foreign leaders who could not believe that American society was as divided as it evidently was, and may have linked with older reputations about American naivete and stupidity which had encouraged actions against the United States, as at Pearl Harbor. It created links between disparate events, such as the skulduggery of International Telephone and Telegraph involving funds to CREP (Committee to Re-elect the President, inaccurately called CREEP by its enemies), FBI monitoring of private conversations, the Vietnam War, the indictment of Spiro T. Agnew, the *Pentagon Papers* and burglarization of Daniel Ellsburg's psychiatrist's office, among others. Its final result was to unseat a President, though this would not have occurred but for the discovery that there were tapes which bore upon the Watergate "caper" or "conspiracy"—the distances between the two concepts were the distance between the contending forces. Central, too, was the hatred which President Nixon evoked in his foes as the massive figure in an anti-liberal point of view, which drove his foes to pursue him as they had not his predecessors who engaged in similar monitoring of political opponents without rousing concerted attacks; see Victor Lasky, *It Didn't Start with Watergate* (1977). The key fact divulged by passages in the tapes, notably that of March 21, 1973, was that Nixon had known of the unauthorized Watergate break-in by White-House associated persons, June 17, 1972, and agreed to a "cover-up." The tapes thus gave authenticity to the free recollections of a young White House attorney, John Dean, before a Senate investigating committee; see his *Blind Ambition* (1976). Indeed, the quality of some of the White House habitues, though not unprecedented, was a count against the Administration. That so grotesque a figure as G. Gordon Liddy should have had access to the White House was unnerving; see his *Will* (1980), which describes a person scarcely in touch with American reality. That Nixon thought him "kind of nuts" was accurate but not helpful. Yet E. Howard Hunt, the former C.I.A. agent central to the Watergate break-in, and a more intelligent person, thought Liddy a fine fellow; see Hunt's *Undercover* (1974). Had Nixon destroyed the tapes his Administration would have continued, though under fire; instead he made an appeal to his "Heartland" constituents with an edited-version of "Presidential Transcripts" which upset them with his informal conversation and profanity as Chief Executive, and weakened his ability to conduct his battle for Executive Privilege. With his "silent majority" tired of the war with anti-Nixon forces, and eager to have it ended on any terms, and with the legal forces arrayed against Nixon, his Republican party leaders demanded that he resign. His "political base" gone, Nixon acceded. A series of White House personalities received prison terms, notably John Mitchell, former Attorney General, and White House aides H. R. ("Bob") Haldeman and John Ehrlichman. For the spirit of the indictments, John Sirica, *To Set the Record Straight* (1979) and Leon Jaworski, *The Right and the Power* (1976). See also R. Ben-Neruste, Hugh Frampton, *Stonewall* (1977); James Doyle, *Not Above the Law* (1977); J. Anthony Lukas, *Nightmare* (1976); W. B. Dickinson, Jr., ed., *Watergate: Chronology of a Crisis* (1973). (*Qq.v.* for above.) See also Cover Up, Leaks.

WATER POWER, a major natural resource, inadequately used for lack of necessary facilities. It entered into the problem of land reform (*q.v.*). Its potentialities helped direct public concern to the Ballinger Affair (*q.v.*). It was a prime factor in the Muscle Shoals (*q.v.*) development, and given major harnessing by T.V.A. (*q.v.*). Its strategic place in the modern debate over energy and its uses was unclear, though it obviously demanded consideration along with coal, gas, solar energy, and wood in the concern over oil (*q.v.*).

WATSON, THOMAS E. (1856-1922), a lost hope of the southern poor whites, the "Abraham Lincoln of Georgia," he worked his way up from poverty to the bar, led the militant Populist forces of his state, even countenancing cooperation with the Negroes in his demand for laws protecting and aiding his people. By 1905, he was issuing *Tom Watson's Magazine*, which sounded in many respects like the muckraking (*q.v.*) magazines of the period, but was virulent in its anti-Negro program. Watson later helped incite mob action in the murder of Leo Frank (*q.v.*). A strange development was his appearance in Jimmy Carter's (*q.v.*) campaign autobiography, *Why Not the Best?* (1975) in which Watson was portrayed as a "populist" admired in the Carter family, his virulent qualities passed over or forgotten: a startling revelation, unnoticed by the public or its commentators, of Carter's feeble grasp of American continuity. Although this lapse must have been apparent to the Yale historian C. V. Woodward, if only because he was the biographer of Watson (1938), he did not protest the absurd admiration by a Presidential candidate who professed hatred of racism probably because Carter was a Democrat and, like Woodward, from the South.

WAYLAND, JULIUS A. (1854-1912), outstanding grassroots (*q.v.*) socialist, born in Indiana; after many vicissitudes founded the *Coming Nation* (*q.v.*), in 1893, which was a striking success. He began the Ruskin Cooperative Association in 1894 in Tennessee, taking the *Coming Nation* with him. The Association deprived him of power over his own paper and he left and went to Kansas, where, in 1895, he founded *The Appeal to Reason* (*q.v.*), which became even more famous, especially when the Reform Era became a national phenomenon in the 1900's. Wayland's success stemmed from his earthy and indigenous approach. He refused to permit the *Appeal* to become a mere function of the Socialist Party, even though he preached socialism in it. He admired Altgeld and "Golden Rule" Jones (*qq.v.*), even though they were not of the socialist brotherhood, and expressed regard for the unpredictable Hearst (*q.v.*). He was interested in an effective socialism, rather than an orthodox one, and made more of an impression on Americans than any other American socialist editor. In 1902-4, he made an effort to rescue the ailing *Coming Nation*. He committed suicide in 1912.

WEATHERMEN, significant as a last writhing of the youth

(*q.v.*) upsurge of the 1960s. With ready support for mass confrontation with police and troops falling away, this handful of loosely organized terrorists (*q.v.*) October 1969, in Chicago during a trial of youth conspirators, staged four "Days of Rage" against the police of the city: a last effort to marshall revolutionary forces against the government. Thereafter, they fell apart or went into long exile, as in the case of Bernardine Dohrn, changing their places and appearance. Anthony Esler, *Bombs, Beards, and Barricades* (1971).

WEAVER, JAMES B. (1833-1912), Populist leader of stature and distinction. He attained the rank of general during the Civil War, and returned to Iowa to develop into a spokesman for the increasingly troubled and rebellious farmers. He served in Congress, and was Greenback Party candidate for President in 1880. As Populist Party candidate, in 1892, he received over a million votes, and twenty-two electoral votes. His *A Call to Action. An Interpretation of the Great Uprising, Its Source and Causes* (1892) is a valuable analysis of political developments. Weaver's reasonableness and eloquence has been inadequately considered by critics of Populism.

WEAVERS, REVOLT OF THE, an insurrection which took place in the industrial region of Silesia, Germany, as a result of onerous social conditions, the theme of Hauptmann's (*q.v.*) *The Weavers* (1892).

WEBBS, THE, major founders of the Fabian Society (*q.v.*). Sidney James Webb, who became the first Baron Passfield (1859-1947), and his wife, Beatrice Potter (1858-1943), became famous for their authoritative studies on the social conditions of Great Britain, trade union history, and socialistic programs for change. Their work, prepared with great deliberation and moderation, took on a quasi-official character, as in their *A Constitution for the Socialist Commonwealth of Great Britain* (1920), and a literature developed around them as well as about their work. Their visit to the U.S.S.R. in 1932 was watched by the world's press, and their positive view of that land represented an influential endorsement; see their *Communism: a New Civilization* (1935).

WEBSTER, DANIEL (1782-1852), his long and distinguished career was that of a sectionalist, partisan to New England's interests, and a nationalist; it was also that of a conservative who did not scruple to receive stipends from the Second Bank of the United States, whose interests he defended, and from private interests as well. Nevertheless, his profound grasp of American history and law and his rich oratorical gift drew respect from his foes and pride from reformers chagrined by his unwillingness to depart from political and conventional trammels. His defense of the Compromise of 1850 (*q.v.*) shocked a North which was reorganizing to resist further southern demands that slavery be given equal treatment under the law with freedom. Yet his death called forth universal respect and recollections of a great life. His defense of the Union in the course of the Webster-Hayne debates (1830), was a milestone in the creation of an American nationalism, his greatest orations were models of American expression.

WELD, THEODORE DWIGHT (1803-1895), one of the outstanding abolitionists of the 1830 period, organizer of the Lane Seminary Debate (*q.v.*), and of a formidable corps of abolitionist speakers, "The Seventy," who agitated the northern countryside to good effect. He himself was a speaker of outstanding qualities. His *American Slavery as It Is* (1839) influenced both Harriet Beecher Stowe and Charles Dickens (*qq.v.*). However, his voice gave out, and he developed a desire for private life, and, having married Angelina Grimké (1805-1879) (*q.v.*), they retired, early in the 1840's to uneventful pursuits. Gilbert H. Barnes, *The Antislavery Impulse* (1935) was a curiously successful academic effort to demean William Lloyd Garrison (*q.v.*) and make Weld central to the antislavery crusade, but failed to persuade the general public; see Filler, "Consensus," in J. Waldmeir, *Essays in Honor of*

Russel B. Nye (1978); R. Abzug, *Passionate Liberator* (1981).

WELFARE CAPITALISM, see American Plan.

WELFARE STATE, one which ministered to its citizens's basic wants, from proper birth to decent burial; Great Britain became the leading example of it, in the post-World War II era, but American critics of the New Deal and the Fair Deal (*qq.v.*) who noted that the succeeding Republican Administration made little effort to cut back from earlier legislation asserted that the Welfare State was well developed in the United States. Extreme critics argued not only that the Welfare State was socialism, but that it was communism. Defenders of the Welfare State argued, in response, that it left large areas of life and enterprise to individualism and private risk not envisioned in the communistic system. The *details* of welfare increasingly concerned citizens and government. In Great Britain socialist measures all but carried recipients from cradle to grave. The Tory government of 1979 undertook to dismantle aspects of it which it deemed harmful to sound government, family life, and social health. In the United States affluence and lack of concern permitted the growth of carelessly administered funds which raised unfortunate children in poverty and hopeless prospects, in destroyed neighborhoods and eroded education, and allowed food stamps to reach hordes of notoriously unworthy recipients; a major premise of included "giveaways" had been that money would change the human nature of the benefitted: an expectation which did not materialize. Yet administration after administration could devise no program to break the cycle of social decay. Although all agreed on the need for and legitimacy of Old Age Dependency, Aid to Dependent Children, and to the blind and handicapped, medical aid and social security, the problem lay with those welfare elements not in such categories. Not until inflation and industrial crisis forced a reconsideration of long-established routines were the basic premises of welfare thrown into focus. In 1978 President Carter asked for the abolition of the welfare system, and proposed instead one of interim work, job incentives, direct money grants, tax relief, reduction of fraud—one of the most blatant scandals of the then-current system, producing welfare (and welfare administrator) "kings" and "queens." However, Carter had by then lost all credibility in such areas, and his ideas were passed over by his party faithfuls as well as scorned by others as just a big expansion of welfare disguised as a work program. The Reagan Administration came into power in 1981 pledged to give aid to the "truly needy" and to further "enterprize zones" to restore wrecked neighborhoods. It was hoped that a decent social work establishment would emerge to direct such programs. (*Qq.v.* for above.) Robert H. Haveman and J. V. Krutilla, *Unemployment, Idle Capacity and the Evaluation of Public Expenditures* (1968); John E. Tropman et al., *Perspectives on Social Policy* (1971); A. D. Tussing, *Poverty and the Dual Economy* (1975); K. Heise, *The Chicagoization of America* (1976), and Heise et al., *How to Survive in Chicago and Enjoy It* (1975); Edith Abbott, *Some American Pioneers in Social Welfare* (1937); W. A. Robson, *The Welfare State and Welfare Society* (1976); L. A. Salamon, *Welfare: the Elusive Consensus* (1978); M. Anderson, *Welfare: the Political Economy of Welfare Reform* (1978); C. K. Rowley and A. T. Peacock, *Welfare Economics: a Liberal Restatement* (1975); Betty R. Mardell, *Welfare in America: Controlling the "Dangerous Classes"* (1975); R. H. Haveman, ed., *A Decade of Federal Antipoverty Programs* (1977).

WELLES, ORSON (1915-   ), theatrical innovator, whose briefly creative career was touched off by the Federal Theater Project (*q.v.*). In 1937, he opened the Mercury Theater and produced Shakespeare's *Julius Caesar*, using black shirts (*q.v.*), Fascist salutes, and other *décor* of Mussolini's Italy. His radio adaptation of H.G. Wells's *The War of the Worlds*, the next year, was presented as actually happening, and frightened many people who thought Martians had landed on the earth. Welles's motion-picture, *Citizen Kane* (1941) was modeled on William Randolph Hearst (*q.v.*) and once again showed a creative sense of the relation between art and life. Thereafter, Welles became a mere integer in the entertainment world.

WELLS, HERBERT GEORGE (1866-1946), literary figure and social thinker, who had intellectual relations with George Bernard Shaw *(q.v.)*, on the one hand, and with such middle-class chronicles as the novelist Arnold Bennett, on the other. He began his career as a writer of science-fiction, some of which had striking social implications; see, for example, his *The War of the Worlds* (1898) and *When the Sleeper Awakes* (1899). See also *A Modern Utopia* (1905). Some of his work had elements in common with that of Edward Bellamy *(q.v.)*. Other writings by Wells suggested Charles Dickens *(q.v.)* in his whimsical vein; *Love and Mr. Lewisham* (1900) was one of a number of writings which emphasized the human, rather than the reformer. *The New Machiavelli* (1911) struggled, though not too successfully, for a fresh view of society. Wells accepted the war, disappointing some of his admirers, and emerged from it more determined than ever to create a scientific approach to human problems. His *Outline of History* (1920) and *The Science of Life* (1929) were among formidable writings intended to draw mankind into contemplation of world knowledge and world problems, in order to serve what Wells called "the open conspiracy": man's struggle with nature and human disorder. The project inspired his fictional masterpiece, *The World of William Clissold* (1926), the experiences and ideas of a social dreamer much like Wells himself. His *Experiment in Autobiography* (1934) was the record of a generation, as well as of the writer, and many other works filled out the record of observations and suggestions. Nevertheless, his works plummeted into silence and disuse when he died.

WEST INDIES, see British Emancipation, Caribbean Nations and American Reform.

WESTERN FEDERATION OF MINERS, organized in 1893, associated a particularly impressive core of militants—made so by their high individualism, which was challenged by an equally spirited type of employer—who met in bitter strikes in Cripple Creek, Colorado, Coeur d'Alene, Idaho, and elsewhere. They were led by such rugged fighters as "Big Bill" Haywood *(q.v.)*, who were impatient of the conservative policies preferred by the A.F. of L. *(q.v.)*, and in 1897 organized a Western Labor Union which Gompers *(q.v.)* and others of the A.F. of L. denounced as a dual union *(q.v.)*. Although the effort to organize an opposition to the A.F. of L. was a failure, the W.F.M. continued its vigorous course, in 1905 helping to organize the I.W.W. *(q.v.)*.

WHEATLEY, PHILLIS, see Peters, Mrs. Phillis [Wheatley].

WHEELER, BURTON K. (1882-   ), Montana political figure, he made his reputation as a vigorous Democratic Progressive who fought along side of Thomas J. Walsh *(q.v.)* to expose frauds in government oil lands. As Vice-Presidential candidate on the Progressive Party ticket of 1924, he ran with Robert M. La Follette *(q.v.)*. In the 1930's, he exposed a reactionary facet to his personality; see John Roy Carlson's *(q.v.) Under Cover*. See his autobiography, *Yankee from the West* (1962).

WHIGS, for antecedents, see Tories. Dr. Johnson, the Lexicographer, told Boswell that he had always said that the first Whig was the Devil. As a firm conservative, he was expressing his views of their liberal propensities. When they were reconstituted in the United States, in the 1830's, it was as political conservatives who sought to resist Democratic popular tactics. Emerson *(q.v.)* thought the Democrats had the better program, the Whigs the better men. This was only partially true on both sides of the epigram. What the Democrats did have was a firmer association with slavery. Moral reformers tended to prefer the Whig Party. Democratic stalwarts accused them of preferring philanthropy for the Negro to justice for the white man. Although by 1840, in the Log Cabin and Cider campaign *(q.v.)*, the Whigs had learned to match the Democrats in demagogy, they had a less firm stand than the latter, who supported nationalism, slavery, and imperialism with increasing determination. Whig disintegration therefore proceeded to the gain of anti-slavery and other elements representing moral issues, but also capitalist issues, notably protectionism *(q.v.)*; they formed the Republican Party. See also Politics and Reform.

WHISKY REBELLION, THE (1794), an incident in the development of a firmer central authority through the Federal government set up under the Constitution of the United States *(q.v.)*. Settlers in western Pennsylvania were suspicious of both the state and national government, and with little regard for their laws which seemed to them calculated to aid the wealthy. They distilled their grain and corn, which made it easier to transport to market, and no less valuable for being late. Hamilton placed a tax on these products, which looked to the frontiersmen like taxation *(q.v.)* without representation. They resisted the tax-collectors, insulted and harmed them, and thus raised the question of Federal authority. Militia was sent west to disperse the rebels, led by David Bradford; the uprising dissolved as the militia approached the Pittsburgh area. Bradford escaped, but other leaders were seized and transported to Philadelphia. Although they could have been severely punished, the government felt there was no need for underscoring its point and making martyrs of the defendants, who were eventually released. L. D. Baldwin, *Whiskey Rebellion* (1967 ed.)

WHISKY RING (1875), a group of revenue officers in St. Louis, Missouri, and Washington, D.C., who connived to defraud the government of its taxes. The exposures involved members of President Grant's official family, and represented some of the disgrace of what Vernon L. Parrington *(q.v.)* called "the Great Barbecue." John MacDonald, *Secrets of the Great Whisky Ring* (1880).

"WHISTLEBLOWING," an effort to fight bureaucratic corruption and waste by public-spirited employees which was often ill-repaid, thanks to public languor and cynicism. Thus a highly-paid employee of the Air Force, Ernest Fitzgerald, involved in cost-cutting, in 1968 testified in Congressional committee respecting "over-runs" on the estimated cost of a cargo plane, the C5A, which mounted as high as $2 billion. Relieved of his job by Air Force authorities, he went to court and by 1973 had won a court decision reinstating him and approving paying of the enormous legal fees. Although the Air Force complied, it gave the "Whistleblower" nothing to do. Further court action dragged into 1981, during which time Fitzgerald's position improved little. See also Nader, Ralph.

WHITE, in the United States used, sometimes unconsciously, as a term of praise: "That's white of you." This obscures the implied superiority of Caucasians to people who are black, red, yellow, or some other color having invidious connotations. White, in the 1920's, was a symbol of reaction, referring to the White Guards in Russia, the White Terror in several places. White as a sign of discrimination was rebuked by reformers, as with white, or "lily white," unions, clubs, or communities. *"White guilt"* emerged as a phenomenon of American prosperity mixed with youth agitation, the propaganda of partisans, and a sense of American well-being having been undeserved, so much of it having been "given" by nature and the struggles of prior generations. Also relevant was the need of some social elements to overcome their antipathies, especially toward Negroes by excessive and uninformed appreciation of black virtues. "White" guilt and "liberal" guilt—there was no minority or black guilt—attracted sentimentalists rather than responsible people working for solutions to ever-changing conditions in the several parts of the nation, and the nation as a whole. The guilt complex also served irresponsible elements, especially in the Negro community, which it was rarely able consistently to resist. Earnest S. Cox, *White America* (1967); George P. Jackson, *White and*

Negro Spirituals (1944); Angus Campbell, *White Attitudes toward Black People* (1971).

WHITE, WALTER (1893-1955), Negro leader and writer who, because of his light complexion was able to move about freely in spots where trouble had broken out between Negroes and aggressive white people, until he became too well-known to risk being recognized. He was long-time secretary of the N.A.A.C.P. (*q.v.*). Among his notable works were *Rope and Faggot—a Biography of Judge Lynch* (1929) and his autobiography, *A Man Called White* (1948). He also wrote novels.

WHITE, WILLIAM ALLEN (1868-1944), famous in his time as an outstanding small-town editor, of Emporia (Kansas) *Gazette*. He made his reputation with a picturesque editorial in 1896, entitled "What's the Matter with Kansas?" in bitter derogation of the Populists. Although his lively journalism seemed to make him a feature of the Reform Era (*q.v.*), and although he supported the Progressive Party (*q.v.*) in 1912, he was essentially a party regular of the Republican Party, and representative of uneventful middle west thought. His early fiction was over-rated; his later studies make suggestive reading; see his *Masks in a Pageant* (1928) and his *Autobiography* (1946).

"WHITE MAN'S BURDEN, THE," title and theme of verses by Rudyard Kipling (1899), treated with irony and dislike by reformers, who resent this view of colonial peoples as "Half-devil and half-child," and who take it to be hypocrisy to believe that the imperialists who are being honored by the verses have the well-being of the nations they dominate by force at heart. The verses are useful for their simple rationale of imperialism (*q.v.*), which no longer has any value to its former proponents.

WHITLOCK, BRAND (1869-1934), American reformer and literary figure, a disciple of Altgeld and "Golden Rule" Jones (*qq.v.*). His The 13th District (1902) and *The Turn of the Balance* (1907) were contributions to the reform, as well as the fiction, of the era. He served as mayor of Toledo, 1905-13; his *Forty Years of It* (1914) was memorable as autobiography as well as social commentary. He became disillusioned with reform, to some degree. His *Belgium: a Personal Record* (1919) stemmed from his experience as Ambassador to that country. Written in his best vein, it seemed a masterpiece to those who believed in the necessity of American intervention in World War I. His *Letters and Journal* (1936) are invaluable for the light they throw on the Progressive mind.

WHITMAN, WALT (1819-1892), one of the greatest literary figures in American history, and often identified with American reform aspirations. He was a liberating force though his goals required pursuit through devious byways. Born of ordinary people on Long Island, he worked at carpentry, school teaching, and printing, and became a well-regarded editor of papers which followed the Democratic Party line. Although he expounded generous principles, his prose lacked distinction, and his verse was inconsequential, sometimes striving to imitate Whittier (*q.v.*). He was probably deeply frustrated by his sexual inclinations, which may have been heterosexual. He discovered a way in a novel by George Sand (*q.v.*) which depicted a prophetic figure of democracy; see Esther Shephard, *Walt Whitman's Pose* (1938). His *Leaves of Grass* (1855) broke with conventional verse and conventional ideas, Whitman glorifying himself, his body, with intimate details which ultimately caused scandal, all men and things, and national destinies. Emerson, though wholly opposed to Whitman's method and principles, saluted his achievement, though Whitman was a stranger to him, in words which Whitman hastily reproduced in a second edition. It has been conjectured that Whitman's services as a male nurse during the Civil War enabled him to activate repressed desires to be near men, but the record shows a warm and dedicated attendant to wounded soldiers who needed one.

As Whitman seemed to Emerson an answer to his call for a natural man and poet, so Lincoln seemed to Whitman an answer to his call for a thorough democrat, and he mourned deeply for him, writing, in "When Lilacs Last in the Dooryard Bloom'd," one of the world's great poems. His *Leaves of Grass* grew in volume and in notoriety, constituting a major issue in freedom of speech and press, as well as art. Whitman attracted followers, though none of stature and distinction. His *Democratic Vistas* (1871) was a prose testimony of faith. He inspired libertarians and poets in the next several decades, and acquired academic status which smoothed away the complexities of his personality and career. By 1950, much of the admiration for him was in the form of lip-service for his ideals and verse which included little real understanding of the complex nature of his campaign and his achievement.

WHITTIER, JOHN GREENLEAF (1807-1892), a famous name in American academic literary history, little read in practice. His libertarian verse was an influence during the entire reform era, 1830-60. Largely forgotten has been the fact that he was a notable prose writer and commentator of the time, and a highly regarded editor of, among other publications, the *Pennsylvania Freeman,* and also of the *National Era*. His public life, and life as a poet and personality, are yet to be adequately integrated. Albert Mordell, *Quaker Militant* (1969 ed.)

WILBERFORCE, WILLIAM (1759-1833), Evangelical Christian of extreme conservative cast, who became internationally famous for his struggle against the slave trade. Awakened to the cause by Thomas Clarkson, about 1787, he began to work in Parliament, with the aid of William Pitt, the younger. Although the battle to curb and diminish the influence of the slave-traders was largely maintained by others, Wilberforce's oratorical style and piety were calculated to appeal most deeply to the cautious custodians of British policy. The slave trade was opposed by businessmen using relatively free labor, as well as by some slaveholders. The slave trade was abolished in 1807. The battle against the slave system in the British West Indies was led by Thomas Fowell Buxton, but such was Wilberforce's fame that he was even popularly credited with its overthrow, shortly following his demise. John Pollack, *Wilberforce* (1978)

WILDE, OSCAR (1856-1900), Irish poet, playwright, literary figure, and leading personage in a notorious scandal of the 1890's. Although an exponent of "art for art's sake" and the irresponsible life, a "decadent" whose ideals of "beauty" have not inspired reformers, he was also author of *The Soul of Man under Socialism,* an essay which echoed sentiments to be found in such writers as William Morris (*q.v.*), but with touches of the famous Wilde paradox, such as that the virtue of socialism would be that one would not have to concern himself for his neighbor. Following his catastrophic fall and service in prison, Wilde wrote his immortal *The Ballad of Reading Gaol* and *De Profundis* (From the Depths), the latter published after his death. Charles Ryskamp, *Wilde and the Nineties* (1966).

WILEY, HARVEY WASHINGTON (1844-1930), chief chemist of the United States Department of Agriculture (1883-1912), and reformer. He agitated during the 1890's for inspection of food to ensure its purity, and stirred interest and controversy, though little action. His "poison-squad" experiments in 1902 helped educate the public to the effect produced upon the body by different substances. They even inspired an effort to pass a law requiring companies to label food products in interstate traffic which passed the House of Representatives, but failed in the Senate. Dr. Wiley's work was influential in the campaign which resulted in the passage of the Pure Food and Drug Act of 1906 (*q.v.*); afterwards, he fought for adequate implementation of the Act, to such effect that he felt forced to resign in 1912; see his *History of* *a Crime against the Food Law* (1929). O. E. Anderson, Jr., *The Health of a Nation* (1958).

WILKES, JOHN (1727-1797), English parliamentarian and democrat; as a member of Parliament, his alleged libelling of the Throne in his famous *The North Briton*, No. 45 (23 April 1763) resulted in his imprisonment in London Tower and the ransacking of his private papers. His subsequent suit, and its successful conclusion, with damages of £1000 was hailed as a victory for personal rights. His subsequent essays in the same field won him great enthusiasm and support on both sides of the Atlantic. "Wilkes and Liberty" was a slogan in opposition to arbitrary rule. Wilkes's picturesque personality and defiance of conventions enchanted his admirers. Among other libertarian actions in which he participated were his defense of the city charter of London against Parliamentary invasion, his protests against ill-treatment of prisoners, his proposals for a redistribution of seats in Parliament, his demand for tolerance toward religious dissenters, and his sympathy with the American point of view, during the long struggle of the colonists with Parliament. George Rude, *Wilkes and Liberty* (1962).

WILLARD, FRANCES E. (1839-1898), noted temperance reformer, educator, and woman suffrage advocate, and aunt of Josiah Flynt (*q.v.*). Her related causes made her the recipient of much love and adulation, and created a reputation which quickly deteriorated after World War I. See her *Women and Temperance* (1883) and *Glimpses of Fifty Years* (1889). M. Earhart, *Frances Willard* (1944).

WILLIAMS, ROGER (1607-1684), pioneer of civil liberties in America; while serving as minister in Salem, Massachusetts, he protested the operations of the theocracy (*q.v.*) and was banished; in 1636 he founded Rhode Island at Providence, and in 1644 received a Royal Charter for the colony. Although opposed to Quakers in principle, he maintained separation of church and state, encouraged friendship with the Indians. John Garrett, *Roger Williams* (1970).

WILLKIE, WENDELL (1892-1944), a phenomenon of the 1930's, he was an Indiana lawyer who became president of the Commonwealth and Southern Corporation, and, as such, made efforts to oppose the creation or development of T.V.A. (*q.v.*). In 1940, he was the Republican nominee for President, and offered anticipated appeals for free enterprise in opposition to the New Deal (*q.v.*) program of the incumbent President Roosevelt. On foreign policy, however, Willkie refused the isolationist stand and stood by the President's policy. Willkie grew rapidly in perspective. He accepted Roosevelt's invitation to make a tour of the world as his personal representative, and returned with a vision which he embodied in his *One World* (1943). Although the Republican Party rejected him for a second try for the Presidency, he appeared on the way to organizing a strong and resourceful following which would accept the necessities of modern life while holding on to ideals of individuality. Willkie's death was a shock to them. A Foundation maintains the program which they perceived in his work. E. Barnard, *Wendell Willkie, Fighter for Freedom* (1966).

WILMOT PROVISO, a step on the way to organizing the forces in the North favoring Free Soil (*q.v.*), it was first introduced in the House of Representatives as an amendment to a bill requesting funds with which to purchase land from Mexico, with which the United States was then at war. The Proviso stipulated that no land so purchased should be permitted to tolerate slavery. Although the Proviso was less the result of principled anti-slavery views, and rather derived from political intrigue and fear of southern expansionist aims, it rallied northern opinion and helped divide northerners and southerners in Congress.

WILSHIRE, GAYLORD (1861-1927), capitalist and socialist editor, whose *Wilshire's Magazine* (1900-3, 1904-15) boasted three hundred thousand subscribers during the Reform Era.

Wilshire was a successful businessman, and ran for Congress on the socialist ticket in the United States, and for Parliament in England and Canada. He was one of the "millionaire socialists" who contributed serious energies, rather than money, in that era, and who seemed to provide evidence that socialism was not exotic or fanciful, but an impressive fact; see his *Socialism Inevitable* (1907), and *Wilshire's Editorials* (1906).

WILSON, HENRY (1812-1875), Massachusetts anti-slavery figure, a northern Know-Nothing (*q.v.*), elected U.S. Senator in 1853; he helped to divide the Know-Nothings and lead the northern contingent into the Republican Party (*q.v.*). He was an active Radical Republican, and, as such, sharply opposed President Johnson (*q.v.*). Wilson was elected Vice-President of the United States, in company with Grant (*q.v.*), in 1872. See his *History of the Rise and Fall of the Slave Power in America* (1872-5).

WILSON, WOODROW (1856-1924), a late-comer to national politics, a Virginian who was a college teacher and President of Princeton University, largely conservative during the pre-World War I Reform Era (*q.v.*) he made a mild reputation as a "liberal" because of his fight for democratizing policies at his elite academic institution. He was chosen by the New Jersey political machine as its gubernatorial candidate in 1910 as a figure-head, but defied the machine and rallied liberal politicians to his side. The split in the Republican Party, plus the cancelling out of Democratic stalwarts made him President of the United States. His first Administration was reputed to have accomplished more reform than any to that time; yet it was only partly due to Wilson, as with the Seamen's (*q.v.*) Act of 1915, which was a bi-partisan achievement. With the heart of the reform movement—the muckraking magazines—stopped, much that went on in Wilson's first term was efficient, rather than substantial: a kind of Taylorization (*q.v.*) in government. Thus, a Clayton Act (*q.v.*) was attained, though trusts were little affected; a free-trade (*q.v.*) tariff was achieved, with no free trade possible during the war, or permitted afterwards. A beginning was made on farmers' loans, railroad employee administration, and other topics. Wilson sincerely wanted peace to the extent that, as a Virginian, he feared that the Caucasian race might be destroying itself in internecine struggles, but his sympathies were early for the British, as compared with the Germans. His friendship for Col. House (*q.v.*) helped reveal the limits of his vision. He mixed a sense of superiority with an ability to offer the public "heart warming" appeals to hearth and home. They enabled him to seem above the bitter struggle during which the many forces which opposed intervention in the European War were crushed. He called America to a Crusade for Democracy, in terms which seemed to link intervention with the recent reform movement. Having once asked for peace in thought as well as in deed, he now demanded war to the uttermost, carried by a vision of a League of Nations (*q.v.*). Wilson offended American opinion in 1918 by asking for a Democratic Congress and emphasizing Democratic followers in his post-War entourage to Europe to make the peace; Republicans had also died in furtherance of his crusade. (Franklin D. Roosevelt (*q.v.*) later sought to avoid this policy.) His Fourteen Points (*q.v.*) for peace stirred the French Premier Clemenceau's irony: God himself, he observed, had been satisfied with ten. But Wilson forced the League of Nations upon his fellow-victors; he then returned home to repudiation. Pleading that the United States join up, he was stricken and incapacitated for the remainder of his term. Some took him to be a prophet of world cooperation; others saw him as a master of rhetoric; see "He Kept Us Out of the War," "Open Covenants Openly Arrived At," Steel Strike of 1919, "Red Scare." Arthur Link, ed., *Woodrow Wilson: a Profile* (1968); E. H. Buerig, *Woodrow Wilson and the Balance of Power* (1955); J. M. Blum, *Woodrow Wilson and the Politics of Morality* (1956); Herbert Hoover, *The Ordeal of Woodrow Wilson* (1958) T. A. Bailey, *Woodrow*

Wilson and the Lost Peace (1944); Filler, ed., *The President Speaks* (1982).

WINES, ENOCH COBB (1806-1879), a Congregationalist clergyman, educator and prison reformer. He became secretary of the Prison Association of New York, and made an epochal inspection tour of northern prisons (1865). His *Report on the Prisons and Reformatories of the United States and Canada* (1867) was filled with recommendations which inspired others and resulted ultimately in such reforms as the parole and the indeterminate sentence (*qq.v.*). Wines was largely responsible for the Cincinnati Congress of reformers of 1870 which issued a "Declaration of Principles." As a result of his efforts, too, the first International Penitentiary Congress was organized at London, 1872; it resulted in a permanent organization. See also his *The State of Prison and of Child-Saving Institutions in the Civilized World* (1880). His son, *Frederic Coward Wines* (1838-1912), was a Presbyterian clergyman who turned to institutional and prison reform. He brought back from Europe the idea of a detached ward, or cottage, for housing the insane, eliminating chains and other cruel measures and restraints, and publicized hydrotherapy, the water cure. See his *Punishment and Reformation, an Historical Sketch of the Rise of the Penitentiary System* (1895), and *Report on Crime, Pauperism and Benevolence in the United States* (1895-6).

WISCONSIN IDEA, see La Follette, Robert M., McCarthy, Charles.

WISE, JOHN (1652-1725), early American Congregationalist clergyman of democratic principles, he refused to pay taxes which contradicted charter principles, and denounced the plans of such influential clergymen as Cotton Mather to create a church authority higher than that of the individual congregation. His pamphlets, which set forth the principles underlying his opposition to authority, entered into libertarian and revolutionary thought. He led an effort to reverse the sentences which had been obtained during the witchcraft (*q.v.*) persecutions; see his *The Churches Quarrel Espoused* (1710), and *A Vindication of the Government of New England Churches* (1717).

WITCHCRAFT, see Salem Witchcraft Trials.

WITCH HUNT, title of books by George Seldes (*q.v.*) ("The Technique and Profits of Redbaiting") (1940), and by Carey McWilliams ("The Revival of Heresy") (1950). Both works were curious in comparing "hysterias" of their eras with the hysteria attending charges of witchcraft (*q.v.*). Neither faced the question of whether there had been witches, during the earlier excitement, in the sense of there having been communists during the later troubles. Seldes concerned himself with redbaiting, Coughlin, the Liberty League, and Dies (*q.v.*). McWilliams was disturbed by the Loyalty Oath, the "persecution" of Hollywood writers for radicalism, McCarthyism (*qq.v.*), and other phenomena of later vintage. At bottom, the problem in both cases concerned the realities **of democracy** (*q.v.*), as well as the alleged privileges it carried. See also Sidney Hook, *Heresy, Yes—Conspiracy, No* (1953). See Arthur Miller's play, *The Crucible* (1953) which, though it imputed psychology to its Puritan characters which the Puritans did not have, because of its implicit analogy with McCarthyism was a ringing theatrical success at home and abroad.

"WOBBLIES," see Industrial Workers of the World.

WOMAN, has been treated in all reform and radical programs, in terms of her individuality, and also as an element in humanity. Theoreticians have assumed her need for greater equality; there has been no comparable treatment of *Man* as an element requiring additional justice, on the single ground of his sex. Treatment of woman's rights breaks down into privileges necessary to her fulfillment, including the right to birth control privileges and maternity privileges, and equal rights engrossing education, the suffrage, equal pay for equal work, (*qq.v*) and entree into most fields of endeavor. Whether bearing arms in the service of the country is a privilege, a right, or a burden, is subject to interpretation. "Woman's work" and "man's work" are also controversial. In the 1960s, beginning with the plaintive, personal protest with her lot of Betty Friedan, *The Feminine Mystique* (1963), which tied in with the general social turmoil and malaise of the time, a wide movement of female voices, actions, and organizations proliferated which seized and held the headlines, created confrontations and manifestoes, and reached almost into every home. It created ERA, the Equal Rights Amendment, and marched across the states demanding affirmation. It resulted in boycotts of states which hesitated to ratify, or rejected ERA. An army of women were made articulate on platforms and campuses, and in social and political organizations, often crying "tokenism" in furtherance of their ambitions, for themselves and other women. Their declarations reached, finally, into the Carter White House, which subsidized women's meetings, publications, and preferred personalities, emphasizing the "radical" viewpoints and giving them a semi-official endorsement. The President's Advisory Committee for Women issued *Voices for Women*, a mouthpiece which seemed threatened with indifference or non-subsidy in 1981 by the incoming Reagan Administration. Part of the Carter-sponsored point of view could be noted in the comment of Ann Ramsey, an Advisory Committee member, who feared for its future even though "we represent half the population of the United States." Although the Committee had concerned itself for rape, violence in the home, teenage pregnancy, female poverty, and children it clearly ignored the female viewpoint of anti-abortionists, anti-homosexuals, and anti-ERA women, who held the more permissive women in disrespect. Undetermined was the range of *human nature* among women which would have to be put in perspective to administer grievances equitably. Thus, among the torrent of books about women in the 1960s and 1970s was one by Marabel Morgan, *Total Woman* (1973), which was sweepingly indifferent to reforms and interested only in pleasing a loved man. It was analyzed and abused in such imitative titles as "Out-totaling the Total Woman" and *Total Woman? I Work;* but it obviously struck a response in some large, undefined segment of womanhood. Women's *weaknesses*, too, needed candid definition, for example with respect to rape and "wife abuse," which karate exercises could not stop or law wholly control. The woman's *body* being different from the man's—for example, caffein could hurt pregnancy, birth control pills were not entirely controllable, sexual freedom spread venereal diseases which not only threatened health but fertility—it seemed evident that laws and attitudes had to be socially adjusted accordingly. A major percentage of the public approved equality for women in jobs and opportunities, and "sexual harassment" anywhere was disapproved in and out of court. Yet women who wished to be attractive to, and to attract, males continued to make adjusting laws and traditions difficult. One man who killed another who "insulted" his wife with advances was given a suspended sentence, but warned to be less sensitive; his wife was attractive, and would invite such attention whether she wished it or not. Men were subject to *reverse discrimination*. A court found for men who had been refused admission to a restaurant for not wearing ties, a stipulation not applied to women. Men were refused jobs available to women. Although women were said to be losing ground in job competition with men in 1981, according to a World Conference of Women sponsored by the UN in Copenhagen, books by women argued that there *were* jobs for adroit and sincerely interested women, at least in America. B. Schickerman and C. H. Green, eds., *Notable American Women: the Modern Period* (1980) discerned in their biographies that notable women including Eleanor Roosevelt and Janis Joplin married less often, had fewer children and divorced more frequently. One woman student of women in 1980 observed that women generally were becoming lackadaisical about women's rights, but there seemed more women active and visible in social and public affairs than ever. Several of the most important jobs in the world were held by women, none of the "activist" breed. Mrs. Margaret Thatcher headed the British Conservative Party, Indira Gandhi the Indian government. Gro Harlem Brundtland, Norway's Premier, confided that she put her husband second to her work. At the Copenhagen meeting, pro-Palestinian delegates shouted down Mrs. Jehan Sadat, wife of President Sadat of Egypt. Communist Bulgaria in 1981 expected its next head of state to be Lyudmila Zhivkova, the daughter of its long-time President. Though the world's first woman prime minister, Sirimavo Benderanaike of Sri Lanka, was ousted from her place and parliament and stripped of her civil rights, she still remained the head of her Freedom Party. Such a list could have been extended indefinitely, and in America, and not taking into account queens, powerful first ladies, and otherwise authoritative wealthy, talented, or preferred females. An enigma unsettled was the question of women who were alone, some making of their separateness works of genius after the case of Emily Dickinson, others becoming "abandoned women," in the nineteenth century cliche, that is, half or defenseless women, as in the modern novel by Judith Rossner, *Looking for Mr. Goodbar* (1973). In 1980 the Democratic Party convention determined to allot one-half its seats to women. How such an organization would assess its male-female program in terms of winning combinations was undetermined. How women would estimate their leaders in the light of their past social experiences with the Suffrage and Reform also remained to be seen. (*Qq.v.* for above.) The literature on women is close to endless; the following are suggestive: Hope Chamberlin, *A Minority of Members: Women in the U.S. Congress* (1973); Nancy Seifer, *Nobody Speaks for Me!* (1976); Selma Fraiberg, *Every Child's Birthright: in Defense of Mothering* (1977); B. Millstein and J. Bodin, *We, the American Women: a Documentary History* (1980); William L. O'Neill, *The Woman Movement* (1971); Iris M. Tiedt, ed., *Women and Girls* (1973); Uta West, *Women in a Changing World* (1975).

WOMAN AS FORCE IN HISTORY: A STUDY IN TRADITIONS AND REALITIES (1946), by Mary R. Beard (*q.v.*), a work tracing women's accomplishments in many fields, and emphasizing general assumptions and attitudes which interfere with awareness of their actual history of economic and social significance, their status in law, the classes of questions which involve their well-being and self-expression.

WOMAN SUFFRAGE, a major reform issue of the post-Civil War period; it was earlier submerged in a more general demand for Woman's "Rights," including the right to speak at public meetings, to own property, to divorce unsavory or otherwise inadequate mates, and otherwise to affect society. Such persons as Susan B. Anthony, Elizabeth Cady Stanton, Lucy Stone (*qq.v.*) made the issue a perennial of social affairs. Belva A. Lockwood (*q.v.*) with dignity, and the Claflin (*q.v.*) sisters without gave depth and color, respectively, to the issue. Charlotte Gilman, Rheta Childe Dorr, Carrie Chapman Catt, and Anna Howard Shaw (*qq.v.*) were among many women who carried the campaign through to passage of the Nineteenth Amendment to the Constitution, in 1920, in time to enable the women to help vote into the Presidency Warren G. Harding (*q.v.*).

WOMAN WHO TOILS, THE... (1902), see Labor and Women.

WOMEN, SUBJUGATION OF, see Mill, John Stuart.

WOMEN AND ECONOMICS (1898), see Gilman, Charlotte Perkins Stetson.

WOMEN, NEGRO, have been, like men, concerned for social reform in the nature of their circumstances. Though Mrs. Phillis Wheatley Peters, like Benjamin Banneker (*q.v.*), was no reformer, her ability as a versifier served the purposes of reformers, who sought to prove that Negroes had the capacity to produce distinctive work. Sojourner Truth personified the Negro's need for consideration and respect; Harriet Tubman (*q.v.*) had the temperament of a revolutionist, rather than a reformer. Hallie Q. Brown, *Homespun Heroines and Other Women of Distinction* (1926) offers a spectrum of Negro women, from women of accomplishment

to reformers; others are found in Carter G. Woodson, *The Negro in Our History* (1922).

WOMEN'S CLUBS, somewhat active as a forum for women concerned for reform in the 1910's, they became less significant as a whole: at best, a meeting place for career women, at worst, an activity for female persons with time on their hands or with pretentious interests. See, however, the League of Women Voters of the United States.

WOMEN'S INTERNATIONAL LEAGUE FOR PEACE AND FREEDOM, founded 1915, by Jane Addams, Rosika Schwimmer (*qq.v.*), and other noted and distinguished personages. It activated many women throughout the world, and was a liaison agency for plans and purposes organized by radical and political movements.

WOODHULL, VICTORIA (1838-1927), born Claflin, adventuress and reformer, sister of Tennessee Claflin. As young women they claimed clairvoyant gifts and sold a patent medicine, as well as negotiated sex adventures. They became speculators in Wall Street, and as "Queens of Finance," they enlisted the interest of Stephen Pearl Andrews (*q.v.*) and George Francis Train. *Woodhull & Claflin's Weekly* (1870-1876) mixed idealistic offerings with a primitive form of muckraking (*q.v.*). It supported Victoria Woodhull for President of the United States. Her memorial to Congress in 1870, praying it to grant women the vote was seriously supported by woman suffragists, and she herself was given status among them. The "Equal Rights Party" which nominated her for the Presidency in 1872 has no status in political history. She pressed her crusade for emancipated sex to little social purpose. She transferred her eccentric causes to England, and is said to have suggested Henry James's *The Siege of London*. Her sister accompanied her in many of her efforts. Both married affluent persons and continued to express idealistic sentiments. M. M. Marberry, *Vicky* (1967).

WOOLMAN, JOHN (1720-1772), Quaker anti-slavery figure, who traveled among his people in the United States and England attempting to persuade them to give up the keeping of slaves, a step they ultimately took; see Society of Friends. He wrote a number of influential pamphlets on slavery and on human conduct, but is best known for his *Journal*, published after his death; it has its place in literature, and reflects his admirable character. See also Benezet, Anthony. Phillips P. Moulton, *The Living Waters of John Woolman* (1973).

WORK RELIEF, distinguished from relief (*q.v.*); see Outdoor Work, W.P.A.

"WORKER'S STATE," a way of looking at the Soviet Union, sometimes, more emotionally, as "the worker's fatherland." This view of affairs put the U.S.S.R. into a special category, as being of personal importance to workers everywhere. It permitted such slogans as "Defend the Worker's Fatherland," and would ultimately justify treason in the interests of the U.S.S.R. However, the manifest development of a Soviet bureaucracy and favored classes revealed that however regarded at home, the U.S.S.R. did not necessarily serve the interests of non-Russians. The Moscow Trials (*q.v.*), Soviet adventures abroad during the 1930's, and the Russo-Finnish War (*q.v.*) substantially ended use of the phrase, the "worker's state," in America, except among the communists.

WORKERS, see Unorganized Workers, Unemployed, Labor.

WORKHOUSE, an institution created under the old Poor Laws (*q.v.*) of England in which able-bodied paupers were compelled to labor; also thought of as a charitable establishment, where those without means acquired sustenance, in the form of "indoor relief." It made no sharp distinction between criminals and the poor. The workhouse served similar purposes in the United States. "Outdoor relief," (*q.v.*) had perhaps a slightly less invidious connotation, referring to labor on roads and other places less associated with incarceration. The workhouse functioned into the twentieth century. The wide-spread nature of "relief" in the 1930's gave the word a slightly less contemptible connotation, and the dwindling away of workhouses, under that name, aided its status.

WORKING CLASS, a shibboleth of revolutionary groups, and also of reformers affected by Marxism (q.v.). It had some descriptive value in Europe, where a portion of the population was substantially confined to operations and opportunities relevant to manual labor. In the United States, frontier opportunities, prosperity eras which created demands for services rather than production, war prosperity, and other conditions permitted a fluidity of hope, and some fluidity of actual opportunity which made the "working class" a fetish, rather than a fact. It had some agitational use, and deluded a few enthusiasts, but created more frustration than it did action.

WORKINGMEN'S PARTY, first organized in Philadelphia, in 1828: a product of the increased suffrage (q.v.). Similar parties were organized in Boston, New York, and elsewhere. The leadership was not so much drawn from among the workers as from craftsmen, reformers, and other essentially middle-class elements. The New York party had notable reformers leading them, including Robert Dale Owen, Frances Wright, George H. Evans, and Thomas Skidmore (qq.v.). The party was a factor in local and state elections, and was especially courted by Jacksonians before being dissipated, by 1834, by Democratic politics, on the one hand, labor organizing efforts, on the other; see National Trades Union.

WORKINGMEN'S PARTY OF CALIFORNIA, see Kearney, Dennis.

WORKMEN'S COMPENSATION, an element in welfare legislation (q.v.) intended to provide a measure of security for workers who might be injured while on the job, under circumstances for which the employer could be held liable. The passage of laws covering such contingencies was resisted, and the laws, when passed, were flouted whenever possible. Nevertheless, they not only multiplied, but were strengthened. The first such law was passed in Maryland, in 1902. By 1919, thirty-nine states had passed workmen's compensation laws, and the remainder adopted it by 1948, Mississippi being the last state to do so. The year 1947 was a banner year for legislation enlarging the scope of workman's compensation, and establishing elaborate machinery to process cases. In the 1960s and after American litigation produced a rash of cases based on industrial negligence, in which workers and others could demand unprecedented sums for legally found negligence which cost life or limb. So drastic were the penalties that it appeared limits would have to be determined in law or expectations which would permit the worker a sense of security and a business the ability to plan and go forward. H. Gutman, *Work Culture and Society in Industrializing America* (1977); Daniel T. Rodgers, *Work Ethic in Industrial America* (1978); J. M. Stillman and S. M. Daum, *Work Is Dangerous to Your Health...Hazards...and What You Can Do about Them* (1973); Barbara A. Curran, *Legal Needs of the Public* (1977).

WORKS PROGRESS ADMINISTRATION, later Work Projects Administration, successor to the Federal Emergency Relief Administration (q.v.) as a relief measure with which to meet the economic crisis of the 1930's. Administered by Harry L. Hopkins (q.v.), W.P.A. was set up in the summer of 1935 and instituted a program of building and public and personal services which in six years employed some eight million individuals. In order to underscore the intended temporary aspect of the work, W.P.A. employees were required by law to disassociate themselves from time to time from the project in order to seek work, but most of them were driven back to relief for lack of other opportunity. In order to receive their fifty to sixty dollars per month, union wages were maintained, but the number of hours work allotted to them cut down accordingly. Some $86 of the W.P.A. $100 went for wages, $10.50 for materials, $3.50 for administra-

tion. The government furnished the labor, states and localities most of the materials and other necessities. W.P.A. was administered by the Federal government until 1939, returning to the states thereafter. Its work transformed the nation in terms of roads, schools, dams, postoffices, playgrounds. Nevertheless, conservatives protested the cost. They protested that much of the work—including the famous Federal Arts Projects (q.v.)—was unnecessary, though the alternative would have been straight relief and no return in labor. They were also bitter over the fact that W.P.A. workers tended to vote for the Democratic Party, though why they would have wished to vote for the Republican Party was not clear. W.P.A. was one indicator of the continuing depression. Its funds were trimmed under protest, but its available opportunities were thoroughly filled by persons dependent on it for a livelihood. Its work did not cease until its units were absorbed by war services. D. S. Howard, *WPA and Federal Relief Policy* (1943); Arthur W. MacMahon et al., *The Administration of Federal Work Relief* (1941). See also Hopkins, Harry L.

WORLD COURT, see Permanent Court of International Justice.

WORLD FEDERATION, a plan for settling strife among nations which was bruited about in the period preceding formation of the United Nations (q.v.). The plan, by a bridge expert Ely Culbertson, who had lived a versatile life, essentially tried to cope with the problem of power politics which might result in further strife. It set up a group of Regional Federations, and a scheme of police intended to make sure that no power or group of powers could undertake to precipitate war; see Culbertson's *Summary of the World Federation Plan* (1943), and "Union Now."

WORLD WARS were greeted in 1914 by American reformers with an alarm they had not felt in connection with the Balkan War which had been raging in 1912 and 1913; presumably this was a more localized, if regrettable, affair. They took it that it was imperialism opposing imperialism for commercial reasons, and that Americans were fortunate to be separated from Europe's "madness." Elements either favoring Germany, as in the case of the German-Americans, or hating the English, as in the case of the Irish, or hating England's ally Czarist Russia, as with the Russian Jews, tended to be satisfied with isolation from the war. Sympathizers of England and lovers of France and Italy were eager to help their preferred nations, and were advocates of aid and "preparedness for any eventuality." The drive to unify the nation for intervention on the Allied side meant a smashing up of the opponents of war. Vigilantes (q.v.) worked to good effect in this situation. The Socialist Party (q.v.) split on the issue. Such reformers as Charles Edward Russell, Upton Sinclair, A.M. Simons, and others in and out of the Creel Committee (qq.v.) cooperated in the war effort. Samuel Gompers (q.v.) was a significant force for "lining up labor" for the war, in the United States and abroad, promising them every manner of improvement in status and conditions as a result of their help. Dissidents included sympathizers of the Bolshevik Revolution, intransigents like Randolph Bourne, followers of the Women's International League for Peace and Freedom, Wobblies (qq.v.), and others whom oppression only rendered more grim and vengeful. When the war ended, the "Red Scare" (q.v.) kept some vigilantes active, but most Americans preferred a return to a general state of ignorance about American affairs, a state into which many of their former antagonists could join them with enthusiasm. World War I became a largely forgotten war, except among attendants at national monuments, concerned elements of the American Legion (q.v.), and other types or individuals with a special interest. The Munitions Investigation (q.v.) threw invidious light on its purposes, as did renewed pacifist and socialist-communist interpretation. The burgeoning of fascism created a cause which could unite all its foes, and which did, after Hitler (*q.v.*) had turned against his partner in the Nazi-Soviet Pact of 1939. Save for a few religious pacifists, American intervention in World War II was popular and seemed promising to those who foresaw "One World" of peace and plenty, untainted by fascism. The breaking up of the alliance of the "Great Democracies," which had presumably included the western democracies and the U.S.S.R. produced a new military competition between West and East. The phrase "Russia and her satellites" gave a sense of eastern unity which those undesirous of a third world war disliked; they hoped there was not enough of a community of interest between the U.S.S.R., Red China, Poland, Czechoslovakia and other "Iron Curtain" (*q.v.*) areas to underwrite Russian plans for war. Most ominous for the future was the phenomenon of "Genocide" (*q.v.*) which was applied to German and Japanese "war criminals," but not to Soviet Russia, despite her Katyn Forest murders and slave labor camps (*qq.v.*). This suggested that accusations of genocide and war crimes could be levelled by victors at any time. Also ominous were the "saturation bombings" of major cities which were featured in the European war engagements and world shaking at Hiroshima (*q.v.*). Avoiding another such holocaust became one of the main thrusts of the "Nuclear Question" (*q.v.*). A new isolationism (*q.v.*) complicated approaches to it.

W.P.A., see Works Progress Administration.

WRIGHT, CARROLL DAVIDSON (1840-1909), a pioneer in fact-gathering on the labor question, U.S. Commissioner of Labor (1885-95), and later a professor of political science in Catholic University and president of Clark University. Among his works were *The Factory System of the United States* (1882), *Convict Labor* (1886), *Strikes and Lockouts* (1887), and *Battles of Labor* (1906).

WRIGHT, ELIZUR (1804-1885), a brilliant and strategic abolitionist of the 1830's, who had been turned against colonization (*qq.v.* for this and following items) by Garrison, but who, as an associate with the American Anti-Slavery Society of William Jay, and Arthur and Lewis Tappan, among others became sharply critical of Garrison and sought to unseat him in his New England stronghold. He and his associates failed to do this through an abortive Massachusetts Abolition Society and its attempted publication, the *Massachusetts Abolitionist*. They were also defeated in an effort to oust Garrisonian principles from the national Society, in 1840, and left the organization. Wright helped launch political abolitionism, through the Liberty Party, and later honored his leader in the effort in a biography, *Myron Holley: and What He Did for Liberty and True Religion* (1882). However, he left the reform movement, and became an agnostic and distinguished as the "father of life insurance in America"; see the biography of him by P.G. and E.Q. Wright (1937).

WRIGHT, FRANCES (1795-1852), a Scottish girl who became notorious for her freethinking and libertarian ideas. She visited the United States in 1818 and again in 1824, on her second visit being impressed by New Harmony (*q.v.*) and other cooperative colonies. She attempted one at Nashoba in Tennessee in 1827, but her permissiveness with respect to the presence of Negroes among her associates and their informal relations were among the reasons for its failure. Her lectures in behalf of free opportunities for women, in opposition to restraints imposed by churches, and in furtherance of humanitarian causes made "Fanny Wright" a byword. She issued the *Free Enquirer* in New York, in 1829, and helped organize the Workingmen's Party (*q.v.*). Her marriage to a French aristocrat, D'Arusmont, in 1831, was unhappy, and they were divorced in 1850. T. Wolfson, *Frances Wright, Free Enquirer* (1939).

WRIGHT, HENRY CLARKE (1797-1870), radical abolitionist, Swedenborgian, and social theoretician. He formulated for W.L. Garrison (*q.v.*) many of the latter's extreme views. He was a children's minister, reform lecturer and pamphleteer, and an early eugenicist (*q.v.*). He was an extreme pacifist, opposing all resistance to violence, and helped form the Non-Resistant Society in 1838, which was, however, little more than a banner; see his *Autobiography of Henry C. Wright* (1849). Lewis Perry, *Childhood, Marriage and Reform: Henry Clarke Wright* (1980).

WRIGHT, RICHARD (1908-1960), Mississippi-born Negro writer of rebellious temperament. In the 1930's, he worked in Chicago on the Federal Writers Project (*q.v.*) and had experiences which he later recounted in his essays for the *Atlantic* (August-September, 1944), under the title of "I Tried To Be a Communist." He published a collection of stories, *Uncle Tom's Children* (1938), and then had a sensational best-seller, *Native Son* (1940) which argued the bitter thesis that a Negro treated like a rat could act only like a rat. The novel repeated its success as a play, the next year, being prepared by Wright in collaboration with Paul Green. Wright later wrote an autobiographical *Black Boy* (1945). He became an expatriate (*q.v.*) and died in Paris. Constance Webb, *Richard Wright* (1968).

WRITS OF ASSISTANCE, general search warrants which were issued early in the 1750's to customs officers to facilitate their search for "uncustomed" or otherwise illegal commodities. Although there was concern about the infringement of privacy involved, it was not until the crisis of Empire relations arose in the next decade that colonists demanded that their courts refuse the issuance of Writs of Assistance. James Otis (*q.v.*) was eloquent in his denunciation of them as being unconstitutional. The Townshend Revenue Act (*q.v.*) authorized customs officials under Writs of Assistance, to "enter and go into any house, shop cellar, warehouse, or room or other place and, in case of resistance, to break open doors, chests, trunks...to seize... any kind of goods or merchandise whatsoever prohibited. . ." Colonial courts, under pressure of angry colonists, largely stopped issuing the Writs, which agitators made infamous.

X

Y

XENOPHOBIA, distaste for foreigners, a product of parochialism, a disease which threatens reformers as well as anti-reformers.

XEROX, like certain other business names—formica, frigidaire, Phillips screwdriver—had come to stand for a process which has multiplied writings, memos, propaganda, art works; Xerox circulated a "xerox" of a Picasso line drawing to underscore the quality of its reproduction. The xerox, more than the ditto or mimeograph machine, freed people to own whatever works they preferred, to such an extent that fearful authors, publishers, and librarians sought laws to curb ready reproduction, at least for profit. Despite limits placed on xeroxing, it should technically have expanded knowledge and understanding. There is no evidence that the desires of researchers or others created an enriching level for society, perhaps because of the specializing services xerox provided, as distinguished from broad, liberal arts goals reached by individual explorations.

XYZ AFFAIR (1797-8), a disgraceful effort on the part of French representatives to elicit the payment of loans and bribes by the United States in order to allay French feelings, which had been ruffled by United States unwillingness to help France in her battle with Great Britain, and by Jay's Treaty of 1794 (q.v.). An unofficial war had been on at sea between France and the United States. Revelations of this demand by the French roused American patriotism, from which the Federalists profited at the expense of the Jeffersonians. The United States began to prepare for full-scale war: an operation which was stymied by John Adams's negotiations with the French; see also Barbary Pirates. W. Stinchcome, *The XYZ Affair* (1980).

YALTA CONFERENCE (1945), controversial meeting of Franklin D. Roosevelt, Winston S. Churchill, and Joseph Stalin which reached secret agreements which were bitterly debated when revealed. In exchange for the Soviet Union's promising to enter the war against Japan several months after the surrender of Germany, the Soviet Union was to receive territories and privileges in the Far East, rights in Manchuria, an autonomous Outer Mongolia which she was certain to dominate, and, in Europe, an eastern tier of states under communist control, part occupation of Germany and other strategic gains. With the war soon over, it appeared that the western powers had bartered a promise for a gigantic concession which ensured the fall of the Chiang Kai Shek (q.v.) government in China and endless trouble in Europe. The argument in defense of Roosevelt was that the atom-bomb was not yet a certainty, that a long campaign against Japan was still envisioned and the possibility of aid in that theater desirable, and that Russia's perfidy, or her capacity for implementing treachery, could not be realized. The Yalta Conference agreed, too, to establish what became the United Nations (q.v.). D. S. Clemens, *Yalta* (1970); A. Theoharis, *Yalta Myths* (1970); F. H. Rodine, *Yalta—Responsibility and Response* (1974).

"YANKS ARE NOT COMING, THE," a slogan created in 1940 by the communist Mike Quin to fight tendencies for enlisting America on the side of Great Britain, then at war with Hitler's Third Reich. It became the basis of a national campaign which was, however, immediately abandoned when Germany overthrew its pact with Soviet Russia, invading her June 22, 1941. Thereafter, the communists agitated for aid to the U.S.S.R.

"YARDSTICK" FOR POWER RATES, see Tennessee Valley Authority.

YAZOO LAND FRAUDS, see Fletcher v. Peck.

"YELLOW DOG CONTRACT," see Norris-La Guardia Anti-Injunction Bill.

"YELLOW JOURNALISM," sometimes popularly thought to refer to the cowardliness of newspapermen seeking sensations at the expense of private reputations; the term, in fact, derived from the popularity of Richard F. Outcauld's cartoon, "The Yellow Kid," first, in 1894, drawn for Pulitzer's *New York World*, and featuring actual yellow ink. Outcauld soon joined William Randolph Hearst's *New York Journal*, where his Yellow Kid, who disported himself in *Hogan's Alley*, was striking enough to became a symbol of the popular journalist's efforts to arrest public attention.

"YELLOW PERIL, THE," see Minority Groups.

YELLOW PRESS, see Journalism and Reform.

"YELLOWBACK," a word of scorn, directed at "slackers" of World War I, men who had not voluntarily enlisted, and thus earned the contempt of patriots. See "Hey! Yellowback!"

YORK, ALVIN C. (1887-1964), a soldier who, during the Battle of Argonne, captured almost single-handed an entire German machine-gun battalion of one hundred and thirty-two men. His is one of the most notable of American soldierly exploits, and of the type with which American social reform has never found any means of being able to identify itself.

YOUMANS, EDWARD LIVINGSTONE (1821-1887), scientist and Social Darwinian (q.v.), who believed that the dissemination of scientific principles must result in the progressive evolution of society. He founded the *Popular Science Monthly* in 1872 in order to advance that cause. See also his *The Culture Demanded by Modern Life* (1867).

YOUNG, an obvious component in the Youth Movement (*q.v.*), widely used in the nineteenth century, to herald imperialism (*q.v.*) in the United States, to signalize nationalist aspirations in Europe: "Young Italy," "Young Germany," etc.

YOUNG, ART (1866-1944), greatest of the socially conscious cartoonists, thanks to his keen eye for the contrasts in human nature, the pathetic as well as the cruel. His grassroots qualities kept his satire and anger from slipping into doctrinaire dissatisfaction with the *status quo*. *On My Way* (1928), *The Best of Art Young* (1936), and *Art Young: His Life and Times* (1939) capture much of his achievement.

"YOUNG AMERICA," a movement developed in the 1840's which emphasized America's manifest destiny to expand. It had its strength in the Democratic Party and aggressive proponents in its pro-slavery leadership which saw increased territory as creating new opportunities for expanding the slavery system, for example into Mexico.

YOUNG COMMUNIST LEAGUE, dedicated to fulfilling Lenin's dictum: "He who has the youth has the future." Thanks to the high integration of the communist movement, the youth worked very closely with "The Party" leadership, and were part of one monolithic structure. One of the main tasks of communist youth was to infiltrate other youth organizations, and take over their direction while preserving a facade of free choice and democracy.

YOUNG PEOPLE'S SOCIALIST LEAGUE, youth organization of the Socialist Party, it offered opportunities for young idealists who, during the 1930's, were given particularly keen competition by the "YCLers," members of the Young Communist League, the youth branch of the Communist Party. Known as "Yipsels," the young socialists faded as a social force with World War II. Their informal name probably inspired that of the paper "Youth International Party," which featured Jerry Rubin and Abbie Hoffman, who dubbed themselves "Yippies."

YOUTH CONSERVATION CORPS, proposed in 1961 by the Kennedy Administration to put male teen-agers to work on conservation projects across the nation. Envisioned by a Department of Labor study was a combined education-work program for 150,000 boys aged seventeen to nineteen. Applicants would volunteer for a year's service as laborers, technicians's helpers, and light construction workers, and serve in such agencies as the National Park Service, the Forest Service, and the Bureau of Reclamation. It would thus help employ "drop-outs" from schools who were unable to acquire work, and help take care of necessary conservation work. The Corps was closely modeled on the Civilian Conservation Corps (*q.v.*) of the 1930's.

YOUTH MOVEMENT, THE, a late bloom in the United States, unlike Europe, which in the nineteenth century produced libertarian circles which attracted youth seeking self-expression and idealistic programs (see Bohemians) and who mixed individualistic living and artistic experimentation with a willingness to serve republican and revolutionary movements and shed blood during nationalistic or labor uprisings. In the United States, the Youth Movement emerged in the 1910's, and was characterized by artistic experiments, a social conscience which, however, was impatient with the "half measures" of reformers, a romantic view of the potentialities of people, and resentment of authority. Randolph Bourne (*q.v.*) represented much of the youthful program, in his idealization of youth, his interest in a revised education which emphasized the child's point of view, his loss of regard for tradition and classics, his ardent pacifism and pro-worker, pro-socialist attitude, and in his desire to experience many things and ideas, rather than to settle down to a specialty. Other youth leaders were Floyd Dell, an irresponsible lit-

terateur, John Reed (*q.v.*), who moved from careless bohemianism to a committed revolutionary position, Max Eastman, Walter Lippmann (*q.v.*), and others who formulated social, political, and cultural tenets intended to transform the country. The youth inadequately appreciated that the reason for their freedom of expression was partly sociological—the rise of the impersonal city, which loosened family ties—and partly the result of the work which the reformers had accomplished through exposures of crime and chicanery and demands for free expressions of opinion. The youth imagined that their wit and daring awed critics and observers. They were disillusioned when the government entered World War I (*q.v.*) and made them subject to conscription. In the 1920's, those who made a "Flapper Age" (*q.v.*) of the time studied flippancy and personal pleasure; writers like Henry Miller did essentially the same thing on a more pretentious level. Some youth, like John Dos Passos (*q.v.*) sought more serious goals. The economic depression of the 1930's created hungry youth as well as ambitious youth. The National Youth Administration recognized that young people needed practical help just as unemployed adults did. N.Y.A., under Aubrey Williams, offered work to unemployed youth who were no longer in school, and also to students in need of financial assistance. Such government aid did not keep others from agitating among the unemployed, or from joining the Young Communist League or the Young People's Socialist League (*qq.v.*). Both tended to look with suspicion at the Civilian Conservation Corps (*q.v.*), which they feared might be a step toward regimenting youth. The Youth Movement was given a sharp setback when conscription went into effect in 1940. In 1939 there were 1,350,000 college students. In 1974 there were 10,137,065. This contrast of enrollment described the difference in the role and effectiveness of the two youth generations in post-World War II developments. Both the increasing youth and their elders put the Depression (*q.v.*) behind them. Affluence (*q.v.*) made for aimless fun and adventures for both generations; and a species of idealism arose among more discontented youth frustrated by the "military-industrial complex" (*q.v.*). Frustration expressed itself in apathy (the "Beats" *q.v.*), a fascination with random music mixed with ballads, some with a social-critical base. The youth read J. D. Salinger's *Catcher in the Rye*, and soon after Jack Kerouac's *On the Road*. They experimented with drugs and sex, and made gestures toward Negro causes. All these impulses were intensified in the early 1960s as Beats gave place to "Hippies" (*q.v.*) who admired Lenny Bruce and were moved by the emotional quasi-verse of Allen Ginsberg. Dissatisfaction exploded in a campus revolt which extended sensationally from the Berkeley, University of California, campus to Columbia University in the East, and caused sit-ins, "teach-ins" (*qq.v.*), assaults upon teachers and administrators, and turned campuses into forums on "Black Studies," demands for withdrawals of investments in Union of South Africa (*q.v.*) business, student representation, curriculum, and other issues. Vital was the support which aggressive students received from friendly or daunted teachers, their aggrieved aides, administrators and staff, and even parents. The empathetic journalists, camera people, and radio and television personalities who followed and reported on their adventures were also basic to their growth and unfolding. President Johnson (*q.v.*) changed the nature of student and other protest by escalating the war in Vietnam (*q.v.*). Thereafter "Hippies" and "Peaceniks" shared visibility with a variety of others, including "Yippies" and the more somber "Weathermen" (*qq.v.*). As demonstrations, take-overs, and assaults mounted against the Pentagon (*q.v.*) and the political parties, the country faced a measure of civil war disruptive of national unity and education. The Kent State tragedy (*q.v.*) constituted a climax in confrontation. Stepped up government activity against sabotage and the winding down of the war in Vietnam loosened the youth coalition, as more and more youth turned to job possibilities and awareness that more courses and "credits" gave no guarantee of work. A movement toward communes and religious fundamentalism (*qq.v.*) attracted an element of the surviving youth adherents. Some fled as necessary to the underground, from which Abbie Hoffman, for one, operated magisterially. He reviewed a motion-picture, *The Fix* (1978) in the New York *Village Voice,* which took off not too inaccurately on his role and future. Many former activists found places and position in the social and educational establishment. "New Left" historians, for example, had been prominent in the actual turmoil. Tom Hayden was one of those who went on to be influential in Democratic and other liberal circles. Others made their outlooks respectable in a diminished historical profession. In 1980 they elected as president of the Organization of American Historians, W. A. Williams, whose main concern had been to prove that the American nation had been dedicated to imperialism (*q.v.*) from its very inception. The youth activists of the 1960s and 1970s, and their abettors, were central to the "new" history such figures taught and defended; see, for example, Paula Foss, *American Historical Review* (December 1979, and October 1980). See also the account of an activist turned "Marxist" sociologist, Todd Gitlin, *The Whole World Is Watching* (1980). Although in 1980 the *Berkeley Barb,* once prime "underground newspaper" of youth, suspended publication for lack of student support, the protracted youth movement had changed the nation: its clothing, its outlook on family and singles (*qq.v.*), its loyalties, and attitudes toward race. Youth seemed likely to play a smaller part in up-coming events, thanks to the growing number of older people, who included the angry youth movement members themselves. The post-Baby Boom youth no longer constituted a youth movement. For youth bibliography, see Filler, *Vanguards and Followers: Youth in the American Tradition.*

YUCATAN, a province of Mexico (*q.v.*), but, like the Ukraine in Russia, a nation in its own right with songs and traditions of ancient origin. It provided American apologists with an answer to the Mexican charge of having been subjected to Yankee imperialism (*q.v.*) by Texan (*q.v.*) adventurers. Yucatan was also a land of contract labor difficult to distinguish from slavery (*q.v.*).

YUGOSLAVIA, see Tito, Marshal.

Z

ZANGWILL, ISRAEL (1864-1926), an Englishman, one of the outstanding Jewish writers in English, his work won international regard for its literary qualities and influenced non-Jewish opinion. His novels included *Children of the Ghetto* (1892), *Ghetto Tragedies* (1893) and *King of the Schnorrers* (1894); his play, *The Melting Pot* (1908) gave wide circulation to a significant phrase (*q.v.*).

ZENGER, JOHN PETER (1697-1746), German-born printer who published, in his *New-York Weekly Journal* attacks on the local administration, for which he was arrested (1735) and charged with criminal libel. An antagonistic court sought to hold him culpable independently of whether or not his libel was true, but Zenger's distinguished counsel, Andrew Hamilton, held the question of the truth of the libel up before the jury, and won acquittal for his client. The latter published *A Brief Narrative of the Case and Tryal of John Peter Zenger* (1736). The case became established as a landmark in the struggle for freedom of the press (*q.v.*).

ZIMBABWE, formerly Rhodesia, a classic instance of adjustment of African nationalism to world relations, including the East-West struggle for influence in black-dominated governments. Rhodesia, colonized by Cecil Rhodes and built by white capitalism, bordered white-dominated South Africa, as well as "Marxist" Mozambique which was supported by Soviet agents and funds in the post-World War II period of political maneuvers. Rhodesia took the road of white control away from Great Britain's Labour Government, thus juxtaposing its quarter million white rulers against a native population of over five million. Increasingly besieged by guerrillas armed and trained in Mozambique and also neighboring Zambia, and subject to United Nations economic sanctions, Rhodesia declared its independence of Great Britain in 1965. Under a determined Premier, Ian Smith, it sought to quell its guerrillas with an armed citizenry and military forces. Aided only by South Africa, with its own world and black government accomodations, Rhodesia fought a losing battle, diplomatic and economic, between 1972 and 1976, when South Africa was forced to give up its indispensible aid. Rhodesia then negotiated for a transitional government which would ensure the place and properties of the white minority. Its best hope lay in a moderate black leadership headed by Bishop Abel Muzorewa, but the guerrilla leaders Joshua Nkomo and Robert Mugabe were able to use the voting machinery to give Mugabe's faction the victory. Ironically, it was the new Conservative government in London which arranged this finale. The best hope for the new Zimbabwe nation lay in its ability to use the expertise of its white population, the funds provided by the British government, aid from the United States, and internal relations which would permit the rebuilding of an economy eroded by warfare and transition. It needed also to control the formerly guerrilla troops, restive for action and recognition. The rate of whites leaving the country also bore watching, as did differences between Mugabe and Nkomo, both claiming socialist goals but needing the benefits of the free market and the services of South Africa. E. E. Mlambo, *Rhodesia: the Struggle for a Birthright* (1972); A. J. Bruwer, *Zimbabwe: Rhodesia's Ancient Greatness* (1965); N. Sithole, *Zimbabwe's Year of Freedom* (1978); *Zimbabwe Independence Movements: Select Documents* (1979).

ZIMMERWALD MOVEMENT, instituted in 1915, it brought together labor and socialist elements to a conference in Zimmerwald, Switzerland, to discuss the outbreak of war, and to protest the support of their own governments by much of the leadership of the Second International (*q.v.*). In

1917, the conference met in Stockholm, where it reached decisions which foreshadowed the creation of the Third International (q.v.).

ZIONISM, a Jewish-nationalist concept which saw the Jews, though dispersed in many lands, as constituting a distinct people with a destiny identified with Jerusalem, where the Bible was born. The word "Zionism" was coined by Nathan Birnbaum in 1890, it was later forged into a vital slogan by another Vienna idealist, Theodor Herzl. A major incentive for planning the rebirth of a Jewish state was the persecution suffered by European Jews; however, strong elements of religion and tradition were also involved in Zionism as a movement. It attracted reformers and socialists, would-be farmers and persons interested in cooperative living. Land purchases, fund-raising activities, the agitation and work of such major figures as Chaim Weizmann and David Ben-Gurion culminated in the establishment of the State of Israel (q.v.). The movement accomplished reformist ends in providing alternatives to Jewish persecution and raising the vision of a democratic civilization in the Middle East. It offended anti-semitic, anti-religious elements who resented the thought that Jews were resisting assimilation in the various countries in which they resided, and who were un-impressed by the lengthy records of patriotism and service Jews built up wherever they were permitted to do so. In the United States, the idea that Zionists harbored "dual loyalties" was repudiated by Jews friendly to Israel, asserted by the American Council for Judaism (q.v.).

ZOAR SOCIETY, like the Amana Community, a religious enterprise which provided an example in the field of coop-erative living. The Zoarites were German separatists who set-tled in Ohio in 1819 under the leadership of Joseph M. Bimeler, who proved an excellent organizer. They built dis-tinctive homes and enterprises and flourished, continuing through most of the century as a unified body.

ZOLA, ÉMILE (1840-1902), leader of the naturalist (q.v.) school of writing which sought to depict reality in defiance of the preferences of pampered and insincere readers and critics. The goal Zola sought was truth, which he believed could only be attained by recording the detail, sordid and otherwise, which entered into the lives of poor people, disturbed people, prostitutes, and other types. In *Le Roman Experimentale* (1880) and *Les Romanciers Naturalistes* (1881), he explained and defended his methods. His novels maintained a sympathetic attitude toward the needy and harassed which reformers found satisfying in their work. His defence of Dreyfus (q.v.), in the famous *J'Accuse* (1898) won him the admiration of liberals everywhere.

ZUEBLEN, CHARLES (1866-1924), sociologist and settlement house pioneer, concerned for municipal reform; see his *American Municipal Progress* (1902), and *A Decade of Civil Development* (1905).